SO-AVS-481

A History of Christendom
Vol. 4

Warren H. Carroll

The Cleaving
of Christendom

Warren H. Carroll

Christendom Press
Front Royal, Virginia

All inquiries should be addressed to:
Christendom Press
134 Christendom Drive
Front Royal, VA 22630

To place an order visit www.christendom.edu/press/

ISBN: 0-931888-75-1 PAPER
ISBN: 0-931888-76-x CLOTH

Contents

DEDICATED
to my beloved wife,
ANNE
whose bright example and unceasing prayer
brought me to the grace of faith
and membership in the Church of Christ

1
Martin Luther's Revolt
1517-1521
Pope Leo X (1513-1521)

"Mindful of the compassion of God Who desires not the death of a sinner, but that he be converted and live, we are ready to forget the injury done to us and to the Holy See. We have decided to exercise the greatest possible indulgence and, so far as in our power lies, to seek to induce the sinner to enter into himself and to renounce the errors we have enumerated, so that we may see him return to the bosom of the Church and receive him with kindness, like the prodigal son in the Gospel. We therefore exhort him and his followers through the love and mercy of our God and the Precious Blood of Our Lord Jesus Christ, by which the human race was redeemed and the Church founded, and adjure them that they cease from troubling with their deadly errors the peace, unity and truth of the Church for which the Savior prayed so fervently to His Father. They will then, if they prove obedient, find us full of fatherly love and be received with open arms."—Pope Leo X on Martin Luther in the bull *Exsurge domine*, June 15, 1520[1]

"Now farewell, you unhappy, lost, and blasphemous Rome; the wrath of God has come upon you at last, as you have merited, for in spite of all the prayers that have been said for you, you have become worse each day. We would have healed Babylon, but she is not healed. Let us forsake her then to become a dwelling place of dragons, evil spirits, goblins, and witches, and her name an eternal confusion, filled to the brim as she is with the idols of greed, with traitors, apostates, beasts, lechers, thieves, and simoners, and an infinity of other monsters, something new in the way of a pantheon of iniquity! . . . If we punish thieves with the gallows, robbers with the sword, and heretics with fire, why should we not all the more assail with arms these masters of perdition, these cardinals, these Popes, the whole dregs of the Roman Sodom, who have been corrupting the Church of God without intermission, and wash our hands in their blood?"—Martin Luther, "On the Papacy at Rome," June 25, 1520 and "To the Christian Nobility of the German Nation"[2]

---

[1] Hartmann Grisar, *Luther* (St. Louis, 1913), II, pp. 48-49.

[2] Robert H. Fife, *The Revolt of Martin Luther* (New York, 1957), pp. 505-506; Ludwig von Pastor, *History of the Popes from the Close of the Middles Ages* (St. Louis, 1950), VII, p. 393.

"Unless I am overcome by means of the Scriptural passages that I have cited, and unless my conscience is taken captive by the Word of God, I am neither able nor willing to revoke anything, since to act against one's conscience is neither safe nor honest. God help me, amen!"—Luther to the Diet of Worms, April 18, 1521[3]

"It is certain that a single monk must err if he stands against the opinion of all Christendom. Otherwise Christendom itself would have erred for more than a thousand years. Therefore I am determined to set my kingdoms and dominions, my friends, my body, my blood, my life, my soul upon it."— Holy Roman Emperor Charles V in reply to Luther at the Diet of Worms, April 19, 1521[4]

In 1517 it had been just ten years short of one and a half millennia since the baptism of Jesus Christ by John the Baptist.[5] During those fifteen centuries the Church Christ founded had grown from a band of twelve Galilean rustics into a highly organized hierarchical body of tens of millions of believers, the cornerstone and reason for being of an entire civilization: Western Christendom. During those centuries the Church had survived the collapse of the Graeco-Roman civilization, bridging the abyss from the old order to the new, synthesizing the wisdom of the pagans with the truths of revelation first in the cosmic world-view of St. Thomas Aquinas, then reaching out confidently in the Renaissance and the Age of Discovery that accompanied it. Along the way there had been struggles with great heresies and the tragic, needless schism that separated most of the Eastern believers from the Church led by the Pope. But in all these struggles the Church had prevailed, her losses minor compared to her victories; and now, following Columbus and Vasco da Gama and Afonso de Albuquerque, the Church was about to move into previously unimagined new realms where more millions of potential converts awaited her. For all those fifteen hundred years, even when temporal and cultural conditions were at their worst, the Church had gone from strength to strength, turning adversity into triumph. When Rome fell to the barbarians, the Church converted the barbarians. When the heretics captured the Pope, the Church recaptured the heretics. When the ancient civilization fell, the Church replaced it with a Christian civilization. When Christian Emperors sought to subjugate the Pope, the Church found Emperors who would be faithful and loyal. When the Papacy itself was riven into three contending factions, the Council of Constance and the true Pope found a way to end the potentially fatal division before it was too late.

Such are some of the high points of the story we have told in the first three volumes of this history—the story of the founding, building, glory and triumph of the Christian Church, against human odds so great as to have made it utterly impossible without the never-failing aid of God Who founded it.

---

[3] *Ibid.*, p. 666.

[4] Karl Brandi, *The Emperor Charles V* (Atlantic Highlands NJ, 1965), p. 131.

[5] See Volume I, Chapter Fifteen of this history.

But in the scant four years from 1517 to 1521 the turning point came. Throughout the 479 years separating 1521 from the end of the second Christian millennium, the Church had to fight unceasingly for its survival. Her people could still dream great dreams and launch great enterprises; she could still convert and reconcile millions, establishing strongholds beyond the West; she could still produce saints whose holiness and total commitment to Christ could match any of their predecessors. Her triumphs were still legion, and her faithful could not only hear the assurance but see the proof that the gates of Hell could not prevail against her, that there would be a Church of Christ on earth until the end of the world. But never again, after that fell moment when Martin Luther of the University of Wittenberg in Electoral Saxony in eastern Germany tacked his 95 theses against indulgences on the door of the Wittenberg palace church, has the Church known full unity and peace in any of its lands and peoples. The hammer and nails of Martin Luther clove Christendom in twain. It has remained cloven ever since. Whatever progress has been and may be made in mutual tolerance and understanding and cooperation with the separated brethren so many generations later, there is still hardly a glimmer of realistic hope that this greatest wound in the Mystical Body of Christ can be healed in the foreseeable future.[6]

Who was Martin Luther?

There is no lack of evidence to answer that question. He left an enormous corpus of writings of every kind—books, pamphlets, sermons, debates, public speeches, and letters by the thousand. He was perhaps the greatest master in the use of the German language in the entire history of the German-speaking peoples. Writings about him by his contemporaries are almost equally voluminous. The flood of books for and against him continued unabated until the twentieth century, when their number has declined with the spreading loss of real Christianity of any kind among people of our time. However great and passionate the differences of opinion about him—and they are both great and passionate—with so much data there can hardly be much mystery in him.

Martin Luther was born in November 1483, the first-born of Gross-Hans Luder, son of a farmer who, in the year of Martin's birth, had just left his ancestral Thuringia to go to work as a copper miner in the county of Mansfeld near the city of Eisleben, where Martin was baptized the morning after his birth and named for the saint of the day. Over the next thirty years his father rose to become part-owner of six copper mines and two metal foundries. Not many successful businessmen come out of the shafts of a mine even now, to say nothing of at the turn of the sixteenth century. Gross-Hans Luder, evidently, was a man who combined a burning ambition with a dogged perseverance. So did his son.[7]

---

[6] I regret having to state so pessimistic a conclusion, with which I expect many good Catholics to disagree, but in all honesty can come to no other. Despite numerous individual conversions, not one Western nation has changed its majority religious affiliation, from Protestant to Catholic or Catholic to Protestant, since the seventeenth century, or come close to doing so.

[7] Henrich Boehmer, *Martin Luther: Road to Reformation* (New York, 1957), pp. 3-6.

Martin was a diligent and talented student, and in 1501 his father decided to send him to the University of Erfurt, then highly regarded, using the money obtained from the remarkable success of his business ventures to finance Martin's education. Luther received his master's degree in 1505 and he and his father decided he should study law. There is nothing to show that he had any thought of a religious vocation at this time. In June 1505 he took a leave of absence to visit his parents' home. He travelled on foot, as was his custom, though it required a journey of several days. On July 2, as he was returning, he was caught outside in a heavy thunderstorm. Lightning struck immediately in front of him, so close that the surge of air knocked him to the ground. He cried out a prayer to St. Anne, and in the same breath, a vow to become a monk.[8]

Luther felt no joy in his vow or its fulfillment. He spoke later only of deep sadness and regret. He consulted friends and advisors, who told him he need not keep a vow taken under such circumstances. He rejected that advice. He had made up his mind, for whatever reason, with the adamant stubbornness that was to mark him all the rest of his life. Just two weeks and one day after the thunderstorm, on July 17, 1505, he joined the Augustinian order at Erfurt.[9]

He advanced rapidly in his new life. In September 1506 he took his final vows; in the fall of 1508 he was sent to the University of Wittenberg in Electoral Saxony to teach moral philosophy; in 1512 he became a doctor of theology who lectured extensively on the Bible, which he had made the focus of his studies as a religious and a theologian. In the course of his earlier studies he had absorbed the philosophical outlook of William of Occam, the nominalist, who divorced faith from reason, and learned to despise the scholastic philosophy of St. Thomas Aquinas and his successors.[10] He had studied the theological works of John Gerson and Cardinal Peter d'Ailly, written at the height of the frustration and desperation in the Church over the Great Western Schism,[11] which tended toward the conciliarist heresy—regarding an ecumenical council as having equal or greater authority than the Pope. He also read and was impressed by some of the sermons of John Hus, though he soon put them aside because Hus had been condemned as a heretic and Luther was then still loyal to the Church.[12]

During his entire life as a religious Luther underwent repeated spiritual struggles, as he often tells us in his later writings. He hated confession and, after he was ordained, never liked to say Mass.[13] His profound sense of personal

---

[8] *Ibid.*, pp. 20-21, 32-34.

[9] *Ibid.*, pp. 34-36.

[10] *Ibid.*, pp. 39, 41, 46; Grisar, *Luther*, I, 38-39, 133-134. With a violence of expression later to become endemic in him, Luther was already calling scholastic philosophers and Aristotle "grubs," "dregs," and "putrid" (Grisar, *op. cit.*, I, 22).

[11] See Volume III, Chapter Eleven of this history.

[12] Grisar, *Luther*, I, 13, 25. For the teaching and actions of John Hus and his followers as precursors of the Protestant revolt, see Volume III, Chapter Twelve of this history.

[13] Luther write to his Augustinian superior Staupitz in May 1518: "The word which I hated most in all the Scriptures was the word penance" (Grisar, *Luther*, I, 296). In a letter

unworthiness made his later doctrine of justification by faith alone a kind of spiritual refuge for him, ending the necessity for grappling with it by assuming God's "imputation" of the divine virtues of Christ to cover over the sinfulness in him which he felt irremediable.[14]   In July 1517, just three months before his public challenge to the Church on indulgences, Luther preached a sermon in Dresden, capital of ducal Saxony, declaring that "the mere acceptance of the merits of Christ insured salvation, and that nobody who possessed this faith need doubt of his salvation." Duke George of Saxony was present for the sermon. The noblest lay leader in Germany during these shattering years, his integrity praised by Catholic and Protestant historians alike, who had been trained in theology and prepared for a Church vocation before the death of his elder brother made him the successor to the dukedom, Duke George—who had probably never met Luther before—took his measure that night. "I would have given a great deal not to have heard this sermon," he said, "which would only make the people presumptuous and mutinous."[15]

Undergirding and permeating all of Luther's other personal qualities, some of them clashing and contrasting, was the one he held in common with all the great history-makers for both good and evil: a stupendous power of will. When Martin Luther fixed on a goal, it seemed that nothing could stop him. Contemporaries noted especially the brilliance of the black eyes deep-set in his beefy face, which could glow with inspiration or burn with anger, dominating and attracting his followers and cowing his adversaries.[16] How terrible was Luther's anger can be seen both in his characteristic violence of expression (of which the second quotation at the introduction of this chapter is one of the most ferocious examples) and in his remarkable ability to dominate an audience, which lends so sharp an edge to the drama of his confrontations with John Eck at Leipzig in 1519 and with Emperor Charles V at Worms in 1521.

On October 31, 1517 Luther's 95 theses, nailed to the door of the Wittenberg palace church, denounced the granting by the Church of indulgences remitting the time and punishment in purgatory due for sins committed by the soul receiving the indulgences, in the specific context of donation of money to the Church. He declared that the indulgences were not recognized by God and that the Church had no "treasury of grace" from which it could dispense them. Luther had told no one of his intention to make this challenge. He sent one copy of the

---

to another Augustinian superior, Johann Lang, on October 26, 1516, he said he avoided saying Mass whenever possible because he felt especially tempted when doing so (*ibid.*, I, 275).

[14] In his lectures on the Epistle to the Romans in 1515 and 1516, Luther said: "The elect are not saved by the cooperation of their free will, but by the Divine decree; not by their merits, but by the unalterable edict from above by means of which they conquer all the difficulties in the way of salvation." (Grisar, *Luther* I, 204)

[15] Johannes Janssen, *History of the German People at the Close of the Middle Ages* (London, 1910), III, 89.

[16] Grisar, *Luther*, I, 279.

theses to Archbishop Albert of Mainz, who had approved the granting of indulgences for contributions to help pay for the building of the new St. Peter's Church in Rome, preached by a Dominican named Tetzel;[17] and another copy to Bishop Hieronymus Scultetus of Brandenburg, ordinary of the University of Wittenberg where Luther taught. The latter took no action, but Archbishop Albert forwarded the 95 theses to Rome in mid-December 1517 with a request that Luther be silenced; but he also called for less publicity and showmanship in the granting of indulgences and a tighter control over the funds collected by this means.[18]

Pope Leo X received Archbishop Albert's letter in January 1518 and responded with a mild request to Gabriele della Volta, Vicar-General of the Augustinians, to have Luther admonished. Della Volta passed on the papal request to Johann Staupitz, Luther's immediate superior in the order, who was a strong supporter of his. It is therefore not surprising that no admonition is recorded, but Luther learned immediately of the Pope's message. He began preparing a written defense of his position on indulgences, while at the same time asking Elector Frederick of Saxony, his sovereign, for protection in general, and specifically for a safe-conduct for travelling to and from the upcoming triennial Augustinian chapters convention at Heidelberg. Frederick replied immediately, giving Luther the safe-conduct and a flattering letter of recommendation, and writing to Staupitz directing him to make sure that Luther was not "carried off or restrained."[19]   At Heidelberg Luther supported—and probably inspired—a resolution denying freedom of the will:

> Free will in man, after Adam's fall, is merely a name and therefore no free will at all, at least as regards the choice of good; for it is a captive, and the servant of sin; not as though it did not exist, but because it is not free except for what is evil.[20]

The early emergence of Luther's concern for and receipt of personal protection from the Elector of Saxony calls for a brief explanation of the complex political situation in Germany at that time, which Luther and his friends skillfully used to thwart the Church and Catholic rulers from ever bringing him to trial before the Church. Germany in the sixteenth century was a patchwork quilt of more than 200 legally sovereign states, some of minute size (like Liechtenstein, their only survivor on the map of Europe today), some almost large enough to be significant powers (notably Brandenburg in the northeast and Bavaria in the

---

[17] The slogan attributed to Tetzel, possibly but not certainly authentic, does regrettably represent the tone of much of the preaching of indulgences in Germany at this time: *Sobald das Geld in Kasten klingt, die Seele aus dem Fegefeuer springt* ("As soon as the coin in the box clinks, the soul out of purgatory's fire springs").

[18] von Pastor, *History of the Popes*, VII, 351-353; Grisar, *Luther*, I, 330-331; Fife, *Revolt of Martin Luther*, pp. 251-256.

[19] Fife, *Revolt of Martin Luther*, pp. 257-258, 264; Grisar, *Luther*, I, 333.

[20] Grisar, *Luther*, I, 318.

southwest), some (notably Salzburg in Austria) the temporal possessions of bishops like the papal states in Rome, and most interlaced with their neighbors by serpentine borders and dotted with enclaves from other sovereignties. Two excellent examples of this political crazy-quilt were the halves of the ancient province of Saxony, Electoral (under Elector Frederick) and ducal (under Duke George), the former a strong sympathizer with Luther, the latter a rock-solid Catholic. If Luther had been on the faculty of the University of Leipzig in Duke George's Saxony rather than on the faculty of the University of Wittenberg in Elector Frederick's Saxony, the whole history of Christendom would probably have been different. Duke George would have turned him over to the Church and to the Emperor on request and he would have been little more than a footnote to history.

One of the main reasons this anarchy of sovereignties had been allowed to continue so long was the presence of the Holy Roman Emperor (to whose title was often added "of the German nation"), who was seen to possess a certain overarching, appellate authority while not governing most of Germany directly. Traditionally the Holy Roman Emperor led Christendom against infidels from without and heretics from within; facing these threats, Germany and Christendom were expected to be united. But if Germany was sundered by heresy, the Emperor had no direct authority under German law to bring into line princes who were heretics or protected heretics.

Some time during the early spring of 1518 Luther had received a letter from his former professor of philosophy at the University of Erfurt, Jodocus Trutfetter, a man whom he deeply respected and who had expected great service to the Church from so able a mind and so strong a personality as Luther. Now Professor Trutfetter solemnly warned his former student against the path he was taking, urging him to turn back before it was too late. On May 9 Luther replied: "To speak plainly, my firm belief is that the reform of the Church is impossible unless the ecclesiastical laws, the papal regulations, scholastic theology, philosophy and logic as they at present exist, are thoroughly uprooted."[21] Such uprooting, he said, had now become his fixed purpose, "a resolution from which neither your authority, although it is certainly of the greatest weight for me, much less that of any others, can turn me aside."[22]

This is one of the most important of the thousands of letters Luther wrote in his long, full lifetime. It reveals that as early as May 1518 he was essentially committed to the destruction of the Church as he knew it, though he had not yet proceeded to total public defiance of all Church authority. It shows his revolutionary temper, his purpose to "uproot" rather than simply to reform, which is the goal of every revolutionary. It provides our first evidence that the upheaval to come was rightly to be called a revolt or a revolution, not a "reformation." It also shows Luther in the act of coldly and deliberately breaking a bond whose

---

[21] *Ibid.*, I, 320.
[22] Fife, *Revolt of Martin Luther*, p. 267.

quality and strength only the dedicated teacher and his former student know: the love and loyalty that emanate from their memories of each other.

Luther wrote this letter just before completing his defense in Latin of his position on indulgences. He sent a copy to the Pope with a cover letter, later printed with it as a preface. In the preface he says that he "cannot recant" from his position on indulgences, yet still insists on his willingness to listen to Leo X "as to the Voice of Christ, who presides in him and speaks through him . . . enliven me, kill me, call me back, confirm me, reject me, just as it pleases you"— despite the fact that in the text itself, sent with this letter, he had flatly and insultingly declared: "I do not care what pleases or displeases the Pope. He is a man like other men. There have been many Popes inclined to errors, vices, and even very strange things."[23]

In mid-June the papal procurator, Mario de Perusco, made a formal charge of heresy against Luther—not for condemning the granting of indulgences for money, which the Church itself, through the Council of Trent, was later also to condemn, but for denying the existence of the treasury of grace and questioning the authority of the Pope. In early July Luther was summoned to appear at Rome for trial within sixty days. He responded with his characteristic defiance, declaring he would not accept excommunication if the Church decreed it for him. On July 25 he reiterated that defiance, along with references to "eternal predestination," in another sermon before Duke George of Saxony and his court. Shouting matches broke out afterward between Luther and professors defending scholastic theology.[24] Undoubtedly the entire academic brawl deepened Duke George's concern about the damage Luther was already doing and the much greater damage he was capable of doing. One wonders if he might have communicated such thoughts to the aging Emperor Maximilian; for on August 5 this light-minded and erratic sovereign, not otherwise known for spiritual discernment,[25] wrote to Pope Leo X saying that Luther's doctrines, "if not strenuously opposed, would imperil the unity of the faith, and private opinion would take the place of traditional dogma" (exactly what was to happen in Protestant Christianity) and "that out of love for the unity of faith he would support any measures the Pope might take against Luther."[26]

On August 23, correctly concluding that Luther had no intention of coming to Rome in response to his summons, Pope Leo X ordered Cardinal St. Tommaso de Vio Gaetani (better known by the Latinized form of his name as Cajetan),

---

[23] *Ibid.*, p. 270; Grisar, *Luther*, I, 335-336. The total contradiction between preface and text was not unusual for Luther, never a systematic thinker. Contradictions abound in his writings, often as here in the same publication.

[24] Von Pastor, *History of the Popes*, VII, 363-366; Janssen, *History of the German People*, III, 96; Fife, *Revolt of Martin Luther*, pp. 275-276.

[25] Though he was a Habsburg, a scion of that family which gave twenty Emperors to Christendom, only one of whom ever fought the Church.

[26] Grisar, *Luther*, I, 340 (first quote); Janssen, *History of the German People*, III, 95 (second quote).

currently his legate to Germany, directing him to declare Luther a notorious heretic and bring him, by arrest if necessary, to Augsburg, where the German Diet (a kind of parliament including both bishops and great noblemen) was meeting. If he did not recant at Augsburg, Cajetan was to send him to Rome for trial. If Luther did not come to Augsburg, the Pope directed, he was to be excommunicated as a heretic and all temporal authorities ordered to assist in apprehending him, on pain of excommunication and interdict. The Pope's strongest weapons were thereby deployed against Luther.[27]

Pope Leo X was not in the best position to use these weapons and gain obedience to his authority in a Germany where vehement anti-clericalism was rampant. In the preceding fifty years the Church at Rome had become deeply corrupt, as every German knew, since their geographical position and close relations with Italy brought them into frequent contact with it, and as the great Catholic papal historian Ludwig von Pastor frankly admits.[28] Several recent Popes, notably Alexander VI Borgia (1492-1503), had given grave scandal by their personal life as well as by conducting so many of their public affairs in the same manner as temporal princes.[29] Leo himself was a member of the ruling Medici family of Florence and, though personally chaste, was famous (or infamous) for his opulent court and entertainments (such as his lavish dinners featuring peacocks' tongues, even though he himself did not eat them) and his often frivolous attitude toward his papal responsibilities, summed up in his comment to his brother Giuliano on his election as Pope: "God has given us the papacy; let us enjoy it."[30] Even the most loyal Catholics did not think of Leo X as a spiritual man. It has always been Church teaching that the authority of any ecclesiastical office is not affected by the personal shortcomings of the man who holds it, but this is not a doctrine easy for men to accept fully, especially in the face of a propagandist of the shattering power of Martin Luther. In fact, the Catholic historian may state without qualification that the course Pope Leo X followed with regard to Luther was remarkably wise, fully canonical, prudent, deliberate, and necessary; St. Pius X or John Paul II could hardly have done better. But as men have known since the fables of Aesop, a poor reputation hinders belief even when a man speaks the simple truth.

Immediately on receiving his difficult instructions, Cardinal Cajetan contacted Elector Frederick, Luther's sovereign and protector, urging him not to "disgrace the good name of his ancestors" by supporting a heretic. Frederick responded that Luther had not yet been proved a heretic to his satisfaction; a

---

[27] Fife, *Revolt of Martin Luther*, p. 283; von Pastor, *History of the Popes*, VII, 369; Grisar, *Luther*, I, 340.

[28] Von Pastor, *History of the Popes*, VIII, 122-125.

[29] Julius II, Leo X's immediate predecessor, was a notable example of the latter. See Volume III, Chapters Fifteen and Sixteen of this history.

[30] Christopher Hibbert, *The House of Medici; its Rise and Fall* (New York, 1980), p. 218.

Church declaration alone was not enough for him. He refused to arrest Luther and send him to Rome.[31]

On October 12 Luther and the Cardinal met. Cajetan specifically directed Luther to recant two propositions: (1) that the Church does not hold a treasury of graces from Christ and the saints from which to dispense indulgences; (2) that the sacraments of the Church are efficacious only by faith, not by their own operation. In explaining why these propositions were heretical, Cajetan, a great authority on St. Thomas Aquinas, relied on the Angelic Doctor, whom Luther despised, for much of his argumentation. Luther scornfully rejected it, saying he must be convinced by Scripture, the Fathers, papal definitions, or sound reason. Cajetan promptly cited the bull *Unigenitus* by Pope Clement VI affirming the doctrine of the treasury of graces. Luther as promptly condemned *Unigenitus*, withdrew his stated willingness to accept papal definitions, and on October 14 presented a written defense of his position based solely on Scripture, though accompanying it with a statement that he would submit if Pope Leo X pronounced him in error (he later stated that his friends persuaded him against his will to insert this concession). Cajetan evidently did not believe it, and was so incensed by Luther's provocative manner and diatribes against St. Thomas Aquinas, to whom he was devoted, that most uncharacteristically he began shouting at him. Luther replied even more loudly (the man did not live who could outshout Martin Luther) and finally Cajetan dismissed him with: "Go, and do not return unless you are ready to recant!"[32]

Shocked by the violence of this encounter, Luther's Augustinian superior Staupitz urged him to apologize to Cajetan, and for once in his life Luther actually did apologize. He wrote to Cajetan that he had "spoken too violently and disrespectfully against the Pope, for which he asked pardon and promised amendment." He said he would keep silent on indulgences until the Pope gave his decision, if his adversaries did likewise (he knew how unlikely this was), but refused to retract anything he had said, and went out of his way to repeat his contempt for the intellectual authority of St. Thomas Aquinas. Cajetan, probably believing the whole letter insincere, did not reply. On October 25 Cajetan again urged Elector Frederick to send Luther to Rome or at least banish him from Wittenberg. Frederick sent the letter to Luther, who replied warning that action against him would lead to the destruction of the University of Wittenberg, of which Frederick was inordinately proud. He added that his enemies wanted to make Frederick play Pilate, by implication putting himself in the place of Christ.[33]

On November 9 the Pope sent Cajetan a bull on the doctrine of indulgences, declaring that by the power of the keys given to St. Peter the Pope could remit

---

[31] Von Pastor, *History of the Popes*, VII, 371-372; Fife, *Revolt of Martin Luther*, pp. 284-285.

[32] Fife, *Revolt of Martin Luther*, pp. 292-295, quote on 295; Von Pastor, *History of the Popes* VII, 374; Grisar, *Luther*, I, 357.

[33] Von Pastor, *History of the Popes*, VII, 376-378; Fife, *Revolt of Martin Luther*, pp. 295-298.

both the guilt and the punishment due for sins, and draw on the treasury of the merits of Christ and His saints to grant remission of temporal punishment for the dead, and that all must teach this under pain of excommunication. The document did not mention Luther's name, but did refer in general to Germans who had been disseminating false doctrine about indulgences. Luther replied by the end of the month with a flat rejection of the authority of this document, giving the lie to all that he had said to Cardinal Cajetan and others promising to accept the Pope's decision on this issue. He appealed from that decision to a future general council, though such appeals had been forbidden by canon law since the conciliarist heresy of the previous century. Elector Frederick had forbidden Luther to publish this reply, of whose contents he had evidently learned before its publication, but Luther defied his sovereign as he defied the Pope. For once Frederick wavered in his support of Luther, and suggested that he would prefer for him to leave Saxony, but was not ordering him out. Luther did not go. On December 8 Frederick wrote to Cajetan that no one in his lands had found Luther's teaching on indulgences heretical. Five days later Cardinal Cajetan published the papal bull of November 9 supporting indulgences. It gained little support in Germany because of the great unpopularity of the fund-raising campaigns there which had used indulgences. Elector Frederick was emboldened to write to Cajetan December 18 saying again that he was not convinced that Luther was truly a heretic.[34]

In the midst of this, a private letter December 11 from Luther to an Augustinian friend, Wenceslaus Link, again revealed, like his letter in May to Professor Trutfetter, that he knew where he was going and was pushing steadily and rapidly along the way:

> The cause, to my thinking, has not yet commenced in earnest and much less can these gentlemen from Rome look to see the end. I shall send my little works to you so that you may see if I am right in surmising that the real Antichrist whom Paul describes (2 Thess ii 3ff) rules at the Roman Court. I think I can prove that today he is worse than the Turks.[35]

Early in that same month of December 1518, Luther had joined one of his earliest and most persistent critics, the Dominican John Eck, in asking Duke George of Saxony to approve a disputation at the University of Leipzig in ducal Saxony on indulgences, penance, and freedom of the will between Eck and Andreas Rudolph Bodenstein, known as Carlstadt, a follower and fellow professor of Luther at Wittenberg. At this point in his life Luther, despite his growing rebellion against the Pope, had not yet lost all respect for everyone who disagreed with him (as he was soon to do). He still respected Eck, as most scholars in Germany did. Eck's baptismal name was Johann Maier, but for his

---

[34] Fife, *Revolt of Martin Luther*, pp. 299-302, 306-307; von Pastor, *History of the Popes*, VII, 379-380, 387; Grisar, *Luther*, I, 359.

[35] Grisar, *Luther*, I, 359.

scholarly work he used the name of his town (like his opponent Carlstadt). Eck
was just a year younger than Luther. He was unquestionably a genius; he entered
Heidelberg University at the age of twelve and received his master's degree from
the University of Tübingen at the age of fifteen. He was ordained at 22, with a
papal dispensation waiving the age requirement, and became a Doctor of
Theology at 24, two years before Luther. Appointed professor of theology at the
University of Ingolstadt in Bavaria, within two years he was its vice-chancellor,
along with acting as pastor of a parish and canon at the cathedral at Eichstätt. A
geographer and philosopher as well as a theologian, Eck's scope of knowledge,
mastery of language, and incisive, analytical mind made him probably the best
debater in Germany.[36] His style in controversial writing was crisp and hard-
hitting but rarely disfigured by the personal attacks or obscenity all too
characteristic of polemic in that age. Eck had been one of the first to write
against Luther on the issue of indulgences, identifying immediately the
similarities in Luther's arguments with those of John Hus. Eck was a man of
compassion as well as Catholic doctrinal conviction, and no man of compassion
can believe in absolute predestination. In answer to Carlstadt he had written:
"God cannot withhold grace from him who does the best he can."[37] Not "does
not"; *cannot.* God's own nature makes it impossible for Him to impose
damnation on any soul.

On December 29, 1518 Eck published twelve theses he was prepared to
defend at Leipzig. They specifically criticized Luther's doctrine on indulgences,
penance, and purgatory, though without attacking or even mentioning Luther by
name. His twelfth thesis firmly proclaimed the Pope's supreme authority in the
Church as successor of Peter and Vicar of Christ, and denied that his authority
derived from any grant to Pope Sylvester I by Emperor Constantine such as the
alleged "Donation of Constantine," which had recently been proved a forgery.[38]

Luther would not find this opponent easy to overawe, insult, stare down or
shout down. Indeed, by the end of 1518 John Eck seems to have come to believe
that the mission for which God had given him such great intellectual talent
combined with so strong a faith was to demonstrate clearly at its beginning the
true nature of the heresy that was to cleave Christendom. He spent most of the
rest of his life trying, and nearly every Catholic who understands what he did
thinks he succeeded. But unfortunately for mankind, such issues are not usually
decided by rational argument, however cogent.

Duke George of Saxony, whose discernment and judgment were the best
among the lay sovereigns in Germany, dismissed with scorn the timorous doubts
of Bishop Adolf of Merseburg, Chancellor of the University of Leipzig, who was
afraid of all the commotion that would accompany the disputation. If we cannot
or dare not defend our faith in public, Duke George in effect told the Bishop, we
are not worthy of it. In February 1519 Luther, understanding that Eck's twelve

---

[36] *The Catholic Encyclopedia* (New York, 1909), V, 271-272.
[37] Fife, *Revolt of Martin Luther*, pp. 335-337, quote on 337.
[38] *Ibid.*, p. 339.

theses were directed much more against his teaching than Carlstadt's, asked to join the disputation, while writing insultingly to Eck that he no longer regarded him as a friend. The faculty senate at the University of Leipzig was horrified at the thought of Luther's participation in the disputation, and petitioned Duke George not to allow him to come. Totally undeterred by Luther's new personal hostility, Eck said he wanted very much to debate him. At the end of April Carlstadt published 17 theses against Eck, calling him a liar and a "miserable stentorian howler." On May 23 Duke George consented to Luther's participation in the disputation at Leipzig since Eck had asked for it.[39]

On June 22 Luther published a pamphlet against Papal supremacy in the Church in support of a thesis he was prepared to defend against Eck. In it he said that "the primacy of the Pope was set up to check heretics and schismatics, but the decrees and proofs which have been used to support it lack any foundation in Scripture." To the obvious citation of Matthew 16:18-19 he responded with the claim that faith, not Peter, was the rock upon which the Church was built—an exegesis so absurd, especially in view of the fact that Simon was at that moment given the name Peter, meaning "rock," which had never before been used as a personal name, that not even today's highly permissive Scripture scholars can defend it.[40]

Two days later several wagonloads of Lutherans arrived at Leipzig, including Luther, Carlstadt, the rector of the University of Wittenberg, the able young Greek professor Philip Melanchthon, Luther's friend Johann Lang, and others, with 200 armed students as a bodyguard. In front of St. Paul's Church the wagon containing Carlstadt tipped over, dumping him out on the ground. Bishop Adolf of Merseburg had posted a proclamation prohibiting the disputation from taking place; Duke George nevertheless directed it to proceed. At a meeting chaired by Duke George's chancellor, ground rules for the disputation were drawn up. Hieronymus Emser, who had entertained Luther at his home in Dresden the year before and urged him to moderate his challenge to the Church, now repeated his admonitions, to which Luther angrily responded with strange words: "The devil take it! The affair was not begun on God's account, neither shall it end on God's account!" Emser believed this reply deeply significant, though he was not sure just what it meant, nor has any later historian or commentator been sure.[41] To this writer it suggests at least that Luther did not feel close to God at this critical moment in his life and career.

In the morning of June 27 the faculty of the University of Leipzig marched in procession to St. Thomas' Church, where Mass was sung with a 12-voice choir, and a great procession with banners and trumpets went from the church to the hall of Duke George's ancient castle of Pleissenburg, hung with splendid tapestries and protected by a substantial guard. Eck's desk was decorated with a tapestry

---

[39] *Ibid.*, pp. 340-343, 346.

[40] *Ibid.*, pp. 346-348.

[41] *Ibid.*, pp. 350-351, 403. Luther's words in the original German were *Die sach ist umb Gots willen nith angefangen, sol ouch umb Gotes willen nith auf hören.*

showing St. George slaying the dragon, while Carlstadt's and Luther's desks had tapestries showing St. Martin, on whose feast day Luther was born. Professor Peter Mosellanus gave an introductory speech recalling other famous theological debates in the Church's history such as St. Paul's with St. Peter and St. Jerome's with St. Augustine, and urged the disputants to remember that all Christendom was watching and listening. The musicians played "Come, Holy Ghost" three times. Then, after a break for dinner, the debate itself began.[42]

Eck spoke first. A tall and imposing man with a strong gravelly voice, at the summit of his powers at age 33, full of energy, clear and composed, with an immense stock of authorities and quotations at his fingertips, he soon made it evident that Carlstadt, short and sallow with a weak and wavering voice and a large stack of books through which he had to leaf before answering his opponent, was not nearly a match for him. Carlstadt denied that the human will had any part in salvation; in confutation Eck cited St. Bernard of Clairvaux and other Fathers of the Church, and the common sense of mankind. After four days most of the spectators saw Eck as prevailing. On June 29 Luther spoke, not as part of the disputation but in a sermon on the feast of Sts. Peter and Paul, using it as an occasion for denying papal primacy, interpreting "the gift of the keys of Peter as conferring no personal power or privilege but as an office to administer the Church." Luther's disputation with Eck began on the afternoon of July 4. A much shorter and then less bulky man than Eck, he was equally articulate, with an equally strong voice, a cheerful and confident manner, dominating his audience with his dark "falcon eyes," contemptuous and insolent on the attack, yet showing scholarship in Scripture to match Eck's. They began immediately debating Luther's view of papal primacy.[43]

Drawing on his encyclopedic knowledge, Eck could see very clearly that many of the doctrines Luther was now propounding were virtually identical with those taught by the condemned heretics John Wyclif and John Hus in the fourteenth and fifteenth centuries. He also knew there was no better place to expose this link than the University of Leipzig, founded by Bohemian Germans who had fled for their lives from the Hussites in the days of One-Eyed John,[44] where people still remembered Czech raids during the Hussite wars. Nor was it a "red herring," an intellectually illegitimate issue; the consequences of the heresy of Hus were a vivid reminder of the consequences of permitting any similar heresy to take root, as Luther's was to do on a scale Hus never dreamed of. So, the next morning, Eck charged Luther with reviving the heresies of Wyclif and Hus, and asked if he thought them to have been justly condemned. Luther does not seem to have yet realized the virtual identity of his views with theirs, and well knew the opprobrium with which they were remembered; he denied any link, but would not retreat from his positions. By afternoon Luther realized Eck had

---

[42] *Ibid.*, pp. 352-354; Grisar, *Luther*, I, 362-363.

[43] Fife, *Revolt of Martin Luther*, pp. 354-360; Grisar, *Luther*, I, 363.

[44] The Oliver Cromwell of the Hussite wars. See Volume III, Chapter Twelve of this history.

trapped him, and felt obliged to say that some of the Hussite propositions condemned at the Council of Constance "are plainly very Christian and evangelical, which it is not possible for the Church to condemn."[45]

From the audience Duke George, shaking his head and planting his hands on his hips, roared out: "A plague on it!"[46] Eck cried in a mighty voice that Luther was defending Hus and had spoken against the Council of Constance, which had reunited the Church and Christendom and was revered by almost every Catholic. Luther shouted at equal volume: "I protest before you all and publicly that the excellent doctor in speaking thus about me is an impudent liar!"[47] The next day Luther renewed his protest against being charged as a heretic, denied that the Council of Constance had condemned Hus' denial of the Roman primacy, and declared that he was not calling for disobedience to the Pope, only arguing that the papacy was not established by Christ and that Matthew 16:18-19 did not prove it. Eck replied devastatingly that the Council of Constance had specifically declared anyone denying the Catholic understanding of Matthew 16:18-19 to be a heretic. Whether he had not known that, or forgotten it in the heat of the debate, Luther now had no choice but to deny the authority of the Council of Constance as confirmed by the Pope, leaving no final authority in the Church at all. His revolutionary purpose stood revealed.[48]

John Eck had made his point and proved his case. He drew himself up to his full height, looked straight into Luther's black "falcon eyes," and said: "I will tell you, honored father, if you say that a council, properly convoked, can err and has erred, you are for me a heathen and a publican."[49]

After that, there was really little more to be said.

When the disputation was finally over, Duke George called Luther in to confer with him alone. He warned him that the Bohemian heretics were becoming his followers and that he was bringing "confusion to many hearts." He probably urged him to desist from his assault on the Church before it was too late.[50]

But Eck had now taken Luther's full measure, and knew it was already too late for reconciliation. There remained only the defense of Christendom. On July 22, a week after the disputation ended, he wrote to Elector Frederick of Saxony, summarizing what had been said at Leipzig, telling him that Luther had described many of Hus' articles "Christian and evangelical" and denied papal primacy, and reminding him "of his sacred obligation to Christ, to Christian faith, and to his own land" to protect the Faith against Luther and his errors, by at least burning

---

[45] Fife, *Revolt of Martin Luther*, p. 361.
[46] Grisar, *Luther*, I, 364.
[47] Fife, *Revolt of Martin Luther*, p. 362.
[48] *Ibid.*, pp. 362-363.
[49] *Ibid.*, p. 363.
[50] *Ibid.*, p. 366.

Luther's books which spread them. Elector Frederick did no more than pass the letter on to Luther for reply.[51]

The lines were being drawn for the mighty struggle to preserve the unity of Christendom, which was to continue for more than a hundred years.

In the first years of that struggle an essential role was marked out for the very young man in line to become the temporal head of Christendom, the Holy Roman Emperor. When Luther tacked his theses on the Wittenberg church door this young man was only seventeen years old and had just inherited the kingdom of Spain, which by the Catholic dedication and moral integrity of Queen Isabel, the political genius of King Ferdinand, and the discoveries of Christopher Columbus had become the greatest power in the world. His name was Charles; he was the son of Ferdinand and Isabel's daughter Juana and of Emperor Maximilian's only son Philip. Now Philip was dead and Juana was mad and Charles was heir apparent to his grandfather's office, though to attain it he must still secure the votes of the seven electors designated by the Golden Bull of Emperor Charles IV in 1355. When young Charles was born and baptized at Ghent in Flanders, his grandmother Queen Isabel, who never saw him, said with a premonition of his destiny: "The lot falls on Mathias."[52]

When Charles' father died in Spain when he was six, Emperor Maximilian brought Charles' Aunt Margaret from Savoy to act as regent of the Low Countries for the little prince. Margaret, one of the soundest and most refreshing personalities in the whole history of European royalty, had been married for just six months to Crown Prince Juan of Spain before his tragic death at the age of 18, then for just three years to Duke Philibert of Savoy before he too died suddenly, in his 25th year. Margaret had loved both her husbands passionately. But she was so stable that she survived both tragedies whole and apparently unchanged—except that she refused to consider another marriage, ever again. She was small and captivating, with bright golden hair, contrasting light brown eyes, and a sparkling, infectious smile. She did not look at all like a statesman (stateswoman?) but she was, remarkably combining prudence, persistence, and resilience. She was a Habsburg, an Emperor's daughter, Catholic to the marrow of her bones.[53] When she first embraced her seven-year-old nephew—a quiet, reserved, unprepossessing boy with narrow pinched features, a long adenoidal

---

[51] *Ibid.*, pp. 372-374.

[52] Ramon Menéndez Pidal, ed., *Historia de España*, Volume XX ("La España del Emperador Carlos V," by Manuel Fernández Alvarez), p. 42.

[53] Karl Brandi, *The Emperor Charles V* (Atlantic Highlands NJ, 1965), pp. 44-47. There is no adequate scholarly biography of Margaret in English. The best we have is Jane de Iongh, *Margaret of Austria, Regent of the Netherlands* (New York, 1953), which at least gives a vivid impression of her personality. Her resilience is memorably shown by a letter she wrote to her father the Emperor at a particularly difficult moment in 1511, saying she did not know which way to turn and wished she had never been born—whereupon she immediately crossed the despairing sentence out (Brandi, *op. cit.*, p. 54).

nose, and a jutting pendulous jaw, who could not remember his mad mother—she knew it was her responsibility to be his second mother. (She had stood as godmother at his baptism, which made that responsibility all the clearer, though she had never had any children of her own, except a daughter by Juan whom she miscarried.) What she could not know—for Martin Luther had just completed his novitiate, and nobody outside of Erfurt and Eisleben had ever heard of him—was that in this boy, the Emperor-to-be who would challenge Luther face to face, she held in her hands the future of Christendom.

Abandoned royal children are prey for the prowlers in the jungles of power. European history is shadowed by the tales of their terror. Ivan the Terrible, Peter the Great, James VI of Scotland and I of England, Louis XVII of France are only some of the most striking examples. Princess Margaret Habsburg would preserve young Charles from that terror, and give him all the love that fate had otherwise denied her and him. Her love, like that of every good mother, would give the future Emperor a reason to live and a reason to die, beyond himself. And whatever Margaret might lack in preparing his mind to heed the Catholic dictates of his heart and soul, his teacher, Adrian Dedel of Utrecht, engaged when the prince was eleven, would provide. Dean of the University of Louvain (a position to which Margaret had promoted him from parish priest),[54] a man of saintly humility, unshakable faith, and total integrity, he was to be Leo X's successor in a brief, tragic pontificate. He was Prince Charles' second father. No man could have had a better one.

Though we have few intimate glimpses into their relationship, there can be little doubt that Margaret Habsburg and Adrian of Utrecht gave young Charles much that he had to have in order to stand virtually alone for more than thirty years against a tide of history and bring Catholic Christendom through it.[55]

In January 1515, at the strong request of the Estates-General of the Low Countries, supported by a large subsidy and encouraged by Prime Minister William de Croy, lord of Chièvres, Emperor Maximilian agreed to let Charles be designated ruler of the Low Countries as an adult, though he had not yet reached his fifteenth birthday. This disreputable and irresponsible action was taken by the Emperor behind his daughter's back and before she knew about it. She knew that Charles was not yet old enough to rule and that Chièvres' motive was to feather his own nest. How Charles felt about it we do not know, but we know what he did: he studied every book and state paper he could get his hands on that showed promise of explaining what was going on in his government and in the world, so that he would be able sooner to understand the discussions and actions at his court. In the summer of 1515 Adrian of Utrecht was sent to Spain to prepare for Charles' succession there, since his grandfather Ferdinand was in failing health.[56] Since Adrian was not the type of man to recommend himself to Chièvres, we may well conclude that Charles himself directed that appointment.

---

[54] Menéndez Pidal, *Historia de España*, XX, 47.

[55] Brandi, *Charles V*, p. 47.

[56] *Ibid.*, pp. 54-55, 59-60; Menéndez Pidal, *Historia de España*, XX, 48-49, 51.

The news of Ferdinand's death came to the court at Brussels in February 1516, three weeks before Charles' sixteenth birthday. After hesitating until almost the last moment, since he favored his namesake, Charles' younger brother, who had been born and grown up in Spain, Ferdinand had named Charles his heir. Perhaps at the suggestion of Margaret, to give him more time to grow up, Charles did not leave Flanders, the only home he had ever known, until September 1517, a year and a half later. Somehow his gorgeously accoutered ships lost their way off the north coast of Spain, landing not at the commodious Castilian port of Santander but at a little cove on the coast of Asturias on which perched the rustic fishing village of Tazones, whose people had no idea what the foreign flotilla was and flew to arms against invasion. There were neither horses, mules, nor wagons to be had in any quantity on this rock-bound coast; Charles and his party had to wait a week for them and still did not have enough. Forlornly they plodded through the precipitous terrain where Pelayo had stood against the Muslim world-empire eight hundred years before. Charles, who could not speak a word of Spanish and was therefore totally dependent on his Flemish entourage—most of whose members did not speak the language either—fell ill and had to stop on the way to recover. It was November before he reached Tordesillas, where Ferdinand had shut up Charles' mother Juana in its frowning castle when her insanity had become evident to everyone in Spain.[57]

Juana feared the day and the light. She lived by choice in dirt and squalor, clinging to her only contact with reality, her ten-year-old daughter whom she had never allowed to be separated from her. Charles entered the dark room where his mother crouched, with feelings which may barely be imagined. When one of his party brought a light, he waved it away. Only Chièvres was with him. Volubly he assured Juana that her son would govern well in her name. If she still remembered the French she had learned at her husband's court, she understood him, but said no word.[58]

Four days later the great Cardinal Cisneros, who had held the country together for Charles during the year and a half Spain had waited for him, died at the age of 81. Charles, who knew little of Cisneros, had not planned to continue him as prime minister at his advanced age, but contrary to later hostile reports had not refused to see him or thank him for his services; after he had recovered from his maritime misadventures and his illness on the journey from the coast, he had simply and understandably given priority to seeing his mother and assuring himself with his own eyes that she was unfit to govern, before he took the crown of Spain. But then, yielding to Chièvres, whom he had just made his prime minister, he nominated Guillaume de Croy, Chièvres' boy nephew, to succeed Cisneros as Archbishop of Toledo and primate of Spain, to the fury of the Spaniards who had much loved and deeply respected the man who had reformed

---

[57] Roger B. Merriman, *The Rise of the Spanish Empire in the Old World and the New* (New York, 1918), III, 27-29; Menéndez Pidal, *Historia de España*, XX, 89, 140-142.

[58] Merriman, *Rise of the Spanish Empire*, III, 29-30; Brandi, *Charles V*, p. 81; Menéndez Pidal, *Historia de España*, XX, 143-144.

the Church of Spain so completely that Protestantism could never gain a foothold there.[59]

At the meeting of the Cortes (parliament) of Castile at Valladolid in January 1518, outspoken Juan Zumel of Burgos vigorously protested the presence and power of the foreigners around Charles, urged that no foreigner be allowed to sit in the Cortes, and stood firm against threats by Chièvres to execute him or confiscate his property. Many petitions supported Zumel. Charles refused to pledge not to appoint foreigners to office, but did promise to choose only Spaniards as attendants in his royal household. In the end the Cortes nevertheless voted him the considerable sum of 600,000 ducats, and on February 7 he was formally crowned King of Castile. In May he made solemn entry into Zaragoza, capital of Aragon, where he swore to uphold Aragon's local rights and was confirmed its king.[60]

Just before his departure from Valladolid to go to Aragon, Charles heeded a request from Juan de Aranda, a member of the *Casa de Contratación* in Sevilla which handled Spain's developing colonies in the New World, to give audience to a Portuguese navigator named Ferdinand Magellan. He had sailed with the great Afonso de Albuquerque[61] to Malacca at the eastern gateway to the Pacific from the Indian Ocean, and continued with his close friend Francisco Serrano all the way across Indonesia to the Spice Islands of Ternate and Tidore, almost halfway around the world east from Portugal. Magellan had none of the arts of the courtier. Short, broad, dark-complexioned, glowering, with thick unattractive features, 37 years old, he was a man of few and blunt words. But after the death of Christopher Columbus he was the best seaman on the planet. Scornfully dismissed from Portuguese service by King Manuel the Fortunate, who personally disliked him, he was now offering himself to Spain for a projected voyage to fulfill Columbus' dream of reaching the East by sailing west.[62] Magellan brought out "a well-painted globe showing the entire world, and thereon traced the course he proposed to take, save that the Strait [in southern South America] was purposely left blank."[63] Magellan said he left it blank so that nobody could get there before him; actually he did not know where the strait was, but still believed it must be there. The Treaty of Tordesillas had divided the world outside Europe into Spanish and Portuguese spheres, by a line of demarcation running through

---

[59] Merriman, *Rise of the Spanish Empire*, III, 30; Brandi, *Charles V*, p. 81; Menéndez Pidal, *Historia de España*, XX, 77; H. L. Seaver, *The Great Revolt in Castile; a Study of the Comunero Movement of 1520-21* (New York, 1928, 1966), pp. 32-33.

[60] Merriman, *Rise of the Spanish Empire*, III, 33-34, 37; Seaver, *Great Revolt in Castile*, pp. 38-41; Brandi, *Charles V*, p. 87.

[61] See Volume III, Chapter Sixteen of this history.

[62] Samuel Eliot Morison, *The European Discovery of America; the Southern Voyages, 1492-1616* (New York, 1974), pp. 316-319, 333, 336. See also Volume III, Chapter Sixteen of this history.

[63] *Ibid.*, p. 319, quoting Bartolomé de las Casas, an eyewitness, who also describes Magellan's unimpressive personal appearance.

the middle of the Atlantic Ocean and cutting off the bulge of Brazil, the Portuguese sphere being east of the line and the Spanish west. But Magellan, here supported by his partner, cosmographer Ruy Faleiro, claimed that if the demarcation line was extended around the world, the Spice Islands would fall on the Spanish side. This was not true, and even if it had been no one then could have determined it, because no accurate means of measuring longitude was developed for more than two hundred years. But in exploration and discovery, possession is nine points of the law. Francisco Serrano was still in the Spice Islands. If Magellan's expedition could reach him there by sailing west, Spain could tap their legendary wealth.

The bold venture caught Charles' imagination. On March 28 he issued a document giving his sponsorship to the expedition, committing himself to providing for Magellan a fleet of five ships with about 250 officers and men. It took well over a year to prepare it, the inevitable delays that had plagued Columbus and da Gama compounded by Portuguese subversion, Spanish distrust of the foreigner Magellan, and the mental breakdown of Ruy Faleiro. On September 20, 1519 it set sail at last from San Lúcar de Barrameda at the mouth of the Guadalquivir River below Sevilla in the south of Spain.[64] Three years later, one ship and 21 men were to return—from the other direction, and without Magellan—to complete the first voyage around the world.

By August 1518 Holy Roman Emperor Maximilian, though not yet sixty, was beginning to feel intimations of mortality; he was to die just five months later. Habsburgs had held the imperial office for the past three generations, but there was no guarantee of hereditary succession; votes had to be obtained from the majority of the seven electors designated by the Golden Bull of 1355. These were the Archbishops of Mainz, Cologne, and Trier; the Electors of Saxony, Brandenburg, and the Palatinate; and the King of Bohemia. Emperor Maximilian bribed five of them to vote for his grandson, all but the francophile Archbishop of Trier and Elector Frederick of Saxony. The young and ambitious king of France, Francis I, was conducting a desultory campaign for the imperial office himself, though without much expectation of success since the electors were all German; on November 26 he told the papal legate in France that he would give up his candidacy and support Frederick if the Elector would make a serious attempt to gain the office.[65]

Emperor Maximilian died on January 12, 1519. When the news of his death reached Rome, Pope Leo X took an action which starkly reveals how deeply the Renaissance Popes had sunk into the swamp of political intrigues at the expense of the reputation and the long-range good of the Church. He directed his saintly legate in Germany, Cardinal Cajetan, just three months after his bruising

---

[64] *Ibid.*, pp. 337-350.
[65] R. J. Knecht, *Francis I* (New York, 1982), pp. 72-73; von Pastor, *History of the Popes*, VII, 262, 266-267; Fife, *Revolt of Martin Luther*, p. 285n. Knecht erroneously identifies the Elector of Saxony as the Duke of Saxony.

encounter with Luther, to oppose Charles as Emperor and support the candidacy of Elector Frederick of Saxony, Elector Joachim of Brandenburg, or King Sigismund I of Poland. The reason for this appears to have been the long-standing principle of papal foreign policy that the Holy Roman Emperor, whose jurisdiction included much of northern Italy, should not also rule the kingdom of Naples in the south of Italy, which for some fifty years had been an appendage of the Spanish crown. Reasonable as this policy had been in other circumstances, for the Pope now to favor Luther's protector Frederick of Saxony over the uncompromisingly Catholic Charles was folly. A few days later the Pope concluded that his alternative candidates could not win, that only Francis I might be able to overcome the Habsburg influence. He told his legate in France to promise Francis his full support, while repeating that he favored the election of anyone other than Charles. Meanwhile the Pope, in his capacity as temporal lord of the Papal States, had simultaneously negotiated treaties of alliance with both monarchs.[66]

Early in March the Pope authorized Francis I to promise the Archbishops of Cologne and Trier cardinal's hats if they would vote for him as Emperor, and himself promised to make the Archbishop of Mainz permanent papal legate in Germany if he voted for Francis. When pressure was added to these blandishments in early April the bishops backed away from the Pope, and by mid-April Leo realized that Charles' election could not be prevented. German national feeling was aroused against papal and French interference in the imperial election, and support for Charles at all levels in Germany was rapidly growing. After a last flurry of messages to Elector Frederick urging him to become a candidate, Luther or no Luther, which received no response, and King Francis I's formal withdrawal of his candidacy, the contest was over. On June 29, at Frankfurt, at the very moment the disputation at Leipzig of Eck with Carlstadt and Luther was underway, 19-year-old King Charles was elected Holy Roman Emperor at Frankfurt with the support of all the electors but Joachim of Brandenburg and the reluctant approval of Pope Leo X.[67]

By such devious and unworthy means was the greatest Holy Roman Emperor since Charlemagne made the guardian of a Christendom about to be assaulted as never before both from within and without.

On Good Friday, April 22, 1519, a prophecy was fulfilled half a world west of Europe, at a place on the coast of Mexico which was to be named Veracruz, the True Cross. Its fulfillment began one of the strangest and most gripping dramas in all history, as a Christian army in King Charles' service marched into an empire ruled by Satan and freed its people from the demonic grasp.

---

[66] Von Pastor, *History of the Popes*, VII, 270, 272-275.

[67] *Ibid.*, VII, 278-279, 284, 286; Brandi, *Charles V*, pp. 109-112; Knecht, *Francis I*, pp. 75-76; Fife, *Revolt of Martin Luther*, pp. 323-324; Menéndez Pidal, *Historia de España*, XX, 176.

There were about fifteen million people in the empire of the Mexica (who came much later to be known to historical writers as the Aztecs), with their capital at an island city with a population of 250,000 or more: Tenochtitlán, Cactus Rock, where salt Lake Texcoco and fresh Lake Chalco joined. Every Aztec city and large town had a central square, from which a pyramidal temple rose, and four gates opening upon four roads approaching the town in straight lines extending at least five miles, each ending at one side of the temple pyramid. On each side of the temple pyramid was a steep stairway to its top. Month after month, year after year, in temple after temple, the sacrificial victims came down the roads to the steps, climbed the steps to the platform at the top, and there were bent backwards over large convex slabs of polished stone by a hook around the neck wielded by a priest with head and arms stained black, never-cut black hair all caked and matted with dried blood, and once-white garments soaked and stained with innumerable gouts of crimson. An immense knife with a blade of midnight black volcanic glass rose and fell, cutting the victim open. His heart was torn out while still beating and held up for all to see, while his ravaged body was kicked over the edge of the temple platform where it bounced and slithered in obscene contortions down the steps to the bottom a hundred feet below. Later the limbs of the body were eaten.[68]

Many primitive peoples have practiced occasional human sacrifice and some have practiced cannibalism. None has ever practiced them on a scale remotely approaching that of the Aztecs.[69] The law of their empire required a thousand human sacrifices every year in every town with a temple, and there were 371 subject towns in the Aztec empire, though not all of them had temples. The total number of sacrifices was at least 50,000 a year, probably much more.[70] In 1487, when an immense new pyramid-temple of Huitzilopochtli was dedicated in Cactus Rock (later Mexico City), more than *eighty thousand* people were sacrificed in four days and four nights, at fifteen seconds per man. The two chief gods of the Aztec pantheon, to which most of the sacrifices were made, were Huitzilopochtli, the Hummingbird Wizard, called Lover of Hearts and Drinker of Blood, and Tezcatlipoca, the Lord of the Dark, the Smoking Mirror, god of phantoms and monsters, demiurge of creation, "He Who Is at the Shoulder" as the tempter. An almost universal symbol in Mexican religion was the serpent. Sacrifices were heralded by the prolonged beating of an immense drum made of the skins of huge snakes, which could be heard two leagues away. Nowhere else

[68] R. C. Padden, *The Hummingbird and the Hawk* (New York, 1970), pp. 24-25, 32-34, 72-73, 99; T. R. Fehrenbach, *Fire and Blood; a History of Mexico* (New York, 1973), pp. 79-80, 83, 96; Warren H. Carroll, *Our Lady of Guadalupe and the Conquest of Darkness* (Front Royal VA, 1983), p. 8.

[69] Maurice Collis, *Cortés and Montezuma* (New York, 1954), pp. 51-52.

[70] *Ibid.*, p. 49; Padden, *Hummingbird and Hawk*, pp. 34, 96; Fehrenbach, *Fire and Blood*, p. 80.

in history has Satan so formalized and institutionalized his worship with so many of his own actual titles and symbols.[71]

Five hundred years before the mass sacrifice of 1487, a priest named Ce Acatl Topiltzin, who served the god Quetzalcoatl, had been forced out of central Mexico because he opposed human sacrifice. He had sailed across to the Yucatán peninsula to live among the Mayas there. There was a prophecy, attributed to Ce Acatl Topiltzin himself, that he would return from the eastern sea to reclaim what had been his and to resume the leadership of his people and their descendants, and abolish human sacrifice. It dated his return, in the extraordinarily accurate Mayan-Mexican calendar, to his name year, 1-Reed, which recurred only once ever 52 years, and his name day, 9-Wind. In that calendar, the year 1519 of the Christian era was a 1-Reed year, and Good Friday of 1519 was the 9-Wind day.[72]

On that day a band of about 500 Spaniards, carried on eleven ships, landed at Veracruz. They had been recruited in Cuba (colonized after Columbus' discoveries) by Hernán Cortés, first and best of the conquistadors, a Christian knight memorably described by the soldier Bernal Diaz who marched with him to the gates of Hell:

> He was of a good height and body and well proportioned and of strong limbs and the color of his face was somewhat ashy and not very merry and had his face been longer he would have been handsomer, and his eyes had a somewhat loving glance yet grave withal; his beard was dark and sparse and short and . . . his chest was high and his back was of a good shape and he was lean and of little belly and somewhat bow-legged and his legs and thighs well set and he was a good horseman and skillful with all weapons on foot or on horseback and knew very well how to handle them, and above all a heart and a courage which is what matters. . . . [He wore] just a thin chain of gold of single pattern and a trinket with the image of Our Lady the Virgin Saint Mary with her precious Son in her arms . . . he prayed every morning with a [book of] Hours and heard Mass with devotion; he had for his protector the Virgin Mary our Lady (whom all Christians must hold as our intercessor and protector) as well as the Lord St. Peter and St. James and the Lord St. John the Baptist . . . even at times when very angry he threw up a lament to heaven and he never said an ugly or offensive word to captain or soldier and he was most long suffering . . . and I always saw him in battle stepping in along with us. . . . God pardon him his sins and me mine.[73]

---

[71] Padden, *Hummingbird and Hawk*, pp. 73-74; Fehrenbach, *Fire and Blood*, pp. 70, 78-80, 94; Carroll, *Our Lady of Guadalupe*, pp. 8-10.

[72] Collis, *Cortés and Montezuma*, pp. 54, 56, 60; Fehrenbach, *Fire and Blood*, pp. 43-46; Carroll, *Our Lady of Guadalupe*, pp. 19-20, 24.

[73] Bernal Diaz, *Chronicles*, as translated by Maurice Keatinge (New York, 1927), II, 529 and by Salvador de Madariaga in *Hernan Cortés, Conqueror of Mexico* (Chicago, 1955), pp. 103-104.

Cortés had two banners made for the expedition, red and black with gold trim, with the royal arms of Spain and a cross on each side, and the words: "Brothers and companions, let us follow the sign of the Cross with true faith and in it we shall conquer."[74] It had been Emperor Constantine's slogan, flashed to him in the sky, when he went forth to found Christendom upon what had been the pagan empire of Rome.[75] Cortés was going forth under that same sign to found a Christian order upon what was the Satanic empire of the Aztecs. When he landed at Veracruz, unknowingly fulfilling Ce Acatl Topiltzin's prophecy, he wore black as Spaniards then did on Good Friday to commemorate the Crucifixion; and Topiltzin, like all Mexican priests, was always garbed in black.[76]

The Spaniards were greeted by emissaries from the Aztec Emperor Montezuma II. Cortés took them to Easter High Mass, and explained that he represented King Charles, a great ruler across the sea, who wished friendship and trade with Montezuma, and had sent Cortés to penetrate his domain. (In fact Charles as yet knew nothing of this expedition; after his landing at Veracruz, Cortés sent one of his ships to report his venture directly to the King for the first time.) Cortés made an Easter dinner of the presents of rich food the emissaries brought, and reacted with horror and fury when they tried to season it with human blood. His reaction caused them and Montezuma to believe all the more that he was Quetzalcoatl's priest returned from beyond the earth.[77]

Early in August, after informing himself as much as he could about the strange and terrible world he had entered, Cortés was ready for his march inland to Cactus Rock. He divided his little army, leaving a third of it at Veracruz and taking the rest with him.[78] Then, in the act of astounding boldness which has ever since been associated with his name, Cortés scuttled nine of his ships, and came before his men to say:

> We already understand the expedition we are to make, and with the help of Our Lord Jesus Christ we must win all of our battles and encounters. If we are ever defeated, which God forbid, we can never raise our heads again, for there are so few of us, and we can expect no other help but His. Now that we no longer have ships in which to return to Cuba, we must depend on our stout hearts and strong blows.[79]

---

[74] Bernal Diaz Chronicles as translated by Madariaga, *Cortes*, p. 97.

[75] See Volume I, Chapter Twenty of this history.

[76] Carroll, *Our Lady of Guadalupe*, p. 24.

[77] Madariaga, *Cortes*, pp. 122-123; Collis, *Cortés and Montezuma*, pp. 62-64; Padden, *Hummingbird and Hawk*, pp. 122-124; Miguel Leon-Portilla, ed., *The Broken Spears; the Aztec Account of the Conquest of Mexico* (Boston, 1962), pp. 26-28; Carroll, *Our Lady of Guadalupe*, p. 25.

[78] Madariaga, *Cortes*, p. 167. He had about 300 men, 13 horses, and seven cannon.

[79] Bernal Diaz, *Chronicles*, tr. & ed. Albert Idell (New York, 1956), p. 88 (put in direct address).

As for the faint-hearted, there was one ship left; they could go back to Cuba in that. Naturally no one wanted to select himself for such a group, so Cortés scuttled the last ship as well.[80]

Hernán Cortés and his three hundred Spaniards turned their backs to the shores of nightmare and their faces to the keep of the Hummingbird Wizard. If one estimates twenty per cent of the fifteen million people of the Aztec empire as men capable of bearing arms, the odds against them were precisely ten thousand to one. Bernal Diaz, who was there, put it best: "Let the curious reader see whether there is not much to ponder over in this which I venture to write, and whether there were ever in the universe men who had such daring."[81]

As they climbed into the high interior, they reached the town of Zocotlán, which had a temple. By the temple were enormous racks for skulls, with regular rows making it easy to count them by multiplication. Each skull represented a victim of sacrifice. Their number, Bernal Diaz said, "might be one hundred thousand, and I say again, *one hundred thousand.*"[82]

In September, after his first battle, Cortés sent his first message back to Veracruz since the epic march began. It was to order up extra altar wine and hosts for Mass. Hernán Cortés had no intention of pushing on into the domain of the Hummingbird Wizard without the Body and Blood of Christ.[83]

Aztec resistance was still tentative, since Montezuma and many of his advisors at least half believed the invaders to be Quetzalcoatl's supernatural legion come to stop the human sacrifices. After winning another battle at Cholula, early in November Cortés and his three hundred came down at last from the high slopes to the great central lake, the standard of the Cross and the motto of Constantine flying in the van, then infantry, horsemen, crossbowmen, horsemen again, and musketeers, their steps resolutely forward, "the beard over the shoulder" as Bernal Diaz says, still against the odds of ten thousand to one. On November 8 they marched out upon the broad eastern causeway leading to the city of Cactus Rock in the middle of the lake. Immense crowds had gathered; every tower and terrace was black with people, and the waters of the lake were covered with canoes. Where a second causeway joined that upon which the Spaniards approached, a thousand prominent citizens in brilliant array greeted the strangers. Leading into the city was a long, wide, straight and beautiful avenue, lined with houses and temples. Along it, to meet Cortés, came Emperor Montezuma II. Cortés dismounted from his horse to greet him.[84]

Christ had now come, in the person of His champions, to claim His own in a land that had never known Him and had been dedicated to the service of His

---

[80] Madariaga, *Cortes*, pp. 155-157; Collis, *Cortes and Montezuma*, pp. 79-81.

[81] Bernal Diaz Chronicles as translated by Madariaga, *Cortes*, p. 232.

[82] *Ibid.*, p. 170.

[83] Madariaga, *Cortes*, p. 195; Carroll, *Our Lady of Guadalupe*, p. 37.

[84] Madariaga, *Cortes*, pp. 213-215, 222-229, 231-244; Collis, *Cortes and Montezuma*, pp. 121-131; Padden, *Hummingbird and Hawk*, pp. 131-132, 166-168; Carroll, *Our Lady of Guadalupe*, p. 42.

ancient enemy. His conquest of Mexico would not be achieved by swords and crossbows, political craft and diplomacy, nor even by the magnificent valor of the soldiers of Catholic Spain, for His kingdom is not of this world. But these men, by these means, would prepare and open up His way, make His paths straight through what had been a wilderness of horror and hellish sin, transforming Mexico into a place which His mother could visit. In the eloquent words of Salvador de Madariaga:

> Thus on that fateful Tuesday, November 8th, 1519, third day Quecholli, 8th Ehecatl of the year 1-Reed of the eighth sheaf, the two men stood before each other, looking into each other's eyes. But the eyes of the Mexican were closed lakes, soon to dry up under the sun of another knowledge, while in the eyes of Cortes there lived the endless sea.[85]

The Spanish were quartered in the palace of Axayacatl directly across the street from the great temple of the Hummingbird Wizard, dedicated 32 years before by cutting out the hearts of eighty thousand men. The daily sacrifices took place at dawn. On their first morning there, the Spaniards could actually see the blood running down the steps of the temple pyramid. On the other side of the palace of Axayacatl from the temple was the zoo. Its carnivores were fed daily on the trunks of the bodies of the sacrificed men. The beasts saw and heard and smelt their breakfast. A cacophony of hideous noise broke out. "I might as well tell all the infernal things now," says Bernal Diaz, visibly screwing up his courage—few men ever had more—"when the tigers and lions [jaguars and pumas] roared, and the jackals [coyotes] and foxes howled, and the snakes hissed, it was horrible to hear; it seemed like Hell."[86]

Yet all around was a clear blue morning; the sun shone, the air was cool and bracing, the lake gleamed, the golden corn tassels waved in the breeze. God was still good, and He still ruled the cosmos. But His enemy ruled Cactus Rock—and the Christian army was inside.

The Spaniards slept in their clothes, their weapons by their side. All the rest of his life Bernal Diaz kept the night habits acquired during his weeks in the keep of the Hummingbird Wizard, sleeping in his clothes, without a bed. But he would get up from time to time, "to look at the sky and stars and walk a little in the night dew," reassuring himself that he was, thanks be to God, a free man alive under the open sky, that he really had escaped the obsidian knife of sacrifice that was to claim the lives of so many of his fellows.[87]

On Sunday, November 13, after attending Mass, Cortes and most of his men climbed the 114 steps to the top of the temple pyramid and beheld the hideous images of Huitzilopochtli and Tezcatlipoca, to whom more than five million

[85] Madariaga, *Cortes*, p. 239.
[86] Bernal Diaz, *Chronicles*, tr. Idell, p. 153.
[87] *Ibid.*, p. 197.

human sacrifices had been made during the past century alone. Cortes turned to Montezuma and said:

> I cannot understand how so great a lord and wise a man as you are has not yet thought it out that these idols are not gods, but very bad things known as devils; and so that you may come to know them as such, and all your priests see it clearly, grant me as a favor that we set up a Cross on top of this tower, and we shall set aside one part of these chapels, where Huichilobos [the Spanish version of Huitzilopochtli, meaning "Witchywolves"] and Tezcatlipoca now are, for an image of Our Lady, and you shall see what fear these idols will then feel.[88]

Two days later Cortés arrested Emperor Montezuma in his own chambers. He felt sure that prolonged close contact with the Spaniards by the Mexicans would convince them they were not supernatural beings, and when that happened, unless they held the emperor as their hostage, they would simply be set upon and killed. But the human sacrifices continued. In January 1520 Cortés secured permission from his imperial captive to place an altar, a cross, and an image of the Blessed Virgin Mary in a room within the temple itself. But soon the temple priests demanded its removal, threatening war if this was not done. Cortés called his men to arms. They climbed the high steps of the temple to the platform at the top, slashing with their swords the veil that screened the monstrous idols from view.[89]

"Oh God!" cried Cortés, "why dost Thou permit the Devil to be so grossly honored in this land?" He bowed his head, and added, as though in prayer: "Accept, O Lord, that we may serve Thee in this land."[90] Then he turned and faced the Hummingbird Wizard. Its obscene bulk rose up before him as though to fill the earth and all the sky.

Cortés saw a metal bar. He seized it and swung it over his head. "I pledge my faith as a gentleman, and swear to God that it is true," wrote Andres de Tapia, a young Spanish officer who has left us the best record of this supreme moment, "that I can see now how the Marquess [Cortés] leapt up in a supernatural way and swung forward holding the bar midway till he struck the idol high up on its eyes, and broke off its gold mask, saying: 'We must risk something for God.'"[91]

A few days later the priests removed the idols from the great temple, in deathly silence. Cortés ordered their shrines cleansed, and two altars erected. Escorted by heavily armed men, a cross, followed by images of the Blessed Virgin Mary and of St. Christopher, were carried up the great staircase, scene of

---

[88] Bernal Diaz Chronicles as translated by Madariaga, *Cortes*, p. 254.

[89] Madariaga, *Cortes*, pp. 259-260, 290-291; Collis, *Cortes and Montezuma*, pp. 159-164; Burr C. Brundage, *A Rain of Darts; the Mexican Aztecs* (Austin TX, 1972), pp. 214-215, 267-269; Carroll, *Our Lady of Guadalupe*, pp. 50-54.

[90] Padden, *Hummingbird and Hawk*, p. 185 (first quote); Madariaga, *Cortes*, p. 292 (second quote).

[91] Madariaga, *Cortes*, p. 292.

the matchless horror of the sacrifice of the eighty thousand in 1487. The Spaniards sang *Te Deum laudamus*, and took off their helmets. Their priest, Father Olmedo, stepped forward. Holy Mass was said: Jesus Christ came, body, blood, soul, and divinity, to His altar now standing, like a meteor fallen from Heaven, in the very heart and center of what had been the keep of the Hummingbird Wizard.[92]

For three months no human sacrifice took place at the great temple. Tension grew in Mexico City, augmented by the necessary absence of Cortés when a new Spanish force sent by the governor of Cuba to take over from him arrived on the coast and he had to go there to confront its commander Narváez and win its men over to him. He accomplished this with ease, but in his absence his lieutenant Pedro Alvarado, alarmed by warnings of an impending Mexican attack on the Spanish, slaughtered several hundred Mexicans at a rain dance. Returning to Mexico City in June with Narváez's men, Cortés had to face a Mexican assault almost immediately. When he brought out Montezuma to try to quell the attackers, the Aztec Emperor was killed by his own people with a stone. Cortés then had to leave Mexico City, which had become a death trap, but the Mexicans broke the bridges on the causeways, and in a ghastly night of battle and flight across the lake on June 30, half the Spanish army was lost.[93]

The survivors gathered on the Hill of the Turkey Hen, which they fortified. From its top they could look across the lake to Cactus Rock where, atop the great pyramidal temple where Cortés had flung his iron bar into the face of the Hummingbird Wizard, the Spaniards captured the previous night were being sacrificed, one by one to the Hummingbird Wizard and the Lord of the Dark.[94]

Almost any other commander in history would, at this point, have taken the remnant of his battered and beaten army out of the country as soon and as fast as he could, boarded Narváez's ships, and sailed for safety. But Hernán Cortés would never call retreat.

He resolved to withdraw only as far as the territory of the Indians of Tlaxcala, hereditary enemies of the Aztecs, who had already supported him against them, and with their help, return and take Mexico City. But at Otumba on the way to Tlaxcala, just a week after his flight from Mexico City, he had to face the whole Aztec army under the new emperor, Cuitlahuac. The Spaniards—now reduced to little more than the number that had originally marched with Cortés from Veracruz—could not evade the Mexican host or flee. They had to fight their way through or perish—and not only that, but win a victory in the process, because in their condition they could not endure a vigorous pursuit by so great an

---

[92] *Ibid.*, p. 294; Padden, *Hummingbird and Hawk*, p. 192; Carroll, *Our Lady of Guadalupe*, pp. 54-55.

[93] Madariaga, *Cortes*, pp. 307-309, 315-318, 325, 330-343, 526-529; Collis, *Cortes and Montezuma*, pp. 173-177, 186-196; Padden, *Hummingbird and Hawk*, pp. 194-196, 201-202; Carroll, *Our Lady of Guadalupe*, pp. 56-64.

[94] Collis, *Cortes and Montezuma*, pp. 197-200; Madariaga, *Cortes*, p. 344; Brundage, *Rain of Darts*, pp. 276-277; Carroll, *Our Lady of Guadalupe*, p. 65.

army. They had no guns left. All that remained of their vaunted technological superiority, to which so many later writers have attributed all their victories, were their small troop of jaded horses, a few coats of mail, and cold steel.[95]

Said Cortés:

> There came to meet us such a multitude of Indians that the fields all around were so full of them that nothing else could be seen. We could hardly distinguish between ourselves and them, so fiercely and closely did they fight with us. Certainly we believed that it was our last day, for the Indians were very strong and we could resist but feebly, as we were exhausted and nearly all of us wounded and weak from hunger. But Our Lord was pleased to show His power and mercy, for with all our weakness we broke their arrogance and pride.[96]

Cortés addressed his men. His soldier Francisco de Aguilar tells us there were tears on his cheeks; he was contemplating not only his own death and that of all the men entrusted to his care, but the apparent ruin of all his magnificent achievements, which were to have been crowned by the Christianization of Mexico—the triumph of the Devil, the defeat of the army of Christ. But, says Aguilar, "he drew himself up and exhorted and encouraged us like a brave captain."[97] He and his men commended their souls "to God and to Holy Mary" and called upon Santiago, St. James the Greater, Apostle and Son of Thunder, the ancient patron of Spain, whom legend said had appeared in person at desperate moments of Spain's history to fight beside her Catholic soldiers when most hard beset. These men were heirs of thirty generations of Christian warriors who had forever refused to surrender Spain to the infidel. All the 770 years of the longest crusade were needed to make men to meet the demands of this hour. The odds against the Spaniards on this battlefield of Otumba had to be at least two hundred to one. The battle swayed to and fro. Spaniards fell, or were captured and dragged off for sacrifice. Yet, Bernal Diaz says, "it seemed as though we all acquired double strength." Cortés saw an Aztec priest-general ahead of him, conspicuous in a huge feather crest and carrying a billowing standard, whom the Mexicans believed to be the incarnation of the serpent-woman Cihuacoatl. Cortés charged. Juan de Salamanca by his side struck the priest-general dead with his lance. The enemy host began to melt away. Incredible as it may seem, it was the

---

[95] Madariaga, *Cortes*, pp. 334-335; Collis, *Cortes and Montezuma*, pp. 201-203; Fehrenbach, *Fire and Blood*, pp. 143-144; Carroll, *Our Lady of Guadalupe*, p. 66.

[96] Hernán Cortés, *Letters from Mexico*, ed. A. R. Pagden (New York, 1971), p. 142.

[97] Patricia de Fuentes, ed., *The Conquistadors; First-Person Accounts of the Conquest of Mexico* (New York, 1963), p. 156 (for quotation); Carroll, *Our Lady of Guadalupe*, p. 67.

Spaniards and their remaining Tlaxcalan allies who pursued. It was not just survival, nor a draw, but a *victory*.[98]

In Tlaxcala Cortés received a hero's welcome from his Indian allies and began, without a pause, to plan for his victorious return to Mexico City. They built a fleet of brigantines to control the causeways across the lake. In February 1521 he was on the march again to the Aztec capital with a strongly reinforced Spanish army of about a thousand accompanied by more than 20,000 Indian allies—a number that in the ensuing months grew to over a hundred thousand. (By now King Charles, now Emperor, had heard of Cortés' achievements, and three shiploads of fighting men had arrived directly from Spain to join him, accompanied by a Franciscan friar carrying bulls of indulgence for men fighting on crusade.) From May to August, for 93 consecutive days, one of the most terrible war grapples in all history raged street to street and house to house throughout the city of the Hummingbird Wizard. Perhaps a quarter of a million people died. Cortés repeatedly offered to negotiate, but the Mexicans would have none of it. The great temple was stormed twice more, and at last everything on it was put to the torch. On August 13 the current emperor, Cuauhtemoc, was captured. He asked Cortés to kill him, but the conquistador praised his bravery and said he would not do it.[99]

The Satanic empire was destroyed. Christianity could now come to Mexico. Within 25 years virtually the whole realm was converted, primarily through the apparition of the Blessed Virgin Mary at Tepeyac hill near Mexico City in December 1531.[100]

Not until the outbreak of the French Revolution and the great crises of the twentieth century involving the two world wars did so much of such great importance happen in so short a time as in the years 1519-1521. These happenings include not only the sundering of Christendom by Martin Luther, but also the election and coronation of Charles V as Holy Roman Emperor, a widespread rebellion against him in Spain, the conquest of Mexico just covered, and the greater part of the first voyage around the world, up to the death of its relentless captain, Ferdinand Magellan. Since his voyage, "the greatest single human achievement on the sea,"[101] departing in September 1519, took place at an

---

[98] Madariaga, *Cortés*, pp. 344-345; Collis, *Cortés and Montezuma*, pp. 201-203; Fehrenbach, *Fire and Blood*, pp. 193-195; Brundage, *Rain of Darts*, p. 277; Bernal Diaz, *Chronicles*, tr. Idell, pp. 257-258 (for quote); Carroll, *Our Lady of Guadalupe*, pp. 67-68.

[99] Madariaga, *Cortes*, pp. 365-386, 391; Collis, *Cortes and Montezuma*, pp. 215-225; Brundage, *Rain of Darts*, pp. 285-288; Fehrenbach, *Fire and Blood*, pp. 149-156; Bernal Diaz, *Chronicles* ed. Idell, pp. 261, 314, 379-384; Cortes, *Letters* ed. Pagden, pp. 191-192, 485; Carroll, *Our Lady of Guadalupe*, pp. 68-78.

[100] For an account of that conversion and its consequences, see Chapter 13, below.

[101] Edward G. Bourne, *Spain in America* (New York, 1904), cited by Morison, *European Discovery of America; the Southern Voyages*, p. 320. No other guide but

even longer distance from Europe than Mexico was, and except for the garbled tales of the officers and crew of one deserting ship, remained unknown to Europe until the surviving remnant returned in 1522, it will be summarized at this point.

Magellan's was not a happy company. He had only one captain he could trust—Juan Serrano, his dear friend Francisco's brother. The other three captains were Spanish; before he left the Canary Islands he received a written warning that they were planning to kill him. Most of the seamen were Spanish also and suspicious of the Portuguese foreigner, though in time they came to respect him enormously as the best seaman they had ever seen. But Magellan made no concessions to the enemies around him and showed no flicker of fear. When he changed course unexpectedly off the African coast and Cartagena, one of the hostile Spanish captains, demanded why, Magellan snapped back: "Follow me and ask no questions!"[102]

In December Magellan stopped at Rio de Janeiro, then little more than an Indian trading post where despite Portuguese hostility there were no forces nearly strong enough to detain him. There he replaced one of the mutinous Spanish captains. In January 1520 he explored the great bay inaccurately called the Rio de la Plata, on which Buenos Aires now stands, hoping that it would be the necessary strait, but he soon determined its true character. He proceeded down the bleak coast of Patagonia, fortunately for him during the southern summer, exploring every bay in search of the strait, augmenting his supplies with the meat of penguins, which the Spanish called "wingless ducks." On March 31 he reached Port St. Julian, a well protected harbor with a narrow entrance between hundred-foot gray cliffs. There he decided to spend the Antarctic winter, and there he quelled the final mutiny of his Spanish captains with a combination of adamant courage and resolution, brilliant nautical maneuvers, and merciless justice. He hanged Captain Quesada on Easter Sunday and marooned Captain Cartagena on the desolate coast when he departed in September. In late October he at last reached the well-hidden entrance of "the strait that shall forever bear his name" and found it to be the long-sought passageway by his usual perseverance in exploring bays and inlets to their very end.[103]

The Strait of Magellan is 334 miles long; its traverse is one of the most difficult and dangerous feats of navigation in the world for sailing vessels. Magellan accomplished it without serious difficulty or loss, except for the departure for Spain of one of his ships under another mutinous captain. Since he had lost another ship to grounding south of Port St. Julian, he had three remaining: *Victoria*, *Trinidad*, and *Concepción*. With these he threaded his way through the long narrow northwest reach of the Strait from Cape Froward, southernmost point of the South American continent (as distinct from the island of Tierra del Fuego south of the Strait), a spectacular but forbidding region

---

Morison is needed for this voyage; the great sailor-historian covers it at length in this his last book, after surveying its entire route by plane while in his eighties.

[102] Morison, *European Discovery of America; Southern Voyages*, p. 357.

[103] *Ibid.*, pp. 360-383.

uninhabited to this day. Magellan sent the flagship's longboat to scout ahead, and its crew first saw the broad Pacific Ocean opening out before them.[104] At the time it seemed one of the most important geographical discoveries ever made; not until the voyage of Francis Drake sixty years later was it learned that the land south of the Strait of Magellan was only a moderate-sized island with an open though very stormy sea below the spume-slashed gray starkness of Cape Horn.

On November 28, 1520 Magellan emerged into the open Pacific. He sailed north along the Chilean coast until he had passed 40 degrees south latitude and moved out of the region of the endless westerly winds which, south of Cape Horn, circle unchecked around the world. Picking up the southeast trade winds, he turned west into the Pacific. For 81 days his three ships sailed through an empty sea, passing just north of Polynesia with its numerous islands. During that whole time they saw only two small uninhabited islands, which offered no landing place. Scurvy broke out among his starving men; Magellan had said earlier he would reach the Spice Islands if they all had to eat the leather off their masts to get there, and that is exactly what they had to do. Desperately weakened, Magellan and his crews finally sighted the island of Guam on March 6, 1521, where he replenished his stores despite clashes with the natives. On March 15 he sighted the island of Samar in the Philippines. On Holy Thursday, March 28, hailing a boat off the little island of Limasawa in Surigao Strait, Magellan's slave Enrique, whom he had picked up in Malacca many years before, found that the people in the boat understood his native language. The East had at last been reached from the west. Magellan and his men gave thanks at a solemn Easter High Mass on Limasawa.[105]

On April 7 Magellan came to the island of Cebu, whose Sultan Humabon welcomed him and agreed to immediate baptism, along with 500 of his retainers. He was christened Charles after the Emperor. Then Humabon's young and beautiful wife and forty of her attendants were baptized; she was christened Elizabeth, and Magellan gave her a small image of a smiling Christ-child, which was miraculously preserved after Magellan's death and Humabon's apostasy and is still venerated at Cebu as *El Santo Niño.*[106]

But tragedy followed hard on triumph. Lapu Lapu, chief of the neighboring island of Mactan, was an enemy of Sultan Humabon. Magellan, eager to show Humabon the benefits of alliance with Europeans, decided to attack Lapu Lapu in force, embarking sixty men on his three longboats and taking command of them in person. Canoes with fighting men from Cebu accompanied him, but they never got into action. Lapu Lapu charged with his full force of 1,500 as the great navigator landed on the beach at Mactan. Magellan's panicky men quickly discharged all their ammunition. With a small band of devoted companions he held out against growing odds for a full hour, until at last he was overborne and

---

[104] *Ibid.,* pp. 384-392.
[105] *Ibid.,* pp. 402-422.
[106] *Ibid.,* pp. 423-425.

killed. His body disappeared and was never found. No finer seaman ever lived than Ferdinand Magellan, but he was no Hernán Cortés.[107]

On May 1 Humabon turned against his European benefactors, treacherously seizing and killing nearly thirty of them at a banquet, including all three ship captains. The demoralized survivors held a conference at Bohol Island, decided to scrap the teredo-riddled *Concepción*, which in any case they had hardly enough men to sail. Juan Sebastian de Elcano, a very competent Basque mariner who had however been a participant in the mutiny back in Patagonia, became captain of the *Victoria*. After voyaging rather aimlessly through southern Philippine and Indonesian waters for several months, in November *Victoria* and *Trinidad* arrived at last at the Spice Islands, Ternate and Tidore. There they found that Magellan's friend Francisco Serrano, after acting as effective ruler of the islands for nine years, had been poisoned at almost exactly the same time that Magellan was killed. But the natives were eager to trade, and both ships were soon loaded with precious cloves. The officers decided that they should try to return home in opposite directions, *Victoria* to Spain around the Cape of Good Hope, completing the circumnavigation of the world, and *Trinidad* to Mexico, where the discoveries of Cortés had just become known when the Magellan expedition departed. But no one had ever sailed across the North Pacific, and Gómez de Espinosa, the jumped-up captain of the *Trinidad*, was not the man to make maritime history. After six weeks he turned back, fell into the hands of the Portuguese, and lost his ship in a squall. Only four members of *Trinidad*'s crew ever returned to Spain.[108]

Elcano set out from Tidore in *Victoria* on December 21, 1521 with a crew of sixty including thirteen natives. To avoid the Portuguese, he went south to Timor and sailed straight across the full width of the Indian Ocean, rounded the Cape of Good Hope, and then came north to the equator for two months without landing. Scurvy and starvation struck again, as in the crossing of the empty Pacific, killing 25 men. When Elcano finally had to land at the Portuguese Cape Verde Islands and offered to buy provisions with cloves, thereby revealing that his ship had come from the Orient, the Portuguese arrested some of his crew and he barely got his ship away in time. With 18 Europeans and three Asiatics, Elcano returned to Sanlúcar de Barrameda on September 6, 1522, whence he had departed almost exactly three years before. He reported as soon as possible to Emperor Charles V, who gave him deserved rewards. The lone cargo of cloves he brought back from the Spice Islands more than paid the entire cost of the Magellan expedition.[109]

The dream of Columbus had been realized before he was seventeen years in his grave. Men had sailed around the world.

---

[107] *Ibid.*, pp. 427-432, 438.

[108] *Ibid.*, pp. 439-455.

[109] *Ibid.*, pp. 457-463. Elcano was astonished to discover, when he reached the Cape Verde Islands, that though the ship's log and the famous journal of Antonio de Pigafetta had carefully recorded each passing day, they were one day behind the date in Europe. Thus was the need for the International Date Line discovered.

News of his election as Emperor reached King Charles of Spain in Barcelona on July 6, 1519. He decided at once to leave Spain as soon as possible, both for his coronation in Charlemagne's city of Aachen (Aix-la-Chapelle) and to familiarize himself first-hand with the situation and problems of Germany, a land which he had never visited, though his native Flanders was technically considered part of it.[110] Undoubtedly he knew enough about Germany and its divisions to realize that they could go from bad to worse very quickly without the imperial presence and active influence. But there is not the slightest reason to believe that Charles ever considered staying in Germany or Flanders permanently. Spain was, after all, the world's leading power, with an expanding overseas empire that Magellan's impending voyage might enlarge by a whole new order of magnitude. Thanks to the work of Isabel and Ferdinand, Spain, in contrast to Germany, was relatively united. But most of the Spanish did not yet really trust their young sovereign. He was too foreign, appeared too immature and too much a captive of his alien entourage. They expected his advisors to get him away and keep him away, using Spain as a milch cow for their own greed and political ambitions.

On July 12 Charles' new Grand Chancellor Mercurino Gattinara, whom his Aunt Margaret had brought from Savoy with the highest recommendation, presented him with a memorandum on his prospects and duties as the temporal head of Christendom, stressing the importance of unifying Christendom under his leadership and urging that he take care not to entrust too much power in Spain or Germany to fellow natives of the Low Countries.[111] In a memorandum to his ambassador to England August 16, Charles restated the ancient duties of his office and his commitment to them. Upon the Emperor and the Pope, he said:

> . . .the duty was imposed of extirpating all errors among Christian peoples, of establishing universal peace, of undertaking a general crusade against the Turks, and of bringing all things into better order and condition. In war and in peace these two powers [the Empire and the papacy] must be indissolubly bound together, and by their unanimity hold out to all true believers the assurance of a better future.[112]

At the end of October Charles announced that he would leave Spain for Germany the following March to be crowned Emperor and hold a Diet.[113] In February 1520 he summoned the Cortes (parliament) of Castile to meet at Santiago de Compostela to vote funds for his support. Since it was located far up in the mountains of Galicia, in the northwestern corner of Spain, to travel there in this late winter season would be extraordinarily difficult, expensive and time-

---

[110] Merriman, *Rise of the Spanish Empire*, III, 43-45; Menéndez Pidal, *Historia de España*, XX, 176.

[111] Brandi, *Charles V*, pp. 90-91, 112.

[112] Janssen, *History of the German People*, III, 159.

[113] *Ibid.*, III, 155-156.

consuming; no Cortes in the history of Castile had ever been held at Santiago de Compostela. The reason for holding it there was simply that sailing from the north Galician port of La Coruña was the quickest way to reach England, where Charles was going to meet with its King Henry VIII on his way to Germany. Determined to get his requested appropriation with the minimum of delay and to defer all consideration of Spanish local problems until his return, Charles prohibited the towns from sending anyone to Santiago de Compostela to petition him, except members of the Cortes, who were chosen from among the local nobility by lot. After a fierce debate in which daggers were drawn, the city council of Toledo nevertheless sent four petitioners to Santiago.[114]

Charles was in Valladolid, on his way to Santiago de Compostela, when Toledo's defiant petitioners confronted him. He refused to see them. All the Spanish frustrations with and suspicions of their young foreign-born sovereign suddenly boiled up and exploded. Thousands of armed men marched in the streets. Charles, accompanied by Chièvres and his bodyguard, fled the city. The guard held a gate open for him while he and Chièvres galloped away almost alone into the night in a pouring rainstorm, riding for Tordesillas, 19 miles away. At his next stop beyond Tordesillas Charles agreed to listen to the petitioners, but would not respond to them; several days later he met them again, but only to chide them for disobedience. On March 31 he opened the Cortes in Santiago de Compostela with an address read by the Bishop of Palencia, in which he declared that Spain was and would remain "the garden of his pleasures, his fortress for defense, his power for attack, his treasure, his sword, his mount and his seat," but explained that he had to leave now to accept the imperial crown and needed the money he had requested to meet properly his new responsibilities to Christendom as Emperor, "in order to ward off great evils from our Christian religion" (a probable reference to the rise of Luther and his followers) and to coordinate action against the infidel. He added some remarks in Spanish to show his progress in mastering the language (which was considerable) and pledged to return in three years and to appoint no more foreigners to office in Spain.[115]

It is hard to see what more he could have said or done, and he was to return in the allotted time and maintain his primary residence in Spain for the rest of his life. But on Palm Sunday, April 1, he ordered the Toledo petitioners out of Santiago de Compostela. When the news arrived in Toledo, the proud ancient capital of Spain announced itself in rebellion against Charles' government "in the name of the King and the Queen, and of the Community [*Comunidad*]" for Spanish liberties.[116] By the Queen they meant poor mad Juana; the reference to

---

[114] Merriman, *Rise of the Spanish Empire*, III, 46-47; Seaver, *Great Revolt in Castile*, pp. 54-58, 77; Menéndez Pidal, *Historia de España*, XX, 188.

[115] Menéndez Pidal, *Historia de España*, XX, 191, 193 (quotations on 191); Merriman, *Rise of the Spanish Empire*, III, 48-50; Seaver, *Great Revolt in Castile*, pp. 62-65, 67-68, 73-75.

[116] Seaver, *Great Revolt in Castile*, pp. 69-70, 79, 86-87, 120; Merriman, *Rise of the Spanish Empire*, III, 69-70. The reference to rebellion in the name of the Community led

the King presumably expressed their hope to persuade or force Charles to change his own government to their liking. The rebels took control of the city and its castle, the most impregnable in Spain and probably in Europe, which was to hold out for two months in 1936 against the full panoply of modern warfare: artillery, flaming gasoline, aerial bombardment, and two and a half tons of TNT exploded in an underground mine.

At the Cortes Charles faced continuing dogged opposition to voting the funds he had requested. He gradually broke it down with carefully selected bribes and promises of high office, but this took so much time that he moved the Cortes to La Coruña, his intended port of departure. Only there did he finally obtain a plurality of the votes of 16 cities of Castile, eight voting for the subsidy, five against, with one divided and two abstentions. Charles' message of thanks to the Cortes also included the announcement that his holy teacher, Bishop Adrian of Utrecht, now a Cardinal, would govern Spain in his absence. This seemed a breach of his promise to appoint no more foreigners to office in Spain, though it was not a permanent appointment and had probably been decided upon before he made the pledge. Few were prepared to listen to any recounting of Cardinal Adrian's many virtues, nor was Charles in any mood to make concessions after he heard of the revolt in Toledo. He departed from La Coruña May 20 in a cloud of anger and mutual recriminations, an ill augury for his future as King of Spain and Emperor of Christendom.[117]

Charles' haste to leave Spain at this critical juncture was not so much because of his coronation in Aachen—it did not take place until October 23—but because he believed it essential to stop in England on his way to Flanders and confer there with its King Henry VIII and his wife, Charles' aunt Catherine, before Henry went to France for a much-heralded meeting with Francis I on what came to be called the Field of the Cloth of Gold. Francis' hostility to Charles had been evident in his unsuccessful attempt to prevent Charles' election as Emperor. An alliance between France and England could pose a major threat to Charles despite his now far-flung domains. The date of the meeting between Henry and Francis was already set; Charles thought he had to get to England before it. Henry was flattered by his visit and Catherine was delighted to see her young nephew now holding the highest temporal office in Christendom. Charles and his advisors regarded the meeting as a diplomatic success.[118]

Meanwhile behind him, the spark from Toledo had set off a conflagration throughout Castile and in the province of Valencia on the eastern coast of Spain. The Cortes deputies who had voted the funds Charles requested after accepting gifts and offices from his government found their property and even their lives threatened. Andalusia and Extremadura and, more surprisingly, Aragon and

---

to this revolt being called that of the *comunidades* (communities) or *comuneros* (people of the communities).

[117] Seaver, *Great Revolt in Castile*, pp. 74-77, 79, 120; Merriman, *Rise of the Spanish Empire*, III, 50-52; Menéndez Pidal, *Historia de España*, XX, 193-197.

[118] Brandi, *Charles V*, p. 116-118, 123.

usually fractious Catalonia remained generally calm, but Castile was the heartland of Spain, and no Spanish monarch could afford to lose it. Adrian of Utrecht did his best and remained totally untainted by any corruption, but this was a crisis no foreigner, however just and holy, could handle. Charles' retention of authority in Spain, and through that (considering the condition of Germany) his whole future, depended essentially on the loyalty and energy of one man: Iñigo Velasco of Burgos, Constable of Castile. Though this was primarily a revolt of townsmen, many of the nobles were sympathetic, and few were initially willing to risk their assets and properties in a fight to the finish with an aroused populace based on a chain of strongly defended walled cities.[119]

In political Spain there has always been a tendency to anarchy crossing with a tradition of intensely personal loyalty. Queen Isabel could walk into the rebellious city of Segovia with just two companions and expect to be instantly obeyed—as she was.[120] Charles had not yet been able to arouse any such loyalty to his person. But there was still the tradition of loyalty to the royal office, which Isabel had done so much to strengthen. Without a king or queen to serve, the rebels would ultimately be vulnerable to the pressure of that tradition. Consequently the more perceptive of their leaders realized from the beginning that they had to have the sanction, or at least appear to have the sanction, of mad Queen Juana, while convincing people that she was not as mentally ill as had been said. Tordesillas, where Juana was confined, joined the rebellion in August, and rebel leader Juan de Padilla met with Juana, saying that his followers would serve and defend her. She seemed to accept their fealty, but when asked to sign a public declaration to this effect, she would not, even after another delegation September 24 pleaded with her to do so. Indeed, for years she had refused to sign papers of any kind, and would never sign any for the rebels. She was almost wholly out of touch with reality; at one pathetic moment she said to one interrogator: "Believe me, all they tell me and all I see seems a dream."[121]

At this point Adrian was reduced almost to despair, writing to Charles: "As to the affairs of this realm, they are apparently going to total ruin if God lay not His hand specially to the remedy and quieting of them."[122] But Adrian for all his virtues was not a man of war; he had not taken the measure of the iron tenacity in battle of Spaniards committed to a cause. The rebels had some of that, but this was still Isabel's Spain—it had been only sixteen years since her death— monarchist to the core. The loyalists needed only a leader. When Constable Velasco's life and that of his family was threatened and he was besieged for two days in his home in Burgos, the famous Casa del Cordón where Isabel and Ferdinand had received Columbus in 1497, where Prince Juan and Charles' Aunt Margaret had been married and Charles' father Philip had died, Velasco made up

---

[119] Seaver, *Great Revolt in Castile*, pp. 90-122; Merriman, *Rise of the Spanish Empire*, III, 107.

[120] See Volume III, Chapter Fourteen of this history.

[121] Seaver, *Great Revolt in Castile*, pp. 132-144, 147-150.

[122] *Ibid.*, p. 125.

his mind to do his full duty as the chief defender of the kingdom. Informed a few days later, at the end of September, that Charles had appointed him co-regent of Castile with Cardinal Adrian (now imprisoned in Valladolid), Velasco responded with a great surge of loyalty and commitment. On October 15 Cardinal Adrian escaped from Valladolid by climbing over a wall and riding away on a mule; it does not seem that any vigorous attempt was made to catch him. By November 1 Constable Velasco had won back his home city of Burgos; on December 5 his son, the Count of Haro, carried Tordesillas by storm and regained possession of Queen Juana.[123]

By January the rebels were beginning to divide; the more responsible among them were especially horrified by the actions of Bishop Antonio de Acuña of Zamora, who on the 23rd of that month descended on the town of Magaz between Burgos and Valladolid and totally destroyed it, after going to its church and taking all its objects of value, including a cloak which had adorned the image of the Blessed Virgin Mary. Even in Toledo voices were being raised against the revolt, and were not silenced when the council leading the uprising sent Bishop Acuña to keep the city under its control. On February 15 the renegade bishop plundered the churches of Valladolid to get money to pay his troops, taking "chalices, patens, tabernacles, and censers of silver, and dividing them among the soldiers and cavaliers, who went through the streets censing and singing with the tabernacles."[124]

As the Spanish republicans in 1936 found out, it is very dangerous to do this sort of thing in Catholic Spain.

In mid-February a decree of Emperor Charles V was published in Burgos condemning 249 leaders of the rebellion for treason. On February 20 there was rioting in Valladolid between those who wanted to make peace with their king and those still resolved to continue the rebellion. On March 10 Pedro Laso de la Vega, a Toledan who had been president of the rebel council, changed sides and proclaimed his support for Charles. A few days later the revolutionary Bishop Acuña was defeated in battle near Ocaña, with 600 of his men killed. On Good Friday he rode into Toledo fully armed. A crowd of his followers proclaimed him archbishop, but the cathedral chapter heroically refused to elect him canonically, its members crying out to the menacing crowd a typically Spanish defiance: "We have already swallowed death; do what you will!" On April 22 Constable Velasco reviewed a now imposing royal army of 6,000 foot and 2,400 horse, and with it he triumphantly crushed the rebellion at the Battle of Villalar the next day, most appropriately Queen Isabel's birthday, at almost the very moment Charles V was magnificently confronting Luther at the Diet of Worms in Germany—a stand

---

[123] *Ibid.*, pp. 26, 155-157, 161, 181, 186, 202-204; Merriman, *Rise of the Spanish Empire*, III, 77, 80-84.

[124] Seaver, *Great Revolt in Castile*, p. 309; see also *ibid.*, pp. 233 and 331.

which, when the Spanish people came to know of it, enshrined his place in their hearts forever.[125]

In Germany John Eck did not relax but intensified his campaign against Luther after the Leipzig disputation. Evidently he had fully divined from their confrontation just how formidable an enemy of the Church and the Faith Martin Luther was. Up to this point, and through the disputation, Eck had been respectful of Luther, avoiding the personal vituperation so characteristic of sixteenth century debate; but now he let his real feelings show. Luther "sweat with hatred" at Leipzig, he wrote; he was "weak in scholarship but strong in biting and abusing. He is a liar and a Hussite." Not once, during the three weeks he was at Leipzig, had he said Mass.[126]

Eck was regularly in communication with Rome about Luther, constantly urging more action against him. On January 9, 1520 Luther's case was reopened before the papal consistory at the express direction of Pope Leo X. In mid-February Eck left the University of Ingolstadt in Bavaria, where he taught, to go to Rome himself to press its progress. Meanwhile the condemnation of Luther by the theological faculty of the University of Louvain was published with a cover letter from Cardinal Adrian describing the heresies in Luther's writings as "rude and palpable." Luther responded in March repeating in even stronger language the statements the Louvain theologians had condemned and saying that unless and until they could refute him to his satisfaction by Scripture he would "pay no more attention to their condemnation than to the ravings of a drunken man."[127] As always, his private letters were even more revealing; writing to the Augustinian Spalatin February 14, he declared unequivocally "we are all of us Hussites" and said John Hus was a martyr who should be canonized.[128] Very soon now he would drop all restraint, and thunder to the heavens his ultimate defiance of the Church.

In the middle of March the theological commission at Rome reviewing Luther's case recommended condemnation of his works but not of his person. But by now Eck had arrived, determined to obtain condemnation of his person. Pope Leo X agreed with Eck, dismissed the commission, and appointed another. By the end of April it had drafted a bull specifically anathematizing Luther as a heretic. Eck worked closely with the Pope on its final wording. On May 21 he had the acts of the Leipzig disputation and the revised draft of the papal bull read to the College of Cardinals in consistory. Their meeting lasted all day and into the evening. It was agreed that all the challenged articles of Luther were

---

[125] *Ibid.*, pp. 252-254, 273-274, 278-280, 283, 325-326, 332-334 (quotation from the cathedral chapter of Toledo on p. 333); Merriman, *Rise of the Spanish Empire*, III, 85-90. For the Diet of Worms see below, this chapter.

[126] Fife, *Revolt of Martin Luther*, pp. 385, 407 (respectively, for the two quotations).

[127] *Ibid.*, pp. 474-475 (for the quotations), 390, 471, 494; Grisar, *Luther*, II, 45.

[128] Janssen, *History of the German People*, III, 99. For the date of this letter see Fife, *Revolt of Martin Luther*, p. 471.

erroneous and heretical, but that he should be given one final opportunity to retract them. On June 1 they met again to review the language of the final draft of the bull of condemnation, *Exsurge domine*, and approved it as it stood. On June 15 it was published.[129]

It condemned 41 propositions of Luther, based primarily on material submitted by Eck, including the printed minutes of the Leipzig disputation. The condemned propositions concerned the total depravity of man, justification by faith alone, grace and the sacraments, the existence of purgatory, and the authority of the Pope and the hierarchy. Luther was prohibited from preaching and ordered to make his submission in writing before Church witnesses within 60 days, and to burn his books. If he did this he would be forgiven; but he must do it, for the sake of "the peace, unity and truth of the Church for which the Savior prayed so fervently to his Father."[130]

At some time in June, well before he had the text of *Exsurge domine* in his hands (though he had undoubtedly been informed that it was forthcoming) Luther published a pamphlet provocatively entitled "Of the Baptism of Rome" in which he made his first public assertion of the shocking thought he had long played with, that the Pope was "the Antichrist of whom the whole of Scripture speaks."[131] On June 25 he published two more pamphlets against the Pope, counterattacking two defenders of papal primacy, the German Franciscan Alveld and the Italian Dominican and Thomist Silvestro Mazzolini, known from his native city as "Prierias." In his pamphlet against Alveld, Luther repeated his identification of the Pope with Antichrist and for the first time used the phrase describing Papal Rome later repeated by generations of Protestants, the "whore of Babylon." Luther denied that *any* Pope had had "the love of Christ demanded of those who were to perform the shepherd's service."[132] The malignant absurdity of denying the holiness not merely of some Popes but of *all* of them since St. Peter—including St. Sixtus II the martyr of the Mass in the catacombs, St. Leo the Great, St. Gregory the Great, St. Leo IX, and St. Peter Celestine, the transcendent goodness of all of whom had hitherto been recognized by every Christian who knew of them—casts a baleful light on the depths into which Luther was now sinking. His pamphlet against Prierias included the appalling invective quoted at the head of this chapter, calling upon his followers to "wash their hands in the blood" of the hierarchy. It ended:

---

[129] Von Pastor, *History of the Popes*, VII, 387-388, 394-400; Grisar, *Luther*, II, 45-46; Fife, *Revolt of Martin Luther*, p. 390n.

[130] Von Pastor, *History of the Popes*, VII, 400-403; Fife, *Revolt of Martin Luther*, pp. 498, 550-551; Grisar, *Luther*, II, 45-49, with the quotation on 48-49. See the quotation at the head of this chapter.

[131] Grisar, *Luther*, II, 9. This pamphlet was written in May and published in June; we do not know the specific date of publication within the month of June.

[132] *Ibid.*, II, 11.

I have published and I do declare, basing on the words of Peter and of Christ, that if the leaders, the bishops, and all other loyal followers do not admonish, arraign, and accuse the erring Pope, whatever may be his crimes, and hold him as a heathen, they are all blasphemers of the way of truth and deniers of Christ, and are, with the Pope, to be eternally damned. I have spoken.[133]

No wonder he wrote to Spalatin, two weeks before these blazing broadsides were published:

I have cast the die; I now despise the rage of the Romans as much as I do their favor. I will not reconcile myself to them for all eternity, nor have anything to do with them. Let them condemn and burn all that belongs to me. In return, I also will do as much for them; otherwise I could not kindle the fire that is to condemn and burn, before the eyes of the world, the whole Papal system—that Lernaean hydra of heresy. Then there will be an end to this show of humility, which has proved so fruitless.[134]

It is language like this that made, and continues to make, Catholic reunion with the church Luther founded, and all its spawn, so very unlikely in the foreseeable future.

From the forge of this titanic and overmastering rage was next struck Luther's famous appeal "To the Christian Nobility of the German Nation," written in German (unlike most of his earlier writings, which were in Latin), in which he adjured the Emperor, princes and noblemen of Germany to reject the Pope utterly, since most Popes "have been without faith . . . perjurors, traitors, villains" who had made a "devil's nest at Rome." All Christians, he claimed, are priests, with an equal right to interpret and expound Scripture, and councils should be summoned not by Popes or bishops but by temporal rulers. He called for the abolition of holy days, pilgrimages, fasts, canon law, endowed Masses, ecclesiastical punishments, and clerical celibacy, and the gradual elimination of religious orders. He specifically included new Emperor Charles V in his appeal, and seemed to believe that he might respond favorably to it. In just eight months Martin Luther would learn how totally he had misjudged young Charles.[135]

The circulation of the papal bull against Luther in Germany was entrusted to John Eck. Many Catholic historians have seen his selection for this task as a major error of judgment by the Roman authorities, since Eck was known throughout Germany as Luther's most articulate and inveterate foe, and had played a large part in the preparation and issuance of the bull; consequently, it is

---

[133] Fife, *Revolt of Martin Luther*, p. 506.

[134] Von Pastor, *History of the Popes*, VII, 390.

[135] *Ibid.*, VII, 390-393; Janssen, *History of the German People*, III, 116-123; Fife, *Revolt of Martin Luther*, pp. 514-518; Grisar, *Luther*, II, 13, 26-31, 55. On August 30 Luther wrote directly to Charles, asking his protection against his enemies and claiming to have been condemned unheard. We know that Charles did receive the letter (Fife, *op. cit.*, pp. 526-527).

said, the Germans saw it as a kind of self-promotion.[136]   Be that as it may, circulation of this bull in the agitated state of public opinion in Germany, with many cities full of enthusiastic supporters of Luther, was going to be both difficult and dangerous.   Eck surely believed he was the best qualified by determination and courage to carry this enterprise through; the Pope presumably agreed, and there is good reason to hold that he was right.   Who but John Eck, so far, had faced down Luther?

The difficulty and danger of Eck's task were immediately apparent when he arrived in Leipzig at the end of September with the bull.   Though he had seemed to enjoy the support of most in that city at the time of the disputation, now the tide had turned against him; his life was threatened, and for a time he could find no one willing to print and distribute the document.   Early in October, at Erfurt, all copies of the bull were torn up or thrown into the river, and armed students prepared to confront Eck as he left Leipzig secretly by night to go to Erfurt.   The University of Vienna rejected the bull, pretending they needed to check with Emperor Charles first.   But the Bishop of Eichstätt published it within ten days of receipt, and Eck's own University of Ingolstadt stood by him.   By November the papal nuncio Hieronymus Aleander had arrived to help Eck.   At Mainz, whose archbishop seemed paralyzed by fear, he demanded the burning of Luther's books, but the public executioner refused to light the fire and Aleander was threatened with stoning.   Nevertheless he directed the provincial of the German Dominicans to have his friars preach against Luther throughout the province.   The Bishop of Augsburg was reluctantly persuaded to publish the bull November 8, but the Bishop of Bamberg refused, taking refuge in a denial of its authenticity— which the famous humanist scholar Erasmus, without knowing what he was talking about, had recently proclaimed.   Eck strode into the residence of the Bishop of Bamberg and slapped on the table his signed papal commission and written instructions to distribute the bull throughout Germany.   It was not easy to get away with lies about John Eck.[137]

Meanwhile Luther had published early in October "The Babylonian Captivity of the Church," in which he called the papacy "nothing but the dominion of Babylon and the true Antichrist" and the Pope "the man of sin and the son of perdition, who sits in the Church like God and by his doctrines and statutes increases the sin of the Church and the destruction of souls."[138]   In this writing Luther also launched his first general attack on the sacramental system of the Church, denying all sacramental character to confirmation, ordination, matrimony, and the anointing of the sick, accepting penance but denying that it could rightfully be made compulsory, and denying transubstantiation in the Eucharist while affirming a theory of "consubstantiation" whereby Christ was

---

[136] Von Pastor, *History of the Popes*, VII, 406.

[137] *Ibid.*, VII, 408-411, 423-424; Janssen, *History of the German People*, III, 129-130; Fife, *Revolt of Martin Luther*, pp. 540, 543n, 557n, 573.

[138] Fife, *Revolt of Martin Luther*, p. 534.

somehow present in the consecrated bread and wine without changing its nature; in other words, it remained bread and wine.[139]

At the end of October Luther published, in both Latin and German versions, his specific reply to the papal bull condemning him, *Exsurge domine*. Its goal, he said flatly in the Latin version, was "to compel men to deny God and worship the devil"; therefore "all good Christians should trample it underfoot." If its author and supporters would excommunicate him, he excommunicated them. The even more violently worded German version declared it impossible for anyone to be saved who did not reject the bull. In a further response the next month Luther described the Pope as "an unjust judge, hardened and erring, and, by all his writings, a convicted heretic and schismatic" and appealed from him to a general council, concluding with the statement that he had "now freed his conscience in the face of all who persist in obeying the Pope and is prepared therefore to confront the judgment of God on the Last Day." Before the next year was out he was not to feel quite so comfortable in contemplating his Judgment.[140]

On December 10, 1520 Luther climaxed his astonishing escalation of defiance by publicly burning at Wittenberg the papal bull condemning him, saying as he did so: "Because you have condemned the truth of God, He also condemns you today to the fire."[141]

Meanwhile the Holy Roman Emperor had come to the battlefront.

On June 6 he had arrived at his birthplace, the Flemish city of Ghent, where he was warmly greeted by his Aunt Margaret. (We would give much to know something of what they said to each other, as he told her all that had happened to him in Spain.) He remained in Flanders all summer, holding court at Ghent and Antwerp. Late in September the papal nuncio Aleander reached him there, bringing the bull against Luther. Knowing little of the young Emperor, Aleander approached the explosive subject tentatively and gingerly. "To his joyful surprise," as he later reported to the Pope, Charles told him immediately that he was "willing to lay down his life in defense of the Church" and committed himself to the immediate circulation of *Exsurge domine* throughout the Low Countries. On October 23 Charles was crowned at Aachen. In view of his avowal to Aleander, the words he spoke at the hallowed coronation ceremony must have taken on a very special meaning for him:

> "Wilt thou," said the Archbishop of Cologne, according to the ancient usage, "hold fast the holy Catholic faith, as it has been handed down from the Apostles, and show it forth in works that are worthy of it? And wilt thou yield due and loyal submission to the Pope and the Holy Roman Church?"

---

[139] *Ibid.*, pp. 530-538; Grisar, *Luther*, II, 32-34.

[140] Von Pastor, *History of the Popes*, VII, 413-414 (first two quotations on 414); Fife, *Revolt of Martin Luther*, pp. 552-556, 560-561 (third quotation on 561); Janssen, *History of the German People*, III, 130-132; Grisar, *Luther*, II, 49-50. See Chapter Two, below, for Luther's doubts in late 1521 about his Judgment.

[141] Fife, *Revolt of Martin Luther*, p. 580.

"I will," answered the Emperor, and laying two fingers of his right hand on the altar to give formal ratification to his oath, he added the words: "In reliance on divine protection, and supported by the prayers of the whole body of Christians, I will, to the best of my power, truly perform what I have promised, so help me God and the holy evangel."[142]

Martin Luther understood. Just three weeks later, on November 13, he wrote to Spalatin saying that no help was to be expected from Emperor Charles V. But Aleander, writing in mid-December from Worms in Germany to Cardinal de Medici, the future Pope Clement VII, after saying that many of the nobles, most of the jurists and writers, and even many clergy in Germany were infected with Luther's heresies, said he placed his hope in Emperor Charles, for "there has not been, perhaps for the last thousand years, a prince raised up with better dispositions."[143]

The grandson of Queen Isabel the Catholic was ready to throw himself into the breach that was cleaving Christendom.

After Elector Frederick of Saxony had once more rejected the demands of two papal nuncios—Aleander and Marino Caraccioli—that he imprison or hand over Luther, on the grounds that he was not yet convinced that Luther was in error, the Emperor wrote him on November 28 that he should bring Luther with him to the forthcoming imperial Diet at Worms, where he could be "examined by learned and well-informed persons," but that until then he should forbid Luther to publish anything more against the Pope and the Church. At a meeting of the imperial council December 14, Aleander objected to Charles' comments accompanying the invitation to Frederick and Luther, as presuming to hear an appeal from a decision by the Pope on a matter of doctrine and heresy to a temporal body, and urged Charles to issue an imperial edict condemning Luther, whose sixty days' grace had long since expired. For a young Emperor in the first flush of his power (it was only two months since his coronation) Charles accepted this firm correction with remarkably good grace. Just three days later he wrote again to Frederick revoking his invitation of November 28 and stating that Luther must recant before being admitted to the Diet at Worms; Charles added that in any case he wished to discuss the whole matter with Frederick at the Diet. He even gave this letter to Aleander for review before sending it. On December 29 the Council of State for the Empire drafted an edict against Luther and all his followers throughout the Empire, but did not issue it because of the hesitation of the timid Archbishop of Mainz, who was afraid of the consequences and tended to sympathize with Elector Frederick.[144]

---

[142] Janssen, *History of the German People*, III, 158.

[143] Von Pastor, *History of the Popes*, VII, 424-425 (quotation on 425); Fife, *Revolt of Martin Luther*, p. 562.

[144] *Ibid.*, VII, 421, 425-427 (quotation on 425); Fife, *Revolt of Martin Luther*, pp. 572, 587-591.

This December an anguished reply to Luther's "Address to the German Nobility" appeared from the pen of a Franciscan monk named Thomas Murner, accompanied by a fervent appeal to Emperor Charles to stand firm for the Faith against the most dangerous attack on it since the founding of the Holy Roman Empire by Charlemagne more than seven hundred years before. Luther, said Murner, had so "shamefully reviled and abused the Pope" that "even if he were a murderer and the greatest villain on earth he ought not to be treated so scandalously."[145] But it was Luther's attack on the sacrificial character and essential significance of the Mass that moved Murner most deeply. On the Mass, in his pamphlet, he addressed Luther directly and personally:

> I must tear open my heart here in great bitterness, and speak with you briefly in plain German. And I will set aside all priestcraft, doctor's degrees, monkhood, monasticism, vows, oaths, promises, and what not, by which I might seem laid under obligation, and will be simply a pious Christian. Well then, my father taught me from my youth up to show reverence to the Mass as a memorial of the sufferings of Christ Jesus our Lord, and thus all are taught who learn in the Holy Scriptures about our common Savior, Christ, that the Mass is a sacrifice, profitable for the living and the dead; all sacred teachers are of this opinion; it is our holy usage that has grown up with us since the time of the twelve Apostles. See to it now and remember, you high priests of the Faith, that you teach us the truth in this matter of the Mass, for it lies at the heart's core of every Christian man. . . . This I say from my Christian heart and my father's teaching: If all the bishops were silent as death [and indeed, most of the bishops of Germany had been just that silent against Luther so far], so that the worship of the Holy Mass became extinct, still I would testify with this my handwriting that I will die out of this world in the paternal doctrine of the worship of the Mass, and will trust for salvation to the contemplation of the Cross of Christ.[146]

Three days into the new year of 1521 Pope Leo X issued another bull against Luther, formally declaring him excommunicated for his failure to submit to *Exsurge domine* and withdraw his heresies. This bull was accompanied by commissions to Archbishop (now Cardinal) Albert of Mainz, the papal nuncios Aleander and Caracciolo, and John Eck to proceed against Lutherans wherever found, "even Electors," and followed on the 18th by a formal and urgent request to Emperor Charles to publish this bull of excommunication and enforce it throughout Germany, in keeping with the age-old duty of the Holy Roman Emperor to protect Christendom against heresy, when temporal means to that end were needed. Perhaps feeling the pressure, Luther wrote on January 25 to Elector Frederick saying that he wished very much to go to the Diet of Worms, where he hoped to show that all he had written and taught had been "for the salvation of Christianity as a whole, for the benefit of the entire German nation, for the

---

[145] Janssen, *History of the German People*, III, 151 (for the quotation), 153.
[146] *Ibid.*, III, 151-152.

extermination of dangerous abuses and superstitions." Handed a copy of this letter February 6, Emperor Charles scanned it quickly and ripped it to pieces. He drafted an imperial edict against Luther, but Chancellor Gattinara persuaded him to submit it to the Diet before issuing it.[147]

On February 13, Ash Wednesday, papal nuncio Aleander addressed the Diet of Worms, which had been in session since January 27. He first read Pope Leo X's letter of January 18 to Emperor Charles urging the immediate enforcement of the excommunication of Luther. He described Luther as a notorious, obstinate heretic who was inciting the German people to rebellion, and specifically noted the parallel of his revolt with that of Hus in the preceding century. He read to the Diet some of Luther's most violent statements, notably his exhortation to his readers to "wash their hands in the blood of the clergy" (quoted at the head of this chapter).[148]   On the proposed new hearing of Luther at the Diet he declared ringingly:

> All-gracious Emperor, how can a man be heard who has openly declared that he refuses to be taught by any, not even by an angel from heaven; that he desires nothing better than excommunication? Luther has appealed from the decision of the Apostolic See to a general council; yet he says publicly that Hus was unjustly condemned at Constance. Therefore I ask to know by whom he can be heard and judged."[149]

Until Aleander's great speech, many at the Diet had not understood how completely Luther now rejected the basic doctrines of the Church. There was a strong, though far from universal reaction against Luther. The next day the decree against Luther drafted by Emperor Charles (not yet present in person) was laid before the Diet. He was committed, Charles told the princes, bishops and noblemen at the Diet in his cover letter to this document, to support the Faith, the Church, and the Pope. Luther must recant and his books be destroyed and he and his followers punished as criminals if they would not submit. Fierce debates raged. Elector Frederick of Saxony now openly took Luther's part; he and the Elector of Brandenburg nearly came to blows. Many members of the Diet urged the Emperor, in view of the magnitude of Luther's popular support, to bring Luther before the Diet to give him a last opportunity to retract his errors. After five more days of vehement debate, the Diet made this proposal an official request and forwarded it to the Emperor, who took it under advisement.[150] Aleander wrote discouragingly to the Pope:

---

[147] Von Pastor, *History of the Popes*, VII, 416, 427-428; VIII, 22; Grisar, *Luther*, II, 56; Fife, *Revolt of Martin Luther*, pp. 612, 613 (for the two quotations, respectively) and 620-621.

[148] Janssen, *History of the German People*, III, 177.

[149] Von Pastor, *History of the Popes*, VII, 429.

[150] *Ibid.*, VII, 431-431; Janssen, *History of the German People*, III, 178-180; Grisar, *Luther*, II, 61-62; Fife, *Revolt of Martin Luther*, pp. 623-624; Brandi, *Charles V*, p. 130.

Were not the Emperor so well disposed, we must have lost the day. The Chancellor, Gattinara, considers it quite hopeless to fight the heresy without a Council. Charles' confessor, Glapion, dreads a general conflagration; the princes are full of indecision and the prelates full of fear. Everything is in such a state of confusion that, unless God help us, the wisdom of men will be of no avail.[151]

Three days later Aleander believed even the Emperor was wavering. The nuncio's life was threatened; he did not consider it safe to walk in the streets of Worms. On March 2 Charles informed the Diet that he accepted their request that Luther be invited to attend under an imperial safe-conduct, but insisted that once he arrived he be simply required to retract his errors, rather than being given yet another hearing. The strongly Catholic Duke George of Saxony also provided a safe-conduct for Luther to cross his territory. The imperial herald, Kaspar Sturm, was ordered to bring the imperial summons to Luther, though Sturm was known to be personally favorable to Luther.[152]

On March 21 Emperor Charles arrived at Worms in person, and presented the Diet with an argument for their support for military action against France in northern Italy. But Luther's revolt remained uppermost in the minds of the participants. It was now Holy Week. On Tuesday, March 26 Charles issued an edict ordering the destruction of Luther's books on his own authority, without waiting further for the Diet's approval. On Good Friday imperial herald Sturm rode into Wittenberg to deliver the imperial summons to Luther, who said he would depart for Worms immediately after Easter. He left on the Tuesday after Easter, April 2, in a wagon with three companions. On April 4 he stopped in Leipzig, where Duke George refused to see him, but the city council treated him with wine. On April 6 he was welcomed with the greatest enthusiasm at Erfurt, and preached in its church the following day, a Sunday, on his doctrine of justification by faith alone, good works not counting. On April 16, at ten o'clock in the morning, he arrived at Worms, where he was greeted by a crowd of about two thousand, including noblemen and some priests as well as the common people. Descending from his wagon, Luther cried "God is for me!" Aleander, watching from afar, spoke of his "demonic eyes."[153]

On that day, Hernán Cortés was fighting hand to hand with the Mexican devil-worshippers at Xochimilco; two days before, on the other side of the world, Magellan in the Philippines had baptized the King of Cebu; one week later, Constable Velasco won the decisive Battle of Villalar against the rebels fighting Emperor Charles in Spain. Christendom was in the cockpit of history.

---

[151] Von Pastor, *History of the Popes*, VII, 430.

[152] *Ibid.*, VII, 431-432; Fife, *Revolt of Martin Luther*, pp. 625, 627-629, 649-650; Janssen, *History of the German People*, III, 181, 186.

[153] Fife, *Revolt of Martin Luther*, pp. 629, 632, 649-655 (see 655 for Luther's words and eyes); Grisar, *Luther*, II, 63-64, 339; Janssen, *History of the German People*, III, 167-168, 187-189.

The day after Luther's arrival, April 17, imperial marshal Ulrich von Pappenheim came to his lodgings (incongruously at the house of the crusading order of the Knights of St. John) to bring him before the Diet. A large crowd followed him, filling the streets. The small hall where the Diet was meeting was "packed . . . to the point of suffocation." Luther was frightened; observers noted his repeated changes of expression and continual turning of his head. Emperor Charles caught sight of him for the first time. One look was enough. "This man will never make me a heretic!" he declared roundly to his escort.[154]

Luther was led to a bench piled with more than twenty of his books. Johann von Eck,[155] legal consultant of the Archbishop of Trier, a tall man with a strong voice, cried out: "Martin Luther, His Imperial Majesty has summoned you for two reasons: to know whether you acknowledge as by you the books before you, which have been attributed to you; and then, if you do acknowledge them, whether you stand by them or wish to revoke any of them."[156] He then read a list of the books. Luther, speaking "in such a low voice that even those close to him could scarcely hear him, and as if he was paralyzed with fear," admitted to authorship of the books, and asked time to think about his response. He was given just one day, and von Eck proceeded with a lengthy speech warning Luther against dividing the Church and causing the loss of souls, urging him to reconsider and recant, and reminding him that the Emperor had pledged to stand by the Church and the Pope to the end.[157]

On the next day, April 18, came the hour of decision. The meeting of the Diet was moved to a larger hall in the palace of the Bishop of Worms. It was scheduled for five o'clock in the afternoon but delayed for an hour. Luther waited outside, surrounded by a large and generally supportive crowd, which pushed to get inside when the doors opened, making it very difficult for Emperor Charles to enter. Luther began to speak. He admitted that the books in question were his, and divided them into several groups. One group, he admitted, had attacked the papacy—"no one can deny," he said, ". . . that through the laws of the Pope and doctrines of man the conscience of the Christian world is held prisoner and the substance of the German people destroyed with incredible tyranny." Charles held up his hand, ordering him not to speak further on this point but to go on to the next of his categories of books. Some of his books, Luther admitted, might have been too frank, but for him to disavow them now would "strengthen tyranny." Von Eck replied, reproving Luther for "vehemence and bitterness unbecoming the monastic cloth" and for "setting up his own opinions against the sacred orthodox faith established by Christ." He then demanded "a sincere, candid, unambiguous answers, without horns" on whether

---

[154] Fife, *Revolt of Martin Luther*, pp. 658, 659 (for the two quotations, respectively).

[155] Unrelated to John Eck, the great Dominican opponent of Luther.

[156] Fife, *Revolt of Martin Luther*, p. 659.

[157] *Ibid.*, pp. 658-662; Von Pastor, *History of the Popes*, VII, 433-434; Janssen, *History of the German People*, III, 190 (for the quotation).

he would recant his errors.[158] Luther squared his shoulders, set his face, looked Emperor Charles in the eye, and said:

> If then Your Majesty and rulers ask for a simple answer, I will give it without horns and without teeth, as follows: Unless I am shown by the testimony of Scripture and by evident reasoning (for I do not put faith in pope or councils alone, because it is established that they have often erred and contradicted themselves), unless I am overcome by means of the Scriptural passages that I have cited, and unless my conscience is taken captive by the Word of God, I am neither able nor willing to revoke anything, since to act against one's conscience is neither safe nor honest. God help me, amen![159]

The dialogue was at an end, at least for that day; the crowd streamed out, many cheering Luther, who raised his arms and swung them in the German signal of victory, shouting as he came back to his lodgings, "I've come through! I've come through!" But some Spaniards in the courtyard of the bishop's palace, watching him go, cried "To the flames!"[160] Spanish soldiers were to confront German Lutherans on the battlefield again and again over the next 127 years as they fought out the irreconcilable division made clear that day. And Emperor Charles, who had adopted Spain as his country, now knew the full magnitude of the challenge he faced and the duty he bore.

That very night Charles wrote out in his own hand, in French—one of the two languages he had first learned as a child, along with Flemish—his own declaration to counter Luther's. It was read to the Diet the next morning at eight o'clock. Though not nearly as well known as Luther's statement, it certainly deserves to be known and remembered. No more eloquent, impassioned, heartfelt words were ever spoken at a turning point of history.

> You know that I am born of the most Christian Emperors of the noble German nation. of the Catholic kings of Spain, the archdukes of Austria, the dukes of Burgundy, who were all to the death true sons of the Roman Church, defenders of the Catholic Faith, of the sacred customs, decrees and uses of its worship, who have bequeathed all this to me as my heritage, and according to whose example I have hitherto lived. Thus I am determined to hold fast by all which has happened since the Council of Constance. For it is certain that a single monk must err if he stands against the opinion of all Christendom. Otherwise Christendom itself would have erred for more than a thousand years. *Therefore I am determined to set my kingdoms and dominions, my friends, my body, my blood, my life, my soul upon it.*

---

[158] Fife, *Revolt of Martin Luther*, pp. 662-666, quotations on 664, 665, and 666 (last two) respectively.

[159] *Ibid.*, p. 666. All modern authorities on Luther, both Catholic and Protestant, agree that in all probability he did *not* conclude with the celebrated words "Here I stand, I cannot do otherwise," which do not appear in any of the original sources on the proceedings in the Diet of Worms (see *ibid.*, pp. 666-667, and Grisar, *Luther*, II, 75-76).

[160] Fife, *Revolt of Martin Luther*, p. 668.

> For it were a great shame to us and to you, members of the noble German nation, if in our time, through our negligence, we were to let even the appearance of heresy and denigration of true religion enter the hearts of men. You all heard Luther's speech here yesterday, and now I say to you that I regret that I have delayed so long to proceed against him. I will not hear him again; he has his safe-conduct. From now on I regard him as a notorious heretic, and hope that you all, as good Christians, will not be wanting in your duty.[161]

Now the die was truly cast. The continental struggle to save the Church and Christendom had begun.

At Worms many were still trying to find a way to compromise, but no human art could reconcile or bridge the stark confrontation that had taken place there. On April 25 Von Eck gave Luther a formal notice of his dismissal from the Diet and 21 days to return home under the imperial safe-conduct. That evening Luther celebrated with his admirers at a table where malmsey wine flowed freely. Elector Frederick came to him and told him that plans had been made to take him to a hiding place where he would be protected, but he would not be told in advance where it would be or how he would be brought there. At ten o'clock the next morning Luther departed. On May 4 a troop of armed horsemen suddenly appeared on the road he was travelling and took him away with them. Luther's companions, whom he had not told of Elector Frederick's promise, fled in terror, spreading the report that he had been captured by enemies. But Luther knew what his "captors" intended. They took him to Wartburg castle, the ancient seat of the rulers of Thuringia high up on a great wooded ridge. There Luther stayed for nearly a year, taking off his monk's habit, letting his beard grow, dressing as a country gentleman, and calling himself Junker George.[162]

On May 10 Pope Leo X read Charles' great speech against Luther to his cardinals in consistory. A few days later the Pope wrote directly to the Emperor, saying that he had "surpassed all his expectations, and acted as a true champion of the Church."[163]

Back at Worms, on May 8 the Diet finally approved an edict against Luther based on Charles' original draft, with some changes by papal nuncio Aleander. It declared Luther an outlaw under sentence of death, condemned his heresy (specifically mentioning his denial of freedom of the will and his attacks on the sacraments, the Pope, and the Council of Constance, and citing his call for the laity to wash their hands in the blood of the clergy), and declared that "under a semblance of preaching the faith, he tried to destroy the one true faith; under pretence of preaching the Gospel, he destroyed all evangelical peace, love, and order." Charles approved the new draft, saying Luther appeared to him like a

---

[161] Brandi, *Charles V*, pp. 131-132. Emphasis added.

[162] Fife, *Revolt of Martin Luther*, pp. 672-678, 683-689, 691; Henry C. Vedder, *The Reformation in Germany* (New York, 1914), pp. 167-168; Janssen, *History of the German People*, III, 193-195.

[163] Von Pastor, *History of the Popes*, VIII, 32-33.

man possessed by the Devil. What was ever afterward known as the Edict of Worms was signed and formally promulgated on the last day's session of the Diet, May 25. The Pope hailed the Edict, and it seemed to signal victory for the Catholics; but in fact it could never be any more effective than the capability and means for its enforcement, which proved sadly lacking despite all that Emperor Charles could do. Cardinal Archbishop Albert of Mainz would not even co-sign the Edict, though he was the imperial chancellor for Germany, and did all he could to hinder any public proceedings against Luther in his own archdiocese and in his suffragan dioceses of Magdeburg and Halberstadt. It wsa a vivid warning of how far Germany had already gone in the direction that Luther sought to lead it.[164]

A religious vocation, as Catholics understand it, is a call from God. It summons a man or woman to dedicate his life to Christ in this special way of service, to help save his own soul and the souls of others. There are many vocations, and most have no great historical significance despite their indubitable spiritual significance. But in moments of historic crisis a vocation may be far more, summoning a man or woman to play a major part in saving the whole Church. Such was the vocation—the calling—of St. Paul, knocked off his horse on the road to Damascus. Such was the vocation of St. Augustine as the Roman empire descended into the abyss. Such was the vocation of St. Catherine of Siena just before the Great Western Schism of 1378. And such was the vocation that came in the summer and fall of 1521 in the north of Spain, after a young man named Iñigo López of Loyola was struck by a ricocheting cannon ball which severely broke his right leg in several places.

Iñigo was a Basque soldier, thirty years old and quite small of stature. He was vain, ambitious, and roistering. There is nothing to suggest a religious vocation had ever crossed his mind. But he had a talent for leadership; when the French invaded Spain's province of Navarra May 10, 1521—less than a month after the confrontation between Emperor Charles V and Luther—despite his low rank Iñigo took effective command of the resistance at the citadel of Pamplona, capital of the province. On May 21 he was felled by the cannon ball, and he, the citadel and its garrison were immediately captured.[165]

French doctors treated his leg, incompetently. He was sent home to his brother's house in the village of Loyola, but the leg would not heal. It had to be broken again and reset, nearly killing him; he received the last rites, and on June 28 his doctors expected him to die before midnight. It was the vigil of St. Peter's feast day—St. Peter the first Pope, whose successors Luther had so ferociously condemned and rejected. Iñigo prayed to St. Peter to intercede with Christ for his

---

[164] *Ibid.*, VII, 436-438 (quotation on 438), VIII, 37; Janssen, *History of the German People*, III, 196-197, 250; Grisar, *Luther*, II, 68; Brandi, *Charles V*, p. 132.

[165] Merriman, *Rise of the Spanish Empire*, III, 101; Knecht, *Francis I*, p. 105; James Brodrick, *Saint Ignatius Loyola; the Pilgrim Years* (New York, 1956), pp. 56-60; Mary Purcell, *The First Jesuit* (Garden City NY, 1956), pp. 54-58.

life. By midnight, instead of dying, he was beginning to improve and was soon out of danger. But his broken leg had healed in such a way that it was considerably shorter than the other, which would leave him with a severe limp, and an unsightly protuberance of bone. Iñigo demanded that it be broken and reset yet again, and in September it was.[166]

Slowly recovering from this debilitating third operation on his leg, confined to a canopied bed in "a large, bright, low-ceilinged room at the very top of the house,"[167] his right leg painfully hung with weights to stretch it to match his left, this young man who had been physically active all his life now lay helpless, day after slow dreary day. Though he had never been a student or a frequent reader, he asked for something to read. There were only two books in the house, a life of Christ and a collection of lives of the saints. Iñigo devoured them. The saints—especially Francis, Dominic, and a desert hermit of Egypt named Humphrey—caught his imagination as the heroes of the tales of chivalry he had previously loved had never done. He began to ask himself what it would be like to do as these saints had done. In October he received a vision of Our Lady with the Child Jesus, and resolved to dedicate the rest of his life to Christ, to make a pilgrimage to Jerusalem as soon as he was well, and then through prayer and penance to seek God's will for him. His brother argued against his change of heart in vain. In January 1522 Iñigo set out on his way to Jerusalem, his first major objective being the famous shrine of the Blessed Virgin Mary at Montserrat, near Barcelona, where he would make a general confession and begin his life as "a knight of God."[168]

As St. Ignatius of Loyola, he was to found the Jesuit order, the largest and most effective religious order in the history of the Church, which from its inception took on three colossal missions: to restore Catholic education in Europe; to evangelize the newly discovered lands beyond the sea; and to bring Protestants back to the Catholic Faith. To an extent that no one could have dreamed in 1521, with God's unfailing help he and his order accomplished all of those goals. It cannot be a coincidence that he was called at the exact historical moment when the battle lines against Martin Luther and his followers were drawn by Emperor Charles V at the Diet of Worms. No truer champion of Christ ever lived than the little Basque soldier whom God knocked into history and heavenly glory with a bouncing cannon ball. Christian history shows again and again that whenever the Church seems to stand on the edge of destruction, somewhere there is an Iñigo López literally or figuratively lying in a bed, meditating on Christ and His saints and marshalling his will to follow them forever, part of the reinforcement of the Church that will never fail, the substance of Christ's promise that the gates of Hell shall not prevail against it.

---

[166] Purcell, *First Jesuit*, pp. 60-65.

[167] *Ibid.*, p. 60.

[168] *Ibid.*, pp. 73-84, 91-95; Brodrick, *St. Ignatius*, pp. 66-74.

2
The Emperor Keeps the Faith
1521-1530
Popes Adrian VI (1522-1523), and Clement VII (1523-1534)

"It is for Your Holiness to consider whether the occasion justifies you in drawing the sword, which, as a rule, should scarcely be lifted by the chief shepherd even against an enemy of the faith; whether the course you are pursuing is in accordance with justice and right, and whether the liberty of Italy and the Church of Italy will indeed be benefited by it, or whether rather the honor and repute of the supreme shepherd of Christendom will not suffer serious detriment if the protector and defender of the Apostolic Chair himself be dealt with so unrighteously. The whole of Christendom will be thrown into confusion by this measure, and a fire will be kindled which it will not be easy to extinguish. And while the strength of Christendom is in this way shattered, treacherous enemies will drive the Christian flock step by step into false paths; new errors will spring up day by day; the doctrines of the heretics will take firmer and firmer root."—Emperor Charles V to Pope Clement VII, September 17, 1526, protesting the Pope's declaration of war against him[1]

"His conscience would not let him abandon the ancient Christian faith, hallowed by long usage. . . . As a Christian Emperor and Catholic prince he would set his life and all he had on the vindication of his own cause and of the ancient and holy Catholic faith."—from summary of statement of Emperor Charles V to the Protestant princes of Germany, September 8, 1530[2]

During the summer of 1521, while Iñigo López lay on his bed of pain at Loyola, in Wartburg castle on its high wooded ridge bearded "Junker George" was bored. Very few in Germany knew where he was. Only an occasional letter kept him informed of current events of special interest to him, such as the *pfaffensturm* ("priest-storm") in Erfurt, where the students in a few days destroyed more than 60 rectories, with their libraries and archives, and seven other clerical residences, and murdered a Catholic professor named Maternus

---

[1] Johannes Janssen, *History of the German People at the Close of the Middle Ages*, Volume V (St. Louis, 1903), p. 11.

[2] Karl Brandi, *The Emperor Charles V* (Atlantic Highlands NJ, 1965), p. 313.

Pictoris.[3] His feverish energy now had no outlet; the atmosphere of constant crisis that had surrounded him, acting like a stimulant drug that loosed his torrents of vituperative rhetoric, had disappeared. He had much time to think. His thoughts were not pleasing to him.

In August he began work on a new tract, "On the Abuse of the Mass." By November, though it was not yet complete, he had begun another, "On Monastic Vows," which he finished first. He was also working on his translation of the New Testament into German.[4] Both the tracts were published early in 1522, while he was still at Wartburg. They are vintage Luther. In "On the Abuse of the Mass" he said:

> I defy the idols and pomps of this world, the Pope and his parsons. You fine
> priestlings, can you point out to us in all the gospels and epistles a single bit
> of proof that you are or were intended to act as priests for other Christians? .
> . . The abominable and horrid priesthood of the Papists came into the world
> from the Devil . . . The Pope is a true apostle of his master the hellish fiend,
> according to whose will he lives and reigns. . . . The laws of the Pope are
> empty mockery and lies, that the popish priesthood is nothing more than a
> sign and an outward show; the popish Mass, which they call a sacrifice, mere
> idolatry, and worse idolatry even than that of which Jews or heathen are
> guilty, or ever have been guilty.[5]

But an entirely different note sounded in a personalized preface to this tract, part of a dedication to the Augustinians of Wittenberg who had followed him out of the Catholic Church:

> How often did my heart faint for fear, and reproach me thus: You wanted to
> be wise beyond all others. Are then all others in their countless multitude
> mistaken? Have so many centuries all been in the wrong? Supposing you
> were mistaken, and owing to your mistake, were to drag down with you to
> eternal damnation so many human creatures? . . . Are you alone wise?
> Suppose that all who follow you are merely dupes.[6]

On November 11, Luther had written to his old Augustinian friend Spalatin of how he was "going to make war against religious vows," but went on to say: "There is more than one Satan contending with me; I am alone, and yet at times not alone."[7] This was Luther's explanation of his doubts and nascent regrets— that they came from the Devil. But a Catholic would see them as coming from the other side of the cosmic abyss.

---

[3] Hartmann Grisar, *Luther* (St. Louis MO, 1913), II, 340-341; Janssen, *History of the German People*, III, 245-246.

[4] Grisar, *Luther*, II, 84-85, 88-90; Henry C. Vedder, *The Reformation in Germany* (New York, 1914), pp. 169-172.

[5] Grisar, *Luther*, II, 89-90; Janssen, *History of the German People*, III, 231.

[6] Grisar, *Luther*, II, 79-80, 165.

[7] *Ibid.*, II, 84-85.

Evidently Luther did not want to be alone with these contending spirits. He craved action now even more than printed invective. On December 3, 1521 a group of knife-wielding, stone-bearing students at the University of Wittenberg (many of them undoubtedly had been his own) stormed into the chapel as the priests were about to say Mass. They slashed the lectionaries and flung their stones at the priests, who scattered in terror. The next day Luther was there, in disguise. He could not have come from the Wartburg to Wittenberg in twelve hours. Unless it was an extraordinary coincidence, he must have known what was going to happen in advance. He said he disapproved of it, as rioting. But he declared himself well satisfied in general with the "progress" being made at Wittenberg.[8]

Staunchly Catholic Duke George of Saxony saw something very different from progress. Just two weeks before the assault on the Mass at Wittenberg he had written to John Frederick, brother of the Elector of Saxony who had persistently refused to take any action against the Lutherans in his domain, saying that he knew of fellow Saxons who had now rejected all religion, even denying the immortality of the soul. A man had ridden a donkey into church; altars and holy statues and pictures were being defaced and destroyed; priests were marrying; monks were renouncing their vows. The damage was spreading and going out of control. He urged John Frederick to persuade his brother not to continue to allow evil to flourish by doing nothing. "We are all now in the last quarter, as is plainly to be seen," Duke George declared.[9]

His warnings and counsel fell on deaf ears. John Frederick, who was to be the next Elector of Saxony, would become and may already have been a convinced Lutheran, while his brother, despite his inaction, always professed to be and remain a Catholic.

On Christmas Eve at Wittenberg a new liturgy written by Carlstadt (who had now become even more radical than Luther) was used at the university church. All references to the sacrificial character of the Mass were omitted, confession was explicitly not required of communicants, Carlstadt said the Mass without vestments, and the people were allowed to take the consecrated bread and wine directly from the altar. Mobs attacked priests in the town and threatened the priest at the castle church with pestilence and hellfire.[10] Luther seems to have approved of it all; in his work "On the Twofold Species of the Sacrament" in 1522, he said of changing the Mass liturgy to remove all references to it as a sacrifice: "The priest will easily be able to arrange that the common people learn nothing of it, and take no scandal."[11]

---

[8] *Ibid.*, II, 97; Vedder, *Reformation in Germany*, pp. 182, 185.
[9] Janssen, *History of the German People*, III, 258-260.
[10] Grisar, *Luther*, II, 98-99; Vedder, *Reformation in Germany*, p. 182.
[11] Grisar, *Luther*, II, 321.

On the day after Christmas, Carlstadt, a priest vowed to celibacy, announced his betrothal to the 15-year-old daughter of a poor nobleman. A year and a half later he was advocating polygamy.[12]

On March 1, 1522 Luther left the Wartburg, retaining his knight's disguise until he had crossed the territory of Duke George.[13] On the way he wrote to Elector Frederick in a style that showed unmistakably that he had put all doubts behind him:

> Your Electoral Grace is already aware, or if unaware, is hereby apprised of the fact, that I have not received the Gospel from man, but from heaven only, through Our Lord Jesus Christ, so that I might already have accounted myself and signed myself a servant and evangelist, and for the future shall do so.[14]

Well might Ulrich Zasius, professor of jurisprudence, have written in December to a student who had turned Lutheran:

> What unheard-of audacity it is for one solitary individual to set up his interpretation above that of the Fathers, of the Church itself, of the whole of Christendom! What justification can you show for such presumption? But I know what you will answer: the Spirit guides and leads you! The Spirit! Answer me, my Thomas, what spirit?[15]

On March 7 Luther was back in Wittenberg. Elector Frederick had finally been jolted out of his complacency by the violence in the churches there, and Luther condemned it; but he did not condemn Carlstadt's new Mass, which continued to be celebrated along with the old, and he was confident that most of the princes of Germany would eventually support him, under pressure if necessary.[16] He refused to accept criticism even by his friends of his ferocious gutter language, descending more than once into outright obscenity. Answering Henry VIII, whose book against Luther (probably actually written, at least in large part, by St. Thomas More) had won him the title "Defender of the Faith" from Pope Leo X,[17] Luther called him, in two torrential sentences, "a nit which has not yet turned into a louse, a brat whose father was a bug, a donkey who wants to read the psalter . . . a sacrilegious murderer . . . a chosen tool of the Devil, a papistical sea-serpent, a blockhead and as bad as the worst rogues whom

---

[12] Janssen, *History of the German People*, III, 254; IV, 99.

[13] Vedder, *Reformation in Germany*, p. 186.

[14] Grisar, *Luther*, II, 91.

[15] Ulrich Zasius to Thomas Blarer, Dec. 18, 1521, in Janssen, *History of the German People*, III, 202.

[16] Luther to Wenzel Link, March 19, 1522, in *ibid.*, III, 267-268.

[17] Henry VIII in fact did keep the faith until his death, despite perhaps the most spectacular act of disobedience to papal authority in the whole history of the Church, to the great puzzlement of his Protestant subjects and many later historians.

indeed he outrivals, an abortion of a fool, an limb of Satan."[18] Far more significant was his statement later in this screed regarding the fundamental importance of the Mass and his campaign against it.

> If I succeed in doing away with the Mass, then I shall believe I have completely conquered the Pope. On the Mass, as on a rock, the whole of the Papacy is based, with its monasteries, bishoprics, colleges, altars, services and doctrines. . . . If the sacrilegious and cursed custom of the Mass is overthrown, then the whole must fall.[19]

On this point, at least, the Catholic Church and its terrible antagonist were in complete agreement.

On December 1, 1521, Pope Leo X, who had done his best to suppress Luther's heresy without ever understanding how much the Church's own failure to reform itself had played into Luther's hands and given him so many followers, died suddenly. He was only 46 years old but had long been in poor health; there is no evident basis for the rumors of poison which spread regarding his death as they always spread in Renaissance Italy whenever a prominent person died quickly and unexpectedly. The Swiss Guard, recently introduced to papal Rome, kept order splendidly, and the conclave convened before the end of the month, with 39 cardinals present. No less than 36 of them were now Italians, a great change from the days of the Avignon captivity.[20] The powerful Medici family of Florence controlled more than a third of the votes and thus could block any candidate they disliked, but did not have enough votes to carry the election for their candidate, Cardinal Giulio de Medici, who had been the right hand of the dead Pope. On the eighth ballot Cardinal Farnese (the future Pope Paul III), supported by the Medici, gained a majority, but the pro-French and anti-Medici cardinals, Colonna and Soderini, dug in and prevented Farnese from obtaining two-thirds. Deadlock threatened.[21]

It is Catholic belief that the Holy Spirit is present in a special way at conclaves as well as at ecumenical councils, and what happened at this conclave could be deemed one of the most striking items of historical evidence in support of that belief. For most of the cardinals at this conclave gave every indication of being totally caught up in the very worldly political and economic affairs of Renaissance Italy; few had shown any serious interest in reform, fewer still any signs of holiness.[22] None seemed farther removed from either than Cardinal Giulio de Medici. Yet on January 9, 1522 he rose to say:

---

[18] Grisar, *Luther*, II, 153.

[19] *Ibid.*, II, 320.

[20] The others were two Spaniards and one Swiss.

[21] Ludwig von Pastor, *History of the Popes from the Close of the Middle Ages* (St. Louis, 1950), VIII, 64-68; IX, 12-17, 20-21.

[22] One notable exception to both generalizations—in addition to the Cardinal about to be elected Pope—would be Cardinal Cajetan.

I see that from among us who are here assembled, no Pope can be chosen. I have proposed three or four, but they have been rejected; candidates recommended by the other side I cannot accept for many reasons. Therefore we must look around us for one against whom nothing can be said, but he must be a Cardinal and a man of good character." Then he proposed Adrian, Cardinal of Tortosa, "who is generally esteemed for his piety."[23]

This was Cardinal Adrian of Utrecht, the beloved teacher of Emperor Charles V—regarded by many leading Italians as a serious threat to dominate their country. No man could be more different from the typical Italian Renaissance Cardinal than Adrian of Utrecht. No shadow touched his name and reputation. He was scrupulously honest and fearlessly outspoken, almost to a fault. He had never been to Italy.[24] The Italian Cardinals barely knew him. But somehow they realized at this critical moment in the history of the Church and of Christendom that here was a man who towered over them in spirituality and integrity, and that the Church desperately needed such a Pope. Warnings that France would be mortally offended by his election, since he was an intimate friend and counsellor of Emperor Charles V whom the French regarded as their enemy, delayed his election for several more ballots, but his vote total increased on each ballot and on the 26th ballot he prevailed.[25]

Everyone was astonished. There have been few more unexpected elections in papal history. The cardinals themselves, within a few days, seemed surprised and apologetic about what they had done. Charles V was delighted but amazed. The new Pope was the most surprised of all. Not only holy but also a realist—as anyone who had been imperial viceroy through the *comunero* rebellion in Spain would have to be, or at least to have become—he could not imagine why he had been selected or how he was going to work effectively in the moral sinkhole that Italy had become, and he was far too genuinely humble to see himself as the recipient of a special electoral pre-emption by the Holy Spirit. But Charles, after several weeks to contemplate what had happened, understood. Despite his youth, he had already shown his capability in the discernment of spirits.

> The choice [of Adrian as Pope], which fell upon one who was never even contemplated by any party, appears to have been rather the choice of God, than of men.[26]

---

[23] Von Pastor, *History of the Popes*, IX, 22.

[24] He was considered one of the "Spanish cardinals," despite his Dutch origin, since he held a Spanish see.

[25] Von Pastor, *History of the Popes*, IX, 22-26, 34-45.

[26] Charles V to Bernard de Mezza, Bishop of Badajoz, Feb. 5, 1522, in William Bradford, ed., *Correspondence of the Emperor Charles V and His Ambassadors at the Courts of England and France* (London, 1850), p. 35.

God had given the Church its first truly holy Pope since Pius II sixty years before. It remained to be seen whether the Church, barely beginning to be chastened by the Protestant scourge, was ready to be worthy of him.

In his humility Pope Adrian refused to take a new papal name, the first Pope in centuries not to do so. He was at Vitoria in the mountainous Basque provinces of Spain in the middle of the winter; the chamberlain carrying the official message from the College of Cardinals declaring his election as Pope was held up for three weeks by blocking snowstorms. Adrian was still one of Charles' viceroys in Spain; though Charles was planning to return to Spain soon, he had not yet done so. Everyone wanted to congratulate and honor Adrian before he left. When he finally reached the coast there were still insufficient ships ready to escort him across the pirate-infested Mediterranean, and the winds were unfavorable. Extracting himself from Spain and getting to Rome took more than seven months, exceptionally slow even for those times. Some of the fault may have been Adrian's. His many virtues did not include promptness in action, and he was 62 years old and exhausted from his labors in Spain for his young master. It was not a good beginning for his pontificate, for he was head of Christ's Church in a revolutionary age and revolutions wait for no man.[27]

The most immediately evident cost of the delay did not, however, have anything to do with the Lutheran revolt. It concerned the easternmost outpost of independent Catholic Christendom, the island of Rhodes. A Greek island just off the coast of Turkey, it had been occupied for two hundred years by the crusading order of the Knights of St. John of the Hospital, founded in Jerusalem very soon after the First Crusade, whose celibate soldiers dedicated their lives to Christ through resistance to the advancing infidel. They had fought in Palestine until the last Christian stronghold there was taken, then on Cyprus, and then on Rhodes. They had withstood a mighty Turkish siege forty years before.[28] Now they were facing another. During the seven months that the new Pope slowly made his way from the snowbound valleys of Alava province in Spain to Peter's chair at Rome, the Turks had been approaching and then assaulting Rhodes under the personal command of their new and exceedingly able young sovereign, Sultan Suleiman the Magnificent.

The new grand master of the Knights of St. John, Philippe Villiers de l'Isle Adam, 57 years old, "tall, lithe, graceful, alert, with delicate sensitive face, high cheekbones and aristocratic, aquiline nose, soft, flowing white beard and hair . . . a stern ruler, tactful diplomat and sincere Christian," on his voyage from France to Rhodes the preceding September had seen a fire break out on his ship which was only put out when he threatened to hang any man who fled from it, and then had his sword struck by lightning. On Rhodes he found a letter from Suleiman awaiting him, boasting that he had just taken Christian Belgrade and killed its people or sold them into slavery. By the new year de l'Isle Adam learned that

---

[27] Von Pastor, *History of the Popes*, IX, 44-68.

[28] See Volume III of this history, passim, for their extraordinary accomplishments over the centuries.

Suleiman was planning a massive assault upon the great fortress of the Knights at Rhodes. All during the winter and into the spring he gathered supplies and reviewed his troops. He had only 500 Knights and their servants and 1,500 other soldiers against at least 100,000 Turks on 400 ships.[29]

But Philippe Villiers de l'Isle Adam was a crusader of the breed of Raymond of Toulouse and Richard the Lion-Hearted. The whole of history shows no more magnificently heroic struggle than he made at Rhodes against odds of forty to one. The Turks landed on the feast of Corpus Christi, June 26, 1522; a month later Suleiman arrived in person, and the bombardment and siege began in earnest.[30] Emperor Charles V knew what was at stake; on August 25 he wrote:

> If the Turk succeeds in making himself master of this island, the door will be open to him, and the key in his hands (after Hungary has been crippled and well-nigh ruined), to penetrate into Naples and Sicily, and right into the Church territory; and when he has traversed these districts, to conquer the whole of Italy and annihilate all Christendom.[31]

But Charles had just gone in the opposite direction from the action, returning from Germany to Spain in July, and the new Pope had still four days left before he entered Rome. There was no one to act on the desperate appeals from Rhodes for help. On August 24 de l'Isle Adam's emissary had returned with a cargo of food, a few soldiers, a handful of Knights, and many empty promises. This was all the help the Knights ever got in the final siege of Rhodes.[32]

On September 4 the Turks exploded a large mine under the bastion of the knights of England at Rhodes, which shook the whole city and blasted a 367-foot-wide breach in the wall. The Turks rushed for it, and were met squarely in the breach by de l'Isle Adam in person and his English knights, including Henry Mansell who had carried the banner of the Crucified Christ at the Turkish siege of Rhodes in 1480. The wave of attackers rolled back, but another surged in. Mansell was killed, but another crusader picked up the standard. De l'Isle Adam survived and held fast. Five days later another mine was exploded in the same area, followed by another series of infantry attacks extending over five days. All were repulsed. Back in Rome Pope Adrian, formally consecrated August 31, on September 16 called upon Emperor Charles V to make an immediate truce with France in order to be able to give quick help to Rhodes. But it took nearly two weeks for a message to reach Charles, and even if he had been able to persuade

---

[29] Eric Brockman, *The Two Sieges of Rhodes*, 1480-1522 (London, 1969), pp. 111-114, 118-121, 125 (quote on 111); von Pastor, *History of the Popes*, IX, 155-156.

[30] Brockman, *Two Sieges of Rhodes*, pp. 125-127.

[31] Janssen, *History of the German People*, IV, 6.

[32] Roger B. Merriman, *The Rise of the Spanish Empire in the Old World and the New* (New York, 1918), III, 116; Brandi, Charles V, p. 168; Brockman, *Two Sieges of Rhodes*, p. 130.

the notoriously selfish Francis I of France to agree to a truce, there was hardly time to arrange it and then put together a relief expedition. Instant action was needed, but was not forthcoming.[33]

On September 20 the Turks took the damaged bastion of the knights from Aragon at Rhodes and captured five Christian banners. The Knights fought back with swords, pikes, cannon, muskets, crossbows, Greek fire, boiling oil and pitch, and stones, and finally regained the ruins of the bastion, inflicting ten Turkish casualties for every one of theirs. On the 24th the Turks returned to the attack, and after hours of fighting finally took the ruined bastion of Aragon again, only to see it regained once more by the Knights at dusk. De l'Isle Adam fought all day by the banner of the Crucified Christ; Rhodian civilians, even some women, joined in the battle. Suleiman, observing the whole battle in person, was so enraged by the repulse that he dismissed his army commander, Vizier Mustafa, and almost killed him on the spot.[34]

On October 4 a ship from Naples brought the report that a relief force was assembling there, but probably would not be able to sail before the winter season closed down most sea traffic.[35]

But even among the magnificent Knights, in this immoral age treason could still happen. On October 27 the personal servant of Chancellor Andrea d'Amaral, de l'Isle Adam's rival in the recent election for Grand Master, was caught about to fire a crossbow into Turkish lines, with a message attached to the arrow saying that the defenders were in desperate straits and would probably be unable to repel another general assault. Under torture, the servant confessed to having carried several messages to the enemy already, which probably encouraged them to press their attacks despite their defeats. D'Amaral was executed November 8, and on November 30 another general assault by the Turks was repulsed.[36]

But there were now only 180 out of the original 500 knights left alive, and the majority of the survivors were seriously wounded. De l'Isle Adam personally preferred for him and his Knights to die fighting to the last man, but when Suleiman offered to let the civilians of Rhodes go with the surviving Knights if they would give up the island and the fortress, he reluctantly agreed for the civilians' sake. On January 1, 1523 they sailed away, praised by Suleiman himself for their valor, honored by all Christendom, the banner of the Crucified Christ still flying at the masthead of de l'Isle Adam's flagship *Santa Maria*, to settle on Malta where a young knight on the deck of that flagship named Jean de la Valette would command another critical siege forty years later, which that time ended in a Christian victory.[37]

---

[33] Brockman, *Two Sieges of Rhodes*, pp. 131-133; von Pastor, *History of the Popes*, IX, 69, 157.

[34] Brockman, *Two Sieges of Rhodes*, pp. 133-136.

[35] *Ibid.*, p. 136.

[36] *Ibid.*, pp. 139-148.

[37] *Ibid.*, pp. 148-155. See Chapter Six, below.

"Nothing in this world was ever so well lost as Rhodes," Emperor Charles V said, and it was true enough; but lost it was, and Pope Adrian knew what that loss meant and why it had happened. In February he said to the Venetian ambassador, with tears in his eyes: "Alas for Christendom! I should have died happy if I had united the Christian princes to withstand our enemy." On September 1 he received de l'Isle Adam for a personal report on the siege and its outcome—just two weeks before his death, which that report may have hastened. For the Turks had occupied Rhodes on Christmas day, and on that day of love and innocence they had desecrated and mutilated the altars, paintings and statues in the church of St. John at Rhodes, and spat on the crucifixes and dragged them in the mud.[38]

No less were the Protestants soon to do, in Switzerland, in Germany, and at Strasbourg on the Rhine.

From the day of his belated arrival in Rome, Pope Adrian VI had been a voice crying in the wilderness. Most Italians disliked him immediately; they found him too solemn, too self-contained, too much in earnest, too obviously uninterested in lavish entertainments and celebrations. The Italians are a theatrical people, and particularly in this age they expected showmanship from their Popes. There was no showmanship whatever in Pope Adrian VI. In a quieter, less dangerous age he might perhaps have learned how to cultivate it, or at least to pretend to it. But facing the now massive Protestant revolt, spreading with the speed and energy and destructive force of an erupting volcano, and the burgeoning Turkish threat, he could think only of his duty to rally Catholic Christendom against its two sworn enemies; and Christendom would not rally.

He denounced the corruption in Rome in the tones of an Old Testament prophet, saying to his first consistory of cardinals meeting September 1, 1522 that "the evil had reached such a pitch that, as St. Bernard says, those who were steeped in sins could no longer perceive the stench of their corruption. Throughout the whole world the ill repute of Rome was talked of."[39] He said Mass every day, the first Pope in a long time to do so. The Italians mocked his German accent and scorned his lack of appreciation for Renaissance art and sculpture, which he considered excessively pagan. Even his beloved former student, the Emperor, seemed estranged from him. He ignored the Pope's pleas to make peace with his enemy, Francis I of France. He sent to Rome an ambassador, Juan Manuel, who despised the Pope as an unworldly dilettante. There could have been no greater misjudgment; Pope Adrian may have hoped for too much from Europe's Catholic leaders, but there was iron in the soul of this man, now Vicar of Christ in one of the darkest hours in the history of the Church, who had faced death at the hands of revolutionaries on the walls of Valladolid during the *comunero* uprising in Spain. In December 1522 he excommunicated

---

[38] *Ibid.*, p. 155 (first quote); von Pastor, *History of the Popes*, IX, 174, 211-212 (second quote on 174); Janssen, *History of the German People*, V, 12.

[39] Von Pastor, *History of the Popes*, IX, 92.

Juan Manuel; in February 1523 he appointed a committee of cardinals to prepare proposals for drastic reductions in the size of the papal staff. One of those whose income was threatened tried to kill him, later that month, with a knife. His life was saved by one of the two genuine reformers in the College of Cardinals, Lorenzo Campeggio (the other was Cajetan). Adrian VI carried on, unwavering, unyielding—but unsupported.[40]

Early in the new year he made a surpassingly eloquent plea to the Diet of the German Nation assembled at Nuremberg, urging them to reject Lutheranism while acknowledging that it was rampant sin within the Church that had brought it forth:

> We cannot even think of anything so incredible as that so great, so pious a nation [as Germany] should allow a petty monk, an apostate from that Catholic faith which for years he had preached, to seduce it from the way pointed out by the Savior and His Apostles, sealed by the blood of so many martyrs, trodden by so many wise and holy men, your forefathers, just as if Luther alone were wise, and alone had the Holy Spirit, as if the Church, to which Christ promised His presence to the end of all days, had been walking in darkness and foolishness, and on the road to destruction, until Luther's new light came . . . We adjure you to lay aside all mutual hatreds, to strive for this one thing: to quench this fire and to bring back, by all ways in your power, Luther and other instigators of error and unrest into the right way. . . .
>
> We frankly acknowledge that God permits this persecution of His Church on account of the sins of men, and especially of prelates and clergy; of a surety the Lord's arm is not so shortened that He cannot save us, but our sins separate us from Him, so that He does not hear. . . . We know well that for many years things deserving of abhorrence have gathered round the Holy See; sacred things have been misused, ordinances transgressed, so that in everything there has been a change for the worse. . . . Each one of us must consider how he has fallen and be more ready to judge himself than to be judged by God in the day of His wrath. Therefore we, in our name, give promises that we shall use all diligence to reform before all things the Roman Curia, whence, perhaps, all these evils have had their origin; thus healing will begin at the source of the sickness. . . . We desire to wield our power not as seeking dominion or means for enriching our kindred, but in order to restore to Christ's bride, the Church, her former beauty, to give help to the oppressed, to uplift men of virtue and learning, above all to do that which beseems a good shepherd and a successor of the blessed Peter.[41]

In another document sent to this Diet, Pope Adrian specifically warned that Luther's teaching would inevitably led to civil as well as religious revolution, and that all German authorities should therefore unite in its suppression.[42]

---

[40] *Ibid.*, IX, 70-74, 106-107, 113, 163-164, 167.

[41] *Ibid.*, IX, 130-131, 134-135.

[42] *Ibid.*, IX, 132-133.

It was all in vain. The age was unworthy of Pope Adrian VI, would not hear him. The Diet at Nuremberg actually cited his own admission of the scandal given by the Church as an excuse for not enforcing the Edict of Worms. On March 3 Pope Adrian flatly ordered Charles and Francis to make at least a truce, so that they could both send armies against the Turks. He adjured Francis to do so "by the vengeance of God, before Whose tribunal you must one day stand." But Francis refused to consider it until he had secured Milan, while Charles did not respond at all.[43]

In late June Francis broke off all communication with Rome and prohibited all transmission of funds from the French church to Rome, denied the Pope's authority to demand a truce, and actually threatened him with the fate of Boniface VIII at Anagni. Francis was known to be planning an invasion of Italy. Consequently on August 3 the Pope joined a defensive alliance with various Italian powers, the Holy Roman Empire, and England against France, to try to protect Milan and prevent another Anagni.[44] But the alliance meant that he was now captive to the very forces he had tried to disband and redirect against the real enemies of Christendom. It may have been necessary, but it was sign and proof of his failure.

He did not long survive it. On September 3, just two days after his interview with de l'Isle Adam, the defeated but glorious Grand Master of the Knights of St. John, he fell mortally ill. On September 14 he died at the age of 64. The inscription above his tomb reads: "Alas! how much do the efforts even of the best of men depend upon time and opportunity."[45]

It was true, but did not go far enough. No man of power and influence had made any serious effort to create opportunities for the leadership of Pope Adrian VI. And he had been despised especially by the proud, corrupt, worldly and debauched society of Renaissance Italy, whose contempt of his virtues corroded any possible opportunity for them to work with him.

The leaders and trend-setters of Rome had scorned the holiest Pope in two generations. For most of that period, that same proud and corrupt society in Rome had scandalized Christendom, thereby doing much to rouse the great revolt that was to cleave Christendom in half. God did not fail to notice. Renaissance Rome would pay for that, within just five years—even as Jerusalem, the holy city, had paid for offending the Almighty in the time of Nebuchadnezzar of Babylon.[46]

Three days before the death of Pope Adrian VI, the Franciscan Provincial with custody over the holy places in Jerusalem had sternly refused permission to the obscure little Spanish pilgrim in sackcloth who begged to be allowed to remain for the rest of his life on the soil his Lord Jesus had trod. Profoundly disappointed, the future St. Ignatius resigned himself to returning to Spain, still

---

[43] *Ibid.*, IX, 169-170, 181; Brandi, *Charles V*, pp. 184-185.

[44] Von Pastor, *History of the Popes*, IX, 197-202, 206-207; Brandi, *Charles V*, p. 208.

[45] Von Pastor, *History of the Popes*, IX, 212-218; quote on 218.

[46] See Volume I, Chapter Six of this history.

not understanding what God wanted him to do, never presuming to think that the spiritual company he would found and lead would in just twenty years undertake the restoration of Christendom so nearly destroyed.[47]

The conclave to elect a new Pope met in the Sistine Chapel on October 1, 1523 with 35 cardinals present and a furious thunderstorm raging. (Did any sense an omen in the state of the sky?) They waited before voting until the three French cardinals, riding hard from France, had arrived. For more than a month there was deadlock, the pro-French Colonna faction of the Italian cardinals arrayed against the Medici. Politics and patronage dominated the debate. They had tried a holy Pope; he seemed to have failed. Cardinal Farnese, one of the contenders, was to be a great and holy Pope; but he had been appointed by Alexander VI because he was the brother of the Pope's mistress (for years he was called "the petticoat cardinal") and had four illegitimate children. Few if any were yet aware of the spiritual transformation already at work in him; he certainly did not campaign on it. In the end Cardinal Giulio de Medici—he who had so splendidly and surprisingly led the move to Pope Adrian at the last conclave—prevailed by lavish promises of Church offices, of which his wealthy and powerful family controlled more than the rival Colonna. The new Pope was only 45 years old, tall, handsome, courtly, charming, experienced, and unusually moral in private life for the age. His appointment was hailed all over Italy. The stodgy, awkward, humorless Dutchman would be succeeded by a genuine prince of the Renaissance church.[48]

He took the name of Clement VII. He seems to have meant well. He even had occasional thoughts of reforming the Church, though none of them were ever carried out. For Italy and for Rome, for whose people Adrian VI had been too good, the pontificate of Clement VII brought the greatest disaster since the Lombards devastated the country in the time of Emperor Justinian a thousand years before—and it was mostly his fault. Yet there remains one star in his crown: his defense of the marriage bond of Queen Isabel's daughter Catherine, wife of Henry VIII of England, against the worst the world could do to him and to her.

By 1524 in Germany the Lutheran assault on the monasteries was in full swing, the German universities which had spawned the Lutheran revolution were collapsing from its backlash,[49] and the final assault of the Mass had begun; while

---

[47] Mary Purcell, *The First Jesuit* (Garden City NY, 1956), pp. 141-142; James Brodrick, *St. Ignatius Loyola, the Pilgrim Years, 1491-1538* (New York, 1956), pp. 142-143.

[48] Von Pastor, *History of the Popes*, IX, 233-235, 241-248; XI, 18-22.

[49] There was a precipitous drop in enrollment at the now Lutheran University of Erfurt, from 311 students matriculating in 1521 to 34 in 1523. There were substantial though not wholly comparable declines in enrollment at the universities of Basel, Freiburg,

in Switzerland a new religious revolutionary had appeared who went even further than Luther, and soon gave his approval to the physical destruction of objects of Catholic devotion in and around his city of Zürich: Ulrich Zwingli.

Catholics victimized by these attacks found little help in their bishops. Throughout Europe, in this gigantic religious crisis, almost every bishop proved a broken reed. Only one was to stand fast for the Church in England, likewise just one in Denmark;[50] in Germany and Switzerland not one stood out as a champion of the Faith, and several deserted it (notably Bishop Erhard von Queis of Pomerania, who marked his arrival in his diocese in January 1525 by the immediate abolition of the Mass, and later the Archbishop of Cologne, Hermann von Wied, long a secret and finally an announced Lutheran).[51] In Italy virtually all the bishops were morally compromised. Profoundly Catholic Duke George of Saxony explained why, in instructions to his ambassadors drawn up by his own hand in 1524:

> It is as clear as daylight that the origin of all this heresy, which God is visiting us with, lies in the way in which the prelates enter into the Church; for God says, 'he that entereth not in at the door is not the shepherd.' Now it is, alas! not the least scandal of Christendom, that we laymen of high and low degree do not take heed to those words. For when we appoint our own children, brothers, and friends to bishoprics and other Church dignities we are not concerned about the door, but only how we can manage to push our own people in, whether under the threshold or through the roof we do not care. These gentlemen, moreover, who get in in this manner behave as if they had bought their benefices for their own heritage, and had full rights to them. . . .
>
> Every day scurrilous pamphlets and booklets to further Luther's gospel are printed everywhere, in which those who continue in their obedience to the Christian Church are slandered. There is no cessation of the endeavors which go on day by day to induce religious men and women to leave their cloisters; sermons and threats of everlasting hell torments if they remain in them, with promises of carnal prosperity and happiness if they leave them. . . . Those who cannot be got out by preaching are bought out by money, and where money does not succeed in moving them, they are accused of so much wrongdoing that they are obliged to come away. And these lords and princes who have thus managed to turn them out by fraud and by force take possession of their property as if it were a lawful inheritance. . . .
>
> People should be made to understand that because one bad covetous priest has transgressed, that is no reason why all priests and rulers appointed by God should be driven away, and their places filled up by scoundrels; that if one man abuses the service of the holy Mass, that is no reason why all Masses should be abolished; that if any have understood from the Canon that

---

Heidelberg, and Vienna, though these were not entirely Lutheran as Erfurt had become (Janssen, *History of the German People*, III, 356-363).

[50] See Chapter Three, below.

[51] Janssen, *History of the German People*, V, 107-110.

God is crucified afresh at every Mass, they should be instructed in the right way of understanding this mystery, the way that the Christian Church understands it. We must not sacrifice the whole body for the sake of one festered finger, but we must see that the diseased finger does not cause the death of the body; in like manner, if in one monastery there should be one or two wicked monks, all monastic orders must not be exterminated on that account.[52]

Most of the monasteries in Germany and many in Switzerland perished quickly, in the years from 1524 to 1530, in the manner Duke George describes. But some survived. In Switzerland, divided into self-governing cantons without a central government legally empowered to coerce them, a block of cantons in the mountainous heartland of the country, led by Lucerne, held out then and ever since against all pressure and inducements to abandon their ancient faith, and maintained all the monasteries within their boundaries, most notably the ancient Benedictine house at Einsiedeln. In Germany, the greatest fight was made a by group of 80 women without help from anyone and anywhere but their beloved Christ: the Poor Clares of Nuremberg under their indomitable abbess Charity Pirkheimer.

By 1524 Nuremberg had become thoroughly Lutheran, and the city council required the Poor Clares in their convent in the city to receive no more Catholic priests for spiritual guidance, but to accept Lutheran preachers instead. In their initial protest they explained that, contrary to the rumor that they were not allowed to read the Bible, they had both Old and New Testaments, in Latin and German, in daily use; contrary to the report that they relied entirely on their own merits and good works, they knew well that all good comes from God, Whose Cross they had taken and followed, but that they also knew there could be no true faith without good works, for the good tree must bear good fruit.[53] Later, when Abbess Pirkheimer realized that the city council was determined to impose the Lutherans upon the convent whatever she and the other nuns said, she wrote to one of the councilors, Martin Gauder, her brother-in-law:

We should be poorer than the poorest if we were obliged to confess to those who themselves have no faith in confession; to receive the Holy Eucharist from people who commit such terrible abuses with regard to it that it was shame and disgrace to hear; and to be obedient to men who themselves obeyed neither Pope, bishop, emperor, nor the holy Christian Church; men who abolished the beautiful services of God and instituted others out of their own heads, just as they liked. I would rather be dead than alive in such a case.[54]

---

[52] *Ibid.*, IV, 52-55.
[53] *Ibid.*, IV, 68-69.
[54] *Ibid.*, IV, 70.

Another member of this community, Sister Felicity Grundherr, wrote to her father, also a Nuremberg city councilor:

> With the help of God no one shall drag me out of my beloved cloister while I live. I will go further and will say this much: if they abuse the monastic state as something so terrible, I at least am of this mind: had I still my free will I would again offer myself to God of that free will; let them preach and say what they will, in the state of a nun I desire and intend to live and to die, and in this state, so God gives me grace, to await my Judge.[55]

Nevertheless the priests were kept away and the Lutheran preachers sent, reviling Church and Pope and clergy and religious, repudiating the Mass, and condemning the monastic way of life. For five years the Poor Clares were deprived of penance and the Eucharist. In June 1525 the wives of three of the Nuremberg city councilors informed Abbess Pirkheimer that they were going to remove their daughters from the convent, where two had dwelt for six years and the other for nine, by force. The abbess told the mothers she would not order the young women to leave, and they refused to go. A Lutheran crowd was assembled and they were literally dragged away, with one of the mothers striking her daughter in the face until blood ran. The official city chronicle, in its report of the incident, said the young women "were tired of convent life."[56]

History does not tell us whether any of these three was able to return; but nearly all the others stayed, and as time passed and word of their heroic constancy spread, priests began to come and minister to them in secret. In the end the community survived, along with a house of Observant Franciscans that was similarly persecuted. But all the other monasteries in and near Nuremberg were eliminated.[57]

On November 17, 1524 Luther, who had long criticized the continuation of the Catholic Mass at the last church in Wittenberg which still dared to conduct it, issued a peremptory demand for its immediate cessation. When his demand was not obeyed, he delivered a fiery sermon the following Sunday, calling the Mass "blasphemy, madness and a lie" and its celebration "worse than unchastity, murder or robbery," and urging "all princes and rulers, burgomasters, councilors and judges" to put a stop to it. There was an explosion of popular denunciation and ridicule of the priests and Mass-goers. Their appeals to Elector Frederick for protection went unanswered. They surrendered. For the first time since the founding of the town of Wittenberg, no Mass said on Christmas day 1524, nor for many years afterward.[58]

In July 1523 Ulrich Zwingli, a priest attached to the "great church" (*Grossmünster*) of Zürich in Switzerland for the past four years, who had violated

---

[55] *Ibid.*, IV, 71.
[56] *Ibid.*, IV, 79-83; Grisar, *Luther*, II, 335.
[57] Grisar, *Luther*, II, 335.
[58] *Ibid*, II, 329-330.

his oath of celibacy by a secret marriage early in 1522 and then challenged the Lenten fast in a pamphlet that year after attending a Lenten dinner at which much sausage was eaten, published a general attack on Catholic doctrine in the form of a defense of 67 theses. His position at this time was essentially the same as Luther's, though he later claimed to have known little of Luther when he wrote this treatise. Zwingli declared that no Church law or practice was binding unless explicitly stated in Scripture, and then only as interpreted by each individual believer. He harshly condemned relics, incense, and decorations in churches; processions and pilgrimages; canon law and payments to the Church; the sacrificial character of the Mass; the existence of purgatory; prayers for the intercession of the saints; and the monastic way of life. Two months later the town council of Zürich put him in charge of the Church there and its entire school system, without any semblance of seeking approval from the Bishop of Constance who had jurisdiction over Zürich, to say nothing of the Pope.[59]

In the same month (September 1523) that Zwingli became the official religious leader of Zürich, destruction of its church decorations and religious objects began: an altar retable and various ornaments in St. Peter's church on the 6th, several lamps in the Lady Church on the 13th, an image of Christ on the Mount of Olives in the town, and a miller's crucifix on his own property (allegedly with his consent, though he seems to have been bullied into giving it). The destruction of the two images of Christ (on the Mount of Olives and on the crucifix) was particularly significant in showing that this was full iconoclasm, not merely a protest against over-expensive ornamentation or prayer to saints. The city council at first refused to punish any of the offenders—all of whom readily admitted their acts—until they had decided whether such objects should be used devotionally; then, under criticism for their inaction, they exiled for two years the two men who had destroyed the crucifix. But when in December a group of men seized a donkey with an image of Christ on it, used in Palm Sunday processions, and threw it into Lake Zürich, the city council released them all with no penalty.[60]

At the next Candlemas, February 2, 1524, no candles were lit in the churches of Zürich. Finally bestirring himself, the Bishop of Constance sent to Zürich a detailed defense of the veneration of images, probably from the pen of his able Vicar-General Faber, which was read to the city council in June. The debate on the issue must have been furious, because during the course of it the two leading councilors who at least had doubts about the radical nature of Zwingli's "reforms" were mortally stricken and died. Their replacements were full supporters of Zwingli, and with their votes the council ordered the removal of all images from churches in the city of Zürich, with crucifixes temporarily

---

[59] G. R. Potter, *Zwingli* (Cambridge, England, 1976), pp. 74-81, 104-125, 220-222; William Oechsli, *History of Switzerland* 1499-1914 (Cambridge, England, 1922), pp. 81-82.

[60] Potter, *Zwingli*, pp. 130-131; Lee P. Wandel, *Voracious Idols and Violent Hands; Iconoclasm in Reformation Zürich, Strasbourg and Basel* (Cambridge, England, 1995), pp. 63, 67-80, 83-84, 90-92.

excepted.[61]   The work of removal began July 2.   Here is how it is described by a careful modern student who seems to see nothing wrong with it:

> For the next ten days they moved from church to church in Zürich. Behind closed doors in each church, they took down the sculptures and smashed them up, turning them into cobblestones; they took down the wooden panel paintings and the altarpieces, smashed them and burned them before the churches; they carried out all the objects made of precious metals and stones, broke them up, melted down the metals, and turned them all into money for civic uses, particularly the poor; and distributed to the poor the vestments and various garments of the religious. All the images, the "idols," carved, painted, sculpted, gilded, cast, and all the objects human skill had made beautiful, were returned to the substances from which they had been made—stone, wood, marble, gemstone, metal—and then were put to use as building materials, heating material, and currency for the poor. When the committee members were finally done, they washed the walls white so that none of the paintings of the medieval church would be visible.[62]

At this time the relics of Sts. Felix and Regula, patrons of Zürich, were secretly removed from their shrines in two churches and, according to one report, thrown into the charnel house where unclaimed flesh and bones were allowed to rot.   By November the net had stretched farther.   Now the city council demanded that every family which had gravestones in churchyards remove them, with or without the bones of their dead; any gravestones not removed would be appropriated by the city.   On December 3 all remaining monks and nuns in the canton of Zürich were brought together in an assembly and told that the younger ones must immediately return to secular life.   The older ones were allowed to remain in the religious life if they insisted, but might not recruit new members or wear a habit, and were required to attend Zwinglian sermons.   Meanwhile Zwingli had proclaimed his total rejection not only of the Catholic Mass but of the Presence of Christ in the Eucharist in any way.   In Holy Week of the following year the city council, at Zwingli's request, entirely abolished the Mass in Zürich.[63]

North of the Rhine in Bavaria, John Eck—still fighting day and night against the rampant heresy unleashed among his people[64]—heard of the havoc

---

[61] Potter, *Zwingli*, pp. 138, 140-141; Oechsli, *History of Switzerland*, p. 84; Wandel, *Voracious Idols and Violent Hands*, pp. 96-97.

[62] Wandel, *Voracious Idols and Violent Hands*, pp. 97-98.

[63] *Ibid*, p. 98; Potter, *Zwingli*, pp. 143, 156-158, 208; Oechsli, *History of Switzerland*, p. 85.

[64] Late in June he had met at Regensburg with Archduke Ferdinand, the Duke of Bavaria, and Cardinal Campeggio, now papal legate to Germany, along with several south German bishops, to discuss action against the Lutherans (Potter, *Zwingli*, p. 225). Out of this meeting, on July 7, came a formal association of the participants who committed themselves to enforce the Edict of Worms as fully as possible, to maintain the Mass, to withdraw all students from their territories studying at Wittenberg, to end simoniacal purchase of Church office, and to examine the qualifications and loyalty of all priests (von

wreaked by Zwingli. In August 1524 the Swiss Diet met at Baden north of the Rhine. Eck attended the Diet, attacking Zwingli's 67 theses as manifest heresy and offering to debate Zwingli before a Diet or a committee appointed by it. Zwingli responded by calling Eck a man of "notoriously evil life" and declining to meet him. In November 1525 Eck renewed his challenge to Zwingli for a debate at Baden, but Zwingli maintained his refusal to come, excusing himself by saying he feared the fate of John Hus at Constance.[65]

During this same period, at the famous old city of Strasbourg on the Rhine, Martin Bucer and Wolfgang Capito had established themselves as pastors. They were closer to Zwingli than to Luther, and like Zwingli were enthusiastic iconoclasts. In October 1524 all retables, paintings and relics were stripped from Strasbourg Cathedral, except for the retable on the high altar. The next month the grave of St. Aurelia in Bucer's parish church named for her was opened and everything found within thrown into the charnel house. During 1525, first Holy Week was abolished in Strasbourg, and then the Mass. The destruction was completed in 1526 when the great bell of the Cathedral was smashed to pieces before its doors, and the gilded cross presented by Emperor Charlemagne taken away and never seen again.[66]

Luther seems actually to have believed that he could tear out the whole structure of the Church from German society while affecting no other part of it. But of course there was no way this could be done. The revolutionary spirit Luther had unleashed would not be confined by any fences he later tried to build. The year 1525 brought to Germany a cataclysm which showed everyone with eyes to see what Luther's revolt had really wrought, causing Luther himself— almost certainly because of a suddenly guilty conscience—to denounce the revolution in terms as scathing as he had ever applied to the Church he wanted so much to destroy.

Many had predicted it, perhaps most poignantly Luther's old Augustinian teacher Bartholomew Usingen, who in 1524 wrote bitterly to Luther's associate John Lang: "I recalled you from exile . . . and this is the distinction you have won for yourself; you were the cause of the Erfurt monks leaving their monastery; there had been fourteen apostasies and now yours is the fifteenth; like the dragon of the Apocalypse when he fell from Heaven, you dragged down with you the third part of the stars."[67] Professor Usingen wrote to the preacher Culsamer, in January 1525:

Pastor, *History of the Popes*, X, 115; Janssen, *History of the German People*, IV, 44-47; Vedder, *Reformation in Germany*, pp. 211-212).

[65] Potter, *Zwingli*, pp. 155, 229-234; Oechsli, *History of Switzerland*, pp. 103-106.

[66] Wandel, *Voracious Idols and Violent Hands*, pp. 114-116, 123-124, 142; Janssen, *History of the German People*, V, 143.

[67] Grisar, *Luther*, II, 343-344.

By your demoralizing preaching you make the people seditious, and the result is that they not only revolt against the clergy, against whom you are everlastingly stirring them up, but also against all secular rulers. The latter will come to see, when it is too late, how foolishly they have acted in taking you under their protection.[68]

Hieronymus Emser blamed Luther directly and completely for the revolution of 1525:

Christ is the friend of peace, but this fellow [Luther] calls to arms. He invites the raging mob to wash their hands in the blood of the clergy. He provokes and incites the masses under a screen of false freedom. . . . He persuaded the people to look on him as a prophet, and to set his foolish fancies in a level with the oracles of Heaven. . . . The [German] people, after casting off all the wholesome restrictions of the ancient laws of morality, are bereft of all discipline, of all fear either of God or the authorities; virtue disappears, law and justice totter. . . . The heart of the German race has been hardened to stone; sunk in the mire, and given over to their passions, they despise all the gifts they have received of God.[69]

Luther had not intended these results of his preaching. As early as July 1524 he published a "Circular to the Princes of Saxony Concerning the Spirit of Revolt" in which he explicitly condemned the leading revolutionary, Thomas Münzer, for his incitement to armed rebellion, saying that he had never resorted to arms or favored doing so. Münzer replied promptly to Luther, calling him "Dr. Liar," and in September led a revolt in the city of Mühlhausen in central Germany, not far from Lutheran Erfurt, plundering churches and monasteries as he established a rebel government. In October there was a revolt in Klettgau in southern Germany, stirred up by both the Zwinglians of Zürich and by Münzer and his followers who came there to lead it. In December Münzer abolished the Mass in Mühlhausen, at the exact moment that Luther was doing the same in Wittenberg.[70]

The close association between Lutheran teaching and the revolution was apparent nearly everywhere that rebellion broke out. In southwestern Germany—Swabia and the Black Forest—where uprisings had taken place throughout the summer of 1524, the rebels (usually called "peasants," though actually they included many townsmen) in March 1525 formulated their demands in twelve articles which were quickly published and spread throughout Germany in some 25,000 copies. The first and last of these articles were explicitly Lutheran: that each parish should be allowed to choose its own pastor and that all laws were to be based on Scripture. The second and third articles demanded the ending of

---

[68] Janssen, *History of the German People*, IV, 301-302.

[69] Grisar, *Luther*, II, 221.

[70] *Ibid.*, II, 364-368; Janssen, *History of the German People*, IV, 219-224, 291-294. For Luther's abolition of the Mass in Wittenberg, see above, this chapter.

tithes to the Church; the rest concerned economic and political grievances. Many of these Swabian rebels joined that March in a Christian Union led by the furrier Sebastian Lotzer for "the exaltation of the evangel and the execution of divine justice." The governing articles of this organization stated that all pastors refusing to "preach the evangel" should be expelled from the country. Its adherents plundered churches, monasteries, and castles wherever they went, making no distinction among them. The Christian Union named Luther, Zwingli, and Luther's close associate Philip Melanchthon as "theological referees" to judge by Scripture the new laws the rebels intended to impose, a role which all three men immediately and indignantly rejected because of its association with armed rebellion. Rebels in the Odenwald, near Würzburg in central Germany, led by George Metzler, called themselves "the evangelical army to defend and administer the word of God."[71]

In April Münzer wrote from Mühlhausen to the miners of Mansfeld calling on them to revolt, in language which shows unmistakably how tightly and indissolubly religious and political revolution were linked in his mind:

> Awake and fight the battle of the Lord. It is high time. . . . At Fulda, in Easter week, four cathedral churches were destroyed; the peasants in the Klettgau, the Hegau, and the Black Forest are up, and more than 300,000 strong, and the host increases day by day. . . . Strike, strike, strike! This is the auspicious moment; the wicked ones are quaking like hounds. Do not let yourselves be moved to pity, even though Esau should speak fair words to you. Regard not the lamentation of the godless. . . . Strike, strike, strike! while the iron's hot. Keep your swords warm with the blood of tyrants. It is not possible, while they still live, that you should be freed from the fear of man. One cannot speak to you of God, while they rule over you. Strike, strike, strike! while it is still day.[72]

The German revolution of 1525 climaxed in Holy Week, which came late that year, from April 9 to 16. On the 10th Duke Albert of Brandenburg, Grand Master of the Teutonic Knights who had abandoned his Catholic faith, secularized the extensive lands of his order in order to form the duchy of Prussia, later to play a central role in German history as its leading non-Catholic state. On the 11th, in Bamberg near Nuremberg, fired by a Lutheran preacher named Johann Schwanhäuser, a violent assembly sounded the tocsin, chose leaders, barricaded the gates, pressed peaceful citizens into joining them by force, and summoned the whole region to revolt; they next day they looted the bishop's house. On the 12th Metzler's Odenwald rebels sacked the convent of

---

[71] Janssen, *History of the German People*, IV, 217-218, 220, 229, 233, 261 (for final quote); Vedder, *Reformation in Germany*, p. 236; Peter Blickle, *The Revolution of 1525* (Baltimore, 1981), pp. 19-20, 98-100. Luther had explicitly endorsed congregational government in 1523 (Grisar, *Luther*, II, 111, 114); he was later to change and support full state control of all churches.

[72] Janssen, *History of the German People*, IV, 296.

Lichtenstein and now held captive no less than four counts.[73] On Good Friday the rebels of the Christian Union of Swabia looted and destroyed the abbey church at Kempten. In the mournful words of a contemporary account:

> On the holy Good Friday, April 14, the day which ought to have been kept most sacred, on that day the Devil possessed them entirely. They destroyed the chapel of the rosary and the vault, tore down the pictures and images, and cut off Our Lady's head. . . . They decapitated all the images of God and our Savior and His blessed Mother, broke in two the image of the Child in the Virgin's arms, and other dear images of saints they dishonored, hacked about, threw down and broke in pieces. They emptied out the baptismal font in the church in a most sacrilegious manner, broke in pieces the cover and carried it off; also the sacramental pyx, which had been made at great cost, was quite destroyed. The ciborium also, in which the Blessed Sacrament was reserved, would have been blasphemously carried away if a priest had not protected it.[74]

On that same Good Friday George Metzler and his Odenwald rebels plundered "all that was ecclesiastical" in the town of Neckarsulm, then marched on Weinsberg in the kingdom of Württemberg. They arrived there just as Easter Mass was being said. When their demand for the immediate surrender of the city was refused they stormed it, aided by a traitor who opened a gate to them. They killed the priests who had just finished saying the Easter Mass, along with all others they found in the city, and also Count von Helfenstein and about a dozen nobles. The dead Count's two-year-old son was slashed with a knife and his widow was taken away on a dung cart, begging for Christ to comfort her. Before Metzler's Easter in Weinsberg was done, he was called to nearby Heilbronn to support an uprising there. Arriving with the blood and flesh of the victims of Weinsberg still on the clothing of some of his troops, Metzler took over Heilbronn on Easter Tuesday. On that same terrible Easter the city of Würzburg rose in revolt, capturing its bishop; his chancellor wrote: "No one knows how long we may be left alive. Everywhere they are crying out: 'Strike them dead! Strike them dead!'" On Easter Monday Dr. Gerhard Westerburg of Cologne, a Lutheran and the brother-in-law of Luther's one-time associate Carlstadt, led a revolt which seized control of the large city of Frankfurt on the Main.[75]

On April 25 the Black Forest rebels took Stuttgart, and on the 27th and 28th Erfurt was taken, its churches and monasteries sacked, and all priests and religious driven out or killed. In May the Rhineland rose. But now, in the face of

---

[73] *Ibid.*, IV, 259, 263; V, 112-113. Though not directly connected in any humanly visible manner, it is worthy of note that it was also in this Holy Week that the Mass was abolished by Zwingli at Zürich, with the wholly new "Lord's Supper" commemoration substituted for it at the great church in Zürich for the first time on Holy Thursday, April 13, 1525 (Potter, *Zwingli*, pp. 208-209).

[74] Janssen, *History of the German People*, IV, 234.

[75] *Ibid.*, IV, 263-267, 270-271, 279-281, 287-288; Grisar, *Luther*, II, 198.

this ultimate menace, all too briefly the Catholic and Lutheran princes made common cause. The army of Catholic Duke George of Saxony marched side by side with that of Landgrave Philip of Hesse, who had announced his conversion to Lutheranism in February. On May 4 Luther wrote his four-page pamphlet "Against the Murderous, Thieving Hordes of Peasants," in which he turned all the savage force of his invective on the rebels, calling for them to be hewn down, slaughtered, and stabbed like mad dogs. The next day Elector Frederick of Saxony, who had protected Luther without ever formally rejecting the Catholic Faith, died in despair ("I see neither love nor truth, nor any good thing remaining upon earth"); he was succeeded by his openly Lutheran brother John Frederick.[76]

Only a few days later the tide turned decisively with the arrival in the field of the well-equipped and well-trained armies of the princes of Germany. On May 12 George von Waldburg, general of the Swabian League of nobles, decisively defeated a peasant army of over 10,000 men at the Battle of Böblingen, ending the revolt in the whole of Württemberg. Jäcklein Rohrbach, who had Beem primarily responsible for the killing of Count von Helfenstein at Weinsberg on Easter Sunday and the injury and humiliation of his wife and child, was captured and executed. Three days later at the Battle of Frankenhausen Thomas Münzer drew up his men facing the army of Duke George and Philip of Hesse and the new Elector of Saxony in an exposed position without powder for his cannon, expecting a miracle because a colored circle had appeared around the sun at noon. Instead the rebel army was utterly routed by an artillery barrage followed by a cavalry charge. Münzer was captured hiding in a bed. He admitted he had intended to conquer Germany, capture or kill its nobles, and drive away or kill all who would not preach the "evangel" or join his league. Before his execution he was reconciled with the Church, begged pardon for his sins, made a good confession, and received viaticum with a last plea for mercy for the people and more justice for them in the future. In his death, though never in his life, Thomas Münzer had a lesson to teach Luther and Zwingli that they refused to heed when their time came to face the Judgment.[77]

The revolution was not over yet. On May 21 12,000 armed peasants who had acquired cannon laid siege to the town of Freiburg in Bresgau and bombarded it, smashing the dome of the cathedral. On the 24th the town had to surrender and was required in the surrender terms to develop a plan to suppress all its Catholic churches and monasteries and to "protect the evangel." On May 23 rebel leaders in Bamberg "proclaimed their resolution not to leave standing a single castle or nobleman's seat from which either they themselves or their forebears had suffered injury or oppression, but to pull down and burn them all." On May 25 there was

---

[76] Janssen, *History of the German People*, IV, 274, 302-304, 306; Grisar, *Luther*, II, 192, 201-203, 352, 354; Clyde L. Manschreck, *Melanchthon, the Quiet Reformer* (New York, 1958), p. 101; Vedder, *Reformation in Germany*, pp. 255-256 (quote from Elector Frederick on 255).

[77] Janssen, *History of the German People*, IV, 306-309, 315-316; Grisar, *Luther*, II, 203; Vedder, *Reformation in Germany*, p. 240; Manschreck, *Melanchthon*, p. 127.

a rebellion against the episcopal state ruled by the Archbishop of Salzburg; the rebels there "put godly law at the very center of their written program, demanding the authentic proclamation of God's word and grounding their economic demands in the gospel."[78]

But the armies of the princes were irresistible now, and one by one they defeated the remaining rebel armies and regained the cities they had taken, the rebels having little knowledge of siege warfare. At the Battle of Königshofen June 2 the combined armies of the Swabian League and Elector Ludwig of the Palatinate easily defeated the army of one of the original revolutionary leaders, George Metzler, who fled before the battle began; five days later this victorious army freed Würzburg, where they found that nearly 40 monasteries and 120 castles in the city and the surrounding area had been destroyed during the six weeks of rebel occupation. By early July both Frankfurt and Bamberg had surrendered. In December the Swabian town of Waldshut, where one of the first risings had taken place, was regained and the revolution was over.[79]

On August 23 Pope Clement VII wrote letters to the German princes congratulating them on their victory over the rebels, which he regarded as also a victory over the Lutherans.[80] So logically it should have been; even so realistic an observer as Catholic Duke George of Saxony thought likewise for a time, believing that Philip of Hesse and Elector John Frederick of Saxony must have seen the fearful consequences of protecting heresy in the revolution just put down.[81] But they had not drawn that conclusion. They were not even turned aside from their course by Luther's own bitter discouragement, expressed in a letter to Elector John Frederick October 31, 1525:

> The clergy are in a most wretched plight. Nobody gives anything in charity; nobody pays anything. Offerings and 'soul pennies' are out of fashion. Tithes are never forthcoming, or scarcely ever. The common people care neither for preacher nor for parson, so that unless Your Electoral Highness undertakes a thoroughgoing reform, before long there will not be a single parsonage, school or scholar left in the land, and God's word and service will go to the ground.[82]

Thus did Luther go over completely to the concept of a state-run church, which he upheld for the rest of his life. As for Landgrave Philip and Elector John Frederick, no one can say how religious and political motives mixed in their minds, but neither gave any indication of a change in their Lutheran confession.

---

[78] Janssen, *History of the German People*, IV, 245-246, 327 (Bamberg quote), 338-339; Blickle, *Revolution of 1525*, p. 101 (Salzburg quote).

[79] Janssen, *History of the German People*, IV, 321-323, 327-328, 331-334.

[80] Von Pastor, *History of the Popes*, X, 119.

[81] Janssen, *History of the German People*, V, 49-50. In this expectation he even invited Philip and John Frederick to join the Catholic League of Dessau in July 1525.

[82] *Ibid.*, V, 86-87.

In August John Frederick ordered all priests in his domain to preach "the pure Gospel" and forbade them to hold requiems for the dead or to consecrate salt and water, and announced himself ready to carry out any plan that Luther drew up for the approval and maintenance of the clergy; in the following year Luther repeated to John Frederick that "the duty and responsibility have also devolved on you of setting these things [pertaining to the church] in order, for there is nobody else who either can or will undertake this work."[83] In October 1525 Philip and John Frederick were not only allied with each other, but working to set up an alliance with the Lutheran Dukes of Mecklenburg and Pomerania and the Margrave of Brandenburg and with the independent Lutheran cities in Germany.[84] Luther now declared that the Mass should be outlawed throughout Germany; Elector John Frederick said he would follow his guidance on this.[85] A year later, in October 1526, Landgrave Philip held a synod to discuss church organization in his domains, which called for the seizure of all Church property, prohibition of the Mass, expulsion of the monks, and the banning of processions, pilgrimages, relics, pictures, and statues in the churches.[86]

About a month before Pope Adrian VI died, in mid-August 1523, King Francis I of France was informed that a relative, Charles de Bourbon, one of the great land-owners of France, had signed a secret treaty with Emperor Charles whereby, when Francis made his next expedition into Italy to try to secure the city of Milan and the surrounding area in fertile Lombardy that it controlled, Bourbon would join the Emperor and counterattack France. The report was true. Bourbon just managed to escape from France early in September, whereupon he publicly pledged his service to Charles, and Francis decided not to go in person to Italy that year. The army he did send accomplished nothing before Milan, and had to retreat when winter came on. Its commander, Admiral Bonnivet, clung to his position on the Italian side of the Alps until April 1524 when he was badly wounded by an arquebus bullet and the legendary French warrior Bayard, "the knight without fear and without reproach," was slain. The army left 41 guns behind as it retreated to France with only 350 men remaining out of an original 1,500.[87]

On July 1, 1524 Bourbon led an invasion of southern France. It was only too typical of the bitter hostility between these two great Catholic sovereigns, Charles and Francis, that Charles—known for his chivalry—would disregard the knight's code by employing in so high a capacity a man who had betrayed his lord. Francis had a genuine hereditary claim on Milan, but so did Francesco Sforza whose rights there Charles was defending. Milan was one of the five most

[83] *Ibid.*, V, 87, 89 (for quote).

[84] *Ibid.*, V, 42.

[85] Luther to Spalatin, Nov. 11, 1525; Luther to Elector John Frederick of Saxony, Feb. 9, 1526 and reply by Elector John Frederick Feb. 13, 1526 (Grisar, *Luther*, II, 331-332).

[86] Janssen, *History of the German People*, V, 79-81.

[87] R. J. Knecht, *Francis I* (Cambridge, England, 1984), pp. 148-155, 160-161.

powerful cities in Italy—the others being Rome, Venice, Florence, and Naples—and a rich prize, but by no stretch of the imagination was it worth what both Francis and Charles eventually paid trying to secure it. At first successful, Bourbon's invasion ground to a halt before stoutly defended Marseilles. The Spanish and German components of his army, neither with much liking or respect for each other or for their commander, began quarreling violently, and Bourbon had to retreat from France just as Francis crossed the Alps with a new and powerful army. He secured plague-stricken Milan without a fight and on October 26 laid siege to nearby Pavia, establishing his headquarters in a very large, thickly walled park called the Mirabella. In November Francis detached 6,000 men under the Duke of Albany to march south through Italy to conquer the kingdom of Naples, repeating the tactics of the French army led by King Charles VIII in 1494.[88]

The prospect of France, long an enemy of his Medici family, in control of both Milan and Naples, menacing the Papal State from two sides, unhinged Pope Clement VII. He seems to have ignored completely the evident fact that Charles' officers in Italy were gathering strong forces to oppose the French—forces so strong that they were able to defeat them decisively just three months later. Clement assumed Francis was going to win and that he must make the best terms with him that he could. Consequently on December 12 he made a secret alliance with France and Venice, sealed by a bilateral personal agreement between Francis and the Pope on January 5, 1525, by which Clement implicitly recognized French possession of Milan and consented to the Duke of Albany's army crossing Papal territory to get to Naples, in return for Francis' guarantee of the existing borders of the Papal State and the rule of the Medici in Florence. On the day this bilateral agreement was signed, Pope Clement wrote Charles to inform him for the first time of what he had done.[89]

Charles was bitterly angry, and wrote to his ambassador in Rome February 7 that he would carry on the fight in Italy even if it cost him his crown and his life. He closed the letter with the highly significant statement: "The present situation is not the best in which to discuss the affairs of Martin Luther."[90] It was the closest Charles ever came to making his Church and his faith a victim of politics. At that moment he was undoubtedly tempted to follow the course of all the other sovereigns of his time, whose religious position was primarily dictated by their personal or national political advantage; if he had succumbed to that temptation, under the circumstances of the moment and those that were to come during the next two years, Catholic Christendom would almost certainly have perished. But he never yielded to that temptation; he never broke his pledge given so dramatically in Luther's face at the Diet of Worms. Writing to the German

---

[88] *Ibid.*, pp. 162-164; Brandi, *Charles V*, p. 218. See Volume III, Chapter Fifteen of this history.

[89] Von Pastor, *History of the Popes*, IX, 265-270.

[90] *Ibid.*, IX, 271.

Estates in May 1525, Charles told them he intended to make every effort to persuade the Pope to summon an ecumenical council soon to restore religious unity and reform the Church, after which he would repress all heresy in Germany; meanwhile, he demanded that there be no further religious changes. Writing to them again in February 1526, Charles thanked the bishops and the loyal Catholic nobles for holding firm against the Lutheran revolt, pledged them his unfailing help, and assured them of his uncompromising hostility to Lutheranism. To his brother Ferdinand he wrote in March 1526 that "he did not intend in the slightest degree to deviate from the obedience he owed to the Church."[91] Thus did Emperor Charles V continue to keep the faith.

On January 25, 1525 the imperial army, now 20,000 strong, marched to Pavia. On February 9 it broke through the French siege lines long enough to deliver a large quantity of gunpowder to the garrison of the city. On the 17th the exceptionally able Italian mercenary general known as "Giovanni of the Black Bands," who was fighting for the French, was severely wounded and retreated from the area with about 3,000 troops, who were personally devoted to him. This left the opposing armies at Pavia about equal in size. On February 24 the imperial army, commanded by Duke Charles de Bourbon and the Marquis of Pescara, unexpectedly attacked the French in force at Mirabella park, their approach unseen until they broke down its encircling wall. Francis I led a cavalry counter-charge before his artillery could fire, but a thousand Spanish soldiers who had become expert with the first infantry firearm usable on a battlefield, the arquebus, poured a devastating fire into the glittering French cavalry, the bullets smashing through their plate armor. Many of the French fled, along with many of the Swiss infantry, who were not really sure why they were there. Francis— young, ardent, wholly inexperienced in battle—kept charging and fighting furiously, with a horse killed under him, but never really took command. His aged chief of staff, La Trémoille, was killed by his side, his second horse went down, and about noon he was captured by the Spanish infantry.[92]

It had been nearly two centuries since a European king had been captured in battle. The victory was greater than Emperor Charles had expected or wanted, much as he desired a victory and much as he disliked Francis I. It threatened to distract him seriously from his twin missions as Holy Roman Emperor: the protection of Christendom from the infidel without and the heretic within, since it had nothing whatever to do with either mission. When the news was brought to Charles in Spain:

> He turned as pale as death and for a few moments did not utter a syllable. Then he repeated slowly the words of the messenger, went into his bedroom, and fell on his knees in prayer. The liberation of Europe from the Turkish yoke was the one thought that possessed his troubled soul. 'I will, as far as

---

[91] Janssen, *History of the German People*, V, 3, 54-56 (quote on 55).

[92] Von Pastor, *History of the Popes*, IX, 272-273; Knecht, *Francis I*, pp. 167-172; Merriman, *Rise of the Spanish Empire*, III, 233-236; Brandi, *Charles V*, pp. 222-223.

is in my power,' he said in German to the Polish envoy, 'use all diligence in order that general peace may be established throughout Christendom, and that I may be able to assist the King of Poland, my brother Ferdinand, and others against the infidels.' He allowed no firing of guns to celebrate the victory, but only thanksgiving processions through the streets of Madrid, and prayers for the blessing of God in the war against the Turks.[93]

Yet even while aware of the danger of being drawn away from his duty as Emperor by making his great opponent captive, Charles nevertheless fell into it. If he had simply demanded that Francis agree by treaty to give up his claim on Milan, Francis would probably have done so (as he in fact did four years later), and kept his word, considering all that the futile pursuit of Milan had already cost him. But now the romantic element in Charles' personality came to the fore. The French province of Burgundy had been the ancestral home of his grandmother when it and the Low Countries formed an independent kingdom. It had been taken over by the extraordinary political skills and strategy of King Louis XI of France, the "universal spider," fifty years before. It was now an integral part of France. Charles demanded Burgundy back. Francis, captive or no, would not and probably could not have given it to him; most of the French nobility and most of his family would probably have prevented him from surrendering it even if he had tried to do so. Charles should have known that. But he ignored it.

In June the captive French king was brought to Spain, and in August ensconced in Madrid under close guard. On August 16, as negotiations began, Francis made a secret declaration to two French envoys that he would not be bound by concessions forced on him as a captive contrary to his royal duty, and specifically mentioned the cession of Burgundy as such a concession which he would not honor. In September he fell seriously ill, and was thought by some to be dying; in October he tried to escape by blackening his face so as to be taken for a slave, but his plan was betrayed. After that he told Charles that he would rather spend his life in captivity than give up Burgundy. By the end of the next month he had changed his words, and told Charles he would give it up; but Charles' own ambassador in France had already warned the Emperor that Francis would never actually do so.[94]

By December a treaty had been drafted, later known as the Treaty of Madrid. Sworn by Francis on the gospels and on the faith and honor of a knight, it provided for France to relinquish Burgundy, Flanders, Artois, and all its claims in Italy, not to aid King Henri d'Albret of Navarra (which Spain claimed), to restore Charles de Bourbon to his lands in France, and to marry Charles V's sister Leonor while leaving his two young sons as hostages in Spain for the fulfillment of the agreement. But the day before he signed the treaty, Francis repeated his

---

[93] Janssen, *History of the German People*, V, 4-5.

[94] Knecht, *Francis I*, pp. 174-175, 185, 187-188; Brandi, *Charles V*, p. 235; Ramón Menéndez Pidal, ed., *Historia de España*, Volume XX ("La España del Emperador Carlos V," by Manuel Fernández Alvarez), pp. 378, 381, 383.

disclaimer of August 16 that he would not be bound by it because made under duress, to the Bishop of Embrun, who was French ambassador to Spain, and to his leading counsellor Montmorency and other French officials with him. Charles' astute Savoyard Chancellor Mercurino di Gattinara warned him that Francis would never keep his promises in the treaty, and advised Charles either to release him unconditionally or hold him prisoner indefinitely, but chivalrous Charles preferred to trust in a knight's honor. Surprisingly, his viceroy in southern Italy, Lannoy, who seemed to have taken a liking to the affable and charming Francis, advised Charles that he could be trusted.[95]

Francis I has been called the very type of the Renaissance prince, and never did he prove it so clearly as in the final scenes before his departure from Spain. Charles spent nearly three weeks in Francis' company in late February and early March 1526; at one point he told him "that I should consider him a dastardly and unprincipled man if he failed in his promises," to which Francis responded: "I will fulfill every single condition, and I know that no one in my kingdom will hinder me. If you experience anything else at my hands, look upon me as a base and wicked man."[96] And a base and wicked man, at least on this issue, he proved to be.

On March 17 Francis crossed the border into his own country, as his two little sons were brought across the border in the other direction. Late in April he told the Venetian envoy that he would join in a league with Venice and the Pope "for Italian liberty" even if it meant violating the Treaty of Madrid and consequent captivity for his sons for many years. On May 10 the French royal council told Lannoy, the Spanish viceroy in Italy, that Francis would not be allowed to hand over Burgundy to Charles even if he wished to do so. On May 22 the League of Cognac was formed, including France, Milan, Florence, Venice, and the Papal State. The new allies would support France in repudiating the Treaty of Madrid, and would help ransom Francis' hostage sons, in return for Francis giving up his claim to rule Milan and Naples directly, though he would receive large yearly tributes from both. Though the Pope never explicitly absolved Francis from his oath to observe the Treaty of Madrid, the alliance made it very clear that the Pope did not consider the oath binding, that he was willing to aid and abet another breach of the peace in Christian Europe. The Pope's own ambassador in Madrid, the famous courtier and author Baldassare Castiglione, had warned Clement VII against any such action, saying "that the Emperor really was a loyal son of Holy Church, and really did prefer peace to war" but would fight to the end for what he believed was his by right.[97]

---

[95] Brandi, *Charles V*, pp. 235-236; Menéndez Pidal, *Historia de España*, XX, 378-379; Merriman, *Rise of the Spanish Empire*, III, 241-242; Knecht, *Francis I*, p. 189.

[96] Janssen, *History of the German People*, V, 6-7.

[97] Brandi, *Charles V*, pp. 236, 239-241; Merriman, *Rise of the Spanish Empire*, III, 242-244; Menéndez Pidal, *Historia de España*, XX, 394; Knecht, *Francis I*, pp. 191, 201, 207, 209-210; von Pastor, *History of the Popes*, IX, 304-305; E. R. Chamberlin, *The Sack of Rome* (New York, 1985), pp. 107-108 (quote on 108).

Charles was indeed furious; he felt betrayed by both Francis and the Pope. Since the Pope had in effect declared war on him, he felt justified in aiding the Pope's enemies, the Colonna, to attack Rome; in June he instructed his new ambassador in Rome, Ugo de Moncada, to contact the Colonna for this purpose if the Pope rejected a last appeal to change his policy toward the Emperor.[98] On August 17 Charles exploded with anger against Francis in a meeting with French ambassadors, challenging him to personal combat.[99] The next month saw the issuance of his solemn protest to the Pope which stands at the head of this chapter. It was eloquently and convincingly stated, and every word of its prophecies of the consequences of this action came true. But no one emerged from this sorry episode with any credit. Francis broke his pledged word and abandoned his two sons, Pope Clement VII stabbed in the back the only sovereign in Europe who could be counted on to keep the Catholic Faith as the cleaving of Christendom began, and Charles trusted a man whom all his experience with him should have taught him not to trust. And while all this was going on 100,000 Turks with 300 cannon were marching across eastern Europe like an avalanche and on August 29 delivered a knockout blow to Christian Hungary on a plain by the Danube near the town of Mohacs.

Hungary had fallen far since the days of the heroic John Hunyadi[100] and the centuries when it had been the shield of Catholic Europe against all its enemies to the east. While in Western Europe during the past fifty years kings everywhere had consolidated their power over the great nobles, in Eastern Europe the trend had been in the other direction, with the great nobles becoming stronger and more independent. Royal absolutism has grave dangers, but no monarch in Europe was yet absolute or close to it, and an invasion by 100,000 well-organized and well-led infidels could not be stopped by military private enterprise. A national, indeed international effort was needed under a highly competent commander. Hungary had no competent commander and made no national effort. Its King Louis II, an irresponsible and dissolute young man of 20 who did little more than play at being king, was no help. When Cardinal Campeggio went to Hungary in December 1524 to alert its king and nobles to their peril and to prod them at least to raise an army, he found no response except from one warlike bishop, Tomoro of Kalocsa. When Bishop Tomoro marched off to the southern frontier in February 1525 he had only the 300 troops Cardinal Campeggio had raised for him at his own personal expense. At a diet in July John Zapolya, a leading Hungarian nobleman who aspired to the throne, threw out the whole royal council with only a token protest from King Louis, but did nothing to strengthen the nation's defenses.[101]

---

[98] Von Pastor, *History of the Popes*, IX, 309-310.

[99] Brandi, *Charles V*, pp. 241-242.

[100] The successful defender of Belgrade in the siege of 1456. See Volume III, Chapter Thirteen of this history.

[101] Von Pastor, *History of the Popes*, X, 173-175.

On April 23, 1526 Sultan Suleiman marched from Istanbul with his mighty army. Hearing the report of their departure, Baron Burgio, papal representative in Hungary, wrote to the Pope that once the Turks arrived in Hungary, "Your Holiness may look on this country as lost."[102]

Late in May Louis II belatedly appealed to Emperor Charles V for help, but by the time the letter reached Charles in June, his new war with France and the Pope was impending, and he believed he had to retain all his military resources for that.[103] By July the Turks had reached the Hungarian frontier, where a tiny garrison consisting mostly of troops raised by papal representatives and funds held out heroically for two weeks in the citadel of Peterwarden against the immense infidel host. But when in mid-August Sultan Suleiman reached the Drave River, the principal military obstacle on the road to Budapest, he was astonished to find it undefended. He built a bridge of boats across it in five days and had all his army across it within a week.[104]

On August 29 was fought the decisive Battle of Mohacs.   Upon encountering the Turks, the main Hungarian army under the personal command of King Louis II charged the enemy at once against odds of more than two to one, not even waiting for John Zapolya's army of 15,000 to come up to reinforce them, though they were only a day's march away. Fighting Bishop Tomoro was killed along with most of the Hungarian army. Two thousand Hungarian heads were piled in front of the Sultan's tent, and at least 1,500 prisoners were slaughtered.   King Louis II fled the field, but his exhausted horse stumbled crossing a stream and threw the King into the surging waters, where he drowned in his armor. On September 10 the Turks took, sacked and burned Buda, the capital of Hungary, and then fanned out to ravage the countryside, mostly flat or rolling open land with no natural defenses.[105]

The conquest of the greater part of Hungary was not consolidated by the Turks for three years, and its only immediate result was an unseemly scramble for the tottering Hungarian throne by Archduke Ferdinand, brother of Emperor Charles; Dukes Wilhelm and Louis of Bavaria; and John Zapolya, the leading Hungarian nobleman who had failed to get to the Battle of Mohacs in time. Ferdinand was the strongest of the claimants, and was elected first King of Bohemia (a second crown which Louis II of Hungary had held) in October and then King of Hungary in December.[106] This double royalty, along with the ancestral Habsburg estates in Austria which Charles had given his brother, laid the foundation for the later Austro-Hungarian empire. But at this critical moment

---

[102] *Ibid.*, X, 178 (quote); Roger B. Merriman, *Suleiman the Magnificent* (New York, 1944, 1968), p. 85.

[103] Menéndez Pidal, *Historia de España*, XX, 396.

[104] Merriman, *Suleiman*, pp. 85-87; von Pastor, *History of the Popes*, X, 179.

[105] Merriman, *Suleiman*, pp. 87-94; Brandi, *Charles V*, p. 247; von Pastor, *History of the Popes*, X, 179-180; Janssen, *History of the German People*, V, 14-15.

[106] Janssen, *History of the German People*, V, 18-20; Brandi, *Charles V*, pp. 247-249; Merriman, *Suleiman*, p. 99; *Cambridge Modern History*, 1st ed. (1903), II, 199.

neither he nor any of the other claimants to the throne of Hungary did anything to defend, regain, or revive the country. The Turks were left free to incorporate most of Hungary into their own Ottoman empire, leaving them established only fifty miles from the heart of Europe at Vienna.

On September 20 the Colonna invaded Rome, left almost defenseless by the Pope because of his military commitments elsewhere under the new alliance. Many in Rome welcomed the Colonna and few Romans, angered by Pope Clement's wars and their cost, showed themselves disposed to defend him. The Colonna and their adherents attacked and looted St. Peter's while the Pope fled by the "covered way" running from St. Peter's to the huge, impregnable round fortress of Castel Sant'Angelo, which had once been Roman Emperor Hadrian's tomb. They even took the papal tiara, but that evening Spanish ambassador Moncada returned it to the Pope, simultaneously showing that the Emperor had good relations with the invaders but that he had no intention of trying to depose the Pope. Moncada negotiated a temporary settlement: a four months' truce in the war in Italy, the Pope to bring back his troops to Rome, and a full amnesty for the Colonna, who kept 30,000 ducats' worth of loot from the Vatican.[107] Charles' participation in this affair through his ambassador is very hard even for his admirers (of whom this historian is definitely one) to justify; since the Pope was making war on him he was entitled to defend himself, but hardly to connive at the sack of St. Peter's and its despoilers keeping their loot. Yet still he stopped short of claiming any power not his by right, such as to depose the Pope or to call a council on his own authority (though he did suggest that the College of Cardinals do so),[108] or giving the slightest support or encouragement to the Lutherans.

Pope Clement VII was now advised by several of his cardinals to leave Rome, where he had been shown so vulnerable and so lacking in popular support; but he resolved to stay. In November Giovanni of the Black Bands, the patriotic mercenary, brought his men to Rome to enable the Pope to regain full control of it.[109]

Emperor Charles V's army in Italy now consisted of nearly 50,000 men under the overall command of the traitor and adventurer Charles de Bourbon, who was constantly and desperately short of money to pay so large a force. There were also more than 6,000 imperial cavalry commanded by Philibert, Prince of Orange. The rest of the imperial army was infantry in four different and sharply divided national components. The largest of these was the 18,000 Germans commanded by George Frundsberg, Prince of Mindelheim, a ferocious old warrior who was a convinced Lutheran as were most of his men, and carried with him a silken rope to hang the Pope. Bourbon made no religious distinctions

---

[107] Von Pastor, *History of the Popes*, IX, 333-334; Brandi, *Charles V*, p. 250; Chamberlin, *Sack of Rome*, pp. 111-117.

[108] Von Pastor, *History of the Popes*, IX, 355-356.

[109] Ibid., IX, 337; Menéndez Pidal, *Historia de España*, XX, 402.

among his men; anyone who would come and fight for him was accepted. There is no indication that Charles, still in Spain, knew the religion of the German troops fighting in his name. The rest of the infantry consisted of 10,000 Spaniards commanded by the Marquis del Vasto, 6,000 Italians commanded by Fernando Gonzaga, and 8,000 Swiss. If these men, regardless of nationality, were for long unpaid they would cease to fight and turn on their commanders; among the commanders only Frundsberg aroused strong personal loyalty in his men.[110]

The four-month truce agreed upon after the Colonna raid on Rome was due to expire in January 1527, and Charles' Italian viceroy Lannoy demanded as the price for its renewal for six months a large payment by the Pope and the temporary surrender of four cities in the papal states and two in the domain of Florence (home of the Pope's family, the Medici) as surety for it. On January 25 a new envoy from Charles, Cesare Fieramosca, arrived in Rome with his personal confirmation of this demand. Three days later Pope Clement VII accepted it and signed the treaty, including the extension of the armistice for six months. But the very next day, January 29, after being told that aid was on the way from the French and the English (it was not), the Pope spectacularly broke his word and violated the armistice by sending his troops to attack imperial positions. One may search all of papal history in vain for a more imprudent or irresponsible act by any Pope.[111]

By mid-February Charles de Bourbon had scraped together enough money to keep his army from mutiny, and had taken many of his troops from Milan to join with Frundsberg in the Lombard plain. Attrition, desertion, and leaving a strong garrison in Milan had reduced their total number to about 22,000. On March 8 they camped less than a day's journey from Bologna in the Papal State. With none of the reported French and English aid forthcoming, Pope Clement VII made yet another switch, and signed another truce agreement with imperial ambassador Fieramosca. Each side was to give up its recent conquests, the Colonna would be absolved and restored, and the Pope would pay 60,000 ducats to Bourbon's army which would then withdraw from the Papal State. Viceroy Lannoy would come to Rome in person to ratify the treaty.[112]

The next day the cold, wet, underfed and mostly unpaid army of Charles de Bourbon, which had been dreaming of plundering the rich cities of the Papal State and even Rome itself, hearing reports of the truce negotiations though not yet of their outcome, rose in mutiny. Only Frundsberg had enough prestige to try to retain control of his men; when his exhortations failed to convince them, he collapsed with a stroke. On March 20 Fieramosca arrived at the camp with 30,000 ducats—half the required papal payment for the truce—but this came to

---

[110] Menéndez Pidal, *Historia de España*, XX, 405; von Pastor, *History of the Popes*, IX, 342-343; Chamberlin, *Sack of Rome*, pp. 91-94, 120-123.

[111] Von Pastor, *History of the Popes*, IX, 356-358, 365-366; Brandi, *Charles V*, pp. 251-252.

[112] Von Pastor, *History of the Popes*, IX, 361, 370-371; Brandi, *Charles V*, pp. 252-253; Chamberlin, *Sack of Rome*, pp. 126, 128-129.

less than two ducats a man, not nearly enough to bring the mutiny to an end. Fieramosca had to flee for his life. On March 29 the Pope and Viceroy Lannoy ratified the armistice treaty; but on the same day Bourbon sent a message to Lannoy that he no longer controlled the army and so could not carry out its terms. He reported that the men were ready to advance southward on their own.[113]

The next day the advance began. The composition of the army had changed substantially from what it had been earlier. Nearly two-thirds of the 22,000 were Germans, almost all Lutherans. The remainder were Spaniards and Italians; the Swiss had gone home.[114] Suddenly this was a Lutheran and not an imperial army, dominated by followers of the man who had called upon his people to wash their hands in the blood of the clergy, eager to make Rome their objective. It could no longer be justly called Charles V's army, for neither he nor his officers commanded it. In those days of slow communication, when it took at least two weeks for a message to reach central Spain from Italy (Charles was then at Valladolid on the high plains of Castile)[115] and therefore a full month for a message and its reply, Charles could not have learned about the mutinous army in time to do anything about it even if he had had a loyal army in Italy large enough to stop it, which he did not. While Charles must bear part of the responsibility for the Colonna raid of September 1526, he bears no responsibility whatsoever for the sack of Rome.

Early in April, though warned that Bourbon's army had mutinied and was advancing south, Pope Clement VII disbanded his entire army because the truce had been signed. No wonder some contemporary observers thought he had gone mad. He was not in fact insane, but had evidently suffered almost a complete breakdown in his power of judgment. On April 3 Viceroy Lannoy left Rome with 80,000 ducats to try to buy off the advancing army. Probably realizing this was not enough money, he went first to Florence—another possible objective for the army—and persuaded its rich men and leaders to provide 150,000 ducats for the ransom of their city. The mutinous army was crossing the Apennines to march on Florence when Lannoy reached them with this offer, which Bourbon, now speaking with the voice of his men, demanded be matched for Rome. As Lannoy undoubtedly knew, the papal treasury was exhausted, unable to make such a payment. He could find nothing to say in response to Bourbon, who on April 26 made the final decision, with the enthusiastic agreement of the Germans, to turn away from Florence and march on Rome.[116]

---

[113] Von Pastor, *History of the Popes*, IX, 374-376; Brandi, *Charles V*, p. 253; Chamberlin, *Sack of Rome*, pp. 130-132.

[114] Chamberlin, *Sack of Rome*, p. 152.

[115] "Itinerary of the Emperor Charles V," in Bradford, ed. *Correspondence of Charles V*, p. 492.

[116] Von Pastor, *History of the Popes*, IX, 377, 382-383; Chamberlin, *Sack of Rome*, pp. 132-135. Critics of Emperor Charles V, who claim he wanted the attack on Rome (which he did not and could not have known about before it happened) to take place (e.g. Chamberlin, *op. cit.*, pp. 133-134), say that Lannoy's failure to make a vigorous verbal

On May 2 the mutinous army arrived at Viterbo, just forty miles north of Rome, and Pope Clement VII seems then suddenly to have realized for the first time the magnitude of the peril. French Ambassador du Bellay saw him that morning and described him as in a state of inexpressible terror. Yet he would not flee, though many urged him to do so, and many others did. Rome had strong walls and a reasonable number of soldiers (though many were little more than poorly trained militia) to defend it, under the command of an apparently competent officer, Renzo da Ceri, in whom the Pope had "blind confidence." But Renzo was either a fool or a traitor; when on May 4 Guido Rangone with 8,000 infantry and 500 cavalry arrived at Viterbo the day after Bourbon's army left it, Renzo sent him a message that his army was not needed; Rome was adequately defended. On the evening of the 4th Bourbon's herald appeared at the walls of Rome demanding 300,000 ducats immediately for the ransom of the city. The Pope's excommunication of him was not a response that had much relevance at that apocalyptic moment.[117]

That night the mutinous army camped in the vineyards behind St. Peter's. The ragged, starving men had no place to go but forward. They had no supplies, no support, no place to retreat, no opposing general to surrender to even if they could have had quarter. No one had money enough to pay them. They must storm Rome or die. On May 5 they resolved to attempt it the following day.[118]

All that night the great bell on the Capitoline hill rang the tocsin. Dawn came with thick fog, hiding the attackers from sight. They had no usable artillery, only hand weapons and ladders "hastily constructed out of garden palings and bound together with withes." Their first and second attacks failed; Bourbon led the second attack in person and fell mortally wounded from a ladder. At six o'clock in the morning the Spanish attackers made a breach in the wall near the Vatican with a pickax, so narrow that only one man could pass through it at a time, while the German attackers found a cellar connecting a house outside the wall with one inside. Instead of rushing to block these two very narrow entry points, Renzo da Ceri panicked and fled, crying that all was lost.[119]

In the Vatican there was no warning of the breakthrough before it happened. Pope Clement VII was praying in his private chapel when the distracted Renzo burst in, screaming that he must flee instantly; he had only minutes, perhaps only seconds, to get away. Swords were already swinging and blood running at the high altar of St. Peter's that stands directly over the bones of the Fisherman, where most of the Swiss Guard, in the noblest moment of their long service, were giving their lives to save the unworthy Pope from the cursing, bellowing horde of

---

protest against Bourbon's decision proves their point. Surely the experience with Bourbon and his army had established by this time that words with them were useless; only money talked, and Lannoy could not promise money he and the Pope did not have.

[117] Von Pastor, *History of the Popes*, IX, 383-387; Chamberlin, *Sack of Rome*, pp. 140-152.

[118] Von Pastor, *History of the Popes*, IX, 387; Chamberlin, *Sack of Rome*, pp. 9-11.

[119] See Note immediately below.

armed savages surging into the mother church of Christendom. Still in his glistening white cassock and red skullcap, the Pope ran for his life, accompanied only by the historian Paolo Giovio, who later described the whole fantastic scene. The "covered way" from the Vatican toward Castel Sant' Angelo emerges upon an open wooden bridge giving access to the impregnable fortress. It was now full morning and the fog was gone; the Pope in his white cassock high up on the bridge could be seen from a considerable distance, and the attacking army was full of men who had sworn to kill him. Giovio flung his own purple cloak over the Pope to hide his white cassock, took off his skullcap, and hustled him through the gauntlet. Descending from it into the fortress, he saw a desperate, milling mass of humanity at the main gate, all trying to push through. One of them who succeeded was Cardinal Pucci, who had been thrown from his horse and trampled. One who did not succeed was Cardinal Armellini; he was still trying to get inside when the castellan, knowing Sant' Angelo was full of fugitives (there were three thousand of them) with no room for more, let the portcullis down with a tremendous crash, its huge iron spikes impaling anyone caught beneath. His torn red robe saved the cardinal's life; identifying him by it among the mob, the guards on the walls let a basket down for him. He climbed into it and was hauled up. On the battlements the famous sculptor Benvenuto Cellini manned the cannon, seeing that their iron balls swept the streets around the fortress to keep the attackers at a distance.[120]

It was the only refuge. The nightmare horrors that followed echo down the ages like screams from Hell. The sack went on for more than a week. No one was spared, regardless of age, sex, wealth, or nationality. Those unable to pay ransom were tortured and killed; and when ransoms were paid, more was demanded. Thousands of women of all ages were raped, and many tortured. Priests were murdered and mutilated, nuns dragged through the streets. Every church was plundered, by the Spaniards as well as the Germans. The Blessed Sacrament was desecrated. The Germans proclaimed Luther Pope in a mock ceremony. Much of the city was burned. Tombs were opened and ransacked. The great golden cross of Constantine that had been in St. Peter's for 1,200 years disappeared and was never seen again. The head of St. Andrew was thrown into the street and the veil of Veronica taken and offered for sale. The Vatican Library and the Raphael rooms adjoining it were saved only because Prince Philibert of Orange, the nominal commander of the invading army after the death of Bourbon, made his headquarters there.[121]

A Spanish observer wrote, a few weeks later:

> In Rome, the chief city of Christendom, no bells ring, no churches are open, no Masses are said, Sundays and feast-days have ceased. The rich shops of

---

[120] Von Pastor, *History of the Popes*, IX, 388-389; Chamberlin, *Sack of Rome*, pp. 156-163, 182-183.

[121] Von Pastor, *History of the Popes*, IX, 399-415; Chamberlin, *Sack of Rome*, pp. 165-181.

the merchants are turned into stables; the most splendid palaces are stripped bare; many houses are burnt to the ground; in others the doors and windows are broken and carried away; the streets are changed into dunghills. The stench of dead bodies is terrible; men and beasts have a common grave, and in the churches I have seen corpses that dogs have gnawed. In the public places tables are set close together at which piles of ducats are gambled for. the air rings with blasphemies fit to make good men, if such there be, wish that they were deaf. I know nothing wherewith I can compare it, except to the destruction of Jerusalem.[122]

Emperor Charles received the news of the sack of Rome in Valladolid with grief and sorrow, and at once suspended the public celebrations of the birth of his son and heir, the future Philip II, on May 21. The Archbishop of Toledo and the Duke of Alva urged him to release the Pope from captivity in Castel Sant' Angelo at the earliest possible moment, and the bishops of Spain considered going to the Emperor as a body, clad in mourning, to beg him to set the Pope free.[123]

By extraordinary chance, Charles' imperial chancellor Gattinara was already in Italy; he had gone for a long-delayed vacation to his native Savoy. Hearing of the march on Rome, he had gone quickly there, and on May 7, the day after the successful assault on Rome, he made his way to besieged Castel Sant' Angelo. There the shattered Pope, in tears, told him he flung himself on the Emperor's magnanimity. Gattinara set himself to try to work out a new agreement between Emperor and Pope.[124]

It proved a long and difficult process to disentangle the position of the Pope as head of the Church, desperately in need of help, from his position as the defeated and captured head of a sovereign state which had been at war with the Emperor and his allies. On June 5 the Pope formally surrendered to the Emperor and agreed to pay 400,000 ducats to the imperial treasury, but continued to be held at Castel Sant' Angelo until the first 100,000-ducat payment was made. Nothing could be done to reclaim most of the mutinous army, now scattered all over central Italy, still killing and looting, but dying rapidly of plague generated, appropriately enough, by the decomposing bodies of their victims in Rome. But if Charles were to keep order in Italy and defend his possessions there, he must have an army, and it still seemed to him just that the Pope whose hostile alliance

---

[122] Von Pastor, *History of the Popes*, IX, 422.

[123] *Ibid.*, IX, 449-450; William T. Walsh, *Philip II* (New York, 1937), pp. 14-16; Menéndez Pidal, *Historia de España*, XX, 414.

[124] Von Pastor, *History of the Popes*, IX, 418-419; Brandi, *Charles V*, pp. 254-255. Dark hints from Charles' traducers that Gattinara's vacation was actually a mission contingent upon foreknowledge of the attack on Rome are chronologically insupportable. Gattinara left Charles' court at the end of March, at almost the same moment that the mutiny of the army occurred in Italy. In view of the two weeks' time required to get a message from Italy to Spain, there was no possible way either man could have known of it then. Even imperial chancellors are entitled to an occasional vacation, and Gattinara was born and grew up in Savoy.

had made that army more necessary should pay part of its cost from his State. The Emperor's counsellor Lope de Soria advised that he eliminate the political authority of the Pope, simply taking over the Papal State, while leaving the Pope his religious authority. But Francisco de Quiñoñes, the Spanish general of the Franciscans who had been resident in Rome, appeared before Charles late in July to tell him that if he did not free the Pope he could no longer rightly be called Emperor, but "must rather be regarded as the agent of Luther, since in his name and under his banner the Lutherans had committed all their infamies in Rome." In November Chancellor Gattinara, returned from Italy, declared at a meeting of the Spanish royal council with the Emperor that so long as Charles V regarded Clement VII as the legitimate Pope he had no right to hold him prisoner.[125]

His Catholic conscience stirred by Quiñoñes' rebuke, Charles wrote to the cardinals, the Roman nobles and people, and the Christian princes, expressing deep regret for the sack of Rome and explaining that he had had nothing to do with it. Following Gattinara's recommendation, the Pope was finally released on the night of December 6, and withdrew immediately from Rome to Orvieto, sixty miles away. There he met with a special envoy from England, Dr. William Knight, who first told him of the wish of King Henry VIII of England to annul his marriage with Catherine, Isabel's daughter and Charles' aunt, so that he might marry Anne Boleyn. At the end of the December Knight brought him a draft bull jointly composed by Henry VIII and his prime minister, Cardinal Wolsey, invalidating Henry's marriage on five separate grounds. The Pope referred the draft to Cardinal Pucci (he who had barely reached Castel Sant' Angelo in time on the day of the sack of Rome after being trampled by his horse). Pucci declared that the bull as drafted "could not be granted without bringing indelible disgrace on the Pope as well as on Henry VIII and Wolsey." And it was not granted.[126]

In that same terrible year of 1527 the little Basque pilgrim who was to become St. Ignatius, having decided that in his mid-thirties he must go back to school to learn better how to teach the Faith that he burned to spread and deepen wherever he went, was enrolled first at the University of Alcalá de Henares and then at the University of Salamanca. At both places he was reported for the Inquisition for offering spiritual guidance and inspiration to anyone who would listen to him, despite being neither a clergyman nor the holder of a university degree. In both places the Inquisition soon cleared him of any taint of heresy, though they ordered him to limit his teaching in ways he found unacceptable, causing him to move on. (The Inquisition had jurisdiction only within a

---

[125] Von Pastor, *History of the Popes*, IX, 421-423, 429, 431-432, 446, 451 (quote), 459, 462; Chamberlin, *Sack of Rome*, p. 188.

[126] Von Pastor, *History of the Popes*, IX, 451-453, 466-467; X, 252-254 (quote on 254); Brandi, *Charles V*, pp. 252-253; Chamberlin, *Sack of Rome*, pp. 199-200; Philip Hughes, *The Reformation in England*, 5th ed. (London 1963), Volume I: "The King's Proceedings," pp. 166-167, 172-174. The full story of the annulment proceedings of Henry VIII, so important in the history of Christendom and especially in the modern history of the English-speaking peoples, is told in Chapter Three, below.

particular diocese.) On the last occasion, at Salamanca in August, where he had been actually imprisoned, he objected when the Inquisition released him, saying that he would have preferred to stay in the prison a while longer in order to suffer more for Christ. The next year he set out to enroll in the University of Paris, the most prestigious in Christendom, arriving early in February 1528.[127]

In March 1528 Emperor Charles V once again challenged King Francis I of France to settle their score by single combat, calling Francis vile and dishonorable for violating the Treaty or Madrid. Francis at first accepted, then did not follow through. Pope Clement continued to be caught between them, but now he understood better where his priorities should lie. Still at Orvieto because of continuing disorder in Rome, on Palm Sunday he addressed the cardinals on the need for reform of the Church, "and spoke emphatically of the sack of Rome as a chastisement for their sins."[128] The next month Bishop Stafileo, speaking at the reassembling of the Rota in Rome for the first time since the sack, gave this answer to the question of why the sack had happened:

> Because we are not citizens of the holy city of Rome, but of Babylon, the city of corruption. . . . We have all sinned grievously; let us reform, turn to the Lord, and He will have pity on us.[129]

So it was not only Luther who called Renaissance Rome Babylon, but a spokesman for the Pope. The sins of the city of the Popes had stoked the fires of its own destruction. The carnival of greed and simony and influence peddling, of fornication and adultery and public gluttony, the shameless parading of glittering luxury while so many lived in poverty, which had caused many to imitate these vices and many others to turn to Luther and Zwingli when they said the Church was the Devil's work and not Christ's—perhaps most of all the scornful rejection by the Romans of Pope Adrian VI who lived the virtues that could have healed them—had cried out to Heaven for vengeance; and vengeance had come from the God of Abraham, of Isaac, of Jacob, and of the prophet Jeremiah, who two thousand years before had told the proud and corrupt of Jerusalem who assumed He would never destroy the city that held His temple:

> Thus says the LORD of hosts, the God of Israel, Amend your ways and your doings, and I will let you dwell in this place. Do not trust in these deceptive words: "This is the temple of the LORD, the temple of the LORD, the temple of the LORD!" . . . Will you steal, murder, commit adultery, swear falsely . . . and then come and stand before me in this house, which is called by my name, and say "We are delivered!"—only to go on doing all these

---

[127] Purcell, *First Jesuit*, pp. 154-186, 188; Brodrick, *St. Ignatius Loyola*, pp. 154-179.

[128] Von Pastor, *History of the Popes*, X, 12-16 (quote on 16); Knecht, *Francis I*, pp. 216-217; Menéndez Pidal, *Historia de España*, XX, 431, 433.

[129] Von Pastor, *History of the Popes*, X, 446.

abominations? Has this house, which is called by my name, become a den of robbers in your eyes? I myself have seen it, says the LORD.[130]

Were there any who remembered, when Rome was sacked, the voice of Gianfrancesco Pica della Mirandola, at the Fifth Lateran Council just ten years before?

If [Pope] Leo [X] leaves crime any longer unpunished, if he refuses to heal the wounds, it is to be feared that God Himself will no longer apply a slow remedy, but *will cut off and destroy the diseased members with fire and sword.*[131]

On October 6, 1528 Pope Clement VII finally returned to Rome, a city in ruins, with four-fifths of the houses uninhabited and almost all the churches despoiled. On October 24 he wrote to Charles V:

Our grief for the ruin of Italy, manifest to every eye, still more for the misery of this city and our own misfortune, is immeasurably heightened by the sight of Rome. We are sustained only by the hope that, through your assistance, we may be able to stanch the many wounds of Italy, and that our presence here and that of the Sacred College may avail towards a gradual restoration of the city. For, my beloved son, before our distracted gaze lies a pitiable and mangled corpse, and nothing can mitigate our sorrows, nothing can build anew the city and the Church, save the prospect of that peace and undisturbed repose which depends on your moderation and equity of mind.[132]

If only he had realized that two years earlier, the tragedy and horror surely could have been averted. For the head of Christ's Church to fight a war with the Church's greatest lay champion in the face of maximum assaults by the infidel without and the heretic within was an act of folly unmatched in the whole history of the Church. None of the excuses made for it can stand historical and logical examination. Too much experience, both in his own life and in the lives of his Medici family, with the Machiavellian power politics of Renaissance Italy had blinded Pope Clement VII to his evident duty. In the magisterial words of Ludwig von Pastor:

If, in an age when hardly anything was respected except material power, when political considerations controlled every question, even the purely ecclesiastical, he refused to renounce his secular sovereignty, he certainly was acting intelligibly from a merely human standpoint; but higher and more Christian conceptions were demanded in one holding the office of Vicar of

---

[130] Jeremiah 7:3-4, 9-11. See Volume I, Chapter Six of this history.

[131] Von Pastor, *History of the Popes*, VII, 6. Emphasis added. See Volume III, Chapter Sixteen of this history.

[132] *Ibid.*, X, 30-31.

Christ. The pursuit of temporal power was to a certain extent fully justified, but ought always to have been subordinated to the supreme interest, that of devotion to the supernatural claims of the Church. That Clement only too often forgot this, throws a heavy shadow over his pontificate.[133]

For his blindness Pope Clement VII paid a bitter penalty, while many thousands of the people of Rome paid a still worse penalty for the same kind of blindness. Unlike them, Pope Clement was spared for seven more years, perhaps as an opportunity for repentance and recompense. There was little enough of either,[134] but some;[135] and there were the honor and the Catholic rights of Queen Catherine of Aragon to uphold, which this Pope, who before the sack of Rome never defended anything on principle, in the end did uphold. But how much even of that defense was principle, and how much derived from his new-found deference and fear of the great Emperor Charles V, her nephew, only God knows.[136]

In June 1529, at last, full peace was made between the Emperor and the Pope, in the Treaty of Barcelona, on terms very favorable to the Pope (suggesting genuine repentance in Charles for not having moved more quickly to end his humiliation and suffering after the sack of Rome). The Sforzas were to be restored to Milan (where they had been when the whole great conflict between Francis I and Charles V over Italy began); the Medici were to be restored to Florence; the cities taken from the Papal State were to be returned. The Pope was to crown Charles Emperor and recognize him as king of Naples with the right to move troops across the Papal State when necessary to get them there, in return for Charles' promise not to interfere in the transmission of Church funds from the kingdom of Naples to Rome. Charles pledged once again to do all in his power to suppress Lutheranism in Germany. Immediately Charles set out for Italy, leaving Isabel, his beloved wife of three years, his regent in Spain.[137]

On March 15, 1529 the next great Catholic-Lutheran confrontation began at the Second Diet of Speyer, with Charles V declaring to it by written message that pending the meeting of an ecumenical council (which Pope Clement VII had promised for the next year—a promise he did not keep), there should be no further religious changes and no violent measures or compulsion in religious matters, but that those denying the Real Presence in the Eucharist (Zwinglians and Anabaptists) should be suppressed everywhere. On his imperial authority he formally annulled the article in the final decree of the First Diet of Speyer in 1526

---

[133] *Ibid.*, X, 37-38.

[134] For example, when Pope Clement VII thought himself dying in January 1529, and made the traditional deathbed nomination of a cardinal, it was his 18-year-old kinsman Ippolito de Medici (*ibid.*, X, 39-40, 375).

[135] See *ibid.*, X 378-384.

[136] Again, on this point see Chapter Three, below.

[137] Von Pastor, *History of the Popes*, X, 56-58, 182; Brandi, *Charles V*, pp. 276-277; Menéndez Pidal, *Historia de España*, XX, 447-448, 479-482, 486-487; Janssen, *History of the German People*, V, 235; Merriman, *Suleiman*, p. 104.

stating that each ruler could act on religious matters as he saw fit. Though that continued to be demanded by the Lutherans at the Diet, on April 19 the majority reaffirmed the Edict of Worms, except for areas "where the new teaching had been introduced and could not be abolished without notable revolt, trouble and danger" and declared that even in such areas, Mass was not to be interfered with.[138]

That same day Landgrave Philip of Hesse, Elector John of Saxony, Margrave George of Brandenburg, Dukes Ernest and Francis of Lüneburg, Prince Wolfgang of Anhalt, and the representatives of 14 cities (of which the most important were Nuremburg, Ulm, Constance, and Strasbourg) issued a formal written protest against the Diet decree of April 19, declaring: "We hold your resolution null and not binding and we desire in matters of religion . . . so to live, govern and carry ourselves, in our governments as also with and among our subjects and kinsfolk, as we trust to answer [for] it before God." The next day they issued an expanded form of the Protest which explicitly declared that the Mass would not be said in the domains and cities of the signatories and stated their outright rejection of the Edict of Worms of 1521. On April 22 Landgrave Philip of Hesse, Elector John Frederick of Saxony, and the cities of Nuremberg, Ulm, and Strasbourg made a secret agreement for mutual armed resistance to any attack made on them by Catholics or adherents of imperial authority. On May 5 Philip of Hesse published the Protest. It gave Protestants their name, for it encompassed Zwinglians as well as Lutherans, indeed all the recent religious rebels but the Anabaptists.[139]

Responding in October to a deputation and message from the Protestants, Emperor Charles V told them they should have accepted the decree of the Diet of Speyer, and reminded them that Catholics also have consciences.[140]

On July 1, 1529 Philip of Hesse issued formal invitations to all the Protestant intellectual leaders, including Luther, Melanchthon, Zwingli, Oecolampadius in Basel, and Martin Bucer in Strasbourg, for a disputation September 29 at Marburg in Germany intended to unify the Protestants on the points of doctrine being most strongly disputed among them, notably the Eucharist. This reflected the growing importance of the Zwinglians, who had gained control of the powerful Swiss canton of Bern in 1528 and then of the city-canton of Basel early in 1529, accompanied by a fierce outburst of iconoclasm there. The Swiss party travelled together down the Rhine to sympathetic

---

[138] Janssen, *History of the German People*, V, 197-199, 202-203, 209-210; Grisar, *Luther*, II, 381-382 (quote on 381); Brandi, *Charles V*, pp. 297-300; Vedder, *Reformation in Germany*, p. 290.

[139] Von Pastor, *History of the Popes*, X, 124; Janssen, *History of the German People*, V, 210-211, 213-216, 218-219; Grisar, *Luther*, II, 382; Brandi, *Charles V*, pp. 300-301; Vedder, *Reformation in Germany*, p. 291; Potter, *Zwingli*, p. 318 (quote).

[140] Janssen, *History of the German People*, V, 238-240.

Strasbourg, where they held two weeks of preliminary meeting in September, then rode for Marburg.[141]

The disputation there took place on the first three days of October. Luther and Zwingli found themselves in full agreement on predestination and denial of the freedom of the will. They found themselves in full disagreement on the Eucharist, Luther insisting that the words "this is my body" meant what they said, while Zwingli insisted that they meant "this signifies my body," that Christ was in no way present at the "Lord's Supper," which was merely a commemorative service. The two men were as harsh with each other as they were with Catholics. At one point after Zwingli cited John 6:63 that "the flesh profits nothing" and then declared to Luther "that passage breaks your neck," Luther responded: "Necks are not so easily broken; you are in Hesse here, not in Switzerland!" Neither side would yield, and the discussion ended with Luther saying to the Zwinglians, "Well then, I abandon you to God's judgment." A conference of Protestant leaders at Schmalkald in Germany in December 1529, seeking to set up a general Protestant alliance, broke up over the Eucharistic dispute. The inevitability of infinite subdivision in a church without a source of final doctrinal authority on this earth, which has dogged Protestantism throughout its history, was thus already clearly manifest before it was a decade old.[142]

In July 1529, shortly after signing the Treaty of Barcelona with the Pope, Emperor Charles set out for Italy from Spain with a new army of 12,000 foot and 2,000 horse. Two months before, Sultan Suleiman led a Turkish army five times as large out of Istanbul, consisting of 75,000 men, mostly cavalry, and 300 guns. For the first time in eight centuries the infidel was reaching into the very heart of Christian Europe. In 733 the Arabs of Spain had marched more than halfway from the Pyrenees to Paris before being stopped at Tours by Charles Martel; that was the only precedent. No Muslim in arms had ever set foot on land inhabited by speakers of German; but Suleiman and his Turks were coming now, and they intended to stay. As the grand vizier of the Ottoman empire had told the embassy of Charles' brother Ferdinand the year before: "Wherever the hoof of the Sultan's horse has trod, there the land belongs to him."[143]

---

[141] *Ibid.*, V, 125-127, 139-140; Potter, *Zwingli*, pp. 261-263, 320-323, 377; Oechsli, *History of Switzerland*, p. 107; Wandel, *Voracious Idols and Violent Hands*, pp. 167-173, 188.

[142] Potter, *Zwingli*, pp. 323-329, 333 (327 for quoted exchange between Zwingli and Luther); Vedder, *Reformation in Germany*, pp. 310-311, 314 (311 for quote from Luther's final statement); Janssen, *History of the German People*, V, 229-233. Contrary to popular belief, Calvin was not the first Protestant leader to endorse predestination. In 1525 Luther published a major work, *De servo arbitrio* ("On the Enslaved Will") denying freedom of the will and endorsing predestination (Grisar, *Luther*, II, 266-279). Zwingli affirmed it unreservedly in a sermon preached in the presence of Philip of Hesse at Marburg September 29, 1529 (Potter, *Zwingli*, pp. 324-325).

[143] Menéndez Pidal, *Historia de España*, XX, 448; Merriman, *Suleiman*, p. 104; Janssen, *History of the German People*, V, 211 (quote).

On July 17, before Charles arrived in Italy, Suleiman was in Belgrade. The ominous Turkish advance in such great strength caused him to make major changes in his itinerary and plans for Italy. He gave up his intention to attack Venice, which had consistently supported France and his other enemies in Italy, and decided to receive his imperial coronation at Bologna rather than in Rome, the site of all earlier imperial coronations. Pope Clement VII readily agreed. On August 18, at Mohacs of evil memory, John Zapolya, the self-proclaimed king of Hungary now a traitor to Christendom, joined Suleiman with 6,000 men.[144]

But the summer was well advanced, and Buda, the capital of Hungary, still had to be secured, because Suleiman had not occupied Hungary after Mohacs. He had no doubt of his ability to occupy it whenever he wanted, but it would take time, and time was running short. The operation had been carefully planned, and there would have been enough time, except for the rain. In living memory no man had seen such rains. The flat plain of Hungary was awash in mud. Horses had no great problem with it, but big guns did. Suleiman had to leave them behind.[145]

On September 8 Suleiman took Buda and massacred most of its garrison. On the 18th the Turks crossed the Austrian frontier. Charles was at Piacenza in Lombardy, unable to reach Vienna before the Turks did; its defenders were on their own. There were only 12,000 of them, commanded by Count Nicholas von Salm; but they had their walls, and the certainty of death if they let them be breached. And Suleiman had no cannon to batter them down; they had been left back near Belgrade, in the mud.[146]

The walls of Rome had been penetrated, but the walls of Vienna held fast. On September 27 Suleiman announced that he would not rest until the muezzin of the Prophet Muhammad was heard from the tower of St. Stephen's Cathedral "and the whole of Christendom subdued." On the following day, in response, the defenders launched a sortie that killed 200 Turks within Suleiman's personal view. On October 9 the Turks exploded mines on either side of the Carinthian Gate, but were flung back from the breach by Count von Salm fighting shoulder to shoulder with his men. More mining and fierce fighting continued for the next five days, but the Turks could make no penetration, even when on the 14th Count von Salm was badly wounded when a fragment of stone shattered his thigh. Reinforcements were coming up, winter was approaching, the mines had not worked well, and cannon were unavailable. The Turks retreated and Vienna was saved, though the elite janissaries plundered and slaughtered through Christian

---

[144] Von Pastor, *History of the Popes*, X, 69, 73-75, 182; Menéndez Pidal, *Historia de España*, XX, 448; Merriman, Suleiman, p. 104.

[145] Antony Bridge, *Suleiman the Magnificent, Scourge of Heaven* (New York, 1966), p. 113.

[146] Von Pastor, *History of the Popes*, X, 183; Janssen, *History of the German People*, V, 235-236; "Itinerary of Charles V," *Correspondence of Charles V* ed. Bradford, p. 494.

Austria between Vienna and the Hungarian border as they moved back through it. They would return.[147]

The Treaty of Barcelona meant that Italy was now finally at peace, but the war between France and the Holy Roman Empire continued. But since its main cause had been power-seeking in Italy, there was no good reason for it to continue, despite the still keen personal hostility between Charles V and Francis I. This hostility, however, deterred both men from approaching each other to negotiate a peace. Therefore the mother of Francis and the adoptive mother of Charles, both women of great experience and fine political judgment, stepped in. Louise of Savoy, who had been regent of France during her son's captivity in Spain, and Margaret of Austria, who had been regent of the Low Countries for two decades, met at Cambrai on the border of France and the Empire in July 1529 to negotiate what soon came to be called the "Ladies' Peace." It was essentially the Treaty of Madrid with the surrender of Burgundy by France deleted. France was to renounce all claims in Italy, Flanders, and Artois. The two French princes would be released and sent home for a ransom of two million ducats. Francis would marry Charles' sister Leonor to seal the agreement. It was all that Charles should have asked for in the beginning, and we may well believe that Margaret had always thought it sufficient. On October 20 it was ratified and sworn in Notre Dame Cathedral after a solemn high Mass.[148]

On November 5, 1529 Charles V made ceremonial entry into Bologna, to which Pope Clement VII had just travelled for his coronation. Surprising as it seems, these two men, whose convoluted relationship shaped the whole history of this decade, had never before met in person. Von Pastor states:

> Italian writers of despatches were struck in Charles, who was not yet full thirty years old, by his seriousness, his sense of religion, and a certain slow deliberation of speech. Contarini [the Venetian ambassador], who had followed the Pope to Bologna, was impressed by the Emperor's absorption in affairs while there; he seldom left the palace except to hear Mass.[149]

On February 24, 1530 the ancient ceremony of imperial coronation was performed at the Church of St. Petronius in Bologna, following as exactly as possible the ritual previously used for coronations in Rome.[150] Though Charles had already been Emperor for eleven years, he had been at odds with the Pope for most of that time, accounting for the long delay in his coronation. It was then still universally believed that an Emperor's authority was not quite complete until the hallowed ceremony had taken place. Though not every past Emperor had been crowned by the Pope since that epochal Christmas day in 800 when the office of

---

[147] Bridge, *Suleiman*, pp. 116-120; Merriman, *Suleiman*, pp. 105-107; Janssen, *History of the German People*, V, 236.

[148] Brandi, *Charles V*, pp. 279-280; Knecht, *Francis I*, pp. 219-220; von Pastor, *History of the Popes*, X, 60; Menéndez Pidal, *Historia de España*, XX, 437-438.

[149] Von Pastor, *History of the Popes*, X, 83-84.

[150] *Ibid.*, X, 92-93.

Holy Roman Emperor was created, most of them had; it was part and parcel of Christendom itself, one of the most vivid symbols of its unity. Though few present at Bologna that day could have imagined it, this was the last imperial coronation by the Pope; there would never be another. For Christendom was dividing, and the greatest and holiest efforts to reunite it did not succeed, and still have not succeeded.

With the imperial crown in his hand, the Pope said to Charles:

> Receive this symbol of glory and the diadem of the Empire, even this Imperial crown, in the name of the Father and of the Son and of the Holy Ghost, that thou, despising the ancient enemy and guiltless of all iniquity, mayst live in clemency and godliness, and so one day receive from our Lord Jesus Christ the crown of His eternal kingdom.[151]

Charles responded by pledging to defend the Church and the Catholic Faith, and was anointed with consecrated oil by Cardinal Farnese, who was to be the next Pope, Paul III, with a pontificate far different and better than that of his predecessor. The Pope then said Mass, with Charles assisting, vested as a deacon. During the Mass the Pope gave Charles the sword, the orb, the scepter, and the imperial crown. Immediately after Mass, speaking privately with the Pope, Charles strongly urged him not to grant Henry VIII's request for an annulment of his marriage to his aunt Catherine.[152]

On March 22, 1530 Charles V left Italy for Germany, with greater power in Italy than any Emperor before him. But in Germany his power was weakening with the continued spread of Protestantism in all its burgeoning forms. In faithful Innsbrück nestled amid the spectacularly beautiful mountains of the Tirol he met his brother Ferdinand and his sister Mary, the widow of Louis II of Hungary, victim of the Turks. There his great Chancellor Gattinara died at his sovereign's side; henceforth Charles acted essentially as his own chancellor. On June 15 Charles entered Augsburg where the next annual Diet of the German Nation was soon to be held. Cardinal Campeggio, now again papal legate for Germany, blessed Charles and the princes, but Elector John Frederick of Saxony and Landgrave Philip of Hesse would not kneel for the blessing. They went to the cathedral, where a Te Deum was said with Charles kneeling twice on the bare stone floor, but John Frederick and Philip would neither kneel nor uncover their heads. Archduke Ferdinand later asked the princes to join in the Corpus Christi procession which would take place two days later; all the Protestants vehemently refused, Margrave George of Brandenburg saying that he would rather have his head cut off than go. The earlier Diets, at least up to that at Speyer the year before, had still presented a show of Christian unity. Now even the appearance was lost. The breach seemed irreconcilable. But the Catholic Emperor was not

---

[151] *Ibid.*, X, 94.

[152] *Ibid.*, X, 94-96; Brandi, *Charles V*, p. 288; Menéndez Pidal, *Historia de España*, XX, 454-456.

yet prepared to concede that. At this Diet of Augsburg he would make the last great effort to bring the two sides peacefully together before Christendom divided permanently.[153]

The critical and decisive Diet of Augsburg opened on June 20 with a solemn High Mass in the cathedral. At the offertory Charles himself brought the gifts to the altar. He was followed by all the princes present except Philip of Hesse, but the Protestants among them showed their scorn for the holy ceremony "with derisive laughter."[154] Luther was not present, but under guard at the castle of Coburg in Saxony, where Elector John Frederick had asked him to stay because technically he was still an outlaw under the ban of the Empire, where he had been placed nine years before by the Diet of Worms. Philip Melanchthon, the Greek teacher at the University of Wittenberg and Luther's close friend and ally, spoke at Augsburg for the Lutherans. Personally Melanchthon was a much more moderate and mild-mannered man than Luther, but there was little difference substantively in his beliefs from Luther's, and our extensive records of the relationship of the two men clearly show that Luther dominated it. At the first assembly of the Diet, Charles declared that he wished to end the religious disputes in Germany "by fair and gentle means" and to that end was willing to receive from the Protestants a statement of their beliefs and the grounds for them, which they should prepare and submit within four days.[155]

Melanchthon had already prepared a draft of this statement (later called the Augsburg Confession) and sent it to Luther May 11. Luther approved it, saying intriguingly, "I know not how to improve or change it, nor would it become me, since I cannot move so softly and gently."[156] Melanchthon and his associates, who had already arrived at Augsburg, were making revisions and additions to the Confession during the next month. On June 23 the final draft was presented by Melanchthon and his cohorts to the Protestant princes, who all accepted it and insisted on signing it. The next day the Diet agreed to hear it read, despite the strong protest of John Eck, who believed this too great a concession to heretics. The reading was done the next day in the episcopal palace hall at Augsburg, which would hold only 200 people. It was packed wall to wall, with hundreds more standing outside; it was a warm day and all the windows were open, so most of those outside could hear the reading. Copies in German and Latin were distributed to the notables present. The reading lasted two hours. The Confession condemned private Masses, compulsory confession, monastic vows, priestly celibacy, laws of fasting, and Communion in one kind only. It affirmed justification by faith alone and the Real Presence (while denying

---

[153] Von Pastor, *History of the Popes*, X, 98-99, 125-127; Janssen, *History of the German People*, V, 248-250; Brandi, *Charles V*, pp. 288-289; Menéndez Pidal, *Historia de España*, XX, 459; Manschreck, *Melanchthon*, pp. 185-188.

[154] Janssen, *History of the German People*, V, 250.

[155] Grisar, *Luther* II, 384; Vedder, *Reformation in Germany*, pp. 319-321; Manschreck, *Melanchthon*, p. 177 and passim.

[156] Vedder, *Reformation in Germany*, p. 322.

transubstantiation), and declared that it was legitimate to have bishops in the Church (the Lutherans had been leaning much more in that direction after beholding the chaos of the revolution of 1525). It made no mention of Luther's teaching on the authority of the Pope, predestination, the priesthood of all believers, indelible sacramental ordination, the number of the sacraments, and purgatory, nor of his condemnation of all Masses public or private.[157]

These were enormous omissions, as everyone present knew. The fact that they were not included in the Protestant Confession gave optimists reason to hope that the Protestants might be willing to abandon them; but those who knew them best, knew better. Cardinal Campeggio, now on his second mission as legate to Germany, urged that a committee of Catholic theologians headed by Eck study the Confession, specify its heresies, and demand that the signers recant them. Urged by Melanchthon to "concede to us that which we cannot with a good conscience relinquish," Campeggio shot back: "I cannot! I cannot, for the keys [the Pope] do not err!"[158] Luther wrote to Melanchthon that no compromise was possible with the Catholic Emperor. Charles' advisors urged him to request the Lutherans to state explicitly whether they would accept his adjudication of the religious controversy; if not, they said, Charles should maintain his policy of calling for an ecumenical council but in the meantime enforcing the Edict of Worms. Early in July the bishops presented their complaints to the Diet of the plundering and destruction of churches, seizure of monasteries and hospitals, prohibition of Masses, and attacks on religious processions by the Protestants. When Charles called upon the Protestants to restore the property they had seized, they said that to do so would be against their consciences; Charles responded crushingly: "The Word of God, the Gospel, and every law civil and canonical, forbid a man to appropriate to himself the property of another." He said that as Emperor he had the duty of guarding of the rights of all, especially those Catholics unwilling to accept Protestantism or go into exile, who should at least be allowed to remain in their homes and practice their ancestral faith, specifically the Mass; the Protestants replied that they would not tolerate the Mass.[159]

On July 4 four Zwinglian cities in Germany—Strasbourg, Constance, Lindau, and Memmingen—sent to Augsburg another statement of faith, named for them the Tetrapolitana. On the 8th Zwingli presented to the Emperor a statement of faith in his own name. Neither this nor the Tetrapolitana made much impact on either Catholics or Lutherans; Melanchthon wrote to Luther: "Zwingli has sent a printed confession here. One would think he was completely out of his

---

[157] *Ibid.*, pp. 322-326; Janssen, *History of the German People*, V, 252-253; Grisar, *Luther*, II, 384-385; Manschreck, *Melanchthon*, pp. 192-194; Brandi, *Charles V*, pp. 307-309.

[158] Manschreck, *Melanchthon*, pp. 194 (for quote), 197.

[159] *Ibid.*, pp. 95-96; Janssen, *History of the German People*, V, 256-257, 282-284 (quote on 282); von Pastor, *History of the Popes*, X, 131.

mind. . . . He vehemently defends his views of the Lord's Supper. Bishops he will in no wise tolerate."[160]

By July it was clear that on matters of doctrine the Lutherans at Augsburg were dissimulating, concealing their real beliefs in the hope of avoiding a final breach without making genuine concessions. On July 6 Melanchthon made the incredible statement: "We have no dogmas which differ from the Roman Church. . . . We reverence the authority of the Pope of Rome, and are prepared to remain in allegiance to the Church if only the Pope does not repudiate us." As it happened, on the very same day Luther, in an exposition on the Second Psalm addressed to Archbishop Albert of Mainz, declared: "Remember that you are not dealing with human beings when you have affairs with the Pope and his crew, but with veritable devils!"[161]

On July 8 the unresting John Eck presented to Emperor Charles a 351-page confutation of the Augsburg Confession. Charles sent it back to him with a request to tone it down and omit the uncompromising preface and conclusion. On the 13th Luther announced from Coburg that the Protestants would never tolerate the Mass, which he called blasphemous, and said of the Emperor: "We know that he is in error and that he is striving against the Gospel. . . . He does not conform to God's Word and we do."[162] On the 14th Charles reported to the Pope that the Protestants refused to accept his judgment on religious questions (as Luther's statement made perfectly clear) and that consequently he was convinced that an ecumenical council was the only remaining hope of restoring them to obedience, along with an appeal to them to make no more changes before it was held. Pope Clement, who never wanted to risk a council, replied July 31 that he doubted the need for it, but would hold it if the Protestants would return to obedience first (for which there was no prospect whatever).[163]

On August 3 Charles presented Eck's revised confutation of the Augsburg Confession to the Diet. It flatly rejected the Lutheran position on the seven sacraments, the Mass and transubstantiation, and insisted that the Papacy and the episcopacy were established by the authority of Christ. Charles declared his acceptance of the confutation and urged the Protestants not to press the issue further. Melanchthon seemed to agree, writing to Cardinal Campeggio "that if a few things were kept in the background, these divisions could be healed." On the 6th the most radical of the Protestant princes, Philip of Hesse, suddenly and secretly left Augsburg; clearly he was no longer interested in an agreement.[164]

---

[160] Potter, *Zwingli*, p. 334; Manschreck, *Melanchthon*, p. 198; Janssen, *History of the German People*, V, 271 (for quote).

[161] Janssen, *History of the German People*, V, 254.

[162] *Ibid.*, V, 287-288.

[163] Von Pastor, *History of the Popes*, X, 133-134, 136-137; Brandi, *Charles V*, pp. 310-311.

[164] Janssen, *History of the German People*, V, 258-261; Vedder, *Reformation in Germany*, pp. 326-327; Brandi, *Charles V*, pp. 309-310; Manschreck, *Melanchthon*, pp. 199-202 (quote from Melanchthon on 201).

On August 16 Catholic and Protestant committees headed respectively by Eck and Melanchthon began an article-by-article review of the Augsburg Confession to try to find common ground. Many concessions were made, at least verbally, with irreconcilable disagreement only on justification by faith alone, canonical penances, and the invocation of saints. But the most fundamental issue was avoided by both sides, because on it they were a world apart: the ultimate authority of the Pope and the visible Church that had existed for 1,500 years.[165] By the beginning of September both antagonists had decided there was no alternative to renewing their uncompromising stand at the Diet of Worms. Luther stated in a letter to Melanchthon August 26: "This talk of compromise . . . is a scandal to God. . . . I am thoroughly displeased with this negotiating concerning union in doctrine, since it is utterly impossible unless the Pope wishes to take away his power." In subsequent letters he declared that no religious settlement was possible so long as the Pope remained and the Mass was unchanged.[166] On September 8, before the Diet, Charles once again took his stand uncompromisingly for the Faith, as summarized by his biographer Karl Brandi:

> The Elector of Saxony and his supporters, he declared, had been willing enough to take advantage of his generous efforts at mediation, but they had not abandoned a single one of their articles, appealing always to conscience. He had not expected so serious a rebuff; his opponents would now have to remember that "His Majesty was their Sovereign and immediate overlord and moreover Vicar of all Christendom." He also had a conscience; he also had duties, both to his own honor and to his position as ruler. His conscience would not let him abandon the ancient Christian faith, hallowed by long usage. He also had his soul's salvation to think of, and a greater responsibility towards Almighty God than any of them, the Estates, could boast. It did not sort with his honor to grant any more concessions on the fundamental points of religion, or to agree to independent innovations. . . .
>   "But if His Majesty's goodness and mercy availed nothing," Charles pursued, then as a Christian Emperor and Catholic prince he would set his life and all he had on the vindication of his own cause and of the ancient and holy Catholic Faith. In this he would call on the Electors, princes and Estates, on the Pope himself, and on all Christian potentates to help him. Should the heretics agree to his proposition of a council, their case would be justly heard; otherwise they would have to answer his challenge.[167]

Through all the nine years of strife and stress and fury and upheaval, of ingratitude and injustice even from the Pope himself and temptation to join his religious as well as political enemies, since the Diet of Worms, Holy Roman

---

[165] Janssen, *History of the German People*, V, 262-263; Vedder, *Reformation in Germany*, pp. 329-330.

[166] Manschreck, *Melanchthon*, p. 204 (quote); Janssen, *History of the German People*, pp. 263-264; Vedder, *Reformation in Germany*, p. 332.

[167] Brandi, *Charles V*, p. 313.

Emperor Charles V had kept the Faith. His grandmother Queen Isabel the Catholic of Spain would have been surpassingly proud of him. His substitute mother Margaret of Austria, who had made the Faith living and real for mad Juana's son, surely was proud of him. Like Philippe Villiers de l'Isle Adam at Rhodes and Count Nicholas von Salm at Vienna, Emperor Charles V had stood in the breach almost alone where the enemies of the Faith pressed hardest. Christendom would be cloven despite all he could do; but because of him, with Christ behind him, Christendom would survive.

On September 22 Charles presented the Protestants with the draft of a proclamation declaring that their Confession "had been, on solid grounds, confuted and rejected with arguments drawn from the holy Gospels and sacred Scripture" and gave them until April 15, 1531 to consider whether they would rejoin "the Christian Church, the Pope, his Imperial Majesty, the princes of the Empire, and other chiefs and members of a united Christendom, until a final decision should be rendered by the future Council." Until that Council met, they were not to permit the publication of new writings on religion nor coercion to join "their sect," nor to persecute Catholics or interfere with their churches and religious services. He refused to accept a reply to the Catholic confutation of the Confession of Augsburg which had been hurriedly prepared by Melanchthon.[168] Luther prepared the final Protestant answer:

> The Augsburg Confession must endure, as the true and unadulterated Word of God, until the great Judgment Day. The [forthcoming ecumenical] Council could be accepted only on condition that the Confession be acknowledged as true apart from any conciliar authority. Not even an angel from Heaven could alter a syllable of it, and any angel who dared to do so must be accursed and damned. Still less might Emperors, Popes, or bishops sit in judgment on it. The stipulations made that monks and nuns still dwelling in their cloisters should not be expelled, and that the Mass should not be abolished, could not be accepted; for whoever acts against his conscience simply paves his way to Hell. The monastic life and the Mass covered with infamous ignominy the merit and suffering of Christ. Of all the horrors and abominations that could be mentioned, the Mass was the greatest.[169]

On September 24 the Emperor declared he would not receive any more documents and responses on these questions from the Protestants. On October 13 the Protestants rejected the proposed Catholic decree from the Diet; Charles told them he would issue it anyway, and on November 19 he did.[170] The debate was over. The lines were drawn. The sword must now decide.

---

[168] Janssen, *History of the German People*, V, 294-295 (first quote on 294, second on 295); Manschreck, *Melanchthon*, pp. 206-208.

[169] Janssen, *History of the German People*, V, 297.

[170] *Ibid.*, V, 312-319; Vedder, *Reformation in Germany*, pp. 328, 336; Brandi, *Charles V*, pp. 315-316; von Pastor, *History of the Popes*, X, 140; Grisar, *Luther*, II, 389.

Archduchess Margaret of Austria, Charles' substitute mother, had lived to see it all. When the final decree was issued at Augsburg she was on her deathbed. From it she wrote Charles a letter whose sweet and serene beauty reflects all she gave to him and through him, to Christendom:

> At this hour I cannot write to you with my own hand, for my conscience is now at rest and I am ready to accept all that is yet to come from God's hand. My only sorrow is that I shall not see you before I die. This is my last letter. To you, as my only heir, I leave the lands which were entrusted to me. You will find them not only unspoiled but greatly increased, after a government for which I hope to receive God's reward, your contentment and the gratitude of posterity. I commend to you above all the policy of peace, with England and France in particular, and I beseech you not to forget my servants. With these words I bid you my last farewell.[171]

In December the Lutheran princes of Germany formed the Schmalkald League as a military alliance to fight any attempt by the Emperor to enforce his decrees of November 19 at Augsburg. But full religious war came first to Switzerland, in the following year, 1531. There Zwingli declared that Protestant Zürich and Bern must dominate Switzerland, and to this end blockaded the Catholic cantons lying between them. The Catholics struck back, led by Markwart Zelger from high forested Unterwalden and Golder of Lucerne. They attacked a force from Zürich led by Zwingli himself near the town of Kappel late of an October afternoon and routed it, leaving 500 Zürichers dead or mortally wounded on the field. One of the mortally wounded was Ulrich Zwingli. A Catholic soldier from Unterwalden named Vokinger recognized him by torchlight and offered to bring him a priest. When Zwingli, facing the Judgment, coldly refused, Vokinger killed him. His body was then quartered and burned and the ashes covered with dung, despite strong objections to such treatment from many of the Catholics.[172]

The military struggle for Europe between Catholics and Protestants, thus begun, would last, with only a few remissions, for the next 117 years. Modern historians have called it unnecessary and even criminal. But no Catholic of spirit and courage could be expected, let alone morally required, to give up all his religious rights without a struggle; and few Protestants, at this point, would allow Catholics to exercise those rights if the Protestants were strong enough to deny them. These were the irreconcilable positions taken by the two sides at the Diet of Augsburg in 1530, which made those long and bloody years of conflict inevitable.

---

[171] Brandi, *Charles V*, p. 320. Margaret died November 30, 1530.

[172] Potter, *Zwingli*, pp. 387, 402-403, 405, 412-414; Oechsli, *History of Switzerland*, pp. 120-121.

3
Whom God Hath Joined Together . . .
1527-1536
Popes Clement VII (1523-1534), and Paul III (1534-1549)

"If I had served God as diligently as I have done my King, He would not have given me over in my grey hairs. But this is the just reward I must receive, for in my diligent pains and studies to serve the King, I looked not to my duty towards God, but only to the gratification of the King's wishes."— Cardinal Thomas Wolsey a few days before his death, November 1529[1]

"Your Majesty knows that God gives the victory to those who do in His service works good and deserving of merit, and that among the most deserving is to try, as you have been doing, to end this case [of the validity of King Henry VIII's marriage], which is no longer mine alone, but concerns all those who fear God, as may be seen from the evils it has already entailed, and those it will bring on the whole of Christendom. . . . I am compelled by my conscience to resist, trusting in God and Your Majesty, and begging you to urge the Pope to pronounce sentence at once. What goes on here is so ugly and against God, and touches so nearly the honor of my lord the King, that I cannot bear to write it."—Queen Catherine of England to Emperor Charles V, September 1532[2]

"Christian people, I am come hither to die for the faith of Christ's Catholic Church. And I thank God, hitherto my stomach hath served me well thereto, so that yet hitherto I have not feared death. Wherefore I desire that you help me, and assist me with your prayers, that at the very point and instant of my death's stroke, and in the very moment of my death, I then faint not in any point of the Catholic faith for any fear. And I pray God save the king and the realm, and hold his holy hand over it, and send the king a good counsel."— Bishop St. John Fisher from the scaffold, June 22, 1535[3]

"He [St. Thomas More] was beheaded in the great square in front of the Tower [of London], and said little before execution, only that the people there should pray God for him and he would pray for them. Afterwards he exhorted them and earnestly beseeched them to pray God for the King, so that He would give him good counsel, protesting that he died his good

---

[1] Ludwig von Pastor, *History of the Popes*, Volume X (St. Louis, 1938), p. 271.
[2] Garrett Mattingly, *Catherine of Aragon* (New York, 1941), p. 352.
[3] E. E. Reynolds, *St. John Fisher* (New York, 1955), pp. 284-285.

servant, *but God's first.*"—from the earliest written account of the beheading
of St. Thomas More, July 6, 1535[4]

The mighty struggles in Germany and Italy since Martin Luther began his
revolt and Charles V became Holy Roman Emperor had for the most part passed
England by. Protected by her insular position, her government administered and
much of her policy made by the Chancellor, Cardinal Thomas Wolsey, with King
Henry VIII's rather casual approval, England tended to support her traditional
enemy France rather than Emperor Charles because of Wolsey's influence, but
Henry was vehemently opposed to Luther and all he stood for. Even Thomas
More protested at one pro-papal passage in Henry's book against Luther,
reminding his king that since the Pope was also a temporal prince, he might one
day find himself opposed to him in war (as Catholic Spain was to find itself, more
than once), to which Henry replied: "We are so much bounden unto the See of
Rome that we cannot do too much to honor it."[5] But throughout the period from
1517 to 1536 England was never involved in serious combat on the continent of
Europe, and flourished economically. Neither military necessity nor economic
determinism plays any part in the tremendous drama of those years, when the
King of England repudiated the Pope and so widened the split in Christendom as
to make its reunification impossible unless one of his successors could bring
England back to the Church.

The year 1527, with which this chapter begins, was not only the year of the
sack of Rome but of the death of Niccolò Machiavelli of Florence after
completing the composition of his justly infamous *The Prince.* A thousand
academically arrogant apologies and "reinterpretations" can never lift the stain
from this book which openly declares that the moral law does not apply to the
public acts of a ruler of men. Machiavelli's teaching greatly magnified the
dangers of the strong centralized royal government which had now taken root in
England, France and Spain (though not in Germany and Italy), restrained only
where the official church was still Catholic under the Pope. Where the king could
take over the church—as happened during the years covered by this chapter in
England, Denmark, and Sweden—full totalitarianism was established. Thomas
Cromwell, the minister who engineered England's break with Rome, kept a copy
of *The Prince* by his bedside. It was a manuscript copy, circulated before its
publication in 1532; he had it in his hands in 1527.[6]

Of the three European nations in which the king seized control of the church
during the first twenty years after Martin Luther's revolt, England was

---

[4] E. E. Reynolds, *The Field Is Won; the Life and Death of Saint Thomas More*
(Milwaukee, 1968), pp. 376-377. Emphasis added.

[5] Thomas Maynard, *The Crown and the Cross; a Biography of Thomas Cromwell*
(New York, 1950), p. 29. For his book against Luther, Pope Leo X honored Henry VIII
with the title "Defender of the Faith," which ironically still stands in the royal titulary of
the Protestant kings of Great Britain and Northern Ireland.

[6] *Ibid.*, pp. 8, 185.

incomparably the most important, for Scandinavia would never be rich or strong or populous enough to be a lasting major influence on the future of Christendom. As the period covered by this volume began in 1517, it seemed that England could not be in better hands. Its King Henry VIII was 26 years old, devoutly and outspokenly Catholic, mentally and physically strong, happily married to Queen Isabel's daughter Catherine who was devoted to him, and both King and Queen were immensely popular.[7] Though Catherine had lost several children, the year before she had finally given birth to a child who lived, Princess Mary; and though six years older than Henry, the queen was still young enough to bear more children.[8] Cardinal Wolsey was unpopular and corrupt, but his worst enemies then and now admit the high quality of his statesmanship, nor did he ever give any hint of doubt of the truths of the Faith and the God-given authority of the Pope. As papal legate to England since 1518 and an unprecedented legate for life since 1524, he dominated the church in England as he dominated government policy. His great error was that, despite Luther, he took his ascendancy and the Church's position in England too much for granted, for there was little heresy there; the "Lollard" following of Wyclif had been almost extinguished. John Eck, visiting Bishop St. John Fisher of Rochester in England in 1525, told him that the whole time he was in England he "never once heard the name of Luther mentioned except in malediction."[9]

Not until after his death in 1546 would Luther and his followers become a major influence on religion in England, for through all his stormy and destructive later years Henry VIII never accepted his doctrine. The initiative for the English schism came not from Luther, but from a slim young black-haired girl named Anne Boleyn.[10]

Anne was just ten years old in 1517. On her father's side she was descended from the Butlers, Earls of Ormond, one of the richest families among the English overlords of plundered Ireland; on her mother's side she was related to the great noble family of the Howards. She and her brothers and sisters were therefore entitled to a place at court; but though they claimed a distant kinship with King Edward I who had died two hundred years before, they were not considered of royal blood. Anne had an older sister Mary, married to the son of a royal counsellor, who caught Henry's roving eye in 1521. After the birth of

---

[7] See Volume Three, Chapter 16 of this history.

[8] J. J. Scarisbrick, *Henry VIII* (Berkeley CA, 1970), p. 150.

[9] Reynolds, *Fisher*, p. 109 (for quote); Maynard, *Crown and Cross*, p. 18. See Volume Three, Chapter 11 of this history for Wyclif and the Lollards. The best biography of Wolsey is Charles W. Ferguson, *Naked to Mine Enemies; the Life of Cardinal Wolsey* (Boston, 1958) 2 vols.

[10] Her last name, which looks so strange to modern English eyes, is simply an attempt to spell the plain old English name of Bullen in French fashion. No one read her character better than the Spanish, who knew her as the deadly enemy of Isabel the Catholic's daughter; her name passed into their language as *anabolena*, a common noun for "a designing woman."

Princess Mary in 1516 Catherine had another miscarriage, and then late in 1518 her last child was born dead. No others were ever conceived. The next year Henry took a mistress, Bessie Blount, who bore him a healthy son (known as Henry Fitzroy, he was later ennobled as the Duke of Richmond before dying at 17). Within two years he had tired of Bessie and took up with Mary Boleyn before dropping her as well.[11]

Meanwhile young Anne, fifteen years old, fell in love with Lord Henry Percy, the future Duke of Northumberland, who already had a more lucrative marriage planned for him. ⟮Cardinal Wolsey ordered young Percy and Anne to break up and, when they would not, brought Percy's father the current Duke of Northumberland down to London to threaten his son with disinheritance.⟯ Young Percy buckled; young Anne did not. At fifteen she first showed her vindictive spirit, saying⸜ "if it ever lay in her power, she would do the Cardinal as much displeasure."⸀ She did him more than that; eight years later she saw him dead.[12]

Despite his two major liaisons with other women, and lesser affairs, Henry remained close to Catherine, whom he had once truly loved and who still loved him, until 1525, when all intimate relations between them ceased.[13] She was now forty years old, in that age probably too old to hope for any more children. The next year Henry began his pursuit of Anne Boleyn.

Anne was a woman of fierce pride and vaulting ambition, as her threat to the great Cardinal Wolsey at the age of 15 so clearly showed. Though familiar tales about the flaws in her appearance are vastly exaggerated, by the neutral testimony of the Venetian ambassador she was not beautiful, except for her striking black hair and eyes.[14] But she was extraordinarily vivacious, and above all knew how to excite and enamour the King by dancing just out of his reach. It is evident from the beginning that she had learned from her sister's experience and was

---

[11] Marie Louise Bruce, *Anne Boleyn* (New York, 1972), pp. 9-11; Scarisbrick, *Henry VIII*, pp. 146-148, 150. Most modern medical authorities do not believe Henry ever had syphilis, as some non-specialists have suggested (Bruce, *op. cit.*, p. 252). The idea that Anne was Henry's own daughter, conceived in adultery with her mother, found in Nicholas Sanders' *The Origins and Growth of the Anglican Schism* written later in the century and still darkly hinted by Catholic historians as recently as the early twentieth century, is improbable almost to the point of impossibility. Not only is there no contemporary suggestion of any significant association between Henry and Anne's mother, but if Anne were Henry's daughter she must have been conceived in 1506, when Henry was just fifteen and not yet king. For the prince at fifteen to have committed adultery with a prominent noblewoman more than twice his age is exceedingly unlikely, to say the least.

[12] Bruce, *Anne Boleyn*, pp. 45-52 (quote on p. 50).

[13] Mattingly, *Catherine of Aragon*, pp. 231-232; Scarisbrick, *Henry VIII*, p. 152.

[14] Bruce, *Anne Boleyn*, pp. 38-39, 205. The alleged large "wen" on her neck was actually a small mole, which portraits show did not prevent her from wearing low-necked gowns, and her alleged "sixth finger" was no more than a rudimentary second nail on one of her fingers.

resolved not to be only another trophy of the royal bedroom. She would be Queen; and in the end, she was Queen.

The chronology leaves little doubt that Anne Boleyn demanded to be Queen before Henry took the first step toward annulment of his marriage to Catherine. Anne returned to court after a three-year banishment because of the Percy affair at the end of 1525 or the beginning of 1526, just after Henry VIII's last period of intimacy with Catherine. Henry was pursuing her throughout 1526; she gave him a ring which he wore regularly on his little finger; she flirted with the poet Thomas Wyatt to make him jealous; he appointed her brother George, to whom she was closest of anybody in her family, as his royal cup-bearer on February 26. An undated letter from him to her beginning "to my mistress" probably was written in this year, during a period when Anne had left court to live for a few months in one of her father's country estates. But she would not accept the position of mistress; she insisted on marriage. By early 1527 he was writing to her in a different vein, promising her marriage, in a letter signed "H seeks AB no other R."[15]

There is no doubt that Henry was also concerned about having a male heir, as he made clear on several occasions in 1525, before his affair with Anne began.[16] The concern was understandable but misplaced, and by no means as self-evident at the time as has often been assumed since. After all, Henry could remember Queen Isabel—he had been 13 when she died—and was married to her daughter. No man in his senses could think that Isabel had not been able to rule her kingdom well, or that Spaniards were easier to govern than Englishmen (think of the *comunero* uprising!).[17] The oft-mentioned fact that England had had no reigning queen since ill-fated Matilda in the twelfth century surely should have carried little weight against the balance of Isabel's far more recent memory and record. Then there was Margaret, Charles V's regent in the Netherlands; all Europe knew her record and success. Though Henry's daughter Elizabeth was not nearly so great a ruler as legend would have it, she was a competent ruler; only an exceptional king could have done better. Henry already had a daughter who would also prove to be a strong queen, however controversial.[18] There was no real political need for him to devote most of his energies for the rest of his life to divorcing his wife and wrecking the Church in England simply in order to obtain a son instead of a daughter for an heir, and he was quite intelligent enough to have seen that if his mind had been clear. But Anne Boleyn seized his concern for a male heir and added it to her armory in the coming struggle—history shows how ironically, for she also proved unable to bear him a son.

Early in May 1527 a French embassy was in England to negotiate a marriage between Princess Mary and one of the sons of King Francis I of France. On Sunday evening the 5th, Henry gave a banquet and dance in honor of the

---

[15] *Ibid.*, pp. 55-69, quote on 69.

[16] *Ibid.*, pp. 64-65.

[17] See Chapter One, above.

[18] See Chapter Five, below.

French ambassadors. It began in the afternoon and continued well into the small hours of the morning. The guests of honor appeared at several of the dances in masks, dressed as Venetian noblemen. At the "witching hour" of midnight Henry led Anne Boleyn out upon the dance floor—his first public recognition of her at a state occasion. Cardinal Wolsey was not there.[19]

That very night, a thousand miles away, the mutineers of the imperial army were assembling their ladders from garden palings held together with withes, for the capture and sack of Rome the following day.[20]

Two days later the French ambassador departed; the following day, May 8, Henry VIII called Cardinal Wolsey to meet with him to discuss his desire for an annulment[21] of his marriage to Catherine, and as speedily as possible. No one knows exactly what they said, though it appears that Henry had given Wolsey some indication of his intention a month or two before.[22] What Henry did not say was anything about Anne Boleyn. (Wolsey knew of his pursuit of her, but evidently presumed like everyone else that she was simply another royal mistress; it never occurred to him that Henry wanted to put Catherine away in order to marry Anne.)[23] Of the two stories circulated soon afterward to explain Henry's purpose in seeking to annul his marriage—that his conscience was troubled by the prohibition against marriage to a brother's wife in the Book of Leviticus, and that the French had expressed doubts about Princess Mary's legitimacy—the former was highly dubious and the latter unquestionably false.[24] Both were concocted either by Henry or by Wolsey or both of them, very possibly at this meeting.

---

[19] Bruce, *Anne Boleyn*, pp. 69-70.

[20] See Chapter Two, above.

[21] Though traditionally called "the divorce," in terms of canon law what Henry sought, and eventually by illicit processes obtained, was an annulment. No Christian in 1527 recognized any such thing as divorce. By Church doctrine from the beginning, marriage was indissoluble. Only if a supposed marriage could be found illicit, that is flawed from the beginning, could it be declared null ("annulled")—that is, never having existed.

[22] Von Pastor, *History of the Popes* X,. 243-244. Although von Pastor says that Henry revealed his plans to Wolsey for the first time at this meeting, in April Wolsey had sent a man to examine the aged Bishop Richard Fox of Winchester, who had opposed Henry's marriage to Catherine when it was first proposed after Prince Arthur's death, which suggests that Wolsey had then already begun preparation of his case (Geoffrey de C. Parmiter, *The King's Great Matter; a Study in Anglo-Papal Relations 1527-1534* [London, 1967], p. 12.)

[23] Parmiter, *King's Great Matter*, pp. 18-19. Of all the books examined in the preparation of this chapter, Parmiter's is the most thorough, meticulous, unbiased and accurate on the subject it covers.

[24] For the falsity of the story about the French doubts, see *ibid.*, pp. 17-18 and Scarisbrick, *Henry VIII*, pp. 153-154. A surprising number of historians (mostly Protestant, some secular) have taken at face value Henry's claim that genuine scruples of conscience were aroused in him by discovering or rethinking this passage in Leviticus— perhaps because he talked about it so much. In view of Henry's evident moral disintegration beginning at this point in his life, to attribute his unyielding determination in obtaining his annulment to a genuine concern about the validity of his marriage—which

Whatever doubts Wolsey may have felt or expressed, this was precisely the kind of undertaking in which he excelled. He was in very good standing with Pope Clement VII and as England's only cardinal, had spoken for England on all Church matters throughout Henry VIII's reign. Popes had annulled royal marriages before on very dubious grounds—Louis XII, predecessor of Francis I on the throne of France, had received such an annulment in quite recent memory. Although Pope Julius II had granted a dispensation for Henry's marriage to Catherine precisely to overcome the impediment created by her previous brief marriage to his brother Arthur, some reason could probably be found to override it. Pope Clement VII's record to date had hardly given him the image of a stern unbending enforcer of moral right. Wolsey could now examine the glittering prospect of marriage into the French royal family, anchoring his pro-French foreign policy not through Princess Mary, but through the king himself.[25]

He wasted no time. Just nine days later, on May 17, he assembled in his home the king himself; the Archbishop of Canterbury—old, tired, pliable William Warham; his secretary; a clerk; and three doctors of law, and under his powers as papal legate solemnly convened them as a marriage tribunal. He then brought a charge against Henry (who was presumably smiling his approval) that he was living in sin in an invalid marriage, and requesting him to prepare a response to the charge.[26]

What had been up to that point a secret strictly between Wolsey and Henry could not be kept secret with eight people involved. The Spanish ambassador knew about it the very next day, told the Queen, and wrote to tell Emperor Charles.[27]

But no one knew yet what had happened in Rome May 6; when the news finally arrived, Wolsey saw immediately that it changed everything. The King's purpose might still be achieved, but with much greater difficulty. For the moment the Pope was inaccessible in Castel Sant'Angelo, with no one outside it quite sure whether he was alive or dead. If he survived, only Emperor Charles could free and restore him, which would give the Emperor far more influence with the Pope than any other sovereign or any cardinal. And Charles was Catherine's nephew and had a strong sense of family duty.[28]

---

no one but he had ever questioned since it was solemnized eighteen years before—is at best ludicrously naive, at worst pure bias. In the magisterial words of St. John Fisher to Henry: "Truly, truly, my sovereign lord and king, you may well and justly ought to make conscience of casting any scruple or doubt of this so clear and weighty a matter in bringing it by any means into question; and therefore, by my advice and counsel you shall with all speed put all such thoughts out of your mind" (Reynolds, *Fisher*, p. 138).

[25] Parmiter, *King's Great Matter*, pp. 18-19.

[26] *Ibid.*, p. 12; von Pastor, *History of the Popes*, X, 245; Scarisbrick, *Henry VIII*, pp. 154-155.

[27] Parmiter, *King's Great Matter*, p. 11n; Ferguson, *Naked to Mine Enemies*, II, 95.

[28] Parmiter, *King's Great Matter*, pp. 13-14; Scarisbrick, *Henry VIII*, p. 155.

But the die was cast; the news was out; there could be no drawing back unless the king could be persuaded to admit defeat. And as the terrible history of the next twenty years was to make crystal clear, to admit defeat in any matter important to him—whatever the cost—was something King Henry VIII would never do.

On June 22 Henry first broached the matter to Catherine personally. Even though she already knew his intention, she broke down in tears when he told it to her face to face—for she did truly love him, and whatever Henry might become, she could never forget the devoted husband he had been.[29] But if he thought her tears feminine weakness, he could not have been more wrong. Catherine "of Aragon" was Queen Isabel's daughter. She was a gentler, more self-effacing personality than her mother, fully satisfied by the role of submissive and dutiful wife and queen. But precisely because her marriage had become her life, she would defend it to the death, and with all her mother's magnificent courage. And Catherine did not lack allies. The people of England loved her and would uphold her cause to the end. Her nephew Charles was Holy Roman Emperor and would not abandon her.

On July 3 Cardinal Wolsey left England for the continent as "king's lieutenant and plenipotentiary in France, consequent upon the captivity of the Pope," authorized to "concert measures with the French king to prevent the calling of a general council by the Emperor or at his dictation, and to prevent the deprivation of the Pope, the election of a new Pope, or the translation of the Holy See to Spain, Germany or elsewhere"[30]—a commission which more reflects Wolsey's hopes to become Pope himself in the event of Clement's resignation or death, or to rule the Church as a kind of regent during his captivity, than the real historical situation as explained in the preceding chapter. But Henry cared little for Wolsey's high-flying ambitions or the troubles of the Pope. All he was interested in was the annulment. Just before he left and just after he was on his way, Wolsey wrote to his king assuring him that he was continuing to work assiduously to this end and expressing confidence in a successful outcome once the dust had settled in Rome.[31]

But in view of the desperate conditions in Rome, even Wolsey could not promise quick action on the King's annulment; it was too obvious that Pope Clement VII had many other matters on his mind to which he must give a higher priority. Spurred by his frustrated lust, Henry sent Dr. William Knight, one of his secretaries, to Rome in August without telling Wolsey. Knight bore the astounding instructions to ask the Pope for a dispensation to commit bigamy by marrying again even before his marriage to Catherine was declared invalid, with the children of both marriages to be legitimate, and the dispensation also to permit him to marry a woman with whom he had contracted canonical affinity by

---

[29] Mattingly, *Catherine of Aragon*, p. 250.

[30] Parmiter, *King's Great Matter*, pp. 14-15.

[31] *Ibid.*, pp. 15-17; Philip Hughes, *The Reformation in England*, 5th ed. (London, 1963), I, 163.

having had intercourse with her sister, and who had previously made a contract to marry another (young Percy).[32] In all the two thousand years of the history of the papacy there has not been a more brazenly shameless request of the Vicar of Christ than this one, whose terms belie all talk of "conscience" and show the degree to which Henry had already dispensed himself from the Ten Commandments. Wolsey, no moral paragon, was appalled when he found out about it after meeting Dr. Knight in Compiègne on the way to Rome. Not only was the request for a dispensation for bigamy unconscionable, but now he knew for the first time that Henry intended to make Anne Boleyn his queen, who was not only obviously unsuitable, but Wolsey's personal enemy. But he dared not show the slightest hesitation in doing Henry's bidding, though he did persuade Henry to withdraw the request to be allowed to live in bigamy. Meanwhile Wolsey met with French cardinals to try to set up an alternative Church government outside Italy, with himself as Vicar-General during Pope Clement's captivity; they wrote to the Pope September 16 explaining this plan. The next day Wolsey started for home, hoping he had not lost his influence with the King.[33]

He was too late. When on the last day of September he arrived at Richmond where Henry was residing, and sent one of his servants to request an immediate meeting with the king, he found the king with Anne. She replied to the messenger instead of Henry, informing him that if Wolsey would see the king, he must see him in that room—and she did not leave it. As Marie Louise Bruce memorably put it:

> As he entered the chamber Thomas Wolsey was aware that, after fourteen years of governing the kingdom as Henry's first minister, his star had been displaced by the arrogant, black-eyed Mistress Anne Boleyn, whom he had described to Percy as "a foolish girl yonder in the Court." And Anne, observing the fixed, nervous smile of greeting on her defeated rival's suddenly shrunken face, savored the first sweetness of revenge.[34]

When, a few days later, Wolsey begged Henry on his knees to abandon his demand for an annulment of his marriage so as to marry Anne Boleyn, he was spurned. All through a lowering November Henry's emissary Knight made his perilous way through devastated Italy, narrowly escaping being murdered by highway robbers twelve miles from Rome, and on arriving there was actually able to get a letter through to the Pope in Castel Sant'Angelo including the draft dispensation for Henry to marry a woman with whose sister he had contracted canonical affinity by adulterous intercourse and who had previously contracted to marry another, once his current marriage was annulled. The Pope made no

---

[32] Parmiter, *King's Great Matter*, p. 21.

[33] Von Pastor, *History of the Popes*, IX, 441-442, X, 248-249; Scarisbrick, *Henry VIII*, pp. 159-162; Parmiter, *King's Great Matter*, pp. 21-25.

[34] Bruce, *Anne Boleyn*, pp. 79-80.

particular objection to this currently hypothetical arrangement, but indicated gently that this was not the best time to approach him on such matters, and kindly urged Knight to get out of Rome before he was killed as so many others had been killed there. Meanwhile Wolsey had sent yet another ambassador, Sir Gregory Casale, to Rome to make more immediately practical arrangements for the main objective: the annulment. Casale carried a draft bull invalidating the dispensation of Pope Julius II for Henry's marriage on the ground that Henry (12 years old when it was issued) did not consent to it, and setting up a special legatine marriage tribunal consisting of Wolsey and one other cardinal to decide the case in England.[35] Casale also bore a personal letter from Wolsey which showed that the Cardinal, possessing one of the finest minds in Europe, had now fully grasped the dangers of his master's course but still could see no choice but to yield:

> If the Pope is not compliant my own life will be shortened, and I dread to anticipate the consequences. I am the more urgent as the King is absolutely resolved to satisfy his conscience; and if this cannot be done, he will of two evils choose the least, and the disregard of the Papacy must grow daily, especially in these dangerous times. . . . I am a humble suitor to the Pope to grant this request, not so much as an English subject, as one who has certain knowledge of what the result must be.[36]

The prediction proved accurate; but it need not have been. Cardinal Wolsey had been too long subservient to his king, as he himself was to recognize on his deathbed (see the first quotation heading this chapter), but subservience would help him no longer. Now was the time to make his stand, not on his knees but on his feet, as a priest of Jesus Christ and a prince of the Church. But he lacked the vision and the courage to do that.

Then, once again, he was outstripped by events. Dr. Knight, whose perseverance at least must command respect, actually gained a personal audience with the Pope under the most improbable circumstances, three days after Wolsey sent the above-quoted letter to ambassador Casale. On the night of December 7 the Pope escaped from Rome and fled to Orvieto; the very next day Knight sought him out there, wild-eyed and dishevelled, and pressed his master's case. Wearily, almost pathetically, the Pope pleaded for a little more time—he was not in the best condition to make decisions of this magnitude, and could not afford to encourage Wolsey to think that he could have full control of the case, being so obviously an interested party. Knight responded that he was only asking him to grant the dispensation to marry the person whose sister Henry had violated and who had been engaged to somebody else, which the Pope had already promised while at Castel Sant'Angelo. Clement VII (who probably did not remember quite

---

[35] Von Pastor, *History of the Popes*, X, 250, 252-253; Parmiter, *King's Great Matter*, pp. 26, 28; Hughes, *Reformation in England*, I, 163-164, 166; Scarisbrick, *Henry VIII*, p. 203.

[36] Ferguson, *Naked to Mine Enemies*, II, 138.

what he had said on that occasion, and had no written records at Orvieto to consult) indicated that he would grant the dispensation if Knight would urge the King not to proceed with the annulment case until the Pope should be both free and safe. Nine days later the dispensation was issued.[37]

On Christmas Eve—and a bleak Christmas it surely was for the harried pontiff—Gregory Casale arrived at Orvieto to see him, elaborately disguised. He presented his draft bull, whose essence was designating the two-cardinal marriage court to decide the issue in England. Never had the Pope delegated full authority to decide a royal marriage case to anyone but himself. To have the court take evidence was reasonable enough, but to let them make the final decision would, in the words of Cardinal Pucci to whom the Pope showed the draft bull, and who scornfully rejected a proffered bribe from Casale and Knight, "bring indelible disgrace on the Pope as well as on Henry VIII and Wolsey." On January 13, 1528 the Pope told Casale that he must retain final authority to decide, and under present conditions would not even authorize the two-cardinal court.[38]

Meanwhile an archival search in Spain had turned up a brief from Pope Julius II dispensing any impediments to the marriage of Henry and Catherine, whose wording was somewhat more specific and less open to legal challenge than Julius II's later bull of dispensation which had been the only document known in England. In late January Emperor Charles V announced that he had the document and sent the original to the Pope.[39] Early in February Wolsey drafted instructions for two more ambassadors to Rome, his secretary Stephen Gardiner and Edward Foxe, to make a maximum effort to persuade the Pope to grant full authority to the proposed special two-cardinal marriage tribunal by giving them a "decretal commission" to that effect, and to warn Clement VII if he proved obstinate that if not granted his annulment, King Henry might "cast off an allegiance which in the past he has given so generously to the Holy See."[40] Since the Pope had heard that Henry wanted the annulment to marry a woman of low character, the new ambassadors were to dilate upon "the approved, excellent virtuous qualities of the said gentlewoman [Anne Boleyn], the purity of her life, her constant virginity, her maidenly and womanly pudicity, her soberness, chasteness, meekness, humility, descent of right noble and high through regal blood, education in all good and laudable manners, apparent aptness to procreation of children, with her other infinite good qualities." Wolsey added a personal letter to the Pope pleading that

[37] Hughes, *Reformation in England*, I, 166-167, 172-173; von Pastor, *History of the Popes*, 251; Parmiter, *King's Great Matter*, pp. 28-29, 34; Scarisbrick, *Henry VIII*, p. 203.

[38] Von Pastor, *History of the Popes*, X, 252-254 (quote on 254); Hughes, *Reformation in England*, I, 173-174; Parmiter, *King's Great Matter*, pp. 32-34, 39-40; Scarisbrick, *Henry VIII*, pp. 204-205.

[39] Parmiter, *King's Great Matter*, pp. 72-73; Hughes, *Reformation in England*, I, 177.

[40] Scarisbrick, *Henry VIII*, p. 207.

the King's wish be granted for the sake of his future and even his life, and warning that the King was serious in his threats if his demands were not granted.[41]

Having arrived at Rome, on March 23 Gardiner and Foxe began marathon negotiations with Pope Clement VII at Orvieto, lasting three or five hours a day. The main issue was the decretal commission. Most of the cardinals were strongly against it. On Palm Sunday, April 5, the Pope told Gardiner and Foxe that he could not grant the decretal commission; when they bullied and threatened him, he broke down in tears and said the cardinals would not let him do it. Then Gardiner and Foxe proposed a secret commission, which at first the Pope also rejected. All through Holy Week their bullying continued while the weak, traumatized Pope (it was still less than a year since the sack of Rome) wobbled and wavered. On Easter Monday there was a violent scene, in which Gardiner said the papacy itself would collapse if Clement VII made an enemy of Henry VIII, and "the Pope's Holiness, casting his arms abroad, bade us put in the words we varied for, and therewith walked up and down the chamber, casting now and then his arms abroad, we standing in a great silence." He gave them a bull constituting the marriage tribunal with Cardinals Wolsey and Campeggio, but still leaving the Pope final authority to revoke their decision, though without saying so. Gardiner and Foxe thought they had what they wanted, but when they brought it to London Wolsey saw immediately that the Pope's final authority was still reserved, and sent Gardiner right back to Rome May 6 with instructions to seek again a full decretal commission, but to promise the Pope that if he got it, Wolsey would show it to no one but the King.[42]

On June 8 Pope Clement VII issued a new bull essentially repeating the first except for the significant addition of a clause that if either of the two cardinals were unwilling or unable to join in hearing or deciding the case, the other could act alone (Wolsey obviously hoped that his colleague would so oblige him, but he had mistaken his man—Lorenzo Campeggio, whose mettle we have already seen, was one of the few fully honest and dedicated men in the College of Cardinals in this dark hour), and another clause prohibiting any appeal questioning the competence of the tribunal. But it was still not a decretal commission, and Gardiner pushed even harder. On June 11 the Pope met with Cardinal Campeggio and told him he would grant the decretal commission, separately from the bull of June 8, but that Campeggio was to show it only to Wolsey and Henry, never to anyone else, and to destroy it immediately afterward. So there was to be a secret decretal commission after all, but once it was destroyed the Pope could deny its existence and still retain final authority in the case. He was doing this, Clement said, to try to save Wolsey's life and keep England Catholic.

---

[41] Parmiter, *King's Great Matter*, pp. 41-43 (quote on 41). Whoever drafted this encomium to Anne Boleyn must have had difficulty keeping a straight face as he wrote it.

[42] *Ibid.*, pp. 43-44, 46, 48-50, 52-53, 75 (quote on 49); Von Pastor, *History of the Popes*, X, 254-257, 259-260; Scarisbrick, *Henry VIII*, pp. 207-210; Hughes, *Reformation in England*, I, 176.

Campeggio was to travel as slowly as possible to England and make every effort to delay the proceedings as long as possible after he got there.[43]

It was one of the lowest points in the history of the papacy. Few but Clement VII, who seemed constitutionally incapable of making a firm stand for anything but was still the Vicar of Christ, would have thought of such a way of doing his duty while pretending not to. We would give much to know what Cardinal Campeggio, whose whole career indicates he would never have stooped to such chicanery, said about it to the Pope that day, and thought about it. But Campeggio was far too discreet ever to let it be known.

Aided by the fact that he really was suffering seriously from gout, Cardinal Campeggio managed to take three and a half months to travel from Rome to the English Channel instead of the normal two to three weeks. On October 24 he finally met with Henry VIII and Wolsey, showed them the decretal commission as his instructions directed, and no one ever saw it again. He met with Catherine, suggesting that she might enter a convent, but Catherine told him that matrimony was her vocation, to which God had called her, and she would never abandon it. That fall she stood firm against every pressure and inducement from Henry and others, and in December Henry sent her away to Hampton Court while Anne Boleyn moved into rooms next to his. Wolsey was now pressing for permission to show the decretal commission to others.[44] In an extraordinary interview with John Casale, brother of English ambassador Gregory Casale who had fallen ill, the Pope said that:

> . . . he had granted the decretal commission at Wolsey's most urgent entreaties in order to save him from ruin; he had granted it solely that it might be shown to the king and then burned immediately, but Wolsey now wished to divulge it to the king's councillors, a course to which the Pope had never assented. His Holiness went on to say with much feeling that he now saw what evil was likely to follow from the issue of the decretal commission, and that he would gladly recall what had been done, even to the loss of one of his fingers. When Casale suggested that the Pope was shifting his ground, His Holiness became more angry and more excited, but refused to give way.[45]

In January 1529 Cardinal Campeggio reported to Rome that Henry VIII was more determined than ever to marry Anne Boleyn and could not be diverted from that purpose, even by Wolsey who now saw clearly its dangers. It was all being done by the king's will; and the experienced, worldly-wise but still moral cardinal

---

[43] Von Pastor, *History of the Popes*, X, 257-258, 260-261; Parmiter, *King's Great Matter*, pp. 51, 56, 58; Scarisbrick, *Henry VIII*, pp. 258-259; Hughes, *Reformation in England*, I, 176; Ferguson, *Naked to Mine Enemies*, II, 160.

[44] Parmiter, *King's Great Matter*, pp. 62-63, 66-70, 72, 78-80; Von Pastor, *History of the Popes*, X, 262-263; Scarisbrick, *Henry VIII*, pp. 214-219; Hughes, *Reformation in ENgland*, I, 176, 178-179, 187; Bruce, *Anne Boleyn*, p. 109.

[45] Parmiter, *King's Great Matter*, pp. 70-71.

saw no cause for it but Anne's ambition and Henry's lust. He stated specifically that in his opinion Anne was withholding sexual intercourse from Henry as a way of compelling him to make her queen (Campeggio, a widower ordained after his wife's death, perhaps understood women better than most prelates). "This passion of the King's," he wrote in February, "is a most extraordinary thing. He sees nothing, he thinks of nothing but his Anne; he cannot be without her for an hour, and it moves one to pity to see how the King's life, the stability and downfall of the whole country, hang upon this one question."[46]

By the last day of May even the resourceful Campeggio had run out of excuses for delay. On a freezing cold morning he and Wolsey opened their legatine marriage court at Blackfriars in London to try "the King's great matter." The floor of the impromptu courtroom was thick with rich carpets and the walls adorned with splendid tapestries; four enormous chairs covered with cloth of gold were placed in it, one for each of the cardinals, one for the king, and one for the queen. This first session, purely formal, summoned the king and queen to appear on June 18 at nine o'clock in the morning. The king did not in fact come personally, being represented by his "proctor" Richard Sampson, but Catherine did. She was forty-four years old, she had lost her youthful beauty, but she carried herself bravely, every inch a queen. She read a document solemnly protesting the trial of the case in England where it could not be impartially heard, and asking for its transfer to Rome.[47]

Three days later the court, rejecting Catherine's plea, held its first full session. Not only the two cardinals but the whole bench of bishops in England was present, Archbishop William Warham of Canterbury in their center. But two of the bishops sat separately, by Catherine's side: St. John Fisher of Rochester and Henry Standish of St. Asaph, for they were her counsel. Nothing like it had ever been seen before in Christendom: a reigning king and queen standing before a court in the land they ruled, the king demanding an end to their marriage, the queen demanding its affirmation.[48] All there present knew that the destiny of England hung on this moment; some guessed that the destiny of Christendom hung likewise. None could know that it also encompassed the destiny of four nations yet unborn, scattered far across the globe now being opened up by the Age of Discovery: the United States of America, Canada, Australia, and New Zealand. The religious future of billions of souls was at stake. All history shows us no more dramatic moment than this confrontation at Blackfriars in London between the King and the Queen of England who had both once been so sure of their love for each other, and of their faith.

---

[46] *Ibid.*, p. 84; Mattingly, *Catherine of Aragon*, p. 278; von Pastor, *History of the Popes*, X, 267 (for the quote).

[47] Parmiter, *King's Great Matter*, pp. 96-98; Bruce, *Anne Boleyn*, pp. 132-134; Hughes, *Reformation in England*, I, 186-187.

[48] Mattingly, *Catherine of Aragon*, p. 285.

Catherine, daughter of Isabel the Catholic, was still sure of her faith and her love. She always would be. This was her hour, as well as the hour of the powers of darkness.

The crier intoned his familiar chant.

"Hear ye, hear ye! King Henry of England, come into the court!"

"Here, my lords," his proctor answered.

"Queen Catherine of England, come into the court."[49]

She came. But she did not go to her gorgeous chair, covered with cloth of gold; she did not go to her two judges in their black robes and red hats, nor to the bishops of her adopted country in splendid array. She went around the dais or "tribune" at the center of the room and across to the chair where Henry sat, knelt at his feet, and said:

> I beseech you for all the love that hath been between us, let me have justice and right, take for me some pity and compassion, for I am a poor woman and a stranger, born out of your dominion. . . . I take God and all the world to witness that I have been to you a true, humble and obedient wife, ever comfortable to your will and pleasure . . . being always well pleased and contented with all things wherein you had any delight or dalliance, whether it were little or much. . . . I loved all those whom you loved, only for your sake, whether I had cause or no, and whether they were my friends or my enemies. This twenty years or more I have been your true wife, and by me you have had divers children, although it hath pleased God to call them from this world. . . . And when you had me at the first, I take God to be my judge, I was a true maid, without touch of man. And whether this be true or no, I put it to your conscience. . . . Therefore I humbly request you to spare me the extremity of this new court. . . . And if you will not, to God I commit my cause.[50]

It seemed it would have melted a heart of stone; but if so, then Henry's heart was harder than stone. He said not a word. Witnesses saw no change in his expression, no response. Catherine rose from her knees, bowed to him, and left the room, with the crier calling vainly behind for her to return. At her counsel's desk, tall but painfully thin St. John Fisher looked out from cavernous eyes in a skull-like face[51] upon the burly red-bearded monarch who would kill him six years later. He had taken his stand, but already he could guess how few in the end would stand with him. Four days later he was to have proof of it.

Once Catherine had departed, Henry could resume his play-acting, which even he had not dared to attempt in her presence. She was a wonderful woman, he said, a paragon of all the virtues, with whom he would have been glad to spend the rest of his life, were it not for the scruples of his conscience. It must have

---

[49] *Ibid.*

[50] *Ibid.*, pp. 286-287.

[51] For Fisher's appearance see Bruce, *Anne Boleyn*, p. 177.

turned the stomach of every decent man in that room.[52] Well might the great historian Garrett Mattingly—who usually showed no religious orientation in his writing and teaching[53]—say:

> Since that moment of shameful silence in the hall of Blackfriars, she [Catherine] had known that it was not Wolsey she was fighting, nor for peace with her nephew, nor even for her own and her daughter's rights that she fought; she was fighting the devil and all his minions for her husband's soul and the souls of all his people.[54]

With Catherine gone, it was now the task and duty of St. John Fisher to defend her cause, and he did so with a courage and eloquence almost matching hers. On June 22 he faced Wolsey in an exchange which recalls Christ before Pilate:

> "Yes," quoth the Bishop of Rochester, "I know the truth."
> "How know you the truth?" quoth my lord Cardinal [Wolsey].
> "Forsooth, my lord," quoth he [Fisher], "I am a professor of the truth. I know that God is truth itself, nor he never spake but truth, which said, What God hath joined together let not man put asunder. And forasmuch as this marriage was made and joined by God to a good intent, I say that I know the truth the which cannot be broken or loosed by the power of man upon no feigned occasion."[55]

At the next session of the court, on June 25, Archbishop Warham was called upon to read a list of the bishops who had signed a document supporting the annulment of the King's marriage. Every bishop's name was included. What followed is reported in the contemporary history of George Cavendish, one of Wolsey's staff and probably an eyewitness:

> "If it please Your Highness," quoth the Bishop of Canterbury, "I doubt not but all my brethren here present will affirm the same."
> "No, sir, not I," quoth the Bishop of Rochester [St. John Fisher], "ye have not my consent thereto."
> "No! ha' the!" quoth the king, "look here upon this, is not this your hand and seal?" and showed him the instrument with seals.
> "No, forsooth, sire," quoth the Bishop of Rochester, "it is not my hand nor seal!"

---

[52] Parmiter, *King's Great Matter*, p. 99. Reflecting on that spectacle, one can understand the nameless nineteenth century historian quoted by Garrett Mattingly who called Henry VIII "a spot of blood and grease on English history" (*Catherine of Aragon*, p. 244).

[53] Dr. Mattingly was among my teachers as a graduate student in history at Columbia University.

[54] Mattingly, *Catherine of Aragon*, p. 291.

[55] Reynolds, *Fisher*, p. 152.

To that, quoth the king to my lord of Canterbury, "Sir, how say ye, is it not his hand and seal?"

"Yes, sire," quoth he.

"That is not so," quoth the Bishop of Rochester, "for indeed you were in hand with me to have my hand and seal, as other of my lords had already done; but then I said to you, that I would never consent to no such act, for it were much against my conscience; not my hand and seal should never be seen at any such instrument, God willing, with much more matter touching the same communication between us."

"You say truth," quoth the Bishop of Canterbury, "such words ye said unto me; but at the last ye were fully persuaded that I should for you subscribe your name, and put to a seal myself, and ye would allow the same."

"All which words and matter," quoth the Bishop of Rochester, "under your correction, my lord, and supportation of this noble audience, there is nothing more untrue."

"Well, well," quoth the king, "it shall make no matter; we will not stand with you in argument herein, for you are but one man."[56]

This dialogue, so starkly clear, so deeply significant, needs no comment, lest it be to say that at the last hour of decision, tragically for England and the Church, among all the bishops of England St. John Fisher was indeed but one man, the only bishop who held true to the ancient faith and the Church Christ founded.

On July 5 Catherine's formal protest against the legatine marriage tribunal in London and appeal to the Pope for final judgment, together with her power of attorney for the imperial ambassador there, arrived in Rome. On July 13 Clement VII agreed to halt the proceedings of the legatine tribunal, and on the 18th he wrote to Wolsey, saying "that hitherto he had exceeded the limits of condescension in acceding to the demands of the English ambassadors, but now, in order to avoid giving scandal to the whole of Christendom, he wished to provide for an impartial judgment." The next day he gave official notice to Henry that the case had been remanded to Rome. But before these letters could arrive, Cardinal Campeggio had already closed the court. He had seen more than enough of the evil that lay behind it, and would not be outdone in valor by Queen Catherine and St. John Fisher. He would give no judgment in the case, he said, until he had reported to the Pope.[57]

I will not for favor or displeasure of any high estate or mighty prince do that thing that should be against the law of God. I am an old man, both sick and impotent, looking daily for death. What should it then avail me to put my

---

[56] *Ibid.*, pp. 150-151. Reynolds incorrectly indicates the date to have been June 21, but Parmiter, *King's Great Matter*, p. 100, shows that it was on the 25th.

[57] Scarisbrick, *Henry VIII*, pp. 226-227; Parmiter, *King's Great Matter*, pp. 104-105, 109 (quote).

soul in the danger of God's displeasure, to my utter damnation, for the favor of any prince or high estate in this world?[58]

When he heard the announcement adjourning the court the Duke of Suffolk smashed his hand down on the table and shouted: "By the Mass, now I see that the old saw is true, that there was never legate nor cardinal that did good in England!"[59] Clearly Henry felt the same. On October 9 Cardinal Wolsey was charged with violating the 200-year-old, loosely worded statute of *praemunire* by receiving and putting into effect bulls from the Pope regarding the Church without royal authorization; on October 16 he was ordered to give up the Great Seal of England; on October 19 he signed a confession acknowledging his "guilt" on the *praemunire* charge, and on November 4 he was arrested. St. Thomas More was appointed Chancellor in his place, the first sign in two years that Henry VIII still had some appreciation of a good man with a real conscience. As Cardinal Campeggio left England at the end of October, his baggage was thoroughly searched in hopes of finding the decretal commission the Pope had so unwisely given him; but according to his instructions, Campeggio had long since destroyed it.[60]

In February 1530, after Wolsey's doctors had told the King he would die within days if left in prison without hope, Henry unexpectedly set him free and sent him north to his titular archdiocese of York, in which he had not set foot for fifteen years, to finally perform his episcopal duties there. He did so with surprising enthusiasm and effectiveness, indicating that he could have been as great a churchman as he had been a statesman if he had ever put his priorities in the right order. At Peterborough on Holy Thursday he washed the feet of 59 poor men, one for each year of his life. Finally he had begun to realize what it meant to serve God more than his king, as his dying lament quoted at the head of this chapter so clearly indicates. For the first time in his overbearing career the people began to warm to him, and there was talk that he might be restored to a substantial degree of power and influence. Henry would probably not have done it, particularly if Wolsey was emboldened by his spiritual growth to be more independent; but his old enemy Anne Boleyn could not abide even the possibility. Late in October 1530 she demanded his re-arrest and threatened to leave Henry if he did not order it. On November 1 the arrest warrant was issued, charging Wolsey with treason for intriguing against the king with Rome. The Duke of Norfolk took him into custody at dinner in Cawood Castle in Yorkshire, he set out for the Tower of London, and by the end of the month he was dead at Leicester Abbey, the first victim of Henry and Anne. He was not to be the last.[61]

---

[58] Bruce, *Anne Boleyn*, p. 138.

[59] Scarisbrick, *Henry VIII*, p. 227.

[60] *Ibid.*, pp. 235-236; Ferguson, *Naked to Mine Enemies*, II, 234-237, 239; Von Pastor, *History of the Popes*, X, 270-271.

[61] Ferguson, *Naked to Mine Enemies*, II, 259-263, 266, 268-269, 281-284, 297-298; Scarisbrick, *Henry VIII*, pp. 239-240; Bruce, *Anne Boleyn*, pp. 153-154, 166-167.

In this same month of November when Cardinal Wolsey breathed his last, Thomas Cromwell, the brilliant, corrupt and unscrupulous Machiavellian who had been in Wolsey's service for seven years and now faced ruin because of that association, somehow contrived a personal meeting with the King to discuss his marriage case. Its lack of progress, Cromwell told him, was due to the timidity of his advisors who clung to the established order even to the King's disadvantage. Why should so great a monarch require the sanction of the Pope for annulling his marriage and providing better for the royal succession? He was the head of his country and should likewise be the head of the church in his country. Henry should proclaim himself head of the church in England. His loyal people would accept that and his clergy would have to accept it and grant his annulment themselves.[62]

Henry jumped at this proposal. Though explicit proof is lacking, it is highly likely that his unexpected and drastic action the very next month—December 1530—to indict the entire clergy of England for violating the statute of *praemunire* by accepting the authority of Cardinal Wolsey as papal legate, was advised and drafted by Cromwell. The strongest evidence of this is the provision that clergy pleading guilty to *praemunire* should make specific recognition of the king as head of the church in England—the first mention of this new concept in any official document.[63] And on December 6 Henry wrote to the Pope on the marriage case, not only blaming Clement VII for "complete subservience to the Emperor" but insisting on an alleged "ancient privilege" of Englishmen not to be cited before a foreign court, while instructing his ambassadors in Rome to do nothing "that would acknowledge the Pope's jurisdiction."[64] It was the first time Henry had explicitly challenged ultimate papal jurisdiction over his case; the whole frantic quest for the decretal commission had demonstrated how completely he had still accepted it until Thomas Cromwell appeared.

Few ministers in English history have risen so meteorically as Thomas Cromwell. On the verge of indictment and dismissal or worse in November 1530, by the beginning of 1531 he was actually installed as a member of the royal council, as well as the king's floor leader in the parliament (later known as the Reformation Parliament) which convened January 16. The Southern Convocation of the English clergy also met at this time. England had just two ecclesiastical provinces, administered by the archbishops of Canterbury and York, with the former much the more important; Southern Convocation included most of its bishops and leading clergy. Frightened and disoriented by their mass indictment under *praemunire*, afraid even to be seen speaking with the papal nuncio, the clergy of Canterbury province offered Henry first 40,000, then 100,000 pounds to

---

[62] Roger B. Merriman, *The Life and Letters of Thomas Cromwell* (Oxford, 1902), I, 91-93; Hughes, *Reformation in England*, I, 223-226.

[63] Parmiter, *King's Great Matter*, pp. 153-154; Hughes, *Reformation in England*, I, 226-227.

[64] Von Pastor, *History of the Popes*, X, 277 (first quote); Parmiter, *King's Great Matter*, p. 148 (second quote); Scarisbrick, *Henry VIII*, pp. 261-262.

buy pardon under the charge. On February 7 Henry indicated that he would accept the larger sum but only after the clergy made an explicit confession of *praemunire* guilt and formally proclaimed him the "only supreme head of the English church," to whom "the care of souls" was committed.[65]

No such title had ever been claimed by any monarch in the history of Christendom. Few could doubt that by it he intended to displace the authority of the Pope in England.[66] But neither side was quite prepared for a final confrontation. The clergy were not yet weakened and frightened enough to yield everything to the king, and he did not yet feel strong enough to force them to submit utterly. (After all, Thomas Cromwell had been his chief minister less than three months.) They tried a compromise, qualifying acceptance of the new title with "so far as canon law allows." Henry (undoubtedly on Cromwell's advice) immediately rejected this, for in view of his marriage case the last thing he wanted was an explicit acknowledgment of the authority of canon law. Then Henry tried a lie, assuring Convocation "that by insisting upon this addition to his style and title he had no thought of making any innovation."[67] With that, St. John Fisher rose:

> What if he should shortly after change his mind and exercise indeed the supremacy over the church of this realm? Or what if he should die, and then his successor challenge the continuance of the same? Or what if the crown of this realm should in time fall to an infant or a woman that should still continue and take the same name upon them? What shall we then do? Whom shall we serve? Or where shall we have remedy?[68]

After three days of debate, another compromise formula, recognizing Henry as supreme head of the English church only "insofar as the law of Christ allows," was brought forward. Archbishop Warham of Canterbury presented it to Cromwell, who considered it for 24 hours, then agreed to accept it. When Warham presented it to the upper house of Convocation (bishops and abbots), there was dead silence. After a long and awkward pause, Warham mumbled:

---

[65] Stanford E. Lehmberg, *The Reformation Parliament, 1529-1536* (Cambridge, England, 1970), pp. 110-112, 118, 132; Parmiter, *King's Great Matter*, pp. 155-156; Scarisbrick, *Henry VIII*, pp. 274-226; Von Pastor, *History of the Popes*, X, 278-279; Hughes, *Reformation in England*, I, 227.

[66] Comparisons often made by historians with previous struggles of emperors and kings against Popes are beside the point, for fierce as those struggles had sometimes been, no emperor or king had ever claimed to be head of the church in his lands and in charge of the care of souls.

[67] Parmiter, *King's Great Matter*, p. 156.

[68] Lehmberg, *Reformation Parliament*, p. 113. Here as elsewhere that it is used in the quoted source, contemporary spelling is modernized. It is the writer's firm opinion that no reader can honestly claim not to be distracted from the sense of a quoted passage by spelling that to modern eyes is at best absurdly quaint and at worst wild and hilarious, though in fact at this time no spelling standards for the English language had yet been established.

"He who is silent seems to consent." "Then we are all silent," responded an unidentified cleric. In the lower house, made up of the lesser clergy, many protested, saying that they did not intend the new title "to impugn their loyalty to Rome or the authority of ecclesiastical ordinances and canons." In fact, the qualifying clause would amount to no more or less than the courage and constancy of the English clergy in maintaining its Catholic interpretation might make it. On February 25 the king quietly dropped the reference to his responsibility for "the care of souls."[69]

Just a few days after the debate in Convocation, in the middle of February, Richard Roose, a friend of Bishop Fisher's cook, put poison in porridge prepared for the bishop's household, making nearly all the servants sick; but the abstemious Fisher did not partake of the porridge, so escaped unharmed. Henry, who was terrified of poison, had Roose boiled alive. But Anne Boleyn, if she did not contrive the poisoning, was quite willing to use it; in October she warned Fisher not to attend the next session of Parliament lest he see a repetition of the incident of February.[70]

In May, 17 members of Southern Convocation declared that its recognition of Henry as supreme head of the English church "was not intended to weaken the laws of the Church, or to impeach her liberty, the unity of Christendom, or the authority of the Holy See" and repudiated "as schismatic and heretical anything which in the future they might do or say in derogation of the sacred canons, the integrity of the Church, the primacy of Rome—for this would not be their true mind but the work of the Devil or of their own weakness." Henry immediately reinstated prosecution for *praemunire* against four of the 17; three promptly submitted but the fourth, Peter Ligham, a friend of Fisher, held out.[71] On May 7 Northern Convocation, for the ecclesiastical province of York, also accepted the King's new title as "supreme head of the English church," but over a vigorous protest by Bishop Cuthbert Tunstall of Durham, who said "if these words are understood of spiritual matters, the king is not supreme head of the church, since this is not lawful according to Christ's law."[72]

On June 2 Henry sent the Dukes of Norfolk and Suffolk, with about 30 members of the Privy Council and several bishops, to make an unannounced visit to Queen Catherine to demand that she withdraw her appeal to Rome. In a calm, dignified and unshakable reply, Catherine took note of recent developments and showed that she well understood their purpose. "Where spiritual matters were concerned," she said, "it was not pleasing to God either that the king should intend to exercise a sovereignty or that she should consent thereto; for the Pope was the only true sovereign and vicar of Christ who had power to judge spiritual matters, of which marriage was one." At another point she described the Pope as

---

[69] *Ibid.*, pp. 113-116.

[70] *Ibid.*, pp. 125; Bruce, *Anne Boleyn*, pp. 177-178.

[71] Scarisbrick, *Henry VIII*, pp. 277-278.

[72] Hughes, *Reformation in England*, II, 229-231 (quote on 231); Parmiter, *King's Great Matter*, p. 157.

"he who keeps the place and has the power of Our Lord Christ on this earth, and is in consequence the mirror image of eternal truth."[73] When Bishop Longland of Lincoln urged her submission in the marriage case, she fixed her still beautiful blue eyes on his face and said: "I came to him as a virgin, I am his true wife, and whatever proofs my lord of Lincoln or others may allege to the contrary, I, who know better than anyone else, tell you are lies and forgeries."[74]

She abashed them all; many of them were deeply impressed, but only one dared say so. As they departed from this interview, Sir Henry Guildford, Controller of the King's Household, suddenly flared out: "It would be the best deed in the world if all those who had suggested and supported the affair [the marriage case] were tied in a cart and sent to Rome." Guildford's words were immediately reported to Anne Boleyn, who more than anyone else "had suggested and supported the affair," and she let him know that when she became Queen she would see him deprived of his office. Guildford responded that she would not have to wait for that; he would resign of his own accord, right now. And he did.[75]

About six weeks later, in the middle of July, Henry went off on a hunting trip with Anne without saying good-bye to Catherine, leaving a message that she was not to follow them. The next time she wrote him, he ordered her not to communicate with him further, whether by letter or by emissary. He never saw her again. In August he banished her from court, sending her to Wolsey's old house in Hertfordshire and turning over her apartments to Anne, and in the cruelest cut of all, took Princess Mary away from her and prohibited mother and daughter from seeing each other.[76]

The common people of England almost universally sympathized with Catherine and were furious with Anne. The women felt the most strongly. Early in October a mob of more than seven thousand of them, armed with sticks and stones, gathered to attack Anne at her house on the Thames, crying out that they would kill her; but she escaped across the river in a boat. Undismayed, she presided at a royal banquet later that month.[77]

At Christmas 1531 a traditional uproarious English celebration of the joyful feast was held in the household of St. John Fisher. His servants, who loved him dearly, urged him to join in their merrymaking. Gently the martyr-to-be replied:

> I have other things to do than to cheer my guests, or to be present at their worldly pastimes, for I tell you in secret, I know I shall not die in my bed. Wherefore it behoveth me to think continually upon the dreadful hour of my account.[78]

---

[73] Mattingly, *Catherine of Aragon*, p. 332.

[74] *Ibid.*, pp. 332-333.

[75] Parmiter, *King's Great Matter*, p. 166 (for the quote); Bruce, *Anne Boleyn*, pp. 175-176.

[76] Mattingly, *Catherine of Aragon*, pp. 334-335; Bruce, *Anne Boleyn*, pp. 180-181; Parmiter, *King's Great Matter*, pp. 166-168.

[77] Bruce, *Anne Boleyn*, pp. 182-183.

[78] Reynolds, *Fisher*, p. 128.

As the new year of 1532 opened, in the eloquent words of Garrett Mattingly, "moving as yet in shadows, hidden, behind the scenes, even from Chapuys [the imperial ambassador to England who was Catherine's strongest foreign supporter], a tougher, subtler brain than [the Duke of] Norfolk's was directing the royal operations. Thomas Cromwell had no traditions to make him reverence the past, no sensibilities to be outraged, and no scruples to give him pause."[79] Time was on his side now; the revolutionary new policy he had suggested to the king was beginning to work; but it might still have been checked by a firm stand on the part of more than Queen Catherine and St. John Fisher. So long as Pope Clement VII continued to delay his decision on Catherine's marriage case, it was impossible to draw the lines as clearly as they needed to be to induce such a stand. But Clement, constitutionally hesitant and indecisive and apparently unaware of what Cromwell was doing—though Henry's new title should surely have sent an unmistakable danger signal to him—still hoped somehow to mollify the English king, or that he would tire of Anne. Cardinal Campeggio could have told him now faint such hopes must be, and probably did tell him; but a policy of delay always commended itself above all to Clement. Catherine sent letter after letter urging quick action, supported by the ambassadors of Charles V, but no significant progress was made on her marriage case at Rome during the entire year.

The third session of the Reformation Parliament convened January 15, 1532 and Southern Convocation reconvened the next day. Bishop Fisher, though not invited, came anyway, but at the end of the month fell ill and had to return to Rochester. Late in February Cromwell took his next step: presentation of a bill in Parliament to halt payment of annates to Rome. Annates were the first year's income of a newly appointed bishop, that for centuries had been sent to the Pope following his confirmation of the appointment of that bishop. Cromwell's bill provided that if the Pope refused confirmation to English bishops because of non-payment of annates, the King himself would confirm and seat them—a long step toward practical royal control of the church in England. Since payment of annates had long been unpopular in England, not least among the bishops who had to pay them, it is most significant that the bishops vigorously opposed this measure in the House of Lords. Henry had to go in person to the Lords three times in order to obtain its passage, on one occasion cursing Archbishop Warham for his opposition and saying that he "would be made to repent his words were it not for his advanced age." (Thomas Cromwell chimed in that he should be hanged high as Haman.) In the end the Lords only passed the annates bill after Henry promised not to put it into effect until he reconfirmed it, giving the impression that he would thereby use it as a bargaining counter with the Pope in the marriage case, and then possibly withdraw it. Even then, all the bishops voted against it. When it came to the House of Commons the objections were equally

---

[79] Mattingly, *Catherine of Aragon*, p. 338.

strong, and passage was only obtained by the first division of the House ever recorded, taken in the presence of the king, who ordered all members "who would stand for his success and the welfare of the realm" to go to one side of the chamber to signify their vote for it, and opponents to the other side.[80]

Cromwell's next step was taken March 18, when Parliament sent Henry a petition "against the workings of the ecclesiastical courts, clerical fees, frivolous excommunications and tithes," which he had drafted. Known as the Supplication of the Ordinaries, this document included complaints about convictions of heresy for insufficient grounds, excessive fees charged in church courts, clerical nepotism, and too many holy days. Henry promptly replied that Parliament should proceed with "a redress and a reformation." Convocation prepared a response to the criticisms, which Henry passed on to Parliament with the significant comment: "We think their answer will smally please you, for it seemeth to us very slender."[81]

But Henry did not await further action by Parliament. On May 10 he sent flat orders to the clergy that Convocation should not assemble in the future without royal consent, that all future clerical legislation should receive the King's assent before taking effect, and that all past clerical legislation should be reviewed and any of which the King disapproved be removed from the books. When the clergy resisted compliance with these orders, at Cromwell's suggestion Henry summoned a delegation from Parliament, showed them the oath to the Pope which all bishops took, and said "we thought that the clergy of our realm had been our subjects wholly, but now we have well perceived that they be but half our subjects, yea, and scarce our subjects." At the last meeting of this session of Convocation, on May 15, after five royal councillors came to demand that the clergy yield to the king without reservation, the bishops voted to do so, with only two dissenting, one of whom quickly changed his position. Seven bishops were absent, one of them St. John Fisher, still ill at Rochester.[82]

It was called, appropriately enough, the Submission of the Clergy. The very next day Thomas More resigned as Chancellor of England.[83] He made no public explanation. But a few days later he sent a significant message to Thomas Cromwell.

> If you will follow my poor advice, you shall, in your counsel given unto His Grace, ever tell him what he ought to do, but never what he is able to do. So

---

[80] Lehmberg, *Reformation Parliament*, pp. 132-134, 136-139, 142, 144 (quotations on 144 and 138, respectively); Parmiter, *King's Great Matter*, pp. 185-186; Scarisbrick, *Henry VIII*, p. 301; Hughes, *Reformation in ENgland*, I, 336-337; Maynard, *Crown and Cross*, p. 83.

[81] Scarisbrick, *Henry VIII*, pp. 297-298 (for both quotations); Lehmberg, *Reformation Parliament*, pp. 138-141; Parmiter, *King's Great Matter*, p. 183-185, 187-189.

[82] Scarisbrick, *Henry VIII*, pp. 298-299 (quotation on 299); Lehmberg, *Reformation Parliament*, pp. 149-153; Parmiter, *King's Great Matter*, pp. 190-192; Hughes, *Reformation in England*, I, 237-239.

[83] Scarisbrick, *Henry VIII*, p. 300.

shall you show yourself a true faithful servant and a right worthy councillor. For if a lion knew his own strength, hard were it for any man to rule him.[84]

Never was good advice more uselessly given. For Thomas Cromwell the Machiavellian did not care at all what Henry VIII ought to do, but cared very much what he was able to do, and wanted his lion to know all his strength. In due time, like so many better men, he also was to feel the lash of Henry's hatred, and pay with his life for offending him.[85]

Meanwhile popular agitation against Henry's determination to put Catherine away and marry Anne Boleyn continued at fierce heat. Crowds of women accosted the king and Anne even on their royal hunts to show their support for Catherine. Many homilies were preached against the king's rejection of Catherine despite the obvious risk; at St. Paul's Cross, after a preacher supported Henry's marriage case, a woman in the congregation stood up and cried out "that the king's example would be the destruction of the law of matrimony." She was arrested, along with several of the clergy who had recently preached in Catherine's favor.[86] But the most dramatic scene took place at the Observant Franciscan monastery at Greenwich in the presence of the king himself, in a homily by the Observant Franciscan provincial, William Peto, who was the confessor to Princess Mary. Looking straight at the king, Peto said:

> I must tell thee truly that this marriage [his proposed marriage to Anne Boleyn] is unlawful, and I know that I shall eat the bread of affliction and drink the water of sorrow, yet because our Lord hath put it into my mouth, I must speak it. . . . There are many other preachers, yea too many, who preach and persuade thee otherwise, feeding thy folly and frail affections upon hope of their own worldly promotion, and by that means they betray thy soul, thy honor and posterity, to obtain fat benefices, and become rich abbots, and get episcopal jurisdiction and other ecclesiastical dignities. These, I say, are the four hundred prophets [of Baal] who, in the spirit of lying, seek to deceive thee; but take good heed lest you being seduced, you find Ahab's punishment, which was to have his blood licked upon by dogs.[87]

The Observant Franciscans were known as the strictest and holiest religious order in England, and Henry dared not vent his fury in their midst. Afterwards he sent for Peto and rebuked him, but the friar would not budge. Then Henry sent him to France and arranged for one of his chaplains, Richard Curwen, to preach in praise of the king in the same place. In the course of his sermon Curwen referred to Peto as having "fled for fear and shame," whereupon another Observant, Henry Elstowe, rose from the congregation to denounce this as a lie. When Peto returned he and Elstowe were summoned by Cromwell, who told them

---

[84] Reynolds, *Field Is Won*, pp. 253-254.
[85] See Chapter Four, below.
[86] Parmiter, *King's Great Matter*, pp. 198 (quote), 200.
[87] *Ibid.*, p. 199.

they deserved to be tied in a sack and thrown into the Thames. The fearless Peto returned the memorable reply: "With thanks to God we know that the way to heaven is as short by water as by land."[88]

But the most unexpected resistance to Henry this year came from a man who had been slavishly obedient to him at almost every step until this year, the man who by his own admission forged St. John Fisher's signature on the bishops' statement approving Henry's marriage case: the Archbishop of Canterbury, William Warham, 82 years old.[89] As the king and Cromwell closed in, taking over the church of England, the aged archbishop, facing the Judgment, began to reflect upon his illustrious predecessor, St. Thomas Becket[90] (or was it because Becket was praying for him in Heaven?), asking himself how well he had served the martyred archbishop's memory and heritage. On February 24, before the Supplication of the Ordinaries and the Submission of the Clergy, Warham had made a "formal protestation dissociating himself from any statutes whch Parliament might pass derogating the power of the Pope or the liberties of the Church."[91] Cromwell took note, and marked his man. In April a *praemunire* charge was brought against Warham for his consecration thirteen years before of Henry Standish as Bishop of St. Asaph without obtaining the specific approval of the king—Henry Standish who just happened to have been Queen Catherine's other counsel, with Fisher, at the confrontation at Blackfriars.[92]

This time Warham did not scurry into retreat, as he always had done before when *praemunire* was brandished before him. Early in May, while Parliament was still in session, he informed the House of Lords that at their next convening he would move to repeal all the statutes which this Parliament had passed against the Church since its beginning three years before.[93] As soon as Parliament adjourned May 14 and the clergy had submitted to all the king's demands May 15, Warham turned to preparing his defense against the *praemunire* charge. But it was not really a defense. It was an attack—a magnificent deathbed counterattack against the would-be destroyers of the unity of the Church.

"I intend to do only that [which] I am bound to do by the laws of God and Holy Church . . . and by mine oath that I made at the time of my profession," Warham roundly declared in his draft of the statement he intended to make to the House of Lords at his trial. If he could not consecrate "him by the Pope provided as bishop until the King's own grace had granted and delivered unto him his temporalities, then the spiritual power of the archbishops should hang and depend on the temporal power of the prince and thus be of little or no effect. . . . It were,

---

[88] *Ibid.*, pp. 199-200 (first quotation on 199); Maynard, *Crown and Cross*, pp. 97-98; David Knowles, *The Religious Orders in England* (Cambridge, England, 1967), III, 207.

[89] Mattingly, *Catherine of Aragon*, p. 345.

[90] See Volume Three, Chapter 3 of this history.

[91] Lehmberg, *Reformation Parliament*, p. 144.

[92] *Ibid.*; Mattingly, *Catherine of Aragon*, pp. 344-345.

[93] Mattingly, *Catherine of Aragon*, p. 344.

indeed, as good to have no spirituality as to have it at the prince's pleasure."[94]
The liberties of the Church had been guaranteed by Magna Carta, and St. Thomas
Becket had died for them. Kings who had violated the Church's liberties—Henry
II, Edward III, Richard II, Henry IV—had come to an evil end. He compared the
lords who had said they would defend the king's power over the church with their
swords to the four knights who had killed St. Thomas. As for him, he was ready
to stand with the man who had been cut to pieces at the altar of his own cathedral,
which was now William Warham's cathedral.

> [St. Thomas Becket] was rewarded of God with the great honor of
> martyrdom, which is the best death that can be. Which thing is the example
> and comfort of others to speak and do for the defense of the liberties of
> God's church. . . . I think it were better for me to suffer the same than
> against my conscience to confess this article to be a *praemunire* for which
> Saint Thomas died.[95]

But God did not put William Warham to the test. On August 23 he died.
The draft of his intended speech to the House of Lords, never delivered, was
found among his papers. Now Henry could appoint as Warham's successor
someone he could count on to annul his marriage with Catherine, marry him to
Anne Boleyn, and crown her Queen of England.[96]

That man was named Thomas Cranmer. For 26 years, from 1503 to 1529,
he had been first a student and then a professor at Cambridge University, where a
Lutheran circle met at the White Horse Inn during the very first years of Martin
Luther's revolt. Though we have no explicit evidence that Cranmer was part of
that circle, he may well have been influenced by some of its members; by his own
later statement, he read many Lutheran books during this period despite their
condemnation by the Church, and emphasized the authority of Scripture much
more than most Catholics of his time. At Cambridge he came to know Stephen
Gardiner and Edward Foxe, Henry VIII's emissaries to the Pope at the time of the
struggle for the decretal commission. On August 2, 1529, travelling with the
King, they dined with Cranmer, who was acting as a summor tutor to two boys at
the town of Waltham. The table talk turned to the most discussed subject in
England, "the King's great matter." Cranmer, with a typical intellectual's
arrogance, declared that theologians, not canon lawyers and church courts, should
decide the case, which was at bottom, he said, a theological and scriptural issue.
Henry should act on the advice of his theologians without bothering about what
church courts said.[97]

It was remarkably bold advice for a timid, unknown professor, and Gardiner
and Foxe passed it on to Henry, who is supposed to have responded that Cranmer

---

[94] Hughes, *Reformation in england*, I, 240.
[95] Parmiter, *King's Great Matter*, pp. 196-197.
[96] *Ibid.*, p. 197.
[97] Jasper Ridley, *Thomas Cranmer* (Oxford, 1962), pp. 15-26.

"hath the sow by the right ear." Cranmer then began arguing the King's case openly with his colleagues. Henry summoned him at the end of October 1529, instructed him to write a book supporting his case, and sent him to the house of Anne Boleyn's father to do it. Her father, now Earl of Wiltshire, was much impressed with Cranmer and his skill in marshalling arguments that would allow his daughter to become queen. When the Earl was sent to Italy to attend the imperial coronation of Charles V, at Henry's suggestion he took Cranmer with him, with instructions to introduce him to the Emperor as a "wonderful and grave wise man" who thoroughly understood why Henry had to put away the Emperor's aunt in order to marry the envoy's daughter. Unfortunately there is no record that this introduction was ever made; if it was, remembering the Diet of Worms, we sorely miss an account of the Emperor's response to the "wonderful and grave wise man."[98]

After the coronation, Cranmer and others went about Italy securing opinions from theologians favorable to Henry in the marriage case, usually after a substantial payment which they called a "retainer" but which some would call a bribe. In October 1530 Cranmer returned to England and during the next several months spent much and perhaps all of his time again in residence with the Boleyn family. By June 1531 he was at court as a king's chaplain and religious advisor to Anne. In January 1532 Henry appointed him ambassador to the imperial court. There is still no evidence that Cranmer met Charles personally, but he did make secret contact with the German Lutherans, and soom became so involved with them that he secretly married the niece of the wife of the leading Lutheran preacher in Nuremberg, Andreas Osiander. Shortly afterward, in October 1532, came Henry's offer to Cranmer to make him Archbishop of Canterbury. Travelling conditions were exceptionally bad, with most of the roads in France covered with ice (Cranmer was coming from Mantua in Italy, whither he had followed the Emperor during a campaign against the Turks in Austria). On December 10, in Lyons, Cranmer received an urgent message from Henry to hurry. By January 10, 1533 he was in London; hastening to report to Henry, he found him at a bear-baiting.[99]

Henry had many excellent reasons for hurrying Cranmer. Archbishop Warham had not been a week in his grave, with the scintillating opportunity mow open to Henry of picking the man who would give him his annulment, when he made Anne Boleyn Marquis of Pembroke, with her new lands entailed to heirs male of her body without the usual phrase "lawfully begotten." This has been interpreted as meaning that she had now at last agreed to have sexual intercourse with Henry, and was taking this precaution in case more than nine months should elapse before the actual marriage could take place. But it was very important for popular acceptance of an heir to the throne that the royal parents be married at least by the time of the birth.[100] Cromwell was now drafting a "statute in restraint

---

[98] *Ibid.*, pp. 26-30.

[99] *Ibid.*, pp. 31-53.

[100] Bruce, *Anne Boleyn*, pp. 197-201; Mattingly, *Catherine of Aragon*, pp. 348-349.

of appeals" as the next step toward full royal supremacy in the English church, which would prohibit all appeals of church cases to Rome.[101] The Parliament scheduled to meet early in 1533 could pass it, leaving no higher authority than the Archbishop of Canterbury to decide the King's marriage case and marry him to the new queen. But it would also be helpful in obtaining popular acceptance of the new queen and the expected heir if the Archbishop of Canterbury had been accepted by the Pope as well as the King. Henry and Cromwell thought they might hoodwink Clement VII into doing this, since he knew little about Cranmer and was still reluctant to act definitively in the marriage case because Francis I of France was now more openly taking Henry's side and the Pope was hoping to marry his niece Catherine de Medici to Francis' second son, Prince Henry.[102]

The urgency had become even greater by the time Cranmer met Henry at the bear-baiting, for Anne was now pregnant. On January 25, 1533 she and Henry were secretly married, probably by George Brown, later the Protestant Archbishop of Dublin, but the secret was so closely kept that to this day we cannot be sure of either the celebrant or the place.[103] Well might it be kept secret, for this "marriage" was bigamous by any standard, a legal outrage without even a cover of excuse by dispensation or annulment. No one with any shadow or appearance of authority to do so had yet pronounced the marriage of Henry and Catherine invalid. This now had to be done, and quickly, before Anne's pregnancy became visible. Cranmer was the man to do it, and there was time to obtain papal confirmation of his appointment, if the Pope could be kept in ignorance about him and the proceedings rushed at top speed.

It was a mad moment in history, with a truly Alice-in-Wonderland character, giving a unique twist to the old joke about how a woman cannot be "a little bit pregnant." Questions such as these must have pounded, day after day, through the heads of the few who knew the full truth: When will Anne's pregnancy first be noticed? Will knowledge of the bigamous secret marriage leak too soon? How quickly can the Pope be induced to act? How long does it take the fastest messenger to ride from Rome to the Channel? Is there still ice on the roads in France to hold him up? How many days left before the birth at term? What if it should be premature?

Anne herself could hardly stand the strain. On February 22, meeting her old flame Thomas Wyatt the poet in a crowded hall at court, she burst out with: "Will you send me some apples, Sir Thomas? I have such a longing to eat apples! Do you know what the king says? He says it means I am with child! But

---

[101] Lehmberg, *Reformation Parliament*, pp. 164-165.

[102] Von Pastor, *History of the Popes*, X, 280; Scarisbrick, *Henry VIII*, pp. 307-308; Parmiter, *King's Great Matter*, pp. 202-203; Mattingly, *Catherine of Aragon*, pp. 350-351.

[103] Von Pastor, *History of the Popes*, X, 281; Bruce, *Anne Boleyn*, pp. 211-212; Hughes, *Reformation in England*, I, 245.

I tell him no. No! It couldn't be, no!" Then she burst into wild laughter and ran away down the hall.[104]

Henry's greatest asset turned out to be Cranmer's obscure background, the lack of any knowledge of him on the European continent until his appointment as English ambassador to the Empire, and the skill with which he had concealed his relationship with the German Lutherans and his marriage to Osiander's wife's niece during that service. Cardinal Campeggio, who had never heard of Cranmer during his stay in England, was actually in favor of him, perhaps thinking that he might be better than the many prospective appointees known to him as ready to do anything Henry demanded. Only Eustache Chapuys, imperial ambassador to England, Catherine's constant friend and an extraordinarily acute observer, knew and warned of Cranmer's Lutheran proclivity, and urged the Emperor in a letter dispatched February 9 to tell the Pope not to confirm Cranmer as Archbishop of Canterbury until he had given a final decision in the marriage case and obtained an oath from Cranmer not to interfere in it. But the Pope still hoped to avoid a final breach with Henry, and it was very soon to become clear that Thomas Cranmer could be restrained by no oath the wit of man could devise. Henry may have threatened to invoke the ban on annates at once if Cranmer were not swiftly confirmed. In any case Chapuys' advice almost certainly did not reach the Pope before he made his decision. On February 21—near record time for so important an appointment—the bulls of confirmation were issued by order of Clement VII, as great a mistake as any in his disastrous pontificate.[105]

Two days later Chapuys, writing from England, reported for the first time the widespread belief that Cranmer had already married or betrothed Henry and Anne.[106] Knowledge of the secret marriage was beginning to leak, but Henry and his ambassadors had moved just quickly enough to forestall it.

On March 14 the Statute of Appeals, on which Cromwell had been working ever since Archbishop Warham's death, was introduced into Parliament, forbidding all appeals to Rome, providing penalties in *praemunire* for anyone seeking to obtain action by Rome overriding the actions of English courts, and a year in jail for any clergyman supporting any such actions by Rome. When the papal nuncio, Baron de Borgho, protested, recalling Henry's book of 1521 in support of papal authority which had given him the title (now so bitterly ironic) of "Defender of the Faith," Henry replied that he had "studied the question more deeply and found that the contrary of what he had writtten was true; yet if the

---

[104] Mattingly, *Catherine of Aragon*, p. 354; Bruce, *Anne Boleyn*, p. 213.

[105] Parmiter, *King's Great Matter*, pp. 214-215; Mattingly, *Catherine of Aragon*, pp. 353-355; Lehmberg, *Reformation Parliament*, p. 162; Scarisbrick, *Henry VIII*, p. 310. Taking account of the usual travel time from England to Rome, Chapuys' important letter of February 9 could only have come into Charles' hands two or three days before the Pope's decision to issue the bulls of confirmation, and in all likelihood its information was never brought to Clement's attention. But that simply underlines the folly of the Pope not waiting to find out what he was doing before he did it.

[106] Parmiter, *King's Great Matter*, pp. 228-229.

Pope complied with his wishes he might have occasion to study the matter even further and reaffirm what he had written." By early April the statute had passed and was law.[107]

Meanwhile the bulls of confirmation for Thomas Cranmer had arrived in England, and Sunday, March 30 was set as the date for his consecration. The ancient formula for the ceremony of consecration included an oath of allegiance and obedience to the Pope. Henry VIII was concerned. Was there any chance that his new archbishop would feel a moral obligation to keep such an oath? Even if he did not, might he at least hesitate before breaking it? There could be no hesitation; Anne must be queen before the birth of the new heir; the bigamous marriage of January would not do by then. So Henry decided that Cranmer must take another, contrary oath first, and then repeat it at the consecration ceremony along with the traditional oath to the Pope. Consequently, early in the morning of March 30 Cranmer went to a private room in the Chapter House of Westminster and in the presence of four witnesses swore that the oath of loyalty and obedience to the Pope which he was about to take was "for form's sake only" and would not be "prejudicial to the rights of the king, or prohibitory of such reforms as he might judge useful to the church of England." Cranmer then proceeded to St. Stephen's chapel in the Chapter House, where he celebrated the Mass of his own consecration, and before the Body of Christ took the oath of allegiance to the Pope while also twice reading his previous oath contradicting it, and another oath "to take and hold the said archbishopric immediately and only" of the king "and of none other." Before the altar of God, this shameless man simultaneously and publicly took an oath to be loyal to the Pope and another oath to be disloyal to him. When years later he stood on trial for his life at Smithfield under then Queen Mary, this was one of the principal articles in the charge against him, as well it should have been. Perjury could go no farther.[108]

Jasper Ridley, a Protestant historian who in some ways admires Cranmer, sums up the meaning and historical consequences of this act in a devastating passage:

> Belief in royal supremacy became for Cranmer as fundamental a principle as his belief in the supremacy of Scripture. He acquiesced in every change of religious doctrine during the twenty years in which he, almost alone among the leading statesmen, survived every turn of official policy; on three occasions he granted Henry a divorce on very questionable grounds; he

---

[107] *Ibid.*, pp. 219-224, 232 (quote); Lehmberg, *Reformation Parliament*, pp. 163-169, 175; Hughes, *Reformation in England*, I, 245-246.

[108] Parmiter, *King's Great Matter*, p. 216 (including all quotations); Ridley, *Cranmer*, p. 55; von Pastor, *History of the Popes*, X, 282; Hughes, *Reformation in England*, I, 242-244. Some Catholic historians, following Lingard, have stated or implied that Cranmer's first oath was kept secret and recorded for Henry's benefit only, but Ridley has proved that he stated it twice in the consecration ceremony itself. Cranmer really was as shameless as that.

obeyed and glorified a cruel tyrant who repeatedly had committed every one of the Seven Deadly Sins.[109]

During Holy Week Henry officially announced to his Privy Council that he was married to Anne and intended to have her crowned queen soon. Catherine was further bullied and deprived. Ambassador Chapuys urged Emperor Charles to war for her sake, but the emperor already as many enemies as he could handle—Turks, Lutherans, French—and could not afford yet another war, nor would Catherine countenance armed rebellion against the man she still regarded as her true husband. On Easter Sunday, when the priest at St. Paul's Cross in London substituted Anne's name for Catherine's in the prayer for the King and Queen, most of the congregation walked out. Henry's response was to order the lord mayor of London to take action to punish anyone who should publicly object to his coming marriage in this way or any other. On May 10 Cranmer opened his own tribunal on the king's marriage at the little town of Dunstable, well out of sight. On the 23rd he pronounced the marriage of Henry and Catherine invalid. Five days later, in proceedings as secret as had been the bigamous "marriage" of Henry and Anne in January, Cranmer, with Thomas Cromwell looking on, pronounced that marriage valid. On June 1, Pentecost Sunday, Cranmer crowned Anne Queen at Westminster Abbey, followed by a magnificent banquet in Westminster Hall (which Thomas More refused to attend). But in the street people chanted: "The Queen's Grace is a goggle-eyed whore!" "God save Queen Catherine, our own righteous Queen!" Fearing an attack on his home by the angry people, Thomas Cromwell moved all his goods into the Tower of London.[110]

When news of all this reached Rome, Pope Clement VII on July 11 overruled Cranmer's annulment of Henry's marriage; declared that any children Henry would have by Anne Boleyn would be illegitimate; excommunicated Cranmer, Gardiner, and the other bishops who had ruled on the case; and declared that Henry would be excommunicated unless he left Anne and went back to Catherine by September. But even now he would not pronounce his own final decision on the marriage case. In August Henry made an illegal appeal to the next ecumenical council against the Pope's recent actions against him and withdrew his ambassadors from Rome.[111]

Now it was time for the long-awaited birth. Ambassador Chapuys wrote on September 3 that both Henry and Anne were absolutely certain the baby was a boy; all their physicians and astrologers had told them so. But they were all wrong. When born four days later, the child was a girl, the future Queen

---

[109] Ridley, *Cranmer*, p. 66.

[110] Bruce, *Anne Boleyn*, pp. 216-217, 220, 226-227; Mattingly, *Catherine of Aragon*, pp. 359-362, 364 (for quotations); Parmiter, *King's Great Matter*, pp. 234-237, 240; Hughes, *Reformation in England*, I, 244-245; Maynard, *Crown and Cross*, p. 91.

[111] Von Pastor, *History of the Popes*, X, 282-283; Parmiter, *King's Great Matter*, pp. 253-254; Scarisbrick, *Henry VIII*, pp. 317-318.

Elizabeth. Shocked and angry, Henry stayed away from her christening, though he eventually consoled himself with the thought that sons must come soon. He ordered that only the new daughter be called Princess, and Mary simply Lady Mary, and deprived her of her separate household.[112]

On December 2 Henry ordered the English bishops to prepare an historical justification for rejecting Papal authority over the whole Christian church, while arranging for the preaching of sermons to that effect, declaring that the Pope "hath not, by God's law, any more jurisdiction within this realm, than any other foreign bishop, being of any other realm, hath; and that such authority, as he before this hath usurped within this realm, is both against God's law, and also against the General Council's; which usurpation of authority only hath grown to him by the sufferance of princes of this realm, and by none authority from God." Not only must this doctrine be preached, but no support for papal authority from the pulpit was to be allowed. It was the first time it had been officially proclaimed in England that the Pope's jurisdiction differed in no way from that of any other bishop, and the first time his position in the Church had been called a usurpation.[113]

The next day Thomas Cranmer was formally enthroned as Archbishop of Canterbury. It was traditional for the archbishop to walk barefoot through the streets to the cathedral for the ceremony; Cranmer did take off his shoes, but not before making sure that the rough streets he would walk were well covered with sand.[114]

On December 18 Henry sent the Duke of Suffolk to Buckden, where Catherine was staying, with instructions to require her servants thenceforth to call her nothing but "Princess Dowager" and dismiss those who refused, and to tell her that she must go to Somersham in the Isle of Ely, "a lonely, decaying house in the fens, approached only by a single road, and reported to be very unhealthy." She refused to leave Buckden, locking herself behind a two-inch iron-studded oak door. To remove her, Suffolk would have to break down the door and carry her out of the house. The people of Buckden, who considered themselves immensely honored by the presence in their out-of-the-way village of their beloved queen, to whom they had regularly brought gifts of fruit and vegetables, gathered about the house where Catherine stayed with crude yet formidable home-made weapons, and the great Duke had to leave her there, though he arrested many of her servants.[115]

---

[112] Parmiter, *King's Great Matter*, pp. 254-257; Bruce, *Anne Boleyn*, pp. 235-236; Scarisbrick, *Henry VIII*, pp. 323-324.

[113] Parmiter, *King's Great Matter*, pp. 268-270 (quote on 269); Hughes, *Reformation in England*, I, 247-248, 331.

[114] Ridley, *Cranmer*, pp. 70-71.

[115] Mattingly, *Catherine of Aragon*, pp. 377-380; Parmiter, *King's Great Matter*, pp. 258-259 (quote on 259). Mattingly's account of this confrontation is a literary masterpiece.

On January 15, 1534 the sixth session of the Reformation Parliament convened. Any prospect that it might resist any of the king's measures regarding the church had faded with the long series of retreats and defeats that marked its pusillanimous history. St. John Fisher saw this clearly, and did not attend the session. Nor did most of the few others who might have raised their voices against the completion of Henry VIII's religious revolution. Parliament's work in this session was done through five major bills. The first declared that henceforth no Englishman should be presented to the Pope for appointment as bishop (Cranmer, thus, was to be the last). The king would provide or oversee all future episcopal appointments and elections. The second bill transferred all requests for licenses and dispensations from the Pope to the Archbishop of Canterbury, and made monasteries formerly subject solely to the Pope now subject solely to the king, whom the act defined as "supreme head of the church of England" without qualification by the law of Christ. The third bill legally confirmed the submission of the clergy in 1532.[116]

The fourth and most important statute, the Act of Succession, was the first law of its kind ever passed in England. It reconfirmed the annulment of Henry's marriage to Catherine and declared his issue by Anne Boleyn his only lawful heirs, though it made no specific mention of the legal status of Princess Mary. To write against the annulment of Henry's marriage to Catherine or his subsequent marriage to Anne was defined as treason, for which the penalty was hanging, drawing, and quartering; to speak against it was defined as misprision of treason, for which the punishment was confiscation of all the offender's goods and a long prison term. The whole population was to be liable to take an oath to "the whole effects and contents of this present act"; failure to take that oath was declared also to be misprision of treason.[117] The reference to the full contents of the act meant that the oath included the preamble, which contained a clause explicitly rejecting papal authority:

> The Bishop of Rome and See Apostolic, contrary to the great and inviolable grants of jurisdictions given by God immediately to emperors, kings and princes in succession to their heirs, has presumed in times past to invest who should please them to inherit [not in the sense of inheritance by blood, but simply of succession, as one bishop by another] in other men's kingdoms and dominions, which thing we your most humble subjects both spiritual and temporal do most abhor and detest.[118]

The fifth bill repealed previous legislation making speech against the Pope a capital offense: "No manner of speaking . . . against the said Bishop of Rome or his pretended power . . . nor against any laws called spiritual laws made by his

---

[116] Hughes, *Reformation in England*, I, 256-258; Lehmberg, *Reformation Parliament*, pp. 183-184; Parmiter, *King's Great Matter*, p. 274.

[117] Hughes, *Reformation in England*, I, 258-259; Lehmberg, *Reformation Parliament*, pp. 191-192, 197-199; Parmiter, *King's Great Matter*, pp. 277-280.

[118] Parmiter, *King's Great Matter*, p. 277n.

authority and repugnant to English laws or the king's prerogative, shall be deemed . . . heresy."[119]

By another of the many striking chronological coincidences that stud the history of the English schism, Pope Clement VII at long last, in a secret meeting of his cardinals, declared Henry VIII's marriage to Catherine of Aragon valid on March 23, just a week before all these bills were finally enacted into law, and before news of his action could reach England.[120]

The preamble to the Act of Succession disavowing papal authority made it impossible for men of strong consciences to take, even if they were willing to accept Princess Elizabeth as Henry's heir. Consequently St. John Fisher and St. Thomas More refused the oath in April, More taking advantage of the legal technicality that the Act of Succession had not specified the exact words of the oath to be taken. Both Fisher and More were sent immediately to the Tower of London, but they were not tried for more than a year. Neither Catherine nor anyone in her household would take the oath.[121] Nearly everyone else did, with the significant exception of the Observant Franciscans, whose seven houses in England were immediately seized, while over 140 friars were exiled, imprisoned, or died under torture.[122] When Thomas More's devoted daughter Margaret Roper asked him why so many had taken the oath, the saint explained:

> Some may do [it] for favor, and some may do [it] for fear . . . and some might hap to frame himself a conscience and think that while he did it for fear, God would forgive it. And some may peradventure think that they will repent, and be shriven thereof . . . and some may peradventure be of that mind, that if they say one thing and think the while the contrary, God more regards their heart than their tongue.[123]

During the early months of 1534 Anne Boleyn had two miscarriages. In July she claimed to be pregnant again, but two months later had to admit to Henry that she was not. Henry had been through this before with another wife, and his patience was short. It appeared that she could not provide him with a male heir after all. He took up with a mistress, and when Anne tried to dismiss her from court, he sent her a message telling her to be content with what he had already done for her, "for he would not do it now, were it to begin again."[124]

But the damage was done, and now there remained just one person who might undo it: Princess Mary, eighteen years old, alone, abandoned, separated

---

[119] Hughes, *Reformation in England*, I, 259.

[120] *Ibid.*, I, 261-263Parmiter, *King's Great Matter*, p. 283; Scarisbrick, *Henry VIII*, pp. 332-333.

[121] Parmiter, *King's Great Matter*, pp. 290-291; Reynolds, *Fisher*, pp. 216-217, 220, 224; Reynolds, *More*, pp. 299-300; Mattingly, *Catherine of Aragon*, pp. 387, 389-391.

[122] Knowles, *Religious Orders in England*, III, 210-211.

[123] *Ibid.*, III, 179n.

[124] Bruce, *Anne Boleyn*, pp. 251-253.

from her mother and not allowed to rejoin her, spurned by her father, and bitterly hated by the new Queen who, when she heard that Henry might be going to France in August, told her brother and others that while he was gone she would kill Princess Mary, whether he liked it or not.[125]

August had been for centuries the dying time for old men in Rome. On August 9, 1534 Cardinal Cajetan, the purest soul in the Sacred College, died in the night. On August 18 Pope Clement VII was stricken, and on the 24th he was anointed, in agony from cramp and fever. For a few days he seemed to rally, but on September 25, at three o'clock in the afternoon, he passed from this earth.[126]

He has been called the unluckiest of Popes, and no doubt had more than his share of misfortune; but no Pope has shown worse judgment, and none has suffered so many disasters of the greatest magnitude during his pontificate. Not only did his actions and policies do more than anything else to make possible the ghastly sack of Rome; not only did he make virtually every mistake he might have made in dealing with the English crisis, except the ultimate one of granting Henry's annulment; but he consistently opposed and refused the ecumenical council which the Church and Christendom desperately needed, which alone might have stayed the steady growth of Lutheranism before it split Germany in two. In his last year of Clement VII's pontificate Duke George of Saxony denounced him in apocalyptic terms, as a man more concerned with 10,000 ducats of revenue than with the loss of 100,000 souls. This was probably exaggerated; but Duke George spoke for the best in Catholic Germany, and like Queen Catherine in England, he felt betrayed by this Pope. Even cautious, measured Ludwig von Pastor, whose monumental history of the Popes will offer the best guidance in that subject to every true scholar for the next thousand years, when he reports Duke George's indictment, says coldly: "Under these circumstances it must be considered fortunate for the Church that the Pope's days were numbered."[127]

It is only too true. It would have been better for the Church, in fact, if Clement VII had died during the first year of his pontificate, as a surprisingly large number of Popes in the Church's history mysteriously have. But, for reasons known only to Him, God was allowing, as from time to time He has done through all the four thousand years since Abraham, His people to be put to the test.

The conclave was held quickly and acted quickly. When it met October 11 with 35 cardinals present, about evenly divided between pro-French and pro-imperial factions, it was immediately clear that the overwhelming choice for Pope was the Dean of the College, Alessandro Farnese, a cardinal for forty years, 67 years old, known to be independent of the two political factions. He was unanimously elected in open ballot and took the name Paul III.[128]

---

[125] *Ibid.*, p. 251.

[126] Von Pastor, *History of the Popes*, X, 324-326.

[127] *Ibid.*, X, 321-322 (quote on 322).

[128] *Ibid.*, XI, 6-14.

He had been the brother of Pope Alexander VI's beautiful young mistress Giulia Farnese and consequently known as the "petticoat cardinal" when appointed in his twenties, though not yet ordained a priest. For twenty years he had lived in sin with a woman. But when finally ordained in 1519 he put away the evil of his past; thenceforth "his moral conduct was without reproach." He was very thin and appeared physically weak; many thought he would not live long as Pope. He spoke slowly in a soft voice and had a long white beard.[129]

But appearances, as so often with Popes, deceived. Paul III found strength, or God gave it to him. He had the longest pontificate in a hundred years, reigning fifteen years until 1549, when he died at 82. He was a lion in defense of the embattled Church. He established the Society of Jesus (the Jesuits), launched the Council of Trent, and began real Church reform at last.[130] For Christ had promised Peter on the road to Caesarea Philippi that the gates of Hell should not prevail against His Church, and under Paul III that promise was to be fulfilled once again.

During these same years, national churches headed by the king were established in Scandinavia following Lutheran doctrine and practice. (The church in England was still fully Catholic in doctrine and practice except regarding the authority of the Pope.) The manner in which the Scandinavian national churches were established has many parallels with Henry VIII's religious proceedings in England. The parallel extends even to the one bishop in the country, standing essentially alone, who fought to the end for the Pope while all others fell away. In England it was St. John Fisher; in Sweden, Hans Brask of Linköping; in Denmark, Joachim Ronnow of Roskilde.

Scandinavia at the beginning of the sixteenth century was a poor, sparsely populated, violence-prone region which had never had strong centralized royal government. There was a natural tendency toward unity of the region because, except for Finland, all the people spoke essentially the same language, in mutually comprehensible dialects, and many of the nobility held estates in more than one of the historic political units. A union had been formalized at Kalmar in 1389 under Queen Margaret and was maintained in the form of Danish rule over Norway and Iceland, but Sweden (which also ruled Finland) had effectively governed itself since the middle of the fifteenth century. When the vigorous, domineering Christian II became king of Denmark in 1513, his chief objective was to establish his authority firmly throughout all of Scandinavia including Sweden. His principal ally in Sweden was the country's only archbishop, Gustav Trolle of Uppsala. In November 1517 the Estates (parliament) of Sweden consequently voted never to accept him as archbishop, to seize his castles, and to

---

[129] *Ibid.*, XI, 14-22, 29-31.

[130] In his first consistory (meeting) with the College of Cardinals after his election, Paul III announced his strong and unequivocal support for an ecumenical council, and said not only that there must be Church reform but that it must begin with the Curia and the cardinals (*ibid.*, XI, 41, 135).

stand united against any attempt by the Pope to punish them for rejecting Trolle. Pope Leo X gave full support to Trolle and Christian II, and in December 1519 excommunicated Swedish leader Sten Sture and placed Sweden under an interdict.[131]

The next month Christian II defeated the Swedes in a battle at Lake Asunden, in which Sten Sture was mortally wounded. By September he had occupied Stockholm, where he was crowned king of Sweden as well as Denmark November 4. Within a few days he and Archbishop Trolle took the action which, more than any other single cause, led ultimately to the break of Sweden from the Church. On November 7 Trolle declared 17 of the leading supporters of the dead Sten Sture and the entire city government of Stockholm guilty of "notorious heresy," which by law made their property forfeit to the crown if they were convicted. At once Trolle convened a special church court consisting of himself, three other bishops, and ten other prelates, which the next day pronounced all the accused guilty, not as heretics but as "contumacious excommunicates" because they had supported the excommunicated Sten Sture and mutually pledged to resist the Pope if he maintained the authority of Archbishop Trolle. The archbishop rejected in advance any possibility of reconciliation, and 82 of the condemned were executed that very afternoon, and many more during the next few days, including two bishops, and the father, brother-in-law, and two uncles of the future king of Sweden who overthrew the Catholic Church there, Gustav Vasa. The bodies of the victims were burned on three huge pyres; Sten Sture's body was exhumed and thrown into the flames as well.[132]

It was called the "bloodbath of Stockholm," neither forgotten nor forgiven by the nobles and people of Sweden. Archbishop Trolle was blamed as much or more even than King Christian II. It was clearly indefensible, but had occurred in so remote and wild a region that the full story of what happened seems never to have reached Rome. Pope Leo X and even Pope Adrian VI continued to support Archbishop Trolle in spite of it. Gustav Vasa led an uprising against Danish authority in the Swedish province of Dalarna in April 1521, and in August was elected regent of Sweden by an assembly at Vadstena, home of St. Bridget. He had not yet rejected the Church completely; the able and dedicated Bishop Brask of Linköping was his ally, and Vasa promised him to "defend and protect all the privileges, persons and possessions of Holy Church."[133]

Meanwhile in Denmark Christian II, though married to a sister of Emperor Charles V, was already flirting with Lutheranism. In December 1520 he asked Luther's protector, Elector Frederick of Saxony, to send Lutheran teachers to Copenhagen, and within a month Martin Reinhard, a priest from the diocese of

---

[131] Michael Roberts, *The Early Vasas; a History of Sweden, 1523-1611* (Cambridge, England, 1968), pp. 2-14.

[132] *Ibid.*, pp. 14-19; von Pastor, *History of the Popes*, VIII, 452.

[133] Roberts, *Early Vasas*, pp. 20-21; Conrad Bergendoff, *Olavus Petri and the Ecclesiastical Transformation in Sweden* (New York, 1928), p. 6 (for quote).

Würzburg in Germany who had been converted to Lutheranism at Wittenberg, arrived as royal chaplain.[134]

In January 1522 Christian II issued regulations for the Church on his own authority, without even consulting his council. The clergy were forbidden to make any appeals to Rome, only to the king. Bishops' courts were to hear only cases involving matrimony. The king would determine how much land the Church might own. Priests must be tested for "competence" and required to preach from Scripture. But the next year an assembly of nobles of Jutland in Denmark declared Christian deposed for assuming absolute authority and levying excessive taxes. They replaced him with his uncle, Frederick of Schleswig-Holstein. Christian II had to flee the country, though he never abandoned his claim to the throne and worked unsuccessfully for years to return to power. In his "election charter" as king of Denmark, Frederick I pledged to protect the Church and expressly stipulated that he would never permit a "heretic, whether a follower of Luther or others, to spread his teaching privately or publicly." But the charter also provided that only Danish nobles might be made bishops, and that no foreigner, not even the Pope, should take any action against them—a major step toward a Danish national church.[135]

In June of this same year 1523 Gustav Vasa was elected and crowned King Gustavus I of Sweden by an assembly at Strängnäs, where the Lutheran Olavus Petri[136] was alredy preaching, as Bishop Brask vigorously complained. In September new King Gustavus removed Bishop Peder Sunnanväder from his diocese of Västerås on suspicion of disloyalty and intention to revolt. This left only two sitting bishops in Sweden. Gustavus wrote to Pope Adrian VI presenting him with a list of nominees to the vacant sees and promising the Pope that if they were confirmed, he would take strong measures against heresy, convert the Lapps, encourage the union of Russia with the Church, and help against the Turks. This grandiloquent program, so obviously far beyond Gustavus' means, did not impress this high-minded Pope with the king's honesty, and probably encouraged him to make a very serious mistake. In a reply written just a few days before his death, Pope Adrian told Gustavus he could take no action on his nominees until he had restored Trolle as Archbishop of Uppsala.

---

[134] Von Pastor, *History of the Popes*, VIII, 453; E. H. Dunkley, *The Reformation in Denmark* (London, 1948), pp. 23-24.

[135] Dunkley, *Reformation in Denmark*, pp. 26-28, 30-32, 39 (for quote); Roberts, *Early Vasas*, p. 22; Ole P. Grell, ed., *The Scandinavian Reformation* (Cambridge, England, 1995); von Pastor, *History of the Popes*, X, 289; Karl Brandi, *The Emperor Charles V* (Atlantic Highlands NJ, 1965), pp. 189-190.

[136] Olavus Petri was a native Swede who had been at Wittenberg with Luther during the critical years 1516-18 and had been secretary to Bishop Matts of Strängnäs, one of the victims of the bloodbath of Stockholm, of which Petri was probably an eyewitness. He was a strong critic of devotion to the Blessed Virgin Mary and the saints and to the Catholic understanding and practice of the sacraments (Bergendoff, *Olavus Petri*, pp. 78-80).

Gustavus could not have done this even if he wanted to, because of popular feeling due to the bloodbath of Stockholm, and he certainly did not want to. He fired back a furious letter telling the Pope that if he did not withdraw support for the rebel, traitor and murderer Trolle, Gustavus himself would take over the church in Sweden and install his own bishops.[137]

When this letter arrived in Rome Pope Adrian VI was dead, and his successor Clement VII typically laid it aside without answer, while trying to conciliate Gustavus by confirming one (but no more) of his episcopal nominees. Such tactics were no more successful with the fiery young Swedish king than they were to be later with Henry VIII. During 1524 Gustavus brought the Lutheran preacher Olavus Petri to Stockholm, where he made him city clerk; while Gustavus' chancellor Lars Andreae, a secret Lutheran who had been converted by Petri, wrote to St. Bridget's convent in Vadstena that the Church's wealth ultimately belonged to the whole Christian community (which meant the state) rather than to the Church itself. Bishop Brask declared at once that this was heresy, and wrote an open letter to the people of his diocese of Linköping against Luther and his followers, whose purpose, he said, was "to cause a great division in Christendom." In August Frederick I was crowned king of Denmark at Copenhagen by exiled Archbishop Trolle. The Danish bishops made him promise to resist Lutheranism and to prevent the circulation of a Danish translation of the New Testament Danish Lutherans had prepared.[138]

During 1525 Gustavus began to seize Church property, even using monasteries to stable his cavalry horses. To Bishop Brask's protests he returned the coldly Machiavellian reply: "Necessity overrides the law; and not only the law of man, but sometimes also the law of God."[139] In Denmark in November, Frederick I and his council agreed, just as England's king and council were to do seven years later, that annates should no longer be sent by bishops to the Pope. Nevertheless, that same month, Pope Clement VII accepted the nominee of Frederick I, Jorgen Skodborg, as Archbishop of Lund, the primatial see of Denmark. But the next year Frederick changed his mind and bestowed the archdiocese on Aage Sparre, who paid him 1,000 gulden for it. Papal consent was neither asked nor obtained, and Frederick promised Sparre his full support if he were excommunicated. In October, despite objections from many of the Danish bishops, he licensed Hans Tausen, known as the "Danish Luther," formerly a member of the crusading order of the Knights of St. John of the Hospital (the defenders of Rhodes) who had broken his vows and become

---

[137] *Ibid.*, pp. 7, 9; Roberts, *Early Vasas*, pp. 1-2, 22-23, 55, 64-65; von Pastor, *History of the Popes*, X, 151-152.

[138] Roberts, *Early Vasas*, pp. 49, 65, 68-69, 71; Bergendoff, *Olavus Petri*, pp. 10-11, 13 (quote), 78; Dunkley, *Reformation in Denmark*, p. 40.

[139] Roberts, *Early Vasas*, p. 67.

Lutheran at Wittenberg three years before, to preach in Viborg with the title of royal chaplain.[140]

By the beginning of 1527 in Sweden it was clear that the future of the Church in that country would be decided by the outcome of what had become almost a personal struggle between King Gustavus and Bishop Brask of Linköping. Brask denounced Gustavus both for attempting to control the Church and for leading it into Lutheranism.[141] When Gustavus told Brask in January of that year that he was still not sure whether the Lutherans or the Catholics were right, Brask stoutly replied that he taught the truth as determined by "apostles, saints, church fathers, and ecumenical Christendom's councils" and urged the king to follow in the footsteps of his predecessor St. Eric.[142] By May Gustavus was accusing Bishop Brask of stirring up rebellion against him with the intention of recalling the hated and bloody Archbishop Trolle, and Olavus Petri was circulating a tract in which he said "it does not help to tell us how old the Pope's authority is; the devil is old, but he is none the better for that."[143]

On June 16 the Swedish Estates convened at Västerås. Though nothing was said about Church issues in the royal writs calling the meeting, Gustavus went before the assembly with a theatrical performance in which he bemoaned widespread ingratitude, disloyalty, and contempt of his authority, declared that the Church controlled two-thirds of the wealth of the country (an absurd exaggeration; out of 107,589 homesteads in Sweden the Church controlled only 13,738, not counting parish churches and rectories), denied he was a heretic, and demanded a free hand with the Church and full support throughout the country, or he would abdicate. No one had any alternative to him, and with chaos looming the Estates rushed to placate him. They granted him full authority to appoint bishops and abbots and dispose of their revenues, and required that all property donated to the church since 1454 be taken away from it and either returned to the family of the donor if still surviving, or forfeited to the crown. They declared the Lutherans not heretical and called for "the pure word and Gospel of God"— language characteristic of the Lutherans—to be preached in Sweden. In the next few days Gustavus drew up an ordinance allegedly to give effect to these decrees, but in fact going well beyond them, even giving the king the right to appoint parish priests. All legal privileges were withdrawn from the Church; the king, now irreconcilably hostile to the Catholic bishops, was its complete master.[144]

In July he went to Linköping and expropriated most of Bishop Brask's land and income. There was a great spoliation of churches, monasteries, and convents all over Sweden. In September Bishop Brask fled the country, first to Denmark,

---

[140] Von Pastor, *History of the Popes*, X, 290; Dunkley, *Reformation in Denmark*, pp. 43, 48; Grell, *Scandinavian Reformation*, pp. 79-80.

[141] Roberts, *Early Vasas*, p. 71.

[142] Bergendoff, *Olavus Petri*, pp. 23-24.

[143] *Ibid.*, p. 30; Roberts, *Early Vasas*, p. 70 (quote).

[144] Von Pastor, *History of the Popes*, X, 294-295; Roberts, *Early Vasas*, pp. 75-78; Bergendoff, *Olavus Petri*, pp. 5n, 33-37.

then to Danzig in Prussia. He never returned to Sweden, dying twelve years later in a Polish monastery.[145]

On January 12, 1528 an elaborate coronation ceremony was held for King Gustavus of Sweden. The ancient pledge to safeguard the rights and property of the Church was omitted from his coronation oath. The sermon at the consecration was preached by Olavus Petri, who that year published books rejecting five of the seven sacraments, denying the existence of purgatory, and calling for the abolition of clerical celibacy (an ordained priest, he had taken a wife even before Luther did). The next year he published a new vernacular liturgy in Swedish reflecting the Lutheran denial that the Mass is an unbloody re-enactment of Christ's sacrifice. Though changes in the externals of the Mass were kept to a minimum in order not to arouse the people, many were not deceived.[146]

King Gustavus' actions against the Church and the Mass roused a Catholic rebellion in three provinces in southern Sweden in the spring of 1529, but Stockholm, now substantially a Protestant city, stood firmly with the king against the rebels, and the rising was quickly suppressed. In 1530 the king appointed Olavus Petri his chancellor, the second man in power in the country; the next year he made Olavus' brother Laurentius Archbishop of Uppsala and primate of Sweden, naturally without papal approval. The breach was complete, and Sweden was Lutheran.[147]

In Denmark the important city of Viborg in Jutland had come under firm Lutheran control by 1530, with Hans Tausen illicitly ordaining his associates to take control of the city's churches. When the Danish parliament met at Copenhagen that year, Tausen and his colleagues prepared a Lutheran statement of faith in 43 articles known as the Copenhagen Confession, which they preached repeatedly in Copenhagen's Church of the Holy Spirit. The bishops responded with a list of 27 Lutheran errors.[148] Immediately after the meeting, Frederick I and his council issued a decree which included this distinctly Lutheran provision:

> Concerning God's Word and the Gospel, we will that each one who has the grace may clearly proclaim it and publicly teach the common people in all our towns and elsewhere in this kingdom. . . . Whosoever shall preach or teach anything other than what he can prove is agreeable with Scripture shall be brought to justice.[149]

In November 1531 the long exiled Christian II of Denmark, who after his deposition had announced himself a Lutheran but had now allegedly returned to the Catholic Faith in order to get money from his brother-in-law Emperor Charles

---

[145] Von Pastor, *History of the Popes*, X, 295; Bergendoff, *Olavus Petri*, pp. 38-39; Roberts, *Early Vasas*, p. 85.

[146] Roberts, *Early Vasas*, pp. 69, 84-86, 89-90; Bergendoff, *Olavus Petri*, pp. 45-49; von Pastor, History of the Popes, X, 295-296.

[147] Roberts, *Early Vasas*, pp. 86-87, 91, 112; Bergendoff, *Olavus Petri*, pp. 48-52.

[148] Dunkley, *Reformation in Denmark*, pp. 55, 61-63.

[149] *Ibid.*, p. 63.

V to attempt his restoration, landed with an army in Norway. He was not as much disliked there as he was in Denmark and Sweden. There were as yet hardly any Lutherans in Norway, and the able Catholic Archbishop of Trondheim, Olaf Engelbrektsson, well aware of the recent destruction of the Catholic Church in Sweden and the grave menace to the Church in Denmark, gave the dubiously Catholic ex-king full support. But Christian was unable to advance beyond Norway or even to secure all of it; he lost his fleet; in his frustration he began executing some of his chief Catholic supporters, such as the Swedish nobleman Türe Jonsson. Eventually he was persuaded to accept a safe conduct in the name of Frederick I to come to Copenhagen to negotiate. On Christian II's arrival Frederick spurned the safe conduct and locked him up in a castle for the rest of his life.[150]

Frederick I died in April 1533. His heir was his elder son Christian, who had been a convinced Lutheran ever since seeing Luther take his stand at the Diet of Worms in 1521. The Danish bishops led the opposition to making him king, and were successful because the Danish monarchy was still elective; there was no law or consistent custom for the crown always to pass from father to eldest son. They had no viable alternative, but mainly due to their opposition, no king was designated at this time. Parliament supported the bishops. Bishop Joachim Ronnow of Roskilde took advantage of the favorable situation to put Lutheran leader Hans Tausen on trial before the council for heresy, slander, and preaching without permission. Tausen was convicted, but only told not to preach, a sentence which proved unenforceable. By 1534 civil war had broken out, a three-cornered struggle among supporters of the bishops, supporters of the imprisoned ex-King Christian II, and supporters of Prince Christian (including in addition to all the Lutherans many Catholics who saw him as the only man who could restore order). As the candidate of order, having the services of two generals of great military skill, the Rantzau brothers, and aided by King Gustavus of Sweden, Christian III prevailed, taking Copenhagen July 29, 1536 after a long siege.[151]

When the Danish bishops refused to give or lend him money to pay his army, Christian III arrested them all in the middle of the night of August 11-12 and imprisoned them, holding them captive until they would agree if released not to try to recover their previous position or challenge "the new order in the church." All agreed but Bishop Ronnow of Roskilde, who died in prison after eight years of captivity, still unyielding. Christian III's electoral charter omitted all reference to the rights and privileges of the Church and its bishops. Meeting in the last half of October, a parliament of a size unprecedented in Danish history, with more than a thousand persons sitting, charged the deposed and imprisoned bishops with seeking to rule the country themselves and promoting civil war, and declared their property forfeit to the crown. Henceforth the king was to control

---

[150] *Ibid.*, pp. 33, 65; Roberts, *Early Vasas*, pp. 95-96; Brandi, *Charles V*, pp. 323-324; Grell, *Scandinavian Reformation*, p. 98.

[151] Dunkley, *Reformation in Denmark*, pp. 53-54, 66-70; Roberts, *Early Vasas*, pp. 98-100; Grell, *Scandinavia Reformation*, p. 91; Brandi, *Charles V*, p. 353.

the church, including all monasteries. The choice of whether to continue to have bishops or merely "superintendents" was left open, awaiting the king's will.[152] On December 2 Luther himself wrote to Christian III, offering his full support and saying:

> It delights me that Your Royal Majesty has eradicated the bishops, who refused to halt their persecution of the Word of God and caused confusion in secular government.[153]

The years covered by this chapter also include two major developments in the European discovery and occupation of the New World: the conquest of Peru and the opening up of the St. Lawrence River in what was to be Canada.

Ever since Cortes' epic conquest of Mexico, Spaniards in the New World had been searching for another Aztec empire. Nothing like it was found for a decade. In December 1524, a Spanish soldier of fortune named Francisco Pizarro, whose mother was so poor that she left him on a church doorstep soon after he was born because she could not afford to raise him, led the first significant Spanish voyage down the Pacific coast of South America from Panama. It found nothing in the least promising; the torrid equatorial jungle covering the four hundred miles of what is now the Pacific coast of Colombia contains almost nothing to sustain travellers and remains mostly uninhabited even today. Pizarro, perhaps unable to forget his poverty-stricken childhood, was a man whose overmastering passion in life was getting money. He had few virtues, but among those few were two which can make history: perseverance and courage. Returning to Panama after a total failure, he thought of nothing but trying again, and contracted with another adventurer named Diego de Almagro and a priest named Hernando de Luque to help him. His second expedition found nothing any better ashore, but in February 1527 captured a strange craft: an oceangoing raft made of light, unsinkable balsa logs which carried a cargo of rich trade goods, far superior to anything a jungle tribe of Indians could produce. Its crew said they came from a place called Peru.[154]

After being stranded on and eventually rescued from a broiling little island off the inhospitable coast a few months later, Pizarro went straight to Spain, where his tale of the balsa raft from Peru and his continued display of perseverance and courage gained him authorization in July 1529 from Empress Isabel, regent of Spain during Emperor Charles' absence in Italy, to discover and conquer Peru as Governor and Captain-General, with financial backing to fit out an expedition. At the beginning of 1530 Pizarro's little fleet set sail from Sevilla for Panama. Men and weapons were moved across the isthmus which Balboa had

---

[152] Dunkley, *Reformation in Denmark*, pp. 70-75; Roberts, *Early Vasas*, p. 109.

[153] Grell, *Scandinavian Reformation*, p. 34.

[154] John Hemming, *The Conquest of the Incas* (New York, 1970), pp. 24-25.

traversed to discover the Pacific Ocean seventeen years before,[155] more men were recruited there, and another small fleet sailed south from Panama in December. In January 1531 Pizarro landed at the mouth of the Esmeralda River in Ecuador.[156]

He really had no idea where he was going or what lay before him, only the lure of gold to draw him on. For no less than a year and a half he blundered hither and yon through the mountains and valleys of mostly trackless western Ecuador, seeking his dream. It is amazing that he survived. But by May 1532 he had reached the village of Tumbez on the south shore of the Bay of Guayaquil, where he finally realized that the heartland of the native civilization he was seeking lay not on the coast at all, but high up in valleys amidst the towering mountain chain of the Andes over which the sun rose every morning as he marched. Indeed, he had already passed the Inca frontier in the Andes, at Quito. So he pressed inland, climbing, climbing as Cortes and his men had climbed in Mexico, until he reached Cájamarca, a mile and a half above the level of the sea, on November 15, 1532. He had with him just 106 foot soldiers and 62 cavalry, only one-third the size of Cortes' initial force which landed at Veracruz in Mexico, ever afterwards famous as "the men of Cájamarca."[157]

Or perhaps we should say "infamous." For while Hernán Cortes, the Christian hero who defeated the Devil himself in Mexico, had been living and glorious proof that not all Spanish conquistadors fit their later image of ruthless plunderers and killers, Francisco Pizarro and his men fit it like a glove.

The Inca empire of Peru was less materially developed than Mayan and Aztec Mexico—it is the only civilization in history without writing—but it was highly organized and relatively well governed from its capital city, Cuzco. The Inca emperors ("Inca" was their title rather than the name of a people, since they governed many peoples) ruled for more than 1,500 miles northwest to southeast, from Quito to what is now Bolivia. Their power was absolute and their subjects had no rights, but the preponderance of the evidence shows it to have been a relatively benevolent despotism. There are no records[158] of mass slaughters (until the Spaniards came), and though there was human sacrifice, it was very rare, only a few persons a year, sometimes none.[159]

Pizarro lost no time. Just one day after his arrival he met with Inca Emperor Atahualpa in the plaza of Cájamarca. Though startled and much impressed by the alien newcomers' horses, they were so few in numbers that Atahualpa did not anticipate any serious threat from them. Even so it is astonishing that only a

---

[155] See Volume Three, Chapter 16 of this history.

[156] Hemming, *Conquest of the Incas*, pp. 25-27.

[157] *Ibid.*, pp. 27, 31-37, 45, 287, 501.

[158] Since the Inca civilization lacked writing, it could not keep records in our sense of the word, but some Spaniards—notably the half Peruvian Garcilaso de la Vega—began writing down what they had learned of the oral traditions of Incan history well within living memory of the conquest.

[159] See Philip A. Means, *Ancient Civilizations of the Andes* (New York, 1931), *passim*.

handful of the thousands of Indians thronging the plaza were armed. Pizarro had asked to see the emperor and promised him "no harm or insult." But in the midst of the ceremonies of meeting he suddenly bellowed the ancient Spanish war cry "Santiago! and at them!", charged the totally surprised Atahualpa, and seized him. Mass panic followed as the Spanish waded into the vast crowd swinging bloody swords against unarmed men. Thousands were killed. One estimate says seven thousand.[160]

The very next day Hernando de Soto, who had also marched with Cortes, raided the imperial camp with thirty horsemen, found all the military officers there so frightened and demoralized that they surrendered immediately, and gathered much gold (the Incas, like the Aztecs had no concept of its monetary value, using it only for decoration, but they possessed it in large quantities). But such plunder was not nearly enough to satisfy the avaricious Pizarro. He now told Atahualpa that he could ransom himself if he collected enough gold to fill the room in which he was confined as high as his arms could reach. Atahualpa sent for the gold, it kept pouring into Cájamarca, and soon the room could be filled to the specified level. In the act of despicable treachery which has forever disgraced his name, Pizarro took the gold (worth at least $10 million in today's money) and killed the emperor on July 26, 1533.[161]

Meanwhile Pizarro's associate Almagro had arrived in Cájamarca with a reinforcement of 153 men and 50 horses, and Pizarro had also captured the top-ranking general of the Inca Army, Chalcuchima, tortured him to obtain more gold, loaded him with chains, and eventually burned him to death. Pizarro still had only about three hundred men, but the shock of his advent, his horses, his weapons, his bloodthirstiness, and his treachery seemed to paralyze the whole Inca empire. Little resistance was offered. In December Pizarro occupied Cuzco and crowned Manco, a distant relative of Atahualpa who had aided him in the campaign, as Inca under the rule of Spain.[162]

The conquistadors continued taking over the Inca empire during the ensuing year. Peruvian defenders began withdrawing into the Amazon jungles, where it was almost impossible to follow them. By the beginning of 1535 the news reached Peru that Emperor Charles V, not wishing to leave a man like Pizarro in sole control of an empire 1,500 miles long, had split it between him and Almagro, in such a manner that it could not be determined on whose side of the vaguely drawn dividing line the Inca capital of Cuzco lay. Friction between the two former partners developed rapidly, until it was temporarily resolved by an agreement whereby Almagro would let Pizarro have Cuzco in return for giving Almagro logistic support for an invasion of Chile.[163]

But Peru was not yet unquestionably Spanish. In striking contrast to Mexico, where millions in the conquered empire had accepted Spanish rule with

---

[160] Hemming, *Conquest of the Incas*, pp. 31-45.
[161] *Ibid.*, pp. 46-47, 52, 72-74, 78-80.
[162] *Ibid.*, pp. 69-72, 86-88, 90-95, 106-119, 126-128.
[163] *Ibid.*, pp. 139-140, 156-159, 166-168, 174-177, 502.

hardly any protest after the fall of the devil-gods who commanded massive human sacrifice, the old royal family still had strong support in what had been the Inca empire, and there were no barefoot friars to begin converting the natives to Christianity—Pizarro had no interest in evangelization. In April 1536 Manco, whom Pizarro considered his puppet, and who had learned in two years' close association with Pizarro's Spaniards their evils and vulnerabilities, fooled Pizarro's brother with a story that he was going to get a life-sized gold statute of Atahualpa's father to bring back to him. Four days after leaving the Spaniards he emerged as commander of a revived Inca army, every man of which was sworn to drive all Spaniards out of Peru or kill them. Manco seized the huge megalithic fortress of Sacsahuamán just outside Cuzco and from it laid siege to the city. A furious struggle raged for weeks for control of the fortress, but eventually the Spanish drove the Indian besiegers out of it. Manco's general Quizo Yupanqui ambushed the first two Spanish relieving columns in deep narrow valleys in May and virtually annihilated them. He went to the provincial capital of Jauja and killed all the Spaniards there, then actually attacked the newly founded Spanish city of Lima on the coast; but there he was repulsed and killed in a cavalry charge.[164]

Early in 1537 Almagro returned from Chile and pretended to Manco that he was willing to cooperate with him. Knowing the depth of Almagro's hatred of Pizarro, Manco believed him and let Almagro and a substantial force into Cuzco. Almagro promptly arrested the Pizarro brothers and proclaimed Manco deposed. Spanish reinforcements arrived from the coast and from as far north as Guatemala, and by the middle of the year Manco had withdrawn to the wilds of Vilcabamba on the eastern slope of the Andes, with most of his army scattered or lost. Spanish rule—of the worst kind, with hardly a touch of Christianity—was established over almost all of what had been the flourishing civilization of the Inca empire.[165]

The amount of gold secured by the conquistadors of Peru was large enough to have an immediate effect on the history of Europe. (Even these men never dared tamper with the "royal fifth" of all treasure earmarked for King/Emperor Charles V.) By 1535 1,650,000 pesos' worth (a peso was equivalent to 450 *maravedis*, the usual denomination of Spanish currency) of gold had arrived in Spain from Peru, and was one of Charles' principal sources of funds for the great military expedition which took Tunis on the coast of North Africa from the Muslims in 1535.[166]

The conquest of Peru quickly opened up much of South America to exploration and colonial development. The Atlantic coast of North America above Florida was first explored in a strange voyage in 1524 by the Italian navigator Giovanni Verrazano, sailing for the King of France, an astonishingly

---

[164] *Ibid.*, pp. 187-188, 192-207, 210-212.

[165] *Ibid.*, pp. 223-234.

[166] Ramon Menéndez Pidal, *Historia de España*, Volume XX: "La España del Emperador Carlos V," by Manuel Fernández Alvarez, 4th ed. (Madrid, 1986), p. 531.

incurious and often bewildered explorer who thought Pamlico Sound across the Cape Hatteras sandspit in North Carolina was the Pacific Ocean; missed Chesapeake Bay; sailed into and out of New York harbor, one of the most magnificent in the world, without being apparently at all impressed; discovered Narragansett Bay in Rhode Island, again with little comment; viewed with his casual eye "the rock-bound coast of Maine;" reached Newfoundland without exploring the Gulf of St. Lawrence; and finally sailed home where his report created no more interest in his discoveries than he seemed to have had himself.[167]

But Verrazano's voyage did mark the emergence into the Age of Discovery of France, which except for the single voyage for England from which John Cabot returned, was the first nation other than Spain and Portugal to take part in it. In April 1534 Jacques Cartier set sail for France with two small ships across the Atlantic from the little English Channel port of St. Malo, long the home of fearless Breton seamen like himself. On May 10 he reached Newfoundland (originally discovered by Cabot), encountering much ice. Following the ice as it retreated, he became the first to sail around the northernmost tip of the big island and then down its west coast, facing the Canadian mainland. At the end of June he reached richly fertile Prince Edward Island in the Gulf of St. Lawrence. During July he rounded the Gaspé peninsula and entered the St. Lawrence River. With summer passing and the strong current of the river holding them back, Cartier and his officers decided to return home in August.[168]

Unlike Verrazano, Cartier was enthusiastic about his discoveries and could hardly wait to get back to the promising country he had just begun to explore. On Pentecost Sunday of the next year, 1535, he and his men confessed and received Holy Communion and a bishop's blessing in the cathedral of St. Malo, and three days later sailed again for the St. Lawrence with three ships. After a stormy passage of the North Atlantic, in which his ships were separated, he made landfall at Newfoundland in his flagship July 7 and rejoined the other two ships some days later off the coast of Labrador. On September 8 he discovered the magnificent site of Quebec; proceeding up the St. Lawrence against the current, he arrived at the future site of Montreal early in October. Returning to Quebec later in the month and well aware of the danger of the North Atlantic in this season, Cartier decided to spend the winter there. It was like nothing he had ever experienced in France, for winters in Canada are far more severe; by February 1536 many of his men were down with scurvy, but Cartier—perhaps advised by the Indians, with whom he generally had good relations—was able to relieve them with the leaves and bark of the arborvitae tree. Next spring he sailed home to St. Malo and was honored by Francis I. Cartier's two remarkably well conducted voyages, though they did not immediately result in the planting of a French

---

[167] Samuel E. Morison, *The European Discovery of America; the Northern Voyages* (New York, 1971), pp. 292-312. This remarkable voyage of the obtuse Verrazano had so little impact on Europe, although it was still enthralled with new discoveries, that Verrazano was forgotten for three centuries.

[168] *Ibid.*, pp. 345-348, 355, 364, 366, 371, 375, 377-378.

colony in the New World, established the French claim to the St. Lawrence River region which eventually became the great French province of Quebec.[169]

The news of the death of Pope Clement VII reached England early in October 1534. When it came, the Duke of Norfolk, who despite his consistent support of Henry VIII still retained some Catholic feeling, asked his master if he would seek an agreement with the new Pope. Henry replied shortly that "the regard he would have for any Pope in the world that might be chosen would be no greater than what he had for the meanest priest in his kingdom."[170] When ambassadors came from France requesting the hand of Princess Mary for the Dauphin, heir to the throne of France, Henry coldly replied that Mary was illegitimate, and only year-old Elizabeth could be considered in royal marriage negotiations with England.[171] (There would be no turning back while Henry VIII was king.)

In November 1534 the seventh session of the Reformation Parliament passed the Act of Supremacy, a statute confirming the vesting of all the Pope's former powers over the English church in the King of England as its supreme head. Another law specified the text of the oath that the Act of Succession had required without giving its exact wording, depriving St. Thomas More of his defense that the language of the oath he had been ordered to take earlier in the year lacked statutory authority. A third statute of great importance defined treason for the first time as applying to spoken as well as written words to "deprive" the king and his heirs "of their dignity, title, or name," which was held to include the king's recently assumed title, confirmed by the Act of Supremacy, of supreme head of the church in England. Even the subservient House of Commons would not approve this until the bill was amended to permit these treason prosecutions only if the words which led to them were "malicious." The first martyrs of the coming persecution would soon discover how little that qualification meant in practice.[172]

The new treason act took effect February 1, 1535. In April royal commissioners went out with orders to administer oaths in all religious houses acknowledging Henry VIII as supreme head of the Church in England. At the London Charterhouse the Carthusian monks made a three-day preparation for the arrival of the commissioners there: on the first day a general confession, on the second day each brother asking the pardon of each of the others for all offenses he had or might have committed against them; on the third a Mass of the Holy Spirit and reflection upon it. On April 13 the priors of two other Charterhouses, Robert Lawrence of Beauvale and Augustine Webster of Axholm, went to Thomas Cromwell to explain why they could not take this oath without the saving

---

[169] *Ibid.*, pp. 391-392, 405-406, 411-423, 430.

[170] Parmiter, *King's Great Matter*, p. 300.

[171] Bruce, *Anne Boleyn*, pp. 258-260.

[172] Lehmberg, *Reformation Parliament*, pp. 202-209; Parmiter, *King's Great Matter*, pp. 294-295.

clause "so far as the law of God might allow." Cromwell replied that there could be no qualifications. They told him that St. Augustine had put the authority of the Church above Scripture. Cromwell replied "that he cared naught for the Church and that Augustine might hold as he pleased. All he wished to know was whether they would swear a direct oath or no." When they would not, he threw them into the Tower of London. On the 15th Richard Reynolds of Syon Abbey, author of 94 books, was interrogated in the Tower as to why he refused to swear to the royal supremacy. "He meant no malice to the king, he said, but would spend his blood in the Pope's cause; whoever might oppose him in the England of that day, he had with him a thousand thousand of the past." He also declared that he was convinced that the majority of Englishmen agreed with him, though most did not dare to say so. On April 20 the entire London Charterhouse, led by their prior St. John Houghton, refused the oath.[173]

On April 26-28 St. John Houghton and his Carthusian companions, along with Richard Reynolds, were put on trial under the new treason act. They denied any malice against the king, and since the statute required malice, the jury was ready to acquit them on this basis, but the judges "ruled that it was impossible to deny the supremacy except maliciously." The jury still resisted, until Cromwell threatened them with death; only then did they convict the saints, and it is said that they "were afterwards ashamed to show their faces."[174] On May 4 the three Carthusian priors—Saints John Houghton, Robert Lawrence, and Augustine Webster—and St. Richard Reynolds were brought to the execution place at Tyburn. At the foot of the gallows they were offered a last chance to take the oath and save their lives. Each refused, and each was hanged, drawn and quartered in his habit and his hair shirt, at Henry VIII's personal order. St. John Houghton, the first to die, embraced his executioner and asked the spectators "to witness against the Day of Judgment that he died rather than deny the teaching of God's Church." His severed arm was nailed to the door of the London Charterhouse. From the window of his cell in the Tower of London, St. Thomas More and his daughter had watched the martyrs going to Tyburn; he said to her: "Dost thou not see, Meg, that these blessed fathers be now as cheerfully going to their deaths as bridegrooms to their marriage."[175]

He would follow them soon, as would St. John Fisher, whom the new Pope made a cardinal May 21, astonishingly thinking that Henry VIII would consider this an honor for one of his English subjects.[176] Hearing the news, Thomas Cromwell went immediately to Fisher's cell in the Tower. What followed is told by Fisher's earliest biographer:

---

[173] Knowles, *Religious Orders in England*, III, 217, 230-231, 280.

[174] Maynard, *Crown and Cross*, p. 112 (both quotes); Hughes, *Reformation in England*, I, 280.

[175] Knowles, *Religious Orders in England*, III, 217-218, 232-233 (first quote on 232); Reynolds, *Fisher*, p. 257 (second quote).

[176] Von Pastor, *History of the Popes*, XI, 139-147; Reynolds, *Fisher*, pp. 262-263.

Mr. Cromwell being come into his [Fisher's] chamber and entering into talk with him of many matters, asked him in this manner, "My lord of Rochester, if the Pope should now send you a cardinal's hat, what would you do? Would you take it? " "Sir, said he, "I know myself far unworthy of any such dignity, that I think of nothing less than such matters; but if he do send it me, assure yourself I will work with it by all means I can to benefit the church of Christ, and in that respect I will receive it on my knees." Mr. Cromwell making report afterward of this answer to the king, the king said again with great indignation and spite, "Yea, is he yet so lusty? Well, let the Pope send him a hat, when he will. But I will so provide that, whensoever it cometh, he shall wear it on his shoulders, for head shall he have none to set it on."[177]

And so it was. On May 7 Henry VIII's Solicitor-General Richard Rich had gone to Fisher in prison and told him that the king wanted his true and honest opinion, in confidence, on whether he could truly be supreme head of the Church in England, and pledging that anything he said would not be used against him. Fisher believed him, and responded "that it was very plain by the holy scripture, the laws of the Church, the general council, and the whole faith and general practice of Christ's Catholic Church from Christ's ascension hitherto, that the king was not, nor could be, by the law of God, supreme head of the church in England." On June 17 Fisher was brought to trial, with his statement to Rich, which Rich had promised to keep in confidence and not to use against him, the principal charge. He was convicted (once again Cromwell had to threaten the jury first) and beheaded at Tyburn on June 22, 1535, the feast day of St. Alban, the protomartyr of England, after speaking from the gallows the glorious words that stand at the head of his chapter. His head was mounted on a spike on London Bridge for two weeks and then flung into the Thames.[178]

Now it was St. Thomas More's turn. Rich tried the same trick with him with which he had entrapped Fisher, but More, a great lawyer, was not fooled. He would make no statement to Rich on the royal supremacy in the church. When More came to trial, Rich therefore had to state falsely that he had admitted to him that he did not regard Henry as the supreme head of the church in England.[179] After Rich's perjury, in the scene immortalized by Robert Bolt in *A Man for All Seasons*, the former Chancellor of England, with whitening hair, long beard, and drawn features from his year of imprisonment, rose to his feet and thundered:

---

[177] Reynolds, *Fisher*, p. 264.

[178] *Ibid.*, pp. 258-261 (quote on 261), 276-280, 282-286; Maynard, *Crown and Cross*, pp. 109, 111.

[179] Reynolds, *Field Is Won*, pp. 338-344. A dilapidated document rediscovered in 1963 proves, for anyone who might have doubted it, that Rich lied. It is a memorandum of what took place during the interrogation, and quotes Rich as saying to More at the end of it: "I see your mind will not change which I fear will be very dangerous to you for I suppose your concealment to the question that hath been asked you is a high offense." (*op. cit.*, p. 344).

You were esteemed very light of your tongue, a common liar, a great dicer, and of no commendable fame. . . . Was it likely that I would have spoken words to a visitor, not even a friendly one, that I had refused to speak when time and again the direct question was put to me by the Councillors?[180]

When the verdict of guilty had been given, More was released at last to state to his country and the world what he had always believed:

Seeing that ye are determined to condemn me (God knoweth how), I will now in discharge of my conscience speak my mind plainly and freely touching my indictment and your statute withal. And forasmuch as this indictment is grounded upon an Act of Parliament directly repugnant to the laws of God and his Holy Church, the supreme government of which, or of any part whereof, may no temporal prince presume by any law to take upon him, as rightfully belonging to the See of Rome, a spiritual pre-eminence by the mouth of Our Savior Himself, personally present upon earth, only to St. Peter and his successors, bishops of the same see, by special prerogative granted; it is thererfore in law, amongst Christian men insufficient to charge any Christian man. . . . No more might this realm of England refuse obedience to the See of Rome than might a child refuse obedience to his own natural father.[181]

On July 6, after declaring that he died "the King's good servant, but God's first," More was beheaded in the square in front of the Tower of London, and his head impaled on a spike on London bridge as Fisher's had been; but his devoted daughter Margaret saved it from being thrown into the river. When he was told that More was dead, Henry VIII, in his only recorded expression of regret for the executions he had inflicted, turned coldly to Anne Boleyn, who had led him down into the pit, and said: "This is long of you; the honestest man of my kingdom is dead."[182]

In briefs sent to all Christian princes when the news arrived, Pope Paul III denounced Henry VIII in the language of an Old Testament prophet, thundering that he should be deposed "as a heretic, schismatic, notorious adulterer, open murderer, sacrilegious despoiler, destroyer and transgressor against the majesty of God."[183]

Less than a year passed before Anne's head too was struck from her shoulders on fantastic charges of adultery and incest elaborately cooked up by Thomas Cromwell to free his master for a third marriage to a woman named Jane Seymour. Two days before Anne's execution, in order to give priority in the succession to children who would hopefully be born of the new queen, ever-obedient Archbishop Cranmer pronounced the marriage of Henry and Anne,

---

[180] *Ibid.*, p. 336 (indirect address in the original source changed to direct).

[181] *Ibid.*, pp. 367-368.

[182] *Ibid.*, pp. 376-379 (377 for first quote); Bruce, *Anne Boleyn*, p. 268 (second quote).

[183] Ludwig Von Pastor, *History of the Popes*, Volume XII (London, 1950), p. 460.

which he had personally approved just three years before, invalid on grounds of the canonical impediment created by Henry's previous adultery with Anne's sister Mary, of which he and everyone connected with Henry's case had known for the past nine years. No wonder Cranmer walked his garden all night before her execution, weeping, unable to sleep. He had much to answer for, and no courage to listen to his conscience. As for Henry, he rejoiced when he heard of her death, spent the day with Jane Seymour, and married her eleven days later.[184]

At the beginning of that year, Henry had also rejoiced at the death of another woman, his true wife. Catherine had died January 7 at her house far away in the village of Kimbolton, after writing a letter to him in which she avowed her enduring love, and urged him to tend to:

> . . . the health and safeguard of your soul which you ought to prefer before all worldly matters, and before the care and pampering of your body, for the which you have cast me into many calamities and yourself into many troubles. For my part, I pardon you everything, and I wish and devoutly pray God that He will pardon you also. . . . Lastly, I make this vow, that mine eyes desire you above all things.[185]

Left motherless, utterly alone, just twenty years old, counselled by all— even her one true friend who remained in contact with her, Charles V's ambassador Chapuys—to submit, Princess Mary surrendered at the end of June, recognizing Henry as head of the Church in England, denying the religious authority of the Pope, and accepting the invalidity of her mother's marriage. But she never meant it; within days she was begging Chapuys to write for her to the Pope to ask secret absolution for her sin.[186] In the words of her eloquent biographer H. F. M. Prescott:

> She never could, now or later, weigh reason of state against reason of state; she could only try, groping and fumbling, to find out what was right for her to do, as a single human soul, like any other, before God's judgment seat, and then to do it, regardless of danger, regardless of wisdom, deaf to argument or persuasion, not daring to compromise or turn back, because once in her life she had know what was right, and had not done it.[187]

The previous year Thomas Cromwell (appointed Vicar-General of England by the king for the occasion) had launched a visitation of all the 376 monasteries and convents of England with fewer than twelve inhabitants or an annual income

---

[184] Bruce, *Anne Boleyn*, pp. 293, 299-307, 313-3333; Scarisbrick, *Henry VIII*, pp. 349-350; Ridley, *Cranmer*, pp. 106-111. Anne Boleyn was executed May 19, 1536. She was just 28 years old. On January 29, 1536 she had a last miscarriage, of a boy, which apparently convinced Henry that she would never bear him a son.

[185] Mattingly, *Catherine of Aragon*, pp. 429-430.

[186] H. F. M. Prescott, *Mary Tudor* (New York, 1953), pp. 80-82, 84; Maynard, *Thomas Cromwell*, pp. 128-130.

[187] *Ibid.*, pp. 84-85.

of less than 200 pounds a year (known as the "lesser monasteries").[188] Cromwell's evident purpose from the beginning was to close them down and distribute their assets to himself, his friends, and loyal supporters of Henry VIII. Since small numbers and poverty might not be sufficient to justify their seizure, his visitors took care to browbeat the monks and nuns into admitting numerous sins, mostly sexual, which they duly recorded (and very likely magnified). In February 1536 the visitors presented their final report; in March the ever-obedient Reformation Parliament, now in its last session, quickly enacted a bill for confiscation of all the lesser monasteries, which was probably presented to the House of Commons by the king in person, so that all should understand immediately that its passage was his will. A companion bill created a special Court of the Augmentations of the Revenues of the King's Crown to dispose of all the properties of the dissolved monasteries. It was headed by none other than Richard Rich.[189]

On June 9 William Aleyn, abbot of Waverley, one of the monasteries listed for confiscation, wrote to Thomas Cromwell:

> beseeching your good mastership, for the love of Christ's passion, to help me in the preservation of this poor monastery, that we your bedesmen may remain in the service of God with the meanest living that any poor men may live with in this world. So to continue in the service of almighty Jesus . . . praying you, and my poor brethren with weeping eyes, desire you to help them, in this work no creatures in more trouble, and so we remain depending upon the comfort that shall come from you.[190]

No comfort came from Thomas Cromwell. Waverley was one of the first monasteries he closed down.[191]

All that summer the targeted religious houses were seized and despoiled. Whatever Cromwell's men did not take was looted by some of the neighboring people. Even the tombs of dead monks and nuns were robbed. But some found protectors. Of the 376 monasteries and convents originally listed for confiscation, 123 survived, either due to local protectors or to large bribes paid to Cromwell. Many more monks and nuns than Cromwell expected wished to continue in the religious life; but since places could not be found for all of them in the relatively few remaining religious houses, many had to abandon the religious life against their will. In Lancashire, for example, all but one monastery was suppressed, though 79 per cent of the Lancashire monks wished to continue

---

[188] The modern practice of using the term "monasteries" exclusively for religious houses for men and "convents" exclusively for religious houses for women had not yet been established; the two terms are used interchangeably by contemporary writers.

[189] Merriman, *Thomas Cromwell*, pp. 166, 169-170; Hughes, *Reformation in England*, I, 279, 285; Knowles, *Religious Orders in England*, III, 291-292; Lehmberg, *Reformation Parliament*, pp. 224-229.

[190] Maynard, *Crown and Cross*, p. 142.

[191] *Ibid.*

in the religious life. In Yorkshire 14 of 29 religious houses were dissolved. The people in these northern regions were mostly faithful Catholics, and the seizure of the monasteries and convents—known and loved by most in their vicinity—brought home for the first time to the people of England what was really happening in their country. That fall they rose in revolt, under the banner of the Five Wounds of Christ, which also bore a Host and a chalice. They called it the Pilgrimage of Grace. Their leader was Robert Aske, a Yorkshire lawyer.[192]

But the Pilgrims of Grace could not bring themselves to blame King Henry VIII for what had happened. In the age-old evasion, they blamed his counsellors for misleading him, while in fact he had led all of them—even Cromwell. One of the Pilgrims' most rousing songs reflected their blaming of the counsellors:

Crim [Cromwell], Crame [Cranmer] and Rich
with three L's [Drs. Layton and Legh, two of the visitors of the monasteries,
and Bishop Longland of Lincoln] and the Lich [the Bishop of Lichfield]
as some men teach,
God them amend
and that Aske may
without delay
here make a stay
and well to end.[193]

For a time the Pilgrims of Grace preserved or restored the monasteries on the dissolution list in the northern regions they briefly controlled. But they had no conception of the magnitude of the task they had undertaken, and did not imagine the relentless hostility of their king to them and what they were doing. Though he commanded 30,000 armed men, Aske had no military competence. On October 26 the Duke of Norfolk wrote to Henry that he had no intention of keeping any agreement he might make with these rebels. In December Henry wrote to the Duke that he "must cause dreadful execution upon a good number of the inhabitants, hanging them on trees, quartering them, and setting their heads and quarters in every town." On December 2 leaders of the Pilgrimage, meeting at Pontefract Castle, demanded restoration of papal authority in the Church, restoration of the confiscated monasteries, repeal of the statute of treason by words, the reform of Parliament, and the re-legitimization of Princess Mary. At a conference at Doncaster in York the Duke of Norfolk promised pardon for the Pilgrims and said he would ask the king to hold a parliament at York to repeal the legislation dissolving the monasteries. Aske was foolish enough to think he meant it, and on December 8 declared his loyalty to the king, dissolved his army,

---

[192] *Ibid.*, pp. 139, 142-143; Merriman, *Thomas Cromwell*, pp. 172, 182-185; Knowles, *Religious Orders in England*, III, 310-311, 316-317, 324; Christopher Haigh, *The Last Days of the Lancashire Monasteries and the Pilgrimage of Grace* (Manchester, England, 1969), pp. 43, 45-46.

[193] Merriman, *Thomas Cromwell*, p. 182.

and took off his Pilgrim's badge. A week later Henry invited Aske to court, wined and dined him, and told him the monasteries would never be restored.[194]

The ill-fated Pilgrimage of Grace was the only popular rebellion Henry VIII of England ever faced in all his reign. The people who had loved him so much could never quite believe the degree of evil that now consumed him. He had separated England from the Pope and from Christendom. Only Princess Mary still might, some day, restore it to both.

---

[194] Hughes, *Reformation in England*, I, 303-312, 315-316; Knowles, *Religious Orders in England*, III, 330-331 (quote on 331); Scarisbrick, *Henry VIII*, pp. 344-345.

4
Delay of the Council
1536-1553
Popes Paul III (1534-1549) and Julius III (1550-1555)

"Let him who would fight for God under the banner of the Cross and serve the Lord alone and His Vicar on earth in our Society, which we desire to be distinguished by the name of Jesus, bear in mind that, after a solemn vow of perpetual chastity, he is part of a community founded primarily for the task of advancing souls in Christian life and doctrine, and of propagating the faith by the ministry of the word, by spiritual exercises, by works of charity, and expressly by the instruction of children and unlettered persons in Christian principles. First and foremost he is to have God always before his eyes, and then the constitutions of this his order which are, as it were, a way to God, striving with all his might towards the attainment of this end which God has proposed to him."—summary of resolutions on a new order (to be the Jesuits), presented to Pope Paul III by St. Ignatius of Loyola and five of its other founders, June 25, 1539[1]

"We have bitter experience of the difficulties of our generation and know the appalling changes of fortune to which practically everything is subjected, just as if the world was in its last delirium and about to collapse into nothingness. . . . Is there to be any measure or end to the multitude of stormy mutinies that have now begun? We are borne down and disquieted from every side by a thousand treacheries and evil designs . . . and there is no place of rest and solid peace for us except into the wounds of Our Crucified Lord. . . . In them is our home of refreshment, our harbor, our sanctuary."—St. Peter Canisius to the Jesuit community at Cologne, spring 1552[2]

"I have always wanted it [an ecumenical council]! As far as I am concerned His Holiness may convoke it and open it at any time. . . . Only let him open it! Let him open it—open it!"—Emperor Charles V to papal nuncio Poggio, April 23, 1540[3]

"The love of the various nations for the Apostolic See has grown cold. Bishops depend too much on princes, while the latter are mainly concerned with their own interests. Yet in spite of everything and trusting in the divine assistance the great undertaking [the Council of Trent] must be risked, for the

---

[1] James Brodrick, *The Origin of the Jesuits* (New York, 1940), pp. 72-73.
[2] James Brodrick, *St. Peter Canisius* (Baltimore MD, 1950), p. 176.
[3] Hubert Jedin, *A History of the Council of Trent*, Volume I (St. Louis, 1957), p. 346.

eventual triumph of truth is not in doubt."—Cardinal Marcello Cervini to
Pope Paul III from Trent, August 8, 1545[4]

The Diet of Augsburg in 1530 and the formation of the Protestant military
alliance, the Schmalkald League, at the end of that year, had made it clear that no
ordinary means could bring about a reconciliation with the Protestants. The one
remaining recourse, short of prolonged internecine war in Christendom, was to
call an ecumenical council as quickly as possible. The Protestants had almost all
paid lip service to a council as final arbiter of the religious cleavage they had
created, and some of them at least were sincere in their avowals. In any case, a
council was and had long been desperately needed, well before there were any
Protestants, for the vested interests at Rome were too strong for any but the most
extraordinary Pope to decree and enforce the necessary comprehensive reforms
on his own.[5]

The enduring lesson of the Great Western Schism of the late fourteenth and
early fifteenth centuries had been that no ecumenical council was valid and could
be permanently effective unless convened and endorsed by the Pope. But the
history of the vitally important Council of Constance also held a second lesson,
tragically disregarded in the period we are about to cover: that in a crisis for
Christendom, as had existed at the time of that council and clearly now existed
again, the close cooperation, support and protection of the Holy Roman Emperor
was also essential. At the Council of Constance the great Emperor Sigismund
had provided that cooperation, support and protection.[6] Charles V took it for
granted that he should do the same, particularly since his firm defense of the
Faith in the first decade of Luther's assault had been essential to the survival of
Christendom. Even Pope Clement VII, who had failed the Church in so many
ways, had seen that at the end; two days before his death he sent this message to
Charles:

> I conjure Your Majesty by the love of Our Lord Jesus Christ, in this my last
> hour, that Your Majesty will preserve the same good will towards the Holy
> Church and the whole of Christendom, and will at all times be solicitous for
> the dignity of the Holy See and for the peace of Italy, which are both mainly
> dependent on your power and integrity.[7]

But Pope Paul III, influenced perhaps by the ghastly memories of the sack
of Rome in 1527, carried out by the Emperor's troops even though not with the
Emperor's consent,[8] and/or by an excess concern with power politics, never

---

[4] *Ibid.*, I, 532.

[5] See the discussion of the Fifth Lateran Council, which ran for five years (1512-17)
before Luther appeared but accomplished almost nothing, at the end of Volume Three of
this history, pages 712-713.

[6] See Volume Three, Chapter 12 of this history.

[7] Johannes Janssen, *History of the German People at the Close of the Middle Ages* (St.
Louis, 1903), V, 516.

[8] See Chapter Two, above.

really accepted Charles V's essential role in dealing with the crisis of the cleaving of Christendom. Paul III often behaved as though he would prefer the Council to be held without the Emperor having anything to do with it, or at least kept at a long arm's length. The misunderstanding between these two men, the spiritual and temporal heads of Christendom, grew with the passing years. Periodically both attempted to overcome it, for they were good men dedicated to the same goal: saving the Church and Christendom. But they never really succeeded in doing so. It was their inability to cooperate consistently in the face of continuing Protestant aggression that more than anything else gave the air of bitterness and desperation to these grim years, whose only cure lay in the words of Cardinal Marcello Cervini and St. Peter Canisius quoted at the head of this chapter.

The lack of cooperation between the Pope and the Emperor might have been less harmful had there been any alternative to the Emperor among the kings of Christendom. But there was not. Christendom had only three great united kingdoms: Spain, France, and England. The Emperor was also the king of Spain; the king of England was in total rebellion against the authority of the Church; and the king of France, Francis I, though he remained professedly Catholic, had no real interest in the Council. Worse, he seemed to have no Christian or Catholic conscience. With Machiavellian shamelessness he allied himself with both the German Protestants and the Muslim Turks in order to weaken the Emperor, his political rival. This was a man who had condemned his two sons to years in a dungeon by breaking his word to Charles V in the Treaty of Madrid, and died from the complications of venereal disease contracted from his notorious promiscuity.[9] He firmly suppressed Protestants in his own country because he recognized the revolutionary character and consequences of their teachings, but had no hesitation in using them against his enemies.

The result was that Charles V, along with constantly urging the ecumenical council to be held and held quickly (as in his statement quoted at the head of this chapter), was faced throughout most of the latter part of his reign with either the actuality or the threat of war from three different directions: the Turks on the east, the German Protestants in the center, and the French on the west. There was scarcely a moment when he was at peace with all three of them and some periods when he was at war with all three. It is no wonder that those who wished to persuade him also to go to war with England for the sake of his aunt Catherine while she lived, and then for the sake of his cousin Mary her daughter, were unsuccessful, however strong Charles' private feelings about the white martyrdom Catherine and Mary suffered. Under these extraordinarily difficult circumstances Charles felt he had a right to the support of the Pope, and reacted with genuine anger when he did not get it.

This multiplex challenge to Emperor Charles V first took shape in the summer of 1532, when a quarter million Turks under Sultan Suleiman the

---

[9] See Chapter Two, above; for his venereal disease, see R. J. Knecht, *Francis I* (Cambridge, England, 1982), pp. 418-419.

Magnificent were surging through the Balkans to Hungary. Suleiman wrote to Charles' brother Ferdinand, the second man in the Empire:

> Be it known unto you that by the grace of God and of the Prophet I have set forth with all my nobles and all my slaves, and with an innumerable host, to seek out the King of Spain [Charles]. By the grace of God I am marching against him. If he is of a high and mighty spirit, let him encounter me in the field, and that which God shall decree will then take place. If he will not encounter me, then let him send tribute to my Imperial Majesty.[10]

When Ferdinand's ambassador reminded Suleiman's Grand Vizier of Charles' great power and authority, the Vizier cuttingly replied: "What sort of obedience does he get? Has he made peace with that Martin Luther?"[11]

An ambassador of Francis I named Rincon actually accompanied Suleiman on his march; he had been sent to persuade the Sultan to attack Italy instead of Hungary, but arrived too late to accomplish this. Writing to the Venetian envoy Giustiniani, Francis I candidly confessed: "I cannot deny that I keenly desire the Turk powerful and ready for war, not for himself, because he is an infidel and we are Christians, but to undermine the Emperor's power, to force heavy expenses upon him and to reassure all other governments against so powerful an enemy."[12] In the face of the advancing Turks, Charles could not risk war with the increasingly formidable Protestant military alliance in Germany, the Schmalkald League. Therefore he made a treaty with them in June whose effect was to suspend all laws against them from the Diets of Worms in 1521 and Augsburg in 1530, and to let them continue despoiling the Catholics. Yet even in this treaty Charles pledged every effort to see an ecumenical council opened within 18 months, evidently believing that this provision would please the Protestants.[13]

And the Protestants did, this once, respond, contributing thousands of soldiers to the army of 80,000 which Charles brought to Vienna in September. The Turks, after being held up for three weeks by the magnificent Christian defense of the little fortress of Güns in Hungary, decided not to challenge so large an army. They had occupied Graz in southern Austria, but the German troops drove them out of it.[14]

In January 1534 Francis signed a secret treaty with a group of German Protestant princes led by Landgrave Philip of Hesse to support the deposed Protestant Duke Ulrich in regaining his former territory of Württemberg. In May this French help enabled Philip and Ulrich to defeat an army commanded by Charles' brother Ferdinand and give Württemberg to Ulrich, who proceeded to Protestantize it by force during the ensuing year, driving monks from their

---

[10] Suleiman to Ferdinand July 15, 1532, Johannes Janssen, *History of the German People*, V, 377-378.

[11] *Ibid.*, V, 378.

[12] Knecht, *Francis I*, p. 225.

[13] Janssen, *History of the German People*, V, 385-386.

[14] *Ibid.*, V, 390; Karl Brandi, *The Emperor Charles V* (Atlantic Highlands NJ, 1965), p. 328.

monasteries and nuns from their convents, ransacking churches and seizing church lands. In June 1535 Francis instructed his ambassador to Rome, Jean du Bellay, just appointed cardinal, to assure Pope Paul III of his full support for a council and that he was hard at work to restore the German Protestants to obedience to the Pope. But in fact Francis did not want a council, believing that it would be dominated by Emperor Charles and increase his power.[15]

These years of 1534 and 1535 also provided a terrifying demonstration of just how revolutionary in practice the Protestant teaching could become. Anabaptists seized power in the city of Münster in north central Germany. Their denial of the validity of infant baptism was accompanied at this period by a satanically violent hatred against the beliefs and practices of all other Christians and a conviction that they alone were the elect of God. Those at Münster concluded that they had a divine right to rule all other men. Led by the Dutchman Jan Mathys, who called himself "the Prophet," they levelled all the city's churches, burned its books and records, abolished the Christian calendar, and seized all goods to be held in common. When Mathys was killed in battle, he was succeeded by John of Leiden, a Dutch tailor, who decreed compulsory polygamy and in early September 1534 he had himself proclaimed "king of the world." When one of his wives asked his permission to leave the possessed city, he cut off her head in its central square with his own hand.[16]

Prince Bishop Francis laid Münster under siege and, with the aid of some of the victims inside the city, took it in June 1535. The "king of the world" was executed with a red-hot dagger.[17] Through all the century of turmoil and upheaval to come in Germany, Münster remained a Catholic city, and continued as such down to our own time when its heroic Bishop Conrad von Galen spoke out repeatedly against the atrocities of another John of Leiden, Adolf Hitler, during World War II.

The horrors at Münster shocked the Protestants almost as much as the Catholics; thenceforth for many years one of the few things the followers of both religions could agree on (outside of the divinity of Christ, which kept most Protestants from becoming ultimate revolutionaries) was in total condemnation of the Anabaptists. And the example of Münster may have played some part in the surprisingly favorable initial response of the Lutherans to the Council as vigorously supported by Pope Paul III, who had declared his commitment to it in uncompromising terms in his first meeting with the College of Cardinals after his consecration in October 1534 (while the Münster nightmare was still going on).[18] He sent a nuncio, Pietro Paolo Vergerio, who had long experience in Germany, to that country to preach the Council all through 1535. Vergerio was well received

---

[15] Knecht, *Francis I*, pp. 232, 275; Ludwig von Pastor, *History of the Popes*, Volume XI (St. Louis, 1950), pp. 71-72; Janssen, *History of the German People*, V, 407-409, 415-416, 421-425; Brandi, *Charles V*, pp. 330-331.

[16] Janssen, *History of the German People*, V, 460-463.

[17] *Ibid.*, V, 483-484.

[18] See Chapter Three, above.

in the strongly Protestant cities of Augsburg and Regensburg,[19] and by Lutheran Margrave George of Brandenburg. Though the Germans wanted the council to be held in Germany and Charles V was later to feel he had to insist on that, at this point no great objection was raised when the Pope indicated his preference for the independent Italian city of Mantua in Lombardy. Even Luther surprisingly met with Vergerio in November and declared his willingness to go to a Council at Mantua to defend his doctrine.[20]

But then an unexpected event intervened, which should have had nothing to do with the Council, but did. The most significant single cause for the great struggle between Emperor Charles V and Francis I in the preceding decade had been their dispute over the possession of Milan. This vexed issue had finally been compromised in the Treaty of Barcelona in 1529 by making the surviving scion of the native Sforza family, which had previously governed Milan, its ruler. But on November 1 Duke Francisco Sforza suddenly died without issue at the comparatively young age of 53. Both Francis and Charles at once revived their claims to Milan; Charles' troops, being closer, occupied it in the next few days.[21]

It is likely that the sudden change in the position of the Lutherans regarding the Council, when on December 21, 1535 the Schmalkald League demanded that it be held in Germany rather than in Italy, with the Pope neither controlling its attendance nor acting as judge or president, resulted from French intervention in view of the prospect of war created by the revival of the Milan issue. We know that the French envoy Guillaume du Bellay expended much effort to persuade the Schmalkald League to take a more hostile position toward the Council than its members had expressed earlier in the year. During 1536 the Protestant opposition, further roused by Luther's inimitable rhetoric, hardened until in February 1537 papal legate Peter van der Vorst was laughed to scorn by the leaders of the Schmalkald League when he appealed to them to come to the Council which had now been scheduled for May of that year.[22]

A new war between Charles and Francis virtually guaranteed there would be no French representation at the Council, which Francis was obviously using as just another tool in power politics. Charles might be tempted to do the same; but he had not yet done so. The Pope could not reasonably be expected to take sides in another war over Milan; but he could be expected to support the Council regardless of it. He was now presented with a splendid opportunity to do just that. Charles had scheduled a visit to Rome in Holy Week 1536. On April 5 he

---

[19] The city of Regensburg in southern Germany was called "Ratisbon" (presumably a French version of its name) in most histories written in English during the nineteenth century, and by some in the twentieth. This alternate name is not used today.

[20] Von Pastor, *History of the Popes*, XI, 49-51, 54-55, 60-61; Jedin, *Council of Trent*, I, 294, 298.

[21] Von Pastor, *History of the Popes*, XI, 237; Brandi, *Charles V*, p. 469; Roger B. Merriman, *The Rise of the Spanish Empire in the Old World and the New* (New York, 1918), III, 263.

[22] Von Pastor, *History of the Popes*, XI, 69-72, 87-90; Jedin, *Council of Trent* I, 317-318, 320-321; Brandi, *Charles V*, pp. 404-405.

made ceremonial entry into the Pope's city on a road especially built for the occasion, going past the Colosseum, under the arch of Constantine, through the ancient Forum, and on to St. Peter's where Paul III, wearing his tiara, awaited him, and said Mass over the grave of the fisherman. The next day the Emperor talked privately with the Pope for more than six hours. On April 8 the Pope and cardinals decided definitely to hold the Council at Mantua. During Holy Week (April 9-16) the Emperor attended the glorious ceremonies and services with pious devotion, and had more long talks with the Pope which appeared harmonious and productive. On Easter Sunday he assisted at High Mass in "full imperial state."[23]

The next day, Easter Monday, Charles made an extraordinary speech to the Pope, the cardinals, and the French ambassadors, which continued for an hour and a half without notes. He startled everyone by speaking not in his native language or in Latin, but in Spanish, the language of his adopted country which since his stand against Luther in the Diet of Worms had supported him more faithfully than any other. After thanking the Pope and cardinals for calling the Council which Christendom so urgently required, Charles passionately stated his case against the perfidy of Francis I. For a second time Charles challenged Francis to single combat, and openly asked the Pope's support against him. War between them at this time, he declared only too truly, could be the ruin of Chriustendom. Paul III responded coolly, saying he believed that both monarchs wanted peace and promising every effort to mediate between them for it. The next day Charles made a specific proposal to that end, that Milan be given to the younger surviving son of Francis, with the provision that it never become part of France.[24]

The French ambassadors angrily rejected this, and threatened schism. Representatives of Pope and Emperor agreed that the Pope would continue to be neutral in any war between France and the Empire, but that they would work together for the success of the Council. On June 2 Paul III issued the bull *Ad dominici gregis curam* officially proclaiming the Council and calling it to meet at Mantua on May 23, 1537, for the purposes of defining and extirpating error and heresy, reforming morals and the Church, restoring peace in Christendom, and launching a new crusade. All bishops, abbots, and heads of religious orders were directed to come in person to the Council, and the sovereigns of Christendom were urged to appear in person or at least send representatives.[25]

Later that year a Commission of Reform set up by Paul III began its work. Its president was Cardinal Gasparo Contarini of Venice, known for his total

---

[23] Von Pastor, *History of the Popes*, XI, 77, 241-247, 253; Jedin, *Council of Trent*, I, 311.

[24] Von Pastor, *History of the Popes*, XI, 77, 257-253; Jedin, *Council of Trent* I, 309-310; Brandi, *Charles V*, pp. 377-379; Janssen, *History of the German People*, pp. 443-444; Ramón Menéndez Pidal, ed., *Historia de España*, Volume XX ("La España del Emperador Carlos V," by Manuel Fernández Alvarez), pp. 572-575.

[25] Von Pastor, *History of the Popes*, XI, 79, 255-257; Jedin, *Council of Trent*, I, 311-312.

commitment to reform; in an early address to the commission, Cardinal Jacopo Sadoleto declared his conviction that the sack of Rome was a sign of the anger of God against the great sins in the Church and especially those committed by several recent Popes, whose result had been the loss of much of Germany and of England to the Church and an immense threat to its future. He extolled Pope Paul III for his efforts for the Council and for reform, and praised individual cardinals such as Contarini who had given good example. In mid-February 1537 the commission issued its first recommendations, condemning abuses in the Curia and the Church, particularly the sale of dispensations and the large number of unfit persons being ordained as priests and given benefices. The commission called for bishops to reside in their dioceses and priests in their parishes, and an end to the appointment of Italians to foreign dioceses. It declared roundly that "bishops and benefices with cure of souls attached must not be granted for the purpose of providing a man with a livelihood, but in order to secure shepherds for human souls." It called for more careful regulation of religious orders, with the suppression of corrupt houses and their replacement by zealous communities.[26] It closed with a rousing tribute to and encouragement of the Pope:

> We have satisfied our consciences, not without the greatest hope of seeing, under your pontificate, the Church of God restored to a fair and dovelike purity and to inward unity, to the eternal glory of your name. You have taken the name of Paul. We hope that you will imitate his charity. He was chosen as an instrument to carry Christ's name to the heathen; you, we hope, have been chosen to revive in our hearts and deeds that name long since forgotten among the heathen and by us the clergy, to heal our sickness, to unite Christ's sheep again in one fold, and to avert from our heads the wrath and already threatening vengeance of God.[27]

It was all indeed to happen, but it took too long. For no less than eight more years passed before the ecumenical Council finally met, and no less than 27 years before at last it finished its work, completing both the reform and the definition of doctrine that the crisis brought by Luther so urgently required.

For the war between Charles and Francis over Milan did break out, leading to a two-pronged invasion of France in the summer of 1536, which accomplished nothing except to cause the death of Charles' able general, the Duke de Leyva, and to make Francis and his people even angrier. As expected, Francis seized the opportunity September 5 to tell the papal nuncio that due to the war he would not send his bishops to Mantua, where he said the Council would be too much under the influence of the Emperor (despite the fact that the Emperor had no political authority in that city).[28]

---

[26] Von Pastor, *History of the Popes*, XI, 156-157, 165-169, 171; Jedin, *Council of Trent*, I, 424-426, quote on 424.

[27] Von Pastor, *History of the Popes*, XI, 169.

[28] *Ibid.*, XI, 258; Janssen, *History of the German People*, V, 445-446; Knecht, *Francis I*, pp. 281-285.

As this matter of Charles V exercising or seeking to exercise "undue influence" over the Council was to come up again and again in the ensuing years, it is well to take a moment to examine it critically rather than blindly accepting its truth as most historians have. It became almost an obsession with Francis I (or at least he pretended it to be) and increasingly with Pope Paul III as well. But while there is ample evidence that Francis was always on the lookout for opportunities to delay the Council or use it against the Emperor, there is *no* hard evidence that Charles ever attempted to exert the controlling influence over the Council that he was always suspected of intending to do. Suspicions of his intentions, no matter how often expressed over how long a period, do not prove them evil without recorded statements by him or his intimates that he sought to dominate the Council, or specific examples of actions of his to that effect. Instead he kept saying over and over again that all he wanted was for the Council to meet and succeed,[29] and there is no real reason to believe these statements insincere. He did make numerous suggestions to the Council when it finally met, not all of them wise, and increasingly acted independently of it as his situation in Germany became more difficult. But he never tried to dominate the Council, by force or otherwise. It is no wonder, humanly speaking, that in the end Charles V became so angry over these constantly repeated but always unproved charges that on more than one occasion he spoke to or of the Pope as no Catholic layman should ever address the Vicar of Christ.

Along with this continuing shadow of undue suspicion and misunderstanding, the history of what was to be the Council of Trent, until its final session, encountered more than one instance of sheer bad luck. The first came on April 9, 1537 when Cardinal Gonzaga made a delayed delivery to the Pope of a letter from his brother Federigo, duke of Mantua, saying that he could not guarantee the security of the Council there without at least five thousand armed men paid for by somebody else. The Pope reasonably responded that so many soldiers would give the impression that the Council was acting under coercion. Duke Federigo immediately dropped his demand to 1,500 men-at-arms, but for reasons unknown the Pope refused to negotiate with him further. On April 20 he declared the Council prorogued to November 1 and ten days later decided to change its location to another north Italian city, suggesting Verona or Padua in Venetian territory, or Bologna or Piacenza in papal territory.[30]

There is no evidence to indicate that Duke Federigo Gonzaga had any motives for proposing a 5,000-man garrison of Mantua during the Council other than nervousness at the great responsibility he would bear for its security, with which everyone charged with security at a major international event in the twentieth century—from the Olympic Games to summit conferences—is very familiar. The abrupt abandonment of the widely publicized site roused doubts of the sincerity of the Pope's commitment to the Council and the lack of a specific

---

[29] Again, see the quotation from him at the head of this chapter.
[30] Von Pastor, *History of the Popes*, XI, 97-102; Jedin, *Council of Trent*, I, 326-327; Brandi, *Charles V*, pp. 405-406.

alternative caused confusion and invited additional delay.[31] Venice was notoriously uninterested in anything but expanding its own trade; no Venetian offer of a host city for the Council could really be trusted to be honored. And a city on papal territory would give the impression, in the conditions of that time, of undue papal domination of the Council. Mantua had been the ideal site, but now, for no clear and sufficient reason, it had been abandoned.

In the summer of 1537 the Turks attacked the Venetian island of Corfu, causing Venice to make a quick alliance with the papal states. The Pope and reforming Cardinal Contarini, himself a Venetian, were delighted when a week after signing the alliance Venice agreed to the Council meeting at the city of Vicenza on its territory. In January 1538 Paul III appointed a commission of nine cardinals to make detailed preparations for the Council at Vicenza. But by April 25, the designated date for opening the Council, not a single bishop had arrived there, not even the three legates the Pope himself had assigned, and he had no choice but to postpone its meeting indefinitely.[32]

Meanwhile, on Palm Sunday 1537, just a year after the magnificent entry of the Holy Roman Emperor into Rome, nine ragged men arrived in the papal city after a long and arduous journey begging their way from Venice. They were the companions of St. Ignatius of Loyola, who in his humility had stayed behind in Venice, believing his presence would prejudice their appeal to the Pope since he thought the Emperor's ambassador, Dr. Ortiz of Toledo, and Cardinal Carafa were personally hostile to him. Three years before, on Assumption day at hallowed Montmartre just outside Paris, six of them had pledged the rest of their lives to the service of God and His Church in total poverty, as a company that was to become the Society of Jesus. Now they were in Rome to ask the Pope's permission to go to Jerusalem together, or if that were not possible, to go wherever he might send them to serve the Church. Contrary to St. Ignatius' expectations, Dr. Ortiz gave them a high recommendation (the following year he was to spend the whole of Lent taking the Spiritual Exercises from St. Ignatius); on April 3 the Pope gave them his blessing. But no ships sailed to Jerusalem that year, when Turkish warships and pirates ranged the Mediterranean almost unchecked. All of the Jesuits-to-be not yet ordained (including St. Ignatius) were ordained in June. In November St. Ignatius, Bd. Peter Favre and James Laynez (to be Ignatius' successor as general of the Jesuits), arrived in Rome to offer themselves and their Company of Jesus for unlimited service to him and to the Church.[33]

---

[31] Luther's great opponent John Eck wrote to Girolamo Aleander, the former papal legate to Germany and future cardinal: "Many people are scandalized when they see the Council gone with the wind" (Jedin, *Council of Trent*, I, 334).

[32] Von Pastor, *History of the Popes*, XI, 104-106, 109-110, 112-114, 271-272; Jedin, *Council of Trent* I, 333, 336-337, 340.

[33] Mary Purcell, *The First Jesuit* (New York, 1965), pp. 215, 264-270, 277, 283; Brodrick *Origin of the Jesuits*, p. 60; William V. Bangert, *To the Other Towns; a Life of Blessed Peter Favre, First Companion of St. Ignatius* (Westminster MD, 1959), pp. 47-51, 54.

There were not even as many of them as the original band of Apostles that Christ selected. But they soon proved to be the reinforcement which in that dark hour the Church needed most.

Realizing now that he could never induce a sufficient international number of bishops to come to the Council without peace between Charles V and Francis I, Pope Paul III went to work personally to make that peace. Early in May 1538 he and Charles arrived in the vicinity of Nice, to which Francis had also been invited. The city refused to allow either within its walls, but otherwise made no hostile move, and Pope and Emperor conferred while waiting for the dilatory Francis, who finally arrived on the last day of the month and met with the Pope, though he would not meet with Charles. On June 9 the Pope suggested handing over Milan to Charles' brother Ferdinand under a strict pledge to marry one of his daughters to the younger of the two surviving sons of Francis I, with Milan to revert to this couple in three years. Charles agreed, on condition that Francis drop his alliance with the Turks and accept the Council. (These two immediate conditions imposed by Charles showed clearly where his priorities lay.) But Francis laughed off the terms. The best Paul III could get from him was his assent to a ten years' truce, with no commitment to the Council, whose convocation the Pope now set for Easter of 1539.[34]

On this occasion Pope Paul III had preformed well one of the primary functions of his high office: to act as peacemaker among Christian rulers. But precious time had already been lost, and the situation in Germany was steadily deteriorating. In September 1538 Cardinal Alexander reported grimly from Germany that its religious condition was ruinous: the administration of the sacraments had largely ceased; most of the princes (except Emperor Charles and his brother Ferdinand) were now either Lutheran or, if still Catholic, increasingly hostile to the Church; the bishops lived extravagantly and scandalously, whatever their religious profession; the number of religious was sharply reduced both by confiscations of monasteries and convents and more or less voluntary forsaking of vows, while the number of priests was also declining and their quality remained low. These developments were almost exactly contemporary with the suppression of the remaining monasteries in England by Thomas Cromwell, whose name now inspired such terror that its mere mention usually sufficed to have religious superiors "grant" their lands and houses to the King through Cromwell. In the same month that Cardinal Aleander made his report, Henry VIII of England despoiled the shrine of St. Thomas Becket and burned his bones, as one who had rebelled against his king. He took the largest jewel which had adorned the shrine, a ruby the size of a thumb, and put it on his own thumb.[35]

---

[34] Von Pastor, *History of the Popes*, XI, 115-117, 283-284, 286-291; Brandi, *Charles V*, pp. 388, 406; Merriman, *Rise of the Spanish Empire*, III, 267, 322-323; Knecht, *Francis I*, pp. 291-292; Jedin, *Council of Trent*, I, 340.

[35] Von Pastor, *History of the Popes*, XI, 362-363; David Knowles, *The Religious Orders in England*, Volume III (Cambridge, England, 1961), pp. 350-417; Eamon Duffy, *The Stripping of the Altars; Traditional Religion in England, c1400-c1580* (New Haven CT, 1992), p. 412.

At Easter, which fell on April 6 in 1539, no bishops had come to Vicenza for the Council, any more than they had come the preceding spring; and on April 17 Duke George of Saxony, the pillar of Catholic Germany behind Emperor Charles and his brother Ferdinand, died, staunch to the end. But all his sons had predeceased him, the last only two months earlier, making his heir his jealous brother Henry, who had converted to Lutheranism six years before. Within two months Duke Henry had imposed Lutheranism on his people and purged all the Catholic professors from the University of Leipzig which his brother had striven to make an intellectual defender of the old Faith. Now the Catholic Church in Germany had no major supporter north of Austria and Bavaria. Two days after Duke George's death Charles signed a six-month truce with the Protestant princes of Germany at Frankfurt, and scheduled a "religious conference" of Protestant and Catholic spokesmen to meet in the Protestant city of Nuremberg August 1 with the Pope and his representatives, on the insistence of the Protestants, specifically excluded. The next month Charles suggested that the Council be further delayed until this conference had done whatever work it might be able to do. The Pope did not protest; on receipt of the news from Germany he and his cardinals agreed on May 31 to the indefinite postponement of the Council and on June 10 proclaimed its postponement to the kings and princes of Europe.[36]

The German religious conference was delayed for no less than ten months. No one had much enthusiasm for it or expected much from it. Charles had agreed to it because the Protestants had demanded it; the Pope had acquiesced without endorsing it because Charles made his continued support of the Council conditional upon it; but the Protestants did not really want it either, for they felt the tide of history was with them and were in no compromising mood. In January 1540 Luther, Melanchthon, and Zwingli's successor Bugenhagen signed a statement declaring that religious peace could be established simply by the Emperor and the German bishops renouncing "their idolatry and error," and that "even if the Pope were to concede to us our doctrines and ceremonies, we should still be obliged to treat him as a persecutor and an outcast, since in other kingdoms he would not renounce his errors."[37] It was the first explicit public announcement that the ultimate goal of the Protestants was the total destruction of the Catholic Church throughout the world. The German religious conference finally opened June 12 in the little town of Hagenau, to which it had been moved when plague struck the city of Speyer, where it had been planned to hold another imperial Diet in conjunction with the conference.[38]

The chief Protestant spokesman at the conference was Martin Bucer. Luther had always regarded religious negotiations of any kind with Catholics as bargaining with the Devil. Melanchthon, known like Bucer for his willingness to seek verbal formulas of concord which to some extent would cover up enduring fundamental differences, was absent; he sent word that he was ill. But there is

---

[36] Von Pastor, *History of the Popes*, XI, 129-130, 359; Janssen, *History of the German People*, VI, 40, 49-53, 55-56.

[37] Von Pastor, *History of the Popes*, XI, 375.

[38] *Ibid.*, XI, 391, 393-394; Brandi, *Charles V*, pp. 437-438.

good reason to believe that the cause of his illness was more than simply physical.[39] Melanchthon, a personally honorable man and very fastidious compared to Luther, had with several other German Protestant leaders been plunged that year into a horribly embarrassing situation.

The two chief princes on whose power and armies the Lutherans relied to defy Emperor Charles V were Elector John Frederick of Saxony and Landgrave Philip of Hesse. John Frederick was a stolid mountain of a man with all the charm of a granite cliff. Philip was young, handsome, dashing, glib—and very promiscuous. As far back as 1526 he had written to Luther asking whether a Christian might have more than one wife. Luther replied citing the Old Testament patriarchs but concluding that a Christian should not live in bigamy, unless his wife "had the leprosy or be otherwise rendered unfit." But Philip would not take no for an answer. In November 1539, through the intervention of his doctor, he had obtained the reluctant agreement of Bucer that he might marry Margaret von der Sale, a maid of honor attending the Duchess of Rochlitz, in addition to his existing wife Christina. Margaret's mother was only persuaded to agree to the bigamy if Christina, Elector John Frederick, and two of the German Protestant theological leadership trio of Luther, Melanchthon and Bucer would publicly attend the wedding.[40] Presumably she hoped either that this condition would prove too difficult to fulfill, or that if it was fulfilled it would mute criticism of her daughter's unique marital status.

On December 1, 1539 Philip wrote to Margaret's mother:

> Bucer is of opinion that while public affairs are in such an abnormal unsettled state it would be well, for the sake of some of the weaker Christian brethren, to whom offense might otherwise be given, that this marriage should be kept secret for a little longer, until the preachers shall see their way better to making it known to the people. But at the same time he fully expects that Luther, Melanchthon, Bucer and others will give their consent in public writing (Bucer anonymously).[41]

In December Landgrave Philip persuaded Christina to agree to his bigamy by promising always to regard her as his "first and chief consort" and to "be more faithful to her than hitherto," and that her children alone would inherit his title. Luther and Melanchthon wrote him that they could not declare bigamy permissible for everybody, though they would allow it for him, so his marital proceedings must be kept secret. His "marriage" to Margaret was solemnized March 4, 1540, with Melanchthon attending at Luther's insistence. Philip's personal minister, Dionysius Melander, appropriately bearing the name of a pagan god, performed the ceremony, stating that "it was from misunderstanding of the Holy Scriptures that Christians had hitherto been forbidden to have two wives, just as marriage of the priesthood, eating meat, and other such things,

---

[39] Janssen, *History of the German People*, VI, 109.
[40] *Ibid.*, VI, 76-77; quote from Luther on p. 76.
[41] *Ibid.*, VI, 77. Any comment would be superfluous.

which a few years ago would have seemed to us quite as abominable and unheard of as the present ceremony may now appear." A month later Philip wrote to Luther that after his bigamous marriage he had gone to the Lord's Supper with a "happy conscience," and thanked him for his good advice.[42]

Of course the secret soon got out. By June Philip's sister and the garrulous Duke Henry of Saxony had revealed it, though Elector John Frederick directed his deputies at the Hagenau conference not to mention it, and to refuse to defend Philip if asked about what he had done. Luther and Bucer told Philip to deny his bigamy ("What harm is there in telling a good bold lie for the sake of making things better and for the good of the Christian Church?" was Luther's spiritual reassurance); but Melanchthon, who had consented to and witnessed the bigamy, knowing he should not, was conscience-stricken, and stayed away from the religious conference at Hagenau.[43]

Its discussions soon deadlocked. Emperor Charles had been obliged to go to the Low Countries to suppress a major rebellion in Ghent. His brother Ferdinand ended the futile meeting but promptly scheduled another one for the fall, at Worms of vivid memory. This time Pope Paul III sent spokesmen, Bishops Giovanni Morone and Tommaso Campeggio (brother of the great Cardinal Lorenzo Campeggio, who had just died that year), with instructions to be "swift to hear and slow to speak." They were not excluded, but the conference was opened by Charles' chief minister Granvelle November 25, before they arrived. After nearly two months of quarrelling over procedures, the disputation finally began January 14, 1541, with the tireless John Eck leading off for the Catholics and Melanchthon (his embarrassment over the bigamy of Philip of Hesse apparently dulled by the passage of time) for the Protestants. Just six days later Granvelle announced that Charles had ordered the conference adjourned to the forthcoming Diet at Regensburg, where the Emperor himself would take charge of "the restoration of religious peace to Germany." When this Diet finally opened April 5, two full years had been lost since Charles' decision to delay the Council until a German religious conference had been held.[44]

For this particular delay Charles must bear much of the blame. He had certainly not lost his desire for the Council—it is from the middle of this two-year period that his heartfelt cry for its opening, quoted at the head of this chapter, was given—but it seems evident that he was losing confidence that the Pope would actually bring it about, after the fiascoes at Mantua and Vicenza. Despite all his experience with the German Protestants, Charles still found it hard to believe that they had totally rejected the Catholic Faith, to the point where no human effort could win them back. He should have listened to John Eck, who knew them better than any other German Catholic, when he thundered in the religious discussions at Regensburg:

---

[42] *Ibid.*, VI, 80-86; quote from Philip to Christina, p. 83, and from Rev. Melander on p. 85.

[43] *Ibid.*, VI, 114-118, quote on 118.

[44] Von Pastor, *History of the Popes*, XI, 395-397, 405-409, 417-419, 436-437 (first quote on p. 406, second on p. 419); Brandi, *Charles V*, pp. 426-434, 441.

Those who wish to become one in the faith must submit to the Pope and the Councils, and believe what the Roman Church teaches; all else is wind and vapor, though one should go on disputing for a hundred years.[45]

Reform-minded Cardinal Contarini attended the Diet of Regensburg and its religious discussions, and managed to obtain agreement by both sides on a statement on justification, but only by using the new concept of "duplicate justice," which recognized that God gave justifying grace to men in baptism, but also stated that "a yet higher justice, that of Christ Himself, becomes necessary in order to attain perfect renewal, this latter being given and imputed to men through faith." It seemed an inspired straddle, but the Council of Trent later repudiated it. Jubilation over this paper harmonization of one of the major points of separation between Lutheranism and the Catholic Faith—Luther's doctrine of "justification by faith alone"—soon faded when the conferees took up their differences on the Mass and the sacraments, which were absolutely irreconcilable.[46] The Catholic Faith cannot be practiced without the Mass, and the Protestants had totally rejected the Mass. Just a week after the illusory agreement on justification, Cardinal Contarini wrote that he had beem astonished to discover that the Protestants rejected both the Real Presence and veneration of the Blessed Sacrament outside Mass. On May 16 Contarini wrote to Rome that there must be no yielding to the temptation to state Catholic doctrine in equivocal terms in the attempt to find common ground with the Protestants; rather, every effort should be made "to convince Germany and Christendom at large that the strife proceeds neither from the Holy See nor from the Emperor, but from the obdurate adherence of the Protestants to their errors." Coming to the same conclusion independently, Pope Paul III instructed Contarini in the same vein May 29. In July the German Protestants specifically demanded a German national council over which the Pope would have no authority.[47]

With deadlock again evident, when the Diet of Regensburg recessed at the end of July 1541 Charles made a secret agreement with the Protestants to leave them in uncontested possession of the Church property they had seized and to act on their own interpretation of German imperial law until a final settlement was made. By this means he temporarily obtained their help against the Turks.[48]

During these years of continued delay of the Council and deadlock between Catholics and Protestants in Germany, the Society of Jesus took form as a religious order and was recognized and approved as such by the Pope. Past and some current criticism of St. Ignatius of Loyola, its founder, was reviewed in

---

[45] Janssen, *History of the German People*, VI, 148.

[46] Von Pastor, *History of the Popes*, XI, 442-446, 449 (quote on 442); Jedin, *Council of Trent*, I, 408-409.

[47] Von Pastor, *History of the Popes*, XI, 444-447, 449, 452-453, 473 (quote on 449); Jedin, *Council of Trent*, I, 384-385.

[48] Von Pastor, *History of the Popes*, XI, 473, 478; Janssen *History of the German People*, VII, 154-159; Jedin, *Council of Trent* I, 388-389; Brandi, *Charles V*, pp. 452-453.

Church court at Rome. Inquisitors from Alcalá de Henares in Spain, Venice, and Rome all testified to his complete orthodoxy and trustworthiness, and he was acquitted of all charges against him and his Company—a striking demonstration of the service of the much-criticized Inquisition in clearing the innocent as well as convicting those guilty of false profession of the Catholic Faith. In the spring of 1539 St. Ignatius began drafting the constitutions of the order, providing for a general elected for life and a special vow of obedience to the Pope, which no previous religious order had prescribed.[49] Though for the most part the creation of the Jesuit order was not a direct consequence of the Protestant revolt, it is hard to believe that their insistence on this vow did not derive at least to a significant degree from the notable disobedience to and abuse of the Pope so characteristic of German Protestants. On June 24 the Jesuits-to-be sent a summary of their proposal to Pope Paul III, beginning with the splendid words quoted at the head of this chapter.

In Spain that spring, Emperor Charles' beloved wife Isabel died. The scion of one of Spain's richest families, Francis Borgia, heir to the Duke of Gandia, great-grandson of Pope Alexander VI of evil memory,[50] who had attended her at court and stood guard over her coffin, was overwhelmed when the coffin was opened and he saw the ravages of corruption on the Empress' once-beautiful face. At that moment he resolved some day to enter the religious life. He was later to join the Jesuits and become their third general. Charles was stricken; the light had gone out of his life. He set aside his multitudinous cares and duties for two full months of mourning and prayer for his Isabel at the Jeronymite monastery in rock-hewn Toledo, and after that remained two weeks more mostly hidden behind the walls of a country house near Madrid.[51]

Pope Paul III, very positively inclined toward the Jesuits, assigned Cardinal Contarini to review their founding documents, and in September 1539 the great reforming cardinal gave them his unqualified approval. A full year was required to overcome the opposition of some leading churchmen at the Vatican, notably Cardinal Guidiccioni, who opposed the recognition of any new religious order. But the Pope believed the "finger of God" was on this new, ardent, but highly disciplined company of soldiers of Christ. He confirmed the Jesuits as a religious order on September 27, 1540. In April 1541 St. Ignatius was elected their first general and the ten original members took their vows.[52]

Even before this process was complete, in March 1540 St. Ignatius had been requested by both Pope Paul III and King John III of Portugal to send missionaries into the vast expanses of Asia opened up when Vasco da Gama

---

[49] Von Pastor, *History of the Popes*, XII 29-30; Brodrick, *Origin of the Jesuits*, p. 72; Purcell, *First Jesuit*, pp. 292, 299.

[50] See Volume Three, Chapter 15 of this history.

[51] Brandi, *Charles V*, p. 421; Menéndez Pidal, *Historia de España*, XX, 631; Purcell, *First Jesuit*, pp. 301-302; *Correspondence of the Emperor Charles V*, ed. William Bradford (London, 1850), pp. 511-512.

[52] Von Pastor, *History of the Popes*, XII, 33-36; Brodrick, *Origin of the Jesuits*, pp. 93-94; Purcell, *First Jesuit*, pp. 299-300, 311-312.

finally achieved the dream of Prince Henry the Navigator by sailing to India around the Cape of Good Hope.[53] Though at that time there were only the ten original Jesuits, St. Ignatius chose two of them, Rodriguez and Bobadilla (both Portuguese) to go to the Orient. But Bobadilla fell ill at the last moment, and it happened that the most eager and enthusiastic of all that group of ardent young men, St. Ignatius' fellow Basque St. Francis Xavier, was with St. Ignatius in Rome. On March 14 the founder of the Jesuits called him in and asked him to go. "Here I am, willing and ready!" Francis Xavier cried out in reply. In just one day he made all his preparations for departure to the other side of the world, picked up a document from Pope Paul III naming him papal legate for the East, wrote and sealed his vote for St. Ignatius as general of the order and his vows as a member, and heard Ignatius tell him: "Go! Enkindle and inflame the whole earth!" On the 16th he left Rome, never to see it or St. Ignatius again, beginning the most extraordinary personal mission of evangelization in the history of Christianity.[54]

In September 1541 the Emperor and the Pope met at the Italian city of Lucca. There was a new threat of war between Charles and Francis, which the Pope offered to mediate. The Pope had learned of Charles' secret agreement with the Protestants after the Diet of Regensburg and objected to it. Charles met the Pope halfway by offering to drop his opposition to Vicenza as the site of the Council, but the Pope sorrowfully informed him that Venice, which had recently signed a treaty with the Turks, had withdrawn its offer for the Council to come to that city. It was probably at this meeting that Charles first suggested that the Council meet at the small city of Trent.[55]

The geographical position of Trent made it the best possible site for the Council given the political realities and problems of the moment, despite the inevitable logistical difficulties created by its small size (it had a population of only about 10,000). All German Protestants and many German Catholics had consistently urged and often demanded that the great Council to reform the Church must be held on German/imperial territory. Charles doubted, with good reason, that many Germans would accept the authority of a Council held outside the Empire. Pope Paul III doubted, with good reason, that many German Protestants would accept any true Council no matter where it was held, and preferred a site as close to Rome as possible without being in the papal city itself. Trent was the best compromise between these two positions. Located in the valley of the Adige River, connected by a tributary with the Brenner Pass, at the point where that valley begins to fan out into the Lombard plain, Trent was at the southern edge of the South Tyrol, the wedge of territory inhabited mostly by speakers of German south of the Brenner. That territory had been German and

---

[53] See Volume Three, Chapters 15 and 16 of this history.

[54] Brodrick, *Origin of the Jesuits*, pp. 84-85; Purcell, *First Jesuit*, pp. 318-319. The astonishing story of St. Francis Xavier's mission will be told in Chapter Thirteen, below.

[55] Von Pastor, *History of the Popes*, XI, 126-129, 296; Merriman, *Rise of the Spanish Empire*, III, 328-329.

imperial from time immemorial (and was to remain so until taken from Austria and incorporated into Italy as one of the punitive provisions of the Treaty of Versailles in 1919). But Trent was an Italian and fully Catholic city, more readily accessible from Italy than from Germany, and far enough away from Germany to escape most of its turmoil. Still, the very fact that it was an imperial city under the ultimate authority of Charles V provided a ready-made excuse for his enemies to stay away.

No decision was made on a new Council site for many months; but when in March 1542 Pope Paul III sent Bishop Morone as his new representative to Germany, his instructions authorized him to accept Trent for the Council if none of four other Italian cities (Mantua, Ferrara, Piacenza, or Bologna) was acceptable to the Germans.[56]

Meanwhile in late August 1541 the Turks had completed their conquest of Hungary (except for mountain-girt Transylvania north of the Hungarian plain) and Charles struck back at them unexpectedly with a massive assault on the Mediterranean port of Algiers, which had been Muslim for more than eight hundred years. On October 23 he began landing an army of 21,000 men near that city. But the next day a fierce storm wrecked many ships in his fleet, and an unexpected Muslim sortie inflicted heavy casualties, so that Charles had to go into the battle personally to rally his troops. Two days later another storm struck, totally disrupting all arrangements for supplying and supporting the Christian army. On October 29 Charles called a council of war. Most of its participants counselled abandonment of the expedition, and their advice was followed.[57]

Outside in that night of October 29 a lone man of 56, who had not been admitted to the council of war, strode from tent to tent. Full of proud confidence and burning anger because he had been excluded from the council, he told any officers who would listen that he was certain Algiers could still be taken. If the Emperor would leave him only a small part of his army, he would guarantee its capture.[58] For Hernán Cortés, after the conquest of Mexico, the military problem of Algiers was child's play. At Veracruz he had burned his ships so that there could be no retreat; even after he had lost half his men on the causeways of Lake Texcoco he had refused to leave the Valley of Mexico, and came back to gain total victory. No other sovereign ever had or ever would have an officer under his command who had conquered an empire against odds of ten thousand to one. Charles V's failure to listen to Cortés that night demonstrated the one great weakness of this splendid Catholic leader of men, which his son Philip was to share: he was too cautious. A resounding military victory over the infidel at that moment could have greatly strengthened him and Christendom in the ordeals that were to come.

---

[56] Jedin, *Council of Trent*, I, 453.

[57] Brandi, *Charles V*, pp. 455-456; Janssen, *History of the German People*, VI, 163-164; Merriman, *Rise of the Spanish Empire*, III, 336-339; von Pastor, *History of the Popes*, XII 125-125, 129-130; Menéndez Pidal, *Historia de España*, XX, 663-664.

[58] Salvador de Madariaga, *Hernán Cortés, Conqueror of Mexico* (Chicago, 1955), p. 477.

In April 1542 the Diet of Speyer in Germany accepted Trent as the site of the Council, extended the truce between Catholics and Protestants for five years, and made a commitment to raise a large army against the Turks, to be commanded by moderate Lutheran Elector Joachim of Brandenburg, whose military experience was very limited. But in May Francis I of France rejected a Council at Trent, and began bringing up no less than six armies to attack the Emperor: one from Cleves with support from France and Denmark to invade the Netherlands; two others from France to invade imperial territory in Artois and Luxembourg; two more from France to attack Italy and Spain in the south; and the Turkish army, heavily subsidized by France, to attack Austria from Hungary. Nevertheless on June 29 Pope Paul III, showing all the boldness Charles V had lacked at Algiers, issued a bull reviewing the whole history of his efforts to convene an ecumenical Council and summoning all bishops, abbots, and heads of religious orders to meet at Trent November 1.[59]

On July 12, 1542 Francis I declared a new war against Charles V, citing the murder in northern Italy of two of his ambassadors to Turkey as the principal cause for it. That same summer the armies of the three most powerful German Protestant leaders, Elector John Frederick of Saxony, Duke Maurice of Saxony (son and successor of Duke Henry), and Landgrave Philip of Hesse, with considerable support from their allies in the Schmalkald League, launched an unprovoked invasion of the still Catholic duchy of Brunswick and conquered it, driving out Catholic Duke Henry, who protested in vain to anyone who would listen. The conquerors ended the practice of the Catholic Faith in Brunswick or drove it underground, as they also did in the nearby cities of Bremen, Hildesheim and Mühlhausen. In Hildesheim the casket containing the bones of its St. Bernhard were used in satanic parodies of Catholic rites. The campaign against the Turks in Hungary commanded by Duke Joachim of Brandenburg fizzled out with no significant victories and no territory regained.[60]

Charles was now fighting on four fronts against six armies raised or aided by Francis I, which required him to refrain from fighting against the Protestants in Germany who were robbing and persecuting German Catholics or against Henry VIII of England who was doing likewise to Catholics in his own country. There was nothing the Pope could do about the Lutherans, Henry VIII, or the Turks, but Francis was still a professed Catholic and Charles quite reasonably believed him as guilty of the betrayal of the Church and Christendom as Luther or Henry VIII and no less an enemy than Sultan Suleiman. In a bitter letter to the Pope August 25, 1542 he sharply criticized him for his neutrality between Charles and Francis in view of Francis' support of the Turks, encouragement of the Protestants, opposition to the Council, and repeated aggression. He declared

---

[59] Jedin, *Council of Trent*, I, 453, 455-456, 459; Janssen, *History of the German People*, VI, 171-173, 179-180; Brandi, *Charles V*, p. 467; von Pastor, *History of the Popes*, XII, 144-145.

[60] Brandi, *Charles V*, pp. 475-476, 483; Knecht, *Francis I*, pp. 303-304; Janssen, *History of the German People*, VI, 176-177, 202, 207-213, 216-217.

that for the duration of the war with France he was suspending his support of the Council and would not allow any bishops from the Empire to attend it.[61]

Paul III was following the long-standing papal policy of not aligning himself with one Catholic power against another, and he also feared a schism by Francis I comparable to that of Henry VIII if he were denounced by the Pope. Francis was a popular king as Henry had been, but France was "the eldest daughter of the Church," and might not have followed Francis into schism as readily as England had followed Henry. But it was a great risk to take, especially in the condition of Christendom at that time. Both the Pope's and the Emperor's positions had merit, but they should not have made the Council a part of their disagreement. Previous experience had shown that it could not be held during a war between the Empire and France, so there was no need to make threats about it or affix blame. The great need was peace; but Francis I never seemed comfortable with peace for long.

As if all this were not trouble enough for the Church in one year, in that same summer of 1542 came the deeply disturbing news that two Italian Church leaders, Bernardino Ochino, superior-general of the Capuchin Franciscans, and the famous preacher Peter Martyr Vermigli, had embraced Protestantism and fled from Italy, Ochino to Calvin's Geneva where he declared the Pope the Antichrist.[62] Claudio Tolomei wrote to Ochino giving the Catholic answer to his pretensions:

> Are we really to believe that Irenaeus, Origen, Cyprian, Athanasius, Gregory, Basil, Ambrose, Augustine, Bernard, and so many other holy and admirable teachers of the law of Christ all erred, and instead of showing us the light wrapped us in darkness, instead of teaching us truth ensnared us with falsehood? No reasonable man can open his mind to such a false conclusion. The Church cannot have been deserted by Christ until Luther arose, for we have His promise that He would be with us to the end of the world. Believe me, on this dark and stormy sea of conflicting opinions a star is shining to which we can look up, which can show us the way to bring us to God. This is, and alone can be, as many holy and learned men have testified, the Roman Church, which, founded by Peter, whom Christ chose to be the rock of His Church, has through an unbroken line of Popes come down to these our own days.[63]

Yet another shocking apostasy developed during 1543 when Catholic Archbishop Hermann von Wied of Cologne called in Protestant leader Martin Bucer to Protestantize the Church in his archdiocese. But Cologne was a

---

[61] Von Pastor, *History of the Popes*, XII, 150-151; Jedin, *Council of Trent*, I, 457; Brandi, *Charles V*, pp. 452-453.

[62] Von Pastor, *History of the Popes*, XI, 492-497.

[63] *Ibid.*, XI, 496-497. That Christ could not, without violating His explicit promises to be with His Church always, have deserted it for more than a thousand years until Protestantism came, is one of the most powerful Catholic apologetic arguments based on history.

strongly Catholic city with a university full of orthodox Dominicans where several of the new Jesuits also resided. Led by Chancellor Johann Gropper, who developed a plan for a Catholic reform of the Church in the archdiocese which Archbishop von Wied ignored, many of the Catholic clergy in Cologne put up a stout resistance to their apostate archbishop. On Easter von Wied used an unauthorized vernacular liturgy and distributed Communion under both species without papal permission. In May Melanchthon visited Bonn at his invitation. In August he had a guest of a very different sort, the Emperor himself. In saying Mass for him, von Wied took great care to follow the rubrics precisely. Charles was not deceived. In a personal interview Charles ordered him to remove Bucer and all Lutheran preachers from Cologne.[64]

In an age of apostasy, one man who died that year had given lifelong witness of unshakable fidelity: Professor John Eck, aged 56, for 32 years head of the theology department of the University of Ingolstadt in Bavaria, the untiring, unyielding, uncompromising opponent of Luther for 24 years since the two men so memorably confronted each other at the disputation in Leipzig.[65] And another man, of different academic profession, died likewise at peace with the Church that year, whom the Church had never challenged or curbed in his scientific work: the Polish astronomer Nicholas Copernicus, whose new book *On the Revolution of the Heavens*, explaining the evidence that the Earth is a planet revolving about the sun, was dedicated to Pope Paul III.[66]

In the summer of 1543 Francis I brought his Turkish allies much closer to home, in August launching an assault on Nice (then an Italian city under imperial authority) by land and sea, led by "Barbarossa," the red-bearded Christian renegade whose Muslim name was Chaireddin. Before the end of the month he took the city, sacking and destroying much of it, killing most of the men he found within and selling the women and children into slavery. In September the Turks withdrew from Nice and went to the French Mediterranean port of Toulon, where Francis I displaced most of Toulon's own citizens (also his subjects) to make room for 30,000 Turks to live while Barbarossa refitted and resupplied his fleet. The 30,000 Turks stayed in Toulon until the following spring. When they departed May 22, 1544 it was to sail back home via the coasts of southern Italy which they repeatedly raided, carrying off into slavery anyone they could catch.[67]

The new war between Francis I of France and Emperor Charles V continued inconclusively into the year 1544. The six armies Francis had assembled to attack Charles and his domains two years before had made little progress, but he showed no sign of giving up. Charles had been driven to seek military help against France from Henry VIII of England, to the Pope's fury. In

---

[64] *Ibid.*, XII, 205; Brodrick, *St. Peter Canisius*, pp. 49, 51-52; Brandi, *Charles V*, p. 502. Archbishop von Wied continued toying with disobedience and heresy until he was excommunicated and deprived of his archdiocese by Pope Paul III in April 1546, during the early sessions of the Council of Trent (Brodrick, *op. cit.*, p. 80).

[65] Brodrick, *St. Peter Canisius*, p. 133. See Chapter One, above.

[66] Von Pastor, *History of the Popes*, XII, 550.

[67] Knecht, *Francis I*, pp. 365-366; Janssen, *History of the German People*, VI, 135.

April the French defeated imperial forces at the Battle of Ceresole in northwestern Italy near Turin; in June the army of the kingdom of Naples in southern Italy, of which Charles was king through his Spanish inheritance, defeated an army in the service of France at the Battle of Serravalle. The Diet of Speyer met in Germany and decreed in June that the Emperor was to be helped against the Turks, but that a council was to be held in Germany even though the Pope had not agreed to it, while the Protestants were to keep everything they had taken from the Catholics. Charles privately disliked these terms, but even the German Catholic leaders resignedly accepted them.[68]

Both the Pope and the Emperor had been frustrated year after year, above all by the failure to open the Council on which both had set their hearts. The Council could not be held while the war between Francis and the Emperor continued. The Pope seems to have believed that Charles could have had peace with Francis at any time if he really wanted it, while Charles believed that the Pope could compel Francis to make peace by speaking out in the Emperor's favor. It was a legitimate and understandable difference of opinion, but should never have been allowed to override the essential unity of purpose between the spiritual and temporal leaders of Christendom, both absolutely dedicated to its preservation in the face of the greatest threat to the Church since the conversion of Constantine. But on August 25, 1544 Pope Paul III gave way to his anger and denounced the Emperor in a solemn admonition for his alleged unwillingness to make peace with France and for not moving militarily against the Lutheran princes after the Diet of Speyer, threatening him in consequence with the wrath of God.[69]

It was one of the worst mistakes of papal history. In the near-desperate situation of Christendom in 1544, Charles was the last man the Pope should have attacked. Without his unshaken fidelity and twenty-three years of unremitting effort to do his duty as the defender of Christendom against the heretic within and the infidel without—and the ambitious Machiavellianism of Francis I to the bargain—Christendom would in all probability already have collapsed into not much more than central and southern Italy, Spain and Portugal. Not only were the Pope's charges against Charles unreasonable and unfair, but they were effectively disproved before his bristling admonition could even be delivered. For on September 14, with Charles' army at the gates of Paris and the English having taken the great fortified French port of Boulogne on the English Channel, Francis did at last offer peace, and Charles accepted it with alacrity. The Peace of Crépy was a great victory for Charles, limited only by the fact that Francis could not be trusted to keep his word if breaking it came to be in his personal interest. The treaty provided that France would give up all its territorial claims in Piedmont-Savoy and Naples in Italy, and in Flanders, Artois, and Gelderland in the Netherlands; in return, Charles would give up his cherished claim to

---

[68] Brandi, *Charles V*, pp. 512-514; Knecht, *Francis I*, pp. 366-367; von Pastor, *History of the Popes*, XII, 189-190. 207; Janssen, *History of the German People*, VI, 252-255.

[69] Von Pastor, *History of the Popes*, XII, 195-198; Jedin, *Council of Trent*, I, 497-501; Brandi, *Charles V*, pp. 513-514; Janssen, *History of the German People*, VI, 256-257.

Burgundy. Long-disputed Milan would go to Francis' second son on condition that he marry a daughter of Charles or of his brother Ferdinand. Of special significance was a secret clause by which Francis, who up to this point had ignored the Council when he did not actively oppose it, finally guaranteed his support for it, accepting Trent as its meeting place despite its being on imperial territory, and promising to help Charles against the Protestants if they refused to accept the Council. By this treaty Charles had essentially done what the Pope had condemned him for not doing, even before he received the Pope's letter of admonition. If the Pope could only have restrained his anger three weeks longer, he would no longer have had even apparent cause to express it.[70]

With great wisdom, charity, and humility Charles decided to make no written response to the Pope's admonition, now so evidently out of date, when it came to him. Verbally he declared, in measured but humble tones, "that the incentive to the evils and misfortunes which had overwhelmed Christendom had not proceeded from him, but that on the contrary he had persistently endeavored to avert them, in conformity with the duty he owed to his own imperial dignity and to the Apostolic See. If everybody, according to his rank and capacity, had acted similarly, the present calamities would not have occurred. He solicited a speedy reopening of the Council."[71] His words were incontestably true and just.

But Charles had suffered too many betrayals. Henceforth, in dark moods and moments, he would hark back to what he remembered as a stab in the back by the Pope himself. What had been only a personal incompatibility and difficulty of communication between the two men now became a profound distrust. For the five remaining years of Paul III's long pontificate, so critical in the history of the Church and of Christendom, Pope and Emperor were almost always deeply suspicious of the other—a situation made doubly tragic because at that moment in history they were the only sovereigns in Christendom (except for John III of Portugal) whom any well-informed and committed Catholic could trust.

As for the Protestants, they knew their enemy better than Pope Paul III knew his friend. In October 1543 Martin Bucer had written to Calvin in Geneva:

> The Emperor delights in superstitious nonsense which is only fit for old wives. He repeats long prayers daily on his knees. He tells his beads, lying on the ground with his eyes fixed on an image of the Virgin. He is now openly striving against Christ.[72]

On October 28 Francis I made good on his promise in the secret clause of the Peace of Crépy by instructing his ambassador in Rome to ask the Pope to convene the Council in three months in Trent or any other place that he and the

---

[70] Brandi, *Charles V*, pp. 520-522; Knecht, *Francis I*, pp. 370-371; von Pastor, *History of the Popes*, XII, 199-200; Jedin, *Council of Trent*, I, 501-502; Janssen, *History of the German People*, VI, 258-259.

[71] Janssen, *History of the German People*, VI, 259.

[72] *Ibid.*, VI, 241.

Emperor could agree upon. The Pope was gracious enough to send a legate to Emperor Charles to thank him for the Peace of Crépy while stressing the necessity to open the Council just as soon as possible, and to clear the field for it by having no more discussion of religious issues at German Diets. On November 30 the bull *Laetare Jerusalem* summoned bishops, abbots, and heads of religious orders to Trent for the Council on March 15, 1545 to discuss "the removal of religious discord, the reform of the Christian people, and the liberation of the Christians under the yoke of the Turks." In February the Pope named three legates to preside at the council: Cardinals del Monte, Cervini (a passionate reformer), and Reginald Pole of England, descended from the last Plantagenets, a scholar who was studying in Rome when Henry VIII broke from the Church and was made a Cardinal in December 1536 in the hope that he would lead opposition to him. A secret bull empowered the legates to move, dissolve, or continue the Council at their discretion, even without consulting the Pope, if they felt it necessary. As the future would show, this was not a wise delegation of authority in a matter of such transcendent importance.[73]

The prospect that the long-awaited Council would actually soon be held roused Luther, now past sixty, to a final outburst more terrible than any of his that had come before. Despite all his fulminations Luther had a conscience, and could not altogether rid himself of its reproach that he was responsible for the disasters, spiritual and physical, that had come upon Germany since he nailed his 95 theses on the church door in Wittenberg twenty-eight years before. He wrote:

> Who among us would have thought of preaching as we have done, could we have foreseen how much misery, corruption, scandal, blasphemy, ingratitude, and wickedness would have resulted from it? . . . Only see how the nobles, the burghers, and the peasants are trampling religion underfoot, how they are driving the preachers away by sheer starvation! . . . I have had no greater or severer subject of assault [by the Devil] than my preaching, when the thought arose in me: Thou art the sole author of all this movement.[74]

But the heroic virtue to admit and confess his sins, great as they were, and try to make recompense—the heroic virtue that Georges-Jacques Danton was to display at the height of the Reign of Terror in the French Revolution[75]—was not in Martin Luther. He convinced himself that the call for repentance was coming from the Devil rather than God. And, as tragically often happens with men far gone down a wrong road, the more his conscience beset him, the farther and faster he went down that road, as though fleeing from it. In March 1545 he published his last pamphlet for circulation among his followers at a new Diet at Worms. It was entitled "Against the Pontificate at Rome, Founded by the Devil." Its language was so savagely vile that a fellow Christian (and it should never be forgotten that Luther always remained a committed believer in Christ as God,

---

[73] Von Pastor, *History of the Popes*, XI, 162-163; XII, 207-211; Jedin, *Council of Trent*, I, 504-505, 509 (quote on 505).

[74] Janssen, *History of the German People*, VI, 276-277.

[75] See my *The Guillotine and the Cross* (Manassas VA, 1986), pp. 111-164.

Savior and Judge of mankind) almost hesitates to quote it. But it must be done. The full extent of the horror that had come to Germany in the first half of the sixteenth century cannot be understood without it.

> The Popes are the descendants of the regicide Emperor Phocas, their founder. They are a set of desperate, thoroughgoing arch-villains, murderers, traitors, liars, and the most utterly debased and depraved beings on earth. . . . Therefore it would be best for the Emperor and the Estates to leave these abominable, villainous scoundrels and their accursed devil's crew at Rome to go headlong to the devil; for there is no hope for amelioration; there is nothing to be done by Councils. . . . Therefore he [the Pope] should be seized, he and his cardinals and all the scoundrelly crew of His Holiness, and their tongues should be torn from their throats and nailed in a row on the gallows tree, in like manner as they affix their seals in a row to their bulls, though even this would be but slight punishment for all their blasphemy and idolatry. Afterwards let them hold a council, or whatever they please, on the gallows or in Hell with all the demons. . . . [Luther says that he wishes to curse the Pope and his supporters] so that thunder and lightning would strike them, hell-fire burn them, the plague, syphilis, epilepsy, scurvy, leprosy, carbuncles and all manner of diseases attack them. . . . Whenever I say, "Hallowed be Thy Name," I am forced to add, "Cursed, damned, dishonored be the name of the Pope."[76]

Less than a year later, in February 1546, a month after preaching against reason ("the most dangerous harlot the Devil has") and a few days after calling for the burning of the homes of Jews and their expulsion from Germany, Martin Luther died of a stroke, at three o'clock in the morning after a long session of his famous "table talk" at supper. He made no confession, and probably spoke no word after being stricken.[77]

In mid-May 1545 Emperor Charles, shaking off a painful attack of gout, arrived in Worms for the Diet. By this time only ten bishops had come to Trent in addition to the papal legates; the Council could not be taken seriously without a substantially larger attendance. Cardinal Alexander Farnese, the Pope's grandson[78] and special envoy to the Emperor, was waiting for the Emperor at Worms. Charles gave him audience almost immediately, reiterating his full support for the Council. This was followed by a visit from Charles' prime minister Granvelle. To Farnese's astonishment (for he was well aware of his grandfather's suspicions of Charles), Granvelle presented him with a plan for a massive surprise attack on the German Protestants in alliance with the Pope, followed by a letter in the Emperor's own hand confirming this as his intention. On the night of June 27, with just one companion, Farnese rode out of Worms

---

[76] Janssen, *History of the German People*, VI, 271-273. Many of these same quotations, in a somewhat different translation, appear in von Pastor, *History of the Popes*, XII, 215-216. There can be no question of their authenticity.

[77] Janssen, *History of the German People*, VI, 278 (for quote), 280-282.

[78] By his illegitimate son Pier Luigi, born before his ordination as a priest, who became Duke of Parma.

through a raging storm to bring the news to Trent and to Rome. The young cardinal—he was only 25—rode like the wind. In six days he had passed through the greater part of Germany and over the Alps to Trent, where he reported to the legates that the Emperor had confirmed his full support for the Council. Then he galloped on to Rome, where he arrived on June 8 with the great news of the Emperor's plans at long last to strike hard at the Protestant rebels. Within ten days the new papal-imperial alliance was sealed.[79]

As Charles V's military enterprise in Germany began to take shape, it soon became evident that it would take longer than he had originally expected. He had to postpone it to the following year, informing the Pope of this change by an envoy sent to Rome July 6. Meanwhile Charles promised to defend German Catholics against Protestant attacks and urged that the Council go forward, but not until the Diet of Worms had ended. This only resulted in a brief delay, since the Diet adjourned August 4. There was a potentially dangerous development in September when the second son of Francis I, the Duke of Orléans, died suddenly of a "brief and mysterious illness," thereby undoing one of the most important compromises of the Peace of Crépy by which he was to become the sovereign of Milan after marrying a daughter of Emperor Charles or of his brother Ferdinand. As the number of bishops at Trent slowly grew during the summer of 1545, there was a good deal of imprudent talk about transferring the Council to another place. Informed that one of the arguments being used was lack of proper accommodation, Charles flashed back by wondering aloud if it was "really asking too much from the prelates that for the sake of a great and sacred purpose they should be satisfied with one room instead of a whole house."[80]

But on November 6 Pope Paul III, speaking to his cardinals in consistory, declared that the Council would convene at Trent and nowhere else, and the next day ordered that prelates still in Rome should leave immediately or be imprisoned in Castel Sant' Angelo. The Council was really going to happen at last, after eleven years of waiting for the fulfillment of Pope Paul III's commitment at the beginning of his pontificate to convene it. Such was the enthusiasm now at Trent that even two of the three French bishops whom Francis I had recalled after the death of his son who was heir to Milan, were persuaded to remain at Trent in hopes that he would change his mind once the Council was actually in session. On December 13, at the Trent cathedral (which still stands, looking little different than it did that day), Cardinal del Monte, chief of the three legates, opened the Council with the Mass of the Holy Spirit. The Council Fathers met in a square enclosure, facing an altar under an immense Flemish tapestry representing the Resurrection. The attendance was barely sufficient to begin: four archbishops, 21 bishops, five heads of religious orders, a representative of Charles' brother Ferdinand (Charles' own representative, the Spaniard Diego Hurtado de Mendoza, was detained in Venice by illness), and 42

---

[79] Von Pastor, *History of the Popes*, XII, 219, 222-226; Brandi, *Charles V*, pp. 527-528.

[80] Von Pastor, *History of the Popes*, XII, 227-228, 234, 236; Jedin, *Council of Trent* I, 529-532, 536 (for quote); Brandi, *Charles V*, p. 529; Knecht, *Francis I*, p. 371.

theologians.[81] Bishop Cornelio Musso of Bitonto preached the inaugural homily, reviewing the long wait for the Council, and declaring as its goals:

> . . . to defend the faith and the sacraments, to restore charity among Christians, to eliminate from the body of the Church the poison of covetousness and ambition, and to ward off the "scourge of God," the Turks.
> . . . Gathered as it is at the gate of the Empire, may it effect the reunion of Germany with the Roman Church. To the realization of so high a purpose all must contribute—Latins and Greeks, Spaniards and Frenchmen, Germans and Italians, every one must give of his very best.[82]

It was a noble beginning. But this Council, so indispensable for the true reform of the Church and for the salvation of Christendom, had been delayed more than twenty years beyond the time it should have been called, when the Emperor's inability to enforce the decree of the Diet of Worms in 1521 against Luther showed that he alone could not suppress Luther's heresy; and it was to be eighteen years more before its work was finally done. The long, long delay raised the odds that in the end the division of the Church and of Christendom that Luther had wrought, would endure for centuries—as it has. There was still, and long remained, a chance to win back Germany and Great Britain; that was the purpose, respectively, of the Thirty Years War and the Spanish Armada. But there was no chance now for Scandinavia; by 1550 the last Scandinavian Catholic voices were silenced. Those last voices are faint as a whisper now, unheard and unknown outside their native lands; but there, even a now apostate people preserves their memory. Let Catholics honor two men who fought to the end for the Faith, in dark forests and upon a rock-bound coast, beyond all outside aid, true unto death: Nils Dacke, woodsman of Smaland in Sweden, and Jon Aresson, Bishop of Holar in Iceland.

In Sweden King Gustavus Vasa had by 1542 established his absolute rule, replaced every Catholic bishop with men of his own choosing, and eliminated all practice of the ancient faith. In May of that year, in the heavily forested province of Smaland, Nils Dacke rose in revolt, believing that "it was an intolerable presumption that the king should interpose his meddling not only between a man and his market, but between a man and his God." In the thick woods Gustav Vasa's German troops with their long pikes were almost useless; the pike is a weapon that can only be used in open country, while Dacke and his men were armed with crossbows they had made themselves, whose arrows shot at 100 yards or less could pierce anything a man could wear but plate armor, now rarely used. In two months 3,000 farmers had joined Dacke, despite its being haying time, the busiest season of the year for farmers in the far north. By August he was marching on the city of Linköping, where heroic Bishop Brask had held out so long for the Church two decades before. Brask was dead now, but fugitive

---

[81] Von Pastor, *History of the Popes*, XII, 237, 241-243; Jedin, *Council of Trent*, I, 538, 541, 574-579.

[82] Jedin, *Council of Trent*, I, 577.

Swedish Bishop Magnus Haraldsson of Skara, living in Mecklenburg in Germany, sent Dacke a message of encouragement—all he could do, for he had no access to material help and Mecklenburg was mostly Lutheran. Early in September Dacke won a resounding victory near the village of Kisa, ambushing and virtually annihilating a large force of Germans. That fall the proud king was forced to make a truce with Dacke; but on the day Gustav Vasa signed it he wrote a letter declaring he did not intend to keep it.[83]

That winter Nils Dacke ruled Smaland from Kronborg Castle. He restored the Catholic Church and the Latin Mass, bringing back 16 refugee priests to say it. Emperor Charles V wrote him a letter of congratulation, urging him to fight on. But by March troops from Denmark, ruled by the totally Lutheran Christian III and available because Denmark was at peace, came to Gustav Vasa's aid. They defeated Dacke on the ice of frozen Lake Hjorten, but only after he had been shot through both thighs and carried from the field. His men broke up into small groups and continued the fight in guerrilla fashion. In two months Dacke had recovered from his wounds and took command once again in the field. But he had lost his military advantage, and the greatly reinforced army of the Lutheran king pressed him hard. Early in August he was betrayed in the forest near the Danish border. Disdaining surrender, he went down fighting, to the great regret of Vasa, who wanted him alive to torture. The Catholic faith hardly exists in Sweden today, but his countrymen have not forgotten Nils Dacke. After a furious controversy with admirers of Vasa as the founder of Sweden's ruling dynasty and of national unity, in 1956 a monument was raised near Lake Hjorten to Dacke, battle-axe in one hand and crossbow in the other. But it does not bear what he surely would have wanted most: a cross.[84]

In remote Iceland there were two bishops. Both resisted the Lutheran takeover. The older, in his eightieth year, was captured and taken away to Denmark. The younger, Jon Aresson of Holar, fought two years for the faith with whatever loyal Catholics would follow him. Somehow word of Aresson's defiance came to Pope Paul III, who sent him a magnificent cope now displayed in the cathedral at Reykjavik—the only Catholic church in Iceland. Eventually betrayed like Dacke in 1550, Aresson was beheaded at a desolate spot on the barren south coast of Iceland. For three hundred years afterwards there were no Catholics in Iceland at all. But tourists today are brought by agnostic Icelanders to see the site of his martyrdom, also commemorated by a monument.[85]

---

[83] Michael Roberts, *The Early Vasas; a History of Sweden 1523-1611* (Cambridge, England, 1968), pp. 132-133, 135 (quote on 133); Wilhelm Moberg, *A History of the Swedish People*, Volume II (New York, 1973), pp. 222-223, 235-236, 243, 248-249, 251, 254, 256. Moberg, though he has no use for any religion, greatly admires Nils Dacke, who grew up not far from Moberg's boyhood home in Smaland.

[84] Moberg, *History of the Swedish People*, II, 224, 254, 256, 259-263; Roberts, *Early Vasas*, pp. 135-136.

[85] Von Pastor, *History of the Popes*, XII, 481-482. I was on one of the tours which visited Aresson's monument in 1971.

The fate of Nils Dacke and Jon Aresson awaited the last loyal Catholics in many nations of Europe if the Council of Trent could not rescue, reform, and reinvigorate the Church before it was too late.

At Trent nearly a full month passed before the Council held its second session. The further delay was probably partly due to the Christmas holidays and partly to the hope that more bishops would arrive to augment the small number present at the opening session. But only five more bishops had come by January 7, 1546 when the second session took place, and little happened at it but further exhortations. Finally discussion groups were formed around each of the three papal legates on January 20 and it was decided on the 22nd to take up doctrine and Church reform simultaneously rather than giving either one preference over the other. Pope Paul III, though he preferred acting on doctrine first, deferred to their decision—the first of many examples of his refusal to direct the Council and his determination to preserve its independence of debate and action.[86]

On February 3 the Council formally declared "the Nicene-Constantinopolitan Creed to be the common foundation of all Christian belief and the presupposition on which all future definitions of faith must depend,"[87] thereby making clear that the Church would never surrender to the Protestant demand that it reject or ignore its tradition in the deposit of faith and justify itself by Scripture only. At the fourth general session on April 8, the Council declared Scripture and tradition received from the apostles to be equally authoritative sources of Church doctrine, rejecting a few who wanted the authority of tradition to be described as "similar" to Scripture rather than equal to it.[88] On February 15 the Council declared the existing canon of Scripture—the books rightfully included in Scripture as authoritative and specially inspired by the Holy Spirit—to be confirmed without further discussion of the issue. The vote was 24-16; the minority believed that an effort should be made to counter Protestant arguments against those books which they did not include in their Bible.[89] In April the Council declared the Latin Vulgate a fully authentic translation of the Bible without doctrinal error, to be used at all public ceremonies, after also calling for publication of the best original Hebrew and Greek Biblical texts.[90]

Moving to one of the principal issues of Church reform, on April 10 the three cardinal legates wrote to Pope Paul III that they believed—and expected the

---

[86] Jedin, *Council of Trent*, II, 24-26, 29-36, 53-54; von Pastor, *History of the Popes*, XII, 248-249, 251-254.

[87] Von Pastor, *History of the Popes*, XII, 254.

[88] Jedin, *Council of Trent*, II, 82-83, 90-92.

[89] *Ibid.*, II, 55-56. Though some Protestant commentators attempted negative critiques of the books in the Catholic Bible which they excluded, the standard actually used for exclusion was strictly linguistic: all books in the Catholic Old Testament for which Hebrew texts then existed were accepted; all those which had only Greek texts were excluded. No change was made in the Protestant Bible even when Hebrew texts of some of the excluded books were later discovered.

[90] *Ibid.*, II, 70-72, 90-92; von Pastor, *History of the Popes*, XII, 258-261.

Council eventually to require—that no one should be consecrated bishop without proper qualifications of age, worthiness and learning, and willingness to reside in his diocese, so that no man could hold more than one diocese. The multiplication of underage and non-resident bishops and episcopal pluralities had been one of the worst scandals of the Renaissance church. In June the Council discussed at length a residence requirement for bishops, and though support for it was strong, its final approval was delayed for months by behind-the-scenes opposition (presumably by those who had something to lose by it) and procedural arguments over whether the Pope rather than the Council should take this action. Even on January 13, 1547 it failed by three votes to gain a majority, but was finally approved on March 3 of that year.[91]

The Council expended its greatest efforts during 1546 on formulating decrees on the doctrines of original sin and justification, pivotal issues in the Lutheran revolt. Detailed discussion of original sin began June 4 with Council members generally agreeing that the tendency to sin which survives baptism, termed "concupiscence" by Catholic moral theologians, is not in itself sinful, though yielding to it is. Therefore man is not irremediably evil as the Lutherans taught. On June 17, at the fifth general session of the Council, a decree was adopted to this effect.[92]

Justification was a much thornier issue. Discussion of it began June 21 and continued throughout the next week with presentations by no less than 34 of the theologians at the Council, whose expert opinion was sought though they had no vote. All but four of these theologians agreed that persons who had attained the use of reason could and must cooperate with God's grace to obtain justification before Him. On July 8 Dominican Bishop Pietro Bertano of Fano in Italy made an outstanding presentation to the effect that faith comes from God but must be accepted by men and put into practice with charity, whose essential role had been explained by St. Paul in the well-known passage in his second letter to the Corinthians on the necessity of love. On July 17 there was a dramatic drop in the level of discourse when Bishop Sanfelice of La Cava, who had taken a position close to Luther's on justification by faith alone and was consequently called "either a knave or a fool" by Bishop Zanettini of Crete, grabbed the Greek bishop by the beard and pulled out some of its hairs. (The Council confined Bishop Sanfelice to his room until he was released by the intercession of Bishop Zanettini.) A draft decree on justification late in July was widely criticized and not adopted. Cardinal Cervini asked Seripando, general of the Augustinians, to prepare another draft, which he presented to the papal legates and a four-bishop committee on August 11. On August 28 there was a long debate on whether to condemn the Lutheran view that a man could be certain of his salvation, which lost on a tie vote of 21-21. Asked if the justified can merit salvation by good works done in a state of sanctifying grace, 30 of the Council's 36 theologians answered in the affirmative on October 15, the most impressive presentation

---

[91] Jedin, *Council of Trent*, II, 153-154, 340-345, 366; von Pastor, *History of the Popes*, XII, 262-263, 340, 344-346.

[92] Jedin, *Council of Trent*, II, 145, 150-151, 155-157, 160-163.

being made by the Jesuit James Laynez. On October 26 the Council rejected by a decisive vote of 32-5 the theory of imputed rather than merited justification—sometimes called "double justification" or "duplicate justice," the first justification being provided by sanctifying grace through baptism and the second deriving from the faith of the baptized, which had been the formula of the illusory compromise with the Lutherans at the Diet of Regensburg crafted by the late Cardinal Contarini[93] and was supported at Trent by Seripando and Cardinal Pole. On January 9, 1547 the Council decided that "no one can be certain of his being in a state of grace with a certitude of faith that cannot be subject to error." The decree on justification finally adopted at the sixth general session of the Council on January 13 declared that grace sanctifies all who cooperate with it and that faith alone is not sufficient for justification, but must be accompanied by hope and love and show itself through works. Approval was almost unanimous, with only minor reservations by a few bishops.[94]

Meanwhile Charles V's plan to make all-out war on the Protestants in Germany had been developing. At the Diet of Regensburg in June 1546 petitions were received from the Bishop of Hildesheim, whose diocese had been forcibly taken over by the Protestants, its buildings ravaged and its communities dispersed; from the Bishop of Regensburg itself against the forcible change of religion in that city; and from the burghers of Mühlhausen in Thuringia, standing firm in the Catholic faith after their ghastly experience twenty years before with the mad revolutionary Thomas Münzer but rendered unable to maintain Catholic worship by coercion from Saxony and Hesse. All these petitions and many other grievances provided clear justification for the war—it was not a matter of Catholics marching against peaceful Protestants to suppress their form of worship by force, but of protecting their own freedom to worship and even their lives.[95] Charles wrote to his sister Mary June 9:

> Unless some means are found, without further delay, to put down these Protestants, all the Catholics everywhere will be exterminated. I have very great sympathy with the complaints that they are raising in all directions. After long consultation with my brother and with the Duke of Bavaria, our cousin, we have decided that no other means will serve than to use force against the seceders and to compel them to submit to reasonable terms.[96]

As this letter indicates, Charles had already made a formal alliance with the Duke of Bavaria, now the only strong Catholic prince remaining in the whole German-speaking world outside Charles himself and his brother Ferdinand. On June 16 Charles declared that to restore order and justice in Germany he must

---

[93] Unfortunately for the Church, this high-minded and beloved reformer had died in 1542 at the age of 59.

[94] Jedin, *Council of Trent*, II, 172-174, 176-177, 184-185, 190-195, 234-235, 240, 242-244, 253-254, 256-257, 297 (for quote), 304-311; von Pastor, *History of the Popes*, XII, 340-346; Brodrick, *St. Peter Canisius*, pp. 94-95.

[95] Janssen, *History of the German People*, VI, 302-305.

[96] *Ibid.*, VI, 306.

take up arms against the rebellious Protestants who used God and Christianity as their excuse for conquest and robbery, and were now directly challenging his imperial authority. On the 19th he also signed a fateful secret treaty with one of the chief Protestant princes, ambitious Duke Maurice of Saxony, the 25-year-old nephew of Catholic Duke George but a Lutheran since childhood, by whose terms Maurice would remain neutral in Charles' upcoming war with the Protestant Schmalkald League (of which he was a leading member) and would pledge to allow Catholics under his rule to practice their faith freely.[97] It is probable, though it cannot be proven, that Charles obtained this agreement from Maurice by promising, or at least hinting at the likelihood of granting him rule over the whole of Saxony, electoral as well as ducal, through the displacement of Elector John Frederick of Saxony, who along with Landgrave Philip of Hesse led the Schmalkald League. This was to be the reward Maurice eventually received for his cooperation with the Emperor. On June 25 General Schärtlin von Burtenbach arrived at Augsburg with 4,000 troops to fight the Emperor, and was soon declared commander-in-chief of the Protestant armies in south Germany. The next day in Rome Pope Paul III signed the final draft of his treaty of military alliance with Charles V. On July 9 General Schärtlin seized the Catholic city of Füssen, where he abolished Catholic worship and destroyed all statues in the churches. The first full-scale religious war between Catholics and Protestants had begun.[98]

The next day the Lutheran army took Ehrenberg Pass in the Alps which brought it within striking distance of Trent, and General Schärtlin threatened to march on the city, which had no significant army to defend it, and disperse the Council. A German Protestant wrote that their army would surely overwhelm the forces of Emperor Charles, "who was become the hangman and beadle of Antichrist," and after that "we shall set up a new order of things in which there will be no place for all the swarm of priests and their followers." There was even a rumor that Landgrave Philip of Hesse had said he would crucify Charles if he captured him. But in fact the Lutheran army was not nearly so strong as enthusiasts for its cause wanted to believe, and on July 14 the council of war of the Schmalkald League withdrew it from Ehrenberg Pass to defend its city of Augsburg against an attack by Bavaria. The Emperor's alliance with Bavaria had been kept secret, so despite this hostile move the Lutherans still hoped to get Bavaria on their side, and Charles was able to assemble his army in Bavaria without the knowledge of the Schmalkald League. The core of his army was Spanish, the only troops whose loyalty he felt he could completely trust, led by the Duke of Alva, who was to become the best general in Europe; by mid-August the papal army, led by Ottavio Farnese, had arrived in Germany to reinforce Charles with 10,000 infantry and 700 cavalry. Cardinal del Monte was now able

[97] *Ibid.*, VI, 310-314; Brandi, *Charles V*, p. 547.
[98] Janssen, *History of the German People*, VI, 315-316; von Pastor, *History of the Popes*, XII, 291; Brandi, *Charles V*, p. 545.

to tell the Council Fathers at Trent that they were no longer in danger and should continue their deliberations.[99]

On August 20 Charles published a decree drafted the previous month placing the two principal Lutheran leaders, Elector John Frederick of Saxony and Landgrave Philip of Hesse, under the ban of the Empire for their unprovoked attack on and conquest of Brunswick, for robbing Catholics of their property, for making it impossible for the Imperial Court to function, and for consistently nullifying all Charles' attempts to bring religious peace to Germany. A few days later he joined his army in camp near Ingolstadt in Bavaria, where he told Cardinal Farnese that he regarded the campaign now underway as "the greatest undertaking of his whole life." Its goals, he said, were "the restoration of the unity of the Empire and the suppression of the power of the Protestants" and "the presence of the Council in Trent was exactly the one thing essential to the assured success of his operations in the field." After two limited engagements with Charles' army near Ingolstadt August 31 and September 2, the Lutheran forces withdrew from the area. On September 15 fifteen thousand troops from the Low Countries joined Charles there, giving him overwhelming superiority. Recognizing this, the Schmalkald League sought help from France, and quickly obtained a promise from Francis I of a large financial subsidy. But no money actually came from France; England would not help unless and until France did; and at the end of September Charles still further increased his strength by transferring the electorate of Saxony from John Frederick to Duke Maurice, who thereby entered the war against his fellow Lutherans.[100]

Morale was low in the Lutheran camp that fall, and attempts to arouse religious enthusiasm among the soldiers were to no avail. In the memorable words of Theobald Thamer, field preacher to Landgrave Philip of Hesse:

> They gorged and they soused, they gambled and caroused, they quarrelled and swore and blasphemed to such an extent that I think the Devil in Hell could not have invented such execrable curses against God and His dear Son Christ. They robbed and plundered the poor people of the land, friends as well as foes. In short, there was nothing from morning to night but sins and abominations which were nothing short of diabolical. I was grievously distressed within me, and in my sermons I exhorted them most earnestly, reminding them that we called ourselves evangelical, and that we ought to be like good seed from which other Christians might grow up and attain to the right faith; but if the seed was of such a degenerate kind what would the fruit that sprang from it be like? But one swore at me; another jeered at me, calling me a fool and a chatterbox; a third shot at me with my own arrows, saying: "You yourself teach us that men can do nothing good, nothing which

---

[99] Janssen, *History of the German People*, VI, 316, 322 (for quote), 332-337; Brandi, *Charles V*, pp. 551, 554; von Pastor, *History of the Popes*, XII, 294, 296, 304, 311.

[100] Janssen, *History of the German People*, VI, 324-327, 337, 339-341, 345-346; Brandi, *Charles V*, pp. 551-554, 556; Knecht, *Francis I*, p. 407; J. J. Scarisbrick, *Henry VIII* (Berkeley Ca, 1970), p. 467; von Pastor, *History of the Popes*, XII, 296-298, 313 (for second quote); Jedin, *Council of Trent* II, 233 (for first and third quotes).

can justify them in the sight of God; and that it is only by the merits of
Christ, which are reckoned to our account through faith, that we can be saved
and become children of God."[101]

Some of the same evils were manifested in the Catholic camp; one day
Emperor Charles himself struck some of his own soldiers with a club and pricked
others with his sword, because of their language and behavior. But the Catholic
army at least held firmly together, while by the end of the year 1546 the Lutheran
army was withdrawn from the whole of southern Germany and beginning to
disintegrate. The city of Ulm, a Protestant stronghold where the churches had
been so totally stripped as to be "bare as a barber's basin," submitted to Emperor
Charles without a fight on December 23, as did the Duke of Württemberg a few
days later. On January 7, 1547 Frankfurt surrendered to Charles; at the end of the
month Augsburg surrendered and General Schärtlin von Burtenbach was forced
to flee the city. The war seemed to be won, though the Lutheran army had not
actually been beaten in the field, and if reunited could still be dangerous. On
January 22 Pope Paul III refused to renew his alliance with Emperor Charles and
ordered the withdrawal of all papal troops from Germany. In his letter informing
Charles of this decision the Pope declared that the war had already been won and
thanked and congratulated Charles for his victory, but it was known that the Pope
was angry at not being consulted on Charles' terms of surrender for Protestant
cities and princes, which at this point required no change of religion. Charles
regarded the Pope's withdrawal as another betrayal. When informed of it by the
papal nuncio, Charles lost his temper completely. His voice rising to a shout, he
said he was glad to be rid of the Pope's army because his name "was so hated in
Germany and many other Christian countries on account of his evil deeds" and
raged on that he was "conscious of having performed his own duty as a Christian
prince better than the Pope had done his, and he hoped that the day would yet
come when he should be able to tell the pontiff so to his face." Then he turned
on his heel and left the audience chamber, saying it was time to for him to go to
Mass. It was the lowest point in Emperor Charles V's public life as a Catholic.[102]

Victory over the German Protestants was far from assured when the
temporal and spiritual leaders of Christendom quarrelled openly in such fashion,
nor did it bode well for the future of the Council at Trent. When at the end of
February 1547 the Pope cut by more than half his promised financial subsidy to
Charles for his war against the Protestants, the imperial ambassadors at Rome
actually.threatened his person. The Pope responded that he was ready and eager
to die a martyr (to *Charles V*, who had defended the Faith unwaveringly for 28
years?) On March 3 the Council held its seventh solemn session, with its largest
attendance to date—four cardinals, nine archbishops, 52 bishops, five generals of
orders and two abbots). It approved and ordered published a decree on the

---

[101] Janssen, *History of the German People*, VI, 343.

[102] *Ibid.*, VI, 344-346, 350, 354; Von Pastor, *History of the Popes*, XII, 221 (first
quote), 298, 327-332 (second and third quotes on 331); Brandi, *Charles V*, pp. 556, 560,
562, 566.

sacraments, which emphasized that their effectiveness was not dependent on the state of the soul of the priest or bishop dispensing them, and the reform decree requiring bishops to reside in their dioceses and not to have more than one of them. But the papal army returning to Italy—much of it through Trent—had brought with it the dreaded typhus, called "spotted fever," which several bishops had contracted, though only one died of it. On March 9 Cardinal del Monte, the president, told the council that well-regarded physicians had warned him that the typhus could quickly become epidemic and bring plague in its wake. Most of the Council Fathers wanted to leave Trent immediately, and several did so that very day without waiting for permission. On March 11 the Council voted 44-14 to move to Bologna in papal territory. After the vote Cardinal del Monte showed the Council Fathers for the first time Pope Paul III's bull of February 22, 1545 empowering the legates to move the Council if a majority favored it. On this authority, del Monte confirmed the decision just made, forbade any further argument about it, and ordered all present to appear April 21 for the first session at Bologna.[103]

Once again the Emperor felt betrayed by the Pope, despite the good medical reasons for the transfer of the Council. On March 17 he instructed his ambassador to Rome to convey to the Pope his great displeasure at the move of the Council and to demand its immediate return to Trent. On April 13 he took personal command of his army (now again largely Spanish under the Duke of Alva) in the invasion of Saxony against John Frederick, against the advice of his doctors because he was suffering severely from gout.[104] With his pain further inflaming his anger, Charles lashed out again to the papal nuncio April 14 against the Pope, going so far as to call him "an obstinate old man who is working for the destruction of the Church" and declared that he would lead the Council if the Pope did not.[105] These terrible words brought Charles to the very edge of schism—but not over it, for at Constance in 1415 Emperor Sigismund had convened a council which was only afterwards ratified by the Pope.[106] And in the end this Council would return to Trent, and triumph after both Pope Paul III and Emperor Charles V, now so tragically at odds, were dead.

By April 21, the designated day of reconvening the Council at Bologna, only 17 bishops had arrived there, approximately one quarter of the attendance at the last solemn session at Trent March 3. Fourteen of the Council Fathers had

---

[103] Jedin, *Council of Trent* II, 366-367, 391-394, 407, 416-419, 421-423, 426-434, 437-444; von Pastor, *History of the Popes*, XII, 333, 349-350, 352-354. Jedin, writing in the 1950's, consulted several distinguished physicians who attested to the medical correctness of the doctors' warning to Cardinal del Monte. Typhus is highly contagious and in those days was often fatal. The usual plethora of conspiracy theories then and now about the transfer of the Council of Trent cannot stand against this solid consensus of medical opinion.

[104] Von Pastor, *History of the Popes*, XII, 356-358; Merriman, *Rise of the Spanish Empire*, III, 358.

[105] Von Pastor, *History of the Popes*, XII, 358-359.

[106] See Volume Three, Chapter 12 of this history.

remained defiantly at Trent, all but one of them Spanish or from Spanish-ruled southern Italy, Sicily and Sardinia, following the lead of their Emperor rather than their Pope. To avoid a schism, Pope Paul III wisely prorogued the Council of Trent indefinitely. It did not meet again for more than four years.[107]

On April 24 Charles' army finally met the army of John Frederick of Saxony in full battle at Mühlberg, and won a crushing victory. The Lutherans lost 2,000 men, all their banners, 21 guns, and 600 wagons; Charles' army lost only 50 men. John Frederick was captured. Recalling Julius Caesar's famous *veni, vidi, vici* message to Rome from eastern Asia Minor after winning an overwhelming victory, Charles proclaimed: "I came, I saw, and God conquered." The next month Charles was in Wittenberg, where John Frederick renounced his office of Elector and pledged to abide by future rulings of the Emperor and Diet. In Wittenberg's cemetery lay all that was mortal of Martin Luther. Some zealot in his company urged Charles to have his bones dug up and thrown to the dogs, as Luther's followers had done with saints' bodies taken from shrines in the towns they had seized. Charles nobly replied: "I war [only] with the living."[108] Martin Luther was in God's hands now; the Judgment he had so long feared had come.

At the end of May Landgrave Philip of Hesse attempted to open negotiations with the Emperor, but Charles demanded his unconditional surrender, telling him bluntly that he had no reason to trust his word. Philip gave himself up. Charles demanded a personal apology from him on bended knee; astonishingly, Philip burst out laughing during the ceremony. Coldly furious, Charles told him "wait, wait, and I will teach you how to laugh," refused to shake his hand, and held him hostage for the maintenance of the peace.[109]

On September 1 an imperial Diet convened at Augsburg in the presence of the Emperor, who was treated with the highest honor. There were still three Protestant Electors (Joachim of Brandenburg, Frederick of the Palatinate, and now Duke Maurice of Saxony) but they were all allied with Charles. However, they remained unquestionably Lutheran, and urged a Council at which all bishops would have to abjure loyalty to the Pope, laymen (including Protestants) would be admitted with votes, and the decrees already made at Trent would be opened for reconsideration. Charles could not dispense with the political and military support of the three Electors, so he temporized, persuading them to leave the issue of the Council entirely to him. The next month in a proclamation he called

---

[107] Von Pastor, *History of the Popes*, XII, 360-361; Jedin, *Council of Trent*, II, 436. Pope Paul's decision to prorogue the Council rather than fight for its continuance at this time, so clearly for the good of the Church rather than serving his own pride, is the best possible proof of how incorrect and unfair were Charles' charges against him in February and April 1547.

[108] Brandi, *Charles V*, pp. 567-570; Janssen, *History of the German People*, VI, 361-364 (first quote on 362); William T. Walsh, *Philip II* (New York, 1937), pp. 77-79 (second quote on 79).

[109] Janssen, *History of the German People*, VI, 368-370, 372-374; Brandi, *Charles V*, pp. 572-573.

for the return of the Council to Trent, without mentioning the Pope, but saying it should proceed under Scriptural and patristic authority. Pressed by the papal legate on his failure to mention the Pope or the restoration of confiscated Catholic property, Charles explained that in his view papal supremacy in the Church was clearly recognized both by Scripture (Matthew 16:13-19) and the Fathers, and that he would restore the lost Church property whenever he possibly could—it was not feasible now. In this he was undoubtedly correct; Catholicism in Germany had been so weakened that without Protestant allies Charles could not maintain his authority, even after his great victory at Mühlberg.[110]

On March 12, 1549, after much effort, a draft was completed at Augsburg of a "declaration of His Roman Imperial Majesty [Charles V] on the observance of religion within the Holy Roman Empire until the decision of the General Council," which came to be known as the 'Augsburg Interim.'" The principal author was Julius Pflug, Bishop of Naumburg, who had repeatedly worked (with little success) to find common ground and areas of compromise with the Protestants. The Interim maintained Catholic doctrine on the sacraments (but with considerable vagueness regarding the nature of the Mass), the veneration of Mary and the saints, monastic vows, fasts, and the Pope and bishops, but it did not mention purgatory and its definition of justification was vague. It did, however, firmly require that at least two Masses be said daily in every church, on altars, with vestments and sacred vessels, crosses, pictures, and images, and the celebration of all Catholic feasts. Priests were allowed to marry and to distribute Communion under both species, pending decision by the Council on these matters. There was no reference to the restoration of confiscated Church property. Electors Joachim of Brandenburg and Frederick of the Palatinate accepted the Interim; Duke-Elector Maurice of Saxony did not. Duke Ulrich of Württemberg coupled his acceptance with the not very conciliatory public statement that political and military circumstances compelled him "reluctantly to let the Devil have his way in this matter." Augsburg, Nuremberg and Ulm accepted the Interim; Strasbourg did not. Late in April Charles belatedly showed the draft to Cardinal Sfondrato, stating coldly that he was not asking the Pope's opinion on it, but simply informing him of what he was doing. Sfondrato reminded Charles of what he must have known, that no layman and no temporal authority could authorize marriage of the clergy and Communion under both species without permission of the Church. Nevertheless, Charles proclaimed the Augsburg Interim as law on May 15, without Church approval.[111]

There was much indignation in Rome when news of the Interim arrived, but Pope Paul III wisely bided his time rather than issuing an immediate condemnation. On June 23 all German bishops accepted the Interim, following an assurance by Charles that he still recognized their authority and hoped eventually to be able to restore their confiscated property. Despite official

---

[110] Von Pastor, *History of the Popes*, XII, 389-392; Janssen, *History of the German People*, VI, 383-386; Brandi, *Charles V*, pp. 576-577.
[111] Von Pastor, *History of the Popes*, XII, 413-423; Janssen, *History of the German People*, VI, 403 (for the quote).

acceptance of the Interim by most of the Protestant leaders, there was vehement popular opposition to the restoration of Catholic worship in the strongly Lutheran areas. The provisions of the Interim were never effectively enforced in Saxony. When the Mass was restored in the Church of St. Elizabeth at Marburg "acts of gross indecency were committed"; a bishop coming into the cathedral at Strasbourg to say Mass was stoned and driven away by a mob.[112] Chastened by this evidence of how very difficult it would now be for even the best disposed Catholic sovereign to eliminate Lutheranism in Germany, the Pope and his spokesmen in Germany became less critical of the Emperor. By October the glow of Mühlberg, won two and a half years before, was gone; Charles expressed to his brother Ferdinand his fear "lest all his efforts for the pacification of Germany might be in vain." In November a new papal legate to Germany, Bishop Pighini, travelling through the country to reach Charles who was now residing in Brussels, reported to the Pope that he "found an outward show of religion, occasioned by the Emperor's victory and his ordinances, but the temper of the people was more than ever in sympathy with the movement of innovation. Mass was said almost everywhere, but in empty churches."[113]

The long delay of the Council was bearing its bitter fruit. At last Pope Paul III began to realize the folly of resisting, rejecting, and condemning the dedicated Catholic Emperor. On April 26, 1549 he granted an indult to Catholics in Germany to obey the Interim, including specific permission for marriage of clergy and Communion under both species (both disciplinary rather than doctrinal issues), until the Council reconvened and decided these matters. In June he sought compromise of their long-festering dispute over the rule of the Italian city of Piacenza near the border of the papal state.[114]

The venerable pontiff had now reached the age of 81, as rare in that age as a centenarian today. In October he declared in writing that all that Michelangelo had done on the rebuilding of St. Peter's basilica in Rome was approved, that he was to remain in charge of its construction for the rest of his life, and that after his death his model was to be strictly adhered to in completing the great edifice. A few days later he issued a bull confirming and renewing all the privileges he had granted to the Jesuit order, including exemption from jurisdiction of the bishops in whose dioceses they worked, and a provision (greatly desired by St. Ignatius, who wanted his order free of the temptations and corruptions of high Church office) that no Jesuit might accept appointment as bishop or any other Church dignity without specific permission by the general of the order. On November 9 Paul III made his last confession, received viaticum, and publicly acknowledged and begged pardon for his nepotism. The next day he died.[115]

His pontificate had been a strange mixture of hope and rally on the one hand, and misunderstanding and disaster on the other. After great and often

---

[112] Von Pastor, *History of the Popes*, XII, 426-431, 433-434; Janssen, *History of the German People*, VI, 414-420 (quote on 417).

[113] Von Pastor, *History of the Popes*, XII, 437.

[114] *Ibid.*, XII, 440-441, 445-446.

[115] *Ibid.*, XII, 38, 452-453, 644.

unnecessary delays he had convened the desperately needed Council, only to see it slip away with its work less than half done. He had stood fast for the Church in the face of schism in England and a revolt full of bitter hatred in Germany and Scandinavia, but never found a way to cooperate consistently with the great Emperor, grandson of Isabel the Catholic, who with him kept the Faith. He had approved and granted essential privileges to the Jesuit order, which was to do so much to rescue and extend the Church, but left them to begin on the smallest scale, because of their lack of resources, the revival of Catholic schools and universities required to produce clergy to stem the Protestant tide. He lacked imagination and appreciation for the feelings of others, especially the Emperor. Yet like St. Peter (who also had many failings), he was a rock. During the fifteen years of disintegration during which he governed the Church, he often seemed to be sustaining it only by his own indomitable will, which was the mind of Christ. There was no man in Christendom who could not learn a lesson in courage and constancy from Alexander Farnese, Pope Paul III, once known as the "petticoat cardinal."

He had outlived not only the Church's supreme enemy, Luther, but also the king who had taken his country out of the Church, Henry VIII of England, and the Church's frequent betrayer, Francis I of France. These two monarchs died within two months of each other in the winter of 1547. Henry, so grossly obese that he could barely walk and was usually carried about in a chair by several strong men and hauled up stairs by machinery, signed the death warrant of the Duke of Norfolk on the last day of his life. By the time he faced the fact that he was dying and called for Archbishop Cranmer, he could no longer speak. According to a contemporary estimate, he had executed 72,000 persons during his reign, some three per cent of the population of England. Francis died of the complications of venereal disease. In his last days he declared publicly that he had committed many sins, made what we may hope was a good confession, and received viaticum; but he did not specify anything that he was sorry for, except possibly in private to his confessor. He was succeeded by his son Henry II, the younger of the two little princes whom his violation of his sworn word to Charles V condemned to years of harsh imprisonment, creating in him a fierce and bitter hatred of the Emperor resembling the feeling of the Lutherans toward him.[116]

During the last decade of his reign Henry had tried to maintain the doctrines and practices of Christianity in England very much as they had been before his schism, except for the total elimination of the authority of the Pope and the suppression of the monasteries. Many—probably a majority—of Englishmen were still Catholics at heart, though also loyal to their king. Only a few saw clearly, with the martyrs Fisher and More, how essential the Pope was to the

---

[116] Scarisbrick, *Henry VIII*, pp. 486, 495-496; Jasper Ridley, *Thomas Cranmer* (Oxford, 1962), p. 217 (for the number of Henry's victims); Knecht, *Francis I*, pp. 418-419; Frederic J. Baumgartner, *Henry II, King of France* (Durham NC, 1988), pp. 18-25. Henry VIII died January 28, 1547, and Francis on March 31 of that year. The Duke of Norfolk was reprieved to avoid beginning the new reign of Henry's young son Edward VI in England with an execution.

Church. The suppression of the monasteries had shaken them, but they came to terms with it. Some—notably Bishop Stephen Gardiner, who had been one of Henry VIII's ambassadors to Pope Clement VII seeking the annulment of his marriage to Catherine—were enthusiastic for the excision of the Pope and endorsed the suppression of the monasteries, but were strongly resistant to other changes in liturgy and doctrine, especially regarding the Eucharist.[117]   But a determined and growing minority were committed to making the Church of England truly Protestant, and they had a powerful secret ally in Archbishop Cranmer, whom Henry always favored and protected throughout his reign. Thomas Cromwell was also generally regarded as their ally, but Cromwell was an essentially amoral and irreligious man who believed in nothing but power. Eventually his unrelenting pursuit of power probably made Henry himself uneasy. When Cromwell, to cement an alliance with the German Protestant Duke of Cleves, chose his daughter Anne as a fourth wife for Henry and she did not please him, Cromwell's doom was quickly sealed. Declared traitor and heretic, on July 28, 1540 he died under the axe he had ordered for so many others, including Fisher and More. Henry proceeded on his way. His fourth wife was given a pension and an estate, after Cranmer had for a third time declared a marriage of Henry VIII invalid; he had the head of his fifth wife, Catherine Howard, struck off a year and a half after he married her; his sixth wife, Catherine Parr, managed to survive him, though she had one narrow escape. Such was the man the English were required, on pain of death, to hail as head of their church.[118]

Henry's main effort to preserve doctrinal orthodoxy and liturgical continuity in the Church of England was the so-called "Six Articles" of 1539. On June 16 he abruptly presented to Parliament a set of six questions on church matters: (1) Is transubstantiation the true explanation of the Eucharist? (2) Should the laity receive Communion in both kinds? (3) Should vows of celibacy be observed? (4) Should private Masses be said? (5) Should priests marry? (6) Is confession of personal sins required by divine law? It soon became clear that Henry wanted all the questions answered "yes" except the second and fifth, while upholders of Protestant doctrine disagreed with him on all questions but the last, where a compromise was reached declaring confession desirable but optional. In a three-day debate in the House of Lords, with Henry present in person for two of the days, Archbishop Cranmer argued vigorously for the Protestant view, while Bishop Gardiner upheld the Anglo-Catholic position. Once they knew what Henry wanted and demanded, Cranmer and the bishops with him dropped their

---

[117] Cf. James A. Muller, *Stephen Gardiner and the Tudor Reaction* (New York, 1970), passim.

[118] Scarisbrick, *Henry VIII*, pp. 368-380, 429-433; Thomas Maynard, *The Crown and the Cross, a Biography of Thomas Cromwell* (New York, 1950), pp. 266-275. In the last year of Henry's life charges of heresy were drawn up against his sixth queen, Catherine Parr, who tended to favor the Protestants, but she manage to cool his wrath by a copious flow of tears and a promise henceforth to abide strictly by his will in religious matters. Otherwise her neck too would have gone under the axe (Scarisbrick, *op. cit.*, pp. 479-480).

opposition. After the House of Commons passed legislation on these points conforming to the King's will, all the bishops voted for it in the House of Lords, along with the rest of its membership.[119]

However, during the debate in the House of Lords the King had asked Cranmer for a written statement of his objections, and he had prepared a (surprisingly outspoken and detailed critique.) He gave it to his secretary, Ralph Morice, to take to the King during the evening at Hampton Court Palace, across the Thames from the building where Cranmer was residing. They were not near storied London Bridge, and London did not at that time have any other bridges over the Thames; Morice would have to go by boat. He found a kind of rowboat called a wherry, manned by a group of soldiers who agreed to take him across the river. But before they could pull out from the dock, they were distracted by a familiar entertainment in London of those days: a bear-baiting. They went off to look at it, while Morice waited in the wherry. Suddenly he heard a commotion. The tormented bear had broken loose and was heading toward the river, hotly pursued by its keeper. With a snuffling bellow it reached the dock and plunged directly into the wherry. Morice understandably hurled himself over the gunwale into the river. The splash dislodged Cranmer's manuscript, which bobbed unnoticed on the surface while Morice pulled himself out of the water and sought to put as much distance as possible between himself and the bear.

The bear-keeper panted to a halt on the dock, trying to decide what to do next (how *does* one get a bear out of a rowboat, anyhow?). His roving eye caught the floating sheaf of papers. He pulled it out of the river. The majority of people in England in 1540—very likely a large majority of bear-keepers—could not read. But either this bear-keeper was an exception, or he recognized Morice as Cranmer's secretary. (And literate or not, he was a Catholic, in the service of Princess Mary (to whom the bear belonged). He promptly showed the dripping papers to a priest standing conveniently nearby. The priest scanned them and declared their contents indubitably heretical. The author, he said, deserved death for his heresy.) That was all the bear-keeper needed to hear. When sodden Morice discovered his loss and who had taken his master's manuscript, and demanded it back, the bear-keeper refused to return it to him; it was evidence of a crime. Morice asked friends to invite the bear-keeper to dinner and try to persuade him to give up the manuscript, but he would not.

Next morning the bear-keeper went to Hampton Court Palace, looking for Bishop Gardiner to give him the manuscript. Gardiner could have made devastating use of it against Cranmer, for (most people in England did not realize just how Protestant Cranmer was.) But before the keeper could find Gardiner, he was intercepted by Thomas Cromwell, who took the paper away from him and delivered it to Henry, who would listen to no accusations of heresy against

---

[119] Ridley, *Cranmer*, pp. 178-184; Philip Hughes, *The Reformation in England* (London, 5th rev. ed., 1963), I, 365-366; Muller, *Gardiner*, p. 81; Scarisbrick, *Henry VIII*, p. 367.

Cranmer. So ends the tale of London's Catholic bear-keeper and his errant bear and their fleeting opportunity to change the course of English religious history.[120]

The Six Articles remained law for the rest of Henry's reign, but after the first year or two following their passage they were not much enforced. By 1541 Henry showed himself increasingly hostile to the veneration of images of the saints and their shrines. By February 1543 Cranmer had prevailed upon him to authorize a project to review and change the liturgy in the English church along with putting it into the vernacular, which was eventually to become the Book of Common Prayer. Probably reacting to this prospect, Anglican clergymen upholding orthodox doctrine drew up formal charges of heresy against Cranmer, including violation of the Six Articles. Henry ignored this, giving Cranmer his full support. But at the end of May 1543 a new statement of official religious doctrine, largely written by Bishop Gardiner, was published and widely circulated under the name of the "King's Book." It explicitly affirmed transubstantiation and all seven sacraments, condemned Communion in both kinds as "pestiferous and devilish," defended clerical celibacy, and upheld the veneration of images while condemning pilgrimages to saints' shrines. But despite this victory, Gardiner was not dominant in the Church of England; he could not save his nephew and secretary Germayne from being hanged at Tyburn for heresy in March 1544. Only at the last moment, in Lent of 1546, was Gardiner able to persuade Henry not to take Cranmer's advice to abolish the ancient practice of covering images and veiling the Cross during Lent, kneeling before the Cross on Palm Sunday, and "creeping to the Cross" on one's knees on Good Friday. The attraction of Cranmer for Henry is one of the mysteries of that monarch's complex character. It is hard to imagine two more dissimilar men. But it was an indubitable fact; no one was ever able to discredit Cranmer with Henry.[121]

In the last months of his life it appeared for the first time that Henry VIII might be contemplating doctrinal heresy as well as schism. After a banquet at Hampton Court for French Admiral d'Annebaut, the now grossly fat Henry struggled to his feet and gave a speech, leaning heavily on the shoulders of Cranmer and Admiral d'Annebaut. He suggested that he and Francis I—whose lack of strong Catholic belief he had long since grasped—might agree to abolish the Mass and replace it with a communion service in both their countries, as a preliminary to jointly repudiating papal supremacy in the Church and demanding that Emperor Charles V do likewise. Henry directed Cranmer to put his proposal in writing for Francis. Cranmer did so, but Francis never replied.[122]

---

[120] Ridley, *Cranmer*, p. 185; Maynard, *Crown and Cross*, pp. 238-239. These sources cover all the three preceding paragraphs.

[121] Ridley, *Cranmer*, pp. 148, 219, 236-240, 251, 254-255; Duffy, *Stripping of the Altars*, pp. 429, 431, 443-444; Muller, *Gardiner*, pp. 106-107, 135-137; Hughes, *Reformation in England*, II, 62, 64; Scarisbrick, *Henry VIII*, p. 472.

[122] Ridley, *Cranmer*, pp. 252-256; Ernest C. Messenger, *The Reformation, the Mass and the Priesthood* (London, 1937), I, 326-329.

Henry VIII left three children from his six marriages. By Catherine he had a daughter Mary, a staunch and fervent Catholic like her mother, whom he had long since repudiated, while retaining just enough paternal feeling to save her from the executioner's axe. By his second wife Anne Boleyn he had a second daughter Elizabeth, who could never be regarded as legitimate by Catholics since she was born while Catherine still lived. By his third wife Jane he had a son Edward, legitimate even in Catholic eyes because Catherine had died before Henry's marriage to Jane. By the law of male preference, found in every European monarchy of that age, Edward was the heir; but he was only nine years old when Henry died. Therefore a regency council must rule. A few days before his death Henry designated its members, fifteen in number, without a head, and with Bishop Gardiner (originally on the list) removed. The future of Christianity in England was now in the hands of this council.[123]

Francis I of France had kept his Catholic profession becaused it served his interests to do so. He had no need of a marriage annulment—he had a fertile wife and a long procession of mistresses—nor of anything else the Pope alone could provide. Ever since Philip IV in the late thirteenth century the King had possessed excessive power over the church in France.[124] He maintained it and it maintained him. Therefore within his own country Francis was a firm defender of the Church and a ruthless enemy of any heresy which might undermine it. But outside his borders he freely encouraged and supported both heretics and infidels to weaken his opponent Charles V and to put pressure on the Pope. He seems to have been a popular king, as Henry VIII was, though not as much toward the end of his reign, when the glitter had faded and Frenchmen began to wonder what they had really gained from their glamorous but utterly unprincipled ruler, who had never won any of his many wars. Well-informed Frenchmen were aware of the vast religious changes taking place in other countries, and wondered—some with hope, others with alarm—whether they would soon come to France as well.

One man, a genius, made this his life's work. He came from Picardy in the far northeast of France, and probably not until 1533 did he emerge from the career of a typical humanist classical scholar to become a militant Protestant.[125] He went on to systematize Protestant theology, organize the Protestant movement, and direct it for the first time explicitly toward the government of states and nations. He harnessed the forces Luther had unleashed but had not known how to control. His name was John Calvin.

---

[123] Scarisbrick, *Henry VIII*, pp. 488-494; Muller, *Gardiner*, p. 142.

[124] See Volume Three, Chapter 8 of this history.

[125] See François Wendel, *Calvin; the Origins and Development of His Religious Thought* (London, 1963), p. 42 for reasons for dating his conversion to Protestantism to this year. Supporting evidence includes Calvin's participation in scheduling and organizing a religious procession in his native Noyon that summer to avert plague (*ibid.*, p. 39) and an interview with an abbess to try to arrange for the admission of a sister of one of his friends to a convent in June (John T. McNeill, *The History and Character of Calvinism* [New York, 1967], p. 112)—both very Catholic actions which it is hard to imagine the Protestant Calvin taking.

In the fall of 1533 Calvin's friend Nicolas Cop was made rector (in American terms, president) of the University of Paris. In his inaugural address November 1, Cop stressed the primary authority of Scripture and justification by faith, well-known Lutheran themes. His remarks on the Beatitudes were taken almost word for word from a sermon by Luther. Since Cop's friendship with Calvin was well known, it was widely believed then and afterward that Calvin wrote the speech, and he may have done so, though it cannot be proved. The University of Paris was still strongly orthodox in the tradition of its one-time professor St. Thomas Aquinas. Reaction against Cop and Calvin because of this speech was so strong and threatening that Calvin left Paris the very next night, climbing out of his window with a rope made from his bed curtains. About fifty other friends and associates of Cop were arrested by government authorities, reflecting Francis I's vigilance against heresy which he regarded as a serious danger to orderly government. Three weeks later Cop also fled when formal charges of heresy were filed against him in the *Parlement* (high court) of Paris.[126]

During 1534 Calvin wandered through France as a fugitive, at one point leading a few companions in the Protestant "Lord's Supper" (which they had substituted for the Mass) in a cave. On Sunday, October 18 numerous placards denouncing the Mass as "horrible" and "insufferable" appeared in Paris and many other cities of France. Francis I and the *Parlement* of Paris ordered a full-scale manhunt for the perpetrators. Whether Calvin was personally involved is not known, but he may well have been. In November over 200 arrests were made of persons thought to have participated in "the affair of the placards," of whom twenty were burned at the stake. In January 73 French "Lutherans" who had so far managed to evade discovery were commanded to give themselves up. Persons harboring these and other heretics were also made liable to death by fire and informers were promised a quarter of the property of anyone they denounced. Calvin left the country and fled to Basel in Switzerland.[127]

There, in August, he completed the first edition of his famous summary of Protestant theology, *Institutes of the Christian Religion*, which he had probably begun writing while still in France. It was published in Basel in March 1536. Its dedication to Francis I shows that Calvin still hoped that inconstant monarch could be converted to his new faith. The book went through a series of ever-expanding editions until it became the best known and most influential compendium of Protestant religious thought, stressing the central Protestant themes of the pervasiveness of sin and the impossibility of overcoming it; further

---

[126] Wendel, *Calvin*, pp. 40-42; McNeill, *Calvinism*, pp. 110-112; Williston Walker, *John Calvin, the Organiser of Reformed Protestantism* (New York, 1906), pp. 106-107; Knecht, *Francis I*, pp. 244-245. For the earlier history of the University of Paris see Volume Three, Chapter 7 of this history. The *Parlement* of Paris will appear frequently in this history henceforth. It will be italicized in its French form to help avoid confusion with the English Parliament, whose equivalent in France was not the *Parlement* but the Estates-General.

[127] Knecht, *Francis I*, pp. 248-252; T. H. L. Parker, *John Calvin* (Philadelphia, 1975), p. 32; Walker, *Calvin*, pp. 119-123, 126.

developing the doctrine of the unmerited salvation of a few individuals (the "elect") whom God had predestined for salvation from the beginning of time; condemning the Catholic Church and its practices almost as harshly though much more coldly than Luther had done—Calvin's passion burned in hidden fires while Luther's had exploded like a volcano.[128] On the Eucharist Calvin took a position which appeared to be midway between Luther and Zwingli, but inclined more and more to Zwingli's side with the passing of time:

> We say that the body and the blood of Christ are presented to us truly and effectively, but not naturally. By that we mean that this is not the substance itself of the body, nor the true and natural body of the Christ that is given us there, but all the benefits that the Christ offers us in his body.[129]

After taking advantage of a six months' amnesty for heretics granted by Francis I to return to France to say farewell to his family and friends, Calvin set out again for Switzerland. He was persuaded by the Protestant preacher William Farel to join him in Geneva, where he had built up a strong following for the new religion, with the goal of making Geneva a showcase Protestant city. Calvin was reluctant to take on this mission; he still thought of himself as a scholar rather than a preacher and controversialist. But Geneva, where Calvin's native language was spoken rather than the German of Basel, attracted him. He yielded to Farel's pleading, and spent most of the rest of his life building up Geneva as a Protestant stronghold.[130]

Geneva had recently become a fully independent, self-governing city-state. Formerly attached to the duchy of Savoy in Italy, it had shaken off Savoyard rule during the 1520's by means of an alliance with the Swiss cities of Bern and Fribourg. The word officially used to denote the Swiss Confederation in the German that most of its members spoke was *Eidgenossen*. Those in Geneva who sought alliance with the Confederation were therefore called in French *Eidguenots*. This is the probable origin of the strange word "Huguenots" later used to identify the followers of Calvin in France. The city was small (about 10,000 people) and, pinched between its great lake and the high Alps, it lacked a hinterland. But it was comparatively wealthy and very well fortified.[131]

Calvin's road to total domination of Geneva was a long one, full of obstacles and with one major detour. His first stay there lasted only a year and a half; in April 1538 he was expelled and did not return until September 1541.[132] But after that he never left the city again. With relentless perseverance, cool clarity of mind, and the power of will that marks a history-maker, he gradually gained control not only of its religion but also of its government, law, and daily

---

[128] Parker, *Calvin*, p. 33; Wendel, *Calvin, passim.*

[129] Wendel, *Calvin*, p. 341.

[130] *Ibid.*, pp. 48-50; Parker, *Calvin*, pp. 52-53.

[131] Parker, *Calvin*, pp. 54, 56; McNeill, *Calvinism*, p. 133; Walker, *Calvin*, pp. 164-165, 171.

[132] Parker, *Calvin*, pp. 66, 80-81; McNeill, *Calvinism*, pp. 143, 158; Wendel, *Calvin*, pp. 70-71.

life, until he became its dictator. In the end he and his followers, whom he firmly believed to be the Elect of God, totally dominated the society and economy as well as the government and church of Geneva. It gave Protestants all over Europe who sincerely believed in the religious revolution they had made, a beacon to point at showing that they could create an orderly and "godly" society, contrasting vividly with the chaos of divided Germany, where even Luther had at times despaired of the havoc wreaked in his name. Calvin followed the great religious conflict in Europe with the closest attention, frequently giving both solicited and unsolicited advice to his fellow Protestants, and founding an academy—later the University of Geneva—to educate and inspire young Protestants from many countries to follow in his footsteps. He never specifically advocated the violent overthrow of Catholic governments, though before his death in 1564 his followers had already begun to do so.[133]

Calvin's creation was certainly not a place where any Catholic could ever feel at home. He justified all that he and his people did by his interpretation of Scripture, which no one was permitted to challenge. He was a very able exegete, and his Biblical commentaries are still read. But this hardly gave him a legitimate basis to claim total authority in both the spiritual and the temporal order. Nevertheless he proceeded steadily and with impressive consistency to establish it. In November 1536, less than three months after arriving in Geneva, he presented the city council[134] with a "confession of faith, which all the citizens and inhabitants of Geneva . . . must promise to keep and to hold."[135] In the course of the following year all were ordered to sign it, though some refused. In January 1537 Calvin produced "Articles on the Organization of the Church and its Worship at Geneva," which defined the Elect as those participating in a Lord's Supper each month, with overseers (not specifically designated) to decide who was worthy by their moral conduct to share in it. The council accepted Calvin's articles the next month, except for reducing the frequency of the Lord's Supper from monthly to quarterly; but they insisted on keeping ultimate control over the exclusion of citizens from the Lord's Supper (tantamount to excommunication) in their own hands. At Easter 1538 the council directly intruded on Calvin's religious authority by ordering the use of unleavened bread at the Lord's Supper, rather than the leavened bread Calvin used to distinguish it from the Mass. Calvin refused their order and left the city.[136]

He spent the next three years variously in Basel, in Strasbourg with the international Protestant leader Martin Bucer, and in Germany attending several of the futile religious conferences between Lutherans and Catholics sponsored by

---

[133] See Chapter Five, below.

[134] Geneva had three city councils, the most important consisting of 25 members which acted as a kind of executive committee, a larger body of 60, and a still larger body of 200. Unless otherwise identified, references to the "city council" hereinafter refer to the 25-member "Little Council" (Parker, *Calvin*, p. 56).

[135] Parker, *Calvin*, p. 63.

[136] *Ibid.*, pp. 62-65; Walker, *Calvin*, pp. 185-192, 204-206; Wendel, *Calvin*, p. 52; McNeill, *Calvinism*, pp. 138-140, 142.

Emperor Charles V. Aided by the wide circulation of his book *Institutes of the Christian Religion* and by the sponsorship of Bucer, who had a flair for publicity and was probably the best known living Protestant after Luther, Calvin became famous. When Italian Cardinal Sadoleto, known for gentleness and charity in an age of poison-pen pamphleteering, wrote to the council of Geneva in March 1539 urging the city to return to its ancestral faith, Calvin from his exile was asked to reply to him. In June 1539 Calvin wrote an uncharacteristically conciliatory letter to the church in Geneva deploring their divisions since his departure and urging support for their new pastors. His supporters grew in political strength until in June 1540 the anti-Calvinists rioted and two men were killed in the fighting. Two leaders opposed to Calvin had already been exiled, a third was executed for stirring up the riot, and a fourth fell to his death while trying to escape from prison by climbing out a high window. In September the council invited Calvin back to Geneva and a year later, after winding up his many affairs in Basel and Strasbourg, he made a triumphant return. The very day of his return he demanded and obtained authorization from the council for a committee under his direction to draw up governing ordinances for the church in the city. A week later Calvin presented the ordinances (the committee was obviously a sham and he must have drawn them up before he returned to Geneva). On November 20, 1541 they were adopted, with a few changes to give the council some control over the selection of ministers.[137]

These ordinances established the form of church government which came to be known as Presbyterianism, because final authority was supposed to reside in a committee of elders (in Greek, *presbyteroi*), who were not ministers but were chosen from among the membership of the three city councils and confirmed by the ministers. The elders and the ministers formed the Consistory, a church court which met weekly to admonish and chastise offenders and excommunicate on the fourth offense, without the appeal to the city council formerly permitted. The next year Calvin published a liturgy for Geneva, which contained no word of Latin and provided for much congregational singing.[138]

Early in 1543 Calvin recodified the temporal law of the city; by then it was clear that he was aiming at full fusion of the spiritual and the temporal order in Geneva. By 1545 he had extended the jurisdiction of the Consistory to wholly private acts. When in January 1546 Pierre Ameaux, a member of the Little Council of Geneva, criticized Calvin at a supper party in his own home, Calvin demanded that he be punished by the government. On March 2 the Council of Two Hundred ordered Ameaux to appear before it in Calvin's presence and ask pardon on his knees "of God, the government, and Calvin"—a punishment which Calvin condemned as insufficient. Obediently the Council reconsidered its sentence, and ordered Ameaux to walk all around the city carrying a lighted torch, bareheaded and dressed only in his shirt, three times falling on his knees

---

[137] Parker, *Calvin*, pp. 78-82; Walker, *Calvin*, pp. 249-252, 256-257, 261-262; Wendel, *Calvin*, p. 71.
[138] Parker, *Calvin*, pp. 82-84, 86-87; Wendel, *Calvin*, pp. 71-78; Walker, *Calvin*, pp. 266-275; McNeill, *Calvinism*, pp. 160-165.

and begging for mercy. A gallows was set up in front of his home to remind him of his likely fate if he continued to be contumacious. On March 21 Ami Perrin, who had been a leading supporter of Calvin, and his vivacious and outspoken wife Franchequine were imprisoned for dancing at a wedding. When the couple were brought before Consistory for this offense, Franchequine Perrin defied Calvin to his face, causing him to declare her "in contempt of God." In July Calvin and his ministers prohibited all theatrical productions in Geneva, a decree which remained in effect for decades. In November Calvin drew up a list of acceptable Christian names for children and prohibited children whose names were not on his list from receiving baptism. These acts of police state tyranny led to a new challenge to his rule during 1547 culminating in violence at a meeting of the Council of Two Hundred in December. Though his opponents went on to win some elections, they were far from strong enough to force Calvin out of the city again. In the end his unshakable perseverance wore them down and established his total power, which he held until his death.[139]

On November 29, 1549 the conclave assembled in Rome to elect a new Pope in succession to Paul III. Forty-one of the 54 members of the College of Cardinals were present, with ten more arriving during the conclave; only two French cardinals and Cardinal Henry of Portugal never participated. The conclave was evenly divided between supporters and opponents of Emperor Charles V. No one person stood out as outstandingly qualified to be Pope or especially likely to be elected. The cardinals voted for a secret ballot. When the first ballot was taken December 3, most were surprised to find the leader to be the only English cardinal, Reginald Pole.[140]

He was the third son of Sir Richard Pole and Margaret Plantagenet, elder daughter of the Duke of Clarence who had been the brother of Kings Edward IV and Richard III, executed for rebelling against Edward IV by being drowned in a barrel of Madeira wine. After the execution in 1499 of the Duke of Clarence's only son, the sons of his sister Margaret became the heirs to the Plantagenet dynasty which Henry VII Tudor had supplanted by force in 1485 with a very questionable title.[141] When Henry VIII took England out of the Church in 1534, Reginald Pole was studying theology and teaching literature in Italy. Early in 1535 Henry VIII wrote to Pole asking him to write his frank opinion on the validity of Henry's marriage to Catherine and his newly assumed title of supreme head of the Church in England. Clearly the king wanted to put his potential rival on record against him, and the forthright Pole obliged him. After fourteen months of scholarly and literary labor, he completed a ringing condemnation of

---

[139] Walker, *Calvin*, pp. 276-277, 281-283, 295-297, 301-304, 306, 309-310; McNeill, *Calvinism*, pp. 167, 169, 171; Wendel, *Calvin*, pp. 83-84, 86, 88-89. For Calvin's last years in Geneva see Chapter Five, below.

[140] Von Pastor, *History of the Popes*, XIII, 3-13.

[141] Martin Haile, *Life of Reginald Pole* (London, 1910), pp. 1-5. For the replacement of the Plantagenet dynasty by the Tudors with the overthrow of Richard III, see Volume Three, Chapter 14 of this history.

the Henry VIII's policy on both matters, entitled "In Defense of the Unity of the Church." At first he hesitated to send it to Henry or to publish it, for fear of reprisals against his family in England, but when Anne Boleyn was executed he concluded it was safe to do so. But he was not so naive as to accept Henry's unctuous invitation, immediately after reading Pole's book, to return to England.[142]

Pope Paul III was deeply impressed by Pole's book. In December 1536 he made him a cardinal and papal legate to England, hoping to reconcile Henry VIII with the Church or to support a Catholic uprising against him. Henry and Thomas Cromwell immediately marked Pole as an enemy whom they must do everything possible to thwart, even to the point of assassinating him. In December 1538 Henry executed Cardinal Pole's two elder brothers, despite a total lack of evidence of any designs against him on their part, mainly on evidence that they deplored his religious changes in England. Seven months later he committed Cardinal Pole's aged mother to the Tower of London and two years later sentenced her to execution by the axe after she had offered total, unbreakable resistance to all questioning. Later Pole was one of the three papal legates who presided over and directed the Council of Trent.[143]

Few men had more reason to hate Henry VIII and his Protestant advisors than Reginald Pole, but he was not a man capable of hate. In the jungle of invective that was disputation in the first sixty years of the sixteenth century Cardinal Pole was an island of reason, charity and sanity, a gentle, soft-spoken man who yet had an iron will and would never compromise with evil. He was to become Queen Mary Tudor's strong right arm, who almost single-handedly made the church in England Catholic again, though he did not have enough time to prepare it to survive his and his mistress' almost simultaneous deaths. He would have made a great Pope, perhaps one of the greatest of all. On the second ballot at the conclave he received 24 votes, just four short of the required two-thirds majority. That night three more cardinals promised him their votes if his total reached 26, and his supporters confidently expected his election in the morning.[144]

It was not to be. Once again the pro-French faction was working hard against the good of the Church. The reform-minded but terrible-tempered Cardinal Carafa attacked Pole for supporting the theory of "double justification" which the Council of Trent had condemned (he had supported it earlier, but loyally abandoned it when the Council rejected it). Cardinal Cervini, his fellow legate at Trent and a champion of reform, declared his intention to vote for Pole. On the third ballot he received 25 votes, within one of the total which would trigger the switch of three more cardinals to give him victory; but he never

---

[142] *Ibid.*, pp. 123-131, 137-138, 152, 158-160, 171.

[143] *Ibid.*, pp. 187-190; von Pastor, *History of the Popes*, XII, 210, 465-467, 470; Roger B. Merriman, *The Life and Letters of Thomas Cromwell* (Oxford, 1902), I, 204-205; Maynard, *Crown and Cross*, p. 187; Scarisbrick, *Henry VIII*, pp. 364-365; H. F. M. Prescott, *Mary Tudor* (New York, 1953), pp. 92-94.

[144] Von Pastor, *History of the Popes*, XIII, 13-15.

attained that last vote. The fourth ballot showed no change; on the fifth ballot Pole lost one vote. Then on December 12 four French cardinals arrived, strengthening the party opposed to Pole, and the young and very able Cardinal Guise, a member of what was now emerging as the leading Catholic family in France, assumed the leadership of that party. The required two-thirds majority was now 31 and unattainable for Pole against the French opposition, though he continued regularly to receive at least 23 votes on all of the first 52 ballots.[145]

It should have become obvious long before that many ballots were taken that neither the imperial nor the French party could secure a two-thirds majority. A compromise candidate had to be found who was not closely affiliated with either. But none came forward, and the endless ballots had hardened the position of both hostile factions. On January 26, 1550, nearly two full months after the conclave had assembled, the folly of such proceedings in the face of the immense crisis of the Protestant revolt was finally recognized. Cardinal Domenico de Cupis gave a powerful speech excoriating as a disgrace to the College of Cardinals the hardening of the factions and the utter disregard of the rules of enclosure (nearly 400 persons besides the cardinals were in the building where the conclave was being held, while others passed in and out through holes made in the walls and trap doors in the roof, and some cardinals even held periodic banquets for their burgeoning though illegal staff). Shamed, the conclave appointed a committee of six, one from each nation represented (Italian, Spanish, Portuguese, French, German, and English), to clear the building, which they did five days later. After the candidacies of little known Cardinals Ridolfi and Salviati failed, in early February support began to build for Cardinal del Monte, the senior legate at Trent who had chaired most sessions of the Council. Del Monte was noted neither for prudence nor for leadership ability, and had not handled well the departure of the Council Fathers from Trent and its consequences. But everybody knew him; he was somewhat unfriendly to the Emperor yet not closely linked with the French; so on February 7, after ten exhausting and increasingly odoriferous weeks, he was finally elected with 41 votes, and took the name Julius III. Visiting on February 3 the building where the conclave was held, Rome's leading physician found the stench so bad that he feared an immediate outbreak of plague.[146]

Julius III's first act as Pope, on February 16, 1550, was to send friends and confidants of the two great Catholic monarchs to them as his emissaries, assuring both that he intended to cooperate with them and to work for Christian unity; but only the envoy to Charles V was instructed to discuss renewal of the Council. At his first meeting with the cardinals as Pope, Julius III declared his commitment to Church reform. On February 24 he ceremonially opened the Golden Door to begin the traditional mid-century jubilee year.[147]

But the pilgrims who came to Rome that jubilee year were almost all Italians. Elsewhere in Christendom there was little to celebrate. In Germany the

---

[145] *Ibid.*, XIII, 15-20.

[146] *Ibid.*, XIII, 32-43.

[147] *Ibid.*, XIII, 55-57.

Lutherans were openly mocking and in some areas directly violating the Augsburg Interim; in England schism was becoming heresy on a grand scale; and King Henry II of France, with his intensely personal hatred of Charles V even more deadly than his father's insouciant alteration of friendship and betrayal, was developing a plan to undo all that Charles had gained by his victory in the Schmalkald War and at the Battle of Mühlberg and throw Germany into even worse chaos.

On February 26, 1550 Duke Albert of Prussia, Margrave Hans von Brandenburg-Cüstrin, and Duke John Albert of Mecklenburg—all Protestants—formed an alliance for mutual defense if the Emperor attacked any of them for either religious or secular reasons. In June Duke Maurice of Saxony, who had fought with the Emperor against his fellow Protestants in the Schmalkald War, sent an ambassador to Paris to offer himself to King Henry II as a "friend and servitor" and asked if Henry II would help him in a war against the Emperor. Though he received only a vague reply, the Protestant general Schärtlin von Burtenbach wrote from Paris that he had information that Henry was ready to support German Protestant princes with both money and troops.[148]

General Schärtlin's information was correct. Henry was simply waiting to be sure that the Lutherans had a good chance to prevail. By May 1551 Maurice of Saxony, while still pretending to be Charles' ally and even commanding imperial troops at the siege of Protestant Magdeburg while negotiating privately for an alliance with its defenders, had built up his secret Protestant coalition into a formidable force. New ambassadors sent to Henry II of France returned with that king's promise of a treaty with Duke Maurice and his allies. In September Henry declared war on Charles V, unprovoked; on October 3 the promised treaty was signed on Lochau Heath, with France paying 240,000 thalers immediately to Duke Maurice and the German Protestant princes allied with him, and 60,000 more promised to follow every month.[149]

Meanwhile, on January 1, 1551 Pope Julius III had published a bull summoning the Council to meet again at Trent, and at the close of the Diet of Augsburg Charles V reiterated his commitment to its support and protection. Pope and Emperor were at last acting in harmony; in instructions that March to his secretary of state who was going to the Emperor's court at Augsburg, the new Pope declared his firm intention "to sail in the same ship with the Emperor and to share the same fate as his, for he knew how closely his interests, especially those concerning religion, were bound up with those of Charles." On April 29 the three new papal legates to the Council—Cardinals Crescenzi, Pighino and Lippomano—made solemn entry into Trent, where four archbishops and nine bishops awaited them along with Trent's own cardinal bishop. On May 1 the reconstituted Council was declared open, but in view of the small attendance the next session was postponed until September.[150]

---

[148] Janssen, *History of the German People*, VI, 425-428.

[149] *Ibid.*, VI, 437-438, 440, 442-444; Merriman, *Rise of the Spanish Empire*, III, 369-370; Brandi, *Charles V*, pp. 603-605; Baumgartner, *Henry II*, pp. 147-148.

[150] Von Pastor, *History of the Popes*, XIII, 90-91, 95 (for quote), 99-101.

But by September French troops were in Italy, supporting Ottavio Farnese who had rebelled against the Pope and seized the city of Parma, and there had been a furious exchange of letters between the hot-tempered Pope and the King of France in which the Pope threatened Henry II with hellfire and Henry called the Pope "among the worst and most ungrateful of men." At the September meeting of the Council (now attended by seven archbishops and 26 bishops in addition to the three cardinal legates and 25 theologians) a letter from the French king was read stating that while he was at war in Italy it was not safe for any of his bishops to come to Trent, that under these circumstances he regarded the Council not as ecumenical but as "a private assembly," and that neither he nor the French nation and church would be bound by its decisions (though he did add that despite all this he was not refusing obedience to papal authority). Nevertheless the renewed Council for the time being continued to meet. At a general session October 11 the Catholic doctrine of the Eucharist was confirmed by a dogmatic decree specifically affirming transubstantiation and the continuing presence of Christ in the consecrated Host after Mass. For the first time some Protestants appeared—specifically, two representatives of Elector Joachim of Brandenburg, conveying his promise to abide by the decrees of the Council. How many other Protestant princes might have submitted to the Council had it not been so long delayed?[151]

Late in November the Council confirmed Catholic doctrine and practice regarding the sacraments of penance and extreme unction (anointing of the sick). On January 9, 1552 its orderly progress was harshly interrupted with the arrival of two militantly Protestant representatives of Duke Maurice of Saxony, who refused even to speak to the cardinal legates, demanded that the Council stop all work until the arrival of a group of Lutheran theologians being sent by Maurice, and demanded that when the Council resumed work it should annul all the decisions it had already made and declare the superiority of its authority over the Pope. Six days later Duke Maurice publicly confirmed his alliance with Henry II of France and most of the other Protestant princes of Germany and declared war on the Emperor.[152]

The agreement at Lochau Heath in October 1551 was kept secret for several months, though rumors about it were flying. The weary Charles, unwilling to face the prospect of another major war with the German Protestants, refused to believe them. On January 15, 1552 the Lochau Heath agreement with its alliance of Henry II of France with Duke Maurice of Saxony was publicly proclaimed as the Treaty of Friedwald.[153] On January 28 Charles wrote to his sister Mary that he was on the brink of financial ruin and had not the means to fight a new war in

---

[151] *Ibid.*, XIII, 102 (quote), 105-107, 109-112; Baumgartner, *Henry II*, p. 118.

[152] Von Pastor, *History of the Popes*, XIII, 113-116; Janssen, *History of the German People*, VI, 449; Baumgartner, *Henry II*, p. 149.

[153] Brandi, *Charles V*, pp. 605-606; Janssen, *History of the German People*, p. 449; Baumgartner, *Henry II*, p. 149.

Germany; if it should be forced upon him, he said, "he would indeed be driven to the extremity of despair."[154]

In March Charles attempted to negotiate with Maurice, but the traitorous Saxon duke was not interested. Instead he marched south in person against Charles, taking Augsburg on the way and restoring full Protestant control in that city. Charles was residing in the Austrian city of Innsbrück not far from Trent. He had no army with him nearly large enough to match Maurice's. On May 18 came the dread news that Maurice had taken Ehrenberg Pass and was about to descend into an almost undefended Innsbrück. Charles, so ill with gout that he could not ride, had to be carried out of Innsbrück in a litter in pouring rain, which changed to sleet as his escort crossed the Brenner Pass at nine o'clock in the evening to reach safety in the small, isolated town of Lienz. Behind him Maurice looted his palace in Innsbrück. It was the greatest humiliation of Charles' life.[155]

The Protestant army at Innsbrück was now in a position to threaten Trent directly. The German bishops had all left Trent to return to their war-torn homeland, and no French bishops were present or coming. The Council was reduced to a gathering of Italian and Spanish bishops which would be hard pressed to call itself ecumenical with credibility. The war might go on for months or even years. In April, with Maurice of Saxony on the march, Pope Julius III reluctantly concluded that the Council must again be suspended, as Emperor Charles V had already recommended the previous month. The Council Fathers as reluctantly concurred. The Council was not to meet again for eleven years.[156]

Maurice of Saxony now demanded of Emperor Charles that he abandon the Augsburg Interim and permit a return to the situation before the Schmalkald War, when the sovereign of each German territory decided the religion of that territory, without even a mention of the Council. At first Charles bravely tried to resist this, aided by Henry II's abrupt withdrawal of most of his French army from Germany. But no Catholic counteroffensive was possible because of Charles' military and financial weakness. On July 31 a weary, disheartened Emperor, severely crippled by gout and in great pain from it, accepted a peace agreement with the German rebels, published August 2 as the Treaty of Passau. It specifically annulled the Augsburg Interim and said nothing about the religious question except to refer it to future Diets, as had so often been done with futility before. This meant that nothing had been decided or permanently changed by Charles V's great effort culminating at Mühlberg. Now turning his back on Germany, ignoring the brutal ravaging of the German countryside by the Protestant Margrave Albert of Brandenburg-Cülmbach, Charles marched into Lorraine, imperial territory which had been mostly conquered for France by Henry II while Charles was trapped in Austria, where he could readily draw support from his native Low Countries, still loyal to him. There in October he sat

---

[154] Janssen, *History of the German People*, VI, 471.

[155] *Ibid.*, VI, 456-, 475-478; Brandi, *Charles V*, pp. 606, 608, 610-611; Menéndez Pidal, *Historia de España*, XX, 863.

[156] Von Pastor, *History of the Popes*, XIII, 125, 127-128.

down before the great fortress of Metz and laid siege to it. France's best soldier, the Duke of Guise, commanded there. Consequently the siege made no progress.[157]

Charles' long, tremendous effort to save the Faith in Germany had not completely failed, but overall was far from successful: a substantial majority of the country was Lutheran, and in those territories the Catholics were exiled or driven underground. The Council for which he had worked so hard had made a significant beginning, but had twice been frustrated by the alliance of professedly Catholic France with German Protestants in arms. He had been the temporal leader of Christendom against the infidel without, the heretic within, and traitorous France for no less than 33 years of toil, travel, trouble and disaster, during which he had found almost no one to trust and was subject to constant suspicion and frequent detraction from the Pope. It is no wonder that by 1552 Charles was at the end of his physical and mental strength. Few if any men in all of Christian history have given more to Christendom and been honored less for it, not only in their own time but ever since, than Emperor Charles V.[158] But at least Charles had one to love and appreciate him: his son and heir Philip, who when he built the splendid basilica of San Lorenzo de El Escorial on the slopes of Spain's Guadarrama Mountains, placed there a statue of his father kneeling bathed in the radiance of the glorified Christ Whom he had always wished above all to serve. At the Diet of Worms, facing Luther's challenge, the 21-year-old Emperor Charles V had pledged his kingdoms and dominions, his friends, his body, his blood, his life, and his soul to do his duty. Despite the inevitable mistakes and misdirections deriving from his fallen humanity, he had truly and fully redeemed that pledge.

The kingdom of Scotland, small and poor but resolute, had maintained its independence from England ever since the heroic days of William Wallace and King Robert Bruce at the end of the thirteenth century and the beginning of the fourteenth.[159] But because of its limited resources and despite its "auld alliance" with France, Scotland had suffered many defeats by England since then, notably the disaster at Flodden in 1513 early in the reign of Henry VIII, where King James IV of Scotland and most of his noblemen died on the field. James IV's only surviving son, James V, was only in his second year when he inherited the throne. His mother Margaret, sister of Henry VIII, never cared for him, and during much of his minority he was a captive of the powerful Douglas family.

---

[157] Janssen, *History of the German People*, VI, 395-396, 480-486, 490-492, 498; Brandi, *Charles V*, 613-615, 618-621; Baumgartner, *Henry II*, pp. 153, 156-157.

[158] A few have nevertheless honored him as he deserves, in his time and now: his adopted Spanish people, for whom he became and remained a national hero, to make up for his betrayal by his own German people, and by his many Dutch and Flemish countrymen soon after his death; and notably the great Neapolitan churchman Girolamo Seripando, cardinal legate of Pope Pius IV at the Council of Trent (Hubert Jedin, *Papal Legate at the Council of Trent, Cardinal Seripando* [St. Louis, 1947], pp. 512-516).

[159] See Volume Three, Chapters 8 and 9 of this history.

His deprived childhood probably damaged him, for he was never a strong or effective ruler. But he was strong in his faith; when in 1536 his uncle Henry sent the distinctly Protestant Bishop William Barlow to try to persuade James to reject the Catholic Church and a thunderstorm broke during the interview, James crossed himself and said he did not know which he feared more, the thunder in the heavens or the blasphemy of Bishop Barlow.[160]

The primate of Scotland was the Archbishop of St. Andrews. During most of James V's reign he was James Beaton, who died at a great age in 1539. He was succeeded by his remarkably able nephew David, who had developed close connections with leading families in France, notably the Guises, and had arranged two French marriages for his king, the first with a daughter of Francis I who soon died, the second with Marie de Guise, a strong woman who left her mark on history though in a losing cause. David Beaton made so good an impression in France that he was proposed for the red hat, and in 1538 became the first Scot ever made a cardinal.[161]

In 1542 Henry VIII sent an army to invade Scotland. Cardinal Beaton wrote to Pope Paul III that the main cause of the invasion was James V's refusal to follow Henry out of the Catholic Church. James was planning a counterattack into the north of England and Beaton suggested publishing the Pope's bull of 1535 against Henry from a church there, where the strength of surviving Catholic sentiment had been shown by the Pilgrimage of Grace six years before. But the battle that ensued at the end of November, at Solway Moss just over the English border, was a re-run of Flodden. The Scots army panicked and fled from the field almost without fighting; most of their losses were by drowning as they floundered across the Esk River. The English took 1,200 Scots prisoners at the cost of only seven killed. King James V was mortally wounded and died December 14. Marie de Guise had borne him two sons, but both had died in infancy the previous year. His only heir was a daughter just six days old: the future Mary, Queen of Scots.[162]

Since Henry VIII's son Edward was five years old at this time, a future marriage between him and the little princess seemed the ideal way to attain the centuries-old English goal of uniting the two nations under the King of England, and Henry immediately began pressing hard for it. Such a union would of course mean the destruction of the Catholic Church in Scotland. Cardinal Beaton opposed it with all his power, which was considerable (he was Chancellor of Scotland as well as primate). Beaton was backed by Queen Mother Marie de Guise. But the Earl of Arran, heir presumptive (next in line for the succession after Mary) inclined toward Protestantism and was bitterly hostile to the Cardinal, actually drawing his sword on him at a meeting shortly after James V's death. Early in January 1543 Arran was able to remove Cardinal Beaton from the

---

[160] Caroline Bingham, *James V, King of Scots* (London, 1971), p. 111 and *passim*.

[161] Margaret H. B. Sanderson, *Cardinal of Scotland; David Beaton* (Edinburgh, 1986), pp. 56-72.

[162] *Ibid.*, pp. 151-152; Bingham, *James V, King of Scots*, pp. 177-191; Antonia Fraser, *Mary Queen of Scots* (New York, 1983), p. 11; Scarisbrick, *Henry VIII*, p. 436.

five-man regency council set up to govern during Mary's minority and have him imprisoned. But the Cardinal's anti-English policy was strongly supported by most of the Scottish people, and the government had to release him in time to celebrate Mass at the cathedral in St. Andrews that Easter. When in July Arran and the government signed the Treaties of Greenwich with England, providing for the future marriage of Prince Edward and Mary and for Mary to be brought up at the English court, there was a furious uprising in Scotland. Cardinal Beaton marched to Stirling Castle with 7,000 troops to prevent the little queen from being taken to England. When in early September a Protestant mob stirred up by English agents attacked friaries and images in Edinburgh, the people rallied and drove them away. The Earl of Arran did penance for apostasy and the government was reconstituted with Cardinal Beaton as Chancellor. It repudiated the Treaties of Greenwich in December, at the same time strengthening the laws against heresy.[163]

Well aware of how essential Cardinal Beaton had become to the survival of the Catholic Faith in Scotland and having received most favorable reports on him from Patriarch Grimani who was temporarily acting as his legate in that country, in January 1544 Pope Paul III appointed Beaton permanent papal legate to Scotland. This office, together with his being primate and Chancellor, gave him even greater powers than Cardinal Wolsey had possessed in England before Henry VIII began proceedings to annul his marriage, since due to the longevity of Archbishop Warham Wolsey never held the primatial office. In April the Scottish laird of Brunston sent a letter to Henry VIII by the Earl of Hertford offering, with the help of a group of discontented Scots, to kill or capture the Cardinal. Henry gave preliminary approval by sending money to the conspirators. In that same month came another English invasion of Scotland to obtain restoration of the Treaties of Greenwich for the future marriage of Prince Edward and Queen Mary (the Scots wryly called it "rough wooing"). Edinburgh was taken, except for the almost impregnable castle, and much of the city was burned. Cardinal Beaton had to flee, with the English in pursuit; but they did not catch him. His abandonment of the Scottish capital considerably damaged his prestige and led to the rehabilitation of the Earl of Arran and a reconciliation between him and Marie de Guise.[164]

But Cardinal Beaton remained Chancellor and effective leader of Scotland. On Christmas Eve 1544 he wrote to Pope Paul III assuring him of Scotland's continued loyalty ot the Pope and asking the Pope's support against the continuing English aggression. In February 1545 the Scots defeated a force of English border raiders at Ancrum Moor. In June, after a French army of 3,000 arrived to help, a Scots convention at Stirling supported the French alliance and

---

[163] Sanderson, *Cardinal of Scotland*, pp. 154-156, 158, 163, 167-168, 170-172, 175-176, 190; Fraser, *Mary Queen of Scots*, pp. 18-21; Scarisbrick, *Henry VIII*, pp. 436-437, 439, 442.

[164] Sanderson, *Cardinal of Scotland*, pp. 114-115, 181-184, 187-188, 194-195; von Pastor, *History of the Popes*, XII, 423; Fraser, *Mary Queen of Scots*, pp. 23-24; Scarisbrick, *Henry VIII*, p. 452.

the war against England in a document signed by 54 noblemen and called for a nationwide muster of armed men. In June the laird of Brunston again proposed the assassination of Cardinal Beaton and again received money from the English government.[165]

In early 1546 Cardinal Beaton called a synod of the Scottish church to raise money to send Scots bishops to the Council of Trent, though the Cardinal himself felt unable to go due to the critical situation in Scotland. On January 13 of that year Cardinal Beaton finally was able to secure the arrest of George Wishart, who had become the leading Protestant preacher in Scotland. Wishart was charged with preaching without episcopal permission and with a veritable litany of heresy: condemning vows of chastity; denying the necessity and validity of the Mass, infant baptism, and confession; denying free will; rejecting any distinction between priests and laity; and denying the existence of purgatory and the value of prayer to the saints. In reply, at his trial, he would only say that he was true to Scripture. Cardinal Beaton pronounced his death sentence and he was burned at the stake March 2, 1546.[166]

Wishart appears to have been personally a gentle and genial man, in contrast to Luther and Calvin and his successor in Scotland, John Knox, but his ideas if not his personality were certainly revolutionary. He had fled to England in 1538 and had preached such radically Protestant doctrine that Henry VIII's church had accused him of heresy. Thomas Cromwell liked him and sent him out of England to avoid prosecution. He lived for several years in Germany and Switzerland, where he picked up Zwinglian and Anabaptist ideas. When he returned to England he taught at Cambridge, Archbishop Cranmer's university, long under strong Protestant influence.[167] Then he came to Scotland, where he surrounded himself with enthusiastic and angry young men of whom John Knox, who joined him in December 1545, was typical.[168] Since there has been so much modern sympathy for Wishart and condemnation of Cardinal Beaton for executing him, extending even to the point of regarding Beaton's murder as a justified reprisal, it must be emphasized once again that Protestants were executed in sixteenth century Europe not for their private beliefs but for promoting revolution and massive violation of the rights of Catholics. If Wishart and his followers became dominant in Scotland, it would be impossible for a Catholic—even a Queen—to live and work there, as Mary Queen of Scots was to learn to her sorrow.

On May 28, 1546 Cardinal Beaton returned to his residence in the castle of St. Andrews after a month's absence. A group of about fifteen conspirators headed by Norman Leslie of Fife, most of whom had known the Cardinal for years, were lying in wait to kill him. They had evidently suborned many of the hundred-man garrison, for few of the garrison were present when Leslie and his

---

[165] Sanderson, *Cardinal of Scotland*, pp. 195, 198, 200-202; Scarisbrick, *Henry VIII*, p. 452.

[166] Sanderson, *Cardinal of Scotland*, pp. 212, 214-220.

[167] *Ibid.*, pp. 192-193.

[168] Jasper Ridley, *John Knox* (New York, 1968), pp. 38-44.

men attacked the castle between five and six o'clock the following morning. Whether they were motivated primarily by religious zeal, political ambition, English gold, or the desire to avenge Wishart we cannot say; presumably all these motives were present in different mixtures in each conspirator. That hour is well past dawn in the high northern latitudes of Scotland at this season; the castle drawbridge had already been lowered and building materials were being brought in, and the attackers mingled with the workmen. Nevertheless Ambrose Sterling, porter of the outer gate, sensed something amiss; abruptly he halted traffic and tried to raise the drawbridge. The conspirators cut him down, took his keys, and locked the gate. They climbed up the circular staircase to the Cardinal's chambers, blocked by a thick barred oaken door, too massive to batter down; but Leslie called for fire and the Cardinal opened it. James Melville told him he was to die because he executed Wishart "and remain[s] an obstinate enemy against Christ Jesus and his holy Evangel." Cardinal Beaton looked him in the eye and said simply, twice: "I am a priest." Swords flashed; in an instant his body was full of bleeding wounds, and in a minute or two he was dead and horribly mutilated.[169]

John Knox, disciple of Calvin and later leader of Protestant Scotland, was not among the group of murderers, but joined them soon afterward,[170] thoroughly approved of what they had done, and never changed his opinion. Years later, in his *History of the Reformation in Scotland,* he wrote:

> How miserably lay David Beaton, careful Cardinal! And so they departed, without *Requiem aeternam* and *Requiescat in pace* sung for his soul. Now, because the weather was hot . . . and his funeral could not suddenly be prepared, it was thought best, to keep him from stinking, to give him great salt enough, a cope of lead, and a nook in the bottom of the Sea Tower (a place where many of God's children had been imprisoned before) to await what exequies his brethren the bishops would prepare for him. These things we write merrily.[171]

Here speaks the voice, not of "reformation," but of hatred, revolution, and death.

Cardinal Beaton had no successor. His murder destroyed Catholic Scotland. Few in the country were eager to punish his killers, who held the castle of St. Andrews for more than a year, although they were offered a full pardon by Regent Arran if they surrendered it. On July 31, 1547 the castle was finally taken by a French army and fleet; the few noblemen captured there were confined in French castles while the commoners, including John Knox, were sentenced to row galleys, a service in which few survived for long. But John Knox did survive, and was freed in March 1549 in a prisoner exchange arranged by the King of Denmark, while in the summer of 1548 six-year-old Queen Mary was sent to France for safety, to be brought up by her Guise relatives with an

---

[169] *Ibid.*, pp. 45-48; Sanderson, *Cardinal of Scotland*, pp. 226-228 (quotes on 227); Fraser, *Mary Queen of Scots*, p. 26; von Pastor, *History of the Popes*, XII, 473.

[170] Ridley, *Knox*, pp. 52-57.

[171] *Ibid.*, p. 47.

agreement that she would marry Francis, the Dauphin (crown prince) of France, when they were of age. Marie de Guise remained in Scotland, but she could not control it; the power was now in the hands of the Protestants, who looked to Calvin's Geneva for guidance.[172]

England was now fast moving in the same direction. After Henry VIII's death at the end of January 1547, England like Scotland was under the titular rule of a child, Henry's nine-year-old son Edward VI. The regency council was led by the boy king's uncle Edward Seymour, Earl of Hertford and soon Lord Somerset, called the Protector; within six weeks he was declared sole regent, though the council continued to advise him. At young Edward's coronation February 20 Archbishop Cranmer declared that the new king should see "idolatry destroyed, the tyranny of the Bishops of Rome banished from your subjects, and images removed." Since during the reign of Henry VIII images were retained in most English churches, this was a clear signal of major new changes to come. Three days later, on Ash Wednesday, Protestantizing Bishop Nicholas Ridley spoke against the veneration of saints, still widely practiced in England. During Lent Bishop Barlow, "a known and ardent Protestant," called for such sweeping changes in the belief and practice of the English church that Bishop Gardiner, the leading defender of orthodoxy in that church, vigorously objected.[173] William Paget, a leading minister under Henry VIII during his last years and now in the Somerset government, an old friend of Bishop Gardiner, warned him immediately:

> I malign not bishops . . . and much less I malign your Lordship, but wish ye well; and if the estate of bishops is or shall be thought meet to be reformed, I wish either that you were no bishop or that you could have such a pliable will as could well bear the reformation that shall be thought meet for the quiet of the realm.[174]

But, as Paget well knew, Bishop Gardiner was not a pliable man. When in June 1547 Cranmer asked him to participate in preparing a book of homilies for the English clergy, Gardiner refused, reiterating his opinion that there should be no religious changes during the King's minority, and saying there was enough material for homilies in the "King's Book" issued under Henry VIII's authority four years before (much of which had probably been written by Gardiner). Cranmer replied that he did not agree with parts of that book and thought Henry had been "seduced" into accepting it. Gardiner replied pointedly that this was "very strange speech" since Cranmer had never disagreed with the King's Book before or expressed any doubt about Henry's approval of it. But of course

---

[172] *Ibid.*, pp. 48-49, 61-64, 66-69, 80-81; Fraser, *Mary Queen of Scots*, pp. 30-34.

[173] Wilbur K. Jordan, *Edward VI, the Young King; the Protectorate of the Duke of Somerset* (London, 1968), pp. 52-53, 65, 67, 73, 155-156 (second quote on 155); Scarisbrick, *Henry VIII*, p. 496; Ridley, *Cranmer*, pp. 262-263 (first quote on 263); Hughes, *Reformation in England*, II, 81, 86.

[174] Paget to Bishop Gardiner, March 2, 1547, in Muller, *Gardiner*, p. 147.

Cranmer had always taken the greatest care never to cross Henry on religious or any other matters, which was why he had kept his head and was still primate of England. Soon afterward Gardiner wrote to Protector Somerset against Cranmer's project; he received no reply.[175]

Paget's and Cranmer's letters show that Henry VIII's break from the Catholic Church, though not at first doctrinal, had opened the gates to an influx of Protestant opinion from the continent, and that many influential men in England had simply been waiting for Henry's death to make England heretical as well as schismatic. It does not appear that the initiative lay with Protector Somerset, though he certainly made no objection to the changes. How much of the initiative lay with the cautious but increasingly Protestant Cranmer, and how much with bishops such as Ridley and Barlow, cannot be surely known, but there is good reason to regard Cranmer as the prime mover. Hilaire Belloc believed him primarily responsible, and much of the evidence assembled by Cranmer's recent most thorough biographer, Jasper Ridley (though he does not write from the Catholic viewpoint and traduces Belloc) supports Belloc's conclusion. For example, Ridley points out that during the summer of 1547 Cranmer's secretary Morice (he who had the misadventure with the bear in the rowboat) suggested to him that Henry's death made more religious change possible, whereupon Cranmer replied that Henry's death was unfortunate because he and Francis I had been about to abolish the Mass, while under the Somerset regency it would be more difficult to do this because of its unpopularity. Evidently abolition of the Mass was Cranmer's long-standing goal.[176]

On July 31, 1547 Cranmer's new Book of Homilies was published, showing how right Gardiner had been in predicting its character. It advocated justification by faith alone, though with the qualification that it must be "true and lively" as manifested by good works; it declared Scripture the sole authority on religious controversies; it made almost no mention of the sacraments, and condemned relics, rosaries, holy bread, holy water, palms and candles in church. On the same day a set of "injuctions" ordered the destruction of all shrines, images which had been incensed, and even stained glass windows, and prohibited religious processions, the ringing of bells at Mass, and saying the rosary in public. The Mass, however, was still maintained and the consecrated Host declared to be "the very body and blood of Christ." We know from Cranmer's words to Morice that he would not be satisfied until that too was changed.[177]

Bishop Gardiner's vehement objections to the Book of Homilies and the Injunctions were ignored, and at the end of September he and Bishop Bonner of London were sent to prison for refusing to abide by them. On October 7 Gardiner was brought out of jail for a conference with Cranmer and Bishop Ridley (now his principal religious advisor) at St. Paul's. Gardiner said he would

---

[175] Ibid., pp. 154-155; Hughes, Reformation in England, II, 88.

[176] Hilaire Belloc, Cranmer (Philadelphia, 1939), passim; Ridley, Cranmer, pp. 1-12, 259-260.

[177] Jordan, Edward VI, the Young King, pp. 159-162; Ridley, Cranmer, pp. 266-267; Hughes, Reformation in England, II, 92-94; Duffy, Stripping of the Altars, pp. 450-453.

yield to them if they could show him a single passage from Scripture or the Fathers "affirming faith to exclude charity in justification." They could not. Cranmer offered not only to free Gardiner but also to readmit him to the Royal Council if he would accept the Book of Homilies and Injunctions; Gardiner replied scornfully that if he did he would deserve "to be whipped in every market town in the realm, and then hanged for example, as the veriest varlet that ever was bishop." Cranmer angrily sent him back to prison.[178]

Early in November the government of Protector Somerset made only too clear what kind of man they preferred to serve them. They appointed Richard Rich, the betrayer of St. Thomas More, Chancellor of England. By the end of November all images had been removed from every church in the city of London. In December the two leading Italian Protestants, Peter Martyr Vermigli and Bernardino Ochino the former general of the Capuchin Franciscans, after spending several years in Calvin's Geneva, arrived in England to preach their faith. For some time they lodged with Archbishop Cranmer. Henry's doctrinally conservative Six Articles were abolished by act of Parliament when it met that month. Parliament also passed the Chantries Act, authorizing the confiscation of funds and properties set aside to endow prayers and Masses for the dead, and the abolition of all religious guilds.[179]

In Lent of 1548 the destruction of images began throughout most of England. For the first time in centuries there were no candles at Candlemas and no ashes on Ash Wednesday anywhere in the city of London, and in many other cities and parishes as well. Clerical marriage was authorized by the House of Lords, though eight bishops voted against it. In April Cranmer authorized divorce for adultery, and at Easter a new "order of communion" was introduced which prohibited elevation of the Host at Mass. All those taking communion were required to receive under both kinds.[180]

In the face of this blizzard of religious change Bishop Gardiner had begun to retreat. He, after all, had played a major part in England's break from the Catholic Church; despite his outspoken courage, he lacked the heroic virtue to repent of fifteen years of his life and surrender on his own the schismatic episcopal seat which Henry VIII had given him. Released from prison into house arrest, he pondered the changes and let Cranmer and Somerset know he could go along with most of them. They demanded an explicit statement of his support for them, on St. Peter's day before the boy king Edward VI. Gardiner agreed, but would not give them a copy of his sermon in advance. Since they had not yet acted specifically against the Mass, though they were contemplating such action,

---

[178] Jordan, *Edward VI, the Young King*, p. 163; Muller, *Gardiner*, pp. 165-167 (first quote on 166, second on 167).

[179] Jordan, *Edward VI, the Young King*, pp. 148, 169, 183-187, 191-193; Duffy, *Stripping of the Altars*, pp. 454-456; Hughes, *Reformation in England*, II, 144. See Chapter Three, above, for Rich.

[180] Duffy, *Stripping of the Altars*, p. 459; Ridley, *Cranmer*, pp. 277-279; Jordan, *Edward VI, the Young King*, pp. 184-187, 311-312; Messenger, *Reformation, Mass and Priesthood*, I, 360-364.

they could not require him to repudiate it; but they did not want him speaking out for the Real Presence.   Protector Somerset sent a sober, industrious, very Protestant young man of 26 named William Cecil to tell him that he must not include "doubtful matter" on the Eucharist in his sermon.[181]

Gardiner looked straight into young Cecil's cold, inscrutable face, and asked him what doubtful matter was he talking about.

"Transubstantiation," Cecil replied.[182]

Stephen Gardiner drew himself up.   He had separated himself from the Vicar of Christ, but he still believed that Christ really and truly gave His Body and His Blood in Holy Communion.

> I will preach the very presence of Christ's most precious Body and Blood in the Sacrament [of the altar], which is the Catholic faith, and no doubtful matter . . . I will not forbear to utter my faith and true belief therein, which I think necessary for the King's Majesty to know; and therefore if I wist to be hanged when I came down, I would [still] speak of it.[183]

Young William Cecil went away, and made his report to Protector Somerset.   We shall hear of him again—and again, all through the next fifty years.[184]

Gardiner gave the sermon, in an open-air pulpit in the King's garden at Whitehall, with the boy king watching from a window in the gallery overlooking the garden.   He vigorously defended the Real Presence and transubstantiation. The next day he was sent to the Tower of London, where he remained for five years—the rest of Edward VI's life.[185]

On September 23, 1548 Archbishop Cranmer laid before a conference of bishops and theologians at Chertsey Abbey a draft of his new English liturgy, the Book of Common Prayer, which was to replace completely the old Latin liturgy. It eliminated all reference to the Mass as a sacrifice, and made a subtle alteration in the language of the English Mass currently in use, by omitting a single word from the prayer before the consecration, which had asked that the bread and wine "may be made unto us the Body and Blood of Thy most dearly beloved Son our Lord Jesus Christ."   The omitted word was "made."[186]

When Cranmer's draft was circulated to all the English bishops (except those in jail, like Gardiner), all agreed with it but two.   One of the two, George Day of Chichester, specifically based his negative on the omission of that one critical word in the prayer before the consecration.   In December the Book of Common Prayer was debated in the House of Lords.   The aged Cuthbert Tunstall, who had been a bishop before the schism, declared for transubstantiation;

---

[181] Muller, *Gardiner*, pp. 170-172, 174-176; Conyers Read, *Mr. Secretary Cecil and Queen Elizabeth* (New York, 1961), pp. 47-48.

[182] Read, *Cecil*, p. 47.

[183] Muller, *Gardiner*, p. 176.

[184] See Chapters Five, Six, Seven, and Eight, below.

[185] Muller, *Gardiner*, pp. 178-182; Jordan, *Edward VI, the Young King*, pp. 213-214.

[186] Ridley, *Cranmer*, pp. 285-287 (quote on 287).

Cranmer replied with the clearest statement he had yet made of his view of the Eucharist: that it was only "the remembrance" of Christ's sacrifice, that "this is my body" means "this is a figure of my body"—not even the Lutheran, but the Zwinglian position. Bishop Barlow strongly agreed with Cranmer's language, but Bishop Thomas Thirlby of Ely vigorously objected to it and was rebuked by Protector Somerset. On January 15, 1549 the Lords passed the bill mandating the Book of Common Prayer, with no negative votes from the secular lords; but the bishops approved it by only 10-8. We hear of no opposition in the House of Commons; final passage was on January 21. [In May, on Pentecost Sunday, the new liturgy was introduced throughout England.[187]

Changes of the magnitude of those imposed on the English church in 1548 and 1549 could not be concealed from the least educated and least observant layman. Up until this time, except for the seizure of the monasteries, the government and the new church had done little visibly to change the traditional way of worship, and it had been possible for many ordinary Englishmen to overlook or disregard the changes which had occurred as a quarrel among distant though powerful men of which simple people knew nothing, and which would hopefully soon be resolved and the old Church restored. Now the full revolutionary extent of the change could be seen, heard, and felt. All celebrations of Eucharistic piety were abolished; only a handful of feast days remained—only one for the Blessed Virgin Mary; no votive Masses were allowed; the liturgy was different and strange.[188] Though the Catholic faith was still strong in the north, its people had been chastened by the total failure of the Pilgrimage of Grace. But in the west of England, Devon and Cornwall, where the faith was equally strong, there were no fearful memories, only shock and fury. Humphrey Arundel led a Catholic rising there, throwing in the teeth of the government and the official church: ("We will have all the general councils and holy decrees of our forefathers observed, kept and performed; and whosoever shall gainsay them, we hold them as heretics.") He and his followers demanded restoration of the old liturgy and ceremonies, the Six Articles, even half of the monasteries; significantly, they also demanded the return of Cardinal Pole from Rome. By June 23 the rebels were besieging Exeter, the principal city in Devon.[189]

It was magnificent, as the saying goes, but it was not war. Two counties alone had no hope of defying the might of the English government. The rising was spontaneous, unplanned; no outside aid had been sought and none was received. There was a July rising in Norfolk, led by a man named Robert Kett,

---

[187] *Ibid.*, pp. 288-289, 293; Jordan, *Edward VI, the Young King*, pp. 313, 315-321, 324 (quote on 315); Messenger, *Reformation, Mass, Priesthood* I, 388-401, 404-407, 409-411; Hughes, *Reformation in England*, II, 106-113.

[188] Duffy, *Stripping of the Altars*, pp. 464-465.

[189] See Julian Cornwall, *Revolt of the Peasantry 1549* (London, 1977), *passim* and especially pp. 49-63 and 114-116 (quote on 115, full text of Arundel's 16 demands on 115-116); Ridley, *Cranmer*, pp. 293-295; Hughes, *Reformation in England*, II, 166-169; Jordan, *Edward VI, the Young King*, pp. 456-460.

but the grievances of his people seem to have been primarily economic (against the enclosure of farm and common land into sheep pastures), and Kett had no direct link with the west country. Only the incompetence of the government's general, Lord John Russell, permitted the Western Rising and to continue through August, while the much abler Earl of Warwick crushed Kett's rebels at the Battle of Duissindale near Norwich on August 26, killing 3,500 of them. Both Kett and Arundel were captured and executed.[190]

The Earl of Warwick promptly used the reputation he gained by his quick suppression of Kett's rebellion; the fear of his large army, personally loyal to him; and the resentment of Somerset by many noblemen who thought him insufficiently vigilant in protecting the interests of their class, to supplant Somerset as the leader of England, though he did not take Somerset's title of Protector.[191] The change of leaders meant no change in the religious revolution, as Cranmer made clear in a Christmas letter in 1549 to the bishops which ordered the destruction of all liturgical books other than the Book of Common Prayer by the forthcoming April.[192]

On January 25, 1550 a new act of Parliament absolutely prohibited the use of any image in any church. There is no record of any opposition to it in the House of Commons, but there were eleven votes against it in the Lords—six from orthodox bishops and five from secular lords. On January 30 and 31 both Houses of Parliament approved in advance a new Ordinal (procedure and language for ordaining priests) to be drafted by a committee of six bishops and six others appointed by the government. Only five bishops voted against it. On February 1 Parliament was dismissed and did not meet again for two years.[193]

As had happened before under Cranmer, the committee on the Ordinal was a sham. It met just a few days after its creation only to accept a draft he had obviously already prepared, for on February 8 Bishop Nicholas Heath of Worcester, the only Anglo-Catholic on the committee, was reproved by the Royal Council for not agreeing with it. The new Ordinal was published in March. It made no mention of the priest re-enacting Christ's sacrifice at the Mass and referred to priests only as "the messengers, the watchmen, the pastors and stewards of the Lord, to teach, to admonish, to feed, and to provide for the Lord's family." The Ordinal authorized them only "to execute an office" without

---

[190] Cornwall, *Revolt of the Peasantry 1549*, pp. 130-159, 222-223, 231-232; Jordan, *Edward VI, the Young King*, pp. 461-462, 470-474, 479-490, 492; Hughes, *Reformation in England*, II, 167-172.

[191] Jordan, *Edward VI, the Young King*, pp. 508-521; Barrett L. Beer, *Northumberland; the Political Career of John Dudley, Earl of Warwick and Duke of Northumberland* (Kent State, Ohio, 1973), pp. 72-91. Warwick did not take the title of Duke of Northumberland until 1551 (Beer, *op. cit.*, p. 119).

[192] Ridley, *Cranmer*, pp. 304-305; Duffy, *Stripping of the Altars*, p. 469.

[193] Jordan, *Edward VI, the Young King*, pp. 45, 265-266; Duffy, *Stripping of the Altars*, p. 469; Hughes, *Reformation in England*, II, 113-115; Messenger, *Reformation, Mass, Priesthood*, I, 448-449.

mentioning the conveyance to them of any supernatural power to consecrate.[194] Its language was much too vague to provide a basis for claiming that those ordained with it knew and accepted the nature and duty of a priest and his power to change bread and wine into the Body and Blood of Christ. Bishop Gardiner declared at his trial in January 1551 that he believed this Ordinal had broken the chain of apostolic succession in England.[195] In a book about the Eucharist published in July 1550, Cranmer left no possible doubt that he had totally rejected not only the sacrificial character of the Mass but also the Real Presence:

> Christ called bread His Body, and wine His Blood, and these sentences be figurative speeches; and Christ, as concerning His humanity and bodily presence, is ascended into heaven with His whole flesh and blood, and is not here upon earth; and the substance of bread and wine do remain still, and be received in the sacrament, and although they remain, yet they have changed their names, so that the bread is called Christ's Body, and the wine His Blood; and the cause why their names be changed is this, that we should lift up our hearts and minds from the things which we see unto the things which we believe and be above in heaven; whereof the bread and wine have the names, although they be not the very same things in deed. . . . In plain speech it is *not true* that we eat Christ's Body and drink His Blood.[196]

In May 1550 the Privy Council agreed to the appointment of John Hooper as Bishop of Gloucester, though he was an open Calvinist who refused even to wear vestments—the beginning of the prolonged controversy over vestments which was to vex the Church of England for the next hundred years. Since all bishops and priests in the English church then still wore vestments, much pressure was put on Hooper to conform; but in August the young King wrote personally to Archbishop Cranmer requesting that Hooper not be required to do anything "offensive to his conscience." Edward was still only thirteen, but he was intellectually precocious and totally committed to Protestantism, presumably mainly through the influence of his teachers, possibly partly because of the influence of his Protestant stepmother Catherine Parr. On Christmas day 1550 Edward publicly attacked his half-sister Mary in the presence of his court for continuing to have Mass said in her private quarters. Meanwhile Hooper, encouraged by the royal support, now condemned any use of vestments by anyone, and had to be silenced temporarily by Archbishop Cranmer.[197]

On November 23, 1550 the Privy Council ordered all altars in England destroyed and replaced by communion tables. This order was conveyed to the

---

[194] Messenger, *Reformation, Mass, Priesthood*, I, 451, 456, 470-471, 483, 492 (quote on 471).

[195] Messenger, *Reformation, Mass, Priesthood*, I, 500. See Chapter Five, below, for the break in apostolic succession in the English church early in Queen Elizabeth's reign.

[196] Messenger, *Reformation, Mass, Priesthood*, I, 429.

[197] Wilbur K. Jordan, *Edward VI, the Threshold of Power* (Cambridge MA, 1970), pp. 294-296; Hughes, *Reformation in England*, II, 117-118; Prescott, *Mary Tudor*, pp. 150-151.

bishops and priests with a cover letter from Cranmer explicitly rejecting the sacrificial character of the Mass. Bishop Day of Chichester refused to obey this directive and was therefore imprisoned and deprived of his diocese.[198]

One might think that all this would have been quite enough in just three years for anyone not an Anabaptist. But in January 1551 Martin Bucer sent Cranmer a comprehensive criticism of his Prayer Book, calling for further changes: the total elimination of the words "may be to us the Body and Blood of the Lord," along with omission of the sign of the cross at the consecration, and the abolition of vestments as Hooper had demanded. John Calvin also wrote to Cranmer urging him to move faster and go further: "Do not slumber at ease! Do not imagine you have reached the goal!" In April the young king added his voice, calling for a revision of the Book of Common Prayer.[199]

Cranmer made no response for almost a year; then in March 1552 the Second Act of Uniformity, calling for revision of the Book of Common Prayer, was introduced in Parliament. Calvin pressed Cranmer again on April 1, 1552, saying that "the remaining popish corruptions in the present Book [of Common Prayer] were so many as almost to overwhelm the pure worship of God." But Cranmer already had what Calvin wanted. On April 6 Cranmer laid before the Lords his radically Protestant Second Prayer Book. All references to the sacraments of confirmation, extreme unction (anointing of the sick), and marriage were dropped, along with all references to altars and prayers for the dead, marking a complete change in traditional burial ceremonies. Most vestments were eliminated. The Mass was called the Lord's Supper throughout and the Real Presence effectively denied by the rubrics. The words "this is My Body" and "this is the chalice of My Blood" were omitted. The prescribed words on reception of Communion were changed from "the body of Our Lord Jesus Christ, which was given for thee" to "take and eat this in remembrance that Christ died for thee, and feed on Him in thy heart by faith." For the first time it was explicitly required that everyone attend Anglican services with the new prayer book every Sunday in church, where their presence could be recorded. Those attending unapproved services were liable to imprisonment from six months to life. Still faithful Catholics were to have no escape. The bill became law April 14. Only two bishops voted against it.[200]

---

[198] Ridley, *Cranmer*, pp. 311-312; Duffy, *Stripping of the Altars*, p. 472; Hughes, *Reformation in England*, II, 120-121; Jordan, *Edward VI, Threshold of Power*, pp. 267-268.

[199] Messenger, *Reformation, Mass, Priesthood* I, 510-515 (first quote on 513); Jordan, *Edward VI, Threshold of Power*, pp. 343 (second quote), 364-365. Martin Bucer's appeal for a revision of the Book of Common Prayer in January 1551 was his last public act. He died the next month, having been a central figure in the Protestant revolt in four nations— Germany, Switzerland, France, and England (Jordan, *op. cit.*, p. 326).

[200] Jordan, *Edward VI, Threshold of Power*, pp. 325 (first quote), 347-350; Messenger, *Reformation, Mass, Priesthood*, I, 519-527 (second and third quotes on 526); Hughes, *Reformation in England*, II, 122-124, 126; Duffy, *Stripping of the Altars*, pp. 473-475; Ridley, *Cranmer*, pp. 326-327.

One important change in the new Book of Common Prayer was made soon after its issuance. John Knox, back from the galleys and now an active Protestant preacher in England, brought to court in London by Warwick/Northumberland, noted that despite elimination of all language attesting to the Real Presence, it still required kneeling at Communion. He demanded removal of this requirement. The Privy Council sought a compromise. On October 27 it voted to retain the requirement for kneeling at Communion but to add a statement (probably drafted by Cranmer) to the revised Prayer Book explicitly denying the Real Presence—the only explicit denial of it in the Book of Common Prayer. Catholics and Anglo-Catholics called it "the black rubric":[201]

> It is not meant thereby [by receiving communion kneeling] that any adoration is done or ought to be done either unto the sacramental bread or wine there being bodily received, or unto any real or essential presence there being of Christ a natural flesh and blood. For as concerning the sacramental bread and wine, they remain still in their very natural substances, and therefore may not be adored.[202]

On November 1, 1552 the Second Act of Uniformity came into effect throughout England. Edward VI was now fifteen years old, but there was almost nothing of the boy in him; already he was cold and merciless, and showed every sign of developing into as absolute a tyrant as history has ever known. For several years he had kept a detailed, remarkably literate and intelligent diary which demonstrated, in the words of his admiring modern biographer, that his "root concern" was "with the maintenance of the structure of royal power." But his last entry was November 28. Suddenly his tomorrows had become yesterdays, his glittering prospects of unlimited rule over his countrymen for a full lifetime transformed into a fading dream. For Edward VI was mortal; he had tuberculosis, and it would kill him, soon.[203]

There are distinct indications, though no explicit statement, that the leaders of England's government were aware of the gravity of young Edward's condition as soon as he was. In January 1553 the Duke of Northumberland, effectively the head of state, wrote to Cecil saying he intended to stay away from court for some weeks, and that he had little reason to wish to live longer. When Parliament met later that month, Cecil rather than Northumberland or the Royal Council prepared its agenda. William Cecil was beginning to reveal his skills, which he would so often demonstrate during the ensuing forty-five years, in operating coolly and decisively behind the scenes, of taking charge in someone else's name without appearing to the public to be doing so.[204]

---

[201] Ridley, *Knox*, pp. 104, 107, 112-114; Ridley, *Cranmer*, pp. 336-338; Hughes, *Reformation in England*, II, 124-125, 137; Jordan, *Edward VI, Threshold of Power*, pp. 351-352; Messenger, *Reformation, Mass, Priesthood*, I, 530-531.

[202] Jordan, *Edward VI, Threshold of Power*, p. 352.

[203] *Ibid.*, pp. 23, 26 (for quote), 352.

[204] *Ibid.*, pp. 497, 501; Read, *Cecil*, p. 80.

In May Edward's doctors predicted his death within three months. Preparation of a successor was urgently necessary. On May 21 Northumberland arranged the marriage of his son Guildford Dudley to 16-year-old Lady Jane Grey, granddaughter of Henry VIII's late sister Mary. Cecil refused to support her as queen, believing (rightly, as events were to show) that few of the nobles and people of England would accept her. On June 11 Edward himself appeared upon the scene, utterly determined to deny the succession to his half-sister simply and solely because she was a Catholic. Wracked with coughing, spitting black phlegm, this boy of sixteen called in Cecil to help him draft a decree altering the royal succession to exclude both his half-sisters and convey the throne to Jane Grey. Cecil would not do it; such a law must be enacted by Parliament (which had adjourned), not by the King and his staff on their own. Edward would not listen to him. He had the decree drafted by someone else and ordered Cecil to sign it on pain of death, which he did. The dying Edward then called a meeting with the Royal Council and several judges and similarly bullied them into assenting to the illegal decree. Cranmer signed it after being assured that all the others had.[205]

On July 4 Northumberland summoned Princesses Mary and Elizabeth to court. Elizabeth did not respond. Mary started, but moved very slowly. Two days later Edward died. Mary learned of it that very night, and set out in the darkness with an escort of only six men, riding north to the Newmarket-Thetford road, which skirts London widely and goes straight to Yarmouth, where she could easily embark for the continent. All night she rode up the long straight road, covering twenty miles until stopping to rest at the home of a loyal Catholic, John Huddleston, where she arranged for a Mass at dawn. She rode on in disguise, guided by a servant of Huddleston, covering forty miles that day. On the 8th the death of Edward was publicly announced for the first time. The following day was a Sunday; Bishop Ridley of London denounced Mary in an "intemperate and almost hysterical sermon" while John Knox in the Chiltern Hills cried "woe against England if she allies herself with the enemies of the Gospel." On the 10th Jane Grey was crowned Queen under heavy guard at the Tower of London. On the same day, still on the road north, Mary Tudor, daughter of Henry VIII and Catherine of Aragon, granddaughter of Queen Isabel the Catholic of Spain, proclaimed herself Queen.[206]

Mary Tudor had lived with tragedy and terror ever since her father put away her mother and proclaimed her a bastard. Anne Boleyn had hated her and wanted to kill her. As England moved more and more toward radical Protestantism, Mary had been pressured and persecuted for her faith, especially since the adoption of the Book of Common Prayer effectively eliminated the Mass in England. Despite repeated attempts by Emperor Charles V to protect her, the government would not guarantee Mary's right even to a Mass inside her own dwelling, and repeatedly threatened to deny it to her. When in May 1550

---

[205] Jordan, *Edward VI, Threshold of Power*, pp. 326-327, 503-504, 513-516.
[206] *Ibid.*, pp. 519-523 (quotes on 521); Prescott, *Mary Tudor*, pp. 170-173.

Charles V recalled his able ambassador to England, van der Delft, it was intended for him to take Mary secretly out of the country with him; when that plan failed, an elaborate attempt was made to get her away by sea, but various misadventures befell the rescuers, Mary lost her nerve, and the escape attempt had to be abandoned. In March 1551, when she made a rare appearance at court, Edward told her to her face that he was revoking her permission to have Mass in her house, though late in April Bishops Cranmer and Ridley persuaded the young king to renew the permission temporarily so as not to give still greater offense to the Emperor.[207] Emperor Charles well knew the peril in which his cousin stood; on June 30, 1551 he suddenly rounded on the English ambassador at his court in blazing anger:

> Ought it not to suffice you that you spill your own souls, but that you have a mind to force others to lose theirs too? My cousin, the Princess, is evil handled among you; her servants plucked from her, and she still cried to leave Mass, to forsake her religion in which her mother, her grandmother, and all her family have lived and died.[208]

But the coalition that was to bring Charles so low the following year was already building, and the English government knew it. Since France under Henry II was about to go to war with the Emperor, France was less likely to attack England and England therefore had less need for the Emperor's support and less reason to avoid offending him. On August 29 Chancellor Rich (he who had betrayed St. Thomas More) carried a letter to Mary from young King Edward VI ordering her to end all Masses at her residence. Perusing the letter, Mary said: "Ah, good master Cecil took much pains here." She was evidently aware of Cecil's growing though silent influence in the government in favor of the Protestant cause. She resisted as strongly as she could, Charles again intervened vigorously on her behalf, and finally an arrangement was made whereby she was allowed to continue having Mass said in her residence, but without public notice and none but she allowed to attend it.[209]

Now she was free and ready to challenge her tormentors, not only for herself, but for the whole future of the Catholic Faith among the English-speaking peoples; and the people were with her. Few had even heard of Lady Jane Grey before that summer; the public had only recently learned of Edward's mortal illness, and they assumed Mary to be the rightful heir, putting no stock in the law declaring her illegitimate. Furthermore, Northumberland as regent had become very unpopular. In a village near Grantham in Lincolnshire July 11 Constable Richard Troughton, told by a man just returned from London of the death of the king and that Northumberland was about to pursue Princess Mary,

---

[207] Prescott, *Mary Tudor*, pp. 124-129, 137-149, 154-155; Jordan, *Edward VI, Threshold of Power*, pp. 257-260; Ridley, *Cranmer*, p. 318.

[208] Prescott, *Mary Tudor*, p. 158.

[209] *Ibid.*, pp. 161-163; Jordan, *Edward VI, Threshold of Power*, pp. 138, 261-263 (quote on 262); Ridley, *Cranmer*, p. 319.

later gave testimony that "I drew my dagger in the sight of the said John Dove and James Pratt, and wished [it] at the villain's [Northumberland's] heart, with my hand at it, as hard as I could thrust, suddenly, face to face, body to body . . . and prayed God to save the Queen's Majesty and deliver Her Grace from him."[210]

On the 14th Northumberland marched from London, but with only two thousand men, and as he himself despairingly commented, "the people press to see us, but not one saith God speed us."[211] Cecil helped prevent reinforcements from reaching Northumberland. More and more leaders endorsed Mary— amazingly, even the vehemently Protestant foe of vestments, Bishop Hooper. On the 17th, shortly after his departure from Cambridge, Northumberland's troops refused to march further with him. The Earl of Oxford joined Mary with a substantial force of armed men. On the 19th the Royal Council abruptly changed sides, Jane Grey's father surrendered the Tower of London without a fight, and Mary was proclaimed Queen in London before an enormous crowd. Convinced that God had called her to restore the Catholic Faith to England, her first act as queen was to order the erection of a crucifix in the chapel of Framlingham Castle where she was temporarily lodged.[212]

Northumberland was arrested, stoned in the streets of London, and imprisoned in the Tower, where he was executed a month later after declaring his return to the Catholic religion.[213] There was rejoicing especially in Ireland, where the priests at Kilkenny joined the faithful in the taverns to celebrate.[214] After nineteen years during which England had broken from Christendom, gone from schism to heresy, stripped its centuries-old altars and martyred their last defenders, she now had a chance to restore what had been lost. But England had gone far astray, and the road back would be very hard. Would Mary, for so long a lone and frightened woman protected only by her distant cousin Charles V, whom she had never even met, be equal to the daunting task of leading her people along that road?

---

[210] Prescott, *Mary Tudor*, p. 175.

[211] Beer, *Northumberland*, p. 156 (for the quote); Jordan, *Edward VI, Threshold of Power*, p. 527.

[212] Jordan, *Edward VI, Threshold of Power*, pp. 176-177, 527-530; Prescott, *Mary Tudor*, pp. 178-180, 182; Read, *Cecil*, p. 99.

[213] Jordan, *Edward VI, Threshold of Power*, pp. 363-363, 530; Prescott, *Mary Tudor*, p. 181. Whether Northumberland's conversion was sincere or an attempt to secure a last-minute pardon is still debated.

[214] Myles V. Ronan, *Reformation in Dublin 1536-58* (New York, 1926), pp. 391-393.

5
The Calvinist Revolutionaries
1553-1562
Popes Julius III (1550-1555), Paul IV (1555-1559), and Pius IV (1559-1565)

"As for the certainty of our faith, whereof the story of the Church does speak, it is a thing of all others most necessary; and if it shall hang upon an Act of Parliament, we have but a weak staff to lean unto. . . . For we see than oftentimes that which is established by Parliament one year is abrogated the next year following, and the contrary allowed. And we see also that one king disallows the statutes made under the other. But our faith and religion ought to be most certain, and one in all times, and in no condition wavering. . . . This we know, that this doctrine and form of religion, which this bill propounds to be abolished and taken away, is that which our forefathers were born, brought up, and lived in, and have professed here in this realm [England] without any alteration or change, by the space of nine hundred years and more, and has also been professed and practiced in the Universal Church of Christ since the apostles' time. And that which we go about to establish and place for it is lately brought in, allowed nowhere nor put in practice but in this realm only, and that but a small time, and against the minds of all Catholic men."—Bishop Cuthbert Scott of Chester, speaking to the House of Lords against the bill to abolish the Mass in England for a second time, April 27, 1558[1]

"I must confess that I am thereof guilty but not thereby at fault and thereto I will stand as long as I shall live."—William Cecil, Secretary of State of England, to Nicholas Throckmorton regarding statements by the Spanish ambassador to England that he was "the author of the change in religion" of England in 1559, July 15, 1561[2]

"If we regard the distance of things (as we must, when there is a question of His corporeal presence, and of His humanity considered separately), we say that His body is as far removed from the bread and wine as is heaven from earth."—Theodore Beza (Calvinist) to the Colloquy of Poissy in France, September 9, 1561; "Oh, that he had been mute or we had been deaf!"—

---

[1] Ernest C. Messenger, *The Reformation, the Mass, and the Priesthood* (London, 1937), II, 208-209.

[2] Conyers Read, *Mr. Secretary Cecil and Queen Elizabeth* (New York, 1961), p. 128.

comment of the Cardinal of Lorraine on these words of Beza, September 10, 1561[3]

By 1553 John Calvin had been in full control of the city of Geneva for a decade, and was to maintain unchallenged mastery there for more than another decade to come. From the beautiful lake city at the crossroads of Europe, close to the line separating speakers of French from those of German, his influence fanned out all across the continent through the ardent young men who came to Geneva to see and study in what they believed to be the ideal Protestant commonwealth, and Protestant refugees seeking a safe haven from which they could recoup their fortunes and try again to destroy the ancient faith in their homelands. Calvin always counselled against violent popular revolution, though he was willing to consider the overthrow of a reigning king if a case could be made for it under existing law, and accept a revolutionary regime after it took power. Many of his followers were not so scrupulous. Calvin might privately reprove them, but usually did not publicly condemn them. He was perhaps a reluctant revolutionary, but his impact upon Christendom was indubitably revolutionary, and provides the key to understanding the critical last nine years before the long-delayed final session of the Council of Trent began. By that time, not only had Lutheranism triumphed in more than half of Germany, but still more radical Calvinism had triumphed in Scotland and was bidding strongly for power in both France and England. The crippled, exhausted Emperor Charles V had abdicated and died in a monastery in Spain, but his son Philip II of Spain had taken up the torch of leadership for the Catholic cause and begun his forty-year duel with William Cecil for the future of Christendom. At this period it was still possible for either side in the immense religious struggle to win complete, or nearly complete victory. There was nothing fated about the cleaving of Christendom that finally resulted.

Indeed, in 1553 Catholic prospects seemed to have brightened immensely with the advent of Mary Tudor as Queen of England. No soul in Europe, man or woman, lay or religious, was more totally devoted to the Catholic Faith than this small red-haired granddaughter of Isabel the Catholic, who saw her mother Catherine of Aragon as a martyr for the Faith, and had herself suffered for it all her adult life.[4] Nor did she stand alone. Despite the maximum efforts of Protestant propagandists against her, she had far more popularity in England than

---

[3] Donald Nugent, *Ecumenism in the Age of the Reformation; the Colloquy of Poissy* (Cambridge MA, 1974), pp. 99-100 (first quote), 104 (second quote).

[4] See Chapter Four, above. The best description of Queen Mary Tudor comes (as so often in the history of the 16th century) from an ambassador of Venice, Giacomo Soranzo, in a report written during 1554: "She is of low stature, with a red and white complexion, and very thin; her eyes are light and large, and her hair reddish; her face is round, the nose rather low and wide, and were not her age on the decline, she might be called handsome . . . . She is of very spare diet, and never eats till 1 or 2 p.m., although she rises at daybreak, when, after saying her prayers and hearing Mass in private, she transacts business incessantly, until after midnight." (Martin Haile, *Life of Reginald Pole* [New York, 1910], pp. 434-435)

most historians since have appreciated. She had the full support of the Emperor and of Pope Julius III. She would never yield an inch on any fundamentally Catholic issue while breath remained in her body. But she was 37 years old and had never married. She must marry and conceive quickly (for women in those days often reached menopause in their early forties), or her half-sister Elizabeth, daughter of Henry VIII and Anne Boleyn, would succeed her—and Elizabeth's title to the throne depended on the validity of a marriage which no Catholic could ever recognize. If she were to reign, it could only be as a Protestant.

Charles V and his son Philip understood the situation perfectly. Almost immediately on the arrival of the news of Mary's enthronement, from Brussels where he was currently residing, Charles wrote to Philip suggesting that he marry the new Queen of England. "The advantages of this course," he said, "are so obvious that it is unnecessary to go into them." Obviously he was confident that his son would understand and agree, as indeed he did, in just three weeks. As for Mary, on August 2 she told the imperial ambassador in England that she had long regarded Charles "as a father" and in her marriage would "follow his advice and choose whomsoever he might recommend." Consequently there was never any real doubt that the marriage would take place, despite the disparity in age (Philip was eleven years younger than Mary), nationalistic objections from English leaders and some of the people, and intrigues by the French who were at war with Spain and did not want England allied with Europe's leading power. On October 29 Queen Mary summoned the imperial ambassador to her oratory and pledged her troth to Prince Philip before the Blessed Sacrament, declaring her conviction that this marriage was inspired by God.[5]

Later historians have felt very much otherwise. In the words of Queen Mary's most recent biographer, "if there has been one unanimous judgment upon the reign of Mary, it has been that the Spanish marriage was an unmitigated disaster."[6] Now let this negative unanimity cease: this historian firmly believes that Queen Mary's acceptance of Philip II of Spain as her husband was the best possible decision she could have made under all the circumstances. If only she had been able to conceive a child, it would have changed the whole history of Christendom and the world, very much for the better from the Catholic standpoint. Hear her generally sympathetic biographer H. F. M. Prescott make the solid case for Queen Mary's Spanish marriage, though perversely he rejects his own excellent arguments:

> Only Spanish orthodoxy, she believed, was sufficiently untainted to rid
> England of heresy; only the power of Spain was enough to defend her against
> France and that other enemy at England's back door—Scotland. More
> legitimately she reasoned that to bear a child would rid her from the fear of

---

[5] David Loades, *The Reign of Mary Tudor*, 2nd ed. (London, 1991), pp. 58-61 (second quote on 60); Philip Hughes, *The Reformation in England* (London, 1953), II, 203-204 (first quote on 203n); E. Harris Harbison, *Rival Ambassadors at the Court of Queen Mary* (Princeton, 1940), pp. 87-88.

[6] Loades, *Reign of Mary Tudor*, pp. 396-397.

rival claimants, and that a husband would relieve her of the intolerable burden of suspicion and bewilderment under which she labored in public business, and would stand between her and treacherous or quarrelsome councillors. . . . The advantages which [imperial ambassador] Renard had hymned to her, were not so chimerical in the eyes of the sixteenth century as they seem to us. Besides the support of a husband, the close protective alliance of Spain, the son to succeed her and confirm her work, he promised to that son a mighty inheritance—England and the Low Countries for certain; if Philip's son Don Carlos died, then Spain, Naples and the Indies as well.[7]

On August 5 the news of Mary's enthronement came to Rome. Pops Julius III wept for joy, and immediately appointed Cardinal Reginald Pole—exiled by Henry VIII at the time of the martyrdom of More and Fisher and subsequently threatened with assassination by English agents, almost elected Pope in 1550—as legate to England to bring his nation back into the Church.[8] On August 27 he wrote her that renunciation of her title as head of the Church in England and submission to the authority of the Pope was her first duty as queen, coming before even her marriage and political settlement of the kingdom.) Charles V did not agree with that, and neither even did Mary, who wrote to the Pope September 11 saying that the time was not yet ripe for Pole's coming, and a few days later told Pole's emissary Henry Penning that "she would give half of her kingdom to have a legate in the country, but that the heretics were capable of anything" and it was not yet safe to have him. Regarding her title of "supreme head of the church in England," she said to Penning: "I do not wish it, even though by it I could gain three other kingdoms" and said she had resolved to ask/Parliament to suspend the law of royal supremacy in the church along with the laws which had deprived her mother of the queenship.[9] Parliament convened October 5 and quickly repealed the annulment of Henry VIII's marriage to Catherine (with a scathing aside on the conduct and character of Cranmer, now confined in the Tower of London where he had put so many others). Though Mary was not yet able to persuade the House of Commons to take up the issue of her headship of the church in England, Parliament did repeal all the religious legislation in the reign of Edward VI, allowing Mass to be said again in England, with only 80 out of the 350 members of the House of Commons voting against it.[10]

No better proof of the value of the much-abused Spanish marriage of Queen Mary could be adduced than her inability, even when at the height of her early popularity, to divest herself of the sacrilegious title "supreme head of the church

---

[7] H. F. M. Prescott, *Mary Tudor* (New York, 1953), pp. 255-256.

[8] Ludwig von Pastor, *History of the Popes*, Volume XIII (St. Louis, 1924), pp. 248-250. For the earlier history of Cardinal Pole see Chapter Four, above.

[9] Loades, *Reign of Mary Tudor*, pp. 67, 125-126; Hughes, *Reformation in England*, II, 216-217; Haile, *Pole*, pp. 392-394; von Pastor, *History of the Popes*, XIII, 253 (first quote); Messenger, *Reformation, Mass and Priesthood*, II, 37 (second quote).

[10] Loades, *Reign of Mary Tudor*, p. 104; Jasper Ridley, *Thomas Cranmer* (Oxford, 1962), pp. 355-356; von Pastor, *History of the Popes*, XIII, 255; Messenger, *Reformation, Mass and Priesthood* II, 41-42.

of England" until Prince Philip had arrived to help her do so. The Spanish marriage treaty was made public in mid-January 1554. There was considerable public opposition, abetted by hostile France, culminating in a rebellion, named for Thomas Wyatt of Kent since his force actually reached London, where it was soundly defeated on Ash Wednesday by Mary's own undaunted courage in refusing to leave the city and personal appeal to the people of the city to come to her aid, which they did with no less than 20,000 armed men. After some delay Philip arrived at the English port of Southampton July 20, and three days later met his bride for the first time in a second-story gallery in Winchester during an evening of pouring rain, where they conversed, she in French which he understood but did not speak well, he in his native Spanish which she understood (from her mother) but did not speak. Two days later they were married. Queen Mary, starved for love since her mother's death eighteen long years before, was totally devoted to Philip; he did not love her in return, and did not like England, but resolutely did his duty by this marriage so important for the Catholic Church. By November Mary believed she was pregnant. When Parliament convened November 12, Pope Julius III had agreed to make no effort to recover the Church property seized and sold by Thomas Cromwell, and Parliament was ready to proceed to the great reconciliation.[11]

Its session began with a Mass of the Holy Spirit at Westminster Abbey, in which prayers were officially made for the Pope for the first time since Henry VIII broke with him. Bishop Stephen Gardiner, whom Queen Mary had released and made her Chancellor, proclaimed that it had been summoned "for confirmation of true religion."[12] Prince Philip, probably speaking in Latin, made his first major address to his wife's countrymen and their representatives:

> Your ancestors lived and died in the profession of the Catholic religion, and in obedience to the Roman Church, that Christian brotherhood whose multitude are joined as witnesses of the same Jesus Christ in unity of faith, legitimately ordained, which unites the people to the priest as the flock of sheep to the shepherd. This, according to the evidence of the New Testament, is our Catholic Church, which had its origin in Jerusalem, and scattered through the world, increased, glorious and manifest, mingling the good and the bad, holy in faith and sacraments, of apostolic origin and succession, with catholic amplitude, one by union of its members, of perpetual duration . . .
>
> The temporal government is not fit for divinity, like the divine worship and the keeping of the heavenly precepts, which make the being and power of the king participants . . . of the being and power of God; and he, to sustain it worthily, asks favor of Heaven, and to keep it obeys the Vicar of Jesus Christ, the Roman pontiff. Of the king's ruling function and office the only

---

[11] Loades, *Reign of Mary Tudor*, pp. 74-75, 79-80, 95, 158, 163-165, 266; Prescott, *Mary Tudor*, pp. 247-248, 251-254, 279-283, 294; Harbison, *Rival Ambassadors*, pp. 108, 125, 132-134.

[12] James A. Muller, *Stephen Gardiner and the Tudor Reaction* (New York, 1970), p. 262.

end is not majesty, wealth and dominion; but rather God and His holy law, and the accomplishment of his precepts, dying for it if necessary.

The mercy of God now calls you to return, through obedience to the Roman pontiff, to the flock of Jesus Christ, incorporating yourselves in His Catholic Church. Vote for this measure, and may God enlighten your understanding and move your hearts.[13]

By these words Prince Philip also indicated the kind of king he intended to be, for Spain and the other lands he ruled, and for England as husband of the Queen.

On November 20 Cardinal Pole landed at Dover with his legatine commission from Pope Julius III. On the 24th the aged Bishop of Durham, Cuthbert Tunstall, the last survivor still in office of Henry VIII's bishops when he broke from the Catholic Church, presented the legate with a golden impression under the Great Seal of England certifying the repeal of all laws passed against Pole in the two preceding reigns. Prince Philip met Pole at the top of the steps from the Thames River to Westminster, embraced him, and bearing a silver cross, led him through the King's Hall where Queen Mary awaited him at the top of the stairs, "radiantly happy," to bow to him and then kiss him, and walked away with Philip at her left hand and Pole at her right. On the 28th the Cardinal Legate addressed Parliament, urging reunion with the Pope, reviewing England's long history of loyalty to the Church, the loss of that loyalty due to "a criminal passion," and its imminent restoration by a faithful queen. The next day Parliament voted to rejoin the Catholic Church and ask absolution from the legate for their schism—unanimously in the House of Lords, and with all but two of the members of the House of Commons present voting yes as well. Speaking before blazing torches on the last evening of November, Cardinal Pole read his bull from the Pope giving him authority to absolve and reconcile and then exercising that authority, thanking God for this moment. Mary and Philip knelt before him; tears of joy streamed down Mary's face. It must have seemed that all her cross-bearing life had pointed to this moment.[14]

The following Sunday, December 2, Bishop Gardiner preached at St. Paul's Cross, the principal preaching church in London, to an audience estimated at 25,000. For all his courage in defying the religious revolutionaries during the reign of Edward VI, for all his unyielding defense of the Real Presence at Mass, Stephen Gardiner had much to answer for. He had been one of the architects of the English schism, one of the most enthusiastic supporters of Henry VIII's "great matter"—the project of ridding himself of his lawful Catholic wife to marry Anne Boleyn.[15] Gardiner was a proud man, considered by his many critics proud to a fault. Yet he could apologize and repent, though all history shows

---

[13] William T. Walsh, *Philip II* (New York, 1937), pp. 145-146.

[14] *Ibid.*, pp. 146-148; von Pastor, *History of the Popes*, XIII, 284-286; Hughes, *Reformation in England*, II, 225-226; Haile, *Pole*, pp. 444-452; Loades, *Reign of Mary Tudor*, pp. 265-267; Prescott, *Mary Tudor*, pp. 294-295; Muller, *Gardiner*, p. 263.

[15] See Chapter Three, above.

how rarely leaders in human society are willing to apologize and repent. He preached on the text "now is the time to arouse from sleep."

> Now also it is time that we awake out of our sleep, who have slept or rather dreamed these twenty years past. For as men intending to sleep do separate themselves from company and desire to be alone, even so we have separated ourselves from the See of Rome, and have been alone, no realm in Christendom like us; as in sleep men dream of killing, maiming, burning, and such beastliness as I dare not name, so among us one brother has destroyed another. . . . Even now hath the Pope's Holiness sent unto us this most reverend father, the Cardinal [Pole], not to revenge injuries done by us against His Holiness, but to give his benediction to those that defamed and persecuted him. Rejoice in this day, that such a noble birth is come . . . It is time for us also to awake—not for the Queen, nor the King, nor my Lord Cardinal, who have never fallen asleep—but for us, us—I do not exclude myself from the number. I acknowledge my fault, and exhort all who have fallen into this sleep through me or with me, with me to awake![16]

On December 14 the great news reached Rome. Pope Julius III embraced its bearer, and fell immediately on his knees to say the Our Father, followed by a Mass of thanksgiving in the chapel of St. Andrew, on whose feast the great event had occurred, and proclaimed many celebrations of it.[17]

Three months later he was dead at 67, having been much afflicted by gout and fatally weakened by a "starvation cure."[18]

The conclave to elect his successor began April 5, with only 37 of the 57 cardinals present, many of the absentees being from France. News of Pope Julius' death had not yet even reached England, and even if it had Cardinal Pole, being seriously ill, could not have come, though Emperor Charles V had instructed his ambassador in Rome to seek support for Pole over all other candidates for the Papacy. In any case Pole, a few days later, declared that his conscience would not allow him to attend the conclave in view of the enormous importance of his presence in England as it re-entered the Catholic Church.[19]

Attempts at the conclave by Cardinal d'Este of Ferrara, known both for his negotiating skills and for his lack of principle, to secure election as Pope were futile, and on April 9 Cardinal Marcello Cervini, an active reformer (he was president of the commission on Church reform appointed by Pope Julius III) who had been the leading legate at the first session of the Council of Trent, was

---

[16] Muller, *Gardiner*, pp. 265-266.

[17] Von Pastor, *History of the Popes*, XIII, 288-289.

[18] *Ibid.*, XIII, 154.

[19] Ludwig von Pastor, *History of the Popes*, Vol. XIV (St. Louis, 1924), pp. 4-6; Haile, *Cardinal Pole*, p. 461; Loades, *Reign of Mary Tudor*, p. 295. The type of historian who always tends to think the worst of Emperor Charles V, or to regard him as more Machiavellian than Catholic, and consequently highlights his occasional clashes with Cardinal Pole (whom no one could possibly call Machiavellian) is at a loss to comprehend this instant total support for the high-minded and pure-hearted Cardinal by Charles V, and so can only ignore it, as virtually all of them do.

elected Pope by an overwhelming margin. Like Adrian VI 33 years before, he kept his own name as Pope, declaring that he would be known as Marcellus II.[20]

The election of a man so well known for his probity, charity, learning, and commitment to reform was welcomed by nearly everyone, and with the greatest enthusiasm by those most dedicated to Catholic reformation. Great things were expected of him, and he began to fulfill the expectations by refusing special favors to the cardinals following his election and by letting it be known that he would demand the residence of all bishops in their dioceses (and therefore an end to pluralism of dioceses) and would give no high Church office to any of his relatives. But suddenly, shockingly, his supremely but dauntingly high office proved beyond his strength. Just eleven days after his consecration he became unable to conduct religious ceremonies or hold audiences; a week later he was unable to engage in any serious work; on April 30 he hd a stroke in his sleep. The next day he died. He was only 53 years old.[21]

Just eight days after Pope Marcellus II's death, Queen Mary of England went into seclusion to await the birth of the child she was convinced she carried in her womb, and remained out of sight of the public (except for occasional appearances at a window) for the next three months). But her womb was empty; she was never to conceive a child. Unless she were completely unbalanced, her periods must have temporarily ceased; but it is known that false pregnancies can cause this, when they are the result of powerful psychological stress. Not only was the birth of an heir absolutely essential to preserve the newly restored Catholicity of England, but it was psychologically necessary for Mary, so long deprived of love, who knew that in the end she could hold Philip only with a child. Her subjects wanted an heir almost as much as she did; on April 30 a false rumor had swept London and even spread to the European continent that she had actually delivered a son that day. Everything depended on the coming of a child; but none came.[22]

The second conclave in two months convened May 15, with 43 of the 57 cardinals present, and two more allowed to enter on the next two days, for a total of 45. Once again, and for the same reason, Cardinal Pole did not feel that he should come. Though there was considerable support for him, it was not enough to elect him in his absence. Cardinal Jacopo Puteo, supported by the adherents of Emperor Charles V but opposed by the French and Alessandro Farnese, gained 25 of the necessary 30 votes but could get no more; as his total fell, that of Gian Pietro Carafa, Cardinal Archbishop of Naples, began to rise, supported by the French and Farnese and also by the able and highly regarded Cardinal Morone. By May 22 he had 28 votes. Farnese and Morone worked all night to get the last

[20] Von Pastor, *History of the Popes*, XIV, 7-11, 27.

[21] *Ibid.*, XIV, 13-14, 33-53.

[22] Prescott, *Mary Tudor*, pp. 297, 305, 312, 315; Harbison, *Rival Ambassadors*, p. 245. When she finally admitted there had been no pregnancy and returned to court in early August, William Cecil noted the fact in his journal, and his biographer Conyers Read believes that it was then that he concluded she would have no heir and Elizabeth would succeed her as Queen (Read, *Cecil*, pp. 111-112).

two votes, and by the morning of the 23rd they had finally succeeded. In the coming years they rued this day—especially Morone, whom Carafa as Pope held in prison for three years on false charges of heresy.[23]

Carafa took the name of Paul IV. As a man, he was a mass of contradictions. An extraordinary physical specimen, 79 years old, tall and thin but with a massive head, he was bursting with immense, protean energy despite his years. It was said he had hardly ever in his life so much as seen a doctor. Co-founder of one of the quietest and most retiring of religious orders, the Theatines, he was nevertheless a man of violent temper, given to explosive outbursts of rage and uncontrolled emotion of all kinds. Ever since the revolt of Luther he had been a dedicated, outspoken champion of thoroughgoing reform in the Church; his reputation as a reformer was the main reason for his election, for the relative weakness of Pope Julius III's commitment to reform was seen by many as a reproach on the Church, and Marcellus II had been elected primarily because he was known to be committed to reform. Paul IV's commitment to reform was real, but all too soon it became evident that he had the worst judgment of men and situations of any Pope since Urban VI in the time of the Great Western Schism. The evil consequences of his often spectacular lack of judgment were greatly compounded by his iron will and resistance to most outside persuasion. St. Ignatius of Loyola, in a clairvoyant moment, felt a trembling in every bone of his body when he heard of Carafa's election, fearing that his latent hostility to the Jesuits, which the saint had long sensed, would come out into the open and destroy their Society. It almost did.[24]

On May 26 Paul IV was crowned in a lavish ceremony, with much more pomp and display than had been expected in view of the new Pope's known abstemious nature. He declared his motto, the most militant chosen by any Pope: "Thou shalt walk upon the asp and the basilisk, and thou shalt trample underfoot the lion and the dragon." On June 7 he stunned the reformers by appointing his nephew Carlo Carafa a Cardinal, and soon also made him Secretary of State, controlling access to him. Carlo Carafa was an adventurer of scandalous personal life, a man recalling the Borgias, yet not until the last year of his near-disastrous pontificate did the Pope discover this. On June 26 he secretly began an investigation of Cardinal Morone for heresy; on July 14 he took severe and unjust measures against the Jews in Rome.[25]

Meanwhile the physically broken Emperor Charles V was preparing to lay down, one by one, the immense burdens of state he could no longer bear. Early in January 1555 his younger brother Ferdinand finally realized that Charles meant it when he said he could not attend the upcoming imperial Diet at Augsburg, that Ferdinand must represent him there and obtain a religious peace

---

[23] Von Pastor, *History of the Popes*, XIV, 56, 60-67; Loades, *Reign of Mary Tudor*, p. 179. See Note 60, below.

[24] Von Pastor, *History of the Popes*, XIV, 65-72, 246-247. For Urban IV see Volume III, Chapter 8 of this history.

[25] *Ibid.*, XIV, 73-74, 77 (the motto), 81-84, 272-273, 292n.

for Germany. Ferdinand opened the Diet February 5 with a moving speech deploring the profound and rapidly proliferating religious divisions in Germany, but no Protestant would now listen any plea for religious reunion; the failure of the Augsburg Interim had convinced them and most Germans that religious reunion was now impossible. On March 11 the Archbishop of Mainz, one of the seven imperial electors, instructed his representative at the Diet to accept Protestant demands for control of the churches under their political jurisdiction. A few days later all three Bishop-Electors joined in calling for a "perpetual peace" even without religious accommodation, thereby providing for the permanent religious division of Germany. Cardinal Truchsess of Augsburg walked out of the Diet in protest against this surrender, to no avail. By May most of the Catholics at the Diet had agreed to recognize the Lutheran seizure of all Church property in regions under their political jurisdiction, while still demanding, with Ferdinand, the prohibition of such seizure in the future (the so-called Ecclesiastical Reservation).[26]

This agreement was formalized on September 25 as the Religious Peace of Augsburg. Lutheran states were for the first time explicitly recognized as of equal legitimacy and sovereignty with Catholic states, and Catholic bishops were denied all authority in Lutheran states. All Church property seized by Protestants up to 1552 was to remain in the hands of those who had taken it, or their heirs and assigns. The religion of every state in the Empire was to be chosen by its sovereign. Those not willing to accept his religion could sell their property and leave their state, but if they remained within it they must conform. Catholic bishops and abbots who became Protestant in the future were to lose their positions, lands, and income (but the Protestants later refused to consent to this). An hour before all this was to be proclaimed as an imperial decree, a messenger arrived with a letter from Charles V declaring that he would soon abdicate, but until he did so, the Religious Peace with its recognition of Protestant sovereignty was not to be issued in his name. Ferdinand suppressed his brother's letter but stated that he needed to consult with him further before ratifying the Religious Peace, and adjourned the Diet. Though it long remained officially unratified, and was never accepted by the Pope, the Religious Peace of Augsburg was quickly accepted throughout Germany and became *de facto* law there.[27]

Just one month later came Emperor Charles' magnificent farewell, in the great hall of the palace at Brussels from which he governed the land where he had been born. Dressed head to foot in black, deathly pale, his beard snow-white, his sunken eyes strangely brilliant, wracked by pain, scarcely able to stand—he had to lean, while speaking, on the shoulder of William of Orange, who was later to betray his son and heir Philip II by leading the Dutch revolt

---

[26] Johannes Jansen, *History of the German People at the Close of the Middle Ages* (St. Louis, 1903), VI, 540-549, 556-562; Paula Fichtner, *Ferdinand I of Austria* (New York, 1982), pp. 210, 214-215.

[27] Von Pastor, *History of the Popes*, XIV, 341-343; Johannes Janssen, *History of the German People at the Close of the Middle Ages* (St. Louis, 1903), VI, 562-565, VII, 1-4; Fichtner, *Ferdinand I*, p. 216.

against him—the temporal head of Christendom, grandson of Isabel the Catholic, gave up the rule of his native Low Countries, recalled the mighty works of his long reign, expressed sorrow that he had not done even more and better, and called upon his son always to keep the Faith that he had kept.[28]

> I have gone nine times to Germany, six to Spain, seven to Italy, and I have come ten times here to Flanders; I have travelled, in war and in peace, four times to France, twice to England, and twice to Africa; making in all forty expeditions . . . I have journeyed eight times upon the Mediterranean, three times on the Ocean, and this will be the fourth, when I return to Spain to find my sepulchre . . .
> I have had to bear the burden of many wars, and this, as I can testify, against my will. Never have I undertaken them except under compulsion and with regret. Even today I grieve that I cannot on my departure leave you in peace and quiet . . . You may easily imagine that I have not undergone all this without feeling the burden and the fatigue. It is easy to judge of thee by the condition to which I am reduced. I have done what I could, and am sorry I could not do better. I have always known my insufficiency and incapacity .
> . .
> I beg you not to read into this resignation any thought of withdrawing myself from the eventualities of trouble, danger and toil; believe me, I have no other motive than the inconvenience attached to my powerless and crippled condition. I leave my son in my place, and commend him to you. Render to him the love and obedience which you have already shown towards me; preserve zealously that union among yourselves that you have never abandoned; sustain and maintain justice. Above all, do not permit the heresies which surround you to penetrate these lands, and if any such there are, let them be rooted out. . . .
> [Then, turning to Philip] My son, always honor religion; keep the Catholic Faith in all its purity; respect the laws of the country as sacred and inviolable, and never attempt to trespass on the rights ad privileges of your subjects.[29]

Tears streamed down the great Emperor's careworn cheeks as Philip fell on his knees before him to kiss his hand. Philip himself, and nearly everyone in the assembly, was weeping uncontrollably.[30] Well might Karl Brandi, Charles V's finest biographer, say:

> We may search the annals of history in vain for such another scene, for such another generation of princes as these of the Hapsburg dynasty, who were ready of their own free will to retire from the scene of their sovereignty. . . .

---

[28] Walsh, *Philip II*, pp. 166-167; Karl Brandi, *The Emperor Charles V* (Atlantic Highlands NJ, 1965), pp. 633-634; Ramón Menéndez Pidal, ed., *Historia de España*, Volume XXII (1), "España en Tiempo de Felipe II," by P. Luis Fernández y Fernández de Retana (Madrid, 1988), pp. 375-382 (see the portrait of Emperor Charles V at this time on p. 379).

[29] Walsh, *Philip II*, pp. 167-168.

[30] *Ibid.*, p. 168.

At what other time, in what other continent, was so great a scene so greatly played?[31]

Even after this, Charles had still two more royal renunciations to make. On January 16, 1556, in his private apartments in Brussels, he abdicated the thrones of Castile, Aragon, Sicily and the Indies to his son Philip II. On September 12, by private letter, he gave up the imperial throne to his brother Ferdinand, leaving him to choose the best time to announce it publicly. On September 28 Charles disembarked in Spain from his last voyage. On November 21 he arrived at the monastery of Yuste, where he would spend the brief remainder of his life in study, prayer and penance. His requiem came while he yet lived. In the imperishable words of St. Paul, he had fought the good fight, he had finished the course, he had kept the faith.[32]

In England, almost exactly contemporary with Charles V's abdications, Thomas Cranmer was dragging his compromised, sinuous life to its bitter end. Rarely has a man who once possessed such power and influence experienced so merciless a reckoning at the hands of the law and the church which his perjury had sullied and his apostasy had scourged.

On September 12 and 13, 1555, at St. Mary's Church in Oxford, he came to judgment. As a duly consecrated archbishop and metropolitan he was supposed to be tried by the Pope himself, but Paul IV delegated the trial to Cardinal Puteo, who in turn delegated it to Bishop Brooks of Gloucester. The charges against Cranmer included the perjury of his consecration oath, his defiance of the Pope, and his heresy regarding the Real Presence. The prosecution was conducted by an attorney named Martin, who eviscerated Cranmer on the witness stand in one of the classic cross-examinations in legal history, concerning his contradictory oaths at his consecration in 1536, one to obey the Pope, the other not to obey him if Henry VIII so ordered.[33]

> MARTIN. Sir, you that pretend to have such a conscience to break an oath: Pray you, did you never swear, and break the same?
> CRANMER. I remember not.
> MARTIN. I will help your memory. Did you never swear obedience to the See of Rome?
> CRANMER. Indeed I did once swear unto the same.
> MARTIN. Yea, that you did twice, as appeareth by records and writings here ready to be shown.
> CRANMER. But remember I saved all by protestation that I made by the counsel of the best learned men I could get at that time.
> MARTIN. Hearken, good people! what this man saith. He made a protestation one day, to keep never a whit of that which he would swear the

---

[31] Brandi, *Charles V*, pp. 634-635. Two of Charles' sisters, Mary who had ruled as regent of the Netherlands and Eleonor who had been Queen of France, were retiring also and returning to Spain with him.

[32] *Ibid.*, pp. 635-644. Charles died September 21, 1558.

[33] Ridley, *Cranmer*, pp. 371-372. See Chapter Three, above.

next day: was this the part of a Christian man? If a Christian man would bargain with a Turk, and before he maketh his bargain solemnly, before witness readeth in his paper that he holdeth secretly in his hand, or peradventure protesteth before one or two, that he mindeth not to perform whatsoever he shall promise to the Turk; I say, if a Christian man should serve a Turk in this manner, that the Christian man were worse than the Turk. What would you then say to this man that made a solemn oath and promise unto God and his Church, and made a protestation before quite contrary?

CRANMER. That which I did, I did by the best learned men's advice I could get at that time.[34]

(On December 4, 1555 Pope Paul IV pronounced Cranmer deposed as Archbishop of Canterbury and excommunicated, and handed him over to the state for due punishment.) On January 28, 1556 Cranmer sent for his jailer at Oxford, Woodson, telling him he was ready to recant. All day they argued over the terms of his recantation; by evening Cranmer told Woodson he still could not make up his mind what to say, and Woodson told him this was but another example of his dishonesty and insincerity. Cranmer fainted, then wept through the night and the next morning produced his first recantation, which said only that he would accept papal supremacy in the Church because the Queen ordered it. Informed that this was no true recantation (since it implied he would deny the Pope again if a Protestant succeeded to England's throne), he wrote a second recantation early in February accepting papal supremacy unconditionally. But when he was formally degraded from the archbishopric of Canterbury at Christ Church in Oxford February 14, he protested his sentence on the grounds that the Pope had no jurisdiction in England, in flat contradiction to his second recantation, and appealed to a future council in violation of canon law. Two days later he tried to persuade Bishop Bonner of London to accept a return to the terms of his first recantation. When Bonner refused, Cranmer wrote out a third (fourth?) recantation affirming his belief "in all articles and points of the Christian religion and Catholic faith, as the Catholic Church doth believed and hath ever believed." Totally unconvinced by this vague general assertion, Bishop Bonner (who was nobody's fool, and had been held in jail by Cranmer for many years) offered no objection when the royal council ordered Cranmer burned at the stake as an unrepentant heretic.[35]

But Brother John de Garcina, a gentle Spanish friar from the University of Valladolid recently appointed Regius Professor of Divinity at Oxford, still thought there was hope for Cranmer's soul. He now wrote out yet another recantation for Cranmer, declaring belief in the Real Presence and

---

[34] Hughes, *The Reformation in England* (5th ed.), I, 244n. John Foxe, the Protestant martyrologist, found this cross-examination of his hero so devastating that he insisted it must have been forged. Not a scintilla of evidence supports his claim, as modern Protestant historian and biographer Jasper Ridley admits (*Cranmer*, p. 376).

[35] Ridley, *Cranmer*, pp. 387-395 (quote on 394); von Pastor, *History of the Popes*, XIV, 376.

transubstantiation, in the other six sacraments, in papal supremacy, and in purgatory, and repudiating all Lutheran and Zwinglian heresies. Cranmer signed it on February 26; it was printed and copies distributed less than a week later. But suspicion lingered; the language of the document was not, after all, Cranmer's own. It would appear that the government postponed his scheduled execution after he had petitioned it that he was preparing yet another recantation, presumably this time of his own composition. Considerably more to the point than this parade of dubious documents was a dream Cranmer told of having on a troubled early March night, in which he saw Jesus Christ and Henry VIII contending for his soul.[36]

In mid-March the English government discovered the conspiracy of Henry Dudley, a relative of the Duke of Northumberland, Edward VI's last regent, to set fire to London, seize the royal treasury, flee to the Isle of Wight where French aid would be obtained (the French ambassador was involved in the plot and King Henry II of France hd approved of it), and from there promote a rising against Queen Mary with the goal of killing her and all foreigners with her and putting Elizabeth on the throne. Though there is no evidence that Cranmer was involved in the Dudley conspiracy, it is likely that its discovery helped cause the royal councillors to decide that no more recantations could save the former Archbishop of Canterbury. On March 18 he was told he would be executed in three days.[37]

Queen Mary let justice be done. This was the man whose illegal decision on her mother's marriage case had made her a bastard and taken England out of the Church, with world-shaking consequences that would echo down the centuries. Now he would pay the penalty.[38]

The news of the decision for his execution arrived just as Cranmer had finished drafting his next recantation, admitting grave offenses against the Church, responsibility for the illegal annulment of Henry VIII's marriage to Catherine, and blasphemy against the Holy Eucharist. He signed it, then drafted (with the aid of Brother John) a speech to be delivered at the stake, repudiating his "untrue books and writings" on the Eucharist and affirming the Real Presence. However, Cranmer refused to insert an Ave Maria after the Our Father at the beginning of the speech. For hours on March 20 the indefatigably charitable Brother John worked to persuade Cranmer to put the Ave Maria in. Finally he agreed, but then stopped signing copies of his final recantation.

---

[36] Ridley, *Cranmer*, pp. 395-399. It is significant that the fullest and best documented telling of this unedifying story comes from a historian who has little good to say of the Catholic Church, but knows and respects the facts in this case. The postponement of Cranmer's execution while preparing a last recantation is indicated only in a letter from the French ambassador.

[37] *Ibid.*, p. 379; Loades, *Reign of Mary Tudor*, pp. 182-184; Prescott, *Mary Tudor*, pp. 339-346; Haile, *Pole*, pp. 490-491; Harbison, *Rival Ambassadors*, pp. 286-287; Frederic J. Baumgartner, *Henry II, King of France* (Durham NC, 1988), p. 180.

[38] This is, of course, not a defense of the exceedingly painful method of execution— burning at the stake—but only of the justice of the death sentence, then universally used to punish the greatest crimes.

During his last night on earth he secretly drafted a new speech from the stake, repudiating all the recantations (which he said he had made only to try to save his life), excoriating the Pope and the Real Presence as a doctrine Christ would condemn at the Last Judgment. Then, at first light on the 21st, Cranmer arose and signed the remaining fourteen copies of his last recantation, delivering them to jailer Woodson with a promise that he would not retract them and a statement that they would serve as his defense if anyone said he had! Perhaps he was still hoping for a last-minute stay of execution; perhaps he actually did not yet know which speech he would read from the stake. The trimmer of Canterbury, until now always able to change sides in time, played both sides to the very end. But in the granddaughter of Isabel the Catholic he had at last found someone in authority whom he could not manipulate.[39]

It was raining hard that morning in Oxford, so the preliminary proceedings were held inside St. Mary's Church rather than at the stake. Brother John of Garcina, still believing Cranmer repentant, walked beside him in procession up the aisle, Cranmer with his beard falling nearly to his waist and tears running down his cheeks. The priest, Father Cole, received him as a genuine penitent and gave a homily welcoming his repentance but explaining why the sentence had to be carried out nevertheless. In the breast of his ragged gown Cranmer carried both his speeches, one of Catholic recantation and the other of Protestant defiance. When the homily ended, Cranmer made his decision, pulled out the Protestant speech, and proceeded to read it. The two statements were mostly the same up to the last paragraphs, so most of the audience had no idea at first what he planned to do; but Brother John knew something was amiss when he omitted the promised Ave Maria. But when he came to the words "as for the Pope, I refuse him as Christ's enemy and Antichrist, with all his false doctrine" a roar rose from the congregation, drowning out his denial of the Real Presence. Lord Williams shouted that he must be out of his mind (a possibility deserving of consideration at this point). Cranmer then literally ran out of the church toward the stake, pursued by Brother John alternately pleading for his reconsideration and reproaching him for his double tongue. On the way Cranmer gave out the texts of *both* his speeches, the Catholic and the Protestant; both were recovered and have survived, without signs of rain or mud, indicating that he put them directly into someone's hands as he ran past (why would he have wanted *both* to be preserved?). When the fire was kindled, Cranmer did indeed put into it first the hand which had signed his last recantation, but the fact that he had still been signing copies of it that very morning puts a somewhat different light on that celebrated act of his than the light in which it is usually seen.[40]

So died Thomas Cranmer at the age of 67, after Henry VIII the principal architect of the English schism and heresy, which in turn (as will be seen in the course of this volume) was the principal reason for the permanent cleaving of Christendom. On the following day Cardinal Pole was consecrated Archbishop

---

[39] Ridley, *Cranmer*, pp. 399-404.
[40] *Ibid.*, pp. 404-408.

of Canterbury by Archbishop Heath of York and Bishop Bonner of London, in the presence of the five now Catholic bishops of the province of Canterbury.[41]

During this year and the next (1556-57) occurred most of the executions for essentially religious reasons that brought down on Queen Mary's head the opprobrious nickname of "Bloody"—though few called her that during her lifetime except for the Calvinist revolutionaries, mostly in exile, who were working night and day for her overthrow.[42] Cranmer's parade of recantations, all false, had brought into disrepute the practice (followed consistently by the Spanish Inquisition) of sparing the lives and even restoring the liberty of heretics convicted for the first time if they would abjure their heresy.[43] Furthermore, the Spanish monarchy was far more stable at this point in history than the English; Wyatt's rebellion of 1554 and the Dudley conspiracy of 1556 were the most dangerous attempts to overthrow Queen Mary's government during her brief reign, but not the only ones. Her religious opponents, combining with those whose nationalism blinded them to the advantages of her Spanish marriage,[44] created a clear and present danger of revolt against her, just as Spain had faced in 1480 when Isabel the Catholic founded the Inquisition there.[45]

In this situation some executions of religious revolutionaries were inevitable and, by the standards of the time, justified. But Mary allowed too many of them. She was frightened and felt abandoned, especially after Prince Philip left England at the end of August 1555—with no indication when or even if he would return—to join his father in the Low Countries to accept their throne from him when he abdicated it in October, as already described. Her great chancellor Stephen Gardiner died of dropsy in November 1555 and no man of nearly comparable ability could be found to take his place.[46] Poor, isolated men—mere village ranters who could pose no serious threat to Queen Mary— were burned along with irreconcilable revolutionaries of the cloth such as former Bishops Ridley, Latimer, and Hooper. The total number of those burned has been reliably counted at 273, but the principal (and strongly biased) source for their story, Protestant John Foxe's *Book of Martyrs*, spends no less than two-thirds of its space on just 17 of them. Only 30 of the 273 were either clergymen

---

[41] Haile, *Pole*, pp. 484-485.

[42] See Hughes, *Reformation in England* (5th ed.), II, 277-285 for a thorough refutation of the widely held belief that the executions for heresy under Queen Mary led to a strong popular reaction against her. Virtually no historical evidence supports this belief, a striking example of the tendency of modern historians to assume that earlier ages would react to events as modern men would.

[43] Ridley, *Cranmer*, p. 384. For these procedures of the Spanish Inquisition, see Volume Three, Chapter 14 of this history.

[44] A type whose numbers among historians remain legion to this day; see Note 7, above.

[45] The seriousness of the danger of revolt was spelled out in detail in the report of the Venetian ambassador to England, Giovanni Michiel, in May 1557 (Haile, *Pole*, p. 508). For the founding of the Spanish Inquisition, see Volume Three, Chapter 14 of this history.

[46] Loades, *Mary Tudor*, pp. 166, 175; Prescott, *Mary Tudor*, p. 318; Muller, *Gardiner*, pp. 291-292.

or gentlemen. Of nearly 200 we know little if anything more than their names and occupations: of 59 reported by Foxe as burned in Kent, we know no more than the names of 52; of 52 burned in Essex, we know no more than the names of 30. A serious persecution aims at leaders, men of renown. And in the absence of information, we cannot be sure why the obscure victims were executed. But we do know that no defense was accepted that the accused had been raised and instructed as a Protestant, though there had been ample time since Henry VIII's break with the Church for a large number of English men and women in their twenties and thirties in the mid-1550's to fall into this category. The Spanish Inquisition had never had authority over practicing, publicly declared Jews and Muslims, but no such exception was made for equivalent English Protestants. On the other hand, it may well be that most of the victims were known in some way as revolutionaries.[47]

In any case, the total number of persons executed as heretics during Queen Mary's reign does not compare with those executed as loyal Catholics during the last dozen years of the reign of Henry VIII or during the 45-year reign of his daughter Elizabeth, despite the fact that Protestant historians have dubbed her "Good Queen Bess" in contrast to "Bloody Mary."

During the first year of his pontificate, from his coronation on May 26, 1555, Pope Paul IV generally seemed to be discharging his enormous responsibilities well. Though he showed no interest in reviving the Council of Trent, he pushed ahead vigorously with reform on his own, stepping up efforts to compel most of the bishops residing in Rome to return to and reside in their dioceses (though many still found excuses not to go) and establishing a 62-member commission to reform the Curia, with special instructions to get rid of simony. He also showed a particular interest in the work of the Inquisition in Rome and the papal state, frequently attending its weekly meetings. Though he several times displayed a passionate personal dislike of Spaniards in general and Emperor Charles V in particular, he allowed himself to be persuaded by his advisors not to challenge them openly.[48] He did everything for the Church in England that Queen Mary and Cardinal Pole asked him to do, and when he confirmed Pole's appointment as Archbishop of Canterbury in December 1555 he spoke "with the greatest praise of the Queen and the Cardinal, testifying to Pole's doctrine, goodness and integrity, which His Holiness said had been known to him for many years, and exalting his merits in the highest terms."[49] But in that same month he signed a secret treaty with France to cede Naples and Milan, now belonging to Charles V, to one of the sons of French King Henry II, and Sicily to Venice, and to expel the Medici (allies of Charles V) from Florence and annex Siena to the papal state.[50]

---

[47] Hughes, *Reformation in England* (5th ed.), II, 255-274, 288-293; Loades, *Reign of Mary Tudor*, pp. 273-288.

[48] Von Pastor, *History of the Popes*, XIV, 103-106, 186-187, 193-194, 234, 262-263.

[49] Haile, *Pole*, p. 479.

[50] Von Pastor, *History of the Popes*, XIV, 108-109; Brandi, *Charles V*, p. 632.

Then suddenly, explosively, on June 20, 1556 Pope Paul IV loosed a veritable tirade to the Venetian ambassador against Charles V—apparently oblivious to his recent abdications and his repeated declaration that he was about to lay down also the imperial authority which alone remained after he had given up the crowns of Spain and of the Low Countries. The Pope called Charles:

> . . . this heretic and schismatic who has always favored false doctrine in order to oppress the Holy See, and make himself master of Rome, for he not only regards this city as his own, but the whole of the States of the Church, and indeed all Italy, Venice included. . . . we shall then raise the whole world against him, deprive him of his imperial dignity and his kingdom, and let him see what we are able to perform by virtue of the authority of Christ.[51]

A few days later he actually went so far as to say that no worse man than Charles V had lived for a thousand years, and that the Devil had chosen him as his tool to prevent reform of the Church.[52]

Hardly anything could have been further from the truth; it is one of the ugliest moments in the whole history of the papacy.[53] On July 3 Pope Paul IV even mocked Charles V's physical condition, calling him "this miserable and sorry creature, this cripple in body and soul." It appears that he was encouraged to indulge his hatred by his evil nephew Cardinal Carlo Carafa, the principal architect of the French alliance, who hoped to profit from the Pope's recent denunciation of the pro-imperial Colonna family in Italy and expropriation of their lands. On July 7 a Spanish courier was captured near the Neapolitan frontier, carrying a letter recommending that a Spanish army march on Rome. Two days later the Pope arrested the Spanish ambassador, and on July 11 called all the cardinals and ambassadors together at the Vatican, told them war with the Emperor and his son Philip was imminent, and declared that they "shall be made our vassals, deprived of all their kingdoms, their subjects released from their allegiance, and their dominions divided among those who occupy them."[54]

How the suffering Charles, after all he had done for the Church and for Christendom, must have felt on hearing of these words, beggars the imagination.

Philip II, king of Spain for less than a year, Catholic to the marrow of his bones, now faced the totally unexpected situation of an impending military assault on him (for his critically ill father was obviously no longer capable of defending himself) by the Pope himself. Spain's greatest commander, the Duke of Alba, led the Spanish army in southern Italy, and counselled Philip most wisely in this crisis. On August 21 Alba wrote to the Pope that after what he had said, "nothing else was possible for the Emperor and the King of Spain except to

---

[51] Von Pastor, *History of the Popes*, XIV, 126.

[52] *Ibid.*

[53] Since no doctrinal pronouncement *ex cathedra* was made, the issue of papal infallibility does not arise here. It had been clear at least from the pontificate of Liberius (352-366) that papal judgments on individuals, even when exercising full papal authority, were subject to error. See Volume Two, Chapter 1 of this history.

[54] *Ibid.*, XIV, 121-122, 127-131 (first quote on 127, second on 131).

do what was permitted to every obedient son, whose father attacked him with a naked weapon, which was to take the weapon out of his hand."[55]

Philip agreed, after obtaining a legal opinion from the University of Louvain that such action was justified. On September 5 Alba crossed the frontier of the papal state with his army. Two days later Cardinal Carlo Carafa arrived in Rome with promises from Henry II of France, a large sum of money, and 1,500 troops—not nearly enough. On September 10 Queen Mary of England wrote her last letter to Charles V, begging him to urge Prince Philip to return to England— obviously impossible at this time. Two days later came Charles' unannounced abdication as Emperor in favor of his brother Ferdinand. On the 14th Cardinal Pole wrote to Paul IV asking for guidance on how to conduct himself regarding the war between Philip II and the Pope. He received no reply.[56]

The Pope began negotiations with Alba, then broke them off. Irony piled on irony as 350 German Lutheran mercenaries, mocking the Mass and pictures of the saints, arrived in Rome at the end of September to help defend it from the very Catholic Spaniards, and soon afterward Cardinal Carlo Carafa urged his French friends to bring up the infidel Turkish fleet for the same purpose. After considerable hesitation, Henry II of France finally ordered a French army of 12,000 foot, 600 horse, and 24 cannon to Italy under the command of the Duke of Guise. The crossing of the Alps at the beginning of winter took considerable time, so that the French army did not arrive in Turin until the end of the year. Meanwhile on October 18 the Duke of Alba took Ostia, the port of Rome, and six days later the stubborn Pope reluctantly agreed to a truce while negotiations were undertaken.[57]

They made little progress for a long time. Late in March Cardinal Pole wrote a beautiful letter to the misguided Pope about the tragic situation into which he had brought himself and Christendom:

> Had I no other tie of obligation, the singular piety he [Philip] showed at the beginning of his reign [in England] . . . in bringing back these people to the obedience of the Holy See, would suffice. . . . On this account, Your Holiness likewise showed that you held him most dear, until Satan sowed these seeds of dissension which, if now uprooted, I cannot doubt he will be much dearer to Your Holiness . . . and the King's obedience towards yourself and the Church will become the more conspicuous. The mode of uprooting is taught by Him who taught us to pray; for when Satan demanded the sons of the Church, that he might sift them like wheat, He resisted with the sole remedy of prayer, and commanded us to use the same remedy. This is what we hope will come to pass . . . so much the more easily that those things which estranged the minds of Your Holiness and the King arose not from

---

[55] *Ibid.*, XIV, 136.

[56] *Ibid.*, XIV, 137-141; William S. Maltby, *Alba* (Berkeley CA, 1983), pp. 100-101; Loades, *Reign of Mary Tudor*, pp. 185, 296-297. For the imperial abdication see above, this chapter.

[57] Von Pastor, *History of the Popes*, XIV, 142-148; Maltby, *Alba*, pp. 101, 103; Baumgartner, *Henry II of France*, pp. 185-187.

yourselves, but from your ministers, and seem to me so recent that they cannot have taken deep root in your minds in so short a time.[58]

Pope Paul IV's only response was to order on April 9 the recall of all his nuncios, legates, and other agents in countries ruled directly or indirectly by Philip II—including England and Cardinal Pole, justifying it because Philip had ordered all Spaniards to leave Rome (not surprisingly in view of the war). No one knew why Pole was not exempted, since his presence in England was obviously essential to the Church, and on the plea of the English ambassador the Pope did suspend the decree in his case for a time. On May 29 Paul IV had the Roman Inquisition arrest and imprison the able, conspicuously virtuous Cardinal Morone on charges of heresy, never proved. All his books and papers were seized and he was held in close confinement, not allowed to say or hear Mass. He remained in prison throughout the remainder of the pontificate of Paul IV. A few days later the Pope told the Venetian ambassador that the College of Cardinals was infected with heresy, and declared his intention to prosecute Cardinal Pole for heresy as well. But Queen Mary would not permit him to be taken from England.[59]

In March 1557 Philip II finally returned to England after an absence of more than a year and a half. His primary purpose was to help Queen Mary bring England into the Spain's war against France which the Pope had provoked. Her council resisted, but a madcap April raid on the Yorkshire coast by none other than a nephew of Cardinal Pole, sailing from France, persuaded them to change their minds and agree. On July 5, having attained his objective, Philip departed once more; Queen Mary never saw him again. He has been blamed for callous treatment of her, but in fact he had other responsibilities greater than those in England, and by now he had undoubtedly concluded that their marriage was almost certain never to bear fruit. After his departure Queen Mary suffered another tragic false pregnancy.[60]

The war between France and Spain had now spread to the border country between France and the Low Countries, and on August 10 Duke Emmanuel Philibert of Savoy, commanding the imperial army, won a decisive victory over the French army of Constable Montmorency near St. Quentin. At least 2,500 French troops were killed and more than 7,000 captured, including the Constable. Only half the French army escaped, in a state of complete demoralization. Under these circumstances Henry II of France had no choice but to bring back the Duke of Guise and his army from Italy, and the Pope no choice but finally to make peace with Spain after Guise's departure. He yielded with bad grace, after threatening to shut himself up in Castel Sant'Angelo and die instead. When the

---

[58] Haile, *Pole*, pp. 502-503.

[59] *Ibid.*, pp. 504, 509; von Pastor, *History of the Popes*, XIV, 156, 289-292, 298-299, 395-396; Hughes, *Reformation in England* (5th ed.), II, 325; Loades, *Reign of Mary Tudor*, pp. 365-367.

[60] Loades, *Reign of Mary Tudor*, pp. 191, 304-305, 332; Prescott, *Mary Tudor*, pp. 362-364, 385; Harbison, *Rival Ambassadors*, pp. 323-326.

treaty was proclaimed in September, it displayed the extraordinary forbearance of Philip II and Alba, so embarrassed at having had to fight the Pope: they agreed to ask his pardon in return for his assurance that he would give it if asked, and to restore all the lands they had taken in the papal state in return for the Pope's dropping his alliance with France. Bishop Seripando of Salerno called the war thus ended "the most execrable of conflicts because it had set father against son" and called the peace "the work of God, not of man." This Catholic historian can only echo that judgment.[61]

By November the Duke of Guise, none the worse for his Italian adventure, was back in his favorite fighting ground: northern France and the Belgian border. He sent a trusted commander, Marshal Piero Strozzi, to reconnoiter Calais, held by the English since the Hundred Years War and now the only part of France remaining in their possession. Strozzi reported that despite its formidable-looking defenses it was vulnerable, and would be more vulnerable in January when the marshes surrounding the city were frozen hard. In the middle of December the Duke of Guise marched on Calais with 20,000 troops, concealing his moves brilliantly from the English garrison, which disregarded all warnings until his troops actually appeared before the city on the last day of 1557. Despite the proud boast posted over the city gate, "then shall the Frenchmen Calais win, when iron and lead like cork shall swim," the garrison crumpled before the great duke's attack. By January 5, 1558 Guise's guns had blasted a huge breach in the walls; the next day the French took the castle, and the next day the English governor surrendered the city.[62]

On top of all her other misfortunes, the loss of Calais struck Queen Mary a shattering blow. Her oft-quoted words to a man of her household named Rice, "when I am dead and opened you shall find Calais lying on my heart," sum it up.[63]

The sands were running out for the great Cardinal Pole as well. In March 1558 the discerning Spanish ambassador to England, the Count of Feria, wrote of him: "The Cardinal is a dead man. I have been able to warm him up a little by talking to him every day . . . [but] the result is not all I could wish." He wrote to the Pope, who continued to repudiate him, saying he felt like Isaac about to be sacrificed by his father Abraham, yet still hoped that God would deliver him as He had delivered Isaac. At the end of that month Queen Mary drafted her will, still dreaming of heirs of her body and making no provisions in case there should be none. By September both the Queen and the Cardinal were seriously ill. Late in October Queen Mary added a codicil to her will, finally admitting that she might not have issue, and declaring that if she did not, "the Crown is to pass to the next heir by the laws of the realm." Though the laws of England then on the

---

[61] Von Pastor, *History of the Popes*, XIV, 164-168; Baumgartner, *Henry II of France*, pp. 194-198, 202; Hubert Jedin, *Papal Legate at the Council of Trent: Cardinal Seripando* (St. Louis, 1947), pp. 503-504 (quotes on 503).

[62] Baumgartner, *Henry II of France*, pp. 202-205; Loades, *Reign of Mary Tudor*, pp. 316-317; Prescott, *Mary Tudor*, pp. 369-371.

[63] Prescott, *Mary Tudor*, p. 381.

books were in conflict on the rights of Princess Elizabeth, she was the obvious heir and accepted as such by most of the people. On November 7 Mary made her choice official, writing to Elizabeth (whom she had always disliked) accepting her as her successor, while pleading with her to maintain the Catholic faith in England.[64]

The Spanish ambassador did not believe that she would do so. Writing to Philip II on November 10, he said: "I greatly fear that in religion she will not go right, as I perceive she is inclined to govern by men who are held to be heretics." The chief man he mentioned in this category was William Cecil, whom he said was certain to be secretary of state to Elizabeth as Queen, as he had been to Edward VI and his regents. He had established a personal relationship with her as early as 1548, when she was only fourteen, and had carefully maintained it ever since; he had her complete trust.[65]

At dawn November 17 Queen Mary died while Mass was being said before her. Cecil and his staff were ready, and acted instantly. Cecil's aide Nicholas Throckmorton removed a black enamelled ring from Mary's finger to bring it to Elizabeth to show that her half-sister was really dead. Within three hours Cecil had taken over the government and Parliament had declared Elizabeth queen in a proclamation Cecil had drafted beforehand. None of Cecil's documents referred to Mary's last request that the Catholic faith in England be preserved. At noon heralds proclaimed the new Queen at the Tower of London and in central places throughout the city.[66]

The news was soon brought to Cardinal Pole. He remarked on the parallelism of his own life with that of his queen. Both had been persecuted for many years because of their unshakable Catholic faith; both had suffered acutely, in different ways, after their elevation to the high offices of queen and primate; both died in the bosom of the Church. But from Queen Mary's death, Pole concluded sadly, great evils would come. The prospect overwhelmed him; he suffered a convulsion, and at six o'clock in the afternoon he died, exactly twelve hours after Mary.[67]

At her first meeting with her council, on November 20, the new young Queen Elizabeth announced that it would be substantially smaller than Mary's, with only eleven members. Six were held over from Mary's council; five new members were added, one of them being Cecil. He controlled two of the other new appointees and three of the holdovers, thus giving him from the beginning a majority of the council.[68] He had stage-managed the whole transition and now

---

[64] Loades, *Reign of Mary Tudor*, pp. 333, 335-336 (second quote on 336), 371 (first quote), 387; Haile, *Pole*, p. 522; Hughes, *Reformation in England* (5th ed.), II, 330n.

[65] Winthrop S. Hudson, *The Cambridge Connection and the Elizabethan Settlement of 1559* (Durham NC, 1980), pp. 12-18, 90 (for quote).

[66] *Ibid.*, p. 11; Read, *Cecil*, pp. 117, 119; Loades, *Reign of Mary Tudor*, p. 334; Prescott, *Mary Tudor*, p. 390.

[67] Haile, *Pole*, pp. 529-530; Loades, *Reign of Mary Tudor*, p. 334; Prescott, *Mary Tudor*, p. 390.

[68] Hudson, *Cambridge Connection*, pp. 9-11, 27-28, 39, 41, 90; Read, *Cecil*, p. 119.

controlled the new government—and, as he was soon to demonstrate and later in an unguarded moment to declare,[69] the English church as well. For the next forty years, behind the glittering facade of the bejewelled, red-haired Elizabeth and the burgeoning myth of the "Virgin Queen," William Cecil made England the mainstay of the division of Christendom.

Who was William Cecil? His grandfather David was a longbowman from the Welsh border who fought with Henry Tudor against Richard III at the Battle of Bosworth. David Cecil married the daughter of an alderman in the prosperous cloth-producing town of Stamford in Lincolnshire, not far from Cambridge and its university, and acquired land, most of which passed to his eldest son Richard at his death in 1537. Richard was "Groom of the Wardrobe" for Henry VIII when he was breaking with the Catholic Church. In that position he personally prepared Henry for five of his six marriages and watched two of his queens go to the executioner's block. Few memories have survived of the life of Richard Cecil, but one recalls the day he sprang to the defense of a fiery Protestant preacher attacked by the congregation in a church in Stamford in 1535. He married Jane, daughter of William Heckington of Bourne, whose principal contribution to her famous son was longevity. She lived to be no less than 87, almost unheard of in her time, dying as the Spanish Armada was approaching England in the spring of 1588.[70]

William grew up highly intelligent, ambitious, observant and alert, but never one to have pulled the longbow like his grandfather on Bosworth Field. He was short and thin, and "seldom or never played any game for he could play at none."[71] As an adult he weighed just 135 pounds. From all we know of him, William Cecil seems as though born old, "cautious, deliberate, with great self-control, enormous industry, and an almost diabolical knowledge of human nature and of the faults and secret scandals of particular men. . . . To say the truth of him, he worshipped power rather than money. He was a figure such as Annas must have been, cold, ingratiating, far-sighted, skeptical, implacable, full of such worldly wisdom as appears in those precepts to his son, which may have suggested the maxims of Polonius to Shakespeare; thoroughly devoted to Machiavelli's principles, and more successful than most in covering his traces."[72]

At a critical moment in the history of England and the Faith, in May 1535 when Sts. Thomas More and John Fisher were awaiting martyrdom in the Tower of London, William Cecil entered Cambridge University at the early age of fifteen. His tutor was John Cheke, who though just six years older than Cecil was already distinguished as a Greek scholar, and an enthusiastic supporter of Henry VIII's schism. In 1542, a year after leaving Cambridge before obtaining a

---

[69] See the second quotation heading this chapter.

[70] Read, *Cecil*, pp. 17-21.

[71] *Ibid.*, p. 24.

[72] Walsh, *Philip II*, pp. 215-216. It is worth remembering that Shakespeare was a contemporary of Cecil and Philip II. This was an age in many ways the most personally dramatic in all the history of the West.

degree, Cecil married Cheke's sister Mary, who bore him a child and then died the following year. Shortly afterwards Cecil sat in the House of Commons as a member for Lincolnshire. At the end of 1545 he married Mildred Cooke, whose father fled abroad during Queen Mary's Catholic reign. Mildred was stern, hatchet-faced, very learned, and very Protestant, probably indeed a full Calvinist ("Puritan" in the terminology of a later age).[73]

When Henry VIII died in 1547 and his son Edward became king at the age of nine, John Cheke was selected as his tutor. Cheke and Cecil were still close friends, and Cecil's new father-in-law was also influential at the court of the young king. Within a year Cecil had written an introduction to a pamphlet by the distinctly Protestant Queen Dowager Catherine Parr, which emphasized justification by faith and the importance of widespread reading of the Bible, and strongly condemned the Pope, the saints and the Blessed Virgin Mary as "vain and counterfeit saviors."[74] Cecil was now solidly and permanently committed to the Protestant cause. Whether he accumulated his vast powers to serve that cause, or used it to justify that accumulation for his own gratification, is known only to his Maker and Judge. But the historian may note the consequence: no more dedicated, brilliant, indefatigable and deadly enemy of the Catholic Church ever lived than William Cecil.

As soon as the news of Mary Tudor's death reached France, its King Henry II formally proclaimed his daughter-in-law, Mary Stuart of Scotland, Queen of England, as by Catholic standards she unquestionably was. She was the granddaughter of Henry VIII's elder sister Margaret; presuming Elizabeth illegitimate (as every Catholic must), she was therefore next in line for the succession. But she was also the wife of the Dauphin Francis, the heir to France, with which Spain had been so many times at war for the past sixty years; and her mother, the queen dowager and regent of Scotland, was Mary of Guise, whose family was generally considered the most powerful in France. Mary Queen of Scots was still very young—she had not quite reached her sixteenth birthday—and appeared to be docile to her family and adopted country (she had lived in France for ten years). The French had shown little inclination during the reign of Charles V to place religious considerations over their own immediate political advantage. Philip II could not bring himself to favor a royal claimant in England who appeared to be completely under the control of his enemies. So he backed Elizabeth, to his lifelong regret.[75]

Queen Mary's funeral took place in Westminster Abbey December 14, 1558. Bishop John White of Winchester praised her for repudiating royal supremacy in the Church, and warned: "The wolves be coming out of Geneva and other places of Germany and have sent their books before, full of pestilent doctrines, blasphemy, and heresy to infect the people." The royal council

---

[73] Read, *Cecil*, pp. 24-35. For Mildred Cecil's appearance, see the striking portrait facing Read's page 34.

[74] *Ibid.*, pp. 37-40 (quote on 40).

[75] Antonia Fraser, *Mary Queen of Scots* (New York, 1969), p. 83; Walsh, *Philip II*, pp. 201-205.

(dominated by Cecil) immediately reprimanded him for these words and put him under house arrest. Protestant Edwin Sandys, writing to Zwingli's successor Bullinger in Zürich a few days later, reported with delight that "the Queen has changed almost all her councillors, and has taken good Christians into her service in the room of Papists." On December 22 Cecil appointed his strongly Protestant brother-in-law Sir Nicholas Bacon to the royal council and made him Keeper of the Great Seal of England. On Christmas day, Queen Elizabeth ordered Bishop Owen Oglethorpe of Carlisle, who was saying the Christmas Mass, not to elevate the Host after the consecration. He refused to obey her, so she left church after the reading of the Gospel, before the liturgy of the Mass had begun. Two days later she ordered the omission of the elevation of the Host at all Masses thenceforth said in England.[76]

The bishops, most of whom had been appointed by Cardinal Pole as papal legate and were staunch Catholics, knew what this meant. In grim consultation they resolved that none of them should crown the heretic queen. But Bishop Oglethorpe broke ranks, convinced that someone would crown her and not wanting her to become even more hostile to the Catholic Church because no Catholic bishop would do so. The coronation took place January 15, 1559 in a ceremony in which the traditional Mass of the Holy Spirit was omitted, the liturgy was sung by a married Protestant clergyman, the Host was not elevated, and Bishop Oglethorpe had essentially nothing to do but place the crown on Elizabeth's head.[77]

Ten days later Parliament met. Candidates for the House of Commons had been carefully chosen from lists drawn up by Cecil and his associates; at least a quarter of them were vocal, committed Protestants. The lay lords were about evenly divided between Catholics and Protestants, but the Catholic lords lacked leadership and determination. Of the 26 spiritual peers (25 bishops and the abbot of Westminster Abbey), only ten were present throughout. There were no less than nine episcopal vacancies, for four bishops had died in the last year of Cardinal Pole's life along with Pole himself, while four more had died in the brief period since then. The other seven bishops were absent for various reasons, and although most of them gave proxies to Archbishop Heath of York, they do not seem to have been used.[78] All but one of the bishops present, in striking contrast to those of Henry VIII, would resist manfully the second destruction of the Catholic Church in England now about to begin, and came close to winning one critical vote; but in the long run they could not prevail against Cecil's

---

[76] Hughes, *Reformation in England* (5th ed.), III, 16-17; J. E. Neale, *Elizabeth I and Her Parliaments, 1559-1581* (New York, 1958), p. 57 (first quote); Henry N. Birt, *The Elizabethan Religious Settlement* (London, 1907), pp. 12 (second quote), 14, 19, 26; von Pastor, *History of the Popes*, XIV, 403.

[77] Hughes, *Reformation in England* (5th ed.), II, 17; von Pastor, *History of the Popes*, XIV, 404; Messenger, *Reformation, Mass and Priesthood*, II, 189. Bishop Oglethorpe later deeply regretted his decision and his sanction for Queen Elizabeth's coronation.

[78] Birt, *Elizabethan Religious Settlement*, pp. 46-55; Neale, *Elizabeth I and Her Parliaments, 1559-1581*, pp. 38-41, 58.

political machine, and everybody knew it. Count de Feria, the Spanish ambassador, reported to Philip II that Cecil was leading the change of religion;[79] Calvin congratulated him for it even before it happened, in a letter written from Geneva January 29:

> It is well known that . . . you have diligently used that influence which you possess, in no slight degree, with your most serene Queen, to the end that the sincere worship of the Gospel and the pure and uncorrupted worship of God should again flourish by the exclusion of those popish superstitions which for four years have prevailed throughout your country.[80]

From the day Parliament convened that momentous January, the second severance of the English church from the Pope was decided. The only question was how far Cecil and the Protestant activists could push the religious change, when by nearly all estimates a substantial majority of the people of England were not doctrinally Protestant, though willing to take the road of schism once again.

Early in February the English ambassador in Rome was instructed to break off diplomatic relations with the Pope. On the 4th the Lords voted, with only the nine bishops present in dissent, that Church revenue from first fruits and tenths, which Queen Mary had renounced so that it should go to the Pope as of old, be restored to the Crown of England. On Ash Wednesday John Scory, a bishop under Edward VI who had fled the country during Queen Mary's reign, preaching at court by order of Queen Elizabeth, harshly attacked the Pope, bishops, monks, the Mass, and the entire Catholic faith before a congregation of 5,000 including the Queen and her council. On February 9 Cecil's father-in-law Sir Anthony Cooke introduced a bill in the House of Commons to eliminate papal supremacy in the Church. In a letter February 12 to Protestant leader Peter Martyr in Zürich, Cooke said "we are moving far too slowly . . . but the result of . . . Parliament will, as far as I can judge, confirm my hope." On February 21 provisions restoring the Second Prayer Book of Edward VI—the liturgy that explicitly rejected the Mass—were added to the bill on royal supremacy to create an Act of Supremacy and Uniformity, passed by the House of Commons February 25.[81]

---

[79] Birt, *Elizabethan Religious Settlement*, p. 39; Hudson, *Cambridge Connection*, pp. 100-101; Hughes, *Reformation in England* (5th ed.), III, 17-20; Read, *Cecil*, pp. 129-130. Hudson concludes that "there is little reason to question Cecil's claim that, in collaboration with others, he was the chief architect of the Elizabethan religious settlement" (*op. cit.*, p. 100).

[80] Messenger, *Reformation, Mass and Priesthood*, II, 172.

[81] *Ibid.*, II, 190; Von Pastor, *History of the Popes*, XIV, 405; Neale, *Elizabeth I and Her Parliaments 1559-1581*, pp. 45, 52-54, 59-62; William P. Haugaard, *Elizabeth and the English Reformation* (Cambridge, England, 1968), pp. 84-85, 89 (quote on 85); Birt, *Elizabethan Religious Settlement*, pp. 60, 73-74; Hughes, *Reformation in England* (5th ed.), III, 21-22; Hudson, *Cambridge Connection*, pp. 117-119. See Chapter Four, above, on the Second Prayer Book of Edward VI.

On March 1 Philip Melanchthon, Luther's partner and widely regarded as his successor, wrote to Queen Elizabeth urging her to establish Protestant doctrine and rites in England "at once." The bearer of the letter was William Barlow, an ardent Protestant who had been a bishop under Edward VI, but resigned soon after the accession of Queen Mary and fled to Europe.[82]

At the middle of March the bill to alter religion in England was revised in the Lords so as only to restore royal instead of papal supremacy in the English church, not to abolish the Mass. It required an oath of loyalty to Queen Elizabeth from all holders of ecclesiastical or teaching positions, and changed her title to "chief governor of all spiritual and ecclesiastical affairs" rather than "Head of the Church," which some even among her supporters thought inappropriate for a woman. This indicated that Cecil was not yet sure of a majority in the Lords, over the unanimous opposition of the bishops present, to eliminate the Mass, deny the Real Presence, and restore the Edwardian "communion service." It is also likely that Elizabeth herself wanted to preserve much of the old liturgy, as J. E. Neale, the great authority on her Parliaments, believes; she distrusted and may have feared the militant Protestants. But no more than the Catholic bishops could she ultimately prevail against Cecil.[83]

The supremacy bill passed easily, despite the opposition of all the bishops present in the House of Lords. Archbishop Nicholas Heath of York, the ranking churchman of England following the death of Cardinal Pole, declared that this action involved the abandonment of all the ecumenical councils, especially Ephesus and Chalcedon, and the unity and all the laws of the Church. He asked who was head of the Church between the Ascension of Christ and the conversion of Constantine, if not the Pope. He recalled that England had received her Christian and Catholic faith directly from the Roman Church via St. Augustine of Canterbury, and warned that "by leaping out of St. Peter's ship, [we] hazard ourselves to be overwhelmed and drowned in the waters of schism, sects, and divisions."[84] It was only too true, as the English Civil War of the next century would most dramatically attest. But great speeches did not matter; William Cecil had counted his votes.

Meanwhile, on the continent, peace negotiations between France and Spain had begun in early February at the little town of Cateau-Cambrésis near the French-Belgian frontier. Until Queen Elizabeth was secure on her throne, neither she nor Cecil wanted foreign war, and they were especially eager to avoid

---

[82] Haugaard, *Elizabeth and English Reformation*, p. 97; Messenger, *Reformation, Mass and Priesthood* II, 173. For Barlow see *Dictionary of National Biography*, I, 1149-1151. Melanchthon died the following year, bitterly disillusioned by the ferocious controversies within Lutheranism (Janssen, *History of the German People*, VII, 141-142).

[83] Neale, *Elizabeth I and Her Parliaments 1559-1581*, pp. 64-71; von Pastor, *History of the Popes*, XIV, 407; Birt, *Elizabethan Religious Settlement*, pp. 75-80; Hughes, *Reformation in England* (5th ed.), III, 23-26.

[84] Birt, *Elizabethan Religious Settlement*, p. 80. Birt calculates the vote in the Lords in favor of the supremacy bill as 52-20. For the mission to England of St. Augustine of Canterbury, see Volume Two, Chapter 7 of this history.

continuance of the war with France since France was the sponsor of Elizabeth's rival Mary Queen of Scots. So eager were they for peace that they even communicated their willingness to let France continue to hold Calais if necessary as part of its price. By mid-March a preliminary agreement had been reached, which was known in England by Palm Sunday, March 19. Finalized at the beginning of April, one of the most significant and enduring treaties in European history, it ended at last the long conflict between France and Spain, generated primarily by French ambitions in Italy and Belgium, which had torn Christendom apart for more than sixty years. France gave up its claims to Milan and Naples and its holdings in Tuscany, and restored Piedmont-Savoy to the Duke of Savoy. France was given Metz and Verdun in Lorraine and given back St. Quentin where the Duke of Savoy, commanding a largely Spanish army, had won the striking victory over the French in 1557 which had convinced French King Henry II to make the peace. Both Henry II and Philip II agreed to give full support to an ecumenical council of the Church, though Pope Paul IV had shown little interest in it. The treaty was to be sealed by the marriages of Philip II to Princess Isabelle (Elizabeth) of France, the 14-year-old eldest daughter of King Henry II, and of the Duke of Savoy to Henry II's sister Marguerite. As for Calais, France was to retain it for eight years with the option of then purchasing it from England for 100,000 crowns—which was done, and it has remained part of France ever since.[85]

There were no marriage provisions for Queen Elizabeth. Though pursued by numerous suitors (including, briefly, Philip II, before he realized she was committed to heresy) she had showed no inclination to marry any of them—and never did marry.[86] It would be unprofitable to enter the thicket of speculation, then and since, as to why she did not, because no available evidence provides a clear or even a probable answer.

As soon as the good news of the peace treaty arrived in England, Protestant pressure mounted to proceed immediately with the abolition of the Mass in England and the restoration of the Second Prayer Book of Edward VI. A bill to that effect passed the House of Commons March 20. But opposition to it was still strong in the House of Lords, and it was generally expected that the Queen would end the session of Parliament on Good Friday, March 24, with no further action on this matter other than an order that communion in both kinds be universally administered on Easter. During the evening of Holy Thursday Elizabeth seems to have changed her mind. She cancelled an audience with the Spanish ambassador on Good Friday morning and went before Parliament at one o'clock in the afternoon (during the time of the special three hours' devotion to the Passion which had been traditional with Catholics) to declare only a ten days' recess instead of an adjournment. English was interpolated into the Easter liturgy

---

[85] Baumgartner, *Henry II*, pp. 225-229; Neale, *Elizabeth I and Her Parliaments 1559-1581*, pp. 70-71; Haugaard, *Elizabeth and English Reformation*, pp. 95, 99.

[86] Birt, *Elizabethan Religious Settlement*, p. 35; Menéndez Pidal, *Historia de España*, XXII, Part 1, p. 483. In mid-February Queen Elizabeth prophetically told Spanish ambassador Count de Feria that she did not expect ever to marry.

attended by the Queen, thereby prejudging a religious disputation on March 31, arranged by Cecil, on the use of the vernacular in the liturgy. When this disputation was resumed April 3, now on the critical proposition that any national church might change its rites and ceremonies as it wished, Bishops White and Watson, after vigorously denouncing procedural rules that favored the Protestants, were confined in the Tower of London by order of Cecil's government.[87]

His reason would soon become apparent. William Cecil was still counting votes.

On April 18 an amended Act of Uniformity, restoring the Second Prayer Book of Edward VI with some alterations in a conservative direction (abolition of prayers against the Pope, who was no longer mentioned at all; restoring some of the language of the First Book of Common Prayer relating to the Real Presence, eliminating the prohibition on kneeling at communion, and permitting the use of traditional Mass vestments) and giving Elizabeth full authority to make further changes in it as she might think necessary, was presented to the House of Commons and passed two days later by voice vote. It was quickly followed by a bill once again abolishing all monasteries and convents in England, which became law in May. On April 27 the Act of Uniformity came before the House of Lords.[88]

Into the breach stepped Cuthbert Scott, Bishop of Chester, appointed by Cardinal Pole and Queen Mary in 1556, the year of Cranmer's execution, a Catholic true unto death. After the thundering denunciation of the Act of Uniformity and all it signified, which stands at the head of this chapter, Bishop Scott cut even deeper, to ultimate consequences and moral responsibilities in the cleaving of Christendom:

> Note, I beseech Your Lordships, the end of these men's doctrines, that is, to set us without God. And the like opinion they hold touching the consecration; having nothing in their mouths but the Holy Communion, which after the order of this book [the new Elizabethan Prayer Book which would be mandated by the Act of Uniformity] is holy only in words and not in deed. For the thing is not there which should make it holy—I mean the Body and Blood of Christ. . . . For the only way whereby It is present is by

---

[87] Neale, *Elizabeth I and Her Parliaments 1559-1581*, pp. 66-72; Birt, *Elizabethan Religouis Settlement*, pp. 31, 77-78, 81-82, 88, 108-111; Haugaard, *Elizabeth and English Reformation*, pp. 90-91, 102-104; Hudson, *Cambridge Connection*, p. 120. In an important letter to Protestant leader Peter Martyr Vermigli on March 20, English Protestant John Jewel wrote: "The Queen . . . openly favors our cause, yet is wonderfully afraid of allowing any innovations [in the liturgy]. . . . She is, however, prudently and firmly and piously following up her purpose, though somewhat more slowly than we could wish" (Messenger, *Reformation, Mass and Priesthood*, II, 172).

[88] Neale, *Elizabeth I and Her Parliaments 1559-1581*, pp. 77-79; Birt, *Elizabethan Religious Settlement*, pp. 71, 87-89; Hughes, *Reformation in England* (5th ed.), III, 27-29; Haugaard, *Elizabeth and English Reformation*, pp. 105-107, 110; Hudson, *Cambridge Connection*, pp. 93-94.

consecration, which this book hath not at all, neither doth it observe the form prescribed by Christ nor follow the manner of the Church. . . . (It is dangerous enough, Our Lord knows, for a man himself to err; but it is more dangerous not only to err himself, but also to lead other men into error. . . . Take heed, my lords, that the like be not said by you; if you pass this bill, you shall not only, in my judgment, err yourselves, but you also shall be the authors and causers that the whole realm shall err after you. For which you shall make an account before God.[89]

Two days later the question was called. The Act of Uniformity passed the House of Lords by just three votes. Every bishop present voted against it, and so did nine lay lords. Most of the latter were not known as strong Catholics; but perhaps they had paid attention to the words of Bishop Scott—and thought about Judgment Day.[90]

And perhaps William Cecil had calculated beforehand how many of them might do so. By confining Bishops White and Watson to the Tower of London, he had removed their votes from the House of Lords at this critical moment. With them, the margin for the Act of Uniformity in the Lords would have been just one vote—much too close for comfort.

Fifteen years later, early Puritan Thomas Sampson, in a letter to Cecil urging further changes in the Calvinist direction, recalled the chief minister's role in this critical Protestant victory:

> Remember what you did, and could do, in the beginning of the reign of the Queen's Majesty [Elizabeth], in the repairing of religion; what your authority, credit and doing then was, you know, God knows, and there are many witnesses of the same.[91]

In May Queen Elizabeth signed the Acts of Supremacy and Uniformity, Parliament adjourned, and Cecil's government launched Thomas Cromwell's procedure of requiring leading persons in the realm, including all the bishops, to take oath to accept the royal supremacy over the church in England. In Henry VIII's time only one bishop dared refuse the oath: St. John Fisher. In 1559 only one bishop took it: Anthony Kitchin of Llandaff in Wales. Bishop Edmund Bonner of London spoke for all the rest. Called before the royal council controlled by Cecil and ordered to take the oath, Bonner replied magnificently: "I possess three things: soul, body, and property. Of the two you can dispose at your pleasure, but as to the soul, God alone can command me." He refused the oath and was immediately removed, along with all the others but Kitchin. Every one of them remained staunch to the end. Aged Bishop Cuthbert Tunstall, 85, who had taken the oath of supremacy for Henry VIII, refused it for Elizabeth and

---

[89] Messenger, *Reformation, Mass and Priesthood*, II, 211-212.
[90] Neale, *Elizabeth I and Her Parliaments 1559-1581*, p. 80; Read, *Cecil*, p. 133; Hughes, *Reformation in England* (5th ed.), III, 27-29; von Pastor, *History of the Popes*, XIV, 410.
[91] Haugaard, *Elizabeth and English Reformation*, p. 111.

Cecil, and died a Catholic. Thomas Watson, the brilliant young Bishop of Lincoln, one of the two bishops Cecil locked up in the Tower of London to guarantee passage of the Act of Uniformity, spent no less than twenty-five years in prison under Elizabeth and died there, unyielding. So Cecil had to install a whole new episcopate, headed by Matthew Parker as Archbishop of Canterbury (where the last Corpus Christi procession ever held in that ancient cathedral city had taken place May 28, attended by three thousand people).[92]

Parker was a very reluctant archbishop. Cecil knew him—he had studied at Cambridge, Cecil's alma mater, like so many of the other Protestant clergy—and presumably seeing in him all the necessary attributes of a puppet, had selected him from the beginning as primate of England, letting him know as early as December 9, 1558 that he would be given high church office. Suspecting what Cecil had in mind, Parker refused a call to London, pleading bad health and saying he should not be given a post "above the reach of mine ability." He asked to be made head of obscure Benet College, failing which that he "be quite forgotten." But no better could friend than enemy evade William Cecil. On December 30 he summoned Parker to London in the Queen's name, where, he said, "I shall declare unto you Her Majesty's further pleasure, and the occasion why you are sent for." In due time Cecil declared unto Parker that he was to be Archbishop of Canterbury. He was brought in as one of the court preachers in the critical Lent of 1559—the only one who had not exiled himself during Queen Mary's reign, not having been prominent enough to face prosecution. On March 1 Parker wrote a long, pathetic letter explaining in great detail why he was unworthy to be Archbishop of Canterbury. In June he wrote in desperation to the Queen herself, still trying to beg off; his only reply was a second order (undoubtedly drafted by Cecil) to assume the office.[93]

After being "elected" by a minority of the Canterbury cathedral chapter—seven of the twelve canons were absent—and moving to the primate's traditional residence in Lambeth, just south of London, Parker (or rather, Cecil) still faced a difficult hurdle: consecration. The anointing and consecration of the primate of England was done in a solemn, ancient ritual which required four consecrating bishops. Protestant bishops had been appointed to several dioceses from which Catholic bishops refusing to take the oath of supremacy had been removed, but none had yet been formally consecrated in those dioceses. By December 1559 the only consecrated sitting bishop in England was Kitchin of Llandaff, who

---

[92] Birt, *Elizabethan Religious Settlement*, pp. 86 92-93, 125, 208-231 (quote on 212); Neale, *Elizabeth I and Her Parliaments 1559-1581*, pp. 80-83; Hughes, *Reformation in England* (5th ed.), III, 29-36, 123n, 245n-246n; Messenger, *Reformation, Mass and Priesthood*, II, 129. Of the 14 bishops of the restored Catholic Church in England living at the end of 1559 who refused the oath—several had died during that stressful year—no less than twelve were kept in confinement for the rest of their lives and two escaped to the European continent. None ever took the oath (Messenger, *op. cit.*, II, 230n).

[93] V. J. K. Brook, *A Life of Archbishop Parker* (Oxford, 1962), pp. 65-68 (first and second quotes on 65, fourth on 67); Birt, *Elizabethan Religious Settlement*, pp. 232-234 (third quote on 233).

would have nothing to do with the whole proceeding. Cecil therefore selected as chief consecrator William Barlow, who had been validly consecrated a bishop under Henry VIII but then deprived of his see by Queen Mary and Cardinal Pole, and was not yet installed in his new diocese. Of the other three consecrators, one (Hodgkins) had been validly consecrated under Henry VIII but had never been more than an auxiliary bishop; the other two, Scory and Coverdale, had been made bishops under King Edward VI, deprived by Mary, and were now appointed to new dioceses but not yet formally installed in them.[94]

From the Catholic standpoint the fundamental issues in the consecration of Matthew Parker as Archbishop of Canterbury were *form* and *intention*. For the passing on of the apostolic succession through bishops, as with the seven sacraments, both form and intention are canonically defined. The form of Parker's pretended consecration (like that of Scory and Coverdale) was the "Edwardian Ordinal" adopted by the radical Protestants who controlled England during the later years of the reign of Edward VI. Ordinations and episcopal consecrations in this form were not considered valid by the Catholic Church during Mary's reign, because it included no reference to the Real Presence or to the priest's power to make the Host into the Body and Blood of Christ; consequently 16 priests "ordained" under it who were reconciled to the Catholic Church were reordained.[95] The inability of the Edwardian Ordinal to convey priestly powers or apostolic succession was reiterated centuries later by Pope Leo XIII in his statement declaring orders in the Church of England "absolutely null and utterly void."[96] As for intention, the chief consecrator, Bishop Barlow, another radical Protestant, had long before declared his lack of belief in any special, unique character of the episcopal state. In 1540 he had stated, in answers to questions put by Henry VIII, that bishops gained authority only through their appointment by a Christian prince, that it was unnecessary to consecrate them, and that laymen could ordain priests. He had also explicitly rejected the Real Presence on two separate occasions early in the reign of Edward VI.[97] A man who did not believe that a bishop had to be consecrated at all, could hardly consecrate the Archbishop of Canterbury.

---

[94] Brook, *Parker*, pp. 68-69, 76-86; Birt, *Elizabethan Religious Settlement*, pp. 236-250; Messenger, *Reformation, Mass and Priesthood* II, 235-236, 240.

[95] Messenger, *Reformation, Mass and Priesthood* II, 45-63. Since Catholic doctrine holds that ordination, like baptism, permanently marks the soul, this means that the Edwardian "ordinations" were seen as invalid. For a general discussion of the Edwardian Ordinal and the reasons for its invalidity, see Messenger, *op. cit.*, I, 448-506.

[96] Pope Leo XIII, *Apostolicae Curiae*, issued Sept. 13, 1896. This document describes the Anglican Ordinal, which is based on the Edwardian Ordinal, as follows: "In the whole English Ordinal, not only is there no clear mention of sacrifice, of consecration, of the *sacerdotium*, of power of consecrating and offering sacrifice, but every trace of these things which had existed in those prayers of the Catholic rite not wholly rejected was deliberately removed and struck out." (Messenger, *Reformation, Mass and Priesthood*, I, 492).

[97] Messenger, *Reformation, Mass and Priesthood*, I, 285, 333, 406.

Let poor Parker have the last word, in his private journal: "On the 17th of December, in the year 1559, I was consecrated Archbishop of Canterbury. Alas! alas! O Lord God! for what times has thou kept me!"[98]

But William Cecil was well satisfied.

In France that spring the first national Calvinist[99] synod was held in Paris under the leadership of François Morel. Eleven churches were represented, all but two led by ministers sent from Geneva. The synod adopted a statement of faith almost identical with Calvin's Geneva Confession, and called for church discipline and government as at Geneva, under "consistories" of ministers and "elders" eventually to be grouped in "colloquies" and provincial synods meeting at least once a year. It was the first creation of a national church independent of the state. At that point there were about 50 organized Calvinist churches in France, and Geneva was regularly sending ministers to them, over a hundred from 1555 to 1562, operating secretly. Despite Calvin's warnings against violence, it was already being used by some French Calvinists; on May 31 they attacked a Eucharistic procession in the streets of Rouen. On June 2 King Henry II, who regarded all Calvinists as total heretics and militant revolutionaries, issued the Edict of Écouen ordering the French judicial system to give high priority to disposing of them, either by bringing them back to the Church, by exile, or by execution. On June 10 he personally ordered the arrest of eight members of the *Parlement* (chief court) of Paris for Calvinist heresy; their trial began nine days later. He was resolved to strike decisively against these revolutionaries before they felt strong enough to attempt the capture of the Catholic monarchy in France (which they were to attempt, with near success, through six wars over the next 33 years).[100]

But the King of France also had to go through a splendid round of wedding festivities at this time, preparing for the two royal marriages called for by the Treaty of Cateau-Cambrésis. The wedding of Henry's daughter Isabelle and Philip II was to take place in Spain, but there was much to do to honor young Isabelle before she departed for that country; while the marriage of his sister Marguerite to Duke Emanuel Philibert of Savoy was set for July 4 in Paris. All

---

[98] Brook, *Parker*, p. 86.

[99] The familiar but misleading term "Huguenot" will not be used henceforth in this history, except in quotations from other authors. This term, probably a French mangling of the Swiss German *Eidgenossen* referring back to a long-ago early Protestant alliance of no lasting historical significance, has no intrinsic meaning for the English reader (unlike the parallel term for England, "Puritan") and therefore only distracts attention from the belief these people professed, which as was demonstrated in this synod, was Calvinist root and branch.

[100] John T. McNeill, *The History and Character of Calvinism* (New York, 1967), pp. 246-247; Williston Walker, *John Calvin, the Organiser of Reformed Protestantism* (New York, 1906), pp. 385-386; Robert M. Kingdon, *Geneva and the Coming of the Wars of Religion in France, 1555-1563* (Geneva, 1956), pp. 46-49; Baumgartner, *Henry II*, pp. 244-245; H. Outram Evenett, *The Cardinal of Lorraine and the Council of Trent* (Cambridge, England, 1930), pp. 65-66.

great court festivities in France traditionally included tournament jousting—the dangerous game inherited from the Middle Ages, when fully armored men with lances rode against each other at the full speed of trained war horses, to see which could knock the other off his saddle. Henry II revelled in tournaments. No less than five days of them were scheduled in the interlude between the formal betrothal of Marguerite and the Duke of Savoy June 27 and their marriage July 4.[101]

On the third day of the tournaments Henry II arrived to take part in person, as was his custom. He was just forty years old and in excellent physical condition. Under normal circumstances, even in the medically perilous sixteenth century, he could expect fifteen to twenty more years of life and reign, which would have spanned the most critical period of the Calvinist revolution.

Riding a Turkish stallion, wearing the colors of his famous mistress Diane de Poitiers despite the presence of his Queen, Catherine de Medici, King Henry II broke lances with the Duke of Savoy and the Duke of Guise. Then he turned to the Count of Montgomery, captain of his Scottish Guards, a huge red-haired man tough as the ledges of the Grampian Mountains in the heart of his native land, and challenged him to the next fall. Montgomery hit hard; the king barely kept to his saddle. Angered by this blow to his pride in his prowess as a tournament rider, Henry demanded another fall with Montgomery. Queen Catherine, devoted to Henry despite his lack of feeling for her, begged him to refrain. So did both Dukes and Montgomery himself. Henry brusquely refused. He must restore his pride. It was five o'clock in the afternoon, the sun still high and bright on the last day of June in Paris. The swarthy, compact, long-nosed king faced the towering ruddy Montgomery down the long lane of packed earth where tournament jousts were run. If the destiny of England had ridden on Queen Mary's ability or inability to bear a child, now the destiny of France might ride with its unyielding, lance-bearing king.[102]

Two metal visors clanked down. Each man was now protected head to foot in solid iron. Only a tiny slit in the visor allowed them to see. The horses thundered along the lane of earth; their riders levelled their lances, and the tremendous impact broke both of them. Montgomery's broken lance shot upward, catching the king on his visor as he rode furiously by, still firmly seated on his horse. The visor popped open, "whether simply because of the force of the blow, or because Henry in his eagerness to joust again had forgotten to have it fastened, or because an inexperienced page had not fastened it right." The broken end of Montgomery's lance, sharp as a dagger, drove straight through Henry's eye and into his brain. Catherine screamed, and their fourteen-year-old son Francis, heir to the kingdom, collapsed in a dead faint.[103]

---

[101] Baumgartner, *Henry II*, pp. 248-249.

[102] *Ibid.*, pp. 249-250; James W. Thompson, *The Wars of Religion in France 1559-1576* (New York, 1909), p. 1.

[103] Baumgartner, *Henry II*, pp. 250-251 (quote on 250); Thompson, *Wars of Religion in France*, pp. 1-3.

A full thirty years later, when that dread anniversary came round, Catherine de Medici was to say: "This was the day when the king . . . was wounded—a wound that brought to me principally and to all the kingdom so much evil that I cannot think on that day I can do anything good."[104]

Henry was almost as tough as Count Montgomery. For several days it actually seemed that he might recover from his terrible injury; the famous doctor and anatomist Vesalius, after riding all day and all night from Brussels to treat him, predicted that he would. The king forgave Montgomery and rescheduled his sister's wedding for July 9. But that age could not prevent or effectively combat infection from severe wounds, and on the fifth day after the fatal joust, infection set in. By the 9th the king's condition was hopeless. The marriage of his sister with the Duke of Savoy was solemnized in funereal gloom. Henry called in his son for some last words of advice, only to see the boy faint again, moaning when he recovered: "My God, how can I live if my father dies?" On the morning of the 10th Henry was anointed, and at one o'clock in the afternoon he died.[105]

Queen Catherine de Medici was prostrated by grief. Mary Queen of Scots was now also Queen of France, and the young and helpless king was entirely under the control of his wife's strongly Catholic Guise family, as English ambassador Nicholas Throckmorton promptly reported to Cecil.[106] But temporary Catholic domination of a weak young king was not at all the same as rule by a strong Catholic king in the prime of life. France was now in deadly danger, and from across the Channel William Cecil began his long and persistent efforts to make that danger deadlier.

In January 1559 Pope Paul IV at long last learned the truth about the corrupt intriguing of his nephew Cardinal Carlo Carafa, and spent hours in tearful prayers of regret and repentance before the altars of St. Peter's. At a consistory of all the cardinals on the 27th he recited the crimes of the three nephews to whom he had given high Church office, called God to witness that he had not until then known of their crimes, deprived them of all their offices except Carlo's cardinalate, and ordered them to leave Rome within twelve days. When they were gone and he went to take custody of the Borgia apartments where they lived, he said he intended to bless their rooms with holy water, since evil spirits had dwelt there.[107]

Gradually, as the eventful year 1559 unfolded, Paul IV began to realize that his mistakes had gone far beyond putting too much trust in his nephews. For all the evil he had done, Gian Pietro Carafa was not an evil man; he had sincerely wished and genuinely sought to reform and strengthen the Church. But what reform he had personally accomplished had been almost cancelled out by his measures against the reformers. The great and good Cardinal Morone languished

---

[104] Baumgartner, *Henry II*, p. 254.

[105] *Ibid.*, pp. 251-253 (quote on 252); Thompson, *Wars of Religion in France*, pp. 3-4.

[106] Baumgartner, *Henry II*, pp. 253-254; N. M. Sutherland, *The Huguenot Struggle for Recognition* (New Haven CT, 1980), p. 74.

[107] Von Pastor, *History of the Popes*, XIV, 224-229.

in prison by his order. He had disastrously crippled Cardinal Pole by his absurd charges against him. After giving great favor to the Jesuits in the first three years of his pontificate, he had suddenly turned on them in September 1558, calling St. Ignatius a "tyrant" and the order "rebellious," requiring them to sing in choir together in their houses every day (which greatly limited their ability to carry on their special apostolate, and consequently had been rejected by St. Ignatius with the approval of all previous Popes who had dealt with the Jesuits) and to limit the term of office of their general to three years instead of life. He had excoriated Emperor Charles V, the lifelong defender of Christendom, refeused to recognize his brother Ferdinand as Emperor, and made war on his son Philip II, the most Catholic sovereign in Europe. Nephew Carlo had encouraged him in these policies; knowing now how Carlo had deceived him, he began to see how much damage had been done. The Pope's previously superb health collapsed; dropsy set in. By the feast of the Ascension in May 1559 he could no longer walk, and had to be carried to Mass.[108]

He began to try to make amends. On June 22 he conducted a meeting of the Inquisition from his bed, highly praising Philip II for his vigorous efforts against heresy. He wrote to Emperor Ferdinand saying that he would soon summon the cardinals to join him in confirming his imperial title.[109] On August 15, on his deathbed, he called the new Jesuit general James Laynez[110] to him to say:

> "How bitterly flesh and blood have deceived me! My relatives have plunged me into an unhappy war, from which many sins in the Church of God have arisen. Since the time of St. Peter there has been no such unhappy pontificate in the Church! I repent bitterly of what has happened; pray for me, because I love your society with all my heart! . . . You see that coffer? In it I have accumulated funds for the endowment of the [Jesuit] Roman College."[111]

On hearing that the Pope was now helpless, the people of Rome stormed the building of the Inquisition which he had misused, beat some of its officials caught there, destroyed many of its documents, set its prisoners free, and later burned down the building. On August 13, 1559 Paul IV died. That night a mob stormed the Capitoline Hill and cut off the head of the his statue which had been erected there, dragged it through the streets, and threw it into the Tiber. His body was secretly buried in St. Peter's at night, and kept under guard; he had, after all, still been the Vicar of Christ.[112]

---

[108] *Ibid.*, XIV, 237, 256-258; James Brodrick, *The Progress of the Jesuits* (New York, 1947), pp. 26-30.

[109] Von Pastor, *History of the Popes*, XIV, 412; James Brodrick, *St. Peter Canisius* (Baltimore MD, 1950), p. 429.

[110] St. Ignatius of Loyola had died in the odor of sanctity July 31, 1556.

[111] Von Pastor, *History of the Popes*, XIV, 417; Brodrick, *Progress of the Jesutis*, p. 31 (for different parts of the quotation).

[112] Von Pastor, *History of the Popes*, XIV, 414-416.

On September 5 the conclave began with 40 cardinals present, soon raised to 44, and divided into three parties: French (16), Spanish (17), and followers of the disgraced Cardinal Carafa (11). Philip II of Spain and Catherine de Medici for France both suggested Cardinal Gian Angelo de Medici of Milan for Pope. This Milanese Medici was (to the endless confusion of history students) totally unrelated to and unconnected with the famous Medici family of Florence (to which French Queen Catherine belonged). Partly because he was not part of a famous and ambitious family, he had avoided entanglement in the worst intrigues of the age; as Pope he was to prove that he not only had the best interests of the Church at heart, but, unlike his predecessor, knew from the beginning what they were. But not being especially powerful and ambitious, he was not well known to many of the cardinals, and the first ballots showed no leading candidate.[113]

Thirty-one votes were needed to elect a Pope in this conclave, and on September 22 the respected but aged Cardinal Tournon of France received 24 votes; but when Cardinal Carlo Carafa shifted his vote and that of his faction to Tournon, his disgusted colleagues turned away from him despite the lack of any evidence that Tournon owed anything to Carafa. The next strong candidate to emerge was Cardinal Gonzaga of Mantua, who had support from both Spanish and French cardinals, though not all of either nationality, but was strongly opposed by most of the Italians and was not on Philip II's list of preferred candidates. So he was likewise unable to garner more than 24 votes. Carlo Carafa continued busily promising and intriguing, and Gonzaga's backers had not given up. Finally Philip II took an open stand against him, and Gonzaga withdrew. In November the unworthy Cardinal d'Este of Ferrara, allied with the French party, made his move; but Spanish ambassador Vargas stood outside shouting through a hole in the wall that the conclave would make a great mistake if they elected a man so much opposed by his very Catholic king, and d'Este did not even come close. By this time it was December and the conclave had been in session for three months without a decision. After the disastrous pontificate of Paul IV and the rapid consolidation of Cecil's power in England, Christendom did not have three months to waste.[114]

A last effort for Cardinal Gonzaga engineered by Carlo Carafa having failed, and with the French now totally disillusioned with the slippery Carafa (who was bitterly denounced by Cardinal Guise), the former Pope's nephew tried to get back in the good graces of the Spanish, promising (for whatever his promises were worth) no longer to support any candidate whom Philip II opposed. Two French cardinals had died on the premises (conclaves were notoriously unhealthy) and another had to leave because of illness, reducing their vote total. Spanish Cardinal Pacheco, who was close to Philip II, on December 18 reached 27 votes of the now required 30, but could get no more, and Cardinal Guise ordered workmen to block up the hole in the wall through which Spanish ambassador Vargas had been shouting or crawling to gain illegal admittance to

---

[113] *Ibid.*, XV, 6, 13-19.
[114] *Ibid.*, XV, 10-11, 20-22, 34, 36-37, 41-43, 50.

the conclave (one wonders why this had not been done earlier). By this point (December 20) Vargas wrote that the cardinals were so weary of the conclave and its interminable political maneuvering that they would have elected a piece of wood to be Pope if that showed promise of bringing their ordeal to an end.[115]

On December 22 the Spanish and French parties, finally convinced that neither could prevail over the other or trust Cardinal Carlo Carafa and his faction to do anything they promised, at last began serious negotiations with each other to agree on a common candidate, which would deprive the Carafa faction of its balance of power role. It was now that Cardinal Gian Angelo de Medici of Milan re-emerged, and Cardinal Carafa concluded he was going to win and leaped on his bandwagon. Through Christmas day, support built up steadily for the previously obscure cardinal. In the small hours of December 26 he was elected Pope, taking the name Pius IV. He was not intellectually brilliant or notably talented, but he had a straightforward mind. He knew the damage that had been done, and the only way it could be repaired. On December 30 he told the cardinals that the election of Emperor Ferdinand should not be further contested, for Catholics as well as non-Catholics had taken part in it, and Ferdinand was zealous for the Faith and had done much to defend Christendom against the Turks; all but one cardinal agreed to his immediate recognition as Emperor. The following day he told the imperial ambassador that the primary objective of his pontificate would be to complete the work of the Council of Trent, a determination which he reiterated to the cardinals in consistory on January 4, 1560.[116]

Truly it was time and past time to do just that. Martin Luther was dead and his followers in disarray, but the Calvinist revolutionaries had the bit between their teeth and saw nothing but victory ahead. Allied with Cecil, they had pressured Elizabeth into making the Church of England more Protestant than her father had ever dreamed of, despite the heroic opposition of all but one of the sitting English bishops. With the removal of the threat of Henry II's uncompromising opposition, the French Calvinists were growing explosively. As early as August they began planning an uprising with King Antoine de Bourbon of Navarre and his brother the Prince of Condé, to seize control of the very young King Francis II from the Guises; in December they assassinated Vice-President Minard of the *Parlement* of Paris.[117] And from Scotland John Knox, whose firebrand revolutionary spirit made even Calvin look gentle by comparison,[118]

---

[115] *Ibid.*, XV, 47-53.

[116] *Ibid.*, XV, 53-63, 124, 180.

[117] Sutherland, *Huguenot Struggle*, pp. 75-79; Kingdon, *Geneva and Coming*, p. 68; Henri Naef, *La conjuration d'Amboise et Genève* (Geneva and Paris, 1922), pp. 75-77; Thompson, *Wars of Religion in France*, p. 15.

[118] His biographer Jasper Ridley says: "Knox is one of the most ruthless and successful revolutionary leaders in history. He was more ruthless, at least in theory, than any revolutionary of more recent times. Dictators ancient and modern have killed their opponents whenever they considered that this was expedient. Revolutionary mobs have kileld oppressors out of a desire for vengeance and justice. But Knox and his Puritans are

was writing Cecil that more English aid could persuade the Scots nobles to overthrow the power of the French troops there, which was all that was still sustaining the Catholic Church. Cecil agreed entirely; he saw "that civil dissensions abroad offered an alternative, which would incapacitate potential enemies for external wars and at the same time establish England everywhere as the champion of forces opposed to Rome." In October the army of the Scottish Protestant Congregation took Edinburgh despite the presence of 3,000 French troops at nearby Leith, and the flow of money to them from Cecil began.[119]

John Knox was very unpopular in England, and especially with its queen, since he had had the misfortune to write and circulate his vehement pamphlet "First Blast of the Trumpet Against the Monstrous Rule of Women" just a few months before she came to the throne. He had directed it against the two Maries who were queens of England and Scotland when it was published in the spring of 1558. But he had not confined his slashing attack to the rule of Catholic women, but applied it to rule by any woman, and Elizabeth hated him for it.[120] So Cecil could not allow circulation of his works in England, but he proposed to use him nevertheless: "I like not his audacity," he wrote November 3, 1559. "His writings do no good here [in England], and therefore I do rather suppress them, and yet I mean not but that ye should continue in sending them."[121]

A few days later the French at Leith attacked Edinburgh and drove out the Protestant army, to the rejoicing of the people of the city, who called them heretics and traitors, as Knox himself admits in his history of the "reformation" in Scotland.[122] But revolutions are not made by popularity, but by persistence, blood and terror, as Knox well knew and as the Communists in the twentieth century were to make very clear indeed. The growing weakness of France under Calvinist pressure and the almost complete dependence of Scots Catholics on French support created an historical opportunity that Knox and Cecil swiftly and brilliantly exploited. At the end of February the Treaty of Berwick was signed by the English government with the Protestants Lords of the Congregation in Scotland to expel the French from Scotland. Cecil saw to the dispatch of no less than 11,000 English troops—three times the number of the French army in Scotland—to assist the 2,000 Scots troops of the ragtag Congregation army. In April young King Francis II and his wife Mary Queen of Scots sent a three-man

---

the only modern revolutionaries who proclaimed that it was sinful not to kill their enemies. The sin of Saul was his decision to spare Amalek. No Jacobin or Bolshevik spoke so often of 'foolish pity' as did Knox." (*John Knox* [New York, 1968], p. 527)

[119] *Ibid.*, pp. 346-347, 351-353, 357; Read, *Cecil*, p. 152 (quote).

[120] Ridley, *Knox*, pp. 265-285. In his title for this pamphlet, Knox used the word "regiment"—now spelled "regimen"—for rule. Almost every writer of history has found the image of a "monstrous regiment" of women—suggesting a legion of amazons marching in full military array—irresistible. But logically, Knox's worst enemy must admit this is unfair. The language of the time conveyed no such image. Consequently the word "rule" is used here instead of "regiment."

[121] *Ibid.*, p. 361.

[122] *Ibid.*, p. 358.

commission to try to negotiate peace. But no one could negotiate with John Knox, who had so delighted in the murder of Cardinal Beaton. The only hope of Scots Catholics now was the constancy of the Queen Mother and regent, Mary of Guise, and at the end of April she fell ill with dropsy. On June 11 she died, "horribly swollen and in great pain."[123]

The day before, Cecil, knowing she was dying, had decided to go to Edinburgh himself to supervise the destruction of French influence and of the Catholic Faith in Scotland. He arrived within a week. While conferring with the commissioners Francis II and Mary Queen of Scots had sent, he arrested the secretary of the dead Mary of Guise and forced him to decipher all the ciphered dispatches in his files on negotiations with France and England, thereby giving him not only valuable information but the key to the cipher (Cecil never forgot the needs of his intelligence service, which soon became by far the best in Europe and one of the best in all history). Cecil demanded first of all the abandonment of Mary's claim to the throne of England; the commissioners reluctantly agreed. On July 6 the Treaty of Edinburgh was agreed to, declaring England and Scotland to be allies and England the "protector" of Scotland. All French troops were to be promptly withdrawn, a committee consisting entirely of Calvinists was appointed to rule for the absent Mary, and all questions of religion were referred to the Scottish Parliament, which unmistakably demonstrated its position when it met two days later in St. Giles' cathedral for a thanksgiving service led by John Knox celebrating the Protestant victory.[124]

It was a quick, complete, and virtually bloodless revolutionary conquest, one of the most adept in history, showing Cecil at his most effective in his favorite place behind the scenes, while Knox was out front denouncing the enemy and collecting the laurels. In August the Scottish Parliament abolished papal jurisdiction over the church in Scotland and adopted a Calvinist confession of faith drawn up by Knox. The Mass was outlawed. The clergy of Scotland, leaderless since the murder of Cardinal Beaton, extensively corrupted, and woefully lacking in courage, did little or nothing. Only two lay lords voted against the Calvinist confession—one of them from the Highlands, where most of the people still remained Catholic and were too good fighters to be converted by force. But lowland Scotland was lost to the Catholic Church; by the beginning of 1560 Knox, operating out of St. Andrews, the traditional religious center of Scotland, was requiring every adult inhabitant to listen to Calvinist sermons every Sunday, with severe penalties including refusal of baptism for their children if they did not.[125]

The Guises could do nothing; their hands were very full in France. The Calvinist plot hatched at Vendôme with the King of Navarre and his brother Condé had taken shape during the fall under the dubious and erratic leadership of

---

[123] *Ibid.*, pp. 364-365, 373; Fraser, *Mary Queen of Scots*, pp. 97-98 (quote on 98). For the murder of Cardinal Beaton see Chapter Four, above.

[124] Read, *Cecil*, pp. 180-182, 188-193; Ridley, *Knox*, p. 375; Thompson, *Wars of Religion in France*, p. 49.

[125] Ridley, *Knox*, pp. 375-377, 400; Fraser, *Mary Queen of Scots*, p. 97.

Jean du Barry, Sieur de La Renaudie, also known as La Forest, whom Calvin dismissed as "frivolous, vain and presumptuous" and refused to endorse or help in any way (which did not stop La Renaudie from claiming that he had done so). With possible support in the background from Condé and Cecil's ambassador Nicholas Throckmorton, La Renaudie had gathered an assembly of militant French Calvinists at Nantes February 1, outlining to them a plan "to seize the tyrants, assemble the estates and provide the king with a suitable council"—that is, arrest the Guises and capture the young king—with a striking force of 500 cavalry on March 6. There were too many people at the assembly to keep the plan secret; in less than two weeks the Guises knew about it and fortified themselves and the king in the chateau of Amboise, where the Cardinal of Guise taxed Throckmorton to his face with complicity in the plot. March 6 came and went without incident, despite great apprehension in the chateau. Eight days later the Calvinist cavalry finally arrived, to find the defenders ready and waiting. They fled, but many were captured and soon executed by hanging, beheading, or being thrown into the Loire in sacks. On March 18 La Renaudie was killed in a forest resisting arrest. Documents found on his secretary described the conspiracy and its objectives, linking it clearly to the Calvinists and providing strong evidence of Condé's complicity. Calvin, receiving the first news of these events, said that "having failed to prevent the enterprise, he hoped it would succeed."[126]

Three days after the death of La Renaudie, the Guise Cardinal of Lorraine wrote to the new Pope saying that his conspiracy had revealed the great extent of the Calvinist revolutionary threat in France, which necessitated immediate corrective action, without waiting for the ecumenical council. He asked the Pope to send Cardinal Tournon to France as legate to investigate and reform the French church, and to convene an assembly of bishops to consider questions of faith and morals—in effect, a national council. He made the same points in another letter about this time to Bishop Lenzi of Fermo, estimating the number of active Calvinists in France at 200,000, stating that Catholic pastors were shamefully neglecting their flocks, and calling for the national council to be held no later than November. At this critical moment Chancellor Olivier of France, a friend of the Guises, died and was succeeded by Michel de l'Hôpital, a member of the royal council and only "a nominal Catholic who had brought up his children as Protestants."[127]

---

[126] Sutherland, *Huguenot Struggle*, pp. 95-96, 99 (second quote on 95, third on 99), 105; Thompson, *Wars of Religion in France*, pp. 28-31, 34-38; T. H. L. Parker, *John Calvin* (Philadelphia, 1975), pp. 148-149 (first quote on 148); Donald R. Kelley, *François Hotman, a Revolutionary's Ordeal* (Princeton, 1973), pp. 108-112; Evenett, *Cardinal of Lorraine*, pp. 90, 92; Walsh, *Philip II*, pp. 281-282. If Cecil did not help instigate the plot, he at least kept well informed about it. A poster describing the conspiracy which was nailed to the gates of Antwerp was found among Cecil's papers (Walsh, *op. cit.*, p. 344).

[127] Evenett, *Cardinal of Lorraine*, p. 98; Thompson, *Wars of Religion in France*, p. 43; Brodrick, *Progress of the Jesuits*, p. 55 (quote).

It was the conspiracy of Amboise that persuaded the Duke of Guise that he could not continue to maintain French troops in Scotland, and caused him to tell Francis II and Mary to send the negotiating commission to that country (mentioned above). He asked Philip II to help his sister in Scotland, but Philip, who had just suffered a naval defeat by the Turks, decided on the Duke of Alba's advice that he lacked sufficient available ships to do so.[128]

The news of the calling of a national council by the French government reached Rome on Good Friday in April. Pope Pius IV was horrified, calling it "veritable schism." From the beginning of the Protestant revolt, the Popes had consistently and strongly opposed any national councils, which could not be kept under the control and within the system of the universal Church and might easily be dominated by the rebels. He wrote the Cardinal of Lorraine agreeing to the request to send Cardinal Tournon as legate while declaring his total rejection of the national council, but saying that for the time being he would assume that the proposed council was only a "tactical feint intended to assuage public feeling but not to be translated into action."[129] On June 3 the Pope told a special meeting of all ambassadors to Rome:

> We wish for the Council. We wish for it emphatically, and we wish it to be both free and general; did we not wish for it, the world would delay it for three or four years, on account of the difficulties as to the place. In order to avoid all disputes as to the place and the manner of holding the Council, it is best to continue it in Trent; later on it can be transferred, if necessary, to another and more suitable place, but it is impossible to spend more time in conferring upon that question how, for the progress of heresy in almost every country of Christendom makes immediate action necessary. . . . Whatever is decided upon by the Council, your princes must assist us in carrying out. We wish the Council to meet as soon as possible, and shall only wait for the replies of your princes before announcing it publicly and sending the legates.[130]

In France the crisis escalated with shocking speed. During the summer of 1560 the rapid growth in the numbers of the French Calvinists made it impossible for them to continue to meet only in secret. Many local noblemen joined with them and protected them, both out of actual sympathy and because they hoped to obtain local church properties as their counterparts had done in England in the time of Thomas Cromwell. Calvin's teaching of non-resistance was increasingly rejected, in practice and explicitly by the revolutionary propagandist François Hotman who left his long-time residence in Strasbourg in July to join King Antoine of Navarre. In some areas of the Rhone valley Calvinist strength increased to the point that they were able to eliminate both Catholic worship and the authority of the central government; Cardinal Tournon, passing through that

---

[128] Ridley, *Knox*, pp. 374-375.

[129] Evenett, *Cardinal of Lorraine*, pp. 98-100, 102 (first quote), 106-107 (second quote on 107).

[130] Von Pastor, *History of the Popes*, XV, 186-187.

region on his way from Rome to Paris, had to hide his legatine cross. Writing in August from Picardy in northern France, English ambassador Throckmorton said that "all in this country seem marvelously bent to the new religion."[131]   The ferocious attacks on the Catholic Church which were the stock in trade of Calvinist preachers now bore their bitter fruit.

> The [Calvinist] faithful had been taught so extravagant a hatred of Catholicism that it became difficult to check its practical expression when such expression became feasible. To mutilate statues, to deride religious and priests, to insult the Host, to seize Catholic churches and desecrate them with Calvinist worship—these were temptations of peculiar and almost irresistible strength, and they were temptations to which, as the consciousness of power increased, and as the craven pusillanimity of the Catholics in regions where they were outnumbered came to be regarded as axiomatic, many of the faithful ultimately succumbed.[132]

On August 21 an Assembly of Notables met at the palace of Fontainebleau near Paris, including most of the royal council and provincial governors. Admiral Gaspard de Coligny, a Calvinist, urged legal permission for public Calvinist worship in France. The Cardinal of Lorraine objected strongly to that, but said he would support a suspension of persecution of Calvinists who came to their assemblies unarmed. Coligny demanded that the Guises allow more access to the young king, and said he could provide 50,000 signatures on Calvinist petitions; the Duke of Guise vehemently replied that the Admiral should show more respect for the king and that he could get a million signatures on petitions to maintain the Catholic Faith. The Notables eventually recommended a meeting of the Estates-General, the French equivalent to England's Parliament, for December and the national church council in January 1561 unless the ecumenical council had begun by then. The government agreed to call the Estates-General and to "show leniency towards heretics not implicated in sedition," and five days later called the national council as well.[133]

The day the Assembly of Notables adjourned, a courier was captured carrying papers from the Prince of Condé revealing the existence of a new plot involving him and his brother, the king of Navarre, for the seizure of the city of Lyons in the Rhone valley September 5, whereupon the Estates-General would be assembled there to overthrow the Guises. Condé and his agents had been raising troops even in Geneva, despite Calvin's proclaimed opposition, and appealing for help to the Lutheran princes of Germany. The Guises ordered a general mobilization and began arresting the known conspirators, while Philip II of Spain sent a special ambassador to France to offer military help against the Calvinist revolutionaries. Pope Pius IV continued to denounce the French

---

[131] Evenett, *Cardinal of Lorraine*, pp. 114-115, 142, 156; Kelley, *Hotman*, pp. 120-121; Thompson, *Wars of Religion in France*, p. 50.

[132] Evenett, *Cardinal of Lorraine*, pp. 115-116.

[133] *Ibid.*, pp. 142-144, 147-149 (quote on 149), 151; Sutherland, *Huguenot Struggle*, pp. 115-119; Thompson, *Wars of Religion in France*, pp. 52-55.

national council and to insist that the ecumenical council would be held, come what may, and to urge the strongly Catholic Guises to follow him in this.[134]

But he doubted that they would; and on October 9 he spoke words to Spanish ambassador Vargas that would have gladdened the heart of Queen Isabel the Catholic:

> I no longer count on France, and believe that the Emperor will continue to hold back, from fear of complications in Germany. The Spanish king is my only support. I shall therefore request his agreement to the opening of the Council of Trent, as a continuation of the former assembly there . . . I hope that after the opening the Emperor and others who still hesitate, will give their adherence.[135]

On October 24 papal ambassadors in Spain conveyed these words to King Philip II. Most of the cardinals strongly supported the Pope's intention to continue the Council of Trent rather than declare the upcoming council a new one. On November 1 Francis II and the Cardinal of Lorraine unexpectedly wrote to Pope Pius IV that the French national council would not be held after all, and that if Emperor Ferdinand accepted Trent as the site for the ecumenical council, the French would accept it as well. In fact, the Emperor had already done so, and on November 15 Pope Pius IV triumphantly announced to his cardinals in consistory that the three great Catholic sovereigns—Philip II of Spain, Emperor Ferdinand I, and Francis II of France—had agreed on the reconvening of the ecumenical council at Trent. The bull formally calling the council was issued at the end of November. It reviewed the history of the Council of Trent under Popes Paul III and Julius III, taking for granted the validity of its acts. Its continuing tasks were declared to be "the eradication of heresy, the removal of schism, and the reform of the Church." The date for its convocation was set for Easter 1561.[136]

It was done barely in time. On November 16 Francis II was suddenly assailed by a violent headache while hunting. It was caused by a rapidly developing mastoid infection in his left ear. The young king's health had never been good, and he was physically frail. The infection overwhelmed his body's feeble defenses. On December 5 he died, never having reached his sixteenth birthday. It had been legally pretended that Francis was ruling in his own right, but he had never really done so. Now he was succeeded by his ten-year-old brother Charles IX, unquestionably too young to rule. His mother Catherine de Medici was made regent, and thereby the Guises lost most of their power. The Prince of Condé, who had been arrested and condemned to death, was spared. Chancellor l'Hôpital made a speech at the convening of the Estates-General begging for peace and harmony. On Christmas day Jeanne d'Albret, the Queen

---

[134] Evenett, *Cardinal of Lorraine*, pp. 149-151, 155, 158-161; Kelley, *Hotman*, p. 121; Kingdon, *Geneva and Coming*, p. 75.

[135] Von Pastor, *History of the Popes*, XV, 202.

[136] *Ibid.*, XV, 203-204, 207-208, 210-211, 213-215; Evenett, *Cardinal of Lorraine*, pp. 179-180, 182-183, 185-195.

of Navarre, openly embraced Calvinism (as neither her husband Antoine nor her brother-in-law Condé had yet done, despite their many intrigues with the French Calvinists) and attended a Calvinist communion service instead of the Mass of Christmas.[137]

Queen Regent Catherine possessed her fair share of the legendary political skill of her family, the Medici of Florence; but she was poorly educated, especially for theological controversy, and no more a crusader than her relatives Leo X and Clement VII who had sat in the chair of Peter earlier in the century and done so little to combat the Protestant revolt. She was a devoted mother, and none of her sons were strong; Charles IX was definitely unbalanced. The threat of the revolutionaries cowed her. Encouraged by Chancellor l'Hôpital, she could only think of making peace with them. But it is part of the definition of a revolutionary that he cannot and will not make peace.

William Cecil wanted no peace in France. In January 1561 he wrote instructing his ambassador Throckmorton to call upon "those Protestants who in fearful times were so busy with their pen *and weapons* to be now forward, for surely courage will abash the Papists, so well I know their cowardice . . . Now is the time for Calvin and all such noble men as have fetched their knowledge from thence to impugn and suppress the tyranny of the Papists."[138]

Throckmorton wrote to Queen Jeanne d'Albret of Navarre conveying Queen Elizabeth's congratulations on her conversion and urging her to be strong and committed to Protestantism. Late in January Catherine de Medici, acting alone and against the advice of Cardinal Tournon, the papal legate, ordered the release of all persons imprisoned as Calvinists in France, even those who had assembled in arms or contributed money to rebellion, except for a few unspecified "leaders of sedition." Far from bringing peace, these measures simply brought on what became known in France as "the Huguenot Lent," full of rioting by Calvinists against Catholics, the Calvinists becoming more aggressive as they became more confident of victory. On March 7 Theodore Beza, one of Calvin's principal associates who was to be his successor, wrote to Johann Sturm in Strasbourg: "Everything in France tends to revolution."[139]

In April the Cardinal of Châtillon, Bishop of Beauvais, who was about to leave the Catholic Church to become a Calvinist, held a Calvinist communion service in his chapel, followed by a Calvinist riot in the town of Beauvais. At Fontainebleau Admiral Coligny installed a Calvinist minister in his apartments and invited members of the court to attend his sermons; even Catherine de Medici accepted the invitation, and brought her royal children. This was too much for old Constable Montmorency, a staunch Catholic and encouraged to be

---

[137] Nancy Roelker, *Queen of Navarre; Jeanne d'Albret* (Cambridge MA, 1968), pp. 149, 151-153; Evenett, *Cardinal of Lorraine*, p. 197-200; Thompson, *Wars of Religion in France*, pp. 70-71, 75-76, 120; J. Russell Major, *The Estates-General of 1560* (Princeton, 1951), pp. 73, 78-79, 82.

[138] Read, *Cecil*, p. 241. Emphasis added.

[139] Roelker, *Queen of Navarre*, pp. 153-154; Sutherland, *Huguenot Struggle*, p. 121; Evenett, *Cardinal of Lorraine*, pp. 209, 220-221; Kelley, *Hotman*, p. 133 (for quote).

so by his deeply Catholic wife Madeleine of Savoy; on Easter Sunday he formed a triumviral alliance with the Duke of Guise and Marshal St. André to save the Faith in France. Civil war was very close.[140]

The renewed Council of Trent was supposed to convene on that Easter, but by then only four bishops had arrived, and none even of the papal legates. The first two legates, Cardinals Gonzaga and Seripando, made their solemn entry into Trent April 16. On May 4 Emperor Ferdinand, finally putting aside his long-lasting doubts and hesitations on the passionate pleas of his religious advisor, Polish Bishop Stanislaus Hosius, agreed to send representatives to Trent. Philip II, who had been waiting for proof that the Council did really have the reluctant Emperor's support, thereupon committed himself to sending the bishops of Spain. The French bishops were summoned to assemble in Paris in July to select representatives to attend the Council and discuss what proposals to make there.[141]

On August 14, 1561 Mary Queen of Scots, ex-Queen of France, who had not yet herself abandoned her claim to the throne of England, departed from France to try to establish her rule in Scotland, of which she was unquestionably the rightful queen.[142] She had been born and spent the first six years of her life there, long enough to be able to speak the language well; but she had only limited memories of the country, for all the rest of her life had been spent in France in the bosom of the Guise family, who had helped to give her an unshakable Catholic faith. She was in the early bloom of young womanhood, tall, very fair-skinned, articulate, exceptionally beautiful[143]—and she was walking, alone and unprotected, into a nation where a religious and political revolution had been made with complete success exactly one year before by John Knox and William Cecil. Even the great Isabel the Catholic, at Mary's age, had a bold and resolute young husband and a wily, experienced father-in-law to help and protect her. Mary had no husband, and her once powerful family in France would soon be fighting for their lives, unable to do anything for her. The world-famous drama of Mary Queen of Scots takes on even greater dimensions of epic tragedy when one is fully conscious of the character and skill of her two great adversaries. Caught between the searing fire of Knox and the glacial ice of Cecil, the lovely young Queen of Scots never had a chance.

She landed at Leith near Edinburgh on the 19th of August, a dark day of fog and rain, which Knox thought appropriate for the arrival of a Catholic queen. The Scots people at first thought otherwise; they gave her an enthusiastic welcome, crying: "Heaven bless that sweet face!" It did not take long for her to discover what she was facing. On the first Sunday after her arrival she had Mass

---

[140] Sutherland, *Huguenot Struggle*, pp. 172-174; Thompson, *Wars of Religion in France*, pp. 95, 98-100; Evenett, *Cardinal of Lorraine*, pp. 222-223; Roelker, *Queen of Navarre*, pp. 156, 158.

[141] Von Pastor, *History of the Popes*, XV, 250, 252-253; Evenett, *Cardinal of Lorraine*, pp. 254, 256-257; Hubert Jedin, *Papal Legate at the Council of Trent; Cardinal Seripando* (St. Louis, 1947), p. 573.

[142] Fraser, *Mary Queen of Scots*, pp. 130-131.

[143] *Ibid.*, pp. 34-40, for Mary's childhood and appearance.

celebrated in the royal chapel at Holyroodhouse. A group of militant Calvinists attempted to force their way into the chapel to kill the priest, who was so frightened he could hardly elevate the Host. Knox thoroughly approved; the next Sunday, August 31, he delivered a violent sermon against Mary, in which he declared "that he feared one Mass more than if 10,000 armed enemies had landed in the realm to suppress the whole religion."[144]

Before another week had passed, Knox met with Mary in Holyroodhouse. Mary asked him to explain why he had incited revolt against her mother and herself, why he had written "First Blast," and what his goal was. He replied that his goal was to abolish "popery" and defend true religion, and that his doctrine in "First Blast" was true. She asked him if he would make war against her, to which he gave the hardly conciliatory response that he was as content to live under her as St. Paul to live under the Emperor Nero. She asked him how he could justify his teaching that subjects were entitled to overthrow their rulers by force; he replied that kings and queens must also obey God.[145]

It must have been a terrifying interview. John Knox was forty-seven years old. He had spent two and a half years as a galley slave, and survived. His most probably authentic portrait shows a man with a face like corrugated iron, with large fierce eyes under a furrowed brow. He was tough as nails, and a maximal revolutionary. She was eighteen, gentle, charming, often compared to a swan. Before long they reached the ultimate issue. Mary told the glowering figure before her: "Ye are not the Kirk that I will nurse. I will defend the Kirk of Rome, for I think it is the true Kirk of God." Knox replied: "Conscience requires knowledge, and I fear right knowledge ye have none." Mary replied quickly "but I have both heard and read"—and burst into tears.[146]

English ambassador Thomas Randolph wrote Cecil, three days later, that there was nothing to worry about. Of Knox he said "the voice of one man is able, in one hour, to put more life in us than 500 trumpets continually blustering in our ears." A month later Randolph told Cecil: "His severity keeps us in marvelous order; I commend better the success of his doings and preachings than the manner thereof, though I acknowledge his doctrine to be sound."[147]

Meanwhile in France, a major new policy initiative by the government of the beleaguered Catherine de Medici was taking place at a small town just outside Paris called Poissy. A group of French Calvinists headed by Theodore Beza had been invited to present the case for their religion to the bishops assembled to prepare for the Council of Trent and decide which of them would attend it. Opening this colloquy on July 31, Chancellor l'Hôpital declared the purpose of the meeting to be the pacification and the realm and the healing of

---

[144] *Ibid.*, pp. 75-77, 137-138, 152-153 (first quote on 75); Ridley, *Knox*, pp. 389-391 (second quote on 391).

[145] Fraser, *Mary Queen of Scots*, pp. 154-155; Ridley, *Knox*, pp. 392-393.

[146] Fraser, *Mary Queen of Scots*, pp. 155-156; W. Stanford Reid, *Trumpeter of God; a Biography of John Knox* (New York, 1974), p. 215. For the probable portrait of Knox see Ridley, *Knox*, facing p. 64.

[147] Ridley, *Knox*, p. 396.

religious divisions, which could not wait for the ecumenical council. Cardinal Tournon, the papal legate, was taken by surprise; l'Hôpital would not even give him a copy of his speech. On the same day the government made public a series of edicts drawn up three weeks earlier, which while continuing to forbid public Calvinist worship, allowed it in private homes, recommended that judges be more lenient with Calvinists, and granted a general amnesty to those in prison charged with heresy.[148]

On August 1 Cardinal Tournon assembled all bishops present and gained their unanimous approval for a statement of loyalty to the Pope and refusal to act contrary to his wishes. But on Sunday the 3rd the Calvinist-leaning Cardinal Châtillon and two like-minded bishops refused to attend pontifical High Mass with the other bishops, instead attending a service at which communion was illicitly given in both kinds. Three weeks later Beza arrived from Geneva, representing Calvin, who would not come for fear of arrest; Catherine de Medici required the French bishops to accept Beza's participation in the colloquy. Soon afterward Jeanne d'Albret, the Calvinist Queen of Navarre, arrived, "resolved to do all the harm she can to religion, and even to her husband, because he goes to Mass" in the words of the Spanish ambassador. Early in September a dozen theologians from the University of Paris appeared, denouncing the invitation to heretics to speak before the boy king, to no avail.[149]

The colloquy itself began September 9 with another speech by l'Hôpital urging religious unity and pledging that the government would no longer persecute the Calvinists. But despite the title of a modern study of it, the Colloquy of Poissy was no exercise in "ecumenism." Even less than the Lutherans were the Calvinists interested in ecumenism. Like all revolutionaries, they would accept it only on their own terms. On this first day of discussion Beza threw down the gauntlet with the explicit and shocking denial of the Real Presence quoted at the head of this chapter. The Real Presence, like the Incarnation, is a doctrine on which there can be no compromise for a serious Catholic. Cries of "he blasphemes!" burst out from all over the refectory of the abbey where the meeting was being held. Admiral Coligny buried his face in his hands; Beza's words had laid bare the true nature and purpose of the Calvinist revolutionaries, more clearly than he and his cohorts had intended. Cardinal Tournon rose from his place, shaking with rage, to fling in Catherine's face: "Will you, Madame, permit yourself to hear these horrible blasphemies, in the presence of the King and your other son, both of such tender age and so innocent?" Catherine replied that she only wanted peace, and that she and the king would live and die in the Catholic faith.[150]

---

[148] Evenett, *Cardinal of Lorraine*, pp. 280-282, 284-286; Brodrick, *Progress of the Jesuits*, pp. 59-60.

[149] Evenett, *Cardinal of Lorraine*, pp. 286-289, 295, 303-306; Sutherland, *Huguenot Struggle for Recognition*, p. 129; Brodrick, *Progress of the Jesuits*, p. 60; Walker, *Calvin*, p. 387; Roelker, *Queen of Navarre*, p. 162 (for quote).

[150] Donald Nugent, *Ecumenism in the Age of the Reformation; the Colloquy of Poissy* (Cambridge MA, 1974), pp. 94-103 (quote on 100); Evenett, *Cardinal of Lorraine*, pp.

A week later the Guise Cardinal of Lorraine delivered an eloquent and effective speech at the colloquy defending the Catholic doctrine of the Real Presence, basing his defense on Scripture (particularly the very explicit sixth chapter of the Gospel of John), history, and the Fathers and Councils of the Church, rather than on scholastic philosophy. He showed that the whole Church for more than 1,500 years had believed in the Real Presence; even the Greek schismatics believed in it. He appealed to young Charles to hold fast to it, the faith of all his predecessors and ancestors since Clovis. Up to this point some had doubted the Cardinal of Lorraine's full loyalty to the Church, since he had earlier supported the French national council; no one doubted it after this speech. Beza asked to make a reply; the French bishops refused—they had heard enough. Still Catherine de Medici and l'Hôpital set up a committee of twelve Catholics and twelve Calvinists to continue the discussions. In a meeting of this committee, Beza attacked the doctrine of papal primacy and papal succession from Peter, using the absurd fable of "Pope Joan" to support his argument, and denied that Scripture depended on the authority of the Church or that there was any infallible source of religious truth. Catholic theologian l'Espence responded by pointing out that the Calvinist ministers lacked any claim to authority whatsoever.[151]

By now the discussion had degenerated into a shouting match; in the words of Jesuit general Laynez, the participants were "all talking at once and ambushing and sniping one another like so many implacable enemies." The Cardinal of Lorraine declared that without agreement on the Real Presence no other agreement was possible. Beza appealed to Catherine; she remained silent. Weak and confused she might be, but like most Italian Catholics she would never deny the Real Presence. Efforts to find a compromise formula of language for the Real Presence were torpedoed by Peter Martyr Vermigli, a radical Calvinist whom Catherine had invited as a fellow Italian even though he could not speak French. Jesuit general Laynez arose to tell Catherine to her face that matters of faith were not her province, and that all such meetings as this should yield to the upcoming council reconvening at Trent. Nevertheless she made a last attempt to break the impasse with a committee of ten, which made no progress at all. On October 18 the Cardinal of Lorraine ended the assembly at Poissy.[152]

With the Calvinist revolutionaries now active almost everywhere throughout France and none of the laws against them being any longer enforced—in mid-December a public Calvinist service conducted by Beza in strongly Catholic Paris was attended by more than six thousand people, and the

---

306-310; Brodrick, *Progress of the Jesuits*, p. 92; Sutherland, *Huguenot Struggle for Recognition*, p. 130.

[151] Evenett, *Cardinal of Lorraine*, pp. 313-324, 334-336, 343-351; Nugent, *Colloquy of Poissy*, pp. 108-115, 128-141; Brodrick, *Progress of the Jesuits*, pp. 92-93; Thompson, *Wars of Religion in France*, pp. 112-113. For the fable of "Pope Joan" see Volume Two, Chapter 14 of this history.

[152] Evenett, *Cardinal of Lorraine*, pp. 351-356, 358-388; Nugent, *Colloquy of Poissy*, pp. 141-160, 162-176; Brodrick, *Progress of the Jesuits*, pp. 93-96 (quote on 93).

Parisian Catholic church of Saint-Médard was seized and pillaged[153]—the whole country was a tinderbox awaiting the spark. It came on March 1, 1562 when a French Calvinist assembly met and clashed with the Duke of Guise and his personal troops near the little town of Vassy, and the first of six religious civil wars broke out in France.[154]

But by then the Council of Trent was again in session. By early December the count of bishops at Trent had risen to 79 (64 Italians, 11 Spaniards, three Portuguese and one English). The French bishops, recalled to their Catholic loyalties by the clash with Beza and the Calvinists at Poissy, were ready now to join them. On December 31 Pope Pius IV set Sunday, January 18, 1562, the feast of the Chair of St. Peter, as the appropriate day for the long awaited, much postponed, desperately needed council to resume its work after the lapse of almost a full decade. For this there were 104 bishops present in addition to four papal legates: Cardinals Gonzaga, Simonetta, Seripando, and Hosius of Poland. They met first in the oldest church of Trent, long ago dedicated to St. Peter. Then they moved to the cathedral, and Cardinal Gonzaga read the Pope's bulls of convocation.[155]

It was a triumph of perseverance, and of the clear thinking, good sense, and inspired diplomacy of Pope Pius IV. It should have been convened forty years before; once belatedly convened, it should have finished its work fifteen years before. But much of its work still remained to be done. While it was delayed, Martin Luther's revolt had developed into Calvinist revolution. But enough of Europe still remained Catholic so that, if the Council listened to the promptings of the Holy Spirit, much of Christendom could still be saved.

---

[153] Roelker, *Queen of Navarre*, p. 169; Louis Batiffol, *The Century of the Renaissance* (*The National History of France*) (New York, 1916), p. 201.

[154] For further information on the so-called "massacre of Vassy" see Chapter Six, below.

[155] Jedin, *Seripando*, pp. 570, 577; von Pastor, *History of the Popes*, XV, 262, 264-265; Evenett, *Cardinal of Lorraine*, p. 421.

6
The Council Fulfilled
1562-1572
Popes Pius IV (1559-1565), and St. Pius V (1566-1572)

"If people say, 'No Council can help us any more, the evil has gone on too long,' I answer, it is never too late, if we set to work in a spirit of godly hopefulness, true faith, and ardent love. In all such desperate emergencies as the present one, the Catholic Church has always had recourse to the one remedy of a General Council, against which the Devil, the sects, the heretics and schismatics have invariably opposed their cleverest wiles, their utmost strength and wickedness, but have always been mightily overcome by Catholic truth."—Cardinal Truchsess of Augsburg to Duke Albert of Bavaria, July 13, 1560[1]

"The difficulties and dangers which beset the third and final meeting of the Council of Trent from its opening on the frosty morning of January 18, 1562, to the December day in 1563 when Cardinal Morone pronounced the '*Andate in pace*,' were so great that the final success is one of the strangest and most unaccountable events in history. Each of the three great Catholic powers, France, Spain, and the Empire, contributed its share of trouble, and that the Pope and his four legates, defenseless in a material sense and mere children at diplomacy compared with some of their opponents, should have piloted the Church to safety through two terrible years of almost incessant darkness and storm argues something more than human skill or prudence behind the scenes."—James Brodrick, *St. Peter Canisius*[2]

"His Catholic Majesty [Philip II] has not persuaded himself, nor can he ever persuade himself, that trifling and dissimulation in this matter of faith can be just or fitting, or can fulfill the obligation imposed. Not only should the heart conceive it and the mouth confess it, but the very hands should perform and guard it."—King Philip II of Spain to Emperor Maximilian II, winter 1569[3]

"The North is full of tangled things and texts and aching eyes,
And dead is all the innocence of anger and surprise,
And Christian killeth Christian in a narrow dusty room,

---

[1] Johannes Janssen, *History of the German People at the Close of the Middle Ages*, Volume VII (St. Louis, 1905), p. 204.
[2] James Brodrick, *St. Peter Canisius* (Baltimore MD, 1950), p. 472.
[3] William Thomas Walsh, *Philip II* (London, 1937), p. 472.

And Christian feareth Christ who wears a newer face of doom,
And Christian hateth Mary whom God kissed in Galilee,
But Don John of Austria is riding to the sea!
Don John calling through the blast and the eclipse
Crying with the trumpet, with the trumpet of his lips!"
—G. K. Chesterton, "Lepanto"

In the winter of 1562 it was still not clear how much—if anything significant—the new session of the Council of Trent would be able to accomplish.   National divisions and jealousies were deep and suspicions abounded; some of the bishops and most of the royal representatives present tended to put the worst construction on every action of everyone not of their own nationality and faction.   The Protestants were invited and assured safe-conducts, but few really expected them to come; most of the German bishops so feared the Lutherans that they stayed away themselves, despite the best efforts of Emperor Ferdinand I, the Catholic brother of Charles V who was as firm in the Faith as he had been, to persuade them to attend.   There was continuing, often bitter disagreement over whether this session should be regarded as a continuation of the earlier sessions at Trent, or a new council; and whether the requirement that bishops reside in their dioceses—which all accepted, at least in principle—was a prescription of divine law or simply part of the proper operation of the Church under the authority of the Pope.   The only issue on which the renewed Council could unite in its first two months was the need to revise the excessively strict Index of Forbidden Books compiled by Pope Paul IV.[4]

Meanwhile the tinderbox in France had exploded.[5]   When hostile tensions reach breaking point, any small spark can bring the detonation.   The propaganda of both sides concentrates immediately on the incident which provided the spark, and the truth about it quickly becomes obscured behind clouds of propaganda.   Such is definitely the case with the events at the little village of Vassy, about 120 miles east of Paris near the sources of the Marne, on the morning of March 1, 1562, a Sunday.   As best we can reconstruct it, what happened was this: the Duke of Guise, the Catholic military leader of France, a famous warrior of Herculean stature, once a handsome man but for many years disfigured by a great scar which slashed across his face from eye to chin, was attending Mass in the

---

[4] Ludwig von Pastor, *History of the Popes*, Volume XV (London, 1951), pp. 267-268, 271-273; Janssen, *History of the German People*, VII, 239; Hubert Jedin, *Papal Legate at the Council of Trent: Cardinal Seripando* (St. Louis, 1947), pp. 588-589, 594, 596, 605; H. Outram Evenett, *The Cardinal of Lorraine and the Council of Trent* (Cambridge, England, 1930), pp. 440-441, 451-452. Pope Pius IV responded promptly to the Council's call for a revision of the Index at its second session February 26, with a decree for this purpose on March 4 (Brodrick, *St. Peter Canisius*, pp. 494-495).

[5] It is a striking though little noticed fact that during each of the last three great ecumenical Councils of the Church, a war particularly dangerous to Christendom has broken out during the sessions: the First French War of Religion during the final session of the Council of Trent, the Franco-Prussian War during the First Vatican Council, and the Vietnam war during the Second Vatican Council.

parish church of Vassy, accompanied by a large number of armed retainers. Nearby some 600 Calvinists were holding an illegal religious service in a barn. After Mass the Duke went to the barn to enforce the law against public Calvinist services. Verbal insults escalated until the Calvinists began throwing stones. At least one struck the Duke; others must have struck some of his men. They opened fire, as they had a perfect right to do under such circumstances, though the Duke always insisted he did not order it. But he did not move very quickly to stop the firing, which took a heavy toll. Estimates of the number killed in generally reliable histories literally range from 12 to 1200. H. Outram Evenett, a careful scholar and one of the few writers on this period who does not reveal a strong bias in favor of the Huguenots (French Calvinists), is probably as nearly correct as anyone now can be with his estimate of 30 killed and 150 wounded.[6]

The Duke and his action were hailed in strongly Catholic Paris when he marched in two weeks later with the Constable of France, the redoubtable Anne de Montmorency, and three thousand well-armed soldiers. The Calvinist military leader, the Prince of Condé, promptly withdrew from the city and called his fellow believers to arms. Queen Mother Catherine de Medici and her twelve-year-old son, King Charles IX, had gone to the royal palace at Fontainebleau just before the news of Vassy arrived. On March 27 Constable Montmorency arrived with a thousand cavalrymen to escort the boy king and his mother to safety. She protested, for she had feared and hated the Guises ever since they had dominated the government so completely during the brief reign of her oldest son Francis II.[7] But it was not the Duke of Guise who had come for her; it was the Constable of France, charged above all with the protection of the person of the king, formerly associated with the party opposed to the Guises, but who knew rebellion when he saw it. In his 69 years he had seen plenty of it. He told the Queen Mother she and her son would come with him or Charles IX would lose his throne.[8]

Sullenly, on the next day—Good Friday that year—they agreed to accompany him. Montmorency was only just in time. On Easter Sunday, March 29, Condé and the other principal French Calvinist military leader, Admiral Gaspard de Coligny, appeared before Paris with 3,000 cavalry, before Montmorency could get there. Consequently he took the royal family to the fortified town of Melun for protection, while Coligny and Condé, facing a fiercely hostile city, withdrew to Orléans in central France. A Calvinist national synod was meeting there. On April 8 Condé issued a manifesto, and three days

---

[6] James W. Thompson, *The Wars of Religion in France 1559-1576* (New York, 1909), pp. 134-135; Walsh, *Philip II*, p. 291; Evenett, *Cardinal of Lorraine*, p. 446; *The Cambridge Modern History*, ed. A. W. Ward, G. W. Prothero and Stanley Leathes (New York, 1934), III, 1; Donald R. Kelley, *François Hotman; a Revolutionary's Ordeal* (Princeton, 1973), p. 155; E. R. Chamberlin, *Marguerite of Navarre* (New York, 1974), p. 12.

[7] See Chapter Five, above.

[8] Thompson, *Wars of Religion in France*, pp. 136-138; *Cambridge Modern History* III, 1; Evenett, *Cardinal of Lorraine*, pp. 440, 447; Irene Mahoney, *Madame Catherine* (New York, 1975), pp. 90-92.

later a "Treaty of Association," declaring that he and his associates had taken up arms "to maintain the honor of God, the peace of the kingdom, and the liberty of the king under the government of the Queen his mother." On April 12 he formally took command of a rebel army of 20,000 men, declaring that their only purpose was to liberate the king and stop idolatry, blasphemy, and violence.[9]

During April the Calvinist rebels also seized Rouen in Normandy, along with much of the rest of that province, and much of southern and central France including the large cities of Lyons and Toulouse. They soon demonstrated that they would indeed act to "stop idolatry" (as they regarded it) by the most direct means. On April 25 the churches of Orléans—only a little more than a century removed from St. Joan—were ravaged, stripped of every image of Christ, the Blessed Virgin Mary and the saints. At Angers not far away, Catholic images were dragged through the streets, whipped, and burned, along with consecrated Hosts taken from the tabernacles. At Rouen on May 3 and 4, "armed Huguenots went systematically from church to church, confiscating objects of precious metal, smashing or defacing sculpture, altars, and baptismal fonts, and dragging all tapestries, pews, coffers, and music books into the streets, where they were consumed in great bonfires. The city's scarred churches still bear witness today to the thoroughness with which the entire operation was carried out." On May 4 in Rouen, a large consecrated Host was first trampled and then stuck on the point of a dragon-headed lance. Calvin's lieutenant and future successor Theodore Beza approved of all this, if somewhat reluctantly, stating in a letter to Jeanne d'Albret, the Calvinist Queen of Navarre, that "in so widespread a movement there may be some secret action of God, who by this means chooses the humble to shame the great and the proud."[10] Was it really only "the great and the proud" who loved the representations of the Mother of God in the parish churches of France?

In the midst of this bloody turmoil, on April 14 three ambassadors from the French government departed for Trent, all Gallicans, opposed to the Pope's authority over the Church in France and well regarded by many French Calvinists. Their instructions directed them to try to move the Council to Constance or some other German city, farther from Italy than Trent, and to demand that the Council declare itself not a continuation of the previous meetings at Trent and deny the Pope's authority to confirm, amend or reject Council decrees. But just five days later Catherine de Medici realized that in the

---

[9] Thompson, *Wars of Religion in France*, pp. 137-141, 224; *Cambridge Modern History*, III, 1; Mahoney, *Madame Catherine*, pp. 92-93 (for quote); Evenett, *Cardinal of Lorraine*, p. 447; A. W. Whitehead, *Gaspard de Coligny, Admiral of France* (London, 1904), pp. 107-108, 110-111; Robert M. Kingdon, *Geneva and the Coming of the Wars of Religion in France, 1555-1563* (Geneva, 1956), pp. 87-88.
[10] Philip Benedict, *Rouen during the Wars of Religion* (Cambridge, England, 1981), pp. 96-98 (first quote on 97); Whitehead, *Coligny*, pp. 114-116; Thompson, *Wars of Religion in France*, p. 142; Mack P. Holt, *The French Wars of Religion, 1562-1629* (New York, 1995), p. 53; Nancy Roelker, *Queen of Navarre, Jeanne d'Albret* (Cambridge MA, 1968), p. 191 (second quote).

immediate crisis she must put her trust in the Catholics (the fact that she was still a Catholic herself seemed to have had curiously little influence on her deliberations on, before, and after this occasion). She summoned the Duke of Guise, Constable Montmorency, King Antoine of Navarre (who after a long flirtation with Calvinism had finally decided to remain Catholic), and Marshals Brissac and St. André, saying that she had been badly advised before but would now rely on them. Together they agreed to ask help from Spain, which was done May 8 and promptly promised by Philip II. Reproached by Coligny for making himself a "tool" of the Guises, Constable Montmorency responded by summoning him to consider "the evil which had fallen on the kingdom since the troubles had begun" and help him to make an end of it instead of perpetuating it.[11]

French Catholics were fighting back. All known Calvinists were expelled from Paris and from Toulouse, where there was a pitched battle with thousands of casualties before they could be driven out. But in Normandy the Calvinists took the great port of Le Havre near the mouth of the Seine; all Catholics were driven out of Rouen, and Mass was no longer said there. In Paris a solemn Eucharistic procession moved through the streets to mark the reconsecration of the Church of St. Médard, desecrated by the Calvinists, with an armed guard stationed before each house on the processional route; a week later there was another great procession with the relics of Ste. Geneviève, patroness of Paris, praying for her help against the destroying heretics. On Corpus Christi day in early June the Cardinal of Lorraine, brother of the Duke of Guise, took his stand for the eldest daughter of the Church: "It were better to die, and to give the last drop of blood, than to permit . . . another religion to be established in France." Indeed, if France were lost, there would be little left of Christendom.[12]

At Trent, after the long weeks and months of hesitation and delay, serious discussion at last began June 10 on the true doctrine of the Mass and Eucharist, the most fundamental of all the differences between Catholics and Protestants.[13]

The Eucharistic question first discussed was an old one: whether the laity should be allowed to drink the Precious Blood from the chalice in addition to receiving Christ in the Host. This debate went back to the Hussites in Bohemia a century and a half before, and had been renewed when Luther endorsed Huss. The Church had always taught that Christ was received full and entire, Body and Blood, in the Host alone, so there was no need for the laity to receive the chalice, but it could be granted to them as a special privilege, as it was for a time in Bohemia. On June 15 the Jesuit St. Peter Canisius rose at Trent to expound this doctrine once more, recommending that the chalice should only be given to loyal Catholics living among heretics if this would really help to keep them in the

---

[11] Evenett, *Cardinal of Lorraine*, pp. 453-454; Thompson, *Wars of Religion in France*, pp. 133, 143; Whitehead, *Coligny*, p. 118 (for quotes).

[12] Thompson, *Wars of Religion in France*, pp. 148-150; Holt, *French Wars of Religion*, p. 54; Barbara B. Diefendorf, *Beneath the Cross; Catholics and Huguenots in Sixteenth-Century Paris* (New York, 1991), p. 65 (for quote).

[13] Jedin, *Seripando*, p. 630.

Faith. From his experience of re-evangelization in Germany, he concluded that the chalice for the laity was not needed there, but only in Bohemia. Emperor Ferdinand emphatically disagreed; he had become convinced that this concession would win back many Lutherans in Germany. On June 23 the Council's theologians unanimously agreed that communion under both species was not spiritually necessary nor usually desirable, while reserving to the Pope the question of allowing it under special circumstances in particular regions. On July 16 the full Council approved the statement of the theologians, but declared that the Council should take action of its own on the issue of the chalice for the laity at a later date. But Cardinal Seripando, one of the papal legates, continued to urge that the Council defer entirely to the Pope on this matter, and eventually his advice prevailed.[14]

More fundamental issues regarding the Eucharist were then examined. On August 6 a draft decree on the Mass as an unbloody perpetuation of Christ's sacrifice on the Cross was presented to the Council. The able Cardinal Stanislaus Hosius of Poland sharply criticized it for not specifically identifying the Last Supper as the first Mass. A revised draft made this identification. A further revision (approved by a vote of 83-57) declared both the sacramental and "spiritual" interpretations of John 6 permissible (St. Peter Canisius had strongly argued in his June 15 address that this chapter should be central in the apologetical defense of the Mass, since it provided clear Scriptural authority for a sacrament which many Protestants regarded as un-Scriptural). At the sixth general session of the renewed Council—attended by five papal legates, three patriarchs, 22 archbishops, 144 bishops, and host Cardinal Madruzzo—these formulations were given final approval, along with a declaration that the liturgy of the Mass in the West should be in Latin rather than in the vernacular, and a specific relegation to the Pope of the decision on whether and when to permit the chalice for the laity.[15]

The essentially minor but contentious issues of whether the Council should be regarded as a continuation of the two earlier sessions at Trent or a new assembly, and whether the obligation of bishops to reside in their dioceses was a matter of divine law, continued to be agitated throughout most of the year. In May Pope Pius IV had tried to take these issues off the table by simply declaring the Council a continuation of its predecessors and reserving decision on the nature of the episcopal residence requirement to himself. But the legates were unable to prevent further discussion of these issues, which tended to become very acrimonious. The Spanish bishops were the primary source of the demand to declare the Council a continuation and episcopal residence a matter of divine law; on July 6 Philip II, in one of the wisest (and least noticed) actions of his

---

[14] *Ibid.*, pp. 634-636; Von Pastor, *History of the Popes*, XV, 280, 285-288, 290-291; Brodrick, *St. Peter Canisius*, pp. 498-500. For the Hussite demand for Communion under both species, see Volume Three, Chapter 12 of this history.

[15] Von Pastor, *History of the Popes*, XV, 294-295, 297-298; Jedin, *Seripando*, pp. 639, 649-652; Brodrick, *St. Peter Canisius*, p. 499.

reign,[16] urged his bishops to cease agitating these issues, since they had already made their position clear. That the Council of 1562-3 was in fact a continuation of the previous sessions at Trent gradually became tacitly accepted, without a formal declaration to that effect. The debate on the origin of the bishop's obligation of residence was enlightened by a brilliant address by Jesuit General Laynez on October 20, drawing a clear distinction between the bishop's power of ordination which he obtains directly from God, and the authority of his office which he obtains from the Pope. Cardinal Seripando similarly distinguished between the necessity of the office of bishop in the Church as established by Christ, and its jurisdiction which the Pope determines. Following up on this, on December 9 Jesuit General Laynez proposed that the existence and inherent power of bishops should be declared part of the unalterable constitution of the Church, but that no mention should be made of the origin of their jurisdiction. This solution eventually prevailed.[17]

Meanwhile in France, faced with the Catholic rally in most of the country, the Calvinists turned to their natural ally, Protestant England, where William Cecil was eager to help them. On July 20 he prepared a memorandum entitled "The Perils Growing upon the Overthrow of the Prince of Condé's Cause," which clearly showed that he viewed the struggle in Europe not in simple nationalistic terms, but in terms fundamentally religious, the mirror image of Philip II's own view of it:

> When the matter is brought to these terms, that the Papists shall have the upper hand, then will it be too late to seek to withstand it, for then the matter shall be like a great rock of stone that is falling down from the top of a mountain, which when it is coming no force can stay. Whosoever thinking that relenting in religion will assuage the Guisans' aspirations, they are far deceived; for two appetites will never be satisfied but with the thing desired, the desire to have such a kingdom as England and Scotland may make united, and the cruel appetite of a Pope and his adherents to have his authority reestablished fully.[18]

Consequently an agreement (finalized in October as the Treaty of Hampton Court) was made between the Prince of Condé, speaking for the French Calvinists, and Cecil, speaking for Queen Elizabeth, by which the port of Le

---

[16] The prejudice against Philip II of Spain is indeed virulent, shared by many good Catholic historians as well as nearly all non-Catholic historians (the recent biography by Henry Kamen, *Philip of Spain* [New Haven CT, 1997] is a notable exception), and even to some extent by the great Ludwig von Pastor, who tends to overrate the significance of the jurisdictional controversies between Philip II and the later Pope St. Pius V as he implemented the decrees of Trent and launched the Catholic Reformation. The fact was that, as St. Pius V repeatedly pointed out (see below), Philip II was the only sovereign upon whom the Church could consistently depend; fortunately for the Church, in this epoch he was the most powerful of them.

[17] Von Pastor, *History of the Popes*, XV, 277-279, 283, 294, 301-302, 305; Jedin, *Seripando*, pp. 608-609, 621-622, 665-666; Brodrick, *St. Peter Canisius*, p. 518.

[18] Conyers Read, *Mr. Secretary Cecil and Queen Elizabeth* (New York, 1961), p. 249.

Havre at the mouth of the Seine, which the Calvinists were holding, would be turned over at least temporarily to England in return for 140,000 crowns and 6,000 men. English troops landed at Le Havre October 4, and some were sent immediately to Rouen, besieged by the Duke of Guise. Despite this reinforcement of the defenders, he took and sacked Rouen October 26. King Antoine of Navarre, the double turncoat (from Catholic to Calvinist and back again) was mortally wounded during the siege of Rouen. He accepted Catholic anointing, but in his last hours turned his coat for a third time, declaring himself neither Catholic nor Calvinist, but Lutheran![19]

By early November 1562 the Calvinist nobles were bringing in thousands of German mercenaries. Philip II's promised Spanish troops began arriving in December. On November 8 Condé left Orléans for Paris with an army of 10,000 foot and 5,500 horse. In the town of Pithiviers through which they passed three days later, they killed every priest they found. Checked at Corbeil on the Seine November 16, they were met by the Duke of Guise and his men. The two armies marched down the Seine on opposite sides of the winding river. On November 25 the spires of the Cathedral of Notre Dame and the walls of Paris rose before them. Constable Montmorency commanded the defenses of the city. He and Catherine de Medici met with Admiral Coligny; with the grand old Constable to stiffen her usually pliable backbone, Catherine would not give an inch. Coligny offered battle. Montmorency and the Duke of Guise refused it; Paris was too great a prize to risk by combat when its defenses were so strong and the enemy had little artillery. By December 10 Condé was running out of money to pay his Germans and food for his army, since most of the readily available food stocks around Paris had been removed or destroyed. He withdrew toward Chartres. The Duke of Guise and Montmorency pursued too closely to give him time to attack it, thereby probably saving the world's most renowned and beautiful stained-glass windows from Calvinist destruction. On December 18, crossing the Eure River by night, the Catholic army caught up with Coligny and Condé and their army.[20]

There followed the next day the Battle of Dreux, the first major engagement of the 32-year Wars of Religion in France. The Catholics had the advantage in numbers (17,000 to 11,500) and of 22 well-placed cannon. Constable Montmorency, in his seventieth year but fighting in the ranks with his men as he always did, was captured, and one of his sons was killed, along with Marshal Saint-André. But as his wing scattered before charges by the Calvinist cavalry, the Duke of Guise from a nearby height gave a tremendous cry of "Now, friends, the day is ours!" and launched a downhill charge which nothing could stop, capturing Condé. Coligny's attempted counter-charge was repelled by the Spanish infantry in square, the best foot soldiers in the world. Coligny, an

---

[19] *Ibid.*, p. 250; Thompson, *Wars of Religion in France*, pp. 164-171; *Cambridge Modern History*, III, 3; Mahoney, *Madame Catherine*, pp. 95-97; Benedict, *Rouen*, p. 100; Roelker, *Queen of Navarre*, pp. 200-202.

[20] Thompson, *Wars of Religion in France*, pp. 176-177; Whitehead, *Coligny*, pp. 130-135, 137-139; *Cambridge Modern History*, III, 4; Diefendorf, *Beneath the Cross*, p. 68.

excellent general, saved the bulk of his men and withdrew them once again to Orléans. Of the Duke of Guise this day, the Catholic-hating English special envoy Nicholas Throckmorton—also captured by the Duke on the battlefield—said: "He behaved like a great and valiant captain; the victory is to be ascribed to him alone."[21]

William Cecil's strategy was ruined. Now for the first time, facing that ruin, he displayed the relentless perseverance which made him so deadly an enemy to Catholic Christendom. "This web is undone," he wrote to Thomas Smith, English ambassador to France, ". . . and new to begin."[22] While life was left in William Cecil, he would never stop weaving webs against the Catholic Church.

On November 13, as Condé and the Calvinists were marching on Paris, the Guise Cardinal of Lorraine arrived at Trent, young, vigorous, resolute. He received a brilliant welcome. He brought with him 13 more French bishops to join the five already at the Council, along with 18 theologians mostly from the University of Paris, still a stronghold of orthodoxy as it had remained ever since, three centuries before, St. Thomas Aquinas was on its faculty.[23] In his first speech to the Council the Cardinal of Lorraine gave advice befitting a true prince of the Church and statesman: they should refrain from useless disputes, legislate sweeping reforms in the Church, and always respect the supreme authority of the Pope. No Gallicanism in these words! He asked aid for his threatened Catholic people. Cardinal Seripando, a generation older, deeply discouraged by the relative lack of progress in the renewed Council's first year, took heart. This man might not only save the Church in his native land, but play a major role in saving Christendom.[24] So he was to do.

On January 3, 1563 a solemn Mass of thanksgiving was held in Rome for the Catholic victory at Dreux. On January 12 Cardinal Seripando and the Cardinal of Lorraine met and agreed on the compromise formulation of the origin of the power of bishops that Seripando and Laynez had formulated earlier. Over the next few weeks, under pressure from some of the other French bishops, the Cardinal of Lorraine backed away from his position, even refusing for a time to recognize the Pope as "universal bishop." Hearing of this, on January 31 Pope Pius IV sent unequivocal instructions to his legates at the Council (including Seripando) that the designation of the Pope as "universal bishop" must be upheld at all costs. Cardinal Gonzaga, head of the papal legates at the Council, at this

---

[21] Thompson, *Wars of Religion in France*, pp. 178-181; *Cambridge Modern History*, III, 4-5; Holt, *French Wars of Religion*, p. 55; Whitehead, *Coligny*, pp. 139-145 (first quote on 143); Mahoney, *Madame Catherine*, p. 97 (second quote).

[22] Read, *Cecil*, p. 257.

[23] See Volume Three, Chapter 7 of this history.

[24] Von Pastor, *History of the Popes*, XV, 302-303; Jedin, *Seripando*. pp. 671-672, 674-675, 678-680.

point wisely proposed a long recess, during which draft declarations on the sacrament of matrimony would be prepared. It was agreed to.[25]

Taking advantage of this break in the action at Trent, Cardinal Gonzaga, the Cardinal of Lorraine, and St. Peter Canisius all travelled across the winter Alps in February to Innsbrück in Austria to confer with Emperor Ferdinand I. Despite his strong personal commitment to the Catholic Faith and Church, Emperor Ferdinand had been harshly critical of the Pope and the Council thus far, insisting that they take up reform before doctrine, give the chalice to the laity, and even allow priests to marry. Of all the visitors, the patient but unyielding Jesuit made the greatest impact. St. Peter Canisius carefully explained to the loyally Catholic but not particularly intelligent Emperor that even if the Council made some mistakes, it was better to support its continued meeting than to suspend it again or allow it to break up, further fragmenting the Church and Christendom; that it would be good for the Emperor to meet personally with the Pope, but not in Trent; that bishops should most definitely be compelled to reside in their dioceses, both by the Pope and by their Catholic princes, but that this should not be declared to be divine law; that discussions of doctrine and reform at the Council should proceed side by side, with neither given precedence; that Ferdinand, as a layman being for all his temporal powers "a sheep subject to the Supreme Shepherd," should not press the Council to impose itself on the Pope or judge him, since Church tradition made clear that no man or group has authority to judge the Pope. Not every ruler—not even every Catholic ruler—in that age would have taken kindly to being described as the Pope's sheep, but Canisius knew his man; Ferdinand was genuinely humble in spirit, and had been raised in Spain—it was what he needed to hear, and would accept. After that the Emperor did not continue to press his demands on the Council.[26]

On February 5 the Duke of Guise had led his army to Orléans and laid siege to it; not for long would he allow the declared enemies of the Catholic Faith to occupy the city St. Joan of Arc had liberated. February days are very short in northern Europe. On February 18 the grizzled, scar-faced old veteran, victor of Dreux and the mightiest warrior in France, was riding back to his camp headquarters from Portereau, a suburb of Orléans on the south bank of the Loire. From behind him, in the shadows, stepped Jean Poltrot, Sieur de Meré, a 26-year-old fanatically Calvinist kinsman of that La Renaudie who had led the conspiracy of Amboise against the Guises three years before in 1560. Admiral Coligny employed Poltrot as a spy. He was carrying an arquebus, and shot the Duke in the back of his right shoulder with a poisoned bullet. He was captured two days later and named Coligny as the planner of the murder, who had engaged him to commit it. The Duke's wound festered quickly because of the poison on the bullet, and Francis of Guise died a holy death on Ash Wednesday, six days after he was shot. The distracted young king wept and Catherine de Medici fainted

---

[25] Von Pastor, *History of the Popes*, XV, 307-308, XVI, 186; Jedin, *Seripando*, pp. 682-684, 686-687.

[26] Von Pastor, *History of the Popes*, XV, 308-310; Jedin, *Seripando*, p. 608; Brodrick, *St. Peter Canisius*, pp. 524, 531-541.

before his bier. The great Catholic Duke had meant more to her than she had ever been willing to admit. There was great grief and lamentation among the Catholics of Paris.[27]

Coligny and the Calvinists, on the other hand, welcomed the news, and openly rejoiced. Coligny admitted employing Poltrot as a spy and hearing him say he could easily kill the Duke of Guise, but denied asking or paying him to do it. Poltrot, desperately trying to bargain for his life, confirmed his story of Coligny's direct complicity in the assassination March 7, retracted it on the 15th, was condemned to death on the 18th, renewed his accusation after the condemnation, then withdrew it again just before he was torn by red-hot pincers, pulled apart by four horses, drawn, and quartered. Not much reliance can be placed on testimony given under such circumstances. We will never know for sure whether Coligny was guilty; but he might have been. The murdered Duke's relatives—especially his ardent young son and heir Henry, a central figure in the forthcoming French wars of religion—were totally convinced of his guilt. Young Henry and his uncle, the duc d'Aumale, swore vengeance over Duke Francis' body in the church at Blois, and d'Aumale later told Henry he would have killed him if he had not sworn.[28] So Catholic a family should have known what kind of evil this was calling down upon their heads, but Henry did not realize it until he himself became a victim of assassination.[29]

On March 8 the two most distinguished prisoners held by the two sides in the French religious war, Constable Montmorency and the Prince of Condé, were exchanged, and immediately began negotiating at Orléans with Catherine de Medici; Coligny, who wanted to continue the war, was not there. Within a few days the negotiators had reached agreement on peace terms, which were formally signed and proclaimed at Amboise on March 19. All official condemnations and general legal disabilities were removed from French Calvinists, their toleration was decreed in the King's name, and Condé was appointed lieutenant-general of the realm. Public Calvinist worship was to continue wherever it was currently occurring, and allowed further in one city in each administrative district, except for Paris and in or near the royal court. The government even agreed to pay the costs and debts of the Calvinist army. These were remarkably favorable terms for rebels who had just lost a major battle, attesting to the deep penetration of Calvinism among the French nobility in a country where the nobility remained exceptionally powerful right up to the French Revolution; to the chivalrous spirit of Constable Montmorency, who still trusted a nobleman's word; and to the shifty timidity of the Queen Mother. But they were not good enough for Calvin,

---

[27] Thompson, *Wars of Religion in France*, pp. 188-189; *Cambridge Modern History*, III, 5; Mahoney, *Madame Catherine*, pp. 98-99; Walsh, *Philip II*, p. 293; Whitehead, *Coligny*, p. 153-154; Diefendorf, *Beneath the Cross*, p. 70. For the conspiracy of Amboise see Chapter Five, above. The poison on the bullet is not mentioned in all accounts, but the report of it is rendered highly plausible by so rapid a death from a mere shoulder wound.

[28] Whitehead, *Coligny*, pp. 149, 154-156, 166-170; Diefendorfer, *Beneath the Cross*, p. 71.

[29] See Chapter Eight, below.

who condemned them almost as vigorously, though obviously for opposite reasons, as Pope Pius IV and King Philip II of Spain; and they were much too good for the people of Paris. When the criers went through the City of Light at the end of the month announcing the terms of the peace, the people threw mud at them and threatened their lives. The *Parlement* of Paris would not register the peace agreement without expressly limiting it to the duration of the King's minority, which now that he had reached thirteen could under French law be ended at any time.[30]

In Trent at the beginning of March 1563, worn out by the constant struggle to keep the Council in being, ward off or moderate the excesses of criticism and party spirit, and make progress on its still largely untouched agenda, the head of the five papal legates, Cardinal Gonzaga, was dead and the great Cardinal Seripando was dying. (During that first week of March, it was impossible to hold any meetings of the Council because of repeated bloody combats among the retainers of the French, Spanish, and Italian bishops.) In a stroke of genius, Pope Pius IV—underestimated in his own time and ever since—appointed as the new chief legate Cardinal Giovanni Morone, the finest diplomat in papal service, a dedicated reformer whose imprisonment by the erratic Pope Paul IV on a groundless charge of heresy had scandalized the whole Church. Morone had worked and suffered all his life for the Church. He was a young 54, vigorous and dedicated, utterly resolved that this time the Council should not stop short of complete success. He was the best possible choice.[31]

Cardinal Morone arrived at Trent on Holy Saturday. Later in April he was in Innsbrück, conferring with Emperor Ferdinand along with the Cardinal of Lorraine and St. Peter Canisius, once again playing successfully on the aging emperor's fundamental Catholic loyalty annealed in his Spanish childhood against the pessimistic and anti-papal advice he was getting from most of Germany where he had spent his whole adult life. By May 12 a full understanding had been reached. The Emperor had decided he would trust Morone and the Pope to reform the Church without constant pressure and ultimata from him. He dropped his request that the Council approve the marriage of priests. At the same time the Emperor and all his theological advisors rejected the Cardinal of Lorraine's position denying the Pope the title of universal bishop and pastor. On May 19 St. Charles Borromeo, the Pope's secretary, wrote him

---

[30] Thompson, *Wars of Religion in France*, pp. 190-191; Holt, *French Wars of Religion*, pp. 55-57; von Pastor, *History of the Popes*, XV, 329-330; XVI, 187-188; T. H. L. Parker, *John Calvin* (Philadelphia, 1975), p. 149; Whitehead, *Coligny*, p. 150; Diefendorf, *Beneath the Cross*, p. 72.

[31] Von Pastor, *History of the Popes*, XV, 310-311, 315-316; Brodrick, *St. Peter Canisius*, pp. 541-544; Jedin, *Seripando*, pp. 688-689, 694, 698-701. Seripando, who had himself been unjustly accused of heresy, made a splendid dying statement, concluding with: "I believe what the Church believes, that we can glory in no one but in Jesus Christ and the grace of God, so that in dying I am in the Church, of the Church, and through the Church." (Jedin, *op. cit.*, p. 699)

that the Pope was highly pleased with his work in Innsbrück—as indeed he had reason to be.[32]

During June the Cardinal of Lorraine became temporarily much less cooperative, declaring that papal reform so far had been wholly insufficient, and exploding in anger when the Pope gave precedence to the Spanish bishops in all ecclesiastical functions at the Council of Trent, since "Philip II must at that time be looked upon as the principal support of the Catholic religion." It was true, and the truth hurt, since from the days of Charlemagne France had seen herself in that position. Lorraine lashed back, denouncing the Pope, questioning the lawfulness of his election due to simony, and threatening to appeal to the Council against him. But the Council's disapproval of his intemperate outburst must have been evident, and his own conscience active, for Spain had indeed become the bulwark of Christendom while France, riven with heresy, had just had to ask help from virtually every surviving Catholic state. Lorraine rose above his human frustrations and resentments. Early in July he again offered full support to the Pope, publicly supported letting him make the final decision on the chalice for the laity, and asked pardon of the Spanish envoy whom he had insulted.[33]

He and Cardinal Morone then pulled the whole Council together to settle, once and for all, the fractious issue of the place of bishops in the Church and their duty of residence. At the seventh general session of the renewed Council on July 15—attended by six cardinals, three patriarchs, 25 archbishops, 193 bishops, three abbots, and seven generals of orders, the largest attendance so far—a decree on ordination was adopted with only six dissenting votes. It described the bishops as those "who have succeeded to the place of the Apostles, and as the Apostle says, have been set by the Holy Spirit to rule the Church of God." It anathematized all who denied that the hierarchical structure of the Church was divinely ordained, that bishops have no power to confirm or ordain or that others share that power, or that "the bishops who are chosen by the Roman Pope are . . . but a human institution." Bishops were required to reside in their dioceses, and to establish a seminary in each diocese for the better training of priests wherever it was in any way financially feasible. This landmark decree owed much to the diligent work and persistent advocacy of the Jesuit general Laynez and St. Peter Canisius.[34]

Cardinal Morone did not rest on his laurels. Just four days after the seventh general session he gave the Cardinal of Lorraine and the envoys of the secular powers a draft of a proposed comprehensive decree of reform, and the following day he and the other legates laid before the Council 11 canons on the sacrament

---

[32] Von Pastor, *History of the Popes*, XV, 316-318, 321, 323-325; Brodrick, *St. Peter Canisius*, pp. 530-531, 546, 552, 556-558; Paula S. Fichtner, *Ferdinand I of Austria* (New York, 1982), p. 234.

[33] Hubert Jedin, *Crisis and Closure of the Council of Trent* (London, 1967), p. 110; von Pastor, *History of the Popes*, XV, 331-332, 335-336 (quote on 332).

[34] Jedin, *Crisis and Closure*, pp. 111-112; von Pastor, *History of the Popes*, XV, 336-338, quotes on 337; Janssen, *History of the German People*, VIII, 263-264; Brodrick, *St. Peter Canisius*, p. 563.

of matrimony, completing its last major area of action in doctrine. An important feature of the reform decree was its requirement for temporal sovereigns to leave the Church free, to exempt it from taxes, to respect its property, and not to impose their will in purely spiritual matters or in appointments to Church office. Some Catholic monarchs were almost as great offenders on these matters as the Protestants; the decree marked a major change for the Church. There were vehement objections to its wording and even its concepts. Throughout the long hot month of August, Rome's perennial dying time, six cardinals led by Morone and including Lorraine and Hosius of Poland worked day and night on the reform decree, revising and adding, incorporating suggestions from other Council Fathers and the representatives of the sovereigns in full or in part, while rejecting others deemed unsuitable. On August 27 the Archbishop of Prague demanded in the name of Emperor Ferdinand that the whole discussion of limitations on the powers of kings and princes over the Church in their domains be abandoned. Cardinal Morone replied sternly that even emperors had no authority to dictate to Councils of the Church, and sent a long letter to Ferdinand explaining why the issue had to be taken up and why good Catholic sovereigns should defend the independence of the Church.[35]

On September 22 French envoy du Ferrier addressed the Council, declaring that the proposed reforms would destroy the freedom of the Gallican church and the God-given authority of the French king. But in the face of mortal danger the ancient Church of France had at last begun to shed its Gallican conceits; du Ferrier was roundly denounced the very next day by numerous bishops including several who were French; the Archbishop of Sens told him not inappropriately that he sounded exactly like Henry VIII of England. When a week later the Cardinal of Lorraine arrived in Rome (having left Trent just before du Ferrier's speech), he assured Pope Pius IV—who received him with the greatest honor— that du Ferrier had not been instructed by his king to speak as he had. Of course the poor boy King of France was not instructing anyone, despite the fact that he had just been declared of age to rule at only thirteen, so that the Peace of Amboise could be legally violated and the rebel Prince of Condé not appointed lieutenant-general of the realm. But what mattered was that the Cardinal of Lorraine had taken it upon himself to say this to the Pope. Pius IV promprly informed his legates at Trent to pay no further attention to du Ferrier's speech, since the Cardinal of Lorraine had assured him it was unauthorized, and gave high praise to Lorraine at the consistory of cardinals meeting October 8.[36]

On October 19 Lorraine left Rome to return to Trent, preceded by a letter from the Pope to his legates at Trent saying "his interests are so closely bound up with ours, that there is no room for doubt" and instructing them to treat him like another papal legate. Soon after his arrival at Trent, Lorraine paid high tribute to the Pope, praising his zeal for reform (which many had previously doubted). At the eighth general session of the renewed Council on November 11 twelve

---

[35] Jedin, *Crisis and Closure*, pp. 122-123; von Pastor, *History of the Popes*, XV, 339, 341-346; Janssen, *History of the German People*, VII, 262-271.

[36] Von Pastor, *History of the Popes*, XV, 348-351; *Cambridge Modern History*, III, 6.

canons on matrimony were adopted, specifying the impediments to marriage and prohibiting clandestine marriage, one of them with a startlingly modern ring which shows, perhaps more clearly than any other statement on marriage at the highest level of the Church, that the arranged marriages and child marriages so common among the European aristocracy were and always had been a deformation of this sacrament: all persons, however great their power and wealth, were ordered, "under penalty of excommunication to be incurred *ipso facto*, that they do in no way whatever, either directly or indirectly, lay any compulsion on their subjects, or on anyone else, to prevent their marrying according to their own free will."[37]

On October 20 Cardinal Morone introduced a revised decree on the reform of religious orders, both men's and women's, which required the maintenance of a common life, the abolition of the holding of private property by religious, a minimum age for professing vows and protection of full personal freedom in taking them, and closer regulation of novitiates[38]—a blow against the common practice of assigning children of the wealthy to the religious life who were thought otherwise useless or a potential embarrassment, without regard to whether they truly had a vocation. Neither this measure nor the decree on free will marriages was by any means fully effective. Great and very widespread abuses are not abolished in a year or a decade. But the Church had taken its stand.

At the end of November the Pope fell suddenly and seriously ill, but recovered in a few days. On December 3 the final session of the Council of Trent was held, the ninth since its renewal in January 1562. Doctrinal decrees affirming the existence of purgatory and praising the invocation of saints and the veneration of relics and images, and the disciplinary decree on the reform of the religious orders (originally presented October 20), were approved by overwhelming margins. A reform decree abolished the payment of expectancies in Church benefices, condemned the levying of high burial fees by the Church, recommended caution in imposing excommunications (which had become the first rather than the last resort of some clerics dealing with disobedience), and required a formal profession of Catholic faith by bishops, other Church officials, and professors in Catholic universities. A final decree declared that "the authority of the Apostolic See must be held inviolate against all the decisions of the Council." It too was almost unanimously accepted.[39]

Because the majority of the Council clearly indicated a desire for a decree on indulgences—since the dispute over them had started the whole revolt against the Church—the final session was extended to December 4, and on that day the Council approved a decree authorizing the granting of indulgences, but not in return for money donations. All the decrees of the previous sessions were re-read

---

[37] Von Pastor, *History of the Popes*, XV, 351 (first quote), 353-357, 376; Jedin, *Crisis and Closure*, pp. 114, 124-127; Janssen, *History of the German People*, VII, 257 (for second quote).

[38] Jedin, *Crisis and Closure*, pp. 134-136.

[39] *Ibid.*, pp. 148-157; Von Pastor, *History of the Popes*, XV, 361-364 (quote on 364).

and their approval was confirmed. All 225 Council Fathers present signed them, and 39 proxies from absent Fathers were recorded in their favor.[40]

When all the signatures had been written and all the proxies collected, the Cardinal of Lorraine—who had done so much to make agreement possible— declared:

> This is the belief of us all, this is our unanimous conviction, to which, in token of our agreement and acceptance, we now sign our names. This is the faith of St. Peter and the apostles; this is the faith of the Fathers [of the Church] and of all true believers.[41]

The Council Fathers answered: "So do we believe. So do we judge. So do we append our names."[42]

The homilist at the opening Mass of this last day of the final session of the Council of Trent directly addressed the Protestants:

> We have chosen this city, at the entrance into Germany, on the very threshold, so to speak, of their house; in order to remove all suspicion from their minds, we have refused to be guarded by troops, we have issued letters of safe-conduct which they themselves have framed; we have waited long for them, we have begged and implored them to come and gain knowledge from the light of the truth.[43]

Yet they had not come; without significant exception, they had indeed showed not the slightest inclination to come; they had cut themselves off from the Church Christ founded. There could be no more attempts at negotiation or compromise with them, which over almost half a century had been given every possible opportunity to happen and to succeed. There must then be, in each country, a fight to the finish. For nearly everyone in that age, Catholic or Protestant, believed unquestioningly that in the end all churches of a nation must preach the same doctrine and acknowledge the same head. Toleration, when requested, was never more than limited, temporary, and tactical.[44] With no compromise or reconciliation possible, the great issue could therefore only be settled on the battlefield, and to the battlefield it was now committed.

Such a decision, on an issue of religion, horrifies modern man; and it can be reasonably argued that some among the sons of the Prince of Peace should have at least proposed the alternative of permanent religious pluralism, as better than

---

[40] Von Pastor, *History of the Popes*, XV, 364-367.

[41] *Ibid.*, XV, 367.

[42] *Ibid.*

[43] *Ibid.*, XV, 366.

[44] In his recent history of the French wars of religion, Mack P. Holt makes it very clear that the support of toleration by the so-called *politiques* in the French Estates-General and elsewhere was strictly temporary: "To suggest that these *politiques* were sympathetic to any permanent religious coexistence, much less any modern notion of religious toleration, is simply inaccurate. . . . In any case, their voices were drowned out . . . by the majority of the deputies who favored a return to war." (*French Wars of Religion*, p. 109).

the century of bloodshed which in fact was to follow. But if permanent religious pluralism had been proposed, it would certainly have been rejected. Given the premises of the age, war was inevitable; and war came, in its most terrible fratricidal form, civil war, dividing families and friends, more than eighty years of it, in the end almost as fruitless as the attempts at compromise and reconciliation had been. Christendom was saved, but would never be again what it had been in the days of its glory.

Pope Pius IV was profoundly gratified by the results of the Council of Trent, as he had every reason to be. This apparently rather ordinary, uninspired and uninspiring Pope had succeeded, with God's help, in bringing this great undertaking to fruition while men of such spiritual and material might as Pope Paul III and Emperor Charles V had failed to do so. Almost miraculously, those still loyal to the Church had in the end spoken with virtually one voice in proclaiming both doctrine and reform, despite all the differences and mutual suspicions dividing them. The contrast with the bitter divisions that had developed among the Protestants—between Lutherans and Calvinists especially, but also between Flacius Illyricus and his followers in Germany and other Lutherans, as well as among Anabaptists, mainline Protestants and Unitarians— was very impressive and well noted. The Catholic Church was essentially reborn at the Council of Trent, resurrected from the dead; now the true Reformation, the Catholic Reformation, could and did begin.

On December 6, 1563 Pope Pius IV declared in consistory in the presence of the imperial, Spanish, Portuguese, and Venetian ambassadors that the Council of Trent had been the most important council in the past five hundred years, praised its work to the highest, and pledged to enforce its decrees fully, particularly the requirement that bishops reside in their dioceses.[45] Speaking again in consistory on December 30, he reiterated these themes, emphasized his total commitment to reform, and said he would go even beyond the Council requirements. He appointed two commissions of cardinals, one to prepare the official papal confirmation of the work of the Council (without which it would have no force of law in the Church) and another to plan how best to carry out its decrees.[46] Uncompromisingly he declared:

> This day ushers in new life and calls for new manners. By the authority of the Council, Church discipline, which had lapsed into decay among the masses, has been restored. but it is on the clergy above all that a new order of life has been enjoined, and from the regulations laid down they may learn that when once they have taken on themselves the dignity of holy orders, necessity is laid on them to shape their conduct according to the plan set forth with divine clearness in these most salutary decrees.[47]

---

[45] Von Pastor, *History of the Popes*, XVI, 1-2.

[46] *Ibid.*, XVI, 3-4, 86; Jedin, *Crisis and Closure*, pp. 157-158.

[47] Janssen, *History of the German People*, VIII, 271-272.

On January 26, 1564 the cardinals in consistory advised unconditional confirmation of all the acts of the Council of Trent, and Pope Pius IV gave verbal assent. A full collection of all the decrees of Trent was published in March, and on June 30 Pius IV issued the bull formally confirming the decrees, which indicated that by his oral approval they had actually been in effect since January 26. On November 14 he promulgated the profession of faith which the Council had recommended for all persons holding positions involving the care and cure of souls, also to be made by all professors in Catholic universities, along with an oath of obedience to the Roman Church.[48]

On July 19, 1564 King Philip II of Spain endorsed and gave full force of law to all the Council's decrees in all his domains, including not only Spain itself but also southern Italy and Sicily, Sardinia, Milan, and the Low Countries. Thereby he made himself the champion of the Council of Trent, of the doctrines it defended and the reforms it called for, the Catholic lay commander in the struggles to come. Because of the encroachment of the state upon the Church, even in Catholic countries, Philip II's full and unequivocal endorsement of the Council's decrees was of the very highest importance.[49]

Portugal followed his example that same year. So did Poland, under its previously lukewarm Catholic king Sigismund II Augustus, urged on by the irresistible zeal of the Polish Cardinal Stanislaus Hosius, one of the prime movers at Trent, and the papal legate to Poland, Commendone. After hearing their eloquent appeals for religious unity, knowing that his country was still basically Catholic but was increasingly threatened by the division created by Protestants and Unitarians, Sigismund II on August 7 accepted the decrees of Trent and gave them the force of law in Poland. The Polish Catholic historian Oscar Halecki calls this "the decisive turning point in the history of the religious crisis in Poland, opening the door to a complete Catholic restoration in that country." That fall legate Commendone travelled throughout the country, explaining to the Polish bishops—many of whom had paid little attention to the Council of Trent, where only Cardinal Hosius represented their country—what the Council demanded, and persuading them to carry out its decrees. The proposal for a Polish national council was dropped, and more and more of the Protestant converts began to return to the Church of their fathers during the year 1565.[50]

In France there was never much chance that the decrees of the Council of Trent would gain official approval any time soon; the miracle was that the Cardinal of Lorraine not only upheld them but had done so much to achieve them. After his return to France he loyally urged their acceptance, but Chancellor L'Hôpital and the Gallicans opposed them, the Gallicans because they continued to resist recognizing the governing authority of the Pope over the

---

[48] Von Pastor, *History of the Popes*, XVI, 5-9, 11-12; Brodrick, *St. Peter Canisius*, p. 609.

[49] Von Pastor, *History of the Popes*, XVI, 364-366; Henry Kamen, *Philip of Spain* (New Haven CT, 1997), pp. 104-105; Walsh, *Philip II*, pp. 365-366.

[50] Oscar Halecki, *From Florence to Brest (1439-1596)*, 2nd ed. (New York, 1968), pp. 151-152 (quote on 152); von Pastor, *History of the Popes*, XVI, 149-151.

Church in France, and L'Hôpital because his main objective was still an agreement with the Calvinists who would have nothing whatever to do with the Council of Trent. Catherine de Medici, as always eager to keep all options open, would make no commitment.[51]

In Germany Emperor Ferdinand I died a holy death in July 1564. There had long been doubts about the Catholic loyalty of his eldest son and successor, Maximilian II. His father shared these doubts, and pleaded with his son on his deathbed to be faithful and obedient to the Catholic Church. One of Maximilian's first acts as Emperor was to withdraw the requirement at the University of Vienna that all professors must proclaim their adherence to the Catholic creed when appointed, despite the Council's recommendation of the exact opposite. In October he refused to publish the Council decrees in Austria or Hungary. But on September 5 Duke Albert V of Bavaria, a dependable Catholic, and the Archbishop of Salzburg and most bishops in Bavaria endorsed and agreed to carry out the decrees of Trent. In the fall of 1565 the great Jesuit theologian, teacher, and re-evangelizer St. Peter Canisius was given the difficult and dangerous task of bringing the instructions on Tridentine reform to the bishops of Germany in secret, under cover of visiting Jesuit colleges in Germany.[52]

In April 1564 the committee of cardinals working on establishing a pilot seminary in Rome, in accordance with the decree of the Council that all dioceses which could possibly afford a seminary should found one, decided to entrust the seminary in the papal city to the Jesuits. That same month the Archbishop of Mainz called for the establishment of a Jesuit-run seminary in his city. In May 1564 the Pope, ordering the visitation of parishes and local clergy in Rome which the Council had required for all dioceses, also entrusted the Jesuits with this task. In November the Bishop of Eichstätt in Bavaria founded the first seminary in Germany in accordance with the Tridentine decree, and the Chancellor of Bavaria summoned St. Peter Canisius to help reform the University of Ingolstadt there, which was infected with heresy. By the end of April Pope Pius IV was able to congratulate the Dominicans on their general chapter held to plan how to carry out the decrees of Trent. A year later the Cistercians did likewise.[53]

No man was watched more closely as a bellwether of reform than St. Charles Borromeo, the Pope's nephew and personal secretary whom he had

---

[51] Von Pastor, *History of the Popes*, XVI, 196-197; Thompson, *Wars of Religion in France*, pp. 209-210.

[52] Fichtner, *Ferdinand I*, pp. 257-258; von Pastor, *History of the Popes*, XVI, 109, 130, 139-140; Janssen, *History of the German People*, VIII, 294-296, 320-321; Brodrick, *St. Peter Canisius*, pp. 610, 624-626. The magnitude of the danger had been made clear the previous November when Anton Cauchius, in the service of papal envoy Delfino, carrying instructions on the Tridentine reform to the bishops in Germany, was attacked on a lonely road in Thuringia. All the men with him were killed, and Cauchius alone escaped with the loss of all his baggage (von Pastor, *op. cit.*, XVI, 108-109).

[53] Von Pastor, *History of the Popes*, XVI, 82, 86-87, 101-102, 139-140; Brodrick, *St. Peter Canisius*, p. 606.

appointed Cardinal and Archbishop of Milan at the age of only 21. Despite his youth St. Charles had played a major role working with the Council by letter, though he remained in Rome throughout it. His early high promotion had been originally due much more to nepotism than to any ability yet proven; though now his ability was generally acknowledged, it remained to be seen if he would practice what he preached. Most emphatically he did: St. Charles Borromeo had vowed to make himself a living symbol of the Catholic Reformation, and by so doing to win his way to Heaven. He began in June 1564 by greatly reducing his court and state, dismissing 150 servants and all his horses. He established a Jesuit-run seminary in the archdiocese of Milan in December 1564, even before Rome did. In September 1565 he arrived in Milan to fulfill his episcopal residence requirement, remaining there for the rest of his life, and making Milan a model reformed diocese.[54]

In Germany (outside Bavaria) Trent had little immediate effect; only the patient labors of St. Peter Canisius and his fellow Jesuits and others, seeking and obtaining individual conversions from Lutheranism over the years, were slowly but steadily to increase the proportion of Catholics to Protestants in Germany. The concession of the chalice to the laity, which Pope Pius IV was eventually persuaded to make against his better judgment (and the strong contrary recommendations of Peter Canisius), to please the dying Emperor Ferdinand who was sure it would help win back his wayward people to the true faith, accomplished less than nothing, merely fueling the expectation of the weak Catholics who had demanded it for still more concessions, such as permission for priests to marry and for everybody to eat meat on Friday. The Archbishop of Salzburg told Cardinal Truchsess in July 1565 that this concession "has been the ruin of my people." Consequently Pope Pius IV instructed his legates in Germany that month to make every effort to persuade Emperor Maximilian II to withdraw his request for permission for the marriage of priests in Germany, which was never granted.[55]

Calvinism advanced steadily during the first three years after the Council of Trent. It was still growing rapidly in France.[56] Through Elector Frederick III it

---

[54] Von Pastor, *History of the Popes*, XVI, 90-91, 119, 394-395; XVII, 77n. Strangely enough, there is no really good scholarly biography of this giant figure in Catholic history available in English. The best (though without adequate documentation) are Cesare Orsenigo, *Life of St. Charles Borromeo* (London, 1945) and Margaret Yeo, *Reformer: St. Charles Borromeo* (Milwaukee, 1938).

[55] Von Pastor, *History of the Popes*, XVI, 122-130, 132-133, 136-137; Brodrick, *St. Peter Canisius*, pp. 602-603, 608 (quote); Fichtner, *Ferdinand I*, p. 235; Janssen, *History of the German People*, VII, 244-245.

[56] Queen Jeanne d'Albret of Navarre had fully Calvinized the church in Béarn in the southwest of France, and was consequently declared a heretic by Pope Pius IV in September 1563 and summoned to trial before the Inquisition, with excommunication and deprivation of her kingdom to follow if she did not come (Roelker, *Queen of Navarre*, pp. 215-221); former Cardinal Châtillon, after being deprived of his Church dignities, openly joined the Calvinists in December 1564 and married (von Pastor, *History of the Popes*, XVIII, 146).

had taken over the region known as the Palatinate in Germany (constituting a substantial part of the Rhineland)[57] and was spreading underground through the Low Countries, where it was to explode in 1566.[58] It was strong enough in England to be a substantial irritant to Queen Elizabeth as governor of its church.[59] In 1564 enrollment at Calvin's Academy in Geneva topped 1,500 and Calvinist writers in France were openly advocating rebellion and revolution.[60] Calvin himself, who until then had always shied away from specifically preaching violence, finally took the plunge in his sermons (posthumously published) on the Book of Daniel, stating that princes "are no longer worthy to be counted as princes . . . when they raise themselves up against God . . . it is necessary that they should in turn be laid low."[61] Afflicted with tuberculosis, kidney stones, and piles, Calvin preached his last sermon February 6, 1564 and died in May at the comparatively young age of 54, a poor man, buried at his own request in the common cemetery without a tombstone. He designated Theodore Beza as his successor, who was accepted as such in Geneva virtually by acclamation.[62]

John Calvin was in large part a revolutionary in spirit, even if not until the end of his life an advocate of revolutionary violence. Like his future countryman Robespierre[63] and the supreme revolutionary, Lenin, he sought nothing for himself, giving all he had to the cause. And though he and his followers wreaked destruction on a gigantic scale (their record in this respect had barely begun by the time of his death), he at least tried to build something still Christian on the ruins. Because he still believed in God and proclaimed the Incarnation, even John Calvin could never be a total revolutionary.

Philip II of Spain continued to be deeply concerned about the growing power of the Calvinists in France despite their military defeat at Dreux, protected as they were by the terms of the Peace of Amboise (though these were by no means always observed). His concern was enhanced by his link by marriage with France through his third wife, Isabelle de Valois, the very young (she was less than half Philip's age), lovely and beloved "Isabel of the Peace." From mid-June to early July 1565 a conference was held at Bayonne near the French-Spanish border, attended by the young King Charles IX, his sister Queen Isabelle of Spain, their mother Catherine de Medici, and Spain's greatest general, the Duke

---

[57] Janssen, *History of the German People*, VII, 320-323.

[58] See below, this chapter.

[59] See Chapter Five, above. In March 1566 one-third of the clergy of London refused to obey Archbishop Parker's orders to wear full vestments (William P. Haugaard, *Elizabeth and the English Reformation* [Cambridge, England, 1968], pp. 224-225).

[60] Williston Walker, *John Calvin, the Organizer of Reformed Protestantism* (New York, 1906), p. 366; Holt, *French Wars of Religion*, p. 78.

[61] Holt, *French Wars of Religion*, p. 78.

[62] Parker, *Calvin*, pp. 151-155; Walker, *Calvin*, pp. 436-440; Robert M. Kingdon, *Geneva and the Consolidation of the French Protestant Movement, 1564-1572* (Madison WI, 1967), p. 17.

[63] Maximilien Robespierre, architect of the Reign of Terror in the French Revolution (see Volume Five, Chapter 8 of this history) came, by a fascinating historical coincidence that may not be entirely coincidental, from Calvin's own province of Picardy.

of Alba. Even the most pro-Calvinist historians are now obliged to admit that the once widely held idea that the massacre of St. Bartholomew was planned at this conference, seven years in advance, is absurd.[64] In fact little happened at Bayonne, other than the Duke of Alba and even young Isabelle making it clear that Spain would not stand idly by and see France taken over by revolutionary Calvinists. Catherine reproached her daughter for becoming so Spanish. At the end of the conference Catherine promised to accept the decrees of the Council of Trent after they had been duly examined and studied, and to suppress public Calvinist worship in France, banish Calvinist ministers, and require judges and other important officers to take an oath of Catholic orthodoxy. She never did any of these things and probably never intended to do any of them.[65]

The deepening divisions within Christendom were watched with eager greed by its unsleeping 900-year enemy: Islam. The Ottoman Turks, turned back from the gates of Vienna in 1529 and held at bay for the next quarter of a century by Emperor Charles V despite all else he had to do, were now on the move again. Their mighty leader, Sultan Suleiman the Magnificent, had reigned for 45 years of conquests, ravages and rapine. One long-ago frustration and grievance cankered in his proud heart. At the very beginning of his reign he had been defied for long gruelling months on the island of Rhodes by a tiny force of the crusading military order of the Knights of St. John of the Hospital. Even when he had finally gained their island he had been forced to let them all go, arms in hand with the full honors of war, to establish themselves on another island, Malta.[66] Now 70, full of years and experience, sole master of a great empire, Sultan Suleiman the Magnificent would have his revenge at last. In October 1564 the Ottoman royal council, the Divan, proclaimed his decision for a massive attack on Malta the following spring. No longer physically vigorous enough to take personal command of the expedition, Suleiman gave it to young Piale Pasha, who was married to the daughter of the Sultan's son and heir Selim, with instructions to follow the advice of the most famous pirate admiral of the Mediterranean, 80-year old Dragut Rais. The army commander under Piale was Mustafa, 65 years old, who had fought at the siege of Rhodes and was directly descended from the standard-bearer of the Prophet Muhammad. On March 29

---

[64] The hard fact is, given the almost infinite variability of human souls and affairs, that no major historical event can be planned seven years in advance, even by planners of the high capability of Philip II and William Cecil.

[65] Kamen, *Philip of Spain*, pp. 102-103; Ramón Menéndez Pidal, ed., *Historia de España*, Volume XXII (1), "España en Tiempo de Felipe II," by P. Luis Fernández y Fernández de Retana (Madrid, 1988), pp. 606-618, 636-649, 673-682; von Pastor, *History of the Popes*, XVI, 202-203; Mahoney, *Madame Catherine*, pp. 114-118; N. M. Sutherland, *The Massacre of St. Bartholomew and the European Conflict, 1559-1572* (London, 1973), pp. 40-45; Holt, *French Wars of Religion*, p. 64; William S. Maltby, *Alba; a Biography of Fernando Alvarez de Toledo, Third Duke of Alba* (Berkeley CA, 1983), pp. 127-128; Walsh, *Philip II*, pp. 382-383.

[66] See Chapter Two, above.

the Turkish argosy set sail from the Golden Horn at Istanbul, once Constantinople, with 160 war galleys, forty thousand soldiers, and nearly a hundred giant siege guns like those which had smashed through the forty-foot walls that had guarded Christian Constantinople for a thousand years.[67]

Awaiting them were just seven hundred Knights, supported by about eight thousand Maltese, sons of the dry rocky island whose people proudly traced their Christianity back to the shipwrecked St. Paul thirty years after the Resurrection. The Grand Master of the Knights of St. John in this grim hour was a man who seemed to stand outside time and history and change, because he would not let them touch him: Jean Parisot de La Valette, 70 years old like Suleiman, fifty years a knight, veteran of the siege of Rhodes, for a full year a galley slave of the Muslims, a crusader in the original mold of Raymond of Toulouse.   Ernle Bradford calls La Vallette "that rarest of human beings, a completely single-minded man."[68] As the Turks approached, La Valette addressed his men:

> It is the great battle of the Cross and the Koran which is now to be fought. A
> formidable army of infidels are on the point of investing our island. We, for
> our part, are the chosen soldiers of the Cross, and if Heaven requires the
> sacrifice of our lives, there can be no better occasion than this. Let us hasten,
> then, my brothers, to the sacred altar. There we will renew our vows and
> obtain, by our faith in the sacred sacraments, that contempt for death which
> alone can render us invincible.[69]

On May 18 the Turks arrived. La Valette held a solemn procession with the Blessed Sacrament, followed by forty hours' adoration, drew up a gigantic chain to block the entrance to the great harbor of the little capital of Mdina (later to be renamed for him), and sent word by fast galleys to the Pope and King Philip II that the enemy had come.[70]

No help appeared. The military capability of the Papal state was negligible against so great a force, Philip II's governor of nearby Sicily was full of excuses, and France and Venice were still allies of the Sultan. La Valette, his seven hundred Knights, and the poor people of Malta all now facing death or slavery, were on their own.[71]

The first blow fell on the recently constructed fort of St. Elmo, placed to deny anchorage in Marsasirocco inlet to an enemy fleet. A Spanish officer, Juan de la Cerda, came before La Valette May 26 to tell him that the small fort could hold out no more than eight days. La Valette swept him with blazing blue eyes. If that was the best he could do, the Grand Master would come himself with a

---

[67] Jack Beeching, *The Galleys at Lepanto* (New York, 1982), pp. 76-79; Ernle Bradford, *The Great Siege* (New York, 1961), pp. 38-40; Walsh, *Philip II*, p. 381. For the fall of Constantinople to the Ottoman Turks see Volume Three, Chapter 13 of this history.

[68] Bradford, *Great Siege*, pp. 9-24 (quote on 18); Walsh, *Philip II*, p. 384.

[69] Bradford, *Great Siege*, p. 43.

[70] *Ibid.*, pp. 44, 50; Walsh, *Philip II*, pp. 383-384; von Pastor, *History of the Popes*, XVI, 367.

[71] Bradford, *Great Siege*, pp. 81-82.

volunteer force and hold St. Elmo far longer. Old Dragut took charge of the first assault, with a devastating bombardment followed by a charge of the best Turkish troops, the janizaries; the defenders hurled them back June 3 with two thousand casualties. Another massive attack four days later met the same fate. But now there were only 53 knights left in St. Elmo; they sent word to La Valette that the fort had become almost indefensible and that they wished to sortie against the enemy and all die fighting amidst his host. La Valette had no more patience with useless heroic gestures than with defeatism; he sent back the steel-toothed reply: "The laws of honor cannot necessarily be satisfied by throwing away one's life when it seems convenient. A soldier's duty is to obey. You will tell your comrades that they are to stay at their posts."[72]

On June 10 the Turks tried a night attack, in a rain of fire bombs, and lost 1,500 more of their best troops to no avail. On the 16th a new daylight attack first by drug-crazed berserkers called layalars, then by dervishes, then by janizaries, failed again. Chevalier de Madran, the Christian commander at St. Elmo, was killed that day. The last contingent of reinforcements reached the doomed fort that night, 330 volunteers going to certain death. On the 18th Dragut was mortally wounded; on the 21st the Knights held the traditional Corpus Christi procession under fire. The next day, with the walls of St. Elmo almost totally in ruins, the defenders fought hand-to-hand in the breaches with swords, pikes, battle-axes and even daggers, and drove back yet another Turkish assault. Before dawn on the 23rd the remnant of the garrison set fire to all their religious objects and decorations so that they would not fall into infidel hands, rang the chapel bell for the last time, and went to the breaches. Their two surviving officers, both too badly wounded to stand (in the siege of Malta no one was considered wounded who could still walk), had chairs pulled up for them into the breaches where they could sit to swing two-handed swords. All the surviving defenders fought and died, to the last man. Watching a scene of heroism such as all history cannot surpass, looking across the embattled inlet to the main Knights' fortress of St. Michael the Archangel, as yet untouched on its high ridge, Turkish General Mustafa cried: "Allah! If so small a son has cost us so dear, what price shall we have to pay for so large a father!"[73]

On this very day some help came at last from Sicily—42 more Knights who had been caught away from Malta when the siege began, and 600 of the splendid Spanish infantry. But Suleiman back in Istanbul would not hear of retreat, and his army on Malta began systematic assaults on the forts of the Archangel Michael and the walls El Burgo protecting the town of Mdina. In mid-August La Valette told his men that they must not count on any help from the rest of Christendom, and must fight to the finish whatever happened; he read them a bull from Pope Pius IV granting a plenary indulgence to all who fell in this siege. On August 18 the besiegers exploded a mine under the walls, with a thunderous roar and fountains of debris. For once the defenders panicked, fleeing in all directions

---

[72] *Ibid.*, pp. 57-58, 63-69, 82-87, 95-97 (quote on 97).
[73] *Ibid.*, pp. 102-103, 106-112, 115-124 (quote on 123); Walsh, *Philip II*, pp. 384-386; von Pastor, *History of the Popes*, XVI, 367.

before the Turks surging into the breach. La Valette called on the knights he could still see around him. He took his sword from its sheath and prepared to lead a counter-charge in person, crying: "How is it possible for a man of my age to die more gloriously than in the midst of my friends and brothers, in the service of God?" His loyal men did it for him, hurling the Turks back eleven separate times, with so great an expenditure of ammunition that La Valette had to order a daily collection of spent enemy shot, with no man to receive his ration of food unless in exchange for at least one ball.[74]

On August 23 La Valette's council urged him to quit the fortifications around Mdina and withdraw all his remaining fighting men to the fort of St. Michael. But he refused to abandon the women and children in Mdina to Turkish rape and slavery. "Here we must all perish together," he declared, "or finally, with the help of God, succeed in driving off our enemy." Already he sensed that the Muslims' fire and fury was weakening against the prodigious heroism of the defenders. When the main Spanish relief fleet at long last arrived from Sicily carrying ten thousand men, it seemed quite likely that even in their decimated condition the Knights could have won without them. After a last resounding defeat, the Turks evacuated. They had lost in all 30,000 men, three-quarters of their attacking force.[75]

However many and deeply infiltrated its enemies, Christendom was not ripe for destruction while it still had such defenders.

On the other side of the world that year, Spain had sent a new exploring expedition across the Pacific from Mexico to the great archipelago Magellan had discovered and died in, which had been reached only twice by Spaniards since 1520, with disastrous results both times. But Philip II was determined to try again, calling from his retirement in an Augustinian monastery Andrés de Urdañeta, survivor of the Loaysa-Elcano expedition of 1526, who had developed a plan to seek westerly winds in the Pacific at the latitudes where they prevailed in the Atlantic, and thereby find a way to return from Asia to Mexico, which none of the previous expeditions had been able to do. He let Urdañeta pick the captain-general (all the earlier expeditions had been marked by violent disputes between the captain-general and his officers, developing into mutinies) and he wisely chose the calm, able and resolute Miguel López de Legazpi. On April 27, 1565—just after the Turks arrived at Malta—Legazpi anchored in the harbor at Cebu, near the site of Magellan's killing, took possession of it for Spain, and named the islands for King Philip, whose name they have ever since borne as the Philippines. Colonization and the conversion of the people began immediately. Legazpi soon found a small statue of the Christ Child ("*El Santo Niño*") left by Magellan, now the most venerated religious treasure of the Philippines. It is most

---

[74] Bradford, *Great Siege*, pp. 131, 140-144, 154-158, 160-162, 166-171 (quote on 169); Walsh, *Philip II*, pp. 386, 389-390.
[75] Bradford, *Great Siege*, pp. 178-179 (quote on 179), 189-193, 198-203, 206; Walsh, *Philip II*, p. 390; von Pastor, *History of the Popes*, XVI, 368.

fitting that this archipelago named for the great Catholic champion should today be the only Catholic nation in Asia.[76]

Legazpi remained with his colony, while Urdañeta set sail to the north in June 1565, found the westerlies, and so was able to return to Mexico via California on October 1. The two-way sailing route across the Pacific was opened: the route of the annual ship laden with the most valuable products of the Orient, which became legendary in sea lore as "the Manila galleon." The first Manila galleon sailed in 1567.[77]

The other principal Spanish colony in the Americas, Peru, faced the Pacific. There a Spanish official named Pedro Sarmiento de Gamboa had deduced from Inca legends (which have been mined for stories of men arriving in Peru from across the Pacific ever since, up to Thor Heyerdahl) that a great southern continent must lie about two thousand miles southwest of Peru. The immensely long voyages of the Polynesians and the existence of the strictly American sweet potato in the South Pacific islands when the first Europeans arrived there make it highly probable that the Inca legends had some basis in truth, but how anyone could have deduced distances and sailing directions from them is quite another matter. Nevertheless Sarmiento convinced the viceroy of Peru, who authorized an expedition to seek out the purported southern continent. Command was given to the viceroy's young nephew, Alvaro de Mendaña, who was to be the gentleman head of a Spanish colony on the southern continent; Sarmiento, sulking because he had not received the command, was taken along because of his knowledge of the Inca legends; and an experienced old seaman named Hernan Gallego was commissioned as pilot. They left Callao, the port of Lima in Peru, on November 19, 1567.[78]

It was one of the most fantastic voyages in history, a wild mingling of ambition, folly, farce, endurance, and horror. The flotilla had to sail six thousand miles, not two thousand. Somehow they managed to miss most of the multitudinous blooming islands of the South Pacific, and the few they did find they refused to land on (the continent or nothing!); finally, at the end of their strngth after 81 consecutive days at sea, they sighted high land ahead of them, immediately and universally assuming that it must be the southern continent. But there was no such continent (unless one counts dead-frozen Antarctica or still far away Australia); it was only one of the Solomon Islands, malaria-haunted tangles of jungle and swamp, offering few edible fruits and no meat but birds and people

---

[76] Samuel E. Morison, *The European Discovery of America; the Southern Voyages, 1492-1616* (New York, 1974), pp. 436, 475-494; Frank Sherry, *Pacific Passions; the European Struggle for Power in the Great Ocean in the Age of Exploration* (New York, 1994), pp. 68-77, 85-86, 95-97.

[77] Morison, *European Discovery of America: Southern Voyages*, pp. 494-495; Sherry, *Pacific Passions*, pp. 97-99; William L. Schurz, *The Manila Galleon* (New York, 1939), pp. 22-28. The Manila galleons carried valuable Chinese silks and porcelain goods as well as the inevitable spices, especially cinnamon which grew in the southern Philippines.

[78] J. C. Beaglehole, *The Exploration of the Pacific* (Stanford CA, 1966), pp. 39-41; Sherry, *Pacific Passions*, pp. 102-105.

(the natives were habitual cannibals). Gradually the overconfident continent-seekers learned these unwelcome facts. They tried first to settle on an island they named Santa Isabel, then on an island they named Guadalcanal (and who could then have dreamed that this pestilential hell-hole at the end of the world would be, nearly four hundred years later in the Second World War, the site of six months of titanic combats between Americans and Japanese that bore more than a little resemblance to the siege of Malta?). Eventually the distracted Mendaña was persuaded by the realistic Gallego—over Sarmiento's vehement objections—that they must return; but how? Gallego knew of Urdañeta's success with the northern route, but it seemed too far to Mendaña, so for a time the two men adopted the Alice-in-Wonderland compromise of sailing north when the winds were favorable in that direction, and east when they were favorable in that direction. Sanity finally prevailed and they settled on the northerly course. The two remaining ships separated, but both finally reached Mexico at the end of 1568, with substantial losses among the crews to scurvy. Sarmiento, commanding one of the ships, was imprisoned for deserting his captain-general, who returned—not exactly in triumph—to Peru in the following year. Mendaña wanted to try again, but had to wait 26 years for his chance.[79]

Early in December 1565 Pope Pius IV fell ill, and on the 9th he died at the age of 66, after being anointed and receiving viaticum from his holy nephew St. Charles Borromeo. The conclave convened on the 20th, with 48 cardinals present. Full enclosure was completed by midnight; for once it was strictly enforced. All present knew the importance of the choice of the new Pope. The cleaving of Christendom was creating the most desperate crisis in its history; the Council of Trent might well have come too late. In the words of Spanish Cardinal Pacheco, writing to Philip II: "If a Pope were to be chosen who was unworthy and not sincerely Christian, I am convinced that all that remains of Christendom would fall to pieces."[80]

Cardinal Morone, respected by all for his superb performance at Trent, was the early leader in the voting, but he could not gain the necessary two-thirds; Cardinals Farnese and d'Este, known for lack of commitment to reform, received just enough support to block him. But the pro-reform majority would not be denied; led by the Spanish, they swung their votes to the head of the Roman Inquisition, Cardinal Antonio Ghislieri. On January 7, 1566 all went to the chapel, Ghislieri protesting that he was not fit for such honor. Instead of the usual secret ballot, a roll was called. Every cardinal present knew Ghislieri's passionate devotion to Christ and the Church, his iron courage, relentless perseverance, and spotless reputation. The open vote left no room for secret grudges to operate. Every cardinal voted for Ghislieri.[81]

---

[79] Beaglehole, *Exploration of the Pacific*, pp. 41-57; Sherry, *Pacific Passions*, pp. 105-116.

[80] Von Pastor, *History of the Popes*, XVI, 399-401; XVII, 5-6, 8, 17 (for quote).

[81] *Ibid.*, XVII, 14, 24-29, 36-46.

Because of the unique character of their office, in the eyes of the Catholic historian all Popes make history, by commission or omission. But even the secular historian must see Antonio Ghislieri, Pope St. Pius V, as a history-maker. By any standard, from any viewpoint, he is one of the giants in the whole history of the Western world. He became the father of the Catholic Reformation and, with the indispensable assistance of Philip II of Spain, the savior of Christendom. Son of a muleteer who shipped grain across the Alps while the boy Antonio tended his sheep, ten days short of his 62nd birthday when elected Pope, of middle height and thin with a bald head, a beak of a nose, and a long white beard, who owned only two coarse woollen shirts and dined on an egg and a few vegetables, he had inspired awe even before he was Pope. He was a Dominican monk who prayed the rosary every day. In the words of Ludwig von Pastor, everyone who saw him "felt that he was in the presence of a man of unshakeable firmness and of a profound seriousness, which, far removed from anything of this world, was fixed entirely on spiritual things." In the words of William Thomas Walsh, he was "one of those rare Christians who take all the words and examples of Christ literally, without exception or reservation, and so move through the world like light in a dark place." The people loved him; at the ceremony of his taking possession of the Lateran palace, "they hailed him with such manifestations of joy as have not been seen for ten pontificates."[82]

Five days after his election Pope St. Pius V addressed the cardinals, exhorting them to reform themselves and their households and avoid the kind of life that had given so much scandal in the past to the humble members of the Church, and declaring that he intended to carry out the decrees of the Council of Trent to the letter. He promised to seek peace among Christian princes, the extirpation of heresy, and victory over the Turks. He instructed the imperial ambassador, who was also present, not to give him any more requests from the shifty Emperor Maximilian II for concessions to heretics, because he had no intention of granting any of them. On January 23 he appointed a special commission of cardinals to reform the clergy, headed by St. Charles Borromeo who had already done so much to that end in his archdiocese of Milan.[83]

On March 13 the new Pope dispatched Cardinal Commendone on a mission to Germany, with instructions to reject all religious disputation at the forthcoming Diet (the time for religious disputation with the Protestants had passed), to publish and execute the decrees of Trent wherever Catholic obedience could be found in Germany, to insist on thorough reform of the Church there, to administer the Catholic profession and oath to the slippery Archbishop von Wied of Cologne, whom many believed to be no longer Catholic at all, and to fill the vacant sees of Magdeburg and Strasbourg—both almost entirely Protestant— with good Catholic bishops. On May 23 Commendone met at Augsburg with Cardinals Truchsess and Sittich; the three bishop-electors of Germany; the strongly Catholic Dukes of Bavaria and Brunswick and the dubiously Catholic

---

[82] *Ibid.*, XVII, 52-54 (first quote on 53), 71 (third quote); Walsh, *Philip II*, p. 374 (second quote); Beeching, *Galleys at Lepanto*, p. 124.

[83] Von Pastor, *History of the Popes*, XVII, 67-69, 71-72.

Duke of Cleves; and representatives of most of the German states still Catholic. All accepted the dogmatic decrees of the Council of Trent but requested some exemptions from the disciplinary decrees. So large a gathering and such quick action was a remarkable tribute to Pope St. Pius V's leadership.[84]

On April 6 he sent a new nuncio to France, Bishop Michele della Torre, with instructions to press for the publication and enforcement of the decrees of Trent, an end to abuses in the granting of benefices, and punishment of the deposed Cardinal de Châtillon, who had left the Church and married. Until he was punished, the Pope said, he would appoint no more cardinals from France. Following up on this, at the end of the year he deprived six bishops of their office and all their dignities and privileges, as proven heretics. Five of them defiantly remained in their dioceses, continuing to act as bishops. The sixth, Bishop Jean de Chaumont of Aix, rose from his episcopal chair in the cathedral of Aix on Christmas day 1566, denounced the Pope, threw down his mitre and staff, stalked out of the church, mounted a horse, and rode away to join the Calvinist army as Captain Saint-Roman.[85]

To insure rigorous reform in the older religious orders, many of which had been divided into branches of more or less strict observance of their Rule, Pope St. Pius V placed all under the control of the stricter branch. However, he firmly upheld the privileges and independence of the mendicant orders, which some had challenged. In May 1567 he gave St. Charles Borromeo full authority to reform a wealthy religious order in Milan misnamed the Humiliati, requiring all the superiors of the order to resign. The Humiliati appealed to the Spanish government of the city, which defended them. St. Charles consequently excommunicated several government officials. The officials appealed to Philip II, but he supported St. Charles, and Pope St. Pius V summoned them to Rome to account for their actions personally to him. The Humiliati were later suppressed entirely after they were involved in firing a shot at St. Charles while he was praying in his chapel. The bullet bounced harmlessly off his unprotected back in a manner generally regarded as miraculous.[86]

In September 1566 the catechism of the Council of Trent was published in Latin, a landmark in the history of Church doctrine. St. Peter Canisius and another German Jesuit were directed to make a German translation immediately, other Jesuits a French translation, and Cardinal Hosius a Polish translation.[87] Lutheran leader Tillman Hesshus paid it reluctant tribute:

---

[84] *Ibid.*, XVII, 249-250, 254-255.

[85] *Ibid.*, XVIII, 105-106, 108-109; Janine Garrisson, *A History of Sixteenth Century France* (New York, 1995), p. 285.

[86] Von Pastor, *History of the Popes*, XVII, 245-246, 251-252, 170; XVIII, 18-21; Orsenigo, *St. Charles Borromeo*, pp. 125-128. The assassination attempt occurred on October 26, 1569.

[87] Von Pastor, *History of the Popes*, XVII, 192-193; Brodrick, *St. Peter Canisius*, pp. 651-652.

[It is] the most artful book that had been written by the papists for centuries, for the Pope and his consistory made it appear as if they were willing to do the right thing and to take up God's Word and the Catechism instead of befooling the people with Masses for souls, processions, indulgences, and idols. The authors of this book might almost pass as Lutherans.[88]

In November 1567 St. Peter Canisius was instructed by the new general of the Jesuits, St. Francis Borgia, to set to work on a general history of the Church, to refute the distorted Protestant history appearing in volumes called the "Magdeburg Centuries."[89]

In these ways and many others there is not space to record, did Pope St. Pius V, with the indispensable aid of the sons of St. Ignatius of Loyola, press forward in the reform of the Church during the first two years of his pivotal pontificate. There would be much more of the same to come, for the Catholic Reformation was a gigantic undertaking that would require more than a full generation to complete.

When St. Pius V was consecrated Pope in January 1566, the bell was tolling for Mary Queen of Scots. With every month that had passed since her arrival in Scotland as its unquestionably rightful Queen in 1561, her situation grew more desperate. Her chief reliance was on her half-brother, Lord James Stuart, Earl of Moray; but this man, as foul a traitor as history records, cared nothing for her or his duty to her; he only wanted the crown of Scotland for himself. John Knox thundered against her every Sunday in the churches of Edinburgh; by the winter of 1563 he was declaring explicitly that she should either convert to Calvinism or be executed. And William Cecil never forgot that her claim to the throne of England—unquestionably a rightful claim under the Catholic law of marriage, by which Queen Elizabeth was illegitimate—was the greatest potential threat both to Elizabeth's rule and to his position and life. Mary knew only too well that there were enemies all around her. But it was years before she understood that *everyone* around her was an enemy, present and potential. Not one among the high nobility could she count on in a crisis, and John Knox had already destroyed the Catholic Church in Scotland. Since Mary had no legitimate rival, her enemies had to proceed cautiously lest they reveal the full extent of their revolutionary spirit and their treason; in that age, to overthrow an undoubted king or queen was the worst of all secular crimes, which not even most Protestants would openly countenance (the outspoken Knox was a rare exception in that regard).[90]

---

[88] Janssen, *History of the German People*, VIII, 276.

[89] Brodrick, *St. Peter Canisius*, p. 685. The compiler of the "Magdeburg Centuries" was the half-mad Croat Matija Vlacic, who went by the Latin name of Flacius Illyricus, author of some 300 virulent Lutheran pamphlets, who had been hailed at one time by Luther as his successor (*ibid.*, pp. 676-680).

[90] Von Pastor, *History of the Popes*, XVI, 281-282, 286. Mary's desperate situation is fully explained in a report to Pope Pius IV from the Jesuit Nicholas of Gouda during a visit to Scotland in the summer of 1562.

Mary's only hope, as Pope Pius IV's Jesuit emissary Nicholas of Gouda reported to him, was marriage to a strong Catholic prince who could protect her. Mary was certainly well aware of this herself. But no strong Catholic prince was available—only the boy brothers of her late husband Francis II of France; Philip II's tragic son Don Carlos, who was about her age but already showing signs of the mental disease that was to destroy him; and Archduke Charles of Austria, who as a Habsburg looked for greater realms than Scotland. In June 1563, preaching to most of the leading nobles in the Scots Parliament, Knox insisted that Mary must never marry a Catholic. Mary called him for an interview, crying "What have ye to do with my marriage? *What are ye within this commonwealth?*" Coldly Knox intoned: "A subject born within the same, Madam . . . to me it appertains no less to forewarn of such things as may hurt it, if I foresee them, than it does to any of the nobility; for both my vocation and conscience crave plainness." Mary burst into a storm of weeping (Knox scornfully called it "howling" in his account of the interview). At last she dismissed him. On the way out he made a last thrust by condemning the bright dresses of her maids of honor. In December, after he had publicly defended an attempt to break into her chapel while Mass was being said there, she haled him before the royal council, crying that he had made her weep, and now she would make him weep; but John Knox was not a man for tears. He had arrived with an escort of hundreds, and the council did not dare act against him.[91]

In June 1564 there was a formal disputation (not open to the public) before the General Assembly of Scotland between Knox and Maitland of Lethington, who was at first a defender of Mary before fear and worldly respect finally overcame him. Knox called Mary a rebel against God and a "slave of Satan"; Maitland objected in vain to such epithets flung at an anointed queen. Maitland then challenged Knox's doctrine that rulers he deemed evil could rightly be overthrown by violence. Knox replied by citing the killing of Queen Jezebel by Jehu of Israel, then demanded whether Maitland would obey an order by Mary to kill him. Maitland weakly replied that he would not obey such an order, but would not object if others did. Knox called for a continuation of the debate in public; Maitland refused. He was no match for the Scots prophet.[92]

Now it was time for William Cecil to take a hand. If Mary was resolved upon a Catholic marriage, but no suitable Catholic prince was available, perhaps she could be induced to marry some other Catholic who would be of little real use to her, or could later be turned against her. Matthew Stuart, Scot Earl of Lennox, had always served the English interest, and had lived in England for twenty years. He had married the daughter of Henry VIII's sister Margaret. Their son Henry, Lord Darnley, had been born in England. He was Catholic. Through his mother, the young lord (he was 18) had some drops of royal blood in his veins. He was tall—taller even than the notably tall Queen Mary—and

[91] *Ibid.*, XVI, 282; Antonia Fraser, *Mary Queen of Scots* (New York, 1969), pp. 211-213, 215-217; Jasper Ridley, *John Knox* (New York, 1968), pp. 425-431, quotes on 426. Emphasis added in the quotation from Mary.

[92] Ridley, *Knox*, pp. 435-437.

strikingly handsome. Cecil would have known such a man as Lennox through and through, and would have made it his business to analyze the son as well. An almost faultless judge of men, Cecil would very likely have known of Darnley's inconstancy, greed and cowardice. Knox was opposed to bringing any Catholic lords into Scotland, and certainly to Mary's marrying one. But Cecil's plans ran deeper—too deep even for the usually astute historian Jasper Ridley, who describes Cecil's decision to send the Earl of Lennox and his son to Scotland as "a rare diplomatic blunder." On the contrary, it was one of the most brilliant strokes of his life.[93]

Lennox arrived in Scotland in September 1564 and Darnley in the following winter. Mary met Darnley at Wemyss castle in Fife in February 1565 and was immediately smitten with his good looks. By the end of the month the two were inseparable; in April Mary nursed him personally in his recovery from measles. It was a classic case of infatuation; the very feminine Mary saw in the 18-year-old lord all that she had been hoping for and dreaming of in the husband whose protection and support she so desperately needed. Because Darnley was a Catholic, the Scots Protestants vehemently opposed the marriage; taking Darnley at face value as a prospective king, the Earl of Moray opposed the marriage; perhaps seeing Darnley for what he really was, Mary's devoted friends and companions, the "four Maries," opposed it also. Even Cecil made a show of opposing it, to win favor with the Scots Protestants, and Queen Elizabeth refused her royal permission for it. Nobody favored the marriage but David Riccio, the Queen's new Italian secretary.[94]

But Mary would not hear anyone's counsel on this decision. Her heart suppressed her mind. She truly believed her knight errant had come for her. She did not even wait for the necessary papal dispensation, though it did arrive shortly after the marriage, which took place July 29, 1565. Darnley gave an ominous indication of how little his purported faith meant to him when he refused to attend the nuptial Mass.[95]

Moray immediately led a rebellion, while Knox preached a sermon in St. Giles cathedral August 19 in which he not only recalled again the story of Jehu's revolt against Ahab and Jezebel, but described how the dogs ate their flesh and drank their blood. The royal council ordered him not to preach again in Edinburgh while Mary and Darnley were there; the Edinburgh city council refused to enforce the order. At the beginning of September Moray occupied Edinburgh, but other nobles drove him out, and Mary and Darnley returned. Some time that month they conceived a child.[96]

---

[93] *Ibid.*, pp. 437-438; Fraser, *Mary Queen of Scots*, pp. 218-220. Fraser, Mary Queen of Scots' finest biographer, upholds the interpretation given here of Cecil's support of the return of Lennox to Scotland, accompanied by Darnley.

[94] Fraser, *Mary Queen of Scots*, pp. 218-221, 223-227, 229-230; Read, *Cecil*, pp. 307, 315; Ridley, *Knox*, p. 438. Riccio's name is often spelled Rizzio, apparently on the authority of Knox, whose knowledge of Italian was rudimentary.

[95] Fraser, *Mary Queen of Scots*, pp. 227-228, 230-233; Ridley, *Knox*, p. 438.

[96] Ridley, *Knox*, pp. 438-443; Fraser, *Mary Queen of Scots*, pp. 233-234, 240.

In February 1566 Scots nobles, believing rumors of David Riccio's great personal influence over Mary, persuaded Darnley that Riccio was Mary's lover. He became furiously jealous and hostile to Mary, who consequently delayed giving him royal authority (the "crown matrimonial"), though he was already generally called "king." He sought solace in the bottle, held a series of wild drunken parties, and finally did something so disgusting at a party on Inch Island that Mary stopped sleeping with him.[97] On the 13th English ambassador Thomas Randolph sent an ominous report to the Earl of Leicester in London:

> I know for certain that this Queen [Mary] repents her marriage, that she hates Darnley and all his kin. I know there are practices in hand contrived between father and son [Lennox and Darnley] to come by the crown against her [Mary's] will. I know that if that take effect which is intended, David [Riccio], with the consent of the king [Darnley] shall have his throat cut within these ten days. Many things more grievous and worse than thse are brought to my ears, yea, of things intended against her own person.[98]

On February 25 Randolph wrote to Cecil, for the eyes only of the Queen, the Earl of Leicester and Mr. Secretary:

> You have heard of discords and jars between this Queen and her husband, partly as she hath refused him the crown matrimonial, partly for that he has assured knowledge of such usage of himself as altogether is intolerable to be borne [the imagined sexual affair of Riccio with the Queen]. . . . To take away this occasion of slander, he is himself determined to be at the apprehension and execution of him whom he is able manifestly to charge with the crime, and to have done him the most dishonor that can be to any man, much more being as he is.[99]

Well might Spanish ambassador to England de Silva say later that he understood that "the whole conspiracy had been engineered from England."[100]

On March 2 a bond was drawn up by the conspirators against Queen Mary, including Moray (just returned from England), Morton, George Douglas, Ruthven, Lindsay, and many others, by which they agreed to support one another in upholding the Protestant religion, obtaining the return of the exiled rebels, and giving the crown matrimonial to Darnley, who also signed the bond. Maitland of Lethington, previously friendly to Mary but now in regular communication with Cecil, did not sign, but clearly knew of it yet did not tell her. On March 7 Mary, without Darnley, opened the Scots Parliament, calling upon it to pass an act of attainder against all rebels who had fled to England after the recent uprising, and

---

[97] Fraser, *Mary Queen of Scots*, pp. 245-246.
[98] *Ibid.*, p. 247.
[99] Read, *Cecil*, p. 348.
[100] *Ibid.*

confiscating all their property. She also called upon the parliament to permit free exercise of the Catholic religion.[101]

Two days later Queen Mary, now six months pregnant, was having a supper party in her apartments at Holyroodhouse, with her half-brother Lord Robert Stuart, her half-sister Countess Jean of Argyll, her equerry, her page, and her Italian secretary David Riccio, who was playing music for the group. The Queen's bedroom adjoined the dining room, and directly below it were Darnley's rooms, from which a narrow staircase led up to Mary's bedroom. Suddenly Darnley, coming up the staircase, appeared at Mary's bedroom door. Behind him loomed the terrifying figure of Lord Ruthven, "with a steel cap on, and with his armor showing through his gown, burning-eyed and pale from the illness of which he was generally thought to be dying on his sick-bed in a house close to Holyrood." In a sepulchral voice Ruthven intoned: "Let it please Your Majesty that yonder man David come forth of your privy chamber where he hath been overlong." Mary replied that Riccio was there by her invitation, and asked Ruthven if he was in his right mind. Then she turned to Darnley and asked if this was his doing. He made no reply; but Ruthven launched into a denunciation of the Queen for her alleged affair with Riccio and for exiling the rebels. Then he drew his dagger and lunged at Riccio. Mary's guards, who had so far done nothing, moved toward him. "Lay not hands on me!" cried Ruthven. Five of his followers, armed to the teeth, now rushed into the room from the private staircase, knocking over the table. Riccio ran to the Queen and clung to her skirts. Ruthven's men physically restrained the Queen, one of them pointing a pistol at her pregnant womb. Kicking and screaming, Riccio was dragged away to the head of the main staircase ascending to the royal apartments, where he was cut to pieces by more than fifty dagger strokes. With magnificent courage Queen Mary, alone, with no one around her willing to raise an arm or a weapon in her defense, turned on Darnley and accused him of trying to murder her and their child by inducing a miscarriage, then usually fatal to a woman as far advanced in pregnancy as she was, so that he might reign alone. Otherwise, why was the attack made in her own chamber? Riccio could easily have been killed elsewhere.

Crowds were now gathering outside, some for and some against the Queen. Darnley went to the window to try to persuade them that all was well. Mary tried to reach the window herself; Lord Lindsay snarled that he would "cut her in collops" if she moved any closer to it. At dawn Darnley came to Mary begging her pardon, and she pretended to grant it. She hoped to escape from menacing Edinburgh with his help. On March 11 she promised pardon to the murderers of Riccio and greeted Moray, just returned from England. Not knowing of his involvement in the bond and the plot, she flung herself into his arms, saying: "Oh my brother, if you had been here, they had not used me thus!" The stone-hearted Earl responded only with a lecture on the virtue of clemency.

---

[101] Fraser, *Mary Queen of Scots*, pp. 247-249; Ridley, *Knox*, p. 446; Read, *Cecil*, p. 346; von Pastor, *History of the Popes*, XVIII, 354.

That night Mary and Darnley made their way out of Holyroodhouse through the servants' quarters and a cemetery just outside, passing Riccio's newly dug grave. A few supporters awaited them with horses, which they mounted to ride for Dunbar Castle where the Earl of Bothwell, an opponent of the conspirators, had promised to protect them. Darnley, in an extremity of terror, whipped his horse to a mad gallop, shouting: "Come on! Come on! By God's blood, they will murder both you and me if they can catch us!" Mary told him she could not ride so fast because of her pregnancy; Darnley responded that if their baby died, they could have another. Such was Henry, Lord Darnley as husband and father. The knight errant had dissolved into a panic-stricken coward.[102]

Back in London ten days later, William Cecil's clerk was filing the copy retained for Cecil's meticulous records of a letter written March 21 to Ambassador Randolph discussing the murder of Riccio. Cecil trained his clerks in his own thoroughness. So the clerk attached a memorandum to the record copy of the letter, entitled "names of such as were consenting to the death of David." Included in the list was the name of John Knox.[103]

Emperor Charles V had been born in the Low Countries, at Ghent in Flanders. He learned both French and Flemish in childhood. When he became king of Spain, the Spanish almost would not have him because he seemed so foreign.[104] Though he adopted Spain as his country more than any other, loving and honoring its people who in turn came to love and honor him, to the Flemings and Dutch and Walloons of the Low Countries he was always one of their own, and they never gave him serious trouble. When he abdicated his many thrones, he feared for them, aware already of the dangerous growth of Calvinism in all the lands surrounding them, and included a special warning against heresy in his abdication speech to them.[105]

But Philip II was Spanish born and bred. Though as a prince he spent considerable time in the Low Countries, and was there for the greater part of two years during the war with France that was ended by the Peace of Cateau-Cambrésis in 1559, after he went home to Spain that year he never returned. With every passing year he seemed more distant and more alien to a people who had never been his own. This did not concern him: legally his title to the Low Countries was impeccable, as the only legitimate son of a father who was born their crown prince; and he had left their government in the hands of his half-sister Margaret of Parma, a native of the Low Countries, and of Cardinal Granvelle who had spent most of his adult life there.[106] In normal times this would have

---

[102] For these fantastic events of March 9-11 in Edinburgh, see Fraser, *Mary Queen of Scots*, pp. 249-257 (containing all quotes) and Ridley, *Knox*, pp. 446-449.

[103] Ridley, *Knox*, p. 447.

[104] See Chapter One, above.

[105] See Chapter Five, above.

[106] Geoffrey Parker, *The Dutch Revolt*, rev. ed. (London, 1985), pp. 41-46.

been sufficient. Kings were not elected and did not have to be popular if they knew how to rule, as Philip II most certainly did.

But these were not normal times; the Calvinist revolutionaries were afoot, in increasing numbers. The French-speaking Walloons were obvious targets for the propaganda being circulated all through France from French-speaking Geneva. The Flemings and Dutch were great traders accustomed to dealing with Protestants; their best customers were the English. They had heard horror stories about the Spanish Inquisition, and were aware of Philip II's unwavering support for it; every few months a new rumor spread, often with every appearance of authority, that Philip intended to impose the Spanish Inquisition on the Low Countries. (He never did, and never intended to.)[107] But he did intend, and clearly declared, his intention to maintain and enforce the laws against heresy. He became the object of increasing fear and suspicion, so that even what should have been self-evidently desirable initiatives, such as increasing the number of dioceses in the Low Countries with their booming population, came under intense criticism.[108]

The first object of the criticism was his chief minister, Cardinal Granvelle. An increasing barrage of ill-founded but vitriolic attacks, culminating in the ostentatious withdrawal from the Council of State of two of the greatest nobles of the Low Countries, Counts Egmont and Hoorn, until Granvelle should depart, eventually induced Philip, seeking peace, to remove him as chief minister in January 1564, while still giving him full honors. Egmont and Hoorn promptly returned to the Council, but the hostile atmosphere did not change. Now Philip was being pressed to relax the laws against heresy and give more power to the Council of State. In the winter of 1565 Egmont was sent to Spain to charm and lobby him to accede to this.[109]

But where the preservation of the Catholic Faith and the maintenance of his royal powers were concerned, Philip II could not be charmed or lobbied. In October he drafted letters in the Wood of Balsain near Segovia ordering more rather than less strict enforcement of the laws against heresy, and appointed to the Council of State in the Low Countries the Duke of Aerschot, who had been an active supporter of Cardinal Granvelle and was a foe of William of Orange, as influential a nobleman in the Low Countries as Egmont and Hoorn and even more wealthy. On November 2 and 3, before news of these orders reached the Low Countries, but anticipating them, a group of minor noblemen of openly Calvinist belief, including William of Orange's brother Count Louis of Nassau and the brothers John and Philip Marnix, who had spent some time in Calvin's Geneva, met at the house of Count Culemborg of Brussels to form a league

---

[107] In 1562 Philip II told Baron Montigny that "never in my imagination have I thought of introducing into Flanders the Inquisition of Spain." In 1565 he told Cardinal Granvelle "that the Spanish model of Inquisition was unsuitable for export to the Netherlands." (Kamen, *Philip of Spain*, pp. 93, 112)

[108] Parker, *Dutch Revolt*, pp. 47-48, 57-63; Walsh, *Philip II*, pp. 338-339, 347.

[109] Parker, *Dutch Revolt*, pp. 53-55, 63-65; Wedgwood, *William the Silent*, pp. 58, 63, 65; Kamen, *Philip of Spain*, p. 90.

against the existing heresy laws. Two days later, when the Balsain Wood letters of Philip II came in, this group was ready and waiting to act. Taking up the letters November 30, the Council of State decided they must put them into effect right away (as they did by proclamation December 20), despite the anger of Count Egmont who insisted that Philip had assured him in person that he would not do this. (Philip had given no such assurance, but Egmont misinterpeted the friendly words which Philip had exchanged with him to mean this.) Several leaders of the Calvinist group now drew up in complete secrecy an agreement to oppose openly the enforcement of the anti-heresy laws, later known as the "Compromise" of the Nobility.[110]

By 1566 there were about 300 active Calvinist communities in the Low Countries, up from no more than 20 just five years before, and their influence was increasingly felt. The heresy laws obviously applied directly to them. They had not been strictly enforced, but this was what Philip II was now demanding. Confrontation was imminent. In mid-March 1566 the signers of the Compromise of the Nobility met at William of Orange's palace in Breda. They agreed to present a petition against enforcement of the anti-heresy laws to Regent Margaret of Parma in April, with as many more signatures obtained as possible in the intervening time. However, Egmont and Hoorn declared they would have nothing to do with this petition. On April 1 Counts Brederode and Louis of Nassau arrived in Brussels with 200 armed retainers. During the next three days, meeting at the house of Count Culemborg, the petition was drawn up and signed "in an atmosphere of unsuitable hilarity" and free-flowing drink (at one point Louis of Nassau harangued the group from the top of a kitchen table). On April 5 the petitioners, followed by a large crowd, entered the presence of Regent Margaret in Brussels. Frightened by their numbers and boisterousness, she began to weep. Councillor Berlaymont tried to reassure her by mocking the petitioners as "beggars" (*les gueux*). The word was overheard, and immediately adopted by the petitioners and their supporters as their own. The petition was presented. Margaret called a meeting of her council that evening. The petitioners, 300 strong, were having another party at Culemborg's house. William of Orange, Egmont, and Hoorn most imprudently went to the party to fetch another Councillor, Hoogstraaten, for the council meeting. As soon as the three magnates were seen, drunken men surrounded them demanding a toast to "the beggars." They gave the toast. They were only at the party for five minutes, but by the next day the whole city of Brussels had heard about their presence there and their toast.[111]

On April 8 Regent Margaret responded to the petition by promising to send a new deputation to Spain to urge Philip II to change his position, and meanwhile to suspend the "extremer measures of the religious program." On the 10th Count

---

[110] Parker, *Dutch Revolt*, pp. 55, 63-64, 66-69; C. V. Wedgwood, *William the Silent* (New Haven CT, 1944), pp. 63, 65; Walsh, *Philip II*, p. 360; von Pastor, *History of the Popes*, XVIII, 81-82.

[111] Wedgwood, *William the Silent*, pp. 75-76, 78-81 (quote on 78); Parker, *Dutch Revolt*, pp. 58, 69-70; von Pastor, *History of the Popes*, pp. 82-83.

Brederode—obviously a born propagandist—left Brussels with his men firing pistols in the air, all dressed in gray or brown (the colors of mendicant friars) with begging bowls around their necks. He went to Antwerp, where soon after his arrival the Calvinists of the city came out into the open, demanding the right to preach freely. When the city council refused their demand, they went out to conduct their services in the open fields outside the walls. By the end of June the total attendance at these services each Sunday was estimated at 30,000. So large were the congregations that preaching began on weekdays as well. During the long midsummer evenings, open-air Calvinist preaching was heard through more and more of the Low Countries, usually just outside cities as at Antwerp, notably outside Amsterdam and Haarlem in Holland. Since these services were all still forbidden by law, many of those attending came armed. The militia at Tournai, when ordered to break up one such meeting, refused, "seeing that some of their relatives and friends might be there." In July both Pope St. Pius V and Regent Margaret wrote to Philip II expressing serious concern about these meetings, their growing attendance, and their inflammatory sermons.[112]

Philip II stood firm. After discussing the situation with his council and with the envoy from the Low Countries, Baron Montigny, he announced July 26 he would not change his policies, but would make a personal visit to the Low Countries the following year to examine the situation there in person. In a private interview, Montigny had the audacity to explode with anger against his king, calling his decision "ill-advised, unwise and un-Christian" and declaring that it showed total disregard for the welfare of the Low Countries, the advice of their nobles, and even of the Catholic religion! But as alarming reports about the open-air sermons continued to flow in (their daily attendance had now risen to 20,000 at Ghent and 10,000 each at Tournai and Valenciennes), Philip decided that since he could not enforce the laws without an army willing to obey orders, he would have to suspend the operation of the anti-heresy laws until he had such an army in the Low Countries.[113]

But the Low Countries were now out of control; the flash-point had come. On August 10 a Calvinist hatmaker of Ypres named Sebastian Matte led his congregation from an open-air service to the monastery of St. Lawrence at Steenvorde. About twenty men led by another Calvinist preacher, Jacob de Buzère, a former Augustinian monk of Ypres, broke into the monastery and smashed all religious images inside. Three days later Buzère led the sack of another monastery near Bailleul; the next day hatmaker Matte preached another iconoclastic sermon at Operinghe, after which about a hundred men spread out to break images in many towns and villages. On August 15 the Calvinists heckled the Assumption procession in Antwerp, shouting at the image of Our Lady:

---

[112] Wedgwood, *William the Silent*, pp. 81-83 (first quote on 81); Parker, *Dutch Revolt*, pp. 72-74, 86 (second quote on 72); Pieter Geyl, *The Revolt of the Netherlands* (London, 1932), pp. 90-91; Jonathan Israel, *The Dutch Republic: Its Rise, Greatness, and Fall* (Oxford, 1995), pp. 146-147; von Pastor, *History of the Popes*, XVIII, 88-89.

[113] Parker, *Dutch Revolt*, pp. 85-87; Andrew Pettegree, *Emden and the Dutch Revolt* (Oxford, 1992), pp. 114-115; Walsh, *Philip II*, pp. 401-402.

"Mollykin, Mollykin, this is your last walk!" It was; on August 20 came the "Calvinist fury" in Antwerp. Almost all the religious images and paintings in the 42 churches of Antwerp were destroyed without opposition by gangs working through the day and night. The iconoclasm was planned by Calvinist leaders and carried out by young men mostly paid by them or their supporters. The little dark Madonna carried in the procession was cut to pieces. Monasteries and convents were also despoiled and their libraries burned. William of Orange had left the city just hours before the assault began. Though most of the people of Antwerp did not participate, none raised a hand to defend their churches.[114]

The fury spread like wildfire. More than 400 churches, monasteries, and convents in Flanders alone were sacked during the next three or four days. Tabernacles were broken open, Hosts taken out and trampled, and the bones of saints disinterred and dragged through the dirt. Great crowds watched, but made no move to intervene, nor did the city guard except in a few places. In Ghent, just before its churches were ravaged, 1,767 well-to-do citizens were asked whether they would physically defend their churches against attack. Only 332 (18 per cent) said they would, and none of them did. But in beautiful Bruges, to its everlasting credit, at the first news of the danger every church was locked and put under guard, the gates of the city were closed, and not a single church was touched. In Brussels, a lone Spanish soldier armed only with a pike saved one church.[115]

In Amsterdam the mayor and the city council attempted to resist the iconoclasts, but were overwhelmed. In Utrecht "great heaps of art treasures and vestments, including the entire library of the Friars Minor [Franciscans], were put to the torch." In Delft the iconoclasm was directed by Adrian Menninck, a leading businessmen, who went on to direct more of the same at The Hague. (Evidence is strong that the iconoclastic attacks were very well organized and coordinated.) The Count of Culemborg chopped down the altar in his own chapel with an ax, ordered his servants to bring tables into the wrecked church, sat down to dinner there, and fed consecrated Hosts from the ciborium to a parrot sitting on his wrist.[116]

Historians eager to find causes other than the obvious one for this systematic and horrible devastation have striven to develop an "economic interpretation" of the Calvinist fury of August 1566. Let a Jewish historian, the most recent at this writing to cover these events, answer them:

> Economic distress and insecurity probably played some part in kindling the iconoclastic fury. Yet the iconoclastic outbreaks of 1566 involved no

[114] Parker, *Dutch Revolt*, pp. 74-75, 78; Wedgwood, *William the Silent*, pp. 86-88 (quote on 86); Geyl, *Revolt of the Netherlands*, p. 93; Israel, *Dutch Republic*, p. 148; von Pastor, *History of the Popes*, XVIII, 85-87.
[115] Parker, *Dutch Revolt*, pp. 77-79; Pettegree, *Emden and the Dutch Revolt*, p. 123; Walsh, *Philip II*, pp. 405-408; von Pastor, *History of the Popes*, XVIII, 81.
[116] Israel, *Dutch Republic*, p. 149 (quote); Parker, *Dutch Revolt*, p. 78; Wedgwood, *William the Siilent*, p. 87; Pettegree, *Emden and the Dutch Revolt*, pp. 126, 128.

assaults on government officials or town halls, or against tax-farmers, and no plundering of shops and food stores. In form the *beeldenstorm* was purely and simply an attack on the Church and not anything else.[117]

Philip II became physically ill when he heard of the mass sacrilege. After reading the letters from Regent Margaret describing the Calvinist fury in Antwerp he fell into a severe fever, suffering seven convulsions over the next two weeks. He was responsible before God above all to protect the Church and the faith of his people; he had now spectacularly failed in that duty, in the Low Countries. Surprise at the rapid escalation of hostility was in his eyes no excuse. He had not done his duty, and God would hold him accountable.[118]

During the next few days William of Orange gave permission for unlimited Calvinist services in Antwerp, Count Egmont allowed them in Ghent, and Count Hoorn in Tournai. Regent Margaret disavowed these permissions, but could no longer enforce her authority. On September 13 she wrote Philip that the Calvinists seek "to provoke a general revolution, dethrone sovereigns, ruin the house of Austria, and bring it about, finally, that the other heretics do the same in France and England." It was only too true.[119]

On September 22 Philip II met with his royal council in Spain to decide what should now be done about the Low Countries. All agreed that an army must be sent. At a later meeting of the council on October 29 Ruy Gómez, a leader in the council, and Cardinal Espinosa and others urged Philip to go in person to the Low Countries the next year, as he had promised before the disaster, with a relatively small force, counting on his prestige to restore order. The venerable Manrique de Lara disagreed, pointing to their king's immense value to the whole of Christendom as well as to Spain, insisting that his person should not be risked. The Duke of Alba, sixty years old, the finest soldier in Europe, spare, ascetic, with hard black eyes, said the time for concessions had passed; only condign punishment for the rebels would wipe out the stain of sacrilege. Manrique de Lara said that a general should go first, and Alba was their best. So, like the prophet Isaiah, the iron Duke said: "Here I am; send me."[120]

His appointment was formalized November 29, after he had already delivered a formal request to the French ambassador to Spain for permission for a

---

[117] Israel, *Dutch Republic*, p. 148.

[118] On May 9, 1568 he wrote to the Pope: "Often I have looked upon the burden which God has laid upon my shoulders in the states and kingdoms of which He has called upon me to undertake the government, as being laid upon me in order that I might keep safe therein the true faith and subjection to the Holy See, that I might maintain peace and justice there" (von Pastor, *History of the Popes*, XVIII, 43-44).

[119] Parker, *Dutch Revolt*, pp. 81-82, 87; Wedgwood, *William the Silent*, p. 89; Walsh, *Philip II*, pp. 403-405, 407-410 (quote on 409).

[120] Parker, *Dutch Revolt*, pp. 87-90; Maltby, *Alba*, pp. 133-134; Walsh, *Philip II*, pp. 413-415.

Spanish army to cross France to go the Low Countries the next year, from Savoy through Franch Comté and Lorraine to Luxembourg.[121]

Alba and his army cast a long shadow. Very belatedly, it began to dawn on responsible citizens of the Low Countries just what they had done, and had allowed to happen, and how little defense most of them could make at the bar of justice when called before it. Support for the rebels began crumbling rapidly during December. Regent Margaret was able to put a royal army into the field under Baron Noircarmes, which on December 29 defeated a Calvinist army of about 3,000 at Lannoy near the Calvinist stronghold of Valenciennes, killing six hundred. Though Valenciennes still held out, this drove the Calvinists underground in the rest of West Flanders, restoring obedience to the government and Catholic worship throughout the area. Public Calvinist preaching virtually ceased, and many Calvinists returned to the Catholic fold. Only Count Brederode among the major nobles wanted to continue armed resistance. In March he took Amsterdam, and John Marnix, one of the original Calvinist rebels, marched on Antwerp with 4,000 men. But William of Orange would not admit Marnix's men to the city, and as they camped outside, Count Egmont descended upon them with only 800 men and killed half of them, including John Marnix. On March 24 Valenciennes, besieged since the Battle of Lannoy, surrendered. William of Orange resigned all his offices in the Low Countries and fled to his estates in Germany. Count Brederode fled to Emden in Germany. In April Regent Margaret wrote to Philip II that his army was no longer needed. By mid-May the Calvinist revolt in the Low Countries had been completely crushed by the people of the Low Countries themselves.[122]

It was too late. The greatest general in Europe was ready to march, with ten thousand of the best soldiers in the world, to find and punish those guilty immediately and proximately of the ravaging of the churches of the Low Countries, and to make such an example of them that no "Calvinist fury" would ever happen again anywhere in the domains of King Philip II.[123] The tragedy of Alba's rule in the Low Countries will never be truly understood so long as it is only viewed (as it usually is) as an exercise in bloodthirsty brutality by a power-hungry general. Alba's mission and cause were just, and he sought nothing for himself. But like most generals he was a poor civil administrator; and though not personally cruel, he lacked charity.

The march of the Duke of Alba across central Europe from south to north enthralled all Christendom. Conspiracy theories swirled around him: he would attack the Calvinists in Geneva, he would attack the Calvinists in France, he would attack Burgundy in France to vindicate Charles V's ancestral claim. These rumored targets of his splendidly equipped army trembled in fear and recruited

---

[121] Parker, *Dutch Revolt*, p. 90; Thompson, *Wars of Religion in France*, pp. 305-306.

[122] Parker, *Dutch Revolt*, pp. 93-99, 101-102; Wedgwood, *William the Silent*, pp. 92-96; Geyl, *Revolt of the Netherlands*, pp. 97-98.

[123] Walsh, *Philip II*, pp. 418, 421.

Swiss soldiers for their protection.[124]   But the Duke of Alba was not going anywhere but where his king sent him, to the Low Countries, by the shortest and quickest route possible, to punish those guilty of rebellion and sacrilege.

A strange, distressing incident had marked his departure from Spain, harbinger of deep trouble within Philip II's household. When Alba came to bid farewell to his king, Philip's only son, Don Carlos,[125] was with his father. The boy (he did not seem fully mature yet, despite his chronological age of 22) had always been moody, mercurial, and passionate—in a word, unstable. His father and his teachers kept hoping that increasing years would steady him. Now, suddenly, Don Carlos cried out to Alba that he must not go to the Low Countries. When Alba ignored him, or made some dismissive reply, Don Carlos whipped out a dagger and struck at his heart. In forty years of military service the Duke of Alba had mastered the techniques of fighting with every weapon of his age; the dagger never touched him as instantly he pinioned the prince's dagger arm. When released, Don Carlos struck at him again, and again the Duke pinioned him.[126]

We do not know what happened afterward.

Alba left Asti on the border of Spanish Lombardy (the state of Milan) with his army on June 18. Six days later he crossed Mont-Cenis Pass through the Alps on a narrow, steep and rocky road still covered with snow, and on June 29 arrived at Chambéry, capital of Savoy. Pope St. Pius V had been urging Philip II to go to the Low Countries in person, and now that the country had already been pacified there was no more risk to his person. During June he wrote Regent Margaret that he was preparing a trip to the Low Countries and desired nothing more than to get there. He notified Don Carlos and the two Habsburg imperial princes currently residing in Spain (Rudolf and Ernest) to be ready to accompany him. He appointed the commander of the fleet that would transport him. He closed the meeting of the *Cortes* of Castile so that he would be free to go.[127]

On July 25 Alba and his army celebrated in French Lorraine the greatest Spanish feast day of the year in honor of Santiago (Saint James the Apostle, reputed to be buried in Spain). Four days later he crossed the border into his king's Low Countries domains, in Luxembourg. He had maintained almost perfect discipline throughout the forty-day march. No foraging had been allowed; the passing army took nothing without paying for it. It was exemplary

---

[124] Von Pastor, *History of the Popes*, XVIII, 95; Kingdon, *Geneva and Consolidation*, p. 164.

[125] No one seems to know why this prince was called "Don Carlos." The Spanish word for prince is *principe* or *infante*. "Don" was a vague general honorific so widely used by Spanish nobles and officers that English who dealt with them jocularly called all Spaniards "Dons." No other legitimate prince in Spanish history was called only by the title of "Don."

[126] Walsh, *Philip II*, pp. 431-432.

[127] *Ibid.*, p. 423; Parker, *Dutch Revolt*, pp. 102-103; von Pastor, *History of the Popes*, XVIII, 92; Menéndez Pidal, *Historia de España*, XXII (1), 738-739.

military leadership, typical of Alba. On August 22 he made his formal entry into Brussels as military governor of the Low Countries.[128]

William Cecil marked the historic moment, in a letter to Henry Norris, the English ambassador to France, on August 3: "Our whole expectation . . . rests upon the event and success of those matters in the Low Countries, which as they shall fall out so are likely to produce consequences to the greater part of Christendom."[129]

On August 11, with all preparations complete for the departure of Philip II to the Low Countries, his fleet and military escort ready, a safe-conduct obtained from France, and all arrangements made for the government of Spain in his absence, it was suddenly and unexpectedly announced that his departure would be postponed. At the time he gave no reason. About six weeks later, in letters to his ambassador in Rome and other officials, he stated that having sent Alba to the Low Countries he wanted to give him the opportunity to rule for a time on his own. But Alba had been on his way to the Low Countries when Philip decided to go himself, and soon. Something must have happened to change his plans.[130]

Two of Philip's principal biographers, Catholic historian William Thomas Walsh and non-Catholic Henry Kamen, both believe that the cause of his change of plans involved the turbulent Don Carlos—that he had intended to bring Don Carlos with him, but began to doubt that this was wise. The contemporary Spanish court historian Cabrera said later that the prince had been encouraged by several of the leaders of the Low Countries, including Count Egmont while he was in Spain and Baron Montigny who was in Spain at this time, to come there even against his father's will. During that summer Philip II had given secret orders to Ruy Gómez that Montigny was not to be allowed to leave Spain under any circumstances, while Don Carlos was to be told nothing of this (the implication being that Montigny might have been planning to take Don Carlos with him). William Cecil, directing the best intelligence service in Europe, seems to have had information pointing in the same direction. On August 19, almost certainly before he could have learned of Philip's decision of the 11th to postpone indefinitely his trip to the Low Countries,[131] Cecil anticipated it, writing most significantly to ambassador Norris: "We begin to doubt of the King of Spain's coming out of Spain, finding it more likely for his son to come." Two days later the French ambassador in Spain wrote King Charles IX that Philip II

---

[128] Parker, *Dutch Revolt*, p. 103; Thompson, *Wars of Religion in France*, p. 311; Walsh, *Philip II*, p. 419. For Saint James in Spain, see Volume Two, Chapter 13 of this history.

[129] Read, *Cecil*, p. 424.

[130] Parker, *Dutch Revolt*, p. 105; Walsh, *Philip II*, p. 424; Menéndez Pidal, *Historia de España*, XXII (1), 741-742, 749.

[131] The normal time for the transmission of a letter from Spain to the Low Countries was ten days to two weeks, longer to England.

was much disturbed by the behavior of Don Carlos "and that some thought he would shut him up in some tower to make him more obedient."[132]

On September 5 Alba established a special court to try those accused of direct or indirect responsibility for the wave of iconoclasm in August 1566 and for violent resistance to the King's law or officers, or for bringing in foreign Calvinist preachers. No phrasemaker, he simply called it "the Council of Troubles." (Considering this far too tame, Calvinist propagandists soon began calling it the "Council of Blood," and the name has stuck.) Four days later he arrested Counts Egmont and Hoorn and impounded their papers, which contained numerous incriminating documents about their dealings with the rebels. For though Egmont had never actively supported the rebellion and had played a major role in eventually suppressing it, before the Calvinist fury he had often been in close contact with its leaders, and had never denounced them.[133]

Though it lasted only nine years, the Duke of Alba's Council of Troubles has been the subject of an historical propaganda barrage comparable to that against the Spanish Inquisition, at least in the inflation of the number executed. This is now at long last being corrected by honest historians regardless of religion. During the entire span of operation of the Council of Troubles (1567-76) about 12,000 people were put on trial before it, of whom 8,957 were convicted and sentenced to lose some or all of their goods, but only 1,083 were executed. A significant number of the others convicted were sentenced to death in absentia, but had already fled the country.[134] Such totals were far from unusual or excessive in that day for a major revolt, even when not marked by heresy and sacrilege.

On September 13 Philip II accepted the resignation of Regent Margaret of Parma, making Alba's authority as military governor complete. The first trials before the Council of Troubles soon began. On January 4, 1568 the first 84 executions were carried out, and William of Orange was formally summoned to trial as a participant in the rebellion, which quite clearly he had been, while pretending a kind of neutrality. Before the end of the month he was condemned to death if he could be caught.[135]

---

[132] Walsh, *Philip II*, pp. 423-432 (first quote on 432, second on 424); Kamen, *Philip of Spain*, p. 120; Menéndez Pidal, *Historia de España*, XXII (1), 749.

[133] Parker, *Dutch Revolt*, p. 106; Maltby, *Alba*, pp. 145, 153-154; Walsh, *Philip II*, p. 421. Egmont was eventually executed by Alba and for centuries was regarded by virtually all Protestant historians as totally innocent and totally wronged. The documentary evidence now available showing his early and long-continued friendly exchanges with the rebels and his requests for support for them from Germany is still soft-pedalled (Parker, for example, buries it in a lengthy but exceedingly important footnote at the back of his book, *op. cit.*, pp. 293-294, and Maltby slides over it with the reluctant admission "they [Egmont and Hoorn] had also, it seems, been remarkably indiscreet" [*op. cit.*, p. 164]).

[134] Parker, *Dutch Revolt*, p. 108; Maltby, *Alba*, p. 156. These totals are much less than earlier estimates. Neither Parker nor Maltby is Catholic, and Maltby's biography of Alba is noticeably hostile to its subject, but they are honest and accurate historians.

[135] Maltby, *Alba*, p. 145; Wedgwood, *William the Silent*, p. 102; Parker, *Dutch Revolt*, p. 108.

Meanwhile, later in September, Philip II had arrested Dutch Baron Montigny at his court, shutting him up in the Alcázar of Segovia, from which he never emerged alive. There are reports that Montigny had been talking with Don Carlos, who now showed signs of preparing for flight, trying to borrow large sums of money. He began asking various nobles for help in some mysterious unidentified enterprise of his own which he would not explain. Some promised him their help unconditionally, others who knew him better qualified their promise by excluding anything against the King or against the Catholic Faith. He prepared letters to Emperor Maximilian II, some kings and princes, and the cities of Castile listing grievances against his father, especially for allegedly delaying his marriage. Finally on Christmas Eve 1567 he closeted himself with Don Juan of Austria, Charles V's illegitimate son and therefore King Philip's half-brother. Don Juan and Don Carlos were close to the same age and had long been friends. Assuming his friend would sympathize with him, Don Carlos revealed to him that he was planning to leave Spain in defiance of his father and to take over at least part of his kingdom. He promised Naples and Milan to Juan. He did not mention the Low Countries, but all the available information suggests that he intended to lay claim to them himself with the support of the former rebels. Juan tried to persuade Don Carlos of the folly of any such attempt. When the prince would not listen to any argument, Juan shrewdly asked for 24 hours to think it over. The next day, Christmas, he went to Philip in his chamber at El Escorial and told him everything.[136]

There can have been nothing at this point that Philip feared more than an escape by Don Carlos to the Low Countries. The sheet-anchor of his position there, unpopular as he was in that region, was the unquestioned legitimacy of his rule. But one of the weaknesses of monarchy as a political institution is that it can always entertain the claim of a son against his father, especially when that son is the rightful and designated heir to the kingdom. Only through Don Carlos could the Calvinists of the Low Countries legitimate their quest for power through violence.

On the feast of the Holy Innocents, December 28, the Spanish royal family always took communion together in public, and consequently went to confession beforehand, as before Easter communion. (Confessions were not made and Holy Communion was not taken nearly as frequently by Catholics in the sixteenth as in the twentieth century.) Whatever Don Carlos' state of mind and soul, whatever influence the Calvinist rebels had gained over him, he was still a Spanish Catholic and he would not lie to God in the confessional. He told the priest that there was a man he hated and meant to kill, and that he could not repent of it; soon he revealed that this man was his father. Consequently he could receive neither absolution nor Communion, though the fact that he was not receiving was adroitly concealed in the public ceremony.[137]

---

[136] Walsh, *Philip II*, pp. 424, 428, 432-434, 455-456; Menéndez Pidal, *Historia de España*, XXII (1), 751-752.

[137] Walsh, *Philip II*, p. 434; Menéndez Pidal, *Historia de España*, XXII (1), 753. The seal of the confessional was not broken; Don Carlos later blurted all this out himself.

During the next few days Philip II, whose feelings in this crisis may barely be imagined, sought advice from all those he trusted most. We know the response of one, Dr. Navarro Martín Dazpilcueta, who told him:

> If Don Carlos fled from Spain, the dangers to Spain and to all Christendom would be serious: the greatest of them the possibility of a civil war on a grand scale, not merely in Flanders but even in Spain, with the king on one side and his own son set up as leader on the other. The Protestant factions, with a royal personage as a figurehead, would gain enormously. The cause of God would be injured; all the more so, in view of the distance of the King's estates, the unstable character of the Prince, "who has not given proofs of such obedient, quiet, prudent and military qualities as there was need of, but wishes to be free and to command in everything," and the fact that he was the only heir-apparent. His going would plunge Europe into war and perhaps ruin the Spanish empire and its people. Therefore it was not only His Majesty's right, but his solemn duty, to take whatever steps might be necessary to avert these dangers.[138]

On January 13, 1568 Philip II, still at El Escorial, asked prayers that God would guide him "in a certain deliberation and design that he had in his heart." In Madrid Don Carlos, having obtained some money from Sevilla, ordered horses for a journey to the port city of Cartagena. The horse-master reported the order to the king, who came at once from El Escorial, appearing calm as always. Don Carlos closeted himself again with Don Juan of Austria, accusing him of betraying him to Philip. He drew his sword. Don Juan tried to withdraw peacefully; finding the door locked, he drew his own sword and disarmed Don Carlos.[139]

January 18 was a Sunday. Philip went to Mass with Don Carlos and Don Juan. The flight to Cartagena was to begin at dawn on Monday. Night fell. A normal person could hardly have slept on such a night, but Don Carlos was sound asleep, with a sword, a dagger, and a loaded arquebus by his bed. It was now or never.[140]

Shortly after midnight on January 19 King Philip II of Spain donned helmet and breastplate and buckled on his sword. He had summoned his councillors Ruy Gómez and the Duke of Feria, prior Antonio of Toledo, and old soldier Luis Quixada, and told them what was happening. He now called five other nobles and a guard of twelve, and they made their way to Don Carlos' room. The wayward prince was still deeply asleep. Someone shook his shoulder. He jerked

---

[138] Walsh, *Philip II*, pp. 435-436, summarizing a passage in the official court history of the reign of Philip II by Cabrera de Córdoba, Book Seven, Chapter 22. This vital source has been shamefully neglected by non-Spanish historians. In the introduction to the notes for his great biography of Philip II, William Thomas Walsh says devastatingly that, when he began his research for the biography by going to the Library of Congress to examine Cabrera's history, he found that in the 54 years since its acquisition no historian before him had ever cut the pages to read its third volume (Walsh, *op. cit.*, p. 727).

[139] Walsh, *Philip II*, pp. 435-436; Menéndez Pidal, *Historia de España*, XXII (1), 754.

[140] Menéndez Pidal, *Historia de España*, XXII (1), 754-756.

awake with a cry: "What is all this?" (*Qué es esto?*) "The Council of State," came the grim reply. "What does the Council look for here, at this hour?" Don Carlos asked, fumbling for his sword. His father stepped forward and took the weapon, along with the dagger and the loaded arquebus. "Does Your Majesty mean to kill me?" the distracted son shouted. "I only wish to make you well," his father said. Don Carlos seized a burning lantern and flung it, but it went out; then he swung a candelabrum, screaming "Kill me or I will kill myself!" followed by a torrent of curses. On his desk was a small gold-inlaid box. Philip opened it, finding documents connected with his projected flight, including some describing his future plans, and a list of his friends and enemies. No one ever saw the documents again; it appears almost certain that Philip himself destroyed them, so that posterity should not know the full extent of his son's madness or treachery or both. Philip directed that he be held in close confinement and never left out of the sight or hearing of trusted officials, whom he listed by name. He was allowed to receive no visitors and no mail.[141]

The next day Philip wrote to the Pope, explaining that he had to confine his son because of his mental and moral irresponsibility, which seemed incurable, and one specific manifestation of this which was a serious threat to Church and state (presumably his plan to escape to the Low Countries). On January 21 Philip, in a letter to Empress Maria, wife of Maximilian II, said all that he would ever say about what he had done and why:

> The grief and pain with which I have done this, Your Majesty can well estimate from what I know you would feel in similar circumstances. But at last I have chosen to make a sacrifice to God of my own flesh and blood, and to place His service and the universal welfare and happiness before all other human considerations. The old causes, like the new ones which have supervened, forcing me to take this resolution, of such a nature that I could not relate them, nor Your Majesty hear them, without renewing our anguish and sorrow. I will only say that the fundamental cause of my determination does not depend on any one fault or lack of respect, nor is it merely a means of punishment, which (sufficient though the grounds would be) could have its time and termination. Nor have I taken this step as a means to reform his disorders. This business has another origin and root, whose remedy does not lie in time or in measures; which is the chief and most important consideration, to satisfy my obligations to God.[142]

Though all who commented at the time on this extraordinary event, in Spain and at Rome, praised Philip II's calm, moderation, and virtue, he must have known from the start that his enemies would put the worst construction

---

[141] *Ibid.*, XXII (1), 756-759, all quotations in the original Spanish on 757 (my translations); Walsh, *Philip II*, pp. 437-439. In March 1568 Cardinal Espinosa, Ruy Gómez the Prince of Eboli, and a lawyer named Briviesca drew up a legal document giving a full explanation of the reasons for the imprisonment of Don Carlos. Court historian Cabrera said he later saw it in a green box in the Simancas archives; there is no record that anyone else ever saw it after that (Walsh, *op. cit.*, p. 444).

[142] Walsh, *Philip II*, pp. 439-440.

upon it. Early in March he tightened his son's imprisonment even further, so that he was never to be allowed to leave his room, whose door was to be always locked, with two guards always on duty before it while at least one man was still to be always in the room with Don Carlos. Writing to Emperor Maximilian in May, he said that what had been done regarding Don Carlos "is not temporary nor susceptible to any change in the future." No more was heard of Philip's previously announced plan to go to the Low Countries in the spring, though Cardinal Espinosa had told the papal envoy in September that "nothing but his death or the end of the world" would prevent Philip from making the journey then. It seems very likely that he felt he could not leave Spain because that would require giving up his personal supervision of the strict confinement of Don Carlos.[143]

The effect of such close confinement upon such a nervous, excitable, and increasingly deranged personality as Don Carlos may readily be imagined. He had always had an inordinate appetite, and with little to do in his locked room to amuse himself but eat (he was not fond of reading), he gorged himself repeatedly until he seriously damaged his digestive system. In the searing heat of midsummer in Spain (his prison room must have been stifling), he consumed one day an entire highly spiced partridge pie along with large quantities of snow-water, bringing on vomiting, diarrhea, and severe fever. The doctors urged his father not to see him because it would agitate him still more; but Philip came to his son while he was asleep and gave him his blessing. On July 24 Don Carlos was anointed, made a good confession, and died a faithful Catholic. He was only 23 years old.[144]

Philip's enemies lost little time in charging him with the murder of his son. William of Orange, his leading opponent in the Low Countries, was the first to make the charge. It has been repeated endlessly, not so much by historians— who, however hostile to Philip, know there is not a scintilla of concrete evidence to support it—but by literary lights, popular historical commentators, and propagandists of many kinds and agendas. It is the theme of a famous opera. Even G. K. Chesterton, the great Catholic essayist and apologist, believed it and made it the subject of an execrable stanza in his otherwise magnificent poem "Lepanto."

But the probability is overwhelming that it is not true. If Philip were really going to kill his son, he would have done so on that grim midnight raid with helmet and breastplate and sword on January 19, as Don Carlos thought he was then going to do. Surely even Philip's enemies—though their name is legion— should recoil from the thought of this man blessing the forehead of his sleeping son in his last hours if he himself had ordered him poisoned. Few men known to history would have done such a thing—it would be hard to imagine it even of

---

[143] *Ibid.*, pp. 438, 445; Kamen, *Philip of Spain*, pp. 121-122 (first quote on 122); Von Pastor, *History of the Popes*, XVIII, 93 (second quote); Menéndez Pidal, *Historia de España*, XXII (1), 759.

[144] Von Pastor, *History of the Popes*, XVIII, 42, 45; Menéndez Pidal, *Historia de España*, 774-777; Walsh, *Philip II*, pp. 448-449.

William Cecil—and Philip II of Spain was assuredly not one of them. The only reasonable conclusion is that Don Carlos died a natural death, accelerated by his psychological condition.

And even yet Philip II had not drained his cup of sorrow to the dregs. For in September of this year of agony for the Catholic champion his beloved young wife, Isabelle of France, the one bright and shining light of all her star-crossed family, fell seriously ill. She was in her fourth pregnancy; each one had been difficult, and an earlier miscarriage of twins life-threatening. She loved her solemn, reserved, care-worn husband—so bitterly traduced by his own and every subsequent generation, outside of Spain—with a passion deep and pure, which he fully returned. On October 1, with Philip at her bedside, she was anointed. She told him how sorry she was to leave him when she knew how much he needed her, and all the more because she was leaving him without a son to replace the one just lost. She begged him to help her mother and her brother against the Calvinists, and never to go to war with Catholic France. He promised her; and through all his forthcoming years of strife and stress, he kept his promise. With tears streaming down his face, his famous imperturbability overwhelmed by grief, Philip told Isabelle that he had hoped she would never be touched by care or trouble and would be his companion until the end of his days; now that she must go, he would remember her forever.[145]

On October 3 she delivered a five-month-old daughter, who lived long enough to be baptized, and died whispering the name of Jesus. She was just twenty-two, one year younger than Don Carlos had been when he died. Philip wore mourning for her all the rest of his life, a full thirty years. Yet so bitterly was he hated that some men were found to say that he had poisoned her too.[146]

During the four years which had passed since the end of the First War of Religion in France, the French Calvinists had been preparing religiously, politically, and financially for a renewal of the conflict. Calvin's posthumously published commentary on Daniel seemed to show that their master had finally endorsed armed resistance to evil (read Catholic) monarchs; his successor Beza had always been more inclined to do so, and had accepted violent iconoclasm as probably a work of God.[147] In March the Prince of Condé had offered no less than 30,000 foot and 8,000 horse to Charles IX to make war on Spain. Charles declined to do it, but could hardly have failed to be alarmed by the numbers offered. And in April a Calvinist spokesman sent from France to Geneva told a secret committee of its governing Small Council, with Beza, that his comrades had a war chest of 240,000 *écus* and would loan 50,000 of them to Geneva at a low rate of interest to build up their defenses against a possible attack by the Duke of Alba on his way to the Low Countries. They also proposed to offer

---

[145] Walsh, *Philip II*, pp. 457-458.

[146] *Ibid.*, pp. 458-459; von Pastor, *History of the Popes*, XVIII, 46.

[147] See above, this chapter.

similar loans to Berne and the Calvinist Palatinate in Germany as the basis for a Protestant alliance.[148]

When the Duke of Alba marched through eastern France to the Low Countries, the royal government summoned a Swiss Catholic force to help protect France if Alba's army should turn on it. This alarmed the Calvinists, who believed the Swiss might be used against them. During August they decided to raise an army strong enough to expel the Swiss and seize several cities where the Calvinists were strong, and to use it first to gain control of the person of the king, as they had hoped to do in the conspiracy of Amboise against Francis II. Coligny, the most cautious of their leaders, for long argued against these plans, but by mid-September had finally accepted them. A striking force of 1,500 cavalry was assembled to try to seize the royal family at their country residence at Monceaux near Meaux, where they were then staying. On September 22 some of them incautiously let themselves be seen in a wood where the king (an inveterate hunter) was to hunt the next day.[149]

The royal family promptly moved into the fortified city of Meaux and summoned their 6,000 Swiss. Asked if he could get them back to Paris through an enemy army, Colonel Pfeiffer stoutly replied that he could, urging the young king "to confide your person and that of the Queen Mother to the valor and fidelity of the Swiss."[150] A great tradition had begun which was to be maintained in France until the 700 Swiss guards protecting Louis XVI were cut to pieces before the Tuileries in Paris on August 10, 1792, the day the reign of terror in the French Revolution began.[151]

Thus splendidly escorted, but with Catherine de Medici terror-stricken and Charles IX "hot, famished, and so angry that his fierce disposition never lost the memory of that humiliation," the royal family reached Paris in safety September 29 after sixteen hours on the road. The Second War of Religion began immediately. Condé tried to besiege Paris, but the forces he could immediately assemble were not enough to do so effectively. For the first time he claimed royal honors, minting coins bearing the words "Louis XIII by the grace of God, first king of the faithful of the Gospel." On October 1 Condé issued his demands: free exercise of the Calvinist religion throughout France; expulsion of all foreigners, including Catherine de Medici's favorite Italians; all taxes imposed since the reign of Louis XII at the beginning of the century abolished; convocation of the Estates-General; all those removed from office on account of religion to be reinstated; dismissal of the Swiss and Spanish regiments; four fortified towns to be given to him for the Calvinists and as security. The royal government found these terms totally unacceptable. On October 7 the royal

---

[148] Sutherland, *Massacre of St. Bartholomew*, p. 48; Kingdon, *Geneva and Consolidation*, pp. 177-178.

[149] Kingdon, *Geneva and Consolidation*, pp. 164-165; Whitehead, *Coligny*, p. 182-183; Mahoney, *Madame Catherine*, p. 122; Thompson, *Wars of Religion in France*, p. 319.

[150] Whitehead, *Coligny*, p. 184.

[151] See Volume Five of this history, forthcoming.

herald went to St. Denis, blew a triple blast of his trumpet, and read three times an order commanding Condé, Coligny, and their chief companions to appear before the king for judgment. When they tried to resume negotiations, Constable Montmorency ordered them all to submit within three days or be liable to execution if captured.[152]

William Cecil was well pleased with this new demonstration of Calvinist strength in France. In late October he wrote a letter to English ambassador Norris in France that reveals as clearly as any in all his correspondence the extent to which his power equalled that of his Queen, and how independent his will was of hers: "Her Majesty much mislikes of the Prince of Condé and the Admiral [Coligny]. . . . I think the principle is that Her Majesty being a prince is doubtful of giving comfort to subjects. Nevertheless you shall do well as occasion shall serve to comfort them." Note the "nevertheless."[153]

In November Pope St. Pius V levied a general tax on the papal states to help pay for military aid to the French Catholics, and the Duke of Alba sent 1,400 Belgian cavalry to help the French royal army against the Calvinist rebels. They arrived just in time for the Battle of St. Denis on the 10th. The Catholics had a large numerical advantage, but received a severe blow when Constable Montmorency, a loyal Catholic unto death, now 74 but still fighting in the ranks as always, conspicuous in a gorgeous red-gold doublet, was shot in the back by the Scotsman Robert Stuart, a mortal wound. Two days later he died. His heart was taken from his body, embalmed, and placed in an urn with the inscription: "Here lies the heart which was our confidence, a heart of valor, a heart of honor . . . the heart of three kings."[154]

The loss of Montmorency was a heavy one in many ways, not least because, after the assassination of Duke Francis of Guise, he was the only good commander the royal army had left. He was replaced by Charles IX's younger brother, Prince Henry, Duke of Anjou, at the tender age of sixteen. Though an elaborate pretense was maintained that Prince Henry really commanded the army, it seems highly unlikely that he could have done so at that age; and the royal army showed no significant initiative during the remainder of this brief war. Its one further important military event was the Calvinist seizure in February 1568 of the western port city of La Rochelle, which was strongly defensible. Its churches were ravaged, local Catholic leaders jailed, and the city was put under the rule of the Prince of Condé.[155]

---

[152] Thompson, *Wars of Religion in France*, pp. 320-321 (first quote on 321), 326-328, 331; Mahoney, *Madame Catherine*, p. 123 (second quote); Holt, *French Wars of Religion*, p. 64; Whitehead, *Coligny*, pp. 184-186; Kingdon, *Geneva and Consolidation*, p. 165.

[153] Read, *Cecil*, p. 394.

[154] Von Pastor, *History of the Popes*, XVIII, 114; Parker, *Dutch Revolt*, p. 123; Thompson, *Wars of Religion in France*, p. 332; Whitehead, *Coligny*, pp. 187-189; Diefendorf, *Beneath the Cross*, p. 81; Mahoney, *Madame Catherine*, pp. 123-124 (quote on 124).

[155] Thompson, *Wars of Religion in France*, p. 342; Whitehead, *Coligny*, pp. 191-194; Mahoney, *Madame Catherine*, p. 125; *Cambridge Modern History* III, 10; Kingdon,

Though Charles IX talked of continuing the war to punish his enemies, Catherine de Medici appears to have imposed her will and begun peace negotiations at the town of Longjumeau at the end of February. On March 23 the Peace of Longjumeau was signed, essentially reaffirming the terms of the Peace of Amboise five years before. Once again the strong advocates of both sides, notably the Guises and Coligny, were angered by the weak and inconclusive terms. Philip II was furious about it, and his Queen Isabelle, Catherine de Medici's daughter, was deeply distressed. The treaty included a promise by the Calvinists to return Catholic cities they had taken, but they refused to do so. It was not altogether effective even in ending the fighting; armed clashes continued at many points in the south of France and never entirely stopped until the next War of Religion began. The ink was hardly dry on the peace treaty of Longjumeau before both sides were actively planning to break it.[156]

And the tale of those two astounding years in the history of Christendom, 1567 and 1568, is still not done; for we have yet to behold the evil they bore to the foredoomed royal victim, Mary Queen of Scots—a story of such tragedy and horror as a writer of fiction would hardly dare invent, yet it all happened. The lovely young Queen, still only 24, was caught like a bird in a net. All her struggles and cries only wound the net more closely about her, until finally, in an act of desperation and supreme folly, she delivered herself into the merciless hands of William Cecil.

A little more than three months after her wild midnight ride with the murderous but cowardly Darnley from Edinburgh to Dunbar Castle, Mary had delivered a healthy son after a long and difficult labor. He was given the traditional Scots royal name of James. When the news came to London, Queen Elizabeth loosed her famous cry: "The Queen of Scots is lighter of a fair son, and I am but a barren stock!" On September 30, 1566 Darnley publicly rejected Mary before the Privy Council. The following month Mary became so ill that she was anointed. By the next month she had physically recovered, but was in a state of profound depression, wishing she were dead. While she was in this condition her half-brother Moray and Maitland of Lethington, both of whom had been involved in planning the murder of Riccio, offered to help her get an annulment of her marriage to Darnley if she would pardon the murderers of Riccio. If her mind had been clear she would surely have seen the hidden meaning of their offer, but in her depressed state she simply agreed. Then Maitland went further, saying that "other means" of dealing with Darnley,

---

Geneva and Consolidation, pp. 172-173. In May 1568 a council was held in Catherine de Medici's sick-room at which two of Constable Montmorency's sons advanced "certain oppositions" against young Prince Henry's exercise of command (Sutherland, *Massacre of St. Bartholomew*, p. 67).

[156] Thompson, *Wars of Religion in France*, pp. 344-348, 350; Holt, *French Wars of Religion*, p. 65; von Pastor, *History of the Popes*, XVIII, 116; Kingdon, *Geneva and Consolidation*, p. 172; Mahoney, *Madame Catherine*, pp. 126-127; Sutherland, *Massacre of St. Bartholomew*, pp. 64-65; Walsh, *Philip II*, p. 463.

beyond annulment of his marriage to the Queen, might be needed. Moray would "look through his fingers" to find them. At last beginning to suspect them, Mary said they must do nothing "against her honor." Maitland blandly reassured her: "Let us guide the matter among us, and Your Grace shall see nothing but good, and approved by Parliament." In the next few days he brought together a group of Scots nobles at the town of Craigmillar to sign another death bond, like that for Riccio. Maitland signed it, and so did the Earl of Bothwell whom Mary also believed to be her friend.[157]

On December 17 the baby Prince James received a splendid Catholic baptism in the chapel of Stirling Castle, the most impregnable stronghold in Scotland. Mary was able to attend it, but Darnley did not come. On Christmas Eve Mary kept her promise to the conspirators by pardoning the murderers of Riccio. In mid-January 1567 she moved her son from Stirling Castle to be with her in Holyroodhouse (despite its evil memories) after hearing a report of a plot by Darnley to seize him. But when she heard that Darnley had fallen seriously ill (allegedly of smallpox, actually of syphilis), some last embers of her love for him were rekindled, and she went herself to his sick-room in Glasgow to bring him back to Edinburgh. Arriving there on February 1, he chose to lodge in a pleasant house of moderate size adjoining the city wall, near an old church called Kirk o'Field, about three quarters of a mile from Holyroodhouse over hilly streets. Almost immediately a detailed sketch of the house and grounds was on its way to Cecil in London.[158]

Mary and Darnley were now apparently reconciled again, and on February 7 Darnley wrote to his father to say how well she was treating him and how rapidly he was improving. He was planning to leave the house by Kirk o'Field and return to Holyroodhouse on the 10th. On February 8 "French" Paris, a servant of Queen Mary in league with Bothwell, obtained keys to the house where Darnley was convalescing. The next day, the 9th, was a Sunday. There was a wedding that morning, of Mary's French valet Bastian Pages and a Scots girl, with the wedding banquet at noon, followed by a state dinner at four in the afternoon for the returning ambassador of Savoy, which Bothwell and several other signers of the Craigmillar murder bond attended along with Mary. After the state dinner the house by Kirk o'Field filled with noble revellers, drinking and gambling. Bothwell was resplendent in black velvet and satin. About ten o'clock someone reminded Mary that she had promised to attend Bastian Pages' wedding dance, after which it would be inconvenient and unnecessary for her to return to the house by Kirk o'Field since Darnley was leaving it to join her at Holyroodhouse the next morning. Mounting her horse to ride to the dance, she saw "French" Paris skulking about covered with dirt, but thought little of it. (All day he and several others had been digging a hole in the cellar to fill with barrels of gunpowder.) After a brief appearance at the dance, Mary returned to Holyroodhouse, where Bothwell conversed with her in the presence of the

---

[157] Fraser, *Mary Queen of Scots*, pp. 266-269, 272-279 (all quotes after the first on 278); Read, *Cecil*, p. 350 (first quote).

[158] Fraser, *Mary Queen of Scots*, pp. 280-285, 288-291; Ridley, *Knox*, p. 459.

captain of her guard for about half an hour until midnight, when she went to bed. The evening was cold, with a dusting of snow.[159]

After Mary had retired, Bothwell went to his room at Holyroodhouse, changed from his velvet and satin to plain dress, came back to the house by Kirk o'Field, met Archibald Douglas with several armed men, and was told that the gunpowder was ready. Inside the house, Darnley ordered horses for his departure the next morning, drank a nightcap of wine, sang a song, and went to bed. Bothwell and his men laid a powder train and prepared a fuse. The noise of all their previous work had been covered by the revelry in the house, but now the winter's night was silent, and Darnley—not yet asleep—heard them. Looking out of his window in alarm, he saw Bothwell and his armed ruffians standing in the garden below. Stark terror gripped Darnley. Dressed only in his nightgown, he called a servant, seized a furred cloak and a dagger, told the servant to bring a chair and a a rope, and let himself down on the outside of the city wall to the chair set below, a distance of fourteen feet. This man could not even flee for his life without taking furniture along.[160]

At two o'clock in the morning the whole city of Edinburgh rocked to a thunderous roar as Bothwell's gunpowder reduced the house by Kirk o'Field to rubble. Outside, at the foot of the wall, Henry Lord Darnley came to Judgment. Ignoring his desperate cry of "Pity me, kinsmen, for the sake of Jesus Christ who pitied all the world!" the murderers strangled him on the spot. He was only twenty years old.[161]

Now Mary Queen of Scots, though there is every reason to believe her innocent of the murder of Darnley,[162] was helpless in the grasp of his murderers. But she was at least able to get her baby son to safety. On March 19 James was taken back to Stirling Castle under the guardianship of the upright Earl of Mar, who was not involved in any of the conspiracies against Mary and Darnley.[163]

The evidence against Bothwell as the man primarily responsible for the murder was overwhelming, and on April 12 he came to trial; but as the president of the court was a signer of the Craigmillar bond and Bothwell had 4,000 soldiers loyal to him in Edinburgh, he was promptly acquitted. He insisted on his innocence, and on April 20 asked Mary to marry him; she refused. Two days later she went to Stirling Castle to visit her son, now ten months old, whom she would never see again in this world. From the castle she wrote to the Bishop of Mondovi, who had been a papal envoy to Scotland, "protesting her devotion to

---

[159] Fraser, *Mary Queen of Scots*, pp. 292-293, 295-300.

[160] *Ibid.*, pp. 300-304.

[161] *Ibid.* (quote on p. 304).

[162] Antonia Fraser's brilliant analysis of all the circumstances surrounding Darnley's murder, in her biography of Mary Queen of Scots (*ibid.*, pp. 288-308), provides in my view convincing proof of her innocence. See also Note 166, below.

[163] *Ibid.*, pp. 310-311.

Scotland, to the Pope, and to the Holy Catholic Church—in which she intended to die."[164]

On April 23 she started back to Edinburgh from Stirling, accompanied by Maitland of Lethington and another signer of the Craigmillar murder bond, with a guard of thirty. Overcome by sudden violent pain, she had to rest in a roadside cottage. When the next day she reached the Bridge of Almond, six miles from Edinburgh, Bothwell appeared with 800 armed men. He seized her bridle, said that danger awaited her in Edinburgh but that he would protect her, and that she should come with him to Dunbar castle. It is fruitless to speculate on what she really felt about him at this dark hour; probably she hardly knew herself. Once she was in his power at the castle he forced himself upon her, and twins were conceived.[165]

On May 6 he brought her back to Edinburgh. The next day the craven Catholic Archbishop Hamilton annulled Bothwell's existing marriage, despite the fact that he himself had given Bothwell the dispensation for it just a little over a year before. Eight days later Mary and Bothwell were proclaimed married by the Protestant Bishop of Orkney, using the Protestant marriage rite, at Holyroodhouse, after John Knox refused them St. Giles cathedral. The next day, Mary told her faithful equerry that she wanted to commit suicide (though she was too good a Catholic ever to do so). Agony and desperation had so altered her countenance that she was almost unrecognizable.[166]

James Balfour held Edinburgh Castle. Though he had supervised, under Bothwell, the actual execution of the murder plot against Darnley, he now joined Bothwell's enemies on condition of confirming his possession of the castle. He called on Bothwell and Mary, who had retired again to Dunbar, to return to Edinburgh. They came with an army, as did rebel nobles now supported by Balfour, and on June 15 the two forces faced each other at Carberry Hill. But there was no battle; the troops of Bothwell and Mary simply melted away. At the end of the day Bothwell urged that they go back to Dunbar, but Mary could endure his presence no longer. He departed at sunset, and she surrendered to the rebels, who had promised earlier in the day to support her as Queen if she would leave Bothwell. It was a lie; they seized her and made her prisoner, their soldiers shouting "Burn the whore!" Piteously she begged Maitland of Lethington, whom she had once thought her friend, for help; he turned his face away. The next morning she appeared at the window of her prison room in the house of the laird of Craigmillar, with her hair hanging down in wild disarray, her clothes torn, her face distorted, screaming for help; but the people in the street outside only mocked her. That night she was taken by Lord Ruthven, son of the most terrible of the murderers of Riccio, and Lindsay, another of her worst enemies, to an island in the middle of Lochleven, the largest lake in lowland Scotland, where

---

[164] *Ibid.*, pp. 310-312, 314 (for quote); Ridley, *Knox*, p. 464; von Pastor, *History of the Popes*, XVIII, 172-173; Read, *Cecil*, p. 376.

[165] Fraser, *Mary Queen of Scots*, pp. 314-317, 319-320, 343.

[166] *Ibid.*, pp. 319-324; Ridley, *Knox*, p. 464; von Pastor, *History of the Popes*, XVIII, 174, 182n.

she was flung into an unfurnished room in the castle on the island which was held by the Douglases. There she collapsed, speechless and much of the time motionless for the next two weeks. From then on through the summer, every Sunday in St. Giles' cathedral John Knox demanded her execution.[167]

In mid-July Mary miscarried her twins by Bothwell, and on July 24 Lord Lindsay presented her with a document of abdication from the throne of Scotland. Some of her spirit was coming back now; she demanded an inquiry by Parliament at which she could testify before signing it. Lindsay had to manhandle her personally and threaten to cut her throat before she would sign. If ever a document were signed under duress, this one was. Baby James was named king, with Moray regent—his objective from the start. On July 29 the infant was crowned. In mid-August Moray returned from London and Cecil to take over the government of Scotland. The day he formally assumed power, he took all of Queen Mary's jewels. In September Bothwell, who had fled to Norway, was arrested there by his creditors, imprisoned at Bergen, and then moved to Copenhagen Castle, where he spent the rest of his life and died raving mad. In December the Scots Parliament passed 19 new laws on religion, which established Calvinist Presbyterianism firmly in Scotland over the signature of Moray. All holders of public office and all teachers were required to be Calvinists. Mary's abdication was held "lawful and perfect." The "Casket Letters," allegedly written by Mary to Bothwell proving her complicity in the murder of Darnley, were unveiled for the first time. The letters, which seemed to show a love affair between Mary and Bothwell before the murder, were in all probability written by another woman. The forged parts of the letters were probably produced by Maitland of Lethington, supervised by Moray under the guiding hand of William Cecil. They had won.[168]

But Mary Queen of Scots was a daughter of the Guises, and above all a daughter of Christ and of His Church, who had kept the Faith. With faith goes hope. And chivalry was not dead. Not all even among the dour Scots were insensible to the romantic appeal of the beautiful, betrayed, abandoned 24-year-old queen shut up on an island in the midst of a lake in the midst of her deadliest enemies. George Douglas, brother of Mary's principal jailer, Sir William Douglas, laird of Lochleven, and his bold young cousin Willy arranged her escape from the island castle on May 2, 1568. Willy knocked holes in all the boats but the one he intended to use, Mary's chief guard went off to play handball, Willy stole the keys to the main gate of the castle from Sir William's belt as he handed him a drink at supper, and Willy and Mary crossed to the shore

---

[167] Fraser, *Mary Queen of Scots*, pp. 328-337; Ridley, *Knox*, pp. 465-466, 470. I have been to Lochleven. It is not a place one forgets. A small boat with an outboard motor brings the tourist to the island with its castle, now in ruins. One can walk all around it in less than an hour. Through gaps in the crumbling battlements of the castle the cold gray rippling waters of the lake can be seen in every direction.

[168] Fraser, *Mary Queen of Scots*, pp. 345-348, 350-352; Ridley, *Knox*, pp. 472-473, 476-477. See Fraser's brilliant analysis establishing the incredibility of the Casket Letters, *op. cit.*, pp. 391-408.

where George Douglas was awaiting her with horses to ride to safety with Lord Seton, a supporter of the Queen. Within a week she was joined by nine earls, nine bishops, 18 lords, and 6,000 men.[169]

On May 13 at Langside this force, holding a strong numerical advantage, confronted the army of Regent Moray. In a disastrous error, Mary was persuaded to give the command to the Earl of Argyll because he had supplied the largest single group of soldiers to her army, rather than to the faithful Lord Seton. The Earl of Argyll (probably unknown to her) was a signer of the Craigmillar murder bond and therefore a former comrade of Moray. By this time virtually everyone in that sinister group had betrayed at least some of the others, and might show up on either side of any combat at any time as suited their personal interests, but no one of sense would want to have any of them in command of his army. Whatever his agenda at the moment, the Duke of Argyll did not fight; it was later claimed in his behalf that he fainted, or had a fit. His troops abandoned the field, thereby providing the advantage of numbers to Moray, who won a complete victory and cut Mary off from her only possible nearby refuge, loyal Dumbarton Castle. She had to flee southwest over country trails, sleeping on the ground for three successive nights and drinking sour milk for sustenance.[170]

On May 15 the fugitive Queen of Scots reached the castle of Terregles, ninety miles southwest of Langside. It was small, poorly defended, very vulnerable; she could not stay there long. But it was close to the sea. She knew she could not now remain in Scotland. She had two choices: to return to France and her Guise family, beleaguered and with lowered prestige after the recently signed Peace of Longjumeau, but still well able to protect her and perhaps in better times to help her return to her rightful kingdom; or to go to England and try by personal appeal to gain support from Queen Elizabeth, whom she had never met but had always hoped to meet and make her friend, counting on the impact of her charm. No rational, dispassionate analysis could possibly have led to any decision other than the first; but Mary Queen of Scots had never been noted for analytical reason or good political judgment. Incredible as it seems, she must have forgotten entirely in that fearful moment that by every Catholic standard of law and right, she was the true Queen of England as well as of Scotland, and therefore in her very existence a looming threat to Elizabeth's throne. She decided to go to England and charm the charmless Elizabeth. On May 16, just two weeks after Willy Douglas had rowed her across Lochleven to liberty, just three days after the final betrayal at Langside, she cut off all her beautiful red hair to disguise herself and, accompanied by only 20 faithful retainers, crossed Solway Firth in a fishing boat and at seven o'clock in the evening arrived at the little port of Workington in the English shire of Cumberland.[171]

---

[169] Fraser, *Mary Queen of Scots*, pp. 355-360, 363-364; Ridley, *Knox*, pp. 479-480.

[170] Fraser, *Mary Queen of Scots*, pp. 364-366; Ridley, *Knox*, p. 480.

[171] Fraser, *Mary Queen of Scots*, pp. 366-368, 373. Mary never did meet Elizabeth in her life; William Cecil saw to that.

She was recognized almost immediately, even without her hair. The next morning 400 cavalry under the deputy governor of Cumberland arrived as her "escort." She sent a message to Queen Elizabeth saying that she had come to England to seek her assistance against her rebellious subjects so as to restore her to her throne. On the next day Elizabeth issued instructions (probably drafted by Cecil) that she would help Mary only if convinced of her innocence of complicity in Darnley's murder, and if she would pardon all those who had risen against her. Meanwhile Mary would stay in Carlisle castle, and not be permitted to leave England.[172]

About a week later Cecil presented a memorandum to Queen Elizabeth in council. He recommended that Queen Mary be held incommunicado, then "settled" in England. The charge of involvement in the murder of Darnley should be thoroughly investigated, with Queen Elizabeth to make the final determination of her guilt or innocence. In doing so Elizabeth should remember that Mary had once challenged her right to the throne of England; that the alliance of Scotland and France was contrary to English interests; and that it was her duty "to strengthen 'religion' [Protestantism] against 'the usurped power of Rome.'"[173]

From that moment William Cecil was dedicated to bringing Queen Mary to the execution block. It took him eighteen years, during all of which he held her prisoner. In the end he succeeded; but in the immortal words of the motto which Mary Queen of Scots embroidered to hang over her head during her long years of captivity, "in my end is my beginning."[174]

In mid-November 1568, five Spanish ships carrying about 400,000 florins or ducats[175] in gold to pay the Duke of Alba's soldiers in the Low Countries were driven into the English ports of Plymouth and Southampton by French Calvinist pirates and an autumn gale. The money aboard had been lent by a banker of Genoa named Benedetto Spinola, in association with some Genoese merchants, to Philip II's government in Brussels. Hearing of this, William Hawkins, whose brother John had been illegally trading in slaves with the Spanish colonies in America and had consequently lost most of his ships in those waters at San Juan de Ulúa, promptly wrote to Cecil suggesting that he communicate with Spinola "to the end there might be some stay made of King Philip's treasure in these parts till there be sufficient recompense made for the great wrong offered" to his brother by the destruction of his ships. Either from Hawkins or from some other source Cecil learned that the loan contract specified that the money remained the property of the lenders until it was actually delivered at Brussels. Cecil therefore held the ships in port, unloaded their gold, stored it in the Tower of London, contacted Spinola and offered to assume the loan for England at a higher rate of interest. During the next two critical years the Duke of Alba, a man of honor,

---

[172] *Ibid.*, pp. 368-369; Ridley, *Knox*, pp. 480-481.
[173] Read, *Cecil*, pp. 397-399.
[174] Fraser, *Mary Queen of Scots*, p. 555.
[175] The Netherlanders measured coined money in florins, the Spanish in ducats.

refused to believe that Cecil and the English government would engage in such barefaced robbery, whatever the legal excuse. He kept requesting and demanding the return of the money, actually expecting Cecil to turn it over. Of course he never did.[176]

The amount of money involved was very large, and Alba desperately needed it. His belief that he might really get it back if England were not further offended by Spain may well have influenced his advice to both Philip II and Pope St. Pius V against supporting the Catholic rising in the north of England in 1569 and against implementing the Ridolfi plot to overthrow Queen Elizabeth in 1570.

On November 25, 1568 the inquiry commission on Mary Queen of Scots' alleged participation in the murder of Darnley reopened at Westminster, with Cecil now sitting with the judges. Mary's traitorous half-brother Moray, now regent of Scotland for the infant James VI, presented to this commission a formal accusation against Mary as an accessory in Darnley's murder, documented by the highly dubious "Casket Letters." Mary was not allowed to appear in her own defense; Cecil and his men blandly ignored her indignant protests. On January 11 the Westminster inquiry was officially ended, but no judgment was given. Only after its adjournment were Mary's agents even shown copies of the Casket Letters.[177]

Now at last she realized her folly in coming to England, and the deadly danger in which she stood. She began seeking help and rescue wherever it might be found. Early in January 1569 Spanish ambassador to England Guerau de Spes reported that she had told him "that if Spain would help her she would be Queen of England in three months and restore the old faith." Early in February she was moved to closer and more onerous confinement in dank, crumbling Tutbury Castle in central England. Her jailer was the Earl of Shrewsbury, Protestant son of a Catholic father, dominated by his wife Bess (he was her third husband) who treated the royal prisoner shamefully. In three months the conditions at Tutbury Castle made Mary critically ill. Late in February a Florentine businessman named Roberto Ridolfi brought a message to the Spanish ambassador from the Duke of Norfolk and the Earl of Arundel saying that they hoped soon to set up a Catholic government and imprison Cecil, whom they condemned for stirring up revolt in other countries, for seizing the money for the pay of the Spanish soldiers in the Low Countries, and for increasing ill treatment of the English Catholics.[178]

By April Ridolfi was in Rome, describing to Pope St. Pius V his plan to bring Spanish troops to England to overthrow Queen Elizabeth in favor of Queen

---

[176] Read, *Cecil*, pp. 432-433, 435; J. R. Black, *The Reign of Elizabeth* (Oxford, 1936), p. 97 (for quote); Maltby, *Alba*, pp. 190-191; Walsh, *Philip II*, pp. 478-479; Parker, *Dutch Revolt*, p. 123.

[177] Fraser, *Mary Queen of Scots*, pp. 339, 388-391; von Pastor, *History of the Popes*, XVIII, 186-187, 191. See Note 166 on the Casket Letters.

[178] Read, *Cecil*, p. 406, 414, 440-442 (quote on 406); Black, *Reign of Elizabeth*, pp. 98-99; Fraser, *Mary Queen of Scots*, pp. 409-412; Philip Hughes, *The Reformation in England* (London, 1953), III, 261-263. Guerau de Spes said of Cecil that "there was no greater heretic or greater adversary to the Catholic religion than he" (Read, *Cecil*, p. 439).

Mary. He had indeed developed such a plan, but as yet had obtained no specific agreement to carry it out from any of the principals involved—Philip II, the Duke of Alba, Queen Mary, or the Duke of Norfolk. But the Pope, who had come to admire Mary greatly for her constancy in the Faith under adversity—after a noticeable cooling toward her during the Bothwell affair—was favorably inclined, and so was Philip. Both knew that Elizabeth had never been the legitimate queen of England, and her government was the leading supporter of the Calvinist revolutionaries in both France and the Low Countries. Her government had supplied ships and troops to the French Calvinists in the First War of Religion and had now stolen 400,000 gold florins from the Spanish army in the Low Countries. There was no reason for the Catholic powers to pretend any longer that she was the rightful queen, and every reason to act against her.[179]

In May 1569 the Dukes of Norfolk, Leicester, Arundel, and Pembroke pledged to support Queen Mary, restore her to the throne of Scotland, and declare her Elizabeth's heir if she accepted the existence of an established Protestant church in both countries and married Norfolk. At the beginning of June she agreed. A few days later it appeared that Norfolk revealed his interest in marrying Queen Mary to, of all people, Cecil. It is not clear whether he also told Cecil that he intended to make Mary heir to Elizabeth, but Cecil almost certainly knew anyway. As usual he bided his time, to draw into his net as many as possible of the present and potential enemies of the regime which he headed as much in fact as Elizabeth did in name. Elizabeth was publicly furious, swearing in August that she "would have the heads of the councillors who supported" Mary. It was probably not coincidental that it was exactly at this time that Elizabeth told Catherine de Medici in France that she would like a marriage alliance with the French royal family. The only available husbands for her in that family were Charles IX's two younger brothers, fifteen and eighteen years younger than she. Her protracted, on-again off-again negotiations with Catherine and Henry, the elder of these two princes, over the next three years do not suggest that she really intended such a marriage; but since at 34 she was obviously still capable of bearing a child, they kept alive the prospect that she would have a successor of her own body.[180]

---

[179] Von Pastor, *History of the Popes*, XVIII, 197, 229. In a memorandum of February 1569, probably intended for Queen Elizabeth, Cecil had described the Calvinists in France and the Low Countries as "the parties that do now stay the fury of the two monarchies from establishing the absolute tyranny of Rome" and called for still more support of them as "the continued feeding of the fires in neighbors' houses." In the words of Cecil's biographer Conyers Read, "the whole argument is based on the assumption of an alignment of western Christendom into two camps, and the identification of English interest with the Protestant interest." (Read, *Cecil*, p. 439)

[180] Hughes, *Reformation in England*, III, 263-264; Fraser, *Mary Queen of Scots*, pp. 417-418; Read, *Cecil*, pp. 447-448 (quote on 448); Conyers Read, *Mr. Secretary Walsingham and the Policy of Queen Elizabeth* (Cambridge MA, 1925), I, 100, 132, 158. Because Elizabeth in all probability never seriously intended to marry either of the available French princes, her extensive marriage negotiations with them and their mother will not further be discussed here.

In September Elizabeth declared flatly that under no circumstances would she allow the Duke of Norfolk to marry Mary Queen of Scots, saying that if this happened "she [Elizabeth] would be in the Tower [of London] within four months." She commanded Norfolk to drop the project and forced Mary to return to Tutbury Castle under close guard. Then she had Norfolk arrested and imprisoned in the Tower of London on October 11. That same day the Catholic Earls of Westmorland and Northumberland in the north of England, site of the Pilgrimage of Grace against Henry VIII's schism and still much more Catholic than the rest of the country, decided upon rebellion. On October 15 Mary Queen of Scots wrote to Pope St. Pius V asking for his help. Within a day or two of receiving her letter he wrote to Philip II and the Duke of Alba, asking them to help Mary and the Duke of Norfolk and saying they could do nothing more pleasing to God.[181]

The rebellion in the north of England began November 9 when the ancient Catholic banner of the Five Wounds of Christ, borne in the Pilgrimage of Grace, was unfurled. The Catholic army occupied Durham five days later. Mass was said again in its venerable cathedral, and the Book of Common Prayer was trampled. The Catholic Earls of Westmorland and Northumberland issued an appeal, but it was not directed against Queen Elizabeth personally, but only against evil counsellors (read Cecil) who were said to be plotting the destruction of the ancient nobility and had introduced a false religion. It was read at the ruined abbey of Ripon November 18. Though Mary was not specifically proclaimed Queen, Northumberland's cousin Leonard Dacres offered to lead an expedition to free her—Tutbury Castle was just fifty miles from territory controlled by the Catholic rebels—but she refused. Perhaps she feared that they could not in fact reach her, or that they could not prevail, as proved to be the case; but with her among them their chance for victory would have been substantially greater, and even in defeat they ought to have at least been able to get her away safely to France.[182]

Cecil, with the best organizational mind in Europe, set to work at once. He never saw a battle on land or sea, but no man of his time knew so well how to prepare for one. Within just thirty days he had raised no less than 30,000 men and sent half of them north under the militantly Protestant Earl of Sussex, who had had only 400 when the revolt broke out—an almost incredible feat in view of the slow communications and transportation of the sixteenth century. Sussex's army outnumbered that of the northern Catholics two to one, and the Catholic army "melted away" before his advance. The two Catholic earls fled to Scotland. By December 20, 1569 the main Catholic army had dispersed, and Cecil was

---

[181] Von Pastor, *History of the Popes*, XVIII, 197, 199; Fraser, *Mary Queen of Scots*, p. 419; Read, *Cecil*, pp. 448-450 (quote on 448), 460, 465; Black, *Reign of Elizabeth*, pp. 105-106; Hughes, *Reformation in England*, III, 265, 273n. For the Pilgrimage of Grace in 1536, see Chapter Three, above.

[182] Hughes, *Reformation in England*, III, 266-270; von Pastor, *History of the Popes*, XVIII, 206-207; Black, *Reign of Elizabeth*, pp. 107-108; Fraser, *Mary Queen of Scots*, pp. 420, 422; Read, *Cecil*, p. 467.

preparing a long list of those marked for death, and others to be induced, by torture if necessary, to betray their associates. Hundreds were offered pardon if they would take the oath of supremacy proclaiming Queen Elizabeth supreme governor of the Church in England. About 800 who refused were executed.[183]

Even if Philip II had decided in advance to help the Catholic rebels in England—which he had not—there would not have been time to do so. In any case the Duke of Alba, still believing he might get the money for his troops' pay back from Cecil if he did not offend England, strongly opposed any such aid. But Pope St. Pius V wanted immediate and decisive action. Leonard Dacres, cousin of the Earl of Northumberland, still had a Catholic army in the field in Cumberland, across the Pennine Mountains from Durham and York. It was defeated at the Battle of Naworth on February 20; Dacres, like the earls, fled to Scotland. But communications between the north of England and Rome were exceedingly slow, usually requiring a month in transit. Long before he could have heard of the Battle of Naworth, on February 25, Pope St. Pius V issued his bull *Regnans in excelsis,* excommunicating Queen Elizabeth for heresy and absolving the English people of the normal obligation of subjects to obey their sovereign, thus giving moral sanction to the dying rebellion.[184]

It was the last time this power of the Pope, first proclaimed and used by Pope St. Gregory VII against Holy Roman Emperor Henry IV in 1076—which eventually brought him to Canossa—was ever invoked. It came too late for its purpose, and Cecil at once fastened on it as the ideal legal tool to proclaim Catholics traitors by the very fact of their religious allegiance, since accepting the Pope as head of the Church implicitly recognized his authority to dispense a ruler's subjects from their moral duty of obedience, as St. Pius V had done with the subjects of Queen Elizabeth. This became the basis for the pursuit, arrest, conviction and execution of many hundreds of Catholics over the next two centuries in the British Isles.[185] Consequently it has been condemned by almost all subsequent historians, both Catholic and Protestant. But if the rising had a chance of success, it was worth trying in view of the immense consequences of the permanent separation of England from Catholic Christendom. And it did have a chance of success. Few could have foreseen that quiet, apparently mousy little William Cecil could raise 30,000 soldiers in a month.

In August 1570 Queen Elizabeth released the Duke of Norfolk from the Tower, no longer feeling threatened by him after the failure of the northern rising. But he was soon again intriguing with the ubiquitous Florentine Roberto Ridolfi. In early March 1571 he agreed to support Ridolfi's plot to remove Elizabeth from the throne in favor of Mary (which even the Catholic rebels of 1569 had not openly endorsed) and at the same time announced his conversion to Catholicism. In April a Scotsman named Charles Bailly was arrested at Dover

---

[183] Read, *Cecil,* pp. 458, 461-464 (quote on 461), 467; Black, *Reign of Elizabeth,* pp. 108-109, 111-112; Hughes, *Reformation in England,* III, 270-271.

[184] Von Pastor, *History of the Popes,* XVIII 209, 214; Walsh, *Philip II,* p. 506; Black, *Reign of Elizabeth,* pp. 100-111; Hughes, *Reformation in England,* III, 272-276.

[185] See Volume Two, Chapter 19 of this history and Chapter Seven, below.

and found to be carrying letters in cipher for Bishop Leslie of Ross, Queen Mary's personal representative at the English court. Though the letters were spirited away and sent on to the Bishop, Cecil—recently appointed Lord Burghley by Queen Elizabeth—put an agent in Bailly's jail cell and found out that he often carried such messages. Cecil now personally interrogated Bailly, threatened him with death and disfigurement, and tortured him until he revealed the contents of the letters, which were from Ridolfi discussing a plan to be concerted with the Pope for a Spanish invasion of England. At the end of March Ridolfi left England to try to implement his plot to depose Queen Elizabeth, rescue and enthrone Queen Mary, and restore the Catholic Church and Faith in England with the aid of Spain. Pope St. Pius V continued favorable to this enterprise, writing to Philip II recommending it and to Queen Mary telling her that he was doing so. The Spanish ambassador to England, Guerau de Spes, was strongly in favor of it, writing to Philip II that 15,000 men should be landed with their first objective to capture Queen Elizabeth, and their second to capture Cecil.[186]

Ridolfi reached Spain at the end of June 1571, giving Philip II the Pope's brief in his favor and his letters of recommendation from Mary Queen of Scots, the Duke of Norfolk, and Ambassador Guerau de Spes. On July 3 he was granted a royal audience. Philip was enthusiastic about his plan, telling papal nuncio Castagna that the time had come for a second Catholic restoration in England. He even ordered the Duke of Alba to do it, while still saying that details of executing the plan would remain subject to his approval. Alba had been consistently hostile to any such action since it had first begun to be discussed two years before, and he had not changed his views. Responding to Philip's directive on August 3, he declared roundly that the Duke of Norfolk had neither resolution nor courage, that Ridolfi was a frivolous intriguer who could not keep secrets, that English national pride would not admit rescue by foreigners, and that it was impossible simultaneously to capture Queen Elizabeth, seize the Tower of London, and burn the English fleet in the Thames, as Ridolfi was proposing. Meanwhile the Spanish Duke of Feria, representing Philip II, had made a monumental blunder by approaching the vehemently anti-Spanish navigator John Hawkins with a 50,000-pound bribe to join in the invasion. Hawkins and his family had close links to Cecil (they had suggested the seizure of the ships carrying the pay for Alba's troops) and informed him at once; in all probability it

---

[186] Von Pastor, *History of the Popes*, XVIII, 227-228, 230, 233; Fraser, *Mary Queen of Scots*, p. 424; Black, *Reign of Elizabeth*, p. 118; Conyers Read, *Lord Burghley and Queen Elizabeth* (New York, 1960), pp. 33-34, 38-40; Hughes, *Reformation in England*, III, 278-279. For the sake of continuity and clarity, William Cecil will continue to be identified herein by his own name rather than by his new title of Lord Burghley. Kamen (*Philip of Spain*, p. 134) says that "it is likely" that Ridolfi was a double agent of Cecil. Though Cecil's vigorous efforts to uncover the plot would seem to be unnecessary if that were the case, he may have simply been spreading his net still further; Kamen's supposition is possible, but to me does not seem likely.

was Cecil's idea that Hawkins pretend to agree to the proposal in order to find out all about it, which he did.[187]

Unwilling to proceed without his great commander but also unwilling to give up the enterprise, saying that it was his duty before God to restore England to the Catholic faith and liberate Queen Mary, Philip tried to compromise at the end of August by modifying his orders to permit Alba to postpone the invasion if he thought it would endanger English Catholics. On September 14 Philip declared that "I am so keen to achieve the consummation of this enterprise, I am so attached to it in my heart, and I am so convinced that God our Savior must embrace it as His own cause, that I cannot be dissuaded from putting it into operation." But by then not only the purpose but also the details of the Ridolfi plot were being discussed in the streets of both London and Antwerp. After the Duke of Norfolk was caught sending a letter in cipher to Scotland, Cecil's agents searched his mansion and found the key to the cipher under some tiles and another ciphered letter, from Queen Mary about Ridolfi, under a mat. Two of Norfolk's secretaries were put on the rack and confessed all. On September 19 the Duke of Alba decided, in view of the total loss of secrecy, to abandon the project and urged that all documents referring to it be burned. It was far too late for that; a month later Cecil revealed it all publicly, and Philip had to give it up. In November Bishop Leslie of Ross, terrified by Cecil and deprived of his ambassadorial immunities, admitted the whole plot and Norfolk's involvement in it, turning on Mary Queen of Scots by accusing her of poisoning her first husband, King Francis II; murdering Darnley, her second husband; and deliberately exposing Bothwell, her third husband, to defeat at Carberry Hill. In February 1572 Charles IX of France declared he could do no more for Mary. The Duke of Norfolk was sentenced to death, and executed in July.[188]

In France, warned of a plan by the Guises to seize them, Admiral Coligny and the Prince of Condé fled for refuge to the newly Calvinist city of La Rochelle at the end of August 1568. Other Calvinist leaders soon joined them there, and on September 9 Condé issued a proclamation declaring that he had again taken up arms "to protect those of the religion [Protestantism] from the tyranny and oppression of their enemies." Catherine de Medici and her Chancellor L'Hôpital nevertheless tried to stave off a new war, but in a furious scene at a meeting of the French royal council September 19, the Cardinal of Lorraine shouted that L'Hôpital was responsible for all the evils that had recently befallen France. When L'Hôpital shouted back that the Cardinal himself was responsible for those evils, Lorraine said the Chancellor should be executed and assaulted him

---

[187] Von Pastor, *History of the Popes*, XVIII, 231, 234-235, 237; Sutherland, *Massacre of St. Bartholomew*, pp. 194-196; Maltby, *Alba*, pp. 201-202; Parker, *Dutch Revolt*, p. 124; Hughes, *Reformation in England*, III, 279.

[188] Von Pastor, *History of the Popes*, XVIII, 235-236, 238; Maltby, *Alba*, p. 203; Read, *Burghley*, pp. 42-43; Read, *Walsingham*, I, 186; Black, *Reign of Elizabeth*, p. 120; Fraser, *Mary Queen of Scots*, p. 420; Sutherland, *Massacre of St. Bartholomew*, pp. 195-196; Parker, *Dutch Revolt*, p. 124 (for quote).

physically, but was blocked by one of the sons of Constable Montmorency. It was the end of L'Hôpital's political career; he was dismissed as chancellor a few days later and replaced by the strongly Catholic and anti-Calvinist Bishop Morvilliers of Orléans. The next day Charles IX went to St. Louis IX's Sainte-Chapelle in Paris to march in procession with the relics of St. Denis as St. Louis had done before going on crusade, and the armed struggle of Catholic against Calvinist in France was renewed for the third time.[189]

After six months of inconclusive maneuvering, the Catholic and Calvinist armies met at the Battle of Jarnac March 13, 1569. Marshal Tavannes, actually commanding the royal army whose nominal commander was young Prince Henry, Duke of Anjou, surprised the Calvinists by a night march across the Charente River by an old stone bridge and a line of boats. In an early morning cavalry charge Condé was thrown from his horse which then fell on him, breaking his leg. He was shot on the spot, by whom history is not sure, making Admiral Coligny the leader of the French Calvinist cause. (Later in the year the Parlement of Paris condemned Coligny for treason, ordered him hanged in effigy, and put a reward of 50,000 crowns on his head, dead or alive.) Jarnac was a great Catholic victory; twelve captured Calvinist standards were sent to Pope St. Pius V and put up in St. Peter's.[190]

Nevertheless the war continued. In September 1569 the Catholics successfully defended Poitiers against Admiral Coligny, who suffered 3,000 casualties in the siege. In October there was another major battle at Moncoutour. The Catholics prevailed by a series of spirited cavalry charges followed by a decisive charge by the steady Catholic Swiss infantry. Nearly 10,000 French Calvinist soldiers were killed, and Admiral Coligny's jaw was shattered, putting him out of action for some time. But once again the irresolute Catherine de Medici and the inconstant young Charles IX were unable or unwilling to take advantage of their successes. In December Charles actually disbanded the army that had won the Battle of Moncoutour (some said he was becoming jealous of his brother, the titular commander, though in fact the battle had been won by Duke Henry of Guise). General jealousy of the Guise influence rose again until almost all the royal council in France favored peace despite the objections of the Cardinal of Lorraine. Duke Henry of Guise fell out of the royal favor by having an affair with Marguerite, the most beautiful of the French princesses. Two Calvinist victories at Saint Gemme and Arnay-le-Duc in June 1570, though on a

---

[189] Thompson, *Wars of Religion in France*, pp. 365-367; Holt, *French Wars of Religion*, p. 65; *Cambridge Modern History*, III, 10-11; Whitehead, *Coligny*, pp. 198-199; Sutherland, *Massacres of St. Bartholomew*, pp. 79, 91; N. M. Sutherland, *The Huguenot Struggle for Recognition* (New Haven CT, 1980), p. 169 (for quote).

[190] Thompson, *Wars of Religion in France*, pp. 376-378; *Cambridge Modern History*, III, 12; Whitehead, *Coligny*, pp. 204-210; Sutherland, *Massacre of St. Bartholomew*, p. 103; von Pastor, *History of the Popes*, XVIII, 120-121.

much smaller scale than Jarnac and Moncoutour, increased the pressure for peace.[191]

On August 8 the Peace of St. Germain was signed, providing amnesty and restitution for the Calvinist leaders and freedom for Calvinist worship for all nobles except in Paris or at court. The most important concession was to recognize and accept full Calvinist control over four heavily fortified French towns, one a seaport and the other three located on rivers: La Rochelle on the Atlantic Ocean, La Charité on the Loire River, Cognac on the Charente, and Montauban on the Tarn. Thus a Calvinist "state within a state" was created, and for decades Catholic France held within itself these enemy bases for its own military destruction.[192]

During the years immediately following the Council of Trent several of the older religious orders were systematically reformed, notably the Franciscans, the Cistercians, and the Carthusians;[193] but in none was the reform so thorough and complete as that of the Carmelites. It was primarily the work of one most holy woman, St. Teresa of Avila, one of only two women honored as Doctors of the Church, the other being the glorious St. Catherine of Siena. Beautiful, vivacious, charming, and passionate by nature, St. Teresa had lived for years in the Carmelite convent of the Incarnation in Avila a religious life of no particular distinction. Suddenly realizing that God had called her to a level far higher, she responded by leaving the Incarnation to found a small but much stricter Carmelite convent at Avila dedicated to St. Joseph, where the primitive rule of the order—with full seclusion, silence, and poverty—was practiced unmitigated.[194]

Five years later, supported both by Juan Bautista Rubeo, general of the Carmelites, and by Philip II in person, she founded two more reformed Carmelite convents (they became known as "Discalced" because their nuns wore no shoes). She founded another at Valladolid in 1568. At the end of that year the first men's community of Discalced Carmelites was established by just three monks in a dilapidated house in the tiny village of Duruelo. One of them had been known of John of St. Matthias, but renewing his profession at the new monastery, he took

---

[191] Thompson, *Wars of Religion in France*, pp. 387-391, 415-416; *Cambridge Modern History*, III, 13-14; Whitehead, *Coligny*, pp. 216-224, 226-227; von Pastor, *History of the Popes*, XVIII, 126; Sutherland, *Massacre of St. Bartholomew*, p. 116; Sutherland, *Huguenot Struggle*, p. 175; Chamberlin, *Marguerite of Navarre*, pp. 60-63.

[192] Thompson, *Wars of Religion in France*, pp. 416-418; Holt, *French Wars of Religion*, pp. 69-70, 77; von Pastor, *History of the Popes*, XVIII, 130-131; Sutherland, *Huguenot Struggle*, pp. 175-177; Whitehead, *Coligny*, p. 228.

[193] Von Pastor, *History of the Popes*, XVII, 243, 256-257, 259.

[194] Marcelle Auclair, *St. Teresa of Avila* (Garden City NY, 1959), pp. 85-157. For St. Catherine of Siena see Volume Three of this history, Chapters 10-11.

the name of St. John of the Cross. He too was to be, like St. Teresa, a profound mystical writer and a Doctor of the Church.[195]

In 1569 St. Teresa founded Discalced Carmelite convents in Toledo and at Pastrami near Madrid, with a Discalced Carmelite monastery for men also founded at Pastrami. Every new foundation of hers in this early stage encountered opposition from influential people in the places where they were established and from members of the existing Carmelite order who did not want to be reformed. But Philip II stood firmly behind the reformers; Ruy Gómez, Prince of Eboli and a leading figure in the royal council, was patron of the Pastrami monastery. Finally in October 1571 the Carmelite general assigned St. Teresa to take over the large convent of the Incarnation in Avila, where she had originally resided and where the nuns were very hostile to her personally. Some of them actually came to blows with St. Teresa's supporters at her induction as superior. But by her unique combination of merry charm, iron will, and above all transcendent goodness and holiness, she soon brought them to obedience, and this community which had given much scandal became the jewel in her heavenly crown.[196] It still exists and flourishes today, a lodestar of vocations. Carmelites are rarely noticed by the world, and when they are noticed they are often mocked and condemned, since they "do nothing" but pray. But the contemplative vocation is essential to every truly Catholic society, calling forth and channeling graces invisible yet immensely potent. The worldly cannot imagine why anyone would live such a life, but all those privileged actually to know any of those who do, are aware of how much joy and fulfillment they find in it.[197]

During the remaining years of his pontificate St. Pius V continued vigorously to enforce the reforms mandated by the Council of Trent. In March 1568 he actually imprisoned behind the grim circuit of the ancient fortress of Castel Sant'Angelo several bishops who remained in Rome despite repeated direct orders from the Pope to go to live in their dioceses as the Council of Trent had commanded. He insisted on regular religious instruction in the parish churches of Rome every Sunday, and regular attendance by the parish children at those sessions, again as Trent had commanded. He saw to the establishment of diocesan seminaries as Trent had so strongly urged, and likewise on bishops' visitation of their parishes.[198] In 1570 he proclaimed a common liturgy and

---

[195] Auclair, *St. Teresa of Avila*, pp. 181-187, 199, 202-204; *Butler's Lives of the Saints*, edited, revised and supplemented by Herbert Thurston and Donald Attwater (Westminster MD, 1956), IV, 412-414.

[196] Auclair, *St. Teresa of Avila*, pp. 207-221, 234-237.

[197] I consider myself immensely privileged to have had the opportunity to teach eight young women later called to the Carmelite vocation. Most of them are members of the Carmelite community in Buffalo, New York, and one is at the convent of the Incarnation in Avila where St. Teresa once lived.

[198] Von Pastor, *History of the Popes*, XVII, 96, 189, 213-214, 294-295.

missal, obligatory for all Latin rite churches which had not had a special liturgy of their own for more than two hundred years.[199]

Pope St. Pius V concluded his trail-blazing, action-packed pontificate, which fulfilled in so many ways the promise and intent of the Council of Trent, with a magnificent victory over the infidel whose fame rang down the centuries all the way to the beginning of our own, inspiring G. K. Chesterton's great poem "Lepanto," some lines of which stand at the head of this chapter. Sultan Suleiman of Turkey had died on campaign against Christians in Hungary in 1566. He was succeeded by his much inferior and increasingly alcoholic son Selim II, who despite his indolent and pleasure-loving character still wished to establish a record of military success which would bear some comparison to that of his famous father. In September 1569 a fire in the maritime city-state of Venice, which traded extensively with the Turks and still held the old crusader kingdom of the island of Cyprus, blew up all the powder and munitions in the city, disabling Venice for some time from carrying on large-scale warfare. On March 15, 1570 Selim sent Venice an ultimatum: surrender Cyprus or war. By the not very resounding margin of 220-199 the Senate of Venice voted for war rather than surrender. Pope St. Pius V immediately began attempting to set up an alliance to help Venice against the Turks, and in April Philip II of Spain agreed to join it. Young King Sebastian of Portugal indicated interest, but Charles IX of France flatly refused to participate.[200]

Early in July 1570 the Turks landed on Cyprus with a huge army of more than 60,000. Two months later the greatly outnumbered defenders of the Cypriote capital of Nicosia capitulated on terms, which the Turks promptly broke, killing thousands of Christians—both soldiers and civilians—and selling most of the women into slavery. One of these victims, Amalda de Rocas, put on a ship with 800 other Christian women to go to Istanbul where each would be sold to the highest bidder to do whatever he wished with her, managed to get to the ship's powder magazine with flint and steel and blew up the ship with everyone on it. Sultan Suleiman had enough sense of honor usually to keep signed peace terms, and required his generals to do the same (as in the first siege of Rhodes). Selim II had no honor.[201]

---

[199] *Ibid.*, XVII, 196-197. In promulgating this common liturgy, which the Council of Trent had called for and has subsequently been called "Tridentine" (the rather awkward adjective for Trent), Pope St. Pius V declared that it should be "perpetual." Though this word was occasionally used in Church documents at the time, and undoubtedly reflected the intention of Pope St. Pius V, today's Catholic readers must be reminded that no Pope has the authority to bind his successors, except in *ex cathedra* teaching on faith and morals where, according to obligatory Catholic belief, the special charism of papal infallibility prevents any contradiction. In matters of Church governance such as the liturgy, any Pope can change it and cannot be prohibited by his predecessors from changing it.

[200] Beeching, *Galleys at Lepanto*, pp. 140, 158-159; Bradford, *Great Siege*, p. 210; von Pastor, *History of the Popes*, XVIII, 63, 362, 372, 374, 380; Walsh, *Philip II*, p. 507.

[201] Beeching, *Galleys at Lepanto*, pp. 160, 164-166; von Pastor, *History of the Popes*, XVIII, 391.

A small Christian fleet had been dispatched to help Cyprus, but they retreated on the news of the capture and horrors at Nicosia, perhaps concluding (as undoubtedly the Turks did) that no other city on Cyprus would now dare to resist the merciless infidel conquerors. But the city of Famagusta maintained the fight. A bold Italian squadron brought reinforcements, food and munitions to its defenders. On March 7, 1571 Pope St. Pius V signed the treaty of alliance against the Turks, creating the Holy League and placing the Christian cause in the hands of the Blessed Virgin Mary. It pledged 200 galleys, 100 supply ships, and 50,000 troops from Spain, Venice, and the Papal states for service against the Turks, at a ratio in numbers of 3:2:1 respectively. The supreme commander was to be Don Juan of Austria, Philip II's half-brother, who had recently distinguished himself in suppressing a large-scale revolt of former Muslims (called Moriscos) in and near the old Muslim kingdom of Granada in southern Spain.[202]

In April 1571 a huge new Turkish army of 100,000 under Lala Mustafa landed in Cyprus and pressed the siege of Famagusta, digging great trenches through the rock toward the city wall, whose defenders now numbered little more than 4,000. In May the Turks opened a bombardment with no less than 74 heavy guns, of which four threw 200-pound balls. On May 27 the Holy League against the Turks was proclaimed in St. Peter's. On June 16 Don Juan arrived at Barcelona to assume his command and sail with the Spanish fleet. But after repelling four massive Turkish attacks, with his garrison reduced to only 1,800 men and his powder almost gone, Marcantonio Bragadino, the Venetian commander at Famagusta, surrendered the city August 1 on the Turks' written pledge that they would grant life and liberty to all inside its walls. The next day Don Juan was invested by Cardinal Granvelle, in an impressive ceremony in Naples, with the insignia of his command of the fleet of Christendom against the Turks. He received from the Cardinal the golden banner with the figure of Christ Crucified that he was to fly on the day of battle, which now hangs in Santa Cruz Museum in Toledo.[203]

Two days later the surrender terms at Famagusta were violated just as those at Nicosia had been. Lala Mustafa, the Turkish commander, flayed the heroic garrison commander Bragadino alive, stuffed his skin, dressed it in a Venetian uniform, and dragged it through the streets of Famagusta, while ordering the massacre of all the prisoners and most of the remaining inhabitants in the city.[204]

---

[202] Beeching, *Galleys at Lepanto*, pp. 164, 166, 171; Walsh, *Philip II*, pp. 509, 512. The Morisco revolt broke out on Christmas day 1568 and was finally crushed after savage fighting three years later. The Christian victory was to a large extent due to the remarkable military abilities and inspirational character of Don Juan, despite his youth (he was only 22 when he took command against the Morisco revolt). See Beeching, *op. cit.*, pp. 99-123.

[203] Beeching, *Galleys at Lepanto*, pp. 174-177; von Pastor, *History of the Popes*, XVIII, 405, 414; Walsh, *Philip II*, p. 515.

[204] Beeching, *Galleys at Lepanto*, pp. 177-179; von Pastor, *History of the Popes*, XVIII, 417-418; Walsh, *Philip II*, p. 513.

As Don Juan's fleet assembled at the Sicilian port of Messina, no one could now possibly doubt the nature of the enemy they were facing or the apocalyptic quality of the coming battle. Defeat would render every Christian city on or near the Mediterranean Sea vulnerable to the fate of Nicosia and Famagusta. The full strength provided for by the treaty of alliance had for once been made good: over 200 war galleys were present. The whole of Christian Europe had been asked to pray the rosary for victory. As the fleet departed from Messina September 16 with the papal nuncio blessing each ship as it passed the harbor entrance, every man aboard carried a rosary so that he might pray with those he was defending. On September 27 the Christian fleet arrived at the Greek island of Corfu, which the Turks had just raided, wrecking churches, desecrating altars, and slicing religious paintings, showing the men of the fleet with their own eyes that all they had heard of infidel rapacity was true. They left Corfu determined to bring the Turks to battle within a few days.[205]

The Turkish fleet, nearly 300 strong, was anchored in the harbor of Lepanto in what was then called the Gulf of Lepanto, but now bears again its ancient name of the Gulf of Corinth, separating the Peloponnesus from the rest of Greece. At two o'clock in the morning of October 7, 1571, a favorable wind sprang up, enabling the Christian fleet to enter the Gulf. At dawn the Turkish fleet emerged, taking its customary crescent formation (the crescent moon being the symbol of Islam) which extended all the way across the gulf from shore to shore. Mass was said on the Christian ships and the priests gave general absolution to the men aboard. The ships then gathered in a formation shaped like a cross, with the bulk of them in the central column. Two large and heavily armed warships called galleasses were placed in front of the formation, commanded by two brothers of Bragadino, the commander of the garrison of Famagusta whom the Turks had flayed alive. All rams were unshipped to provide a better field of fire for the guns. Turkish Grand Admiral Muesinsade Ali flew a great green banner copied from one carried by the Prophet Muhammad and long kept at Mecca, with the name of Allah inscribed 28,900 times upon it in letters of gold. Don Juan of Austria flew the blue flag with the figure of the Crucified Christ. Don Juan went from ship to ship to speak to the men, holding up a crucifix and telling them: "Live or die, be conquerors; if you die, you go to Heaven." Then he hung the crucifix on the forward mast of his flagship.[206]

Under a cloudless sky the two fleets made their final preparations: the Turks with a great noise of gongs, cymbals, conchs and yells; the Christians in almost complete silence until Don Juan had fired the first shot. Then his flagship

---

[205] Beeching, *Galleys at Lepanto*, pp. 189-191, 194-195, 198, 200-201; von Pastor, *History of the Popes*, XVIII, 416-417; Walsh, *Philip II*, pp. 515-518. Confronted with last-minute doubts and hesitation from his chief subordinate commander, Gianandrea Doria—often incorrectly called the real victor in the Battle of Lepanto—Don Juan replied to his council of war: "Gentlemen, the time for counsel has passed; the time for fighting has come!" (Beeching, *op. cit.*, p. 209).

[206] Beeching, *Galleys at Lepanto*, pp. 206-213; Walsh, *Philip II*, pp. 519-520 (quote on 520); von Pastor, *History of the Popes*, XVIII, 418-420.

charged straight at Ali's; he danced to the music of fifes as he approached. The galleasses commanded by Bragadino's brothers opened fire, followed by the whole attacking column when they were close enough to see the faces of the enemy. The two flagships met with a tremendous crash, and a woman called Maria the Dancer, disguised as a man and burning to avenge the contempt for womanhood so cruelly characteristic of Islam, led the Christian charge to the Turk's deck. Hundreds of men followed, reinforced by more from other ships nearby. The struggle for the Turkish flagship went on for two full hours. The Venetian commander-in-chief, white-bearded Sebastian Veniero, 75 years of age, wearing carpet slippers to give him a better grip on the deck, methodically picked off one enemy after another with an old-fashioned crossbow. Don Juan was slightly wounded in the ankle, but Muesinsade Ali took an arquebus bullet in the brain. The green flag with the 28,900 names of Allah came down; the blue banner of Christ Crucified was brought from the Christian flagship to be raised over the flagship of the infidel, and there was not a hole nor a cut in it. The Turkish right wing turned the Christian flank and loomed as a major threat until the Christian slaves at the oars of the galleys, many of whom had filed their chains to the breaking point in anticipation of this opportunity, broke free in a wild assault on those who had beaten and abused them for so long. Two of Spain's greatest future commanders on sea and land, Alvaro de Bazán the Marquis of Santa Cruz and Alessandro Farnese the Prince of Parma, greatly distinguished themselves. By mid-afternoon what remained of the Turkish fleet was seeking only to escape.[207]

A storm prevented pursuit, but the Christian victory was overwhelming: 8,000 Turks were killed and 10,000 captured, and 117 of their ships were captured and 50 destroyed. The Christian losses were 7,500 men killed but only 12 ships lost; 12,000 Christian galley slaves were liberated. Cervantes, the later author of *Don Quixote*, was there; he called it "the greatest day's work seen in centuries." Pope St. Pius V was there in spirit. At the hour of victory, in the midst of a meeting with his treasurer, he suddenly rose to his feet, opened the window, looked up at the sky, and said: "This is not the moment for business; make haste to thank God, because our fleet this moment has won a victory over the Turks." Never again were the Turks to threaten Christendom at sea.[208]

On October 21 the first written report of the triumph arrived in Rome; Pope St. Pius V wept for joy, and repeated to God the words of Simeon: "Now dismiss your servant in peace." The following Sunday he celebrated a Mass of thanksgiving in St. Peter's; the next March he designated the day of the Battle of Lepanto as a permanent feast day of the universal church commemorating Our Lady of Victory. The news came to Philip II while he was at prayer in the basilica at El Escorial; in Madrid the Mass of thanksgiving was celebrated on All

---

[207] Beeching, *Galleys at Lepanto*, pp. 213-218; Walsh, *Philip II*, pp. 521-523; von Pastor, *History of the Popes*, XVIII, 420-421.

[208] Von Pastor, *History of the Popes*, XVIII, 421-423, 449 (second quote); Beeching, *Galleys at Lepanto*, pp. 216 (first quote), 220-221; Walsh, *Philip II*, p. 523.

Saints day.[209]   Along with fulfilling the Council, reforming the Church, and leading a counterattack upon the spiritual rebels who had riven Christendom, Pope St. Pius V had revived the crusading spirit which had seemed completely dead, and marshalled it to attain as complete and decisive a battle victory as Christendom ever won.

It was enough and far more than enough for one Pope in a pontificate just six years in length, though it seemed a lifetime. His responsibilities bearing down upon him more heavily than ever—for only a small part of them were discharged by the victory at Lepanto, splendid as it was—in mid-March 1572 he collapsed from kidney stones, a long-time ailment of his, but now much more severe. In excruciating pain, he never complained; once he was heard to say, "Lord, increase my pains; but increase my patience too." He died May 1 at the age of 68. In just fifteen years the process for his canonization began. He was beatified in 1672 and canonized in 1712. In more ways than one he had saved Christendom.[210]

---

[209] Von Pastor, *History of the Popes*, XVIII, 424-425, 443, 451; Walsh, *Philip II*, pp. 523-525.

[210] Von Pastor, *History of the Popes*, XVIII, 452-454, 456-460 (quote on 456).

7
The Struggle for the Low Countries
(1572-1585)
Pope Gregory XIII

"I would go myself [to the Low Countries] if my presence were not indispensable to these kingdoms, to raise the money here which is needed to sustain all the others: otherwise, surely I would have devoted my person and my life, as I have often wished to do, to an affair of such high importance and so close to the service of God. It is necessary for me, therefore, to avail myself of you, not only for what you are and the good qualities God has given you, but for the experience and knowledge of affairs which you have gained. . . . I am confident, I say, that you will dedicate your strength and your life and all that you hold most dear to an affair so important and so much concerned with the honor of God as well as the welfare of His religion; for on the conservation of that of the Low Countries depends the conservation of all the rest, and since they are in peril, there is no sacrifice one ought to avoid to save them."—King Philip II of Spain to his half-brother Don Juan of Austria, April 8, 1576[1]

"I could reckon unto you the miseries they [English priests] suffer in night journeys in the worst weather that can be picked, peril of thieves, of waters, of watches, of false brethren; their close abode in chambers as in prison or dungeon, without fire or candle lest they give token to the enemy where they be; their often and sudden rising from their beds at midnight to avoid the diligent searches of heretics; all which and divers other discontents, disgraces and reproaches they willingly suffer . . . all to win the souls of their dearest countrymen."—William Allen, rector of Douai seminary, to Rev. Maurice Chauncey, prior of the English Carthusians at Bruges, August 10, 1577[2]

The conclave to elect the successor to the great Pope St. Pius V was one of the quickest and smoothest in memory. It convened May 12, twelve days after the death of St. Pius V, with 51 cardinals present (44 Italians, four Germans, two Spaniards, and one Pole). The leading figures were Alessandro Farnese, the ambitious and able nephew of Pope Paul III, and Cardinal Granvelle, representing King Philip II of Spain. Philip had instructed Cardinal Granvelle to request Farnese to withdraw because of the strong hostility of his political rivals in Italy (he was the eldest son of the Duke of Parma), which would make war in

---

[1] William T. Walsh, *Philip II* (New York, 1937), pp. 552-553.
[2] Martin Haile, *An Elizabethan Cardinal: William Allen* (London, 1914), pp. 119-120.

Italy likely if he became Pope. Both Farnese and Granvelle, speaking for Philip, agreed on the necessity for continuing vigorously to carry out the reforms of Trent. Each proposed several other candidates, as did the cardinals appointed by Pope St. Pius V and also those appointed by Pope Pius IV, led by St. Charles Borromeo. The one candidate who found favor immediately with Farnese, Granvelle, and both groups of cardinals was Ugo Boncampagni, a vigorous 70-year-old canon lawyer. He was elected May 13 with no reported dissenting votes. He took office as Pope Gregory XIII and reigned for thirteen years.[3]

At his first consistory (meeting with his cardinals) on May 30, the new Pope emphasized his "resolute determination to carry on the reform work of his predecessor," confirmed Pope St. Pius V's bull against nepotism, and tightened enclosure requirements for nuns. The next month he informed both Emperor Maximilian II and King Charles IX of France that he would not approve their nominees for bishops if unworthy, declared that bishops holding office but not having received approval from the Pope must gain his approval or be removed, and required all bishops to make the Tridentine profession of faith. On September 19 he insisted that all cardinals assigned to dioceses must go and live in them, with only rare exceptions. He maintained this position despite many protests, to the great satisfaction of St. Charles Borromeo. Leading by example as well as by decree, early in 1573 Pope Gregory XIII appointed seven distinguished bishops as apostolic visitors for the dioceses of the papal states to make sure that the reforms of Trent were being fully carried out in them, especially with regard to the renewal of religious life and the defense of Church liberties against the powers of the secular nobles.[4]

St. Charles Borromeo, Cardinal Archbishop of Milan, continued to demonstrate in his large archdiocese[5] just how the Council of Trent had intended a diocese to be run, rejecting all other Church offices to concentrate for the rest of his life on making the fullest possible reform of the region entrusted to his spiritual care, which included 15 dependent dioceses as well as the archdiocese itself. In addition to the regular seminary called for by the Council of Trent, he established another for country priests, a third for late vocations, another for the Swiss borderlands, and two junior seminaries. He strongly supported Sunday religious instruction, which by 1595 was being provided for more than 20,000 young people in the city of Milan alone. He founded two colleges of his own at Milan and Pavia, and one for the Jesuits and another for the Theatines. When he died in November 1584, at the early age of 46, he had accomplished as much or more in his abbreviated lifetime as any bishop (exclusive of Popes and patriarchs) in the whole history of the Church.[6]

Throughout his long pontificate Pope Gregory XIII greatly favored the Jesuits. He reconfirmed the Society of Jesus and renewed all its privileges,

---

[3] Ludwig von Pastor, *History of the Popes*, Volume XIX (St. Louis, 1930), pp. 11-26.
[4] *Ibid.*, XIX, 67-68, 70, 73-75, 323-324.
[5] There were 2,220 churches, 3,200 clergy, 100 monasteries, 90 convents, and nearly 900,000 parishioners in the archdiocese of Milan alone (*ibid.*, XIX, 87).
[6] *Ibid.*, XIX, 86-94, 104-105.

including exemption from regular choir and permission to receive holy orders after taking the first three simple vows. Tempted to intervene in the election of their fourth general after the death of St. Francis Borgia, to avoid the choice of another Spaniard (the first three Jesuit generals had all been Spanish), he withdrew when shown that such outside interference in the choice of their leader, even from the Pope, was fundamentally contrary to their papally approved constitutions; but his wish was heeded when a Belgian, Everard Mercurian, was elected in April 1573. The new general enthusiastically supported the Jesuits' extraordinary work in Germany and in England. By Mercurian's death in August 1580 the Jesuit order had 21 provinces, 110 houses and more than 5,000 members; the Italian Claudio Acquaviva, the fifth general, was even more accomplished and successful. In the fall of 1584 the Pope blessed the opening of the new Roman college of the Jesuits, later called in his honor the Gregorianum, and consecrated the splendid Jesuit church in Rome, to this day a wonder to all visitors, the Gesù.[7]

He also took an active interest in the reform of the Carmelites, which St. Teresa of Avila took the lead in promoting for the women and St. John of the Cross for the men. When the Pope's well-meant order of 1575 prohibiting the establishing of new convents against the orders of the Carmelite general led to an actual persecution of the stricter Carmelites known as "discalced," and King Philip II himself and the papal nuncio in Spain interceded in their favor, the Pope in June 1580 established the Discalced Carmelites as a canonically separate order, no longer under the authority of the original Carmelites. At this point the Discalced had 22 houses and about 300 friars and 200 nuns.[8]

Gregory XIII's pontificate is noted also for the beginning of the publication of the first great modern Catholic history of the Church, by Caesar Baronius, and for the glorious new Church music to accompany the Mass of Trent, mostly written by the musical genius Pierluigi da Palestrina.[9]

Pope Gregory XIII was very ecumenical, establishing a Greek college in Rome, operated by the Jesuits, to try to undo the consequences of the Great Eastern Schism and the conquest of Constantinople by the Turks. With his encouragement, two Jesuits took part in a synod held in 1580 by the Catholic Maronites of the Middle East in Lebanon to discuss the decrees of the Council of Trent; the Maronites showed total loyalty to the Pope. An attempt was even made at reunion with the Monophysite Coptic Christians of Egypt in 1583, but this was unsuccessful.[10]

Pope Gregory XIII will always be remembered for his reform of the calendar. With the increased attention to dates characteristic of the modern age

---

[7] *Ibid.*, XIX, 234-235, 238-239, 250-253, 379, 382-384, 388-390; XX, 579-580; James Brodrick, *St. Peter Canisius* (Baltimore MD, 1950), p. 726.

[8] Von Pastor, *History of the Popes*, XIX, 152-153, 156-158; Walsh, *Philip II*, pp. 572-573.

[9] Von Pastor, *History of the Popes*, XIX, 265, 273.

[10] *Ibid.*, XIX, 247; XX, 493-494, 497; Oscar Halecki, *From Florence to Brest (1439-1596)*, 2nd ed. (New York, 1968), p. 196.

now fully launched, it had become more and more noticeable that the calendar dates did not coincide with the seasons. During the slightly more than 1,600 years since Julius Caesar had reformed the calendar of imperial Rome, which Christendom had used ever since, the slight error involved in its assumption that the length of the year is exactly 365 days and 6 hours, when the correct figure is 365 days, 5 hours, 48 minutes, and 46 seconds, had grown to an error of ten days by which the calendar was behind the seasons. The error could be corrected almost perfectly by dropping the ten extra days and providing for the future that century years should not be leap years unless divisible by four (thus 1600 and 2000 would be leap years but 1700, 1800, and 1900 would not). Pope Gregory so decreed in a bull published in March 1582, directing that the ten days be dropped in October, so that October 5, 1582 would become October 15.[11]

No rational man could deny the need for and value of this change, and the whole world now uses the Gregorian calendar. There is no better proof of the irrational ferocity of the times, where any religious institution or leader was concerned, than the rejection of this new calendar by every non-Catholic country in Christendom, simply because it came from the Pope. Wholly Catholic Italy, Spain, Portugal, and Poland accepted it before it went into effect, mostly Catholic Hungary a few days afterward, officially Catholic France in December, and partly Catholic Bohemia and the Catholic states of Germany and Switzerland in 1583 and 1584. But no Protestant state nor Eastern Orthodox community would use it; Patriarch Jeremiah II of Constantinople rejected it despite special efforts by Pope Gregory XIII to cultivate his good will.[12] England held out against the "papist calendar" for no less than 170 years, and Russia until the twentieth century, when the Gregorian calendar was at long last installed by none other than Lenin![13]

That ferocity which rendered even a nearly perfect calendar anathema if it came from the Pope was the hallmark of the late sixteenth century, as of the first half of the seventeenth century. It was both cause and product of the general religious war between Catholic and Protestant in which most of Christendom was now embroiled. As pointed out above,[14] the total refusal of the Protestants to have anything to do with the Council of Trent, their flat rejection of every Catholic effort to reach them and find common ground during the course of their revolt against the Catholic faith as it had been known and practiced since the time

---

[11] Von Pastor, *History of the Popes*, XIX, 287-289.

[12] Halecki, *Florence to Brest*, p. 215.

[13] The result is a chronological nightmare for historians, with dates used in the Protestant countries and in Russia diverging by first ten (until 1700), then eleven, then (in Russia) twelve and thirteen days from the Gregorian dates. Most historians have thrown up their hands and settled for the coward's solution of giving only the dates found in their sources. All dates used in this history after 1582 will be Gregorian, with apologies for some errors likely to creep in from dates taken from other histories without clear indication of whether they are Julian or Gregorian.

[14] In Chapter Six.

of the apostles,[15] had rendered that war inevitable, given the firm belief of nearly everyone in that age that religious uniformity was a prerequisite for national unity. Not until 1648 on the European continent, not until 1660 in Great Britain, was it finally realized that under the prevailing conditions religious uniformity could no more be achieved by war than by persuasion. During the late sixteenth century, with the significant exceptions of Italy, Spain, and Portugal, there was no country in Europe whose religious orientation might not change overnight, often at the cost of the lives of the losers if they would not conform or could not leave the country. The atrocities of these years, both Protestant and Catholic, must be examined with this stark alternative constantly in mind. (Wartime psychology is different from that of peacetime. Many people, who would never do so under normal circumstances, will in wartime cheer the death and suffering of the enemy.[16] And in these years, with the exceptions noted, all Europe was at war.)

Such was the heritage of Martin Luther, who far back in 1520 had called upon the nobility of Germany to wash their hands in the blood of the Catholics.[17]

In the sixteenth century nearly everyone thought that peace and a royal marriage went together, though this was usually applied to international relations rather than civil conflicts. In the winter and spring of 1572 the Queen Mother of France, Catherine de Medici, that inveterate intriguer, negotiator and promoter of dynastic politics, decided that the only solution to the ten years' strife of Catholic and Calvinist within France was the marriage of Henry, son of the Calvinist Queen of Navarre, to Marguerite, Catherine's exceptionally beautiful marriageable daughter. That the couple heartily disliked each other—the fastidious Marguerite found Henry's rank body odor and habit of chewing garlic disgusting, while Henry saw her as a hothouse flower of a corrupt court who had nothing whatever in common with him—was regarded as totally irrelevant. The fact that Henry's mother, the vehemently Calvinist Jeanne d'Albret, strongly objected to the marriage because Marguerite would not even consider giving up her Catholic Faith was somewhat more of a problem, conveniently resolved when Jeanne died in June 1572, though by then she had given her reluctant consent to the marriage.[18]

---

[15] The revolt was not only, nor even primarily, against the Pope and the Church hierarchy, as is commonly believed. The Protestant rebels in every country sought to abolish the Mass. They called it idolatry. The Mass is the heart of the Church's worship. No Catholic could ever accept the abolition of the Mass.

[16] This was clearly the case even during that most just of wars, World War II, and led to most Americans accepting without complaint and even with approval the internment of tens of thousands of innocent Japanese-Americans and the ghastly nuclear bombing of Hiroshima and Nagasaki. I can vividly remember just how we felt about such matters at that time, and the recollection is not pleasant.

[17] See Chapter One, above.

[18] Irene Mahoney, *Madame Catherine* (New York, 1975), pp. 143-146; Philippe Erlanger, *St. Bartholomew's Night* (New York, 1960), pp. 103-105; E. R. Chamberlin,

Immense preparations were made for the Paris wedding of Henry and Marguerite, which would involve the introduction of thousands of Calvinists among the militantly Catholic population of Paris. Pope St. Pius V had said he would not even consider a dispensation for this marriage and Pope Gregory XIII held equally firm against it. But on August 16, two days before the wedding, Catherine de Medici told old Cardinal Bourbon, who was to solemnize the marriage, that the dispensation had been granted and was on its way, while ordering all couriers from Rome stopped at Lyons until after the wedding, so that no notice of the truth could reach Bourbon. Gullible or suborned, the Cardinal agreed to proceed with the marriage. Royal weddings were held at Notre Dame, but since heretics were not allowed to pass through its ancient portals, the ceremony took place on a dais in front of one of the cathedral doors. The next day a play was presented called "The Mystery of the Three Worlds," featuring Henry of Navarre and his friends trying to invade Heaven but being repulsed by angels and hurled into Hell by King Charles IX and his brothers, but then rescued from Hell by now friendly angels.[19]

Paris would have need of a legion of friendly angels during the horrors of the next week, but none were forthcoming.

Meanwhile a new confrontation was building in the Low Countries. The Duke of Alba, strictly a land warrior in the old Spanish tradition, had neglected his sea flank; on April 1 a 25-ship fleet of Dutch Calvinist pirates calling themselves "Sea Beggars" descended upon the defenseless coastal town of Brill and captured it. They celebrated their victory by sacking all the churches in the town and torturing 13 priests to death. Their commander, Count Lumey de la Marck, an adherent of William of Orange, decided to remain, fortify and defend the town, and use it as his new base of operations since Queen Elizabeth had just expelled his pirates from their former bases in England. Soon afterward 800 "Sea Beggars" in eight ships came to the aid of rebels in the important port of Flushing in the province of Zeeland and helped them secure that town and most of the surrounding island of Walcheren. The next month the "Sea Beggars" similarly took the port of Enkhuizen on the Zuyder Zee, and Cecil sent a memorandum to Queen Elizabeth on the necessity of giving large-scale support to them.[20]

Marguerite of Navarre (New York, 1974), pp. 70-77; Nancy Roelker, *Queen of Navarre; Jeanne d'Albret* (Cambridge MA, 1968), pp. 367-381, 390-391.

[19] Von Pastor, *History of the Popes*, XVIII, 140, XIX, 484, 495; Sylvia L. England, *The Massacre of St. Bartholomew* (London, 1938), pp. 54, 56-64; Erlanger, *St. Bartholomew's Night*, pp. 128-132; A. W. Whitehead, *Gaspard de Coligny, Admiral of France* (London, 1904), pp. 256-257; Mahoney, *Madame Catherine*, pp. 152-154; Chamberlin, *Marguerite of Navarre*, pp. 78-79.

[20] Geoffrey Parker, *The Dutch Revolt*, rev. ed. (London, 1979), pp. 117, 126, 132; Jonathan Israel, *The Dutch Republic; Its Rise, Greatness and Fall 1477-1806* (Oxford, 1995), pp. 170-173; William S. Maltby, *Alba* (Berkeley CA, 1983), pp. 224-225; N. M. Sutherland, *The Massacre of St. Bartholomew and the European Conflict 1569-1572* (London, 1973), pp. 271-272.

In May Louis of Nassau, brother of William of Orange, commanding an army consisting mostly of French Calvinists, took Mons and Valenciennes near the French border in what is now Belgium. He was soon forced to fall back into France, where he and the French Calvinists began to press hard for direct French involvement in the struggle on the side of the Calvinist rebels, with the full support of the formidable French Calvinist political and military leader, Admiral Coligny. On June 6 Coligny rode into Paris with a bodyguard of 300 horsemen, the Catholic Parisians watching in hostile silence as he rode through their streets, "already a legend, with his grey beard, his toothpick, his cold, masterful and gloomy eye." On the 19th the royal council met and heard Coligny call for all-out support of the Calvinist rebels in the Low Countries and full alliance with William of Orange, arguing that the risk of war with Spain could be taken because Spain was overextended and not as strong or as dangerous as many believed. Bishop Jean Morvillier of Orléans replied for the Catholics, saying that the majority of the people of the Low Countries were not Calvinists or rebels and would not welcome the French, that war with Spain would be long and bloody and very costly. On June 26 Coligny's proposal was rejected.[21] Coligny was defiant, telling King Charles IX to his face:

> I may no longer oppose your will, but I am certain that you will be sorry for it. However that may be, Your Majesty will not think it amiss if, having promised the Prince of Orange aid and support, I do my best to furnish him with both, with the help of all my friends, relatives and servants and even, if need be, with my own person.[22]

Charles IX, 22 years old, was now ruling in his own right, though still much influenced by his mother, Catherine de Medici. Like all four of her sons, he had something wrong with him. E. R. Chamberlin memorably describes him:

> Physically he was not very impressive, a lopsided young man with enormous shoulders and spindly legs, who looked fixedly at his feet, or at the ceiling, when speaking to anyone. . . . His sanity was balanced on a knife edge; no one knew when, or for what cause, he would topple into raging madness. . . . His language was habitually laced, and at times rendered almost incomprehensible, by the vilest, most obscene of oaths. The violence with which he would throw himself into his ironwork, hammering hour after hour until he was bathed in sweat, was equalled by the immoderation of his hunting. At times he would spend twenty hours at a stretch in the saddle, his exhausted attendants following him in relays until the kill. And the kill itself—that purely technical end of the hunt—was conducted with a disgusting brutality that shocked even his unimpressionable huntsmen: as often as not he preferred to club the beast to death.[23]

---

[21] Erlanger, *St. Bartholomew's Night*, pp. 94-95, 98-99 (quote on 94); Whitehead, *Coligny*, pp. 248-251; Sutherland, *Massacre of St. Bartholomew*, pp. 241, 248, 261-262; Parker, *Dutch Revolt*, p. 132; Israel, *Dutch Republic*, pp. 171-173.

[22] Erlanger, *St. Bartholomew's Night*, p. 100.

[23] Chamberlin, *Marguerite of Navarre*, pp. 83-84.

⌐Such a man was easily influenced by others, yet essentially uncontrollable because of his disordered nature.⌐ This renders illusory the many learned arguments about whether his mother or Coligny had the upper hand with him in the critical summer of 1572. Neither could be sure of it. But Charles had incautiously committed to paper a promise of French support for Louis of Nassau, and after the Duke of Alba's son had routed a French Calvinist army under the Count of Genlis at St. Ghislain near Mons on July 17, that written promise was found on Genlis' person. Spain now had a clear justification for war if Philip II wanted to use it. Catherine de Medici was as eager to avoid war with Spain over the Low Countries as Coligny was to have it. She overwhelmed her royal son with reproaches, and he backed off, claiming (contrary to the words of his own letter) that the French Calvinists under Genlis had gone to the Low Countries against his orders.[24]

On August 9 a long and stormy meeting of the French royal council discussed whether to go to war in the Low Countries. Coligny continued to favor it, promising to contribute 15,000 foot and 4,000 horse from his Calvinist associates, while Catherine de Medici wept (her tears always had a special impact on her son) and said repeatedly "there shall be no war." She was supported by the principal military man in the council, Marshal Tavannes. Though it appears that when the meeting convened a majority favored war, Catherine and Tavannes won over enough of them to reject it. Coligny left the meeting in cold anger, Catherine in mortal fear of him and of French Calvinist power.[25]

Catherine was already in touch with Anne d'Este, widow of Duke Francis of Guise, who had subsequently married the Italian Duke of Nemours. The whole Guise family remained convinced that Coligny had planned the assassination of Duke Francis nine years before. Anne d'Este had been devoted to her magnificent first husband. She was the granddaughter of Lucrezia Borgia and had the Italian spirit of vendetta. On August 17 Catherine met with her again. There is good reason to believe that the two women, probably in collaboration with other members of the Guise family, now decided to use Charles de Louviers, Sieur de Maurevert, who had already tried to kill Coligny in 1569 and had taken service with the Guises, to assassinate him.[26]

---

[24] Parker, *Dutch Revolt*, p. 137; Maltby, *Alba*, p. 231; Erlanger, *St. Bartholomew's Night*, pp. 106-108.

[25] Erlanger, *St. Bartholomew's Night*, p. 121 (for quote); Whitehead, *Coligny*, pp. 245-255; Mahoney, *Madame Catherine*, p. 156; Sutherland, *Massacre of St. Bartholomew*, p. 304; Conyers Read, *Mr. Secretary Walsingham and the Policy of Queen Elizabeth* (Cambridge MA, 1925), I, 216-217.

[26] There is no specific testimony to this effect, but the meeting of Catherine with Anne d'Este definitely took place this day, and Maurevert was later to lie in wait for Coligny in a house belonging to a former tutor of Duke Henry of Guise, which Anne d'Este had just vacated, and to ride a Guise horse in his subsequent flight from Paris (Erlanger, *St. Bartholomew's Night*, pp. 127, 129, 133; England, *Massacre of St. Bartholomew*, pp. 70-71).

In the morning of August 22, during a month of severe heat when "the Seine ran brown and sluggish," Admiral Coligny, staying in Paris after the royal wedding to present a list of violations of the last Catholic-Calvinist peace agreement (that of St. Germain), was walking back to his lodgings from the Louvre palace where he had just met with the king in council. Crouched behind an upper lattice-window covered with a cloth, Maurevert the assassin took careful aim with a long-barrelled arquebus set on a crutch at the black-clad figure approaching in the street. The arquebus was a notoriously inaccurate weapon, but the long barrel and the crutch improved its accuracy. Maurevert waited until Coligny was close enough so that he was confident he could put a bullet through his heart. He fired two shots. But just as he fired, Coligny made a sudden move, "variously reported as bending to adjust a shoe, stopping to open a letter, or turning to spit in the street." Consequently Maurevert's first bullet struck his left arm instead of his chest, lodging in the elbow, while the second took off the index finger of his right hand and ricocheted away. The imperturbable Coligny snapped "bad shot!" and then: "There is the window whence came the shot—you can see it by the smoke . . . Yolet, go tell the king what has happened." But Maurevert was away on a fast horse before he could be apprehended. He picked up a second horse later from a Guise follower, and then went to a house at Joinville belonging to the Guises (all of which indicates their complicity in the assassination attempt). It is clear that Charles IX knew nothing of the plot, since his first action on learning of it was to prohibit citizens from taking up arms and to command Catholics living close to the house where Coligny was taken for medical care, to give up their houses to his Protestant attendants.[27]

King Charles showed great anger at the assassination attempt and pledged Coligny protection. The wounded Calvinist leader refused to leave Paris, despite the advice of some of his associates that he do so, though he may simply have been too ill to travel (his wounds, though not life-threatening, were debilitating and very painful). The Calvinists who had come to Paris for the wedding and still remained, were seething with anger. According to a reliable report from a physician of Mantua in Italy, who had no stake in either party in France, soon after the wounding of Coligny (probably the day of the attack on him or the following day) a group of them met in a room just below his under the leadership of his son-in-law Téligny and decided to bring up a force of 4,000 cavalry by August 26 and seize the Louvre palace, where they would kill everyone they believed had advised or promoted the attempted assassination, notably the Dukes of Guise and Nevers, and possibly some members of the royal family as well. In the emotional and frantic atmosphere of that moment, it was exceptionally hard to keep secrets; the plan was probably revealed to the royal family quite soon after it was made. Charles later said he was told on the 23rd that French

---

[27] Erlanger, *St. Bartholomew's Night*, pp. 138-139; England, *Massacre of St. Bartholomew*, pp. 71-73 (third quote on 73); Barbara B. Diefendorf, *Beneath the Cross; Catholics and Huguenots in Sixteenth-Century Paris* (New York, 1991), pp. 91-93 (second quote on 93); Whitehead, *Coligny*, pp. 258-259; Mahoney, *Madame Catherine*, p. 152 (first quote).

Calvinists were marching on Paris and intended to seize him in the Louvre that very night, while Catherine de Medici said she received three separate letters warning that the Calvinists had decided to kill her, the king, and all the court. The frightened young king and his equally frightened mother met with the royal council on the afternoon of the 23rd, discussed the danger with them, and decided to strike first by killing about thirty of the Calvinist leaders then in Paris, including the wounded Coligny. Marguerite of Navarre later said in her memoirs that on that evening Catherine revealed to Charles IX for the first time that she had been involved in the plot to kill Coligny, and that this could be exposed if the Calvinist leaders were not silenced. Other evidence confirms her statement.[28]

It was now Saturday evening, the 23rd, the eve of the feast of St. Bartholomew. At about seven o'clock Téligny went to the Louvre to ask for a guard to be stationed outside Coligny's house. Prince Henry heard his request and sent Cosseins, a fierce Catholic and known enemy of Coligny, with some men allegedly for this purpose. About eleven o'clock Charles IX summoned the provost, Jean Le Charron, who was responsible for safety and order in Paris. The king told him that the Calvinists were planning to seize the Louvre (as they had proposed, but not that night) and ordered him to lock all the gates of the city so that no one could enter or leave, and chain all boats on the Seine for the same purpose. He also ordered Le Charron to distribute weapons to all citizens able to bear arms and to alert the militia officers. However, no orders were given for the armed citizens to attack or kill anyone; their calling out can be explained by Charles' belief that a Calvinist attack impended. Le Charron went back to City Hall and began preparations, but was unable to get out orders for the assembly of armed citizens until early the next morning.[29]

An hour or two before dawn, Duke Henry of Guise and about a hundred men went to carry out the killings of Calvinist leaders ordered by the king and council. They went first to the house where the wounded Coligny was staying, to which they were immediately admitted by Cosseins. The handful of guards loyal to Coligny were quickly overwhelmed, but their brief resistance gave time to barricade the door to Coligny's room with furniture. Coligny told all those with him to save themselves by fleeing by way of the roof. But the wounded admiral himself could not do that, and a few minutes later he faced a Czech ruffian named Simanowitz armed with a pike. From his bed Coligny addressed him: "Young man, you should respect my old age and my infirmity." Simanowitz's response was to run him through with his pike and then throw him out of a window ("defenestration," the traditional method of killing important people in

---

[28] Sutherland, *Massacre of St. Bartholomew*, pp. 333-335 (for report of the physician of Mantua), 341-342; Erlanger, *St. Bartholomew's Night*, pp. 139-141; England, *Massacre of St. Bartholomew*, pp. 60, 75-79; Diefendorf, *Beneath the Cross*, pp. 95-96; Whitehead, *Coligny*, pp. 261-263, 278; Donald R. Kelley, *François Hotman, a Revolutionary's Ordeal* (Princeton, 1973), pp. 211-213.

[29] Diefendorf, *Beneath the Cross*, pp. 96-97; Sutherland, *Massacre of St. Bartholomew*, pp. 338-339; England, *Massacre of St. Bartholomew*, pp. 86-87, 94-96; Chamberlin, *Marguerite of Navarre*, pp. 93-94, 96.

Bohemia). Below on the pavement, Duke Henry of Guise bent over to make sure the battered body was indeed Coligny's, kicked him in the face, and then let his men hack him to pieces. As he left the area, perhaps in answer to murmurs or questions, Duke Henry shouted: "It is the king's command!" Almost certainly he meant that killing Coligny had been the king's command, which was true. But those in the rapidly gathering crowd outside Coligny's house understood him to mean that the king had commanded them to kill every Calvinist they could lay their hands on, which was not true.[30]

At dawn's first light the orders to assemble and arm the militia went out from City Hall. By then almost everyone assumed that the purpose of their arming and assembly was to kill Calvinists. Louvre de Nançay, captain of the palace guard, began by undertaking the massacre of the approximately 200 Calvinists who had taken what they imagined to be refuge in the Louvre palace where the royal family was living. Queen Marguerite of Navarre was awakened by a man at her door shouting "Navarre! Navarre!" Her nurse opened the door, believing that it was her husband outside, and a man covered with blood shot through it with four guardsmen in pursuit and threw himself into Marguerite's bed. De Nançay allowed her to save him, but a few minutes later another helpless fugitive was cut down with a halberd right in front of her. Charles IX, himself inside the palace, did nothing to stop the killing, and there are persistent reports that he watched it and even urged it on, firing an arquebus wildly into crowds of victims in the courtyard. Henry of Navarre and his brother the Prince of Condé were brought before the wild-eyed king, who brandished a dagger and screamed: "Mass, death or the Bastille!" Henry immediately chose the Mass, but Condé refused, saying that if he were killed he would be avenged. Charles was ready to kill him, but Catherine was by now on the scene, threw herself between them, and finally persuaded her berserk son to give Condé three days to change his mind.

Meanwhile, Hell was in the streets outside. The mob, hating and fearing the Calvinists as revolutionaries and blasphemers, having heard reports of a Calvinist conspiracy to kill the royal family and believing the king had ordered a massacre, attacked everyone known to be Calvinist with horrendous fury and ghastly atrocities, to a thunderous din of "To arms! Kill! Kill! Glory to God and the King!" Even women and children were not spared. Blood ran in the streets; corpses were stacked in courtyards and gateways. At least 2,000 were slain. Some were saved by the occasional pity that always appears at such times, proving that charity never disappears altogether from the bloody human race; some were saved for reasons of state, like Briquemaut, who had once led Calvinists into battle wearing a necklace of priests' ears, and who found refuge in the English embassy; and some escaped on fast horses, notably Montgomery the Scot, the man who had killed Henry II in the tournament (because he had since become a French Calvinist leader, some now believed that had not been an

---

[30] Diefendorf, *Beneath the Cross*, pp. 97-99 (second quote on 99); Erlanger, *St. Bartholomew's Night*, pp. 145, 156-157; England, *Massacre of St. Bartholomew*, pp. 102-103, 108 (first quote on 103); Whitehead, *Coligny*, pp. 266-267.

accident after all), who was pursued all day by the Guises, and in an epic race finally outdistanced them on a tireless little mare.[31]

By eleven o'clock in the morning of St. Bartholomew's day, August 24, Charles IX issued an order to stop the killing, and also orders to his provincial governors to maintain peace in their regions.   His orders were widely disregarded; the killing and looting in Paris went on for several more days.) But the Guises, returning from the unsuccessful pursuit of Montgomery, made a point of disengaging, and Duke Henry even gave sanctuary to about a hundred Calvinists. On August 25 Charles IX ordered lists made of known Calvinists in Paris and their addresses so that they might be individually protected. The next day he came before the *Parlement* of Paris to say that "everything that had occurred was done by his express commandment" and to declare Coligny and his chief adherents guilty of high treason. Though, in view of his belated efforts to stop the massacre, Charles probably did not mean that he had willed that, when he emerged from the *Parlement* building and saw a crowd killing a Huguenot, instead of stopping them he cried: "Ah, if only he were the last of the Huguenots!" This was naturally taken by those who heard it to mean that he wanted all the rest of the Huguenots killed too, and many more were slain that day.[32]

By August 28 similar massacres, imitating that at Paris, had already taken place at Meaux, Troyes, Orléans, Bourges, Lyons, Angers and Saumur.[33]   That Charles was to some extent personally involved in these massacres as well is suggested by the curious order he sent out to all his provincial governors that day:

> Whatever verbal command I may have given to those whom I sent, whether to you or to others, my governors, lieutenants general and officers, when I had just cause . . . to fear some fatal occurrence, having learned of the conspiracy planned against me by the said Admiral [Coligny], I have revoked and do revoke all that, not wishing that anything should be executed either by you or by any other.[34]

Two days later he sent our a clearer and firmer message strictly prohibiting, on pain of death, all attacks on Calvinists, and cancelling all orders given for their punishment. But during September several hundred Calvinists were killed

---

[31] For both paragraphs: Erlanger, *St. Bartholomew's Night*, pp. 158-168 (second quote on 164); England, *Massacre of St. Bartholomew*, pp. 96-97, 114-128; Diefendorf, *Beneath the Cross*, pp. 100-101; Chamberlin, *Marguerite of Navarre*, pp. 98-101, 103-104 (first quote on 103-104); Whitehead, *Coligny*, pp. 267-269.

[32] Erlanger, *St. Bartholomew's Night*, pp. 169, 171-172, 174-176 (second quote on 175); England, *Massacre of St. Bartholomew*, pp. 128-130; Diefendorf, *Beneath the Cross*, p. 98; Sutherland, *Massacre of St. Bartholomew*, pp. 342-343; Mack P. Holt, *The French Wars of Religion, 1562-1629* (New York, 1995), p. 88 (first quote).

[33] Holt, *French Wars of Religion*, pp. 88-94; Erlanger, *St. Bartholomew's Night*, pp. 184-190; England, *Massacre of St. Bartholomew*, pp. 158-162, 169-171.

[34] England, *St. Bartholomew's Massacre*, p. 140.

in prison in Bourges and Rouen, and early in October several hundred more were massacred in the large southern cities of Toulouse and Bordeaux when persons there claimed orders from Charles IX to do so. The total number killed outside Paris was about 3,000, more than had been killed inside it.[35]

In all probability we come closest to the real truth about Charles IX and what he had done in his confession to his doctor, the famous Ambroise Paré, about a week after the massacre in Paris:

> Ambroise, I do not know what has been happening to me for the last two or three days, but I find my mind and body greatly disturbed, as if I were fevered. It seems to me at every moment, whether waking or sleeping, that those massacred bodies are presenting themselves before me, with their faces hideous and covered with blood. I wish they had not included the simple and the innocent.[36]

One hard fact emerges clearly from this welter of horror: contrary to generations of Protestant historians, the St. Bartholomew's Day massacre was not premeditated. The intent of the king and council was to kill only thirty people, not two thousand. After the attempted assassination of Coligny there had been at least serious talk of, and quite possibly a specific plan for a Calvinist attack on Paris and seizure of the royal palace of the Louvre, which seemed to justify action against the leaders. But the total disregard of all forms of law in the killings; the merciless butchery of the helpless, unarmed, undefended Coligny; and the complete disregard of the impact of these bloody nocturnal proceedings upon a volatile and angry populace, made massacre the inevitable result. Since the general massacre actually began in the royal palace, Charles IX could hardly claim ignorance of it. From dawn until eleven o'clock on the fatal morning he did nothing to stop it, and there are reports that he encouraged it. When later he tried to pull back, it was much too late. The responsibility and the guilt were his. Unbalanced as he was, he was not insane; he must bear it. What he said to Dr. Paré indicates that he knew it.

An event such as this, whose true story has taken four hundred years to disentangle, was sure to be wildly misrepresented in the first news reports of it. No one really knew what had happened, except that a great many French Calvinists had been killed by Catholics in Paris. A shudder of horror and a burst of anger passed over Protestant Europe. The massacre seemed to prove that the Catholics really wanted to kill them all. Catholics, on the other hand, could not forget that many of these Calvinists had been entirely willing to kill at least priests and religious with no more compunction than the Paris Catholics had shown in striking down the Calvinists in their midst. The massacre of St. Bartholomew was an event of war, not of peace. For years the Pope and Philip II

---

[35] *Ibid.*, pp. 158, 164-168; Holt, *French Wars of Religion*, pp. 93-94; Erlanger, *St. Bartholomew's Night*, p. 181; Philip Benedict, *Rouen during the Wars of Religion* (Cambridge, England, 1981), pp. 127-128.

[36] England, *St. Bartholomew's Massacre*, p. 138.

of Spain had been urging the French government to crack down on the Calvinist revolutionaries, to proceed against them with the utmost rigor. It was all too easy to see what had happened in Paris as the infliction at last of the much-needed condign punishment, a victory in the great religious war sweeping Christendom.

But in a civilized state, condign punishment is the function of law. To have it inflicted by a mob in the streets is anarchy, not justice.

The greatest scandal of the massacre of St. Bartholomew's Day is not the massacre itself, which was a product of fear and panic and the psychological weaknesses and ills of King Charles IX, but the satisfaction taken in it and the celebration of it by Catholic leaders who should have known better. Wartime psychology may partly excuse them, but cannot excuse them fully, any more than it can fully excuse the Americans who took satisfaction in and even celebrated the nuclear bombing of Hiroshima and Nagasaki.

The first news of the massacre came to Rome on September 2, in a garbled report from the secretary of the governor of Lyons, stating that Coligny had been wounded and subsequently died, that the Calvinists had in consequence begun to assemble in arms, whereupon the Catholics had attacked them and killed their principal leaders, Montgomery alone escaping.[37] Three days later a full report was available from papal nuncio Salviati in Paris and from a special envoy who was the nephew of the French ambassador. The envoy bore a message from Charles IX declaring the massacre to have been done in "the interests of religion, and that many other things would follow in due course for the same end, since as time went on the Queen intended, not only to revoke the edict of St. Germain, but to restore the ancient observance of the Catholic faith by force of law."[38] The Guise Cardinal of Lorraine, who was in Rome, rejoiced; Pope Gregory XIII ordered a *Te Deum* said in thanksgiving for the deliverance of the French royal family and Christendom from Coligny's alleged plot to murder the king, seize the crown, support the rebels in the Low Countries, and march on Rome.[39]

However, the Pope was horrified by the cruelties of the massacre, shedding tears and saying: "I am weeping for the conduct of the king [Charles IX], which is unlawful and forbidden by God." Spanish ambassador Zuñiga described him as "struck with horror" at the details of the massacre. Later the Pope said he wept for the many innocent dead, and refused to receive the assassin Maurevert in audience. The ambassador of Savoy wrote from Rome that what had happened in Paris "has been extolled insofar as it affects the good of the king and of his kingdom and of religion, but it would have been far more highly extolled if His Majesty had been able to act with clean hands." Nevertheless on September 8 a procession of thanksgiving for the events of St. Bartholomew's Day took place in Rome, at which the Cardinal of Lorraine likened Charles IX to "a persecuting angel sent forth from God" who had "in one killing" removed "nearly all the heretics from his kingdom." On September 11 the Pope celebrated the event in a special bull, though it was worded to praise only the execution of

---

[37] Von Pastor, *History of the Popes*, XIX, 499-500; Whitehead, *Coligny*, pp. 271-272.

[38] Von Pastor, *History of the Popes*, XIX, 501-502.

[39] *Ibid.*, XIX, 502-507; England, *St. Bartholomew's Massacre*, pp. 185-186.

the leaders, not the slaughter of the two thousand. But as late as December, when much more of the story was known, one Marc-Antoine Muret, in a commemorative oration in the presence of the Pope, declared—without known rebuke from the Holy Father—that on St. Bartholomew's Eve "the stars gave out a brighter light than usual, and the Seine swelled more than ordinarily in order the quicker to carry the bodies away and unload them into the sea."[40]

The news of the massacre arrived in Madrid September 6. Philip II welcomed it with great satisfaction, disregarding the number killed and focusing on the elimination of the French Calvinist leaders who were doing him so much harm in the Low Countries. When on September 14 the French ambassador reported to him in detail what had happened, the usually taciturn Philip laughed aloud. Wartime psychology was again at work; but Philip II would never have allowed anything like the St. Bartholomew's Day massacre to happen in his well-governed and law-abiding realm.[41]

The Inquisition and the Crusades, for which the Catholic Church is so often reproached, were far better and are far more defensible than their popular image today suggests. The St. Bartholomew's Day massacre is not in that category.

In the Low Countries the destruction of so much of the French Calvinist leadership greatly strengthened the position of the Duke of Alba; as the battle commander directly helped by this event, he is more easily forgiven for rejoicing, as he did. He received the news while besieging Mons, the one Belgian city now held by the Calvinists. William of Orange came up with his army and bombarded Alba's camp early in September, but did not dare risk an infantry attack against superior numbers and a great general, and retreated. Alba, pursuing, caught up and launched a night attack on William's camp. William was saved only by being awakened just in time by the barking of his little white pug dog, Kuntze. The survivors fled in maximal confusion, and Mons capitulated on September 21.[42]

Alba still faced serious trouble in the provinces of Holland and Zeeland, then the only provinces in the Low Countries where the Calvinists had substantial popular support, and whose half-submerged geography allowed the victorious "Sea Beggars" to play a major role. But the rest of the Low Countries seemed at Alba's mercy—and mercy is what Alba should have given them. But he was bitterly angry at the sullen hostility and recurring rebellion of these people, and he was almost out of money. So he resorted for the first time (despite all the previous mostly unfounded accusations against him) to systematic terror. He promised his soldiers the spoils of the town of Mechelen near Brussels and let

---

[40] Von Pastor, *History of the Popes*, XIX, 506, 508 (first three quotes on 508); England, *St. Bartholomew's Massacre*, pp. 185-190 (quotes from the Cardinal of Lorraine on 188, from Muret on 190); Erlanger, *St. Bartholomew's Night*, p. 199.

[41] Henry Kamen, *Philip of Spain* (New Haven CT, 1997), p. 141; England, *St. Bartholomew's Massacre*, p. 191.

[42] Maltby, *Alba*, pp. 233-234, 236-238; C. V. Wedgwood, *William the Silent* (New Haven CT, 1944), p. 125.

them sack it for four days, killing many of its citizens. This was not the great Duke of Alba who had so splendidly marched his tightly disciplined army from Italy to the Low Countries five years before.[43]

In the middle of November Alba moved on Zutphen, a small city on the Ijssel River which was a strategic key to the approach to the northeastern provinces where William of Orange had his largest following. Its people tried to resist, but its medieval walls proved totally inadequate. The garrison fled, panic struck, no surrender terms were offered or accepted, the Spaniards surged in, and the city was sacked and burned, with hundreds killed. Alba then turned the command over to his son Fadrique, who crossed into the province of Holland and demanded the surrender of the town of Naarden on the south shore of the Zuyder Zee. The city council held out against surrender for a week, and when after that they tried to surrender, Fadrique would not accept it. Naarden was sacked and razed and almost all its inhabitants were killed; "not a mother's son escaped," Alba grimly declared.[44]

On December 12 the Spanish army laid siege to Haarlem, a substantial city on the narrow strip of land connecting North Holland with the rest of the Netherlands. On the 15th a Spanish assault was repelled with heavy losses, and another on January 31, 1573. This time there was no talk of surrender; it was war to the death. Old soldier Alba, until now always careful with the lives of his men, in his bitterness and frustration had forgotten how dangerous it is to deprive brave men of all hope. The defenders of Haarlem, remembering the fate of Mechelen and Zutphen and Naarden, were resolved to fight to the last man, convinced that their only alternative was death at the hands of the Spanish. On January 30 Philip II had relieved Alba in favor of Luis de Requesens, who had been Viceroy of Milan. He was just too late, and unfortunately Requesens took a very long time to arrive.[45]

Alba told his son that he would disown him if he raised the siege of Haarlem without the surrender of the town. When the ice melted in March, the Spanish launched a fleet to tighten the siege. Still Haarlem held out, its defenders resolved to sell their lives dear. Two attempts by William of Orange to challenge the Spanish fleet at Haarlem were unsuccessful. But by July Alba was writing "I can't go on," and there was still no sign of Requesens; Philip II sent him peremptory orders to leave Milan for the Low Countries at once. Finally Fadrique took Haarlem on July 12, killing the entire surviving garrison of 2,300 men. They sold their lives at four to one, for more than 10,000 Spanish soldiers

---

[43] Parker, *Dutch Revolt*, pp. 140-141; Maltby, *Alba*, p. 240; Israel, *Dutch Republic*, p. 178; Kamen, *Philip of Spain*, pp. 144-145. When incoming civil governor the Duke of Medinaceli suggested to him in November a pardon to encourage the innocent, Alba said he did not know who the innocent in the Low Countries might be (Kamen, *op. cit.*, p. 145).

[44] Maltby, *Alba*, pp. 241, 243-244; Parker, *Dutch Revolt*, pp. 142 (quote), 163; Israel, *Dutch Republic*, p. 178.

[45] Maltby, *Alba*, pp. 245-246, 249-250; Parker, *Dutch Revolt*, p. 163; Kamen, *Philip of Spain*, pp. 146-147.

fell in the siege. At least no civilians were killed this time. Hearing of the slaughter of the garrison, Requesens was distressed. "Mercy is very necessary," he said. In October Philip directed Requesens to treat the people of the Low Countries "with love and good will."[46]

Alba now sent his son on to the little town of Alkmaar in North Holland, declaring that none of its defenders would be spared. They resisted desperately, with all the resolution of the defenders of Haarlem. Alba had learned nothing from the Spanish losses before Haarlem. But his men still loved him; although unpaid for more than two full years, they rallied to him when he came to camp to end a mutiny in August. But then he departed, and Fadrique was not nearly so popular as his father. Early in October the Spanish troops twice refused Fadrique's orders to assault the stubborn town. Alkmaar's people now cut the dikes. As the water rose (most of the land around Alkmaar was below sea level) Fadrique and the Spanish abandoned the siege. Just three days later, in a decisive naval battle in the Zuyder Zee, the Dutch defeated the Spanish fleet and captured its commander. The tide had turned.[47]

In November 1573 Requesens finally arrived in Brussels to take up his duties, almost a full year after his appointment. Alba tried to convince him that the all-out war must be continued and could still be won, but Requesens did not think so. A month later Alba departed, a defeated commander in the cause closest to his king's heart. He thought his career was at an end, but he still had one great service to perform for his royal master.[48]

The new governor's health was poor; the obstacles confronting him were daunting, and he had no plan for dealing with them, nor was he able to develop one. Spanish soldiers were besieging the large Dutch city of Leiden but making no progress. Late in January 1574 the Dutch fleet inflicted another defeat on Spanish warships in the estuary of the Scheldt River leading to Antwerp. On April 14 the Spanish army won a signal victory at Mooker Heath over German mercenaries invading the Low Countries under Louis of Nassau, brother of William of Orange. Louis was wounded, left in a charcoal burner's hut in the confused aftermath of the battle, and never seen again. But the very next day the Spanish troops mutinied and marched on Antwerp to hold the city hostage for payment of their huge arrears in pay (one million florins). Six weeks later Requesens somehow found all this money for them and they returned to duty, resuming the siege of Leiden. On August 3 William of Orange opened the dikes on the Meuse River, and gradually the water level rose around Leiden. At the beginning of October a strong northwest wind combined with a high tide raised the water level to three feet, enough to float the shallow-draft Dutch ships, which steadily approached the Spanish besiegers across the flooded fields accompanied by wading men. Discouraged, and perhaps unnerved by this weird spectacle,

---

[46] Maltby, *Alba*, pp. 251, 253-254; Kamen, *Philip of Spain*, pp. 145-147 (first quote on 146, second on 145, third on 147).

[47] Maltby, *Alba*, p. 258, 260; Parker, *Dutch Revolt*, pp. 161-162; Wedgwood, *William the Silent*, pp. 134-135; Kamen, *Philip of Spain*, p. 147.

[48] Maltby, *Alba*, p. 261; Kamen, *Philip of Spain*, p. 148.

with no effective military leadership, the Spanish troops gave up and retreated. In November they mutinied again and left the whole province of Holland to the rebels.   Three months later a Calvinist university was founded at Leiden, modelled after Calvin's Academy in Geneva, to commemorate the city's successful resistance during the siege.[49]

In January 1575 Requesens wrote to Philip II: "Matters here are in such a terrible state, and so impossible to sustain, that we will have to give in to all they want, so long as religion is excepted."[50] But religion could not be "excepted," for it had always been at the heart of the struggle. When negotiations began between representatives of the Spanish government and the States-General of the Low Countries in March, little progress was made because neither side would consider toleration of the religion of the other. In June the former provinces of Holland and Zeeland united under William of Orange as chief executive, or *stadtholder*; the law of the new state flatly prohibited the Mass. By November Requesens had again run out of money, his health was broken, and he died in March 1576.[51]

Almost as soon as he had the news of Requesens' death, Philip II appointed none other than his famous half-brother Don Juan of Austria, the victor of Lepanto, governor of the Low Countries, investing and instructing him with the words quoted at the head of this chapter. He stressed that Don Juan must go to his new post quickly—"I would wish that the bearer of this dispatch had wings to fly to you and that you had them yourself, to get there sooner."[52]   For the situation in the Low Countries was now both highly threatening and exceedingly volatile, and could collapse at any moment. But Don Juan, receiving Philip's letter May 3, did not even reply for twenty-four days. His reply, when he finally made it, was a lucid exposition of the problems in the Low Countries, and contained a proposal to put an end to present and prospective English support of the rebels by an invasion of England in which Don Juan would liberate Mary Queen of Scots. But when Philip sent him a second letter again urging that he go immediately to the Low Countries, Don Juan replied that he had decided he must come to see Philip first. We have no idea what he had to say to Philip that required personal contact; and after they had met, Don Juan decided to reach the Low Countries by crossing hostile France disguised as a Moorish slave, causing still more delays.[53]

By the time Don Juan finally arrived in Luxembourg November 3, much of the Spanish army had mutinied and sacked Maastricht, and delegates from most of the provinces of the Low Countries, meeting at Ghent, had decided to unite

---

[49] Von Pastor, *History of the Popes*, XX, 3-4; Parker, *Dutch Revolt*, pp. 145, 164; Israel, *Dutch Republic*, p. 181; Wedgwood, *William the Silent*, pp. 138, 141-143, 146-148; Kamen, *Philip of Spain*, pp. 154-155.

[50] Kamen, *Philip of Spain*, p. 155.

[51] *Ibid.*, pp. 155, 160; Parker, *Dutch Revolt*, pp. 145-146, 166-170; Israel, *Dutch Republic*, pp. 197-198; Wedgwood, *William the Silent*, p. 159.

[52] Walsh, *Philip II*, p. 553.

[53] *Ibid.*, pp. 554-555, 557-559; Charles Petrie, *Don Juan of Austria* (New York, 1967), pp. 269, 273.

against the Spanish troops and call a meeting of the full States-General to decide the religious and political organization of the entire region, without reference to Spain, while recognizing full Calvinist rule of Holland and Zeeland. On the very next day mutinous Spanish troops assaulted and took the great and rich Flemish commercial city of Antwerp, looting the big warehouses, burning over a thousand houses, and killing several hundred people.[54] From Luxembourg Don Juan penned an almost despairing letter to his friend Rodrigo de Mendoza on November 5:

> I reached this place on the 3rd of this month, and found the worst possible tidings of these provinces, for only this one in which I am and Friesland, of which Robles has charge, can certainly be said not to be in revolt. The rest are leagued together and calling out troops and seeking foreign aid against the Spaniards, and making and repealing laws in their own fashion, all these things being done under the name and in behalf of the King, whose name is also used while they are taking steps to admit Orange into Brussels and fitting up a house for him there. I have written to the Council in general, and to some of its members in particular, of my having come. I know not what the reply may be, nor whether they will receive me . . . Such is the miserable condition of affairs here, which may God remedy, for He only can do it.[55]

In France during these four years the massacre of St. Bartholomew's Day had brought no benefits to its instigators. The surviving Calvinist leaders took refuge in the cities granted them by the Peace of St. Germain, particularly the strongest, La Rochelle, which, not unnaturally under the circumstances, rejected a governor appointed by Charles IX and defied a demand from his general to surrender, inaugurating the Fourth War of Religion in France. La Rochelle was besieged, but easily held out because the French navy was too weak to blockade it effectively by sea. After several assaults on La Rochelle failed, yet another peace agreement was signed in July 1573, which preserved the special privileges of La Rochelle and three other cities as Calvinist sanctuaries.[56]

Meanwhile a curious charade had been acted out involving King Charles IX, his ambitious brother Henry, and the elective monarchy of Poland. There was no love lost between the two brothers (Charles said prophetically in 1573: "If my brother obtains my crown, which he covets, the fine expectations that people have formed respecting him will soon be dissipated; my brother's character will alone be appreciated when he rules")[57] and the fact that Charles'

---

[54] Parker, *Dutch Revolt*, pp. 177-178; Israel, *Dutch Republic*, p. 185; Wedgwood, *William the Silent*, p. 166; Kamen, *Philip of Spain*, p. 160; Walsh, *Philip II*, pp. 560-562.

[55] Petrie, *Don Juan of Austria*, p. 285.

[56] Mack P. Holt, *The Duke of Anjou and the Politique Struggle during the Wars of Religion* (Cambridge, England, 1986), pp. 28, 33, 96-98; Erlanger, *St. Bartholomew's Night*, pp. 217-218; James W. Thompson, *The Wars of Religion in France 1559-1576* (New York, 1909), pp. 458-460.

[57] A. Lynn Martin, *Henry III and the Jesuit Politicians* (Geneva, 1973), p. 62.

first-born child was a girl left Henry, at least for the time being, his designated successor. Their mother Catherine de Medici thought it best to separate them, but this could only be done by providing some glittering, irresistible prize for Henry. That prize was the crown of Poland. The death of Poland's King Sigismund II in 1572 without heirs brought the old Polish tradition of elective monarchy back into force, and a well-managed campaign among the self-seeking and hardly nationalistic Polish nobility obtained the election of Prince Henry as king of Poland in May 1573. An exotic-looking delegation of some 200 Poles in colorful eastern finery arrived in Paris in mid-August to convey official notification of the election to him.[58]

Henry was happy to be a king, but had no interest in Poland. By milking one excuse after another he managed to delay his departure from France until December, after his brother had contracted smallpox at severe cost to his already precarious health. It is said that his mother Catherine whispered in Henry's ear during their leave-taking at the French border (he had always been her favorite son): "Do not worry; you will soon be back!" As Charles became increasingly ill, plots against him were made by both the Calvinists and the king's youngest brother, the Duke d'Alençon.[59] On May 30, 1574 King Charles IX died of rapidly developing tuberculosis. When the news reached Henry in Cracow, he wasted no time; three days later he departed secretly for France in the middle of the night. But he was seen as he left the city, and pursued by 200 horsemen and a troop of Tartar archers. They almost caught him. He crossed the frontier bridge at full gallop in sight of his pursuers, who were crying out to him: "Serene Majesty, why do you flee?"[60]

In August 1574 an alliance was formed in southern France between the Calvinists and the Catholic Marshal Damville, one of the sons of the late great Constable Montmorency, whose objectives were to limit the powers of the monarchy, leave each religion in control of the areas it currently dominated, convoke the national Estates-General, reduce taxes, and abolish the sale of

---

[58] Norman Davies, *God's Playground; a History of Poland* (New York, 1984), I, 322-336, 413-414; Sutherland, *Massacre of St. Bartholomew*, p. 283; Thompson, *Wars of Religion in France*, pp. 464-465; Mahoney, *Madame Catherine*, p. 182.

[59] This prince's name is a nagging problem for every historian who must deal with him. He was baptized Hercule, but in common with most French princes was given a long string of royal names among which he could pick and choose. When his oldest brother Francis, briefly King Francis II, died in 1560, Hercule was given his name. Later he was made Duke d'Alençon. When his brother Charles IX died and Henry became King Henry III, Hercule/Francis/d'Alençon took over Henry's former title and revenues as Duke of Anjou. So he went by no less than four different names at different periods in his life. The majority of historians have settled on d'Alençon as the most distinctive, and with some reluctance (since his only true personal name was Hercule) he will be so called herein throughout.

[60] Thompson, *Wars of Religion in France*, pp. 469-470, 476-484; Holt, *Duke of Anjou*, pp. 36, 38-42; Mahoney, *Madame Catherine*, pp. 185, 190-195, 199-201 (first quote on 185); Chamberlin, *Marguerite of Navarre*, pp. 119-121; Read, *Walsingham* I, 280, 282; Davies, *God's Playground*, I, 414-418 (second quote on 418).

government offices. New King Henry III vowed "unremitting war" against this alliance, but already his weaknesses were becoming apparent.[61] Italian observer Fabio Frangipani commented:

> The true salvation of France would be a king who knew how to be a king indeed. We can look for nothing from this young man. His tastes are all for ease and amusement, his body is weak and sickly, so that only a short life can be predicted for him.[62]

It was all true, except for the last clause. Despite his debilities Henry III reigned as king of France for fifteen tumultuous, disordered years, and then died by the sword.

On December 26, 1574 long-time Catholic champion the Cardinal of Lorraine died at the early age of 49, leaving no one to take his place. Henry III, who had come first from Poland to Lyons in southern France, found it very difficult in the face of Montmorency-Damville's hostile forces even to reach Paris, but finally got to Reims for his coronation in February 1575. In September the Duke d'Alençon escaped from the house arrest in which Henry had been holding him and issued a manifesto calling for a reorganization of the government, convocation of the Estates-General, and a national council on religion. Catherine de Medici tried to make peace between her two surviving sons, but had to be satisfied with a brief truce. During 1576 Henry III became increasingly eccentric and effeminate, surrounding himself with perfumed young men with long curly hair, and dressing more and more weirdly. In February Henry of Navarre escaped house arrest and rode to join the Duke d'Alençon.[63] Looking back toward Paris from the Loire River, he said to his companion, the famous Calvinist Agrippa d'Aubigné:

> They killed the Queen my mother in Paris and murdered the Admiral and all my friends, and would have done the same to me had not God protected me. I'll never return there unless they drag me back.[64]

By April 1576 Henry III was reduced to controlling little more than the area around Paris and the provinces immediately eastward, Burgundy and Champagne. D'Alençon controlled central France, Montmorency-Damville and Henry of Navarre the south, Coligny's son the province of Dauphiné, Henry of Navarre's brother Condé Picardy, and the Scot Montgomery Normandy, while the German Calvinist Prince John Casimir of the Palatinate had just arrived with

---

[61] Thompson, *Wars of Religion in France*, pp. 489-491 (quote on 491); Martin, *Henry III and the Jesuit Politicians*, p. 58; Holt, *Duke of Anjou*, pp. 46-47; Franklin C. Palm, *Politics and Religion in Sixteenth-Century France* (Gloucester Ma, 1960), pp. 98-100.

[62] Von Pastor, *History of the Popes*, XIX, 523.

[63] Holt, *Duke of Anjou*, pp. 48, 52-56, 59, 62-63; Mahoney, *Madame Catherine*, pp. 212-215, 217, 232-233; Thompson, *Wars of Religion in France*, pp. 495-496, 514; Martin, *Henry III and the Jesuit Politicians*, p. 61.

[64] Chamberlin, *Marguerite of Navarre*, p. 155.

20,000 Germans to join the French Calvinist forces of about 10,000 at Moulins, leaving Henry III no choice but to capitulate. He bought peace from John Casimir for 40,000 francs, full pay for his German troops, two duchies and nine lordships. On May 6 he signed the Peace of Beaulieu, popularly called the Peace of Monsieur (the traditional title of the heir to the throne, now referring to d'Alençon, who was the heir since Henry III remained childless) which allowed Calvinist worship throughout the country except within two leagues of the court and four leagues of Paris, made Calvinists eligible to hold any public office, and placed eight more cities under their exclusive control. The St. Bartholomew's Day massacre was condemned. The Duke d'Alençon received three rich central French provinces. The Calvinists had finally achieved full equality if not superiority over the Catholics in France. Their triumph seemed imminent; only Paris held out against them with furious demonstrations.[65]

In the Low Countries the States-General, meeting with representatives of William of Orange on November 8, 1576, agreed on the union of 17 provinces (all but Limburg and Luxemburg, where Don Juan of Austria was) and demanded the immediate removal of all Spanish troops. Religious toleration was promised for 15 of the provinces, but there was to be absolute Calvinist domination in Holland and Zeeland, where William was recognized as stadtholder. The ultimate authority of Philip II was not yet explicitly denied, but Archduke Matthias of Austria rather than Philip's choice, Don Juan, was recognized as governor. However, on becoming aware of Don Juan's arrival and determination to carry out his duties, the next month the Estates-General offered to recognize him as governor and to maintain the Catholic religion (outside Holland and Zeeland) if all Spanish troops were removed, all prisoners released and a general amnesty granted, and the union of Ghent confirmed by Spain. This reflected the fact (often obscured in later histories) that a strong majority of the people of the Low Countries were still Catholic, despite the war, the depredations of the unpaid Spanish troops, and the activity of militant Calvinists throughout the region. Don Juan, so recently arrived, probably did not yet see this clearly, but Philip II did. He ordered Don Juan to accept these terms (which William of Orange had not believed he would accept, and which he was ready to reject before he had Philip's orders). On January 27, 1577 Don Juan obeyed these orders, accepting these terms (except for the Calvinist rule of Holland and Zeeland), with the proviso that the Estates-General must pay a large part of the expenses of removing the Spanish troops. He confirmed this in what he grandly called a "perpetual edict" issued February 17.[66]

---

[65] Thompson, *Wars of Religion in France*, pp. 515-521; Holt, *French Wars of Religion*, pp. 104-106; Johannes Janssen, *History of the German People at the Close of the Middle Ages* (London, 1906), VIII, 204-205; De Lamar Jensen, *Diplomacy and Dogmatism; Bernardino de Mendoza and the French Catholic League* (Cambridge MA, 1964), pp. 36-37.

[66] Von Pastor, *History of the Popes*, XX, 5-6; Kamen, *Philip of Spain*, pp. 160-161; Walsh, *Philip II*, pp. 563-565; Petrie, *Don Juan of Austria*, pp. 291-293; Parker, *Dutch*

Meanwhile the French Estates-General was also meeting, with a surprisingly large Catholic majority in all three Estates. The Duke d'Alençon, once he got his rich provinces in central France, had separated himself from the French Calvinists, and Duke Henry of Guise had set up a Catholic Association to protect French Catholic interests. King Henry III, in an unexpected access of firmness and decision, put himself at the head of the Catholic Association, declared the Peace of Beaulieu had been signed under duress and repudiated it, and announced that religious uniformity would now be restored by law in France. The Estates-General accepted his newly militant policy but voted no money for the military effort necessary to enforce it. Marshal Montmorency-Damville in the south was reconciled with Henry III and declared his allegiance to the crown. The French royal army laid siege to one of the smaller Calvinist strongholds, a place incongruously called La Charité, and took it early in May 1577. The unpaid troops looted it thoroughly and killed many of its people. In June the Calvinist fortified town of Issoire in the Auvergne suffered the same fate. But in July the French royal army had to be disbanded for lack of pay, so another peace was made in September at Bergerac, reducing permission for Calvinist worship to just one town in each administrative district and prohibiting any "League, association or brotherhood" on either side.[67]

Having temporarily stabilized the situation in the Low Countries, Don Juan was looking to England in the early months of 1577. In the castle of the Earl of Shrewsbury at Sheffield in the heart of England languished Mary Queen of Scots, 35, now nine years a prisoner, the rightful heir to the throne of England and a Catholic who had clung to her faith under the worst conditions, ever since she first entered Protestant territory sixteen years before.[68] In the Low Countries the large Spanish army could as well depart by sea as by land. Its troops, troublesome as they had been to others, would follow the hero of Lepanto anywhere. Don Juan was 30 years old, one of the handsomest as well as one of the most resourceful leaders in Christendom, available and ready to act—and unmarried. Why should he not go to Mary's rescue, save and marry her? It could change the whole Protestant-Catholic balance of power at one blow. Win or lose, it would be a romantic story to ring down the ages, just what the gallant Don Juan loved.

This was not the hare-brained, impossible project that most later historians have imagined. The romantic is not always the impractical. It could have been done. From the Catholic standpoint it may be strongly argued that it should have been done. It had originally been suggested by none other than Pope St. Pius V as early as 1570, with the enthusiastic agreement of the Cardinal of Lorraine, Mary's uncle. Pope Gregory XIII favored it in his turn, and Philip II, though

---

Revolt, p. 181; Israel, *Dutch Republic*, pp. 185-187; Wedgwood, *William the Silent*, pp. 166, 168-169.

[67] Von Pastor, *History of the Popes*, XIX, 530, 532, 540; Holt, *French Wars of Religion*, pp. 106-108, 111; Holt, *Duke of Anjou*, pp. 76-81, 83-84, 87-91; Mahoney, *Madame Catherine*, pp. 221-223, 229-230.

[68] Antonia Fraser, *Mary Queen of Scots* (New York, 1969), pp. 432-454.

cautious and dubious, was not actively opposed. Duke Henry of Guise favored it. Cecil, that eminently practical man, was so concerned about such an enterprise that he wrote a long memorandum to Queen Elizabeth in December 1577 on the danger it presented to her. It was Cecil's superb intelligence service which frustrated these plans at the one critical point when they might have succeeded. The secret of the project was not well kept—indeed, such a plan would have been exceptionally hard for anyone knowing of it not to talk about!—and both Cecil and William of Orange were fully informed about it by the beginning of 1577. William saw to it that the Estates-General of the Low Countries demanded as a condition for their agreement with Don Juan, which he confirmed in February 1577, that he withdraw his troops by land rather than by sea.[69]

A sudden cavalry raid on Sheffield Castle under dashing and resolute leadership might still have succeeded in rescuing Mary. But developments in the Low Countries during 1577 soon put it out of the question for Don Juan to leave his post. His hour of popularity there, gained from the peace and the withdrawal of the Spanish troops, was brief; by summer he felt enemies pressing in from every side, and on August 24 he seized the citadel at Namur, pistol in hand, to bring it under his personal command. The Estates-General charged him with renewing the war by this act, and invited Archduke Matthias to come and govern the Low Countries in his place. The recently departed Spanish troops were recalled in December. With them, and the aid of their extraordinarily able commander, the young Alessandro Farnese, Prince of Parma (the son of Charles V's illegitimate daughter and governor of the Netherlands, Margaret of Parma), Don Juan won a striking victory at the Battle of Gembloux near Namur in January 1578, under his banner of the cross with the legend: "In this sign I conquered the Turks; in this sign we conquer the heretics." William of Orange, Archduke Matthias, and the entire States-General of the Low Countries had to flee from Brussels to Antwerp. With the Catholics of the Low Countries now divided between supporters of Don Juan and of the States-General, the Calvinists had a new opportunity, and they seized it by taking control of the principal cities of Flanders—Antwerp, Ghent and Bruges—in the spring of 1578. On the feast of Corpus Christi in June Calvinists attacked Catholic religious processions in Brussels and Liège, desecrating the Blessed Sacrament, smashing crucifixes and images, and killing many worshippers. On June 10 there was a Calvinist uprising in Utrecht, with more iconoclasm; on June 28 six Catholic religious were burned to death in Ghent.[70]

In the last months of his young life Don Juan of Austria walked with death. A plot to assassinate him was made in the house of the Duke of Leicester in

---

[69] Von Pastor, *History of the Popes*, XIX, 407-409; Petrie, *Don Juan of Austria*, pp. 233-235, 239; Conyers Read, *Lord Burghley and Queen Elizabeth* (New York, 1960), pp. 185-187; Read, *Walsingham*, II, 357-359.

[70] Parker, *Dutch Revolt*, pp. 181, 183-184, 186, 188-190; Petrie, *Don Juan of Austria*, pp. 296-297, 307-308, 312-317; Kamen, *Philip of Spain*, p. 161; Walsh, *Philip II*, pp. 568-571 (quote on 570); von Pastor, *History of the Popes*, XX, 9; Israel, *Dutch Republic*, p. 192; Wedgwood, *William the Silent*, pp. 186-187; Read, *Walsingham*, I, 351.

England, with Queen Elizabeth's consent. The assassin was to be a soldier of fortune named Egremont Radcliffe. For once Spanish intelligence was as good as the English; Spanish ambassador to England Bernardino de Mendoza learned of the plot and the assassin and found a portrait of Radcliffe which he sent to Don Juan along with a letter of warning. So when Radcliffe appeared outside Don Juan's tent bearing a poisoned dagger, Don Juan recognized him, refused to come out of the tent at his call, and had him arrested and executed. All accounts agree that during the summer of 1578 Don Juan became far more serious, dedicated and religious than ever before in his life. His unpaid soldiers remained devoted to him; there were no mutinies. Both England and France were now actively aiding the rebels, the nominally Catholic Duke d'Alençon having become once again the friend of Calvinists, at least in the Low Countries, leading an army to their relief in July. The States-General had demanded that Don Juan leave the country once and for all. But even his dedicated enemy Francis Walsingham, Secretary of State for England, was enormously impressed when he met him in late August ("surely I never saw a gentleman for personage, speech, wit and entertainment comparable to him"). On September 17 Don Juan fell suddenly and seriously ill in his camp near Namur. On the 28th, knowing he was dying, he called the Prince of Parma to his side and appointed him his successor. He was anointed, received viaticum, asked to be buried at El Escorial, and died a holy death on October 1.[71]

He was only 31, but the evidence indicates that his death was natural, the result of peritonitis from the rupture of a typhoid ulcer.[72] Mary Queen of Scots was devastated by the news; for two days she refused to eat.[73] This man whom she had never met had been the first in years to give her real hope. Now she could no longer dream of his riding up to the gates of her prison in a cloud of dust and a glitter of steel, to force them open and set her free.

As Mary Queen of Scots' hopes for physical rescue faded, a spiritual rescue operation for England was already underway. When Gregory XIII became Pope it was clear that no internal change in the religious policy of the English government could be expected so long as Queen Elizabeth lived; and since she was still only 36, that might be (as it was to be) a very long time. Therefore, if there were to be a change, Elizabeth had to be overthrown from the outside, which was possible but very difficult; or the English Catholics deprived of all practice of their faith had to be reached by priests with the sacraments at the constant risk of martyrdom. This was the mission taken up by the seminary for English Catholic exiles originally founded at Douai in French Flanders and later transferred to the grand old French cathedral city of Reims, financed by the Pope

---

[71] Von Pastor, *History of the Popes*, XIX, 448; Haile, *Elizabethan Cardinal*, pp. 165-167; Walsh, *Philip II*, pp. 587-588; Petrie, *Don Juan of Austria*, p. 326 (for quote); Parker, *Dutch Revolt*, p. 191; Holt, *Duke of Anjou*, pp. 101, 104; Read, *Burghley*, pp. 188-189; Read, *Walsingham*, I, 387, 408-411.

[72] Petrie, *Don Juan of Austria*, p. 327.

[73] Haile, *Elizabethan Cardinal*, p. 167.

and Philip II of Spain, founded and conducted by Dr. (later Cardinal) William Allen, whom the Pope in August 1575 gave extensive faculties for absolution and dispensation and authorized to communicate those faculties to priests going into England. It was a mission whose character is unforgettably described in the second quotation that heads this chapter, and best summed up in the four words of the title of Robert Hugh Benson's historical novel about these heroic young priests: *Come Rack, Come Rope.* The rack was the chosen instrument of torture of William Cecil's government of England; the rope was that from which priests were hanged at London's execution site of Tyburn. By the fall of 1576 the seminary at Douai already had 120 students.[74]

The first of their martyrs, now canonized, was St. Cuthbert Mayne, hanged, drawn and quartered at Launceston on November 29, 1577. The charges against him were denying Queen Elizabeth's headship of the church in England, carrying a brief of indulgence, and wearing a rosary. Asked to swear on a Bible that Queen Elizabeth was supreme head of the church in England, Mayne "took the Bible in his hands, made the sign of the cross on it, kissed it and said: 'The Queen never was, nor is, nor ever shall be head of the church!'"[75] The next year Cecil took one Richard Topcliffe of Lincolnshire into his service as a priest-hunter, as which he continued, gaining infamy as a merciless torturer, for the twenty years that remained of Cecil's life.[76]

In 1579 Jesuit General Mercurian agreed to a proposal of Cardinal Allen to send Jesuits to England, and designated a group led by Edmund Campion, a young Englishman known for his literary and rhetorical brilliance, and Robert Parsons.[77] In his instructions to them, Pope Gregory XIII explained that the bull of Pope St. Pius V against her bound only her and her officers, not Catholics generally—that is, that though it permitted revolt against her it did not require her Catholic subjects to revolt; they could still profess obedience to her if they wished to. This had always been true of papal bulls depriving rulers of the moral obligation for their subjects obey them, but the point was often (sometimes willfully) misunderstood, then and now.[78] But when Campion and Parsons arrived at Reims, Dr. Allen had to tell them of a series of events in Ireland which would cast a shadow over their mission and make it easy for Cecil and his men to impute political motives to it.

The people of Ireland had from the beginning almost universally rejected the change of religion in England. Only a tiny minority, prompted in almost every case by love of gain or desire for office, had adhered to the Protestant

---

[74] *Ibid.*, pp. 126-127, 130, 137, 139, 143.

[75] *Ibid.*, pp. 140-141.

[76] *Ibid.*, p. 201; Philip Hughes, *The Reformation in England* (New York, 1954), III, 363n.

[77] His name is often spelled Persons; but Elizabethans were as careless about spelling their names as their words, and it seems better to spell it phonetically, as does E. E. Reynolds, author of the joint biography of the two Jesuits (see Note 79, below) since there is no doubt that it was pronounced "Parsons."

[78] See Volume Two, Chapter 19 of this history.

church in Ireland, whose bishops were mere place-men who rarely if ever ventured out among the overwhelmingly Catholic people. In Irish-speaking areas there were no Protestants at all, for hardly any Protestants could be found who spoke their language. But the Irish were, as ever, cursed by political disunity. Their chieftains could not seem to comprehend bringing the Irish people together as Catholics to fight to preserve the religion they professed.[79]

The first Irish leader to consciously aim for that end was James Fitzmaurice Fitzgerald of the Desmond country in Munster, the southwestern quarter of Ireland. The not over-friendly English historian J. B. Black says that he "first rose to the dimensions of a really great figure in Irish history, and provided his race with a policy and a rallying-point. . . . In Ireland Fitzmaurice constituted himself the apostle of an all-Catholic island under the patronage of the Pope and the king of Spain."[80] Fitzmaurice was involved in an uprising in Munster in the years 1569-73, but was upstaged by the English adventurer Thomas Stukeley, who developed a series of plans for a Spanish-assisted invasion of Ireland which looked impressive but were never followed through. In February 1575 Fitzmaurice sailed from Glin in County Limerick to seek aid from France and the Pope. Henry III gave him an audience, but this was the period when the rejection of his royal authority by Calvinists, Marshal Damville, and his brother d'Alençon made him hardly able to save himself, let alone the Irish. The Pope gave Fitzmaurice a subsidy in June. In 1576 he went to Spain, where he met Dr. Nicholas Sanders, a vehement and literary English Catholic who represented the English Catholic exiles to Philip II. In February 1577 Pope Gregory XIII gave Fitzmaurice a brief of support, but then his old nemesis Stukeley reappeared, and in October the Pope shifted his support to him, leaving Fitzmaurice with only a single ship whose Spanish captain and crew stole it from him while he was at Epiphany Mass in January 1578. In the summer of 1578 Stukeley diverted the entire expedition for Ireland which he was leading, to the disastrous venture of King Sebastian of Portugal in Morocco, where the king was killed and so was Stukeley.[81]

Fitzmaurice would not allow himself to become discouraged. He joined formally with Dr. Sanders and they obtained some slight support from Philip II. More was promised from Portugal, but when news of it leaked out, the aged and

---

[79] Cf. Myles V. Ronan, *The Reformation in Ireland under Elizabeth, 1558-1580* (London, 1930), *passim*. In the winter of 1576 Lord Lieutenant Sydney passed through Munster, where the first Catholic rebellion was soon to occur. All the bishops, though willing to accept Queen Elizabeth as temporal ruler, totally rejected her claim to supremacy in the church. Sydney described the people of Munster as "for the most part all papists, and that of the maliciousest degree" (*ibid.*, pp. 529-530). On the extreme rarity of Irish-speaking Protestant ministers see *ibid.*, pp. 532-534.

[80] J. B. Black, *The Reign of Elizabeth 1558-1603* (a volume in the Oxford History of England) (Oxford, 1936), pp. 396-397.

[81] Von Pastor, *History of the Popes*, XIX, 409-410; Ronan, *Reformation in Ireland*, pp. 325-327, 348-350, 372-379, 509, 560-563, 567-568, 577-580; Brian Fitzgerald, *The Geraldines* (New York, 1952), pp. 274-276; Read, *Walsingham*, II, 360. See below, this chapter.

timid Cardinal Henry, now king of Portugal, cut it off. In June 1579 a tiny force sailed from Spain in a single ship carrying just fifty Spanish soldiers along with Fitzmaurice and his faithful wife who had followed him on all his journeys, Dr. Sanders, Bishop O'Hely of Killala, four priests and four Franciscan friars, carrying a banner of Christ Crucified which Pope Gregory XIII had blessed. They landed at Dingle Bay July 17 and Fitzmaurice issued a ringing proclamation, explicitly invoking Pope St. Pius V's bull against Queen Elizabeth.[82]

> This war is undertaken for the defense of the Catholic religion against the heretics. Pope Gregory XIII has chosen us for Captain General in this same war, as it appears at large by his own letters patent, which thing he did so much rather because his predecessor Pope Pius V had before deprived Elizabeth, the patroness of the aforesaid heresies, of all royal power and dominion, as it is plainly declared by his sentence, the authentic copy whereof we also have to show. Therefore now we fight not against the lawful scepter and honorable throne of England, but against a tyrant who refuses to hear Christ speaking through His Vicar.[83]

The Earl of Desmond joined them along with some 3,000 men, and for a moment it appeared the rising had a chance; there was near-panic among some of the English officers in Ireland. [But Cecil and Walsingham never panicked; they responded quickly and efficiently. The coasts were closed off to prevent further outside help from entering; Bishop O'Hely was captured on the way to Limerick, tortured, and executed; and the English under Sir Nicholas Malby roused the Burkes of Mayo and Connemara, traditional enemies of Desmond. On August 18 Malby's men and the Burkes met Fitzmaurice's army at Castleconnell, Fitzmaurice shouting "Papa Abu!" ("Forward the Pope!") and Burke "God save the Queen!" It was a ferocious combat; Fitzmaurice killed eighteen men with his own hands including clan leader Theobald Burke, but was mortally wounded in the moment of victory, made his confession, and died a holy death. After the battle, the Earl of Desmond fought on, despite an old wound which required him to be lifted into the saddle; he adopted Fitzmaurice's war cry of "Papa Abu!" The Earl of Ormond, one of Elizabeth's favorites, was appointed military governor of Munster in March 1580 and immediately began ravaging the countryside, making it very difficult to raise and harvest crops that year.[84]

It was at this point that Campion and Parsons arrived at Reims and were told of the documents Pope Gregory XIII had given to Fitzmaurice, which had been read at Dingle Bay, reviving the whole issue of the papal bull against Elizabeth and Catholic involvement in attempts to overthrow her. They were dismayed, but still resolved to go ahead with their strictly spiritual mission to

---

[82] Ronan, *Reformation in Ireland*, pp. 594-595, 604-605, 608-610, 615n; Fitzgerald, *Geraldines*, p. 277.

[83] Fitzgerald, *Geraldines*, p. 278.

[84] *Ibid.*, pp. 279-283; Ronan, *Reformation in Ireland*, pp. 629-633; Read, *Burghley*, p. 242.

England. In June 1580 they arrived secretly in England.[85] Almost immediately Campion wrote his famous "Brag,"[86] all over the country during the next few months:

> Many innocent hands are lifted up to heaven for you daily by those English students, whose posterity shall never die, which beyond the seas, gathering virtue and sufficient knowledge for the purpose, are determined never to give you over, but either to win you heaven, or to die upon your pikes. And touching our Society, be it known to you that we have made a league—all the Jesuits in the world, whose succession and multitude must overreach all the practice of England—cheerfully to carry the cross you shall lay upon us, and never to despair your recovery, while we have a man left to enjoy your Tyburn, or to be racked with your torments, or consumed with your prisons. The expense is reckoned; the enterprise is begun; it is of God.[87]

Cecil's government responded instantly. Queen Elizabeth made a proclamation, drafted by Cecil, condemning Catholic rebels and urging the people to stand with her against them. On July 15 an order was issued that all Englishmen with sons studying overseas must recall them within four months. The penalties on Catholics refusing to attend Church of England services were sharply increased, and whole castles were set aside as prisons for those who would not or could not pay the fines. Yet during that one year, some 20,000 Englishmen were converted to the Catholic faith.[88] Meanwhile in Ireland, a Spanish force of 1,300 men in six ships sent by Philip II to aid the Desmond Catholics was shut up in Smerwick with insufficient supplies and forced to surrender in November. The famous Elizabethan courtier Sir Walter Raleigh, in command, ordered everyone found in Smerwick killed except the Spanish officers, including Irish men and women also taken there; the two Irish priests captured with them were hanged, drawn and quartered.[89]

The English Parliament met in January 1581 a few days after Queen Elizabeth had put out another proclamation (undoubtedly the work of Cecil) ordering all English Catholic students abroad to return immediately, prohibiting their parents or anyone else from sending them money or other means of support if they remained abroad, and requiring special licenses henceforth to depart from the kingdom. Anyone who received or assisted a Jesuit in particular, and did not turn him over to the government on sight, was declared to be aiding and abetting rebellion. On hearing of this decree, 19 seminarians at Reims volunteered to go to England immediately, saying "they were brought up and made especially for

---

[85] Von Pastor, *History of the Popes*, XIX, 388-390; Haile, *Elizabethan Cardinal*, pp. 192-193; E. E. Reynolds, *Campion and Parsons; the Jesuit Mission of 1580-1* (London, 1980), pp. 34-35, 65, 68, 71-72; Hughes, *Reformation in England*, III, 304-306.

[86] So called by the Protestants, but Campion never disowned the name, perhaps remembering the words of Scripture: "Let him who boasts, boast in the Lord."

[87] Reynolds, *Campion and Parsons*, p. 80.

[88] Von Pastor, *History of the Popes*, XIX, 393, 416, 458; Read, *Burghley*, pp. 244-246.

[89] Von Pastor, *History of the Popes*, XIX, 412; Fitzgerald, *Geraldines*, pp. 285-287.

such days." (In March Parliament passed and the Queen signed a law "for obedience to the Queen's Majesty against the see of Rome," which declared anyone who converted Englishmen to the Catholic faith guilty of treason and increased the fines for "recusancy" (refusal to attend Church of England services) to a level prohibitory for all but the most wealthy noblemen.) In July, just over a year after he had entered the country, Campion was betrayed and captured. A few weeks before, lost in a Munster bog, Dr. Nicholas Sanders had starved to death, but the Earl of Desmond still fought on.[90]

St. Edmund Campion now experienced "come rack, come rope" in all its horror. Whatever his persecutors might have pretended or honestly believed, he had nothing whatever to do with planning for armed uprisings in Great Britain or Ireland, or with political or military undertakings against Queen Elizabeth. He always maintained full loyalty to her as his sovereign, though never as head of the English church. He met her face to face at the Earl of Leicester's house in London, telling her that he accepted her as his Queen, whereupon she offered him freedom and public office if he would become Protestant, which he firmly refused to do. When he would not answer questions about the bull of Pope St. Pius V against Elizabeth, he was racked, and his fingernails torn off. In his agony he revealed the names of some of the people he had stayed with, but still refused to say anything about his Masses and the confessions he had heard. In mid-August, still weak from the torture and denied any books or notes, he nevertheless conducted a brilliant public debate on religion with the Calvinistic deans of St. Paul's and Windsor. The next month, somewhat recovered, he had a second debate with two scholars at Cambridge, long a hotbed of Protestantism, who insisted that no man could love God with all his heart, all his soul, and all his strength, to which Campion replied that he could and did. A third disputation followed, and a fourth, at which William Charke, who had written against Campion, insulted him repeatedly and had the doors locked so that no one in the audience could leave while he was speaking; he was repeatedly hissed. There were still Englishmen who believed in fairness and justice.[91]

Four days later Campion was racked again, much more severely than the first time. He was indicted for treason for having met with persons in Europe suspected of designs against Queen Elizabeth, though his prosecutors had no evidence of what was said at the meetings. At his trial, the prosecutor in his opening speech condemned him and his co-defendants for having come to England to reconcile men to the "Romish religion . . . by saying of Mass, by administering the Sacrament, by hearing confessions." The jury was bribed to insure conviction, and they convicted.[92] At the close of the trial, Campion said:

---

[90] Haile, *Elizabethan Cardinal*, pp. 188-190 (first quote on 190); J. E. Neale, *Elizabeth and Her Parliaments, 1559-1581* (New York, 1958), pp. 386-390 (second quote on 386); Reynolds, *Campion and Parsons*, pp. 97, 107-110, 113-125; Fitzgerald, *Geraldines*, pp. 287-288.

[91] Von Pastor, *History of the Popes*, XIX, 400-401; Reynolds, *Campion and Parsons*, pp. 131-134, 138-145.

[92] Reynolds, *Campion and Parsons*, pp. 146-147, 161-165, 167-194 (quote on 170).

In condemning us, you condemn all your own ancestors—all the ancient priests, bishops and kings—all that was once the glory of England, the island of saints, and the most devoted child of the See of Peter. For what have we taught, however you may qualify it with the odious name of treason, that they did not uniformly teach? To be condemned with these old lights—not of England only, but of the world—by their degenerate descendants, is both gladness and glory to us. God lives; posterity will live; their judgment is not so liable to corruption as that of those who are now going to sentence us to death.[93]

On December 1, 1581 St. Edmund Campion went from rack to rope. With the layman St. Ralph Sherwin and the priest St. Alexander Briant, he died at Tyburn, praying for Queen Elizabeth. In Ireland John, elder brother of the Earl of Desmond, was killed in an ambush in County Cork in January 1582 and his body hung in chains from a tower in Cork for three years. But the old crippled Earl still held out, all through that year and into the next.[94]

Having kissed Countess Eleanor [his wife] farewell, the last of the Munster Geraldines wandered from glen to glen, mountain to mountain. He knew not where to lay his head. His retinue had shrunk from eighty persons to twenty; from twenty to five—two horsemen, a priest, a kerne, and a boy. These would not desert him. Yet almost all Ireland was Catholic; certainly, all Ireland was pro-Geraldine. But brute ferocity had triumphed. But even Desmond's devoted little band was to be further diminished. The priest was captured, brought handcuffed to Cork, and hanged. MacSweeny, loyalest of friends, fell next; and it was an Irish dagger that killed the leader of the Kenmare mountains. Desmond knew that his turn was coming. But he was the great Earl of Desmond, and he would not give in.[95]

In the end he was betrayed by one Owen O'Moriarty, who on a moonlit night climbed to the top of a ridge overlooking a deep glen and saw a fire burning in a cabin below. His men surrounded the cabin at dawn. It contained only an old man, a woman and a boy. The old man was the Earl of Desmond. They cut off his head and sent it to Queen Elizabeth, who had it mounted on London bridge, where her father had placed the head of St. Thomas More.[96]

At this same period, further compromising the cause of the Jesuits coming to England to try to restore the Faith there, an apparently very promising political opportunity came for Catholics in Scotland, where their prospects suddenly improved so much that it was even possible to entertain the hope that it could be used as a base for a Catholic restoration in England as well as in Scotland. In

---

[93] *Ibid.*, p. 194.

[94] Von Pastor, *History of the Popes*, XIX, 401-402, 449; Hughes, *Reformation in England*, III, 314-315; Reynolds, *Campion and Parsons*, pp. 150-151, 154-156, 199-204; Fitzgerald, *Geraldines*, pp. 288-289.

[95] Fitzgerald, *Geraldines*, p. 292.

[96] *Ibid.*, pp. 292-293.

September 1579 a handsome Frenchman in his thirties of partly Scottish descent, Esmé Stuart d'Aubigny, arrived in Scotland, sent by Duke Henry of Guise to gain the favor of the 13-year-old King James VI, Mary's son, and draw him closer to France. D'Aubigny succeeded spectacularly, since James had strong homosexual tendencies which caused him to be immediately and intensely attracted to him. James made him Duke of Lennox.   By the end of 1580 d'Aubigny had consolidated his power position to the extent of being able to have Regent Morton arrested as an accessory in the murder of Darnley thirteen years before (which he was, in common with several other leaders of the Scots nobility). The English sent a special ambassador, Thomas Randolph, to make vigorous protest and to denounce d'Aubigny, to no avail; Morton was executed in June 1581. By August English Secretary of State Francis Walsingham, in Paris, had learned from his best agent in Rome that the Pope and Philip II had approved plans for an invasion of Scotland to restore the Catholic Faith there, and that these plans had been prepared by a Scottish Jesuit, William Creighton.   That same month Campion's original companion, the Jesuit Robert Parsons, sent the Jesuit William Watts to Edinburgh to try to convert James VI to the Catholic Faith, soon followed by the Jesuit William Holt for the same purpose. At the end of the year Jesuit General Acquaviva, after consultation with the Pope, sent Jesuits Creighton and Edmund Hay to Scotland as well. Campion was martyred that December, and though there is nothing to show he had any knowledge of plans for political and military action in Scotland involving the Jesuits, his reference to the united commitment of the Jesuits in his "Brag" made it seem that he might know of them.[97]

In February 1582 Parsons and Creighton met with Duke Henry of Guise at Rouen.   Creighton went on at once to Scotland, where on March 7 he told d'Aubigny (now Duke of Lennox) that Philip II and the Pope would fund an army of 15,000 to invade first Scotland and then England. D'Aubigny agreed to lead this army, saying that he would convert James VI, restore Catholicism in Scotland, and then proceed into England to free Mary Queen of Scots from prison "or die in the attempt." In April Creighton returned to France and reported to Duke Henry of Guise, who was very enthusiastic for the project; but Spanish ambassador to England Mendoza warned that the enterprise was moving too fast and said no one had authorized any specific number of troops, to say nothing of 15,000.   At a May conference in France of Creighton, Parsons, the Jesuit provincial for France Mathieu, the Duke of Guise, and Dr. Allen, the plan was revised to provide for only 8,000 troops, but otherwise remained essentially unchanged. It was to be executed soon; the Duke of Guise, who now intended to accompany the army, said at the end of May "in a month or two we will be either conquerors or dead." Pope Gregory XIII said he favored the project, but wanted

---

[97] Antonia Fraser, *King James VI of Scotland and I of England* (London, 1974), pp. 36-37; Black, *Reign of Elizabeth*, p. 310; Read, *Burghley*, pp. 232-234; Read, *Walsingham*, II, 155-156, 164-165, 172, 373-374; von Pastor, *History of the Popes*, XIX, 427; Hughes, *Reformation in England*, III, 317, 319-320; Martin, *Henry III and the Jesuit Politicians*, pp. 68-69.

to be sure it was actually undertaken before giving support; Philip II, short of money because of the long struggle in the Low Countries and not wishing to offend King Henry III, no friend of the Guises, hesitated. The Pope and the king of Spain were each waiting for the other to act first. (So during the summer of 1582 they marked time.[98]

Their delay was fatal to the enterprise. On August 22, 1582, when 15-year-old James VI was hunting in the country without d'Aubigny/Lennox or his other principal supporter among the nobility, the Earl of Arran, he was seized by a group of Scots nobles influenced by the Calvinist ministers, hostile to d'Aubigny and backed by the English, and locked up in impregnable Stirling Castle—a coup known from the family name of its leader, the Earl of Gowrie, as the "Ruthven raid." The whole Catholic undertaking, which had depended totally on d'Aubigny's presumed control of young James, collapsed at once. D'Aubigny fled to France and soon died there. The great opportunity had been missed, and served only to provide more ammunition for Cecil when he published in 1583 a defense against the execution of Campion and other missionary priests in England entitled "The Execution of Justice in England, not for Religion but for Treason."[99]

Nevertheless their work went on, "come rack, come rope." Twelve of them were martyred during the year 1582 and 40 imprisoned, but by March 1583 Dr. Allen could say that no less than 230 had been sent to England. None had fled and none had given up their faith. In just six months during 1583 they converted more than four hundred people in one small shire. In 1582 the first Catholic translation of the New Testament into English, prepared at Douai by Gregory Martin, was published, to be followed some years later by an English translation of the Old Testament. The "Douai-Reims Bible" continued in widespread use by English-speaking Catholics over the whole world until the middle of the twentieth century.[100]

But the conspiracies also went on, and continued to involve the Jesuits. Early in June 1583 there was a conference at the house of the papal nuncio in Paris of several who had been active in planning the abortive invasion of Scotland and through it, of England. Duke Henry of Guise was present, and the Archbishop of Glasgow, the Spanish ambassador Mendoza, Jesuit provincial for France Mathieu, and the Jesuit Parsons. The Duke of Guise now had a specific plan for the assassination of Queen Elizabeth, though he admitted that Mary Queen of Scots "would not hear of it." The Pope's secretary, Cardinal Como,

---

[98] Von Pastor, *History of the Popes*, XIX, 430-432 (second quote on 430); Martin, *Henry III and the Jesuit Politicians*, pp. 70-74, 81-82; Hughes, *Reformation in England*, III, 320-322; Haile, *Elizabethan Cardinal*, pp. 222-223 (first quote on 223); Black, *Reign of Elizabeth*, pp. 312-313; Read, *Walsingham*, II, 374-375.

[99] Fraser, *James VI*, p. 38; Fraser, *Mary Queen of Scots*, p. 458; von Pastor, *History of the Popes*, XIX, 432-433; Martin, *Henry III and the Jesuit Politicians*, p. 105; Black, *Reign of Elizabeth*, p. 313; Read, *Burghley*, pp. 251-254; Read, *Walsingham*, II, 180-181.

[100] Von Pastor, *History of the Popes*, XIX, 378, 387-388; Haile, *Elizabethan Cardinal*, pp. 217, 258; Hughes, *Reformation in England*, III, 299-301.

was informed, but the Pope was not to be told. In August it was decided to send Charles Paget to rouse the support of the English Catholic nobility, and Duke Henry drafted instructions for Parsons to take personally to Rome to inform the Pope of the new plans for the invasion of England, asking him to provide money, renew his predecessor's decree against Queen Elizabeth, issue a bull supporting the invasion, and appoint Allen Bishop of Durham. The Duke would cross the English Channel, land at the port of Arundel in Sussex, and go immediately to liberate Mary Queen of Scots. In October Francis Throckmorton, who had discussed the plan with Charles Paget in Paris, was arrested in London carrying a list of leading Catholics and of the chief ports of England. Racked three times, he broke down and confessed the whole plot to Cecil's men, including the plan to assassinate Queen Elizabeth and the leading role of the Spanish ambassador in the whole project; Mendoza was promptly thrown out of the country.[101]

The final debacle of this misbegotten project came almost a full year later, in September 1584, when Jesuit William Creighton was captured on his way to Scotland by a Dutch ship (probably hired for the purpose by Walsingham), carrying a paper describing in detail the projected invasions of England and Scotland in 1582 and 1583. (Why he was still carrying such a document, when the projects had already been revealed and abandoned, is impossible to explain.) Standing on the quarterdeck of his captured ship with this highly incriminating paper in his pocket, Creighton tried to tear it up and throw it overboard. But he threw the torn-up fragments into the wind instead of with it. Consequently most of them blew back on deck, where they were carefully collected, pieced together, and forwarded to Walsingham and Cecil.[102]

Though there is no proof that Pope Gregory XIII ever learned of, much less approved the assassination of Queen Elizabeth, and evidence (already mentioned) that he did not, this "Throckmorton plot" of 1583 played straight into Cecil's hands. He did not hesitate to use his thorough advance knowledge of the plot not only to frustrate it, but also to blacken the reputation of every Catholic in England and every missionary priest who came to England. It might be possible to justify the assassination of Queen Elizabeth under the doctrine of tyrannicide, but it should never have been linked with the Jesuits and Dr. Allen. The Jesuits in particular suffered ignominy and hatred throughout the English-speaking world for the next four hundred years, and much of it grew out of this plot which never even began to be carried out.

The conspirators were trying to do far too much. England had not been successfully invaded from the continent of Europe since William the Conqueror, and in fact was never to be. If such an invasion were ever to be accomplished, it could only be by the full exercise of the might of a great power—as Philip II was soon to undertake with the Spanish Armada. What could and should have been

---

[101] Haile, *Elizabethan Cardinal*, pp. 231-233, 241; Hughes, *Reformation in England*, III, 324-325, 327; Martin, *Henry III and the Jesuit Politicians*, pp. 106-107; Black, *Reign of Elizabeth*, pp. 315-316; Fraser, *Mary Queen of Scots*, pp. 469-470; Read, *Walsingham*, II, 382-387.

[102] Von Pastor, *History of the Popes*, XIX, 453; Read, *Walsingham*, II, 398.

done was to at least try to rescue Mary Queen of Scots. Sole concentration on this one objective might have succeeded. Mary, free, would have been a rallying point for every English Catholic and a mortal threat to Queen Elizabeth, as Cecil well knew. But plans for her liberation were always entangled with other projects and died with them. When William Creighton threw his torn-up paper into the North Sea wind that September day in 1584, she had less than two and a half years to live.

From 1578 to 1580 a surprising series of events brought Portugal, with its vast overseas empire established in the glory days of the Age of Discovery,[103] under the control of Philip II of Spain, substantially increasing the wealth and power of the nation which already had more of both than any other in Europe. King John III of Portugal, son of King Manuel and Queen Maria, third daughter of Fernando and Isabel the Catholic, had died in 1557 after his son and heir, Prince John. John III's heir was therefore Prince John's posthumous baby son, Sebastian. In 1578 Sebastian was 21, ruling on his own, still unmarried, and full of romantic, crusading enthusiasm. Against all advice he led a military expedition into Morocco, which was destroyed at the Battle of Alcaçer-Quivir near Tangier. Few survived the disaster. King Sebastian disappeared—his body was never found. John III had no other living children, and all his brothers were dead without legitimate issue except Cardinal Henry, a sick man of 67. He became king, but lived only a year and a half. Next in line for the throne, according to the laws of monarchical succession in Spain and Portugal, were the sisters of John III, the eldest of whom had been Isabel, the mother of Philip II of Spain. Since Empress Isabel was long since dead, Philip was the rightful heir, and Cardinal Henry so proclaimed him before his death in January 1580.[104]

Philip's claim to the Portuguese royal succession was legally unassailable, but Portugal was a proud nation after its fantastic success in the Age of Discovery, and many of its people were most unwilling to be taken over by their larger neighbor. They had only an illegitimate son of a dead brother of former King John III to rally around, Antonio of Crato, a man of very limited ability and appeal. But the support of many of the Portuguese people—and that of England, whose government obviously did not wish to see its great enemy made even greater by gaining control of Portugal and its Indian and South American colonies—gave him strength. Philip needed to move quickly and decisively before resistance to his rule in Portugal could coalesce. In February he turned to the Duke of Alba, now 73 and in retirement. That tough old soldier was no diplomat and had lacked the imagination to deal effectively with the supremely difficult situation in the Low Countries, but he was still the best general in Europe, and this time would be operating in a climate and terrain just like home. There were no dikes to be opened in Portugal. Reviewing his troops in June,

---

[103] See Volume Three, Chapter 16 of this history.

[104] Von Pastor, *History of the Popes*, XIX, 357-359, 410-411; Kamen, *Philip of Spain*, pp. 169, 173; Walsh, *Philip II*, pp. 579, 597-598.

when the army was fully assembled, Alba seemed rejuvenated, in his element again.[105]

For action at sea, essential in Portugal with its long seacoast and outlying islands, Philip had the Marquis of Santa Cruz, one of the best admirals in Europe. Santa Cruz sailed from Cádiz in July, after Alba had crossed the frontier. So Philip II moved on Portugal with overwhelming force, on land and sea. Antonio challenged him at Alcántara near Lisbon on August 25. The battle was over in half an hour; Alba not only outnumbered but totally outgeneralled his inexperienced opponent. By the end of the year all resistance in Portugal had ceased (except for the Azores Islands, which were not fully secured until 1583) and Philip II came to take residence in his new domain. In April 1581, in a splendid ceremony, the Portuguese *cortes* accepted him as king, and he took an oath confirming the privileges and liberties of the country. He remained there until March 1583, convincing the Portuguese that he intended to maintain their laws and customs as he had sworn to do, and to rule them no differently from past Portuguese kings. His fourth and last wife, Anna of Austria, accompanied him to Portugal and died there. Philip had been devoted to her, and she had finally provided him with sons—four of them. But she was his own niece, and though they were dispensed by the Pope for a marriage so far within the normally prohibited degrees of relationship, the biological consequences could not be avoided. Three of the four boys died in childhood, and the fourth, his namesake, was never more than a pale shadow of his father as king. Upon Philip III's grandson the laws of genetics were to do their worst.[106]

The death of Don Juan of Austria was far from bringing an end to the struggle for the Low Countries. Though William of Orange and the Calvinists seemed to have the upper hand, the Calvinists were still very much a minority in the region as a whole, and William of Orange had publicly identified himself as one of them as early as 1573.[107] The Prince of Parma, just 33 years old, soon proved as able a general as the Duke of Alba and a much more effective diplomat. Increasingly the Catholics of the Low Countries rallied to him. England aided the rebels only indirectly and sporadically, and the French aid repeatedly promised by the Duke d'Alençon had far more show than substance. In the seven years from the death of Don Juan to Parma's great triumph in the capture of Antwerp in August 1585, the Spanish cause in the Low Countries recovered and gained much strength, though still far from total victory. Increasingly the northern and southern portions of the Low Countries began to diverge, with the north (the future Netherlands) more Calvinist and the south (the

---

[105] Kamen, *Philip of Spain*, pp. 173-175; Walsh, *Philip II*, pp. 602-605; Maltby, *Alba*, pp. 283-288; Read, *Burghley*, pp. 223-224.

[106] Kamen, *Philip of Spain*, pp. 175-177, 205-208, 210, 248, 252; Walsh, *Philip II*, pp. 604, 606-607, 616; Maltby, *Alba*, pp. 297-299. See Volume Five, forthcoming, for Philip III's grandson, King Charles II, who lacked half the normal complement of ancestors, and was known by his distressed subjects as *el hechizado*, "the bewitched."

[107] Von Pastor, *History of the Popes*, XX, 2.

future Belgium) more Catholic. In the south was formed the Union of Arras to protect the Catholic Faith and seek reconciliation with Philip II; in the north the Union of Utrecht took shape under William of Orange, the nucleus of the future Dutch Republic.[108]

In August 1580 the States-General of the Low Countries (now quite clearly not representing nearly all of the region) offered their crown to the Duke d'Alençon instead of Philip II, though the two were entirely unrelated: an action breaching the entire monarchical tradition of Europe. Archduke Matthias, only 21 years old and wholly ineffective, was summarily dismissed. The next month d'Alençon entered the Low Countries and occupied the city of Cambrai near the French border, but declared he could not proceed further without money, having as yet received none from the States-General. He soon did get some funding from both his brother Henry III and from England, enabling him to keep a foothold in the Low Countries but no more; exasperated by this lack of support, he withdrew temporarily to France in September.[109]

But William of Orange had now convinced himself that d'Alençon was essential to the victory of the rebels over Parma. It was the biggest misjudgment of his life, for the pockmarked little man with the enormous nose[110] never had distinguished and never would distinguish himself in any of his numerous enterprises, and made a fool of himself wooing the aging Queen Elizabeth, eighteen years his senior.[111] William was far more competent, and already the effective leader of the rebels. But William made the installation and support of d'Alençon as king of the Netherlands his main political objective for the rest of his life—an objective he could not attain, and which would have done him and his cause no good if he had. On February 19, 1582 he crowned d'Alençon Duke of Brabant in Antwerp and proclaimed him "prince and lord" of the seven northern Dutch provinces in revolt against Spain. Only afterward did d'Alençon, still professedly Catholic, discover that the Mass had been prohibited in Antwerp. He was satisfied when the law was modified to permit its celebration in one church.[112]

By July, despite periodic infusions of French and English money, d'Alençon's army had dwindled to only 7,000 men through desertion because of

---

[108] Parker, *Dutch Revolt*, pp. 193-196, 202, 208, 215; Israel, *Dutch Republic*, pp. 199-202, 206-207, 212.

[109] Holt, *Duke of Anjou*, pp. 133-141, 155-159; Parker, *Dutch Revolt*, pp. 197-198; Israel, *Dutch Republic*, pp. 208-209; Wedgwood, *William the Silent*, p. 222; Kamen, *Philip of Spain*, p. 254.

[110] For d'Alençon's physical appearance see Chamberlin, *Marguerite of Navarre*, p. 184.

[111] These strange amours, which bulk large in the diplomatic correspondence of the time and in many later histories, and even seem to have been taken seriously by Cecil, were all bluff and show, probably on the part of both protagonists and certainly on the part of Elizabeth, who could not afford to make herself a laughing-stock, but enjoyed a pretended flirtation. Therefore no space need be given them in this history.

[112] Wedgwood, *William the Silent*, pp. 226-227; Holt, *Duke of Anjou*, pp. 166-170; Kamen, *Philip of Spain*, p. 254.

lack of pay and supplies, while Parma had 60,000, including over 11,000 Spanish and Italian veterans. Calvinist expansion had virtually ceased; Brussels, a city of 40,000, had only six Calvinist ministers, and Bruges in Flanders only one. In January 1583 d'Alençon, after reminding the remnants of the States-General that they were 600,000 pounds in arrears on their promised payments to him, attacked Antwerp. Its people, who had experienced too many sacks, fought back furiously, and half d'Alençon's men were killed, many jumping or falling from the walls or drowning in the moat. Despite William of Orange's incredible continued defense of d'Alençon (which caused his leading Calvinist supporter, Philip Marnix, to break totally with him), Antwerp and Brussels would have nothing more to do with him. The last remnants of his army dissolved in May; by July d'Alençon was back in France begging help from his distracted mother, Catherine de Medici, to revive his dream of kingship.[113]

There was still plenty of fighting to be done in the Netherlands, but the initiative had passed to the Prince of Parma and his Spaniards. They pushed inexorably into Flanders, where the population was about evenly divided between Catholics and Protestants (a census in Antwerp in 1584 showed 3,011 Catholic families, 2,131 Calvinist families, and 940 Lutheran families, with about a third of the population not declaring their religion). In April Parma took Ypres after a six-month siege. In May he took overwhelmingly Catholic Bruges without resistance. In June the discredited d'Alençon died of the same tuberculosis that had killed his brothers Francis and Charles. In July William of Orange was assassinated by Balthazar Gérard, whose plan was known to Parma and who collected the price which Philip II had long ago placed on rebel William's head. In September Parma took Ghent, giving its numerous Calvinists two years to decide whether to return to the Catholic Church or leave the city, and began building an enormous dam across the broad Scheldt River to cut Antwerp off from the sea. In just five months it was completed: 2,400 feet long, resting on piles set in holes drilled 75 feet deep by a special machine, defended by 200 siege guns. The Duke of Alba had done nothing like this. In a desperate attempt in April 1585 to break the dam, a flotilla of fireships from the besieged city blew open a 200-foot span, killing 800 Spaniards and dazing Parma himself; but the breach was closed before a relieving fleet could arrive from the north. Antwerp would fall now, and Flanders be secured for the Catholics. Whether the whole of the Low Countries could be regained, no man could say; but if they could be, the end of the Protestant revolution might be in sight.[114]

In Germany, all through the years covered by this chapter, the Catholic Church was reviving wherever it was allowed to do so, the Lutherans falling into

---

[113] Parker, *Dutch Revolt*, pp. 202, 206, 209; Israel, *Dutch Republic*, pp. 212-213; Holt, *Duke of Anjou*, pp. 173-174, 180-184, 188-189, 191-192; Wedgwood, *William the Silent*, pp. 237-240; Kamen, *Philip of Spain*, p. 254.

[114] Parker, *Dutch Revolt*, pp. 202-203, 207, 214-215; Wedgwood, *William the Silent*, pp. 249-250; Holt, *Duke of Anjou*, pp. 208-209; von Pastor, *History of the Popes*, XX, 19; Kamen, *Philip of Spain*, p. 255; Walsh, *Philip II*, pp. 618-619.

furious and often bloody faction, and the Calvinists set against everyone else. The contrast between Catholic unity fostered by the Council of Trent and Protestant division and hatred was very striking, revealing to many the real nature and consequences of tearing the seamless robe of Christ. The Jesuits, following in the footsteps of St. Peter Canisius, were particularly active in the Catholic reclamation of large parts of Germany. As early as April 1573 the Jesuit Georg Schorich was able to report that almost all the formerly Lutheran nargraviate of Baden-Baden in southwestern Germany was now Catholic again, with 38 churches repossessed—the first entire province regained for the Church. In May 1573 the German congregation of cardinals at Rome sent Abbot Bartolomeo Portia to Upper Germany (Bavaria and much of present Austria) to investigate the progress of reform, and the support or lack of it given by bishops and princes, with emphasis on the establishment of Catholic seminaries and printing presses, and active assistance to Catholic scholars and preachers. In October 1573 papal nuncio Gaspar Gropper reported to Rome that Archbishop-Elector Jakob von Eltz of Trier is "in his life, his habits, his dress and in every act, a true bishop"— which could certainly not have been said of several of his recent predecessors in that see. When the bishop of Würzburg died in November 1573, the great reformer Julius Echter was elected to succeed him.[115]

Bishop Echter was only thirty years old, and he served as head of his important southwest German diocese for no less than 43 years, always a strong supporter of the Jesuits.[116] Ludwig von Pastor says of him:

> Equally great as a civil ruler and as a prince of the church, and endowed with extraordinary shrewdness, vast prudence, an iron will and a great power of administration, he restored the diocese of Würzburg from a state of complete disorganization and bankruptcy to a healthy condition, and from the religious point of view, brought it back permanently to the old Church.[117]

In March 1575 Flacius Illyricus, whom Martin Luther had once declared his successor, died in poverty at Frankfurt, hunted as a heretic by Elector Augustus of Saxony, successor of Luther's protectors. In June 1576 Elector Augustus sponsored a meeting of 17 Lutheran theologians at Torgau to draft a Lutheran creed, which would reject Philip Melanchthon and attempt to convey "the spirit of Luther," while proclaiming the ubiquity of Christ in His human nature "in every stone, plant and rope" (to which a critic replied: "Christ must be sought for in His words and sacraments, not in ropes and stones"). The "Torgau Book" was accepted by most Lutherans in nine provinces, but firmly rejected in four provinces, including the important Hesse. A later revision called the "Bergen Book" fared little better, being still rejected by Hesse and also by the large Protestant cities of Nuremburg, Frankfurt, Speyer, Worms, Bremen, and Danzig. In the Palatinate the vehemently Calvinist Elector Frederick III died in 1576,

---

[115] Von Pastor, *History of the Popes*, XX, 48-49, 66-70, 82, 354 (quote).

[116] *Ibid.*, 193-194.

[117] *Ibid.*, XX, 194-195.

leaving two sons, Lutheran Ludwig and Calvinist John Casimir. In the space of just seven years the province went from Calvinist to Lutheran to Calvinist again, when Ludwig died relatively young and his brother assumed the regency for his boy son.[118]

In 1576 Emperor Maximilian II, once thought a Protestant sympathizer but who now refused to yield to any Protestant demands, died of long-standing heart disease, and was succeeded by his son Rudolf II, 24, a convinced Catholic who had Jesuit confessors, was very learned (he spoke six languages) and a connoisseur of art, but was weak, irresolute and suspicious, subject to long periods of depression, and delegating most of his authority, an Emperor who most of the time did not reign, but when he did exert his authority was always in favor of the Catholics.[119]

In October 1579 Duke Albert of Bavaria died and was succeeded by his son William V, who "proved himself, by his personal and deep piety, even more than his father, the supporter and protector of the Catholic religious revival" in Germany. Duke William was a great benefactor of the Jesuits. He and his wife Renée of Lorraine supported and strengthened each other in the Faith, visiting churches and giving alms together, and receiving Communion together much more often than was usual in that period. It was said that neither ever committed a mortal sin. By 1582 the Catholic community at Augsburg, where the original Protestant Confession had been written but where St. Peter Canisius had so often spoken, had grown so much that it was possible to establish a Jesuit college there, endowed by the wealthy Fugger merchant family.[120]

It remains to survey the east and the north. Poland had been deeply penetrated by Calvinism and even Unitarianism during the later years of King Sigismund II, who died in 1572. Though always Catholic himself, Sigismund refused to act against the Calvinists and Unitarians. During the charade of the election of Prince Henry of France as king of Poland and his abrupt departure in 1574 to assume the crown of France, the Polish Protestants kept their free hand. But by 1575 the Jesuits had gained substantial influence in the Polish church, and in December of that year Stephen Bathory, prince of Transylvania (northeastern Hungary) was elected king over Emperor Maximilian II, on condition that he marry Anna Jagellon, sister of the late Sigismund II. He did so on May 1, 1576, his coronation day, thereby continuing the dynasty that went back to Jagiello and Jadwiga.[121] On July 5 King Stephen informed Pope Gregory XIII of his election and coronation in a humble letter, asking the Pope's blessing and protection and offering him obedience. In November the Pope recognized Stephen Bathory as king of Poland and sent a nuncio to his court. During the first year of his reign,

---

[118] Janssen, *History of the German People*, VIII, 187, 394, 406-409 (quotes on 407), 412-421, 428-429; IX, 82, 93.

[119] *Ibid.*, VIII, 366-367 (quote on 367); Von Pastor, *History of the Popes*, XX, 222, 251, 262, 264.

[120] Von Pastor, *History of the Popes*, XX, 52-53; Brodrick, *St. Peter Canisius*, p. 767.

[121] For their story see Volume Three, Chapter 11 of this history.

Stephen restored to Catholic use all churches under royal patronage which had been taken over by the Protestants. He was bound by his coronation oath not to proceed against Polish Protestants generally, but acted as a strong Catholic ruler throughout his reign.[122]

King John III of Sweden, who had ruled since 1569, was married to Catherine Jagellon, a sister of Sigismund II of Poland. Her right to continue to practice her Catholic faith in totally Lutheran Sweden had been guaranteed in their marriage agreement. Through her, John III had a claim on the Polish throne, and in May 1573, before the election of Prince Henry of France, his ambassadors in Poland informed Rome that he would be willing to become Catholic and open Sweden to Catholic missionaries if he could get Catholic support for his candidacy for king of Poland. The next month Pope Gregory XIII directed Polish Cardinal Hosius to send Polish Jesuit Stanislas Warszewicki from Vilnius, Lithuania to Stockholm as a priest to attend Queen Catherine, but with instructions to find out if John III might possibly be sincere in his offer. Communications and transportation in northeastern Europe were poor, slow, and risky; Warszewicki did not reach Stockholm for more than a year, travelling by way of Estonia and barely evading capture by pirates and sinking by a storm in the dangerous waters of the Baltic Sea. Once he had arrived, Warszewicki found that the king of Sweden was sincere in his interest in the Catholic Faith. After only about two weeks of discussion, John III pronounced himself convinced "in principle" of the truth of Catholic doctrine, but said it could only be introduced into Sweden gradually; any attempt at a quick and complete conversion would cost him his throne. (In this he was undoubtedly correct, as later events were to show.) He strongly requested dispensations from the Pope to permit the chalice for the laity, married priests, and the use of the vernacular in the liturgy, which would make a change of faith appear more gradual to the Swedes.[123]

At the end of August Warszewicki returned to Poland to report what the king had said to him, and John III himself confirmed it in September in a letter to the Cardinal Secretary of State in Rome. In December he compelled the reluctant Archbishop of Uppsala, Lutheran primate of Sweden, to accept the king's Seventeen Articles (also known as the New Church Ordinances), which contradicted Lutheran doctrine by declaring faith and works equally necessary for salvation, emphasized the Eucharist, permitted veneration of the Blessed Virgin Mary and the saints, and encouraged celibacy in the ministers, the restoration of monasteries, the reintroduction of confession and anointing of the sick, and the use of mitre and crook by bishops. Impressed by these promising developments, in September 1575 the Pope sent a Norwegian Jesuit, Laurentius Nicolai (known from his nationality as "Norvegus"—the Norwegian) to Stockholm as another chaplain to the Catholic Queen, but with instructions to

---

[122] Von Pastor, *History of the Popes*, XX, 389-393; George Vernadsky, *The Tsardom of Moscow, 1547-1682* (New Haven CT, 1969), I, 149.

[123] Oskar Garsten, *Rome and the Counter-Reformation in Scandinavia* (Bergen, Norway, 1963), pp. 62-63, 74-77.

begin the reconversion of Sweden. At that time he was the only member of the Society of Jesus who could speak Swedish.[124]

In 1576 John III published a new liturgy for the Swedish church, popularly known as the "Red Book," with Catholic elements predominating and many similarities to the Mass, except for the omission of the commemoration of saints by name and references to purgatory. He established a new theological college at a former Franciscan friary in Stockholm and put Laurentius the Norwegian in charge of it, while obtaining an oath from him that he would not reveal that he was a Catholic. By fall, 60 students were enrolled in the new college. In October John sent Peter Fecht, who had compiled the liturgy of the Red Book, and General Pontus de la Gardie as official ambassadors to the Pope to explore a reunion with the Catholic Church and to press for the dispensations he had requested earlier. On the way they were shipwrecked on the island of Bornholm. Fecht was drowned, but General de la Gardie survived and finally arrived in Rome in April 1577. On Easter Sunday of that year, John III ceased to take communion from Lutheran ministers, convinced that they and their church did not have valid sacraments.[125]

On May 10, 1577 Pope Gregory XIII announced to his cardinals that General de la Gardie had professed obedience to the Catholic Church and had conveyed his king's request for missionaries to reconvert the people of Sweden. There was much rejoicing in Rome (so poor were the communications of the time, especially to distant Scandinavia, that we have no record of any report of this ever getting back to Sweden). On Pentecost Sunday Jesuit General Mercurian and his secretary Antonio Possevino met with the Pope regarding the appeal from Sweden. They decided that Possevino should go there himself to supervise the missionary work. In December Possevino arrived after a very difficult journey through the snowbound northern countryside, accompanied by two other Jesuits, and was warmly welcomed by John III. Just after their arrival, Laurentius said a Christmas Eve midnight Mass at the new theological college and distributed consecrated Hosts to students whom he now obviously believed to be Catholic. He had already sent six seminarians to study in Rome; they were personally welcomed by the Pope in January 1578. The prospects for the reconversion of Sweden looked bright.[126]

But John III was not as compliant as he seemed; and even if he had been, the difficulties of reconverting a people so deeply penetrated by Lutheranism in the forty years since Nils Dacke died fighting for the Catholic Faith in the heart of Sweden,[127] were enormous. Strong monarchical authority was historically

---

[124] *Ibid.*, pp. 78-81, 84-86, 90; Michael Roberts, *The Early Vasas; a History of Sweden 1523-1611* (Cambridge, England, 1968), pp. 280, 282-283.

[125] Garsten, *Counter-Reformation in Scandinavia*, pp. 94-97, 119-120, 124-127; von Pastor, *History of the Popes*, XX, 422-423, 425; Roberts, *Early Vasas*, pp. 282-285.

[126] Von Pastor, *History of the Popes*, XX, 423-424; Garsten, *Counter-Reformation in Scandinavia*, pp. 100-101, 104-105, 107, 129, 131-132; Roberts, *Early Vasas*, pp. 284-285.

[127] See Chapter Four, above.

new in Sweden; it had been first established by Gustavus Vasa, John III's father, as he broke Sweden away from the Church. John III, though resolute, had neither his father's genius nor his popularity. He believed that some compromises with Lutheranism must be made if the Catholic Faith were to be restored in Sweden. So in March 1578 he wrote to Pope Gregory XIII in effect demanding, as his price for the reunion of Sweden with the Church, the chalice for the laity, the marriage of priests, Mass in Swedish, the retention of lands taken from the Church in his father's reign, permission to attend Lutheran as well as Catholic services, and recognition that veneration of saints and prayers for the dead were not obligatory. His distant, indirect dealings with the Pope had not given him any sense of how exorbitant these demands would seem to him. Therefore John III was genuinely astonished and very angry when, after he had made a secret profession of faith and been formally received into the Church by Possevino in May, he received word late in October that most of his requests to the Pope had been denied. By July 1579 the Swedish king was again receiving communion from the Lutherans, and for some time refused to give audience to Possevino when he returned to Stockholm after a trip to Poland. When John III did meet him, he threatened literally to beat him up; in the midst of their violent argument a gust of wind blew out several panes of glass in a window next to them and Possevino collapsed in a dead faint.[128]

But Queen Catherine still provided a Catholic base in Sweden; Laurentius the Norwegian was a missionary powerhouse; and the king, though angry with the Pope, still admired the Jesuit priests who had come to Sweden and had no thought of expelling them. When he moved his court out of Stockholm at the end of September due to plague, the Jesuits took advantage of the opportunity to print and distribute a recently prepared Swedish edition of St. Peter Canisius' catechism. Seventeen young men—14 Swedes, two Finns and a Lapp—were sent to German seminaries to prepare for the priesthood. On Christmas Eve Father Warszewicki said a private Mass for John III's son by Polish Queen Catherine and heir, young Prince Sigismund, who made a good confession and pledged never to forsake the Catholic Church and never to receive the Eucharist from Protestants. That winter, John III agreed to restore the famous convent of St. Bridget at Vadstena and to allow the use of St. Peter Canisius' catechism there.[129]

Early in February 1580 all the Jesuits in Sweden decided to reveal themselves as priests, though not as Jesuits. In a dramatic sermon at his theological college beginning with that revelation, Laurentius the Norwegian called upon the entire congregation to embrace the Catholic faith. The response was overwhelmingly enthusiastic. Over the next few days there emerged from

---

[128] Garsten, *Counter-Reformation in Scandinavia*, pp. 135-144, 160-161, 166, 176, 178-179, 188; von Pastor, *History of the Popes*, XX, 426-427, 429. Pope Gregory XIII was willing to concede the retention of most lands taken from the Church. Veneration of saints and prayers for the dead were never obligatory for laymen, but they were for priests.

[129] Garsten, *Counter-Reformation in Scandinavia*, pp. 178-184, 188-192, 195, 197-198.

the surrounding countryside some old people who had grown up as Catholics fifty years and more before; forty of them volunteered to make a public profession of their long-held, silent faith.[130]

But now John III's secret was out. The Swedish *riksdag* (parliament) met, declared almost unanimously for Lutheranism, and called on the king to replace the Catholics at his theological college with Lutherans and to withdraw Prince Sigismund from Catholic influence. In April a Lutheran mob attacked the theological college and set fire to it. After a heroic defense the ill-armed religious and students were overwhelmed; the buildings were ravaged and many of the faculty and students imprisoned. John III ordered punishment of leaders of the mob, but also arrested Laurentius the Norwegian, charging him with breaking his oath to the king that he would not reveal his priesthood. He deprived him of his office in the theological college and banished him from the country. He and Possevino departed in August, still hoping that the Queen's chaplains and a few Jesuits King John III had allowed to stay, might carry out the mission; but it was doomed. Possevino and Laurentius each blamed the other for its failure—they had never liked each other nor cooperated well despite their great common purpose, which was probably one reason for the disaster. All hope for the reconversion of Sweden, at least during the lifetime of John III, ended when Queen Catherine died suddenly in October 1583.[131]

Meanwhile, Poland under King Stephen Bathory had become more and more solidly Catholic. In May 1577 a synod at Piotrkow, presided over by the primate of Poland, Archbishop Uchanski of Gniezno, and the papal nuncio Laureo, condemned the Protestants, unanimously accepted the decrees of the Council of Trent, and issued decrees for Catholic reform; all its acts were sent to Rome for confirmation. In 1581 Archbishop Stanislaus Karnkowski, the new primate of Poland, established two seminaries directed by the Jesuits and had a Polish translation of the Bible prepared by the Jesuit James Wujek.[132]

In the summer of 1579 King Stephen Bathory went to war against his big neighbor, Russia (then usually called Muscovy, since Moscow was its capital) which had been encroaching more and more on Livonia, the region including the modern states of Latvia and Estonia which bordered the Polish-Lithuanian union to the north. King Stephen took the city of Polotsk from the Russians at the end of August (they had seized it without justification 16 years before) and the next year founded a Jesuit college there. The Tsar of Russia, Ivan the Terrible, raged and mobilized. In November, the traditional month when Russian peasants lacking land of their own could leave the estates where they had been working through harvest time and seek other estates to work on for the next year, Ivan decreed that at least for the duration of the Livonian war, no peasant should move

---

[130] *Ibid.*, pp. 201-204.

[131] *Ibid.*, pp. 204, 207-209, 211-217, 219, 255; Roberts, *Early Vasas*, p. 287, 290; von Pastor, *History of the Popes*, XX, 433.

[132] Von Pastor, *History of the Popes*, XX, 393-394, 403, 406; Halecki, *Florence to Brest*, pp. 196-197, 199-201, 204.

from where he was, the better to mobilize them as needed. It was the beginning of legal serfdom in Russia.[133]

It was natural that this ruler should be the first in Russia to virtually enslave his subjects who worked the land. Ivan's father, Grand Duke of Moscow Vasily III, died when he was three years old; his young mother, Elena Glinskaya, died in great pain, probably from poison, when he was seven. Greedy nobles seized power and fought among themselves for it while young Ivan watched helpless and afraid for six years, until at 13 he ordered the arrest and execution of the then dominant noble Andrei Shuisky. Three years later he was persuaded that an old friend named Fyodor Vorontsov and his brother were plotting against him; Ivan ordered them to lie flat on the ground where he had their heads chopped off by axes, a grim foretaste of what was to come. Though it did not become clear until after his brilliant capture of the Tartar stronghold of Kazan in eastern Russia in 1552 and the death of his beloved first wife in 1560, Ivan the Terrible had developed during his dreadful childhood a blazing fire of fear, anger, and hatred against the world that nothing could quench. He went from crime to crime, from atrocity to atrocity. In 1565 Ivan divided his kingdom, keeping part for his personal use and allowing the rest to be governed by nobles, but in constant fear of his personal troops, the *oprichniki*, who took an oath to break totally away from family and friends to serve the Tsar only, and were empowered to kill anyone whom the paranoid Ivan thought might be a traitor. They wore black clothes, rode on black horses, and carried broomsticks and dogs' heads on their saddles. They looked like devils, as Ivan no doubt intended. Their depredations led to an act of religious heroism unmatched in the whole history of the Russian church, when Archbishop of Moscow Philip Kolychev, who had been abbot of the monastery on the Solovetsky Islands in the White Sea, refused the Tsar his blessing at Uspensky Cathedral in Moscow in March 1568,[134] saying:

> To what limits have you gone, O Tsar, to place yourself beyond the reach of a blessing? Fear the judgment of God, O Tsar! We are now offering up the bloodless sacrifice to the Lord, while the blood of innocent Christians is being spilt beyond the altar! Since the day when the sun first shone in the heavens, no one has ever seen or heard of a God-fearing Tsar persecuting his own countrymen so ferociously! . . . You sit high on your throne, but here is

---

[133] Von Pastor, *History of the Popes*, XX, 397, 403; Halecki, *Florence to Brest*, p. 204; Vernadsky, *Tsardom of Moscow* I, 105, 153-154; Robert Payne and Nikita Romanoff, *Ivan the Terrible* (New York, 1975), pp. 205, 375.

[134] Vernadsky, *Tsardom of Moscow*, pp. 21, 24-25, 109-112, 162-165; Payne & Romanoff, *Ivan the Terrible*, pp. 9-10, 20, 39, 62-64, 221, 224-228, 234-236. The Solovetsky Islands were the site of the first large death camp in Communist Russia. Legend told of a monk-priest named Job, long years before, whom the Blessed Virgin Mary visited during an all-night vigil at the foot of a hill on this island, telling him that the hill should be named for Golgotha, and a church and monastery built there dedicated to the Crucifixion. Then she added: "It will be whitened by the sufferings of countless multitudes" (see my *Rise and Fall of the Communist Revolution* [Front Royal VA, 1995], p. 246).

a God who judges us all. How will you stand before His judgment seat, stained with the blood of the innocent and deafened by their screams under torture! Even the stones under your feet cry out for vengeance! I speak, O Tsar, because I am a shepherd of souls and I fear only the one and only God![135]

In response, Ivan snarled: "Up to now I have spared you traitors to no purpose. From now on I shall behave as you depict me!" Philip replied: "I am a stranger and a pilgrim on earth, like all priests, and I am ready to suffer for the truth. If I remained silent, where would be my faith?"[136]

Soon Philip was assaulted by the Tsar's men while saying Mass at Uspensky Cathedral, tearing his vestments from his back. He was tried, convicted on false evidence, and imprisoned in chains. After the chains fell off his body and a half-starved bear put into his cell was found sleeping quietly in a corner, Ivan was sufficiently impressed to spare his life, but he remained a prisoner until he died. And Ivan still would not change his ways, for God or man.[137]

Poland was full of refugees from Ivan's terror, and King Stephen Bathory was a highly competent warrior and despised the Tsar. During the summer of 1580 he secured most of Livonia and invaded Russia itself, taking the town of Velikie Luki. This made Ivan willing to discuss peace. Pope Gregory XIII decided to intervene as a mediator, hoping (incredible as it sounds, but very little about Ivan was known in Rome at this time) to win the Tsar to the Catholic Church in the process. Ivan had opened the door by letters to the Pope, Emperor Rudolf II, and the Doge of Venice that year asking them to help him against Stephen. There was even a possibility of restoring good relations with John III of Sweden by a just peace, since Sweden also had claims to Livonia and Swedish soldiers were fighting there. So the Pope sent the much-travelled Antonio Possevino as legate and peacemaker, with instructions to enter Russia and make a personal approach to Ivan the Terrible.[138]

On August 12, 1581 Possevino presented his credentials to Ivan in person, with a letter from the Pope urging peace with Poland to make possible an alliance against the Turks, and a copy of the decrees of the Council of Florence, which had attempted to reunite the Eastern Orthodox churches with the Catholic Church in the mid-fifteenth century.[139] During the next six weeks Possevino had six meetings with the Tsar. Most of them were very short; Ivan refused to discuss religious reunion until peace was made with Poland, and refused to consider peace with Sweden. He was willing to consider peace with Poland, however, as was King Stephen when he failed to take the Russian border city of Pskov after a

---

[135] Payne and Romanoff, *Ivan the Terrible*, pp. 254-255.

[136] *Ibid.*, p. 255.

[137] *Ibid.*, pp. 258-261.

[138] *Ibid.*, pp. 382-383; Von Pastor, *History of the Popes*, XX, 435-437; Vernadsky, *Tsardom of Moscow*, I, 159-161; Garsten, *Counter-Reformation in Scandinavia*, pp. 243-244.

[139] See Volume Three, Chapter 13 of this history for the Council of Florence.

long siege extending through most of the winter of 1581-82. In November 1581 Ivan, furious at a petition calling for his son and namesake to lead the Russian troops into battle against the Poles, brought the crook of his heavy iron staff down on the young man's head with lethal force. Rare indeed is the criminal, however depraved, who kills his own child; this ghastly murder seems to have brought Ivan at last to the beginnings of repentance. During the two and a half years of life and reign that remained to him, he tried to make amends to the families of his victims, but there were so many of them that it was impossible for him to compile even a nearly complete list. The memory of Ivan and his terror remained in Russia for centuries. After him no one questioned the total autocracy of the Tsar nor, for seventy years, the totalitarian rule of the Communists in the twentieth century.[140]

In January 1582 Possevino made the Peace of Jam-Zapolski between Russia and Poland. Poland got most of Livonia; Velikie Luki was returned to Russia but Poland kept Polotsk; Sweden was not included. With peace made, Possevino returned to Moscow in February, hoping that the Tsar would now be willing to discuss religious reunion. Ivan called the Pope a wolf, to which Possevino replied that it was strange for Ivan to have sought the mediation of a wolf. Unfamiliar with this kind of repartee, Ivan seized the iron-tipped staff with which he had killed his son; but Possevino sat calmly, and later Ivan asked his pardon, while refusing his requested permission to build a Catholic church in Russia. By now Possevino had a much better idea of the manner of man he was dealing with, and quietly left Russia in March. In 1583 Russia also made peace with Sweden, recognizing its control of the whole Estonian coast of the Gulf of Finland, up to the Neva River where St. Petersburg now stands. In March 1584 Ivan the Terrible died unmourned, to be succeeded by his retarded son Fyodor.[141]

In 1584, as the pontificate of Gregory XIII drew toward its end—he was now 82—the question of the French succession loomed large. The death of the Duke d'Alençon in June and the childlessness of King Henry III of France meant the end of the Valois dynasty. The prince most closely related to Henry III was none other than Henry of Navarre, a Calvinist and Jeanne d'Albret's son. The prospect of a heretic king was anathema to many Catholics in France, especially in Paris. With King Henry III's incompetence now well established, Duke Henry of Guise assumed the leadership of the Catholic cause, vowing that Henry of Navarre should never be king and establishing a Holy League with members all over France to try to ensure that this would never happen. A fourth Henry, the Cardinal of Bourbon, was proclaimed successor to Henry III by the Holy League and recognized as such by Spain in January 1585. By April, French Catholics and Calvinists had assembled their forces and launched yet another religious war.

---

[140] Von Pastor, *History of the Popes*, XX, 439-441; Vernadsky, *Tsardom of Moscow*, I, 163-165; Payne & Romanoff, *Ivan the Terrible*, pp. 386-392, 394-395.

[141] Von Pastor, *History of the Popes*, XX, 441-444; Vernadsky, *Tsardom of Moscow* I, 165-166; Payne & Romanoff, *Ivan the Terrible*, pp. 401-405; Roberts, *Early Vasas*, pp. 264-265; Garsten, *Counter-Reformation in Scandinavia*, p. 248.

In that same month the aged Pope Gregory XIII died quietly, in striking contrast to his stormy and often bloody pontificate.[142]

He is not an easy Pope to assess. He was not an exceptionally holy man like his predecessor; no one has ever seriously proposed his canonization. His judgment of men and their enterprises was poor. He showed more zeal than reflection. He was devoted to the Catholic reformation, and forwarded it by every means in his power. He reformed the calendar so well that it will last as long as the Christian era. His patronage of Jesuit education was vital to the future of the Church. But too often he lost sight of the truth that he was Pope of *all men*, not just Catholics, whether they recognized him or not, even when they reviled and cursed him. He was the Holy Father of the women and children who died screaming in the streets of Paris during the St. Bartholomew's Day massacre. He was the Holy Father even of Queen Elizabeth and of William Cecil. They had to be fought; they could be, and should be overthrown, but not by the assassin's bullet or poisoned dagger. The Pope may not have known of the plans to assassinate Queen Elizabeth, but his Cardinal Secretary did, and Jesuits devoted to him did. If he did not know, he should have known. This Pope came perilously close to believing that the end justifies the means. He never taught that, for the Holy Spirit Who guards the infallibility of the Vicars of Christ neither slumbers nor sleeps. But sometimes he practiced it.

As for the struggle itself, the great war between Protestant and Catholic had not yet reached its climax. During the next five years the climax came. The religious fate of two great Christian countries—England and France—would be decided in battle, on the sea for England and at the walls of Paris for France.

---

[142] Von Pastor, *History of the Popes*, XIX, 542-544, XX, 635-636; Martin, *Henry III and the Jesuit Politicians*, pp. 126, 134; Jensen, *Diplomacy and Dogmatism*, pp. 66-67.

8
Decision By Battle
1585-1598
Popes Sixtus V (1585-1590), Urban VII (1590), Gregory XIV (1590-1591), Innocent IX (1591), Clement VIII (1592-1605)

"'As the hart panteth after the fountains of water, so my soul panteth after Thee, O God. My soul hath thirsted after the strong living God; when shall I come and appear before the face of God?'"—psalm repeatedly recited by King Philip II of Spain on his deathbed, September 13, 1598[1]

"Serve God by serving of the Queen, for all other service is indeed bondage to the Devil."—from the last letter of William Cecil, Lord Burghley, to his son Robert, July 10, 1598[2]

"Rue not my death, rejoice at my repose
"It was no death to me but to my woe;
"The bud was opened to let out the rose,
"The chain was loosed to let the captive go."—ode by St. Robert Southwell, S.J., on the execution of Mary Queen of Scots, February 18, 1587[3]

"The martyr began in this order. First, in the hearing of them all, she prayed for the Catholic Church, then for the Pope's Holiness, the Cardinals, and other Fathers that have charge of souls, then for all Christian princes. At which words the tormentors interrupted her, and willed her not to put Her Majesty among that company; yet the martyr proceeded in this order, 'and especially for Elizabeth, Queen of England, that God turn her to the Catholic faith, and that after this mortal life she may receive the blessed joys of heaven. For I wish as much good to Her Majesty's soul as to mine own."—St. Margaret Clitherow just before she was pressed to death under 800 pounds of weight upon a sharp stone, Good Friday, April 4, 1586[4]

Pope Gregory XIII breathed his last on April 10, 1585, at the age of eighty-four.[5] The Church's ordeal by battle was at hand; in view of all the circumstances of the time, there was no way to avoid it without destroying the

---

[1] William Thomas Walsh, *Philip II* (New York, 1937), p. 725.

[2] Conyers Read, *Lord Burghley and Queen Elizabeth* (New York, 1960), p. 545.

[3] Antonia Fraser, *Mary Queen of Scots* (New York, 1969), quoted on p. 523.

[4] Rev. John Mush, "A True Report on the Life and Martyrdom of Mrs. Margaret Clitherow," quoted in Mary Claridge, *Margaret Clitherow* (New York, 1966), p. 174.

[5] Ludwig von Pastor, *History of the Popes* (St. Louis, 1952) XX, 636.

confidence in the Church of many of those most fervent in the Catholic Faith. The wars were just, and generally fought by just means. Catholic victory would have changed the whole course of history.

The times called for a fighting Pope, and a fighting Pope was chosen by the conclave and anointed by the Holy Spirit. His given name was Felice Peretti and he took the papal name of Sixtus V.

He had no political or family influence in his favor; he was the fourth son of a poor farmer from the rocky, thin-soiled March of Ancona. As a boy he had dug in the garden, tended pigs, and cut logs in the woods. A nearby Franciscan priest paid for his education. He became a Franciscan and eventually a doctor of theology; in 1552 he gave Lenten discourses in the churches of Rome and attracted the eye of then Cardinal Ghislieri, the future Pope St. Pius V, who appointed him cardinal in 1570 at the age of only 48. Now he was 63, still full of volcanic energy and passion for the cause of the Holy Roman Catholic Church. He carefully observed all the Church's festivals, carrying the Blessed Sacrament bareheaded in the annual Corpus Christi procession, frequently making the pilgrimage to the Seven Churches of Rome, and going on retreat throughout every Lent. He combined the profound piety of the Italian peasant with the simplicity and poverty St. Francis had taught. He was stocky, of middle height, not handsome, with a large head, a thick beard, prominent cheekbones, a large nose, a furrowed forehead, and thick eyebrows over piercing eyes. His anger could be terrifying. He was born to command. The parties of the Farnese of Parma and the Medici of Florence wilted before his relentless advance in the conclave, and on April 24 he was elected Pope, taking the name Sixtus because it had been held by an earlier Franciscan Pope.[6]

On the very next day after his election the new Pope showed his decisive, hard-hitting character. Crime had gone out of control in the papal states in Gregory XIII's enfeebled last years. Brigands and highwaymen infested the countryside. Pope Sixtus V told his cardinals entrusted with keeping public order, his military commanders and his chief barons that he would hold them personally responsible for suppressing crime and administering justice. If they failed, he would execute the generals and the barons and lock up the cardinals in the prison cells of Rome's impregnable fortress, the Castel Sant'Angelo.[7]

Ten days later he led a procession through the streets of Rome to take formal possession of the Church of St. John Lateran, but did not hold the customary banquet on this occasion, "on account of the miserable state of the population." At his first consistory (meeting with his cardinals) he stressed the restoration of law and order and the provision of sufficient food for the people as his immediate priorities. In July he assigned two experienced bishops to make a formal visitation of every parish and college in Rome, and before the end of the year renewed the requirement of Pope St. Pius V that all bishops make regular visits to Rome and the Pope, every three years for those relatively nearby, at

---

[6] *Ibid.*, XXI, 8-9, 15-30, 39-47, 54-57.
[7] *Ibid.*, XXI, 72.

longer intervals for those further away. He began almost at once moving the old pagan obelisk which had stood at the center of the Circus Maximus, where St. Peter and so many other Christians had been martyred by the Emperor Nero, to the magnificent courtyard of the new St. Peter's, now nearing completion. In January 1586 he issued a vigorous condemnation of astrology, the most influential and widely believed superstition of that age.[8]

But most revealing of all were the words of the new Pope to the new Spanish ambassador to Rome, that during his pontificate he hoped to carry out some "outstanding enterprise" for the Church, such as the conquest of Muslim Algiers, or a Catholic invasion of England.[9]

King Philip II of Spain was now 58 years old. He had reigned over Spain, the Low Countries, Sicily, Sardinia, Naples, Milan, and the Indies for thirty years, and over Portugal, its island and Indian territories, and Brazil for five years. Since the death of his uncle Ferdinand in 1564 he had acted in effect as Holy Roman Emperor, since neither of the two Emperors since Ferdinand I had really been fit and competent to rule.[10] Periodically crippled by gout, worn by his incessant labors, having outlived no less than four wives and now alone except for his devoted daughters (his sons were all small children and only one was to survive him), Philip's once golden hair had gone completely white, but his mind was as keen and his will as firm as ever, or more so.[11] When he sent his new ambassador, Olivares, to Rome (to whom Sixtus V had spoken of his desire to perform an "outstanding enterprise" for the Church), Philip instructed him to make clear to the new Pope that Spain was the greatest power in the world, not only because of the extent of its dominions but also because of its complete internal peace, and that Philip was ready "to place the whole power of Spain at the disposal of the Pope for the defense of the Church and the Holy See." Spanish rule had brought peace and tranquillity to all the parts of Italy under it, and should therefore be continued. But Philip wanted no more territory, though he was deeply concerned with the situation in France where by the normal laws of French royal succession the crown would pass to a Calvinist, Henry of Navarre, upon the death of present King Henry III.[12]

During 1585 Philip moved at last into his permanent apartments at the monastery-palace at El Escorial on the lower slopes of the mighty Guadarrama

---

[8] *Ibid.*, XXI, 75 (for quote), 90, 127, 195; XXII, 248-251.

[9] Colin Martin and Geoffrey Parker, *The Spanish Armada* (New York, 1988), p. 110. Neither enterprise would have been an act of aggression. Raiding ships from Algiers were constantly preying on Christian shipping, routinely sending every man they caught aboard into slavery. For the acts of aggression by England against Spain which fully justified Spain in going to war, by any reasonable standard of international law, see below, this chapter.

[10] Ferdinand's son Maximilian II was crippled by a bad heart which brought him to an early death; Maximilian's son Rudolf II was an eccentric recluse, plagued by depression and occasionally slipping into actual insanity.

[11] Henry Kamen, *Philip of Spain* (New Haven CT, 1997), pp. 269-270.

[12] Von Pastor, *History of the Popes*, XXI, 262-263 (quote on 262).

Mountains rising high above Madrid, which he had been building for more than twenty years. Two years later the basilica there was completed, and the bodies of the past kings of Spain, Castile and Aragon moved to a new royal mortuary under its high altar.[13] Its immense stone mass thrusting out from the slope and looking over the plain of Madrid, with the Real Presence of Christ at its heart and the prayers of its Augustinian monks storming Heaven—this was the spiritual fortress which Philip saw as his base for the restoration of Christendom.[14]

Throughout his reign Philip II had been known in Spain as "the prudent king." His caution was proverbial. He never hurried, considering and evaluating a project from every angle before he undertook it. But he could feel the crisis approaching, the time for decision by battle. His weakening body might not sustain him for many more years (though in fact he lived no less than thirteen more); he must strike at the country which had now become the last resort and best help of the enemies of Christendom. He knew that he had both right and reason to do so. On October 24, 1585 he wrote to Pope Sixtus V that he was definitely committed to the invasion of England.[15]

Cardinal Este from Ferrara, an ancient foe of Spain, spoke to the Pope at once. While he granted that the invasion of England was probably justified, he did not want Philip to lead it, because "there is no possible doubt that he is aiming at the domination over the whole of Christendom." The Pope's dark eyes took on a far-away look. "It would be a long and wearisome journey to that point," he said, and then, we are told, he "remained thoughtful and said no more."[16]

Argument about Philip II's motivations has been going on ever since. For Protestants he has always been a fanatical Catholic demon. They at least do him the honor of taking him at his word when he said the preservation of the Church, the restoration of Catholic Christendom, and aid to oppressed Catholics was his primary concern and motivation, overriding all others. They assuredly believe he meant it when he made a formal vow of obedience to Pope Sixtus V in March 1586.[17] For Spanish Catholics, at least until very recently, he has always been, like his father Emperor Charles V, above all the champion of their faith. But for Catholics elsewhere, especially in the English-speaking countries where there has been relentless, often vicious propaganda against him ever since the Armada,[18] there is a general tendency not to take him at face value, not to see him as the

---

[13] Kamen, *Philip of Spain*, pp. 187, 266-267; William T. Walsh, *Philip II* (New York, 1937), p. 625.

[14] I spent many inspiring hours at El Escorial, looking from the magnificent building across the plain, or up at the mountains and the bright blue sky, and listening to the bells, during five summers spent there with an American Catholic program in the 1970's.

[15] Martin and Parker, *Spanish Armada*, p. 111.

[16] Von Pastor, *History of the Popes*, XXI, 272.

[17] *Ibid.*, XXI, 265.

[18] The recent fine biography of Philip by Henry Kamen is a welcome exception to this. Kamen is not a Catholic, but he is an honest man. His is the first study of Philip by a non-Catholic written in English in this century to be even reasonably fair to him.

dedicated Catholic that he was—as the monastery-palace at El Escorial above all showed him to be.

It is true that he interfered more in the Church than a lay sovereign should, even the sovereign of the most powerful Catholic country in the world. He frequently insisted on maintaining ancient privileges or practices in episcopal appointments and the use of Church funds which did not fit the Church as reformed by the Council of Trent, though for the most part no Catholic ruler supported the Tridentine reforms more ardently than he. Philip had a very great, probably excessive respect for precedent and tradition, and a correspondingly insufficient respect for the absolute sovereignty of the Pope in his governance of the Church. His arrogant ambassador to Rome Olivares would sometimes actually get into shouting matches with the tempestuous Pope, making relations worse. But Sixtus V, in his calmer moments, saw the undeniable truth: that Philip II of Spain, great-grandson of Queen Isabel the Catholic, was totally committed to the Church and the Faith, willing to die for them, and would champion them everywhere that he possibly could, until his last hour on earth. Because of his material power, he could stand alone against the whole of Protestant Europe; and without his unfailing willingness to do just that, Christendom would probably have been destroyed in the sixteenth century instead of not until the twentieth. Despite their public arguments, on all fundamental matters Pope Sixtus V supported Philip II as he bore the sword for Christendom on both land and sea. The two men were well matched.

As we approach the tremendous drama of the Spanish Armada, the most important naval battle fought in the whole history of Christendom, it is essential to keep in mind that, despite the indelible image of the smaller English warships heroically resisting and overcoming the big Spanish galleons, and despite the fact that the purpose of those galleons was to convoy an army to take over at least a substantial part of England, the aggressors in this war were not the Spanish, but the English. The Low Countries belonged to Spain; Philip's father had been born and baptized there. English support for the Dutch rebels against Philip II, even if only financial, was already an act of war—though one which might be prudently overlooked. To send English troops in substantial numbers to the Low Countries was an even more obvious act of war, which no one could overlook. Attacking Spanish ports both in Spain and in her American colonies was beyond question an act of war, which no self-respecting government could ever be expected to tolerate. For a captain to be honored by the Queen of England and her government for capturing numerous Spanish ships on the high seas was also an act of war. And all these acts of war had been committed in or shortly before the year 1585, the year when Philip II told Pope Sixtus V that he was now committed to the invasion of England, to put a stop to them, as well as to end the persecution of English Catholics.

The English provocation of war with Spain begins with that swashbuckling, ardently Protestant adventurer Francis Drake, the greatest seaman of his age, fittingly the successor of Magellan (an even greater seaman two generations before) in being the next after him to sail around the world. "Drake he was a

Devon man," as Henry Newbolt says in his stirring poem "Drake's Drum," son of the chaplain of the royal dockyard of Chatham. His home town was Plymouth, the best port in the west of England, from which the *Mayflower* set out to settle New England forty years later, and where his statue stands today looking out over the harbor. Drake enters history as a junior officer on John Hawkins' expedition of slave trading and piracy to the Caribbean in 1568. In 1572 Drake attacked Panama and seized a mule-train of Spanish silver, later another. It was simple robbery, with no trace of legal justification. In December 1577 he left from Plymouth on his voyage around the world. He got through the Straits of Magellan in just 16 days, less than half the time Magellan had required. Loose in the Pacific Ocean, where the Spanish along the coasts of Peru, Panama and western Mexico had never faced any maritime threat, Drake raided and plundered at will, taking from one ship alone 25 tons of silver bars, 13 chests of silver coin, and 80 pounds of gold. He brought it all back to England and turned much of it over to Queen Elizabeth, who knighted him on the deck of his ship, the *Golden Hind*, in April 1581, making her a receiver of stolen goods on a grand scale.[19]

On July 11, 1585 Queen Elizabeth signed a commission for Drake to command an English fleet to go to the West Indies for the specific purpose of intercepting the annual Spanish treasure fleet. Drake's ships and men were paid for by the government of England; his vice-commander was the third of the triad of great Elizabethan "sea-dogs," Martin Frobisher (the others being Drake himself and Hawkins). Drake and Frobisher sailed September 24 and raided Vigo and Bayona in northern Spain on the way October 17, sacking their churches in particular. Surely it was no coincidence that just one week later Philip II wrote to Pope Sixtus V committing himself to the "enterprise of England." From there Drake went on to ravage the Canary Islands, the Cape Verde Islands, and Santo Domingo, the first Spanish colony in the New World. But when he informed the blacks of Hispaniola, the island where Santo Domingo was located, that they would no longer be allowed to practice the Catholic religion, they drove him out. He returned again to England with much loot.[20]

Meanwhile the steady advance of Parma in the Low Countries had convinced Queen Elizabeth that the Spanish were probably going to defeat the rebels there if she did not intervene directly. On March 22, 1585 she told two Dutch envoys that she would take the Netherlands under her military protection if they would turn over several of their port towns for security. In May she rejected an offer from the Dutch to accept sovereignty over them, but continued to negotiate for a military alliance and the sending of English troops to help raise Parma's siege of Antwerp. On August 12 a treaty was made to this effect, with

---

[19] Samuel Eliot Morison, *The European Discovery of America; the Southern Voyages* (New York, 1974), pp. 634-638, 645, 650-657, 684; John Cummins, *Francis Drake; the Lives of a Hero* (New York, 1997), pp. 90-104.

[20] Conyers Read, *Mr. Secretary Walsingham and the Policy of Queen Elizabeth* (Cambridge, England, 1925), III, 102; Cummins, *Drake,* pp. 135-137, 141, 146-152; Kamen, *Philip of Spain,* pp. 263-264; Martin and Parker, *Spanish Armada,* p. 111; von Pastor, *History of the Popes,* XXII, 45.

4,000 English infantry commanded by Sir John Norris to go to Antwerp with all their expenses paid by the English government for three months. Antwerp fell on the 17th, long before the four thousand English could get there, but Elizabeth kept them in the Netherlands and reinforced them. By the end of August they numbered 6,350 foot and 1,000 horse, commanded by her favorite the Duke of Leicester.[21]

The raiding and looting by Drake and its acceptance, encouragement, and eventual financing by Queen Elizabeth, and her sending of more than 7,000 English infantry and cavalry to fight against Spain in the Netherlands had taken place before Philip II decided on the invasion of England. He probably made the decision only after Drake attacked Spain itself on October 17, 1585. The Armada was a counterattack, as justified as the Allied D-day armada counterattacking Hitler's "Fortress Europe" on June 6, 1944.

Yet the Armada in all its immensity was not sent simply or even primarily for these reasons. It was sent because of Philip II's Catholic commitment and his vivid awareness of what his fellow Catholics were suffering in England. For, though he met with the Prince of Parma and the great Spanish Admiral Santa Cruz at the very end of 1585 to develop the first concrete plans for what the Armada and Parma's troops would do to England,[22] he was slow to implement the plans, which made little progress except on paper during the whole of 1586. All that was changed by the execution of Mary Queen of Scots in February 1587. The heroic story of her last hours was told and retold all over Europe, and made abundantly clear what was ultimately at stake in Philip's "enterprise of England." But in the year before, the quiet year 1586, a martyrdom occurred in England which, more than any of the other martyrdoms under Queen Elizabeth, demonstrated just what the Armada would sail to stop.

The martyr was a woman of York, St. Margaret Clitherow. York had been a Catholic stronghold ever since King Henry VIII broke with the Pope. From York and its neighboring shires had come the Pilgrimage of Grace in 1536 and the great northern rising of 1579. The premier nobleman of York, Bd. Thomas Percy, Earl of Northumberland, had died on a traitor's scaffold in 1572, giving public testimony to his faith, speaking of "that church which, throughout the whole Christian world, is knit and bound together. . . . In this same faith I am about to end this unhappy life. But as for this new English church, I do not acknowledge it." A Protestant minister broke in: "You are dying an obstinate papist; a member, not of the Catholic, but of the Roman church."[23] The martyr had replied:

---

[21] Conyers Read, *Lord Burghley and Queen Elizabeth* (New York, 1960), pp. 311, 323; Read, *Walsingham*, III, 109-110; Jonathan Israel, *The Dutch Republic; its Rise, Greatness and Fall 1477-1806* (Oxford, 1995), p. 219. The Anglo-Dutch military alliance was sealed by the Treaty of Nonsuch.

[22] Martin and Parker, *Spanish Armada*, pp. 111-112.

[23] Claridge, *Margaret Clitherow*, pp. 48-49.

That which you call the Roman Church *is* the Catholic Church, which has been founded on the teaching of the Apostles, Jesus Christ Himself being its cornerstone, strengthened by the blood of martyrs, honored by the recognition of the holy Fathers; and it continues always the same, being the Church against which, as Christ our Savior said, the gates of Hell shall not prevail. . . . If I had a thousand lives I would give them up for the Catholic faith."[24]

Margaret Clitherow, a young wife and mother just sixteen years old, who had recently given birth to her first child, was probably present, for the execution took place only a hundred yards from her home in York. She had been brought up a Protestant, and her husband John was a Protestant. He called her "the best wife in all England," and indeed she seemed to be and to have everything good: devotion to her husband and children, overflowing kindness and consideration which drew everyone to her, remarkable beauty of face and form, lively conversation and a ready wit, and comfortable financial circumstances. She was noted for her mirth; almost everyone who wrote of her later recalled how "merry" she was. She did not seem the type of which the world thinks martyrs are made.[25]

Though we have no proof that Percy's martyrdom brought her to the Church, it seems likely since it happened so close to her, and she began to take secret instructions in the Catholic faith only a few weeks afterward. (Percy was martyred November 29, 1572, and Margaret became a Catholic before the end of 1573.) She went to work immediately spreading the Catholic Faith in York city, particularly among the wives of its tradesmen whom she knew (her husband was a butcher). By 1576 she appeared on a list of "recusants" (persons refusing to attend Anglican services) given to the governor of the north, the Puritan Earl of Huntingdon, who reported to Cecil in September of that year that "the declination in matters of religion is very great, and the obstinacy of many doth shrewdly increase. . . . those that are in these matters most peevish, so far as I yet see, are in this town [York] women." The next year she was sent to prison, released the following year, sent back again in 1580 until released for childbirth in 1581, and imprisoned for a third time in 1583 and 1584. In each of her prisons she participated actively in a close community of Catholics giving witness to their faith. Wherever she went, she inspired and emboldened Catholics and converted Protestants. In 1583 she saw her confessor, Father William Hart, martyred.[26]

By 1585 she was the best-known lay apostle in York, who arranged for the priests who came underground to the city to be maintained and guarded, and to have rooms to say Mass. In that year Parliament passed new legislation making sheltering priests a felony punishable by death. Margaret asked her new confessor (and later biographer), Father John Mush, if she should obey such laws, or ask her husband's consent before defying them; Mush told her she should not

---

[24] *Ibid.*, p. 49. Emphasis added and last sentence put in direct address.

[25] *Ibid.*, pp. 44-48 (quote on 45).

[26] *Ibid.*, pp. 56-70 (quote on 67), 79-83.

obey them, and need not tell her husband because it would endanger him. She was overjoyed, saying: "I thank you, Father. By God's grace, all priests shall be more welcome to me than ever they were, and I will do what I can to set forward God's Catholic service." In Father Mush's words: "All her actions were tempered with all inward tranquillity and comfort, with discreet and honest mirth, with mild and smiling countenance."[27]

Margaret Clitherow had harmed no one. She had been involved in no assassination or invasion plots; she had never left England nor communicated with any foreigners; she was universally beloved by the people who knew her. She had brought light into many lives. She had done nothing but good. Father Mush wrote later that he believed she would have become a saint even without martyrdom. But for having a Catholic teacher for her own children, and maintaining a room for sheltering priests where vestments were kept, she was indicted under the new law on March 12, 1586. Informed of her indictment, she laughed and said to the messenger: "'I would I had some good thing to give you for these good news. Hold, take this fig, for I have nothing better.'" She totally denied the jurisdiction of the court over what she had done, and refused to plead either guilty or not guilty. It places quite a new light on the alleged glories of the English common law to find that in 1586 it prescribed—and still enforced—a penalty of pressing to death by heavy weights for anyone, man or woman, who refused to plead. That penalty was imposed upon St. Margaret Clitherow. On Good Friday by the calendar of Pope Gregory XIII she delivered up her bright spirit with the words quoted at the head of this chapter.[28]

To end atrocities like this was why the Spanish Armada sailed.

By 1585 Mary, Queen of Scots, had been a prisoner of Queen Elizabeth for seventeen years, more than a third of her lifetime. William Cecil had her in his grip and would never let her go. Because Elizabeth had never married, Mary was her next of kin; because Mary was as staunch a Catholic as St. Margaret Clitherow, her accession to the throne of England would indubitably restore England to the Catholic Faith as Mary Tudor's accession had done, and bring down the whole Protestant establishment so much enriched by the land taken from the monasteries. Because she was a queen in an age with great respect for monarchy and those of royal blood, she was not kept in the very closest confinement, being allowed a number of privileges that less distinguished prisoners lacked. Though she was under constant watch and tight control, Cecil was haunted by the possibility of her escape. Like John Knox who had so often avowed it from the pulpits of Edinburgh, he wanted her dead. Elizabeth held out against her execution. It was not well for kings or queens to shed the blood of royalty. Their own blood might come next.

But so long as Mary lived, her very existence was a beacon to every persecuted Catholic in England and Scotland. To all the normal feelings of love

---

[27] *Ibid.*, pp. 106-128 (first quote 122, second quote 120-121); von Pastor, *History of the Popes*, XIX, 454-455.

[28] Claridge, *Margaret Clitherow*, pp. 131-153 (quote on 136), 173-176.

and loyalty Catholics felt for an imprisoned queen and royal heir who would never give up her Catholic faith, were added the romantic appeal of a woman of storied beauty,[29] separated from her son during his first year and never seeing him again, locked away in a castle where the public was almost never allowed to see her, held by jailers who cared nothing for her but her political significance. And then there was the powerful Catholic Guise family of France—her family. Duke Henry of Guise had the ability himself to launch an expedition against England-not big enough to take over the country, but big enough to reach Mary's castle-prison and liberate her. Plans and plots to help or free her were constantly being hatched and aborted. But it only took one to succeed, to transform the whole situation.

One who conspicuously made no effort to help her was her son James, now "reigning" in Scotland at the age of 19, surrounded by designing noblemen, in peril of his life since before he was born (Mary always believed that the murder of Riccio in her chambers[30] was done in the hope of causing a miscarriage), whose whole life story was wrapped around self-preservation, putting a premium on cowardice and lack of charity, since James never found a strong faith. As late as the winter of 1585 Mary, from prison, was still trying to find a way to work with her son in an association; in March of that year the Council of Scotland coldly declared, with reference to their king, that "the association desired by his mother should neither be granted nor spoken of hereafter." James, who could not remember his mother personally, made no protest whatever. Mary raged, then wept inconsolably when this news was brought to her. In her desperate anger she vowed to give the crown of Scotland to the greatest enemy he had, rather than allow him to enjoy it as the fruit of his rejection of his mother. In May 1586 she bequeathed the crown of Scotland and her succession to the crown of England to King Philip II of Spain, if upon her death her son James still remained a Protestant.[31]

Philip II had never met Mary Queen of Scots, but she had been on his mind ever since the death of his second wife Mary Tudor, three years into his reign. The Scottish queen was the rightful queen of England as well, since Queen Elizabeth, daughter of Anne Boleyn, was illegitimate in the eyes of Catholics. But Philip, dedicated Catholic though he was, let the demands of power politics cloud his moral vision and refused to endorse Mary Queen of Scots' claim. He

---

[29] By 1585 Mary had lost most of that beauty in her 17 years' confinement. In the words of Antonia Fraser: "Mary is now very far from being the laughing Goujon-like belle of the French court; this is a woman with a drawn face, a beaky prominent nose almost Roman in its shape but cut finely at the end, with a small rather pinched mouth; the smallness of the whole face is in contrast to the fullness of the body, which is now matronly in its proportions." (*Mary Queen of Scots*, p. 450)

[30] See Chapter Six, above.

[31] Fraser, *Mary Queen of Scots*, pp. 462, 490; Walsh, *Philip II*, p. 642; Martin and Parker, *Spanish Armada*, p. 123; De Lamar Jensen, *Diplomacy and Dogmatism; Bernardino de Mendoza and the French Catholic League* (Cambridge MA, 1964), pp. 83-84.

had known the young Princess Elizabeth when he was consort to the Queen of England, her half-sister. He believed (or persuaded himself) that she had Catholic inclinations and preferences. (No one, not even the supremely shrewd Cecil, not even her long-time personal favorite the Duke of Leicester, could ever read Elizabeth's inclinations and preferences, which seemed as changeable as moonbeams—though a hard core of self-interest always ran through them. All we can say in matters of religion is that she definitely preferred a more elaborate ritual and the use of vestments by the clergy, in contradistinction to the Puritans.) Philip II did not think Elizabeth would become a hardened enemy to the Faith and to himself. He was wrong; he knew it now. The confinement of Mary Queen of Scots for 17 years had been the price of his mistake. With all the resources of the world's greatest power at his command, during all that time he could most probably have arranged her escape. He had been willing to let Don Juan of Austria try it before he died, but had not encouraged it.

Philip II was far too realistic to believe that many would accept Mary's authority to bequeath her crown; nor did he want any more crowns, he had all he could do to maintain those he had and still seek to use them to aid his fellow Catholics all over Europe. But her offer touched him, and probably roused the reproaches of his conscience for his earlier neglect of her. On July 18, 1586 he wrote to his ambassador to France, Bernardino Mendoza, who had received Mary's letter offering to bequeath him her royal rights and forwarded it to him:

> I was happy to receive the copy of the letter written to you by the Queen of Scotland, along with your own of June 26. She has certainly risen a great deal in my estimation as a result of what she says there, and has increased the devotion which I have always felt for her interests—not so much because of what she says in my favor (though I am very grateful for that too), but because she subordinates her love for her son, which might be expected to lead her astray, for the service of Our Lord, the common good of Christendom, and that of England. You may write and tell her all this from me and also assure her that if she perseveres in the path she has rightly chosen, I hope that God will bless her by granting her rightful possessions. You will add that I shall be very pleased to undertake the protection of her person and interests, as she requests.[32]

The importance of this letter of Philip II has not been sufficiently appreciated. By it he had put Mary Queen of Scots under his personal protection. Just seven months later the English government struck off her head. Philip would have found this totally intolerable; and he responded with an attack by the greatest fleet ever assembled up to that time in the history of the world.

Already the nets were closing tighter around Mary Queen of Scots. Cecil's old intelligence service, already the finest in Europe when he was still Secretary of State, had been improved even more by his successor Francis Walsingham, with whom Cecil worked very closely. In October 1585, if not earlier, Walsingham recruited to his corps of spies one Gilbert Gifford, a professed

---

[32] Jensen, *Diplomacy and Dogmatism*, pp. 84-85.

Catholic who had been studying at the seminary in Reims headed by Dr. (soon to be Cardinal) William Allen. Carrying a letter of recommendation to Mary from her agent in Paris, Thomas Morgan, Gifford went to London and saw Walsingham, who put him in touch with an expert forger and decipherer named Thomas Phelips, and worked out a plan whereby Gifford would act as a courier for correspondence between the French embassy in London and Mary at Chartley castle. Gifford would pick up the letters for Mary at the French embassy and the letters from her to the French embassy. To avoid suspiciously frequent appearances by Gifford at Chartley, Phelips suborned a local brewer who provided beer for those living at Chartley. Incoming and outgoing letters would be sent in a watertight bag which could be passed through the bunghole of a beer barrel. They would then be delivered to someone in Mary's household and sent out likewise. All letters would be intercepted, steamed open, read (if necessary after decipherment by Phelips), copied, and then sent on to their destination. The whole fantastic system was in place and working perfectly when Mary wrote her letter to Spanish ambassador Mendoza thanking his master for seeking to liberate her by his planned invasion of England. Phelips steamed it open, read it, and sent a copy on to Walsingham.[33]

Now enter Anthony Babington—young (25), rich, charming, romantic, and foolish, for whom liberating Mary was a chivalric imperative. Through his wealth and charm he had made favorable contacts, and managed to obtain a letter of recommendation from that same Thomas Morgan who had sent her Gilbert Gifford (Morgan seems to have been very free with his recommendations). Hearing, probably from Morgan, that Babington wanted to help her escape, Mary wrote to him herself, inviting him to communicate directly. A few days later he did, all letters continuing to be pulled through the bunghole of the beer barrel and read enroute. Babington's letter to Queen Mary of July 6, 1586 outlined a full plan: (1) an invasion from abroad, by whom not stated; (2) the invaders to be joined and supported by "a strong party at every place" of English Catholics; (3) the liberation of Mary by Babington and a hundred men; (4) "the dispatch of the usurping Competitor [Elizabeth]" by six assassins selected by Babington.[34]

It was pure lunacy (indeed, though the human capacity for folly is almost limitless, one must wonder if Babington were not a little mad). He had no invaders (Philip II's invasion might be coming, but no one including Philip knew when, and certainly not Babington). He had no strong party of English Catholics at any place, to say nothing of every place. He might have been able to liberate Mary with a hundred men, if he really had a hundred and they took her guards completely by surprise, but hardly if there had to be a national uprising first. By the time the invasion and uprising took place—if they did!—Mary would be

---

[33] Read, *Walsingham*, III, 1-14. The reader may wish to know what happened to the perfidious Gilbert Gifford. He was actually ordained a priest at Reims in March 1587, a month after Queen Mary's execution, the directors of the seminary not yet knowing of his betrayal; but soon afterwards he was arrested in a house or prostitution in Paris, imprisoned, and died in prison in 1590 (von Pastor, *History of the Popes*, XXII 9, 21n).

[34] Fraser, *Mary Queen of Scots*, pp. 484-487.

under maximum security if not already dead, and Elizabeth would be so protected that a mere six assassins could never get within miles of her. What can he possibly have been thinking of? The sole practical objective of such an undertaking should have been to get Mary out of her prison and off free to France. That a young and ardent local strike force might have accomplished— nothing more.

Walsingham and his team were not at all worried about Anthony Babington, nor did they have any cause to be. But in his letter they saw their chance to convict Mary at last of seeking the death of Elizabeth, who lived in fear of assassination, and for this might finally overcome her scruples about executing a fellow queen. "We await her very heart in the next [letter]," Phelips said; one can almost hear him smacking his lips. The beer barrel posting continued to work as designed; on July 17 Walsingham's men had Mary's reply to Babington, accepting his plan. There is a tone of desperation in her references in this letter to her desire for liberty that shows she had thrown prudence (never her strong point) to the winds; and it is important also to realize that she had just received another shattering blow to her maternal feelings by the news that on July 6 England and Scotland had signed the Treaty of Berwick in which her son in effect formally repudiated her. Mary's faithful secretary Nau advised her to make no reply to Babington; she rejected his advice.[35] Though her reply nowhere explicitly states that she wants Elizabeth killed, the following passage can hardly be interpreted any other way:

> The affairs being thus prepared and forces in readiness both within and without the realm, then shall it be time to set the six gentlemen to work, taking order, upon the accomplishing of their design, I may be suddenly transported out of this place.[36]

Phelips drew a gallows on the outside of this letter when he passed it on to Walsingham. Trying to bring the alleged assassins also into his net, Walsingham had a forged postscript added to the letter before sending it on to Babington, in which Mary was made to ask him for their names. But Walsingham needed nothing more. With regard to Mary, acquiescence in the assassination threat was more than enough to convict her; for centuries English law had prescribed the death penalty for "imagining the death of the king." Mary's actual moral guilt is by no means so clear; she was a captive, unjustly held, with not only the right but the duty to escape. If someone else offered to kill her jailer, she was not necessarily required to protest. But when the proposed victim was the sovereign, the law was and would be merciless. Mary Queen of Scots was doomed.[37]

Babington and his associates were executed at the end of September and the beginning of October; by Elizabeth's direction their deaths were "protracted to the extremity of pain," with the full ghastly ritual of hanging, drawing and

---

[35] *Ibid.*, pp. 487-491.
[36] Read, *Burghley*, p. 344.
[37] Fraser, *Mary Queen of Scots*, pp. 488-492.

quartering. Mary was sent from Chartley to Fotheringhay castle for better security, under close guard by the iron Puritan Amyas Paulet, who despised her. She was brought to trial October 24 by a commission presided over by her ancient enemy William Cecil ("here are many counsellors, but not one for me," she said sadly—and later, to Cecil: "Ah! You are indeed my adversary!"). At the end of the first day the judges "attacked her like furies, sometimes one by one, sometimes all together, all shouting that she was guilty." They convicted her unanimously of "compassing and imagining since June 1 matters tending to the death and destruction of the Queen of England" and sentenced her to death. Both Houses of Parliament voted unanimously for her execution, but Elizabeth still held back.[38]

On hearing of her sentence, Mary thanked Cecil's court "for the honor they did me in considering me to be such a necessary instrument for the re-establishing of religion in this island." Soon afterward she wrote to Pope Sixtus V (it no longer mattered whether Walsingham's men were pulling the letters through the bunghole to read them), pledging that she would testify to her Catholic faith by her death "for my sins and those of this unfortunate island" and asking the Pope to secure her rights to the crown of England to Philip II of Spain rather than to her heretic son.[39] At the same time she wrote to Duke Henry of Guise, her cousin and the leader of the French Catholics, that she now believed she was born to offer her blood for the Faith:

> Although no executioner has ever before dipped his hand in our blood, be not ashamed of it, my dear friend, for the condemnation of heretics and enemies of the Church (and who have no jurisdiction over me, a free Queen) is profitable before God for the children of His Church.[40]

On December 14 Queen Elizabeth confirmed and proclaimed the death sentence against Mary Queen of Scots, but still refused to sign her death warrant. Secretary Walsingham left court in disgust for the entire winter. But Cecil stayed, one of the supreme goals of his life being now so close to attainment. He persuaded Elizabeth at the end of December to authorize him to draw up the death warrant. He did, and she held it for six weeks. Finally she signed it on February 11, 1587 and gave it to Cecil, who, to make it legal, had to take it to the Lord Chancellor to affix the Great Seal of England to it. But she had not yet authorized its use. First she directed that she be told no more about the execution until it was done; then she said it might help if a loyal subject killed Mary for her rather than having her officially executed, and wrote her jailer Paulet asking him

---

[38] *Ibid.*, pp. 501, 508-519 (second quote on 510, third on 514, fourth on 518); Martin Haile, *An Elizabethan Cardinal, William Allen* (London, 1914), pp. 279-280 (first quote on 280); von Pastor, *History of the Popes*, XXII, 23; J. E. Neale, *Elizabeth I and Her Parliaments*, Volume II (London, 1957), pp. 113-114.

[39] Fraser, *Mary Queen of Scots*, pp. 519-521.

[40] *Ibid.*, p. 521.

to do it.[41]   Cold-hearted Puritan though he was, there were depths to which Amyas Paulet would not sink. He replied:

> My good livings and life are at Her Majesty's disposition and I am ready to so leave them at this next morrow if it shall so please her. . . . But God forbid that I should make so foul a shipwreck of my conscience or leave so great a blot to my poor posterity as to shed blood without law or warrant.[42]

Unabashed, Elizabeth condemned Paulet for excessive "daintiness" (surely "dainty" was a word never before applied to Mary's harsh and dour jailer) and now proposed that one Robert Wingfield smother her with a pillow.   Even Elizabeth's fervent admirers admit that this was the moral low point of her entire reign.[43]

That very day Cecil, with the full support of the Privy Council, sent the now signed and sealed death warrant to Paulet at Fotheringhay Castle, without telling the Queen he had done so.   It arrived two days later, on February 17, 1587, and Mary was told that night that she would die the next morning.   Paulet denied her a priest.   The very Protestant Lord Kent told her bluntly: "Your life would be the death of our religion, your death would be its life."   Her face lit up; this was the call to martyrdom!   She replied: "Oh, how happy these words make me; this at last is the truth!"[44]

All through the night she heard the hammering as her scaffold was erected and her guards tramped up and down before her door.   At dawn she prayed in her small oratory until the sheriff of Northampton called her into the great hall of Fotheringhay castle, her groom bearing a crucifix before her.   "All this world is but vanity and full of troubles and sorrows," she said.   "Carry this message from me and tell my friends that I died true to my religion, like a true Scottish woman and a true French woman."   She was dressed in black satin, but with red undergarments for her martyrdom, a crucifix and a prayer book in her hand, two rosaries hanging from her waist, and an Agnus Dei around her neck.   She kissed the crucifix, crossed herself, and said: "Even as thy arms, O Jesus, were spread here upon the cross, so receive me into Thy arms of mercy, and forgive me all my sins."   She lay down and placed her chin on the block.   At ten o'clock in the morning the executioner cut off her head.   The blow dislodged her auburn wig to reveal close-cropped snow-white hair.   So died Mary Stuart, Queen of Scots, who had lived 44 years and 18 of them in captivity.   She died better than she had lived, thereby fulfilling her motto during her captivity: "In my end is my beginning."   Everything she had worn to her execution and the block on which

---

[41] *Ibid.*, pp. 521, 528-529; Neale, *Elizabeth I and Her Parliaments*, II, 136-137, 244; Read, *Burghley*, pp. 363-367; Read, *Walsingham* III, 236.

[42] Read, *Burghley*, p. 367.

[43] *Ibid.*, pp. 367-368 (Read is generally a fervent admirer of Queen Elizabeth); Fraser, *Mary Queen of Scots*, p. 530.

[44] Fraser, *Mary Queen of Scots*, pp. 530-533 (first quote on 532, second on 533); Read, *Burghley*, pp. 367-369.

she died were burned so that no relics containing her blood would remain. But her memory would not be effaced that way, nor by any other.[45]

El Escorial in Spain stands at a high altitude, with peaks a mile and a half high just to the north. Summers are hot but winters can be bitterly cold. Easter came early by Pope Gregory XIII's new calendar in 1587; but Philip, despite his precarious health, could never let himself miss the glorious liturgy and processions of Holy Week, beginning with Palm Sunday which fell that year on March 22. There was snow in the air. The next day a courier from Spanish ambassador to France Mendoza arrived with the tragic news of the execution of Mary Queen of Scots. Philip had not rescued her after all; his offer of protection had been empty; he had left her to die. Some of her martyr's blood, he probably felt, was on his hands. He went into isolation to pray, doing no business for an entire week.[46] Then:

> Suddenly, in the evening of March 31st, the secret heart of the Escorial pulsed with action. There was a volley of curt missives. Santa Cruz must try to be ready to sail before spring was over. The ships and stores at Cartagena and Málaga must hurry to Lisbon. The Biscayan shipwrights should have the 25,000 escudos advance they asked for, only let them make haste. The arsenal of the galleys at Barcelona was to review its ordnance and stores and release everything it could spare to equip the Atlantic armada. A similar order to Naples. An emphatic query as to what was delaying the saltpeter expected from Genoa. A brief veiled note to Parma: The plans already agreed on would be carried out with increased speed in view of recent events. One almost equally curt to Mendoza. He was to condole with the Scots ambassador in Paris over the Queen's death.[47]

Philip II of Spain, great-grandson of Queen Isabel, son of Emperor Charles V, protector of Christendom, the "prudent king," was going to war with everything he had, with the future of the faith among the four hundred million people on the face of the earth who speak English today, and all their forbears between then and now, and uncounted generations yet unborn, at stake.)

During the preceding year two different plans for the "enterprise of England" had been developed by Admiral Santa Cruz, who had secured the Azores Islands far out into the Atlantic when Philip II took over Portugal, and the Prince of Parma, Philip's commander in the Netherlands. Santa Cruz proposed bringing a mighty, overwhelming fleet from Lisbon with enough troops aboard to invade England; Parma proposed sending 30,000 men from his army across the Straits of Dover to England in seagoing barges, which could cross that famous 22 miles of open water in a single day. In July Philip's senior advisor Juan de Zúñiga combined the two plans. Santa Cruz would sail from Lisbon, stopping first at Ireland where many of the troops he carried aboard would be landed in

---

[45] Fraser, *Mary Queen of Scots*, pp. 534-541 (first quote on 535, second on 538); Garrett Mattingly, *The Armada* (Boston, 1959), pp. 1-5.

[46] Kamen, *Philip of Spain*, p. 269; Mattingly, *Armada*, pp. 54, 69, 80.

[47] Mattingly, *Armada*, pp. 80-81.

Munster, where Catholic rebels had been active just seven years before. Then the Armada would go on to convoy Parma's barges across the Straits. But neither commander was very enthusiastic about the enterprise. Santa Cruz knew that the navigational difficulties would be great; there was no port on the French and Flemish shores of the Straits of Dover that could hold a large number of ships (except Antwerp, and to get to that required following a long and winding channel through the estuary of the Scheldt River, which no large fleet unfamiliar with the coast could manage). Coastal waters there were shallow and sandy, where deep-draft galleons could easily go aground. We know that the problem of the lack of an adequate port was brought specifically to Philip's attention early. And Parma was understandably reluctant to risk most of his peerless army on barges at sea where they would be virtually helpless if the fighting ships could not protect them.[48]

Now all doubts were swept aside and all objections dropped. Santa Cruz began working night and day to assemble and load every ship that could be obtained, pressed constantly and often harshly by Philip who at first wanted the Armada to leave by June, then reluctantly agreed to a series of postponements through the rest of the year and into the next. Parma "not only wrote but acted as if the death of the Queen of Scots had made a decisive change in his plan of operations." From March, "the maps in his study were all of the mouths of the Scheldt, and the first orders had been written for the southwest shift of his battalions and the movement of munitions toward Flanders." Parma was the best general in Europe. If he could get the majority of his men across the Straits in good order, England had nothing nearly sufficient to stop them. They could take London easily. Everything depended on the defense offered by the English navy.[49]

During the whole of the year 1587 and on into the winter of 1588, the Marquis of Santa Cruz, a fine seaman and brave fighter but no administrator, slowly sank under the burdens of assembling, supplying, and manning the largest war fleet in history up to that time.[50] On February 9, 1588, with Philip prodding him relentlessly now to sail within a week, he died, drained and despairing, at age 61. It was a portent. To replace him, Philip chose one of the principal noblemen of Spain, the Duke of Medina Sidonia, much younger than Santa Cruz (37) and known for his administrative abilities, kindly and devout, whose estates then

---

[48] Martin and Parker, *Spanish Armada*, pp. 112-119, 134; Kamen, *Philip of Spain*, pp. 264-265.

[49] Kamen, *Philip of Spain*, pp. 164, 265; Martin and Parker, *Spanish Armada*, p. 114; Mattingly, *Armada*, pp. 50-51 (first quote 50, second 50-51). Parma, formerly called Prince, was now Duke because of the death of his father and his succession to the ducal title.

[50] A typical letter from Philip II to Santa Cruz during this period, sent October 10, 1587, says: "There is no more time to waste on requests and replies; just get on with the job and see if you cannot advance the agreed departure date [October 25] by a few days." (Martin and Parker, *Spanish Armada*, p. 140)

produced most of the world's sherry.[51] He was a descendant of the legendary
Guzmán the Good who had held Tarifa against the Moors even after they
captured his son and demanded his surrender at the price of his son's life.[52] Let
him explain in his own words, writing to Philip II, why his appointment was such
a disastrous mistake:

> My health is not equal to such a voyage, for I know by experience of the
> little I have been at sea that I am always seasick and always catch cold. . . .
> Since I have had no experience either of the sea or of war, I cannot feel that I
> ought to command so important an enterprise. I know nothing of what the
> Marques of Santa Cruz has been doing, nor of what intelligence he has of
> England, so that I feel I should give but a bad account of myself,
> commanding thus blindly, and being obliged to rely on the advice of others,
> without knowing good from bad. . . . I write with all frankness and truth,
> which is my duty; and I have no doubt that His Majesty in his magnanimity
> will do me the favor which I humbly beg, and will not entrust to me a task in
> which I could certainly not succeed; for I do not understand it, know nothing
> about it, have no health for the sea, and no money to spend on it.[53]

Two days later he not only wrote Philip II another letter reiterating his
conviction of unfitness to command, but urging that the whole enterprise be
abandoned. Nevertheless Philip wrote Medina Sidonia saying that he remained
his choice, reminded him of the tradition of Guzmán the Good, said God would
not allow the failure of an enterprise so dedicated to him, and ordered him to be
in Lisbon ready to sail by March 1.[54]

It is one of the most inexplicable command appointments in all of military
history, for which there was no possible justification. No matter how admirable
the Duke's piety and loyalty, no matter how skilled an administrator he was, one
does not give the command of the largest armada ever assembled to a man who
has never held any sea command and has only very rarely gone to sea. Philip
does not seem to have been altogether himself during the months after he learned
of Mary Stuart's execution. Nothing mattered to him but speed, as though he had
only to get the Armada on the sea and God would do the rest. God expects His
servants to be "wise as serpents and innocent as doves." The Duke of Medina
Sidonia was only a dove.

Meanwhile the English navy took up the gauntlet with a spirit which
already pointed to what the future held. Its ships were new, fast, well-armed and
magnificently commanded.[55] In Francis Drake, John Hawkins, and Martin
Frobisher it had three of the best captains who ever lived. By the end of March

---

[51] Mattingly, *Armada*, pp. 201-205; Martin and Parker, *Spanish Armada*, pp. 21, 147;
Kamen, *Philip of Spain*, p. 271.

[52] See Volume III, Chapter 8 of this history.

[53] Mattingly, *Armada*, p. 205; David Howarth, *The Voyage of the Armada: the
Spanish Story* (New York, 1981), p. 25.

[54] Martin and Parker, *Spanish Armada*, p. 148; Howarth, *Voyage of the Armada*, p. 25.

[55] Mattingly, *Armada*, pp. 195-198.

1587 Drake had already persuaded Queen Elizabeth to commission him to take a fleet to Spain to attack it before it could attack England. On April 12 his strike squadron of 23 ships left Plymouth harbor; hardly a one of the many histories of the Armada does not quote the electrifying words of Drake's letter as he weighed anchor at Plymouth: "The wind commands me away; our ship is under sail!" The winds stayed fair across the Bay of Biscay. Queen Elizabeth had second thoughts about his mission and sent an order that he was not after all to attack Spain, but Drake sailed too fast for the pinnace with the message to catch up with him. Every ship but one reached its destination, the port of Cádiz in the south of Spain, upon which he descended at the end of April. The harbor of Cádiz is at the end of a long narrow bay; he sailed right into it without pausing to reconnoiter or to consult with his other captains, achieving total surprise. In the next 24 hours he destroyed almost half the sixty ships he found there, and then went on to burn a mighty galleon just being completed for the Armada. As he described it in a phrase that became legendary, he had "singed the King of Spain's beard."[56] But early in May he wrote to Walsingham:

> I assure Your Honor the like preparation was never heard of nor known as the King of Spain has and daily makes to invade England . . . which if they be not impeached before they join will be very perilous . . . all possible preparations for defense are very expedient. . . . I dare not almost write of the great forces we hear the King of Spain has. Prepare in England strongly and most by sea! Look well to the coast of Sussex![57]

On July 29 Philip II made a treaty with Pope Sixtus V by which the Pope deposited one million ducats in gold with two bankers instructed to turn it over to Spain if Spanish forces had landed in England before the end of 1587. Philip was to nominate a king for England who would be acceptable to the Pope and invested by him. Still hoping to dispatch the Armada before the end of the year, Philip in September dropped the plan for landing troops in Ireland and ordered the Armada to "sail in the name of God straight into the English Channel and go along it until you have anchored off Margate head, having first warned the Duke of Parma of your approach." He wrote to Parma that the Armada would be coming soon and he should be prepared to send his whole army across the Straits of Dover in the barges he had prepared, but gave no details of how and where the Armada and the barges were to meet. On October 19 the English Privy Council met. Old William Cecil, now back in the royal favor after being excluded from court for months after sending the death warrant for Mary Queen of Scots to Fotheringhay Castle for her execution without telling Elizabeth about it, presented a detailed plan for the mobilization of the navy and carried much of it through himself, despite gout so severe that he was often unable to walk. On December 21 Lord Howard of Effingham, a high-ranking nobleman who loved

---

[56] *Ibid.*, pp. 88-91, 93-108 (first quote on 90-91, second on 108); Cummins, *Drake*, p. 163; Martin and Parker, *Spanish Armada*, p. 127.
[57] Mattingly, *Armada*, p. 109.

the sea, was appointed commander-in-chief of the English navy. (Drake, Hawkins and Frobisher were commoners who could not, by the standards of the time, aspire to the supreme command; but Lord Howard was wise and humble enough to listen to them and not interfere with them.)[58]

On April 25 the Duke of Medina Sidonia went to Lisbon cathedral, where after Mass he took from its altar the blessed standard of the expedition, with figures of Christ Crucified and of the Blessed Virgin Mary and the words: "Arise, O Lord, and vindicate Thy cause!" The crusading indulgence from the Pope was read, and all the thousands of men sailing with the Armada were to have confessed and received Holy Communion before their departure. On May 9 a general muster was held of the approximately 130 vessels in the Armada, including twenty of Spain's famous, intimidating galleons, commanded by Diego Flores de Valdés; four galleasses (big awkward ships which could be propelled, though very slowly, by oars, and were excellent gun platforms) commanded by Hugo de Moncada; forty heavily armed merchantmen arranged in four ten-ship squadrons commanded by four of their best seamen: Juan Martínez de Recalde, Miguel de Oquendo, Pedro de Valdés, and Martin de Bertendona; two huge carracks, one from Venice and one from Genoa; and many smaller ships. The Armada carried 238 officers, 146 gentlemen, nearly 19,000 soldiers, 8,000 sailors, and 2,000 oarsmen, 2,431 cannon and 123,790 shot. This meant that during each day at sea nearly thirty thousand men had to be supplied with food and drink. In England, Lord Howard's squadron at the mouth of the Thames sailed west down the Channel to anchor off Plymouth Hoe. Thanks to Walsingham's extraordinary network of spies, the English knew not only the exact strength of the Armada but every detail of its operational plan. In mid-May Parma sent word that he could only provide 17,000 men instead of the 30,000 he had originally promised for the invasion force against England, but Philip II told the Duke of Medina Sidonia that the men Parma had withdrawn could be replaced from the 19,000 soldiers carried on the Armada ships.[59]

On May 28, 1588 the giant fleet set sail. It took three whole days for its 130 ships to clear Lisbon harbor. On every ship an explanation of the causes and character of the war was read to the men, placing at the center the persecution and liberation of the English Catholics—the Margaret Clitherows. Mocked by modern historians, despite the inevitable tendency to overstatement in wartime propaganda this really did reveal the basic reason Philip II was fighting this war:

> Onward, gentlemen, onward! Onward with joy and gladness; onward to our glorious, honorable, necessary, profitable and not difficult undertaking! Glorious to God, to His Church, to His saints, and to our country. Glorious to God, Who for the punishment of England has allowed Himself to be

---

[58] Von Pastor, *History of the Popes*, XXII, 51; Martin and Parker, *Spanish Armada*, pp. 20, 126, 137 (quote), 140; Read, *Burghley*, pp. 410, 418-420, 423-424; Read, *Walsingham* III, 295-297.

[59] Mattingly, *Armada*, pp. 215, 245-249; Howard, *Voyage of the Armada*, pp. 11-17; Martin and Parker, *Spanish Armada*, p. 155; Read, *Walsingham*, III, 292-293, 302.

banished from the land, and the holy sacrifice of the Mass to be abolished. Glorious to His Church, now oppressed and downtrodden by the English heretics. Glorious to the saints, who have there been persecuted, maltreated, insulted and burned. Glorious for our country, because God has deigned to make it His instrument for such great ends. . . . There also will await us the groans of countless imprisoned Catholics, the tears of widows who lost their husbands for the faith, the sobs of maidens who were forced to sacrifice their lives rater than destroy their souls, the tender children who, suckled on the poison of heresy, are doomed to perdition unless deliverance reaches them in time; and finally myriads of workers, citizens, knights, nobles, and clergymen, and all ranks of Catholics, who are oppressed and downtrodden by the heretics and are anxiously looking to us for their liberation. . . . Let us live Christian lives, without offense towards our God, in brotherhood with our fellow soldiers and in obedience to our captains. Courage! Steadfastness! And Spanish bravery![60]

After being partly driven into the harbor of La Coruña by a storm, the Armada had to reassemble there, with some ships reporting alarming shortages of food and water already, due to spoilage in casks. On June 24 the Duke of Medina Sidonia again wrote to Philip II urging that the whole enterprise be called off, saying the storm was a sign of God's displeasure, there was not enough good food and water, and that many of the officers were incompetent. Few handicaps are worse in a military operation than a commander who does not have confidence in the operation he is conducting. But Philip was as determined as ever: "I have dedicated this enterprise to God. . . . Get on, then, and do your part!" On July 11 he and his son prayed for four hours for the Armada, on bare pavement with hands joined or raised. Ten days later the Armada sailed again from La Coruña with a fair wind at dawn.[61]

On the morning of July 26 the wind dropped, and for several hours the huge fleet lay almost becalmed. Then a hard north wind began to blow, with blinding rain squalls. The galleys could not cope with it, and had to return to port. The wind developed into a full gale, very unusual during July, but the Armada kept moving northward under storm canvas. The next day, Thursday the 28th, dawned bright and clear with no more than a stiff breeze, and the Armada made good progress.[62]

Friday, July 29, 1588. The stage is set. The hour has struck. The lookout on a humble English trading bark, bringing home a cargo of salt from across the Channel, sees suddenly looming upon the western horizon an array of huge sails in crescent formation, each bearing a red cross, the Spanish naval emblem. The Armada—which all England had been talking about for many months—is upon them. The salt trader claps on sail and hurries to the safety of his home port. Breathlessly he tells his news. A horse is found. The trader or his messenger

---

[60] Howard, *Voyage of the Armada*, pp. 46-47.

[61] *Ibid.*, pp. 72, 74, 78-86; Martin and Parker, *Spanish Armada*, pp. 21, 159-162 (quote on 162), 195-196, 200-209; Mattingly, *Armada*, pp. 252, 254-255.

[62] Mattingly, *Armada*, pp. 268-269; Howarth, *Voyage of the Armada*, pp. 107, 111.

mounts and rides furiously for Plymouth, Drake's home town and headquarters, where virtually the whole English navy is now based. Drake is there. He is playing a game of bowls in a field. [He is given the overwhelming news. In a reply which has become legend, but is attested within living memory by people who were there and surely would never have forgotten it, he drawls: "We have time enough to finish the game, and beat the Spaniards too."[63]

Drake and many other officers of the English fleet know every twist and cranny of the convoluted coast of Devon with its unique, age-hallowed names: the Lizard, the Start, the Sleeve, the Hoe, and the Eddystone. Off the Lizard the Duke of Medina Sidonia hoists his battle ensign of Christ Crucified, the Virgin Mary, and Mary Magdalene, and fires three guns. The high, hard-running tides of the Channel keep the English fleet in Plymouth harbor until ten o'clock that night. The days are still long in England in July, but darkness falls at last. Moving to the edge of the harbor nearest the open sea to be in the best position to emerge on the morrow, the English warships anchor under the lee of Rame Head.[64]

It is well to remember, as we watch the unfolding of the most important naval battle ever fought in Christendom, not only the Catholic purpose and resolution of the men of the Spanish Armada, but also that every man has a natural right to defend his home from foreign invaders, whatever kind of government he has or whatever kind of man he is.] Devon and Plymouth were Drake's home, and he had a right to fight for them, just as the Armada had a right to come in response to English aggression, and to stop the persecution of the Margaret Clitherows of England.

The next day, Saturday July 30, at about three o'clock in the afternoon, with a fresh southwest wind on an ebb tide, the English fleet beat out to sea, 54 strong, each tall ship swinging round the Eddystone, the massive low-lying boulder that broke the surface just outside the entrance to Plymouth harbor. Upon it stood the legendary Eddystone Light. The lighthouse keeper had a ringside seat as the English fleet maneuvered around him. We may imagine him cheering wildly as each ship tacked past the Light and raised its battle flags. Off the Eddystone in the late afternoon the English captains and sailors could all see "the long line of the Spanish fleet, like a floating wall, black and menacing, crowned with a multitude of towers. They could not count them or distinguish separate ships, but the gentlemen who swung themselves up the shrouds to look could reflect that never since the beginning of the world had any eyes before theirs beheld so vast an array of hostile sailing ships of war." But they soon found they could outsail them. Before nightfall, they were well ahead of them, upwind, allowing them to take maximum advantage of their maneuverability in the battle that was certain on the morrow.[65]

---

[63] Mattingly, *Armada*, pp. 265-266; Howarth, *Voyage of the Armada*, pp. 119-120; Cummins, *Drake*, p. 183.

[64] Howarth, *Voyage of the Armada*, p. 114; Mattingly, *Armada*, pp. 266-267.

[65] Mattingly, *Armada*, pp. 266-267, 270-274 (quote on 174); Howarth, *Voyage of the Armada*, pp. 114-118, 121; Martin and Parker, *Spanish Armada*, pp. 164-165; personal

On Sunday, July 31, in medieval fashion each admiral challenged the other to battle, about nine o'clock in the morning. The English attacked in line against the Spanish crescent, the first use of line-of-battle tactics in naval history. Drake in *Revenge*, Hawkins in *Victory* and Frobisher in *Triumph* led the attack on the rear of the Armada. One of the large Spanish ships was severely damaged by an explosion of gunpowder, another by a collision; both were soon captured, one by Drake himself. All day the English had shown themselves able to evade grappling and boarding by the big Spanish ships with their large contingents of soldiers, while pouring a steady fire into them, though at a range too long to be decisive. On August 2 all four of the big galleasses attacked Frobisher, but he fought like a tiger, using his knowledge of the coast and the currents, holding out until other ships came to help him, in a continuous roar of cannon fire and blinding smoke. On August 3 the wind dropped almost completely. Neither side could move, and the English held a council of war aboard Lord Howard's flagship *Ark Royal* at which it was decided to divide the whole fleet into four squadrons commanded by Lord Howard, Drake, Hawkins, and Frobisher. On August 4 there was still almost no wind. The Spanish threatened to enter the protected waters of the strait called the Solent, north of the Isle of Wight. Hawkins and Frobisher had their ships towed in to block the Solent, while Drake waited for the wind to rise in the late afternoon, as he knew it usually did, and when it did he attacked, seeking to drive the Armada on the rocks known as the Owers. The Armada avoided the trap, but at the price of forcing it to turn away decisively from Selsey Bill at the entrance to the Solent.[66]

After another calm August 5, by the 6th the wind had picked up, and by four o'clock in the afternoon Calais on the Straits of Dover was in sight. The Armada anchored that evening between Calais and Dunkirk; neither had a port nearly large enough to accommodate all its ships. Medina Sidonia sent a not very encouraging message to Parma saying: "I am anchored here, two leagues from Calais, with the enemy's fleet on my flank. They can cannonade me whenever they like, and I shall be unable to do them much harm in return." Late that night Parma replied saying that now that the Armada had arrived, he would bring up his forces and load them on the barges, but it would take six days. Medina Sidonia had expected that Parma would have his troops ready to sail immediately on the barges. By now he had learned enough about sea warfare to be quite sure that he could not simply lie at anchor for six days while Parma brought up his barges. The English had stayed within range of his fleet for an entire week, bombarding them every day, and had been reinforced by 35 ships including five more galleons. And there was a Dutch fleet in the offing, consisting of small but

---

observations by the author of Plymouth and its harbor in June 1994. Eddystone Light was so famous that when centuries later it had outlived its usefulness and been replaced by a much bigger lighthouse, it was brought ashore, reassembled piece by piece, and stands today as a British national monument at Plymouth Hoe.

[66] Mattingly, *Armada*, pp. 275-301, 303-309; Martin and Parker, *Spanish Armada*, pp. 166-178, 208-209, 212-213; Howarth, *Voyage of the Armada*, pp. 121-137, 140-143, 155; Cummins, *Drake*, pp. 184-188.

dangerous shallow-draft warships called flyboats, ready to attack the barges in inshore waters which the Armada's big galleons could not penetrate.[67]

With most of the Armada at anchor in the unprotected waters off Calais, it was a perfect target for fireships, and Drake called for their use at once, the very next night after they anchored there. Wooden ships are highly inflammable; by setting a ship afire and directing it into the midst of an anchored enemy, many enemy ships could be burned or at least forced by fear of fire to scatter. At midnight August 7, before a freshening south wind with cloud-scud flying across the face of the moon, driven by a spring tide and a strong Channel current, eight fireships bored down on the anchored Armada, with guns double-shotted to shoot by themselves as the heat from their fires built up. Six of them got through. Most of the Armada captains cut their anchor cables and fled. Those with two anchors out now had none left, because most ships carried only two. In the remaining hours of the night they scattered to the four winds.[68]

At dawn the Duke of Medina Sidonia found only five galleons still with his own, and a crippled galleass. The English fleet moved in for the kill. But the Duke—miscast, misplaced, outmaneuvered—could still fight. With magnificent courage he held out, while the English became diverted by the task of taking the damaged but enormous galleass, and by nine o'clock enough of the Armada had reassembled to make a defensive formation. Then the ultimate Armada battle was joined off the little French fishing port of Gravelines. It lasted all day. For the first time the English ships closed to small arms range. Drake and Frobisher took position just a hundred yards on either side of the Spanish flagship *San Martín* and made more than 200 hits on her, including a 50-pound shot that went right through her, in one side and out the other. *San Mateo* was "riddled with shot like a sieve" and literally came apart at the seams, sinking before the day was done. Bertendona, one of the Spanish division captains, observed a lowly supply hulk which had fought so hard that he could see blood spilling out of the scuppers, with musketeers still firing back from her tops and quarterdeck. *Maria Juan* went down with 275 men aboard. Two sinking Spanish ships had to be beached, and two ran aground. The Spanish suffered about 600 killed and 800 seriously wounded. By six o'clock in the afternoon both sides had used up most of their powder and shot, but the English could easily replenish theirs at their

---

[67] Mattingly, *Armada*, pp. 309-315, 318 (quote), 320-321; Martin and Parker, *Spanish Armada*, pp. 178-183, 186; Howarth, *Voyage of the Armada*, pp. 149-152, 156-158, 162. The physical and military obstacles to the successful accomplishment of the operational plan at this point were formidable, but not prohibitive. The marked lack of confidence in the operation by both commanders is self-evident. It was almost as though they were merely going through the motions of carrying out a plan they had both become convinced was doomed to fail. Both were loyal to Philip; they would not disobey his orders. But they would do no more than the bare minimum to fulfill them. The Duke of Medina Sidonia did not even understand most naval operations, and Parma never really wanted to leave the Low Countries, where he had been born and brought up—they were home to him—and risk his veteran army in such dangerous waters.

[68] Mattingly, *Armada*, pp. 323-326; Martin and Parker, *Spanish Armada*, pp. 185-187; Howarth, *Voyage of the Armada*, pp. 168-174; Cummins, *Drake*, pp. 188-189.

nearby ports, while the enormous Armada could not get into any port. The English ships had suffered very little damage, possibly because poorly made Spanish round shot shattered on impact, without penetrating the English hulls.[69]

The next morning many of the Spanish captains had had enough, refusing to respond to Medina Sidonia's signal to assemble around him. There was angry shouting between ships about who was to blame for the rapidly developing disaster. Medina Sidonia relieved 19 captains of their commands. While their leaders were arguing, the Armada passed the mouth of the Scheldt River leading to the one port which could have accommodated the Armada, at Antwerp, though they would have needed a local pilot for each ship to reach it (Parma had sent only two). Late in the morning the whole Armada almost went aground on the sandy shelving shore of Flanders, with only six feet of water under the big galleons, but a fortunate wind shift at the last minute took them out of danger. A council of war voted to try again to rendezvous with Parma and his barges (he had now loaded 8,000 men aboard them) over the next four days. But the wind continued to blow steadily from the southwest, dead foul for a return to the Straits of Dover, and on August 13 Medina Sidonia ordered the Armada to return to Spain around the northern tip of Scotland and the rocky west coast of Ireland, a route wholly unfamiliar to most of the Spanish captains—and 2,625 nautical miles long.[70]

Many of the remaining ships were barely seaworthy because of their battle damage, and cask after cask of both food and water was found virtually empty or spoiled. Some ships had already cut the daily ration to one pint of water, half a pint of wine, and half a pound of biscuit per day—only a thousand calories, not enough to sustain life. As they made their laborious, tortured way along the forbidding northern coasts, the thousands of soldiers and sailors aboard the Armada ships were literally starving to death, or dying of thirst. Some who could stand it no longer simply sailed ashore, preferring the chance of survival from a wreck to sure death at sea; others fell afoul of the coastal navigational hazards. No less than 26 Armada ships were wrecked on the west and north coasts of Ireland. The Irish Catholics would often plunder the castaways but rarely killed them; the English officials and troops killed them whenever they could catch them. A splendid old Irish chief, past 80 years old, Sorley Boy McDonnell, who held Dunluce Castle on the north coast of County Antrim, worked out a regular procedure for getting Spanish castaways out of Ireland and into neutral Scotland.[71]

It was during this dolorous Spanish retreat, on August 18, that Queen Elizabeth appeared before her troops at Tilbury and gave her speech highlighted

---

[69] Martin and Parker, *Spanish Armada*, pp. 187-192, 199; Mattingly, *Armada*, pp. 327-336; Howarth, *Voyage of the Armada*, pp. 176-182, 190-191.

[70] Martin and Parker, *Spanish Armada*, pp. 192-193, 227-229; Mattingly, *Armada*, pp. 336-341, 364-365; Howarth, *Voyage of the Armada*, pp. 182-187, 196-198.

[71] Martin and Parker, *Spanish Armada*, pp. 229-233, 235-236, 242-243, 245; Howarth, *Voyage of the Armada*, pp. 201-203, 210, 216-218; Mattingly, *Armada*, pp. 365-366.

by the famous line: "I know I have the body of a weak and feeble woman, but I have the heart and stomach of a king, and a king of England too!"[72]

The Duke of Medina Sidonia survived, bringing just eight ships with him into the northern Spanish port of Santander on September 21. His flagship *San Martín* was leaking so badly that three great hawsers had to be tied around it to keep it from sinking; half his men were dead or dying; he himself had a high fever and was only semi-conscious, too weak to stand. Gradually, over the next several weeks, about fifty other Armada ships came straggling in to north Spanish ports at their last extremity. The last of them, in mid-October, had aboard the best of the captains, Juan Martínez de Recalde, who was probably the man who should have had the command. He was carried ashore on a litter and died nine days later, spending his last hours in a monastery in the tradition of the great Spanish warriors of the Reconquest. The Duke of Medina Sidonia lived 22 more years, but he was a broken man. About half of the Armada ships and at least three quarters of the Armada men never returned.[73]

By the end of August Philip II knew he had suffered the greatest military defeat in Spanish history since the Moors killed King Roderick on the Guadalete River in 711 and conquered the country in just three years. His secretary Juan de Idiáquez wrote to Parma: "His Majesty feels the blow more than you would believe. . . . Although he felt the news very much at the beginning, he feels it more every day. . . . It hurts him immensely that he failed to render a great service to God, after doing more than you could have asked or imagined."[74]

But, with a mighty effort of will, King Philip II humbled himself to the Will of God, Who must have had some good purpose for allowing this to happen. And in honor of that unknown purpose, Philip commanded a "Te Deum" to be sung in thanksgiving to God for allowing the destruction of the enterprise of England. He was still the king of Spain. His country was still Catholic. England might be lost to the Faith (in fact she was, though Philip would never admit it), but the Church was endangered everywhere but in Spain and Portugal. Duty called; as ever, he would answer. Catholic France was disintegrating, and for the Church to lose both England and France at virtually the same time would indubitably destroy Christendom. If he could not save the Faith in one, he must save it in the other. Sixty-one years old and looking much older, ravaged by gout, in almost constant pain, His Most Catholic Majesty returned to the struggle with hardly a pause. This most powerful ruler in the world always knew what it means to serve the King of Kings.[75]

When all is said and done, we should never forget that, as with other battles on which the destiny of centuries turned, it might have gone the other way, changing the history of Christendom almost beyond recognition. In the judicious words of the most recent historians of the Spanish Armada:

---

[72] Mattingly, *Armada*, p. 350.

[73] *Ibid.*, pp. 370-371, 373; Martin and Parker, *Spanish Armada*, pp. 257-260; Howarth, *Voyage of the Armada*, p. 244; Kamen, *Philip of Spain*, p. 275.

[74] Kamen, *Philip of Spain*, p. 275.

[75] Mattingly, *Armada*, pp. 388-390; Walsh, *Philip II*, pp. 664-665.

It is always easy to be wise after the event. By emphasizing the unrealistic aspects of the "armchair" strategy devised by Philip II, or the perhaps excessive caution of Parma, or the naval inexperience of Medina Sidonia, it is easy to present the whole Armada project as a futile, crack-brained, over ambitious adventure. But that is unjust. If an accurate and balanced assessment of the 1588 campaign is to be made, it must take into account the strengths as well as the weaknesses: the selection of an ideal invasion area; the formidable planning and immense resources which brought the fleet from Spain and the army from the Netherlands so close together; the patient and successful diplomatic efforts which secured both the paralysis of France and the complete isolation of England throughout 1587 and 1588; the carefully fostered divisions within the Dutch Republic; the enormous benefits that the occupation of even a part of Kent—carefully exploited—could have brought to Spain. It must also leave room for luck—that, somehow, one of Medina Sidonia's messengers might have reached Parma before the fleet arrived at Calais; that the Armada might have been able to regroup after the fireship attack; that the wind might have swung round and allowed the re-formed Grand Fleet to sail back into the straits, while Parma's forces remained embarked on the barges and the English shot-lockers were still empty. Any or all of these contingencies might have occurred, and who can now tell what the consequences might then have been? Only one thing is certain. If, during the second week of August 1588, the Army of Flanders had been marching towards London, everyone today would regard the Invincible Armada, despite all its deficiencies, as Philip II's masterpiece.[76]

When his pathetic, disfigured, three times renamed brother succumbed to the hereditary tuberculosis of the Valois family in 1584, King Henry III of France had been married ten years without issue, nor had he fathered any illegitimate children. It was all but certain that he could have no children. In a monarchy the question of the royal succession is all-important; for fundamental stability it is necessary always to have a designated and generally accepted successor for the incumbent monarch. But by France's immutable Salic Law (forbidding a woman to rule or even to pass on a royal title), with all his brothers dead and no children, Henry III's heir was separated by no less than nine generations from the last reigning king ancestral to him, none other than St. Louis IX. The heir's name was also Henry. He was known as Henry of Navarre because his father and then he had ruled the French fragment of the ancient kingdom of Navarre, straddling the Pyrenees (King Ferdinand, Isabel's husband, had taken over the Spanish side early in the century). And Henry of Navarre was a Calvinist, son of Jeanne d'Albret, the most vehement Calvinist in the history of European royalty, who had died twelve years before.[77]

To its north (England), northeast (the Low Countries), and east (Germany and the Calvinist cantons of Switzerland), the leaders and people of France had

---

[76] Martin and Parker, *Spanish Armada*, p. 277.

[77] For Queen Jeanne d'Albret of Navarre, see Chapter Six, above.

seen what the Protestant rebels did when they gained power. They closed all Catholic churches and abolished the Mass. They tore every vestige of the ancient Church out of the government of the state, the life of the community, and the devotion of the people. Wherever they gained power, they hung on like bulldogs, especially after they had taken over all Catholic Church lands, mainly those of monasteries and convents which they seized as one of their first acts. No one could feel confident that Protestant power, once established, could ever be overthrown (in fact it never was, except in some of the small German states, and in indestructibly Catholic Ireland in the twentieth century). The only way to preserve Catholic France was to prevent the initial takeover by any means necessary and moral, whatever the cost.

For this purpose the Catholic League of France (also called the Holy League) was formed by Duke Henry of Guise with the active assistance of Philip II of Spain, beginning with the Treaty of Joinville between Philip and the Guises, signed on the last day of the year of Henry III's brother's death, in 1584, and made public in March 1585.[78]

Few national organizations in history have been so scathingly and repeatedly denounced by historians with so little warrant, as the Catholic League in France in the 1580's and 1590's. All the denunciations heaped on Philip II of Spain are extended to it, with the additional charge of treason and the taken-for-granted conclusion that all Philip was interested in was more power and a bigger empire, of which France would be a part. In not one of his voluminous writings and in no paper preserved by anyone who served him or was friendly to him is there any avowal or even implication that ruling France was Philip's goal. Again and again he stated that he had enough or more than enough dominions already; the last thing he wanted was more of them, and to have to borrow more money to maintain them. The historians who draw these conclusions about Philip II and the Guises of France seem totally unwilling even to consider the possibility that genuine attachment to the Catholic Faith, and a well-justified fear of a repetition in France of the outlawing of the Mass, which had actually happened in England, Scotland, the Netherlands and half of Germany, might have motivated the Catholic League, which found supporters all over France, especially in Paris.[79]

At long last a more reasonable reaction has set in, as expressed by a recent historian of France's religious wars:

---

[78] Mack P. Holt, *The French Wars of Religion, 1562-1629* (New York, 1995), p. 122; Jensen, *Diplomacy and Dogmatism*, pp. 54-55; von Pastor, *History of the Popes*, XIX, 543.

[79] David Buisseret, the most recent biographer of Henry of Navarre (*Henry IV* [London, 1984], p. 21) acknowledges that the Catholics of the League did fear the fate of the Catholics in England, but says superciliously: "Four hundred years later this argument may not seem very convincing." Why not? It happened in every country the Protestants took over, and the unquestionable fact will stand for four hundred years or four thousand years.

What is the final judgment on the Catholic League? It would be a mistake to treat it, as so many historians have, as nothing more than a body motivated purely by partisan politics or social tensions. While political and social pressures were doubtless present, and even significant in the case of the Sixteen in Paris [commoners who gained a substantial share in the leadership of the Catholic League in that city], to focus on these factors exclusively overlooks a very different face of the League. For all its political and internecine wrangling, the League was still very much a Holy Union. Its religious role was significant, as the League was the conduit between the Tridentine spirituality of the Catholic Reformation and the seventeenth-century *dévots*. Often overlooked is the emphasis the League placed on the internal and spiritual renewal of the earthly city. Moving beyond the communal religion of the later Middle Ages, the League focused on internalizing faith as a cleansing and purifying agent. New religious orders and confraternities were founded in League towns, and the gulf separating clergy and laity was often bridged as clerics joined aldermen in the *Hotel de Ville* where both became the epitome of goodly magistrates. To overlook the religious side of the League is to overlook the one bond that did keep the Holy Union holy as well as united.[80]

On March 31, 1585 the Catholic League of France issued a manifesto at Péronne declaring that no heretic should be allowed to assume the crown of France, whatever his hereditary claims; consequently, the succession should devolve upon Cardinal Charles of Bourbon, uncle of Henry of Navarre; and that the Catholic Faith should be fully restored in France and the revolutionary Calvinist church eliminated.[81]

This manifesto was not even presented to the king, for French Catholics had long since learned that he was a broken reed. The causes of Henry III's degeneration have been much debated. It was both physical and mental, possibly deriving from the family tuberculosis or venereal disease or both in some kind of ugly combination. Suffice it to say that by the time of the formation of the Catholic League the King of France had reached the point where he obviously felt no obligation to consider the future of Catholics or the Catholic Faith in his country, which he was sworn by his coronation oath to protect. In the unforgettable word-portrait of Garrett Mattingly:

> Those thirteen years [since Henry was elected king of Poland, before becoming king of France] had sufficed to turn the buoyant, self-confident young man into a flaccid, hesitant old one. The hands, the beautiful slender hands, were as restless as ever, forever shaping arabesques of meaning to accompany the fluent, melodious voice, forever, when the king was silent, toying with something, with a marmoset, a sweetmeat, a lap dog, a muff, or the hair and ears of a handsome young man. But, although defiantly painted into a red and white mask of health, like some triumph of the embalmer's art, the face had a shrunken stillness. The eyes, peering out from sockets yearly

---

[80] Holt, *French Wars of Religion*, pp. 149-150.
[81] *Ibid.*, pp. 123-124; Jensen, *Diplomacy and Dogmatism*, pp. 66-67; von Pastor, *History of the Popes*, XIX, 544.

deeper and more corpselike, were sick, sullen, distrustful. The last of the
Valois looked like a man secretly at grips with death.[82]

With a cold and corrosive jealousy, King Henry III of France hated Duke
Henry of Guise and his family, despite—and perhaps even partly because of—
their common faith. For the Duke of Guise was recognized, as his father had
been, as the true leader of militant French Catholics, while Henry III never was
and never would be. Reputedly the handsomest man in France when he was
young, now with a whiplash battle scar on his face that underscored his martial
prowess, with a commanding presence and charism which inspired passionate
personal loyalty, Duke Henry of Guise was a man's man, born to lead and
knowing it. Henry III was a failure; his dynasty would end with him. But so
long as he lived he would fight to hold every royal prerogative he had, by any
means he could find, totally without regard to morality.

His first reaction to the manifesto of Péronne was to send his elderly
mother, Catherine de Medici, in late May 1585 to try to negotiate with the Duke
of Guise (Henry III hated him so much that he intensely disliked even meeting
with him). But the two sides really had nothing to negotiate; Henry III had long
preferred the succession of the Calvinist Henry of Navarre, while the League had
settled on the Cardinal of Bourbon and was committed never to recognize a
heretic king. Then at the beginning of July, Henry III humiliatingly surrendered
to all the League's Péronne demands, unquestionably meaning to abandon his
promises as soon as he could (as he had done before). He did not even go in
person to sign the Treaty of Némours embodying his capitulation to the hated
Guise, but sent Catherine in his place. Meanwhile Henry of Navarre met with
Montmorency-Damville in southern France, near Toulouse, and made a close
alliance with him to help Henry of Navarre maintain an armed force in the field.[83]

The straightforward Pope Sixtus V took the Treaty of Némours at face
value, as a commitment of the king with the Catholic nobility and people of
France to preserve the Faith and eliminate heresy, and so followed it up on
September 21 with the formal excommunication of Henry of Navarre, absolving
his subjects present or future from all allegiance to him, and declaring that no
heretic could ever be recognized as king of France (a law which most countries
of Christendom already had on their books, though it was evidently not being
enforced in the Protestant countries). Henry III refused to publish the bull,
though he did command that all French Calvinists lay down their arms. Naturally
they refused. A desultory war broke out in 1586, called the "war of the three
Henries" because the three principal protagonists (the King, Guise, and Navarre)
all shared this name. In December Catherine de Medici (miscast as an
evangelist) went to Henry of Navarre to try to convert him to the Catholic Faith,

---

[82] Mattingly, *Armada*, pp. 32-33.

[83] Irene Mahoney, *Madame Catherine* [de Medici] (New York, 1975), pp. 290-292;
Holt, *French Wars of Religion*, p. 124; Buisseret, *Henry IV*, pp. 18-19; Jensen, *Diplomacy
and Dogmatism*, pp. 69-71; N. M. Sutherland, *The Huguenot Struggle for Recognition*
(New Haven CT, 1980), pp. 279-280.

as the only way to reunite the nation. Though he was later to come to agree with that position, at this time he rejected it.[84]

In June 1587 Pope Sixtus V appointed Giovanni Morosini, Bishop of Brescia, as nuncio to France. He had been a good friend of St. Philip Neri in Rome and was an experienced diplomat. In writing to the Pope, he commented most perceptively on King Henry III:

> [He] is one man, yet acts like two persons . . . he wishes for the defeat of the Huguenots [Calvinists] yet fears it; he fears the defeat of the Catholics, yet desires it; these interior conflicts within himself afflict him, so that he lives in constant mistrust of his own thoughts and wishes . . . he does not trust himself, and trusts only in an Épernon [his favorite]; the envy of the latter for Guise has changed into hatred, and the poison has made its way into the heart of the infatuated monarch; greed for possessions and honors tyrannize over the favorite, liberality and humanity hold sway in the heart of Guise, adored by the people and hated by the king.[85]

In view of the strength of the Catholic League, with the power of Spain behind it, the prospects of an excommunicated and unaided Henry of Navarre resisting it successfully seemed slight. Therefore William Cecil appeared on the scene again in late July 1587, with a lengthy memorandum to Queen Elizabeth and her privy council urging financial and military aid for Henry of Navarre along with the financial and military support they were already giving to the Dutch Calvinists. The recommendation was approved and acted on in just two months. In October 1587 Henry of Navarre gave the first demonstration of his considerable military skill by winning the Battle of Coutras on the road north from Bordeaux with 5,600 men against 7,300 in a royal army led by the Duke of Joyeuse, who died trying to surrender but finding no takers. The next month the Duke of Guise matched Henry of Navarre by defeating an army of mercenaries from the German Palatinate paid for by Queen Elizabeth, at Auneau near Chartres.[86]

The next year was 1588, the Armada year. Early in February a Guise family council agreed on a list of demands to be presented to King Henry III: that he give active support to the Catholic League, remove from his council anyone suspected of heresy, publish and put into effect the decrees of the Council of Trent, establish a nationwide Inquisition, restore lands the Catholic Church had been forced by earlier treaties to sell, increase taxation especially on Calvinists, and seize their property of heretics and execute any found in arms against the king. Henry said he would take these proposals under consideration,

---

[84] Von Pastor, *History of the Popes* XXI, 282-285; Holt, *French Wars of Religion*, p. 124; Jensen, *Diplomacy and Dogmatism*, p. 72; Michael Wolfe, *The Conversion of Henri IV* (Cambridge MA, 1993), pp. 35-36; Buisseret, *Henry IV*, p. 21; Mahoney, *Madame Catherine*, pp. 301-303.

[85] Von Pastor, *History of the Popes*, XXI, 294-295.

[86] Read, *Burghley*, pp. 383-384; Mattingly, *Armada*, pp. 146-148, 150-157, 168-170; Jensen, *Diplomacy and Dogmatism*, pp. 90-92; Buisseret, *Henry IV*, pp. 21-25.

while trying unsuccessfully to buy off Duke Henry of Guise. The king's only specific response was to send his favorite Épernon, who was particularly objectionable to Catholics and suspected of heresy, from Paris to Normandy as provincial governor. In late April the Duke of Guise asked Mendoza, the Spanish ambassador to France, "how much longer he should delay before he should make his move" in conjunction with the Armada. He had long planned to seize Paris just as the Armada sailed. One of the goals of this operation was to draw troops loyal to Henry III away from Boulogne so that the Armada might use it as a port.[87]

On May 9 Duke Henry of Guise arrived in Paris about noon, greeted by crowds bearing arms and shouting: "Long live Guise, the pillar of the Church!" Guise went first to Catherine de Medici, whom he thought (correctly, as it turned out) that he could influence despite the fact that she was reputed to hate him passionately. And she did intercede for him with her son, whom he saw angrily later that day. It was known that one of Henry III's guards had told the king he would gladly kill Guise if ordered, but Catherine feared another St. Bartholomew's day if this happened, and by declaring that she had invited Guise to Paris (actually nobody at court had invited him) she made such an act impossible for the time being. The next day the two Henries met again, surrounded by heavily armed guards. On the 11th an attempt by Henry III and his guards to expel some two thousand Catholic League soldiers now in the capital failed farcically, most of the guards having little desire to fight for their feeble and erratic monarch. By evening the guards had melted away, and Henry called 4,000 Swiss and 2,000 French guards whom he believed more reliable to enter Paris at the coming dawn.[88]

That day, May 12, 1588, became known as the "Day of the Barricades." Paris' narrow streets had always lent themselves to a unique kind of war by barricade, whereby impromptu walls were put up to block the streets, to keep unwanted troops out and large sections of the city in the possession of rebels—in this case Catholic rebels. Henry III immediately issued orders to his newly arrived troops not to injure the person or property of anyone in Paris. Once these orders became known, many Parisians not only joined the defenders of the barricades and helped build more, but cut off or seized the supply wagons of the soldiers. The tocsin began to ring—church bells rung continuously and very fast, a warning of danger to the city. Shots were fired and stones thrown at the soldiers in the ever-volatile Latin Quarter on the left bank of the Seine; the barricades were brought within fifty yards of the royal residence at the Louvre. After suffering 300 killed and many more wounded the Swiss guards began to surrender, pulling out crucifixes, rosaries and scapulars to show the hostile Leaguers that they were Catholics, most being from the strongly Catholic Swiss canton of Lucerne. Henry III now went to Guise and asked him to save the lives

---

[87] Jensen, *Diplomacy and Dogmatism*, pp. 133-134, 137-140 (quote on 139); von Pastor, *History of the Popes*, XXI, 296.

[88] Mattingly, *Armada*, pp. 225-233; Jensen, *Diplomacy and Dogmatism*, pp, 137-138, 140-142; Mahoney, *Madame Catherine*, pp. 313-315.

of his men; the Duke stopped the fighting by his supporters immediately. Henry could only sit in his audience chamber "like the image of a dead man," tears streaming down his cheeks, sobbing: "Betrayed! Betrayed! So many treacheries!" His coldly realistic old mother told him the truth: he would have to promise Guise a Catholic heir to the throne and a much larger role in the government, dismissing Épernon and other officials whom the League opposed. Desperate to avoid a decision, Henry III fled that night to Chartres. Philip II of Spain and the Duke of Parma were very angry at Guise for letting him get away.[89]

In Paris the Guises and the Catholic League set up a government, headed by a 16-man council including some commoners, all very active and convinced Catholics. On July 11 Henry III agreed to all the demands of Duke Henry of Guise, including accepting the Cardinal of Bourbon as his successor and excluding the Calvinist Henry of Navarre, restoring the Treaty of Némours, accepting the Council of Trent, promising to suppress heresy and to convene the Estates-General. All these and other demands were incorporated into the Edict of Rouen which was officially promulgated eight days later. On August 4 he appointed the Duke of Guise commander-in-chief of the French army. On that day the Armada was off the Isle of Wight, almost trapping Frobisher in the Solent, and the outcome of the desperate struggle in the Channel could not be predicted. The Duke of Guise could be expected to provide much help to a victorious Armada.[90]

Since the Duke of Guise was formally allied with Spain by treaty,[91] his fortunes tended to rise and fall with those of Spain. The Armada disaster weakened him as much as the "day of the barricades" in Paris had strengthened him. Though the Catholic League controlled the Estates-General when it met October 16, Henry III—in a rare access of spirit—denounced it in his introductory speech, blaming them and not the Calvinists for France's suffering. The Estates-General actually did relatively little, but the denunciations of the king during its meetings, mainly from priests, were so vehement that his life was endangered. In the words of DeLamar Jensen: "Henry's hatred of Guise deepened into loathing and malevolence as the gloom of winter descended on the stately chateau at Blois and turned its cold stone walls into a gray and silent mausoleum."[92]

---

[89] Mattingly, *Armada*, pp. 233-244 (quote on 241); Jensen, *Diplomacy and Dogmatism*, pp. 142-145; Holt, *French Wars of Religion*, pp. 127-128; Mahoney, *Madame Catherine*, pp. 315-320.

[90] Jensen, *Diplomacy and Dogmatism*, pp. 146-147, 152; Holt, *French Wars of Religion*, pp. 128-129; Mattingly, *Armada*, p. 326; Buisseret, *Henry IV*, p. 25; Mahoney, *Madame Catherine*, pp. 326-327; Read, *Walsingham*, III, 214-215. See above for the battle in the Solent, between the Isle of Wight and the English mainland.

[91] This was the Treaty of Joinville of December 31, 1584, summarized above.

[92] Jensen, *Diplomacy and Dogmatism*, pp. 161-163, 165-167 (quote 167); Mahoney, *Madame Catherine*, p. 329.

On December 22 Henry III spoke with the Duke of Guise, telling him that he and the Queen would be leaving the chateau of Blois for Christmas, but that he wanted to have a royal council meeting early next morning, before they left, at eight o'clock. So Guise rose at dawn of a drear midwinter day, cold, wet and sleeting. He arrived at the council chamber to find that no fire had been lit there, and lit one himself. Then he was told that the King wished to see him privately. A long corridor led to the royal apartments. As the duke strode along it, the king's hand-picked guard of 45 men fell into line behind him. That morning Henry had given each of them a dagger and sacrilegiously had a Mass said for their intentions. Guise whirled about and grasped his sword-hilt, but it became entangled in his cape. Before he could free it the killers were upon him, pinioning his arms and stabbing him. Henry of Guise was a magnificent physical specimen of extraordinary strength. He dragged several of his murderers with him the full length of the king's antechamber until he collapsed at the foot of the king's empty bed. Then somehow he rose to his feet again, took one last step, cried "This is for my sins!" and died. (Was he thinking of how he and his own assassins had treated the wounded Coligny at the beginning of the St. Bartholomew's Day massacre?) Then King Henry III crept out of his hiding place to ask: "Is it done?" Assured that it was, he entered the blood-spattered room and looked down upon his enemy and victim. His next remark tells us much about the psychology of this unworthiest of all the kings of France: "How tall he is! I had not thought he was so tall. He is even taller dead than alive."[93]

The next day Henry III also had Duke Henry's brother Louis, Cardinal of Guise, waylaid and killed by royal guardsmen in a narrow corridor in exactly the same manner as the Duke had been, and arrested the Cardinal of Bourbon, the preferred Catholic heir to the throne whom he had agreed to support. On Christmas Eve he gave the news to his dying mother, telling her: "Now at last I am king of France! Guise is dead!" For much of his life he had been the apple of her eye, her favorite son; now she looked at him as though from a death's head and said, cold as a tomb: "You have ruined the kingdom. Pray God that you not prove to be king of nothing." Eleven days later she was dead.[94] How long ago it must have seemed to Catherine de Medici, in her last hours, that day 29 years before when the sun shone brightly over a festive tournament, and Montgomery the Scotsman drove his lance through the unfastened visor of King Henry II, her husband, and smote him dead, loosing his—and her—sick and disordered sons, one after another, on a France that desperately needed leadership, but was never to find it from any of them.

The news arrived in Paris on Christmas Eve. Naturally, there was an explosion of fury. Homilies at Notre Dame cathedral at midnight Masses called

---

[93] Mattingly, *Armada*, pp. 381-384 (first and third quotes on 384); Jensen, *Diplomacy and Dogmatism*, pp. 168-169 (second quote on 169); Desmond Seward, *The First Bourbon; Henri IV, King of France and Navarre* (Boston, 1971), p. 68; Mahoney, *Madame Catherine*, pp. 331-332.

[94] Jensen, *Diplomacy and Dogmatism*, p. 170; Von Pastor, *History of the Popes*, XXI, 304 (both quotes); Mahoney, *Madame Catherine*, pp. 333-334.

down God's vengeance on "the wicked Valois race." The royal arms were torn from the churches and all public places.[95] On Christmas day a procession of thousands marched through the city and heard Henry III comprehensively condemned as "a perjurer, an assassin, a murderer, a perpetrator of sacrilege, a spreader of heresy, a simoniac, a magician, an infidel, and a man accursed."[96] Pope Sixtus V spoke out just as strongly, though more against the murder of the Cardinal of Guise than the murder of his layman brother, Duke Henry:

> He has been butchered without trial, without sentence, by the civil authority, unknown to us, without the sanction of the Holy See, to which he was so closely united, as though we had not existed, and as though there had been neither Apostolic See, nor God in heaven or earth. The divine law binds all men, nor is anyone excepted. The divine law commands that "thou shalt not kill."[97]

In May 1589 the Pope excommunicated Henry III for the murder of the Cardinal of Guise. The beleaguered king sought to increase his rapidly dwindling strength by a secret alliance with Henry of Navarre, including him again in the royal succession. The alliance was made public at the end of April 1589 when the two men met at Plessis-les-Tours and united their armies against the Guise Duke of Mayenne, now leading the army of the Catholic League after Duke Henry's death. Two months letter their combined army crossed the Seine and laid siege to Paris with 42,000 men. The garrison in the city was only 5,000 men. The besiegers took the bridge of St. Cloud, where they encamped, and planned an all-out attack for August 2.[98]

At seven o'clock in the morning of August 1, when Henry III, in the camp at St. Cloud, was in the process of dressing, a mentally defective monk named Jacques Clément, who for weeks had been telling anyone who would listen that he intended to kill the king, approached him with a dagger and plunged it into his bowels, causing his death from peritonitis before the next dawn. The dying king called Calvinist Henry of Navarre to his bedside and recognized him as a successor, while urging him to take Catholic instruction immediately with a view to his prompt conversion. Henry III confessed his sins, but made no public mention of his excommunication by the Pope or any repentance for the Guise murders. On the day of the death of the last of the Valois dynasty, Calvinist Henry of Navarre proclaimed himself Henry IV of France. About two-thirds of the Catholic nobles and princes accompanying him accepted him as king on his promise "to seek religious instruction from a national church council within the next six months." But a full third of his Catholic supporters left his army at this time, forcing him to raise the siege of Paris, while Spain promised continued

---

[95] Jensen, *Diplomacy and Dogmatism*, p. 176.

[96] Seward, *First Bourbon*, p. 69.

[97] Von Pastor, *History of the Popes*, XXI, 309.

[98] Jensen, *Diplomacy and Dogmatism*, pp. 179-180, 188; Buisseret, *Henry IV*, p. 27; Wolfe, *Conversion of Henri IV*, p. 43; R. B. Wernham, *After the Armada*; *Elizabethan England and the Struggle for Western Europe*, 1588-1595 (Oxford, 1984), pp. 142-143.

active support for the Duke of Mayenne and the Cardinal of Bourbon.[99] Philip II
wrote to Mendoza, his faithful and diligent ambassador to France:

> Because it is of the greatest importance to Catholics, I am infinitely pleased
> with what you have counselled in my name, and I hold your service in
> particular esteem and ask that you continue in the future to advise and help
> the Catholics of France as much as possible, that their cause may prosper. . . .
> They can be assured that when they have need for assistance, for whatever
> matter concerning religion, I will gladly help with whatever is agreed upon.
> For their cause is such that I am honored to befriend and protect them.[100]

Henry of Navarre, supported by only about one-sixth of France,[101] could not
survive long if left alone to fight both the Catholics of France and the might of
Spain, still the world's greatest power despite the defeat of the Armada. It was
time for 69-year-old William Cecil, the shrewdest and most successful enemy of
the Catholic Church in Europe for the 31 years of Elizabeth's reign, to step in
again. In mid-September, in the parlor of his house in Covent Garden, Cecil
declared, with Walsingham and Lord Admiral Howard as witnesses, that the
government of England was prepared to lend Henry of Navarre 20,000 pounds
and to give him a considerable quantity of powder and shot. Queen Elizabeth
had to sell some of her royal lands to get the money. Henry made a hurried trip
to London to pick it up personally. Cecil invited him to his Covent Garden parlor
and handed it over. Henry of Navarre later said it was the largest amount of
money he had ever seen collected in one place. In addition, Cecil with the
Queen's consent made funds available to pay 4,000 Swiss and German
mercenaries to fight for Henry of Navarre in France. They were sent into action
almost at once, landing on October 8, 1589 at Dieppe under the command of
Lord Peregrine Willoughby, a veteran of the wars in the Netherlands. It was just
three months since the assassination of King Henry III.[102]
     With this potent force added to his now growing army, Henry of Navarre
brought up nearly 30,000 men to besiege Paris again in late October, reaching it
before the slow-moving Duke of Mayenne. He seized two sections of the city on
the left bank of the Seine, but could not cross the river; his famous Calvinist
captain, François de la Noue *"Bras de Fer"* ("Iron Arm") nearly drowned in the
rampaging stream. Two days later the dilatory Duke of Mayenne finally arrived

---

[99] Von Pastor, *History of the Popes*, XXI, 320-321; Wolfe, *Conversion of Henri IV*, pp.
43, 53-54, 56-57 (quote on 57); Jensen, *Diplomacy and Dogmatism*, pp. 188-193; Seward,
First Bourbon, p. 73; Buisseret, *Henry IV*, p. 29.

[100] Jensen, *Diplomacy and Dogmatism*, p. 194.

[101] Because he had only minority and factional support at first, without formal
coronation and approval by the Church, Henry of Navarre was not really king yet, and will
consequently be referred to herein only by that name, not as Henry IV of France, until
after his conversion to Catholicism at Saint-Denis in July 1593 he was crowned in the
traditional ceremony at Chartres in February 1594.

[102] Wernham, *After the Armada*, pp. 150-152, 156-157, 160-161; Read, *Burghley*, p.
459.

with 20,000 men, and Henry had to withdraw again from the capital city that steadfastly refused ever to submit to him while he remained a Calvinist.[103]

In November Pope Sixtus V sent word to Philip II that he was ready to conclude an alliance with him to save the Catholic Faith in France. In the increasingly probable event of the death of the aged Cardinal of Bourbon, a prisoner of Henry of Navarre since Henry III's murder of the Cardinal of Guise the preceding Christmas Eve, the Pope promised to accept whatever succession to the French throne was supported by Philip, and endorsed unlimited Spanish support of the League. Of all the Popes since the Council of Trent, it was Sixtus V who most fully understood and appreciated Philip II's unwavering support of the Catholic Church and the Catholic people of all Europe during all of the forty-two years of his reign.[104] Philip accepted and enthusiastically welcomed this alliance in January 1590. However, angered by his request that the Pope excommunicate all cardinals, princes and nobles supporting Henry of Navarre, which the famously hot-tempered Pope took as a threat, and was in fact neither necessary nor wise, Sixtus V pulled back for reconsideration. Disrespectful and boorish pressure from Spanish ambassador to Rome Olivares widened the breach. Though in April Philip II ordered his ambassador to moderate his behavior toward the Pope, the damage was done and the treaty never received final approval.[105]

This infighting among Catholics came at the worst possible time, for Henry of Navarre won his greatest victory at the Battle of Ivry, just 35 miles from Paris, on March 14, 1590. Calling on his men to follow his famous white plume, he routed the plodding Duke of Mayenne and his army in the open field with furious cavalry charges, leaving them with nearly 4,000 casualties compared to only a handful among his men. By the end of April he was besieging Paris for the third time with an army of 15,000 against little more than half that number of defenders. The priests of Paris inspired the people to total resistance, calling on them to be "true Maccabees" carrying "a crucifix and image of the Virgin Mary on their banners." Spanish ambassador Mendoza, though sick and almost blind, was the mainstay of the defense, "visiting outposts, exhorting soldiers, feeding the hungry, and encouraging the people." On May 9 the aged Cardinal Charles de Bourbon died in his cell. By all normal laws of hereditary succession, Henry of Navarre was now king. But the Catholics of Paris still held out against him. On their constancy rode the future of Christendom.[106]

---

[103] Wernham, *After the Armada*, pp. 159-160, 165-166; Buisseret, *Henry IV*, p. 31; Seward, *First Bourbon*, p. 79.

[104] Von Pastor, *History of the Popes*, XXI, 341-342, 347. Unfortunately von Pastor, great Catholic historian though he is, also fails to understand and fully appreciate Philip II as a defender of the Faith.

[105] *Ibid.*, XXI, 355-356, 360.

[106] Jensen, *Diplomacy and Dogmatism*, pp. 206-208; Seward, *First Bourbon*, pp. 80-83; Buisseret, *Henry IV*, pp. 33-34; Holt, *French Wars of Religion*, pp. 137-138; Wernham, *After the Armada*, p. 182; Wolfe, *Conversion of Henri IV*, pp. 97-98 (first quote on 98); Walsh, *Philip II*, p. 677 (second quote).

By the beginning of July most of the food in Paris had been eaten and starvation was setting in among the poor; some 13,000 starved to death during that month. Ambassador Mendoza drew upon his own funds to buy bread and flour and distribute them among the starving. When his money was exhausted he melted down his silver plate and struck Spanish coins and passed them out to the poor. Meanwhile he was sending plea after plea to Philip II, reminding him how much was at stake, saying that Paris must be relieved at any cost. Largely because of the breach between Philip and the Pope, no strong Spanish army, such as Philip had earlier promised from Spain, was available in France. The only man who could bring relief was the ever-victorious Duke of Parma, commanding the Spanish army in the Netherlands. In mid-July Philip ordered Parma to march for Paris. Parma protested; all Flanders might be lost, and more, in the absence of the greater part of his army. The risk was too great. Philip responded, like the flash of a Toledo blade: "If Flanders is lost, it belongs to me!" He would risk all he had, all he was, for Catholic France and Christendom. He gave Parma explicit orders to march to Paris at once.[107]

The Duke of Parma was forever loyal. He did march at once, with no attempt to make excuses or court delays. He left Flanders July 27, the very day the Parisians heroically repulsed a midnight assault which seemed sure to overwhelm them. Parma was the fastest marcher in Europe. In less than a month he arrived at Meaux, just thirty miles from Paris, where he joined the League army of the Duke of Mayenne, giving him a grand total of about 24,000 men. Before the end of August he had opened a corridor to supply Paris. On September 7, covered by a thick morning fog, Parma moved his army across the Marne River by a bridge of boats and took the key stronghold of Lagny by storm before Henry of Navarre even knew he was there. On September 19 he entered Paris in triumph, the siege ended. The majority of Henry of Navarre's outmaneuvered army had already disintegrated under the shock of Parma's advent; its numbers had declined to 2,000 horse and 6,000 foot, and for a third time Calvinist Henry had to pull back from the unconquerable "city of light."[108]

What the Duke of Parma had not been able to do in England, because of the failure of the Spanish Armada under its landsman commander, he had now done in France. England was lost to Catholic Christendom, but France was saved for it. All the credit belongs to Philip II, whose decision and orders alone made it possible.

Pope Sixtus V did not quite live to see it. The sultry heat of August, the ancient dying time in Rome, felled him without warning after only a week's illness, at the age of 69, just two weeks before Parma crossed the Marne.[109]

---

[107] Jensen, *Diplomacy and Dogmatism*, pp. 207-208; Holt, *French Wars of Religion*, p. 138; Wernham, *After the Armada*, p. 185; Kamen, *Philip of Spain*, p. 297; Walsh, *Philip II*, p. 677 (quote).

[108] Geoffrey Parker, *The Dutch Revolt* (London, 1977), p. 227; Seward, *First Bourbon*, pp. 83-84; Buisseret, *Henry IV*, pp. 36-37; Wernham, *After the Armada*, pp. 185-186; Walsh, *Philip II*, pp. 677-678.

[109] Von Pastor, *History of the Popes*, XXI, 373; XXII, 178-180.

The conclave assembled September 7 with 54 of the 67 cardinals present, all Italians but two Spaniards, two Germans, one Frenchman and one Englishman. Despite the small number of Spanish cardinals, the constancy of Philip II to the ancestral faith had made so great an impression that the conclave elected as the new Pope Giovanni Battista Castagna, 69, who had been papal nuncio to Madrid and was on the best of terms with Philip II. He took the name Urban VII—and was dead in twelve days, of Rome's scourge of malaria.[110]

The conclave reassembled October 6 with 52 cardinals present. This time, for whatever reason, there was much more opposition to the Spanish interest. The debates and maneuverings ran on through the whole month of November and into December. On the 4th of that month Cardinal Paleotto received 33 votes, only three less than the required two-thirds. Then Cardinal Niccolò Sfondrato stepped in, and was elected the next day. He had been one of seven cardinals specifically declared by Philip II to be fully acceptable, and he was only 55 years old. More importantly, he was known for his moral purity and personal holiness, a favorite of St. Philip Neri. He was also a great admirer and supporter of Philip II. He took the name Gregory XIV.[111]

In January 1591 Pope Gregory XIV told Philip II that Catholic Paris must be held and that he would grant a monthly subsidy of 15,000 gold scudi to help hold it. He told Philip and his nuncio in France that France must have a Catholic king. He renewed all former decrees against Henry of Navarre as a relapsed heretic, who because of that status had lost his right of succession to the French throne, and told the French bishops they must withdraw all support from Henry within fifteen days or be excommunicated and lose their dioceses. On March 14, 1591 he provided the enormous sum of 400,000 scudi from the papal treasury to aid the French Catholics. He pressed all French Catholics supporting Henry of Navarre to abandon him immediately. Correspondingly, the English increased their aid—financial and military—to Henry and his followers. Queen Elizabeth proposed that he try to take the important and strategically located city of Rouen, the capital of Normandy. In April she sent a fleet under Lord Howard to try again to embarrass and damage Spain at sea. When Howard's fleet attacked the Azores Islands in September, its finest ship, the *Revenge*, was cut off and hammered into pieces by Spanish galleons lying only a few feet away. Its commander, Sir Richard Grenville, though stricken by two mortal wounds, defended her to the last in the famed engagement of "the one against the fifty-three." At the beginning of July Queen Elizabeth committed herself to full financial and military support of the assault on Rouen; just a few days later, Philip II called the Duke of Parma once more to march from the Low Countries into France to rescue Rouen.[112]

---

[110] *Ibid.*, XXII, 315-316, 322-323, 325-327, 330-332.

[111] *Ibid.*, XXII, 338-349, 353-356.

[112] *Ibid.*,Von Pastor, XXII, 369-373; Kamen, *Philip of Spain*, p. 298; Wernham, *After the Armada*, pp. 291-292, 294, 302, 305, 307-308, 310-314, 317, 340-343; Peter Earle, *The Last Fight of the* Revenge (London, 1992), pp. 52-54, 77, 106-148.

Despite his unusually young age for a Pope (56), Gregory XIV had been in poor health throughout most of 1591, and by the end of September he was dying. After a final allocution urging a quick, harmonious conclave to elect his successor, and continued insistence that the King of France must be Catholic, he died October 16. For the conclave, Philip II had sent instructions to Spanish Cardinal Mendoza in Rome that this time there was to be no pressure for any specific candidate, only a list of cardinals to be opposed. There were 56 at the conclave, which convened October 27. Cardinal Antonio Facchinetti received 23 votes on the first ballot and Cardinal Giulio Santori 14. Mendoza then persuaded Cardinal Santori, who was at the top of Philip II's list of unacceptables, to withdraw, and Facchinetti was elected and took the name of Innocent IX. But he was 72 years old, "only skin and bone . . . the shadow of a man." He was crowned November 3 and died December 30. For the fourth time in just over two years, it was again necessary to elect a Pope.[113]

The new conclave assembled January 10, 1592 with 52 cardinals present, and Santori the leading candidate despite Philip II's continued opposition. By the next morning a sharp division had emerged in the College between those for and against Santori—so sharp that each group had a separate Mass of the Holy Spirit said before voting. An irregular ballot was taken at the break of dawn in a room lit only by a few candles, in which it took three hours to count the votes, mainly because of the poor lighting. When finally tallied, it showed Santori with 35 votes and 17 in opposition, just one short of the required two-thirds. The conclave then returned to regular procedure and the first official ballot gave Santori 30 votes. The loss of five votes between morning and evening established a trend, and Santori dropped out of contention, leaving Cardinals Girolamo della Rovere and Ippolito Aldobrandini the leading contenders. After della Rovere died in his conclave cell January 25, Aldobrandini was unanimously elected, taking the name Clement VIII.[114]

The new Pope was "a man of great stature, majestic bearing, pale complexion, with white hair and a well-trimmed white beard." He was kindly, well-liked and very devout, noted for his strict personal mortifications. He was the confessor of the great Catholic historian Baronius, and even as Pope would hear confessions in St. Peter's during Holy Week for up to three hours consecutively. His election at this time was particularly beneficial to the Church because he had represented Pope Sixtus V in Poland and knew that country thoroughly, enabling him better to see the importance of, and act quickly upon the request of several bishops of the Greek rite in eastern Poland to rejoin the Catholic Church with all their people, which led to the Union of Brest-Litovsk in 1596, the largest accession to the Catholic Church at one time since the beginning of the Protestant revolt.[115]

---

[113] Von Pastor, *History of the Popes*, XXII, 384-386, 411-412, 414-416, 418-419, 426-427.

[114] *Ibid.*, XXIII, 10-18.

[115] *Ibid.*, XXIII, 24-30, quote on 32. See below for the Union of Brest-Litovsk.

Meanwhile Henry of Navarre had sent an army to besiege Rouen, held by the Catholic League with Spanish aid. The defenders responded immediately by a fierce sally which was only beaten back with difficulty. On November 23 Henry arrived in person. English militia arrived early in December to reinforce the besiegers, while the Catholic League split down the middle that same month when the Duke of Mayenne, brother of the late Duke of Guise, marched on Paris, arrested most of the Council of Sixteen who had governed Paris for the League, and executed four of them for misusing their power through summary executions. By January Parma was in France, winning a battle at Aumâle but losing a cavalry skirmish at Bures. Meanwhile negotiations were in progress between the Duke of Mayenne, the military leader of the League forces, and Villeroy, a high state official under both Henry III and Henry of Navarre. The Duke of Mayenne told Villeroy that he would accept Henry of Navarre as king the moment he converted to the Catholic Faith, if he agreed to treat Mayenne honorably; but both refused to make their positions public, and on April 11 Henry told an English envoy that he would never give up his religion.[116]

Then Alessandro Farnese, Prince of Parma, showed again why he was the best general in Europe. On April 20, marching at top speed, without baggage, taking the besiegers of Rouen by surprise, he struck with 16,000 men. The besiegers barely escaped, and Parma pinned the greater part of Henry of Navarre's army in the great loop made by the Seine River dear Pont de l'Arche. There was only one bridge by which the army could retreat, and Parma could have destroyed them; but the Catholic League, so often condemned for treason and terror, pleaded with him not to do so. He agreed and took his army back to the neighborhood of Rouen, where, after delivering large quantities of food and other necessities to the city, he decided to seize the fortified town of Caudebec, which was hampering delivery of the supplies. Riding up to reconnoiter Caudebec, he was shot in the arm. The wound required long and painful surgery, and Parma was still in bed two days later when Henry moved to block his retreat across the Seine with 26,000 troops against his 15,000. Parma rose from his bed to evacuate his troops across the tidal Seine, three hundred yards wide, at night, a brilliant operation "far beyond the capacity of most sixteenth-century armies." Further exhausted by this endeavor, unable to rest as he supervised the withdrawal of his army through an increasingly hostile France back to the Low Countries, Parma contracted a lingering infection in his wound which, after months of suffering, spread through his body and killed him in December. The one man who could consistently defeat Henry IV in the field was gone. But he had saved both Paris and Rouen from being conquered by Henry, ensuring that if

---

[116] Wernham, *After the Armada*, pp. 356, 358-359, 364-365, 367-368, 372, 376, 378-379, 387-388; Wolfe, *Conversion of Henri IV*, pp. 108-109; Seward, *First Bourbon*, p. 92; Jensen, *Diplomacy and Dogmatism*, p. 215.

he was to win the French monarchy, it would only be by his conversion, not by force.[117]

On July 10, 1592 Pope Clement VIII had condemned Henry of Navarre with "the utmost severity" and called on all his Catholic followers to withdraw their support from him.[118] Though most of them were not willing to obey immediately, they increased the pressure on Henry to convert and become Catholic. On November 10 many members of the *Parlement* of Paris,[119] which had refused to recognize Henry as king, declared that they recognized his royal title, but could not actually serve him unless and until he became a Catholic. Thirteen out of the sixteen city districts of vehemently Catholic Paris took the same position. On calling an Estates-General at the end of December to discuss the royal succession, the Guise Duke of Mayenne similarly declared that Henry of Navarre was king by hereditary right, but must become a Catholic before he could be acknowledged and served as king. By January 1593 there was increasing agreement among Henry's Catholic supporters that he must take Catholic instruction and proclaim his conversion, but that if he did so, it was not necessary to wait for the Pope to absolve him and formally receive him back into the Church. On February 15 Henry conferred for much of the night with the Protestant Sully, one of his chief advisors, on the pros and cons of converting. Sully advised Henry to make his decision immediately, and to convert if he found himself able sincerely to believe in and practice the Catholic Faith, but not otherwise. Henry responded with a decision to convert, declaring this to be "a course of action by which I will easily achieve all I have fought for, without upsetting anyone"—a comment which certainly underlines the worldly motives for his conversion.[120]

On May 17 Henry of Navarre publicly declared that he was ready to be instructed in the Catholic Faith at an assembly to be convoked in July. Many Paris preachers responded vehemently to this announcement, charging that he was clearly insincere and hypocritical, and as a relapsed heretic could never be trusted to speak truly in matters of faith. Though Henry was technically a relapsed heretic because he converted to save his life after the St. Bartholomew's day massacre, and later, after getting out of Paris, returned to the Calvinism in

---

[117] Howell A. Lloyd, *The Rouen Campaign 1590-1592* (Oxford, 1973), pp. 185-188; Wernham, *After the Armada*, pp. 389-395; Buisseret, *Henry IV*, pp. 38-39 (quote on 39); Seward, *First Bourbon*, pp. 92-93.

[118] Von Pastor, *History of the Popes*, XXIII, 64.

[119] This curious institution, which must never be confused with the similar English word "parliament" (the French equivalent of the English Parliament was the Estates-General), was an hereditary court of nobles charged not only with the responsibility of deciding major legal cases, but also of "registering" royal decrees intended to become permanent laws, and also treaties of peace between France and other nations. A decree or treaty was generally not regarded as in effect or enforceable if it had not been registered by the Parlement of Paris. Other *parlements*, though much less powerful than the one in Paris, were found in several other large cities of France.

[120] Wolfe, *Conversion of Henri IV*, pp. 112-114, 116-120, 123-124 (quote on 124); von Pastor, *History of the Popes*, XXIII, 69-70.

which he had been raised, clearly this conversion was under duress and therefore invalid; though now a heretic, he was not actually relapsed. A proposal by Philip II to elect young Duke Charles of Guise king of France and have him marry Philip's daughter Isabel Clara Eugenia, who was the granddaughter of French King Henry II, came too late to forestall the surging movement to recognize Henry of Navarre as king of France if he converted. A decree of the *Parlement* of Paris June 28 prohibited enthroning a foreigner and reaffirmed the Salic Law against rule of France by a woman, thereby rejecting on both counts the legitimacy of Isabel Clara Eugenia as queen.[121]

By July 1593 Henry had committed himself to conversion, disregarding the strong protests of Queen Elizabeth of England and the 15 arguments against it prepared by ageless William Cecil. He began his instruction, as he had promised earlier to do, on the 15th, and on the 22nd he went to Saint-Denis near Paris, accompanied by about 40 prelates and doctors, writing to his mistress Gabrielle d'Estrées that "tomorrow I shall make a perilous leap." On that day he met all morning and into the afternoon with four Catholic clerics, led by Archbishop Renaud de Beaune, primate of Aquitaine, who were longtime supporters and advisors. The meeting was private; a later official document emphasized the explanation to Henry of the errors of Calvinism, and his acceptance of it. Emerging from the meeting, Henry issued an order that no meat be served at his table that night, which was Friday, nor on any Friday in the future, marking the court's return to traditional Catholic Friday abstinence. He ordered final drafts of his abjuration of Calvinism and his profession of Catholic faith to be prepared by evening, and they were signed the next day.[122]

On the following day, July 25, Henry of Navarre met at dawn in his bedroom with the Calvinist minister La Faye, who promised to pray for him and to serve him in the future as in the past, regardless of his conversion. In return Henry promised to protect the Calvinists from any use of force against them on account of their religion. La Faye then left through a rear door to avoid being seen. At nine o'clock a clerical procession made its way to the abbey church of St. Denis, followed an hour later by a resplendent lay procession in which Henry marched, simply clad in white (the color of purification and innocence), with no emblems of his rank but his royal sword, which he unbuckled as he knelt on the abbey steps before Archbishop de Beaune, accompanied by a group of archbishops, bishops and abbots. De Beaune received him with the ritualistic question: "Who are you?" "I am the king," Henri replied. "What do you want?" the Archbishop then asked. "I want to be received into the bosom of the Roman Catholic Church." "Do you wish to do so freely?" "Yes, I desire it freely." Henry gave him the texts of his abjuration of heresy and profession of faith which he had signed the previous day.[123] Then, turning to the people in the plaza

---

[121] Holt, *Conversion of Henri IV*, pp. 130-136; von Pastor, *History of the Popes*, p. 71; Holt, *French Wars of Religion*, pp. 148-149; Jensen, *Diplomacy and Dogmatism*, p. 217.

[122] Wolfe, *Conversion of Henri IV*, pp. 140-145, 148; Seward, *First Bourbon*, pp. 97-98 (quote on 98); Wernham, *After the Armadas*, pp. 494-498.

[123] Wolfe, *Conversion of Henri IV*, pp. 147-151 (dialogue quotes on 151).

in front of the abbey, with his hand on a Bible, Henry recited a summary of these documents:

> I, Henry, king of France and Navarre by the grace of God, do hereby recognize the Roman Catholic Church to be the true Church of God, holder of all truth and without error. I promise before God to observe and uphold all decrees established by its saintly councils and all canons of the Church, following the advice given to me by prelates and doctors as contained in statements earlier agreed to by me wherein I swear to obey the ordinances and commands of the Church. I also hereby disavow all opinions and errors contrary to the holy doctrines of the Church. I promise as well to obey the Apostolic See of Rome and our Holy Father, the Pope, as have all my predecessors. I will never again depart from Catholicism, but instead persevere in its profession with the grace of God until I die. For this I implore his assistance.[124]

By now an enormous throng had gathered in the plaza, which vociferously acclaimed the king and his statement. Archbishop de Beaune blessed him. He remained kneeling for some time, his head bowed in prayer. Eventually de Beaune lifted him to his feet and led him into the church to the cadenced beat of the drums of the Swiss Guard, with some difficulty since the church was so full of people that some had even climbed up to the windows and the rafters. Henry knelt before the altar and renewed his pledge to live and die a Catholic. A special confessional had been set up behind it, and there Henry made a 20-minute confession to de Beaune, who pronounced him absolved. Then he was led to the royal pew for High Mass. Henry alone received communion in both kinds, then a special privilege of new converts. At this moment a flock of white doves was released in the belfry. Henry left the church with all the insignia of royalty he had put aside when he arrived as a penitent. Dinner followed, then vespers at the abbey church at four o'clock. At five o'clock Henry went to Montmartre, the Hill of Martyrs, where the Jesuit order had been founded, to give thanks to God. Cannonades thundered and fireworks flashed into the evening sky.[125]

Exactly seven months later, at the glorious cathedral of Chartres, Henry of Bourbon, king of Navarre, was crowned King Henry IV of France according to the ancient ritual. Though the Catholic League still held Reims, the traditional coronation city (where St. Joan of Arc had taken Charles VII for his coronation), and at that time still vowed to hold out against the new king, their defeat was highlighted when less than a month later, on March 18, Henry IV took over Paris, heart of the League. There was no opposition, the Spanish garrison of five thousand men quietly marching away. Just four days earlier the Catholic League had sent a remarkable memorial to Pope Clement VIII, saying that their military victory was now almost impossible because of the great desire for peace among the French people and their general acceptance of Henry IV as king, and urging the Pope to support peace on the conditions that Henry should promulgate the

---

[124] *Ibid.*, p. 151.
[125] *Ibid.*, pp. 151-155.

decrees of the Council of Trent and guarantee a Catholic education to his then heir, the Prince of Condé.[126]

In December 1594, conferring with an envoy of Henry IV, Pope Clement VIII made these demands, along with another for the restoration of the Catholic Church in Navarre, conditions for his acceptance of the sincerity of Henry's repentance and conversion. In June 1595 the Pope met at night on a deserted country road with Jacques du Perron, Bishop of Evreux, a convert from Calvinism, to discuss whether he should reconcile Henry IV fully with the Church, and ordered forty hours' devotion in several Roman churches to pray for his enlightenment by God in making this decision. The Spanish and some of the Catholic League in France continued to urge him against reconciling a monarch who had given so many indications of hypocrisy in religion. On August 2 Clement VIII presented the matter to his cardinals, urging them to "weigh well a matter of such great importance as had not occurred for centuries, and not to be guided in their decision by human considerations, by their sympathies for Spain or France, but only as their consciences should direct them for the cause of God and the good of souls." But he made clear that he was in favor of granting absolution to Henry, noting the great danger of schism if it were not granted, and that canon law should not be allowed to stand in the way of this absolution if it was for the good of the Church. He then proceeded to meet with the cardinals individually to discuss the matter. On August 30 he called them together again to announce that more than two-thirds were favorable to Henry's absolution, and to take note of the words of his holy confessor, the great historian Baronius, who reminded him, with reference to Henry IV's sincerity, that only God can read the secrets of the human mind and heart. Keeping that in mind, he had decided to welcome Henry IV back into the Church. This he did, at an impressive ceremony in St. Peter's September 17, in the presence of 34 cardinals.[127]

France had been saved, for the Church and for Christendom, by a very narrow margin. The extent of Henry's sincerity, as Cardinal Baronius[128] so well said, could be known only to God. The historian is in no position to deny it without much clearer evidence than he in fact possesses. Though Henry never said the words so often attributed to him, "Paris is worth a Mass,"[129] the Church might well say that even a king of France personally indifferent to religious truth was a price worth paying to keep France Catholic. Though Henry later gave special privileges to French Calvinists in the Edict of Nantes in 1598,[130] and

---

[126] *Ibid.*, pp. 174-175, 177-178; Seward, *First Bourbon*, pp. 100-105; Buisseret, *Henry IV*, pp. 50-51, 53-54; Holt, *French Wars of Religion*, pp. 158-160; von Pastor, *History of the Popes*, XXIII, 97-98, 100-101; Jensen, *Diplomacy and Dogmatism*, pp. 218-221.

[127] Von Pastor, *History of the Popes*, XXIII 107-108, 112-115, 119-126 (quote on 124), 128-130, 133-141.

[128] The great historian was appointed cardinal by Pope Clement VIII in June 1596 (*ibid.*, XXIII, 46, 207).

[129] Holt, *French Wars of Religion*, p. 153; Seward, *First Bourbon*, p. 98.

[130] Von Pastor, *History of the Popes*, XXIII, 157-161; Holt, *French Wars of Religion*, pp. 162-166; Sutherland, *Huguenot Struggle*, pp. 328-332.

protected them from persecution, he remained actively and visibly Catholic throughout the remaining fifteen years of his reign, and the prospects of another successful Calvinist rebellion in France were essentially nil. Henry did not decide to become Catholic quickly or easily—not until four years after he first claimed the kingship following the assassination of Henry III. Though not a man marked by any strong sense of filial duty, he could hardly have forgotten the passionate Calvinism of his mother, Queen Jeanne d'Albret of Navarre,[131] and how shocked and betrayed she would have felt by his conversion. Whatever his sincerity when he made his decision to convert, there was much in his earlier life to keep him from the Catholic Church. It is unlikely, barring very special graces, that he would have converted only by his own inclination. A substantial element in his motivation seems likely to have been sheer necessity, created by the deep-rooted strength of the Catholic tradition of most of the French people, the magnificent heroism of the Parisians during the great siege of 1590, and the military genius and loyal service of Alessandro Farnese, Duke of Parma. Like the Spanish Armada, the decision of King Henry IV to preserve the old religion in France was primarily a battle decision, but this time in favor of Christendom and the Catholic cause.

After his coronation and unification of France in 1594, on January 16, 1595 Henry IV declared war on Spain, to unite the country more strongly and to forestall further invasions from Belgium.[132] England was still continuing the war with Spain which Queen Elizabeth had begun by supporting rebels in the Low Countries and by plundering Spanish ships and colonies in the Caribbean and the Pacific, and which Philip II had tried to answer with the Armada. Henry had received a great deal of English aid in his fight against the League, and continued to work with the English although no longer of their religion. Much was expected from the prowess of the English navy, especially after its Armada victory, but little resulted from its three great expeditions over the next three years: the first led in the fall of 1595 by Drake and Hawkins to the West Indies, where both of them died;[133] the second led by Lord Admiral Howard, who had

---

[131] See Chapter Six, above.

[132] Seward, *First Bourbon*, p. 107; Jensen, *Diplomacy and Dogmatism*, p. 221; Holt, *Wars of Religion in France*, p. 161.

[133] R. B. Wernham, *The Return of the Armadas; the Last Years of the Elizabethan War against Spain, 1595-1603* (Oxford, 1994), pp. 47-49, 51-53; Cummins, *Drake*, pp. 236-241, 244, 246-248, 250, 252-257. Even a Catholic historian, for whom Francis Drake must always represent the enemy, can pay tribute to his valor and his right to defend Plymouth, his home, by quoting the immortal poem of Henry Newbolt, "Drake's Drum": "Take my drum to England, hang et by the shore, / Strike et when your powder's runnin' low; / If the Dons sight Devon, I'll quit the port o' Heaven, / An' drum them up the Channel as we drummed them long ago. / Drake he's in his hammock till the great Armadas come, / (Capten, art tha sleepin' there below?), / Slung atween the round shot, listenin' for the drum, / And dreamin' arl the time o' Plymouth Hoe. / Call him on the deep sea, call him up the Sound, / Call him when ye sail to meet the foe; / When the old trade's plyin' and the old flag flyin' /They shall find him ware and wakin', as they found him long ago." (Cummins, *op. cit.*, p. 298)

commanded against the Armada, to the coasts of Spain in 1596, which ravaged the town and churches of Cádiz, but did little else;[134] the third, led to the Azores Islands by the bombastic and incompetent Earl of Essex in 1597, the biggest fiasco of all.[135]

Despite his rapidly declining health, being badly crippled by gout spreading all over his body, Philip II of Spain was sufficiently aroused by these forays and distressed by memories of the failure of the Armada, to make one last effort at a major naval assault on England. On September 18 Admiral Padilla left the north Spanish port of Ferrol with 98 ships and 17,000 men, had orders to seize and hold the port of Falmouth and make Plymouth untenable as a naval base, though there was no longer any thought of seizing London and overthrowing the government. After being forced back by storms, Padilla sailed again from La Coruña a month later, with additional instructions to try to intercept Essex's fleet returning from the Azores. On October 22 this second Spanish armada was approaching the English coast, just a few leagues away, on a gentle wind. The English had no idea they were there and almost no ships left in home waters to resist them. But then a sudden northeasterly gale blew up, which continued all through the night. One ship began to break up and another lost her foremast. Padilla, no doubt remembering the fate of the Armada and with a far less comprehensive and historic mission, took his 96 remaining ships and went home. The verdict of battle and storm in 1588 stood.[136]

During 1597 the Spanish, with still some support from diehards of the Catholic League, succeeded in taking the important town of Amiens in northern France in March, while also holding strategic Calais near Belgium. By September, after a long siege, Henry IV repulsed a Spanish relieving army from the Low Countries and regained Amiens. The war between France and Spain then stagnated, and both monarchs wanted to be rid of it. Peace was made in May 1598 by the Treaty of Vervins, a small town near the Belgian border. Philip II returned Calais to France, and parts of Brittany which Spanish troops had occupied, and abandoned his daughter's now moribund claim to the throne of France, while Henry IV gave a bit of Burgundy, the ancestral realm of Philip's father Charles V, to Philip. It was a fair and reasonable peace. Though the war of Spain with England went on until Queen Elizabeth died five years later, it was essentially confined to Ireland where the Nine Years War was raging.[137]

---

[134] Wernham, *Return of the Armadas*, pp. 56, 58, 93-94, 96-104, 106-112; Read, *Burghley*, pp. 520-521, 526; Kamen, *Philip of Spain*, pp. 306-308; Walsh, *Philip II*, pp. 712-713.

[135] Wernham, *Return of the Armadas*, pp. 159-160, 162-164, 171-179, 181-182; Read, *Burghley*, pp. 533-535.

[136] Kamen, *Philip of Spain*, pp. 306, 308-309, 311; Walsh, *Philip II*, p. 718; Wernham, *Return of the Armadas*, pp. 184-187.

[137] Wernham, *Return of the Armadas*, pp. 150-152, 185-186, 196; Seward, *First Bourbon*, pp. 116-117; Buisseret, *Henry IV*, pp. 66-67; Holt, *Wars of Religion in France*, p. 162. For the Nine Years War see below, this chapter.

It will be recalled that King John III of Sweden had been obviously attracted to the Catholic Church during his marriage with Princess Catherine Jagellon of Poland, who died in 1583, but his attempts to reintroduce the ancient faith into Sweden, which had not known it for forty years, were unsuccessful.[138] John III died in November 1592, leaving a son by Catherine who was now king of Poland, Sigismund, and a brother Charles, who took effective control of the country while Sigismund was still in Poland.[139] To Sigismund, English historian of Sweden Michael Roberts pays this striking tribute:

> The dominant interest of his life was his religion; the core of his character was a profound seriousness and a fundamental integrity. In the last resort he could contemplate without any sense of personal sacrifice the loss of two kingdoms, provided that he were assured of gaining the kingdom of Heaven.[140]

Pope Clement VIII had been in Poland when he was Cardinal Aldobrandini. He knew the passionate Catholicity of the Poles. Under a half-Polish king who was also king of Poland, there were potentially even better prospects than in the time of John III for bringing Sweden back to the Catholic Church. In January 1593, on receipt of the news of John III's death, Clement VIII set up a special committee of six cardinals to work to maximize those prospects. At almost the same time, Duke Charles and the Swedish royal council established, without first seeking Sigismund's permission, a joint interim government which pledged itself to maintain religion in Sweden according to the Lutheran Confession of Augsburg. On January 19 Sigismund III sent an open letter to the people of Sweden guaranteeing his protection to the established Lutheran church there and promising that he would not persecute it, and Duke Charles summoned a Lutheran national church council to meet in the archepiscopal city of Uppsala.[141]

Despite his sterling character, young Sigismund (the third king of that name in Poland, the first in Sweden), only 26 years old, did not prove a strong leader, showing a distinct tendency to procrastinate. His uncle Duke Charles was thorough, meticulous, shrewd and determined to keep Sigismund's hands off all the levers of power. Sweden's loyalty to the political principle of succession to the monarchy by the eldest son, taken for granted in the rest of Western Europe, was not well established; Sigismund's own father had deposed his elder brother Eric XIV, though Eric does appear to have been insane, and his grandfather Gustavus Vasa had established the principle for the first time in Swedish history. Poland's elective monarchy rejected hereditary succession altogether. Politically speaking, Sigismund's only hope of prevailing in Sweden lay with the

---

[138] See Chapter Seven, above.

[139] Michael Roberts, *The Early Vasas; a History of Sweden 1523-1611* (Cambridge, England, 1968), p. 326; Oskar Garstein, *Rome and the Counter-Reformation in Scandinavia*, Volume II (1583-1622), p. 95; von Pastor, *History of the Popes*, XXIV, 84.

[140] Roberts, *Early Vasas*, p. 330.

[141] Ibid., pp. 328, 331-333; Garsten, *Rome and the Counter-Reformation in Scandinavia*, II, 71, 95; von Pastor, *History of the Popes*, XXIV, 84.

redoubtable governor of Finland, Klas Fleming, whose loyalty to his true king never wavered. In February 1593 Sigismund ordered Fleming to take orders only from him, not from Duke Charles or the interim government—orders Fleming faithfully obeyed until his death.[142]

The Lutheran national council called by Duke Charles met at Uppsala at the beginning of March, attended by over 300 clergy, nine members of the royal council, and the chancellor of the kingdom, and chaired by the radical Lutheran Petrus Jonae, just appointed bishop. The chancellor, Nils Gyllenstierna, declared that Swedish religious unity must be maintained to avoid the fate of France and the Low Countries, and that the council would support the maintenance of Lutheranism; Sigismund III must not be allowed to become "lord and master of our faith and our consciences." Within a week the council had unanimously rejected the "red book" liturgy King John III had compelled them to use, which notably resembled Catholic liturgy; unanimously adopted the original Lutheran Confession of Augsburg as Sweden's creed; and called for the destruction of the last remaining convent in Sweden, St. Bridget's at Vadstena; for the expulsion of all Catholics in Sweden who criticized Lutheranism; for excluding all Catholics from government office; and for requiring all ministers and teachers to adhere publicly to the Augsburg Confession. On March 18 the council publicly stripped the clerical garb from Petrus Paulinus Gothus, who had been court chaplain to John III, and on the 25th they elected the most bitterly anti-Catholic prelate in Sweden, the puritanical Abraham Angreae Angermannus, as Archbishop of Uppsala (a seat currently vacant) and primate of the Swedish church.[143]

It was not until mid-September that the slow-moving Sigismund finally embarked for Sweden from Danzig in Poland, on ships provided by Governor Fleming of Finland. But he took only 400 Polish soldiers with him, naively believing that most Swedes would welcome him and be offended if he brought a large foreign military force. In fact, to bring so few exposed him to the contempt of many Swedes, while also placing him in real personal danger. He was accompanied by the papal nuncio to Poland, Germanico Malaspina, and also by Governor Fleming. After a stormy voyage, he arrived in Stockholm October 10. He quickly realized the difficulties of his position. When Malaspina urged him not to recognize Angermannus as Archbishop of Uppsala and install a Catholic prelate in his place, Sigismund "sighed deeply and said that such an appointment was quite out of the question in the circumstances." Four days later Duke Charles and the royal council told him bluntly that he could not even be crowned if he did not endorse the Uppsala resolutions and accept Angermannus as Archbishop.[144]

---

[142] Roberts, *Early Vasas*, pp. 337-338 and *passim*.

[143] Garstein, *Rome and the Counter-Reformation in Scandinavia*, II, 97-101 (quote on 99), 103-104, 106-107; Roberts, *Early Vasas*, p. 334; von Pastor, *History of the Popes*, XXIV, 85.

[144] Garstein, *Rome and the Counter-Reformation in Scandinavia*, II, 92 (for quote), 122; Roberts, *Early Vasas*, pp. 338-339; von Pastor, *History of the Popes*, XXIV, 90.

At the beginning of December the Swedish Lutherans demanded that Sigismund pledge to bring up his eldest son as a Lutheran, limit the number of priests at his court to ten, transfer the convent at Vadstena to a Lutheran minister, re-establish the University of Uppsala under Protestant control, permit the holding of church councils without his permission, and drop his power to make church appointments. Sigismund asked his uncle Charles if there were any prospect for at least the toleration of Catholics in Sweden; Duke Charles refused to answer him. On February 11, 1594, following a delayed funeral for King John III at which Angermannus preached the sermon, the Estates of Sweden (the *riksdag*) met in anger, demanding that Sigismund confirm the acts of the Lutheran council at Uppsala before his coronation and that he make no buildings available to Catholics nor allow Mass to be said anywhere but in his royal chapel—the same conditions imposed by the Calvinists in Scotland on Mary Queen of Scots. They declared they would "never" permit the free preaching and practice of the Catholic Faith in Sweden, and would rebel against Sigismund if he did not accept their demands. The pressure on Sigismund became intolerable, not least by the fact that the Estates had 2,000 soldiers to "guard" them, while he had only 400—five to one odds against him. He capitulated, agreeing to the confirmation of Angermannus as Archbishop of Uppsala according to the Lutheran ritual, on the very morning of the day of his own coronation, and to an accession charter in which he pledged to give no office to anyone not Lutheran nor to any foreigner, to accept a Lutheran monopoly on education, and to govern with the "advice" of Duke Charles, who refused to kneel before his king when he swore fealty to him.[145]

A more unpromising beginning for a reign can hardly be imagined; but, above all, these conditions imposed on King Sigismund for his coronation show how difficult it would be for even a much more energetic, persistent and capable ruler than he to supplant Protestantism in a country where it had become so deeply entrenched. By the advent of King Sigismund only the oldest inhabitants could remember the Catholic Sweden of seventy years before, or the heroic resistance of Nils Dacke sixty years before.[146] And the bitter, almost universal hostility to the Mass, inexplicable by any strictly political or economic analysis, shows once again the real fundamentals of the struggle: whether or not Christ should continue to appear on the altars of Christendom and be taken in communion by the faithful.

Following the advice of his nuncio Malaspina, Pope Clement VIII forgave Sigismund for these concessions, which the king later took oath before Malaspina were extracted from him under duress. Sigismund had promised his Polish subjects that he would return within a year, but he made a substantial effort to retain some authority in Sweden before he left. He refused to recognize his uncle as regent during his absence, and when informed that he might be captured and

---

[145] Garstein, *Rome and the Counter-Reformation in Scandinavia*, II, 122, 128-130, 132, 141, 144-147, 188-189; Roberts *Early Vasas*, pp. 339-340, 342-345; von Pastor, *History of the Popes*, XXIV, 98-99.

[146] For Nils Dacke see Chapter Four, above.

imprisoned before he could leave, he sent for ships and more troops from Poland, to which Duke Charles and the royal council vehemently objected when they learned about it. Finally he made Charles and the council joint regents, hoping they would start fighting each other. He appointed Catholic friends or relatives governors of the Swedish provinces, to work closely with Klas Fleming of Finland. He confirmed Karin Olsdotter as the last abbess of St. Bridget's convent at Vadstena. On a stormy night in mid-August 1594 he left Stockholm to return to Poland. On reaching it, he and his wife went to the shrine of Our Lady of Czestochowa, then as now the most famous in Poland, to give thanks to the Blessed Virgin Mary for their survival. Lutheran ministers in Sweden thundered so much against this "public abasement before a graven image" that even Duke Charles protested.[147]

Within less than a month the royal council recognized Duke Charles as head of the government in Sigismund's absence, which Sigismund himself never did. In January 1595 the Lutheran church at Uppsala required and strictly enforced an annual examination of each person in every parish in the archdiocese, to see if he knew the new Lutheran catechism based on the decrees of the council at Uppsala. The ministers went house to house to give the examination, which completed the indoctrination of virtually the whole population of Sweden in Lutheranism. All surviving traces of Catholic rites, ceremonies and devotions were stamped out. In December of that year Duke Charles extended these examinations to the whole country. In mid-October Charles convened the Estates to declare him regent in defiance of the king, who had not consented to the meeting which legally only the reigning monarch had authority to call. Charles now declared that any order from Sigismund would not bind without his approval. Archbishop Angermannus led the Estates in agreeing to meet these demands. The convent at Vadstena was seized and, after all attempts (including an appearance by Duke Charles in person, and torture) to make the nuns reject their Catholic faith were firmly rejected, eight of the eleven of them followed their king to Catholic Poland.[148]

One by one most of the governors installed by Sigismund before he left Sweden were forced out during the next four years, and Duke Charles stirred up rebellion in Finland against Klas Fleming. Sigismund's demand in September 1596 that his uncle resign as regent or obey him went unheeded. In December 1596 the province of Dalarna called for Duke Charles to be king. Klas Fleming, loyal unto death, fought on heroically in Finland against all that Charles could send against him, but died in April 1597. In February 1598 Polish envoy Samuel Laski appeared before Duke Charles to formally warn him that he was in rebellion and if he did not immediately give obedience to King Sigismund, the King would lead a military expedition against Sweden. Charles contemptuously refused. On hearing of this response, the Polish *Sejm* (parliament), angered by

---

[147] Garstein, *Rome and the Counter-Reformation in Scandinavia*, II, 142-143, 149-155, 158-161, 179; Roberts, *Early Vasas*, p. 352; von Pastor, *History of the Popes*, XXIV, 101.

[148] Garstein, *Rome and the Counter-Reformation in Scandinavia*, II, 173, 201-210; Roberts, *Early Vasas*, pp. 353-360; von Pastor, *History of the Popes*, XXIV, 102-104.

the insult to their king, offered to fund a substantial armed force to accompany Sigismund to Sweden. But to conquer a country as large and as militantly anti-Catholic as Sweden was beyond their resources. Arriving at Kalmar in August with only 5,000 men, Sigismund won some initial victories by virtue of surprise, but Duke Charles came quickly from Finland where Klas Fleming's successor Arvid Stalarm was still fighting, and met Sigismund at the village of Stangebro near Linköping. They agreed to a truce, but a fog came up and Duke Charles immediately broke the truce so as to advance under cover of the fog. His surprise attack in violation of his word overwhelmed the outnumbered Poles. Charles captured his nephew and forced him to accept, as a condition of his liberation, the Treaty of Linköping, which reaffirmed his accession charter, required him to disband his army, and forgave Charles his rebellion and all his acts against the royal authority. Utterly discouraged, on November 1 Sigismund sailed away to return to Poland, with only the castle of Kalmar left in his hands in all of Sweden. He never saw his native country again. The next year Duke Charles stormed Kalmar and the Estates formally deposed Sigismund, with a new law that Swedish kings must always be Lutheran.[149]

Duke Charles, hesitating to appear as an open usurper (which of course he was), did not formally take the crown until 1607. He was the father of Gustavus Adolphus, who won the Thirty Years War in Germany for the Protestants.

Despite his defeat in Sweden, Sigismund III became one of the great kings of Poland, where his staunch Catholicity was an asset rather than a liability. He played an essential part in a story unique in the history of the cleaving of Christendom: a reunion of a full million Eastern Christians with the Catholic Church. From it come virtually all Ukrainian Catholics today, especially after Ukraine was moved substantially westward at the expense of Poland during World War II. It was called the Union of Brest-Litovsk, made in 1596.

Poland and Lithuania, united in the person of their common monarch since the late fourteenth century when pagan King Jagiello of Lithuania became a Catholic in order to marry Queen Jadwiga of Poland, had been fully merged in a common realm quite recently, in 1569 under Sigismund II.[150] Lithuania encompassed most of what are today called Ukraine and Belarus, whose people (outside Lithuania proper, the present much smaller state of that name, where Lithuanian is the native language) were known as Ruthenians, the more recent

---

[149] Roberts, *Early Vasas*, pp. 363, 365-366, 371-372, 378-386; Garstein, *Rome and the Counter-Reformation in Scandinavia*, II, 218, 220, 223-224, 227-229, 236, 238-240. When he heard of the danger to his king, Governor Stalarm of Finland gathered a fleet and rushed across the Baltic to Stockholm to rescue him, but arrived a week too late, after Sigismund had signed the Treaty of Linköping (Roberts, *op. cit.*, p. 385). Perseverance was not among Sigismund's many virtues.

[150] Davies, *God's Playground; a History of Poland* (New York, 1984), I, 152-154. For a somewhat tendentious account of the consequences of this closer union for the Ruthenians, whom he anachronistically calls Ukrainians, see Nicholas Fr-Chirinovsky, *An Introduction to Ukrainian History* (New York, 1984) I, 24-26. For Jagiello and Jadwiga, see Volume Three, Chapter 13 of this history.

names not having yet come into use. The Ruthenians spoke a Slavic language related to both modern Russian and Ukrainian. Ukraine was full of migrating Cossacks, its wide-open range consequently being unfavorable to farming despite the superlative richness of its famous "black earth," so that it had a much smaller population than Poland. Poles and Lithuanians were almost all Latin Catholics; the people native to Ukraine and Belarus were almost all Eastern Orthodox. But along the linguistic and ethnic border (never very well defined) there was considerable intermingling, so that several cities had two bishops, one of the Catholic Latin Rite, the other following the Greek Orthodox patriarch in Constantinople rather than the Pope.

The Ruthenians[151] had come closer than any of the other elements of the Greek Orthodox Church to reuniting fully with the Catholics after the Council of Florence in 1439.[152] But the turmoil in the Balkans accompanying the great Turkish sweep northward, which conquered Constantinople in 1453, engulfed Hungary in 1526, and crested at the walls of Vienna in 1529, though it did not quite reach the Ruthenians, largely cut them off from Rome. Through these angry decades Ruthenian loyalty to the agreements at Florence dimmed until it was extinguished. But now the Church, reinvigorated by the Council of Trent and the Jesuits, was increasingly active in Poland and Lithuania through numerous educational missions and especially the writings of the great Polish Jesuit Peter Skarga in favor of religious reunion. Skarga appealed to the Ruthenian church to join the Catholic Church with their traditional rite in their full million-strong body, rather than by individual conversions to the Latin rite.[153]

The Turks had viewed the patriarchate of Constantinople, as much as the city itself, as a prize of war. They made and unmade patriarchs at will. Since the former Byzantine emperors used to do exactly the same thing, the Eastern church had never developed a strong doctrine of patriarchal independence, so it accepted control by the ruling power even when it was Muslim. Within a few years after the Turkish conquest the patriarchs had become—mostly—pathetic puppets. The Eastern Orthodox Church, still theoretically united under them, sank deeper and deeper into corruption, apathy and chaos. When in 1572 a more active and determined patriarch, Jeremias II, tried to exert his authority, the Turks first removed and imprisoned him, then reinstated him, then removed him again, then reinstated him for a second time. In 1589 Jeremias II elevated the Archbishop of Moscow to the status of patriarch, though still insisting that he had the ultimate primacy. But, when invited by many Russians and Ruthenians to leave Constantinople and live with them in freedom and a common faith, he refused. The result was that his series of removals stood as a warning that Muslims now exercised ultimate authority over the Eastern Orthodox church, and fed the

---

[151] Henceforth in this chapter this name will be used for Ukrainians, Belorussians, and Poles descended from them.

[152] See Volume Three, Chapter 13 of this history.

[153] Oscar Halecki, *From Florence to Brest (1439-1596)*, 2nd ed. (New York, 1968), pp. 197-203, 207-209; Davies, *God's Playground*, I, 168, 170.

pretensions of the Russians who held that now only their own patriarch had religious authority over them.[154]

This created a real possibility that Russia, hereditary enemy of Poland and Lithuania, might impose its religious authority on the Ruthenians, who made up a substantial part of the population of Poland and Lithuania. Therefore in June 1594 the Orthodox Ruthenian Bishop of Lutsk, Cyril Terlecki, took the initiative in obtaining the signatures of all but one of the Ruthenian bishops on a statement supporting reunion with Rome, and a petition asking for endorsement of the reunion by King Sigismund and protection from any reprisals that might be attempted by the leading Eastern Orthodox nobleman in the Polish Commonwealth, Prince Constantine Ostrogsky of Kiev, who was adamantly opposed to the proposed Union and reputed to have strong leanings toward Calvinism. A report on Terlecki's initiative was passed on enthusiastically to Pope Clement VIII (who had spent some time in Poland himself) by his nuncio in Poland, Malaspina, and received by the Pope with equal enthusiasm.[155]

At the beginning of December Bishop Terlecki, accompanied by Bishop Adam Pociej of Brest-Litovsk (significantly, a convert from Calvinism), met with Bernard Maciejowski, the Latin Bishop of Lutsk, at the latter's home at Torczyn. There Terlecki—fluent in both Latin and Ruthenian—drafted a new and expanded declaration on reunion that superseded all earlier ones, and was immediately accepted by his companions. Drafts in Ruthenian, Polish and Latin were prepared. It set forth as the chief reasons for the Union the penetration of Protestant sects, even Unitarians, into Poland and Lithuania and the need to combat their influence, and the inability of the Ruthenian church to trust a patriarch under infidel control. The declaration accepted papal primacy not only dutifully but enthusiastically, stating the desire of the signatories henceforth to worship God "with our dearest brethren the Romans, remaining under the same visible pastor of God's Church, to whom such pre-eminence had always been due." By February 1595 Terlecki and Pociej obtained and sent on to Rome signatures to this statement by Archbishop Rahoza of Kiev and Bishops Gregory of Polotsk and Vitebsk, Zbirujski of Chelm, and Pelczycki of Pinsk and Turov, together with his auxiliary Ionas Hohol. King Sigismund III had written to Bishop Pociej congratulating him on his commitment to church reunion with the Ruthenians.[156]

The opposition surfaced in March 1595 with a letter from Prince Constantine Ostrogsky of Kiev to Bishop Terlecki condemning his plan for reunion with Rome, and all the Ruthenian bishops for supporting it. The somewhat timid and hesitant Archbishop Rahoza of Kiev, the primate of the Ruthenians, in response to a second request made by Bishops Terlecki and Pociej, made public in May his support for the Torczyn declaration for reunion. On June 22 he met with Terlecki and Pociej at Brest-Litovsk and together they drew up a letter to Pope Clement VIII stating that in view of the captivity of the

---

[154] Halecki, *Florence to Brest*, pp. 222-235.
[155] Halecki, *Florence to Brest*, pp. 268-269, 271-272.
[156] *Ibid.*, pp. 273-277 (quote on 275), 281-283.

Patriarchs of Constantinople to the Turks, and with the strong agreement of their king Sigismund III, they wished to adhere to the reunion made at Florence but later abandoned, provided they could keep their ancestral liturgy. A few days later, Ostrogsky persuaded two bishops who had previously supported the reunion, Balaban of Lvov and Kopystenski or Przemysl, to withdraw their approval of the reunion, and lashed out in a violent letter to a Protestant member of the powerful Radziwill family condemning the proposal as treason to their ancestral church and the Pope as "the devil himself." He urged a Protestant-Orthodox alliance against Rome and boasted that he could bring up 20,000 men to stop it. The Protestants responded by holding a synod at Toruń in August for this purpose. But Ostrogsky never assembled so much as a thousand men.[157]

On August 12 King Sigismund III, rejecting the request of Prince Ostrogsky, refused to call another Orthodox synod on the question and approved the request of the Ruthenian bishops for reunion with the Catholic Church, declaring that once approved by the Pope, they should have all the rights and privileges of the Latin Church. As it became clear how deep and widespread was the support for the reunion, the weathervane Bishops Balaban of Lvov and Kopystenski of Pinsk changed sides again, renewing their earlier acceptance of the reunion and defying Prince Ostrogsky. Bishops Terlecki and Pociej set out from Cracow to Rome on October 6, notwithstanding reports that on an earlier journey Ostrogsky had sent 150 men to kill them. They arrived in Rome safely on November 17 and were given an audience just two days later by Pope Clement VIII, who was greatly impressed with them and their willingness, even eagerness, to make so arduous and dangerous a journey on their mission of reunion.[158]

On December 23, 1595, in a solemn ceremony before Pope Clement VIII with 33 cardinals, including many diplomats and other officials at Rome, at the Hall of Constantine in the Vatican, Bishops Terlecki and Pociej made a Catholic profession of faith and declared that the other six Ruthenian bishops all joined in it. The profession of faith did not require the Ruthenians to say Creed with the *filioque*, but specified that their bishops nevertheless upheld an orthodox understanding of the procession of the Holy Spirit and of purgatory. They pledged full acceptance of the decrees of the Council of Trent. Declaring that it was licit to use either leavened or unleavened bread in the Eucharist (which had always been Catholic teaching), the Pope proclaimed them—and all others who would follow their example—true Catholics, and granted permission for them to continue to celebrate the Eucharist according to their traditional liturgy. Afterward he invited the two bishops to participate with him in the Christmas Eve vesper service. Later he granted to Archbishop Rahoza of Kiev the faculty

---

[157] *Ibid.*, pp. 277-279, 283-284, 287, 295-298 (quote on 297); von Pastor, *History of the Popes*, XXIV, 130-131.

[158] Halecki, *Florence to Brest*, pp. 298-300, 302, 305-310, 314-316, 321-322; von Pastor, *History of the Popes*, XXIV, 131.

to consecrate bishops, but required him first to obtain confirmation for his nominees from the Pope.[159]

In May 1596 Sigismund III authorized the holding of a formal synod of the Ruthenian bishops in October to confirm the Union, and confirmed them all in the possession of their dioceses (Ostrogsky and his adherents were making vigorous efforts to have them deposed—generally much easier to do with an Eastern bishop than a Latin one). Sigismund took the precaution of declaring that only bishops, clergy, and interested Ruthenian laymen would be allowed to attend the synod, not foreigners or Protestants. Meletius Pigas, the vehemently anti-Catholic Coptic patriarch of Alexandria, wrote to Ostrogsky urging him to fight on against the Union, and sent to him Cyril Lucaris, a Greek "Orthodox" bishop who openly professed Calvinism. Sigismund III in turn designated Prince Nicholas Radziwill, Grand Chancellor Sapieha of Lithuania, and his Grand Treasurer—all strong Catholics—to protect the synod, and made Bishop Maciejowski and the Jesuit Father Skarga his personal representatives there.[160]

The Ruthenian synod opened at Brest-Litovsk on October 16 at the cathedral of Bishop Pociej. Prince Ostrogsky was there for it, accompanied by Cyril Lucaris and another Greek named Nicephorus who claimed to have a four-year-old commission from Patriarch Jeremias II of Constantinople, recently deceased, giving him broad powers of authority and supervision over the Ruthenians. In Ostrogsky's train were also the two chameleon bishops, Balaban of Lvov and Kopystenski of Przemsyl, who had changed sides again; the archimandrite of the famous Monastery of the Caves of Kiev; and several hundred armed men. No church would have them; they had to meet in the house of a Unitarian in the city. Each side claimed its meeting was the only legitimate synod, one under the authority of the king and the Pope, the other under the presumed authority of Nicephorus representing the late Patriarch of Constantinople. Nicephorus drew up a decree of deposition for Archbishop Rahoza of Kiev, who presided at the synod in the cathedral. The king's armed forces prevented it from being delivered in person, so it had to be shouted from outside the closed cathedral door. No one inside paid any attention to it. On October 19, the fourth day of its session, the synod issued a Charter of Union which reviewed the original unity of the Church and the history of the Eastern schism, emphasizing the primacy of the Pope and the Council of Florence. All the church bells of the city rang in celebration of the reunion and a great procession marched through the streets, singing "Te Deum" in Ruthenian, from the cathedral to the Latin church of St. Mary's where the Blessed Sacrament brought from the Greek church was placed on the altar.[161]

---

[159] Halecki, *Florence to Brest*, pp. 327-333, 340; von Pastor, *History of the Popes*, XXIV, 132-136.

[160] Halecki, *Florence to Brest*, pp. 346-347, 359-361, 363-364. The Coptic Church was a relic of the Monophysite heresy of the fifth and sixth centuries, which retained its hold on the dwindling number of Christians remaining in Muslim Egypt.

[161] *Ibid.*, pp. 355-360, 367-371, 374-382, 384-388.

It was a moment well worthy of celebration. Never before nor since in modern history have a million people come into the Catholic Church at once.

In Ireland the merciless crushing of the explicitly Catholic Desmond rebellion in Munster[162] had struck so heavy a blow as to paralyze the spirit of resistance to English Protestant rule—over the whole of Ireland for a decade, and over two generations in Munster. The most Irish part of Ireland was now the north: Ulster and Connaught. The principal family and clan of Ulster, from the earliest remembered or recorded history of Ireland, was the O'Neills, who had supplied many High Kings in the days before the coming of the Vikings and then of the English. The principal family and clan of County Donegal, in northwest Ulster and northern Connaught, was the O'Donnells. Northern Ireland had not yet seen much actual penetration by the English, though England claimed dominion over it. It was still rural, traditional Ireland, where almost no English was spoken, totally Catholic, including St. Patrick's own see of Armagh, site of the arduous pilgrimage mountain climb up Croagh Patrick, and Loch Derg, the lake with its island which hosted—and still hosts—the most rigorous Christian penitential exercise in the world.[163]

Sensing the danger presented by the proud tradition, the fierce independence, and above all the passionate Catholic loyalty of the O'Neills and O'Donnells, the English government both in London and in Dublin kept a wary eye on them. Hugh O'Neill, who had been brought up among the English and knew how to talk their language (literally and figuratively), already at the time of the Armada the wealthiest and most powerful Irish lord in Ireland, had used his English connections to gain him that position. But if he were ever to proclaim himself "the O'Neill"—that is, head of the whole ancient clan—and then act on it, he would be a correspondingly great threat to the English. They thought they had bought him off when Queen Elizabeth in May 1587 made him Earl of Tyrone, authorized to sit in the House of Lords in London, and helped him in expanding his territory.[164] But he was using them—shrewdly and implacably—rather than they using him. No one knows when he first conceived of a free Catholic Ireland, separated completely from the English crown, with him its leader; but the manner of his proceedings before the actual outbreak of war suggests a long-held, carefully developed plan to that end.

"The O'Donnell," Hugh Duv, had never been a strong leader, and was now increasingly enfeebled by age. He waited only for his son Hugh Roe, 14, to reach full maturity before abdicating in his favor. Despite his extreme youth, flame-haired Hugh Roe O'Donnell, known as "Red Hugh," was already famous throughout northern Ireland for his dashing courage, his golden tongue, his high intelligence, his splendid looks, and above all for his outspoken, articulate Catholicity and patriotism. He was already betrothed to Hugh O'Neill's daughter

---

[162] See Chapter Seven, above.

[163] T. W. Moody, F. X. Martin, and F. J. Byrne, eds., *A New History of Ireland*, Volume III (Early Modern Ireland, 1534-1691) (Oxford, 1976), pp. 14-15, 115-117.

[164] *Ibid.*, pp. 115-188; Sean O'Faolain, *The Great O'Neill* (Cork, 1942, 1970), p. 94.

Rose; when the marriage actually took place the two great tribes of northern Ireland, often enemies in the past, would now be bound together, creating an even greater threat to England. Consequently English Lord Deputy John Perrot sent a ship in October 1587 to kidnap young Hugh Roe. Anchoring in Loch Swilly in Donegal and pretending to come from Spain with a cargo of fine wines, its Captain Skinner invited young Hugh Roe aboard with his friends for a drink. When they were sufficiently intoxicated to be unable to offer effective resistance, they were seized without warning, put in chains, and taken to Dublin Castle, where they languished half-starved for three years.[165]

As Christmas of 1591 approached, someone smuggled a file to Red Hugh in Dublin Castle. On a snowy, blustery Christmas Eve when the guards were partying, he used it to file through his chains and those of two of his companions, Art and Henry O'Neill. With a rope made from their bedding they lowered themselves down the castle wall, met a guide sent by a sympathetic chieftain, and headed for open country through the snowstorm. Henry became separated from the others while they were still running through the streets of Dublin. Red Hugh and Art and the guide had to walk through the cold snowy night without warm clothing and without a road. Art collapsed before dawn; Red Hugh and the guide had to carry him. By morning of the brief day, one of the shortest of the year, they were hidden under a rock between Loughs Dan and Glendalough as their guide went off to get help. In the morning their absence from Dublin Castle was discovered and search parties were sent out. The boys had not eaten for more than forty hours, passed the whole of that day without food or shelter, and then had to endure another night and another day without either. By the evening of the third day Art O'Neill was dying; Red Hugh held his hand as he departed from earth. In the last twilight the guide finally returned with helpers, too late for Art, barely in time for Red Hugh.[166] In the words of a contemporary Irish historian:

> They had neither cloaks nor plaids, nor clothing for protection under their bodies, to save them from the cold and frost of the sharp winter season, but the bedclothes under their fair skins and the pillows under their heads were supports heaped up, white-bordered of hailstones freezing all around them, and attaching their light coats and shirts of fine linen thread to their bodies, and their large shoes and the fastenings to their legs and feet, so that they seemed to the men that had come not to be human beings at all, but just like sods of earth covered up by snow.[167]

Eighteen years old, near the peak of his physical vigor, with devoted nursing Red Hugh O'Donnell survived and recovered. But we may safely conclude that he never forgot his three dreadful days in that snow-swept

---

[165] Hiram Morgan, *Tyrone's Rebellion; the Outbreak of the Nine Years War in Tudor Ireland* (Woodbridge, Suffolk, England, 1993), pp. 128-129; O'Faolain, *Great O'Neill*, pp. 95-96; Timothy O'Donnell, *Swords Around the Cross* (Front Royal VA, 2000), Chapter 2.

[166] O'Donnell, *ibid.*; Morgan, *Tyrone's Rebellion*, pp. 131-132.

[167] Lugaidh O'Cleary, *The Life of Hugh Roe O'Donnell*, cited by O'Donnell, *ibid.*

wasteland, with his dear friend dying in his arms. Ireland, which has bred so many implacable foes of the English and their political and religious dominion, never produced one more passionate and more relentless than Hugh Roe O'Donnell, Prince of Donegal.

By February, just a month later, Red Hugh was not only fully recovered, but had gathered an army in Donegal, raised the siege of the castle where his parents were trapped, and expelled the English garrison from Donegal monastery, which they had seized for military purposes. On May 13, in a splendid ancient ceremony, he was formally installed "the O'Donnell" atop the Rock of Doone in County Donegal. He then attacked Turloch O'Neill, a relative of Hugh O'Neill, who had ravaged the O'Donnells' home territory of Tyrconnell during Red Hugh's imprisonment and was closely in league with the British, assigned to keep watch on both O'Donnell and Hugh O'Neill. The attack was successful and Turloch and the English agreed to send Hugh O'Neill to make peace with Red Hugh. They made more than peace; they made a friendship which lasted for the rest of their lives, one of the deepest and closest ever known among national leaders. Red Hugh agreed for the time being to halt his war against England; but it seems most unlikely that he would have done so, or become such close friends with Hugh O'Neill, if he had not known that O'Neill no more intended Red Hugh to keep peace with them than he himself intended to.[168]

Philip II of Spain, despite his declining health and world-wide problems and responsibilities, retained a strong interest in the Irish. In September 1592 he received in audience the Catholic Archbishop of Armagh, Edmund McGauran, primate of Ireland, and gave him a ship, supplies and funds to return to his native country. In a letter to Philip II's secretary in March 1593, Archbishop McGauran explained that numerous Irish lords were ready to give full support to an uprising against English rule in the name of the Catholic Faith, and put Red Hugh O'Donnell at the head of his list. As proof he enclosed a letter from Red Hugh to Irish lords and to the Spanish king in which, after retelling the epic story of his escape from Dublin Castle, he declared his total commitment to the Irish cause and urged Philip to come with troops, take over the country, and free the Church there. Meanwhile Red Hugh had sent the archbishop of northwestern Ireland, James O'Healy of Tuam, to urge Philip II to send aid to the Catholics in Ireland resolved to throw off the English yoke. In May Archbishop McGauran formed the Irish Catholic Confederacy, with Red Hugh at once becoming its military leader. In September the English made war against the Maguires, with Hugh O'Neill, Earl of Tyrone, still pretending to be on their side, but rescuing some 35,000 head of their cattle, while Red Hugh O'Donnell gave refuge to their surviving fighting men after they were defeated on the battlefield.[169]

By February 1594 Hugh O'Neill at last began to come out into the open. He refused an English demand that he go to Donegal and persuade O'Donnell to

---

[168] O'Donnell, *op. cit.*, Chapter 3; Morgan, *Tyrone's Rebellion*, pp. 133-134; O'Faolain, *Great O'Neill*, pp. 122-123.

[169] Morgan, *Tyrone's Rebellion*, pp. 111, 141, 146-147, 154-158; Cyril Falls, *Elizabeth's Irish Wars* (New York, 1970), pp. 174-175; O'Donnell, *op. cit.*, Chapter 4.

make a formal and personal submission to the English, or force him to make it if he could not persuade him. In July the English tried offering him a pardon; he refused to take it until the lands taken from his countrymen by the English in Connaught should be returned. In August Hugh O'Neill's brother Cormac and Hugh Maguire defeated an English force sent to resupply the fort at Enniskillen which they held, at what was called the "Ford of the Biscuits" because bread supplies for the garrison at Enniskillen were scattered all over the ground when the battle was over. Before the battle the two commanders conferred at length in secret with Hugh O'Neill and Red Hugh O'Donnell. Hugh O'Neill had now in fact joined the Irish rebels against the English, but still did not say so, and even assured the English of his continued loyalty; they debated whether to believe him. An English official named Fenton gave it as his opinion that if O'Neill should "publish himself as a protector of the Catholic cause he will shake the Four Provinces." By October 1594 Queen Elizabeth was convinced that he had decided to join the Irish, and issued a peremptory demand to the Irish council to "make one final demand for his submission in person or else he would be proclaimed a traitor." Expecting no genuine submission, about two weeks later she sent famed General John Norris with 2,000 troops from Brittany in France to Ireland.[170]

Early in May 1595 Red Hugh swept through Connaught, killing or driving out all English outside the few fortified towns; General Norris landed with his army at Waterford; on the 25th Red Hugh and Hugh Maguire took long-besieged Enniskillen castle from the English. A proclamation drafted by William Cecil formally charged Hugh O'Neill, Earl of Tyrone, with treason, murder and rebellion; it was publicly proclaimed in Ireland June 22. But even with Norris' men, the English army was now outnumbered two to one, and there was no longer any significant difference in infantry weapons and tactics between the two forces, though the Irish had no warships and few large cannon. On June 23 Hugh O'Neill inflicted a crushing defeat on Marshal Henry Bagenal, commanding a large part of the English army, at Clontibret in County Monaghan, when Bagenal was returning from an apparently successful relief of the town of Monaghan, besieged by the Irish. The battle was highlighted by a personal combat between Hugh O'Neill and a gigantic English officer named Segrave which O'Neill won, followed by a furious Irish cavalry charge. O'Donnell's army had not arrived at the time of the battle and when it did, another English army led by Lord Deputy Russell in person turned around and hurried back to Dublin. But they sallied out again to Armagh in July. Late in September Hugh O'Neill and Red Hugh O'Donnell wrote jointly to Philip II of Spain: "Our only

---

[170] Morgan, *Tyrone's Rebellion*, pp. 159-160, 170-175, 177 (second quote); O'Faolain, *Great O'Neill*, pp. 147-148, 150 (first quote); Falls, *Elizabeth's Irish Wars*, pp. 282-283; O'Donnell, *ibid.*

hope of re-establishing the Catholic religion rests on your assistance. Now or never our Church must be succored."[171]

While waiting for Spanish help (which proved a long time coming) O'Neill and O'Donnell resumed negotiations with the English as a delaying tactic, even going so far as to make another pretended submission. But in January 1596, meeting English representatives in a field near Dundalk, they demanded dismissal of all English officials in Ulster and the removal of all English troops there except for Newry and Carrickfergus, restoration of Catholic lands not only to O'Neill and O'Donnell but also to all their associates, and the establishment of liberty of conscience for all Ireland. That the English, eager as they were for peace, would not accept, and Red Hugh O'Donnell in particular would not give up. In April O'Neill yielded in form in a weasel-worded treaty, which at least made it clear that there would be no suppression of the practice of the Catholic faith in lands controlled by O'Neill and O'Donnell. The next month three Spanish ships arrived on the north coast of Donegal, bearing a letter from Philip II to Red Hugh which said: "I have been informed that you are defending the Catholic cause against the English. That this is acceptable to God is proved by the signal victories which you have obtained. I hope you will continue to prosper, and you need not doubt that I will render you any assistance you may require." Their spirits buoyed by this, the two great Irish leaders and their allies maintained their men in the field and held no further serous negotiations with the English during 1596.[172]

In midwinter, at the end of January 1597, Red Hugh O'Donnell made another sweep through Connaught with more than 3,000 men, storming English-held Athenry and marching south to Galway before returning to Donegal. He was now the effective ruler of Donegal and Connaught as Hugh O'Neill was of most of Ulster. An attempt by new Lord Deputy Brough to advance beyond Portmore and the Blackwater River was repulsed by O'Neill in July, though in the next month another English force burned O'Neill's home town of Dungannon and his mills there. Also in August Red Hugh held his castle against attack by British general Conyers Clifford, who barely escaped from the area as a large force came quickly to aid O'Donnell.[173] In September, responding to Philip II's letter, O'Neill and O'Donnell wrote:

> We cannot express in words the intense joy and delight which the letter of Your Most Catholic Majesty, full of extreme kindness, has caused us. . . .
> We will keep firm and unshaken the promises which we made to Your

---

[171] Morgan, *Tyrone's Rebellion*, pp. 178, 194-195; Falls, *Elizabeth's Religious Wars*, p. 187; *New History of Ireland*, III, 125-126; Wernham, *Return of the Armadas*, p. 23; O'Donnell, *op. cit.*, Chapter 5.

[172] Morgan, *Tyrone's Rebellion*, pp. 193, 197-199, 204-211; O'Faolain, *Great O'Neill*, p. 177; Falls, *Elizabeth's Irish Wars*, pp. 192, 194-195; Wernham, *Return of the Armadas*, pp. 31-32; O'Donnell, *ibid.*

[173] O'Donnell, *op. cit.*, Chapter 4; O'Faolain, *Great O'Neill*, pp. 188-190; Falls, *Elizabeth's Irish Wars*, pp. 204-206.

Majesty to our last breath; if we do not, we shall incur at once the wrath of God and the contempt of men.[174]

In December 1597 O'Neill, at last feeling able to say what he really thought and really wanted from the English invaders, demanded the return of *all* the land they had taken from the Irish by force, and above all for the right freely and safely to practice the Catholic Faith. When the English Earl of Ormonde refused physically to take the documents stating his demands, O'Neill literally stuffed them into his shirt. The furious and embarrassed Ormonde swore to burn them when he returned to his residence, but in fact sent them to London marked "suppressed." Parleying again in June 1598, O'Neill and O'Donnell repeated these demands and said they had sworn to accept nothing less. The English would not consider accepting them; so, the famed Sir John Norris having recently died, Marshal Bagenal, despite his earlier defeat at Clontibret, was sent north to Armagh with a splendidly equipped army of over 4,000. The Irish camped on the nearby Blackwater River. Feareasa O'Cleary, hereditary historian of the Clan O'Donnell, described to the excited Irish soldiers in the camp a vision of St. Berchan 900 years before when he walked in this very area and foresaw a great battle with overwhelming sounds like thunder, in which Ireland defeated its foes.[175]

What followed next day, August 14, was just such a battle, fought at the Yellow Ford of the Blackwater with the roar of the firearms undreamed of in St. Berchan's day. The English marched out of Armagh to fife and drum, in three widely separated divisions. The mobile Irish *kernes* began firing from behind trees. By noon the marching English came up to the main Irish body and the battle reached its climax. Marshal Bagenal was killed. More than two-thirds of his force was lost through death, wounds, or desertion. The remainder fled to the cathedral of Armagh where they were besieged, having lost all their colors, cannon, ammunition and food as well as the Blackwater fort. It was the worst English military defeat in the whole long reign of Queen Elizabeth.[176]

There was panic in Dublin and intense joy in the rest of Ireland. "A wave of feeling that was like one vast geyser of long suppressed discontent gushed up . . . until, within a few months, Tyrone [Hugh O'Neill] was virtual master of Ireland and could see the outline of a rapidly forming Confederate Army. Everywhere [Irish] men were claiming old titles and the [English] colonists abandoning them."[177]

In Spain in late June 1598 Philip II, 71 years old and long in poor health because of gout and dropsy, against the advice of his doctors made a last trip to

---

[174] O'Donnell, *ibid.*

[175] O'Donnell, *op. cit.*, Chapter 5; O'Faolain, *Great O'Neill*, pp. 194-197, 199; Falls, *Elizabeth's Irish Wars*, p. 215.

[176] Falls, *Elizabeth's Irish Wars*, pp. 214-220; O'Faolain, *Great O'Neill*, pp. 199-203; O'Donnell, *ibid.*

[177] O'Faolain, *Great O'Neill*, p. 203 (quote); Falls, *Elizabeth's Irish Wars*, pp. 221-222.

his glorious monastery-palace of El Escorial in intense heat. The journey and the heat exhausted his wasted body; sores and abscesses began to form on it. Far away in England his shrewd, relentless antagonist through exactly forty years, William Cecil, Lord Burghley, 77, was also in his final decline. On July 20 he wrote his last letter to his son Robert, containing the disturbing sentence quoted at the head of this chapter. On August 1 Philip's confessor told him that the doctors no longer held out any hope for his survival. He responded: "Thanks be to God." Within a few days he could no longer move from his position on his back in bed because of the pain any movement or touching caused him. Constant thirst tormented him. Because he could not be moved or even touched, his own excrement lay around him. As he came closer to the end, in agony, he asked to have the Gospel narratives of the Passion of Christ read to him over and over again. On August 28 he called his son and namesake to his repulsive bedside to show him that this is what all the world's pomp and splendor comes to in the end. At the end only the Faith matters, and the souls it saves. His son must uphold and defend the Faith all the days of his life, as his father had tried his best to do.[178]

As Philip lay in torment on his dreadful deathbed, William Cecil was dying quietly at his home in London, in only a little pain, surrounded by his family. The two men who left accounts of his death say he appeared somewhat troubled in his mind toward the end, but they did not know why. In his last words he implored God's mercy. He died at seven o'clock in the morning of August 14, exactly thirty days before his great antagonist of Spain.[179] For forty years Philip II of Spain and William Cecil of England had fought each other, with the future of Christendom at stake. Now they appeared before the judgment seat of the King of Kings almost together.

On the very day of Cecil's death came the tremendous victory of Hugh O'Neill and Red Hugh O'Donnell at the Battle of the Yellow Ford. The news arrived in Spain with unusual speed, presumably by a fast ship, in about three weeks. It was brought to Philip's bedside, a ray of light penetrating the suffocating dark that was engulfing him. He dictated "a warm letter of congratulations and encouragement" to the Catholic victors whom he had so often encouraged and helped, and would have done far more if his physical condition had permitted. Because we do not know the precise date of his letter, we are not sure whether it was his very last official act as king. It may well have been, and if so fittingly, showing him serving the cause of Catholic Christendom to the very end of his life as he had done throughout his 42-year reign.[180]

In his final hours, Philip recited again and again the psalm quoted at the head of this chapter. The deeply Catholic historian William Thomas Walsh gives an unforgettable description of his last day, September 13, 1598:

---

[178] Kamen, *Philip of Spain*, pp. 313-314; Walsh, *Philip II*, pp. 719-724; Read, *Burghley*, p. 545.

[179] Read, *Burghley*, pp. 545-546.

[180] Falls, *Elizabeth's Irish Wars*, pp. 221-222; O'Faolain, *Great O'Neill*, pp. 203, 205; O'Donnell, *op. cit.*, Chapter 5.

The Archbishop of Toledo spoke consoling words to him for about half an hour, and then, at Philip's request, read once more from the Passion from Saint John. . . .

It was all happening there, in the silence of the Escorial, in the soul of the dying king. It was already midnight. The voices continued, some high, some low, reading holy words. Whenever they stopped, the king would whisper: '*Padres, decidme mas*." ["Fathers, read me more"]

About two o'clock Toledo opened the little box and took out one of the blessed candles from Our Lady's altar. But the king said, "*Aun no es tiempo*." ["It is not yet time"]

An hour later Toledo again offered the candle, and Philip said, "*Dad aca, que ya es tiempo*." ["Give it to me, for now it is time"]

With Toledo's help he held the candle in one hand, and the small wooden crucifix of his Mother and Father in the other. . . . He seemed to become unconscious. They thought him dead; but when someone went to take away the candle and cover his face, he opened his eyes, with a sudden paroxysm, and fixed them, with intense longing and devotion, upon the crucifix, around which his fingers still closed. Thus he remained for some time. He remained fully intelligent after that for more than an hour.

It was five o'clock. In the chapel below there was a stirring of footsteps, a flicker of candles, and the murmuring of voices as priests and acolytes began, on the vigil of the Exaltation of the Holy Cross, to say the Mass of Dawn, which they had always offered for the spiritual welfare of the king. Philip gave three little gasps, like a child's. His eyes, still on the crucifix, became stony. At that moment the sun arose over the eastern hill and flooded the white walls of San Lorenzo with the cheerful light of morning.[181]

Philip II of Spain lived during the greater part of the century when Christendom was cloven, and reigned during nearly half of it. Though one more mighty military struggle between Catholic and Protestant lay ahead—the Thirty Years War in Germany, fought to decide whether Christendom would be reunited in the heart of Europe—a full reunion of Christendom was no longer possible. For nearly four hundred years it would stand cloven, until the late twentieth century slipped into apostasy.

This would not have surprised Philip II. He knew his enemy—none better—and the consequences of encouraging the spirits of disunion and revolution. As the long-lived, ever diligent, ever persevering sovereign of the world's greatest power in his time, most Catholic Spain, he knew that his supreme duty was to fight the enemies of the Church Christ founded and do his very best to restore the unity of Christ's people in Christendom, so precious, before it had faded into no more than a holy memory. His reward was misunderstanding, hatred, calumny, a black legend enduring to this day. Except among his own people, whom he protected and kept united and happy and prosperous, his name casts an evil aura. So, down the generations and the centuries, Philip II of Spain pays the price of his heroic sacrifice. All the

---

[181] Walsh, *Philip II*, pp. 725-726.

pleasures the world offers, all the self-indulgence available to royalty, lay before him. He rejected them all to save and restore Christendom. By the world's standards, he failed—though he did much to save France for the Faith, he lost England with the Armada. But he died, offering up his pain, at peace with God, and could have said to his enemies then and since, with G. K. Chesterton:

> On you is fallen the shadow,
> And not upon the Name;
> That though we scatter and though we fly,
> And you hang over us like the sky,
> You are more tired of victory,
> Than we are tired of shame.
>
> That though you hunt the Christian man
> Like a hare on the hillside,
> The hare has still more heart to run
> Than you have heart to ride.
>
> That though all lances split on you,
> All swords be heaved in vain,
> We have more lust again to lose
> Than you to win again. . . .
>
> For our God hath blessed creation,
> Calling it good. I know
> What spirit with whom you blindly band
> Hath blessed destruction with his hand;
> Yet by God's death the stars shall stand
> And the small apples grow.[182]

---

[182] G. K. Chesterton, *The Ballad of the White Horse* (London, 1911, 1927), pp. 63-66.

9
Expansion and Colonization
1598-1618
Popes Clement VIII, 1592-1605, Leo XI 1605, Paul V 1605-1621

"1. That the Catholic, apostolic, and Roman religion be openly preached and taught throughout all Ireland, as well in cities as borough towns, by bishops, seminary priests, Jesuits, and all other religious men. 2. That the Church of Ireland be wholly governed by the Pope. 3. That all cathedrals and parish churches, abbeys, and all other religious houses, with all tithes and Church lands, now in the hands of the English, be presently restored to the Catholic churchmen. 4. That all Irish priests and religious men, now prisoners in England or Ireland, be presently set at liberty, with all temporal Irishmen, that are troubled for their conscience, and to go where they will, without further trouble. 5. That all Irish priests and religious men may freely pass and repass, by sea and land, to and from foreign countries."—demands presented to the English government by the Irish Confederacy led by Hugh O'Neill and Hugh O'Donnell, November 1599[1]

"Upon this day is recorded the Invention [Finding] of the Cross of Christ, and upon this day, I thank God, I have found my cross, by which I hope to end all the crosses of my life, and to rest in the next by the grace and merits of my Savior. As for the treasons which are laid against me, I protest now at my death that I am not guilty of them: neither had I knowledge of the powder but in confession, and then I utterly misliked it and earnestly dissuaded it. Yea, I protest upon my soul I should have abhorred it ever, though it had succeeded. And I am sorry with all my heart that any Catholics had ever any such intention, knowing that such attempts are not allowable and, to my knowledge, contrary to the Pope's mind. And I would therefore wish all Catholics to be quiet, and not to be moved for any difficulties to the raising of tumults, but to possess their souls in peace. And God will not be forgetful of them or of his promise, but will send them help and comfort when it is most to His glory and their good."—last statement of Father Henry Garnet, S.J., before his execution for alleged participation in the Gunpowder Plot, May 13, 1606[2]

---

[1] Timothy O'Donnell, *Swords Around the Cross* (Front Royal VA, 2000), Chapter 6.

[2] Philip Caraman, *Henry Garnet and the Gunpowder Plot* (New York, 1964), p. 436.

In the wake of his great victory at the Battle of the Yellow Ford in August 1598, Hugh O'Neill[3] was master of Ireland, and virtually the whole country was behind him. Only four principal men in Ireland still held back from O'Neill;[4] to one of them, Lord Barry, he wrote:

> You separated yourself from the unity of Christ, His Mystical Body, the Catholic Church. You know the sword of extirpation hangs over your head as well as ours, if things fall out otherwise than well. . . . You might . . . by God's assistance (Who, miraculously and above all expectation, gave good success to the cause principally undertaken for His glory, exaltation of religion, next for the restoration of the ruins and preservation of the country) expel them, and deliver them and us from the most miserable tyranny and cruel exaction and subjection. . . . Enter, I beseech you, into the close of your conscience, and like a wise man weigh seriously the end of your actions.[5]

The English knew that their dominion over Ireland was threatened as never before. Neither their generals in place nor their military and financial commitment at anywhere near its present level could deal with this crisis. Queen Elizabeth was 62 years old, but implacable as ever; Robert Cecil, the "little beagle," had taken over his father William's office with all his aplomb and resolution. They did not even consider retreat. Instead they sent the Earl of Essex, the young idol of court and people, to Ireland with "the largest army ever sent across the Irish Sea." He arrived on May 5 commanding a force, at least on paper, of 16,000 foot and 1,300 horse.[6]

O'Neill was ready for him. In London it was still thought that what was needed was a quick and massive invasion of O'Neill's Ulster homeland, but he had built up too much support in the rest of Ireland to make that possible. Essex had to try first to clear the rebels from Leinster, the most anglicized part of Ireland. He had some success, but was defeated by Owney O'More at a place thereafter called the Pass of the Plumes because of the many white plumes on the helmets of the Englishmen left dead after the battle, and by Phelim O'Byrne near Wicklow. Essex managed to take the important Castle Cahir in County Tipperary after a ten days' siege, but the Irish soon retook it. Sir Thomas Norris, brother of dead English general John Norris and president of Munster, was

---

[3] This name was his own, and the one he preferred; his abandonment of it was actually one of the peace terms the English demanded of him. He will therefore be so designated herein rather than "Tyrone," the anglicized name of his district when he was made an Earl, which in Irish was "Tirowen."

[4] Sean O'Faolain, *The Great O'Neill* (Cork, 1942, 1970), pp. 203-206. In the face of statements like this and the first five demands on the English government, quoted above, it should be hard to maintain the position, taken by most historians, that religion never really mattered to O'Neill. But it does seem to be true that Red Hugh O'Donnell was even more totally committed to the Catholic Faith.

[5] *Ibid.*, pp. 206-207

[6] *Ibid.*, p. 208; John J. Silke, *Kinsale; the Spanish Intervention in Ireland at the End of the Elizabethan Wars* (New York, 1970), pp. 51-52, 57.

mortally wounded in a skirmish in County Limerick. In June 1599 Spanish ships arrived in Ulster with a special envoy, and arms and ammunition for the Irish Catholics.[7]

Early in July Essex told Queen Elizabeth in a discouraged letter that as far as he could see, all the Irish want "to shake off the yoke of obedience to Your Majesty and to root out all remembrance of the English nation in this kingdom."[8] Elizabeth fired back that he was causing international humiliation for England by failing to make progress against O'Neill, the "arch-traitor," for whom she had now developed a consuming hatred, and directed him not to leave Ireland until he had done better. He court-martialled and executed a number of his officers for cowardice and ordered Sir Conyers Clifford, president of Connaught, to relieve the siege of Coolooney Castle and split the home territories of O'Donnell and O'Neill.[9] Red Hugh met him in the Curlew Mountains on the feast of the Assumption of the Blessed Virgin Mary, speaking to his men on the eve of battle:

> Have no dread or fear of the great number of the soldiers from London or the strangeness of their weapons and arms, but put your hope in the God of glory. . . . By the help of the Most Blessed Virgin Mary, Mother of God, we will this day utterly destroy the heretical enemy whom we have always hitherto worsted. We fasted yesterday in honor of the Virgin, and today we celebrate her feast. Therefore in her name let us fight stoutly and bravely the enemies of the Virgin, and we shall gain the victory.[10]

The Irish surged forward shouting their battle cry of "O'Donnell *abu*! [On with O'Donnell]!" The English fired off their powder, and the Irish closed with the pike. Two-thirds of the English force was killed, but only about two hundred Irish; Clifford and the commander of his vanguard, Sir Alexander Radcliffe, were both killed; Coolooney Castle surrendered and O'Connor of Sligo, who had formerly fought with the English, joined Red Hugh. The Irish council met and agreed with Essex to call off the proposed English landing at Lough Foyle in the north of Ulster, intended to pressure O'Neill from the north as well as the south. Essex marched north with an inadequate force of only 4,000 against double that number of O'Neill's Irishmen. When the two armies met on September 13, 1599, Essex called for a parley on the River Lagan. With their horses up to their bellies in water, the two leaders—Essex and O'Neill—conversed without witnesses for thirty minutes. Wild rumors about what they discussed and proposed—either O'Neill or Essex to be king of Ireland, for example—have

---

[7] R. B. Wernham, *Return of the Armadas; the Last Years of the Elizabethan War against Spain*, 1595-1603 (Oxford, 1994), pp. 302-303; Cyril Falls, *Elizabeth's Irish Wars* (New York, 1970), pp. 233-235; Silke, *Kinsale*, pp. 57-59.

[8] Wernham, *Return of the Armadas*, p. 304.

[9] O'Faolain, *Great O'Neill*, pp. 214-217; Wernham, *Return of the Armadas*, p. 307; Falls, *Elizabeth's Irish Wars*, p. 240, 242-243.

[10] O'Donnell, *op. cit.*, Chapter 6.

circulated ever since, but in fact no one will ever know what they said to each other. A truce was agreed upon; one-time hero Essex was a complete failure.[11]

Elizabeth was furious. She condemned Essex in the strongest terms for dealing with the enemy, and commanded him to agree to nothing that had not been previously submitted to her in writing and received her approval. Realizing that he had mortally offended her and given much cause for suspicion of his own motives, Essex rushed back to England (despite Elizabeth's prohibition on his return without her permission) and on October 8 burst unannounced into her bedchamber, covered with mud, while she was arranging the red wig that concealed her nearly bald head. Essex was put into house arrest while Robert Cecil, his enemy, began preparing a legal case against him. The next day Charles Blount, Lord Mountjoy, untested in high command, was named Lord Lieutenant of Ireland. On December 9 the dreaded Court of Star Chamber indicted Essex. Meanwhile O'Neill and O'Donnell presented their demands to the English government, the first five of which are quoted at the head of this chapter. Cecil took one look at them and scrawled "Ewtopia" on the margin. Queen Elizabeth spurned them.[12]

During the winter of 1600 Hugh O'Neill made the grand tour of Ireland that was traditional for High Kings. He had only 2,000 men with him against 14,000 English soldiers, but they hid behind walls and would not face him. The truce ended in February and O'Neill put pressure on the few remaining holdouts. By February 28 he had reached Cork, at the opposite end of Ireland from his native Ulster. The O'Mahony, O'Donohue and O'Donovan clans joined him there, as did Florence MacCarthy, to whom he gave the ancient title of "MacCarthy More," and Donald O'Sullivan Bear, bravest of the brave. He wrote to King Philip III of Spain declaring himself "Your Majesty's most faithful subject." Five days later Mountjoy, the new Lord Lieutenant, set sail across the Irish Sea on a tiny pinnace called the *Popinjay*. He was to prove again, this time against the Catholics, that men make history.[13]

Amid the wild distractions, raids, double-dealing, and heedless enthusiasms of Ireland in 1600, Mountjoy set himself at once to the pursuit of one grim goal: the total destruction of the great Irish rising, the elimination of old Celtic Ireland from history. He achieved that goal. The one aspect of the old Ireland that he

---

[11] Falls, *Elizabeth's Irish Wars*, pp. 242-246; Wernham, *Return of the Armadas*, pp. 311, 313, 315; Silke, *Kinsale*, pp. 61-62; O'Faolain, *Great O'Neill*, pp. 217-221; O'Donnell, *op. cit.*, Chapter 6.

[12] Wernham, *Return of the Armadas*, pp. 316-318, 347; Falls, *Elizabeth's Irish Wars*, p. 247; P. M. Handover, *The Second Cecil; the Rise to Power 1563-1603 of Sir Robert Cecil, Later First Earl of Salisbury* (London, 1959), pp. 196-197, 201; Frederick M. Jones, *Mountjoy 1563-1606, the Last Elizabethan Deputy* (Dublin, 1958), p. 64; O'Donnell, *ibid.* After being pardoned but dismissed from public service, Essex was executed as a traitor after he rebelled against the old queen in February 1601 (Wernham, op. cit., pp. 354-358; Handover, op. cit., pp. 221-228).

[13] O'Faolain, *Great O'Neill*, pp. 223-224; Falls, *Elizabeth's Irish Wars*, p. 252; Jones, *Mountjoy*, pp. 66, 68-69; O'Donnell, *Nine Years War*, Chapter 7.

could not destroy was its Catholic faith, guarded in Heaven by St. Patrick's prayers. That alone survived. In the trenchant words of Sean O'Faolain:

> By nature he [Mountjoy] was laconic, a man whom the corrupt officials could neither persuade nor pump; cold, stern, and silent; often throwing our false scents to deceive, averse to hot language, never swearing, controlling an unruly Board with a glance of his black eye. In fact there was a good deal of Tyrone [O'Neill] in this man in whom Tyrone at last met his match. The days of hard-swearing Bingham and blustering Brough were over. Mountjoy was the one thing that the Irish nature dislikes intensely in an enemy and admires intensely in a leader—a calm, patient man, slow to promise, firm in his word, not without evasion, relentless in his pursuit of any object, and most obstinate.[14]

By sheer perseverance Mountjoy obtained his success. All the conditions he confronted were initially against him. O'Neill outmarched him on his return from Cork to Ulster on March 25; it was not the last time he was to be outmarched in Ireland by its people who knew the land so much better than he. In April Pope Clement VIII granted a plenary indulgence to supporters of O'Neill in Ireland and recognized him as "captain-general of the Catholic army in Ireland." The 68-year-old Earl of Ormond, one of the last noblemen still (dubiously) loyal to the English, was captured that month by Owney O'More. Early in May the Spanish Franciscan Mateo de Oviedo, appointed Catholic Archbishop of Dublin, arrived in Red Hugh O'Donnell's country with arms, 22,000 pieces of gold, a firm pledge of at least 5,000 Spanish troops, and a crown of "phoenix" feathers for O'Neill. Spanish infantry were still by a wide margin the best fighting men in the world. With their steady ruthless competence combined with Irish ardor and fervor, it seemed that nothing could stand against them.[15]

But before the end of May, Mountjoy had forced Moyry Pass, the gateway to Ulster, and returned to the Blackwater River near which the victory of the Yellow Ford had been won. While O'Neill was trying to hold the pass, Sir Henry Docwra landed behind him in Lough Foyle at the Irish town of Derry, which was promptly and heavily fortified. George Carew, the capable but ruthless new English president of Munster, took Limerick and captured Edmund Fitzgibbon, the most important of the Geraldine chieftains, called the "White Knight." In captivity Carew fed Fitzgibbon's pride at the expense of his patriotism and persuaded him to fight for the English. The Earl of Ormond obtained release from his Irish captors.[16]

---

[14] O'Faolain, *Great O'Neill*, p. 226.

[15] Jones, *Mountjoy*, pp. 70-71; Silke, *Kinsale*, pp. 68-69 (quote), 73-74; Falls, *Elizabeth's Irish Wars*, pp. 257, 259-260; O'Faolain, *Great O'Neill*, pp. 224-225; O'Donnell, *op. cit.*, Chapter 7.

[16] Wernham, *Return of the Armadas*, pp. 337-338; Jones, *Mountjoy*, pp. 73, 77; Falls, *Elizabeth's Irish Wars*, pp. 262-263, 282; O'Faolain, *Great O'Neill*, pp. 228-229.

Bishop Oviedo wrote to Philip III of Spain calling for the promised Spanish aid immediately, saying: "This is the best possible opportunity, and if it is allowed to slip by, I do not know when we shall find another."[17] Martin de la Cerda, special Spanish ambassador to Ireland, who had arrived with Oviedo in May and had hurried back to Spain to present the need for Spanish aid to Ireland personally at court at the beginning of July, strongly agreed. Philip III, in one of his few acts of clear-cut leadership, agreed just as strongly. When his council opposed his plans, he said he would pay for the expedition himself, promised 6,000 of the peerless Spanish infantry rather than 5,000, and appointed Diego de Brochero, commander of the Spanish Atlantic fleet, to the naval command of the expedition to Ireland and Antonio de Zúñiga to the army command.[18]

But shortage of money in nearly bankrupt Spain delayed the expedition for months, Admiral Brochero and General de Zúñiga could not agree on how to proceed,[19] and during the latter part of the summer of 1600 both Mountjoy and Carew were devastating Leinster and Munster.[20] In Carew's own words, "no day passes without report of burning, killing and taking prey . . . infinite numbers of their cattle are taken, and besides husbandmen, women and children, of weaponed men there have been slain many."[21] Ireland was a poor country, with few reserves; it would be exceedingly difficult for any army, even the Spanish, to operate in it after such massive devastation. In September Mountjoy suborned Niall Garbh O'Donnell, Red Hugh's brother-in-law and cousin, with the promise of all the O'Donnell lands in the north, and sent him against Red Hugh in a surprise attack on Lifford Castle, which he took. Niall Garbh's wife Nuala, Red Hugh's sister, left him at once. O'Donnell rushed back to retake the castle, and O'Neill, who had been successfully holding strategic Moyry Pass against Mountjoy, had to abandon his position there to support his dear friend. Dermot O'Connor Don, a stalwart supporter of O'Neill and O'Donnell, was murdered in Connaught in November, and Florence MacCarthy, whom O'Neill had made "the MacCarthy More," turned his coat to the English (who repaid him by locking him up in the Tower of London for the rest of his life). The tide was beginning to turn.[22]

At the end of the year 1600 Martin de la Cerda brought more arms and money from Spain to Donegal. Meeting with him there, O'Neill told him that if 6,000 Spanish troops came they should land at Cork in Munster, but in view of what was now the English military predominance there, a smaller number should go north to Ulster, where O'Neill and O'Donnell could immediately support

---

[17] O'Donnell, *op. cit.*, Chapter 7.

[18] Silke, *Kinsale*, pp. 73-76, 79-82; Jones, *Mountjoy*, p. 110.

[19] Silke, *Kinsale*, pp. 84,-89-90, 93.

[20] Jones, *Mountjoy*, pp. 78-79; Falls, *Elizabeth's Irish Wars*, p. 264.

[21] O'Donnell, *op. cit.*, Chapter 7.

[22] Wernham, *Return of the Armadas*, pp. 341-343; Jones, *Mountjoy*, pp. 81-82; Falls, *Elizabeth's Irish Wars*, pp. 265, 269-272, 287-289; Silke, *Kinsale*, p. 88; O'Donnell, *Nine Years War*, Chapter 8.

them.[23] But the Spanish, never known for speed in preparing for a military operation in foreign territory, were still not ready. By July 1601 Antonio de Zúñiga had proved so uncooperative that he was replaced as army commander for the expedition by Juan del Aguila, who had the reputation of an experienced soldier but was taken from a jail cell he had been occupying for peculation of government funds to assume his command—not a very good beginning. To the discussion on whether the Spanish should land in the south or in the north of Ireland, del Aguila contributed a new proposal: to land on the east coast, facing England. Ensign Pedro de Sandoval sailed for Ireland to inform O'Neill and O'Donnell that the Spanish were finally coming, and to ask them where they should come. Sandoval reached both men in August. They told him in no uncertain terms that the military situation in the south of Ireland had definitely turned for the worse, so now the Spanish should land nowhere south of Limerick, no matter how many men they had. But Sandoval was unable to get back to Spain before October. By then the fleet had sailed, after a fateful council of war at which Archbishop Oviedo, who had not been in Ireland for a year, insisted on a landing near Cork despite the opposition of both del Aguila and Admiral Brochero. It seems the military men yielded to the civilian because he knew Ireland and they did not.[24]

Nor was the catalogue of accident and misfortune for this enterprise, so essential to the future of Catholic Ireland and through it to all the English-speaking peoples, yet exhausted. The recruiting fell short; there were only 4,500 soldiers instead of 6,000. A final council of war was held on board, with unchanged result, except that Admiral Brochero managed to persuade the conferees that the Spanish should not challenge the fortifications of Cork, but rather land at the small neighboring harbor of Kinsale. Then, during the last night of their voyage, as they approached the southern coast of Ireland, a gale came up and blew eight Spanish ships, containing 674 soldiers and most of the munitions, out of all contact with the other ships, so far away that they eventually had to return fruitlessly to Spain.[25]

The remaining Spanish army, reduced by attrition to less than 3,500 men, landed at Kinsale with just four cannon (most of the cannon had been blown away in the eight lost ships). They immediately secured the town and the two castles commanding the entrance to the small harbor, but del Aguila was distressed to discover that the Irish earl of Desmond had been captured and Florence MacCarthy had turned traitor. It seemed there was no one left to lead the Munster Irish in aiding the Spaniards, and O'Neill and O'Donnell were at the opposite end of the country. When the heroic O'Sullivan Bear came forward to offer two thousand men, del Aguila, who had never heard of him, ignored his offer.[26]

---

[23] Silke, *Kinsale*, pp. 86-88.

[24] *Ibid.*, pp. 93, 96-97, 102-103; Jones, *Mountjoy*, p. 111.

[25] Silke, *Kinsale*, pp. 104, 108-110; Jones, *Mountjoy*, p. 117.

[26] Silke, *Kinsale*, pp. 110-112; Jones, *Mountjoy*, pp. 112-113, 117-118; Falls, *Elizabeth's Irish Wars*, pp. 292-294.

Word of the coming of the best soldiers in Christendom flew across Ireland. When he learned that the Spanish fleet was on the sea, Mountjoy, coldly realistic as always, wrote to Robert Cecil that if a Spanish army landed in Ireland, "you must believe me, sir, that then it will not be the war of Ireland but the war of England made in Ireland. If we beat them, both kingdoms will be quiet; if not, even the best will be in more danger than I hope ever to live to see."[27] He was meeting with Carew at Loughlin in Carlow when the news came of the Spanish landing. He lost not a moment, which is how Napoleon said wars are won. In exactly one week, across a sodden countryside, he arrived in Cork. Three days later he set out from Cork to Kinsale with just 1,500 men, less than half the Spanish number, and attacked. Of course he was repulsed; but he had taken the initiative. When Robert Cecil wrote to him, instructing him to burn the letter, and authorized him to negotiate with O'Neill if necessary, he ignored it. On October 26, just two weeks after the Spanish landing, now with 5,000 men but without artillery or entrenching tools, he laid siege to the Spanish in Kinsale.[28]

In that same critical month of October the news of the arrival of the Spanish came to Red Hugh O'Donnell and Hugh O'Neill. Travel conditions were abominable for the march of nearly three hundred miles that faced them, for the fall rains had been exceedingly heavy. They had to march through gnawing cold and freezing rain, with all roads awash in cold mud. Red Hugh, more ardent than ever, well knowing that the fate and future of Ireland rode on the issue of this struggle, left first, on November 2. O'Neill followed a week later. Mountjoy detached a substantial part of his forces under George Carew to stop O'Donnell. Carew seemed to have blocked him in County Tipperary, closing the main roads so that he could only continue by marching through the Slieve Phelim Mountains, believed impassable due to bogs. But a hard freeze came and Red Hugh took his army across the bogs on the newly formed ice. Carew called it "the greatest feat of marching of which he had ever heard."[29]

Meanwhile Mountjoy stood fast before Kinsale, repelling vigorous Spanish sallies from the walls. He took the two small castles at the entrance to Kinsale harbor after unrelenting bombardment and attacks. He stepped up the bombardment of Kinsale itself, and called upon del Aguila to surrender. Del Aguila replied proudly that he held Kinsale "for Christ and the King of Spain" and would not yield it. By now Mountjoy had 12,000 men, but Spanish reinforcements also arrived, O'Sullivan Bear had come with over a thousand Irish, and O'Donnell and O'Neill were approaching with 11,000 men of their

---

[27] Jones, *Mountjoy*, p. 115

[28] *Ibid.*, pp. 111, 117, 121, 123; Silke, *Kinsale*, pp. 116-117; Falls, *Elizabeth's Irish Wars*, p. 295; Wernham, *Return of the Armadas*, pp. 379-380.

[29] Falls, *Elizabeth's Irish Wars*, p. 297 (quote); T. W. Moody, F. X. Martin, and F. J. Byrne, eds., *A New History of Ireland*, Volume III ("Early Modern Ireland, 1534-1691") (Oxford, 1976), p. 134; Jones, *Mountjoy*, p. 127; Wernham, *Return of the Armadas*, pp. 382-383; O'Faolain, *Great O'Neill*, pp. 254-255; O'Donnell, *op. cit.*, Chapter 7.

own. Counting the Spaniards, the allies together held a substantial advantage in numbers.[30]

On December 23 the Irish forces of O'Neill and O'Donnell had arrived, and besieged Mountjoy's camp as he was besieging Kinsale. It was a classic military confrontation, such as Julius Caesar had fought and won at Alesia in Gaul—a fortress held by one side, besieged by the other, whose camp was in turn besieged by a relieving force. Few commanders would have allowed themselves to be caught in such an apparent trap (as Caesar had been at Alesia), but would have fled for safety. But Mountjoy, like Caesar, with nerves of ice, never moved. The Irish could simply besiege him, aided by his severe shortage of provisions for so many men; or they could attack. Del Aguila asked them to attack; the ardent O'Donnell instantly agreed; O'Neill hesitated, but finally let his friend's enthusiasm carry him away. The most decisive battle in the history of Ireland was joined.[31]

It was the day before Christmas by the old Julian calendar still used in the British Isles; Red Hugh O'Donnell intended to give the destruction of Mountjoy's army before Kinsale to the Irish people as a Christmas present. There were violent thunderstorms all night. In the misty dawn some of the attackers lost their way, and others unexpectedly met a strong English position at a ford. O'Neill withdrew temporarily to try to reassemble his men. So the Irish did not reach the position which del Aguila was watching, at which their arrival was to serve as a signal for a Spanish sally. There was no sally. Mountjoy, observing the confusion of O'Neill's Irish, launched a cavalry charge. Just then O'Donnell came up, but Mountjoy attacked him at once from another direction. Red Hugh's troops, still lacking the discipline of veterans, broke and fled. The Spaniards, whose iron discipline was world-famous, never came out of Kinsale at all. In three hours the Irish host was gone, fleeing where no man pursued.[32]

Mountjoy proved himself one of the greatest generals in English history by his triumph against the odds at Kinsale. The Irish and the Spaniards certainly should have won. Neither Juan del Aguila nor Red Hugh O'Donnell nor "the great O'Neill" could ever really explain why they had lost.[33]

---

[30] Falls, *Elizabeth's Irish Wars*, pp. 295-300; Silke, *Kinsale*, pp. 123, 127-128, 131-132, 135; Jones, *Mountjoy*, pp. 124-125, 128, 130-131; Wernham, *Return of the Armadas*, pp. 381-383; O'Faolain, *Great O'Neill*, pp. 252-255, 257.

[31] O'Faolain, *Great O'Neill*, pp. 259-261; Silke, *Kinsale*, pp. 136-137; Jones, *Mountjoy*, p. 134; Falls, *Elizabeth's Irish Wars*, p. 302; O'Donnell, *op. cit.*, Chapter 7. For Caesar at the siege of Alesia, see Volume I, Chapter 12 of this history.

[32] Silke, *Kinsale*, pp. 141-145, 151; Jones, *Mountjoy*, pp. 136-137; Wernham, *Return of the Armadas*, pp. 384-386; Falls, *Elizabeth's Irish Wars*, pp. 304-308; O'Faolain, *Great O'Neill*, pp. 260-265; O'Donnell, *ibid.*

[33] A lengthy inquiry into del Aguila's actions at Kinsale was conducted at the highest levels of the Spanish government, the councils of state and of war, and he was acquitted on all counts of the charges against him, charges which were principally pushed by Mateo de Oviedo, who by insisting on the landing at Kinsale instead of further north was at least as guilty as he. Del Aguila was not condemned to imprisonment, as some historians erroneously state. He does seem to have performed in a minimally competent manner.

But lost they had. On January 12, 1602 del Aguila surrendered Kinsale in return for permission to take his men and their arms and go home. (A courier carrying a letter from King Philip III to del Aguila ordering him to stand fast was intercepted.) On January 16 Red Hugh O'Donnell took ship for Spain to try to persuade Philip to send another Spanish expedition—now Ireland's only hope.[34] But this was highly unlikely after such a debacle, and never came close to materializing. George Carew, president of Munster, made sure that it would not materialize by sending an agent named Blake to poison Red Hugh in Valladolid. He died a holy death in Simancas in September 1602.[35] He was only twenty-eight years old. He lives in the memory of the Irish, forever young, bold and high-hearted. His song "O'Donnell *Abu!*" almost became the Irish national anthem.

The last fight was made by Donald O'Sullivan Bear and his captain, Richard MacGeohegan.[36] When its Spanish garrison was ready to turn over his castle of Dunboy to the English as called for by their surrender agreement, O'Sullivan Bear surprised everybody by taking it back from them before they could surrender it. On June 15 George Carew attacked Dunboy Castle, while Mountjoy was penetrating at last into O'Neill's homeland of Ulster where he would soon destroy the ancient ceremonial stone on which he had been proclaimed "the O'Neill." On June 28 the 143 defenders of Dunboy Castle died to the last man in its defense; their commander MacGeohegan, desperately wounded, with his last reserves of strength staggered with a lighted candle toward the magazine, and was stopped just short of blowing it up. With his world crumbling around him, O'Sullivan Bear with deathless loyalty marched a thousand men across Ireland to stand with O'Neill to the end in Ulster. He arrived with only 35 survivors in March 1603, just as O'Neill was forced to surrender.[37]

Not until February 1603 did Queen Elizabeth reluctantly approve negotiations with the beaten O'Neill. Mountjoy personally conducted them. O'Neill gave up everything but his personal property, even his name and the public (though not the private) practice of his faith. After he had agreed to submit, but before the actual ceremony of submission on his knees before

---

But why he did not sally on the fatal day has never been fully explained, not by the absence of the Irish from the dawn rendezvous point or in any other way. The roar of muskets is known to have been heard in Kinsale. Why did del Aguila not "ride to the sound of the guns"? (Silke, *Kinsale*, pp. 146, 162-165, 167-174)

[34] Falls, *Elizabeth's Irish Wars*, pp. 311-313; Wernham, *Return of the Armadas*, p. 386; Jones, *Mountjoy*, p. 139; O'Donnell, *op. cit.*, Chapter 9.

[35] O'Donnell, *op. cit.*, Chapter 7. Despite the obvious desire of English historians to hush up this final horror, Carew himself declared that his man had done the deed. In the words of Sean O'Faolain, "the point has never been conclusively proved but the balance of suspicion is heavily on the side of assassination." (*Great O'Neill*, p. 268)

[36] Pronounced "McGoohan."

[37] Falls, *Elizabeth's Irish Wars*, pp. 321-325, 327-329; Jones, *Mountjoy*, pp. 144-146; O'Faolain, *Great O'Neill*, pp. 267-268; Silke, *Kinsale*, p. 155; Wernham, *Return of the Armadas*, p. 402; O'Donnell, *op. cit.*, Chapter 7.

Mountjoy,[38] Queen Elizabeth died at her castle in Richmond, in stark terror, fighting sleep, speechless at the end, with her finger in her mouth. On April 1, when she could still speak, she at last named James VI of Scotland as her successor, son of Mary Queen of Scots whose death warrant she had signed. To Admiral Lord Howard, victor over the Spanish Armada, who tried to persuade her to go to bed, she said: "If you were in the habit of seeing such things in your bed as I do in mine, you would not persuade me to go there. . . . I am tied with a chain of fire around my neck." And to Lady Scrope, her maid of honor, she said: "I saw one night my own body, exceedingly lean and fearful, in a light of fire. Do *you* see sights in the night?"[39]

The "Virgin Queen," England's "Gloriana," daughter of Henry VIII and Anne Boleyn, thus went to her death and Judgment with visions of Hell, while her great adversary Philip II went with visions of the Cross and the Heaven it had opened to him. And Robert Cecil proceeded at ten o'clock in the morning of April 3 to proclaim the son of Mary Queen of Scots, whom his father had killed—strange, timid James, whom she had never seen after the first year of his life and who was as confirmed a Protestant as she had been Catholic—as king of all the British Isles.[40]

Expectations of an end to the persecution under James I[41] were high among Catholics, since his mother had so long been their champion. But their expectations arose more from wishful thinking than from logic; a child who does not remember his mother cannot be influenced by her. In May he arrived in London, made Robert Cecil a lord, and put him effectively in charge of the government. A plot to kidnap the king and his son Henry and force them to dismiss Cecil was quickly betrayed and thereby frustrated. The ruthless George Carew was appointed Lord Deputy of Ireland in place of the sick and exhausted, but triumphant Mountjoy. James remitted much of the recusancy fine (fine for not attending Anglican church services on Sundays) on Catholics, but not, as they

---

[38] Jones, *Mountjoy*, pp. 153-155; Falls, *Elizabeth's Irish Wars*, pp. 332-333; Wernham, *Return of the Armadas*, pp. 405-406; O'Faolain, *Great O'Neill*, pp. 269-270. O'Neill's final submission on his knees to the dead Elizabeth occurred on March 9. He did not learn of her death until five days later, although Mountjoy had known it at the time of the ceremony. He is said to have wept with frustration, believing he could have obtained a better settlement from the new king than from the implacable Elizabeth.

[39] Theodore Maynard, *Queen Elizabeth* (Milwaukee, 1940), p. 375 (for the two quotations); Handover, *Second Cecil*, p. 295; Edward P. Cheyney, *A History of England from the Defeat of the Armada to the Death of Queen Elizabeth* (London, 1926; Gloucester MA, 1967) II, 575; G. B. Harrison, ed., *The Elizabethan Journals, Being a Record of Those Things Most Talked of during the Years 1591-1603* (London, 1938), pp. 325-327. Though some historians have doubted that Elizabeth actually specifically designated James as his successor, even at the end, it is strongly attested in the contemporary journal, edited by G. B. Harrison, here cited.

[40] Handover, *Second Cecil*, pp. 296-298; Edward P. Cheyney, *History of England to the Death of Queen Elizabeth*, II, 576-577.

[41] We will hereinafter refer to James as I of England rather than as VI of Scotland, England being much the more wealthy and powerful of the two countries he ruled.

fondly believed, as a signal that he intended to stop collecting them, but as a special privilege on the occasion of his coronation, held with all due pomp on August 4.[42]

Both Catholics and Puritans began to gather petitions urging the new sovereign to make changes in the government's religious policy in their favor. James I soon prohibited this gathering of petitions, saying that changes in the church were solely the province of the king its head. Meanwhile he was already negotiating with Spain for an end to its long and unproductive war with England, which had now lasted nearly twenty years. Philip III was favorably inclined. His ambassador in England urged him to put aside, for the sake of peace, the issue of England's outlawing the practice of the Catholic faith. Philip II would never have agreed to that, but after some hesitation his son did. In January 1604 the Puritans stated their case to the unsympathetic James I at the Hampton Court conference. Committed Protestant though he was, James hated Calvinism, which had been dominant in Scotland since John Knox; he found in the subservient Anglican church, of which he was now the head by dint of Henry VIII's legislation, exactly what he was looking for. It was at the Hampton Court conference that he first uttered his famous dictum: "No bishop, no king." It was also at this conference that the King James translation of the Bible was authorized.[43]

At the beginning of March 1604 James I startled those who thought he would remain loyal to the memory of the mother he had never known, by roundly declaring his "utter detestation" of the Catholic Faith, which he persisted in calling "Papist." He ordered all Jesuits out of his kingdom, and restored the full recusancy fines. When his first Parliament met later that month, he made it clear that he had no intention of doing any favors for Catholics, and would not allow any significant increase in their numbers. He called for more restrictive laws against them, which were promptly given him. Six Catholics were martyred in this and the following year, and a committee of the privy council was set up under Lord Ellesmere "to exterminate" the Jesuits and anyone else seeking to withdraw the obedience of his subjects from him, and to collect the recusancy fines which he had remitted on the eve of his coronation. By 1605 it was obvious to every Englishman that James would press religious persecution as hard as Elizabeth ever had.[44]

---

[42] Samuel R. Gardiner, *History of England from the Accession of James I to the Outbreak of the Civil War*, Volume I (London, 1884), pp. 87, 100-101; Handover, *Second Cecil*, pp. 306-308, 310; Falls, *Elizabeth's Irish Wars*, pp. 337-338; Ludwig von Pastor, *History of the Popes* (St. Louis, 1937), p. 75.

[43] David H. Willson, *King James VI and I* (New York, 1956), pp. 203-204, 207; Antonia Fraser, *Faith and Treason; the Story of the Gunpowder Plot* (New York, 1996), p. 78. A collective peace treaty among Great Britain, Spain, and the Netherlands was made in August 1604 (Wernham, *Return of the Armadas*, pp. 413-414).

[44] Willson, *James VI and I*, pp. 249-252; von Pastor, *History of the Popes*, XXIV, 77-79; Fraser, *Faith and Treason*, pp. 83-85, 89, 102.

This was the background of one of the most famous conspiracies in history, the Gunpowder Plot, popularly associated primarily with the name of one of its most active participants, Guy Fawkes, but actually generated by another man named Robert Catesby.[45] Due to plague in London, Parliament was prorogued and scheduled to reconvene in October 1605. In February of that year James I declared to his privy council "that he detested in the highest degree the superstitious religion of the Papists, and that if he thought that his son and heir would show the slightest favor to them, he would rather see him buried before his eyes." He called on his judges to execute the anti-Catholic laws "with all possible severity," and the greater part of the property still owned by Catholics in England was confiscated before the end of the year.[46]

James I's February 1605 declaration of hatred was just what Catesby and Fawkes and their cohorts expected. They looked down a vista of the future and could see nothing but more and more of a persecution which had already lasted forty-five years. Horribly misguided though they were, Catesby and Fawkes were committed Catholics who could not endure the prospect, for themselves and for their children, of a Catholic life lived always in hiding, with no hope of relief. On May 30, 1604 they had already met with three other men of like persuasion, at an inn called the Duck and Drake in the Strand district of London. They swore an oath of secrecy and mutual loyalty on a prayer book, and Catesby shared his plot. Because it was Sunday, Father John Gerard celebrated Mass for them after the meeting, in complete ignorance of their intentions.[47]

Catesby's plot was no less than to blow up Parliament on the day it reconvened, with James I and his son in the building for the ceremonial address from the throne, appealing to the ancient Catholic doctrine of tyrannicide to justify it.[48]

But Catholic moral theologians had always attached strict conditions to the justification of tyrannicide. James I was a rightful king, through his mother; no Catholic could deny the hereditary legitimacy of his rule.[49] Unbearable tyranny could still justify his killing, but only if the would-be tyrant killers could replace the tyrannical regime by a beneficent one of their creation. No such regime was in prospect.[50] Young Catesby had few supporters, and fewer still who would stay

---

[45] Fraser, *Faith and Treason*, pp. 70-75, 91-94. The peculiar-looking name "Fawkes" was a typically English attempt to give a more distinguished spelling to the common and earthy name of "Fox," like Anne Boleyn for Bullen. However, Fawkes had little of the Englishman left in him; he had served for years with the Spanish army in the Netherlands and always signed his first name "Guido."

[46] *Ibid.*, p. 110; Von Pastor, *History of the Popes*, XXIV, 79-80 for all quotes; Willson, *James VI and I*, pp. 219, 223.

[47] Fraser, *Faith and Treason*, pp. 97-101.

[48] *Ibid.*, pp. 98-99.

[49] In contrast to the rule of Elizabeth, by definition illegitimate for any Catholic since they regarded her parents as never having been validly married.

[50] Fraser, *Faith and Treason*, pp. 101, 104-105. Father Henry Garnet, the hunted and outlawed Jesuit superior in England, was always counselling against violence under the circumstances in James I's England. See Caraman, *Henry Garnet and the Gunpowder*

with him through such an undertaking. King James I had four children, two sons and two daughters; even if Crown Prince Henry was blown up with him in Parliament, the other son (Charles, aged four) and then the two daughters would be his legitimate successors and undoubtedly would be generally recognized as such.[51] Furthermore, not only James I and his older son would perish, but all the members of Parliament present, including several still staunchly Catholic lords.[52] The scheme was political madness and morally indefensible—like that of Anthony Babington to use Mary Queen of Scots to overthrow and kill Queen Elizabeth, only worse. It was pure terrorism, which would brand English Catholics as revolutionaries and murderers; far from ending their persecution, it would—and did—make it even more terrible.

So spectacularly did the Gunpowder Plot play into the hands of England's persecutors that there has been a persistent belief among some students of English history that Robert Cecil, true son of his brilliant and relentless father and now holding essentially the same position in the English government his father had held, was the author of the plot. But the historian may never be satisfied with mere suspicion, however seemingly plausible. He must demand proof. And proof in this case, as for so many alleged conspiracy theories, is lacking. In the assassination of Red Hugh O'Donnell in Spain by an agent of George Carew, we have Carew's own word for it. No such confirmation is available for the putative role of Robert Cecil as *agent provocateur* of the Gunpowder Plot.[53]

Plot, *passim* and especially pp. 321-322. Another priest named Tesimond heard the confessions of several of the plotters, learning about the plot for the first time from them. He asked Garnet what he should do. They decided they could not break the seal of the confessional, but could only urge the plotters not to carry out their plans, and seek from the Pope the excommunication of all English Catholics participating in terrorism (von Pastor, *History of the Popes*. XXVI, 133-134; Fraser, *Faith and Treason*, pp. 127-132).

[51] Catesby intended to kidnap nine-year-old Princess Elizabeth and rule in her name, marrying her to a Catholic, and designated one of his fellow conpirators to kidnap young Prince Charles. He never did figure out what to do with James' just-born daughter Mary. But before the fatal November 5 it became known that Prince Henry was not after all going to attend the opening session of the reconvened Parliament. All plans to abduct the children collapsed, without which the plot could not possibly have succeeded. Why Catesby and Fawkes did not abandon it then passes rational explanation. Some of the plotters did suggest it to them, to no avail. See Fraser, *Faith and Treason*, pp. 116-117, 165.

[52] Catesby tried to persuade one of them, Viscount Montague, to stay away from the opening day of the reconvened Parliament, but did not tell him why (Fraser, *Faith and Treason*, pp. 148-149).

[53] This may be seen by a careful comparison of the work of the latest Catholic writer holding Robert Cecil responsible for the Gunpowder Plot, the Jesuit Francis Edwards in *Guy Fawkes; the Real Story of the Gunpowder Plot?* (London, 1969) with Antonia Fraser's meticulously researched *Faith and Treason*, published in 1996 (especially pp. 284-287). Edwards himself admits the dubiety of his conclusions by ending his subtitle with a highly significant question mark.

But we may safely presume that Robert Cecil, as good at intelligence at his father, learned of the plot well in advance, and saw at once its immense propaganda possibilities. He may have played a part in orchestrating its development, particularly its public disclosure by an anonymous letter believed to have been written by Lord Mounteagle at precisely the right moment to catch the plotters red-handed, with Guy Fawkes actually carrying gunpowder into the cellar of the palace of Westminster, where Parliament would meet.[54] Robert Cecil laid the trap and sprang it, and thereby effectively destroyed Catholicism in England. For three hundred years it became inseparably linked in the popular mind with the worst and most spectacular kind of treason.

Guy Fawkes, caught with the gunpowder in the Westminster Palace cellar, was broken on the rack and confessed everything. Robert Catesby died fighting rather than be taken. Henry Garnet was seized and martyred, along with St. Nicholas Owen, known as "Little John," a tiny deformed man who spent most of his time designing and building "priests' holes" for hiding hunted priests in Catholic homes, praying all the while. Both were horribly tortured. Father Garnet denied any sympathy with the plot. All Garnet's expressions of disapproval of the plot were taken out when his statements were read to the jury which condemned him to death. St. Nicholas Owen, who died on the rack, never revealed the location of any of his hiding places for priests.[55]

It was all made much worse by King James I's physical cowardice and terror of assassination, learned from the dreadful experiences of his childhood. His fear and hatred of Catholics, already strong, became consuming. The indelible image of Guy Fawkes skulking through the cellar of Westminster Palace, shrouded in black cloak and hat as he dragged in barrels of gunpowder to blow up king and Parliament, was a propagandist's dream come true. Every November 5 until the twentieth century, English-speaking peoples celebrated Guy Fawkes Day with execration of all Catholics. In June 1606 Parliament passed many new anti-Catholic laws, prohibiting husbands and wives not married by a Protestant minister from inheriting from each other, prescribing severe fines for not having all one's children baptized by a Protestant minister or failing to be buried in a Protestant cemetery. A child sent overseas to be educated was barred from any inheritance or gift, in favor of his Protestant next of kin. Catholics were restricted to a radius of five miles from their residence, and deprived of all rights in court. They were barred from the professions of law and medicine, were subject to searches of their houses and the burning of their religious books or devotional objects, and not allowed to carry arms. Any householder receiving Catholic visitors or keeping Catholic servants was fined monthly. Every Catholic had to swear that James I was his rightful sovereign and head of the church in

---

[54] Fraser, *Faith and Treason*, pp. 150-158, 161, 166-173; Willson, *James VI and I*, pp. 224-226. The date of the reconvening of Parliament had recently been put off from October 3 to 5 by the Julian calendar used in England (Fraser, *op. cit.*, pp. 132-133).

[55] Fraser, *Faith and Treason*, pp. 179-187, 214-218, 244-247, 250-252, 254; von Pastor, *History of the Popes*, XXVI 136, 148, 152-156; Caraman, *Henry Garnet and the Gunpowder Plot*, pp. 348-440.

England, and that the Pope had no power to act against him. This legislation was drafted by an apostate Jesuit turned Protestant, Christopher Perkins, to present Catholics with an oath they could not possibly take in good conscience. The next month King James ordered the expulsion of all priests from Great Britain. For the rest of his reign he remained deaf to all appeals to mitigate these laws.[56]

All these anti-Catholic laws of England were also applied to broken Ireland. No realistic possibility of resistance remained after Kinsale, even though the population remained overwhelmingly Catholic. O'Neill was still feared by the English. He was constantly harassed, charged with new treasons, forbidden to practice his faith even in private, and eventually summoned to London in the summer of 1607. He was convinced, in all probability rightly, that if he went there he would never return. So he boarded a ship sent by his son Henry from the Netherlands to carry him to safety on the continent. With him went his son Conn; Rory O'Donnell, Red Hugh's brother; and many of their nearest relatives, including Nuala, Red Hugh's sister, the long-separated wife of the traitor Niall Garbh O'Donnell. They entered the Seine River in France at the beginning of October and proceeded by slow stages to Rome, where one by one they died, O'Neill last, struck blind, but clinging always to his Lord in St. Peter's city, on July 20, 1616. He is buried in Rome with the heroes of Christendom.[57]

The still extensive lands of the O'Neills and the O'Donnells were seized by the government, and over the next several years planted with colonists, many of whom were fierce Calvinist Scots of the John Knox type, and virtually all of whom were violently anti-Catholic.[58] The effects have endured, creating the troubled Northern Ireland of today, its boundaries drawn to insure a Protestant majority, far different from Catholic Ireland, now an independent nation peaceful and free. England's revenge against O'Neill and O'Donnell resounds through history to the present.

On February 10, 1605 Pope Clement VIII suffered the first of a series of strokes which brought about his death less than a month later. The conclave began March 14 with sixty cardinals present, no less than 53 of them Italians. The two most distinguished Cardinals, venerated throughout Europe, were the Jesuit St. Robert Bellarmine and the great pioneering Catholic historian Caesar Baronius. But even the renewed and reformed Tridentine church found such men too holy to be Popes, especially since neither would lift a finger to gain the papacy. Baronius did receive 32 votes, a majority, but had no chance for two-thirds; the Spanish cardinals, aided by Italian cardinals living in the parts of Italy they controlled, could and did block him, at least partly because as an historian he had proved that some of the documents on which they relied for control of the

---

[56] Fraser, *Faith and Treason*, pp. 169, 283-284; Von Pastor, *History of the Popes*, XXVI, 159-164; James Brodrick, *Robert Bellarmine, Saint and Scholar* (London, 1961), pp. 269-270.

[57] O'Faolain, *Great O'Neill*, pp. 273-274, 281; *New History of Ireland* III, 195-196. The departure of the O'Neills and O'Donnells was called "the flight of the earls."

[58] *New History of Ireland*, III, 196-205.

church in their territories were inauthentic or forged. In back-room negotiations French Cardinal Joyeuse persuaded the late Pope's nephew, Cardinal Pietro Aldobrandini, to yield to the Medici of Florence, whose ecclesiastical leader Alessandro, aged 70, succeeded to the tiara as Pope Leo XI despite Spanish disapproval. Baronius sealed his victory by endorsing him.[59]

Within a month Pope Leo XI was dead, and it all had to be done over again. Virtually the same conclave reassembled in May. Once again supported by the best men, Cardinal Bellarmine told them "that he would not so much as pick up a straw if that alone would obtain" the papacy. He considered resigning as Cardinal, and prayed that God would not make him Pope. The Holy Spirit answered Bellarmine's prayers, through the agency of the Spanish cardinals and their Italian allies. But Bellarmine and Baronius had more than enough votes to block any unsuitable candidate not a credible champion of the Catholic Reformation, and so used them. In the end they agreed on Camillo Borghese, only 54 years old, the youngest Pope in many years. He was enthroned as Pope Paul V.[60]

In late October 1605 Paul V decided to challenge new laws in the immemorially Catholic state of Venice prohibiting the sale, gifts, or even building of a church, monastery, hospital or other Church structure without the consent of the Senate of Venice, and prohibiting the disciplining of Venetian clergy by Church courts without the Senate's consent. Pope Paul V sent a formal rebuke for approving these laws to Doge Grimani, who was dying. The rebuke was therefore not delivered to him, but to his successor Doge Donato, already an "avowed enemy" of the Pope's authority in the Church. When Donato would not yield, the Pope excommunicated him and the entire government of Venice, and put the city under an interdict. The government actually forced some priests to say Mass in defiance of it. Doge Donato declared he had no superior but God. He expelled the Jesuits. The English ambassador to Venice urged its alliance with the Protestant powers; Philip III of Spain ordered the Spanish army of 30,000 in Milan to prepare for war against Venice. A Servite monk in Venice named Paolo Sarpi emerged as the intellectual leader of the rebellion, on excellent terms with the Protestants, and was excommunicated. Under this heavy pressure the Doge began to back down, but the Senate remained defiant. Both it and France sent subsidies to Protestants in the Grisons canton in Switzerland, so positioned geographically as to be able to block movement of Spanish troops from Milan to Germany through the Valtelline Pass.[61]

But converted Henry IV of France rejected alliance with the schismatic Venetians, and in February 1607 leading French Cardinal Joyeuse arrived to act as a mediator of the dispute, a task which he successfully accomplished. The Venetian Senate accepted a statement he drafted saying that Venice did not wish "to depart from its traditional piety and religious spirit in the application of the

---

[59] Von Pastor, *History of the Popes*, XXIV, 434; XXV, 4-17.

[60] *Ibid.*, XXV, 27-29, 32, 33-37 (quote on 32).

[61] *Ibid.*, XXV, 116-122, 126-127, 132, 134-139, 141, 143, 148, 159, 161-162, 164; Roland Mousnier, *The Assassination of Henry IV* (London, 1973), p. 129.

laws." Further negotiation was transferred to Rome, where both sides retreated from the confrontation in such a manner that neither lost face. The offensive laws went quietly unenforced and were eventually dropped. Italy would remain, as it had been since Constantine, with all its governments totally loyal to the Pope, despite individual defections. The attempt of Sarpi in 1608 to set up a Protestant community in Venice was a failure.[62]

In December 1602 a relatively young man of 35, already well known as a preacher in the still largely Catholic area south of Lake Geneva, was appointed Bishop of Geneva, though he could not even enter his episcopal city because of the vehement Calvinism established there. He was St. Francis de Sales. Six years later, after quiet, gentle but ceaseless work among the people of his diocese, he was able to report to Rome that there were no longer any significant numbers of Protestants outside the lands directly controlled by the fiercely Protestant governments of Geneva and Berne. Virtually all had returned to the Catholic Faith. The following year the great saint published the first edition of his *Introduction to the Devout Life*, one of the most effective and beloved guides to personal spiritual growth ever written.[63]

In December 1604 Pope Clement VIII appointed the able young Maffeo Barberini, the future Pope Urban VIII, as his nuncio to France, and gave him detailed instructions emphasizing the absolute necessity of Church reform in France to keep it Catholic. Henry IV, the sincerity of whose conversion was still widely doubted, should not be allowed to appoint any bishops without careful review, and he must be pressed to proclaim the decrees of the Council of Trent as he had promised to do when accepted back into the Church, but had not yet done. In August 1605 new Pope Paul V sent a brief to Henry IV urging him again to proclaim the decrees of Trent, also appealing for the same purpose to Cardinals Joyeuse, Gondi and Sourdis and to two influential members of the royal council, Pomponne de Bellièvre and Brulart de Sillery. In October he reiterated the absolute obligation of all bishops, according to the Council of Trent, to reside in their dioceses. But it was not then possible to reject lay influence entirely in the selection of French bishops, and at Easter 1607 Jean Armand du Plessis, the future Cardinal Richelieu, became Bishop of Luçon at the age of only 23. However, he seemed zealous and devout, and immediately began a thorough Tridentine reform of his diocese, even though the Tridentine decrees had still not been published by the king.[64]

In March 1609 the feeble-minded, childless Duke of Cleves on the lower Rhine in Germany died, and Henry IV intrigued with the German Protestants to control the succession. The southern part of Cleves was Catholic and the northern part Protestant. Archduke Leopold Habsburg of Austria occupied the

---

[62] Von Pastor, *History of the Popes*, XXV, 167-168, 171-173, 176-177, 198; Mousnier, *Assassination of Henry IV*, p. 229.

[63] Maurice Henry-Couannier, *Saint Francis de Sales and His Friends* (New York, 1964), pp. 145-158; von Pastor, *History of the Popes*, XXIII, 425; XXVI, 78-81.

[64] Yves-Marie Bercé, *The Birth of Absolutism; a History of France 1598-1661* (New York, 1992), p. 81; von Pastor, *History of the Popes*, XXV, 218; XXVI 1-5, 7-8, 11, 54.

southern part July 23, but with only 900 men. Henry IV offered the Protestants at least 15,000 French soldiers, well armed with artillery. Archduke Leopold put the Protestant claimants to the duchy under the ban of the Empire. Henry expanded his plans to include a resumption of war with Spain, at least partly because of his lust for the 15-year-old wife of his relative the Prince of Condé, who had fled with her to the Spanish Netherlands (Belgium) to escape his unwelcome attentions. Pope Paul V pleaded in vain for peace between the Catholic sovereigns. Henry IV brought up 34,000 soldiers, with the mission of first taking Cleves, then invading the Spanish Netherlands to secure Madame de Condé. But on May 14, just three days before Henry was scheduled to take the field, the madman Ravaillac, in all probability acting alone, assassinated him.[65]

Suddenly the king of France was young Louis XIII, nine years old, with his formidable mother, Marie de Medici, as regent. Marie de Medici was a better Catholic than former Queen Mother Catherine, a relative, and she appointed an Italian, her favorite Concino Concini, as her chief minister, forcing out the Calvinist Duke of Sully, who had been Henry's chief minister. Early in 1612 France and Spain, so long enemies, made a firm alliance, to the great joy of the Pope who had so long suffered from their enmity. The alliance was to be sealed by a double marriage: France's boy king to Princess Anne of Spain, and Spain's Crown Prince Philip to Princess Isabelle of France. At the end of 1611 a French Oratory, modelled after that of St. Philip Neri in Rome, was established in Paris by the great Catholic reformer Pierre de Bérulle, a close friend of St. Francis de Sales, and Pope Paul V approved its constitutions in May 1613. In 1612 St. Vincent de Paul began his holy work in the Paris area to succor the poor.[66]

On September 27, 1614 Louis XIII attained his majority under French law at fourteen, but delegated most of his power back to his mother to continue, in effect, her regency. An Estates-General was called. The First Estate, the clergy, had 59 bishops and 81 other clerics present; the Second Estate, the nobility, 138 members present; the Third Estate (everybody else) had 187 delegates, mostly officers of the government. The First Estate called unanimously for official publication of the decrees of the Council of Trent. The Third Estate, strongly Gallican, rejected the proposal of the First Estate for common action on this and other issues. The Third Estate declared that the king gains his crown and his power from God alone, and could not therefore be deposed by the Pope. The Parlement of Paris declared on January 2, 1615 that even a heretic king must be

---

[65] Mousnier, *Assassination of Henry IV*, pp. 21-26, 135; Bercé, *Birth of Absolutism*, pp. 18, 27-30, 34-35; Buisseret, *Henry IV* (London, 1984), pp. 171, 174-175; Johannes Janssen, *History of the German People at the Close of the Middle Ages* (London, 1906), X, 426-427, 429, 431, 433, 457; von Pastor, *History of the Popes*, XXV, 399-400, 411-417.

[66] Mousnier, *Assassination of Henry IV*, pp. 134-135, 232-235; Bercé, *Birth of Absolutism*, pp. 31-32, 40-41, 47-48; von Pastor, *History of the Popes*, XXVI, 55, 58-59. In April 1618 Pope Paul V approved the Visitation Order, founded by St. Jeanne de Chantal with the constant encouragement of St. Francis de Sales (von Pastor, *op. cit.*, XXVI, 72-74). For St. Vincent de Paul, see Chapter Eleven, below.

obeyed and could not be excommunicated or deposed by the Pope. Cardinal du Perron, a convert from Calvinism, replied that this was schism or heresy, and in a great speech carried the whole First Estate and a majority of the Second with him. Young Bishop Richelieu of Luçon addressed the Third Estate calling for confirmation of the decrees of the Council of Trent, and this was finally done by the bishops on their own authority during 1615 and 1616. The double Spanish marriages took place in the fall of 1615.[67]

In November 1616 Bishop Richelieu began the long and tragic process of transferring his primary attention and concern from Christ and the faith which he had been called to serve, to worldly affairs. He became secretary of state for France, the principal voice in the government in foreign affairs and war. In February 1517 he prepared a lengthy statement in support of the government and Marie de Medici's Italian favorite Concini, against a background of increasing protests by the nobility at the conferral of so much power on a foreigner. But in April young Louis XIII, still only 18, was persuaded to end the rule of his mother, and had Concini assassinated. When Bishop Richelieu, shocked by the crime, came before him, Louis shouted: "Now at last, Luçon, I am free of your tyranny. . . . Be off, get yourself out of here!" Richelieu had no choice but to obey, returning to his diocese, and Louis XIII also dismissed his mother from court. She was never again to play a role in public life, but Bishop Richelieu was to betray Christendom.[68]

As the seventeenth century opened, most of Europe's Christian intellectuals still held to the old Aristotelian-Ptolemaic view of the universe as a series of concentric spheres in which perfect heavenly lights, consisting of special celestial matter, shone and revolved in perfect circles around a stationary earth. Centuries of effort had brought this theory to the point where it appeared to explain all observations. It fitted especially well with Catholic theology and held nothing to frighten Protestants.[69]

Then a Dutch spectacle-maker named Hans Lippershey, at Middelburg in Zeeland, invented the telescope in 1609.[70]

News of the epoch-making invention soon came to Galileo Galilei, professor of mathematics at the University of Padua, who had resigned from his

---

[67] Bercé, *Birth of Absolutism*, pp. 51, 67-68; Mousnier, *Assassination of Henry IV*, pp. 261-266, 268-269, 274-277; Joseph Bergin, *The Rise of Richelieu* (New Haven CT, 1991), pp. 131-133; von Pastor, *History of the Popes*, XXVI, 28-34; Brodrick, *Robert Bellarmine*, pp. 298-299.

[68] See Chapter Eleven, below. Bergin, *Rise of Richelieu*, pp. 140, 154-155, 161 (quote), 164-165, 168, 172; Bercé, *Birth of Absolutism*, pp. 70-73. Marie de Medici wrote to Richelieu applauding his decision to return to his diocese and his flock, and ordering him not to leave it without express royal permission (Bergin, *op. cit.*, p. 169). If he had stayed in Luçon, how different history would have been!

[69] Jerome J. Langford, *Galileo, Science and the Church*, 3rd ed. (Ann Arbor MI, 1992), pp. 23-32.

[70] *Ibid.*, p. 39.

professorial chair at the University of Pisa because of conflicts with the Aristotelians. He had held for more than ten years to the theory of Nicholas Copernicus, a Polish monk, published in 1543 almost at the moment of his death, that the sun and not the earth was the center of the universe,[71] and the earth revolved around it. The theory was received with considerable scorn by both Catholics and Protestants, though it found some supporters. Early in 1610 Galileo, after making a telescope for himself based on Lippershey's design, published a book called *The Starry Messenger* in which he described his astonishing discoveries with it: the mountains of the moon (proving that the moon was not made of "celestial matter" but of matter like the earth); the phases of Venus (indicating that it revolved around the sun) and the moons of the planet Jupiter which revolved around it (indicating that not all celestial bodies revolved around the earth). All his discoveries gave strong support to the Copernican theory and ran contrary to the theories of Aristotle and Ptolemy.[72]

In understanding what was to come, it is essential at the outset to put ourselves by imagination into a world where science, in the modern conception of the term, was unknown. What we now call physics was then called "natural philosophy" and considered a branch of that discipline. Mathematics was beginning to be understood and given a place in university curricula, and those natural philosophers who emphasized quantitative elements in the universe were called mathematicians. Their main function was seen as providing additional explanations of how the universe worked, expressed in a different medium from words. There was a fundamental distinction—not always perceived—between the truths of faith, held as absolutely and unchangeably true on the basis of revelation, and truths of natural philosophy which changed as knowledge grew. Since Scripture was an important part of revelation, rendered even more important for Catholics in that age by the tremendous emphasis of the Protestants upon it, any scientific theory which seemed to challenge Scripture was suspect. Scientific theories were not heretical, and Copernicus as a religious had remained in good standing with the Church all his life and after his death until this time, but if they seemed to contradict Scripture, then those who held them were easily suspected of heresy. The concept of science as an autonomous field of study barely existed. In fact Galileo has often been called the world's first real scientist, along with his near contemporary William Harvey, discoverer of the circulation of the blood.

Furthermore, the Copernican theory of the earth's rotation on its axis and revolution around the sun, though of course correct, was not provable in Galileo's time. As the great astronomer Tycho Brahe showed, the facts of observation could be explained with a stationary earth as well as with a stationary sun. The telescopic discoveries strengthened the Copernican theory but did not relate directly to the question of whether the earth revolved around the sun or the

---

[71] We now know that neither the sun nor the earth is the center of the universe; indeed, it has no detectable center. The sun is one of uncountable multitudes of stars in the Milky Way galaxy.

[72] Langford, *Galileo, Science and the Church*, pp. 32-40.

sun around the earth. The nearest stars were so distant that no instruments existed accurate enough to measure their tiny parallax which, if found (as it was not until Friedrich Bessel did so in 1838) would have proved the earth's revolution around the sun. Galileo believed that the tides proved the Copernican theory, but in that he was mistaken. The two leading astronomers of the time, Brahe and Johann Kepler (Galileo was more of what we would call a physicist) split on the Copernican theory; Kepler accepted it while Brahe adhered to the Aristotelian-Ptolemaic theory with modifications.[73]

On December 10 Jesuit Father Christopher Clavius, the greatest mathematician of his age and maker of the new "Gregorian" calendar, wrote to Galileo that Jesuit observers of the skies had confirmed his discoveries with the new telescopes and urged him to come to Rome and promote them. Galileo did so in March 1611 and was received with great honor, having a long audience with Pope Paul V and being made a member of the prestigious Lyncean Academy. Father Clavius assured Jesuit Cardinal Robert Bellarmine that the discoveries were real, and confirmed by some telescopic observations of his own. In February 1612 Father Clavius died, after declaring the Aristotelian-Ptolemaic world-view no longer tenable, but not commenting on Tycho Brahe's alternative theory which kept the earth at the center of the universe.[74]

Galileo published *Discourse on Floating Bodies* in 1612 and a book on sunspots in 1613, in both of which he sarcastically mocked the Aristotelians but had the support of Cardinal Maffeo Barberini, later Pope Urban VIII, who played a key role in the Galileo case. In December 1613 Grand Duke Cosimo de Medici of Tuscany, who had been tutored by Galileo as a young man and had given him an important and lucrative position at his court, held a banquet at which his wife Christina declared the Copernican theory heretical because contrary to Scripture. Galileo soon wrote a letter to a friendly priest named Castelli, later circulated as an open letter to Grand Duchess Christina, saying that Scripture should be understood figuratively and not literally when it spoke of the sun rising and setting. A week later the Dominican priest Tommaso Caccini preached against Galileo and the Copernican theory, saying that all mathematicians should be banished from Christian states as fomenters of heresy. As an example of the incompatibility of the Copernican theory with Scripture, Caccini specifically pointed to the command of Joshua to the sun to stand still in the valley of Ajalon, which he said it could not have done according to the Copernican theory.[75]

Thus surfaced the first claim that the Copernican theory was heretical, testifying to the shallow thinking of some men as the age of science dawned. They were unprepared to recognize that a universe generally governed by physical laws could still accommodate miracles due to the direct action of God. The sun standing still at Joshua's command was not an action that could be

---

[73] *Ibid.*, pp. 40-49.

[74] *Ibid.*, pp. 45-46; James Brodrick, *Robert Bellarmine, Saint and Scholar* (London, 1961), pp. 342-345.

[75] Pietro Redondi, *Galileo, Heretic* (Princeton NJ, 1987), pp. 36-37; Brodrick, *Robert Bellarmine*, pp. 351, 355; Langford, *Galileo*, pp. 52, 58, 70-73.

explained by natural laws, but it did not need to be so explained; the miracle could not be seen as disproving a theory about those laws. God can override His laws when it serves His purpose. He could make the sun stand still in the sky over the valley of Ajalon just as he made the sun dance and drop in the sky over Fatima in 1917.[76]

Father Caccini's complaint to the Roman Inquisition, and another by Father Niccolo Lorini objecting to Galileo as presumptuous and engaging in private interpretation of Scripture, were summarily dismissed in February 1615.[77] But Cardinal Maffeo Barberini, the future Pope Urban VIII, urged Galileo to use "greater caution in not going beyond the arguments used by Ptolemy and Copernicus, and finally, in not exceeding the limitations of physics and mathematics. The explanation of Scripture is claimed by the theologians as their field, and if new things are introduced, even by a capable mind, not everyone has the dispassionate facility of taking them just as they are said."[78] The judicious Cardinal Bellarmine wrote that the Copernican theory might be true, but was not yet proved, and should not be applied to the interpretation of Scripture until it was proved—a position that justly accommodated both sides in the Galilean controversy.[79]

Unfortunately the matter did not end there. In December 1615 Galileo again came to Rome, against the advice of many of his friends who believed the Church would maintain a "wait and see" attitude in his case if he did not push matters. Wherever he went he preached the Copernican theory as truth. The theory was unsettling for many because it removed man's abode on earth from the center of the cosmos; and indeed earth's astronomical insignificance was to become a stock in trade of mockers of Christianity, though of course the most important abode of life in the universe need not be at its center even if it had one that we could detect (which we now know it does not). God sanctified the earth by the Incarnation regardless of its size or placement. In February 1616 Pope Paul V decided that "a formal decision on the Copernican system" should be made by the Inquisition, though he was persuaded at the last moment by Cardinal Bellarmine not to make a statement himself on the issue. Cardinal Bellarmine had said it might eventually be proved true; probably the greatest Catholic apologist who ever lived, he surely had some understanding of how disastrous it would be for the Church to have the Pope condemn a scientific theory that later turned out to be true. But the total separation of scientific theories on the material nature of the universe from theological and philosophical teaching was not yet generally understood, and even less could most contemporaries grasp that despite being the guardian of ultimate truth, the Church as such has no authority or competence in science. So a committee of eleven theologians and not one natural philosopher or mathematician was presented with the proposition that the

---

[76] See Volume I, Chapter 4 of this history.

[77] Langford, *Galileo, Science and the Church*, p. 57.

[78] *Ibid.*, p. 58.

[79] *Ibid.*, pp. 60-62; Brodrick, *Robert Bellarmine*, pp. 360-363; Rivka Feldhay, *Galileo and the Church* (Cambridge, England, 1995), pp. 34-36, 232-237.

earth revolves around the sun and unanimously pronounced it false, absurd and heretical.[80]

Heretical it certainly was not, by any rational criterion, and the Inquisition took out the word before publishing its decree against Galileo.[81] But the condemnation of a scientific theory as "false and absurd" was one of the most grievous mistakes in the history of the Church. The Church was not empowered by its Founder to decide scientific questions. St. Augustine had said exactly that more than a thousand years before, but few seemed to remember it.[82]

Pope Paul V directed Cardinal Bellarmine to inform Galileo of the condemnation of the Copernican theory by the Inquisition and to direct him that he could no longer "hold" or "defend" it, which meant to hold or defend it as certainly true. Only if he were to defy the decree would he become subject to a prohibition from teaching it as a theory without saying whether he regarded it as true. Cardinal Bellarmine had always favored teaching it as a theory, because he knew it might turn out to be true, though not yet proven. And the Congregation of the Index of Forbidden Books agreed with him, because they did not ban Copernicus' book but only suspended its circulation until a preface could be added stating that it was a theory and not sure truth. Cardinal Bellarmine later declared publicly in a sworn affidavit that, contrary to rumor, Galileo had not formally abjured or been given a penance by him, but simply told that he must no longer hold the Copernican theory to be certain truth.[83]

But at some time—probably in the spring of 1616, possibly later—an unsigned document dated February 26, 1616 was inserted into the Galileo file enjoining him from teaching it in any way. This originally had been the "back-up" provision if he defied the decree against holding or defending it—which he did not. Galileo always insisted he could not recall ever receiving this injunction. When the controversy revived seventeen years later Cardinal Bellarmine was dead and so could not be questioned on it, though his affidavit did not mention it. Controversy over the authenticity of this document has raged since it was first discovered in 1632. There is not enough information to decide it for sure. But the document is in conflict both with what the Inquisition said Galileo must do and what Cardinal Bellarmine said he had done. Its date of February 26 is suspiciously early, in view of the decision of February 23 to warn Galileo first (which was done on February 25) and only if he proved defiant to be enjoined against teaching it as a hypothesis, without any indication that he ever proved defiant. Since it carries no internal authentication and there is no record of any instructions to give the injunction to a compliant Galileo except this document, the balance of probability lies against its authenticity. Several authorities on

---

[80] Langford, *Galileo*, pp. 79, 87-88 (quote on 88); Redondi, *Galileo*, pp. 37-38; Brodrick, *Robert Bellarmine*, p. 372; Stanley L. Jaki, "The Case for Galileo's Rehabilitation," *Fidelity*, March 1986.

[81] Brodrick, *Robert Bellarmine*, p. 373.

[82] Langford, *Galileo*, pp. 73, 90.

[83] *Ibid.*, pp. 92, 97-99, 102-103; Feldhay, *Galileo*, pp. 28-29, 45-48, 51; Brodrick, *Robert Bellarmine*, pp. 374-376 (text of Cardinal Bellarmine's letter on p. 376).

Galileo believe that it was surreptitiously inserted in the file by a Dominican member of the Inquisition with a particular objection to the Copernican theory or Galileo or both, on no authority but his own.[84]

Galileo was a very good Catholic. He submitted at once, had a 45-minute audience with Pope Paul V, who assured him of his continued admiration and support, and went back to Florence "discouraged and disappointed, but not defeated."[85]

During these years an extraordinary drama was unfolding in faraway Russia. There Tsar Fedor I, the gentle, devout and unworldly son of Ivan the Terrible, had died at the beginning of 1598 without issue. He tried to make his beloved wife Irina his successor, but she would not have it, instead retiring into a convent. The actual leader of the government throughout Fedor's reign had been Irina's brother Boris Godunov, and at the end of February 1598 he was elected Tsar by a special assembly.[86]

Tsar Boris gave good government, but he was never able to overcome the handicap of lack of royal blood, though his sister had been queen. The great nobles, called boyars, were constantly plotting against him. Several of them challenged him at his weakest point by insisting that Dmitri, the last child of Ivan the Terrible, was still alive and had not died by cutting his throat in an epileptic fit in 1591, as he in fact had done. In the summer of 1603 a young man, recently taken into the service of Prince Adam Vishnevetsky of Poland, declared that he was Tsarevich Dmitri. He appears to have actually been a young Russian monk of vaulting ambition named Gregory Otrepyev, who had boasted that he would one day be Tsar. Patriarch Ion reported to Tsar Boris "that the unworthy monk Gregory wants to become the vessel of the devil," and Boris Godunov sent him to the remote Solovetsky Monastery on an island in the White Sea (where later the Communists were to establish one of the first of their infamous GULAG prison camps) to repent. But instead of going to the Solovetsky Islands, Gregory/Dmitri fled to Poland and was baptized a Catholic on Holy Saturday of 1604. He wrote immediately to the Pope declaring submission to his religious authority.[87]

Here was an opportunity for the deeply Catholic King Sigismund III of Poland to achieve the conversion of Russia after failing to bring about the conversion of his native Sweden.[88] He invited the impostor to Cracow and gave him a private audience on March 15, 1604. He was unconvinced by the man's

---

[84] Langford, *Galileo*, pp. 92-97, 103, 135, 138-139, 144-148; Feldhay, *Galileo*, pp. 47-49, 59-61, 210-211; Redondi, *Galileo*, p. 38; Brodrick, *Robert Bellarmine*, pp. 374-375.

[85] Langford, *Galileo*, pp. 92-97, 102-103, 105 (quote); Brodrick, *Robert Bellarmine*, p. 375. For the conclusion of the Galileo case in 1633, see Chapter Ten, below.

[86] George Vernadsky, *The Tsardom of Moscow 1547-1682*, Volume I (New Haven CT, 1969), pp. 204-207; Ian Grey, *Boris Godunov, the Tragic Tsar* (New York, 1973), pp. 131-141.

[87] Grey, *Boris Godunov*, pp. 112-119, 156-167; Vernadsky, *Tsardom of Moscow*, I, 226.

[88] See Chapter Eight, above.

claims and refused him official support, but backed him privately in order to weaken Russia and bring Catholicism into it. Rangoni, the papal nuncio in Poland, was enthusiastic, as was Pope Clement VIII, who had once himself been the nuncio in Poland and so should have known better. A nobleman named Mnishek, who was steward of Adam Vishnevetsky's estate and a strong Catholic, endorsed the impostor's claims and had him marry his beautiful teenage daughter Marina, whose ambitions were as great as her new husband's. It was agreed that once he became Tsar, the pseudo-Dmitri would pay Mnishek a million zlotys and give him the city of Smolensk in return for his help, while giving Marina the cities of Novgorod and Pskov in the northwest, famous for their riches derived from extensive trade.[89]

Tsar Boris conferred with the real Prince Dmitri's mother, now the nun Marfa, to assure himself of the reality of his death, and prepared to fight the false Dmitri, who marched into Russia with an army of Poles and Ukrainians in August 1604. By October 7,000 Russians who believed the pretender's story had joined them. On the last day of the year this army defeated in Severia the loyal Russian army commanded by Prince Fedor Mstislavsky at Novgorod. But Tsar Boris quickly assembled another army, commanded by Prince Vasily (Basil) Shuisky, which turned the tables by defeating the pretender in January 1605. He was rescued by the lawless Don Cossacks, and Prince Shuisky did not push the attack on their stronghold of Kromy. Artillery were withdrawn and the planned assault was never carried out. Before the end of the month Tsar Boris suddenly died, probably from poison. His 16-year-old son Fedor II was his successor, but several of the great boyars immediately betrayed him. In May the pretender was proclaimed in Red Square, and the next month Fedor II was murdered and Patriarch Ion arrested in his cathedral during Mass and deported to a distant monastery.[90]

On June 2 papal nuncio Rangoni sent from Poland a full and favorable account of the false Dmitri's takeover of Moscow. which described the attitude in Poland toward "Dmitri" as much more favorable than it actually was. Pope Paul V, just elected the preceding month and knowing little of Poland and still less of Russia, wrote the pseudo-Dmitri congratulating him on his accession and "exhorting him to hold fast to the Catholic Faith." The nun Marfa, mother of the real Dmitri, now publicly declared the false Dmitri to be her son, convincing many that he must be so; she later said that of course she had known he was not her son, but had been afraid (with much reason) of being killed if she said so. At the end of July the pseudo-Dmitri was solemnly crowned Tsar. The Pope sent rich gifts and urged him not to forget his promise to reunite Russia with the Church.[91]

---

[89] Grey, *Boris Godunov*, pp. 164-167; Vernadsky, *Tsardom of Moscow*, I, 226.

[90] Vernadsky, *Tsardom of Moscow*, I, 222, 227-229; Grey, *Boris Godunov*, pp. 168, 170-171, 173-175; von Pastor, *History of the Popes*, XXVI, 219.

[91] Von Pastor, *History of the Popes*, XXVI, 219-221; Vernadsky, *Tsardom of Moscow*, II, 229.

But Prince Vasily Shuisky, who had betrayed Boris Godunov, now betrayed pseudo-Dmitri, bringing an army into Moscow. He seized and murdered the pretender, horribly mutilated his body, then buried it, exhumed it, burned it, and rammed its ashes into a cannon to be blown into the sky. He proclaimed himself Tsar and was crowned in June. He forced the Russian church (always subservient to the state) to declare the real, dead Dmitri a martyr murdered by Boris Godunov, though there was no good evidence of his murder. These proceedings finally roused the confused and betrayed Russian people to fury. A patriotic army led by one Ivan Bolotnikov laid siege to Moscow and called on the people to rise against the boyars and kill them all. Bolotnikov was driven back, but the anger remained. Tsar Vasily Shuisky never firmly established his rule, and in June 1607, incredibly, a *second* false Dmitri emerged to fight him, and wrote to King Sigismund III of Poland asking for help. Anarchy threatened in this "time of troubles"; Russia seemed ripe for the taking by any adventurer. The former Marina Mniszech capped the climax of her greed by marrying the second false Dmitri, despite his extraordinary ugliness; she must have loved power with a truly consuming passion. Confronted with a choice between this oaf and Vasily Shuisky, who had betrayed two masters, murdered one, and probably murdered the other, 1,500 Russians held out against both at the fortified Trinity Monastery near Moscow in a state of religious exultation, and repelled the attack of 20,000 men. Tsar Vasily called in Swedes from Finland and Estonia to help him; many Poles marched with the second false Dmitri. The Swedes defeated the Poles and Cossacks at the city of Tver, but their troops mutinied when not allowed to sack the city. The Poles abandoned the second false Dmitri; many of his remaining supporters now offered their allegiance to Sigismund III's son Vladislav. A Polish army occupied Moscow and the Kremlin in August 1610, and Sigismund III announced that he and not his son would reign in Russia. For a brief moment it appeared that Catholic Poland might actually conquer Orthodox Russia.[92]

It was not to be. Despite its political collapse, Russia was a great and proud country. It had been totally cut off from the Catholic Church for five hundred years, the two false Dmitris were totally miscast as missionaries, and the Poles were hereditary enemies. In January 1611 the Russian nobleman Prokopi Liapunov rose against the Polish government of Ryazan province. Patriarch Filaret, whose baptismal name was Fedor Romanov, and Prince Golitsyn refused to swear allegiance to Sigismund III, and were arrested and taken to Poland as prisoners. Nizhni Novgorod in the upper Volga region and Kazan on the middle Volga became centers of resistance to Polish rule. A Russian army with strong popular support took Moscow in April, but a Polish garrison held out in the Kremlin. In June the Poles stormed Smolensk, killing most of its defenders. A surviving remnant went to the cathedral and fired the powder stored in its basement, blowing them all up. The Swedes took Novgorod against fierce resistance. After a provisional government fell apart when one of its leaders

---

[92] Vernadsky, *Tsardom of Moscos*, I, 234-244, 246-250, 253-254, 256-257; Grey, *Boris Godunov*, pp. 177-178.

killed another, Kuzma Minin, a former butcher who had become mayor of Nizhni Novgorod, demanded and received a capital levy of 20 per cent from most Russians who had money, including abbots of monasteries and landlords of great estates, and used it to recruit and equip a new army of 20,000 led by wounded war hero Prince D. M. Pozharsky. Late in 1612 the Polish garrison of the Kremlin capitulated after a long and heroic defense worthy of a better cause. The candidacy of one of the two princes of Sweden, Charles Filip and the later famous Gustav Adolf, was considered and a national assembly (*zemsky sobor*) of 800 members met in the Cathedral of the Dormition in Moscow and elected Charles Filip Tsar. But he failed to arrive when expected. Therefore in March 1613 Michael Romanov, 16-year-old son of Patriarch Filaret, was elected Tsar after Cossacks forced their way into the Kremlin and demanded it of the national assembly. His mother warned young Michael that many of the boyars now swearing allegiance to him had betrayed four Tsars in succession, and at first he rejected the election "with ire and tears." But eventually he accepted, and only after that did Prince Charles Filip of Sweden finally arrive, too late. On July 21, 1613 Michael Romanov was crowned Tsar. His coronation manifesto was full of attacks against Catholics. The rejection of the Catholic Church by almost all Russians hardened still more.[93]

Despite all apparent probability, the dynasty of Michael Romanov was to endure until overthrown in the epochal year of the Communist Revolution, 1917.

These opening years of the seventeenth century were also the time of what might well be called the Second Age of Discovery, when bold Europeans followed the track of the original explorers of the fifteenth and sixteenth centuries and began founding colonies in the lands they reached, as only the Spanish and Portuguese in America and the Portuguese in India and the Spice Islands had previously done. Despite its enormous consequences in the history of the world, this new surge of exploration and colonization has been curiously neglected in most histories, perhaps because it involved three different nations— Great Britain, France, and the Netherlands (the northern, Calvinist part)—whose overseas expansion was mostly entirely separate, and therefore tends to be described as part of their national histories or the histories of the colonies they founded, without regard to its contemporaneity. In the twenty-year period covered by this chapter, both Great Britain and France founded their first enduring colonies in North America, in Virginia and Nova Scotia and Quebec respectively; and the Dutch, taking advantage of having prevailed over Spain in the long war with the late Philip II, set sail for every part of the newly discovered world which offered commercial prospects, from Spitsbergen to Brazil, from the Cape of Good Hope to Indonesia. In the end they secured and held only Indonesia, but control of the fabulous Spice Islands was more than enough to

---

[93] Vernadsky, *Tsardom of Moscow*, I, 256, 258-268, 274-280, 285-286; Michael Roberts, *Gustavus Adolphus; a History of Sweden 1611-1632* (London, 1953), I, 77-78; von Pastor, *History of the Popes*, XXVI, 231.

make this small Calvinist country one of the wealthiest in the world for the next century and more.

Since Sir Walter Raleigh's colony at Roanoke in North Carolina had failed at the time of the Spanish Armada, no further effort had been made by England to plant colonies in North America, despite all the explorations of the coast of the great continent by Queen Elizabeth's "sea dogs." But in the summer of 1606 the newly established Virginia Company decided to plant two colonies in America, one in the north (the future New England) and another in the south. More explorers were sent out along the coasts. The first colonizing expedition was captured by the Spanish in the West Indies, but the company persevered, and toward the end of December sent Captain Christopher Newport, with previous explorer Bartholomew Gosnold second-in-command, to Virginia with three ships and 120 colonists. Almost no one noticed, and the ships remained pinned by unfavorable winds in the Downs off the east coast of Kent for a full month. Aboard was a man of no influence, though a protegé of Gosnold, who was not even considered for leadership of the group because of his lowly birth marked by his very common name, John Smith.[94]

But John Smith was as extraordinary as his name was ordinary. Son of a yeoman farmer who died when he was sixteen, he set out at once in the classic manner to "seek his fortune." The quest took him very far indeed from the green fields of England, to distant, exotic Transylvania north of Hungary, ruled (in a manner of speaking) by a king named Sigmund Bathory who abdicated and was brought back on three different occasions. Smith was serving with Sigmund's army in 1602, besieging a city held by the Turks. A Turkish soldier in the besieged army issued a general challenge to Christians for single combat. He had many would-be opponents, among them John Smith. A lot was held to choose among them; Smith won the draw. He killed the Turk with a herculean lance thrust and cut off his head. A friend of the Turk renewed the challenge, and John Smith disposed of him in the same way. A third Turk now challenged, and also lost his head. Smith was brought before his proud general and authorized forevermore to wear three Turks' heads on his shield. The Turks called for help to the Crimean Tartars, and they struck and routed the Christian army. John Smith was captured and sold at auction as a slave, then sent as a gift by his owner to a young and beautiful Greek girl in Trebizond. Passed on to her brother, sent to thresh in his fields in the Kuban steppe of southern Russia, John Smith set upon his master, who was beating him, with a threshing bat and split open his head. He dressed in his master's clothes, hid his body under straw, filled his knapsack, mounted the dead man's horse, and galloped off into the steppe, without the slightest idea of where he was.[95]

A few days later he came to a crossroads. One road was marked by a crescent (the symbol of Islam), the other by a cross. John Smith took the road with the cross. For sixteen days he rode alone until he came to a wooden Russian

---

[94] Philip L. Barbour, *The Three Worlds of Captain John Smith* (Boston, 1964), pp. 99-100, 107-110.

[95] *Ibid.*, pp. 3-10, 42-62.

fort. Its governor and his wife befriended him and took him to Moscow, from which he made his way to Spain, took ship to Morocco, joined the crew of a French pirate, survived and escaped a fierce battle with two Spanish warships, and finally returned to England to find Bartholomew Gosnold and the Virginia Company.[96]

This man was obviously a survivor, and tough as nails. In Virginia he was to prove it again and again, surviving an execution decree by Indian chief Powhatan at the beginning of 1608 and the explosion of a bag of gunpowder in his lap in September 1609. He died in his bed, in 1631, full of years and renown. Captain John Smith made the first successful English colonization in North America, at Jamestown in Virginia where he was president of its governing council for the critical years 1608 and 1609, twelve years before the so-called Pilgrims settled in Massachusetts. Threatened with starvation that winter, he decreed that the often feckless settlers should either work or starve. When the Indians refused to trade for food on Powhatan's orders, John Smith went out and found the second chief Opechancanough, seized him by the topknot, and shook him until he agreed to trade again. Forced out of Jamestown by jealous and ungrateful colleagues, he sailed to the north, explored the coasts of Maine and Massachusetts, but saw his colonizing venture there lost when French Calvinist pirates seized his ships. An earlier English colony planted by the Virginia Company at Popham Beach, Maine failed in September 1608 for lack of any leader like him; he was at Jamestown then, governing it. We have heard too much about the Protestant piety of the settlers at Plymouth in 1620, and not enough about the grit and iron will of Captain John Smith which saved Jamestown in 1608 and 1609.[97]

The founding of Canada occurred at almost exactly the same time, by French Catholics led by the great Samuel de Champlain. He first voyaged there in 1603, exploring the St. Lawrence River as far as Montreal, and helped convince Henry IV to sponsor a colony. In June 1604 he established it, at the mouth of the St. Croix River which now forms part of the boundary between Canada and Maine. Another colony, Port Royal, was established in 1605 across the Bay of Fundy in Nova Scotia. In 1607 it was temporarily abandoned, but in 1608 Champlain returned from France on his third voyage and on July 8 founded the magnificently sited city of Quebec.[98]

That winter was exceptionally severe, and Champlain stayed at Quebec throughout it. When spring came, only eight of 24 settlers were left alive, but Champlain was one of them. In 1609 he went to war against the Iroquois tribes of the Mohawk River valley in what is now New York, who were attempting to exterminate the Canadian tribes along the St. Lawrence. In his southward

---

[96] *Ibid.*, pp. 62-86.

[97] *Ibid.*, pp. 165-169, 231, 243-254, 262-268, 272, 276, 278-279, 311-313, 317-321. The episode with Powhatan was the famous occasion where the chief's eleven-year-old daughter Pocahontas persuaded her father to save Smith's life.

[98] Samuel Eliot Morison, *Samuel de Champlain, Father of New France* (Boston, 1972), pp. 27, 32, 34, 38, 71-72, 77-78, 103, 106; Buisseret, *Henry IV*, pp. 138-139.

campaign against the Iroquois he discovered the great lake which bears his name. On May 28, 1611 he founded Montreal, and in 1613 explored the Ottawa River, gateway to the interior of North America. At the end of 1613 the Canada Company was established, with the Prince of Condé, heir to the throne until Louis XIII should have a child, as its head and Champlain his lieutenant, and an eleven-year monopoly on the lucrative Canadian fur trade. When Champlain came back to Canada from France for the seventh time in April 1615, he brought four missionaries to join several who had come even earlier. They said the first Mass in Montreal.[99]

Champlain resumed his inland explorations that year, following the Ottawa River even farther, to Lake Nipissing and then down the Nipissing River to Lake Huron, discovering the vast extent of the Great Lakes. He continued his war against the ferocious Iroquois. He spent the winter of 1616 with the Huron Indians and was given up for lost. Upon his return he found Quebec on the verge of starvation after another hard winter, but soon had the colony flourishing once again. The French Catholic presence was established in Canada once and for all.[100]

Meanwhile Lord de la Warr (for whom Delaware is named), the new governor of Virginia, had sailed for it in April 1610 with a large reinforcement of colonists, 400 of them, more than the existing population of the colony, and the English explorer Henry Hudson, who earlier had helped to prove there was no Northeast Passage to the Orient around the north of Russia, discovered New York harbor and the Hudson River while sailing in the Dutch service. The next year he found employment again by merchants of his native country interested in a Northwest Passage, north of Canada to the Orient. He became the first man to enter the great subarctic expanse of water named for him as Hudson's Bay, to become one of the principal outlets of the North American fur trade. Reaching Hudson's Bay rather late in the season, mid-August, his ships were frozen in for the winter at James Bay at its southern end. The long night of the arctic winter depressed the men's spirits, and only two weeks of food were left when on July 1, 1611 a seaman with a criminal background named Henry Greene led a mutiny, put Hudson (who wanted to do more exploring) into a small boat, abandoned him and sailed for England. Henry Hudson was never seen again.[101]

In 1612 James I gave a more liberal charter to the Virginia Company, and also chartered a merchant company called the Discoverers of the Northwest Passage, to follow up Hudson. A new expedition by the latter, commanded by Thomas Button, Robert Bylot and the unforgettably named Abakuk Prickett, filled out knowledge of Hudson's Bay, Baffin Bay, and their geographic relationship to the arctic lands north of them. Their work was sufficiently thorough as to strongly suggest that there was no northwest passage practicable

---

[99] Morison, *Champlain*, pp. 108-110, 126, 139, 143, 147-149.

[100] *Ibid.*, pp. 150, 152-153, 157-159, 164, 166-167, 174.

[101] Barbour, *Captain John Smith*, pp. 292-294; Donald S. Johnson, *Charting the Sea of Darkness; the Four Voyages of Henry Hudson* (Camden ME, 1993), pp. 114-115, 149-156, 167, 173-179, 197.

for sailing ships, as is indeed the case, though it is sometimes possible to pass through the seaways north of Canada with the aid of engines and icebreakers. Canada was already making a profit on furs, but the only hope of a cash crop in Virginia was tobacco, the first shipment of which went to England in 1614. James I detested tobacoo; but money talked, and in the end he agreed that it should be grown and exported in large quantities. The English colony in Virginia was now firmly established, with a population exceeding a thousand and no prospect any longer that it would ever be abandoned.[102]

The Dutch would soon (1624) establish their own colony at New York, on Governor's Island just off Manhattan, after their navigator Adriaen Block had sailed to Manhattan in 1613, then explored Long Island Sound and discovered Rhode Island and Block Island, named for him. The development of the best colony site on the east coast of North America was, however, little more than a side-show for the merchant princes and far-ranging sea captains of the Netherlands, who exploded from their tiny and embattled country into the whole world as its greatest voyagers just as the seventeenth century turned.

In 1594 Cornelis de Houtman returned from a voyage of exploration and investigation to Southeast Asia and was equipped by a company of Amsterdam merchants with four ships and 248 men for another voyage. The ships were armed by the government, for they were going into territory historically claimed by Portugal, and Portugal was now merged with their inveterate enemy Spain. Jan Huygen van Linschoten obtained Portuguese sailing directions to Indonesia (sail around the Cape of Good Hope in the track of Vasco da Gama, cross the Arabian Sea to India with the monsoon, go on eastward across the Bay of Bengal and through the Straits of Malacca) and translated them into Dutch. Houtman's voyage took 15 months, five months longer than usual, and nearly a third of the crew died of scurvy on the way. One ship was lost, and the Portuguese soon drove them away. Houtman returned with only 89 of his original crew of 248 and only enough spices to pay the cost of the expedition.[103]

But the way had been opened, and the Dutch showed extraordinary vigor and alacrity in following it up. In 1598 two much larger expeditions set out from Holland for the East Indies, one of eight ships on the Portuguese route under Admiral Van Neck, the other of four ships under Admiral van Noort to the Spice Islands via Magellan's route and his Straits. Van Neck reached the East Indies in seven months, eight months less than Houtman had required, and sent back three ships immediately with full cargoes of spices. While Van Noort was fighting his way through the Straits of Magellan, quelling a mutiny and marooning one of his officers, two more Dutch fleets of four ships each set sail from Holland, one bound for Java and the other for Sumatra. The Portuguese had never had much time and resources for Sumatra; the Dutch were able to make a very favorable agreement with the sultan of its most powerful state, Atjeh. In 1600 the

---

[102] Barbour, *Captain John Smith*, p. 300; Johnson, *Charting the Sea of Darkness*, pp. 200-201; Willson, *James VI and I*, pp. 330-331.

[103] E. S. de Klerck, *History of the Netherlands East Indies* (Amsterdam, 1938, 1975), I, 196-198.

remaining ships of the Van Neck expedition returned home with a 40 per cent profit. The next year, 1601, 65 Dutch ships in 14 different fleets sailed to the East Indies. Most of them returned with fabulously rich cargoes of spices, though eleven were lost along with many men. In August Van Noort completed the fourth circumnavigation of the world, after Magellan, Drake and Cavendish.[104]

In January 1602 five of these redoubtable Dutch ships commanded by Arctic explorer Van Heemskerck put no less than 28 Portuguese to flight, ending most of the weakening Portuguese rule in the East Indies. In the spring Dutch merchants formed the Dutch East India Company, with a monopoly on trade and all Dutch activities in Indonesia, empowered to make treaties, raise troops, build fortresses, and govern, and fully supported by the prime minister of Holland, Jan van Oldenbarnevelt. Two large Dutch fleets sailed for the East Indian archipelago that spring. The leader of the second, Van Waerwijck, gained permission to build a stone factory and to leave behind a permanent representative at the principal Dutch trading center of Banten on Java. In 1604 a 13-ship fleet under Admiral Stephen van der Hagen reached Java, then sailed for Amboina in the Moluccas where the Spice Islands were located, forced the Spanish there to surrender, and signed a treaty of friendship with the native chiefs, assuring them a monopoly of cloves, nutmegs and mace, and installing a Dutch governor at Amboina. But the Spanish could still fight. In 1606 they repulsed a Dutch fleet from the main Portuguese base of Malacca after a bloody battle, and a Spanish force of 3,000 from the Philippines retook Ternate and Tidore, the original Spice Islands. But Dutch Admiral Matelieff set up a substantial colony, with schools and marriages of the Dutch with native women, intended to be permanent. Meanwhile a Spanish captain named Luis Torres, after separating from a lost and confused second Spanish expedition to the Solomon Islands, explored New Guinea and proved it to be a large island.[105]

In the Netherlands, with the death of the Duke of Parma the fire had gone out of the Spanish drive to regain the whole terrritory, though the Genoese Ambrogio Spínola provided competent military leadership for Spain which permitted them to hold most of the southern Netherlands. England under James I stopped all military aid to the Dutch, but they no longer needed it. In April 1606 the effects and possible consequences of Dutch penetration into the East Indies impelled the Spanish to open secret peace negotiations with the Dutch by offering to recognize the independence of the northern Netherlands in return for Dutch withdrawal from Asia and America. At the talks in February 1607, Jan van Oldenbarnevelt refused to put any such commitment in writing, but pledged it orally; however, he found it politically impossible to dissolve the Dutch East India Company as he had promised. Nevertheless there was general agreement in the Netherlands and Spain on a truce, and on April 9, 1609 it was formally

---

[104] *Ibid.*, I, 198-202; Frank Sherry, *Pacific Passions; the European Struggle for Power in the Great Ocean in the Age of Exploration* (New York, 1994), pp. 183-187.

[105] De Klerck, *History of the Netherlands East Indies*, I, 203-209; Sherry, *Pacific Passions*, pp. 174-177, 188, 190.

agreed, for the unusually long period of twelve years. Nothing was said about the rights of Catholics in the Calvinist Netherlands, which Philip III and the Duke of Lerma were apparently no longer interested in defending. At least for the duration of the truce, Spain recognized the independence of the United Provinces of the Netherlands (the northern part of the Low Countries), and both sides were to hold what they had overseas, rather than the Dutch totally withdrawing as had been originally proposed. In fact the truce never applied outside the Low Countries themselves.[106]

In September 1609 the appointment of a governor-general for the East Indies was authorized by the States-General of the Netherlands, with an advisory council of five. Dutch Admiral Hoen took a Spanish stronghold at Batjan in Java in November, and in the following year 1610 the first Dutch trading post was established on Borneo. There was another pitched battle between Dutch and Spanish in Manila Bay, which the Spanish won. The Dutch Governor-General Both arrived at Banten in Java in 1611, set up a council, appointed a Visitor-General, and established his permanent headquarters in the Moluccas while setting up a trading post in Timor. In the course of that year Dutch captain Hendrik Brouwer discovered a much faster route to the East Indies. Noting the strong and steady westerly winds which blew in the region of the Cape of Good Hope, he let them blow him across the southern Indian Ocean until reaching the approximate longitude (it was then not possible to measure longitude precisely, but in this case only an approximation was necessary) of Java, and then turning north. This route came nowhere near India and cut in half the overall travel time to the East Indies.[107]

In the fall of 1611 Spain, through its chief minister the Duke of Lerma, secretly offered the Dutch a full peace, recognizing their independence if they would withdraw from the East Indies. But this was no longer practicable, if it had ever been. Ten Dutch ships attacked and raided the Philippines in 1614. In 1616 Dirk Hartog, sailing Brouwer's new faster route across the southern Indian Ocean to Indonesia, discovered western Australia. In that same year the Dutch established a colony at Surinam on the north coast of South America, and two Dutch navigators named Willem Schouten and Isaac LeMaire discovered the sea route around Cape Horn which, though still very dangerous due to storms and high winds, was significantly safer and much easier than passage of the Straits of Magellan. Its stark and dramatic name is a contraction of the name of the Dutch city of Hoorn. The two Dutch sea captains made their way across the Pacific to the Bismarck Islands and New Guinea, finally reaching the Spice Islands from the east in September 1616. On reaching Jakarta, now the capital of the Dutch

---

[106] Wernham, *Return of the Armadas*, pp. 413-414; J. H. Elliott, *The Count-Duke of Olivares; the Statesman in an Age of Decline* (New Haven CT, 1986), pp. 49-52; Jonathan Israel, *The Dutch Republic and the Hispanic World*, 1606-1661 (Oxford, 1982), pp. 4-9, 11-12, 18, 31; Mousnier, *Assassination of Henry IV*, p. 132; De Klerck, *History of the Netherlands East Indies*, I, 213.

[107] De Klerck, *History of the Netherlands East Indies*, I, 212-215, 230; Israel, *Dutch Republic and the Hispanic World*, p. 15; Sherry, *Pacific Passions*, pp. 193-194.

empire in the East Indies, they were arrested by Jan Pieterszoon Coen for not having a license to sail the Straits of Magellan, Coen refusing to believe they had found a new route. He impounded their ships and cargoes and sent them home as prisoners with another circumnavigator, Joris van Spillbergen. Le Maire died on the homeward journey, but his partner survived and his relatives back in the Netherlands brought suit in his behalf which vindicated his claim and regained his property.[108]

Meanwhile the Dutch had extended their activity to West Africa, building a fort just five miles from the ancient Portuguese fortress of El Mina in Ghana, and to Brazil, establishing a series of strongholds on the Amazon River.[109] In just two brief decades they had reached all the continents of the world but Antarctica and settled in all but Australia. The spice riches which had enticed generations of explorers of the east now belonged to them. Even less than their predecessor Portugal were they large and strong enough to sustain a vast overseas empire. But they clung to Indonesia until the Second World War, and put their mark forever on the history of the sea.

Holy Roman Emperor Rudolf II was a most peculiar man. No one has ever been quite sure what was wrong with him. At first his erratic behavior, consuming interest in and dependence on fortune-tellers and astrologers, periodic retreats out of the sight of men, and inconsistencies and contradictions in behavior and policy were ascribed to mere eccentricity rather than developing psychosis. After all, he had been brought up a strict Catholic in Spain, and had never shown any weakening in the Faith. But by 1608 he was suicidal and increasingly out of touch with reality.[110]

Germany during Emperor Rudolf II's reign was enough to drive anyone mad. The coruscatingly violent confrontation between Lutheran and Catholic in the early to mid-16th century had now become three-cornered: an even more surpassingly violent confrontation among Lutherans, Calvinists, and Catholics, with each of the three totally, vehemently, and terminally hostile to both the other two. At a baptism in Dresden a butcher appeared with his baby and an ax, and told the minister that if he did not perform the baptismal service in the manner the butcher desired, he would chop his head off in the church.[111] Alexander Utzinger, Protestant preacher at Schmalkald, declared the papacy to be "the mother of fornication and of all the abominations on earth . . . a frightful abyss of Hell . . . an execrable den of murderers . . . thieves and robbers" and said this had been "so thoroughly proven, demonstrated, and made public that no right-minded veracious person could contradict it."[112] A Lutheran synod in Hesse declared that

---

[108] Israel, *Dutch Republic and the Hispanic World*, pp. 16-17, 26-27; Sherry, *Pacific Passions*, pp. 203-207; Samuel Eliot Morison, *The European Discovery of America: the Southern Voyages* (Boston, 1974), pp. 731-734.

[109] Israel, *Dutch Republic and the Hispanic World*, pp. 25-26.

[110] Jansen, *History of the German People*, IX, 506.

[111] *Ibid.*, IX, 153.

[112] *Ibid.*, X, 254.

Protestants should not eat and drink with Catholics, or even speak with them.[113] The firm and ubiquitous challenge of the Jesuits in particular roused Protestants of both kinds to paroxysms of fury. Lutherans and Calvinists converted back to Catholicism in growing numbers; Catholics converted to Lutheranism and Calvinism, though in much lesser numbers than when the two founders were alive; Lutherans became Calvinists and Calvinists became Lutherans, sometimes within the same family. With the hundreds of duchies and principalities, some moderate-sized and many tiny, into which Germany was divided, each one of these conversions caused a political crisis if the convert was a ruler or a member of the ruler's family. Dr. Johann Pistorius, a distinguished convert from Lutheranism to Catholicism who in 1591 declared Luther to be "beyond measure unclean, blasphemous, dissolute, untruthful, puffed up, full of doubts, and obscene," converted Margrave James III of Baden-Hochberg to his new faith. Within months of his conversion James III was dead, leaving his lands to two small daughters; his brother Ernest Frederick, a strong Lutheran, moved in, seized the little country, and promptly expelled Dr. Pistorius and all the Catholic priests.[114]

All of this led to almost constant civil war in Germany. But because of the political disorganization, the large number of states, and the three religions, from the Religious Peace of Augsburg in 1555 to the beginning of the Thirty Years War in 1618 there was no general religious war there. There was no one around whom either Catholics or Protestants could generally rally—certainly not the bewildered and bewildering Rudolf II. Sooner or later, however, such a conflict had to come; men cannot go on for two and three generations saying the sort of things about each other and doing the sort of things to each other that German Lutherans, Calvinists, and some Catholics (not as many,[115] but some) had been saying and doing, without making general war a certainty. Contrary to what is often said or implied, the horribly devastating Thirty Years War in Germany was utterly inevitable; no war in history has been more so. Once again, there was to be a decision by battle; but in this case even battle could not in the end make the decision, and Germany was left evenly divided, almost exactly as when the war had started, but so utterly ravaged and exhausted that the struggle was finally given up. With a wail and a whimper the great religious conflict in Europe ended in 1648, and Christendom was sundered as far into the future as man can see.

Emperor Rudolf's escalating mental debility marked him as a target, not only for his Protestant enemies but also for his would-be successors. In January

---

[113] *Ibid.*, X, 254-255.

[114] *Ibid.*, X, 116-127, 130-132 (quote on 132). The Lutheran Wilhelm Holder responded to Pistorius' attack on Luther with a pamphlet charmingly entitled "The Disembowelled Mouse" (from the hypothetical question of what should be done if a mouse ate a Host) saying in effect that if Luther was bad, the Catholics were worse (*ibid.*, pp. 137-138).

[115] The great German Jesuit evangelist St. Peter Canisius, the most successful preacher in Germany, never used the violent language characteristic of the time (see James Brodrick, *St. Peter Canisius* [Baltimore MD, 1950], *passim*).

1608 Calvinist rebels in Hungary, Moravia and Austria declared him deposed and his brother Matthias Emperor in his place. Matthias, like all the Habsburgs, was a Catholic, but a weak man who wanted the imperial title and perquisites even if without much actual power. Though sane, he was hardly better equipped than the psychotic Rudolf II to wield the sword of the Faith. After the Protestants broke up the Diet of Regensburg in late April 1608 because they were in the minority there, they formed an alliance to advance their cause, called the Protestant Union. By the Peace of Leoben that June, Rudolf was compelled to give Austria, Hungary and Moravia immediately to Matthias, while retaining Bohemia and Silesia. Matthias was crowned King of Hungary in November but had little real power, most of it being in the hands of the largely Calvinist nobility. Even in Austria the nobility under Matthias was no more than one-quarter Catholic. Meanwhile in Bohemia, once Hussite and now by a large majority Protestant, Rudolf's rule was allowed only after he promised total religious toleration in what was called his "Letter of Majesty."[116]

On June 10, 1609 a Catholic league was formed as a counterweight to the Protestant Union, led by Duke Maximilian of Bavaria, the strongest Catholic ruler in Germany outside the Habsburgs. Matthias was declared Rudolf II's imperial successor despite disapproval by Pope Paul V, who distrusted Matthias' appeasement of Protestants. In January 1612 Rudolf died as mysteriously and as abruptly as he had lived. Matthias was elected his successor and reluctantly confirmed as such by the Pope. In April the Protestant Union made a defensive alliance with England, to be sealed by the marriage of the beautiful and vivacious Princess Elizabeth, improbable daughter of "the wisest fool in Christendom," with the equally young Elector Frederick V of the Palatinate, who combined inexperience and irresolution with charm of manner and nobility of bearing. Knowing their weakness, deriving from the inevitable religious disunion of every Protestant country, the Protestant allies reached out in the fall of 1614 to the aggressively Calvinist northern Netherlands with its redoubtable leader, Maurice of Nassau, and received his alliance. In a foreshadowing of things to come, they also reached out to young King Gustav Adolf of Lutheran Sweden, then campaigning in Russia during its "time of troubles." Gustav put them off for the time being, but was to listen to them again later.[117]

On October 27, 1615 Pope Paul V issued a brief calling for the immediate designation of a successor to the aging and childless Matthias, now 58. The

---

[116] *Ibid.*, IX, 490-492, 502, 510-511, 517-518; X, 406, 418-419; von Pastor, *History of the Popes*, XXVI, 271, 274, 282, 286-287; Mousnier, *Assassination of Henry IV*, p. 134; Geoffrey Parker, *The Thirty Years War* (New York, 1984, 1987), pp. 11, 39.

[117] Jansen, *History of the German People*, X, 469, 509-513, 515, 587; von Pastor, *History of the Popes*, XXVI, 282, 289, 295, 300-302, 314; *The Cambridge Modern History*, Vol. IV (Cambridge, England, 1906, 1934), pp. 11-12; Parker, *Thirty Years War*, p. 33; C. V. Wedgwood, *The Thirty Years War* (New York, 1961), pp. 55-56; Roberts, *Gustavus Adolphus*, I, 81-82. Henry IV of France, a master of the *bon mot*, was responsible for calling James I of England "the wisest fool in Christendom" (Willson, *James VI and I*, pp. 144-145).

Habsburg family had selected Ferdinand of Styria, the only grandson of Ferdinand I with children, as the approved successor.   At the suggestion of Maximilian of Bavaria, Matthias proposed to call a meeting of the imperial electors.   He and his chief advisor, Archbishop Khlesl of Vienna, were not enthusiastic about this; the Protestants were too strong, and vehemently opposed the pious, strongly Catholic Ferdinand, who had been educated by the Jesuits at the University of Ingolstadt in Bavaria.   The Protestants controlled three of the seven electors provided by the ancient Golden Bull of Emperor Charles IV in 1355, which had never been changed.   They were young Frederick V of the Palatinate, the husband of English Princess Elizabeth, a Calvinist; John George of Saxony, a firm Lutheran; and the elderly John Sigismund of Brandenburg who had in 1614 converted from Lutheranism to Calvinism.   The Catholics were sure of the vote of the three bishop-electors, of Cologne, Mainz and Trier.   The casting vote, that of the King of Bohemia, was held by Matthias himself, who was not at all eager to cast it, since Bohemia, remembering John Hus, was primarily Protestant.[118]

King Philip III of Spain had a claim on the imperial succession through his mother, Anna of Austria, but agreed to abandon it in return for lands in Alsace and probably a pledge of support for the Spanish when the Twelve Years Truce ended in the Netherlands and war resumed there, in 1621.   Lacking any other realistic alternative to Ferdinand's succession, and jogged by a sudden severe illness of Emperor Matthias, he and Archbishop (now Cardinal) Khlesl finally had to advance Ferdinand in 1617.   The Bohemian Estates lacked strong leadership, and fell back on tradition by approving a Habsburg heir to the Bohemian throne.   This guaranteed him the majority of the imperial electors when Emperor Matthias died.   Matthias and the Bohemian Estates asked the newly designated heir to approve and reissue Rudolf II's "Letter of Majesty" for full religious toleration in Bohemia.   Two prominent Bohemian Catholics, Jaroslav Martinitz and William Slavata, strong proponents of the Tridentine Catholic Reformation, urged him not to reconfirm the Letter of Majesty, believing that the practice of Protestantism should not be permitted in Bohemia and the Habsburg domains.   Ferdinand rejected their counsel, but had no intention of keeping his promise of toleration.[119]

While nothing justifies a public lie on such a matter, at least it becomes more understandable when it is remembered that in early seventeenth century Germany, toleration was not a prescription for peace, but for war.   The rulers of every state felt themselves entitled and even required to forbid the practice of more than one religion as soon as they had the power to do so.   Every Protestant

---

[118] Jansen, *History of the German People*, X, 617-621; von Pastor, *History of the Popes*, XXVI, 319, 322; Wedgwood, *Thirty Years War*, pp. 58-61; *Cambridge Modern History* IV, 10, 13.   For the Golden Bull, see Volume III, Chapter Ten of this history; for John Hus and the Hussites, see Volume III, Chapter Twelve.

[119] Wedgwood, *Thirty Years War*, pp. 59, 75-77; Parker, *Thirty Years War*, p. 41; Jansen, *History of the German People*, X, 622; von Pastor, *History of the Popes*, XXVI, 320, 323.

state outlawed the Mass; every new state the Protestants could acquire did likewise. If the Catholic states permitted Protestant practice, they were creating centers of armed rebellion against their rulers and their religion.

In August 1617 Lutheran Elector John George of Saxony pledged his support to Ferdinand as the duly elected heir, and Catholic Duke Maximilian of Bavaria did likewise early in 1618 despite the fact that Electors Frederick V of the Palatinate and John Sigismund of Brandenburg were, without his consent, proposing him for Emperor against the designated heir. It is a remarkable fact that the two Calvinist Electors were reduced to backing the very Catholic Maximilian simply because he was not a Habsburg, and equally remarkable that despite their fears of Ferdinand, which were shared by many Protestants, more opposition had not been mounted to his election as King of Bohemia. On May 16 he was proclaimed King of Hungary, Emperor Matthias standing down from that role.[120]

In April 1617 Emperor Matthias ordered both the Catholic and the Protestant leagues to disband. The Catholics did; the Protestants would not. In March the Bohemian Protestants under the leadership of Count Heinrich Matthias Thurn held a massive gathering in Prague, trumpeting their grievances and their unhappiness with Archduke Ferdinand as their king. Cardinal Khlesl called their assembly rebellious and threatening to the rightful king. Nevertheless Protestant leaders in Bohemia drew up an appeal to be read in all the churches of Prague May 20, and called another rally and demonstration of militant Protestants the next day, which was attended by a crowd of thousands.[121]

It quickly became a mob, led by Count Thurn, demanding the overthrow of Habsburg Catholic government of Bohemia and the execution of the two strongly Catholic Bohemian councillors, Martinitz and Slavata, who were currently in Prague. They sent for help, too late. On May 23 Protestant deputies of the Bohemian Estates led the mob to the towering royal castle of Hradschin. They surged into its courtyard, up the staircase, through the audience hall, and into the room where the council sat. There was no exit other than the door by which the mob was entering, and a single window overlooking the castle moat fifty to sixty feet below. Trapped in the council room, Martinitz and Slavata faced death. The mob was determined to inflict death upon them by the ancient, traditional and unique Czech method (still used on Jan Masaryk when the Communists took over Prague 330 years later) of defenestration, throwing them out of a window.[122]

---

[120] Jansen, *History of the German People*, X, 625-626; von Pastor, *History of the Popes*, XXVI, 325; *Cambridge Modern History*, IV, 14, 17.

[121] *Cambridge Modern History*, IV, 12, 14, 19-20; Wedgwood, *Thirty Years War*, pp . 74, 77-78; Parker, *Thirty Years War*, pp. 36-37; Jansen, *History of the German People*, X, 626. Their principal grievance was refusal of permission to build Protestant churches on what had been royal land (where Protestant churches could be built under the Letter of Majesty) after the King had granted the land to the Catholic Church.

[122] Wedgwood, *Thirty Years War*, pp. 78-79; *Cambridge Modern History*, IV, 20; Parkerm *Thirty Years War*, pp. 48-49; von Pastor, *History of the Popes*, XXVI, 354. For defenestration, see the account of the St. Bartholomew's Day massacre in Paris in Chapter

They fought magnificently for their lives, crying appeals to the Blessed Virgin Mary for help. First Martinitz, then Slavata were thrust battling through the window frame. Their would-be murderers leaned out the window as they fell, taunting "we will see if your Mary can help you!" A few second later another voice cried in astonishment: "By God, his Mary has helped!" The two councillors had fallen on a thick pile of manure. Martinitz actually jumped back up from his fall. Slavata was knocked unconscious and had to be carried away, but recovered. There was no pursuit.[123]

The Thirty Years War had begun.

Seven, above, and my *The Rise and Fall of the Communist Revolution* (Front Royal VA, 1995), p. 373.

[123] Wedgwood, *Thirty Years War*, p. 79.

10
A Cardinal Against Christendom
1618-1640
Popes Paul V (1605-1621), Gregory XV (1621-1623), Urban VIII (1623-1644)

"If there is a God, Cardinal Richelieu has a lot to answer for. If there be none, he certainly has had a successful career." —Pope Urban VIII on Cardinal Richelieu[1]

"France's foreign policy no less than her domestic one was guided by Richelieu in a way that was utterly incompatible with the duty of a Catholic bishop, not to speak of that of a Cardinal. In his foreign policy, the Cardinal was activated by purely national ambitions, to which even the interests of the Church had to yield, while his home politics were based on royal absolutism. . . . He was a Frenchman first and foremost and a realist in politics. As such he pursued his political objectives with cold aloofness and utter indifference to religious and ethical principles. His ideal was the *State* to which all must bow, the King included, and for him the State was not the twenty million Frenchmen which it embraced, but the man who, having gathered all power in his own hand, alone guided its fortunes. This new system . . . was not limited by any constitutional rights or any consideration of religion and ethics. Whatever stood in the way of this mysterious and awe-inspiring conception of the State must be crushed; whatever could serve it was lawful and even commanded, were it falsehood, treachery, harshness and cruelty."
—Ludwig von Pastor, *History of the Popes* XXVIII, 379-380

In the wake of the defenestration of Prague, its militant Protestants immediately gained control of the city. But the defenestration was as clear and total an act of rebellion as anyone could imagine, and Archduke Ferdinand, heir to the empire, was king of Bohemia. On March 27, 1619 he offered to the rebels a general pardon and a confirmation of their privileges if they would end their rebellion and surrender to him, but they did not even deign to reply, instead invading the neighboring province of Moravia which they coerced into joining their rebellion. Count Thurn, leader of the demonstration that had ended in the defenestration, took a Protestant army of 11,000 men to besiege Vienna in June.[2] In the words of Golo Mann:

---

[1] Mary Purcell, *The World of Monsieur Vincent* (London, 1963), p.196.
[2] C. V. Wedgwood, *The Thirty Years War* (New York, 1961), p. 91; *The Cambridge Modern History*, Volume IV (Cambridge, England, 1906, 1934), pp. 26-27; Golo Mann, *Wallenstein* (New York, 1976), pp. 123-126.

No more determined Catholic reformer and no more unbending enemy to heresy existed outside Spain than the Archduke of Styria [Ferdinand]. The world knew it, the Bohemians knew it. If there was one man who did not fit into their seething state of affairs, it was Ferdinand.[3]

That summer Bohemia formed a confederation with Moravia, Upper and Lower Austria, Lusatia and Silesia to uphold Protestantism, which had gained many followers in all these provinces. On August 19 the Diet of the Confederation declared the election of Archduke Ferdinand as King of Bohemia to be invalid and proclaimed him deposed. Anguished the Archbishop of Cologne: "If it should be that the Bohemians are about to depose Ferdinand, let everyone be straightway prepared for a twenty, thirty, or forty years' war."[4] A thirty years' war it was to be.

A week later the Diet elected (by a vote of 146-7) as the new King of Bohemia Frederick, the young Calvinist Elector Palatine, purely by reputation and because he was the son-in-law of the King of England; he had never set foot in the country. Just two days later Ferdinand was unanimously elected Holy Roman Emperor, the crotchety and incompetent Emperor Matthias having died in March. New Emperor Ferdinand II was strongly supported by the most powerful Catholic nobleman left in Germany, Duke Maximilian of Bavaria. In late September Elector Frederick accepted the proffered Bohemian throne, declaring it "a divine calling which I must not disobey." On October 31 he entered Prague; on November 4 he was crowned King of Bohemia. He began his reign by despoiling St. Vitus' cathedral in Prague, destroying all of the images within it. Pope Paul V sent a large subsidy to Ferdinand II, who promptly made an alliance with Spain, whose ruling family was also Habsburg.[5]

Late in July 1620 an army of 25,000 departed from Bavaria to march to Bohemia. Duke Maximilian was a steadfast Catholic and a brilliant diplomat, but no warrior. To command his army he chose an extraordinary man, over sixty years old, who earlier in life had considered a Jesuit vocation and was deeply devoted to the Blessed Virgin Mary. He was called the "monk in armor." His name was John Tzerclaes Tilly. A Belgian, he had risen from the ranks under the great Duke of Parma, and also served under France's Catholic champion, the Duke of Guise.[6] In the twilight of his life, for the defense of the Catholic Faith he flung himself and all he had and was into the bloody maelstrom that was

---

[3] Mann, *Wallenstein*, p. 110.

[4] *Ibid.*, p. 130 (for quote); Wedgwood, *Thirty Years War*, p. 95; *Cambridge Modern History*, IV, 28.

[5] Wedgwood, *Thirty Years War*, pp. 95-96, 98-100 (quote on 99), 113; *Cambridge Modern History*, IV, 25, 28-31; Mann, *Wallenstein*, p. 132-134; Ludwig von Pastor, *History of the Popes* (St. Louis, 1937) XXVI, 355-357, 359-362, 366

[6] Wedgwood, *Thirty Years War*, pp. 119, 121, 142; *Cambridge Modern History*, IV, 34, 65; Carl J. Burckhardt, *Richelieu and His Age* (London, 1970), II, 310-311.

Germany and Bohemia in this devastating conflict, and ultimately gave his life for the Catholic cause.

On November 8, at the White Mountain near Prague, Tilly attacked a Bohemian fort on a foggy morning after a Dominican monk had shown the troops an image of the Blessed Virgin Mary mutilated by the Calvinists. With the battle cry of "Holy Mary!" they won the battle decisively in just one hour, taking 45 standards and Prince Christian of Anhalt, commander of the Bohemian army. Elector Frederick and his family and a few counselors fled from Prague, just in time to escape seizure and killing by its people, who surrendered to Emperor Ferdinand II on November 11. Many of them joyfully welcomed the restoration of the Catholic Faith. In the hallowed ancient church of St. Mary Major in Rome, Pope Paul V gave thanks.[7]

Bohemia had been an important part of the ancestral domains of the Austrian-based Habsburg family, and for more than a century it had been the practice of the imperial heir first to be elected King of Bohemia, as Ferdinand II had been. Rebellion in Bohemia, therefore, was not taken lightly or forgiven quickly, especially because of the brutality of the defenestration, and the Battle of the White Mountain was so complete a victory that little will or capacity for resistance was left in the Bohemian rebels. Catholic leaders knew that the Church had to be strengthened and reformed in Bohemia. The helplessness of the former rebels and the need to be sure of preventing their resurgence, along with the obvious needs of the Church there, tempted Catholic leaders into excesses.

Clearly justified were the trials of 47 leaders of the rebellion and the execution of 27 of them (it was amazing that so many as 20 were not sentenced to death) and placing Elector Frederick under the ban of the empire, depriving him of his electorate of the Palatinate, which was reassigned to Duke Maximilian of Bavaria, who was not previously an Elector. In light of the conditions and assumptions of the times, it was also justified for Emperor Ferdinand II to order on March 30, 1631 that all clergy, professors, teachers, and schoolmasters who taught the doctrines of Calvin or of other non-Lutheran heretical sects in Bohemia must leave the realm within three days. The estates of the rebels were confiscated and most of them ended up in the hands of Albrecht von Wallenstein, a shrewd bargainer influential at court, who made these confiscated estates the foundation of his vast personal wealth as Duke of Friedland.[8] Wallenstein was a strange man, born of Protestant parents but converted to Catholicism by the Jesuits. In the penetrating words of Carl Burckhardt:

---

[7] Wedgwood, *Thirty Years War*, pp. 123-128; *Cambridge Modern History*, IV, 65-66; von Pastor, *History of the Popes*, XXVI, 368-371; Mann, *Wallenstein*, pp. 143-144; Burckhardt, *Richelieu*, II, 309-310.

[8] Wedgwood, *Thirty Years War*, pp. 133, 138-139; *Cambridge Modern History*, IV, 71-73; Mann, *Wallenstein*, pp. 154-155, 166-167, 182; von Pastor, *History of the Popes*, XXVII, 276.

[Wallenstein] vacillated between an exaggerated sense of his abilities and self-doubts so overwhelming that they deprived him of the power of action. Torn between these abnormally powerful impulses, he not only constantly betrayed both himself and the principles and institutions he had elected to serve, but also cancelled out his considerable perspicacity in practical affairs. His trust was blind, his mistrust malicious, and he superstitiously projected onto the stars the consequences of his actions.[9]

Wallenstein was an inveterate astrologer, a superstition condemned by the Church, but widely practiced in his day. It was a serious political mistake of Emperor Ferdinand II to create by these confiscations so wealthy, powerful, and untrustworthy a duke, but there was nothing morally wrong with it; the convicted leaders had, by the universal standards of the time, forfeited their right to land in Bohemia by rebellion against their liege lord.

Unfortunately the Emperor and the Church did not stop with these justified punitive measures. In October 1622 Emperor Ferdinand II ordered all Lutheran churches closed in Prague and all Lutheran preachers expelled from Bohemia, regardless of whether or not they had been involved in the rebellion. Most of them had not been involved; all its prime moving spirits had been Calvinist, like Elector Frederick himself. Protestants remaining in Bohemia were denied all legal rights in May 1624. In October all of them, laymen and clergy alike, were ordered to profess the Catholic faith by Easter 1626 or leave the country. Catholic soldiers were quartered in Protestant homes. A real persecution was launched. On April 29, 1626, on the proposal of papal nuncio Carlo Carafa, Emperor Ferdinand II accepted Cardinal Harrach as the new Archbishop of Prague and instructed his governor of Bohemia, Prince Liechtenstein, "to consult together [with Cardinal Harrach] with a view to discovering a milder way of bringing the Empire back to the faith." In 1627 Cardinal Harrach launched a major reform of the Church in Bohemia, including a substantial effort to convert the Protestants. Count Jaroslav Borzita of Martinitz, one of the victims of the defenestration of Prague, said that since God had miraculously spared his life then, he considered it no longer his own but God's, and wished to spend it spreading the Catholic faith in his homeland. That same year more than 30,000 Protestants were forced to leave the country.[10] But gradually the persecution came to an end and the majority of Bohemians embraced the old faith, though a significant Protestant minority remained. The Catholic majority has kept the faith ever since, even under Communist rule from 1948 to 1989.

Meanwhile Pope Paul V had died at the end of January 1621, at the age of seventy. The conclave began February 8 with 52 cardinals present, all Italians except for two Spaniards. The very next day Cardinal Alexander Ludovisi was elected Pope. Of a similar age, he took the name Gregory XV. He was Jesuit-educated, experienced in the work of the Church, well liked and trusted, of a

---

[9] Burckhardt, *Richelieu*, II, 311.

[10] Von Pastor, *History of the Popes*, XXVII, 280; XXVIII, 117, 125 (quote), 130-131, 151.

placid temperament, and in poor health; he lived only two years.[11] But those two years, 1621 to 1623, included an unusually large number of epochal events.

On March 31, 1621 Philip III of Spain, son of the great Philip II, died at the early age of 43, lamenting the failures and inadequacies of his 23-year reign, succeeding such a father. His heir was Philip IV, only sixteen, legally old enough to rule on his own but not actually able to do so for several years, and then always willing to give way to his prime minister. Baltasar de Zúñiga was his first prime minister, but he died the next year, to be succeeded by the man who really ruled Spain until 1643, the hard-charging Count-Duke of Olivares.[12] The papal nuncio to Spain described him as follows: "The Count of Olivares, although jealous of his office and violent in his conduct, acts with upright intentions, and is endowed with a mind superior to what might be expected of his age and experience."[13] For all the mud thrown at him by his enemies then and (among historians) now, Olivares was no mere royal "favorite," but a great man. In the end he failed, but not until after making a tremendous fight, which he might have won. The Church, engulfed in the war in Germany that developed out of the Bohemian rebellion, owes him much for what he tried to do, to fulfill the role that Philip II had given to Spain—the role of protector of Christendom.[14]

A great question that had to be decided immediately the year Philip III died, which his young son was incapable of deciding on his own, was whether to renew the twelve years' truce with the Netherlands, which expired that year. The relationship of Spain and the Netherlands had changed fundamentally during the twelve years of the truce. Up to the turn of the century the long war which had begun when the Calvinist Dutch ravaged the churches of Antwerp and other Belgian cities in 1566 had all been fought in the Netherlands itself. It had shown clearly that the Spanish could not prevail in the more Protestant parts of the country, notably the provinces of Holland and Zeeland.[15] But now the Dutch were counterattacking. The people of Calvinist Holland and Zeeland in particular had become great shipbuilders, explorers, and colonial developers. They were displacing Portugal (now united with Spain) from its dominions in Southeast Asia, notably in the great archipelago of Indonesia, and were beginning to penetrate the New World as well. The Spaniards depended on their overseas empire for survival, because of the gold and silver it produced, and the majority of Spanish councillors felt it essential to resume the war in order to force the

---

[11] *Ibid.*, XXVI, 373; XXVII, 29-41, 33-50, 86.

[12] *Ibid.*, XXVII, 95-96; *Cambridge Modern History*, IV, 634-635; J. H. Elliott, *The Count-Duke of Olivares* (New Haven CT, 1986), pp. 81, 102, 131, 156, 166, 169.

[13] Elliott, *Olivares*, p. 290.

[14] We have only one full scholarly biography of Olivares in English, J. H. Elliott's monumental 700-page work. Elliott prefers economic to political history, but in this book proves he can do political history very well. He lacks, however, a sense of the impact of personality on history, and certainly has no Catholic sensibilities. But his accumulation of research in rarely used sources about Olivares, a key figure in the Thirty Years War, almost makes up for this.

[15] See Chapters 6, 7, and 8, above.

Dutch to give up their overseas holdings, which Spain considered exclusively her own. Archduke Albert and Philip II's daughter Isabel jointly ruled the Low Countries, and held the loyalty of most Catholic citizens, especially in the south (the future Belgium). Spain had an able general, the Italian Ambrose Spinola, to lead the fight, and the Spanish councillors believed he could win enough victories at least to force the Dutch to curtail their overseas efforts.[16]

Thus when the truce expired April 9, 1621, no real effort was made to renew it. The Cortes of Castile made a large appropriation to the government, mostly for renewal of the war in the Netherlands, and resolved to meet Archduke Albert's requirement for 300,000 ducats per month, a very large sum. The Dutch chartered a West India Company to match their highly lucrative and aggressive East India Company, thus signalizing their intention to move also on Spain's American dominions.[17]

But then Archduke Albert died suddenly in July 1621, and though his widow Isabel Clara Eugenia, Philip II's daughter, bravely carried on, some loss of Spanish authority in the region could not be avoided. In September a Spanish attack on Zeeland from Flanders was decisively repulsed in a night battle, and the Dutch advanced into Flanders instead, ravaging three Catholic churches. General Spinola was forced to abandon the siege of a key Dutch fortified town, Bergen-op-Zoom. On June 30, 1624 the Dutch immensely strengthened their hand by signing a treaty with France, in which the young French King Louis XIII promised to pay a million livres a year to support the Dutch war against Spain, in return for a Dutch pledge to keep on fighting and make no peace or truce without his consent. At about the same time the English, though generally pacific under their rapidly aging King James I, pledged to maintain 6,000 English volunteers in Dutch service.[18]

The Franco-Dutch alliance of 1624 first put the spotlight on the central figure of the age, Armand-Jean du Plessis, Cardinal Richelieu. The wiliest negotiator in Europe, Richelieu became the real ruler of France as the Count-Duke of Olivares was the real ruler of Spain, but unlike Olivares he had no principles—no more than Thomas Cromwell had had in England. He had not the slightest compunction as a prince of the Church in aiding Calvinist regimes, which he did repeatedly, the treaty with the rebel Netherlands being only a beginning. The young king of France, Louis XIII, who had succeeded to the throne as a child when his father was assassinated in 1610, was totally dominated by Richelieu. In the fall of 1619, when the struggle for power at the French court was still working itself out and Richelieu was seething with ambition to become cardinal, St. Francis de Sales touched him on the shoulder and said: "Return to

---

[16] Jonathan I. Israel, *The Dutch Republic and the Hispanic World, 1606-1661* (New York, 1982), pp. 69-70, 73-74; Elliott, *Olivares*, pp. 61-62.

[17] Israel, *Dutch and the Hispanic World*, pp. 80, 84-85, 92; Cornelis Goslinga, *The Dutch in the Caribbean and on the Wild Coast, 1580-1680* (Gainesville FL, 1971), p. 141; Elliott, *Olivares*, pp. 68-69; Wedgwood, *Thirty Years War*, p. 136.

[18] Israel, *Dutch and the Hispanic World*, pp. 18, 100; Elliott, *Olivares*, pp. 68, 221; *Cambridge Modern History*, IV, 71, 87; von Pastor, *History of the Popes*, XXVIII, 68.

your bishopric; turn your back on all this." For a time Richelieu heeded the saint's advice, but not for long. By 1622 he was back at court, wheedling and intriguing. In September of that year he obtained the coveted cardinal's hat, at the comparatively young age of 37. In August 1624 he became officially the prime minister of France.[19] His goal was always to make France the greatest power in the world, supplanting Spain—a goal he had achieved before his death. And it was Cardinal Richelieu who fastened the absolutism upon France that led ultimately to the French Revolution.[20]

During his brief two-year pontificate, Pope Gregory XV became a major figure in both European and Church affairs. At the very beginning of his pontificate he founded the Gregorianum College in Rome, which still exists, issuing doctorates in theology. He supported the Jesuits in France and tried to overcome the hostility of the University of Paris toward them. He strongly supported the Emperor's action against the Calvinist Elector Frederick of the Palatinate depriving him of his electoral vote in favor of Duke Maximilian of Bavaria, and urged Philip IV of Spain to help the Emperor. He gave substantial subsidies to the Catholic League of German states. In January 1622 he established for the first time an organization to coordinate missionary work, called De Propaganda[21] Fide, consisting of 13 cardinals, two bishops and a secretary. De Propaganda Fide prepared missionaries both for non-Western lands[22] and for Protestant countries. It also sent missionaries into lands separated from the Catholic church by centuries of misunderstanding, such as Armenia. On January 1, 1622 the papal Chancery announced that the ancient practice of dating the beginning of each year on March 25 would be ended, and the year's official beginning placed on January 1. On March 12, 1622 he canonized together four of the greatest saints in the Church's history—Ignatius of Loyola, Francis Xavier, Philip Neri, and Teresa of Avila—along with Isidore the Farmer of Spain. On March 20, 1623 he issued the encyclical *Omnipotentis Dei* against magic and witchcraft, but cautioning against excessive punishments for those popularly suspected of practicing them. He wrote to King James I of England urging his conversion; James pretended an interest in it which he did not feel, since his son Charles was then trying to establish a Spanish alliance by courting Princess Maria of Spain, a peculiar affair which neither the Spanish nor the English people wanted any part of. Pope Gregory died quite suddenly, on July 8, 1623—the familiar summer dying time in Rome.[23]

---

[19] Burckhardt, *Richelieu*, I, 101 (quote), 116-117, 123-124; II, 344; von Pastor, *History of the Popes* XXVIII, 27.

[20] See Note 31, below, and Volume Five of this history.

[21] The word "propaganda" in 1622 still had its original meaning of "to spread" or "to publicize"; the very negative connotations now carried by that word due to the ideological and irresponsible modern media had not yet developed.

[22] See Chapters 12 and 13, below, for their work.

[23] Von Pastor, *History of the Popes* XXVII, 105-106, 119-121, 132, 139, 144, 187-188, 191, 220-223, 229-238, 253, 289.

The conclave began on July 19 with 54 cardinals present, but none from France. On the first ballot the votes were much divided, with no candidate receiving more than 13. Various candidates rose and fell. One, named Millini, was vigorously opposed by Cardinal Ludovisi, who was a nephew of the late Pope. Ludovisi became a candidate, as did Cardinal Borghese, a relative of the former Pope Paul V. Then one of the youngest of the cardinals, Maffeo Barberini, aged 55, was proposed as a compromise candidate. Borghese was forced to leave the conclave by an attack of malaria in the heat of summer, and Cardinal Richelieu, though he was not present, let it be known that he supported Cardinal Barberini. On August 6 Barberini was elected with 50 votes, and took the name of Urban VIII. Because of his relative youth he had a long pontificate, no less than 21 years, very unusual in those times. Generally regarded as pro-French and anti-Habsburg, in contrast to his predecessor, he was actually quite fair-minded about the struggle in Germany and deeply concerned to bring peace to it, which his best efforts failed to achieve in all his long pontificate. He was well aware of the corruption of the church in France, writing scathingly to his nuncio there a year after his consecration as Pope that he deplored the small number of vocations in France, the neglect by many bishops of their duty of residence, the bestowing of rich benefices on laymen, laywomen and heretics, the irregular life of country parish priests, the decadence of many monasteries and their resistance to reform, and the Gallican tendencies of the University of Paris and the *Parlements*. And he did more than write criticisms; he acted. One of the holiest men in France, Pierre de Bérulle, who had founded a French Oratory on the plan of recently canonized St. Philip Neri's Oratory in Rome, was given all the privileges of the Rome Oratory in January 1625, and in August of that year he was made Cardinal.[24]

Meanwhile in Germany, the war launched by the defenestration of Prague wore on. German Protestants had rallied to the cause of Elector Frederick, not so much because of his brief tenure as king of Bohemia, but because of his displacement from his hereditary dominions in the Palatinate by the very Catholic, Jesuit-educated Emperor Ferdinand II and the assignment of those lands to the already very powerful Catholic Duke Maximilian of Bavaria. Frederick himself, a young man without the charisma of leadership (the most effective advocate of his cause was his beautiful and intelligent wife Elizabeth, improbable daughter of James I of England), had neither the ability nor the trust to take charge of this Protestant war against the Emperor. And the Bavarian forces, which were occupying the Palatinate, were commanded by Tilly, "the fighting monk," the best general in Europe in the early 1620's, with the possible exception of the Italian-Spanish Spinola in the Netherlands. In the spring of 1622 Tilly brilliantly outmaneuvered the Protestant general Count Mansfeld and

---

[24] *Ibid.*, XXVIII, 2-24, 35, 442; Burckhardt, *Richelieu*, II, 373-377. Once again it needs to be stressed that the *Parlements* were NOT comparable to the English Parliament, despite the similarity of the name. The *Parlements* were a uniquely French institution, composed of nobles who inherited a seat in them. They acted as a court and had to register (that is, approve of) royal decrees and treaties before they could become law.

joined with a Spanish army to strike successfully at the other leading Protestant general, Christian of Brunswick, at the Battle of Höchst. On September 17, after a tremendous artillery barrage, Tilly stormed Heidelberg, the heavily fortified capital of the Palatinate. The next summer Tilly won the Battle of Stadtlohn, defeating Christian of Brunswick near the Dutch border, killing 6,000 of his soldiers and capturing 4,000 including 50 officers, virtually destroying his army. Count Mansfeld had gone to England to recruit an army there on the strength of the people's love for Princess Elizabeth, and raised 12,000 men, but many soon fell ill and he was never able to make effective use of them.[25]

In the wake of these great Catholic victories, Cardinal Richelieu offered his second large subsidy to the enemy, promising King Christian IV of Denmark 600,000 livres a year and a French attack on the Rhineland to check the Catholic army in Germany and reconquer the Palatinate for Frederick. In the winter months of 1625 Christian of Brunswick, his military strength already reduced to a shadow, was badly injured by a fall from his horse which kept him out of action for months, and the remnants of Mansfeld's once imposing army from England straggled back to their homeland. Leaderless and severely mauled, the Protestant leaders agreed to serve under Danish command if Christian IV would help them. But when he mustered his army in Lower Saxony, it was not nearly as large as had been expected, fewer than 20,000 men. In July 1625 Emperor Ferdinand II sent Tilly to march on Lower Saxony "in the name of God and His holy mother." In August Mansfeld joined Christian IV with 4,000 more troops. Both armies had insufficient supplies to keep alive, and began ravaging the countryside for food, a practice that became universal and almost continuous through the remaining years of this ghastly war. It was augmented by the arrival of Wallenstein's mercenary army, recruited primarily by his personal wealth, the majority non-German, who were kept entirely separate from Tilly's army and were even more rapacious. Tilly now had the chance to assess Wallenstein, who fought for the same cause he did, but not from the same motives. In penetrating words, Tilly said: "For as long as I have to deal with the Duke of Friedland [Wallenstein] and keep a watchful eye on him, for so long too does he every hour cause me unrest, one excitement and turmoil after another."[26]

In January 1626 Lutheran Elector John George of Saxony, the strongest Protestant ruler in Germany, "roughly rejected an invitation to join" the Protestant alliance being put together by Christian IV of Denmark. Elector John George did not want to plunge his peaceful land and people into this devastating war. Christian IV made his son Frederick the Bishop of Osnabrück in northern Germany, for which Pope Urban VIII sharply condemned him, urging Emperor Ferdinand II and Duke Maximilian of Bavaria to extend their military operations to the north to regain Osnabrück. Indeed, the war was moving in that direction, as the Protestants in central and southern Germany had been thoroughly beaten.

---

[25] Wedgwood, *Thirty Years War*, p. 147-153, 178-183; *Cambridge Modern History* IV, 80-81, 86.

[26] Burckhardt, *Richelieu*, II, 344; *Cambridge Modern History* IV, 91-94 (first quote on 92); Mann, *Wallenstein*, pp. 269-270, 276, 305-306, 319 (second quote).

Christian of Brunswick died that June, worn out at 28 after having been defeated once again. Mansfeld returned to the fray with a large army and invaded Silesia, but Wallenstein went in immediate pursuit of him, demonstrating some genuine military ability and driving his opponent precipitately back. The possibility of reuniting Germany under Catholic leadership was now very real. It would represent a restoration beyond any that had been contemplated when Ferdinand II became Emperor. The prospects of a Catholic reunion grew suddenly much brighter when Tilly decisively defeated the highly touted Danish army, augmented by thousands of German Protestants, in August 1626 in the Harz Mountains at the Battle of Lutter. Christian IV lost more than half his army killed, wounded, or captured, and all of his artillery. In one blow he was knocked out of the war, never to re-enter it, and the Protestant coalition disintegrated. Before the year ended, Count Mansfeld died at 46 under mysterious circumstances in Bosnia, with only a few mercenary soldiers and Turks with him. He died a Catholic, being reconciled with the ancient faith on his deathbed.[27]

By 1627 the Count-Duke Olivares had heard enough about Wallenstein to arouse his curiosity and some concern. In May 1627 he wrote to his much trusted envoy in Vienna, the Marquis of Aytona, to ask what manner of man this Wallenstein was. Aytona replied cautiously that he appeared loyal and a friend to the Spaniards, but was not a man to take military risks. But the Catholic and imperial forces now had so much the upper hand in Germany that Wallenstein thrust himself into the northern provinces. In May 1627, the same month as Olivares' inquiry, he forced the Protestant Elector of Brandenburg into unconditional surrender to the Emperor. Meanwhile Tilly completed the conquest of the largely Protestant north German state of Brunswick. In August Wallenstein and Tilly marched together down the Elbe, an overwhelming force which took over the peninsula of Jutland, the greater part of the now helpless kingdom of Denmark, which refused humiliating peace terms from Tilly but could now look for nothing better than mere survival. The main body of Christian IV's reduced army was captured in northeastern Holstein on the Danish border, where Wallenstein now commanded. He was beginning to think of a Baltic empire for himself.[28]

On September 20, 1627 the four Catholic electors in Germany publicly declared that since the German Protestants had rejected every attempt to persuade or pressure them to restore Church lands and property which their governments

---

[27] Wedgwood, *Thirty Years War*, pp. 202, 204-206, 208-209; *Cambridge Modern History* IV, 76, 96-98; von Pastor, *History of the Popes* XXVIII, 101-102, 152, 170; Mann, *Wallenstein*, pp. 287, 290-292, 294; Burckhardt, *Richelieu*, II, 323; Michael Roberts, *Gustavus Adolphus; a History of Sweden, 1611-1632* (London, 1958), II, 305, 328. Denmark was never a real threat in Germany again. When the Peace of Lübeck was publicly proclaimed in June 1629, it provided that Denmark should get out and stay our of Germany (Wedgwood, *op. cit.*, pp. 243-244, 246; *Cambridge Modern History*, IV, 109).

[28] Wedgwood, *Thirty Years War*, pp. 212-213, 216-217; *Cambridge Modern History* IV, 101-102; Mann, *Wallenstein*, pp. 348, 352-354, 358-359; Roberts, *Gustavus Adolphus*, II, 339, 345; Elliott, *Olivares*, p. 333.

had seized, the time had come for a general restitution of such lands by imperial authority. The military position was sufficiently favorable to make this possible. Duke Maximilian of Bavaria, now one of the electors, directed his delegate to the Diet of Electors to take counsel with the other electors about the recovery of all dioceses in Germany for the Catholic Church and the restitution of their property. On October 18 this Diet, summoned by the Archbishop of Mainz, met at Mühlhausen and voted that all Catholic property taken by Protestants since the Religious Peace of Augsburg in 1555, no less than 72 years before, be returned to the Catholic Church.[29] (Up to 1555, though there had been much confiscation of Church property by Lutherans, there had been none by Calvinists, who were not then in power anywhere in Germany; however, the Lutherans had increased their loot from the Church in these 72 years.) Rarely has there been a more sweeping attempt to reverse the results of so long a period of history—or one that, when first advocated, seemed to have a better chance of success. On November 29 Carlo Carafa, papal nuncio to Vienna, triumphantly reported to Pope Urban VIII "that, by the grace of God, he had at last obtained that the bishoprics of Lower Saxony and other territories occupied by the imperial forces should be restored to the Catholics without further discussion and as quickly as possible." All that was now required was an imperial proclamation requiring the return of Catholic Church property taken since 1555, and that was issued March 6, 1629. Over 500 churches and monasteries were involved. It was called the Edict of Restitution. Holy Roman Emperor Ferdinand II swore to stand by it. Significantly, the two great Catholic generals split on it. Tilly supported it, while Wallenstein was opposed.[30]

As German Catholics began to move to regain their Church's property and the unity of their fatherland, civil war broke out again in France between the Calvinists and the Catholics. Most of France was now united internally under Catholic leadership; however much Cardinal Richelieu helped Protestants in other countries, he never helped them in the slightest in France itself. The great standing exception to Catholic unity in France was the port city of La Rochelle on the Bay of Biscay, which had for years been a virtually independent Calvinist stronghold. In January 1625 the French Calvinists, led by La Rochelle, revolted once again in many parts of France. In September of that year French government forces seized the islands of Ré and Oleron just outside La Rochelle, and in November King Louis XIII told Protestant deputies that he intended to bring to an end the special status of La Rochelle as a Calvinist island where the laws of Catholic France did not rule. In February 1626 there was a peace mediated by the English ambassador, but it proved very short-lived; the profound hostility of La Rochelle's Calvinists to the Catholic government of France continued. In May 1626 Cardinal Richelieu made peace with Spain, which supported him in his attack on La Rochelle as it fought the Protestant recipients of his subsidies in Germany. In 1627 the French royal army began occupying

---

[29] Von Pastor, *History of the Popes* XXVIII, 172-174.

[30] *Ibid.*, XXVIII, 175-176 (quote), 249-251; *Cambridge Modern History* IV, 111-112; Mann, *Wallenstein*, pp. 462-467, 692; Burckhardt, *Richelieu* I, 243 and II, 353.

strong points around the La Rochelle and laid it under siege August 10. La Rochelle now formally allied itself with England. An English force came to attempt its rescue, but failed totally under the incompetent command of the Duke of Buckingham, for many years the favorite both of King James I in his dotage and young Charles I when he became king in 1625. The English had to flee to their ships and sail back to England in early November 1627. In January 1628 ships were sunk to block its harbor and a French fleet of 250 warships, which Richelieu had created, came up to blockade the city under the command of the current Duke of Guise. An English fleet sent to help sailed home after one futile demonstration against the formidable royal guardships and fortifications, and the Duke of Buckingham was assassinated as he prepared to sail to La Rochelle for the second time. On October 29, 1628 La Rochelle, worn down by starvation, surrendered. The independent dominion of the Calvinists in France was eliminated. But the result was merely to fasten Cardinal Richelieu's absolutism more tightly on the people, and give him more money to subsidize enemies of the Catholics in Germany. His long-range goal, as he explained to France's King Louis XIII before witnesses in January 1629, was to establish the supremacy of the royal government in France while doing anything possible to wear down and eventually surpass Catholic Spain as the world's leading power.[31]

At this point Spain was engaged in no less than four separate but simultaneous wars: helping the Catholics in the Thirty Years War in Germany, helping Richelieu at La Rochelle, continuing the doomed effort to reconquer the northern Netherlands, and an idiotic struggle over the succession to the dukedom of Mantua in Italy that should have concerned only the people of Mantua, not the great powers.[32] For well over a hundred years, Spain's best had been going to the Americas, to explore and rule over much of South America and about half of North America. Spain had consumed the blood of her people and the treasure of her crown in the largest military expedition in history up to that time—the Spanish Armada of 1588[33]—and in over forty years of ferocious warfare in the Netherlands, where the battle still continued with no significant improvement in the Spanish position. The productivity of her people was increasingly impaired by the exodus to America and the heavy burden of taxation. Every year Olivares bargained for months with the bankers of Genoa to obtain a loan large enough to

---

[31] Burckhardt, *Richelieu*, I, 149, 152-157, 160-161, 163-164, 166-167, 180, 182-183, 196-197, 205, 211-213, 257-259, II,15-26; *Cambridge Modern History* IV, 59, 130, 133, 264, 272.

[32] On the War of the Mantuan Succession, see Elliott, *Olivares*, pp., 330, 340, 343-346, 368, 400-401; Wedgwood, *Thirty Years War*, pp. 227-228, 256-257; Burckhardt, *Richelieu* I, 253, 267, II, 366; Mann, *Wallenstein*, pp. 480-481; von Pastor, *History of the Popes* XXVIII, 208, 220, 224-225, 232, 239, 242, 265. Olivares favored this needless war because he thought incorrectly he could easily win it; later he tried to evade responsibility for it. An older and wiser Philip IV declared many years later "although I have always followed the opinion of my ministers in matters of such importance, if I have erred in anything and given Our Lord cause for displeasure, it was in this." (Elliott, *op. cit.*, pp. 344, 360 (for quote).

[33] See Chapter 8, above.

continue his wars.[34] The principal—virtually the only—security he could offer these Genoese bankers was the annual delivery of a large quantity of silver from the American mines. It usually arrived in two unequal fleets, though sometimes only one sailed. Naturally the ships carrying silver had to be heavily convoyed, which meant that they could only make the run once a year. The whole financial structure of Spain, and its capability to act as the world's leading power, depended upon the regular receipt of this silver; so, to a large extent, did all the Catholics in Europe—notably in Germany and in the southern Netherlands—who depended on Spanish aid to fight their enemies. As Spain's four wars raged simultaneously, the stakes grew steadily higher on the safe passage of the silver fleets across the Atlantic.

By now the Dutch, who had begun to establish themselves as a great naval power around the turn of the seventeenth century[35] and were again at war with Spain, were regularly sending plundering expeditions to both Asia and America against the Spanish and Portuguese domains there. In 1624 they established themselves on the great eastward bulge of Brazil, a colony of Portugal (joined to Spain since 1580). The 800-mile Brazilian coastline was too long to be defended, and the Dutch took Brazil's principal city, San Salvador (usually called Bahia) with ease. The Spanish recovered Bahia the next year by sending 50 ships, 1200 cannon and 12,000 men, which they could ill spare from their other conflicts; but the Dutch remained in possession of the Recife-Pernambuco area on the tip of the bulge of Brazil. Meanwhile the Dutch had sent orders to a young vice-admiral of common, not noble blood, with an almost comically foreshortened name, Piet Hein, to raid Portuguese Angola in southern Africa. In 1626 Hein was sent to the Caribbean. In July he reached the West Indian island of Barbados, where he watched in angry frustration as the 40-ship Spanish treasure fleet passed by him on its way to Spain, Hein not having enough ships to engage the escort. In April 1628 Hein was commissioned full admiral and captain-general in the service of the recently formed Dutch West India Company and given a fleet of 31 large ships, with which he sailed from Holland in May and reached the Caribbean in July. By the end of July his fleet was off the coast of Cuba, lying in wait for the 1628 Spanish silver fleet. In early August the treasure fleet arrived in Havana.[36]

By this time there were three Dutch fleets in the Caribbean, Hein's (the largest) and two smaller fleets commanded by Admirals Ita and Bankaert. This greatly confused the Spanish. When they received accurate reports that Ita's fleet was leaving the region early in August, after taking two treasure ships which had been separated from the others in the Gulf of Mexico by storms, they assumed Hein's fleet had left, but it was still there. On September 7 Hein was joined by Bankaert's fleet of seven ships, giving him a total force of nearly 40 warships, fully equal and probably superior to the Spanish escort for the main treasure fleet assembled at Havana. Spanish intelligence could not have been worse; Juan de

---

[34] Elliott, *Olivares*, pp. 253-254, 301, 303, 364.

[35] See Chapter 9, above.

[36] Goslinga, *Dutch in the Caribbean*, pp. 150-156, 167, 176, 180-182, 185.

Benavides, commander of the escort, had no information that any substantial force of Dutch ships was in the area. During the night of September 7-8 the paths of the Spanish and Dutch fleets crossed, and for several hours Benavides actually followed the lights of the Dutch ships without knowing their nationality. When the dawn brought unpleasant enlightenment, Benavides decided to flee to the Bay of Matanzas instead of fighting. Hein, with his opportune reinforcement, promptly blockaded the Spanish ships in the bay. Benavides, with his warships and the treasure ships on which Spain's economy and government depended for the coming year, was trapped.[37]

The debacle that followed reflected the decline in the standards and fighting spirit of the Spanish navy, once the greatest in the world. Though no seaman, the Duke of Medina Sidonia would have been appalled, as would Spain's two greatest sea warriors of the late sixteenth century, the Marquis of Santa Cruz and Juan Martínez de Recalde. The Spanish ships were so encumbered with passengers' baggage that many of their guns could not be fired. Benavides ordered the treasure unloaded. Before unloading could really begin, the men panicked and ran many of the ships ashore. Darkness fell, but it was a clear night with a bright moon. Dutch ships surged into the bay, and some of the Spaniards began to burn their ships, though fire would still leave the silver intact. Hein arrived in person in the bay and ordered his ships to open fire. Demoralized by this cannonade on top of their other woes, the Spanish surrendered without a fight. Hein had captured an entire treasure fleet, the largest monetary haul in the history of sea warfare, 22 ships including four huge treasure galleons, carrying at least a million ducats' worth of silver. The bottom dropped out of the Spanish government's precarious financial balance. The later execution of Benavides for cowardice in the face of the enemy did not bring the silver back. "Deprived of their Mexican revenues at the same time that they had allied themselves with the Catholic League [in Germany], [they] would not be able to consummate their warlike plans against France nor stamp out the heresy of the German countries."[38] To make up for the loss, they had to levy a forced loan of a million ducats on the already overburdened citizens of Castile. Copies of a manifesto accusing the Count-Duke of Olivares of "insatiable ambition to govern" and "mistaken policies" were widely circulated in Spain. Piet Hein went home a national hero. The treasure he had taken equalled two-thirds of the annual military budget for the Netherlands, and the Dutch West India Company paid an enormous dividend to its shareholders. Hein was killed in a naval battle in the English Channel the next June, but his name is still remembered in Holland. *"Piet Hein, zijn naam is klein/Zijn daden benne groot/Hij heeft gewonen de zilvervloot"* ("Piet Hein, his name is small/his deeds are great/he has taken the silver fleet").[39]

---

[37] *Ibid.*, pp. 175, 182-184, 186.

[38] *Ibid.*, p, 197.

[39] *Ibid.*, pp. 173 (second quote), 186, 188-190, 193-195, 197-198; Israel, *Dutch and the Hispanic World*, pp. 174, 194, 197-198; Elliott, *Olivares*, pp. 358, 363-365, 367-368, 374-375 (first quotes).

The hard-pressed Count-Duke of Olivares saw Spain facing "total ruin" as he negotiated another loan from the Genoese banks on very unfavorable terms. There was an acute shortage of credit throughout Spain as a result of Hein's capture of the silver fleet. Immediate financial disaster was avoided by the opportune early arrival of the 1629 treasure fleet from Peru during Holy Week, carrying enough money to save Spain from national bankruptcy. But the enormous financial loss of 1628 was never really made up, nor was Spain's credit standing regained. And in the Netherlands a vigorous new young king, Frederick Henry, had succeeded to the leadership of the rebel provinces, and promptly went on the offensive when he heard Hein's news. The Dutch army was expanded to 77,000 men, and 28,000 of them led by Frederick Henry in person attacked the Spanish-held Flemish frontier fortress of Hertogenbosch at the beginning of May 1629. In just three weeks he surrounded it with a double wall of circumvallation. A relieving army was checked; two key forts were stormed by Frederick Henry late in July, and on September 14 the city surrendered. It was a Catholic town. All priests were forced to leave immediately and all Catholic ornaments and relics removed at once. Spanish government in the Netherlands had virtually collapsed; Archduchess Isabel, Philip II's daughter, was growing old and was ineffective in military matters; General Spinola was in Italy, where he died in 1630; the Spanish Netherlands were virtually leaderless. Olivares wrote that Catholicism in northern Europe was "utterly lost," above all because of French aid to the heretics. In 1630 Cardinal Richelieu renewed his alliance with the rebel Netherlands for seven more years, promising them a subsidy of a million pounds a year in return for their pledge not to make peace with Spain without French consent. He was deliberately using this exhausting war to wear down crippled Spain so that France might supplant her as the world's leading power, not at all concerned that he was thereby strengthening the hands of the deadliest enemies of the Catholic faith. Spain sent her best admiral, Fadrique de Toledo, with a large fleet to escort the 1630 Mexico treasure fleet home, which he did successfully, but the million ducats Piet Hein had taken were gone forever.[40]

When Emperor Ferdinand II issued the Edict of Restitution in March 1629, he had no idea of the long-range effects of Piet Hein's feat on his great power ally, Spain, and only a vague suspicion of the treachery of Wallenstein who was now apparently seeking to build up a Baltic empire for himself. A report from Capuchin Father Alexander von Ales said that Wallenstein planned to deceive both Duke Maximilian of Bavaria and his general Tilly, and to become Holy Roman Emperor rather than Ferdinand II's son and namesake. This was possible, because no written law, only 150-year custom and precedent, provided for the succession of the Habsburg family to that lofty position. Wallenstein had gone to the Baltic coast in June 1628, taking the title of Duke of Mecklenburg, which made him a prince of the Empire. He took the port of Rostock and tried to

---

[40] Israel, *Dutch in the Hispanic World*, pp. 176, 178-179; *Cambridge Modern History* IV, 691-693; Wedgwood, *Thirty Years War*, p. 240; Elliott, *Olivares*, pp. 367 (first quote), 388-389 (second quote on 389), 400; Goslinga, *Dutch in the Caribbean*, p. 215; Roberts, *Gustavus Adolphus* II, 428, 596.

take the port city of Stralsund on the Baltic, but failed. Stralsund appealed for help to Denmark and Sweden; beaten Denmark was unable to give it, but Sweden was only too glad to do so. Wallenstein took advantage of the Danish defeat at the Battle of Lutter to extend his dominions into the northern province of Holstein. Though he still professed loyalty to the Emperor, his accumulation of financial power and uncertain intentions caused substantial uneasiness in Vienna. And he let it be known that he was strongly opposed to the Edict of Restitution, though the Emperor sternly ordered him to enforce it. In April 1630 Ferdinand II ordered him to stop recruiting troops for his army, and to reduce their number.[41]

Despite Wallenstein's opposition, the Edict of Restitution was remarkably effective. The year after it was issued, 1630, saw the reestablishment of six Catholic dioceses in north Germany, with their lands, and about 200 monasteries and convents. There was of course furious opposition from the Protestants, but at this point in the war their resistance would have been useless without outside help.[42]

But outside help was coming, from the greatest general of the age: the Protestant champion, king of Lutheran Sweden, Gustav Adolf.[43] Young (in his thirties), ardent, a born leader of men, he was also a veteran commander who had been fighting wars in Poland, Latvia and Estonia for years. But he had also campaigned in Prussia, and had long had his eye on fractious Germany. Wallenstein's Baltic ambitions deeply concerned him, as did the plight of the German Protestants. There is every indication that Gustav Adolf's concern for Protestants in other lands was genuine, as much as Ferdinand II's and Olivares' concern for Catholics, utterly different from the attitude of Cardinal Richelieu. Sweden produced superb infantry, almost as good as Spain's. But they were a poor nation, mostly agricultural, with a population of only 900,000 (not counting the then primitive Finns).[44] They could not intervene in strength in the German war unless somebody paid them to do it.

Cardinal Richelieu was that somebody. He was already financing the Dutch rebels in their war against Spain, and had financed the intervention of the Lutheran Danes on the Protestant side in the Thirty Years War. The Danish defeat at Lutter had left him with only "the Swedish card" to play. He did not hesitate. In October 1629 he sent his best diplomat, the Duc de Charnacé, to help bring an end to the war between Sweden and Poland, which was tying up most of the Swedish troops. In January 1631 he signed a five-year renewable alliance with Sweden, the Treaty of Barwälde, providing for a French subsidy twice a

[41] Mann, *Wallenstein*, pp. 382-388, 408, 416-418, 431, 333, 446, 462-468; *Cambridge Modern History* IV, 105-106, 111-112, 116; Wedgwood, *Thirty Years War*, p. 202; Burckhardt, *Richelieu* II, 352; Roberts, *Gustavus Adolphus* II, 350-359.

[42] *Cambridge Modern History* IV, 112-113; Mann, *Wallenstein*, p. 533

[43] He will be called herein by the Swedish form of his name, as Michael Roberts calls him in his great biography. Though the Latinized form "Gustavus Adolphus" has become much more familiar, there is no reason for using it, since the names of kings of other European countries than Sweden are never Latinized.

[44] Burckhardt, *Richelieu*, II, 361, 363.

year, large enough to pay most of the cost of a Swedish army of 30,000 foot and 6,000 horse, initially to take possession of as much of the Baltic coast of Germany as they could. His purpose was to weaken the Emperor; he salved his conscience by getting Gustav Adolf to agree not to suppress Catholic worship in any of the territories he should conquer—an agreement which he kept only at first. But the reunion of Germany under Catholic leadership was rendered forever impossible by his intervention, as Richelieu intended. The leadership and the victories in battle were Gustav Adolf's; but the money to pay for them came from a prince of the Church, the cardinal who betrayed Christendom.[45]

Gustav Adolf had already ceremonially landed near his allied city of Stralsund on the north coast of Germany on July 4, 1630, with 28 warships and 28 troop transports carrying 13,000 men, a total quickly augmented to 40,000. The cavalry and artillery and a substantial part of the infantry were Swedish, but a considerable percentage were mercenaries whom Cardinal Richelieu's money was needed to pay. It was a very Lutheran army. Lutheran prayers were held twice daily, and each soldier was given a pocket book of Lutheran hymns.[46] Gustav Adolf let it be known at the outset that he would recognize no neutrals in this religious war:

> What kind of a thing is it, neutrality? It surpasses my understanding. . . .
> Here God and the Devil are in strife. If His Dilection desires to side with God, let him join me. If however he decides to side with the Devil, then verily he must fight me.[47]

Gustav Adolf promptly took Stettin at the mouth of the Oder River, capital of the province of Pomerania, which capitulated virtually without resistance. Before the month of July was over he was conferring with the Duc de Charnacé, demanding a larger subsidy than that which Richelieu had been offering him, which he eventually revived in the Treaty of Barwälde. The four Catholic electors strongly recommended to Emperor Ferdinand II that he dismiss Wallenstein, whom they regarded as primarily responsible for the devastation of Germany through his recruiting of large numbers of mercenary soldiers. His Privy Council, however, urged him to retain Wallenstein in view of the magnitude of the Swedish threat which they thought he alone could cope with. Nevertheless the Emperor continued to discuss Wallenstein's removal with them. Urged by his chancellor, Prince Johan von Eggenburg, to rescind the Edict of Restitution, he absolutely refused to do so.[48]

---

[45] *Ibid.*, I, 244-245, 247-248, 364-368, 385-386; Roberts, *Gustavus Adolphus* II, 466-467; Wedgwood, *Thirty Years War*, pp. 268-269; *Cambridge Modern History*, IV, 198; von Pastor, *History of the Popes* XXVIII, 270-271.

[46] Wedgwood, *Thirty Years War*, pp. 260, 265-266; *Cambridge Modern History* IV, 193; Roberts, *Gustavus Adolphus* II, 417, 442.

[47] Mann, *Wallenstein*, p. 545.

[48] *Ibid.*, pp. 522-526; Wedgwood, *Thirty Years War*, pp. 255-257; *Cambridge Modern History*, IV, 194; Roberts, *Gustavus Adolphus* II, 442, 464-465.

By this time Wallenstein had overdrawn even his enormous accumulation of landed wealth. It was no longer producing the profit he had come to expect. His financial manager had to cut off his subsidy and when Wallenstein cut off his pay, he committed suicide September 2. Thus when Emperor Ferdinand II finally nerved himself to dismiss Wallenstein from command on September 7, he did not object, needing to concentrate on solving his financial troubles. Tilly, now 70 years old, was chosen his successor in command of the imperial army. Tilly accepted reluctantly; he was twice Gustav Adolf's age, as dedicated as ever but no longer sure of his military mastery over such an opponent—presciently so, because Gustav Adolf was one of the great generals of history, while Tilly was only a good one. Meanwhile in France, Cardinal Richelieu assured his continued rule by defeating in the "day of dupes" a conspiracy against him by the Queen Mother and Louis XIII's brother Gaston. The Queen Mother was exiled to Brussels, never to return.[49]

In January Gustav Adolf compelled Elector George William of Brandenburg to grant him the right of passage across his territories, and received the pledge of strong French financial support at Barwälde.[50] Tilly knew crisis was at hand; he wrote:

> The danger, the need and the impoverishment of both armies are growing not only with each day but with each hour and each moment that passes. Consequently, exchanges of letters, reminders and entreaties and comforting words do little to help our cause, and the calling of meetings and discussions does even less. Immediate action is needed. If this does not ensue, then the inevitable and certain consequence will be that the whole avalanche of war will plunge into the lands governed by the princes of the [Catholic] League.[51]

In February 1631 a conference on the Edict of Restitution was held at Frankfort. Protestant Elector John George of Saxony demanded its immediate revocation, and even Catholic Duke Maximilian of Bavaria said he was willing to postpone its enforcement for forty years. Richelieu sent a representative, the Protestant Melchior de Lisle of Basel, who also urged the edict's revocation. But Ferdinand II would not be moved.[52] He regarded Catholic restoration in Germany as the culmination of his life's work, not a plaything of power politics. He was committed to the reunion of Germany in the Catholic faith—a commitment to which he was true unto death. To him it was simple justice: Catholic property had been confiscated and stolen, without the approval of the Emperor or of any Diet. Only one written agreement, the Religious Peace of Augsburg in 1555, had authorized the Lutherans to hold some Catholic Church properties. All other confiscations were unauthorized and illegal. Now, with his military victories, came his opportunity to reverse them, and in the process create

---

[49] Wedgwood, *Thirty Years War*, pp. 256, 258; Mann, *Wallenstein*, pp. 516-517, 526-528, 533, 539; Roberts, *Gustavus Adolphus* II, 439.

[50] *Cambridge Modern History* IV, 197-198. See Note 45, above.

[51] Burckhardt, *Richelieu*, II, 369.

[52] *Cambridge Modern History* IV, 114.

the basis for the return of the Catholic Church in all of Germany. On this issue he would not yield while the slightest chance remained for the reunion he dreamed of.

Later that month 14 German Protestant princes and 26 Protestant cities met to form a league with Gustav Adolf. But Elector John George of Saxony, the most powerful Protestant prince, though urged by his own advisors to join this league, refused to do so; John George wanted neither an imperial nor a Swedish master. But he issued a renewed demand for repeal of the Edict of Restitution. Gustav Adolf swept across Mecklenburg and considered offering immediate battle to Tilly, but decided against it and put his army into winter quarters. Meanwhile Tilly was pressing on toward the important Protestant city of Magdeburg, to which he laid siege at the beginning of April. On April 13 Gustav Adolf stormed Frankfurt-on-Oder in northeastern Germany and killed two thousand of its 5,000-man garrison.[53]

On May 20 Tilly's army stormed Magdeburg after, encouraged by Gustav Adolf, it had twice rejected calls to surrender by Tilly's besieging forces.[54] As so often happened in this kind of warfare, the storming was accompanied and followed by a general destruction for which the Catholic army was blamed; but "most contemporary witnesses, some of them Protestants, stated that when Falkenberg [the Swedish liaison officer in Magdeburg] realized the town was lost, he gave orders for mines to be laid in various places and for the armory and a number of other buildings to be set on fire. Falkenberg himself was killed in the battle."[55] When the horror was over, only about 5,000 of the city's population of 30,000 remained, mostly women. Tilly, deeply distressed, pardoned the survivors and tried with some success to restore the city.[56]

Late in May 1631, Count Thurn of Bohemia, one of the leaders in the defenestration of Prague, met with Gustav Adolf to tell him that Wallenstein, now without a command, might be interested in working with him. Gustav Adolf then had Thurn undertake negotiations with Wallenstein's man Trchka, orally promising him 12,000 troops and recognition as Viceroy of Bohemia in return for his promise to betray his master and overthrow Habsburg rule. There was nothing in writing. For the moment Wallenstein did not agree, and the negotiations were kept secret. But such a secret is hard to keep, and suspicion of the dismissed general continued to grow at Emperor Ferdinand II's court.[57]

Gustav Adolf did not like intrigue such as this. He preferred to win on the battlefield. In late June he appeared before Berlin, the capital of Brandenburg, training his potent cannon on the electoral palace, and imposed a treaty on the

---

[53] *Ibid.*, IV, 197, 199-201; Wedgwood, *Thirty Years War*, pp. 272-273, 276; Roberts, *Gustavus Adolphus* II, 472, 478-481, 484-485, 487-488; Mann, *Wallenstein*, pp. 546, 548.

[54] Wedgwood, *Thirty Years War*, pp. 277-280; *Cambridge Modern History* IV, 201-202; Roberts, *Gustavus Adolphus* II, 495-496.

[55] Burckhardt, *Richelieu* II, 370.

[56] *Cambridge Modern History* IV, 202-203; Mann, *Wallenstein*, p. 552

[57] *Cambridge Modern History* IV, 206-207; Mann, *Wallenstein*, pp. 566-568; Roberts, *Gustavus Adolphus*, II, 678-679.

Electorate by which he was to hold two of its key fortresses for the duration of the war. He then marched to the Elbe River, where he won two battles near the town of Werben. At the end of August the reluctant Elector John George of Saxony finally offered him alliance. Tilly invaded Saxony to try to deter the alliance, but the invasion only made John George the more willing to work with the Swedes. In early September Swedish troops entered Wittenberg, Luther's home town, to great acclaim. On September 12 a formal treaty of alliance between Saxony and Sweden was signed and sealed. On the 16th Tilly took Leipzig, the largest city in Saxony. The two armies hurried toward a clash. It came the next day at a little town called Breitenfeld four miles from Leipzig.[58]

Gustav Adolf had trained his musketeers to fire continuously in alternating ranks, and arranged his forces checkerboard fashion, like the ancient Roman maniples, rather than in a mass at the center and light-armed troops and cavalry on the wings, as was then customary. In fifty years of warfare, Tilly had never seen such a formation. His spirited Croatian cavalry charged the Saxons with wild cries and put them to rout, but the Swedes formed square and repelled the cavalry charges, while their well-trained musketeers kept firing. Then, as the wind shifted and began to blow in the face of the Catholic army, Gustav Adolf led a mighty charge of his own cavalry which cut off the Catholic cavalry from its infantry. It had been many years since Europe had seen such mastery on the battlefield; by this battle Gustav Adolf established himself as one of the great generals of history. Trying to rally his troops, the 72-year-old Tilly took three wounds, one of which shattered his right arm. He had to leave the field and transfer the command to Pappenheim, an able but not inspired general who led an orderly retreat to Leipzig, but with only 3,000 men. No less than 12,000 of his army were killed on the battlefield or in the retreat, and 7,000 were prisoners, most of whom immediately entered Swedish service as mercenaries. There were only about 2,100 Swedish casualties and an unknown number of Saxons, whom Tilly's Croatian cavalry had routed.[59]

A week later Tilly, heroically refusing to retire to a hospital for treatment, had collected 13,000 soldiers of his now scattered army and retreated with them into Brunswick until they should be able to fight again. Gustav Adolf, who had originally intended to pursue him vigorously, changed his mind as a result of this splendid recovery by the old warrior, and went into winter quarters. By October the resolute Tilly had collected 20,000 men. Meanwhile Gustav Adolf occupied the large central German city of Erfurt, one of the most Lutheran cities in Germany, then the central German province of Thuringia, then the south German city of Würzburg, where he massacred the defending garrison, but no civilians. On October 18 he took the castle of Marienburg on the left bank of the Main near Würzburg, with an enormous accumulation of military supplies and ecclesiastical

---

[58] Wedgwood, *Thirty Years War*, pp. 282, 285-286; *Cambridge Modern History* IV, 203-205; Roberts, *Gustavus Adolphus* II, 508-513, 518-521, 532-534.

[59] Wedgwood, *Thirty Years War*, pp. 287-291; *Cambridge Modern History*, IV, 205; Roberts, *Gustavus Adolphus*, II, 535-538; Mann, *Wallenstein*, pp. 554-555; Burckhardt, *Richelieu* II, 377.

and literary treasures, and proclaimed himself Duke of Franconia, a major region in south central Germany. The city of Nuremberg declared for Gustav Adolf. A Saxon army invaded Bohemia; little or no resistance was offered. The indomitable Tilly, recovering from his wounds, proposed an attack on Würzburg, but Duke Maximilian of Bavaria rejected the proposal, unwilling to risk his last remaining army to another blow like Breitenfeld. In Rome, Cardinal Barberini wrote the papal nuncio in France instructing him to point out to Cardinal Richelieu the dangerous position of the Church in Germany and to implore him to stop supporting Gustav Adolf and his army. The appeal fell on deaf ears.[60]

By November 1631 the Saxons had taken Prague and the Swedes were marching on the Rhine, with Protestant cities opening their gates to them. Emperor Ferdinand II ordered Pappenheim, who was his general and not under the command of Duke Maximilian of Bavaria, to detach himself from Tilly with his men, as Tilly was now withdrawing toward the Danube to protect Bavaria, and go to the north. Gustav Adolf took Frankfort and brought in his extraordinarily able Chancellor Axel Oxenstierna from Sweden to administer his now vast conquests in Germany. Tilly arrived before Nuremberg, but the city refused him admission. Reluctantly, Emperor Ferdinand II felt obliged to turn again to Wallenstein, even though intercepted letters from Count Thurn had revealed some part of his attempted intrigue with Gustav Adolf. On December 10 Ferdinand II sent an emissary to Wallenstein to find out his terms for resuming command. On December 13 Pope Urban VIII wrote to the King and Queen of France and to Cardinal Richelieu, urging them not to aid in a Protestant triumph in Germany, and pointing to Gustav Adolf's many violations of his promise not to injure the Catholic religion in territories he conquered. On December 15 he called for special prayers for the Church all over Christendom. These actions cast much doubt on the supposed support of Pope Urban VIII for Cardinal Richelieu. They show no treason to Christendom, but they do show a Pope outstripped by events. He should have condemned Cardinal Richelieu's actions much earlier, perhaps even removed him from his cardinalate.[61]

Wallenstein's new commission as commander from the Emperor was dated December 15, 1631.[62] Tilly agreed to this, despondent; too much had been asked from the old man. Duke Maximilian of Bavaria found him weeping, "entirely perplexed and, as it were, defeated, altogether irresolute in counsel, without any notion how to succor himself, and [he] passes from one proposal to another, reaches no conclusion, sees the great difficulties and extremities but openly admits that he is at a loss for ways and means."[63] Gustav Adolf made a daring

---

[60] Wedgwood, *Thirty Years War*, p. 295; *Cambridge Modern History* IV, 207-209; Roberts, *Gustavus Adolphus* II, 538-539, 542-544, 546-549, 551-552, 682-683; Mann, *Wallenstein*, pp. 557, 572; von Pastor, *History of the Popes* XXVIII, 278.

[61] Wedgwood, *Thirty Years War*, pp. 295, 298; *Cambridge Modern History* IV, 208-209; Roberts, *Gustavus Adolphus* II, 553, 555-556, 588; Mann, *Wallenstein*, pp. 573-574; Burckhardt, *Richelieu* II, 377-378; von Pastor, *History of the Popes* XXVIII, 279-280.

[62] Mann, *Wallenstein*, p. 579.

[63] *Ibid.*, p. 594.

crossing of the Rhine at Mainz and took it and Worms before the year 1631 was ended. He now commanded nearly 80,000 men in seven armies, with 15,000 under his personal command on the Rhine. At the end of the year imperial general Pappenheim appeared in the Rhineland and began to harass the Swedish-German forces there effectively, retaking Magdeburg in north central Germany, but he had no intention of directly confronting the Swedish king. Gustav Adolf rejected any thought of peace, and began to see himself as a prospective Protestant Emperor, who would unite the Lutheran and Calvinist churches. After humbling Bavaria, he now planned a great campaign to conquer Austria. He told Elector John George of Saxony that he intended to annex to Sweden the whole province of Pomerania on the Baltic coast of Germany. Opposition to him began to grow in Germany, due to fear of his ambitions and the power of his army. But the Catholic League broke up in January.[64] Cardinal Richelieu began to wonder if he had created a monster that would threaten France as well as the Empire. He tried to curb his ward, to no avail. Fiercely Gustav Adolf replied:

> Had it depended on mere numbers, it had not been I who beat the Emperor, but he me. Let your king go where he will; but let him have a care not to cross the path of my armies, or he may look for a *rencontre* with me.[65]

The arrogance of power was clearly taking possession of Gustav Adolf. Cardinal Richelieu had thought to use him against his enemies, regardless of the needs and priorities of Christendom; now he realized that all along it had been Gustav Adolf who had used him.

The magnitude of the danger to Catholic Christendom was seen clearly by many in Spain, its ancient defender in the religious wars. At a combined meeting of the Spanish Council of State and the Council of Castile, it was discussed "whether France's attack on the Emperor and Spain's allies constituted an act of war against Spain; whether there was a case for a pre-emptive strike; and whether it was better to 'live at risk,' in view of 'the difficulty or impossibility of finding resources,' or to 'die, expending the last drop of blood to ensure an effective defense.'"[66] In February Emperor Ferdinand II concluded a "close alliance" with Philip IV of Spain, though it was not immediately ratified. The 1631 Mexico treasure fleet was all but destroyed by a hurricane, though the Peru fleet reached Spain safely. But the long-range effects of Piet Hein's spectacular seizure of the 1628 silver fleet were still reverberating down the years, and Spain's financial strength was now declining with each passing year. Nevertheless, in view of the danger to Christendom, the Cortes of Castile voted for taxes sufficient to bring in 2,500,000 ducats a year for the next three years. Pope Urban VIII had recently promised a one-year subsidy of 600,000 ducats for the Habsburgs in Germany,

---

[64] Wedgwood, *Thirty Years War*, pp. 296, 300-303; *Cambridge Modern History* IV, 208, 210; Roberts, *Gustavus Adolphus* II, 557-558, 645, 671, 674-678, 688-690; Mann, *Wallenstein*, pp. 569, 596, 601-602.

[65] Roberts, *Gustavus Adolphus*, p. 587.

[66] Elliott, *Olivares*, p. 436.

but it was to be drawn solely from the Spanish and south Italian clergy.[67] On March 8, 1632 there was a furious scene at a secret meeting of the cardinals with the Pope. Spanish Cardinal Borja accused the Pope in writing of tolerating heresy and aid to it, saying:

> No sooner had the Most Serene Catholic King of Spain received information of the conspiracy of all the heretical powers with the King of Sweden, and of the defeat of the Catholics in Germany, his one anxiety was to meet so great a danger at once, knowing that thus he would walk in the steps of his ancestors who had bequeathed to him so glorious a title, because they too fought for religion even more than for their kingdom. For this reason the King has put on one side his interests in the Indies, in Italy and in the Netherlands and has supported the Emperor with vast subsidies. While thus mobilizing the resources of his kingdom with a view to a yet greater effort, he realized that the combined forces of the heretics could only be driven back by the united armed forces of all Catholics. For this reason he has had recourse to Your Holiness as to the common Father, praying you with all humility, though also most earnestly, that you would deign not only to contribute generous sums of money but, what is even more important, that you would warn all Catholic princes and peoples of their danger and earnestly exhort them to defend the cause of religion. . . . At the same time he [the King] commanded me to protest with all due respect and humility, that any injury suffered by the Catholic religion must be ascribed not to himself, the most pious and obedient king, but to Your Holiness.[68]

Pandemonium erupted. The Pope was livid, demanding to know by what right Cardinal Borja spoke to him thus. Cardinal Antonio told Cardinal Borja to be silent, and seized him by the arm to drag him down into his seat.[69] Cardinal Borja's words have rung down through Catholic history. From then on the Spanish, who stood on their pride and honor as defenders of Christendom, were convinced that Pope Urban VIII favored the French. There is little hard evidence to support this view; rather it appears that this Pope was struggling desperately to remain neutral between the two great Catholic powers, knowing that the fall of either the Holy Roman Empire or the French Catholic government would gravely weaken the Church and Christendom. But Spanish anger was natural enough when Cardinal Richelieu was pouring out the wealth of France to finance Protestant rebels, and the Pope would not give the Catholics comparable support. They forgot that the Pope must always think and act in the long term, for the sake of Christendom; that he cannot ever be tied to any one country and its policy without very bad results for the Church. As between Catholics and Protestants, the decision had already been made: they must fight, because none but a military solution to their rending quarrel was now possible, nor had been possible since

---

[67] *Cambridge Modern History* IV, 211; Roberts, *Gustavus Adolphus.* p. 575; Goslinga, *Dutch in the Caribbean*, p. 222; Elliott, *Olivares*, pp. 439-440; von Pastor, *History of the Popes* XXVIII, 284-285.

[68] Von Pastor, *History of the Popes* XXVIII, 287-288.

[69] *Ibid.*, XXVIII, 286-289; Elliott, *Olivares*, p. 431.

the Council of Trent finished its work. In the Netherlands the Protestants were winning, but in Germany (at least until the arrival of Gustav Adolf) the Catholics were winning. And it was a Catholic power, France, under the Machiavellian Cardinal Richelieu, which had now turned on them. Pope Urban VIII would never support what Richelieu was doing, but he could not afford to try to help his victims much, nor indeed could he match Richelieu's largesse in any case; France was much richer than the Holy See and Cardinal Richelieu was perfectly capable of taking France into schism, to set up a Church of France like the Church of England.

As Gustav Adolf's tremendous army bore down on hitherto unravaged Bavaria with the coming of spring, Tilly returned to the fray since Wallenstein, who strongly disliked Duke Maximilian of Bavaria, would not lift a finger to help him despite all the Emperor's pleas and orders. Gustav Adolf crossed the Danube at Donauwörth and plunged into Bavaria, expelling the Jesuits and plundering their colleges. On the Lech River, Bavaria's boundary, he once again defeated Tilly, and this time the old general was mortally wounded and lost his artillery and baggage. But before he died he managed to get his army away at night and to make a successful retreat to Ingolstadt. On April 29 Gustav, after cruelly ravaging Bavaria on the way, came up to him at Ingolstadt and brought it under heavy cannon fire. Tilly, now 73, who had "never once deviated from the strict path of allegiance," died after terrible sufferings, his eyes fixed on a crucifix. He had commanded his army from his bed until his last hour, a good but not spectacular general facing a genius he could not match.[70]

In the middle of May Duke Maximilian of Bavaria fled to Salzburg in Austria, leaving only 2,000 cavalry as a garrison for München, his capital. Gustav Adolf occupied München without resistance, sacked it, and carried off numerous works of art, manuscripts and books to Stockholm, while ravaging all the countryside around it. On May 21 Wallenstein offered the Saxons peace in return for revocation of the Edict of Restitution; four days later he retook Prague and began the process of clearing Bohemia, where many of his numerous estates were located, of Protestant invaders. Pope Urban VIII sent instructions to his nuncios in Vienna, Madrid, and Paris stressing the necessity of reconciling the Catholic powers and combining their forces against the Swedes. But he said that he was not able to grant more than his current monthly subsidy or 10,000 thalers to the Habsburgs, and his nuncios were not able to make any progress toward a reconciliation. When Cardinal Richelieu wrote to him in May, trying to arouse suspicions of Spain, the Pope wrote back urging an end to his support of Gustav Adolf. Richelieu haughtily replied that he would continue that support, since it was helping the Pope to withstand pressure from the Empire.[71] It was a desperate

---

[70] Wedgwood, *Thirty Years War*, pp. 305-306; *Cambridge Modern History* IV, 214; Roberts, *Gustavus Adolphus* II, 699-701, 703-704; Mann, *Wallenstein*, pp. 608-610, 618-619; Burckhardt, *Richelieu* II, 378-379, 388 (for quote).

[71] Wedgwood, *Thirty Years War*, pp. 309-310; *Cambridge Modern History* IV, 213, 215; Roberts, *Gustavus Adolphus* II, 709-710; Mann, *Wallenstein*, pp. 620-621;

moment for the Catholic Church, and it is understandable that Pope Urban VIII hesitated before so drastic a move as the public condemnation of Richelieu, but timidity wins no wars. Richelieu, the cardinal who betrayed Christendom, proved the stronger personality.

In July the Protestant army of Gustav Adolf and the Catholic army of Wallenstein, now joined by Duke Maximilian of Bavaria, camped near each other near heavily fortified Nuremberg, held by Gustav Adolf. The two Catholic armies outnumbered the Protestant by more than two to one, but there was no immediate battle. Given time, Gustav Adolf quickly brought up reinforcements, so that he had some 28,000 foot and 17,000 horse against Wallenstein's 32,000 foot and 12,000 horse in prepared positions, but because of the fortifications he would not at first accept battle. Wallenstein had never intended to attack; he was no more a match for Gustav Adolf than Tilly had been, though Wallenstein concealed it better. But his defensive position was good, and on September 3 and 4 he repulsed an attack by the Swedish king on his fortifications at Alte Veste near Nuremburg, with 2,400 Swedish and German casualties at the cost of only 600 for Wallenstein's army. Both generals then withdrew, with disease and desertion (mostly of his German soldiers) making considerable inroads on Gustav Adolf's forces. Wallenstein's troops, in their prepared encampments, fared better. Gustav Adolf concluded that he must risk a major battle before his army weakened further, and on September 18 formally challenged Wallenstein to fight. Wallenstein did not respond; Gustav Adolf marched his army in the direction of Transylvania, where a Protestant rebel offered help. Duke Maximilian of Bavaria urged Wallenstein to attack Gustav Adolf on the march, but he refused, breaking camp and marching north, away from the Swedes. In a letter October 9 to Chancellor Oxenstierna, Gustav Adolf outlined plans for the pursuit of Wallenstein, in whatever direction he might go. Just a few days later came the news that Wallenstein's army had divided into three parts, giving Gustav Adolf's army a strong numerical advantage. On November 6 General Pappenheim, who had been commanding an army in the Netherlands, joined Wallenstein, countering that advantage. Wallenstein, who had just sent Pappenheim off again, hastily recalled him, just in time for the major battle which took place November 16.[72]

This was the Battle of Lützen, one of the most important military turning points in the history of the world.

In the morning of November 16, Gustav Adolf had 12,800 foot, 6,200 horse, and 20 field guns, while Wallenstein had 8,200 foot, 7,500 horse, and 24 field guns in a strong defensive position. Pappenheim was riding hard to his rescue with 3,000 cavalry. Gustav Adolf planned to win the battle before Pappenheim could arrive, but a thick fog prevented it from starting until eleven

---

Burckhardt, *Richelieu* II, 393-397; von Pastor, *History of the Popes* XXVIII, 304-307, 310-311.

[72] Wedgwood, *Thirty Years War*, pp. 311-313, 315-316; *Cambridge Modern History* IV, 216-220; Roberts, *Gustavus Adolphus* II, 718, 727-729, 731-735, 738, 744, 764; Mann, *Wallenstein*, pp. 624, 626-628, 633-637, 647, 650.

o'clock. Pappenheim arrived at noon, to find the battlefield still enveloped in a combination of mist and smoke which negated Gustav Adolf's skill by rendering him unable to see what was happening. Wallenstein, also present on the field, was in no better case. Fierce individual and small group combats broke out everywhere. The commanders were in the thick of them. Pappenheim was killed, declaring with his last breath that he was dying for the Catholic Faith. Shortly after noon, Gustav Adolf was struck in the arm by a musket ball as he led a cavalry charge, then overwhelmed by a counter-charge. His men fled or died; he was killed with pistol shots and sword thrusts, stripped of all his rich clothes, and left naked and unidentified on the earth just as the fog descended heavily again. For three hours no one knew where the king of Sweden was. When the Swedish soldiers finally learned of his death, about 3:30, they launched a series of vengeful charges that took 14 guns from the Emperor's army. Both armies then retreated, leaving approximately equal numbers of dead on the field. Both sides claimed victory. But the military genius upon whom the Protestant cause depended was dead. His successor in command, Duke Bernhard of Saxe-Weimar, was a good general but not a great one; Gustav's baby daughter Christina succeeded to the throne, with Chancellor Axel Oxenstierna as regent; and the war was no longer winnable for either side.[73]

On December 14 Pope Urban VIII wrote to Emperor Ferdinand II:

> We offer unceasing thanks to the God of Judgment that He has exercised vengeance against the proud and removed from the neck of the Catholics the yoke of their most pitiless enemy. The greatness of this favor of His bounty is realized by Germany, of which more than one province, now reduced to desolation by foreign arms, will for a long time to come lament the death of its inhabitants, the looting of its towns, and the devastation of its territories; it is realized by us whose heart was ever full of nameless grief because of the anguish and oppression of our sons; and it is realized by the whole of Christendom which heard the boast of this king who made war on Catholicism and who had become exalted by reason of his splendid armies and their triumphs, that he had beaten down with fire and sword and devastation all that stood in the way of his rapid march from the furthermost shores of the Baltic as far south as Swabia. Accordingly, as soon as the report of the desired victory reached us, we offered with infinite joy the Holy Sacrifice in the German national church of Our Blessed Lady of the Anima . . . and when we had thus returned thanks to Him, together with our beloved sons, the Cardinals of the Holy Roman Church, and a vast concourse of the faithful, for so great a benefit, we earnestly besought Him to lead to a happy issue all the splendid efforts which you are making for the defense of the Catholic Church.[74]

---

[73] Wedgwood, *Thirty Years War*, pp. 316-318; *Cambridge Modern History* IV, 221-222; Roberts, *Gustavus Adolphus* II, 765-772; Mann, *Wallenstein*, pp. 649-663; Burckhardt, *Richelieu*, II, 398-402.

[74] von Pastor, *History of the Popes* XXVIII, 320-321.

The death of Gustav Adolf had established that the Protestants could not win the Thirty Years War. But neither could the Catholics win it; with Tilly dead and Wallenstein vastly overrated and not long for this world, their generals were no better, and perhaps not as good as those Gustav Adolf had trained. Yet because of the ambitions of Cardinal Richelieu, no lasting peace could be obtained either, and the French finally entered openly into the war. So for sixteen terrible years the Germans suffered under the merciless ravages of soldiers from both sides, who had no other way to avoid starvation.

Copernicus' book on the revolution of the earth around the sun was taken off the Index of Forbidden Books in 1620 after the addition of a preface explaining that it was theory and not assured fact. Late in 1623 Galileo published a new book called *The Assayer*, dedicated to the Pope, now Urban VIII, his friend Maffeo Barberini. It had nothing more to say about the Copernican theory, but did advocate the atomic theory of the composition of matter, which a few overzealous critics took to be an attack on transubstantiation, though Galileo specifically disavowed any such intention. The book also contained fierce attacks on the Aristotelians, one of whom—a leading Jesuit named Grassi— Galileo described as writhing like an injured snake.[75]

Pope Urban VIII received Galileo with great honor on six separate occasions when he was in Rome in 1624, and stated "that the Church had never declared the works of Copernicus to be heretical and would not do so," though he immediately added "that there was no reason to fear that a proof of its truth would ever be forthcoming." This emboldened Galileo to begin in 1629 writing *Dialogue on the Two Great World Systems* which, as he told his friend Elia Diodati "will provide, I trust, a most ample confirmation of the Copernican system." He completed it early in 1630 and immediately went to Rome to arrange for its publication with the aid of his good friend, the Dominican Father Riccardi, Master of the Palace. Instructing the Inquisitor in Florence who was asked to give the book its imprimatur, Father Riccardi said the *Dialogue* focussed on "the mathematical examination of the Copernican position on the earth's motion, with the aim of proving that, if we remove divine revelation and sacred doctrine, the appearances could be saved with this supposition . . . so that one would never be admitting the absolute truth of this opinion, but only its hypothetical truth without the benefit of scripture."[76]

---

[75] Pietro Redondi, *Galileo, Heretic* (Princeton, NJ, 1987), pp. 40-50, 195, 328; Feldhay, *Galileo*, pp. 29-31; Langford, *Galileo, Science, and the Church,* 3rd ed. (Ann Arbor, MI, 1992), p. 112. The principal thesis of Redondi's book is that Galileo was challenging transubstantiation. There could not be a more obvious example of trying to use a miracle to disprove a scientific theory, which no miracle can do, since miracles override natural laws. But Galileo, as he specifically said, never made that claim. Others claimed it, but not he.

[76] Von Pastor, *History of the Popes*, XXVI, 50, 116 (second quote); XXIX, 46-47 (first quote on 47); Langford, *Galileo*, pp. 131, 209; Redondi, *Galileo*, p. 233; Rivka Feldhay, *Galileo and the Church* (Cambridge, England, 1995), p. 55 (third quote).

But unfortunately Galileo made it entirely clear in the *Dialogue* that he regarded the Copernican theory as absolutely true and ridiculed opposing arguments by placing them in the mouth of a participant in the dialogue called Simplicio, a dunce.   With almost incredible imprudence, he seems to have included among Simplicio's anti-Copernican arguments some which Pope Urban VIII himself had proposed to him. When the *Dialogue* was published in March 1632, the Pope was furious because of this. By a malign coincidence for Galileo, this was just at the moment of Gustav Adolf's great Protestant military victories during the Thirty Years War, when he was ravaging Bavaria, expelling Jesuits and plundering their colleges, invading the Grisons in Switzerland, and threatening to march into Italy. Pope Urban VIII had seemed to favor Cardinal Richelieu of France, the paymaster of Gustav Adolf (though, as we have seen, he had not favored him nearly so much as was believed), and the Pope was consequently, as we have seen, under very heavy critical pressure from Spanish Cardinal Borja, a strong supporter of Gustav Adolf's enemy, Holy Roman Emperor Ferdinand II.[77]

Urban VIII therefore needed to prove his orthodoxy, and his former friendship with Galileo was overlaid by his anger at being accused of supporting heretics. In August 1632, after Galileo's *Dialogue* was publicly denounced by the Jesuits, he set up another special commission of theologians to examine it, and told the ambassador from Florence that "Galileo had dared enter where he should not, into the most grave and dangerous subjects that one could possibly raise at this moment."[78]

This special commission, examining Galileo's file, immediately came upon the mysterious document dated February 26, 1616 purporting to enjoin him from teaching the Copernican theory, and they charged him with disobeying these instructions. Galileo, now 70, was summoned before a three-man committee of the Inquisition in September 1632 to answer the charge. One of the members of the committee was Father Riccardi, caught between his friendship for Galileo and the fact that he had procured the imprimatur for the *Dialogue*; another member was the hard-line Jesuit Melchior Inchofer who, without ever inquiring into its authenticity, insisted that Galileo had *prima facie* disobeyed the injunction given to him.[79]

Cardinal Bellarmine was dead, so no longer able to help. Galileo asked to be excused from the hearing on grounds of age and ill health, but to no avail. His patron, Duke Cosimo de Medici of Tuscany, told him he must attend it. In mid-February 1633 he arrived in Rome. Proceedings against him continued despite the confirmation by a Cardinal of the Holy Office that he had never been given

---

[77] von Pastor, *History of the Popes*, XXIX, 52-54; Redondi, *Galileo*, pp. 229-232; Feldhay, *Galileo*, p. 15; Langford, *Galileo*, pp. 130-131; Stanley L. Jaki, "The Case for Galileo's Rehabilitation," *Fidelity*, March 1986.

[78] Redondi, *Galileo*, pp. 239-245, 256 (quote).

[79] Von Pastor, *History of the Popes*, XXIX, 55; Redondi, *Galileo*, p. 246; Feldhay, *Galileo*, pp. 65-66; Langford, *Galileo*, p. 135. The third member of the committee was Father Zaccaria Pasqualigo, a Theatine close to the Pope (Redondi, *op. cit.*, pp. 250-252).

the injunction not to teach Copernicanism. He was imprisoned in the Inquisition building, and Pope Urban VIII said his trial could not be avoided because the charges concerned "new and dangerous doctrines" and "the Holy Scripture where the best thing is to go along with common opinion."[80]

On April 12, 1633, in his first deposition before the Inquisition, Galileo produced Cardinal Bellarmine's affidavit that he had not been required to abjure any false doctrine nor been given any penance in 1616, and making no mention of any prohibition against teaching the Copernican theory as an hypothesis. The committee responded that this was irrelevant, because he had in fact taught the theory as truth by loading the arguments in the *Dialogue* in its favor and making its opponent, Simplicius, look ridiculous. On April 30, in a second deposition, Galileo admitted that he could now see that his book would give most readers the impression that he believed the Copernican theory certainly true. The charge that he had been forbidden to teach it at all was quietly dropped as doubts began to accumulate about the authenticity of the unsigned document dated February 26, 1616, which Galileo continued to insist he had never seen or heard of until 1632. He appealed for mercy because of his age and ill health. In fact it had long been the practice of the Roman Inquisition to levy no severe punishments even for proven heresy upon persons of Galileo's age.[81]

On June 16, 1633 the Inquisition handed down its verdict, censuring Galileo as "vehemently suspected of heresy"[82] for advocating heliocentrism as truth, which it declared contrary to Scripture. It forbade him once and for all from teaching it even as an hypothesis, banned his *Dialogue* (it remained on the Index for more than two hundred years) and required a public abjuration, followed by imprisonment for three years (which turned out to be a very mild house arrest). In the words of Pietro Redondi (no friend of the Church) "this heresy was inquisitorial—that is, disciplinary, not theological or doctrinal—both according to the words of the manuals of criminal heresiology of the period and as reported by the most serious juridical scholars of the affair."[83] Galileo was actually, therefore, convicted not of heresy but of disobedience. The Church never ruled the Copernican theory a heresy, despite the initial wildly imprudent declaration of the theologians' committee and the Holy Office in 1616 that it was "false and absurd," which in fact they had no authority to decide.

---

[80] Redondi, *Galileo*, pp. 257-258 (quote on 258); Feldhay, *Galileo*, pp. 16, 59; Langford, *Galileo*, p. 137.

[81] Von Pastor, *History of the Popes*, XXIX, 56-57; Langford, *Galileo*, pp. 135-140, 142-144, 146-148; Feldhay, *Galileo*, pp. 59-61, 64; Redondi, *Galileo*, pp. 259-260. A reference to the possibility of torture made in the Holy Office statement in June has been endlessly cited and condemned, but in fact persons of Galileo's age called before the Roman Inquisition were never tortured in this period (Langford, *op. cit.*, pp. 150-152).

[82] Redondi, *Galileo*, p. 260. To be suspected of heresy—however "vehemently"—was by no means the same thing as being convicted of heresy.

[83] *Ibid.*, p. 326 (quote); von Pastor, *History of the Popes*, XXIX, 58; Langford, *Galileo*, pp. 150-151.

Now, shamefully, Galileo was required to abjure in public even the theory, though legend has it that he murmured *sotto voce* immediately afterward, referring to the Earth, *"Eppur si muove!"* ("Yet still it moves!") If he did not, he should have; the Church has neither the power nor the right to deny what are, or may become, facts of science. On June 30, 1633 he was released into the custody of his friend, the Archbishop of Siena, to supervise his serving of three years of mild house arrest, and was not harassed further. At his country house in Florence, where he served the house arrest, he proceeded to write his greatest scientific work, *Discourses Concerning Two New Sciences*. But his erstwhile friend Pope Urban VIII continued to denounce him in absurdly exaggerated terms, telling the ambassador from Florence in September that Galileo's book was "an injury to religion as grievous as ever there was and of a perverseness as bad as could be encountered."[84] As grievous and perverse as Martin Luther's injury to the Church? As grievous and perverse as John Calvin's?

In 1637, a year after the publication of *Discourses Concerning Two New Sciences*, Galileo went blind, probably from too much exposure of his eyes to the burning light of the sun. On January 8, 1642 he died at the age of 77. His patron and former student, Grand Duke Cosimo de Medici of Tuscany, was not allowed to build him a monument because he was said to have given rise to "the greatest scandal in Christendom."[85]

Unlike so many who came after him and eagerly used his case as a club to beat the Church with, Galileo humbly submitted to her judgment. He was a man of faith, not a rebel. That makes the hostility of Pope Urban VIII all the more difficult to account for and to forgive. But in spite of this the Church never ruled Galileo a heretic. The declaration of the Holy Office that the Copernican theory was false was never personally stated, let alone taught, by any Pope; in fact, Pope Urban VIII specifically declared that it was not heretical and never would be, despite the fact that he did not think it would ever be confirmed as undoubted truth.[86] He certainly never taught anything about it *ex cathedra*. Doctrinal infallibility of the Pope was preserved. On a number of occasions in its long history the Church has condemned an innocent man, whether by misjudgment of the evidence or duress on the Pope.[87] The Catholic has no protection against this except the respect for justice by fallible men—and on his judgment of individuals even the Pope is fallible. It is right to condemn the injustice to Galileo. It is wrong to say that it disproves the authority of the Church.

In January 1633 Vice-Chancellor of Austria von Stralenhof, prominent Austrian minister Max Trautmanshoff, and Bishop Antonius together sent a

---

[84] Von Pastor, *History of the Popes*, XXIX, 59-60 (quote on 60); Langford, *Galileo*, pp. 157-158, 204.

[85] Langford, *Galileo*, p. 158.

[86] Von Pastor, *History of the Popes*, XXIX, 47; see Note 19, above.

[87] Notably St. Athanasius, Patriarch of Alexandria in Egypt, by Pope Liberius. See Volume Two, Chapter 1 of this history. Pope John Paul II has officially apologized, in the name of the Church, for the injustice done to Galileo.

memorandum to the still strongly Catholic Emperor Ferdinand II that further implementation of the Edict of Restitution was now impossible unless and until the Catholics won a complete victory in the war in Germany, which did not appear at all likely since there were now six times as many Protestants there as Catholics. Spain, the memorandum said, was their one reliable ally, but Spain had been badly hurt by its lack of success in the Netherlands and consequently probably could not do much more for the Emperor (the authors of the memorandum were profoundly wrong in this assessment, as the history of the next two years was to show). They went on to say, rightly, that the supreme duty of the Emperor in this situation was to make peace on any acceptable terms. The authors of the memorandum recommended that the peace process begin by approaching Cardinal Richelieu, since France still pretended to neutrality.[88]

But the cardinal against Christendom did not want peace; he wanted the Emperor and his family crushed if possible, seriously weakened for sure, so that France would emerge as the world's leading power. To this end he intended France to enter the war openly, rather than just by proxy, at a propitious moment, thus expanding the devastating and now pointless conflict. Meanwhile, his ambassador in the Netherlands urged the rebel Dutch to continue the war with Spain.[89] Pope Urban VIII told his nuncio in Paris that he would on no account make the Capuchin Father Joseph, a right-hand man of Richelieu, a cardinal despite Richelieu's desire that he be given the red hat.[90]

Catholic Spain still refused to retreat or abandon the Emperor. After a ringing call to his Council of State for immediate action in Germany and the Netherlands,[91] the Count-Duke of Olivares wrote on January 23 to Father Quiroga:

> We should repay God for the favors He has shown to us by securing once and for all the Catholic religion in Germany. The way to do this is to unite and incorporate the affairs of Holland and Flanders with those of the Empire. . . . This is our chance to drive the blade home. . . . If things should go wrong this year, everything is lost, and we shall be so debilitated by our heavy expenditures that we shall never recover.[92]

The Count-Duke was a little precipitate; seven years rather than one were required to bring about the result he feared, for which Piet Hein's capture of the silver fleet in 1628 had laid the basis. But Olivares was willing, in what little time he had left, to risk the foreseeable future of Spain to save the faith in Germany and the Netherlands. Nothing the great Philip II ever said showed a more profoundly Catholic commitment than this heroic statement by the Count-Duke of Olivares in January 1633.

---

[88] Mann, *Wallenstein*, pp. 681-683.

[89] Geyl, *Netherlands in the 17th Century*, I, 108-109.

[90] Von Pastor, *History of the Popes*, XVIII, 400-401.

[91] Elliott, *Olivares* p. 457.

[92] *Ibid.*, pp. 458-459.

At the end of that month Elector John George of Saxony and his military commander Marshal von Arnim called for peace and sought to begin negotiations with Wallenstein. Other Protestant princes in Germany, wanting to continue the war, formed the League of Heilbronn with the Swedes under Chancellor Axel Oxenstierna as regent for baby Christina, Gustav Adolf's only child. Oxenstierna declared in mid-February that the aim of the late Gustav Adolf had been "first and foremost to liberate these and all his co-religionists and relatives in the Empire from the popish yoke." He called for unity among the Protestants and better control of looting and ravaging troops—far easier to say than to do. In March a Swedish army under the best German general, Duke Bernhard of Saxe-Weimar, took the field in the Palatinate, intending to invade Bavaria again. On Easter the Spanish Council of State approved new plans by the Duke of Feria in Milan to send 20,000 infantry and 4,000 cavalry to recover Alsace and hold Franche-Comté. In April Duke Bernhard's Protestant army overran Bavaria and joined with another Swedish army under General Horn, who had been a trusted lieutenant of Gustav Adolf. Duke Maximilian of Bavaria pressed for a counteroffensive, but Tilly had been the counter-attacker and Tilly was dead. Wallenstein could not be moved; he insisted on a defensive strategy only. At this time, in April 1633, Habsburg Crown Prince Ferdinand, heir to the imperial throne and already King of Hungary, was officially proclaimed commander-in-chief of the Austrian Catholic army, as his aging father began the process of establishing the succession of his son. At Heilbronn that same month, the chief French ambassador, on instructions from Cardinal Richelieu, told the German Protestants to raise more troops and continue to cooperate with the Swedes, and to be suspicious of any overtures from Vienna and Madrid. They agreed to follow his advice if they got more money, which they did. [93]

In May 1633 the Spanish ambassador told Emperor Ferdinand II that Philip IV of Spain would take over the entire expense of the war in Germany if he could direct it though his brother, Cardinal-Prince Fernando, who arrived in Genoa, Italy in May. That same month there was a meeting with Wallenstein at his residence in Bohemia with Swedish Major-General Johann von Bubna and agent Sezyma Rasin. Both men vehemently attacked the Catholicism of the Emperor and urged Wallenstein to take the crown of Bohemia, which he refused. [94] But he went on to state:

> We who have the armies in our power negotiate and conclude; the others, even though 'tis not what they presently want, must accept and incline to. . . .
> The Emperor shall have naught to do with the matter, but we ourselves shall

---

[93] *Ibid.*, 458, 460; Wedgwood, *Thirty Years War*, pp. 329, 338, 351; *Cambridge Modern History*, IV, 223-229; Roberts, *Gustavus Adolphus* II, 418 (quote); Mann, *Wallenstein*, p. 74; Burckhardt, *Richelieu* II, 408-413.

[94] Wedgwood, *Thirty Years War*, p. 340; Elliott, *Olivares*, p. 460; Mann, *Wallenstein*, pp. 687-688.

direct all the business, and whatever 'tis that we do and direct, thus too it must remain.[95]

Wallenstein was not quite ready yet actually to try to overthrow the Emperor, but this conversation certainly showed him to be no longer (if he ever had been) the Emperor's loyal supporter.

In June 1633 Wallenstein took it upon himself to propose the repeal of the Edict of Restitution in his negotiations with Elector John George of Saxony. As soon as he heard of it, Emperor Ferdinand II explicitly overruled him, which must have rankled Wallenstein's proud heart. Wallenstein was now one of the wealthiest men in Christendom, distinguished neither for piety or loyalty, and guiding his wavering course by repeated horoscopes. No one trusted him; all men feared him. He could raise and lead larger armies than anyone else, even the Swedes, but the worsening state of his health prohibited him from leading his armies from the saddle. Some of his officers were loyal to him, but others he had reason to doubt; and his troops obeyed him only because he paid them more regularly than anyone else. No one could tell where and how he might jump. But Cardinal Richelieu knew what he wanted him to do. In June Wallenstein was presented with a draft treaty from France by which he would repudiate his master the Emperor and invade his lands, and in return be recognized by France as king of Bohemia. Wallenstein read Richelieu's draft treaty but made no response to it, nor did he pass it on to the Emperor.[96] The French ambassador admitted, in a letter to Richelieu:

> The Duke of Friedland's [Wallenstein's] game is too subtle for me. From his silence in the face of all that I have let him have, I can well guess what it is that he really desires, namely, strife between His Majesty and his allies. He is mistaken. His capers deprive him of the help with which the King, my master, and the whole union would be in a position to lend him against those whom he has most reason to fear and whom we also know to be his most dangerous enemies. With his methods he will neither regain their trust nor allay their jealousy and hatred.[97]

At this time Wallenstein and Marshal von Arnim of Saxony met and agreed upon a truce, to begin June 8. Wallenstein was in a foul mood. He snarled to von Arnim: "Does he [the Emperor] not know that my aversion to the scoundrels, these Jesuits, is such that I would Satan had long since taken the rogues! I have a mind to drive them all out of the Empire to the Devil!"[98]

Thus spoke the man who had been generally seen as the Catholic champion in the Thirty Years War.

---

[95] Mann, *Wallenstein*, p. 688.

[96] *Ibid.*, pp. 701-702; *Cambridge Modern History*, IV, 234-235.

[97] Mann, *Wallenstein*, p. 702.

[98] *Ibid.*, pp. 706-707 (quote); *Cambridge Modern History*, IV, 234; Burckhardt, *Richelieu* II, 417.

Duke Bernhard of Saxe-Weimar, now the principal Protestant general, was declared Duke of Franconia in June, but only by the Swedes, who had no real authority (other than that of the sword) to create dukes in Germany. In July the French ambassador promised again that Louis XIII of France would recognize Wallenstein as King of Bohemia if he betrayed his Emperor and fought against him. The annual Spanish treasure fleet from America arrived intact and Philip IV of Spain told Archduchess Isabel in the Netherlands that he would never agree to a truce there limited to Europe, nor suffer Dutch presence in the East or West Indies or Brazil. Cardinal-Prince Fernando planned a march against France and into Flanders, which Wallenstein strongly opposed. But the imperial government supported the march, and it was undertaken. Meanwhile Swedish Marshal Horn laid siege to the key fortress of Breisach on the upper Rhine. In August Wallenstein sent General Holk to Leipzig with 13,000 men to press his demands on the Saxons, but his army was destroyed by hunger and plague before it ever came to battle. A French army invaded Lorraine, a duchy bordering on France but considered part of the Empire, and the Elector of Trier, an imperial city, placed himself under French protection. Prince Frederick Henry of the Netherlands rejected any immediate truce there. A four-week truce was made between Saxony and Brandenburg, but signified little change in the overall situation. At the end of August Pope Urban VIII wrote to Richelieu condemning his subsidy to the Swedes, but still did not dare risk an open break with him, since he suspected that Richelieu intended schism if condemned by the Pope. Whether he was right in this decision, only those who never made or really imagined making such decisions are sure. It is worth noting that it was at this desperately troubled time that Pope Urban VIII was making his unjust decision in the Galileo case.[99]

The Spanish were sure he was wrong, and were very angry, as they had considerable reason to be. For years Cardinal Richelieu had been arming all their enemies, and more recently he had been chiefly responsible for preventing peace in Germany. The Spanish repeatedly jogged the Pope's conscience, and in December 1633 he gave the German Catholic League and Emperor Ferdinand II the enormous subsidy of 550,000 thalers, far more than any previous financial help he had given them. It was needed. The Swedes and many German Protestants were on the march again in Catholic Bavaria under Duke Bernhard of Saxe-Weimar, and Wallenstein was not concerned about Catholic Bavaria's fate, having long found himself bitterly at odds with its Duke Maximilian. Ignoring frantic appeals by Maximilian, he marched north instead, and fought the Swedes in Silesia, winning a battle against them at Steinau. But then he freed the old Bohemian rebel Count Thurn without ransom or penalty. Meanwhile the great city of Regensburg in northern Bavaria fell to the Protestants, who seized the Catholic cathedral and held their services in it. Wallenstein, probably aware that

---

[99] Wedgwood, *Thirty Years War*, pp. 340-341, 344, 387; *Cambridge Modern History* IV, 143, 229-230, 235; Israel, *Dutch in Hispanic World*, pp. 248, 299-301; Mann, *Wallenstein*, pp. 712-715, 717-718; Elliott, *Olivares*, p. 465; von Pastor, *History of the Popes* XXVIII, 324-325, XXIX, 60.

suspicion of him was growing in Vienna, marched for Regensburg late in November, but all the armies went into winter quarters in December without further conflict. Wallenstein ended his campaign against Duke Bernhard without result on December 4.[100]

Despite the relatively small victory at Steinau, Wallenstein had failed in Saxony, abandoned Bavaria, and had several times negotiated with the enemy without telling the Emperor. In December Emperor Ferdinand II appointed a secret commission, consisting of leading ministers Eggenburg and Trautmansdorff and Bishop Antonius of Vienna, to advise him what to do about Wallenstein. Another of the Emperor's principal Catholic advisors, Rev. Johannes Weingartner, S.J., in that same month made a public exhortation to the Emperor to dismiss Wallenstein, calling him insane, arrogant, vainglorious, and superstitious (he seems to have been sane, but all Father Weingartner's other adjectives apply). At the same time two other pamphlets widely circulated in Austria demanded Wallenstein's dismissal from command. And Duke Maximilian of Bavaria instructed his ambassador to Vienna to work with the Spanish to remove Wallenstein. The Spanish ambassador gave full support to the proposed removal. On the last day of the year 1633 Emperor Ferdinand II at last made up his mind to get rid of Wallenstein, though he was still not sure just how he was going to do it. On that same day Galileo went into house arrest near Florence.[101]

On January 1, 1634 a devious officer named Kinsky, veteran of twenty years of intrigue, wrote to the French ambassador the Marquis de Fouquières that Wallenstein was now ready to accept the French proposals made to him during the preceding year, and the Marquis replied that he would take steps to see that Wallenstein was given the opportunity. On January 3 General Ottavio Piccolomini, a German with an Italian name, told two of his colleagues that Wallenstein had told him he was going to hand his army over to the enemy, conquer the Habsburg hereditary lands in Austria, capture the Emperor, exterminate the Habsburg dynasty, and reorganize Europe, dividing up Italy, giving Luxemburg to France, Flanders independence, Silesia to Poland, and Moravia to his friend Count Trchka. It is hard to imagine Wallenstein announcing so many explosive treasons all at once to any of his generals, but he may have mentioned some of them, and Piccolomini may have improved on the story on the basis of his own imagination or hints Wallenstein had given him. On January 9 Wallenstein told the Spanish ambassador Quiroga that Spanish Cardinal-Prince Fernando could not get an army through Swedish-held Germany to the Spanish Netherlands, and he would not help him try, though Quiroga bore a writing of Emperor Ferdinand II giving his full support to the Cardinal-Prince's plans. On January 10 the imperial court was informed of Wallenstein's intent to

---

[100] *Cambridge Modern History* IV, 231-232, 237-238; Mann, *Wallenstein*, pp. 729-730, 737-738; von Pastor, *History of the Popes* XXVIII, 328.

[101] Wedgwood, *Thirty Years War*, pp. 344-345; *Cambridge Modern History* IV, 237, 240; Mann, *Wallenstein*, pp. 741-742, 754-755, 757-758, 760-761; von Pastor, *History of the Popes* XXIX, 59.

become king of Bohemia. Wallenstein now tried a last-minute ploy to secure the support of his principal officers (generals and colonels). He said he would resign unless they all signed a declaration of personal loyalty to him. After an emotional harangue, they all agreed to sign. It is called the Pilsen Oath (for the city where it was done.) The final draft of the Pilsen Oath contained no reference to continued loyal service to the Emperor.[102]

On January 24 the three-man secret commission on what to do about Wallenstein reported to the Emperor that he was a traitor and should be removed from command. The Emperor's confessor, Jesuit Father Lamormaini, concurred. The Emperor acted that very day to remove him, ordering him captured dead or alive, but temporarily kept the orders secret. General Piccolomini's political agent went to Vienna and secretly met the Spanish ambassador outside the walls of the city to discuss how to implement the Emperor's instructions before Wallenstein learned of them. On February 11 Piccolomini, now promoted to Field Marshal (an honor requested by Wallenstein, who considered Piccolomini his friend and supporter), returned to Pilsen. Gallas, the ranking general in the imperial army next to Wallenstein, issued a general order declaring Wallenstein's command vacant, and promptly left Pilsen to escape the fallout. On February 18 the Emperor publicly announced the dismissal of Wallenstein as a traitor, to be replaced by Gallas. He appointed a commission to confiscate all of Wallenstein's estates. The next day Wallenstein, "looking like a corpse," summoned his generals and colonels at Pilsen to his bedside and assured them he had no intention of abandoning the Catholic faith or undertaking anything against the Emperor. The next day he asked for a second oath of loyalty to himself, but this time several officers refused it, and the majority who agreed to take it qualified their commitment by saying they would stand by him only so long as he took no action against the Emperor. Wallenstein swore that he intended no such action, and sent an emissary to Eggenburg promising loyalty to the Emperor and offering peacefully to resign.[103]

But no one believed him any more. By February 22 all of his hard-won army but two regiments had left him. He fled from Pilsen toward Saxony, and possibly appealed to Protestant Duke Bernhard of Saxe-Weimar for help, but got none. Eggenburg refused in writing to receive him. On the 24th, Irish Colonel Butler pretended to give Wallenstein refuge at Eger in Bohemia, but only the more easily to capture and kill him. Butler ordered a splendid banquet for the next evening. His Irishmen surrounded the dining hall, then burst in and killed Wallenstein's three remaining generals after a considerable fight. Wallenstein had not come to the dinner, but was lying ill in bed. The killers broke into his room during a raging thunderstorm. Irish Captain Devereux dispatched his erstwhile commander-in-chief with a sword-slash from chest to abdomen. The huge Butler then picked up his body and tried to throw it out of the window in the

---

[102] Wedgwood, *Thirty Years War*, p. 345; *Cambridge Modern History* IV, 239-240; Mann, *Wallenstein*, pp. 761-762, 764-767, 769-770, 790-791.

[103] Wedgwood, *Thirty Years War*, pp. 345-347; *Cambridge Modern History* IV, 240-242; Mann, *Wallenstein*, pp. 796-797, 799, 802-803, 806, 808, 822, 820-824, 827.

Czech tradition of defenestration, but he was stopped by someone more merciful, and no further violence was done to the body.[104]

It was one of the most famous assassinations of history, and sealed the verdict of the Battle of Lützen, drawn because of Gustav Adolf's death. Wallenstein had earned the suspicion directed against him, but to this day it is not certain that he was actually guilty of treason, since he had never specifically agreed to any of the numerous treasons proposed to him. Because of his military power and wealth, the Emperor had not dared risk a public trial. But in those days the king had the right to take the sword in his own hand when the safety of the realm was at stake. Still one would have hoped to see from a Catholic Emperor a more orderly and just proceeding.

But now Wallenstein was dead, and there was no one to replace him. Without strong command on either side, the war drifted quickly into confusion and chaos, and increasingly hellish misery for the entire population of Germany. In the beginning, especially while Tilly lived, it had been a religious war; Gustav Adolf had always seen it as such; Emperor Ferdinand II and the Count-Duke of Olivares still thought of it so. But the Emperor had only three more years to live, and the ruin that Olivares had foreseen for himself and for Spain came upon them in six years. All the Catholic participants were ruined by this war, except Cardinal Richelieu. He had planned it so, and was now to get his wish.

In March 1634 Pope Urban VIII gathered another large sum from the Church in Italy, Sicily, and Portugal to aid the Habsburg cause. The Count-Duke of Olivares told the Spanish Council of State that France was very likely soon to enter the war, but he did not intend to give Richelieu any good excuse for doing so. In April Cardinal Richelieu more than doubled his financial support to the Dutch rebels under the condition that they would suspend all peace negotiations for the next eight months. Late that month, he refused to participate in a peace conference in Rome with the Pope and the Emperor. The evidence is overwhelming that Cardinal Richelieu wanted all the wars among Christians to continue as long as possible, weakening the Empire and Spain while he and France grew stronger.[105]

In July Richelieu proposed increasing the subsidy to the Swedes in Germany in return for control of the key fortress of Philippsburg on the Rhine for the duration of the war. On August 30 the Swedes turned it over to France, which promptly sent into it an army of 25,000 men, clearly much larger than needed just to hold the town. Meanwhile the Spanish Cardinal-Prince Fernando began his march northward from Milan into Germany. The German Protestant armies under Duke Bernhard of Saxe-Weimar joined Marshal Gustav Horn with 20,000 Swedes at Augsburg. While waiting for the Cardinal-Prince they further ravaged Catholic Bavaria, and on July 22 stormed the fortified city of Landshut.

---

[104] Wedgwood, *Thirty Years War*, pp. 347, 349; *Cambridge Modern History* IV, 242; Mann, *Wallenstein*, pp. 818, 826-827, 834-836, 838-844; Burckhardt, *Richelieu* II, 432; von Pastor, *History of the Popes* XXVIII, 329.

[105] *Cambridge Modern History* IV, 602; Elliott, *Olivares*, pp. 471-473; Israel, *Dutch in Hispanic World*, p. 304; von Pastor, *History of the Popes* XXVIII, 328, 339.

On September 2 Cardinal-Prince Fernando, a very capable general despite his religious vocation (which he took rather lightly), emerged from the Black Forest to join with the imperial army commanded by Crown Prince Ferdinand (the future Emperor Ferdinand III) to create a united force of 33,000, slightly larger than the number of their Protestant opponents.   Duke Bernhard gravely underestimated this Catholic army, which was exceptionally aggressive, and began cannonading the Protestant camp near the town of Nördlingen the day after the two portions of it joined.[106]

There followed on September 6 the Battle of Nördlingen, an unexpected triumph for the Catholics, which Gustav Adolf would never have allowed to happen if he had still been in command. Two Swedish infantry brigades fired on each other, a large part of the Swedish store of gunpowder blew up, the Swedish cavalry became separated from the infantry, and 15 Swedish charges were repulsed in succession by the rock-hard Spanish infantry, still the best soldiers in the world. Marshal Horn finally ordered a retreat after 17,000 of his men were killed, well over half his army. Four thousand more, including Marshal Horn himself, were captured, while Duke Bernhard fled with his surviving Germans no less than 150 miles to escape the relentless Spanish pursuit. The entire Protestant baggage train was taken, including 4,000 wagons, 1,200 spare horses, 6,000 prisoners, and all their artillery.   The Cardinal-Prince marched on to the Netherlands, leaving behind the wreck of Swedish military prestige. As a result of this battle the Swedes could no longer dominate Germany, and Cardinal Richelieu could no longer prevent a Catholic victory by paying them money. Now he would have to bring French troops into action, and before the month of September had ended, that is what he had decided to do. Meanwhile the Catholic victory resulted in the full restoration of the Faith in southern Germany, and Pope Urban VIII held a solemn thanksgiving ceremony at St. Peter's in Rome.[107]

In October 1634 Swedish Chancellor and regent Axel Oxenstierna and the council of the Heilbronn Protestant league had to move their headquarters from Frankfurt to Mainz, as Frankfurt was now threatened by the imperial army. The unpaid troops of Duke Bernhard of Saxe-Weimar—both sides in Germany were using a larger and larger percentages of mercenaries in their armies—ravaged the Palatinate, Protestant at the beginning of the war, now for some years Catholic under Duke Maximilian. At the end of October Emperor Ferdinand II signed an offensive and defensive alliance with Spain, which was kept secret at first. Early in November Cardinal-Prince Fernando forced his way through all opposition and arrived at Brussels in triumph. But Cardinal Richelieu would not permit a Catholic victory.[108]

---

[106] Wedgwood, *Thirty Years War*, pp. 358-363; *Cambridge Modern History* IV, 244, 246; Elliott, *Olivares*, p. 480; Burckhardt, *Richelieu* II, 439.

[107] Wedgwood, *Thirty Years War*, pp. 364-370; *Cambridge Modern History* IV, 245; Burckhardt, *Richelieu* II, 444; III, 64-65; Elliott, *Olivares*, pp. 482-482, 484; von Pastor, *History of the Popes* XXVIII, 334-336.

[108] *Cambridge Modern History* IV, 247; Elliott, *Olivares*. p. 482.

In December he sent a French army to relieve the siege of Heidelberg in the Palatinate by Duke Maximilian of Bavaria. The French were fresh and unbloodied, while the besieging soldiers were exhausted by years of fruitless fighting. Within days the French took Heidelberg from its Protestant defenders and drove off its Catholic attackers. Now it belonged to France.[109]

The vision of a Catholic victory in Germany and the future of Christendom if it should be won, held by the Count-Duke of Olivares in Spain whose soldiers had shed their blood for it at Nördlingen, is described by his biographer:

> His vision was of a Christendom—for the time being religiously divided, but not, he hoped, forever—rejoicing in all the benefits of a *pax austriaca*. This *pax* would be guaranteed by the power of the king of Spain, acting in close collaboration with the Emperor and a Pope who placed the interests of the church above his own narrowly temporal concerns. Richelieu, although a cardinal of the church, had deliberately set out to wreck this noble vision. Since attaining power he had done nothing but challenge the legitimate rights of the House of Austria, aiding and abetting rebels and heretics whose overriding purpose was to destroy the power of Spain.[110]

So strong were the religious feelings invested in this war, despite the growing lack of loyalty to the religious alignment by some of the commanders and especially by Cardinal Richelieu, that in February 1635 it was first proposed that the Netherlands be permanently divided along religious lines into a Catholic south (Belgium) and a Calvinist north. Cardinal Richelieu prepared a new treaty that month between France and the Netherlands, to fight the Spanish there, and offered the Dutch 30,000 troops, which they promptly accepted. In Germany, on the other hand, a truce was made between the Emperor and Saxony which became a general peace, the Peace of Prague. The Palatinate was not to be restored to Elector Frederick's descendants, but the Edict of Restitution was no longer to be applied against Lutherans, except that the Emperor could still do so in his own lands. All formerly ecclesiastical lands were to remain for forty years in the hands of those who held them in November 1627. Both parties were now committed to fight against both French and Swedes. It was clear to any rational German that with Richelieu's France on the verge of massive intervention, the greatest danger to Germany lay there.[111]

At the end of March the Spanish had conveniently provided Cardinal Richelieu with an excuse for war, by marching from Luxembourg into nearby Trier, whose Elector-Bishop had turned it over to the French, totally without warrant from his people or the imperial government. The Spanish carried the

---

[109] *Cambridge Modern History* IV, 249; Burckhardt, *Richelieu* III, 55-56; Elliott, *Olivares*, p. 486; von Pastor, *History of the Popes* XXVIII, 337.

[110] Elliott, *Olivares*, p. 488.

[111] Wedgwood, *Thirty Years War*, pp. 379-382; *Cambridge Modern History* IV, 144, 252-254, 697; Geyl, *Netherlands in the 17th Century* I, 109-110, 117; Burckhardt, *Richelieu* III, 62; Mann, *Wallenstein*, pp. 873-874; von Pastor, *History of the Popes* XXVIII, 337-338.

turncoat elector off as a prisoner, but Richelieu could now claim that French territory had been invaded. He lost no time. In Switzerland he sent a French Calvinist officer to occupy the strategic Valtelline Pass and override its Catholic population, thereby cutting off the easiest road north for the Spanish army and their supplies. Just a month later he and Chancellor Oxenstierna of Sweden signed the Treaty of Compiègne establishing a full alliance between Catholic France and Protestant Sweden, with neither to make peace without the other's consent. The Swedes were to retain Worms and Mainz, the French to get the whole left bank of the Rhine from Breisach to Strasbourg. The Swedes agreed that they would allow the Catholic faith to be practiced wherever it had been in 1618—not subsequently. This slight Catholic gesture of Cardinal Richelieu probably was made because of significant continuing opposition he faced in France from those who, unlike him, put their faith first. Then on May 19, just two weeks before the Peace of Prague was published, France declared war on Spain, "now openly challenging Spain for primacy in Europe."[112] In the words of King Philip IV of Spain:

> The King of France, defying God, law and nature, has opened hostilities against me . . . At a time when I was attempting to rein in the heretics, he has gone to war with me, without challenge or warning, in support of heresy.[113]

That was the simple truth, unfashionable as it may be (because of the strongly anti-Spanish attitude of so many historians, even great ones like Ludwig von Pastor) to say it.

The French armies were first in the field on a large scale in the Netherlands. In June 1635 French and Dutch armies totalling 60,000 men approached Brussels, sacking Belgian Catholic towns. They surrounded Louvain, home of one of the great Catholic universities of the world. But the Spanish and the Belgians stood fast, and the French and Dutch retreated as quickly as they had come. In July Cardinal Richelieu sent 60,000 more livres in subsidy to the Protestant General Duke Bernhard of Saxe-Weimar in addition to 12,000 livres he had already paid to him earlier in the year. The Spanish treasure fleet, storm-delayed but intact, reached Cádiz in June, and a month later the Cortes of Castile voted a subsidy of 9 million ducats over three years to the King and Olivares' government. Near the end of the month, Cardinal-Prince Fernando took the great Dutch fortress of Schenkenschans on the German border in a daring night attack. In August all major German princes and the larger free cities accepted the Peace of Prague. Pope Urban VIII, about to create new cardinals and angry at Richelieu's continued pressure on him to make his ally the Capuchin Father

---

[112] Wedgwood, *Thirty Years War*, p. 381; *Cambridge Modern History* IV, 144, 251; Burckhardt, *Richelieu* III, 62-63, 70-71, 184; Elliott, *Olivares*, pp. 486, 492 (quote); von Pastor, *History of the Popes* XXVIII, 338.

[113] Elliott, *Olivares*, p. 488.

Joseph a cardinal, told Richelieu he would never do so.[114] His reputation of being pro-French does not stand up under close historical examination, but he was never willing to risk condemning Cardinal Richelieu and then seeing him take France out of the Church as Henry VIII had taken England out of the Church. But he did sharply object when Cardinal Archbishop La Valette of Toulouse commanded an army invading Catholic territories in Germany.[115]

In late October 1635, by the Treaty of St.-Germain-en-Laye, Cardinal Richelieu promised to provide a regular subsidy of 4 million livres annually to the Protestant army of Duke Bernhard, which was to make no peace without his approval. He also pledged 12,000 foot and 6,000 horse to campaign in Germany against the Catholics. In March 1636 the much-tried Emperor Ferdinand II finally declared war on France, which was invading his territories and subsidizing his enemies. In April Swedish regent Axel Oxenstierna left Germany, never to return; he no longer saw a future for Sweden in that devastated land. Prince Frederick Henry recovered for the Dutch Protestants the fortress of Schenkenschans on the German border that had been so boldly taken from them, while the Cardinal-Prince Fernando now invaded France from Belgium. Both France and Spain now had about 150,000 men under arms; they were evenly matched. Though French opposition, popular as well as military, slowed and finally stopped the Cardinal-Prince's army on the road to Paris, in September the Spanish successfully accomplished their largest troop-ferrying operation of the war, bringing 4,000 infantry and 1,500,000 ducats of silver in 38 ships past the Dutch blockading fleet. The Spanish treasure fleet for 1636 arrived safely, but only furnished 400,000 ducats for the royal treasury, hardly more than a quarter of the treasure sent to the Netherlands. Spain was being asked to give more than she had.[116]

At the end of December Archduke (Crown Prince) Ferdinand of the Habsburgs was elected King of the Romans, placing him firmly in position to succeed his aging father, who died a tranquil and holy Catholic death on February 15, 1637.[117] He had made a mighty effort to restore Catholicism throughout Germany and reunite it under his authority, but the complexity of German politics, the riches of Richelieu, the military genius of Gustav Adolf of Sweden, and the probable treason of Wallenstein had frustrated him. The attempt was never to be made again.

In October 1637 the Dutch under Prince Frederick Henry recaptured the important city of Breda from the Spanish after twelve years of Spanish

---

[114] *Ibid.*, pp. 485, 492-493, 499, 502; Israel, *Dutch in the Hispanic World*, pp. 252-253; *Cambridge Modern History* IV, 254-255, 365; Burckhardt, *Richelieu* III, 170; von Pastor, *History of the Popes* XXVIII, 401.

[115] Von Pastor, *History of the Popes* XXVIII, 402.

[116] Wedgwood, *Thirty Years War*, p. 391; *Cambridge Modern History* IV, 368-370, 698; Burckhardt, *Richelieu* III, 170-171, 174, 337; Elliott, *Olivares*, pp. 504-505, 509, 517, 520-521; Israel, *Dutch in Hispanic World*, pp. 265-266.

[117] Wedgwood, *Thirty Years War*, pp. 396-398; *Cambridge Modern History* IV, 372-373; von Pastor, *History of the Popes* XXVIII, 356-357.

occupation, forcing Spain to rush more troops into the Netherlands sinkhole. On December 8 a new Jesuit confessor to king Louis XIII of France, Father Nicholas Caussin, finally told him directly that it was his obligation as a Catholic king to make peace, not war in Germany and the Netherlands. That very day Cardinal Richelieu found out what Father Caussin had advised the king, and instantly told the king that he must choose between Father Caussin and himself. Throughout all his reign after he began ruling apart from his mother, the weak Louis XIII had been under Richelieu's shadow. He could not imagine governing without him. Just two days later he banished Father Caussin to Brittany.[118]

Yet at this very moment, and for some years before, a man had been working in France to bring the Calvinists of the central mountain mass of France back to the Catholic Faith, and was having astonishing success. He was hardly a man whom Cardinal Richelieu would have deigned to notice, for his apostolate was to the poor and unlearned of the mountains of Vivarais and the Central Massif, some of the most remote and forgotten areas of France. But he blazed a trail of ardor and love through the darkness, and France and the Church have never forgotten him. He was St. John Francis Regis.[119]

In November 1634 he was professed in the Jesuit order, his Jesuit superior having stated: "I cannot estimate the great number of conversions that have been effected as well by the rare example of his life as by the power of his discourses—a thing that has made him already regarded as the apostle of Vivarais. He is a holy missionary who breathes nothing but the glory of God and the salvation of souls."[120] In January 1635, with just one companion, he began work in the high cold region called the Upper Boutières. In September of that year he was sent by his bishop to the small city of Privas, a hotbed of Calvinism. In the winter of 1636, working in some of the most severe climatic conditions in France, he evangelized the town of St. Agrève, 4,000 feet high and full of Calvinists, converting many of them to the Catholic Faith. (By St. Regis' time, many French Calvinists were already second or third generation.) Vast crowds assembled in the mountains for his sermons in Lent and for Holy Week in 1636. In April he went to Le Puy, and by summer had filled the cathedral in what had been mostly a Calvinist area. The next winter he was back in country where no man would travel in winter except in case of absolute necessity, in the highest parts of the Cévennes, where the cold wind blew with such vehemence that great stones held down the roofs, and the town's cross had to be secured with guy ropes. On one occasion St. Regis became lost in the terrible cold and did not reach shelter until after midnight.[121] He seemed indestructible; but in truth he was expending his very life to help these people, whom the world had shunned or

---

[118] *Cambridge Modern History* IV, 698-699; Burckhardt, *Richelieu* III, 194, 244-245; Elliott, *Olivares*, p. 524; Israel, *Dutch in the Hispanic World*, p. 258; von Pastor, *History of the Popes* XXVIII, 389-391.

[119] Albert S. Foley, S.J., *St. Regis, a Social Crusader* (Milwaukee, 1941), pp. 63-73.

[120] *Ibid.*, pp. 61, 78 (quote).

[121] *Ibid.*, pp. 91-94, 99, 103-110, 115-118, 140-143.

ignored, but who were precious to God. In February 1639 his superior Father Arnoux, rector of the Jesuit college at Le Puy, wrote of him:

> Father Regis conducts public catechism classes in the church that is called Saint-Pierre-du-Monastier, to the admiration of all, and with an almost incredible success. In fact, one could see every Sunday for the past two years, save for Lent and Advent, five thousand persons of both sexes and of all conditions packed in there, filling not only the nave, which is very vast, but also numerous tribunes and the temporary seats that were of necessity constructed; and even under the portico and at all entrances, heads were held cocked to hear him. I add that he is an obedient religious and that he is commonly called a saint.[122]

And a saint he was. In December 1640, two days before Christmas, carrying on his winter apostolate in the mountains, he became lost in the woods and had to spend a very cold night in a deserted hut. He never recovered from the physical effects of that night. His reserves of strength were gone. On the last night of the year, he died at Lalouvesc in the mountains.[123]

For all that Cardinal Richelieu had done and would do, France was still Catholic.

In 1638 in Germany the well-subsidized Duke Bernhard of Saxe-Weimar was carrying all before him, there being few if any good imperial generals left. But by now Germany had been so despoiled that new conquests benefited neither side, only imposing an additional burden. In 1638 Bernhard laid siege to the key fortress of Breisach on the Rhine, said to be impregnable. In July he was joined by a French army, and in December he took it. The Spanish government was furious with Cardinal-Prince Fernando for not having saved it, but in view of dwindling financial support from over-committed Spain and a stream of contradictory orders from Madrid, he had little chance of intervening effectively in the siege. Count-Duke Olivares declared that the capture of Breisach would make the French masters of the world, unless quick action were taken against them in the year 1639. But by May of that year Cardinal-Prince Fernando was still being starved of men and money. The treasure fleet of 1638 had not yet reached Spain, having been forced to winter at Veracruz because of the numerous Dutch ships in the Caribbean. The Spanish Council of State met, and recommended another Spanish invasion of France. But it was the French who invaded Spain instead, in Catalonia, forestalling any Spanish invasion, while a great Spanish fleet of about a hundred ships was met by Dutch Admiral Van Tromp in the Downs under the cliffs of Dover. These were British waters, but they were openly violated. A destructive storm followed the battle. The Spanish lost no less than 70 ships including nine galleons. It was the end of Spain as a

---

[122] *Ibid.*, p. 180.
[123] *Ibid.*, pp. 240-250.

leading sea power. The usually optimistic Count-Duke of Olivares described the naval disaster as "irreparable."[124]

The Spanish were temporarily successful in repelling the French invasion of Catalonia, but quartered their troops extensively in Catalan homes. The people of that ever-restless province rose in a massive revolt in May 1640, crying "Vengeance and Liberty!" Before the month was over the rebels had seized Barcelona. The Spanish Viceroy Santa Coloma was killed and the *corts* sided with the insurgents. The Count-Duke of Olivares raised a new Castilian army. But the treasure fleet for 1640 had not yet come in, and no one knew when or if it would; the Count of Oñate presented a paper to the Council of State declaring in no uncertain terms that it was absolutely impossible for Spain to carry on wars in Germany, the Netherlands, and Catalonia all at the same time. The Count-Duke at last agreed to begin specific peace negotiations with the Dutch, seeking peace at almost any price; but the Dutch, sensing victory, were not dealing. The Catalans appealed for help to Cardinal Richelieu, who was only too glad to supply it. On October 31 he put all the French troops in Languedoc on special alert for action in Catalonia, and in December signed a formal treaty of alliance with the Catalans. Then came the crowning blow. Portugal, once independent, but for sixty years ruled by the Spanish king, also rose in revolt. The Spanish Viceroy Vasconcelos was murdered, like his counterpart in Catalonia, and the Duke of Braganza, of the former Portuguese royal family, was proclaimed King John IV. Count-Duke Olivares of Spain and his government were taken totally by surprise. Facing the almost complete exhaustion of her funds and major rebellion in two of her richest provinces in the Iberian peninsula itself, Spain's days as the world's greatest power were over. Meanwhile the German Protestant commander, Duke Bernhard of Saxe-Weimar, the best general left in the Thirty Years War, had turned on his erstwhile allies the Swedes, encouraged by Cardinal Richelieu, who wanted as much fragmentation in Germany as possible, though he disliked Duke Bernhard's independent spirit. Then the Duke suddenly died in July 1639, just 35 years old, leaving a void that no one could fill. The French government assumed responsibility for the pay of his many mercenaries, and their officers were guaranteed rank, positions and estates if they would swear fealty to France. French officers took command of the army, and henceforth the only effective armies in Germany were the French.[125]

So by the epochal year 1640 France had replaced Spain as the world's leading power, which had been Richelieu's objective throughout his career as chief minister of France. The people of Spain suffered severe privation, and the

---

[124] Wedgwood, *Thirty Years War*, pp. 299-301, 405-407m 413-414; *Cambridge Modern History* IV, 375-377, 645-646, 700-701; Burckhardt, *Richelieu* III, 194-197, 199-201, 207-210; Elliott, *Olivares*, pp. 542-543, 546, 550; Israel, *Dutch in Hispanic World*, pp. 269-270; Geyl, *Netherlands in the 17th Century* I, 125-126; von Pastor, *History of the Popes* XXVIII, 359.

[125] Wedgwood, *Thirty Years War*, pp. 410-413; *Cambridge Modern History* IV, 380-383; Burckhardt, *Richelieu* III, 119-122, 313; Israel, *Dutch in the Hispanic World*, pp. 313-314.

people of Germany suffered mayhem and devastation of every kind, to feed the Cardinal's ambition as it reached its goal. Neither Spain nor Germany would recover for 150 years. The politically foreseeable future belonged to France—and perhaps also to its ancient rival England, whose maritime enterprises flourished as those of Spain declined. But by 1640 England was caught in its historic struggle between king and Parliament, signalized by the convening in November of the Long Parliament, which eventually overthrew and killed the king and was in turn overthrown by Oliver Cromwell.

We must therefore conclude this chapter with a brief account of how England reached this point of collision between its royal executive and its national legislature in the fall of 1640. Though the subject of a vast bibliography, the English Civil War and its preliminaries and consequences are of only limited interest to the Catholic historian, since one of the few things all the major participants in the English Civil War agreed on was total condemnation of the Catholic Faith. A favorite form of attack on King Charles I was to call him pro-Catholic because he supported the ceremonious Anglican liturgy and vestments favored by his appointee Archbishop Laud of Canterbury,[126] had a French Catholic Queen, and disliked Calvinists, who in England were called "Puritans" because their alleged goal was to "purify" Anglican worship of Catholic remnants. Actually Charles I was not pro-Catholic; there was not a Catholic side in the controversy, though the Puritans developed into true Calvinist revolutionaries during it, and the Catholics would always support the king rather than the Puritans, since they had no other choice.

England had stayed out of the Thirty Years War. King James I hated war, and would not engage in it even to save the ancestral lands of his son-in-law, Elector Frederick of the Palatinate, though he allowed some two thousand English volunteers to go to his aid uselessly.[127] In November 1624, after a madcap adventure in Spain trying to woo Philip IV's sister, Charles was betrothed to Prince Henrietta Marie of France, a strong Catholic. The proposed Spanish marriage left bitter memories in Parliament. James I died in April 1625 and was smoothly succeeded by Charles, who was already running the government.[128]

In 1627 Cardinal Richelieu's laid siege to La Rochelle. The English attempted to save it by an expedition commanded by the royal favorite the Duke of Buckingham, but he had to withdraw, losing more than half his men due to battle, capture, and disease. Charles I's third Parliament met in March 1628, with the Duke of Buckingham clamoring for money for another expedition to La Rochelle, which was still holding out, to retrieve his reputation. Parliament was

---

[126] Laud was appointed Archbishop of Canterbury in August 1633 (*Cambridge Modern History* IV, 279).

[127] David H. Willson, *King James VI and I* (New York, 1956), pp. 414-416; Wedgwood, *Thirty Years War*, p. 120.

[128] Von Pastor, *History of the Popes* XXVII, 176, 178, 183-184, 187-188, 191, 194-195; Elliott, *Olivares*, pp. 147, 209-210, 213-214, 217; Wedgwood, *Thirty Years War*, p. 191; *Cambridge Modern History* IV, 641.

lukewarm toward the venture. Eventually, on motion of the highly respected Sir Edward Coke, it did approve much of the king's financial request, but only after he promised no longer to imprison persons failing to make forced loans. In May Coke introduced a bill of grievances against the king which came to be called the Petition of Right. It condemned forced loans, arbitrary imprisonment, the quartering of troops in private homes, and the abuse of martial law by the King's government. On June 7 both houses of Parliament passed the Petition of Right, and after some hesitation Charles signed it, but then repudiated it as he dissolved Parliament in early July 1628. Showing that he was by no means as pro-Catholic as some alleged then and since, in August Charles proclaimed the detention of all Jesuits and strict punishment of those who might receive and aid them. Then on September 2 the Duke of Buckingham was spectacularly assassinated by a man named John Felton in Portsmouth, as he was about to embark on his second expedition for the relief of Protestant La Rochelle. He had no successor as royal favorite.[129]

A young man in his twenties was a little-noticed member of this turbulent Parliament, later to be one of the dominant personalities of English history. His name was Oliver Cromwell, and he was a direct descendant of Thomas Cromwell's sister.[130]

In December 1628 Charles I, in his capacity as head of the Church of England, issued a Declaration on Religion directing all clergymen to promote uniformity and prevent disputes in the Anglican church, hold a literal belief in the Anglican 39 articles of doctrine, accept the existence and authority of bishops and royal supremacy. At the end of January Parliament was called back into session. Sir John Eliot spoke in favor of making the Declaration on Religion more Calvinist. In March 1629 the House passed Eliot's resolutions against Bishop William Laud and his followers who sought to make the Church of England more ceremonious, and against the supporters of a tax called "tonnage and poundage" that was being administered by the king even though never voted by Parliament. A raging Charles stood ready to dissolve Parliament again, but the Speaker was forcibly held in his chair until the resolutions were passed. Then it was dissolved. Just a month later the Peace of Susa ended the English war with France. The French Queen had to accept the exclusion of most of her Catholic entourage, in return for England's ceasing to help the Calvinists in France.[131]

Charles I now decided to rule on his own, without Parliament which had caused him so much trouble. He was able to do this during a time of peace, needing no extraordinary appropriations and able to meet the normal peacetime

---

[129] *Cambridge Modern History* IV, 132-133, 269-272; Conrad Russell, *Parliaments and English Politics 1621-9* (Oxford, 1979), pp. 329-330, 340-341, 344, 360-361, 377, 383, 401; Kevin Sharpe, *The Personal Rule of Charles I* (New Haven CT, 1992), p. 301; Burckhardt, *Richelieu* I, 179-180, 190-191, 205.

[130] Antonia Fraser, *Cromwell, the Lord Protector* (New York, 1973), pp. 7-8, 30-36.

[131] *Cambridge Modern History* IV, 134, 273-275; Conrad Russell, *The Fall of the British Monarchies* (Oxford, 1991), pp. 15-16; Russell, *Parliaments and English Politics 1621-9*, pp. 406, 415-416.

expenses of government with revenue he could raise by means that arguably did not require the approval of Parliament. Sir John Eliot was imprisoned for the rest of his life in January 1630 for his defiance of the king in Parliament. In 1634 Charles I issued his first "ship money" writs, collecting money for expansion of the navy without the consent of Parliament. Also in this year he visited Scotland for the first time in his reign, and ordered that the full Laudian ceremony be instituted at Holyrood Chapel.[132]

In Scotland, where John Knox had abolished bishops, episcopacy was alien as well as contrary to Calvinist doctrine. When a bishop attempted to preside over a Laudian ceremony in Edinburgh's St. Giles Cathedral, a woman of the people named Jenny Geddes threw a stool at him. The Scots never thought of Charles I as one of themselves. A baby when his father went to England as its king, brought up entirely in England, having made only a few visits to Scotland in his lifetime and only one as king, he was to the Scots, though biologically one of them, an English stranger. They would not tolerate his English church and the government of a ruler who called himself head of their church and would try to change their religion. In March the Protestant clergy of Edinburgh drafted and signed the Scottish National Covenant, which defined the Christian faith in strictly Calvinistic terms, excluding more moderate Protestants as well as the much-execrated Catholics. While affirming their "dread sovereign, the King's Majesty," this unique document sharply limited his sovereignty by declaring that the Scottish people would only support him "in the defense and preservation of the aforesaid true religion, liberties, and laws of the kingdom."[133] The Covenant was extraordinarily popular, seen as an almost Biblical commitment of the whole Scottish nation to God; there were "Covenanters" in Scotland for the rest of the seventeenth century. John Knox had been the most revolutionary of all the Calvinist leaders in Europe,[134] and his mark was still on the people he had converted to Calvinism.

In May Charles I appointed the Marquis of Hamilton to negotiate with the Covenanters, but had no faith in his prospects for success. More and more Scotsmen were signing the Covenant. In June King Charles declared to Hamilton: "I expect not anything can rescue that people but only force . . . I give you leave to flatter them with what hopes you please . . . till I be ready to suppress them . . . I would rather die than yield to these impertinent and damnable demands." Thus Charles displayed that fatal stubbornness which was ultimately to bring him to the execution block. But he did withdraw the English liturgy from Scotland and allowed the convening of the Scottish Parliament and the General Assembly of its Calvinist church, the Kirk. It met in November, condemning episcopacy and vestments and excommunicating all the bishops of Scotland, was dissolved by Hamilton in the king's name, but continued to meet

---

[132] *Cambridge Modern History* IV, 281-282; C. V. Wedgwood, *The King's Peace, 1637-1641* (New York, 1955), p. 114.

[133] Wedgwood, *King's Peace*, pp. 198-199, 206-207; Russell, *Fall of the British Monarchies*, pp. 52-53 (quotes on 53).

[134] See Chapter 5, above.

for three more weeks in defiance of the King. Charles I annulled all its acts and officially declared Scotland to be in rebellion.[135]

There followed in 1639 what has been called the First Bishops' War. The Covenanters, took Edinburgh and Stirling Castles and the crown jewels. The garrison of the port city of Dumbarton opened its gates to them. A few days later they took Aberdeen, with Huntly, the Catholic lord of the Gordons, retiring from the city while Charles I entered York to take command of his army. But Charles I had very little military experience, and no resources sufficient to overcome a country as determined in its opposition to him as Scotland. He had not called a Parliament in ten years and had almost no financial reserves. His impoverished treasury could not bear the cost of the war with Scotland. For the Scots, this was emphatically a religious war; but for most English soldiers, it was nothing of the kind. At the end of spring 1639 Charles signed the Pacification of Berwick, which called for the disbanding of both armies, with religious and political matters in dispute to be put before the Kirk Assembly and the Scottish Parliament, which Charles had earlier dismissed in anger.[136]

When the Kirk Assembly met in August, it re-enacted most of the acts it had tried to pass the previous year, including the abolition of episcopacy, and demanded to meet annually, which Charles would not agree to. In September the Scottish Parliament convened with a Covenanting majority, and Charles dissolved it in November. The next month, Charles I and his councillors decided on renewed war with Scotland, despite the evidence of the First Bishops' War that England was unlikely to prevail. Now it was imperative that he obtain funding for the war from Parliament. He called the first session of Parliament since 1629 to meet in April, the so-called "Short Parliament." Soon after it convened it called for a new investigation of the merchant John Hampden's case against "ship money" and also an inquiry into the imprisonment of four members of Parliament. Meanwhile the House of Commons refused to take up any taxation bill. Charles tried to take the initiative by appearing in person before the House of Lords to ask their help, but he was politically outmaneuvered by John Pym, a master parliamentarian and committed enemy of the king. On May 9 Pym carried a series of motions condemning all images, crucifixes, and even simple crosses. May Day rioters in London tried to destroy the house of Archbishop Laud, who fled from the city. With the concurrence of the majority of his council but not of his chief minister Lord Strafford, Charles dissolved the Short Parliament in mid-May, because it had refused to vote the king money and had attacked his religious policy. Rioters broke open several of the prisons of London and a judge charged them with treason.[137]

---

[135] Wedgwood, *King's Peace*, pp. 212-215, 218 (quote), 229; Russell, *Fall of the British Monarchies*, p. 57.

[136] Wedgwood, *King's Peace*, pp. 261-262, 276-277.

[137] *Ibid.*, pp. 292-295, 303-304, 322-326, 330-331; *Cambridge Modern History* IV, 284-285; Russell, *Fall of the British Monarchies*, pp. 92, 110-115, 121-122, 129. John Pym was perhaps the most brilliant Parliamentary strategist in English history. Born in 1584, old enough to remember the defeat of the Spanish Armada, he served in every

In June the Scottish Parliament met without Charles I's authorization. In England ship money collections virtually ceased as many refused to pay. The Convocation of the English Church, in conjunction with the King, issued a statement harshly critical of the Puritans. Rebellion was in the air, with mostly Puritans threatening it. The second campaign aimed at Scotland, the Second Bishops' War, was more ineffective even than the first had been; the Scots struck before the English, invading England before Charles I could lead his army north. When he did he was met in England not Scotland, at Newburn on the Tyne River near Newcastle, by Alexander Leslie, the Scots general who had gained experience as a mercenary commander in the Thirty Years War. The Scots won the battle and took Newcastle. At the same time, early in September, twelve lords (some directly in collusion with the Scots) signed a petition in London complaining against the war with Scotland, what the petition called innovation in religion, insufficient repression of Catholics, a report (false when the petition was issued) that Catholic Irish troops would be used by the king against his English and Scottish people, and calling for another Parliament to meet immediately. A few days later the victorious Scots presented their peace terms to the King: royal confirmation of all the acts of their last Parliament, including the abolition of bishops; Scottish control of Edinburgh Castle; dropping all punishment for signing the Covenant and allowing Scots living in England to sign it; and the English to pay for damages done to Scotland by the two Bishops' Wars.[138]

Charles I would not accept these terms as first presented, but realized that he had not the power to reject them out of hand as he undoubtedly wished to do. He called a special "Great Council" at York to advise him, appointed commissioners to negotiate with the Scots, and agreed to convene a new Parliament. The rumor about Irish troops coming finally gained substance when late in October the Earl of Strafford (who had been Charles' minister Thomas Wentworth, now governor of Ireland) offered to bring his Irish army to Great Britain in just two days if provided with shipping. Though his offer was not accepted by the beleaguered king, it became public knowledge.[139]

At the beginning of November Charles I made another peace with the Scots, the Treaty of Ripon, with the Scots to hold the northern six counties of England until all hostilities ended.[140] On November 13 Parliament reconvened. In its first few days the astute John Pym began a virulent attack on Strafford which eventually led to his impeachment, conviction and execution. Archbishop

---

English Parliament from 1621 to his death in 1643, and was the person principally responsible for the sundering of English government that led to the civil war. See biographies by C. E. Wade (London, 1912) and William W. Macdonald (New York, 1981).

[138] Wedgwood, *King's Peace*, pp. 341, 344-349; Russell, *Fall of the British Monarchies*, pp. 132-138, 143-146, 149-151, 156-157.

[139] *Cambridge Modern History* IV, 285; Wedgwood, *King's Peace*, p. 354; Russell, *Fall of the British Monarchies*, pp. 157, 162.

[140] *Cambridge Modern History* IV, 285; Wedgwood, *King's Peace*, p. 355; Russell, *Fall of the British Monarchies*, p. 162

Laud was also impeached before the year was out. This is known to history as the Long Parliament, and was to sit for no less than twelve and a half years, to lead a rebellion against King Charles I and cut off his head.

11
Christendom Cloven
1640-1661
Popes Urban VIII (1623-1644), Innocent X (1644-1655), and Alexander VII (1655-1667)

"The agreements and decisions arrived at Osnabrück and Münster [ending the Thirty Years War in Germany], the document [a brief of Pope Innocent X] states, have given great pain to the Pope because they gravely curtail and injure the Catholic religion and its exercise, the Apostolic See, the Roman Church and its subordinate churches, the ecclesiastical state, the jurisdiction, liberties, privileges, possessions, goods and rights of the Catholic Church. They surrender for all time to the heretics and their successors the property of the Church seized by them."—Pope Innocent X, November 26, 1648[1]

"Let me see a legal authority warranted by the Word of God, the Scriptures, or warranted by the constitution of the kingdom [England] and I will answer. . . . There is a God in Heaven, that will call you, and all that give you power, to account."—King Charles I of England and Scotland at his trial, January 30, 1649[2]

"You are part of Antichrist, whose kingdom . . . should be laid in blood. . . . I shall not, where I have power, and the Lord is pleased to bless me, suffer the exercise of the Mass . . . nor suffer you that are Papists, where I can find you seducing the people or by any overt act violating the laws established; but if you come into my hands, I shall cause to be inflicted the punishments appointed."—Oliver Cromwell to the bishops of Ireland, January 1650[3]

"I leave my soul to God, my service to my prince, my good will to my friends, my love and charity to you all."—the Earl of Montrose, Scotland from the scaffold, May 31, 1650[4]

"Never forget [that] the memory of these slaughtered jewels . . . the defense and safety of Catholics, the vindication of the Roman religion, the enlarging

---

[1] Ludwig von Pastor, *History of the Popes* (St. Louis MO, 1952) XXX, 130-131.
[2] C. V. Wedgwood, *A Coffin for King Charles* (New York, 1964), pp. 151-152.
[3] D. M. R. Esson, *The Curse of Cromwell; a History of the Ironside Conquest of Ireland, 1649-53* (London, 1971), p. 131.
[4] C. V. Wedgwood, *Montrose* (London, 1952), pp. 153-154.

of your friends' and allies' endurance, is justifiable before God and man."—
Owen Roe O'Neill of Ireland to his soldiers, November 1, 1647[5]

By 1643 the verdict of the Thirty Years' War was in. Cardinal Richelieu
lay in his grave,[6] but he had won. Spain was in decline and Germany was
shattered. France was now the greatest power in the world. The infantry *tercios*
of Spain, invincible on most battlefields for 150 years, were smashed at the Battle
of Rocroi.[7] The Count-Duke of Olivares was dismissed by his king in that same
fatal year and never returned to power, though Spain was not the better for that,
but the worse.[8] The French conquered most of Catalonia,[9] and Spain did not
even seriously attempt to recover Portugal.[10] In Germany, Swedish Marshal
Banér had crossed the frozen Danube at Regensburg in January 1641 and almost
captured Emperor Ferdinand III. The thawing of the river had forced Banér to
retreat. In May he had died and been succeeded as Swedish commander-in-chief
by the still more able Lennart Torstensson, who campaigned through much of
Germany during the next three years (France, still under the rule of Cardinal
Richelieu, had renewed its fatal treaty with Sweden). Marshal Torstensson's
campaigns climaxed with a great victory in the Second Battle of Breitenfeld in
November 1642, in which half the Austrian army was killed or captured, with
most of the captives taking service with the Swedes, who also took 46 cannon, 50

---

[5] Jerrold I. Casway, *Owen Roe O'Neill and the Struggle for Catholic Ireland*
(Philadelphia, 1984), p. 197.

[6] Cardinal Richelieu died in December 1642, apparently unrepentant, having already
declared Cardinal Mazarin, an Italian living in France, his successor. But it is pleasant to
record that Richelieu's will left all his residual property, after payment of debts and
special legacies, to St. Vincent de Paul. See Carl J. Burckhardt, *Richelieu and His Age*
(London, 1970), III, 428-429, 436, 460; von Pastor, *History of the Popes* XXVIII, 378,
386; Wedgwood, *Thirty Years War*, pp. 438-439. Just a few months later Louis XIII, his
puppet king, died a holy death in St. Vincent de Paul's arms. But politically, nobody
missed him; he had never really reigned. See Mary Purcell, *The World of Monsieur
Vincent* (New York, 1963), p. 198.

[7] C. V. Wedgwood, *The Thirty Years War* (New York, 1961), pp. 443-444; *The
Cambridge Modern History*, Volume IV (Cambridge, England, 1906, 1934), p. 594; J. H.
Elliott, *The Count-Duke of Olivares* (New Haven CT, 1986), p. 664; Jonathan I. Israel,
The Dutch Republic and the Hispanic World, 1660-1661 (New York, 1982), p. 317.

[8] Elliott, *Olivares*, pp. 648-652. Olivares died, still out of power, in July 1645.
Contrary to claims that he died insane, he remained in full possession of all his faculties
until a week before his death (*ibid.*, pp. 670-672).

[9] *Ibid.*, pp. 604, 637-638; Burckhardt, *Richelieu*, III, 429. On September 10, 1642
Perpignan in Roussillon surrendered to the French, and the Count-Duke of Olivares, in
tears, went to his king Philip IV and asked permission to kill himself, which Philip
refused. The next month two Spanish armies with a total of 20,000 men were thoroughly
thrashed by 12,000 French and a thousand Catalans at Lérida; a contemporary Spanish
writer declared that "the honor of the nation and the reputation of Spain were lost."

[10] The first significant battle between the two nations was not even fought in Portugal,
but in Spain at Montijo near Badajoz, following a Portuguese border incursion supported
by a Dutch contingent, in May 1644 (Israel, *Dutch and the Hispanic World*, p. 318).

wagonloads of ammunition and the papers and money of the Archduke Leopold who had been in command for Austria.[11]

But now the dominant personalities who had made the Thirty Years War so relentless a struggle were gone: the very Protestant King Gustav Adolf of Sweden (died 1632), the very Catholic Emperor Ferdinand II (died 1637), the Machiavellian Cardinal Richelieu (died 1642), and the faithful Catholic Count-Duke of Olivares (died 1645). They had no immediate successors. The titular ruler of Sweden, Queen Christina, was still a little girl under a regent in 1643, though she had a great destiny ahead of her. Emperor Ferdinand III was a pale shadow of his namesake and father. The Count-Duke of Olivares had no successor. And Cardinal Mazarin in France was to prove incapable of holding the reins of power with anything like the decisive grip of Cardinal Richelieu. It was time to talk real peace at last, and all of the principal powers were now willing to do so. On July 3, 1643 Emperor Ferdinand III gave his imperial sanction for negotiations with France and Sweden for peace in Germany. In October Spanish and imperial delegates finally arrived to begin the talks at the West German city of Münster, where ghastly memories of the horrors of violence remained from the seizure of the city by mad Anabaptist revolutionaries just over a century before.[12]

In June 1644 Pope Urban VIII, 76, began to lose his strength after one of the longest and most troubled pontificates in history. On July 29 he died.[13] The much reiterated charge that he was pro-French is sufficiently refuted by the devastating quotation that heads the previous chapter. In a singularly unpromising environment this Pope had been unable to discover a course of action that would really help the Church in the face of its betrayal by Cardinal Richelieu. Perhaps a greater Pope might have done so. But to this day we cannot really see how it might have been done.

The conclave to elect his successor was held in August. Fifty-six of 62 cardinals were present. A conspicuous absentee was Cardinal Mazarin; he was too busy governing France (in a manner of speaking) to do his supreme duty as a prince of the Church. He gave instructions to his envoy in Rome to work for the election of Cardinals Bentivoglio or Sacchetti, and strongly to oppose Cardinal Pamfili. His efforts were unavailing. Locked up in the hottest season of the year in Rome, the dying time, four cardinals were dead by September, including Bentivoglio. Cardinal Albornoz of Spain pressed the candidacy of Cardinal Pamfili, 70 years old, who was elected despite the persistence of five dissenting votes. He ascended the Chair of Peter as Innocent X, with a reputation of being pro-Spanish as Urban VIII had a reputation of being pro-French, but no more

---

[11] *Cambridge Modern History*, IV, 385-386, 388; Wedgwood *Thirty Years War*, pp. 422, 432-435.

[12] Wedgwood, *Thirty Years War*, p. 445; von Pastor, *History of the Popes*, XXVIII, 372. See Chapter Four, above, for the revolutionaries in Münster.

[13] von Pastor, *History of the Popes*, XXIX, 402, 404.

able than his predecessor to change the course that history was following into a cloven Christendom.[14]

At Münster there was little serious negotiating during 1644. Both sides were waiting to see if they could gain a military advantage first. This Swedish Marshal Torstensson did in March 1645, defeating the imperial army at Jankau near Tabor in Bohemia. The Swedish artillery was as usual superior, the Emperor's Bavarian cavalry were destroyed, and Torstensson marched on Prague, forcing the Emperor to flee to ever-loyal Catholic Tyrol. Torstensson came within thirty miles of Vienna in early May, but did not try to take it; he had made his point. But imperial forces defeated a French army under Marshal Turenne at almost the same time. The verdict of the battlefield was, as always in the Thirty Years War, ambiguous; and on June 11, 1645 peace negotiations finally began in earnest, in Münster between the Empire and the French, and in the nearby city of Osnabrück between the Empire and the Swedes. The French demanded a restoration of the conditions of 1618, and the Swedes a full acceptance of all the Protestant seizures of Catholic property. Emperor Ferdinand III countered with a demand for a restoration of the conditions in 1630 and an end to intervention in the Empire by France and Sweden. At the end of October 1645 six of the seven rebellious Dutch provinces voted, after four years of disagreement and recriminations, to send plenipotentiaries to the conference at Münster.[15]

In December 1645 Count Maximilian von Trauttmansdorf, Emperor Ferdinand III's closest confidante, arrived at Münster as the head of an imperial delegation with plenipotentiary powers, ready to work for peace at almost any price. Sensing the weakness of the imperial position, the German Protestants, fully supported by the Swedes, demanded the free practice of Protestantism in the Catholic states but not of Catholicism in the Protestant states, and restoration of the situation which had existed in 1618, when the war began. In mid-January the head of the Spanish delegation, the Count of Peñaranda, gave a stirring speech on the need to bury past animosities, and declared his country's willingness to recognize the independence of the Dutch (living in the northern part of the Netherlands or Low Countries). Imperial plenipotentiary Trauttmansdorf offered Alsace to France, but the French negotiators, also sensing the imperial weakness, held out for the great German fortress of Breisach as well, which Emperor Ferdinand III soon conceded to them by secret instructions to Trauttmansdorf. At the end of April the papal nuncio to the talks, Fabio Chigi, reported that most of the Catholic delegates at Münster were unwilling to resist the Protestant demands. Elector Maximilian of Bavaria, who had fought all through the Thirty Years War, supported Trauttmansdorf in yielding to a large extent to those demands. At the end of November 1646 the Catholics at the peace conference,

---

[14] *Ibid.*, XXX, 14-17, 19-20, 22-23, 27-28.

[15] *Ibid.*, XXX, 96-97, 99; *Cambridge Modern History*, IV, 389-390, 399; Wedgwood, *Thirty Years War*, pp. 465-466; Israel, *Dutch and the Hispanic World*, p. 357.

led by Trauttmansdorf, finally gave up the Edict of Restitution and conceded to the Protestants all the Church property they held in 1625.[16]

On January 8, 1647 preliminary articles of peace were signed by Spain and the Dutch Netherlands. After some bickering, they received final approval on February 9, 1648. They included permission for the Dutch of Zeeland to close the Scheldt River, ruining the great city of Antwerp, so often a victim in the 80-year war in the Low Countries. In March 1648 at it was confirmed at Osnabrück that Germany would go back to its condition in 1624, with no return of confiscated Catholic properties. Protestants were given parity in the imperial Diet, the imperial Chamber tribunal, and the Imperial Court Council, and Calvinists were for the first time explicitly recognized along with Lutherans. Emperor Ferdinand III salvaged only a permission to prescribe the religion of his own lands in Austria.[17]

On November 3, 1648 the Peace of Westphalia was adopted in its final form, the result of the work of both peace conferences. It was an epochal moment in the history of Christendom. The treaties included in the Peace of Westphalia were based on the assumption that Christendom was permanently cloven. They did not provide, as is so often thoughtlessly repeated, that "the religion of the country was the religion of the ruler." They made no provision for the conversion of rulers. What they said was that all states Protestant in 1624 would remain so, and all states then Catholic would remain so. All hope or prospect of reunifying Christendom was openly and publicly abandoned. Sweden got most of the German Baltic coast, and the territory of Bremen on the North Sea; France got Alsace-Lorraine, that apple of discord for the next three hundred years. The independence of the Dutch Netherlands and of Switzerland was guaranteed. France and Sweden could continue to interfere in German affairs if they wished.[18]

In view of the utter exhaustion of Germany after this long and ruinous civil war, there was probably no alternative to this Catholic surrender. The last of the battle decisions of the religious wars had gone against the Catholics, as had so many others. Papal nuncio Chigi issued a solemn protest against the Westphalia settlement, repeated twice in October 1648. Pope Innocent X waited two years before he published his protest against it, in the brief *Zelo domus dei*. He did not condemn the whole treaty; it was too obviously necessary to end this dreadful internecine war. But he deplored the immense, unrecoverable and irreparable

---

[16] Wedgwood, *Thirty Years War*, pp. 468-471; *Cambridge Modern History*, IV, 406-407; von Pastor, *History of the Popes* XXX, 100-103, 105; Israel, *Dutch in the Hispanic World*, p. 360.

[17] Israel, *Dutch in the Hispanic World*, pp. 370, 373; *Cambridge Modern History*, IV, 410-412, 715-716; Wedgwood, *Thirty Years War*, p. 481; von Pastor, *History of the Popes* XXX, 85, 118-119, 141.

[18] Wedgwood, *Thirty Years War*, pp. 483-484; von Pastor, *History of the Popes* XXX, 120-1241

loss to the Church—not only of property, but above all of the right to practice the Catholic Faith.[19]

Of the 850-year-old Holy Roman Empire, nothing was left but the name and a shell, and the authority of the Emperors in their native Austria and attached Bohemia and part of Hungary. Protestant Germany no longer owed the Emperor even a token obedience. The Protestant states of Germany had been confirmed as independent; they would never allow a Catholic Emperor to guide or lead them. Austria continued to be a great power for 250 years, but only by virtue of extending its rule eastward over the polyglot peoples of a "multinational empire," cut off from the majority of Germans. So meaningless did the imperial title become that when Napoleon Bonaparte decided he wanted it for himself in 1804, no one protested when he proclaimed himself Emperor of the French; Pope Pius VII then proceeded to ceremoniously hold the crown for this son of the bitterly anti-Catholic French Revolution, who lifted it from his hands and put it on his own head in a parody of the ancient ceremony whereby the Pope crowned the Holy Roman Emperor—one of the lowest points in the history of the Papacy.[20]

It was a long way down from the unified Christendom of the turn of the 16th century, when Queen Isabel the Catholic of Spain yet lived.

Yet there were many countries where the Church still lived; and, as always, she was reaching out to evangelize new peoples to replace those she had lost.[21]

In the British Isles the Church had been underground for a century in Great Britain and forty years in Ireland, and the fatal destiny of Protestantism, with its plethora of separated churches and its absence of legitimate religious authority, was working itself out. King Charles I championed the Church of England, but he could not impose it upon Scotland, nor really upon Ireland, where despite having to accept its presence, the great majority of Irishmen remained Catholic. And even in England he faced fierce and growing hostility to his church on the part of the Puritans. There is good reason to believe that they were never a majority of the population of England, but an aggressive and resolute minority who were, as their like have done for both good and evil so many times in history, prevailing over less committed opponents. When in 1640 elections were held for a second Parliament in that year, not a man in England could have dreamed that this Parliament—or, rather, part of it—would still be sitting no less than nineteen years later, after having been in session continuously for twelve and a half years, and seen England rent asunder as badly as Christendom had been by the Thirty Years War. It is most aptly called the Long Parliament—by far the longest in English history.

On November 13, 1640[22] the Long Parliament convened, under the effective leadership of John Pym, perhaps the most skillful Parliamentary

---

[19] von Pastor, *History of the Popes* XXX, 125-126, 130-131.

[20] See Volume Five, Chapter 14 of this history. Two years later the Emperor of Austria, at Napoleon's demand, gave up forever the title of Holy Roman Emperor, which had lasted almost exactly one thousand years.

[21] See Chapters Twelve and Thirteen, below.

manipulator England ever saw. Members began at once to prepare a "remonstrance" against Charles I's policies during the 1630's, including both his taxes and his wars in Scotland, and the ministers who had advised him during that time. Thomas Wentworth, Lord Strafford, King Charles' able governor of Ireland, was impeached and confined by action of Pym within eight days of the Parliament's opening. Before the year was over Archbishop of Canterbury William Laud had also been impeached and confined. Lord Keeper Finch, facing similar action, fled to the Netherlands. And on December 21 the appropriately named "root and branch petition" to abolish all bishops in England was introduced by a member from London, and referred immediately by Pym to the Puritan-dominated religion committee. By January 1641 he had brought a bill to require meetings of Parliament every three years, whether the King wanted them or not, to a third reading, and the reluctant monarch signed it into law the next month.[23]

On February 1 King Charles reprieved a Catholic priest named John Goodman from execution. There was a tremendous outcry from the Puritans, demanding the strictest enforcement of the anti-Catholic laws. The more conservative House of Lords joined with the King in supporting Goodman's reprieve. But in April Strafford was brought to trial before that same House of Lords; Pym had carefully prepared the prosecution, admitting that none of the individual charges against Strafford warranted the death penalty, but insisting that together they showed a pattern of treasonable action. Strafford was accused of planning to bring an Irish Catholic army to England, when all he had said, in the context of the Bishops' Wars in Scotland, was that he could bring such an army to "this kingdom," obviously meaning Scotland. Strafford defended himself so well that the House of Lords cut short the impeachment trial, and it appeared ended. But John Pym was not so easily disposed of. Within 24 hours he had introduced a bill of attainder, that most savage of all forms of legislation, which the United States Constitution so rightly prohibits, by which a national legislature can vote to kill a man whom it deems a threat to the safety of the state. The extent of John Pym's control of the House of Commons was demonstrated by a stunning vote of 204 to 59 to kill Strafford.[24]

The House of Lords, bewildered and unnerved, and probably believing that the King would never allow Strafford to be sacrificed by signing the bill of attainder, voted 37-11 for it, the majority not voting. Crowds demonstrated in the streets for Strafford's execution. The King desperately sought counsel, and was

---

[22] In keeping with the general policy in this history, all dates are in the New Style according to the Gregorian calendar, even though England was still using the Old Style throughout the 17th and into the 18th century. Therefore the dates given here are all ten days later than the dates actually then being used in England. Though no great harm is done by using the Old Style dates for English events as most historians do, an international history must use a uniform dating system or soon degenerate into great confusion.

[23] C. V. Wedgwood, *The King's Peace, 1637-1641* (New York, 1955), pp. 363-365, 368, 371-373, 378-381, 391, 396.

[24] *Ibid.*, pp. 392-393, 398, 405-406, 410-413, 419.

told by Bishop Williams of Lincoln that though the attainder was offensive to his "private conscience," it could still be signed according to his "public conscience." Claiming to be convinced by this incredible argument for a double conscience, Charles signed the attainder. Just two days later—May 22— Strafford went to the scaffold, less than two months after his impeachment trial began. When John Pym wanted to kill a man, he lost no time about it, and managed to make it appear a legal process.[25]

When, eight years later, King Charles I himself was sentenced to death, he said from the block: "An unjust sentence that I suffered to take effect, is punished now by an unjust sentence on me." Before his execution, he repeatedly said that he believed that God was punishing him for not saving Strafford.[26]

The Long Parliament recessed from August to October 1641, reassembling with low attendance to discuss the "remonstrance," now capitalized as the Grand Remonstrance. On Guy Fawkes day Pym made a speech urging totally unprecedented legislation to compel King Charles to gain the approval of Parliament for all his appointments. The next day a 42-year-old member from Cambridge, an ally of Pym named Oliver Cromwell, moved that the Puritan Earl of Essex rather than the King be given command of all the militia ("trained bands") in the south of England: the opening move in Pym's campaign to withdraw the army from the king's control and place it under the control of Parliament, or rather of his Puritan faction in Parliament. But the centerpiece of his program was passage of the Grand Remonstrance, whose harsh and almost revolutionary tone frightened many who had not previously realized where Pym was going, and was brilliantly opposed by Edward Hyde, later chief minister of the Restoration government. It barely passed by a cliffhanging vote of 159-148 at one o'clock in the morning.[27]

King Charles' leader in Parliament, Geoffrey Palmer, was shouted down in a near-riot when he tried to present a minority report, and two days later was sent to the Tower of London by a vote of 169-128, though a motion to expel him from the House was defeated by 163-131. Everything hung on temporary majorities, which John Pym was a master at assembling. On December 11 King Charles received a House deputation bearing the Grand Remonstrance, with the dignified response that he would answer it in his own good time, and requested that it not

---

[25] *Ibid.*, pp. 421-428. The mythology created by Pym's fantastic success was still alive and strong as late as the middle of the twentieth century. The Stuart kings, especially Charles I, were accused of all kinds of tyrannical acts and dark intentions, while Parliament was cast in the role of guardian of the fundamental rights of Englishmen. Actually, as Strafford's impeachment, attainder, and execution so clearly show, it was a naked power struggle whose object was for the Calvinist Puritans to gain control of the English state.

[26] C. V. Wedgwood, *A Coffin for King Charles; the Trial and Execution of King Charles I* (New York, 1964), p. 219.

[27] Wedgwood, *King's Peace*, pp. 450-451, 472-474, 483-484; Antonia Fraser, *Cromwell, the Lord Protector* (New York, 1973), p, 76-77. The term "trained bands" has caused unnecessary confusion. It simply means militia who train occasionally. There were no such things as "train-bands."

be published. Two weeks later Pym published it regardless. Sir Arthur Haselrig introduced legislation, innocuously called the Militia Bill, to place all military and naval appointments under Parliament's control rather than the King's. It passed by 158 votes to 125. At the very end of 1641 an election for city councillors in London was decisively won by the Puritans, who were now politically dominant in England's capital.[28]

On the first day of 1642 the King replied to the Grand Remonstrance, declaring his firm intention to uphold the Church of England with his blood if need be, but also to tolerate other Protestant churches. On January 6 the insatiable Pym threatened the impeachment of King Charles' French Queen Henrietta Maria, and rioters outside Westminster Hall blocked the bishops from taking their seats in the House of Lords. Twelve bishops signed an appeal against this forcible exclusion; all of them were immediately impeached. Charles I tried to buy off Pym by making him Chancellor of the Exchequer, to no avail; Pym wanted all the power, not just one department of government.[29]

King Charles now finally realized that he was facing an ultimate test, and struck back hard for the first time. His Attorney-General accused five prominent members of the House of Commons—Pym, John Hampden, Arthur Haselrig, Denzil Holles and William Strode—of high treason for subverting the laws, alienating the affections of the King's subjects, terrorizing Parliament by riots, and inciting a foreign power (Covenanting Scotland) to invade the country. The evidence in support of all these charges was overwhelming, but the power struggle had gone far beyond the ability and authority of any court to stop it. On January 14 the House of Commons went into session in the morning with the five accused members present. Pym kept them there to bait the king, who in the early afternoon came in person with his guards to arrest them. Pym knew he was coming, and when; his intelligence service was excellent. He and the other four accused members promptly decamped, and Charles searched for them in vain in the House chamber. The newly Puritan London city council refused to order their arrest, and crowds surrounded the King's carriage shouting "Privilege! Privilege!" Unnerved, the king retired, while the House of Commons denounced as public enemies anyone who aided King Charles in attempting to seize its members. Street barricades began to appear, the city council of London established a joint Commitee for Public Safety (a foreshadowing of the French Revolution), and Parliament gave command of the trained bands (militia) of London to Puritan Philip Skippon, a veteran of the Dutch wars. On January 20 the city of London definitively rose for Parliament against the king. That night King Charles and his family fled from London. On January 30 Charles wrote Parliament from Windsor "calling heaven to witness that he had never designed anything against them." They replied only by demanding the abolition of bishops, full control of the armed forces, and the surrender of the Tower of

---

[28] C. V. Wedgwood, *The King's War, 1641-1647* (London, 1958), pp. 22, 29, 41-42, 47-49.

[29] *Ibid.*, pp. 49-55.

London. The next day a large crowd gathered in London to watch the execution of the Catholic priest martyrs Alban Roe and Thomas Greene.[30]

At the beginning of March 1642 Queen Henrietta Maria embarked at Dover on a fleet to try to obtain military help from Denmark (the homeland of Charles' mother) and the Netherlands, where Charles' son-in-law was titular Prince of Orange, though still too young to rule. Charles, who was profoundly devoted to his petite French wife, shed tears at her departure. He refused to sign the Militia Bill; Pym immediately declared it passed as an ordinance, and began military preparations. Oliver Cromwell, though wholly without military experience (later years were to show him nevertheless one of the great generals of history) urged the formation of a committee to put the country in a state of defense, which was done. In the parts of England they controlled, the Puritans began smashing images in churches. Late in March Charles arrived in York, knowing that the north of England had a long record of loyalty to the monarch and resistance to great changes imposed from London. Early in May a delegation of Kentish royalists led by the poet Richard Lovelace tried to present a petition to the House of Commons to restore the army to the King. The defenders of the people's rights voted the petition subversive and threw its chief sponsors in jail, where Lovelace wrote the immortal lines "stone walls do not a prison make, nor iron bars a cage."[31]

On May 18 commissioners from Parliament arrived at York, and King Charles had already been denied entry to the Puritan port city of Hull. Charles responded by calling on the Yorkshire nobility to "attend him in arms." On June 6 the House of Commons declared that the King was making war on it, and that authority for governing the country therefore devolved upon them. They declared no royal order valid without the approval of Parliament, and began borrowing money at 8 per cent to carry on their war. A week later they approved 19 propositions as their reasons for making war on their king. These included demands that Charles' children be educated by and married to only persons approved by the Puritan Parliament, that all official appointments be approved by that Parliament, and that all the Catholic Lords be summarily dismissed. In July the two great English universities, Oxford and Cambridge, voted substantial financial help to their beleaguered king. The money from Oxford reached him; the money from Cambridge was waylaid in the fen country by Cambridge member of Parliament Oliver Cromwell. The strongly Puritan Earl of Essex was appointed commander-in-chief of the nascent Parliamentary army, and the Earl of Warwick, a supporter of Parliament, took control of the navy. Only two ships resisted him in the name of the King. On the 25th occurred the first cavalry battle of the English Civil War, near Manchester. The royalists lost, as they were often to lose more critical combats in the course of the war.[32]

---

[30] *Ibid.*, pp. 56-62, 64-66, 68 (quote on 64); Fraser, *Cromwell,* p. 78.

[31] Wedgwood, *King's War*, pp. 68-70, 72-73, 82-83, 89-90; Fraser, *Cromwell,* p. 79.

[32] Wedgwood, *King's War*, pp. 87-89, 99-101, 104-107, 115; Fraser, *Cromwell*, pp. 82, 84-85.

In Scotland, the dominant heirs of John Knox and the Presbyterian church he had established expanded their horizons. Their country had now become dominated by its clergy to an extent unequalled in any other, including all the Catholic countries. The leading Calvinist ministers of Scotland made policy much more than anyone else. In July 1642 an assembly of the Scots Church (familiarly called "the Kirk") met at St. Andrews, the site of Cardinal Beaton's formerly Catholic cathedral, now falling into ruin. They appointed a commission to work with the rebellious English Parliament to establish a Presbyterian church throughout all of Great Britain. The Duke of Argyll in southwestern Scotland, probably the richest and most powerful of all the earls and dukes of Scotland, gave the ambitious Calvinist ministers his full support, convinced that in alliance with them he could attain his own dream of supreme power over Scotland.[33]

In August 1642 Princes Rupert and Maurice, the young but adult sons of Charles' sister Elizabeth, once briefly Queen of Bohemia and now the widowed and displaced Electress of the Palatinate in Germany, arrived in England with a small group of professional military officers who had learned their trade in the Thirty Years War, ready to fight for the king. On September 2, in what should have been a glorious moment rendered almost farcical by pouring rain, a limp flag and a vague, confusing proclamation, King Charles I "raised his standard" at Nottingham. Few recruits came to join him. John Pym was centuries ahead of his time in his ability to destroy a man's reputation by skillful propaganda. Six days later Oliver Cromwell, who had never previously even borne arms, raised a troop of about a hundred cavalry at Huntingdon, to fight for Parliament against the King.[34]

Early in October the royalists had to abandon the city of Worcester, where they were particularly strong among the people but whose decayed walls and gates were indefensible, and fell back into Wales while the Parliamentary forces occupied Worcester, sacked its cathedral, and destroyed its famous organ. But at the same time Prince Rupert and his cavalry defeated a substantially superior force of Parliamentarians at Powicke Bridge over the Teme River in Worcestershire. It was an overture to the first great battle of the English Civil War, fought at Edgehill between approximately equal armies of 13,000 men each. The Parliamentary army was commanded by the Earl of Essex, son of the already legendary Earl of Queen Elizabeth's later years; the royalist army was commanded by Prince Rupert and his old teacher Sir Jacob Astley. Rupert routed the Parliamentary cavalry, but with a young man's impetuosity pursued them too far, giving the Parliamentarian infantry the opportunity to make a stand. It was crumbling when Oliver Cromwell appeared (he later said "at my first going into this engagement, I saw our men were beaten on every hand") but he succeeded in rallying it, so that the battle was a draw rather than a defeat for Parliament. But Cromwell deplored the low quality of Parliament's soldiers, saying men with more spirit must be found. Essex returned to London with the

[33] Wedgwood, *King's War*, pp. 109-110.
[34] *Ibid.*, pp. 114, 117-118; Fraser, *Cromwell*, p. 85, 91-92.

Parliamentary army, picked up Philip Skippon with some of his "trained bands," and marched out of the city in pursuit of the king. Charles gave up his attempt to take London and retreated to Oxford, where he set up his court. Near the end of the year the Parliamentary cavalry drove royalist cavalry out of Winchester and destroyed the tapestries, vestments, books, and organ in the beautiful ancient cathedral of that city.[35]

In January 1643 Oliver Cromwell was commissioned colonel and began appointing officers by merit rather than social rank, and recruiting Puritan yeomen for his common soldiers. Able royalist general Ralph Hopton defeated a Parliamentary force at Braddock Down near Bodmin in Cornwall. On February 4 emerging Parliamentary general Thomas Fairfax took Leeds in central England for Parliament, supported by local volunteers and singing the 68th Psalm ("Let God arise and His enemies be scattered"). Pym's war party in the House of Commons rejected all negotiations with the King in February, but had to back down and permit them when the Lords declared they would pass no more money bills unless negotiations took place. But Parliament's negotiators continued to demand abolition of bishops, stricter enforcement of the laws against Catholics, and the punishment of Charles' advisors, including Prince Rupert, his best commander. He in turn demanded that the Parliamentary army be disbanded and that Parliament be moved out of London. These positions were entirely irreconcilable and neither party would move away from them. Early in April Pym obtained Parliament's approval for the confiscation of all royalist estates, and Oliver Cromwell gained firm control of his native East Anglia for Parliament. Parliament then recalled its negotiators and set up a special committee against "superstition and idolatry," which ordered remaining stained glass windows in the churches to be smashed and remaining statues of saints to be beheaded. In that month the King at Oxford gave a spirited response to the Scots negotiators, telling them not to meddle between him and his English people.[36]

Then the military news took a turn for the better for the King's cause. At the end of June Prince Rupert with 1,800 men surprised a substantial part of the Parliamentary army in the Chiltern Mountains at dawn. When other Parliamentary forces tried to intercept his retreat he defeated them at Chalgrove Field where John Hampden, an early leader against the king who had become nationally known for his refusal to pay the king's "ship money" tax, was mortally wounded. Royalists from Yorkshire and Cornwall began a steady eastward advance, winning a major battle at Roundway Down, where the Parliamentarians lost 1,400 men killed or captured and all their cannon, ammunition and baggage to a royalist cavalry force less than half their number which had ridden forty miles for two days and two nights. Charles and his queen were reunited at Edgehill. And in Scotland James Graham, the young (30) Earl of Montrose and

---

[35] Wedgwood, *King's War*, pp. 122-124, 141-142, 144, 155.

[36] *Ibid.*, pp. 170-172, 176, 182-189; Fraser, *Cromwell*, pp. 99-100; von Pastor, *History of the Popes* XXIX, 338.

the first signer on the Scottish national Covenant, embraced the royalist cause. He would be heard from again.[37]

In August 1643 the Scots and their kirk proposed a formal alliance with Parliament and drafted a "Solemn League and Covenant" which would impose a strongly Calvinist Presbyterian church on both countries. It was drafted in Edinburgh that month with the Duke of Argyll deeply involved in its preparation. John Pym made an immediate favorable response. Proposals in the English Parliament for renewing negotiations with the King were voted down by a narrow margin, with Pym masterminding the debate and the vote, the Puritan ministers preaching furiously for war, and women who had come pleading for peace were driven away with blows and shots which killed several of them. Meanwhile Prince Rupert took the great city of Bristol after hard fighting, and Gloucester was under royalist siege. Essex marched to raise the siege and was successful in doing so, but then retreated immediately to London. Prince Rupert tried to intercept him, but his ammunition supply was low and consequently the resulting Battle of Newbury was a draw. On October 5 the "Solemn League and Covenant" was signed, establishing a firm alliance of the English and Scots Calvinists. The Scots agreed to send 20,000 soldiers to England to augment the Parliamentary force, to be paid for by the English. On October 20 came the Battle of Winceby, when Oliver Cromwell, now a major cavalry leader, won by charging a royalist force, with his horse killed under him. By now only the Calvinist fire-eaters were left in Parliament; attendance at the House of Commons had dwindled to less than 200 out of its original 600, and the House of Lords to only about fifteen.[38]

At the very end of this year 1643 John Pym died at 59 of cancer of the colon.[39] His job was done, and with it he took his place as one of the major revolutionaries of history. The evil he had unleashed engulfed the British Isles for the next seventeen years. Leadership of the Puritan revolution passed from the great legislative manipulator to the even greater general—Oliver Cromwell—inspiration of the heavy cavalry already beginning to go by the name "Ironsides." In January 1644 Cromwell came in person to break up a choir service in Ely cathedral, sending the congregation flying.[40]

At the end of April the Scots army joined with the English Parliamentarian army under Fairfax, and laid siege to York. Prince Rupert led 15,000 men to relieve the northern city. The Parliamentary army besieging York mined its ancient walls, but the defenders held the breach, counterattacked, and forced the besiegers to withdraw. By a brilliant maneuver Prince Rupert outflanked the besieging army on July 11 and entered York. But royalist troops in York under the Duke of Newcastle, who felt Prince Rupert had slighted him, at first refused to march to his support the next day. Finally they moved up, but they were not

---

[37] Wedgwood, *King's War*, pp. 221-231, 240; Fraser, *Cromwell*, p. 109.

[38] Wedgwood, *King's War*, pp. 232-234, 236, 239-243, 245-253, 256-258, 265-266, 277, 283-284; Fraser, *Cromwell*, pp. 107, 111-112.

[39] Wedgwood, *King's War*, p. 277.

[40] Fraser, *Cromwell*, p. 104.

ready to fight until four o'clock in the afternoon. Prince Rupert decided not to risk an attack with them, and broke ranks for supper on Marston Moor in a thunderstorm with considerable daylight still left in high summer. He was caught literally sitting by a Parliamentary force vastly superior in artillery and Cromwell leading the cavalry, who broke Prince Rupert's cavalry and slaughtered the stubborn Yorkshire infantry. By nine-thirty in the evening when twilight was fading at last, a full moon came out, and by its baleful light Cromwell rallied his "Ironsides" to break the remainder of the royalist cavalry under Lord Goring and pursue them off the field. The victory was all Cromwell's and showed his extraordinary mastery of the art of war, in which he had only been engaged for two years. Four thousand royalists were killed and 1,500 captured at the cost of only 300 Parliamentarians.[41]

The blow to the royalist cause was staggering. The survivors abandoned York and retreated into Lancashire with discipline collapsing. Queen Henrietta Maria, who had just given birth to her last child whom she had to leave behind, barely escaped from Exeter on a Dutch ship, which was fired on by a Parliamentary warship but got away. She was received with honor by Cardinal Mazarin and the French court, but not helped in any way. King Charles spoke at a rally on the bleak plain of Dartmoor, but gained few recruits. But at the end of July Montrose, who had had only very limited success in persuading Scots to fight for their king, received a major and unexpected reinforcement: a giant warrior from Ulster, Alistair Macdonald, six feet six, whose clan were the hereditary enemies of the Duke of Argyll and his Campbells. Macdonald was a devout Catholic who brought both his family and a priest with him.[42] With his natural allies, the Catholic highlanders of Scotland, he provided a potent force of the best infantry in Christendom, who fought in the old style, stripped nearly naked and swinging their enormous broadswords called claymores. Most Celtic hosts had lacked good commanders, but not this time.

Montrose was probably as good a general as Cromwell, though he had much less to work with; history is the poorer because the two men never met on the battlefield. In September he arrived in Scotland disguised as a groom, with only two companions, and joined Macdonald with his royal commission hidden in the lining of his saddle. He raised the royal standard at the Braes of Atholl in Highland dress with a bunch of yellow oats in his bonnet and a claymore in his hand. The Irish fired off the last of their ammunition welcoming him. He convinced 800 Scots who had come to fight the Irish to join him and them instead and swept down on the important Scots city of Perth, defended by an army twice the size of his, whose commander chose the password "Jesus and no quarter." Montrose, who unlike so many of his time had no such conception of Jesus, was enraged. He and his men fought with redoubled strength at a place called

---

[41] *Ibid.*, pp. 117-118, 120-133; Wedgwood, *King's War*, pp. 308-309, 320-321, 327, 332-333, 336-344.

[42] Wedgwood, *King's War*, pp. 343-344, 351, 353-354.

Tippermuir. Having no ammunition, there was nothing left to do but make a claymore charge. With it, they routed the Scottish army and took Perth.[43]

Montrose had superb infantry, but no cavalry at all; at the Braes of Atholl he had only three horses.[44] This was the key to the campaigns that followed; Montrose won several battles with only a small cavalry force, but could never come close to matching his foes in that military department. The only large source of cavalry in Scotland was the Gordon country, home of the Marquis of Huntly, the fantastically attired "Cock o' the North," but he was no fighter, and resented Montrose as supplanting him in the leadership of the Catholic forces. He never gave dependable support.

On September 23 Montrose appeared before the principal northern Scottish city of Aberdeen. Macdonald's Irish again routed the opposing infantry, but after permitting a sack of the town he had to withdraw from it, since he could not spare the men to garrison it. The Duke of Argyll occupied it, posted a reward of 20,000 pounds for Montrose dead or alive, and pursued Montrose's army into the Highlands, chasing him 200 miles without ever sighting him; his Highlanders and Irish, in their own kind of country, had no supply line and needed none. In early November Montrose prepared a position at Fyvie Castle, allowed his pursuers to catch up with him, repelled three major attacks, then disappeared again into the mountains.[45]

Meanwhile in London Parliament passed a bill of attainder against Archbishop Laud after concluding that there were no legal grounds to find him guilty of high treason, but it defeated a bill to make the church in England all Presbyterian; too many of its members now belonged to independent Protestant sects. King Charles rallied his army, now consisting of 15,000 men, and finally gave Prince Rupert sole command of it. He scathingly rejected an offer by the Presbyterian party in Parliament for peace with the aid of the Scots if he would abandon the Church of England.[46] Oliver Cromwell, deeply dissatisfied by the poor performance and leadership squabbling of the Parliamentary army after the Battle of Marston Moor, set himself to raise and train a "New Model army," with the long-remembered words: "I had rather have a plain russet-coated captain that knows what he fights for, and loves what he knows, than that which you call a gentleman and is nothing else."[47]

On January 20, 1645 Archbishop Laud went to the scaffold. The remnant House of Lords had passed his attainder, and under the wartime circumstances Parliament had no compunction about making law or death without the king's

---

[43] *Ibid.*, pp. 364-366; C. V. Wedgwood, *Montrose* (New York, 1952), pp. 60-65.

[44] Wedgwood, *Montrose*, p. 64.

[45] Wedgwood, *King's War*, pp. 375-377, 392; Wedgwood, *Montrose*. pp. 70, 72-74.

[46] Wedgwood, *King's War*, pp. 381-382, 384-386.

[47] *Ibid.*, pp. 419-420; Fraser, *Cromwell*, p. 114, 144 (quote on 114).

consent. Before he died, Laud recalled two of his predecessors, St. Alphege, killed by the pagan Danes, and Simon of Sudbury, killed by Wat Tyler's rebels.[48]

In the Scottish highlands the winter weather was severe. Montrose ostentatiously withdrew from the Duke of Argyll's Campbell country, going around the head of Loch Awe and crossing the Pass of Brander, then crossing Loch Etive in four boats, thence going west into the Lochaber Hills, where the Campbell Duke lost sight of him. Early in February he reversed course, marched night and day with his Irishmen and Highlanders through the bitter cold, several times becoming lost, in perhaps the most extraordinary of the fast marches always associated with his name. Young and strong, he asked his men to do nothing that he himself did not do. In the small hours of February 12 his men ate the last of their oatmeal in a porridge made with snow, which Montrose ate with them. At dawn they launched a claymore charge against the house and headquarters of the Duke of Argyll, who was taken totally by surprise. Three-quarters of his Campbell army was killed, and the Duke fled at top speed in a galley. Montrose wrote to King Charles announcing his victory and urging the king never to negotiate with rebels with arms in their hands, the ancient Roman practice. The Gordon cavalry at last began to join Montrose after this victory, while the Scots parliament proclaimed Montrose a traitor to be hanged, drawn, and quartered if captured.[49]

In April the mercurial Gordon chief withdrew his cavalry from Montrose, who promptly seized the city of Dundee but was driven out by the Scottish army. Once again he eluded pursuit by fading into the Highlands; the successful retreat from Dundee was considered perhaps the most amazing of his many military accomplishments. In May some of the Gordon cavalry rejoined Montrose, and on the 19th he won the Battle of Auldearn, fought in a heavy mist which prevented his enemy from observing how small his numbers were. With Alistair Macdonald's Irish in front and the Gordon cavalry on the flank, he won another complete victory, and in June he wrote the King that with only 500 horse he would be strong enough to invade England. Meanwhile in England Cromwell's New Model Army had taken the field in their red uniforms, which British soldiers were to continue to wear for two hundred years. Prince Rupert was deeply concerned, as well he might be. This was a different kind of army, fired with a genuine religious enthusiasm, however misplaced. These men actually believed, as did Cromwell their commander, that God was fighting on their side and would give them triumph. Their reliance on "special providence" served them well at the time with a great general, but was to lead to total disillusionment when Cromwell was no longer with them.[50]

---

[48] Wedgwood, *King's War*, pp. 400-403; Fraser, *Cromwell*, p. 143. For the martyrdom of St. Alphege, see Volume Two, Chapter 17 of this history; for the murder of Simon of Sudbury, see Volume Three, Chapter 11.

[49] Wedgwood, *King's War*, pp. 412-417; Wedgwood, *Montrose*, pp. 78, 80-85.

[50] Wedgwood, *King's War*, pp. 436-437, 439, 448, 459-461; Wedgwood, *Montrose*, pp. 89-94; Fraser, *Cromwell*, pp. 145, 148-149.

On June 22 Cromwell's New Model army joined Fairfax's Parliamentary army, creating a force of 14,000 men, nearly twice the number the royalists could muster under Prince Rupert. The Prince did not wish to give battle against such odds, but two of the King's civilian advisers prevailed over the counsel of the battle-tested Rupert. Charles ordered an attack, and Prince Rupert obediently charged. The result was the decisive Battle of Naseby. Cromwell and his highly disciplined "Ironsides" cavalry counter-charged with overwhelming force. The King wanted to lead his men against Cromwell, but was persuaded not to try it. The royalist army was routed, with all of its artillery lost. It was all over by mid-afternoon, and the king's cause in England was lost. The verdict of Naseby was confirmed by the Battle of Langport in the west of England on July 20, where the New Model army overwhelmed Lord Goring's royalists even in difficult country, with Cromwell clinching the victory by another great charge of the Ironsides. Two thousand royalists were killed and their infantry was totally broken.[51]

This left Montrose the only consistently successful royalist commander. At Alford in July he drew Scots general Baillie into the hill country above the River Spey and defeated him with another claymore charge. Charles thought of going to Scotland to join him, which would probably have been the best thing he could have done; but, giving way to his fatal indecision, he never made up his mind to go. On August 26 Montrose won his last victory at Kilsyth, the first he had won in Lowland Scotland, once again by a claymore charge; the Duke of Argyll had to flee for his life for a second time. Glasgow and Edinburgh submitted to him, releasing their prisoners who had supported Montrose. He called a new parliament for Scotland in the king's name, and knighted Alistair Macdonald.[52]

But within a few days the new Sir Alistair had left him for a raiding expedition in southeastern Scotland, and the Gordon Lord Aboyne had left him for the Gordon country in the northeast. Cromwell's and Fairfax's Parliamentary army was now carrying all before it, taking the great western city of Bristol from Prince Rupert. They no longer needed the Scots army, which promptly headed home to deal with Montrose. The able Scots General David Leslie, trained in the Thirty Years War, surprised Montrose's depleted forces at Philiphaugh with three to one odds in his favor. Suspecting treachery by the profoundly loyal Prince Rupert, King Charles foolishly revoked his commission and ordered him out of the country. In Scotland the followers of Montrose were being executed whenever caught; when in Glasgow the head of a third successive 18-year-old captive was struck from his shoulders, a Calvinist minister in attendance declared, in the true spirit of John Knox: "The work gangs bonnily on!" Charles now reconsidered going to Scotland, until the news arrived that Montrose had been forced back into the Highlands. At long last Charles tried to send him strong cavalry support commanded by Lord George Digby, but Digby was intercepted by the Ironsides and forced to flee to the Isle of Man. In mid-November Charles returned to Oxford, his army collapsing around him because

---

[51] Wedgwood, *King's War*, pp. 450-455, 465-467; Fraser, *Cromwell*, pp. 154-164, 167.
[52] Wedgwood, *King's War*, pp. 460, 475-477, 479-482; Wedgwood, *Montrose*. pp. 94-98, 101-103.

of his ingratitude and injustice to Prince Rupert and the hopeless military situation. In February 1646 Chester, the only remaining port by which Irish troops might reach England, surrendered to the Parliamentary army. In March Charles' son and namesake, fighting in Cornwall, had to flee to the Scilly Isles and later to the Channel Islands near the French coast.[53]

By April, by indomitable perseverance Montrose had raised a new army of 6,000 men, but Huntly the Gordon clan leader still would not support him with the cavalry he so desperately needed. Meanwhile Charles had finally decided to throw himself on the mercy of his own people—but to those who had been in arms against him, not his heroic defenders. On May 15, after leaving Oxford at three o'clock in the morning with his hair cut, a false beard, drab clothes, and only two companions, he gave himself up to the Scottish army in England, accepting verbal assurances of his personal safety. How much these assurances were worth was soon revealed. After Charles had cooperated with them by ordering the peerless Montrose to disband his army, in a transaction still profoundly disgusting across 350 years, at the beginning of January 1647 the Scots sold their king to the English for 200,000 pounds (including two 30,000-pound grants to the Duke of Argyll and Charles' perfidious Scottish adviser the Duke of Hamilton), with the rest of the blood money to be applied to their army's arrears of pay. Even English boys taunted the Scots for selling their king, and threw stones at them. Montrose disguised himself and set sail for Norway on a fishing boat.[54]

Charles was held in close captivity by Parliament (or rather, the remnant of the House of Commons elected seven years before). His attempt to escape the very day after the Scots sold him was foiled. On January 10 he wrote to his wife in France and to the Queen Regent of France, saying that he could no longer save himself, but must depend on the help of the other kings in Christendom. On January 31 he wrote to Montrose, who had made good his escape to Norway, asking him to go to his Queen and help her in any way he could. But no one could help him now.[55]

At two o'clock in the morning of August 16 the New Model army, 18,000 strong with Cromwell riding at their head, occupied London and removed 11 members of Parliament who were believed to be anti-army. Cromwell declared: "I do not know what force is to be used except we cannot get what is good for the kingdom without force." He stationed a regiment of cavalry at Hyde Park, within striking distance of the House of Commons, which at his demand rejected the Presbyterians in favor of the church independents. Attendance at Parliament fell to about 150 in the House of Commons and to a pathetic seven in the House of Lords. Cromwell was the ruler of England now, and despite some dissensions

[53] Wedgwood, *King's War*, pp. 487-491, 493, 497-501, 504, 538, 540, 542, 549; Wedgwood, *Montrose*, pp. 110-111, 114-115; Fraser, *Cromwell*, pp. 168-169, 175; Antonia Fraser, *Royal Charles* [Charles II] (New York, 1979), pp. 40, 42.

[54] Wedgwood, *King's War*, pp. 554-555, 558-559, 607, 609, 652; Wedgwood, *Montrose*, pp. 118-119, 122, 125-126; Fraser, *Cromwell*, pp. 177, 184.

[55] Wedgwood, *King's War*, pp. 609-611; Fraser, *Cromwell*, p. 184.

the army would follow him anywhere. It conducted prolonged debates on the form the new government should have, which showed that no one, including Cromwell, really had any idea what that form should be. But there was increasing consensus that it was no longer possible to pretend that England was a monarchy. Cromwell cried "thou shalt not suffer a hypocrite to reign." Colonel Thomas Harrison called Charles I a "man of blood" and urged his prosecution. The time was not yet quite ripe for that, but Charles, seeking to divide his triumphant enemies, secretly made an "engagement" with the Scots who had sold him to abolish bishops and establish Presbyterianism, in return for which the Scots said they would restore him by force. How either of these parties could possibly have believed the other at this point staggers the imagination.[56]

On July 18, 1648 the Scottish army invaded England under the shifty Duke of Hamilton, but without artillery. Most of the remaining royalists in England would not fight beside the Scots who had sold their king, even though they came allegedly in the King's name. Cromwell met them with little more than half their numbers and soundly defeated them August 27 at the Battle of Preston. The Scots fled that night, hopelessly outgeneralled, having lost some 2,000 killed and thousands more captured, though many of their troops had never even been brought into action. The King was generally blamed for this useless war, and seen all the more as a "man of blood." On November 30 the army demanded that he be brought to trial, and on December 6 resolved to purge what was left of Parliament, removing all who would not do their will. This was the famous Pride's Purge, the work of Colonel Thomas Pride, who with his men manned the doors of the House of Commons and refused to let anyone in who was not on an army-approved list. Only about eighty members (later called "the Rump") were on the list. The next day Cromwell rode into London from the north, declaring he had known nothing of the purge beforehand, but approved the result. The Puritan preachers thundered against the king from their pulpits, saying there must be no more compromise with him. The council of officers of the New Model army voted to move the king to Windsor "in order to the bringing of him speedily to justice."[57]

On the first day of the New Year 1649 army chaplain Hugh Peter delivered a fire-eating sermon, saying the army would uproot the monarchy and dash it to pieces. The next day the Rump Parliament, without a division, voted to bring King Charles I to trial before a special court of about 150 members. The handful of Lords still meeting rejected this, but the House of Commons took no notice.

---

[56] Fraser, *Cromwell*, pp. 205, 208, 212-213, 215-216, 220, 225-229 (quotes on 229 and 220; Fraser, *Royal Charles*, p. 55. The Presbyterians, mentioned above, organized their church strictly according to the pattern and rules made by John Calvin in Geneva. The independents did not follow any pre-existing plan of church organization, but let each congregation decide who would be its minister and what it would believe. It was Protestant separatism, subdivision, and rejection of religious authority carried to the ultimate. Oliver Cromwell was an Independent.

[57] Fraser, *Cromwell*, pp. 242-246, 248-253, 264-268, 270-272; Wedgwood, *A Coffin for King Charles*, pp. 39-41, 43 (quote on 43); Fraser, *Royal Charles*, p. 59.

Cromwell indicated his agreement, saying characteristically that he must "submit to Providence." His was really the only voice that mattered now.[58]

On January 18 the king's trial began in the Painted Chamber, with only 53 of the 135 persons appointed to be both judge and juror even present (49 of them never put in an appearance at any of these proceedings, and only 59 of them eventually voted for his execution, the remainder staying away on the day of the final vote). Cromwell unhesitatingly declared: "I tell you we will cut off his head with the Crown upon it!" Charles splendidly rejected the jurisdiction of the court, saying: "If power without law may make laws, may alter the fundamental laws of the kingdom, I do not know what subject he is in England, that can be sure of his life, or anything he calls his own." He refused to plead. Even this court respected his status sufficiently not to order him to be pressed to death between two stones, as St. Margaret Clitherow had been for a similar refusal.[59]

After sitting for exactly one week, the special court condemned Charles to death as "tyrant, traitor, murderer and public enemy." His death warrant was drawn up the next day. Court member John Downes rose to denounce this travesty of justice; Cromwell snapped: "What ails thee? Art thou mad? Canst thou not sit still and be quiet?" A recess was called and Cromwell came and berated Downes to his face until he dissolved in tears. Thomas Lord Fairfax, another of the judges who opposed the execution of Charles, did no more than absent himself. But his dauntless wife, wearing a mask, rose in the gallery when Chief Justice Bradshaw was declaiming about how he was acting for the people of England to cry out: "Not half, not a quarter of the people of England! Oliver Cromwell is a traitor!" Muskets were levelled at her, and she was removed. Very temporarily inspired by his wife's courage, Fairfax met with his friends, but quickly concluded that action to save the king was hopeless and a statement in his favor would only result in more bloodshed, so nothing whatever was done.[60] As with similar moments in the history of the French and Russian Revolutions, one longs in vain for a rescue party, such as Don Juan of Austria or the Marquis of Montrose might have led, if only they had had the opportunity.

When it came time to actually do the heinous deed, many hung back. The executioner disguised himself and asked for one of the soldiers to be his assistant. Colonel Hercules Huncks, hitherto an obedient Puritan, refused to sign the order for the execution, despite personal pressure from Cromwell, who called him a "forward, peevish fellow." In a statement from the block Charles forgave his enemies and called on them to make peace. When the executioner severed his head from his body in a single blow, an eyewitness reports that from the surrounding crowd came "such a groan as I never heard before, and desire I may never hear again." On February 19 the decapitated king was buried at Windsor, and on that day royalist Richard Royston published one of the most famous

---

[58] Wedgwood, *Coffin for King Charles*, pp. 88-92; Fraser, *Cromwell*, pp. 272-276.

[59] Wedgwood, *Coffin for King Charles*, pp. 109-116, 135-140, 147-152, 156-159 (second quote on 157); Fraser, *Cromwell*, p. 282 (first quote). See Chapter 8, above.

[60] Wedgwood, *Coffin for King Charles*, pp. 175-189, 198-207 (first quote on 175, second on 180, third on 177).

books in English history, an account of Charles I's last days, slightly disguised by a Greek title, *Eikon Basilike*.[61]

Just the day before the king's execution, the remnant of the Long Parliament had met to prohibit any proclamation of a new king. It had very belatedly dawned on them what is probably the greatest single strength of monarchy as a political system, that each king always has a known successor. Charles I's successor was his 18-year-old eldest son and namesake, now Charles II. But Parliament's writ ran only in England. Charles II was proclaimed in the Netherlands, and even by the Scots. Montrose received the news of his master's killing in Brussels; this still young and battle-hardened general fainted dead away at the shock, and after he recovered, shut himself in his room for two days and two nights. Early in March he came to kiss the hand of Charles II at the Hague and swear allegiance to him, proposing an invasion of Scotland from overseas, so that he might try once again to raise it for its true monarch. Charles seemed to agree. On March 27 the Rump of Parliament declared the monarchy abolished, and two days later did the same with the House of Lords.[62]

Meanwhile, during exactly the same years which saw the temporary overthrow of the monarchy in England and its replacement by a Cromwellian dictatorship, Ireland was in revolt. Few Englishmen recognized what this really meant; they saw it all through pro-English glasses, and were constantly trumpeting fears that a Catholic Irish army would be brought into England by supporters of the King. Some of the King's men in Ireland, notably the Earl of Ormonde, tried unsuccessfully to do that. The only significant Irish contribution to the civil wars in Great Britain was Alistair Macdonald's thousand men who fought for Montrose. But though they came from Ulster, they were more Scots than Irish, led by the Scottish Macdonald clan. The native Irish did not wish to fight for either King or Parliament; they wanted to be free and to freely practice their Catholic Faith. Immediately after their uprising, Phelim O'Neill said as much; its sole motive, he declared, was "the defense and liberty of ourselves and the Irish natives of this kingdom." And from August 1642 they were led by Owen Roe O'Neill, nephew of Hugh O'Neill, one of the two great leaders of the Nine Years War—but unfortunately, already past his sixtieth birthday. Years later Owen Roe wrote to Papal envoy Rinuccini in the same vein, regarding the English royalists and Parliamentarians: "We view both, God knows, with the same hatred and horror."[63]

The 1640's in England were the propaganda years, when myth became truth because so many believed only what they wanted to believe. The Irish uprising

[61] *Ibid.*, pp. 212-216, 218-223, 238-241, 245 (second quote on 223); Fraser, *Cromwell*, pp. 290-293 (first quote on 292).

[62] Wedgwood, *Coffin for King Charles*, pp. 214, 232-234; Wedgwood, *Montrose*, pp. 129-130; Fraser, *Cromwell*, pp. 301-302.

[63] Jerrold I. Casway, *Owen Roe O'Neill and the Struggle for Catholic Ireland* (Philadelphia, 1984), pp. 52 (first quote), 63, 246 (second quote). For the Nine Years War, see Chapters Eight and Nine, above.

of November 1641 is one of the chief examples of that. Within weeks it become a standing Puritan conviction, which it has taken centuries of historical research to disprove, that thousands of Protestants were deliberately massacred in this uprising. The great historian Antonia Fraser says flatly: "There is no actual evidence that this deliberate massacre, as such, took place." Some people were killed, as is inevitable in a revolt; others were turned out of the houses they were occupying into the cold weather of approaching winter, and could not find other shelter quickly enough. Even when Cromwell's courts later began to hand down indictments for the alleged massacre, only 16 of 51 referred to actual killings, while the others were for threatening words only. As for the houses that Catholics turned Protestants out of, these had previously belonged to Catholics and had been taken from them as punishment for the Nine Years War, particularly by Scots Calvinist settlers in Ulster.[64]

The Irish rebels gained possession of most of the country at first, but a strong English garrison held firm in Dublin. King Charles denounced the Irish rebels as traitors. In February 1642, after prohibiting the practice of the Catholic Faith in Ireland, Parliament proclaimed the confiscation of over a million acres of Irish land. London merchants solicited financial contributions to put down the Irish rising, with the promise of the confiscated Irish land as repayment. Many members of the House of Commons made such contributions, including Cromwell for 2,000 pounds. Three thousand English troops were sent to reinforce Dublin. But Pope Urban VIII wrote letters of encouragement and support to the Irish rebels, and sent them a subsidy of 20,000 scudi.[65]

In March the Irish Catholic bishops of Ulster met at Kells and declared that the rising was justified, but that murder and seizure of Protestant lands was not, and that it was the duty of all to fight for their religion, country and king against Parliament.[66] The reference to the King reflected the new situation caused by the failure of Charles' attempted purge of Parliament, which committed him to an anti-Parliamentary position and made civil war in England inevitable. The Irish Catholics had been relatively well governed by Charles I and his representatives and knew only too well how much the dominant Puritans in Parliament hated then. But few Irish Catholics had any real love for the king; to them he was only the lesser of two evils.

By the spring of 1642 the Irish rebellion had become a stalemate. The Irish held most of the country, but the English, in addition to Dublin, held the cities of Kinsale, Cork and Youghal in the south and Drogheda in the north, and half a dozen strong points in Ulster. The Irish appealed for help to the two great

---

[64] Fraser, *Cromwell*, pp. 72-76 (quote on 73); Casway, *Struggle for Catholic Ireland*, pp. 51-52; D. M. R. Esson, *The Curse of Cromwell; a History of the Ironside Conquest of Ireland, 1649-53* (Totowa NJ, 1971), pp. 52, 54-56; Wedgwood, *King's Peace*, pp. 469-470, 473; Wedgwood, *King's War*, pp. 21-22.

[65] Fraser, *Cromwell*, p. 80; Wedgwood, *King's War*, pp. 54-55; Casway, *Struggle for Catholic Ireland*, p. 53; Esson, *Curse of Cromwell*, pp. 58-59; von Pastor, *History of the Popes*, XXIX, 342, 346.

[66] Esson, *Curse of Cromwell*, p. 64.

Catholic powers, France and Spain, and to the Pope. At the end of April Ireland's leading royalist, the Earl of Ormonde (a Protestant originally named Butler), defeated a force of Irish Catholic rebels led by Lord Mountgarret, a veteran of the Nine Years War, at Kilrush. In May a convention of the Irish clergy at Kilkenny voted to support the uprising and urged the currently leaderless rebels to call an Irish parliament which would elect a Supreme Council of 24 to run the war. The assembly decreed that anyone abandoning the Catholic cause and supporting the Protestant enemy was to be excommunicated. In May Robert Munro's army of Ulster Scots massacred 60 prisoners and two priests at Newry, whereupon Phelim O'Neill burned the town of Armagh in retaliation. In the summer of 1642 an Irish Catholic army took Limerick. But also that summer Colonel Thomas Preston, Protestant son of a Norman-Irish nobleman who had fought with the Spanish in the Netherlands, arrived at Wexford to join the rising, at almost exactly the same time that Owen Roe O'Neill of the mighty heritage, sailing from Flanders round Scotland, arrived at Sheep Haven in Donegal with 300 soldiers and several seasoned officers, repelling two English ships which tried to pursue him there by the fire of three hastily emplaced cannon. His kinsman Phelim O'Neill set out immediately with several thousand men to join him in Donegal, and the army proclaimed Owen Roe O'Neill, a veteran soldier, as their commander-in-chief.[67]

In late October the Irish Catholic Confederacy was formed at Kilkenny in accord with the proposals of the Irish Catholic clergy in May. It elected the proposed 24-member Supreme Council and proclaimed itself in favor of the King against Parliament in the civil war already begun in England. But in December the Supreme Council made a catastrophic error when it divided the command in Ireland among the four ancient provinces, giving Owen Roe O'Neill only the command in Ulster, the Protestant Preston in Leinster, and two lesser figures in Munster and Connaught. It was the kind of compromise that always tends to commend itself to civilian legislative bodies, but every real soldier knows that unity of command is vital, especially when facing a powerful foe with few resources.[68]

In January 1643 the beleaguered King Charles I informed the Irish Catholics that, although he would delegate the Protestant Earl of Ormonde to negotiate with them, he would still not allow them legally to practice their faith, nor recognize any Irish parliament. Owen Roe O'Neill summoned a general meeting of Irish Catholic rebels in Ulster. Ormonde, fighting against the rebels, besieged New Ross in March but could not take it, but defeated General Preston in the course of his retreat. At the end of the month the Irish offered King Charles 10,000 men (an offer they were scarcely in a position to fulfill) in return for his recognizing an Irish parliament; but as was his habit, the King temporized,

---

[67] *Ibid.*, pp. 59, 64-66; Casway, *Struggle for Catholic Ireland*, pp. 52, 62-63, 89; Wedgwood, *King's War*, pp. 92-94, 96, 110; Fraser, *Cromwell*, p. 80; von Pastor, *History of the Popes* XXIX, 344, 346.

[68] Casway, *Struggle for Catholic Ireland*, pp. 64-65, 74; Esson, *Curse of Cromwell*, p. 65; von Pastor, *History of the Popes* XXIX, 345.

later secretly instructing Ormonde to raise an army to serve in England from both Irish and English—a scheme which came to nothing. In May the Catholic Irish won their first victory at Fermoy, inflicting a loss of six hundred men on the English, along with all their baggage, cannon and ammunition. In June Owen Roe O'Neill set out to march south from Ulster into central Ireland. His army, still largely undisciplined, was ambushed by the Ulster Scot army near Clones and suffered substantial losses despite a vigorous defense: about 150 Irish were killed, including several important officers. In September a year's truce was agreed upon, after six months of fitful negotiations, with all persons to retain the land they now had, but still without legal permission for the practice of the Catholic Faith. Pope Urban VIII had sent as special envoy to Ireland the distinguished Oratorian, Pier Francesco Scarampi, but no Italian could be expected immediately to grasp the almost fantastic complexity of the Irish political situation. Scarampi opposed the truce, unavailingly.[69]

In November 1643 the Irish parliament met at Waterford and considered pledging that town to foreign powers in exchange for money and aid. Owen Roe O'Neill denounced this plan and it was dropped. The delegates agreed to try to raise an army of 6,000 men, but foolishly did not give Owen Roe O'Neill the command of it. At the same time they appointed seven commissioners to present their grievances to Charles I. Owen Roe, whose only desire was to help the Irish cause in the land where he was born and was to die, dutifully accepted the authority of the inexperienced commander appointed by the Irish parliament, the youthful Earl of Castlehaven. In March 1644 the Irish commissioners reached King Charles I with their requests for free practice of their religion and a free parliament. He refused to respond or negotiate with them further, and turned the conduct of negotiations over to the Earl of Ormonde.[70] In fairness to Charles, it should be noted that any appearance of favoring or making concessions to the Irish Catholics on his part would have been devastating to him politically, in view of the bitterly anti-Catholic attitude of the English Puritans.

In February 1645 Irish leader Connor McGuire was hanged at Tyburn saying "Jesus, Jesus, Jesus!" By March Charles, growing desperate after his defeat by Cromwell at Marston Moor, wrote secretly to Ormonde in Ireland directing him to offer to suspend—not abrogate—the anti-Catholic laws and make peace with the Catholic rebels at almost any cost, so as to get some of their troops to fight in England, dubious as any such project was. King Philip IV of Spain wrote Owen Roe O'Neill words of sympathy rendered totally meaningless by his urging in the same letter that Owen Roe return to Spanish service in the Low Countries, which was the very last thing the nephew of the great O'Neill, now clearly his successor, would ever do. In May the new Pope Innocent X recalled envoy Scarampi and replaced him with another Italian totally unfamiliar with the Irish scene, Juan Battista Rinuccini, Archbishop of Fermo. At Kilkenny

---

[69] Casway, *Struggle for Catholic Ireland*, pp. 74, 78-83, 90-92; Esson, *Curse of Cromwell*, pp. 68-69; Wedgwood, *King's War*, pp. 190, 259-261; von Pastor, *History of the Popes* XXIX, 345-347.

[70] Casway, *Struggle for Catholic Ireland*, pp. 96-98, 101.

in August the Irish entered into a secret agreement with King Charles' commander Lord Glamorgan, a Catholic, by which they would be granted full freedom of worship and possession of all churches not actually occupied by the Protestants, in return for which they pledged ten thousand armed men and two-thirds of their Church property to the king. Papal envoy Scarampi, who had not yet departed, warned that the king would never keep any such agreement. When the titular archbishop of Tuam in Ireland was killed near Sligo in October, a copy of the secret agreement with Lord Glamorgan was found on his person and publicized early in 1646. King Charles immediately denied that he had made the agreement and denounced the Earl of Glamorgan. The Earl of Ormonde arrested him.[71]

In October 1645 the second Papal envoy, Rinuccini, arrived in Ireland and was met by Owen Roe O'Neill. In November he made solemn entry into the Irish rebel capital of Kilkenny in a downpour of rain, and urged the Irish to insist on a complete public and legal restoration of Catholicism in their country. The times seemed favorable; after the Battle of Naseby in June King Charles I faced defeat, and desperately needed the Irish troops to enable him to survive. The Catholic Earl of Glamorgan was rehabilitated and concluded early in April 1646 a peace treaty with the Irish Supreme Council relieving all Catholics from taking the oath of supremacy to the king as head of the Church and removing all penalties on their worship, but not giving them back their church lands. In return they were to send ten thousand men to England. But the treaty proved a dead letter; just a month after it was signed, Charles made his fatal surrender to the Scots who later sold him to the English Puritans.[72]

Early in June Owen Roe O'Neill marched to the Blackwater River in Ulster and, at Benburb on its north bank only a few miles from the site of the great victory of the Yellow Ford in 1598 by Hugh O'Neill and Red Hugh O'Donnell, secured a comparable triumph over the Ulster Scots, fighting in the name of the English Parliament, by leading in person a magnificent charge of his pike-bearing infantry.[73] Father Boetius MacEgan spoke to the soldiers just before the battle, saying they were fighting against:

> those that profane your churches [and have] turned your sweet native country to desolation . . . So let your manhood be seen by your push of pike: and I will engage, if you do so, by God's assistance and the intercession of his Blessed Mother and all the holy saints in heaven, that the day will be your own. Your word is Sancta Maria; and so in the name of the Father, Son and Holy Ghost advance, and give not fire till you are within pike-length.[74]

---

[71] *Ibid.*, pp. 114-115, 121-122; Esson, *Curse of Cromwell*, pp. 70-71; Wedgwood, *King's War*, pp. 421, 424, 534-535; von Pastor, *History of the Popes* XXX, 155-157, 160.

[72] Casway, *Struggle for Catholic Ireland*, pp. 115-116, 120; Esson, *Curse of Cromwell*, p. 73; Wedgwood, *King's War*, pp. 524-525; von Pastor, *History of the Popes* XXX, 157, 161.

[73] For the Battle of Benburb, see Casway, *Struggle for Catholic Ireland*, pp. 129-136; Esson, *Curse of Cromwell*, pp. 74-77; Wedgwood, *King's War*, pp. 562-563.

[74] Casway, *Struggle for Catholic Ireland*, p. 133.

Rarely was it made so clear on the Catholic as well as the Protestant side that in these years of the cleaving of Christendom, the great religious issue in many places was being decided by battle.

Monro, the Ulster Scot general defeated by Owen Roe O'Neill at Benburb, managed to escape, while Papal envoy Rinuccini, trying frantically to make sense of the chaotic Irish situation, began to believe the detractors of Owen Roe and to distance himself from the Irish Catholic champion. By the summer of 1646 no less than five armies were active in Ireland: Owen Roe's Catholic army; a separate Catholic army raised by Rinuccini; the Earl of Ormonde's royalist army consisting of both Catholics and Protestants; Monro's Ulster Scot army; and the official Parliamentary army commanded by Sir Charles Coote. Lord Mountgarret made a separate peace with the Earl of Ormonde. Rinuccini was horrified, protesting vigorously that the peace agreement made no provision for the free and legal practice of the Catholic faith. Most Irish bishops agreed with him, and so did Owen Roe. Nevertheless the Supreme Council at Kilkenny ratified the treaty, thereby greatly increasing the fragmentation in Ireland. A meeting of the Irish Catholic clergy in Waterford, led by Rinuccini, denounced it and excommunicated everyone principally involved in bringing it about. The next month Owen Roe O'Neill and Rinuccini with their separate armies entered Kilkenny in triumph. Owen Roe turned over the castle, the town and all hostages over to Rinuccini. Ormonde was in rapid retreat to Dublin, and the Supreme Council ordered an attack on it. But once again they divided the command between Owen Roe O'Neill and the Protestant Thomas Preston. Early in October the old Supreme Council was dissolved and another one formed with Rinuccini as president. Ormonde finally abandoned the temporarily lost royalist cause and appealed to the English Parliament for help against the victorious Catholics in Ireland.[75]

Despite the flare-up of an old leg ailment, fever, and the increasing burdens of age, Owen Roe O'Neill harried the Earl of Ormonde into Dublin at the end of the year 1646 and besieged him there. Parliamentary reinforcements arrived in January, however, and a now badly outnumbered Owen Roe retreated from it. A new Irish parliament met in Kilkenny in February, but with so many divisions that most of its members did little or nothing but dispute with one another, giving the phrase "quarrelling like Kilkenny cats" to the English language. Rinuccini had now been sufficiently prejudiced against Owen Roe O'Neill that he would not speak to him when they were both at Kilkenny in April 1647. He wrote to the Pope that this lifelong Catholic champion, heir to the leadership of Catholic Ireland, was not sincere in his religious motivations and was seeking only to further his own personal interests. He was even criticized for calling his army Catholic, which it most certainly was. In May, preparing for another attack on Dublin, Owen Roe was stunned to learn that the new Supreme Council intended

---

[75] *Ibid.*, pp. 142, 144-146, 148, 151-152, 154; Esson, *Curse of Cromwell*, p. 77; Fraser, *Cromwell*, pp. 182-183; Wedgwood, *King's War*, pp. 593, 596-597; von Pastor, *History of the Popes* XXX, 162.

to send him to Connaught, the least militarily significant of all the four Irish provinces. At the end of June the Earl of Ormonde turned Dublin over to a Parliamentary army headed by Michael Jones and left Ireland, not to return until the Restoration.[76]

In the summer of 1647 Owen Roe O'Neill led his army on a difficult passage of the Curlew Mountains and attacked Scottish garrisons near Sligo, finally laying siege to it, but he had insufficient support. In August the Parliamentarian Colonel Jones defeated General Preston at the Battle of Dungan's Hill (Preston had never yet managed to win a significant victory; he must have been very good at self-promotion to hold on to his position, but perhaps his Protestantism aided him since he was one of the few Protestants the Irish could claim to be on their side.) As a result of this victory, the new Supreme Irish Council finally realized their need for Owen Roe O'Neill, and sent him back into Leinster to try to undo the effects of the English triumph at Dungan's Hill. In September there was a near mutiny, since most of the men had not been paid for months.[77] Owen Roe O'Neill firmly put it down, with these words:

> I came to this kingdom with the intent to serve the king and the nation in general, and in particular the province wherein I was born, and that no further reason and justice would dictate; and I do tell you no pretense or color, or any notion whatsoever, will dislodge me from discharging to the utmost of my power the many assurances of this kind I gave the Supreme Council, and the nation in general, and you before.[78]

In this age of betrayal Owen Roe O'Neill, like Montrose, was true unto death. In November 1647, as he stood on the battlefield of Dungan's Hill, he spoke to his army the inspiring words quoted at the head of this chapter. He then approached within five miles of Dublin. Michael Jones harassed him with cavalry, but seeing the size of the Irish host, he waited for reinforcements in infantry. Just a week later, however, Parliamentary Lord Inchiquin defeated the disorganized army of Lord Taaffe at Knockanoss in Munster, leaving Owen Roe's the only effective Irish army in the field.[79]

The Irish parliament assembled in Kilkenny that month with only 73 members present, a majority of whom were now determined to throw in their lot with the Earl of Ormonde and abandon the Catholic crusade. On January 3, 1648 the assembly dissolved, after passing whatever authority it had left to a new Supreme Council of 48. Owen Roe O'Neill was vehemently attacked by this body, to move him aside for the Earl of Ormonde, and Owen Roe had to flee from Kilkenny in disguise. In February Lord Inchiquin advanced toward Kilkenny with his victorious troops from Munster, but Owen Roe promptly

---

[76] Casway, *Struggle for Catholic Ireland*, pp. 167-168, 178-179, 181; Esson, *Curse of Cromwell*, pp. 78-79; von Pastor, *History of the Popes* XXX, 165.

[77] Casway, *Struggle for Catholic Ireland*, pp. 184-185, 187-189.

[78] *Ibid.*, p. 193

[79] *Ibid.*, pp. 197-200.

returned and stopped him. The Council made a truce which both O'Neill and Papal envoy Rinuccini opposed. On May 10 Rinuccini met with Owen Roe at camp in Maryborough. The time had surely come for them to join forces; the Italian had now been in Ireland three years and should at last have been able to take its Catholic leader's measure. It seems that he did so. But his own authority was now greatly lessened, and the Ormondist Supreme Council late in May declared Owen Roe O'Neill dismissed from all command. When the letter announcing this suicidal action was delivered to Owen Roe, he finally gave way to his real feelings, and threw it into the fire. Then he marched on Kilkenny, approaching to within three miles. The Supreme Council declared him in rebellion, and he retired to avoid a battle against other Catholic Irishmen.[80]

The Ormondists in the Irish parliament took this as weakness. Convening in general session in September 1648, they vitriolically condemned Owen Roe, saying he and his clerical adherents sought to enslave the nation. They commanded all Irish generals and magistrates to "proceed against and destroy the said Owen O'Neill as an enemy and traitor on pain of being proceeded with themselves in case of their willful neglect." Rinuccini was ordered to depart from Ireland, accused of "transcendent crimes and capital offenses." At the end of the month Ormonde returned to Ireland as Parliament's new viceroy there.[81] All in all, it is as ugly an example of ingratitude as any to be found in history.

Owen Roe was fought out. He was approaching seventy and had been in the field in the cold bogs of Ireland for seven years. His health began a steady decline. Nevertheless he still held out for freedom to practice the Catholic Faith in Ireland, restoration of the ancestral Irish estates, and amnesty for all involved in the rebellion since 1641. Meanwhile in March 1649 the English Parliament asked Oliver Cromwell to lead an expedition to Ireland, which it confirmed three days after abolishing the monarchy in England. Cromwell had long been eager to do this, to teach the Irish, whom he firmly believed had been guilty of atrocious massacres of Protestants, a lesson they would never forget. So he did. Irish today still speak of "the curse of Cromwell."[82]

On August 25 Oliver Cromwell landed at Dublin with 35 ships, proclaiming "that all those whose heart's affections were real for the carrying on of the great work against the barbarous and bloodthirsty Irish, and the rest of their adherents and confederates . . . should find favor and protection from the Parliament of England." Two days later his son-in-law Henry Ireton arrived with no less than 77 ships. The New Model army and the Ironside cavalry, the best in the world in their time, were to be loosed on the now almost helpless Irish.[83]

Even at his best, at the time of his victory at Benburb, Owen Roe O'Neill would have been outclassed. He was a good general, but Cromwell was a great

---

[80] *Ibid.*, pp. 201, 205-207, 210, 212, 219, 221, 224-226.

[81] *Ibid.*, pp. 227-230, 233 (quote on 229).

[82] *Ibid.*, pp. 245-246, 251-252; Esson, *Curse of Cromwell*, p. 90 and *passim*; Fraser, *Cromwell*, pp. 310-311.

[83] Fraser, *Cromwell*, pp. 326-327 (quote on 327); Esson, *Curse of Cromwell*, pp. 102-103.

one. Cromwell had all the wealth of England behind him, since he was already effectively its dictator, and more than any other man he had been responsible for the execution of its king. Ireland had been reduced to dire poverty by eight years of civil war among so many factions that a man could hardly keep count of them. And Cromwell approached his task with a vicious hatred for all Irish Catholics that could hardly be believed if we did not have his own explicit testimony to it, expressed most memorably in the quotation from him at the head of this chapter. Marching out of Dublin on the 10th of September, Cromwell soon reached Drogheda to the north, bombarded it, and summoned it to surrender; but the garrison would not. After his first attack on the 21st was repulsed, Cromwell ordered another which he personally led. He wrote shortly afterward: "Our men getting up to them, were ordered by me to put them all to the sword. And indeed, being in the heat of action, I forbade them to spare any that were in arms in the town." The commander of the garrison was beaten to death with his own wooden leg; about 3,500 people were killed, including women and children. To the House of Commons Cromwell wrote: "This is a righteous judgment on these barbarous wretches, who have imbued their hands with so much innocent blood."[84]

Since he could no longer walk, Owen Roe O'Neill was being carried on a horse litter with his army to County Tyrone when he heard the terrible news. By October Cromwell's Colonel Venables had overrun much of O'Neill's native Ulster, and therefore Cromwell turned south, and summoned the heavily defended city of Wexford, which defied him, to surrender. Its commander, Colonel David Sinnott, heroically refused Cromwell's demand for surrender, despite the ghastly lesson of Drogheda. The Earl of Ormonde came up on Wexford with 3,000 men, but dared not challenge Cromwell, and marched away again without a fight. On October 19 Cromwell began to bombard it, and on the 21st he stormed it and once again put everyone he could find within to the sword. At least 1,500 persons inside Wexford were killed, including some two hundred women. Priests were killed, scourged, and thrown into drains. Cromwell declared that God had "brought a righteous judgment upon them to become a prey to the soldier . . . it were to be wished that an honest people would come and plant here." Paralyzed by fear of yet another such massacre, New Ross surrendered to Cromwell, but begged him to respect the religious conscience of its people.[85] Cromwell replied:

I meddle not with any man's conscience. But if by liberty of conscious you mean liberty to exercise the Mass, I judge it best to use plain dealing, and to

---

[84] Esson, *Curse of Cromwell,* pp. 104-105, 110-113 (first quote 111); Fraser, *Cromwell,* pp. 329, 336-340 (second quote 338). This deliberate massacre took far more lives than any of which the Irish had ever been specifically accused.

[85] Fraser, *Cromwell,* pp. 343, 345-348 (quote on 345); Esson, *Curse of Cromwell,* pp. 117, 120-122, 125; Casway, *Struggle for Catholic Ireland,* p. 256.

let you know, where the Parliament of England have power, that will not be allowed.[86]

Still in camp, Owen Roe O'Neill lay dying, and passed from this embattled earth on November 16, 1649.[87] In one of his last letters he firmly declared:

Being now on my death-bed, without any hope of recovery, I call my Savior to witness, that as I hope for salvation, my resolution, ways and intentions, from first to last in these unhappy wars, tended to no particular ambition or private interest of my own.[88]

Because of the calumnies spread against him and his ultimate failure against insuperable odds, Owen Roe O'Neill to a considerable extent has been denied his place among the Catholic heroes of Ireland. Even Jerrold Casway in his well-researched book about Owen Roe disclaims in advance any intent to glorify him. But no man showed more constancy in the Catholic cause despite all adversity and betrayal, than Owen Roe O'Neill. Can a man do more than die in the field for his cause? His praises should be sung so long as Catholic Ireland endures.

There was now no way left to avert "the curse of Cromwell." In December he took Cork; the Earl of Ormonde fled to the continent of Europe, not to return for twelve years, until Cromwell was safely dead. In the depth of winter 1650 Cromwell completed the conquest of Munster. The Irish could find no one better to command their depleted armies than a bishop with no military experience. In April Cromwell took Clonmel. In June he returned to a hero's welcome in London, leaving his son-in-law Henry Ireton behind to complete the war. Two weeks later Parliamentary general Sir Charles Coote destroyed what had been Owen Roe O'Neill's Ulster army, incompetently commanded by the bishop, who was captured and executed along with most of his officers. The great Irish fort of Charlemont in Ulster made a magnificent defense under Phelim O'Neill, not surrendering until only thirty men out of 150 were left able to fight. (Three years later, Phelim was hanged, drawn and quartered by the victorious English.) One by one, the remaining Irish leaders and garrisons surrendered. Ireton brilliantly crossed the Shannon River and took Limerick after a long siege. He paid for it with his life, dying in the west of Ireland in December at the age of only forty, at least partly due to the rigors of the climate. His death removed the most likely successor of Cromwell from the scene.[89]

There remained the Cromwellian land settlement, one of the most vindictive in all history. In August 1652 all Irish were divided into five categories: (1) those in rebellion before November 1642, all subject to the death

---

[86] Fraser, *Cromwell*, p. 347.

[87] Casway, *Struggle for Catholic Ireland*, pp. 261-262.

[88] *Ibid.*, p. 261

[89] Fraser, *Cromwell*, pp. 348-349, 351-353; Esson, *Curse of Cromwell*, pp. 127, 132-133, 138-141, 143, 145, 148-149, 151-154, 181; Casway, *Struggle for Catholic Ireland*, pp. 264-267.

penalty and total forfeiture of their land; (2) the entire priesthood, all subject to the death penalty; (3) leading noblemen excluded from the pardon; (4) Irish who had killed any civilians, who were to be executed; (5) all the other Catholic people of Ireland, soldiers and civilians, who could not show "constant good affection" to the English Parliament and its army, who were to lose two-thirds of their land and be transplanted to Connaught, Ireland's poorest province, supposedly to get there the equivalent of one-third of their land. Some of the English officers tried to protect some of the Irish from the full rigors of this deportation, especially in the dead of winter; in June 1655 Cromwell's General Fleetwood issued a blistering order condemning and prohibiting any such clemency.[90]

But a generation later, Ireland was to rise again, and almost win its independence under the great Patrick Sarsfield.[91]

When Cromwell returned from Ireland in June 1650, he found himself immediately facing another war with Scotland—with the nation's Calvinist or Covenanting army, not with Montrose. That splendid hero had returned to Scotland in March 1650 despite reports that Charles II was abandoning him in favor of the Covenanters, to whom in May he made sweeping promises of support for their Presbyterian church, which he had no intention of fulfilling if he could possibly avoid it, and approved their much-heralded Covenant. Montrose landed in the remote Orkney Islands to the north after a bad storm, which sank the ships carrying his ammunition. He rallied several hundred young Orkneymen totally unfamiliar with warfare; most of them had never even seen a horse. They were routed by cavalry in the Battle of Carbisdale. A thick mist settled on the bleak landscape of far northern Scotland, and Montrose became separated from his companions, several of whom died of exposure. At length he came to the McLeod country and the little castle of Ardvreck on Loch Assynt, where the young McLeod chief offered him hospitality—and then, prompted by his greedy wife for the sake of the enormous reward, turned him in. On May 28 Montrose was led captive through the streets of Edinburgh while the mob demonstrated against him, and the Duke of Argyll looked on through a shutter held ajar.[92]

At his much abbreviated trial, Montrose declared: "Let me be judged by the laws of God, the laws of nations and of nature, and the laws of this land. If you do otherwise, I do here appeal to you to the righteous Judge of the world."[93] The Scots Committee of Estates sentenced him to be hanged for three hours on a gibbet 30 feet high, then drawn and quartered, with parts of his body to be displayed on the town gates of Stirling, Glasgow, Perth, and Aberdeen, and his

---

[90] Esson, *Curse of Cromwell*, pp. 160-167, 179; Fraser, *Cromwell*, pp. 498-499. The death penalty was applied to any of these Irish who would not move to Connaught. That is the origin of Cromwell's celebrated statement that he was sending them "to Hell or Connaught" (Esson, *op. cit.*, p. 164).

[91] See Volume Five, Chapter 2 of this history

[92] Wedgwood, *Montrose*, pp. 136-142, 147-148, 156-157; Fraser, *Royal Charles*, pp. 80, 89-92; Fraser, *Cromwell*, p. 359.

[93] Wedgwood, *Montrose*, p. 150.

head on the gate of Edinburgh. Let them be posted up, he said; they would serve as lasting monuments to his unbreakable loyalty. He died magnificently on May 31, just 38 years old. All the trained bands of Edinburgh escorted him to the gallows, thousands of armed men against the great general who now had none; he mocked them: "Are you afraid of me still? My ghost will defeat you yet!" To a last visitation by the Calvinist ministers he said: "I acknowledge nothing but fear God and honor the king. I have not sinned against man but God, and with Him there is mercy." He concluded with the words quoted at the head of this chapter. The executioner wept visibly as he tied his hands. The Duke of Argyll also killed all the officers who had served with Montrose and enslaved the Orcadian countrymen who had volunteered for his last army.[94]

On July 4 Charles II landed in Scotland as the puppet of the Duke of Argyll. Montrose was already dead; and although the new young king had not directly betrayed him (he had written in January to Montrose explaining that he judged it necessary to negotiate with the Covenanters, a letter which Montrose received only after he had landed in the Orkney Islands, and Charles did not agree to swear to the Covenant until the very day of Montrose's defeat at Carbisdale),[95] he had come very close to it. Charles II gained nothing and lost much by this evil bargain. But for its unexpected sequel he would almost certainly never have recovered from it.

In mid-July, just six weeks after returning from Ireland to England, Cromwell summoned Scotland to surrender, and on August 1 he crossed the Scottish border. General Leslie commanded the Scottish army, fighting in the name of Charles II but actually for its Presbyterian Covenant and the Duke of Argyll. Leslie was a veteran of long service as a mercenary in the Thirty Years War, where he had learned to lead men competently in battle; but against Oliver Cromwell far more than mere competence was needed. Never did Cromwell's military genius show itself to such advantage as at the epochal Battle of Dunbar on September 13, the greatest of all his victories. Leslie had twice his force and was entrenched atop cliffs along the coast road to Dunbar. The Scots Committee of the Estates, mostly civilian, ordered Leslie to attack so as to use his advantage in numbers. But Oliver Cromwell never waited to be attacked. At dawn he made a surprise counter-attack on the Scots and routed them with his Ironside cavalry. Three thousand were killed and ten thousand taken prisoner. Oliver Cromwell had won another war—his fourth.[96]

---

[94] *Ibid.*, pp. 148-150, 152-156 (quotes on 153).

[95] *Ibid.*, pp. 130, 156-157; Fraser, *Royal Charles*, pp. 86, 89-92; Fraser, *Cromwell*, p. 359.

[96] Fraser, *Cromwell*, pp. 363-365, 367-372. The four wars included the English civil war, the war in Ireland, and two wars against Scotland, the first having been won at the Battle of Preston in 1648. The Battle of Dunbar was preserved in folk memory by my Maine ancestors until the twentieth century, since the first of them, James Warren, was taken prisoner by Cromwell at Dunbar, and sent to Maine as an indentured servant. I have not been able to determine if he was fighting Cromwell as a royalist or as a Covenanter, though the tradition was that he was a "cavalier."

Despite this tremendous defeat, the Scots led by the Duke of Argyll carried out their plan to crown Charles II on the traditional "Stone of Scone" at the beginning of January 1651; the Duke of Argyll put the crown on his head. In March Charles II persuaded the Scottish parliament to permit him to recruit soldiers among the Highlanders, who had proved their worth in Montrose's campaigns, and they agreed that despite his youth he should be commander-in-chief (age and experience had not availed for Leslie). When in August Cromwell marched north of Edinburgh to take Perth, Charles recklessly took a mixed army of royalists and Scots south, from which the Duke of Argyll prudently absented himself. On September 1 Charles, marching fast with no real opposition, reached the strongly royalist city of Worcester, which rose in his favor. He had 16,000 men, but not with many good officers and not accustomed to working together. Cromwell had 31,000 of the best soldiers in the world. On September 13 he struck like a pile-driver. The Duke of Hamilton was killed, General Leslie refused to fight, and the royalists were forced back into the city of Worcester with great slaughter. Two thousand were killed, nine thousand were captured, and in an overwhelming pursuit Cromwell scattered all the remainder and scored yet another resounding triumph (his last) in this Battle of Worcester. Charles, fleeing the doomed city with a party of about sixty, lost his way in the darkness of the night.[97]

Charles II at 21 was neither an army commander, a diplomat, nor a political manipulator. He had not lived long enough to be any of these. But he had nerves of steel and a boyish zest for adventure. He might not be able to defeat Oliver Cromwell in battle, but he was confident that, though caught in the middle of England far from the sea, he could still elude him and escape. And he did.

The story has been often retold,[98] but it has an ever-fresh and ever-new quality, a true romance, almost like a fairy tale. It showed Charles at his very best, making a place for him in the hearts of most Englishmen, wiping away the memory of his craven surrender to the Earl of Argyll and the Scots Covenanters. If it did not lead to his immediate triumph, it was because no man could displace Oliver Cromwell while he still lived. But it laid the foundation for Charles' eventual restoration.

As the royal party sought to find their way in the open country north of Worcester on the night of September 13, one of them, Lord Derby, recommended that they seek refuge and help from the people in England much the most experienced in hiding and helping fugitives: the outlawed Catholics. When they finally got their bearings, a Catholic named Charles Gifford[99] who was with the party urged the king to go to an isolated house they owned about fifteen miles further on, called Whiteladies. The fugitives reached Whiteladies at dawn and

---

[97] *Ibid.*, pp. 378, 383-390; Fraser, *Royal Charles*, pp. 98-100, 103, 108-111, 113.

[98] The best and most thorough modern account is Richard Ollard, *The Escape of Charles II after the Battle of Worcester* (New York, 1966). Almost as good, though shorter, is that of Antonia Fraser in *Royal Charles*, pp. 114-128.

[99] Strangely, this was the same family from which the turncoat Gilbert Gifford, who betrayed Mary Queen of Scots, had come. See Chapter Eight, above.

were welcomed by George Penderel, who was renting the house and had four brothers living nearby, all Catholic recusants. Charles took off his royal clothes and put on the dress of a woodman. One of the Penderel brothers met a priest on the road who had been in hiding with them, Father John Huddleston, and told him the identity of their guest. Father Huddleston at once recommended another local Catholic gentleman, Thomas Whitgreave of Moseley Old Hall, in whose house he had often stayed secretly and who he was sure would help. That night Charles and Richard Penderel walked nine miles to the home of another Catholic, Francis Wolfe, who informed them when they knocked at his door that he dared not help any fugitive at that moment unless it were the king himself. Told that it was indeed the king himself who was asking his help, he invited him in, and found a hiding place for him under the hay in his barn. Charles darkened his skin by an infusion of walnut leaves and set out for Boscobel, a house in which Humphrey Penderel lived. Reaching it at dawn, he found another fugitive from Worcester, Captain Carlis, who told him he had found a very good hiding place in a large and leafy oak tree. Charles joined him there and spent the day, clutching its trunk as soldiers went by underneath searching for him. The tree has ever since been famous as the "royal oak." England built a battleship by that name in the early twentieth century.[100]

At nightfall Charles climbed down from the royal oak and had supper with Humphrey Penderel, learning for the first time that Cromwell had put a reward of a thousand pounds on his head, more money than the average workman could earn in a lifetime (and scorned by all of the fifty or more people who helped Charles II escape). Charles spent the night in the "priest's hole" at Boscobel, a tiny hideaway where he could not stretch out to his full height, which was over six feet. The next day he went to Whitgreave at Moseley Old Hall, whom Father Huddleston had recommended, and stayed in the "priest's hole" which Father Huddleston had used. The priest showed Charles his secret chapel, and Charles said: "If it please God, I come to my crown, both you and all of your persuasion shall have as much liberty as any of my subjects." Two days later Father Huddleston discussed the Catholic faith with Charles and gave him a catechism and a tract written by his uncle entitled "A Short and Plain Way to the Faith and the Church," about which Charles said: "I have not seen anything more plain or clear on this subject. The arguments drawn from succession are so conclusive, I do not see how they can be denied."[101]

Whether Charles was simply being kind and appreciative to Father Huddleston, without real religious feelings involved, has been much debated. If he had proclaimed himself a Catholic convert, Charles would never have regained his throne. But it was his mother's faith, and the faith of those who were saving him from the vengeance of Cromwell. At least, it must have made a real impression on him. Conversion is a grace full of mystery.[102] Whenever it

---

[100] Ollard, *Escape of Charles II*, pp. 22-29, 32-41; Fraser, *Royal Charles*, pp. 113-119.

[101] Ollard, *Escape of Charles II*, pp. 37-49, 53-55; Fraser, *Royal Charles*, pp. 120-121 (first quote on 120, second quote on 121).

[102] As I can testify, as a convert myself at age 36.

came to Charles, he announced it on his deathbed in 1684. When Father Huddleston almost miraculously appeared again when he asked for a priest, Charles said to him: "You that saved my body have now come to save my soul."[103]

Plans were now made for Charles, disguised as a servant called Will Jackson, to accompany a party escorting a woman named Jane Lane, a Colonel's daughter, who was visiting a friend near Bristol who was about to give birth, and had obtained permission for the trip before the Battle of Worcester. Cromwell's soldiers in the vicinity had heard from a captured officer who was tortured, that Charles was nearby. The houses of Whiteladies and Boscobel were thoroughly searched and all the Penderels' provisions were taken, but nothing could be proved against them. Enroute to the Bristol area, Jane Lane's horse lost a shoe; it was the task of "Will Jackson" to get it replaced. Charles chatted with the blacksmith as he put on the horseshoe, saying: "What news?" "There is no news, except the good news of beating those rogues the Scots," the smith replied. Charles then asked if "that rogue Charles Stuart" had been caught, and declared roundly that he deserved to be hanged. "Spoken like an honest man!" declared the smith, never dreaming that he was standing in the presence of "that rogue Charles Stuart" himself. This episode in particular showed how much young Charles was enjoying his perilous adventure.[104]

When Charles reached the Bristol area, he discovered that no ships were available for hire there. He had to make his way to the English Channel coast instead. On September 26 Cromwell's Council of State issued peremptory new instructions to all its officials "to use the best means they can for the discovery of Charles Stuart." He went to Castle Cary, the home of royalist Colonel Frank Wyndham and his Catholic wife in the small village of Trent near Lyme (later renamed Lyme Regis for its part in the king's escape) in Dorsetshire. Colonel Wyndham remembered how his father had warned all his five sons that troubled times were coming, and they must hold fast to the king through all of them. Wyndham contacted a merchant named Ellesdon, who knew of a ship ready to sail to the French coast. Its captain, Stephen Limbry, agreed to take two English fugitives to France (Charles and Lord Wilmot, a high-ranking royalist) without knowing who they were. The ship was supposed to sail at about midnight, but Captain Limbry never appeared. It was later learned that his wife, hearing that he was to transport two royalists to France, feared for his life and locked him in his room to prevent him from making the rendezvous.[105]

The next day the ostler at the inn deduced that Charles was an important person from the expensive shoes on his horse, even suspecting that it might be the king. He went immediately to the local minister, John Westley (great-grandfather of the famous Methodist evangelist), but had to wait for an hour or more while Westley finished his prayers, and then took no decisive action. Also

---

[103] Fraser, *Royal Charles*, p. 454.

[104] *Ibid.*, pp. 121-122 (quotes on 122); Ollard, *Escape of Charles II*, pp. 57-62.

[105] Ollard, *Escape of Charles II*, pp. 64-66, 68-76, 80-82, 84-85; Fraser, *Royal Charles*, pp. 122-125.

put off by a justice of the peace, the ostler finally reported his suspicions to Captain Macy of the Parliamentary army, who sent cavalry in pursuit of the man with the expensive horseshoes. Cutting back to Trent, the party with Charles turned off the main road from Dorchester to London just five minutes before Macy would have caught them. Charles continued to hide out with Colonel Wyndham at Trent Manor for two weeks. Then terms were agreed with royalist Colonel Phelips and a merchant named Horne for the hire of a ship, but it was commandeered by the New Model army now headed for the conquest of the Channel island of Jersey. Charles II now set out for the home of Mrs. Amphillis Hyde, the widow of a cousin of his chancellor Edward Hyde, later Lord Clarendon, where he spent five days. She recognized him but said nothing. Inquiries along the coast finally turned up a third ship, the appropriately named brig *Surprise*, whose captain, Nicholas Tattersall, was willing to take two gentlemen to France to escape the consequences of a duel they had supposedly fought.[106]

The *Surprise* was anchored at Brighton on the Sussex coast. With just three companions Charles set out for Brighton. At the village of Bramber they encountered soldiers, but were not discovered. They took rooms at the George Inn in Brighton, where Captain Tattersall came for supper. He at once recognized the king, who had once given him back his ship in Holland, and fell on his knees before him, begging him to make him a lord when he came into his kingdom. (And Charles did remember all those who helped in his escape, rewarding them in various substantial ways after his restoration as king.) An offshore wind began to blow, and the *Surprise* sailed at dawn. No more than two hours later a Parliamentary ship came searching all along the Sussex coast for the fugitive king. The *Surprise* left the Isle of Wight at five o'clock in the afternoon. In the first light of morning the French coast appeared ahead near the little town of Fécamp. They made a quick secret landing, seaman Richard Carver of Captain Tattersall's crew carrying Charles ashore on his back. The wind began to blow hard from the southeast, so that Tattersall could make a quick return to England undetected. Charles II and Lord Wilmot hired horses to ride to Rouen, and a coach to get to Paris, where they arrived late in the evening of October 30, to be met by Charles' mother Henrietta Maria and escorted triumphantly to the Louvre. From Paris the news of Charles' almost miraculous escape was broadcast to the world. He had indeed outwitted Oliver Cromwell and all his minions.[107]

The France to which Charles II thus dramatically returned was itself wracked by civil war, though not as severe as the civil wars in the British Isles. Following the death of King Louis XIII in 1643 and the accession of his son, Louis XIV, as a minor, the country had been under the regency of the Spanish queen mother, Anne of Austria, and the dominant and highly unpopular figure of

---

[106] Ollard, *Escape of Charles II*, pp. 86-93, 99-106, 112-115, 117; Fraser, *Royal Charles*, pp. 125-127.

[107] Ollard, *Escape of Charles II*, pp. 123-138; Fraser, *Royal Charles*, pp. 127-128.

the Italian Cardinal Mazarin (originally Mazarini). The country had generally accepted the growing autocracy of Cardinal Richelieu, sanctioned as it was by King Louis XIII. But now many were ready to protest absolute rule, even in arms. In the same year that the Peace of Westphalia was signed and the Scots sold King Charles I to the English, the disorganized street rebellion in Paris known as "the Fronde" (from the French word for slingshot) broke out and forced Cardinal Mazarin, the Queen Mother and the boy king to flee their capital. Since then the Fronde had flared up again on several occasions, and eventually was supported by Marshal Turenne who had fought with distinction in the Thirty Years War. The issues at stake were vague and confused, but they revolved around a perception of excessive royal power now in the hands of foreigners, the Spanish Queen Mother and the Italian cardinal. In October 1651, the very month Charles II was escaping from England, the Prince of Condé, leader of what was called the Second Fronde inspired by some of by the French nobility, sent a mission to England asking Cromwell for 100,000 pounds and ten thousand men. Cromwell replied that he would come himself with fifty thousand men if France would overthrow its monarchy. That was far beyond Condé's intentions, and he ended negotiations for English intervention at once. Cardinal Mazarin was now recalled, and in December Condé was attainted by the *Parlement* of Paris. Marshal Turenne changed sides, and Cardinal Mazarin returned to court late in April 1652.[108]

In the background of the developing divisions within Catholic France was a major new heresy, put forward by a Flemish Catholic theologian and bishop named Cornelius Jansen, whose large book on St. Augustine was published shortly after his death in 1638. St. Augustine, the Doctor of grace and the great opponent of the Pelagian heresy that man can save himself by his own efforts, in the course of decades of theological dispute occasionally expressed himself in ways susceptible to a Lutheran and Calvinist interpretation, that good works avail nothing and that saving faith is all due to special grace which does not require personal cooperation. This was the interpretation of St. Augustine's teaching which Jansen gave. Though in many respects a kind of Catholic Calvinism, one key difference was the great Jansenist veneration of the Eucharist, which led them with their incorrect theology to presume that very few believers were ever worthy of receiving It, except perhaps immediately before death. Since Jansen died before his book was published, he could not champion his heresy, but its cause was quickly taken up by Jansen's close French friend, the Abbé de St. Cyran, and by the prestigious family of Arnauld, whose head Antoine in the late 16th century had been a Calvinist until the St. Bartholomew's Day massacre. Antoine's widow and their six daughters all entered the convent of Port-Royal. Joined later by six nieces, they soon dominated this community. Jansen, St. Cyran and the Arnaulds combined their vision of a purified church with strong

---

[108] *Cambridge Modern History* IV, 607, 611-616; A. Lloyd Moote, *Revolt of the Judges; the Parlement of Paris and the Fronde, 1643-1652* (Princeton NJ, 1971), pp. 151-153, 155, 186, 189-191, 193, 210-213, 218, 260, 264, 273, 275, 291-295, 297, 300, 304-305, 324, 338; Fraser, *Cromwell*, p. 409; von Pastor, *History of the Popes* XXX, 67.

hostility to the Jesuits, who had spelled out in detail the truly Catholic doctrine of grace (that men must cooperate with it) in a series of writings over the preceding fifty years. This hostility to the Jesuits was shared by many in France who did not necessarily agree with the heresy, but considered it tolerable and a good way of rallying anti-Jesuit sentiment. And the Jansenist belief fitted in with a long-lasting French tendency (notably shown in the Catharist heresy of the 13th century) to follow people who ostentatiously proclaimed themselves "holier than thou"—a tendency also characteristic of England in these years of the triumph of the Puritans. Like all advocates of the doctrine of the Elect, Jansenists were always sure that they were a part of it, forgetting Christ's scathing discourses against the Pharisees.[109]

Pope Urban VIII was reliably informed of the contents of Jansen's book before its posthumous publication, and on July 19, 1640 prohibited its printing. But he was too late; the printing was done five days before the date of his decree. The University of Louvain, where Jansen had been a much respected professor, insisted that his book had nothing heretical in it, making great point of the fact that Pope Urban VIII had not actually read it before condemning it, but only brief condensations by others. (It was an enormous volume.) In August 1641 the book was condemned by the Roman Inquisition; a month later circulation of the Inquisition's decree of condemnation was prohibited by the council of Brabant, the Belgian province in which the University of Louvain was located. In December Pope Urban VIII condemned the refusal of the University of Louvain to publish and abide by the Inquisition's decision, and in March 1642 wrote the bull *In eminenti* against the book, though it was not published until the following year. The Pope had spoken, and on a strictly doctrinal issue on which even most of the French Gallicans, who believed their church was not always required to obey the Pope in matters of Church government, had recognized his supreme authority.[110]

News of his decision did not arrive in France until after the death of Cardinal Richelieu, when authority of all kinds began to be questioned in that country. In a manner that will be familiar to all who lived through or have studied the 1960's in America, Jansen's ideas became suddenly fashionable despite, or perhaps because of, the Pope's condemnation. Again and again its defenders asserted that the Pope had not understood the book, that there was no basis for the accusations of heresy. In October 1643 Pope Urban VIII sent briefs to the governor of the Spanish Netherlands (Belgium), to Archbishop Boonen of Brussels (who had supported the position of the University of Louvain) and to the University of Louvain itself, calling all the objections to his bull against Jansen's book "futile, frivolous and impotent" and called on the authorities to proceed against the presumptuous professors. But the popularity of the heresy and the reputation of its defenders continued to grow apace in France. In that same month of October the Abbé St. Cyran died, but the leadership of the Jansenist

---

[109] von Pastor, *History of the Popes* XXIX, 66-103. For the Catharist heresy, see Volume Three, Chapter 5 of this history.

[110] *Ibid.*, XXIX, 62-63, 102-105, 114-120.

movement was taken over by Antoine Arnauld Jr., youngest son of his namesake father, brilliant, versatile, committed, a bitter hater of the Jesuits and a fine writer, whose first book, "On Frequent Communion"—which he greatly deplored—had just been published and was being eagerly discussed by most French intellectuals. He was a young man and continued to lead the Jansenists for half a century.[111]

The University of Louvain continued to hold out against the Papal decision and authority. Papal nuncio Bichi in Brussels wrote to Pope Innocent X in July 1645 that Archbishop Boonen definitely favored the Jansenists. In that year many French bishops wrote to him in support of Arnauld's Jansenist book against frequent Communion. Upon hearing in December 1646 that the Papal bull against Jansenism had still not been published in the Spanish Netherlands, King Philip IV expressed astonishment, and indicated its publication was his wish, which he reiterated two years later when informed that many dioceses in the Spanish Netherlands still had not published or circulated it. Probably the most significant intervention in the controversy came from the most famous priest in France, a peasant's son, a man whose name is still attached to one of the principal Catholic charities in the world: St. Vincent de Paul. Such was his fame for humility, love and charity that Cardinal Mazarin actually appointed him to the French "Council of Conscience" to deal with ecclesiastical issues, particularly the nomination of bishops, only to try to remove him when his calls to follow a Catholic conscience became too uncomfortable for the worldly Cardinal. None could see more clearly than this saint of the poor the Satanic pride that animated so many Jansenists. In a letter written in September 1648 he accused the Jansenists of driving good people away from the Body and Blood of the Lord. At the beginning he had taken the Jansenists' measure. When the Abbé St. Cyran told him that God had revealed to him that no true Church had existed for five or six centuries, the saint replied: "Sir, you are going too far. Do you expect me to believe a single doctor of theology like yourself in preference to the teaching Church, the pillar of Truth with whom Christ promised to remain until the end of time?"[112]

In the preceding month the Fronde revolt had broken out in Paris and St. Vincent, without sympathizing with it, urged the Queen Mother and Cardinal Mazarin to leave the city while the Frondeur agitation was at its height. In December 1649 the faculty of the University of Paris, heretofore always a pillar of orthodoxy, refused to condemn Jansen. In 1650 a Jansenist catechism written in a popular style was widely circulated. Though only a minority of the Frondeurs were declared Jansenists, the two movements developed almost simultaneously. In February 1651 St. Vincent circulated a letter to Rome against

---

[111] *Ibid.*, XXIX, 120-140. With the Council of Trent and the development of the Catholic Reformation that followed, great efforts had been directed by Church reformers and particularly by the Jesuits to induce the people, if not bound by mortal sin, to receive Holy Communion more frequently, which the Jansenists hereby set themselves against.

[112] *Ibid.*, XXX, 217-218, 230, 301-306, 308, 310, 313, 315; Mary Purcell, *The World of Monsieur Vincent* (New York, 1963), pp. 176-177 (for quote), 198-200.

Jansenism; in no small part due to his reputation, he obtained the signatures of 88 of the bishops of France (a majority) upon it. At the end of March Archbishop Boonen of Brussels published an apology for Jansen. In April eleven French bishops (one-eighth of St. Vincent de Paul's total) signed a letter to Pope Innocent X in favor of Jansenism, which was dictated at the Jansenist community of Port Royal. Pope Innocent X set up a special commission of cardinals to examine Jansen's doctrines. On May 31, 1653, after the commission of cardinals had returned a split verdict, a second Papal bull (*Cum occasione*) condemned five specific propositions from Jansen's book, four held erroneous and the fifth heretical. This bull was published within ten days.[113]

But the battle with Jansenism had only begun, despite two Papal bulls against it. The University of Louvain ordered all its faculty to submit to the Papal decision. But the center of the heresy had now shifted decisively to France and away from the Spanish Netherlands. At the end of 1653 Pope Innocent X opened an inquiry into a pastoral letter issued by the Archbishop of Sens in favor of Jansenism. In April 1654 all Jansenist writings in the past four years, including about 50 books, were placed on the Index of prohibited books by the Roman Inquisition. In September 1654 Pope Innocent X had to reiterate that he really had meant what he said in the bull *Cum occasione* and that the five condemned propositions of Jansen were essentially what he had stated in his book (many defenders of Jansen were claiming they were not). In February 1655 Antoine Arnauld wrote a pamphlet stating that the condemnation of a person (such as Jansen) for heresy was not an infallible act, since the existence of heresy in his writings was a question of fact rather than of authoritative doctrinal teaching; but he continued to insist on the Jansenist claim that sufficient grace for salvation is not given to all. In October of that year the assembly of the clergy of France, meeting in Paris, submitted to the Papal decrees against Jansen, and threatened to exclude all bishops refusing to enforce its prohibitions from all general meetings of the French clergy. In January 1656 the University of Paris condemned Antoine Arnauld for not being sufficiently respectful of Papal authority, but only by a vote of 124-71, with 15 abstentions.[114]

Within ten days of this vote appeared the first "Provincial Letters" of French scientist and author Blaise Pascal. Pascal had become a Jansenist in 1643, and Antoine Arnauld asked him to write a defense of the Jansenists in a popular style. Pascal's 19 "Provincial Letters" published in 1656 and 1657 remain a masterpiece of ironic French prose and greatly promoted the Jansenist cause. Pascal made fun of the Dominicans and more savagely of the Jesuits, whom he despised for their casuistry, which he considered a watering down of essential morality. By September 1656 the clergy of Paris and Rouen were

---

[113] von Pastor, *History of the Popes* XXX, 70, 220-221, 244-245, 254-256, 259, 265, 272, 277, 280-281, 328; *Cambridge Modern History* IV, 607; Purcell, *World of Monsieur Vincent*, pp. 213, 216; Richard M. Golden, *The Godly Rebellion; Parisian Curés and the Religious Fronde* (Chapel Hill NC, 1981), p. 27.

[114] von Pastor, *History of the Popes* XXX, 292-293, 299, 334 and XXXI, 147, 171, 174-175, 179-180.

circulating charges against the Jesuits of also holding erroneous propositions, and though they submitted to their bishops in October before the general assembly of the French clergy, their animus against the Jesuits continued. In 1657 Cardinal Mazarin's aide Colbert wrote him that "all these sorts of religious affairs are fought with so much ferocity in Paris that we cannot doubt that the Jansenists, the friends of the Cardinal de Retz . . . are deeply involved and carry along the *dévots*." The French bishops berated the priests of Paris for lack of obedience, and in March prescribed a formulary to be taken by all priests upholding the condemnation of the five false propositions and asserting that they were in fact contained in Jansen's book. Young King Louis XIV was firmly opposed to Jansenism, and in December 1657 he formally ordered the hostile *Parlement* of Paris to register (permit publication of) a bull by new Pope Alexander VII against Jansenism, the third of its kind.[115]

The Jesuits fought back hard, for their order had now become strongly established in France and in French missionary work.[116] So bitter did the dispute become that the Pope felt obliged in August 1658 to condemn a Jesuit apology by Georges Pirot and its defenders and to publish his condemnation in Paris. On August 3, 1659 French Jesuit Louis Maimbourg denounced from the pulpit the persecution of his order and accused the Jansenists of simony for taking money for baptisms and burials. The assembly of the priests of Paris demanded that he be silenced, but the *Parlement* of Paris refused to proceed against him. The assembly of the clergy of France decided in February 1661 that all bishops, teachers, and sisters must sign the formulary of March 1657 against Jansenism on pain of losing their clerical office. But this decree was by no means universally enforced. The struggle would not be resolved until almost the end of the century.[117]

Meanwhile in November 1659 the returned Cardinal Mazarin had finally made peace in the long war with Spain which Cardinal Richelieu had started, a peace which officially marked the end of Spain as the world's leading power. France got Roussillon, southern Flanders and Alsace-Lorraine, but had to evacuate Catalonia, where the war had been going against them. Louis XIV was to seal this Peace of the Pyrenees by marrying Maria Teresa, eldest daughter of Philip IV of Spain, who gave up her right of succession to the Spanish throne on condition of the payment of a very large dowry (which was never fully paid due to Spain's increasing poverty). Louis XIV did not wish to marry her, but gave way to Cardinal Mazarin. By this treaty France also promised not to help Portugal in her fight for independence, but with British and Dutch help the Portuguese finally prevailed over an aging Philip IV at the battles of Elvas and Villaviciosa. Cardinal Mazarin died in March 1661 at the age of 58, after

---

[115] *Ibid.* XXXI, 186-187, 203; Golden, *Godly Rebellion*, pp. 81-82, 84, 116, 130 (for quote), 135-136, 138; *Catholic Encyclopedia* (New York, 1913), XI, 511-512. For the election of Pope Alexander VII see below, this chapter.

[116] See Chapter Twelve, below, for the great French missionary work in North America during this period.

[117] Golden, *Godly Rebellion*, pp. 85-86, 91, 118-119.

advising the 22-year-old King Louis XIV to be his own first minister, which he was. Absolute monarchy had come to France, now the world's leading power. It was only to end in history's mightiest revolution.[118]

In England the dictator Oliver Cromwell, after his two great victories at Dunbar and Worcester, held all power in his hands (Milton in the first line of a famous sonnet called him "our chief of men") as young King Charles II worked out his fantastic escape in September and October 1651. The French court of Cardinal Mazarin, who returned only in November after finally prevailing over the Fronde, allowed him to stay for a time at the Louvre, but gave no financial support either to him or to his mother, though she was a French princess; they were dependent on the charity of sympathizers in France. In the spring of 1652 Parliament passed a law annexing Scotland to England, without the Scots having anything to say about it, and dissolved the Presbyterian general assembly in Scotland by force. In April 1653 came the famous scene in which Cromwell marched into the chamber where the "rump" of the Long Parliament, elected thirteen years before, was still officially sitting, and declared: "I say you are no Parliament; I will put an end to your sitting. . . . In the name of God, go!" He took the ceremonial mace from the paralyzed Speaker with the scornful comment, "What shall we do with this bauble?" and had his troops clear the building. He set up a new ten-man Council with himself in charge, and called for a nominated assembly to take the place of Parliament—a word he no longer used. This was the assembly which went down in history under the picturesque Puritan name of one of its members from London: Praisegod Barebone.[119]

But good Puritans though they were, Praisegod Barebone and his fellows were not submissive enough to the dictator. They took their seats in July and were dissolved in December. For the second time in less than a year, musketeers cleared their meeting hall of any who would not depart at Cromwell's order. On New Year's Day 1654 by England's calendar he proclaimed himself "Lord Protector," after it became clear that his army would not accept his coronation as king, and moved into Whitehall. It was a long way up for the man who had once been a minor squire in the Cambridge fens.[120]

He was the target of repeated plots, but his brilliant secretary and intelligence chief John Thurloe, who recalls Cecil and Walsingham in Queen Elizabeth's time, prevented any from harming or even seriously endangering

---

[118] *Ibid.*, p. 65; *Cambridge Modern History* IV, 620-622; von Pastor, *History of the Popes* XXXI, 82-83, 89. For the long reign of Louis XIV, see Volume Five, Chapters 1 and 2; for the French Revolution and its heir Napoleon, see Volume Five, Chapters 7-21. St. Vincent de Paul died, full of years and honors, on September 27, 1660 (Purcell, *World of Monsieur Vincent*, pp. 229-231).

[119] Fraser, *Cromwell*, pp. 391, 418-421 (quotes on 420), 425, 436, 438; Fraser, *Royal Charles*, pp. 129-131; von Pastor, *History of the Popes* XXX, 67.

[120] Fraser, *Cromwell*, pp. 446-451, 455-456, 458.

him.[121] In the summer of 1654 his minions arrested Father John Southworth. When Southworth refused to renounce his priesthood he was hanged, drawn and quartered, while in Scotland the last resistance to Cromwell's rule was crushed. In September Cromwell called the First Protectorate Parliament, which was elected, but only by men worth at least 200 pounds. He welcomed it fulsomely, declaring that "you have upon your shoulders the interests of all the Christian people in the world." But it did not last even as long as Barebone's parliament. Cromwell dissolved it on February 1, 1655 after it had been in session less than five months.[122] In August he divided England into eleven districts, each to be governed by a major-general who was supposed to make society more godly. The New Model army had come to rule, with Cromwell ever its commander.[123]

But as the history of communism in the twentieth century memorably shows, there is one enemy even the most successful manipulator of a totalitarian system, the most absolute and unchallenged ruler, the greatest of generals, cannot defeat: the Grim Reaper. For when man lost his innocence in the Garden of Eden, God put a limit on the harm he could do. From that original sin to the end of the world, all men must die, with only His sinless Son having risen from the dead,[124] until Judgment Day.

Oliver Cromwell, not yet sixty, died in his bed in September 1658, just nine days after one of the worst storms in English history lashed Great Britain from Cape Wrath on Scotland's Minch to Land's End on the English Channel, and it seemed that the howling winds at last had blown away this man who had never been defeated, one of the most terrible enemies Catholic people have ever known.[125]

Oliver Cromwell left a son named Richard, the palest shadow of his father, as his successor. Richard had never served in the New Model army, which had little use for him except as their instrument. But the rule of the major-generals had become very unpopular, and the soldiers' demands for immediate pay of their large arrears created a fiscal crisis for the government. The leading officers in the New Model army, who had been Cromwell's battlefield lieutenants— Lambert, Fleetwood, and Desborough—called what was euphemistically termed

---

[121] *Ibid.*, pp. 493-494, 517-518; Fraser, *Royal Charles*, pp. 140-142. Thurloe had placed a spy, Sir Richard Willys, in the leadership of the principal royalist undercover organization, the Sealed Knot (Fraser, *Cromwell*, p. 585; Fraser, *Royal Charles*, pp. 163-164).

[122] Fraser, *Cromwell*, pp. 438, 489-490, 506-509 (quote on 507), 511, 514-516. For Father Southworth the martyr, see *Butler's Lives of the Saints*, edited, revised and supplemented by Herbert Thurston and Donald Attwater (Westminster MD, 1956) II, 662-664. In 1657 Cromwell violently dispersed another Parliament, his fourth, saying: "I think it is high time that an end be put to your sitting and I do declare to you here that I do dissolve this Parliament. . . . Let God judge between you and me." (Fraser, *Cromwell*, p. 651).

[123] Fraser, *Cromwell*, pp. 555-557.

[124] The Blessed Virgin Mary was also assumed into Heaven body and soul, but we do not know whether she died first.

[125] *Ibid.*, pp. 6733-678.

Richard's Parliament, with 549 members most of whom had no previous experience in government. Its members were nominated, not elected. It convened in February 1659, and quickly became hostile to Richard Cromwell. The general council of army officers vehemently demanded back pay and the suppression of royalists now gathering openly in London, while a House of Commons committee report showed the nation two and a quarter million pounds in debt, its revenue falling short of expenditures by 330,000 pounds a year, and the army owed nearly a million pounds in arrears of pay. Recalling the fate of its predecessors, the House of Commons now attempted to outlaw meetings of the general council of officers held without its consent, and to require every officer to sign a declaration against coercion of Parliament on pain of dismissal. The defiant officers now demanded yet another dismissal of Parliament, and after some hesitation Richard Cromwell surrendered to their pressure and proclaimed its dissolution, turning the effective government of Great Britain over to the general council of army officers.[126]

But there was strong popular resistance to military rule. Great Britain has never had a military dictatorship in all of its history, except for Oliver Cromwell's; and he was one of a kind. His former subordinates had neither the skill nor the will to maintain it. On May 17, 1659 an astonishing development occurred, the product of the Puritan state's increasingly desperate search for a legitimacy which it could never possess. The Long Parliament—or rather, the Rump—nineteen years after its election, was recalled by the general council of army officers. There were only 78 members of the Long Parliament still living who had not been included in Pride's purge, and only 42 appeared at the reconvening. But there were 213 living men who had been excluded by Pride, including William Prynne, who demanded admission but was turned away at the door by the soldiers. Two days letter Prynne slipped unseen into the House and began to denounce the Rump. After being removed again, he began a pamphlet war—of which he was a past master—against them.[127]

In May 1659 the Rump established a new Council of State with 31 members, only ten of whom were generals (the rest being its own members). It voted formal toleration of all Protestant sects, but not for Anglicans and Catholics, while the status of the increasingly numerous Quakers was left equivocal. Early in June it actually voted to sell Whitehall to pay the army—but could find no buyer for the hallowed palace. At almost the same moment the hapless Richard Cromwell resigned, in return for a promise by the Rump to pay his debts; meanwhile it gave him six months' protection from arrest for debt. In August the army easily suppressed a royalist rising led by Sir George Booth. But their government, having no legitimacy—even less after Richard Cromwell's departure, being now based only on an election held nineteen years before—was far weaker than it appeared. Chaos and anarchy threatened, the political condition that every people instinctively recognizes is worse than any other. The

---

[126] Ronald Hutton, *The Restoration; a Political and Religious History of England and Wales, 1658-1667* (Oxford, 1985), pp. 21-29, 31, 35-38.

[127] *Ibid.*, pp. 39-43, 45, 56.

New Model army's commander in Scotland, Sir George Monck, was a professional soldier rather than an ideological Puritan. He had fought for Charles I during the English civil war, was imprisoned by Parliament for three years after the King's defeat, and began working with Cromwell only in the Irish campaign. He now began to consider whether he should move unilaterally to prevent chaos and anarchy.[128]

Early in October a group of junior officers in General Lambert's army drew up a strongly worded petition to Parliament, condemning its delays and calling for more Puritan reforms, with a guarantee that no officer would be dismissed without a military court-martial. Sir Arthur Hesilrige, one of the five leaders of the House of Commons whom Charles I had attempted unsuccessfully to arrest seventeen years before and had come back with the Rump, obtained a copy of the junior officers' petition before it was edited by more cautious spirits, and denounced it on the House floor. The House ordered General Fleetwood to admonish the army and keep them from dismissing yet another Parliament by force. The general council of officers responded angrily, approving a harsh address to Parliament defending the officers, calling for the censure of members denouncing the army, and once again demanding their enormous arrears of pay. On October 28 the council of officers decided to make a new government. On no authority but their weapons, they declared Fleetwood commander-in-chief, Lambert his second, and Desborough and Monck generals of Horse and Foot respectively. They took full control of appointment of officers into their own hands. The script for such action by the army was only too familiar. The last five successive Parliaments had all been thus sent packing. But early in November a letter arrived from General Monck in Scotland declaring for Parliament against the army. A significant number of other officers supported him.[129]

But Monck was not a Parliament man, and had fought against the very Parliament from which the present Rump was taken, in the early days of the English civil war. He took its side at the moment because it was the only alternative to the army and its commanders. Because Monck had fought for Cromwell and the great Oliver had recognized his military ability and promoted him, his colleagues took it for granted that he had accepted the Cromwellian system in which the army ruled. They were wrong.

Within a few days General Lambert, the most Cromwellian of the army leaders, left London to march against Monck, while Generals Fleetwood and Desborough sought negotiations for a settlement. Lambert arrived at Newcastle with 8,000 men on November 30. But the large garrison at Portsmouth, which believed that some of their pay arrears had been diverted to London by the army officers there, defected. On a bitterly cold day in December, some 20,000 apprentices in London—men too young to remember the English civil war—defied the army and demanded government by a real Parliament, newly elected.

---

[128] *Ibid.*, pp. 40, 45, 48-49, 58-59, 68-69; Fraser, *Cromwell*, p. 686; Fraser, *Royal Charles*, p. 165.

[129] Hutton, *Restoration*, pp. 64-67.

They greeted the troops sent to subdue them with barrages of stones, tiles, and pieces of ice. The soldiers fired, killing some of them, the coroner declared their deaths to be murder, and the grand jury prepared to indict them.[130]

The general council of officers now declared for a new Parliament with an elected lower House and an upper house dominated by them. The English navy mutinied, led by Captain John Lawson. It sailed into the Thames and closed the port of London. The London city government declared for a Parliamentary election, not merely support of the Rump. At the beginning of January General Fleetwood buckled, declaring that God had spat in his face, and passed out of public life. General Lambert in Newcastle, receiving this startling and unwelcome news, marched back south. Lord Fairfax, who had been the Puritan commander-in-chief before Cromwell, declared for Monck, who was advancing into England while Lambert's army was disintegrating. The general council of officers, obviously losing hope, issued a document they actually called a "last will and testament" stating that they still adhered to "the good old cause." But almost nobody else did.[131]

The Rump now created a new Council of State, with the Cromwellian army officers purged and Monck, Lord Fairfax and Captain Lawson added. At the beginning of February 1660 Hesilrige arrived in London with the defecting soldiers from Portsmouth, and the New Model army was broken as a political force. Four days later General Monck's tightly disciplined army occupied London, received the thanks of the Rump Parliament on February 16, and pledged to issue writs for the election of a new Parliament within a week. Massive popular celebrations broke out all over London, with bells, bonfires, and the public roasting of beef rumps. The next month General Monck totally reorganized the army command, replacing officers still loyal to the Cromwellian Commonwealth with others whom he could expect to obey his orders. Early in March the beleaguered Rump decided to recall its Presbyterian members expelled by Pride's Purge in 1648. On March 26, at long last, the Long Parliament dissolved itself and accepted the holding of elections for a new one. The government had now divested itself of the last fragments of legitimacy, and General Monck told friends he was ready to restore the king and the House of Lords if the new Parliament asked him to. In London, Samuel Pepys tells us, more and more people were beginning "to talk loud of the king."[132]

This sudden and extraordinary turnabout in Puritan fortunes came as almost as much a surprise to Charles II as to all of Europe. Few had realized how totally the Puritan dictatorship had depended on Oliver Cromwell. Without him, they could not govern. At the end of March General Monck told Charles' envoy Sir John Grenville that he would be satisfied with Charles' promise of indemnity for rebellion against him and his father, payment of the soldiers' arrears, and religious toleration (which Charles was happy to grant). In return he would restore the king. On April 14 Charles issued the Declaration of Breda (named for

---

[130] *Ibid.*, pp. 71, 74, 76-80.

[131] *Ibid.*, pp. 79-84.

[132] *Ibid.*, pp. 84-87, 91, 93-94, 96, 103-104, 106-109; Fraser, *Royal Charles*, p. 170.

the city in the Netherlands where he was staying) accepting these terms, except that there would be no amnesty for the regicide judges who had sentenced his father to death.[133] He concluded with words that indicate that he was much more than the royal playboy he was later assumed by many to be:

> We hope that we have made the right Christian use of our affliction, and that the observations and experiences we have had in other countries hath been such as that we, and we hope all our subjects, shall be the better for what we have seen and suffered.[134]

The elections to what was called the Convention Parliament returned 61 royalists, though they were not supposed to stand as candidates, and rejected three civilians intimately connected with the Long Parliament and the Cromwellian regime: Sir Arthur Hesilrige, Sir Henry Vane, and Speaker Lenthall. General Monck required all his officers to submit to whatever kind of government the new Parliament established. General Lambert, the last of the Puritan commanders with any fight left in him, was imprisoned in the Tower of London, escaped, and fled with a hundred-pound reward on his head. He tried to rally troops, but only secured a few hundred, and was soon captured and returned to the Tower. On May day 1660 by the Julian calendar, a traditional day of celebration in England which the Puritans had tried hard to abolish, the Convention Parliament (officially convened just six days before) overwhelmingly voted to ask Charles II to take the government of the country, entirely without restricting conditions. Charles graciously accepted, and on June 8 entered London, escorted by Monck's army, to almost universal rejoicing. All day gun salutes thundered, bells never stopped ringing, and the people shouted and wept for joy. A thanksgiving service was held at Westminster Abbey. The Church of England was restored. In May 1661 Charles II was magnificently crowned in Westminster Abbey, and a few days later a Parliament elected under his writ convened, confirmed the work of the Convention Parliament, and gave full support to the restored monarchy. It was called the Cavalier Parliament.[135]

Rarely—very rarely—in history is it possible to restore what has been lost. But this time, it was possible and it was done.

There remains one extraordinary story to tell from this tumultuous period, that of the amazing conversion of the queen of the most Protestant country in Europe, Sweden, where simply to be Catholic was to face death or exile[136] (even Cromwell's England did not go that far, except for Catholic priests). Queen Christina was the only child of the great Gustav Adolf. She ascended her father's

---

[133] *Ibid.*, pp. 106-108; Fraser, *Royal Charles*, pp. 172-173.

[134] Fraser, *Royal Charles*, p. 172.

[135] *Ibid.*, pp. 181-182, 189, 191, 197-201; Hutton, *Restoration*, pp. 109-114, 116-118, 125, 145-146, 153-154.

[136] For these Swedish laws against Catholics, see Oskar Garsten, *Rome and the Counter-Reformation in Scandinavia*, IV (Leiden, 1992), p. 700.

throne in 1644 at the age of eighteen. Already she was known as a linguistic genius, an enthusiastic student of the classics, and a budding philosopher, a young woman who above all could think for herself. And the more she thought about the official Lutheranism of Sweden, the less she liked it. Regarding Catholics, she had to divest herself of the mountain of obloquy and myth which the Protestants had piled upon them, some of which is still believed even today. In the immediate wake of the Peace of Westphalia and the Protestant success in cleaving Christendom, this was not easy to do. But Christina brought to the task a relentless perseverance, a love of truth, and a horror of mere conformity. She knew perfectly well that if she were to become Catholic, she would be removed, or must first remove herself, from the Swedish throne. She did not flinch from the prospect.[137]

In the spring of 1647 Queen Christina shocked Sweden and all Europe by declaring that she would never marry. For some time few would believe it, despite the fairly recent example of a similar resolution kept by Queen Elizabeth of England. The married state was simply not for Christina, especially with its requirement of submission to a husband. In late February 1649 she reiterated her uncompromising resolution on this point to the Grand Council of Sweden, and since she would have no heirs of her body, called on the Swedish Estates to declare her cousin Duke Charles Gustav her successor, which with some reluctance it did. In October 1649 the famous French philosopher René Descartes arrived in Stockholm at Queen Christina's invitation to instruct her in philosophy. The rigors of the far northern climate proved too much for Descartes, and he died during his second winter in Sweden. But he taught Christina that virtue was to follow the truth, which should be prized above a crown.[138] She later paid this tribute to him:

> We hereby declare that Descartes contributed greatly to our glorious conversion and that God in His wisdom used him and his honored friend, *le sieur* Chanut [the French ambassador to Sweden], to impart upon us the

---

[137] *Ibid.*, IV, 550-559; Curt Weibull, *Christina of Sweden* (Stockholm, 1966), pp. 60-63, 100-110. These two excellent, thorough and well-documented studies, especially Garsten's, destroy in detail the subsequent Protestant myths that Queen Christina was an evil and/or lascivious woman, a lesbian, a hermaphrodite, and so on and repulsively on. What remains of her body, buried in St. Peter's in Rome, was actually exhumed in the mid-1960's in search of anatomical irregularities, but none whatsoever were found. In his brilliant opening chapter on Queen Christina, Garsten in particular vindicates her from all these fantastic lies about her with overwhelming documentation (*op. cit.*, pp. 525-547). Christina was not a saint; she was a careless dresser and speaker (her flow of obscenities, derived from her soldiers, was notorious), and was too arrogant and too much concerned with money. But she is the only monarch in European history who gave up a crown for the Faith. Queen Elizabeth did not do it, if indeed she were Catholic by inclination, as Philip II of Spain, who knew her personally, believed for many years; and Charles II did not do it until he lay on his deathbed, when worldly considerations no longer mattered.

[138] Weibull, *Christina of Sweden*, pp. 20, 28-30, 46-48, 64-70, 90; Garsten, *Counter-Reformation in Scandinavia* IV, 583-586.

primary enlightenment and to enable us to embrace the truths of the apostolic Roman Catholic religion.   God in His mercy and compassion has subsequently fulfilled this work.[139]

In July 1650 the party arriving in Stockholm with the Portuguese ambassador, José Pinto de Pereira, included a Jesuit priest named Antonio Macedo. By the fall Queen Christina was privately discussing the Catholic Faith with him with no appearance of hostility, though she did ask him acutely about how the Catholic conception of the universe could be integrated with recent scientific discoveries. On June 1651 she notified the heads of her government, her cousin and heir Prince Charles Gustav, and French ambassador Chanut that she intended to abdicate, though she gave no reason. The Swedish Council of State, headed by Gustav Adolf's right-hand man Axel Oxenstierna, was aghast, and rejected any thought of their queen's abdication. She pretended to agree with their position. But in August she told Father Macedo in a confidential discussion that she was contemplating conversion to the Catholic faith, despite all its harsh consequences for her personally. She asked him to carry a letter from her to the general of the Jesuits, written in her own hand, in which she would ask him to send her two learned Jesuit priests. She gave him a passport which she had personally signed. He left her palace by a back gate, boarded a small ship to the harbor of Dalarö, and from there caught a ship to Lübeck in north Germany.[140]

At the end of October Father Macedo arrived in Rome, where he found that Jesuit general Francesco Piccolomini had died in June, and that the order was being directed by Vicar-General Goswin Nickel pending the election of a new general. He gave Father Nickel the Queen's message, which asked him to send two learned Jesuits to her, and told him orally (though, carefully, not in writing) that she was considering conversion to the Catholic Faith. After consultation with Papal Secretary of State Cardinal Fabio Chigi, later Pope Alexander VII, Father Nickel then wrote to Queen Christina promising to send to her Francesco Malines, professor of theology at the Jesuit college in Turin, and Paolo Casati, professor of theology and mathematics at the Gregorianum in Rome. That same month former French ambassador Chanut wrote to Christina to say that he was praying God to "grant her the perspicuity to find the right path in matters religious and thus reach true spiritual fulfillment."   Father Nickel sent instructions to the two theology professors that their primary task was to bring the Queen to the Catholic Church, but they must keep this purpose strictly secret, for their mission was extremely dangerous. A code was set up in which Queen Christina was only to be mentioned as "Signor Teofilo."[141]

In January 1652 a new Jesuit general, Alessandro Gottifredi, was elected, and the very same day he wrote encouragingly to Queen Christina.

---

[139] Weibull, *Christina of Sweden*, p. 70.

[140] *Ibid.*, pp. 70-71, 76, 82-83, 85-87; Garsten, *Counter-Reformation in Scandinavia* IV, 627, 629-630, 633-636, 707-710

[141] Garsten, *Counter-Reformation in Scandinavia* IV, 634-640, 617 (for quote); Weibull, *Christina of Sweden*, pp. 72-73.

Unfortunately he died just two months later, to be succeeded as Jesuit general by Father Nickel. Meanwhile the Jesuit professors Malines and Casati had arrived in Stockholm. Father Malines described her as "a 25-year-old sovereign so entirely removed from human conceit and with such a deep appreciation of true values that she might have been brought up in the very spirit of moral philosophy." At Easter she decided definitively to become a Catholic, and sent Father Casati to Rome with a letter to Pope Innocent X in which she declared this intention. A new embassy arrived from King Philip IV of Spain in August 1652 which included another Jesuit, Father Charles Manderscheydt. In October 1652 the Lutheran consistory meeting in Stockholm took official note of the presence of the Jesuit Father in the Spanish embassy and Queen Christina's evident interest in him. In April 1653 she told Father Manderscheydt and the Spanish ambassador of her intention to become Catholic, because she intended to go to the Spanish Netherlands (Belgium) to be received into the Catholic Church.[142]

In February 1654 Queen Christina reiterated to the top officials of her government that she was resolved to abdicate. Chancellor Oxenstierna urged that she share royal power with Charles Gustav, but she said she would accept no such half measures, and Oxenstierna finally yielded to her. In May she publicly announced to the Swedish Riksdag (parliament) that she had irrevocably decided to abdicate, firmly rejecting all pleas to change her mind. She had not yet told any but the Jesuit Fathers and the Spanish ambassador her real reason. The abdication ceremony was held on June 9. She looked "beautiful as an angel." Many of the spectators wept. That night her designated successor Charles X Gustav was crowned, and Christina stayed for his coronation banquet, then left Stockholm unheralded at about midnight, cutting off her hair and donning men's clothes to avoid being recognized, and set out for the Spanish Netherlands, passing incognito through Denmark and north Germany until she reached Antwerp in Catholic Flanders. There she met with Count Raimondo Montecuccoli of Savoy, telling him that she had left Sweden as she had because she feared being held there by force if her secret should become known, and did not feel safe from arrest until she came to a Catholic country. From Antwerp she went to Brussels, where she wrote to her cousin and successor telling him that she had left Sweden forever and planned henceforth to live in Italy. But she still did not tell him why. And there on Christmas Eve she professed the Catholic Faith in the chapel of Archduke Leopold, pronounced the Tridentine Creed and promised eternal adherence to it, attended midnight Mass, and received the Eucharist.[143]

Before she could proceed to Rome, Pope Innocent X had died. The conclave began on January 20, 1655 with 66 cardinals present. The first ballot

---

[142] Garsten, *Counter-Reformation in Scandinavia* IV, 640-641, 656-660, 664-666, 700-704; Weibull, *Christina of Sweden*, pp. 74-75 (quote on 74); von Pastor, *History of the Popes* XXXI, 48-49.

[143] Garsten, *Counter-Reformation in Scandinavia* IV, 710-712, 716-723, 727-729, 732-734; Weibull, *Christina of Sweden*, pp. 92-94, 97; von Pastor, *History of the Popes* XXXI, 52.

was almost evenly divided between Cardinal Carafa (a clerical manipulator), Cardinal Sacchetti (strongly opposed by Spain), and the relatively young but very able Cardinal Chigi, who had already been in touch with Christina. Ballots continued to be taken, with Cardinal Sacchetti rising to a majority but not close to two-thirds. On February 14 Cardinal Carafa suddenly died, and on April 6 Cardinal Sacchetti, still far from a two-thirds vote, abandoned his candidature. So Cardinal Chigi prevailed, and took the name of Alexander VII.[144]

The new Pope immediately wrote to Christina, urging her to come to Rome, and when he found out that she was indeed coming, prepared a tremendous reception for her. Christina chose the beautiful Catholic city of Innsbrück in the Tyrol to make her public profession of faith on November 3, repeating her profession of faith in Brussels. Jesuit Father Staudacher preached a homily based on the 45th Psalm, especially the passage: "Hearken, O daughter, consider, and incline your ear; forget your people and your father's house; and the king will desire your beauty; since he is your Lord, bow to him." Cannon boomed a salute and all the church bells in Innsbrück pealed out joyously. On November 8 she set out for Rome, stopping at Trent to see the cathedral where the great Council had met. Pope Alexander VII read a letter from her to the entire College of Cardinals. On December 23 she was solemnly and splendidly received at Rome by the entire College of Cardinals and the Pope himself, and prayed at the high altar of St. Peter's, which her magnificent tomb now overlooks.[145]

It is a deeply inspiring story for a Catholic,[146] but it had few consequences in history. Because of her conversion to the hated Catholic faith, former Queen Christina became an "unperson" in her native country for two hundred years. Lies about her were spread all over Europe. In another age so splendid an example would have had power to change men's hearts. But in 1655 Christendom was irreparably cloven into Protestant and Catholic segments, with never the twain to meet. There was not and could not be any religious bridge between them, only secular diplomatic and trade relations. The very concept of Christendom lived on only in the Catholic segment. The Protestants still believed in the Incarnation, thereby unquestionably remaining Christians too. But with the unity of the church destroyed, even faith in the Incarnation weakened, especially with the absence of the Eucharist in nearly half of what had been Christendom. The forces began to build which were later to challenge Christ Himself in the French Revolution, as He had never been challenged since the ancient Roman

---

[144] von Pastor, *History of the Popes*, XXX 377-378; XXXI 1, 4-12. He took the papal name of Alexander in honor of the great Pope Alexander III (1159-1181), who came from Chigi's home town of Siena, apparently not concerned with recalling Rodrigo Borgia who had given so much scandal to Christendom at the turn of the sixteenth century as Pope Alexander VI (see Volume Three, Chapter 15 of this history). No other Pope has ever taken the name Alexander, and it is unlikely that any ever will.

[145] Garsten, *Counter-Reformation in Scandinavia* IV, 742-743, 747, 757-760; Weibull, *Christina of Sweden*, pp. 51-53, 116-118; von Pastor, *History of the Popes* XXXI, 52-55, 57-59; Psalm 45:10-11.

[146] Especially an adult Catholic convert, like this historian.

persecutions of Emperor Diocletian and Julian the Apostate. For those who dared to face the truth about it, this was a profoundly depressing time in which to live.

But in this same year of 1655 came a glorious sign that the Mother of God had not abandoned her people. On July 21 the new king of Sweden, Charles X, invaded Catholic Poland. In six weeks he took Warsaw with almost no resistance, and Polish King John Casimir fled to Silesia. Cracow was besieged and taken, and many towns and estates were burned and plundered. The Polish national army disintegrated. Then the Swedish Lutheran army under General Müller approached the fortified monastery of Jasna Gora, located on a hill outside the town of Czestochowa.[147] What happened there, amply attested in the historical sources, is well known to Pope John Paul II, who has often mentioned it, but almost completely unknown to the world outside Poland and its people. Norman Davies, a recent secular historian of Poland with no apparent interest in its Catholic faith, nevertheless quotes at considerable length from the contemporary Polish chronicle which describes what happened at Jasna Gora. We cannot do better than to excerpt some of what he passes on to us:

> General Müller, who had directed his forces against the monastery of Czestochowa, was now faced with a more severe task, for he was defying the Almighty. . . . The monastery of Jasna Gora is consecrated to the Immaculate Virgin Mary, whose famous and miraculous icon is to be found there, painted on a board of cypress wood by Saint Luke the Evangelist himself. It was this icon, a source of great veneration and of immense treasure amassed from the offerings of three centuries, that inspired the enemy to lay the siege and to offset his war costs by plunder. . . . But the fathers of Jasna Gora, called upon to admit a Swedish garrison, replied boldly that they were bound to God's service by their vows and that to surrender the ancient place of pilgrimage would be sacrilege.
>
> When negotiations brought no result, the Swedes began a violent bombardment of the walls. Then, in order to spread fear among the defenders, they started to hurl in blazing firebrands, setting the monastery's barn alight together with a great quantity of corn. Next, all around the monastery, they set up a camp with wooden palisades and gun emplacements. . . . But their attacks had little effect. The walls were banked with earth on the inside, and only a few bricks were displaced by the cannon. Before long, the defenders opened fire in reply. The aim of their gunners was so accurate that after three hours the Swedes were obliged to pull back

---

[147] *Cambridge Modern History* IV, 580-581; Garsten, *Counter-Reformation in Scandinavia* IV, 739; Norman Davies, *God's Playground; a History of Poland* (New York, 1981), I, 451. Czestochowa was home to an ancient painting of the Blessed Virgin Mary, popularly attributed to St. Luke (though there is no reliable historical evidence that it was that old), and slashed across by a sword-thrust which legend held to have been made by one of the Mongol conquerors of Poland in the 13th century. See Volume Three of this history, pages 446-447. The painting is still venerated there as Poland's "black Madonna." I have seen it, and the worshippers around it, whose fervent faith was like nothing else I have ever seen except at the shrine of Our Lady of Guadalupe in Mexico.

with great loss. Meanwhile, the inhabitants of houses adjacent to the monastery, where the enemy had found shelter, set their homes on fire, not counting the cost. . . .

The Swedes renewed their attack on the 19th of November, the day of the Transfiguration of the Virgin. They had received six mortars from Cracow, and a great store of ammunition . . . The official printed description of this siege records that the bullets and missiles fell so thick on the church and tower that they seemed to be in flames. But . . . the cannon balls bounced off the walls and tiles or flew over the church roof, causing no damage. . . . Müller was most angered by the monks, who would climb to the top of the tower and in full choir pour down pious hymns on his soldiers. . . .

Jasna Gora was not saved by men. The holy place was preserved by God, and more by miracles than by the sword. A thick mist screened the monastery from attack . . . Müller himself saw a Lady in a shining robe on the walls, priming the cannon and tossing shells back in the direction from which they came . . . In the monastery, a grenade which landed and exploded in a baby's cradle did not hurt him, while in the Swedish camp six gunners were blinded by one single explosion. . . .

He [General Müller] launched his last attack on Christmas day, firing off all his guns in one salvo, and sending his entire army to storm the walls . . . But at that very moment, he suffered a fatal accident. He was eating breakfast in a fairly distant house, and cursing Jasna Gora with blasphemies, when suddenly an iron shot penetrated the wall, knocked all the plates, bottles and glasses from the table, scattered the guests, and struck him in the arm. . . .

At last, in the night before St. Stephen's day, the Swedes started to drag the guns from their emplacements, to collect their equipment, and to direct their wagons in the direction of Klobuck. The infantry and cavalry were the last to leave, at nine o'clock in the morning. . . .

Of course, no heretic will believe that cannon balls were repulsed from the walls of Jasna Gora by supernatural means. . . . But all that I have described is true.[148]

If the cleaving of Christendom was a battle decision, the Mother of God had showed herself at Czestochowa to be still the Queen of battles.

---

[148] Davies, *God's Playground*, I, 451-453.

12
Evangelization of a New World
1531-1661

"You must know and be very certain in your heart, my son, that I am truly the perpetual and perfect Virgin Mary, holy mother of the True God through whom everything lives, the Creator and Master of Heaven and Earth. I wish and intensely desire that in this place my sanctuary be erected so that in it I may show and make known and give all my love, my compassion, my help and my protection to the people. I am your merciful mother, the mother of all of you who live united in this land, and of all mankind, of all those who love me, of those who cry to me, of those who seek me, of those who have confidence in me. Here I will hear their weeping, their sorrow, and will remedy and alleviate their suffering, necessities and misfortunes. . . . Am I not here? I who am your Mother, and is not my help a refuge? Am I not of your kind?" —the Blessed Virgin Mary, Our Lady of Guadalupe, to Bd. Juan Diego[1]

Mexico

In 1531 in Mexico it had been twelve years since the landing of Cortés, and ten since the fall of the Hummingbird Wizard. A stratified colonial society was already beginning to develop, with the conquistadors and those who had come in their train the privileged class, and the Indians below them regarded primarily as servants and a labor pool. This was not what Cortés or any of the best of the Spaniards had intended. Their goal had been a united Christian community, truly a new Spain. The cultural amalgamation required would have taken a long time in any case, and was now sure to be strongly resented by those who preferred the master-servant relationship. But the conversion of the Indians was the indispensable starting point. It was retarded by their sheer numbers and the very small number of active missionaries.[2]

Furthermore, it must never be forgotten how their world had been shattered. It had been a fantastically evil world; but that was not the fault of the

---

[1] C. J. Wahlig, *Past, Present, and Future of Juan Diego* (Kenosha WI, 1972), pp. 78-84.

[2] See Lesley B. Simpson, *The Encomienda in New Spain* (Berkeley CA, 1950), pp. 56-110, and Robert Ricard, *The Spiritual Conquest of Mexico* (Berkeley CA, 1966), pp. 15-38, 61-65, 71-72.

macehualtin, the Indian poor; they had been its victims, not its creators. It was all they had known. Liberated from its evil, they were left floating—no longer Aztecs, not yet Spaniards. They needed a whole new ground for their lives. If that ground were to be Christianity, as the missionaries desired so ardently, it must become part of *them—their* faith, not only or primarily the faith of their conquerors.

This was the need of the Indians. As for the Spaniards, they needed to be reminded that the real crushers of Satan are not fallen men, but the perfect God and His sinless Mother, and that they care for all men equally, without distinction of race or culture. In a word, it was time for Juan Diego to receive his visitor.

Few lives have spanned such awesome changes as his. Growing up on the shore of Lake Texcoco, thirteen years old at the time of Tlacaellel's sacrifice of eighty thousand men at the 1487 dedication of the temple of the Hummingbird Wizard, dwelling there all through Cortés' first arrival, the Night of Sorrow, the Battle of Otumba (Cortés on his march to Otumba must have passed within a few miles of Juan Diego's hut), the return from Tlaxcala, and the final Spanish triumph in Mexico City,[3] becoming a Christian in 1525 along with his wife Maria Lucia and his uncle Juan Bernardino, beholding the chaos and terror of the rule of the governors who immediately succeeded Cortés and the explosions of hatred, lust and fear that marked the time of the First Audiencia of Nuño de Guzmán, Juan Diego had seen some of the most extraordinary history of all ages unfold before his eyes. He was now fifty-seven years old, but all of it had left him still simple, kind, loving, childlike in mind and heart.[4]

We have the story of what happened in December 1531 on the hill of Tepeyac overlooking Mexico City from Antonio Valeriano, one of the best Indian scholars at the College of Santiago de Tlatelolco, set up by the Franciscans in 1536 for the higher education of the Indians in the part of Mexico City nearest Tepeyac. Valeriano was proficient in Spanish and Latin, but the Nahuatl language of the Indians of Mexico City was his mother tongue. He knew Juan Diego personally and wrote his account of the apparitions on the basis of Juan Diego's own testimony, before he died in 1548.[5]

At dawn Saturday, December 9, 1531, the day after the feast of the Immaculate Conception, Juan Diego was on his way to Tlatelolco adjoining Mexico City for morning Mass, which he attended every day when he possibly could. His route ran over the hill of Tepeyac and across the Tepeyac causeway.

---

[3] See Chapter One, above.

[4] C. J. Wahlig, *Past, Present and Future of Juan Diego* (Kenosha WI, 1972), pp. 1-77.

[5] This document, in Nahuatl, is known as the *Nican Mopohua* from its first two words. What is either the original or a very early copy, almost contemporary with the original, was recently rediscovered by Jesuit Father Ernest J. Burrus in the New York Public Library. (See Ernest J. Burrus, "The Oldest Copy of the *Nican Mopohua*" and "The Basic Bibliography of the Guadalupan Apparitions," *CARA Studies on Popular Devotion*, Volume IV: *Guadalupan Studies*, No. 4 (Washington, 1981) and No. 5 (Washington, 1983).) It should lay to rest once and for all the claim that there is no adequate contemporary historical record of the apparitions of Our Lady of Guadalupe.

As he came to the top of the hill he heard singing, and saw a brilliant white cloud aureoled in rainbow. A beautiful young woman appeared before the cloud, her clothes shining so gloriously that they seemed to turn rocks into jewels, cactus leaves into emeralds, and cactus trunks into gold. Juan Diego fell to his knees, and the young woman said to him the words quoted at the head of this chapter, concluding with a request that he go to the bishop of Mexico and tell him from her that she desired to have a shrine built there on Tepeyac hill.[6]

The bishop of Mexico was a holy Franciscan and former hermit named Juan de Zumárraga, nominated by Emperor Charles V and approved by the Pope, who had also been officially designated Protector of the Indians in New Spain (Mexico). Almost from the first moment of his arrival in Mexico at the end of 1528, Bishop Zumárraga found himself confronting rapacious men who had taken over after Cortés' return from Mexico to Spain, who were enslaving the Indians and forcing them to labor for their own personal benefit. Meeting total defiance from these Spaniards who had seized power, who also tried to prevent him from even communicating with the government in Spain, Bishop Zumárraga smuggled out a letter to Empress Isabel, Charles V's wife and his regent for Spain and its colonies while he was in Germany, inside a slab of bacon hidden in a barrel of oil. This well-hidden letter reached the Empress, who promptly issued a blistering order to exile from the New World anyone who interfered with the transmission of personal correspondence from Mexico to Spain. In 1530 the dauntless bishop laid Mexico City under an interdict and formally excommunicated the two surviving members (*oidores*) of the First Audiencia. Empress Isabel sent a new Audiencia consisting of men of unquestioned probity, including Vasco de Quiroga, then a layman, later to become Bishop of Michoacán and beloved of the Indians, whom he served until he was ninety years old. Enslavement of Indians was strictly prohibited, and Bishop Zumárraga's office as Protector of the Indians was confirmed and given greater powers.[7]

Juan Diego hastened to do Mary's bidding, and went to Bishop Zumárraga's official residence, asking to speak with him. The truth of his story was doubted, and he was told to return at a more convenient time. Juan Diego came back to the hill of Tepeyac about sunset. The lady of light was waiting just as he had seen her at dawn. He urged her to send someone more distinguished to the Bishop and so more likely to be believed. "I am only a poor man," Juan Diego told her. "I am not worthy of being where you send me. Pardon me, my Queen, I do not want to make your noble heart sad." But Mary told him that it was he, and no other, whom she wished to send, that he should go again to Bishop Zumárraga the following day with her message.[8]

The next day, December 10, was a Sunday. After Mass Juan Diego went again to the Bishop's house, and after much difficulty with the guards, gained admittance. The Bishop questioned him, more impressed this time. But he told

---

[6] Wahlig, *Juan Diego*, pp. 78-81.

[7] See my *Our Lady of Guadalupe and the Conquest of Darkness* (Front Royal VA, 1983), pp. 90-96.

[8] *Nican Mopohua* of Antonio Valeriano, in Wahlig, *Juan Diego*, p. 81.

him that the lady must provide proof that she really was the Mother of God. At sunset Juan Diego was back on the hill of Tepeyac, where Mary was waiting for him and assured him that the next day she would give him the sign the Bishop had asked for. But when he reached home that evening he found his uncle Juan Bernardino very ill. All day Monday, December 11 he cared from his uncle, rather than returning to Bishop Zumárraga or to Tepeyac. Juan Bernardino thought he was dying, and asked his nephew to get a priest to anoint him. On Tuesday morning, December 12, Juan Diego started out to do this, avoiding the top of Tepeyac hill out of fear and embarrassment because he had not kept his promise to return there. But Mary came down the side of the hill to intercept him, asking him where he was going. He explained about his uncle.[9] She responded:

> Listen and be sure, my dear son, that I will protect you; do not be frightened or grieve, or let your heart be dismayed, however great the illness may be that you speak of. Am I not here? I, who am your Mother, and is not my help a refuge? Am I not of your kind? Do not be concerned about your uncle's illness, for he is not going to die. Be assured, he is already well. Is there anything else that you need?[10]

"Am I not of your kind?" With these words the Mother of God gave dignity and hope to the Mexican Indians who had been Satan's captives under the regime of human sacrifice. She was of their kind. She was no alien, no stranger. She was theirs.

Then she told Juan Diego to climb up the hill, saying that he would find flowers blooming which he should pluck and bring to her. The hill was a desert place where only cactus, thistles and thornbrush grew. Juan Diego had never seen a flower there. But when he reached the top, it was covered with beautiful Castilian roses, touched with dew, of exquisite fragrance. Mary took them from him as he gathered them, arranged them with her own hands, put them in his cactus fiber cloak, or *tilma*, and tied a knot in it behind his neck to hold the roses in place. Then she told him that he should take the roses to Bishop Zumárraga, and "in my name tell him that with this he will see and recognize my will and that he must do what I ask."[11]

When Juan Diego arrived again at the Bishop's house he was kept waiting a long time by the Bishop's attendants, who eventually insisted on seeing the roses; but when they tried to take some of them they could not, because it was "not roses that they touched, but [they] were as if painted or embroidered." When they finally admitted him to the Bishop's presence, Juan Diego told him all that had happened, and opened his cloak. The roses cascaded to the floor; and there upon the *tilma* was a full portrait of the Mother of God, in Indian dress, her small hands joined in prayer, her soft black hair falling gently upon her shoulders and

---

[9] *Ibid.*, pp. 81-83.
[10] *Ibid.*, p. 84.
[11] *Ibid.*, p. 83.

under her cape and framing the perfect oval of her face, with half-closed eyes deep as the sea, and the rosebud mouth, slightly smiling, that had kissed the Infant God on Christmas Day in Bethlehem.[12]

That portrait still exists today, just as it was then, still in brilliant color, unchanged, the normally short-lived cactus fiber cloth untouched by the passage of nearly five hundred years. Anyone can go to Mexico City and see it.

Bishop Zumárraga fell to his knees. It had been given to him to see what even his supremely holy master St. Francis of Assisi had never seen in this life: the face and form of the Blessed Virgin Mary, her own portrait. The tears streamed down his worn cheeks as he prayed her forgiveness for having doubted her and her messenger. When he could speak and stand again, he reverently took the cloak from Juan Diego and brought it to his chapel to lay it before her Son present in the Blessed Sacrament. Juan Diego remained with Bishop Zumárraga that night. We would give much to know what they talked about. But no word of Bishop Zumárraga's on this greatest event of his life has survived to our day.[13]

But the best evidence that the Blessed Virgin Mary truly visited Juan Diego on the hill of Tepeyac must always be her portrait itself. In 1979 it underwent a thorough scientific study by Philip Callahan, a research biophysicist at the University of Florida, who is also a painter, photographer, and scientific writer. Photographing it extensively for the first time in infra-red light, a recommended technique in the critical study of old paintings, Dr. Callahan found evidence that some decorations on the portrait—the sunburst around Mary, the gold stars and gold trim on her blue mantle, the dark moon and the angel under the moon, whose paint is clearly cracking and fading—were added or painted over much later by human hands, probably after the great floods in Mexico City during the years 1629-34 which did some damage to the *tilma* which bore the sacred

---

[12] *Ibid.*, p. 86.

[13] Nevertheless we have explicit testimony that Archbishop Garcia de Mendoza had seen in 1601 in the archdiocesan archives of Mexico City a full and circumstantial account of the apparition prepared by Bishop Zumárraga, which Dr. Alonso Munoz de la Torre once found him reading; while Fray Pedro de Mezquia states categorically that he read in the Franciscan monastery at Vitoria in Spain in the eighteenth century an account of the apparitions by Zumárraga which he had sent back to Spain. Both these documents have unfortunately disappeared, but the evidence is solid that they once existed; and the *Nican Mopohua* is enough for full authentication since it was written while Bishop Zumárraga was still alive and in Mexico (he died there in the same year as Juan Diego, 1548) by Antonio Valeriano, who as the best Latin scholar of the students at the College of Santiago de Tlatelolco undoubtedly knew the bishop personally. See Luis Ascensio, S.J., "The Apparitions of Guadalupe as Historical Events," *CARA Studies on Popular Devotion*, Volume II: *Guadalupan Studies*, No. 1 (Washington, 1979); Donald Demarest and Coley Taylor, *The Dark Virgin; the Book of Our Lady of Guadalupe* (New York 1956); Lauro López Beltran, *La Historicidad de Juan Diego* (Mexico, 1981) and *La Protohistoria Guadalupana* (Mexico, 1981).

image.[14] But regarding the rest of the portrait, including every aspect of Mary's own face and form, Dr. Callahan's conclusion is very different.

> The mantle is of dark turquoise blue . . . This presents an inexplicable phenomenon because all such pigments are semi-permanent and known to be subject to considerable fading with time, especially in hot climates. The Indian Mayan blue wall paintings are already badly faded. The blue mantle, however, is bright enough to have been laid last week. [It is this incredible brightness of the colors in the portrait that first impresses and astonishes nearly every visitor to the shrine of Our Lady of Guadalupe in Mexico City today, as I can personally testify.] . . .
>
> The most notable feature of the robe is its remarkable luminosity. It is highly reflective of visible radiation yet transparent to the infrared rays. . . .As in the case of the blue mantle, the shadowing of the pink robe is blended into the paint layer and no drawing or sketch is evident under the pink pigment. . . . The pink pigment appears to be inexplicable. . . . One of the really strange aspects of this painting is that not only is the *tilma* not sized, but there is absolutely no protective coating of varnish. Despite the unusual total lack of any protective overcoating, the robe and mantle are as bright and colored as if the paint were newly laid. . . .
>
> The head of the Virgin of Guadalupe is one of the great masterpieces of artistic facial expression. In subtleness of form, simplicity of execution, hue and coloring it has few equals among the masterpieces of the world. Furthermore, there are no portraits that I have ever observed which are executed in a similar manner. . . .
>
> One of the truly marvelous and inexplicable techniques utilized to give realism to the painting is the way that it takes advantage of the unsized *tilma* to give it depth and render it lifelike. This is particularly evident in the mouth, where a coarse fiber of the fabric is raised above the level of the rest of the weave and follows perfectly the ridge at the top of the lip. The same rough imperfections occur below the highlighted area on the left cheek and to the right and below the right eye. I would consider it impossible that any human painter could select a *tilma* with imperfections of weave positioned so as to accentuate the shadows and highlights in order to impart realism. The possibility of coincidence is even more unlikely. . . .
>
> The black of the eyes and hair cannot be iron oxide or any pigment that turns brown with age, for the paint is neither cracked nor faded with age. The truly phenomenal thing about the face and hands is the tonal quality which is as much a physical effect from light reflecting off the coarse *tilma* as it is from the paint itself. . . . At a distance, where the pigment and surface sculpturing blend together, the overwhelming beauty of the olive-colored Madonna emerges as if by magic. The expression suddenly appears reverent yet joyous, Indian yet European, olive-skinned yet white of hue.[15]

---

[14] In confirmation, the sunburst does not appear in early representations of the sacred image in Indian picture-writing.

[15] Philip S. Callahan, "The *Tilma* under Infra-Red Radiation," *CARA Studies on Popular Devotion*, Volume II: *Guadalupan Studies*, No. 3 (Washington, 2982), pp. 9-11, 14-15.

Furthermore, greatly enlarged photographs of the right eye of the Blessed Virgin Mary in the portrait have revealed three human figures, one of whom appears to be Juan Diego and another his interpreter when speaking to Bishop Zumárraga, Juan González, who later became a zealous supporter of devotion to Our Lady of Guadalupe. We have portraits of both Juan Diego and Juan González, showing a strong resemblance to two of these figures in the eye.[16]

The day after the revelation of the portrait of the Blessed Virgin Mary, Bishop Zumárraga and Juan Diego went to Tepeyac accompanied by a large group. Juan Diego naturally wanted to hurry on to see his uncle, though he must have believed him cured since Mary had said he surely would be. Indeed he was; and he told them that she had come to him, as he lay helpless in his illness, naming herself to him as "Holy Mary of Guadalupe."[17]

Guadalupe was one of the most important shrines to the Blessed Virgin Mary in Spain, but had no visible connection with the apparition in Mexico. However, Queen Isabel and Christopher Columbus had gone there to pray, and Columbus baptized the first American Indians at that shrine. There has been much speculation that Our Lady actually used some Nahuatl word (many suggestions have been made as to what word it might have been) which sounded in Spanish like "Guadalupe," a very Spanish word that would be hard for Nahuatl speakers to pronounce, since their language has no "g" and no "d". All such speculation overlooks the fact that Juan Diego and his uncle, who knew no Spanish, were presenting their accounts of the apparitions to Bishop Zumárraga through a trained interpreter, Juan González, whose native language was Nahuatl but who also spoke Spanish well, and therefore would have been most unlikely to have mis-heard or mistranslated some Nahuatl name or title as "Guadalupe." Therefore this must really have been the name Mary chose—perhaps as another way of showing how she wanted her children in Spain and her children in Mexico to draw closer together.

Juan Diego and his uncle returned to Bishop Zumárraga's house, where they and many others began to plan the quick erection of a simple shrine on the side of Tepeyac hill, where the Blessed Virgin Mary had requested it. The most readily available construction material was adobe—sun-dried clay. Many willing hands assisted in the task, and a small building was ready to house the glorious image in less than two weeks. It was completed just before Christmas. Bishop Zumárraga ordered its dedication with much rejoicing and a great procession on the second day of the Christmas season, December 26, 1531.[18] He sent a special invitation to Cortés and his second wife, recently come from Spain, to attend the dedication and join in the procession. The letter of invitation, from Bishop Zumárraga to Cortés, was discovered some years ago in the Archives of the Indies in Spain by the devoted researches of the great Mexican Church historian P. Mariano Cuevas, S.J. Though not entirely clear because of its allusions to

---

[16] Wahlig, *Juan Diego*, pp. 122-124 and Appendix.

[17] *Nican Mopohua* of Antonio Valeriano, in Wahlig, *Juan Diego*, pp. 88-89.

[18] P. Mariano Cuevas, *Historia de la Iglesia en Mexico*, Volume I (El Paso, Texas, 1928), p. 281; Wahlig, *Juan Diego*, pp. 89-90; Demarest and Taylor, *Dark Virgin*, p. 223.

prior correspondence or conversations between the two men, not now known, it is the nearest we have to a directly contemporary document attesting to the miracle:

> Illustrious and most fortunate lord! Give thanks to the Lord our God, resolving to serve him more fully henceforth. . . . Have patience tomorrow with the play we put on, it will give pleasure on the joyous Nativity of Our Savior and how splendid it will be! Before long I revealed it [Bishop Zumárraga does not say what he revealed; Cuevas thinks this refers to the circumstances of the apparition which at first he had been reluctant to discuss] and at sunset walked my stations of St. Francis first at the Great Church, and then those of St. Dominic. The bishop of Tlaxcala preaches tomorrow. And now I am in charge of my procession and am writing to Veracruz. It is impossible to describe the joy of everyone. . . . All praise to God, and the dances of the Indians; all praise to the name of God on the eve of the fiesta of fiestas.
>
> Say to her ladyship [Cortés' wife] that I wish to give the Great Church the name of the Conception of the Mother of God, since on that occasion God and His mother willed to grant this favor to the land which you won.[19]

Cuevas points out that in the Sevillan missal then used in Mexico, the feast of the Immaculate Conception was not confined to the single day of December 8, but, like Christmas, extended over a number of days, from December 8 to 17.[20] Thus the reference to the great favor from God "to this land which you won" happening on the occasion of the Immaculate Conception could refer to any event during this ten-day period, and would seem to refer to the apparitions which took place December 9, 10, and 12. Were it not for this reference to the special favor (*merced*) from God, the letter could be regarded as alluding simply to Christmas celebrations. The Guadalupan tradition, attested by several of the elderly witnesses at the formal investigation in Mexico City in 1666 who reported what they had heard of the miracle from their parents and grandparents, recalls a great celebration at the first installation of the portrait in the original shrine on Tepeyac hill, December 16, 1531.[21] This tradition receives considerable confirmation from this letter of Bishop Zumárraga.

If this be the meaning of the letter, as seems probable, it is particularly noteworthy that the great bishop made a point of paying tribute to Hernan Cortés, in the immediate context of Our Lady's gift of her own portrait, by speaking of Mexico, the land to which that splendid favor had been given, as the land that he had won. It suggests that Bishop Zumárraga believed, as was proposed above in Chapter One, that the victory of the Catholic army of Cortés over the gods of darkness and death was necessary before the Blessed Virgin Mary could come to Mexico.

---

[19] Cuevas, *Historia de la iglesia en Mexico* I, 281-283.

[20] *Ibid.*, I, 183-184.

[21] Demarest and Taylor, *Dark Virgin*, pp. 169-171.

Indians and Spaniards came together to venerate the surpassingly beautiful image, children together of the Mother of all the faithful. They came on December 26, 1531, and they have been coming ever since—day and night, season after season, decade after decade, century after century. Later the Church was to proclaim Our Lady of Guadalupe the patroness of all the Americas, the whole vast span from Arctic to Antarctic which the sailors and conquistadors of Catholic Spain revealed to the world.

Fray Martin of Valencia, head of the Franciscan party of twelve missionaries who began the evangelization of Mexico in 1524, wrote to Charles V in November 1532 that so far about 200,000 Indians had been baptized[22]—a small fraction, probably about ten per cent, of the total population of Mexico. His letter probably arrived in Spain shortly before Bishop Zumárraga himself, who had been temporarily recalled to give a personal report, and to receive his formal episcopal consecration, at Valladolid in Castile. When he returned to Mexico in October 1534, he found that an unprecedented outpouring of grace among the Indians of Mexico had begun, and was swelling into a tide.

Careful records were maintained by Father Toribio Motolinea, a leading Franciscan missionary, who was already at work on his great history of the Indians of New Spain. Writing in 1536, he reports that he and one other priest had baptized 14,200 Indians in five days. In Mexico as a whole, he declared that there had been no less than five million baptisms since the arrival of the first twelve Franciscans under Fray Martin in 1524. Comparing this total with Fray Martin's 200,000 to 1532, it is clear that the vast majority of these baptisms took place in the four years from 1532 to 1536, when, as Robert Ricard states, "evangelization [in Mexico] made an immense jump . . . it is certain that the average number of baptisms was much greater between 1532 and 1536 than between 1524 and 1532."[23] Wherever the missionaries were, wherever they went, Indians of all ages flocked to them for baptism in overwhelming numbers. These numbers necessitated omission of some elements of the usual baptismal ritual, such as the rites of the salt and saliva, and the use of consecrated oil (supplies of which were limited). But Motolinea is unequivocal that every candidate was individually baptized and every adult presenting himself was given two oral summaries of the catechism. Therefore instruction, though brief, was never lacking. Nor was any pressure, to say nothing of force, employed. On the contrary, it was the missionaries who were pressured and almost unbearably overburdened by the tide of converts, so much greater than they had ever expected so soon. We hear of Indians coming to them for baptism when they approached villages for the first time, before they had even begun to preach.[24]

The flood of baptisms continued during all the remaining years of the life of Juan Diego and of Bishop Zumárraga, who died within a few days of each other in the spring of 1548. By then the total number of baptized Indians in Mexico was approximately nine million. The validity of the baptisms with an

---

[22] Robert Ricard, *The Spiritual Conquest of Mexico* (Berkeley CA, 1966), p. 91.

[23] *Ibid.*,

[24] *Ibid.*, pp. 83-93.

abbreviated liturgy performed during the period 1532-36 was confirmed in the bull *Sublimus Deus* of Pope Paul III issued in 1537, though the Pope directed that there be fewer omissions from the baptismal liturgy in the future.[25]

In Tlaxcala, the territory whose people had allied with Cortés against the Mexican Empire which for decades had fought wars with them deliberately to gather more victims for human sacrifices, Christian fervor reached great heights. Easter of 1536 was celebrated in Tlaxcala with thousands of special offerings by the Indians, decorated with Christian symbols, and by a reverent dawn procession. The celebration of Corpus Christi in 1538 was equally or even more memorable:

> The procession of the Most Holy Sacrament was accompanied by files of Indians bearing crosses and saints' images, worked in gold and feathers. Their route was decorated in the form of a three-aisled church, in which the Host and ministers occupied the center, and the congregation the outer aisles. Over a thousand floral arches simulated the form of an actual religious building. . . . Later, religious plays were given, representing the annunciation of the birth of John the Baptist and other events of Christian history.[26]

The young men of Tlaxcala who had been educated during these years by the Franciscan missionaries went out with a burning enthusiasm to convert and teach their people and make the new faith the center of their lives. Many Indian young women, educated at convent schools, joined them, teaching Christian doctrine in the homes of the Indians. Jerónimo de Mendieta, who arrived in Mexico in 1554 and wrote his ecclesiastical history of the Indians from 1571 to 1596, entitles one of his chapters covering this period "How the conversion of the Indians was done through children."[27]

Though most conventional historians of Mexico today, perhaps embarrassed by so great and still visible a miracle, tend to avoid mentioning the portrait of Our Lady of Guadalupe at the point in time when it appeared, it should be self-evident that this immense surge of baptisms beginning in the year after the apparition, 1532, derived primarily from the impact of the apparition and the portrait, as spread throughout the land by word of mouth. The Franciscans at this time recognized and honored Our Lady of Guadalupe; they organized a procession to her shrine to pray for relief from an epidemic in 1544. The public criticism of the devotion to Our Lady of Guadalupe some years later, in 1556, by the then Franciscan provincial in Mexico, Fray Francisco de Bustamante—of which so much has been made by critics of the historicity of the apparition and

---

[25] *Ibid.*, pp. 93-95; T. R. Fehrenbach, *Fire and Blood; a History of Mexico* (New York, 1973), p. 209; Stafford Poole, *Pedro Moya de Contreros; Catholic Reform and Royal Power in New Spain* (Berkeley CA, 1987), p. 128; *Cuevas, Historia de la iglesia en Mexico,* I, 242.

[26] Charles Gibson, *Tlaxcala in the Sixteenth Century* (New Haven CT, 1952), pp. 37-38.

[27] Ricard, *Spiritual Conquest of Mexico,* p. 101.

the spiritual significance of the devotion—represented only his personal opinion, and probably that of some other Franciscans at the time, who tended to be uncomfortable with the Blessed Virgin Mary portrayed as a Mexican. The Archbishop of Mexico in 1556, Alonso de Montúfar, Zumárraga's successor, was and remained an ardent advocate and defender of Our Lady of Guadalupe.[28]

Juan Diego, who devoted the rest of his life to the constant care of the little sanctuary where the sacred image was kept, became famed among the Indians for his sanctity, and is represented in their contemporary picture-writing with the signs of a holy man. Gabriel Suárez, an Indian, testified at the hearing of 1666 at the age of 110 that his father, Mateo Suárez, had known Juan Diego well, had seen the sacred image while Juan Diego was still living, "and knew many who had gone to the Hermitage to ask Juan Diego to pray for them." Another witness at the 1666 hearings, Pablo Juarez, chief of Cuauhtitlán, whose grandmother had been a close friend of Juan Diego who had grown up in that town, said the apparition of Our Lady of Guadalupe was "a matter so public and well-known, how it all happened, that even the children sang all about it in their games."[29]

Also, we have the will of Juana Martín of Cuauhtitlán, a relative of Juan Diego, a document dated March 11, 1559, which mentions Juan Diego and declares that "through him, the miracle took place over there in Tepeyac, where the beloved Lady Holy Mary appeared, whose lovely image we see in Guadalupe, which is really ours and of our town of Cuauhtitlán. And now, with all my heart, my soul and my will, I give to Her Majesty all that is mine. . . . I give it all to the Virgin of Tepeyac."[30]

The nine million baptisms between the apparition of Our Lady of Guadalupe and the death of Juan Diego and Bishop Zumárraga in 1548 created large Christian Indian communities throughout most of central Mexico, where a substantial majority of the population was now Christian. They were usually separate from the Spanish communities, with Indian dwellings gathered round church-monastery complexes erected by the missionaries. The churches were decorated by Indian artists with frescoes and sculptures a universe removed from the horrors they had painted and carved in the days of the Hummingbird Wizard. The liturgy was celebrated with music played and sometimes composed by the Indians, and dramatized by Nahuatl plays (the earliest known, written by the Franciscan Fray Luis de Fuensalida probably before 1535, dramatizes the Annunciation). The numbers of the new Indian Catholic communities were limited only by the number of the missionaries and of their Indian assistants who could be trusted to lead such communities in the absence of a Spanish priest or lay brother.[31]

---

[28] Ricard, *Spiritual Conquest of Mexico*, pp. 189-191.

[29] Demarest and Taylor, *Dark Virgin*, p. 169 (first quote) and 171 (second quote). See also material compiled by Msgr. Enrique Salazar in support of the cause for Juan Diego's beatification, now achieved.

[30] Herbert F. Leies, *Mother for a New World; Our Lady of Guadalupe* (Westminster MD, 1964), p. 161.

[31] Ricard, *Spiritual Conquest of Mexico*, pp. 135-206.

It is not at all surprising that in later years it was found that some of these new converts had secretly apostatized, or never had really believed in Christianity, and that the old religion was not entirely dead. That could have been expected. The truly significant fact is the vast extent, the general depth, and above all the historical endurance of the conversion. In the fifteen years after the appearance of Our Lady of Guadalupe on Tepeyac hill, the nine million baptisms she inspired created Catholic Mexico—Indian as much as Spanish, devoted, indestructible, surviving devastating epidemics and even the terrible mistake of the Spanish Church (at the Provincial Council of 1555) in refusing to ordain native priests (a prohibition extended to *mestizos*, with only rare exceptions permitted, by the pivotal Third Council of Mexico in 1585).[32] In more recent times Catholic Mexico has survived revolutions and bitterly anti-Catholic persecuting governments, ever continuing to draw strength and grace from the inexhaustible fountain of both whose gentle face has glowed undimmed for more than four hundred and fifty years on Juan Diego's *tilma*.

The conversion of Mexico was by far the greatest and most complete in all missionary history, and Mexico remains one of the most Catholic countries in the world today. And most of that conversion took place in the years from 1532 to 1536—the very same years when Henry VIII was taking England out of the church. What the Church had lost in the old world, she regained in the New.[33]

The consequences of the apparition of Our Lady of Guadalupe stand therefore at the heart of the Catholic history of Mexico and especially of its evangelization. Beyond that, only certain relatively minor episodes and actions of its early colonial history need to be mentioned. There was one native uprising in the name of the old devil-gods, and only one—the Mixton War of 1540. Significantly, it took place not in Mexico itself but in the province of Michoacán (then known as New Galicia), which had been conquered in 1530 by Nuño de Guzmán with all the cruelty and plunder that Cortés had mostly avoided in Mexico.[34] This rising was suppressed with considerable difficulty by the first Viceroy, Antonio de Mendoza, and cost the life of one of Cortés' leading subordinates, Pedro de Alvarado, when his horse fell on him. It also gave the Church two friar-martyrs. But the conquest veterans still knew how to fight, and many Indians who did not want to see the return of the devil-gods and their human sacrifices (which the rebels freely practiced), fought with the Spaniards.[35]

---

[32] Poole, *Pedro Moya de Contreros*, pp. 69, 71-72, 127-129, 145-147, 152. The precise language of the Third Council's decree on this point was: "Neither those of mixed blood, whether from Indians or Moors, nor mulattoes in the first degree are to be admitted to orders without great caution." In the original draft no such ordinations were permitted under any circumstances; the addition of "without great caution" created a loophole, though not a large one, for a priest without the requisite blood-lines.

[33] See my *Our Lady of Guadalupe*, pp. 111-113.

[34] *Ibid.*, pp. 95-96.

[35] Hubert H. Bancroft, *History of Mexico*, Volume II (San Francisco CA, 1883), pp. 493-495, 503-504, 507-509, 546; Arthur S. Aiton, *Antoino de Mendoza, First Viceroy of New Spain* (New York, 1927), pp. 137, 141-145, 148-157.

Later, as Spanish power moved north, Spaniards went to war against the primitive Chichimec Indians, some with a genocidal purpose.[36] The Third Council of Mexico spoke out in ringing terms against this wanton slaughter—"it is pitiful to see how openly they are brought naked to a nation that professes the gospel, chained and yoked, for public sale—and there is no one to stop it. . . . They are souls redeemed by the blood of Christ"—and it was stopped.[37]

The Mexican labor system caused many problems. The Indians had been accustomed to give frequent labor service to their chiefs, and the Spanish took over that custom and made large groups of Indians liable to forced labor under what they called the *encomienda*. The abuses that resulted, especially by men far from home and any real supervision, were deeply disturbing. The great Spanish champion of the Indians, Bartolomé de Las Casas, later Bishop of Chiapas in Mexico, made so strong a point of these abuses in representations to the Spanish court that Charles V decreed a set of "new laws" against the *encomienda* system. At first they proved unenforceable. However, over the years in the 16th century the *encomienda* was gradually changed into what was called the *repartimiento*, in which the forced labor was not supposed to be used for private advantage, but only for real needs of the state, authorized by government officials. This authorization was too easy to obtain whether justified or not, and many of the abuses continued, especially in the mines (primarily in Zacatecas state, first developed in 1548) whose production of silver was absolutely essential to Spain, as we have seen.[38] Meanwhile a succession of terrible plagues resulting from the Mexicans' lack of natural immunity to white men's diseases swept over Mexico and in the end killed the majority of its native population.[39]

Extraordinary exploring expeditions left Mexico by land and sea. Coronado marched north in 1540 to discover New Mexico, the Grand Canyon, and much of the later U.S. Southwest, though he returned a broken man still trying to magnify Indian village pueblos into great cities. For forty years no one followed him into New Mexico; from 1581 to 1593 four small expeditions, in which missionaries played a substantial part, penetrated the Rio Grande River country in far western

---

[36] Poole, *Pedro Moya de Contreros*, pp. 167-169, 171-172.

[37] *Ibid.*, p. 175.

[38] Simpson, *Encomienda in New Spain*, *passim*; Henry P. Wagner, *The Life and Writings of Bartolomé de Las Casas* (Albuquerque NM, 1967), pp. 116-118, 133, 136-138, 157; Bancroft, *History of Mexico*, II, 523-527; Aiton, *Mendoza*, pp. 96-99. The *repartimiento* was condemned by the Third Provincial Council of Mexico in 1585 as "unjust, prejudicial, and harmful to the souls, possessions, health and life of the Indians" (Poole, *Pedro Moya de Contreros*, p. 183). See Poole, *op. cit.*, pp. 176-187, for a general discussion of the evils of the *repartimiento*. For the discovery and development of the silver mines in Zacatecas province, see Bancroft, *op. cit.*, II, 554 and Aiton, *op. cit.*, pp. 75, 83.

[39] The epidemics of 1546 and 1576-77 were particularly severe, and may have taken two million lives. This was strictly a medical catastrophe; the Spaniards may not fairly be blamed for it in any way. Indians at hard labor were no more subject to it than other Indians. See Bancroft, *History of Mexico*, II, 657-659; Aiton, *Mendoza*, pp. 172, 174; Poole, *Pedro Moya de Contreros*, pp. 26, 52-53, 177-178.

Texas and New Mexico.[40] Two hard-bitten, amazingly persevering navigators, Juan Rodríguez Cabrillo in 1542 (a Portuguese who had marched with Cortés) and Sebastian Vizcaino some fifty years later, made their way up the California coast past the Golden Gate, though without discovering it; Cabrillo died on the way, from infection in a broken arm. Thus they laid the basis of Spain's claim to California, later inherited by Mexico.[41] Other voyagers went west to the Philippines on the other side of the world, and from the Philippines to Japan, where a great evangelization and then a great martyrdom took place, in which men and several saints and martyrs from Catholic Mexico played a significant part.[42] The Manila galleon began making its annual way from these distant Asiatic tropical isles to the Pacific coast of Mexico.[43] The University of Mexico, the first institution of higher learning in the New World, teaching grammar, philosophy, rhetoric, theology, law, mathematics, astronomy, medicine, Latin, Greek, Nahuatl and Otomi opened at the beginning of 1553.[44] To the south, Spanish explorers and developers conquered the old Maya peninsula of Yucatán[45] and spread to all parts of Central America, which they found often inhospitable, but with some inviting areas. Pedro de Alvarado had conquered Guatemala just three years after Cortés conquered Mexico.[46]

Hernan Cortés died in 1547; his son by Marina, Martín, inherited his father's title of Marquis del Valle. When the "New Laws" against forced Indian labor were issued, he became involved in an attempt to overthrow Spanish rule in Mexico and become its king. He was exiled forever from America, and three of his partners in the conspiracy were executed.[47] Philip II was ruling Spain now, and there was never a successful rebellion against him. In 1572 he selected one of his most trusted churchmen, Pedro Moya de Contreros, to go to Mexico, with the Pope's approval, as its archbishop (Mexico, by action of the Pope, had become an ecclesiastical province). Like his holy predecessor Bishop Zumárraga, Pedro Moya de Contreros was specifically designated protector of the Indians by King Philip II. Archbishop Moya was also ordered to conduct a *visita* of the viceroyalty, which he did despite the fierce opposition of two viceroys and numerous incumbent officials. He found much wrongdoing and

---

[40] See Herbert E. Bolton *Coronado, Knight of Pueblos and Plains* (Albuquerque NM, 1949) and Arthur G. Day, *Coronado's Quest; the Discovery of the Southwestern States* (Berkeley CA, 1940), also Paul Horgan, *Great River* (New York, 1954), I, 105-147, 153-160.

[41] Samuel Eliot Morison, *The European Discovery of America: the Southern Voyages* (New York, 1974), pp. 624-631, 675-676; Poole, *Pedro Moya de Contreros*, p. 125.

[42] See Chapter Thirteen, below.

[43] See Chapter Six, above.

[44] Bancroft, *History of Mexico*, II, 591-592; Aiton, *Mendoza*, p. 106.

[45] For the Spanish conquest of Yucatán, see Bancroft, *History of Mexico* II, 446-455, 649, 676-677.

[46] See John E. Kelly, *Pedro de Alvarado, Conquistador* (Princeton, 1932).

[47] Salvador de Madariaga, *Hernan Cortes, Conqueror of Mexico* (Chicago, 1955), p. 484; Bancroft, *History of Mexico*, II, 580-581, 608-628.

fearlessly reported it to the King. In striking contrast to the greedy and dishonest officials he exposed, he died a poor man, unable to pay for his own funeral.[48]

Meanwhile missionaries were streaming into Mexico in ever greater numbers. To the original Franciscans were first added Dominicans and Augustinians, and somewhat later Jesuits (in 1572) and Carmelites (in 1586). The three orders first in the country worked closely together as urged by Bishop Zumárraga, meeting together periodically in Mexico City to examine their joint challenges and problems in spreading the Gospel in this alien land. The Jesuits established a college in Mexico City in their second year in the country, in keeping with their emphasis on the educational apostolate everywhere. In 1576 Archbishop Moya asked Pope Gregory XIII for more Jesuits; 155 were in Mexico when he completed his work and returned to Spain in 1586.[49]

It was Archbishop Moya who conducted the landmark Third Provincial Council of Mexico in 1585, which set the basic framework for the Mexican church maintained into the twentieth century. Despite strong local opposition to its reforms, they were fully supported by King Philip II in 1586 and by Pope Sixtus V in 1588.[50] With everything else he had to do, Philip II maintained throughout his reign a constant and deep concern for the welfare of New Spain, and did all in his power to give it good government despite the months that were required to travel there or even send a message, one way.

In April 1598, as Philip II lay dying at El Escorial, an expedition from Mexico consisting of 130 families, 270 single men, 11 Franciscan friars, 83 wagons and carts, and about seven thousand cattle headed north from Mexico to the Rio Grande, commanded by Juan de Oñate, whose wife was a granddaughter of Hernán Cortés and whose father had marched with Coronado. They built an altar beside the river. On the last day of April, in the presence of all the men and the families, the Franciscan priests sang a solemn High Mass. Governor Oñate, invoking the Trinity, "the one and only true God . . . creator of the heavens and the earth . . . and of all creatures . . . from the highest cherubim to the lowliest ant and small butterfly," claimed New Mexico along with western Texas for Spain. The expedition then moved on through the future site of El Paso, Texas and northward into the future U.S. state of New Mexico, traversing the dread *Jornada del Muerto* (Dead Man's March)—ninety miles with only one small spring—and established the town of San Juan de los Caballeros on the Rio Grande near the site of present-day Santa Fe. Before the year ended, the local Indians launched an unprovoked assault on a party headed by Juan de Valdivar at Acoma mesa, and killed eleven of them. The Franciscan friars were consulted and assured Oñate that this act justified war. With only 70 soldiers Oñate vanquished

---

[48] Bancroft, *History of Mexico*, II, 556, 674-675, 678, 682-684, 746; Poole, *Pedro Moya de Contreros*, pp. 39-40, 53-54, 90-91, 93, 99-100, 108, 113-116, 207.

[49] Bancroft, *History of Mexico* II, 700-704, 711, 730n; Poole, *Pedro Moya de Contreros*, p. 78; Ricard, *Spiritual Conquest of Mexico*, p. 285.

[50] Poole, *Pedro Moya de Contreros*, pp. 148-201.

thousands of Indians, killing almost a thousand in the Battle of Acoma in late January 1599 while only two Spaniards were lost.[51]

Franciscan missionaries reached out quickly to Indians all over New Mexico. A number of them were martyred. In the first quarter of the seventeenth century they built approximately fifty churches, all built with the indispensable aid of the Indians, who painted decorative designs on the adobe walls, their designs becoming more Christian as they learned the Faith. Larger and larger numbers were instructed and baptized. In 1629 the new Archbishop of Mexico, Francisco Manza y Zúñiga, told the missionaries that they were to investigate reports from Spain that the superior of a convent at Agreda, Mother María de Jesús, had been miraculously transported from Spain to New Mexico to preach to the Indians. She had described her visits, saying that she was able to speak to the Indians in their own language, though at home in Spain she did not know it, and describing how she was transported by angels. The settlers in New Mexico thought of several visits from a distant Indian tribe called the Humanos, who had somehow found out about Christianity without its ever having been preached to them so far as the missionaries knew, urging them to come and instruct them in the Christian faith. Upon being asked, these Indians said that a white woman attired as a nun had preached to them repeatedly. Two Franciscans were now sent to them, Fray Juan de Salas and Fray Diego López. They crossed the Apache buffalo country for five hundred miles before they reached the Humanos, who came forward crying out for baptism. Then messengers from two other Indian tribes even further eastward came to the missionaries, also asking for baptism. "A white woman," they said, "young, pretty, in gray, black and white robes with a blue cloak, had been among them preaching and urging them to seek the desert fathers."[52]

Fray Alonso de Benavides, the Franciscan provincial of New Mexico then went to Spain to see Mother María of Agreda, sailing from Veracruz in 1630. By the following year he had presented his report, describing her and what he was convinced she had done:

> She could not, he thought, be as old as twenty-nine. Her face was beautiful, white except for a faint rosy tinge. She had large black eyes under heavy, high-arched eyebrows. Her costume consisted of coarse gray sackcloth worn next to the skin, and over that a habit of coarse white sackcloth with a scapula of the same stuff. She wore the white cloth tucked up so that much of the gray showed. Around her neck was a heavy rosary. At the waist she wore the Franciscan cord. Her face was framed in a winding of white cloth over which she wore a black veil. To her feet were tied hemp sandals. Her cloak was of heavy blue sackcloth. If her eyes were darkly calm, her mouth had a little smile of sweetness and humor. She talked freely.
>
> She said that all her life she had suffered for those who did not know God, especially the heathen peoples whose ignorance was not their own fault. She

---

[51] Horgan, *Great River*, pp. 11, 160-174, 199-211.

[52] *Ibid.*, I, 219-234 (quote on 234).

had had made known to her in revelations all those lands which did not know God. To them she had been repeatedly transported by her guardian angels, whom she identified as Saint Michael and Saint Francis of Assisi. As for New Mexico, she had been expressly called for by the custodian angels of that kingdom, who had come to get her by divine command. She went there the first time in 1620, and continued to go ever since. On some days she went three or four times in less than twenty-four hours. . . .

She told in detail about how Fray Juan de Salas and Fray Diego López went from the river to the Humanos nation, and said that it was she who had sent the Indians to fetch them. She described the two priests, and declared that she helped them herself in their work. When the messengers came to them from the other tribes farther out on the plains, it was because she had sent them. Her descriptions of the country were so accurate and detailed that they recalled to Fray Alonso much that he had seen and forgotten. . . .

When the interview was over, Fray Alonso showed her what he had written down of their exchange, and asking her whether it was the truth he "invoked the obedience from our most reverend father general that I carried for this purpose." Her confessor was also present and he called down upon her the same powerful sanction. In her own hand she addressed to the friars of the New Mexican river a confirmation of all that Fray Alonso had put down in his notebooks. "I saw and did all that I have told the Father," she wrote, and in a final summation of his view, the priest declared, "She convinced me absolutely by describing to me all the things in New Mexico as I have seen them myself, as well as by other details which I shall keep within my soul. Consequently, I have no doubts in this matter whatsoever."

In her written statement to the friars, Mother María de Jesús spoke gently of the nature of the Indians, and of the measures to be taken for their salvation. "God," she wrote, "created these Indians as apt and competent beings to serve and worship Him."[53]

It is the fullest, clearest, most substantial account of bilocation in history, provided for us by Paul Horgan's history of the Rio Grande region, meeting the standards of historical truth as well as the apparition and the picture of Our Lady of Guadalupe, or the apparitions of Our Lady of Lourdes and Our Lady of Fatima, meet them.[54] Most histories totally omit it, though the sources are there, and are listed by Paul Horgan. All honor to this man who refused to submit to the conspiracy of silence most historians maintain toward any event clearly supernatural. Of all the evangelizations in the world of the 16th and 17th centuries, that element was most prominent in Mexico.

Spanish South America

Spanish rule in Peru was secured by the defeat of the rebel Inca Emperor Manco after a year-long seesawing struggle in 1537.[55] By that conquest the

---

[53] *Ibid.*, I, 235-237.
[54] See my books *1917: Red Banners, White Mantle* (Front Royal VA, 1981) and *Our Lady of Guadalupe and the Conquest of Darkness*.
[55] See Chapter Three, pages 148-151.

Spaniards had established themselves in a reasonably well developed (by the Inca civilization) central location in the western, or Andean region of the continent of South America, including the modern nations of Peru, Ecuador, and Bolivia (called Upper Peru until the Spanish American wars of independence). Such was the torrential vigor of the *conquistadores* and their hunger for, and willingness to believe rumors of gold in various parts, that in the five years after Manco's defeat they had begun to open up all the rest of the continent, though for a century and more large areas of it remained unknown and unvisited.

To the north, Gonzalo Jimenes de Quesada marched up the broad Magdalena River flowing into the Caribbean to reach the high plateau on which Bogotá, the capital of the modern nation of Colombia, now stands; he named it New Granada. There on that plateau, in May 1538, he met two other *conquistadores*: Sebastian Belalcázar from Quito in Ecuador, and Nicholas Federmann, a German who had established himself in Venezuela. All three sailed back down the Magdalena River to make their discoveries and conquests known.[56] To the east, Francisco de Orellana broke away from an expedition into the jungles of eastern Peru and sailed all the way down the giant Amazon River to its mouth in the year 1542.[57] To the south, Pedro de Valdivia, with only about 125 Spaniards and a thousand Indians, marched from the Inca capital of Cuzco in southern Peru down to the long, narrow, but fertile stretch of land on the western slope of the Andes which is Chile, founding its capital of Santiago in the center of the country early in 1541, and later in that year assuming the position of its governor.[58]

To the southeast, Pedro de Mendoza founded Buenos Aires in 1536, fought off a furious Indian attack that same year, and in the next year sent his lieutenant Juan de Ayolas far up the Paraná and Paraguay Rivers. Ayolas was killed by Indians; Mendoza sailed for home in April 1537 but died at sea. Captain Juan de Salazar de Espinosa founded Asunción on a very defensible site on the Paraguay River far inland, on Assumption Day 1537. The handful of settlers elected Domingo de Irala as their governor—he was later confirmed by Emperor Charles V—and he soon decided (1541) to abandon the settlement of Buenos Aires and transfer it to Asuncion, his men being too few to hold both places. In Asunción relations with the local Indians, the pacific and talented Guaraní people, were at first very harmonious.[59] Thus in this incredible five years, Spanish rule was extended over substantial parts of no less than seven modern countries (Colombia, Ecuador, Peru, Bolivia, Chile, Argentina, and Paraguay) and the

---

[56] Clements Markham, *The Conquest of New Granada* (London, 1912), pp. 95-97, 114-115, 137, 142-143.

[57] John Hemming, *Red Gold; the Conquest of the Brazilian Indians* (Cambridge MA, 1978), pp. 186-194.

[58] Hugh Pocock, *The Conquest of Chile* (New York, 1967), pp. 49, 54, 57, 66-70, 80-82.

[59] Samuel E. Morison, *The European Discovery of America*, Volume II "The Southern Voyages" (New York, 1974), pp. 566-569.

whole of those countries was claimed by Spain and constituted what may be called Spanish South America.

Eastward on the great bulge and long southerly reaching coast was Brazil, which the Portuguese claimed as a result of the discovery of Pedro Alvares Cabral in 1500 and the Treaty of Tordesillas in 1494, and which was then and remained separate from the Spanish colonies, except for the period (1580-1640) when the crowns of Spain and Portugal were united. The "green hell" of the Amazon River region was at first regarded as part of the Spanish sphere, but eventually came to be ruled from Brazil.[60] Brazil and its evangelization will be treated in the next section of this chapter. Venezuela and Guiana remained during the sixteenth century essentially anarchic, open to any and all, as the presence of Germans such as the *conquistador* Federmann in Venezuela, and later of the British, Dutch and French in Guiana, made clear.

In these tumultuous and heroic five years, there was almost no Christian presence in South America—nothing at all like the equivalent period in Mexico. Francisco Pizarro did set aside land for Franciscan missionaries in Lima and Cuzco in Peru, but at first he had only two of them there, and made no effort to get more, as Cortés had done. In Quito a Franciscan house was established in 1538 under the direction of the missionary Jodoco Ricke, and during the next decade over a hundred Franciscan missionaries arrived at Quito. In 1546 Ricke finally established the house in Lima for which the Franciscans had been given land eleven years before.[61]

During the nine years following the defeat of Manco's Inca rebellion in 1537, much had happened in Peru. In April 1538 Pizarro fought a battle just outside Cuzco with the small army of his erstwhile partner and now bitter foe, Diego de Almagro, and defeated and captured him. In July the ruthless *conquistador* had Almagro strangled in his prison cell. Retribution came through Almagro's son, who with a band of 20 followers assassinated Pizarro in 1541. The newly installed Bishop of Cuzco, a friend of Pizarro, fled for his life, but was killed and eaten by cannibal Indians on the island of Puna. Pizarro's brother Gonzalo took over. But when Emperor Charles V issued his "new laws" in 1542 prohibiting forced labor for the Indians, Gonzalo Pizarro revolted, and in January 1546 killed the viceroy Charles had just sent to rule in his name in Peru, Blasco Vela.[62]

---

[60] E. Bradford Burns, *A History of Brazil*, 2nd ed. (New York, 1980), pp. 24-30; Hemming, *Red Gold*, p. 183.

[61] Antonin Tibesar, *Franciscan Beginnings in Colonial Peru* (Washington, 1953), pp. 16-22.

[62] John Hemming, *Conquest of the Incas* (New York, 1970), pp. 233, 262, 267-268, 275; Pocock, *Conquest of Chile*, pp. 43-44; Eugene H. Korth, *Spanish Policy in Colonial Chile; the Struggle for Social Justice, 1535-1700* (Stanford CA, 1968), p. 23n. See the "Mexico" section, above, for further information on the New Laws of Charles V, which unfortunately proved unenforceable anywhere in Spanish America in the sixteenth century.

With extraordinary wisdom and restraint, made necessary by the remoteness and inaccessibility of Peru (to get there, a Spaniard had to sail across the Atlantic to Panama, cross it to the Pacific Ocean, then obtain or buy passage on another ship going south down the Pacific coast, land at Lima, and finally make his way inland to the high valleys of the Andes) Charles V appointed a priest, Father Pedro de la Gasca, as president of the royal *audiencia* in Peru, in place of his murdered viceroy. Father de la Gasca had to deal with ruthless thieves and murderers, but he knew that they all still thought of themselves as Catholics. He gently reminded them of their loyalties to Church and King, which despite their behavior they had not entirely abandoned. He arrived in Peru in July 1546 and steadily undermined Gonzalo Pizarro's support. In October 1547 Gonzalo Pizarro won a battle on the shores of two-miles-high Lake Titicaca, but two months later the loyal *conquistador* Valdivia arrived from Chile with an army to strengthen de la Gasca. In April 1548 Gonzalo Pizarro was utterly defeated in the Battle of Jaquijaguana near Cuzco, after most of his men had deserted him and joined Father de la Gasca. The next day he was captured and executed. Father de la Gasca confirmed Valdivia's position as Governor of Chile in return for his services. In addition to bringing an end to this rebellion and ending domination of Peru by the Pizarros, Father de la Gasca finally brought in a large group of Franciscans to Peru, while Bishop Jerónimo de Loaiza of Lima decreed the building of a hospital and a school for the Indians.[63]

Meanwhile the Spanish expansion through South America continued. In the fall of 1543 the redoubtable Alvar Núñez Cabeza de Vaca, who had journeyed on foot from the Mississippi River to Mexico, explored up the Paraguay River as far as he could go by boat, and much of the surrounding countryside. In Chile Valdivia was concentrating his control, sending expeditions southward down the long Chilean coast, and forcing more and more Indians to work for the Spaniards.[64] Like many Spanish in the New World, he was convinced that this was necessary because of the small number of Spanish colonists, the multitudes of Indians, and the disinclination of most Indians to work regularly for wages. Valdivia was not an evil man, but he allowed much evil to happen. One wonders if he ever saw, or even heard of, the ringing statement by Pope Paul III in 1537 condemning:

> those who go about saying that the Indians of the west and of the south ought to be reduced to our service, as if they were brute beasts, under the pretext that they are incapable of receiving the Faith; and they actually do enslave them, grinding them down with such treatment as they scarcely use with their own beasts of burden. . . . Wishing to provide a suitable remedy for these evils, We, by Our apostolic authority, do hereby determine and declare that,

[63] Hemming, *Conquest of the Incas*, pp. 267-268, 271-280; Pocock, *Conquest of Chile*, pp. 144-148, 155-157; Tibesar, *Franciscan Beginnings in Colonial Peru*, pp. 24-25; Martin, *Intellectual Conquest of Peru*, p. 4; Frances P. Keyes, *The Rose and the Lily* (New York, 1961), pp. 76-79.

[64] Morison, *European Discovery of America*, II, 573-578; Pocock, *Conquest of Chile*, pp. 108-110, 114-117; Korth, *Spanish Policy in Colonial Chile*, pp. 24-25, 27.

notwithstanding what may have been said in the past or what may be said in the future, the aforementioned Indians and all other peoples who may in the future come within the ken of Christians, even though they be infidels, are by no means to be deprived of their liberty or their dominion over their property. Moreover, they may freely and licitly enjoy their dominion and liberty, and they are not to be reduced to slavery; and whatever has happened contrary to this declaration shall be null and void and have no binding force whatsoever.[65]

In January 1550, leading about two hundred Spaniards, most of them mounted, and numerous Indian auxiliaries, Valdivia came to the Bío-Bío River, frontier of the Indian people later called the Araucanians, who put up the longest and most courageous fight against the European invaders in the whole history of the Americas, continued until late in the 19th century. They knew and hated the Spanish system of forced Indian labor. Fifty thousand of them attacked Valdivia on the march, and though he prevailed with his horses and guns, sixty Spaniards, almost a third of his force, were wounded. He returned to the newly established Spanish town of Concepción, and though ordered by Charles V not to try to advance further to the south, he did so, hoping to go all the way to the Straits of Magellan. His way was blocked by an extraordinary young Indian named Lautaro, who had been Valdivia's groom and understood the Spaniards' weaknesses as well as their strengths. Valdivia knew an attack was coming, but entrenched at a place called Tucapel rather than retreating. Lautaro ambushed and routed a Spanish reinforcement sent to Valdivia, and then on Christmas day 1553 he launched four attacks from the woods on Valdivia's force, driving him back from Tucapel. Lautaro had kept a considerable number of warriors in reserve, and with discipline hitherto never seen among Indians, held them back until Valdivia, weakened and in retreat, was most vulnerable. Then they struck, and killed Valdivia and every man with him. Concepción was temporarily abandoned to the Araucanians. Four years later Lautaro died in battle, but the fight went on. In July 1563 the first bishop of Santiago, González Marmalejo, declared the Spanish war against the Araucanians to be a just war, which meant that, regardless of the laws intended to protect the Indians from forced labor, prisoners of war could be in effect enslaved.[66]

But the missionaries never ceased to defend the rights of the Indians. In January 1553 Dominican friar Francisco de Victoria wrote directly to the Council of the Indies, supreme authority over Spanish America under the king, telling them that:

from the reports of two persons recently arrived from Chile . . . it is evident that Christian principles and charity are completely lacking in that colony, and the abominations that occur there cry out to heaven for vengeance. All

---

[65] Korth, *Spanish Policy in Colonial Chile*, p. 16.

[66] Pocock, *Conquest of Chile*, pp. 171-178, 186-188, 204-205, 211, 215-224, 227-228. *Ibid.*, pp. 55-58. For the discovery and character of the Straits of Magellan, see Chapter One, above.

the *encomenderos* send their Indians—men, women, and children—to the mines to work without giving them any opportunity to rest, or any more food than a daily ration of maize during the eight months of the year that they labor there. The Indian who fails to produce the required amount of gold is beaten with clubs and whips. And if any Indian conceals a single grain of gold, he is punished by having his ears and nose cut off.[67]

Across the Andes in Tucumán province of what was to become northwestern Argentina, Nuñez de Prado founded the city of El Barco, which was placed under the *conquistador* Valdivia's rule shortly before he was killed by the Araucanians. A diocese was founded there in 1570. By 1557, when Governor Irala died, Asunción in Paraguay had a Spanish population of 1,500, a bishop, a cathedral, and a textile mill, and was the capital of a vast region including present-day Argentina and Paraguay and the future Brazilian provinces of Santa Catarina, Guairá, Rio Grande do Sul, Paraná and Mato Grosso, which the few Portuguese on the coast had not yet settled. For this region of generally open country, it was laid down as a principle by the Council of the Indies in 1551 that "the Indians should be reduced to towns, and should not live divided and separated by mountains and forests, depriving themselves of all spiritual and temporal benefit, without the aid of our ministers."[68] This was the beginning of a formal Spanish policy of creating communities of peaceful and productive Indians, already Christian or learning the faith, which was to bear fruit in the famous "reductions"—orderly and mostly Christian Indian communities—of Paraguay, northeastern Argentina and southwestern Brazil conducted by the Jesuits.

King Philip II, in one of his first decrees following his assumption of the crown of Spain, wrote to the *Audiencia* of New Granada (Colombia):

> Know that we, desiring . . . the conversion of the natives of those parts and that they may be brought to the knowledge of our Holy Catholic Faith to the end that they may be saved, have tried and each day do try to send religious and learned persons who are God-fearing, in order that they may endeavor to bring the said people to the true knowledge of the Faith; and although in many parts they have accomplished and each day do accomplish . . . great results . . . we are informed that the labor of said religious and learned persons is being hindered because of the impediments that they have had from some Spaniards who have resided and do reside in those parts, especially from those who have held and do possess enslaved Indians. . . . We therefore command that no person nor persons . . . dare to impede any

---

[67] Korth, *Spanish Policy in Colonial Chile*, p. 30.
[68] Pocock, *Conquest of Chile*, pp. 192-195; Fanchon Royer, *St. Francis Solanus; Apostle to America* (Paterson NJ, 1955), p. 94; Philip Caraman, *The Lost Paradise; the Jesuit Republic in South America* (New York, 1976), pp. 16, 25-26; J. Fred Rippy and Jean T. Nelson, *Crusaders of the Jungle* (Chapel Hill NC, 1936), p. 49 (for quote).

religious of whatever order that there may be who shall be travelling with the permission of the prelate [bishop].[69]

During these years the Dominican friar Gil González de San Nicolás, coming from Peru to Chile, emerged as the major defender of the oppressed Indians. He spoke for them at every opportunity, recalling the crusade for Indian rights by the great Bishop Bartolomé de Las Casas in Mexico. In November 1557 the first Dominican monastery was founded at Santiago de Chile. The best that could then be done to curb the exploitation of Indian labor was to limit the number assigned to the mines to no more than twenty per cent of the population, to provide that only twenty per cent more could be forced to work for the *encomendero* at any given time, and that the work should not be so distant as to force them to leave their homes. But these regulations, though approved by the Council of the Indies, were often evaded, and both the Franciscans and Dominicans in Chile were split on whether to endorse the views of Gil González de San Nicolás, which were sometimes exaggerated as a result of his hatred of Indian exploitation. In January 1564 Antonio de Molina, vicar-general of Santiago, wrote to Philip II that in Chile "the authorities are guilty of using great force on the natives, subjecting them to inhumanities unknown among people however barbarous they may be and however ignorant of God."[70]

The next month the current Spanish viceroy in Peru, López de Zúñiga, died after a night of debauchery. A conspiracy then developed among Indians still remembering the Incas to rise up and attack the Spaniards in Holy Week of 1565. The conspiracy was discovered, and peace was made in 1566 with the Inca leader Titu Cusi by the terms of which he agreed to accept Spanish missionaries. The next year there was another plot, involving Spanish *mestizos* as well as diehard Inca supporters, which was also discovered in time to thwart it. Clearly, Peru was not yet fully pacified; it needed a strong hand and a man of good judgment as its viceroy. Peru got both in Francisco de Toledo, appointed in February 1567, who was a good friend of St. Francis Borgia and the Jesuits he directed. The first shipload of Jesuits, under Gerónimo Ruiz de Portillo, arrived in Peru in April of that year and were immediately given a prime site in Lima which became the campus of the first university in South America, the College of San Pablo.[71]

Still very little had been done to evangelize the Indians, who by this time in Mexico were almost all Christian, and had been for at least twenty years. The new viceroy, who sailed from Spain in March 1569 with twelve more Jesuits actually on board his ship, sent into the field most of the order priests and brothers who were living comfortably in Lima, and ordered the Franciscans to assume a permanent commitment in the 59 Indian parishes where they were currently working, including 118,000 Indian converts, about ten per cent of the

---

[69] Rippy and Nelson, *Crusaders of the Jungle*, p. 50. This *cédula* was dated December 10, 1556.

[70] Korth, *Spanish Policy in Colonial Chile*, pp. 34-41, 43-47, 52-55 (quote on 54).

[71] Hemming, *Conquest of the Incas*, pp. 302, 305-307, 313-344, 343-344; Martin, *Intellectual Conquest of Peru*, pp. 12-15.

total population of Peru. In June 1570 the Jesuit Alonso de Barzana delivered a flawless sermon in the Quechua language of Indian Peru in the presence of the viceroy and the *audiencia*. He then made an extensive tour of highland Peru. But a special commission that he set up decided that the mining of precious metals was required by the public interest of Spain, so some Indians could continue to be forced to work in the mines. The archbishop of Lima, who had served on this commission, soon changed his mind and spoke out against its position. The viceroy attempted to justify the Spanish conquest of Peru by pointing out that the Incas had conquered the rest of the country themselves, and that Atahualpa, their last ruler, was a usurper. Meanwhile the remnant of the Incas gathered near Vilcabamba killed the missionary Diego Ortiz and a Spanish ambassador, and forbade Christianity in their isolated region of Peru. Viceroy Francisco de Toledo made war on them, defeated their leader, a descendant of the Incas named Tupac Amaru, and had him executed, despite the strong intercession by Spanish churchmen in favor of mercy for him. With his last breath Tupac Amaru professed Christianity and denounced the Inca religion.[72] It was not really Christianity that the Indians fought against, but Spanish denial of their rights as human beings.

In July 1573 Philip II issued the Ordinance on Discoveries, banning further Spanish conquests in America, and emphasizing missionary work among the Indians and their protection as primary objectives of the Spanish government in America. That same month he abolished the *audiencia* of Chile, which had refused to obey his commands against imposing excessive labor on the Indians, and made Rodrigo de Quiroga Chile's governor, only to find him supporting forced Indian labor as well, and setting out in 1577 on an expedition against the Araucanians, calling for many prisoners to be taken who would be sent to the mines. At the end of 1573 Philip II received petitions from persons related to Tupac Amaru the Inca against Viceroy de Toledo's confiscation of all the goods of their family and expulsion of them from Peru; he ordered a full investigation and later pardoned all who had received this treatment. In 1580 the ordination of *mestizos* was forbidden in Peru, thus extending the tremendous mistake made in Mexico, which has deprived Latin America of sufficient priests to this very day, even though this policy has long since been abandoned.[73]

The vehement protests against forced labor by the Indians continued; their advocates would not rest, or accept the official evasions. In 1580 new Governor Ruiz de Gamboa of Chile abolished personal labor service by Indians, substituting a monetary and produce tax. This too was widely evaded, but added

---

[72] Tibesar, *Franciscan Beginnings in Colonial Peru*, pp. 48-50, 96; Martin, *Intellectual Conquest of Peru*, pp. 16, 49; Hemming, *Conquest of the Incas*, pp. 405, 412-419, 421-423, 432-440, 443-449, 505. In April 1545 the Indian convert Diego Gualpa had discovered the rich silver mines of Potosí in Upper Peru (now Bolivia), which rivalled the mines of Zacatecas in Mexico in value (Hemming, *op. cit.*, p. 369.

[73] Henry Kamen, *Philip of Spain* [Philip II] (New Haven CT, 1997), pp. 150-151; Korth, *Spanish Policy in Colonial Chile*, pp. 63-65; Tibesar, *Franciscan Beginnings in Colonial Peru*, pp. 33-34; Hemming, *Conquest of the Incas*, pp. 453-454.

to the momentum of reform. Later that year, Buenos Aires was resettled. The next year the "gentle" Martin Enríquez de Almansa succeeded the hard-hitting Francisco de Toledo as viceroy of Peru. In 1582 the Peruvian Jesuits decided at a provincial convention to do more missionary work among the Indians, and in the following year the Third Council of Lima ordered the writing of a catechism for the Indians in their own languages. A bilingual catechism in 1584 was published in Peru, the very first printed book produced in South America. Jesuit General Aquaviva told his Jesuits in Peru to give more emphasis to missionary work and less to administration, and to hold themselves apart from the pressures of those in temporal authority. The number of converts was slowly but steadily rising. The Bishop of Tucumán in the future Argentina invited Jesuit missionaries to his vast diocese in 1585, and the first great missionary to the Guaraní Indians of Paraguay, Fray Luis de Bolaños, completed the first grammar of the Guaraní language. A seminary and a university were founded in Quito, Ecuador in 1586. In 1590 the first Jesuits arrived in New Granada (Colombia), and the fearless and far-wandering St. Francis Solanus went out preaching to the Indians in the Tucumán region of the future Argentina, and in the Chaco wilderness which stretches from Paraguay into Argentina and Upper Peru.[74]

But the most important development in Spanish South America in the later years of the sixteenth century was the advent as Bishop of Lima, the primatial see of the whole region, of a saint: Turibius de Mogrovejo. As a professor of law at the University of Salamanca he had come to the notice of King Philip II, who saw that he was made chief judge of the court of the Inquisition at Granada, a very unusual position for a layman, which St. Turibius then still was. When the position of Archbishop of Lima became vacant, Philip II proposed him for it, despite the fact that he was still a layman. The saint protested in vain. He was promptly ordained, consecrated, and sent off to his distant new post in 1581. He found abuses of the Indians everywhere, communications very slow and unreliable, the Catholic faith at a low ebb among the conquerors and still rejected by the majority of Peruvian Indians, largely because of the exceedingly bad example the Spanish were giving to them. And Peru had no Virgin of Guadalupe.[75]

St. Turibius at once undertook a visitation of his diocese, taking particular care to identify and punish the offenses of the clergy. When told he was violating local custom, he replied memorably: "Christ said, 'I am the truth.' He did not say 'I am the custom.'" Everywhere he founded churches, monasteries and hospitals. In 1591 he founded a major seminary at Lima. He learned several Indian languages so as to preach to the native people in their own tongue. During

---

[74] Korth, *Spanish Policy in Colonial Chile*, pp. 68-69; Hemming, *Conquest of the Incas*, p. 505; Morison, *European Discovery of America*, II, 580; Martin, *Intellectual Conquest of Peru*, pp. 49-50, 123-124; Tibesar, *Franciscan Beginnings in Colonial Peru*, pp. 55-57, 61; Caraman, *Lost Paradise*, pp. 26-27; Royer, *St. Francis Solanus*, pp. 95-127; Keyes, *Rose and Lily*, p. 153.

[75] *Butler's Lives of the Saints*, edited, revised and supplemented by Herbert Thurston, S.J., and Donald Attwater (Westminster MD, 1956), II, 176-177.

the twenty-five years that he was Archbishop of Lima, he visited almost every part of his huge diocese, personally confirming thousands upon thousands of young people, Spanish and Indian. He confirmed three saints—Rose of Lima. Martin de Porres, and John Massias. He died in 1606, 68 years old, willing his personal belongings to his servants and all the rest of his property to the poor. Little more than a century afterward, he was canonized.[76]

The impact of such a man in such a position, working continuously for twenty-five years for evangelization and the deepening of faith where it already existed, can hardly be exaggerated. Many, if not all of the rapacious Spaniards were overawed; the Indians were profoundly impressed. The movement began which was to lead to the eventual conversion of the majority of the continent. In 1608 the Jesuit provincial of Paraguay, La Plata, Tucumán, and Chile, Diego de Torres, publicly condemned obligatory personal service by Indians even when they had been captured in wars held unjust by the Spaniards. King Philip III continued his father's efforts to abolish the *encomienda* system. In Chile in 1609, the Jesuit Luis de Valdivia was able to persuade the Council for the Indies and King Philip III to adopt a plan for waging defensive warfare only against the Araucanians, rather than provoking them into more and more wars by raiding into their territory. Philip III appointed him *visitador* of Chile, making him for the duration of his appointment superior to all crown officials in the colony. Viceroy Mendoza of Peru confirmed the Bío-Bío River in Chile as the Araucanian frontier which no Spaniard in arms was authorized to cross, and the enslavement of Indians captured in war was brought to an end. Unfortunately, peace negotiations with the hard-fighting Araucanians foundered when their chief Anganamón killed three Jesuit missionaries because they had told him he should have only one wife. The governor of Chile, Alonso de Ribera, bitterly challenged Luis de Valdivia's demand that the Spaniards abstain from offensive warfare against the Araucanians in light of this triple murder. Luis de Valdivia's policy for defensive warfare only was sustained by Philip III, but after his death and the accession of his young son Philip IV, under heavy pressure from the colonial authorities this policy was abandoned, and once again the enslavement of rebel prisoners of war was authorized. But Indians living peacefully in their villages were generally protected, and the extraction of forced labor from them prohibited, by the orders of Jesuit provincial of Paraguay Diego de Torres, who had been appointed *visitador* of Tucumán, Paraguay, and Rio de la Plata (Buenos Aires) in 1612. The first of the Jesuit "reductions" of Paraguay was set up on the Paraná River in 1610, followed by another in 1615, and by several more over the next ten years.[77]

---

[76] *Ibid.*, II, 179-180. St. Martin de Porres, a mulatto, was professed in the Dominican order in 1603 (J. C. Kearns, *The Life of Blessed Martin de Porres, Saintly American Negro and Patron of Social Justice* [New York, 1937], pp. 127-128). For St. Turibius' confirmation of St. Rose of Lima, see Keyes, *Rose and Lily*, p. 101.

[77] Korth, *Spanish Policy in Colonial Chile*, pp. 100-103, 108, 116, 121, 127, 129, 136-137, 152-157, 163; Caraman *Lost Paradise*, pp. 32-35, 43-45, 47-48, 54; Martin, *Intellectual Conquest of Peru*, p. 57.

Meanwhile, one of the greatest saints in the whole history of the Church had arrived unheralded at the port of Cartagena at the mouth of the Magdalena River in New Granada (Colombia): Peter Claver. He was a Spaniard who had studied at the Jesuit college on Majorca island in the Mediterranean, where a humble and holy brother named Alphonsus Rodriguez was doorkeeper. Alphonsus the doorkeeper became young Peter's spiritual guide and master. He sought persistently to arouse in the best of the young Jesuits at the college a fervent desire for missionary work in America.[78]

> From the outset Alphonsus prayed for this choice soul, of whose great mission he had a foreshadowing. One day, praying for his friend in a moment of crisis, of indecision about the future, Alphonsus was rapt to heaven accompanied by his guardian angel. There he saw innumerable thrones occupied by the souls of the blessed, and among them, the most splendid of all, an empty one. Desiring to know the meaning of that mystery, he was told: "That is the place prepared for your disciple, Peter Claver, as a reward for his many virtues and the innumerable souls he will convert by his toil and sweat in the Indies."[79]

St. Peter Claver arrived at Cartagena in 1610 or 1611, quietly pursuing his studies there and at Tunja near Bogotá, leading up to his ordination, which took place in Cartagena in 1616.[80] The year before, Spanish officials made a contract with a Portuguese named Antonio Delbas to guarantee the delivery of 3,500 to 5,000 black slaves from Africa every year, most of them being sent to Cartagena, with a much lesser number going to Veracruz in Mexico.[81] The increasing restrictions on the use of Indian forced labor had turned the thoughts of the governors of South America's two northern provinces, New Granada and Venezuela, with their tropical climate, to the economic advantages of black slaves, most of whom had already been enslaved by their own people and were easy to buy in quantity at a small fraction of the price they would command in the New World. Consciences were stilled by the hollow argument that these men and women were already in a state of slavery in a pagan land, and that by drawing them out of Africa to a Christian land they could be converted. But no one had set himself to that task—one of formidable difficulty. When they first arrived in Cartagena, unable to speak any Western language, many in a dying condition (slave ships could lose one-third of their human cargo and still turn a profit), most of them diseased and half-starved, the black slaves were kept for weeks in incredibly filthy hovels and then sent off to their New Granadan and Venezuelan buyers, who mostly were interested only in the unpaid labor they

---

[78] Angel Valtierra, S.J., *Peter Claver, Saint of the Slaves* (Westminster MD, 1960), pp. 20-37.

[79] *Ibid.*, p. 26.

[80] *Ibid*, pp. 29, 58-59, 65-66, 70.

[81] *Ibid.*, pp. 83-85.

could provide. In the land that had been conquered for Christ, no one cared for them.[82]

On May 30, 1617 St. Peter Claver wrote the only surely authentic letter of his that has been preserved, to his Jesuit provincial:

> Yesterday there came to land a great ship laden with negroes from the Rivers [of West Africa]. We went there laden with baskets of oranges, lemons and tobacco. We entered their house which seemed like another Guinea, piles of them on all sides; we made our way through till we reached the sick of whom there were a great number lying on the ground, which, as it was damp and liable to flooding, was levelled up with sharp-edged pieces of brick and tiles, and this was their bed, where they lay naked without a stitch of clothing. We threw off our cloaks and went to fetch planks from a store-room and we laid a floor there and carried the sick in our arms, pushing our way through the rest.[83]

In 1622 Peter Claver made his solemn profession as a Jesuit, taking the famous four vows, and writing below his signature on the vows: "Love, Jesus, Mary, Joseph, Ignatius, Peter, my own Alonso [Rodriguez], Thomas, Lawrence, Bartholomew, my saints, patrons and my intercessors and those of my beloved negroes, hear me." He signed himself *"Petrus Claver, ethiopum semper servus"* ("Peter Claver, slave of the Negroes forever").[84]

It was an apostolate like none other there has ever been. Peter Claver had to devote himself, alone except for a few assistants, to the overwhelming burden of providing both physical care and spiritual guidance for people deprived of all worldly hope after experiencing one of the most hellish environments in recorded history for the many weeks it took to cross the Atlantic. He had to assemble and take with him several blacks already living in New Granada who had become conversant in Spanish but knew one or more African languages, to act as his interpreters. He showed the blacks pictures of Jesus and Mary, and of great men in the Church, mitred bishops, rejoicing at the baptism of a black. He brought them refreshment; he wiped the sweat from their faces with his own

---

[82] In recent years, many well-documented studies of the slave trade and its horrors have been published. See especially (among many others) Basil Davidson, *The African Slave Trade* (Boston, 1988); Herbert S. Klein, *African Slavery in Latin America and the Caribbean* (New York, 1986); James A. Rawley, *The Transatlantic Slave Trade, a History* (New York, 1981); and Hugh Thomas, *The Slave Trade* (New York, 1997). Contrary to a widespread impression, most slaves were not kidnapped by the slave traders, though this did sometimes happen. Most of them had already been enslaved by chieftains of their own people who had been successful in war. A decree of Pope Urban VIII on April 22, 1639 expressly prohibited the capture and removal of blacks from their native country by any Catholic (Valtierra, *Peter Claver*, p. 94).

[83] Valtierra, *Peter Claver*, pp. 109-110.

[84] *Ibid.*, p. 71.

handkerchief; he even sometimes licked clean their sores with his own tongue, and baptized the dying.[85] In the words of a contemporary account:

> If anyone were dangerously ill, he baptized him at once, and those who were not in that state he instructed for many days, teaching them the catechism and prayers, and afterwards he made them say the act of contrition very fervently; and then when he was going to baptize them he put on the stole which was so old it had completely lost its original color. For baptism he used a jug and a basin of very fine china, and the interpreters or others present acted as godparents; then he put the medals around their necks.[86]

To the greatest extent possible, St. Peter Claver kept up with the blacks he had instructed in Cartagena, even after they were sent off to their owners. It is estimated that he heard five thousand of their confessions every year. He spent so much time with them that the foul smell of the slave-pens always hung about him, causing the fastidious to avoid him. But he was also concerned with the souls of white men. In 1639 he met a ship carrying 600 English and Dutch prisoners of war brought from two West Indian islands they had occupied, ministered to them, and received the Protestant archdeacon of London into the Catholic Church on his deathbed, which was followed by the conversion of many of the other Englishmen. He even converted several Moors after prolonged efforts, something which almost never happens. Surely at least partly due to his presence and moral example, black slavery in Spanish South America was less totally oppressive than elsewhere. Marriages of slaves were allowed and protected; slave owners were not permitted to separate married partners and their minor children. Those who wonder why St. Peter Claver never urged a slave rebellion need look no farther for an explanation than the ghastly bloodbath in Haiti in the slave rebellion in 1791, stimulated by the French Revolution, in which almost every white man in Haiti was killed. Understandable as revenge under these circumstances may be, vengefulness was totally alien to the character of St. Peter Claver.[87]

As the years passed and the demand for black slaves in Spanish South America increased, as many as ten thousand were being brought into Cartagena every year. St. Peter Claver tried to be there, and usually was, when every slave ship was unloaded. Over the entire span of his apostolate it is estimated that he baptized more than 300,000 blacks, one-third of all the slaves brought into Spanish South America during these years—the fulfillment of Alphonsus Rodriguez's vision.[88] Only a very few could endure his work for long, and were

---

[85] *Ibid*, pp. 124, 132-159; *Butler's Lives of the Saints* as edited, revised, and supplemented by Herbert Thurston, S.J., and Donald Attwater, III, 519-524.

[86] Valtierra, *Peter Claver*, p. 126.

[87] *Ibid.*, pp. 180-183; *Butler's Lives of the Saints*, edited, revised, and supplemented by Herbert Thurston, S.J., and Donald Attwater, III, 519-524. For the slave rebellion in Haiti, see Volume Five, Chapter 9 of this history.

[88] *Butler's Lives of the Saints* as edited, revised, and supplemented by Herbert Thurston, S.J., and Donald Attwater, III, 520-521; Valtierra, *Peter Claver*, pp. 310-311.

available to help him. After St. Peter had been at this work for almost thirty years, the great plague of 1651 in Cartagena killed six Jesuit priests and three brothers. The saint contracted it, and though he recovered, it cost him the splendid physical health that he had been given through all the thirty years that he had been "the slave of the slaves." He lay sick and eventually dying, avoided by almost everyone whose conscience his devoted service had troubled, tended only by a black who did not really care about him and felt no gratitude to him. St. Peter Claver never complained. On September 8, 1654 he died. Suddenly many who had forgotten or ignored him in his last illness—thousands of them—came to pass by his body, touching their rosaries to it, noblemen mingling with slaves. His funeral the next day was marked by a procession including the governor, the lieutenant-governor, all the aldermen of the city, and all the Augustinians (now the largest order in Cartagena, which had never done anything to help St. Peter and his mission while he was alive). People tore off his clothing for relics. On September 14 his body was laid in a tomb, which was formally dedicated by the governor; but the blacks provided the candles and music for the ceremony. His process for canonization began just three years later, though it was not finally completed until 1887. On the same day his mentor, Alfonso Rodriguez, the holy doorkeeper of Majorca, was also canonized.[89]

St. Peter Claver had plumbed the heights and the depths of what it means to be a saint. No saint of all those the Church has honored ever exceeded him in holiness; few have ever matched him. In the words of Pope Leo XIII, who presided at his canonization: "No life, except the life of Christ, has so moved me as that of St. Peter Claver."[90]

In 1627 the Count of Chinchón became Viceroy of Peru, and in 1629 he asked the Jesuits at the College of San Pablo if he might increase the numbers of Indians required to work in the rich silver mine of Potosí. Jesuit provincial Pedro de Oñate replied forcefully that forced Indian labor could never be right, and certainly must not be expanded. The professors at the College fully supported him in refusing to allow forced Indian labor in Tucumán province in the future Argentina. In 1633 King Philip IV of Spain banned all compulsory Indian labor in Chile "whenever and in whatever form it existed." Leading Chileans actually discussed rebelling against the King and the Viceroy because of this decree, but the days of Gonzalo Pizarro had passed; there was no actual revolt. In 1635 the governor of Chile issued 16 specific ordinances intended to do away with compulsory Indian labor; and though some of it still continued, it now had to be done largely in secret. In September 1639 King Philip IV declared: "No Indian of whatever quality he may be, even although an infidel, may be held captive nor placed in slavery in any manner, or for any cause or reason, nor may he be deprived of the natural dominion that he has of his goods, children, or wife."[91]

---

[89] Valtierra, *Peter Claver*, pp. 136-138, 215, 255-256, 273, 287-289, 292-309.

[90] *Ibid.*, p. 266.

[91] Rippy and Nelson, *Crusaders of the Jungle*, p. 53 (second quote); Kenneth Andrien, *Crisis and Decline; the Viceroyalty of Peru in the Seventeenth Century* (Albuquerque NM,

In January 1641 the Pact of Quillin at last made peace between the Spanish settlers in Chile and the Araucanian Indians, recognizing the independence of the latter south of the Bío-Bío River. Unfortunately war broke out again in 1655, when 240 Spaniards were massacred by the Indians and the colonists tried to put in their own governor, only to find his predecessor restored by royal authority.[92] In 1645 a succession of devastating earthquakes struck Quito in Ecuador, followed by epidemics of measles and diphtheria, and then by the eruption of a nearby volcano. An eloquent priest, Father Alonso de Rojas, declared that these were signs that God was angry with the Spanish of Quito. Blessed Mariana, known as "the Lily of Quito," rose from the congregation and offered to give her life in propitiation. Her sacrifice was accepted; she died on Ascension day, though still a young woman, and the city was spared further calamities.[93] In June 1649, a miraculous vision of the Christ Child was seen at the Corpus Christi festival at the Franciscan establishment at Magdalena de Etén in Peru.[94] When the headstrong, domineering Bernardino de Cárdenas, Bishop of Asunción in Paraguay, attempted to close the Jesuit Reductions and expel all the Jesuits from his diocese in 1649, the Spanish governor León y Zárate rose up to defend them, brought up 700 Indians from the Reductions to do battle with the maverick bishop, and expelled him from the country.[95] In 1650 the first Franciscan mission entered hitherto neglected Venezuela. It was reinforced in 1656 and again in 1658.[96]

Against all obstacles, despite the bad example so many Spaniards had given, despite the enormous distances of the new lands and their isolation, the whole of Spanish South America was moving steadily toward conversion by the middle of the seventeenth century. In May 1656 Belgian Jesuit Noel Berthot wrote that there were hardly any infidels left in the province of Santa Fe, upstream on the Paraná River in the center of the future Argentina;[97] in 1659 Jesuits were sent to evangelize the almost impenetrable mountains of New Granada (Colombia).[98] Evangelization was virtually complete by the eighteenth century. A whole Catholic continent resulted, even though the priest shortage caused by the tragic refusal of both Spain and Portugal to ordain Indians, or even most *mestizos*, gravely hindered their practice of the faith outside specifically Christian communities like the Reductions of Paraguay.

1985), pp. 145-149; Korth, *Spanish Policy in Colonial Chile*, pp. 168-174 (first quote on 168).

[92] Korth, *Spanish Policy in Colonial Chile*, pp. 175-176, 182-187.

[93] Keyes, *Rose and Lily*, pp. 213-217. Blessed Mariana was only 27 years old when she died.

[94] Tibesar, *Franciscan Beginnings in Colonial Peru*, p. 63n.

[95] Caraman, *Lost Paradise*, pp. 82-89, 92, 94-96.

[96] Rippy and Nelson, *Crusaders of the Jungle*, pp. 109-112.

[97] Caraman, *Lost Paradise*, p. 52.

[98] Rippy and Nelson, *Crusaders of the Jungle*, p. 303.

Brazil

Just under half of the whole continent of South America is included in the vast expanses of the Portuguese-speaking state of Brazil,[99] for centuries Portugal's huge and fruitful colony. Extending from the "green hell" of the Amazon River region—the Amazon is the largest river in the world—along a coast with many fine harbors which have developed into major ports, and with inland provinces south of the Amazon rain forest which are rich in minerals and open land, it is truly astonishing that the tiny nation of Portugal, with only a little more than one per cent of its area, was able to retain and develop Brazil for nearly three hundred years.[100] The wonder is not that it was often misgoverned or ungoverned, a haunt of outlaw raiders, but that Portuguese government was preserved there at all.

The Indians of Brazil, with whom the Portuguese came in contact from the beginning of their arrival as colonists, were wholly unlike the Indians of Mexico who had derived a true civilization, though primitive and fearfully distorted morally, from the Mayas and the Toltecs,[101] and also unlike the Inca empire of Peru (including the present Peru, Ecuador and Bolivia) and the semi-civilized Indians of Colombia and Chile. The Indians of Brazil were much more like those of North America, except that they were cannibalistic on a much larger scale, and in the subtropical Brazilian climate, they went about stark naked.[102] Divided into numerous hostile tribes, none with a settled agriculture, they could not understand land titles or the rule of law. The first task was to civilize them, and it was a task of enormous difficulty. The Jesuit missionaries sought to do that through their mission villages, called "reductions" in Spanish America and *aldeias* in Brazil.

---

[99] Precisely 3,286,470 square miles compared to 3,408,000 for all the rest of the continent.

[100] The exact area of Portugal is 35,672 square miles compared to Brazil's 3,286,470.

[101] For the culture of pre-Columbian Mexico and its dedication to human sacrifice, see Chapter One, above. For its evangelization see the "Mexico" section earlier in this chapter.

[102] For the culture of the Indians of Brazil, read (with caution) John Hemming, *Red Gold; the Conquest of the Brazilian Indians* (Cambridge MA, 1978). While Hemming established that he could write good South American history in his earlier book *The Conquest of the Incas* (cited in Chapter Three, above), in this book he not only whitewashes but glorifies the Brazilian Indians, mostly ignoring the fact that before the white man came they engaged in almost constant wars to eat each other, and claiming that some tribes were not cannibalistic—which is true, but little as he likes to admit it, they were very much in the minority according to all the contemporary testimony. The Brazilian Indians were, as Hemming repeatedly and angrily points out, badly victimized by the whites. But nothing done to them was any worse than what they had previously done to each other, and continued to do. Their nakedness, though permitted by the climate, was not simply "natural." Most other native dwellers in hot climates throughout the world still wore at least some clothes.

In 1532 Martim Afonso de Sousa planted the first Portuguese colony in Brazil, on the coast at Sao Vicente near present-day Santos, building there a headquarters building, a chapel, and two forts. Later that year King John III of Portugal informed de Sousa of his intention to divide Brazil into separate captaincies, each with fifty leagues of coast. The captaincy system did not work; Brazil was too vast and the Indians too hostile, making the interior ungovernable; and Portugal at this time was deeply committed in Asia, where her ships actually controlled the Indian Ocean.[103] Fortunately for Portugal, Brazil gained economic self-sufficiency (other than its need for military protection) quite soon through the production of sugar, a delicacy increasingly prized in Europe during the sixteenth and seventeenth centuries.[104]

Labor was necessary to work the sugar plantations. The number of Brazilian colonists from Portugal was insufficient to supply it, and in any case most of those colonists disdained manual labor. Black slaves from Africa were rare and very expensive in the first century of the settlement of Brazil. So the Indians were enslaved, on every kind of pretext, despite a brief of Pope Paul III in 1537 specifically forbidding the enslavement of Indians.[105] But as Helen Dominian points out:

> An Indian slave originally was a victim captured in intertribal wars and fattened for the cannibalistic feast. As more enlightened tribes required labor, they forced some captives into service rather than killing all of them; this proved so profitable that intertribal slave raids became the vogue. Among the whites, particularly such backsliding men as Joao Ramalho, slave raids became more businesslike. Ramalho had sanguinary accomplices in his colony of *mamelucos*[106] who were the means of establishing a ruthless slave trade. Bands of armed men went into the wilds and captured Indians, like so many forest animals, brought them to the settlements, and forced them into hard labor.[107]

---

[103] See Volume III, Chapter Sixteen of this history.

[104] E. Bradford Burns, *A History of Brazil*, 2nd ed. (New York, 1980) pp. 30-32; Helen G. Dominian, *Apostle of Brazil; the Biography of Padre Jose de Anchieta, S.J.* (New York, 1958), pp. 30-34. Fifty years after the first settlement in Brazil, it was estimated that there were 118 sugar mills in Brazil, which had become the world's principal supplier of sugar (C. R. Boxer, *Salvador de Sá and the Struggle for Brazil and Angola* [London, 1952], pp. 177-179).

[105] Burns, *History of Brazil*, p. 49; Boxer, *Salvador de Sá*, p. 129.

[106] This odd term, which was probably taken from the Mameluke "slave kings" of Egypt, was applied to the ungoverned and ungovernable population of the interior of Brazil south of the Amazon region, the offspring of cohabitation among whites, Indians, and blacks, who mostly grew up without real families and took what they wanted whenever they could. They were particularly identified with Sao Paulo, the first significant Portuguese settlement in inland Brazil, which was not reachable by any wheeled vehicle until 1661, at the very end of our period. Consequently the *mamelucos* are sometimes called Paulistas.

[107] Dominian, *Apostle of Brazil*, p. 37.

In 1548 King John III of Portugal bought back the captaincy of the principal city in colonial Brazil at that time, on the northeastern coast between Brazil's future capital, Rio de Janeiro, and the eastern bulge of Brazil which was closest to Portugal. This city was officially named San Salvador, but was always called Bahia. In establishing Bahia as a crown colony, King John III declared that he would rule it "for the service of God, and the exaltation of our holy faith, of me and of my people, for the ennoblement of the captaincies, and the betterment of the aborigines."[108]

This required missionaries, none of whom had yet been sent to Brazil. The newly formed[109] Jesuit order, which had made a particularly strong beginning in Portugal, took charge of this formidable task. In March 1549 a fleet of six Portuguese vessels commanded by Tomé de Sousa, newly appointed Captain-General of Brazil, dropped anchor in Bahia harbor with about a thousand colonists and soldiers on board, and six Jesuit missionaries led by the intrepid Manoel de Nóbrega. That Sunday the Jesuit Fathers said the first Mass at Bahia, in the open. Before Pentecost, Nóbrega and his companions had baptized about a hundred Indians and had six or seven hundred under instruction.[110] Nóbrega drew up six principles for evangelizing and civilizing the Indians of Brazil:

> (1) Forbid them to eat human flesh or to make war without permission from the Governor; (2) make them keep only one wife; (3) dress them, for they have plenty of cotton, at least after they are Christians; (4) remove their sorcerers; (5) maintain justice between them and between them and the Christians; (6) make them live quietly without moving to another place unless they move in among Christians.[111]

These principles remained the basis of the evangelization and civilization of the Indians of Brazil. Those who deride them, now that it is so fashionable to do so, simply have no conception of what life with naked, polygamous, cannibalistic savages was really like. The missionaries knew; they regularly went among these savages while they were still in their primitive condition. Their accounts tell the story.

On Christmas day in that same year of 1549 one of the Jesuits, Father Leonardo Nunes, said the first Mass at a newly built chapel in Sao Vicente. A year and a half later Nóbrega was back in Bahia, planning a Jesuit college there with Governor Tomé de Sousa. He then set out with just one companion in a small boat to voyage more than 500 miles to the eastern bulge of Brazil, the province of Pernambuco, where the colonial settlement of Olinda had recently been founded, and began missionary work there at once. Thus the Jesuit missionaries arrived at three major settlements along the coast almost contemporaneous with the first Portuguese colonists, and began immediately

---

[108] *Ibid.*, pp. 37-39 (quote on 38); Burns, *History of Brazil*, p. 34.

[109] In 1540.

[110] Burns, *History of Brazil*, pp. 34-35; Hemming, *Red Gold*, pp. 79-80; Dominian, *Apostle of Brazil*, pp. 40-41, 47-48.

[111] Hemming, *Red Gold*, p. 113.

preaching against the enslavement of the Indians, already widely practiced by the Portuguese settlers. King John III supported the Jesuits, but he was very far off, and except to some extent within the port towns established along the coast, there was no law in Brazil, so the enslavement mostly could not be prevented.[112]

In July 1553 Brazil became the first foreign province of the Society of Jesus, which for more than a century provided the overwhelming majority of its missionaries. Nóbrega was named Provincial. In that same month a new fleet arrived from Portugal with Brazil's second governor, Duarte da Costa, and seven more Jesuits including St. José de Anchieta, a slender young man with curvature of the spine who at first glance seemed wholly unfit for arduous missionary labors among savage Indians, but over the next forty-four years was to prove himself one of the greatest missionaries in the history of the Church. Anchieta wasted no time in getting started. He disembarked in July; by Christmas Eve he was in Sao Vicente, where his superior Nóbrega awaited him and his companions. In January 1554 they ascended a trail from Sao Vicente to the uplands—a trail so undeveloped and precipitous that part of it had to be climbed on hands and knees. There they found an Indian village called Piratininga, where the local chief, Tibiraça, had built a hut for them. They celebrated Mass there the next day, January 25, and named the Indian town Sao Paulo, for the feast of the conversion of St. Paul. This was José de Anchieta's mission base for the next twenty-three years. It eventually became the largest city in Brazil and one of the largest in the world.[113]

Later in 1554, two Jesuits going south from Sao Paulo to the Carijo Indians were killed by Indians—the first martyrdoms in Brazil. The blood of the martyrs bore its usual fruit, and the very next year the Carijo chief whom the Portuguese called Antonio de Leiva had come from Sao Paulo begging them to return to convert his people, who in his own words were "living like beasts." The Jesuits could not then spare two more men, but they remembered the request, and eventually responded to it. In 1555 Anchieta, who had a great gift for languages, completed a grammar of the Tupi language which was the most widely spoken of the many Brazilian Indian languages. His grammar was studied by all the incoming Jesuit missionaries, who were required to be able to speak Tupi not many months after their arrival. In June 1554 Father Nunes set out by sea to Rome to make a personal report to the Pope on missionary prospects in Brazil, but his ship was wrecked on the still largely uncharted coast of Brazil two weeks later. A bishop had also been appointed for Brazil, but in June 1556 he too was shipwrecked, and killed and eaten by Indians. On November 1 a Jesuit church and college in Sao Paulo were solemnly dedicated.[114]

In November 1555 French Calvinists founded a short-lived colony at Rio de Janeiro before the Portuguese could establish themselves there, calling it Antarctic France. In March 1557 three hundred more colonists arrived from France. In May King John III of Portugal died, to be succeeded by his

---

[112] *Ibid.*, pp. 159-160; Dominian, *Apostle of Brazil*, pp. 52, 54, 62, 64.

[113] Dominian, *Apostle of Brazil*, pp. 11, 69-80.

[114] *Ibid.*, pp. 134, 139, 145-146; Hemming, *Red Gold*, pp. 82, 244.

posthumous son Sebastian of tragic fate. But at the end of the year the highly cultured and competent Mem de Sá arrived in Brazil, the best governor colonial Brazil ever had. In March 1560 Mem de Sá attacked the French Calvinist colony and took its fort, named for arch-Calvinist Admiral Coligny. In July 1561 a massive Indian attack struck Sao Paulo, but it was beaten off by the Indian converts, exhorted by the Jesuits and led by Chief Tibiriça. In June 1562 Sao Paulo became an official Portugese municipality.[115]

In May 1563 Nóbrega and Anchieta set off from a fort near Santos to the country of the Tamoio Indians of the Rio de Janeiro area, to make a truce between them and the Portuguese. Tamoio chief Pindobuçi ("Great Sea") attacked and captured them, but was deeply impressed by their kind and unmoved demeanor despite what he had done, and by their Christianity. Therefore he accepted the proffered truce and released Nóbrega to return to the Portuguese, while detaining Anchieta as a hostage for the fulfillment of the truce terms. Anchieta therefore remained among them for three months (June to September). On at least one occasion two Indians were killed in front of him, despite his efforts to persuade their murderers to spare them. In July an Indian grandmother buried her daughter's baby son alive, considering her tainted by the circumstances of her conception. Hearing of this, Anchieta rushed to the grave, dug up the infant, found him still breathing, baptized him, and tried to arrange for his care; but none of the Indian women would nurse him, and he died a month later. False reports of a new Portuguese massacre of the Indians caused Anchieta to be repeatedly threatened with death, but he showed no fear or yielding; and Chief Pindobuçi, impressed anew, took his side. Five canoeloads of Tamoios from Rio de Janeiro came to kill him, but were overawed by his calm and gentle manner and stupendous spiritual courage. In September Anchieta was released and escorted back to Sao Vicente by another admiring chief, Cunhambeba. The two great Jesuit missionaries came to Rio de Janeiro the following year, saying Easter Mass on the site of the abandoned French colony. A large fleet was sent from Portugal to protect it. Rio de Janeiro has remained Portuguese and Brazilian ever since, its Sugar Loaf Mountain a national symbol of Brazil.[116]

In 1566 Jesuit leader Manoel Nóbrega publicly defended the freedom of the Brazilian Indian as a natural right, and the next year he was made rector of the new Jesuit college at Rio de Janeiro.[117] In October of that year the great Pope St. Pius V[118] wrote to Cardinal Henry of Portugal, uncle of the young King Sebastian, urging him to protect new converts from oppression by Portuguese soldiers, to remove scandals which might stand in the way of the conversion of

---

[115] Samuel Eliot Morison, *The European Discovery of America; the Southern Voyages, 1492-1616* (New York, 1974), pp. 591-593; Hemming, *Red Gold*, pp. 83-84, 120, 125-128; Dominian, *Apostle of Brazil*, pp. 146-151, 163-164. For the life and death of Admiral Coligny, see Chapters Six and Seven, above.

[116] Dominian, *Apostle of Brazil*, pp. 177, 182-195, 197-201, 208-209, 217, 220-223; Hemming, *Red Gold*, pp. 130-132; Burns, *History of Brazil*, p. 41.

[117] Hemming, *Red Gold*, pp. 135, 148; Dominian, *Apostle of Brazil*, pp. 232-233.

[118] See Chapter Six, above.

the Indians, and to protect the missionaries and advance the new converts to higher status. At the beginning of 1571, in a brief to King Sebastian, Pope St. Pius V recommended the formation of a native priesthood in Brazil. Tragically this was not done, at untold spiritual coast to what was to become the country with the largest population of Catholics on earth.[119]

In October 1567 Anchieta at Sao Vicente spoke out against the enslavement of the Indians, telling the slave-owners that most of them "with no regard for values . . . consider each human slave as stupid and bestial instead of recognizing in each the image of the Savior." The following year Anchieta went to wild Sao Paulo, center of the Indian slave trade, and denounced the capture and abuse of Indian slaves as rebellion against Christ. In 1569 special Jesuit Visitor Ignacio de Azevedo, who had been several years in Brazil, reported to Pope St. Pius V and Jesuit general St. Francis Borgia in Rome. In July 1570 Azevedo was sent back to Brazil as Provincial, with 39 other Jesuits. On the way they were captured by a French Calvinist pirate and all murdered in cold blood. Soon after this dreadful news arrived in Brazil, the heroic Jesuit missionary Manoel de Nóbrega breathed his last. Father Tolosa became the new Provincial and made Anchieta the Jesuit superior at Rio de Janeiro.[120]

In 1572 the just and able Governor Mem de Sá died in office. Brazil was then divided into two governorships, one at Bahia and one at Rio de Janeiro. These governors declared that any Indian could sell himself into slavery if he wished, and allowed several open slave raids to take place. Portuguese inland planter Diogo Dias seized and enslaved the daughter and sons of the powerful chief of the Potiguar Indians on the bulge of Brazil, leading to war; the Governor of Bahia completely defeated the Potiguar and enslaved thousands. But Anchieta continued his defense of the abused Indians. In 1577 he was made Jesuit Provincial for the whole territory, which was reunited under a single governor, a friend of the Jesuits, in 1579.[121]

In 1585 Provincial Anchieta estimated that since 1549 over 100,000 Indians had been baptized, but only 20,000 of these had remained living Christians, due to European diseases, white rapacity, and Indian nomadic habits. The Jesuits continued with their policy of encouraging the Christian Indians to settle in mission villages where they could lead an orderly life under the leadership of the Fathers and gradually learn the ways both of civilization and of the practice of their new faith. But Indian enslavement continued to be a great obstacle to conversion. In 1585 Anchieta, as Jesuit Provincial, declared flatly that there "can be no remedy for existing obstacles to conversion until His Majesty provides the law that has been requested, that Indians must not be captured, bound or sold." The new Spanish governor who took office in 1583 (young King Sebastian had been killed in battle and, after a brief interlude of rule by his elderly and infirm uncle Cardinal Henry, Philip II of Spain, next in line for the Portuguese throne,

---

[119] Von Pastor, *History of the Popes*, XVIII, 332-333.

[120] Dominian, *Apostle of Brazil*, pp. 248-254, 256 (quote on 248).

[121] Hemming, *Red Gold*, pp. 151, 161-162, 174-175; Dominian, *Apostle of Brazil*, pp. 254-255, 262-266.

took over the country) was distinctly hostile to the Jesuits. But the third bishop of Brazil, António Barreiros, strongly took their part.[122]

The colony was now prospering, having become the largest producer of sugar, increasingly in demand in Europe. It had about 150 sugar-mills. In Pernambuco, the far eastern bulge of Brazil, the sugar-mill owners preferred black slave labor to Indian slave labor, and were able to afford more of it, so that by the turn of the century blacks in that province came to outnumber Indians. Recife in Pernambuco now had three thousand houses, Bahia about a thousand.[123] Brazil was to be the last Christian country in the world where black slavery was abolished, after the emancipation of all black slaves in the United States immediately following the Civil War.

Anchieta finally resigned as Provincial in 1587, only 53 but exhausted by his years of missionary labors and in poor health, no longer able to conquer the effects of his weak and misshapen spine sufficiently to continue to act as head of all the Jesuits in Brazil. Marçal Beliarte replaced him. But it never occurred to St. José to retire from his mission. That year, after resigning as Provincial, he journeyed inland from Rio de Janeiro to mission villages in the interior, living as always in extreme poverty, clad in a faded, mended cassock, with a large rosary around his neck. The Indians were in awe of him, often speaking of how he "talked with God" all through the night, in his prayers. Also in this year, the Jesuits began work among the more peaceful and cultured Guaraní Indians, many of whom lived in the Spanish colony of Paraguay, but a substantial number of whom had come to Guairá province of Brazil, near the mighty Iguassú falls which today mark the boundary between Brazil and Argentina. In 1592 the English pirate Thomas Cavendish, on his way to the Straits of Magellan and around the world, stopped to destroy the port towns of Sao Vicente and Santos, showing particular animus against the Jesuits. Christian Indians formed the bulk of the army that drove him off.[124]

In 1594 Anchieta, appointed special Jesuit Visitor in Brazil, took the opportunity once again to denounce Indian slavery in his reports to Jesuit general Acquaviva. Both King Sebastian (before his untimely death) and Philip II (after he took over Portugal and Brazil in 1580) had issued decrees against Indian slavery in Brazil, but they exempted prisoners taken in a just war (defined with great elasticity), and the *mamelucos* of the Sao Paulo area (who sent out a massive slave raid in 1597, led by the son of the governor of Rio de Janeiro) paid no attention to royal decrees. However, in 1595 Philip II emphasized that at least the Christian Indians in Brazil should all be free, and directed that they be gathered together in the mission communities and protected there. Two years later St. José de Anchieta died at the age of 63, after having spent 44 continuous

---

[122] Dominian, *Apostle of Brazil*, pp. 181, 266, 274-275, 280 (quote), 282; Hemming, *Red Gold*, pp. 144, 152.

[123] Hemming, *Red Gold*, p. 180; Charles R. Boxer, *Salvador de Sá and the Struggle for Brazil and Angola*, 1602-1686 (London, 1952), pp. 177-179.

[124] Dominian, *Apostle of Brazil*, pp. 202, 292-294, 302, 304-305, 310-312; Philip Caraman, *Lost Paradise*, p. 16.

years in Brazil. His body remained incorrupt. The eulogist at his funeral truly called him "the apostle of Brazil." He was canonized by Pope John Paul II. The next year Philip II, lifelong champion of the faith, also died gloriously united with Christ, at his monastery-palace of El Escorial.[125]

New King Philip III of Spain and Portugal attempted to tighten and better enforce the laws against Indian slavery, but the *mamelucos* of the Sao Paulo area more and more carried on their slave raiding even in the Christian Indian communities administered by the Jesuits, notably those in Guairá, out in the wilderness west of Sao Paulo and not strongly defended. In 1611 the Governor of Brazil himself engaged in slave raiding, and in that year Philip III—not a strong monarch—felt he had no choice but once again to allow enslavement of Indians captured by the Portuguese in "just wars" and for ransomed captives of Indian tribes, and allowing Indians to be forced to work for Portuguese colonists at fixed wages. This was not quite slavery, but almost. By now there were an estimated 50,000 white colonists in Brazil, almost all Portuguese, with half of them in the rich sugar-producing province of Pernambuco on the eastern bulge of Brazil.[126]

In 1621 Spain ended its twelve-year truce with the Netherlands.[127] The Portuguese and Dutch had had generally good relations before the union of Spain and Portugal in 1580, but now the Dutch were the deadliest enemies of that union, and the enormously long Brazilian coast was highly inviting to their numerous, far-venturing warships. During the truce the Dutch had already established forts on the virtually unclaimed Amazon River, where the first Portuguese town, Belém, was not founded until 1616. Now, with the renewal of the war, the Dutch West India Company decided for an attack on Bahia, and sent out an armada of 26 ships, 3,300 men, and 500 cannon under the command of Admiral Jacob Willikens, with the formidable Piet Hein as second-in-command. It took the Dutch expedition only one day to storm all Bahia's forts and capture all the ships in its bay, and the city surrendered. But the Catholic population of Bahia and its surrounding area would not accept Dutch Calvinist rule. Bishop of Brazil Teixeira drove himself to his death trying to arouse resistance. The next year an even larger Spanish-Portuguese armada retook the city and withstood a new Dutch fleet sent to the port. In 1627 Piet Hein returned to Bahia, capturing or destroying 30 Portuguese ships with only three, before he went on to his stunning achievement of capturing the entire Spanish silver fleet from Mexico.[128]

---

[125] Dominian, *Apostle of Brazil*, pp. 280, 305. 313-314, 317-319; Hemming, *Red Gold*, pp. 151-152, 248-259, 313. See Chapter Eight, above, for an account of Philip II's holy death.

[126] Hemming, *Red Gold*, pp. 252, 254, 314-315; Caraman, *Lost Paradise*, p. 36; Boxer, *Salvador de Sá*, pp. 16-17.

[127] See Chapter Ten, above.

[128] Jonathan I. Israel, *The Dutch Republic and the Hispanic World, 1606-1661* (New YUork, 1982), p. 25; *The Cambridge Modern History*, Volume IV (Cambridge, England, 1906, 1934), pp. 703-706; Hemming, *Red Gold*, pp. 212-213, 284; Boxer, *Salvador de Sá*,

By 1629 there were 13 Jesuit Christian Indian communities in Guairá province, each with two Jesuit priests. A Portuguese named Rapôso Tavares, leading a *bandeirante* (slaving expedition) of the *mamelucos* of Sao Paulo, descended upon two of these communities, seizing four thousand Indians as slaves, burning the villages, plundering the churches, and desecrating an image of Our Lady. The authorities in Brazil—such as they were—ignored the Jesuits' fervent protests. By the next year the *mamelucos* had enslaved some sixty thousand Indians, and the Jesuits had to evacuate all their communities in Guairá. But they continued to establish similar communities along the coast of Brazil.[129]

In 1630 Dutch captain Hendrik Lonck, who had been second-in-command to Piet Hein in the capture of the Spanish treasure fleet from Mexico, arrived at Pernambuco with a very strong force, landed, and took the city of Olinda by storm. Recife, the largest city in Pernambuco, then surrendered to the Dutch, but Portuguese guerrillas fought on. A Spanish rescue expedition tried to help them, but the skilled Dutch seamen fought them to a draw, and Recife remained in Dutch hands. In the next few years it became a showcase Dutch colony, fiercely anti-Catholic, as the Netherlands (Holland) most emphatically was at this time. In 1638 the Dutch governor of eastern Brazil, Prince Johann von Maurits von Nassau (who had renamed Recife for himself), was repulsed from Bahia, ending the prospect that the Dutch might swallow up all or most of Brazil south of Pernambuco.[130]

Despite the curse of slavery, there were many sincere Catholic converts now among both the Indians and the blacks. When his rescue fleet failed, King Philip IV of Spain and Portugal designated an Indian convert, Antonio Poti (known to the Portuguese as "Camarao," the translation of his Brazilian name which means "shrimp") to command the Potiguar Indians—and many whites as well—against the Dutch, and enrolled him in the famous Portuguese crusading Order of Christ. Poti/Camarao was a fervent Catholic, who heard Mass and prayed the Office of Our Lady every day even when he was on the march, and carried images of Christ and the Blessed Virgin Mary with him at all times. He fully understood what was at stake in the struggle for Pernambuco. In 1637 he conducted an able retreat from the backlands of Pernambuco to Sergipe. The next year a potent Spanish-Portuguese armada sailed from Lisbon with the objective of removing the Dutch from Brazil, but it was commanded by Count La Torre, a man with little experience of the sea (shades of the Duke of Medina Sidonia and the Spanish Armada of 1588!). Not surprisingly in view of his very limited sea experience, the Count found himself unable to land many of his

---

pp. 17, 48-50, 55-57, 60-61. Piet Hein's world-changing capture of the Spanish silver fleet from Mexico in 1628 is described in Chapter Ten, above.

[129] Hemming, *Red Gold*, pp. 256-259, 262-263, 285; Caraman, *Lost Paradise*, pp. 56-60, 63-68; Rippy and Nelson, *Crusaders of the Jungle*, p. 239.

[130] Israel, *Dutch in the Hispanic World*, pp. 202-203, 276-277; Cornelis Goslinga, *The Dutch in the Caribbean and on the Wild Coast, 1580-1680* (Gainesville FL, 1971), pp. 223-224, 241; *Cambridge Modern History* IV, 707-708, 751; Hemming, *Red Gold*, pp. 285, 288; Boxer, *Salvador de Sá*, p. 115.

soldiers in Pernambuco. A Dutch fleet half the size of his came up in January 1640, and at the Battle of Itamaraca prevailed against the odds, for the Dutch were the best seamen in the world of that time, and Count La Torre was not a seaman at all.[131]

The Jesuits in the mission villages, despairing of any immediate help from their own government, now began to arm the Indians, even when it was still against the law; this action was officially approved in 1639. King Philip IV of Spain and Portugal denounced the *mameluco* slave raids in 1639, and in that same year Pope Urban VIII, in the brief *Commission nobis*, proclaimed the liberty of all Indians and prohibited their enslavement for any reason. The brief arrived in Brazil in April 1640, brought by a new group of Jesuits, who demanded its immediate publication without waiting for the royal assent. Governor Salvador de Sá of Rio de Janeiro supported them, and it was published. Riots followed, in which the lives of all the Jesuits in Santos and Rio de Janeiro were threatened, but Governor de Sá continued to protect them, though it was decided to suspend execution of the brief despite the fact that its contents were now known. This calmed the storm only temporarily. Later in the year the Jesuits, blamed for the Pope's action so unwelcome to many colonists, were expelled from Sao Paulo, Sao Vicente, and Santos, though able to remain in Rio de Janeiro because of the fidelity of Governor de Sá. Meanwhile the Jesuits in the mission villages with their Indian soldiers went on the offensive under a banner of St. Francis Xavier and defeated a *mameluco* expedition with 300 Portuguese and 600 Tupi Indians against three to one odds at Mboboré.[132]

In February 1641 the startling news of Portugal's revolt against Spain at the end of 1640 became known in Brazil, which quickly joined the mother country in proclaiming King John IV. The second man to sign the proclamation in Sao Vicente was the ferocious slave raider António Rapôso Tavares, obviously hoping to gain amnesty for his crimes from the new monarch. The surge of Portuguese patriotism that followed reignited the war against the Dutch, with Portuguese settlers in Pernambuco rising in revolt. The slave-raiding *mamelucos* remained bitterly hostile to Salvador de Sá, who decided to step down at the end of his current term as governor of Rio de Janeiro and went back to Portugal, where he gained the support of the new king, which the Jesuits already had. The Dutch, who had had good relations with Portugal before their union with Spain, now removed Prince von Nassau as governor of Dutch Brazil (Pernambuco and north) and reduced their troop commitment there. On Christmas day 1544 de Sá left Lisbon with a strong fleet, bound for Brazil. He arrived at Bahia in February

---

[131] Israel, *Dutch in the Hispanic World*, p. 281; Goslinga, *Dutch in the Caribbean*, p. 249; Hemming, *Red Gold*, pp. 295-296, 304, 307, 309; Boxer, *Salvador de Sá*, pp. 116, 120-121.

[132] Hemming, *Red Gold*, pp. 267-269, 274; Caraman, *Lost Paradise*, p. 17; Boxer, *Salvador de Sá*, pp. 129-138, 150. In a remarkable combination of prejudice and honesty, John Hemming has to admit that "amid all the hypocritical claptrap about the benefits of Christianity, these [Jesuit] missions demonstrated that in the right circumstances something could be done" (*Red Gold*, p. 274).

and immediately set to work to rouse a further uprising against the Dutch in Brazil.[133]

In June 1645 the rising came, and was by no means confined to the Portuguese planters. It was a Catholic uprising against Dutch Calvinism. Its leaders made an extraordinary "racial rainbow": António Vieira, Jesuit and intellectual, the greatest Portuguese writer and preacher of his time; the supreme commander the low-born mulatto Joao Fernandes Vieira (no relation to the writer and preacher); and General Vieira's two principal subordinates, the very Catholic Indian general "Shrimp" (Camarao) and a black general named Henrique Dias. The three generals defeated the Dutch at Monte das Tabocas on August 3. A series of Dutch forts fell. The Dutch remained masters of the sea, but proved entirely unable to suppress the revolt on land. In January 1646 the Indian general "Shrimp" decisively defeated a largely Dutch army outnumbering his own, with brilliant generalship, and in February followed up this victory in the field by another. In June of that year Dutch reinforcements arrived from the Netherlands, the proponents of empire having overcome the doubts of those who wanted to restore good relations with Portugal. In 1647 King John IV firmly ordered that the Indians should be free from enslavement and from forced labor.[134]

On April 19, 1648, despite facing a Dutch force double their strength, the now battle-tested Brazilian army, commanded by the Indian general "Shrimp" and the black general Dias, won a decisive victory at the Battle of Guararapes, taking 33 battle standards and killing some five hundred of their enemies while losing only eighty of their own men. This victory restricted the Dutch to Recife and its immediate neighborhood. Indian General "Shrimp" died that August of natural causes, but was succeeded by his nephew, who with the Portuguese rebels of Pernambuco won a second battle at Guararapes the following year. Despite all the horrors of the slave trade, the Faith had triumphed over its enemies because of the devoted perseverance and leadership of its Indian and black adherents. The whole of history since shows no army quite like that which liberated Brazil at the end of the 1640's.[135]

The Dutch, their war with Spain ended in 1648, began to retrench, while the Portuguese began building galleons in Bahia. The whole of Dutch Brazil was returned to Portugal by the Capitulation of Taborda in January 1654. In the fall of the preceding year António Vieira, after having been several years in Portugal, returned to Brazil as a Jesuit missionary, and at once began denouncing with his incomparable rhetoric the mistreatment and enslavement of the Brazilian Indians, warning that all those regularly guilty of this would go to Hell. Due to Vieira's fame, this to some extent counterbalanced a weak retreat from the issue by King

---

[133] Boxer, *Salvador de Sá*, pp. 145-146, 154-157, 170, 187-189, 200, 203-205; Israel, *Dutch in the Hispanic World*, p. 314; Hemming, *Red Gold*, pp. 275, 279, 290. For Portugal's revolt against Spain, see Chapter Ten, above.

[134] Burns, *History of Brazil*, p. 61; Israel, *Dutch in the Hispanic World*, p. 329; Boxer, *Salvador de Sá*, pp. 196-204, 209-210, 219; Hemming, *Red Gold*, pp. 221, 301, 303, 306-307, 318.

[135] Burns, *History of Brazil*, p. 61; Hemming, *Red Gold*, pp. 308-310.

John IV, declaring that Indians still could be legally enslaved for raiding, persistent non-payment of taxes, failing to obey royal orders to work, cannibalism, or impeding the preaching of the Gospel. But obviously none of these exceptions applied to the Christian Indians in the mission villages. In 1654 the missionary António Vieira and three colleagues penetrated the wild Amazon River region, and were given full authority there by King John IV, who in 1655 sent a new governor with firm orders to support and protect the Jesuits. Unfortunately for the Portuguese, the next year King John IV died. In 1658 Salvador de Sá returned to Brazil as governor of Rio de Janeiro, then departed from it on a lengthy journey southward to regions until then barely penetrated by Brazilian government authority. While he was gone a rebellion broke out in Rio de Janeiro, but de Sá suppressed it in April 1661. In the preceding winter he constructed the first road usable by wheeled vehicles from Sao Paulo to Santos on the coast, building more than 70 bridges.[136]

Despite all wrongs and sins and abuses, Catholic Brazil had come into being—a multi-racial society in which the gift of faith was more important than the color of one's skin, or one's past, present or future condition of servitude.

French North America (1620-1661)

In 1620 the redoubtable Samuel de Champlain, at this time the only man really dedicated to developing French Canada, returned with his young bride to live there for four years, building the first strong fort at the magnificent site of Quebec. King Louis XIII had made the Duke of Montmorency viceroy of Canada, but he employed French Calvinists and seemed only interested in the potential revenue from the province, which proved very sparse despite the abundance of valuable furs, because there were as yet so few Frenchmen there. At the beginning of 1625 Montmorency sold his viceroyalty to his nephew, the Duke de Ventadour, who promptly confirmed Champlain's commission, prohibited the practice of Calvinism in French Canada, and decided to introduce Jesuit missionaries into the fledgling colony. Four ships arrived in June carrying Champlain and three Jesuits—Charles Lalemant, Ennemond Massé, and the later famous St. John de Brébeuf. The colony had almost disappeared during the last winter; only 55 people were found there, and practically no food was being grown. Nevertheless, by September the Jesuits had erected their own habitation and formally blessed it, and in October St. John de Brébeuf set out to spend the winter with mountain-dwellers of the Algonquin Indian tribe.[137]

---

[136] Burns, *History of Brazil*, p. 62; Israel, *Dutch in the Hispanic World*, p. 402; Boxer, *Salvador de Sá*, pp. 167, 303-309, 312-323; Hemming, *Red Gold*, pp. 310, 318-319, 321, 323-332.

[137] Samuel Eliot Morison, *Samuel de Champlain, Father of New France* (Boston, 1972), pp. 176-180, 185-188; Francis Parkman, *Pioneers of France in the New World* (Boston, 1865, 1905), pp. 427-435; Francis X. Talbot, *Saint among the Hurons; the Life of Jean de Brébeuf* (New York, 1949), pp. 16-31, 36-44.

By the following year the French population of Quebec had declined to 43, but in 1627 Cardinal Richelieu and 100 associates established the Company of New France, giving it a claim to all land between Spanish Florida and the Arctic, and from Newfoundland to Lake Huron, with a monopoly on the fur trade and a promise (which turned out to be empty) to place at least 4,000 colonists there within 15 years. A large fleet, mostly transports assembled by this Company, set out for Canada in 1628, but was intercepted by an English fleet commanded by the Scotsman David Kirke, most of whose crew were French Calvinists. All the supplies destined for Quebec were seized. Kirke sailed to Quebec and summoned Champlain to surrender, which he refused to do until starved into submission a year later. Champlain and the Jesuits were sent back to France. However, English King Charles I had married Princess Henrietta Marie of France during this time, and the marriage treaty provided a very large dowry. The French had paid only half of it, with no clear indication when they would pay the balance. In return for their immediate payment in full, Canada was restored to them in the Treaty of St.-Germain-en-Laye, signed in March 1632. The English returned the territories to France in July. Forty more French settlers arrived, along with several Jesuits. Cardinal Richelieu had given them a monopoly of mission work in Canada.[138]

The next year, 1633, Champlain sailed with three ships on his last voyage to Canada, having been recommissioned as governor of New France by Cardinal Richelieu, acting through the king. Paul le Jeune, leader of the Jesuits, set out in October of that year for a far-distant region, the island-studded Georgian Bay of Lake Huron, which despite its distance was readily accessible by canoe up the Ottawa River from the St. Lawrence, across a low watershed at Lake Nipissing, and down the French River to Lake Huron. Here was the homeland of a major Indian tribe, the Hurons, so far almost untouched by Europeans. The journey to and living conditions among the Hurons were extraordinarily difficult, and Father Le Jeune returned to Quebec in April 1634 almost at the point of death. But he was replaced, before the year was over, by Father John de Brébeuf, a man of mighty frame and tremendous endurance, who proved that living among the Indians was possible for a Frenchman. By May 1635 Brébeuf had completed a detailed report for his Jesuit superiors on the Huron Indians and the prospects for evangelizing them, and later that year two more Jesuits joined him in the Huron country.[139]

That fall the great Samuel de Champlain suffered a stroke—he was nearly seventy years old—and died on Christmas day. Father Le Jeune said of him: "Truly, he led a life of great justice, equity and perfect loyalty to his King and towards the Gentlemen of the Company. But at his death, he crowned his virtues

---

[138] Parkman, *Pioneers of France*, pp. 435n, 443, 445, 447-450, 454-459; Morison, *Champlain*, pp. 191-192, 195, 198, 200-201, 213; Talbot, *Saint among Hurons*, pp. 76-78, 82-83, 86; Francis X. Talbot, *Saint among Savages; the Life of Isaac Jogues* (New York, 1935), p. 28.

[139] Morison, *Champlain*, p. 214; Talbot, *Saint among Hurons*, p. 92-97, 108-110, 113-117, 125-126, 130; Parkman, *Pioneers of France*, p. 459.

with sentiments of piety so lofty that he astonished us all. . . . Those whom he has left behind here have reason to be proud of him." At his death, the population of Quebec had finally reached two hundred, a number large enough to be unlikely to disappear.[140]

His successor was as deeply believing a Catholic, Charles de Montmagny, a Knight of Malta. His first act on arriving in Canada was to fall on his knees before a crucifix. He told the Jesuits that their first report on their missionary work—the first volume of the immense *Jesuit Relations*—had aroused unprecedented fervor in France, with thousands wanting to help, the younger by joining the Jesuit mission themselves, the older by contributing financially to its support. In August 1636 another Jesuit, Antoine Daniel, returned to Quebec from the Huron country almost dead of starvation, but another of the future North American martyrs, St. Isaac Jogues, was ordered to the Huron mission that same month, and arrived on the shore of Georgian Bay in September. There he found a severe influenza epidemic in progress, the inevitable result of early contact between the natives of North America and Europeans. Huron sorcerers blamed the foreign "blackrobes" for the disease, but St. John de Brébeuf defended them before the tribal council in his rapidly improving Huron, and many were still hospitable. In May 1637 the first adult Huron man was baptized, and St. John de Brébeuf was allowed to build a "long house" for the mission, which he dedicated to the Immaculate Conception. On August 16 the nephew of a major chief, Chihwatenhwa, was baptized when near death from influenza, but recovered and remained a staunch friend to the missionaries.[141]

There ensued one of the most extraordinary periods of mission history, encompassing just twelve years (1637-49) but leaving a long trail of glory for the sons of France. Canada was a vast wilderness; in 1637 there were only two French towns, Quebec and Three Rivers, both still very small. In the Huron country far away, bordering the Great Lakes, the only white men were the Jesuits and their few companions. The French colony, barely viable, could do almost nothing to help them, only provide refuge for those who had to flee. To protect them was impossible. They were threatened not only by the Hurons who disliked them and blamed them for their plagues, but by the Hurons' traditional enemies, the uniquely ferocious and fearsome confederation of tribes known as the Iroquois, based in northern New York but capable of ranging over the whole St. Lawrence River region, who were made doubly dangerous during these years by firearms purchased from the Dutch colony of New Amsterdam (later New York).[142] As the Spanish and Portuguese missionaries had long since learned in South America, the only feasible way to preserve the conversions they made

---

[140] Morison, *Champlain*, pp. 222-224; Parkman, *Pioneers of France*, pp. 462-463; Talbot, *Saint among Hurons*, p. 149 (for quote).

[141] Francis Parkman, *The Jesuits in North America* (Boston, 1867, 1963), pp. 202-203, 208-211, 241-244; Talbot, *Saint among Savages*, pp. 50-51, 54, 61, 79-82, 98, 107-108; Talbot, *Saint among Hurons*, pp. 170-171, 176-177.

[142] Parkman, *Jesuits in North America*, pp. 305-306; Talbot, *Saint among Savages*, pp. 146-148.

among the Indians was to resettle the Christian Indian converts in villages of their own, called "reductions" in Spanish South America. But, with the exception of one Indian village at Sillery four miles from Quebec, where Blessed Marie of the Incarnation worked with her religious sisters,[143] the colony of New France did not have the resources to do this, and missionaries and converts were both left on their own. The only Europeans who had had much close contact with a totally savage culture were the Portuguese in Brazil, and the French seem to have known little about their experiences. The pungently detailed and appalling descriptions of life among the Hurons and the Iroquois which fill stunning pages of the *Jesuit Relations* are all the more convincing because the missionaries, despite the multitudinous diabolical horrors[144] that they watched and chronicled, still firmly believed that the conversion of these people could be accomplished. With a significant number it was, but not with the majority until the Huron tribe was so decimated by the Iroquois that they abandoned their homeland and joined with the French in Quebec in 1650.[145] The missionaries' vivid accounts of Indian life should destroy forever the Rousseauian myth of the "noble savage" and the modern myth (spawned in the 1990's) of a gentle nature-loving paradise in America before the European came.

In August 1639 a permanent residence for the Jesuits in the Huron country was completed and named Sainte Marie, and also a large wooden church for the Indian converts. St. John de Brébeuf wrote an optimistic report to the Jesuit general on prospects for evangelization of the Hurons. By the fall of the year there were 13 Jesuits and 14 other Frenchmen aiding them, living among the Indians. But a new plague, the deadly smallpox, was spreading among the native peoples, and once again they blamed it on the "blackrobes." In August 1640 only about 25 Huron converts maintained the Faith, and the chief's nephew Chihwatenhwa, their leader, was murdered. Realizing that the Hurons were at least for the time being not open to evangelization, St. John de Brébeuf with one companion set out to evangelize the "Tobacco Nation" which attempted to preserve neutrality toward both the Hurons and the Iroquois, while St. Isaac Jogues went westward to Sault Ste. Marie which links the great lakes of Superior and Huron, making the first approach to the Ojibway Indians of that then very remote region.[146]

In an extraordinary initiative in the spring of 1642 the Sieur de Maisonneuve, leading a party of just forty men and four women religious,

---

[143] Parkman, *Jesuits in North America*, pp. 246, 275-276; Talbot, *Saint among Hurons*, pp. 242-243.

[144] Fingers were literally chewed off; cannibalism was widely practiced; babies were roasted alive in the sight of their mothers (Parkman, *Jesuits in North America*, p. 343; Talbot, *Saint among Savages*, pp. 160-215).

[145] Parkman, *Jesuits in North America*, pp. 496-499, 517-522; Talbot, *Saint among Hurons*, pp. 310-313, 317-320.

[146] Talbot, *Saint among Savages*, pp. 117-119, 122-123, 141-142, 150-153; Talbot, *Saint among Hurons*, pp. 202-206, 216-218, 220-223, 232-234; Parkman, *Jesuits in North America*, pp. 235-236.

reached and settled the large island of Montreal at the confluence of the St. Lawrence and Ottawa Rivers, founding there a mission settlement that was to become the seed of one of the world's great cities. The founders of Montreal were characterized by particularly strong Catholic devotion. On Epiphany 1643 they erected a great cross on the highest point of the island. During the summer of 1642 a full-scale war with the Iroquois broke out. An Iroquois marauding band captured twelve Huron canoes carrying St. Isaac Jogues, two French laymen working with the Jesuits, and two leading Christian Hurons. The captives were subjected to horrific tortures; one of the Frenchmen was killed. Governor Montmagny marched hoping to rescue them, but had to stop at the mouth of the Richelieu River, flowing out of Lake Champlain into the St. Lawrence, to build a fort. Before it was completed the Iroquois were upon him; he barely held out. No rescue could be made. In 1643 the Iroquois attacked the new settlement of Montreal.[147]

The Council of the Five Nations of the Iroquois could not at the last minute agree to the killing of St. Isaac Jogues, famous among the Indians as "Ondessonk," and he remained with him until they took him to the Dutch outpost of Rensselaerswyck. The Dutch helped arrange his escape from them and sent him back to France. He accepted rescue only very reluctantly, despite the effect of his tortures. He landed on the coast of Brittany Christmas Day; his first action was to ask where he could find the nearest church where Mass would be said on the holy day. On January 5, 1644 he returned to the Jesuit house in Rennes, greeted by his brothers with astonishment and reverence. His fingers, fearfully mangled by the Iroquois, made him a living martyr. The Queen Mother of France brought him to court to honor him, and Pope Urban VIII gave him special permission to celebrate Mass despite being unable to hold the vessels and the Host properly, saying "it would be shameful that a martyr of Christ be not allowed to drink the Blood of Christ." After just five months in his homeland, this living martyr returned to the country where he had suffered so much, settling temporarily at Montreal.[148]

That fall St. John de Brébeuf returned to Sainte Marie in the Huron country after an absence of three years; he found it much built up as the rate of conversions increased. The war between the Hurons and the Iroquois continued. When a peace treaty was made in 1645, it included only the Mohawks among the five Iroquois nations and excluded non-Christian Algonquins, who were furious at the discrimination. In September of the following year St. Isaac Jogues returned to the country of the Mohawks, where he had been tortured, pleading for adherence to the peace treaty and, as always, spreading the Faith. But despite his best efforts, the Mohawks repudiated the peace treaty, and on October 18, 1646

---

[147] Parkman, *Jesuits in North America*, pp. 289-303, 307-313, 318-320, 338-340, 359-360, 366-372; Talbot, *Saint among Savages*, pp. 160-215, 220-222, 228, 234-240, 344.

[148] Talbot, *Saint among Savages*, pp. 228, 276-277, 293-326, 335-339, 344-345 (quote on 337).

split St. Isaac's skull with a tomahawk. He was the first and probably the most famous of the North American Martyrs.[149]

During the year 1647, some 1,300 Huron Indians were baptized after careful catechesis. But the pressures of the Iroquois war were unrelenting, and the Hurons, facing the ruin of their tribe, were now seeking help not only from the French, but also from other, distant Indian tribes. In July 1648 the Iroquois burned the Huron town of Tenaustayé, where many of the Huron converts lived, about fifteen miles from the mission headquarters at Sainte Marie. They killed Jesuit missionary Antoine Daniel there. At the same time the Iroquois attacked Hurons living near the French outpost of Three Rivers. On March 16, 1649 came the crowning blow. The Iroquois attacked another largely Christian Huron town and burned it, capturing the senior Jesuit missionary still in French Canada, St. John de Brébeuf, and his companion Gabriel Lalemant. The two Jesuits were tortured; St. John was killed that evening, Lalemant the next day. St. John, who had once been particularly admired by the Indians for his rugged strength and named by them "Echon," was dismembered. The Iroquois literally drank his blood and ate his heart.[150]

For the time being, the Iroquois had won. The French at Quebec, Three Rivers, and Montreal were far too weak to do anything more than defend their own immediate settlements. The Huron nation was largely destroyed; in the spring of 1649 they decided to flee from their homeland on Georgian Bay of Lake Huron. The Jesuit mission headquarters at Sainte Marie was stripped and burned. In December the Iroquois attacked the previously neutral "Tobacco Nation" and martyred two Jesuits living with these people, Charles Garnier and Noel Chabanel. The following April the surviving Jesuits and most of the surviving Hurons left the shores of Georgian Bay forever, heading for refuge under the guns of French Quebec, which they reached at the end of July. After a time a considerable number of them settled on the Isle of Orléans off Quebec, where in 1656 the Iroquois attacked them, taking away many captives. The fugitives were then brought within the palisade of Quebec. At the Battle of the Long Sault in 1660 the Iroquois triumphed again over the Hurons, despite some French military support of the Huron remnant.[151]

Then began a major Jesuit effort to penetrate the Iroquois, which had only limited success; however, it resulted in the conversion of Blessed Kateri Tekakwitha, "the lily of the Mohawks," who was instructed and baptized by the Jesuits in 1676, lived an exceptionally holy life as a Christian, and died in 1680. Despite their shattering defeats and the loss of their best missionaries, the Jesuits persevered. In 1646 Jesuit Father Gabriel Druilletes had first come to the Abenaki Indians of Maine on the Kennebec River, reaching the present site of

---

[149] *Ibid.*, pp. 346-348, 352-362, 366-367, 396-421; Talbot, *Saint among Hurons*, pp. 264-267; Parkman, *Jesuits in North America*, pp. 381-394, 398-403, 438-440.

[150] Talbot, *Saint among Hurons*, pp. 277-278, 281-285, 291-304; Parkman, *Jesuits in North America*, pp. 440-441, 475-479, 480-487, 490-493.

[151] Parkman, *Jesuits in North America*, pp. 496-499, 507-512, 517-522, 534-535; Talbot, *Saint among Hurons*, pp. 310-320.

Augusta. In 1650 he took the long journey to the Abenaki once again, and afterwards went on to the English colonies of Massachusetts Bay and Plymouth, where he was warmly received by Governors Dudley and Bradford, despite their general antipathy to all Catholics and particularly to Jesuits; but the consummate spiritual heroism of the North American martyrs and their fellows could hardly be denied by even the most bigoted Protestant. In Boston and Plymouth, Father Druilletes discovered first-hand the tragic consequences of the Calvinist belief in absolute predestination; according to it, all the heathen were destined to damnation, so there was no point in trying to evangelize them. We know of only one man who challenged this infernal logic in the colonial period in New England: Rev. John Eliot, pastor of Roxbury, who learned several Indian languages and settled with his converts at Natick in 1651. Within a decade he had over a thousand Christian Indians in 13 villages. Surely it is no coincidence that the establishment of his first Christian Indian settlement in Calvinist Massachusetts came the very year after the visit of the French Jesuit missionary, who is known to have talked with Rev. Eliot at length.[152]

Jesuit missionaries in Asia[153] had already proved that they could, and indeed must penetrate the alien culture of a non-Western civilized society to make a significant number of conversions there. But among savages like the Iroquois and the Hurons, such penetration was not possible. The only solution, where the resources of the European colony would support it, was to gather the Christian Indian converts together in villages of their own, separating them from their pagan brethren and the hideous customs they practiced. There is a difference, unfashionable as it may be today to say it, between barbarism and civilization. The French experience in North America proved the need for two entirely different missionary techniques, depending on whether the people to be evangelized had achieved civilization or were still in barbarism. Even in the primitive Aztec and Inca civilizations of Mexico and Peru, evangelization was relatively easy and quite complete. It had been accomplished in Mexico a hundred years before the Jesuit martyrdoms in North America, with the supernatural aid of Our Lady of Guadalupe; its delay in Peru was the result of the self-seeking leadership of the Spanish there until the arrival of St. Turibius of Lima, but the Peruvian Indians also had been mostly converted before the Jesuits came to Canada. In the ancient and cultivated nations of Asia—India, China, Japan, Vietnam—evangelization growing out of cultural penetration made slower though real progress, but generally was not bloody until the nineteenth century. Among savages, on the other hand, the culture could not be penetrated; the converts must be separated from it, or they were unlikely to survive as Christians or even as living men and women. And in the end, the Indians were submerged beneath, and later absorbed into European culture, which had happened throughout most of eastern North America by the end of the eighteenth century.

---

[152] Parkman, *Jesuits in North America*, pp. 419-420, 423-426.

[153] See Chapter 13, below.

13
Missions to the Orient
1540-1873

"Multitudes out here fail to become Christians only because there is nobody prepared for the holy task of instructing them. I have often felt strongly moved to descend don the universities of Europe, especially Paris and its Sorbonne, and to cry aloud like a madman to those who have more learning than good will to employ it advantageously, telling them how many souls miss Heaven and fall into Hell through their negligence! If, while they studied their humanities, they would study also the account which God will demand of them for the talent He gave, many might feel the need to engage on spiritual exercises that would lead them to discover and embrace the divine will, as against their own proclivities, and cry to God, 'Lord, here I am? What wouldst thou have me do? Send me where Thou willest, yea, even to India.' Ah then, with how much more peace would they live and with how much more hope in the mercy of God would they die."—letter of St. Francis Xavier, January 15, 1544[1]

St. Francis Xavier (1540-1552)

In March 1540, six months before the definitive Papal recognition of the Jesuit order, one of its founders, St. Francis Xavier, enthusiastically agreed on just one day's notice to depart for Portugal to catch the next fleet for the still mostly unknown East which had been opened up by the Age of Discovery, to preach Christ to millions who had never heard of him. So began the most extraordinary personal mission in the history of the Church.[2]

Just over a year later, on April 7, 1541, after a private audience with King John III and his wife Maria, the great Queen Isabel's daughter, St. Francis departed for India on a fleet of five ships from the quay on the Tagus River in Lisbon called the Place of Tears. He carried with him the Pope's letter appointing him legate in the Far East and a letter of recommendation "to all princes and lords of the islands of the Red, Persian, and Indian Oceans, and of all the countries on this side and beyond the Ganges." Becalmed off the coast of Guinea for forty days, he arrived in the Indian Ocean too late to catch the

---

[1] James Brodrick, *St. Francis Xavier* (New York, 1952), pp. 157-158.
[2] See Chapter Four, above.

monsoon winds from the west to India, and did not arrive at the great Portuguese stronghold of Goa in India until May 6, 1542.[3]

At the time of St. Francis' arrival, the Portuguese had established themselves at Goa, on the middle west coast of the Indian peninsula, and in several port cities in the far south, near the point of the peninsula. They had also crossed the Indian Ocean to Malacca in Malaya on the wide straits which led to the ultimate Orient, and had voyaged east to the Moluccas or Spice Islands in the great Indonesian archipelago. Some of their traders had reached the outer fringes of the enormous empire of China; Japan had not yet been reached.[4] Almost all the Orient east of India was still unknown and mysterious, and even in India the Portuguese, while surveying the coast and holding strong points on it, had hardly penetrated the interior. China is, and always has been the most populous country on earth.[5] The combined populations of India, China, Japan, and Southeast Asia dwarfed that of Europe. Except for a small enclave of St. Thomas Christians in India, totalling only about 200,000 among millions, there were no native Christians in all of the vast expanse which was St. Francis Xavier's mission territory. The Gospel had been preached so far only in Goa, where the Portuguese held political control. From the standpoint of Christian evangelization, virtually everything needed to be done when St. Francis Xavier came to India, and there was hardly anyone but himself to do it.[6]

The Church had not faced a nearly comparable challenge since the conversion of eastern and northern Europe in the tenth and eleventh centuries, and before that the conversion of the Roman empire.[7] Many of the lessons of

---

[3] James Brodrick, *Origin of the Jesuits* (New York, 1940), pp. 112-113; James Brodrick, *St. Francis Xavier* (New York, 1952), pp. 106-107, 113; Georg Schurhammer, *St. Francis Xavier* (St. Louis MO, 1928), pp. 62-67, 84-85; quote on 62-63). The Portuguese arrival in India, their colonization of Goa and gaining of naval control over the Indian Ocean are covered at some length in Volume Three, Chapter 15 of this history.

[4] *Cambridge History of China*, Volume VIII (2), p. 336; K. G. Jayne, *Vasco da Gama and His Successors* [London, 1910], p. 227.).

[5] An imperial census as early as 2 A.D. showed 57,671,400 inhabitants (*Cambridge History of China* I, 206, 240).

[6] See St. Francis Xavier's fervent appeal for help in this enormous missionary task, quoted at the head of this chapter. The best book on the St. Thomas Christians is George Moraes, *A History of Christianity in India, A. D. 52-1542* (Bombay, 1964). For their total number see Vincent Cronin, *A Pearl to India; the Life of Roberto de Nobili* (New York, 1959), p. 50. For discussion of St. Thomas' apostolate in India and its results, see Volume One, Chapter 17 of this history. The first Bishop of Goa took possession of his vast diocese (then including the whole of the Orient) in 1539. With his support and that of Viceroy Martim Afonso de Sousa, the first colonizer of Brazil, the natives of Goa began to be converted, but only by becoming in effect Portuguese, abandoning their native customs. All Hindu temples in Goa were destroyed by order of the King of Portugal in 1540 (Moraes, *op. cit.*, p. 162); Jayne, *Vasco da Gama and Successors*, p. 193; Carlos Merces de Melo, *The Recruitment and Formation of the Native Clergy of India* [Lisbon, 1955], pp. 14, 66-69, 74.

[7] See Volume One of this history, Chapters 17-20, and Volume Two, Chapters 16-17.

those days had to be relearned, though to some extent they still existed in Christian tradition. The most important was *adaptation*; the missionaries must adapt to the culture surrounding them at every point possible, except for its features which directly contradicted the Christian Faith. The more they were seen as outsiders and foreigners, the smaller would be their spiritual harvest. The early apostles, and still more their successors, had the advantage of a very considerable knowledge of the culture they were trying to penetrate; St. Paul, after all, was fluent in Greek and a Roman citizen. But the cultures of the Orient were almost totally unfamiliar.

Nevertheless Christians could penetrate unfamiliar cultures, and had done so. The Apostle Thomas had come to India and launched the St. Thomas Christians. The shipwrecked boy Frumentius had converted utterly alien Ethiopia. Missionaries from Syria had come to China in the seventh century and made numerous converts (though no one knew it in 1542).[8] St. Francis Xavier was their successor. And he had been sent by St. Ignatius of Loyola to "enkindle and inflame the whole earth."[9]

Late in September 1542, with the torrential rains of the monsoon season in India finally ended, St. Francis Xavier set out from Goa for the Fishery Coast far to the south, carrying only his Mass kit, his breviary, and an umbrella to shield him from the blazing tropical sun. All that fall and into the following spring he preached among the Paravas, who made their living by diving for pearls. Thousands of them had been baptized six years before through the agency of a former page to the Zamorim of Calicut who travelled to Portugal and been converted there. He brought four priests to do the baptizing, who promptly departed almost as soon as the holy water had been poured out. Since then the Paravas had had no Christian instruction at all, nor any opportunity to practice the Faith. Though he knew no Tamil (the language of southern India) and had always to speak through interpreters, St. Francis went up and down the streets of the towns of the Fishery Coast ringing bells, first teaching prayers to children, then explaining the Christian faith to adults, having the Our Father, the Hail Mary and the Ten Commandments translated into Tamil and memorizing the strange polysyllabic sounds.[10]

In the fall of 1543 St. Francis Xavier returned briefly to Goa to obtain help in his mission. He was most honorably received by Viceroy de Sousa, and four priests accompanied him back to the Fishery Coast early in 1544. There, after an

---

[8] See Volume Two, Chapters 1 and 8 of this history.

[9] Mary Purcell, *The First Jesuit* (Garden City NY, 1965), p. 319.

[10] Brodrick, *Francis Xavier*, p. 130-142; Schurhammer, *Francis Xavier*, pp. 90-103; Moraes, *Christianity in India A.D. 52-1542*, pp. 144-145. For the Zamorim of Calicut, see Volume Three, Chapter 15 of this history. The familiar legend that St. Francis Xavier possessed the gift of tongues and could speak in any language as soon as he heard it is no more than a legend, thoroughly refuted by the facts of history. Tamil is a language of immensely long words (see a sample in Brodrick, *op. cit.*, p. 139).

apostolate of less than two years, he attained an unparalleled missionary triumph.[11]

With his pathetic little stock of ill-understood Tamil words, like the loaves that fed four thousand in Galilee, he somehow succeeded in impressing the Catholic faith so indelibly on the souls of that primitive tribe that no manner of violence or cajolery has ever been able to erase it. When the Dutch conquered the Fishery Coast in the seventeenth century, they used every kind of persuasion in their power to win the Paravas to Calvinism, but they failed egregiously and, when they pressed too hard, came near to bringing about a general insurrection.[12]

In June 1544 the great Hindu empire of Vijayanagar, which had been founded in 1343 and was much the strongest of the Hindu states of India which had not been conquered by the Muslims, launched a massive invasion of the southern tip of India including the Fishery Coast. Though he could not arouse much interest among the Portuguese in protecting these fellow Christians, St. Francis Xavier was able to prevent the extermination of the Paravas. Meanwhile a native Indian priest, one of the first to be ordained, came from Goa at St. Francis Xavier's call to bring the Faith to thousands of the Carea people of southern India. St. Francis himself went next to the Macau people of Travancore in far southern India, baptizing some ten thousand of them and leaving them as firm in the faith as the Paravas of the Fishery Coast. The Macaus also "have maintained the Catholic Faith delivered to them by St. Francis Xavier through all the vicissitudes of the centuries" to this day.[13]

St. Francis Xavier next determined to pay his respects to the Apostle Thomas at his shrine and purported grave at Mylapore. He left on Palm Sunday 1545 trying to reach it by sea; when he was unable to do so, he set off on foot in May, the hottest month of the Indian year, to spend the summer in prayer and contemplation at the shrine. St. Francis Xavier appreciated the Thomas Christians better than any other European of his time. On returning to India from lands farther east, he was to write to John III of Portugal in 1549 about Mar Jacob, who had been the only bishop of the Thomas Christians for 45 years, describing him as "a very old, virtuous, and holy man . . . [who] has been working much amongst the St. Thomas Christians, and now in his old age he is very obedient to the customs of the Holy Mother Church in Rome." Mar Jacob had introduced private sacramental confession to his people. Having never been in contact with Rome since St. Peter, the practice of the Faith by the Thomas Christians naturally diverged somewhat from the Roman practice. Where a Roman practice was unknown in India, for example personal confession, it was adopted; other differences were minor and at that time easily compromised. The

[11] Brodrick, *Francis Xavier*, pp. 159-163; Schurhammer, *Francis Xavier*, pp. 104-105

[12] Brodrick, *Francis Xavier*, p. 169n.

[13] *Ibid.*, pp. 174-179, 195, 201-202, 210 (quote); Schurhammer, *Francis Xavier*, pp. 112-116; Vincent A. Smith, *Oxford History of India*, 3rd ed. (Oxford, 1958), p. 304.

only native Oriental Christians for the most part welcomed the European Christians as their brethren in the Faith.[14]

In January 1545 a ship from Malacca had put in at the important south Indian port of Cochin bearing Antonio de Paiva, who told Francis Xavier not only about Malacca, but still more about the vast Malay or Indonesian archipelago to the east of it, extending on for hundreds of miles to the Spice Islands where the Portuguese had established their presence thirty years before. After his summer in retreat at the shrine at Mylapore, St. Francis Xavier took ship for Malacca in September. For four months he preached there among the people, ringing his bell, teaching children to pray, visiting the sick, and charming both Portuguese and Malays. As he had done in Tamil, so he translated into Malay the Creed (with brief explanations), the general confession, the Our Father, the Hail Mary, the Salve Regina, and the Ten Commandments.[15]

Early in 1546 St. Francis Xavier departed for Amboina, at the center of the Spice Islands, where the only priest had died some years before. He first baptized the children born to the Christians on the island since the priest had died, and did his best to instruct the adults, many of whom remembered little about their Faith. Then he went to the island of Ternate, then to wild and dangerous Morotai Island, torn by civil war, where the natives had the reputation of being poisoners. They had accepted Christianity in 1534, but under Muslim pressure the majority had apostatized, murdering their priests and burning their churches, and since then no priest had dared come to them. St. Francis Xavier dared, and was not harmed. Many of the people of Morotai returned to the Faith they had lost.[16]

Thus St. Francis Xavier carried on his mission at the two opposite ends of Southeast Asia, the second of the four vast mission fields opened up by the Age of Discovery (India being the first). He was soon to penetrate the third, just-discovered Japan, and to die at the gates of the fourth and much the largest, the Celestial Empire of China. For other missionaries, a lifetime in just one of these fields was more than enough. But St. Francis Xavier heard and obeyed God's call to bring Christianity to all four of them.

In the fall of 1546 a Japanese named Anjiro left his country on a Portuguese ship, one of the few trading with Japan since the first Portuguese captains had discovered the chain of thickly populated islands just three years before. The Portuguese captain had heard of St. Francis Xavier, as nearly all Europeans in the Orient had by then, and what he told Anjiro of the great missionary fired his

---

[14] Brodrick, *Francis Xavier*, pp. 220-228; Schurhammer, *Francis Xavier*, pp. 124-127; George Schurhammer, *The Malabar Church and Rome during the Early Portuguese Period and Before* (Trinchinopoly, 1934), pp. 21, 37.

[15] Brodrick, *Francis Xavier*, pp. 203-204, 229-230, 233-241; Schurhammer, *Francis Xavier*, pp. 119-120, 129-132. For the Portuguese in Malacca and the Spice Islands, see Volume Three, Chapter 15 of this history.

[16] Brodrick, *Francis Xavier*, pp. 247-250, 253-255, 259-260, 268-274, 278-282; Schurhammer, *Francis Xavier*, pp. 138, 140-141, 147-148, 154-157; Jayne, *Vasco da Gama and Successors*, pp. 205-207.

imagination to such an extent that he went all the way to Malacca to try to find him, only to learn that he had gone to the Spice Islands at the beginning of the year. The Christian community in Malacca (mostly Portuguese) received Anjiro coldly, refusing him baptism. Disappointed and angry, he attempted to return to Japan in the spring of 1547, but was prevented by a typhoon. Then in June St. Francis Xavier sailed back to Malacca to prepare three heroic Jesuits for an apostolate in the Moluccas, in which two of them would be martyred and the third would lose his mind as a result of his sufferings. In the fall Anjiro the Japanese finally found his way to him, and spent eight days telling him about the country and people of Japan and how promising a prospect for Christian conversion they presented.[17]

After surviving a terrible storm lasting three days and nights, during which he prayed fervently to Christ, Mary, all the saints, and every choir of angels, St. Francis Xavier returned to Cochin in southern India, but found there no other Jesuits. No one knew better than he how immense the mission field in the Orient was and how few Europeans had yet come to work it. He wrote about this in angry though respectful tones to King John III of Portugal, at the same time sending a letter urging the chief Jesuit in Portugal, Simon Rodriguez, to "wake up His Highness" by providing India with spiritual foundations which he could point out to his credit when he faced the Judgment. St. Francis spent most of Lent 1548 in Goa, where he preached a memorable Lenten sermon, and returned to Cochin at Easter, having travelled 1,600 miles on native ships. From Cochin he returned briefly to the Fishery Coast, where he found Christianity flourishing and several missionary priests resident among the Paravas, including a Father Anriquez who had acquired such fluent Tamil that he no longer needed an interpreter.[18]

On January 12, 1549, from Cochin, St. Francis Xavier wrote a long and perspicacious letter to St. Ignatius of Loyola. He reported that the missions in India were making significant progress despite the contumacy and barbarism of many Indians, the severity of the climate, the difficulty of the many languages, and the lack of education of most of those to whom they were preaching. But all these hindrances were formidable, and furthermore he had learned enough about India's unique and horrible caste system, which rigidly segregated different groups of people from one another, to know that higher-caste, better educated Hindus would not be open to conversion because of the imaginary defilement they would incur by association with fisher-folk and the foreign, casteless Portuguese, many of whom were giving very bad example of what it meant to be Christian.[19] So more and more he was filled with hope from what Anjiro had told him of Japan, which seemed more European than the rest of the Orient and was highly civilized. St. Francis began to plan a journey there in Anjiro's company.

---

[17] Brodrick, *Francis Xavier*, pp. 243-247, 285-287, 295, 297; Schurhammer, *Francis Xavier*, pp. 165-166, 173-175.

[18] Brodrick, *Francis Xavier*, pp. 301-302, 305-310 (quote on 310), 322; Schurhammer, *Francis Xavier*, pp. 179-180, 184-186, 189-192.

[19] Brodrick, *Francis Xavier*, pp. 326-329.

As a protégé of the great missionary, Anjiro was personally baptized by the Bishop of Goa in his cathedral on May 20, 1548, and was given the name of Paul of Holy Faith. At the request of the Jesuits in India he sent a brief account of his remarkable life and adventures to the Jesuits in Europe that November, saying soon afterward of St. Francis Xavier, "I would lay down my life a hundred times for the love I bear him."[20]

Many of his friends were astonished at his daring in making so long a voyage to a country so strange. St. Francis Xavier replied, in a letter to chief Portuguese Jesuit Simon Rodriguez:

> God our Lord is master of the tempests that blow in the seas of China and Japan, even though they be the worst known to man, and He rules over all the winds and the shoals which, they say, cause the destruction of many ships, and He has in His power and control all the robbers of the sea, appallingly numerous though they are, and most cruel pirates likewise, who torture their victims, principally the Portuguese, in many wicked ways. As the Lord God is omnipotent over all these things, I am afraid of none of them, but only that I may be chastised by God for my negligence in His service."[21]

Surely, in all the history of Catholic sanctity, there has never been a man less negligent in God's service than St. Francis Xavier, apostle to four cultures at the ends of the earth.

At Goa on April 15, 1549 St. Francis Xavier embarked for again for Malacca, taking only his Mass kit and "a few books," and accompanied by six Jesuit priests, a Jesuit brother, a Thomas Christian, and a Chinaman. He received a hero's welcome from the governor of Malacca, Pedro da Silva da Gama, one of the six sons of the great Vasco, who sold five tons of pepper to pay all the expenses of the trip to Japan. After sending three of his companions off to the Spice Islands, St. Francis left Malacca in a Chinese junk hired for a direct voyage to Japan (a journey of no less than three thousand miles), whose captain was reputed to be a pirate and whose crew consisted entirely of pagans. But five tons of pepper could safely hire even a pirate. On August 15 the ship arrived at Kagoshima in the south of Japan, where St. Francis was cordially received, and soon had audience with its prince, who gave him permission to preach the Christian faith in Kagoshima and its environs, and gave his subjects liberty to embrace it. He found many Japanese receptive to Christianity, but most of the Buddhist monks strongly opposed, in part because they paraded the vice of homosexuality whose practice Christian teaching condemned.[22] St. Francis wrote to the Jesuits in Goa that:

---

[20] *Ibid.*, pp. 295-296, 312 (quote), 316-317; Schurhammer, *Francis Xavier*, pp. 186-187.

[21] Brodrick, *Francis Xavier*, pp. 345-346.

[22] Brodrick, *Francis Xavier*, pp. 346-349, 354-356, 360-361; Schurhammer, *Francis Xavier*, pp. 198, 200-202, 204-205, 208, 210-211; George B. Sansom, *History of Japan*, Volume II (Stanford CA, 1963), 218, 264.

> [They were] the best race yet discovered, and I think that among non-Christians their match will not easily be found. Admirable in their social relationships, they have an astonishing sense of honor and esteem it above all other things. In general, they are not a wealthy people, but neither among nobles or plebeians is poverty regarded as a disgrace. . . . A good proportion of the people can read and write, which is a great help towards teaching them quickly the prayers and the things of God. They are monogamists, and they abominate thieving.[23]

The Jesuit brother, Juan Fernandez, turned out to be a fine linguist, mastering Japanese quite well. As usual, St. Francis Xavier began by translating basic prayers, the Creed, and the Ten Commandments into Japanese. After establishing a community of converted Christians in Kagoshima, despite the hostility of the local Buddhist monks, St. Francis and Brother Juan Fernandez, together with his first convert in Kagoshima, who was called Bernard, set out for the Japanese imperial capital of Kyoto in the dead of winter, when the winds blow down upon Japan from Siberia. They stayed for a time in Yamaguchi, then the second city in Japan, more than half way to Kyoto, where Saint Francis converted and baptized his host and hostess, and preached in the streets and crossroads, especially condemning the sodomy and infanticide regrettably common in Japan. He spent Christmas of 1550 on the road with his two companions, carrying a blanket and a few spare shirts, wading through freezing streams and leaving bloody tracks in the snow. The inns had no beds, only sometimes a straw mat and a wooden pillow for their guests. Finally they found a ship sailing for Kyoto on Japan's famed Inland Sea. When they landed they were stoned by mocking children, but were befriended by a merchant who had heard of Europeans, and provided them with a guard.[24] Bernard described how St. Francis rejoiced on this last leg of the journey:

> Francis, the happiest man he ever knew, used every now and then to leap and skip like a frolicsome child as he trotted along behind the horsemen and bearers. He had brought an apple with him, Bernard added, and this he would sometimes throw into the air and deftly catch as it came down. The kind *Kudo* had given him a letter of introduction to a merchant friend of his at Miyako [Kyoto], so why should he not be merry? This was the day he had dreamed of ever since his arrival in Japan. He was going to the capital, the holy city of Japan, where dwelt the *Tenno*, the Son of Heaven, who would surely in his wisdom submit himself to the King of Heaven and bring all his people to the feet, the wounded feet of Christ.[25]

St. Francis Xavier's dream recalled the glorious day in the history of Christendom when Roman Emperor Constantine had been converted to

---

[23] Brodrick, *Francis Xavier*, pp. 361-362.

[24] *Ibid.*, pp. 395-397, 408-409, 413-421, 424-426; Schurhammer, *Francis Xavier*, pp. 214, 216, 222-225. The ancient capital of Japan, Kyoto, was then known as Miyako.

[25] Brodrick, *Francis Xavier*, pp. 427-428.

Christianity, ending three centuries of persecution and bringing about the formation of the first Christian state.[26] It had happened once; why not again? In China, which St. Francis had not yet penetrated, such a conversion would have been possible and would have had many of the same effects as that of Constantine. But in Japan in 1550, the Emperor had been a puppet and a shadow for more than two hundred years, and before then for centuries likewise.[27] A weird system had grown up whereby Emperors were almost forced by social pressure to abdicate in their early twenties, or if they did not abdicate, to defer entirely to their principal ministers, known as *shoguns*. They had become no more than bare symbols, not even maintained in the splendor that would normally surround a king or emperor even if only titular. The current Emperor lived hidden from the world in "a ramshackle wooden palace enclosed by a crumbling bamboo stockade," with so little income that he had to augment it himself by writing verse. The *shogun*, who was himself only 16 years old, was absent from the capital. St. Francis Xavier's dream dissolved in the face of a political structure inconceivable in Europe of the sixteenth century.[28]

So St. Francis Xavier returned to Yamaguchi, where by spring conversions had exceeded five hundred, with more being baptized every day. St. Francis speaks of the appeal of the natural law in Japan, to which the Ten Commandments spoke. One of these converts was a remarkable speaker and debater baptized Laurence. He became a Jesuit lay brother and worked for thirty years to evangelize Japan, victor over the Buddhist monks in numerous arguments, notably on personal immortality, which essential Buddhist doctrine denied. Now understanding the political situation in Japan, St. Francis realized that it was necessary to get the support of at least one of the local warlords, called *daimyos*. He attained this goal by visiting the Daimyo of Bungo in southwestern Japan, who was interested in trade with the Portuguese and entirely willing to

---

[26] Constantine may rightly be called the founder of Christendom as a social and political order. See Volume One of this history, Chapter 20.

[27] The Emperor Go-Daigo (ruled 1318-39) had tried to break this deceitful system and for these years had done so. But his movement died with him, until his cause was to some extent revived in the Meiji restoration of the 19th century. The Emperor had become powerless in the "Heian" period of Japanese history, in the 9th century. See the excellent study by Andrew E. Goble, *Kenmu; Go-Daigo's Revolution* (Cambridge MA, 1996).

[28] Brodrick, *Francis Xavier*, pp. 429-432 (quote on 430); Schurhammer, *Francis Xavier*, pp. 225-226; Charles R. Boxer, *The Christian Century in Japan* (Berkeley CA, 1967), p. 42. In the middle of the eighth century in France, a somewhat similar system temporarily existed, with the powerful Carolingian "mayors of the palace" ruling for puppet Merovingian kings after many royal minorities. Pepin the Short asked Pope Zachary to decide whether this was right. Pope Zachary told him it was not; he who wears the crown should have the power. See Volume Two, Chapter 11 of this history. For the long and tangled history of the loss of imperial power and the role of the *shoguns*, see the first two volumes of George Sansom's *History of Japan*.

authorize St. Francis to preach Christianity and make converts in his domain. New Daimyo Haruhide of Yamaguchi also showed favor to the Christians.[29]

St. Francis Xavier left Bungo on a Portuguese ship, which was almost wrecked on Sancian [Shangchwan] Island off Canton in southern China, which the Portuguese, officially barred from China proper, had made a trading base. There he found another Portuguese ship about to sail for Malacca, and took passage aboard it. By now he had learned, especially during his stay in Japan, that China was the largest and most respected country in the Orient, and therefore the key to its evangelization. China had been closed to foreigners, but no official decree ever stopped St. Francis Xavier. He promised the captain of his new ship, Diogo Pereira, that he would cause the Viceroy in India to make him ambassador to China, with St. Francis to accompany him, thereby gaining entry into the closed country. Pereira readily agreed to defray all the expenses of the embassy.[30]

In January 1552 he returned to Malacca, where he was assured of continued support from friendly governor Pedro da Silva da Gama. Just two days later he left for Cochin in India, finding a letter awaiting him from St. Ignatius of Loyola appointing him Provincial of all the Jesuits in the Orient. He reported the good prospects he had found in Japan, and began exercising his new authority over the Jesuit missionaries in India and the Moluccas. But his mission to China was now uppermost in his mind.[31] On April 9 he wrote to King John III of Portugal that he was resolved to go to China immediately:

> In five days' time I am sailing from Goa to Malacca, which is the route to China. In the company of Diogo Pereira I shall make my way to the court of the Chinese King. . . . My trust in God our Lord is that he will have pity on so vast an empire and mercifully open a way for His creatures made in His image to adore their Creator, and to believe in Jesus Christ, His Son and their Savior.[32]

The future was to show that China was not only the greatest Christian missionary opportunity in the world outside Christendom, but that the fate of the missions to most Oriental countries was linked with it. This was not true of India; but India was full of its own special obstacles to conversion. It was also not true of the Philippines, where Spain was to rule and Chinese were rejected as foreign interlopers. But it was very true of Japan and Southeast Asia.

The ruin of St. Francis Xavier's final and greatest mission began in Malacca, where the youngest and most ignoble son of the great Vasco da Gama, Alvaro Ataide, had just been made co-governor when St. Francis arrived in May 1552. He defied both the instructions of the Viceroy and St. Francis' authority as

---

[29] Brodrick, *Francis Xavier*, pp. 437-442, 446-453; Schurhammer, *Francis Xavier*, pp. 229-241.

[30] Brodrick, *Francis Xavier*, p. 453; Schurhammer, *Francis Xavier*, pp. 242-246.

[31] Brodrick, *Francis Xavier*, pp. 433-437, 457-458, 466-467; Schurhammer, *Francis Xavier*, pp. 249-249, 253, 256-257; Sansom, *History of Japan* II, 291.

[32] Brodrick, *Francis Xavier*, p. 490.

Papal legate by refusing to let Pereira depart on the Chinese embassy, meaning that it could no longer be financed by him as he had pledged. Pereira was to have provided the expensive gifts needed for an audience with the Emperor. St. Francis called on the Bishop of Goa to excommunicate him, but went on alone, back to Sancian Island, where he could not find anyone willing to take him to the mainland, since the entry of foreigners into China was prohibited.[33] On November 13 he wrote his last letter to two leading Jesuit Fathers in India:

> I am greatly hoping that I shall be able to make my way into China. Know this for certain and have no doubt that the devil will do all in his power to prevent our Fathers from entering China . . . but also know equally certainly that with the grace and help of God our Lord the devil will be put to confusion.[34]

A week later he fell ill. He was only 46, but he had already lived the equivalent of several lifetimes. Two weeks later, following a severe fever, he fell into delirium and lost the ability to speak and to recognize people. But three days later he recovered his power of speech, calling upon the Most Holy Trinity and the Blessed Virgin Mary. On December 2, 1552, the greatest apostle the Church has known since Sts. Peter and Paul died on this forsaken island with the name of Jesus on his lips. His body was placed in a wooden coffin. The next year it was returned to Malacca, still incorrupt. In Malacca it was laid in the ground, in direct contact with the earth for five months. In 1554 it was brought to Goa, still incorrupt. In 1694, 142 years after his death, his body was exhumed again, examined for an hour and a half by Bishop Espinosa, Vicar Apostolic of the East, and the French Jesuit Joseph Bayard. They gave a perfect lifelike description of its appearance. By then Francis Xavier had long since been canonized.[35]

India (1517-1661)

The subcontinent of India includes many nations and many peoples, with no common language until English rule had been long established, in the nineteenth century. Native Indian cultures had many characteristics in common, some unique to India such as almost universal belief in reincarnation and acceptance and practice of the caste system which rigidly stratified people into groups only allowed to interact with one another when close in the caste hierarchy. The Thomas Christians had accepted many Indian social practices while rejecting reincarnation because of their enduring faith; but they were only a tiny percentage of the population of India. However, in 1000 A.D. a major Muslim irruption into India took place under the redoubtable Mahmud of Ghazni, and

---

[33] Brodrick, *Francis Xavier*, 499-504, 514-515; Schurhammer, *Francis Xavier*, pp. 277-278, 280-283, 288-290.

[34] Brodrick, *Francis Xavier*, p. 523.

[35] Brodrick, *Francis Xavier*, pp. 524-526, 528-529, 533-534, 537-538; Schurhammer, *Francis Xavier*, pp. 294-306. St. Francis Xavier was canonized in 1622.

Muslim invasions and rule in large parts of India continued for the next seven hundred years.[36]

No two religions could be more unlike than Islam and Hinduism. Islam was vigorous, militant, always seeking converts, and so passionately opposed to idolatry that it banned in its mosques even the representation of anything found in nature, so that only geometrical designs were permitted for decoration. Hinduism was passive, pacific, content to believe that God could be known in a thousand or a million different forms, any or all of which could be represented by the sculpted idols which were found in considerable numbers in every temple. Buddhism was an offshoot of Hinduism, differing from it primarily in that its worship centered around the historical figure of the Buddha rather than some mythical being. But the distinction between myth and history was never clear in India; and Buddhism retained the Hindu view of the universe, its quest for union and absorption in God to end the imagined cycle of reincarnation. But by the time the Muslims arrived, Buddhism remained dominant only in the southern island of Ceylon and the southern foothills of the Himalayas (Nepal and Bhutan); most of the rest of India had reverted to the original Hinduism before Buddha with its many gods, whom he had implicitly rejected.[37]

India had never regarded the history of its various kings and their governments as significant; to a greater extent than any other civilized culture known to history, it ignored them. Only a few areas (such as Ceylon and Kashmir) had anything even resembling Western-style history before the Muslims came. Except for the Buddhist emperor Ashoka in the third century B.C., whose edicts carved in imperishable rock preserved the memory of his deeds and policies, for all practical purposes India had no political history, only religious literature.[38] The smashing advent of the Muslims created it, with them at the center. The result is that we know much more about the history of the Muslim states in India than the contemporary Hindu states. In the sixteenth

---

[36] For early India and Buddha, see Volume One, Chapter 1, pages 30-33, and Chapter 7, pp. 160-163 of this history; for the Apostle Thomas in India, see Volume One, Chapter 17, pp. 407-408, 417-419. For Mahmud of Ghazni and his invasion, see Volume Two, Chapter 17, pages 456-457.

[37] The decline of Buddhism in India began in the later years of the Gupta dynasty, one of whose rulers bore the name of Buddhagupta; he died at the beginning of the sixth century. In the seventh century Chinese Buddhist pilgrim Hiuen Tsang could still report finding over 100 Buddhist monasteries during his travels through India and over 10,000 Buddhist monks, but noted that Buddhists were no longer a majority of the population in any of the Indian nations he visited. The number of Buddhists steadily and rather quickly declined after that. See Ramesh C. Majumdar, ed. *The History and Culture of the Indian People*, Volume III, pp. 30-33, 239-240 and *passim*; Smith, *Oxford History of India*, pp. 180-184, 215, 222.

[38] See Volume One, Chapter 7, note 44 of this history; also A. L. Basham, *The Wonder That Was India* (London, 1954) and Romila Thapar, *Asoka and the Decline of the Mauryas* (New York, 1961). For the history of Ceylon, the *Mahavamsa*, see Majumdar, ed. *History and Culture of the Indian People* II, 241-242; for the history of Kashmir, the *Rajatarangini*, see Smith, *Oxford History of India*, pp. 15, 194.

century, when an adventurer called Babur "the Tiger," coming out of totally Muslim Afghanistan and bringing modern artillery which had never before been seen in India, swept to victory at the decisive Battle of Panipat in 1526, he created the Mogul empire in northern India, whose history over the next two centuries is known in great detail. By contrast we know almost nothing of the history of the mighty Hindu state of Vijayanagar, founded in 1343 and dominant on the Indian peninsula until heavily defeated by an alliance of Muslim states at the Battle of Talikota in 1565. A much lessened part of it survived until 1646.[39]

This meant that the missionaries who followed St. Francis Xavier in India had two completely different apostolic tasks, depending on whether their environment was Muslim or Hindu. In the Mogul empire, the dominant culture was Muslim, and historically of all peoples in the world, the Muslims have been the most resistant to Christian conversion. Missionary work there was possible only because a strain of freethinking ran through the Mogul ruling family, beginning with Akbar the Great who took the throne in 1556 at the age of 13 and held it until he died in 1605. He and his son Jahangir (reigned 1605-1627) did not consider themselves Muslims and therefore were willing to let Christian missionaries into their territory to preach the Gospel and seek converts. Several dedicated Jesuits tried, notably the nephew of the great St. Francis Xavier, Jerome; but they had little success, having no way to get past the religious and cultural prejudices of both the Muslim and the Hindu population of the Mogul empire, while Sultans Akbar and Jahangir, though leading the missionaries on with the hope of their own conversion, never seem to have been really serious about it.[40] Jahangir's son Shah Jahan, though not a fervent Muslim, was willing to go along with Islam at least for appearance's sake; such Christian missionary activity as there was was sharply curbed during his reign (1628-58), with one major persecution (1632-35). His son Aurangzeb overthrew his father and imprisoned him for the rest of his life, and is one of the most fanatical Muslim rulers in any country that history records. The Mogul mission came to an end with him.[41]

---

[39] Smith, *Oxford History of India*, pp. 303-428.

[40] *Ibid.*, pp. 337-375. The best accounts of the Mogul mission are Smith, *op. cit.*, and Edward Maclagan, *The Jesuits and the Great Mogul* (London, 1932). Father Jerome Xavier served in the Mogul mission for twenty years, 1595-1615, during the reigns of both Akbar and Jahangir (Maclagan, *op. cit.*, pp. 50-84). He and his companions and successors never succeeded in developing a Christian community of any size anywhere. In the year 1606, after the Christians had been at the Mogul capital of Agra for a decade, they still celebrated only 20 baptisms; as late as 1632 the whole congregation at Agra numbered no more than 400 (Maclagan, *op. cit.*, pp. 70, 74, 90-92, 283, 286.

[41] For Shah Jahan, builder of the world-famous Taj Mahal and creator of the fabulously rich Peacock Throne, see Smith, *Oxford History of India*, pp. 376-403; for Aurangzeb, see *ibid.*, pp. 404-429; for the persecution of the Christians from 1632 to 1635, see *ibid.*, p. 380 and Maclagan, *Jesuits and the Great Mogul*, pp. 101-105, 175, 315. In 1653 only 30 baptisms were recorded for the whole Mogul mission (Maclagan, *op. cit.*, p. 283.

The second, at least equally difficult task was to penetrate the utterly alien Hindu society and begin conversions to Christ within it.

Portugal, despite the many misdeeds of its officials and fortune hunters in a land six months' travel distant from their homeland, had an abiding commitment to the missionary apostolate, and from the time of St. Francis Xavier had given special favor to the Jesuits.[42] The Portuguese ruled the coasts of India (never the interior) for 150 years. For a long time they could not understand their lack of progress in spreading the faith in Hindu territory. Their national experience with Islam during the wars of the Reconquest in the Iberian peninsula had taught them how hard it was to convert Muslims, but they did not expect equally strong resistance from the Hindus, whose religion for their first century in India they barely understood. The enormous obstacle created by the Hindu caste system was only faintly seen, if at all, during the first Portuguese century. The Portuguese have been much blamed for their slowness in grasping the caste system and the stranglehold it had imposed on Hindu society; but that failure is really not surprising in view of how unique and horrifying this system was,[43] to any Christian (or for that matter to any virtuous man of whatever faith, as Gandhi and Nehru abundantly proved in the twentieth century), and how silently it operated. Native Indians who went to live in Goa or other coastal cities which the Portuguese dominated, lost their caste and could no longer associate with Indians elsewhere. They could only become Portuguese, insofar as they were able to adapt to a culture totally new to them; and Portuguese were considered casteless persons, *Parangis*, at the very bottom of the social ladder, despised even when they could not be physically resisted because of their arms and warships. As for the native Indians converted by St. Francis Xavier and his co-workers, they were all of lower castes, mere fisher-folk, with whom the brahmins and rajas and vaisyas could never associate.[44]

And behind the fantastic rigidity of the caste system there remained the bedrock Indian beliefs in reincarnation, the possible existence of direct contradiction in philosophical premises, the absorption of all personality into a divine essence—that whole complex of ideas and unworldly world-views traceable in so many ways to the Harappa civilization of earliest India.[45] The mind of the Indian, even their wisest, was crippled by these gigantic and

---

[42] See Chapter 12, above, on the Portuguese evangelization of Brazil, notably by Father José de Anchieta, S.J.

[43] No other nation or culture had anything like it. Social stratification was found in most civilized cultures at that time, including the European, but never did it approach the point where every contact by a person of high caste with members of much lower castes, even at considerable physical distances, was considered personal defilement to the person of higher caste.

[44] Cronin, *Pearl to India*, pp. 35-46. The brahmins, though by no means all considered priests, were believed to have a virtual monopoly on religious thought and action. The rajas were secular leaders, political or military; the vaisyas were, as we would say, businessmen.

[45] See Volume One, Chapters 1 and 7 of this history.

fundamental errors, which predisposed them to reject the doctrine of personal salvation central to Christianity. It was as though they slept, dreaming fantasies and nightmares, with no one to awaken them. Fifteen centuries before, there had come to them the Apostle Thomas, he who had demanded to put his finger into the wounds of Christ before he would believe that Christ had risen. Apostle Thomas was a man who believed first of all in physical reality, even before he finally made his commitment to the Risen Christ.[46] That is probably why he was sent to India. He had made his mark there with the 200,000 native Indian Christians who were keeping the faith when the Portuguese arrived. But now India had need of another Teacher of Reality. And that was the name given to the Italian Jesuit Roberto de Nobili after he came to the Hindu interior of southern India, at the great city of Madurai: *Tattuva Bodhakar*, Teacher of Reality. He bore it to his grave, and his converts always used it in remembering him.[47]

De Nobili saw that so long as the inevitable consequence of Christian conversion was loss of caste, the Faith would never make any progress in Hindu India. As an Italian Jesuit, he could declare truthfully that he was not a Portuguese and therefore not a *Parangi*, since this term applied specifically to them. Since he had been nobly born in Europe, he could truthfully claim to be of the raja caste. He found that Hindu India had one small class of men who escaped from the caste system by devoting their lives, mostly in their later years, to the preaching of religious doctrine, who were in effect wandering teachers. These men were called *sannyasis* and were distinguished by wearing a yellow robe. He arrived in Madurai toward the end of 1606, and donned the garb of a *sannyasi* with the approval of one of the most extraordinary bishops in the history of the Church, a Catalan named Ros, who had been appointed Archbishop of Cranganore primarily to serve the Thomas Christians, since he knew Syriac, their liturgical language. He had a breadth of mind and a refreshing absence of the usual European prejudices, and since he was not a Portuguese, he was not tempted by Portuguese nationalism. Without the favor of Archbishop Ros, de Nobili could hardly have survived the firestorm his missionary method created.[48]

In 1607 the occurrence of a solar eclipse toward the end of February, which de Nobili's European astronomy accurately predicted, led to long discussions with a Hindu school teacher. De Nobili convinced him of the unity of God, His

---

[46] A commitment to the attainability of truth and the knowledge of reality must precede any commitment to Christ. I have stated that the heart of a Christian education may be summed up in five words: "Truth exists; the Incarnation happened." One cannot truly believe in the Incarnation, and therefore in Jesus Christ as God, if one does not believe that truth exists and is attainable by the human mind.

[47] Cronin, *Pearl to India*, pp. 126-129. Despite being in many ways the best history of missionary work in India, Cronin's book is disfigured for the orthodox Catholic reader by its often patronizing tone in describing de Nobili's rational arguments against Hindu pantheism, assuming against his own evidence that these arguments from reason and reality rarely convinced his hearers.

[48] *Ibid.*, pp. 35-37, 50-51, 56.

creation of the universe from nothing, and the error of reincarnation. That spring de Nobili baptized him. De Nobili parted from Portuguese Jesuit missionary Gonçalo Fernandez, who in no less than eleven years of effort had not made a single convert, because he did not understand the caste system, going from a Portuguese-style mission house to live in a simple dwelling which he built himself, with rooms for talking with visitors and a small chapel. Like the Hindu holy men, he ate only one vegetarian meal a day. In the summer of 1608 a brahmin named Sivadarma became intrigued by this very different kind of foreigner, and agreed to tell him about the Hindu holy books, the *Vedas*, which had never been shown to foreigners, and to teach him their language, Sanskrit—the first European to read, or even see that ancient hieratic tongue. By the middle of 1609 de Nobili alone had made more than fifty converts, including Sivadarma. He wrote to his immediate superior in the Jesuit order, Albert Laerzio, that he had found in the *Vedas* references to four laws, three of which the brahmins were still teaching, but the fourth, how to find salvation, had been lost. He pledged he would bring it to them, as St. Paul in his sermon on the Areopagus of Athens had magnificently named Christ as the "unknown God" worshipped along with many others by the Athenians.[49]

In 1609 a powerful Indian noble, Erramma Setti, offered de Nobili his full protection against physical threats and calumny. He was put on trial for atheism by an assembly of some eight hundred brahmins, but defended himself splendidly with the aid of Sivadarma, by insisting that his first teaching was that man must know God before worshipping Him—a proposition with which almost all of the eight hundred brahmins agreed. He sent two of his converts, aged 25 and 18, to Cochin, where they were welcomed by Laerzio and gave exemplary proof of their piety and knowledge of Christian doctrine. They fully recognized that despite their different culture and way of life, the Portuguese were their brothers in the faith. Archbishop Ros gave them the sacrament of confirmation on the feast of Saints Peter and Paul, and they declared they were ready for martyrdom should it be God's will. It was in that year that de Nobili gained the name of Teacher of Reality.[50]

In 1610 it was announced that the primatial office of Archbishop of Goa would be transferred from Alexeio de Menezes, probably its greatest and most apostolically minded occupant, who was to be primate of Portugal, to the much more conventional Christovao de Sa, formerly Bishop of Malacca, who knew very little about Hindu India. The Portuguese Gonçalo Fernandez, seeing de Nobili making more and more converts while he had still made none, complained to Jesuit Visitor Pimenta about his unorthodox missionary methods. The Visitor ordered an investigation by Laerzio, who conducted a special inquiry among the new converts at Madurai, asking them fifteen penetrating questions about their new faith. In reply, they assured him that they confessed the Holy Name of Christ, that Father de Nobili had never forbidden them to go to Father Gonçalo's

---

[49] *Ibid.*, pp. 39, 61-74, 78, 85-90, 109, 129. For St. Paul's sermon, see Acts 17:22-31.
[50] Cronin, *Pearl to India*, pp. 98-103, 111-113, 126-132.

Masses or confessions (as he had charged), that they honored the Portuguese as fellow Christians despite the difference in their social customs, and that they accepted the Pope and Archbishop Ros as their spiritual heads. Not all were willing so to commit themselves; eighteen of the new converts apostatized when faced directly with these issues. But the majority held firm in the grace of faith they had been given by the Christian *sannyasi*. In 1611 de Nobili wrote to his friend Cardinal Bellarmine for books against Pythagoras' teaching on reincarnation, by St. Augustine on grace, and explaining the Christian doctrine of personality, developed in the great theological controversies concerning the Monophysite heresy when the dogma was promulgated at the Council of Chalcedon that Christ was one person with two natures, divine and human. On the Feast of the Annunciation he opened a regular church in Madurai, where he said the Mass of the Latin rite. By the end of the year he had 150 converts who worshipped regularly in his church.[51]

In 1612 de Nobili began an extraordinary career of writing in Tamil, the language of southern India in which he had become remarkably fluent, and also in Sanskrit, which he knew less well but still well enough to write in it. He prepared a summary of Christian doctrine and a brief life of the Blessed Virgin Mary in Sanskrit. He wrote in elegant Tamil a whole series of books making the case for the Catholic Faith, entitled "On the Existence of a Supreme Being," "Spiritual Teaching," "Disquisition on the Soul," "The Divine Model," "Refutation of Blasphemies," "Spiritual Medicine," and "Refutation of Rebirth," also called "Dialogue on Eternal Life." No European had ever penetrated so deeply into Hindu life and thought.[52]

At the end of 1611 Albert Laerzio, who had consistently supported de Nobili's missionary tactics along with Archbishop Ros of Cranganore, was replaced as his Jesuit superior by a bigoted Portuguese, Pero Francisco. In December 1612 the aged Jesuit general Claudio Aquaviva wrote to Pero Francisco urging caution in de Nobili's adapting himself to Hindu culture. Aquaviva knew next to nothing about Hindu culture, but he had been a great Jesuit leader, and even in his last years could recognize that much good might come of de Nobili's apostolate even though he thought he should modify it in certain ways. The very hostile Pero Francisco interpreted this letter as authorizing him to require all of de Nobili's converts to give up their caste marks, notably a colored thread to which great significance was attached, and to prohibit him from performing any more baptisms until the prospective converts had complied. But de Nobili noted in the general's letter a statement that "no change should be made which would compromise the mission" and without direct consultation with him in person. He therefore informed Pero Francisco that he would meet him in Cochin. Accepting with ill grace, Pero Francisco ordered him

---

[51] *Ibid.*, pp. 146-147, 149-153, 156-158; M. D'Sa, *History of the Catholic Church in India*, Volume I (52-1652) (Bombay, 1910), pp. 171, 186. For the Monophysites, the Council of Chalcedon, and the Catholic doctrine of the person, see Volume Two of this history, Chapter 4.

[52] Cronin, *Pearl to India*, pp. 176-182.

not to come in *sannyasi* dress. But de Nobili found in the general's letter explicit approval of his use of the yellow robe, so he came in it anyway. The infuriated Pero Francisco refused to receive him in the robe, writing to the general that de Nobili had arrived clad only in a loin-cloth. He journeyed on for a day to Cranganore, where Archbishop Ros offered to accompany him back to Cochin; Pero Francisco could not refuse to speak to the archbishop, but he remained absolutely unyielding. In December 1613 de Nobili wrote out an explanation of General Aquaviva's letter and his compliance with it, pointing out that nowhere in it did the general say that Indian converts would have to remove their caste thread.[53]

There followed a celebrated controversy over missionary adaptation to an ancient civilized culture, highlighted by the problem of the caste thread. Did it carry sufficient pagan religious baggage to be dangerous, or was it simply a mark of social status? Pero Francisco suddenly died in 1615, and his replacement was at least neutral toward de Nobili's tactics. The case went before the Roman Curia. Pending its decision, General Aquaviva removed many restrictions on de Nobili, but would not renew his authorization for de Nobili to perform baptisms while the case before the Curia was still pending. Archbishop Christovao de Sa of Goa petitioned Rome to ban the caste thread for all Christians in India. In one of the wisest documents in the history of the Papacy, Pope Paul V replied that de Sa and Archbishop Ros of Cranganore should examine the thread and similar tokens of caste to see if they could not be set apart from the accidental superstitions connected with them. King Philip III of Spain (which had ruled Portugal also since 1580) urged Archbishop Ros to come to Goa to discuss the problem. The Pope's response reached Goa at the end of 1617 (the ten-month time span required to transmit a message from Europe to India via the Cape of Good Hope route must always be remembered). Archbishop de Sa, goaded into defiance, refused to receive it officially once he found out what it said, and haled de Nobili before the Inquisition.[54]

On February 4 and 5, 1619 a memorable hearing was held in Goa. Five native Indian priests who had long lived in Goa and had given up their caste in Hindu India, three Portuguese secular priests, two Franciscan and Dominican and Augustinian friars, three Portuguese and one Italian Jesuit, two Inquisitors, and the two archbishops were its members. Archbishop Ros, now nearly blind and greatly debilitated, was still able to point out that "Nobili's method was neither new nor absurd, but borrowed from apostolic times; that the Church in the past had allowed even abhorrent rites and ceremonies after stripping them of their perverse and impious significance, and substituting another in keeping with Christianity." Despite de Nobili's vigorous defense and that of Jesuit André Palmeiro and the Second (but not the First) Inquisitor, the majority of this assembly condemned the thread for Christian converts in India. A particularly memorable moment in this confrontation came when one of the Franciscan friars,

---

[53] *Ibid.*, pp. 166, 189-197.
[54] Ibid., pp. 202-208; D'Sa, *History of the Catholic Church in India*, I, 187.

wearing his brown habit, cried out to de Nobili in his yellow *sannyasi* robe: "Did Our Lord wear clothes like yours?" to which the missionary devastatingly replied: "No; nor did he wear clothes like yours."[55] De Nobili concluded his defense with these words:

> I left Rome for Madurai only to preach Jesus Christ. I have not lost all religious sense; my only wish is to be useful to souls. Without any fault on my part, without any shadow of proof, you accuse me of inventing a false and absurd method of spreading the Gospel. That is totally unjust. I preach Christ openly, without fraud or disguise. If this assembly refuses to listen to me and despises me to that extent, elsewhere perhaps I shall find more friendly and attentive ears. Elsewhere perhaps I shall find men to defend my cause. If my arguments carry any weight, I have no doubt that the Holy Father, Vicar of Christ Our Lord, will see that truth triumphs.[56]

Never was such trust better founded. Fernao Martins de Mascarenhas, Grand Inquisitor of Portugal, overruled the decision of the Archbishop of Goa, stating that de Nobili had the better of the argument, and was upheld by King Philip IV.[57] His and Mascarenhas' decision and other documents pertaining to de Nobili's case were forwarded to Rome, where Pope Gregory XV appointed a pontifical commission to settle the matter, including the 79-year-old Cardinal Bellarmine and Archbishop Peter Lombard of Armagh in Ireland, a leading theologian. The documents included de Nobili's pamphlets written in answer to criticisms of the Madurai mission, in which he cited adaptation by the early Church to Greco-Roman culture and by the first missionaries to pagan England. He quoted extensively from Indian books to prove that the thread and other caste marks did not have a religious significance. In December 1622 Lombard wrote the report of the commission. He quoted from St. Augustine's *City of God* that dress and customs need not be changed when converting to Christianity. He pointed out that Archbishop Christovao de Sa's predecessor de Menezes had baptized the nephew of the king of Calicut wearing the thread, with no one objecting; that Thomas Christians in good standing with the Church wore it; that in the China missions converts were not required to change their dress and lifestyle, and that the Grand Inquisitor of Portugal favored de Nobili's methods. In January 1623 Pope Gregory XV fully confirmed Lombard's position, allowing the caste signs to be retained by Christian converts in India so long as they had them blessed by a priest.[58]

---

[55] Cronin, *Pearl to India*, pp. 211-219 (first quote on 217, second on 219).

[56] *Ibid.*, pp. 219-220.

[57] This is one of the most striking examples of the Inquisition's prime function in the Iberian peninsula, almost totally obscured by anti-Catholic polemic, of clearing people falsely accused of heresy or the abandonment of Christianity. At least three-quarters of those accused before the Inquisition were cleared, and given certificates to prove it (see my *Isabel of Spain, the Catholic Queen* [Front Royal VA, 1991], p. 140).

[58] Cronin, *Pearl to India*, pp. 223-230; Ludwig von Pastor, *History of the Popes* XXVII (St. Louis MO, 1952), 148.

The Universal Pastor had ruled; now it was time for the spiritual harvest. In the summer of 1623 de Nobili discussed Christianity before Sellappa, ruler of the principality of Salem, who had been a follower of Vedanta. They debated the Christian doctrine of preservation of the individual soul against the Vedanta doctrine of its absorption into God. Sellappa, though he never converted, declared that de Nobili had won the debate, and gave him full license to preach and make converts in his territory. In February 1624 the heroic Archbishop Ros died after translating the Latin Mass of the Council of Trent into Syriac for the Thomas Christians, and appointing a Thomas Christian archdeacon as administrator of the diocese after his death, thus bringing these people who had kept the faith alone in India for 1,500 years into full communion with Rome. A second assistant came to de Nobili in Madurai, an ardent young Portuguese named Emmanuel Martins,[59] to supplement the work of his first assistant, the Italian Antonio Vico, who penned this glorious tribute to de Nobili:

> However favorable the opinion I had till now regarding his [de Nobili's] aptitude for apostolic work, I must confess that all I had imagined is nothing compared with the reality. If I did not see it with my own eyes and touch it with my own hands, I would call it the ideal but unattainable perfection of the missionary. Shall I speak of that consummate science with which he exposes the most abstruse questions of theology as if they were child's play? Of that subtle talent which, while it enables him to make himself understood by the ignorant, arouses the interest of the most learned and holds them spellbound? Of that matchless eloquence and the richness of expression with which, in spite of the variety and difficulty of the idioms of these people, he astonishes them? Of the gentle art with which he embellishes and renders attractive the most forbidding subjects? Of the ease with which he adopts the ways and manners, however strange, of the people of this country? And finally of that power of persuasion, with which he sways the minds of all?[60]

Vico died in 1638, and was replaced by Baltazar da Costa, who donned a *sannyasi* robe as soon as he arrived. De Nobili, frequently ill but never discouraged, continued to work at Madurai, while Martins worked at the new capital of the Nayak (ruler) of Madurai, Tiruchirapalli. In 1640 a brief persecution began in Tiruchirapalli and Madurai. Martins and de Nobili were arrested, and de Nobili's house was plundered. On hearing of this de Nobili, now 63 and infirm, rose to the occasion by rebuking the despoilers and threatening them with God's anger, whereupon they promptly returned all the sacred objects which they had taken. When de Nobili was finally ordered to leave the Madurai mission due to age and debility in 1644, it had made 4,183 converts—1,208 of the brahmin caste. Shortly before he left, the Nayak asked him to name his persecutors so they could be punished. De Nobili refused, declaring that Christianity is a religion of forgiveness. His eyesight fading, he wrote his last

---

[59] Cronin, Pearl to India, pp. 235-238; D'Sa, *History of the Catholic Church in India*, I, 182.
[60] Cronin, *Pearl to India*, p. 155.

letter in September 1649, typically on the Christian instruction of the young. He died in 1656, at the shrine in Mylapore where the Apostle Thomas had been martyred fifteen hundred years before.[61] Roberto de Nobili was a worthy successor to him. The Madurai mission continued to make converts and was never forgotten, though Hindu religious assumptions were so antithetical to Christianity that only a small minority of Indians are Christians to this day. They are now beginning to work with the Muslims against the modern "culture of death" which both of them abhor.[62]

No religion can take root in a country without native clergy. There were many native Indian priests in Goa—a reported 180 in 1655—but most if not all of them had broken all ties with Hindu India, becoming in effect denationalized. While the Portuguese authorities were quite willing to ordain them, they were reluctant to ordain as priests the kind of men who followed de Nobili at Madurai. A brahmin convert who had taken a Portuguese name, Matthew de Castro, came to Rome to study for the priesthood in 1625, after having been turned down for ordination by the Franciscan college in south India. He made the acquaintance of Francesco Ingoli, secretary to the newly established Vatican congregation for the missions, De Propaganda Fide, founded in 1622, who came to understand that this reluctance to ordain native Indian priests of Matthew de Castro's stature was a very great mistake. For most of the rest of his life, Ingoli continually advocated a greatly expanded native priesthood in India. In 1628 the Papal nuncio in Madrid reported to De Propaganda Fide that he was unable to find any law or official regulation restricting the ordination of native Indians, and pointed out that there were more than 300 priests (mostly natives) in the archdiocese of Cranganore, which included the Thomas Christians. But still there was a shortage of priests. In 1630 the College of Cardinals ordered that more native priests be ordained in India, and in 1631 Matthew de Castro was ordained personally by the influential Cardinal Barberini. He went to India, then back to Rome, where in 1636 he reported an enduring reluctance by the Portuguese to ordain native priests from the Hindu regions. In November 1637 Matthew de Castro was secretly consecrated bishop in Rome and sent to the Muslim-ruled kingdom of Bijapur, where the clash of Muslim and Hindu redoubled the difficulties of his apostolate. In 1645 he returned to Rome and presented a long memorial to De Propaganda Fide emphasizing the aptitude of brahmin converts to the priesthood and the obvious advantages of native priests, who knew the local languages and were closer to their own people than foreigners could be. Furthermore, he pointed out, there was no known case of apostasy by a native Indian priest. In 1648 Ingoli once again petitioned the Cardinals to ordain more native Indian clergy.[63]

---

[61] *Ibid.*, pp. 245-249, 252, 255-256, 262-263, 265, 267-268.

[62] Indian Muslims (the majority of whom have lived in the separated state of Pakistan since partition and the end of British rule in 1947) joined with Christians in opposing a law of Indira Gandhi for forced sterilization which she attempted to impose in the 1970's.

[63] Von Pastor, *History of the Popes*, XXVII, 132; Merces de Melo, *Recruitment and Formation of the Native Clergy of India*, pp. 149, 215-218, 227-234, 230-240, 243; D'Sa,

In 1637 Archdeacon George, administrator of the Thomas Christians, died and was succeeded by his relative Thomas a Campo. In 1641 Stephen de Britto, worthy successor of the great Archbishop Ros of Cranganore, followed him to the reward for his apostolic labors. His successor, Francisco Garcia, did not have nearly as much rapport with the Thomas Christians as had Ros and de Britto. In 1645 Jesuit lay brother Pedro de Basto, famed for his holiness and gift of prophecy, died at Cochin; he foretold that the Portuguese would soon lose their 150-year-old dominion in India.[64]   The Dutch, who had been attacking the colonies of Spain and Portugal during most of the period of their union (1580-1640), since they were at war with the Spaniards during all those years and more,[65] maintained their attacks even when a greatly weakened Portugal regained its independence. They were particularly interested in the large island of Ceylon off the southern tip of India, where they took three important ports in 1639-40. In 1648 they sacked and burned the major port of Tuticorin in south India, where the Portuguese had long been strongly established. In 1653 they took Cananor, another important south Indian port, and the Portuguese Viceroy at Goa for the first time was overthrown by rebels under one Braz de Castro. In 1656 the Portuguese lost the capital city of Colombo and all the rest of Ceylon to the Dutch, who insisted that all Catholics left on the island, including native converts, accept their Calvinist religion.[66]

At this difficult moment, the heretic Jacobite (Monophysite) church in Antioch seized the opportunity created by more frequent overseas communications with India to send a bishop of their sect, Mar Ahatalla, to take advantage of the ancient tradition that Thomas Christians received their bishops from Syria. The Portuguese promptly arrested Mar Ahatalla and sent him to Goa, ignoring pleas by the Thomas Christians for his release, not taking much trouble to explain to them that he was out of communion with Rome. In May 1653 the majority of the Thomas Christians, led by Archdeacon Thomas a Campo, rejected Papal authority to appoint bishops over them.[67]

In 1655 Pope Alexander VII took office, and within a year he had moved decisively to combat the schism of the Thomas Christians. He sent a group of Carmelites headed by Father Joseph of St. Mary to reconcile them, and wrote letters calling for healing of the schism to Archbishop Garcia of Cranganore, to the clergy and laity of his archdiocese, to the cathedral chapter of Cochin, and to the schismatics directly. By 1657 the Carmelite reconciliation was bearing fruit; 44 churches of the Thomas Christians reunited with Rome, though they would

---

History of the Catholic Church in India I, 183; H. Chappoulie, *Aux origines d'une église; Rome et les missions d'Indochine au XVII siècle*, Volume I (Paris, 1943), p. 94.

[64] D'Sa, *History of the Catholic Church in India* I, 184; *Old Catholic Encyclopedia* (1913), XIV, 686; Brodrick, *Francis Xavier*, p. 196n.

[65] See Chapters 6-10, above.

[66] Israel, *The Dutch Republic and the Hispanic World*, 1606-61 (Oxford, 1982), p. 278; Pieter Geyl, *History of the Netherlands in the Seventeenth Century* (New York, 1961), I, 187; *Cambridge Modern History* IV, 744; Cronin, *Pearl to India*, pp. 265-266.

[67] D'Sa, *History of the Catholic Church in India* I, 184-185.

still not recognize the authority of Archbishop Garcia. Through the shattering crash of the Portuguese empire in India these holy men persevered in their task of ecclesiastical peace-making. By 1661 two-thirds of the Thomas Christians had been reconciled. In that very year Portugal and the Netherlands signed a treaty which guaranteed Brazil to the Portuguese but gave the Dutch free rein in India. In the next year the Dutch seized Cranganore, and in the following year Cochin. Wherever their writ ran in India, the Dutch expelled all the European Catholic priests. But just before departing from India, Joseph of St. Mary consecrated native priest Chandy Parambil as vicar apostolic of the Thomas Christians. Ever since the majority of them have remained faithful to the Roman Catholic Church.[68]

As for the Parava fisher-folk to whom St. Francis Xavier had brought the Faith, when told by the Dutch that the must become Calvinists, they responded:

> You say your religion is better than the religion which our great padre taught us. Well then, you must perform more miracles than he. Resurrect at least a dozen dead persons, for Xavier restored to life five or six here; heal all our sick; increase the number of fishes in our sea; and then we shall see what answer we will give you.[69]

But the Portuguese *raj* was no more. The Dutch were not strong enough to replace it all; but they were aided by the English under King Charles II, whose Portuguese wife claimed lands around Bombay in west central India as part of her dowry, conveying her claim to him. The small country of the Netherlands found it necessary to concentrate its imperial ambitions in Indonesia and the Spice Islands; more and more the English involvement in India grew, especially after the death of Aurangzeb at a very advanced age in 1707 led to the breakup of the Mogul Empire.[70] Some Jesuit missionary effort in India remained, but now it entirely lacked official support. The story of British India is an extraordinary one, but does not include Catholic missions.[71] A remarkable beginning had been made, largely inspired by Roberto de Nobili, with thousands of souls brought into the Church without fundamental change in their culture, but they were still a tiny fragment of the hundreds of millions who lived a land where almost no one but the Thomas Christians and the converts had any glimmering of the transcendent value of each human person.

---

[68] D'Sa, *History of the Catholic Church in India* II, iii-v; *Old Catholic Encyclopedia* (1913), XIV, 686; *Cambridge Modern History* IV, 744; Merces de Melo, *Recruitment and Formation of Native Clergy in India*, pp. 38-39.

[69] Schurhammer, *Francis Xavier*, p. 310.

[70] Smith, *Oxford History of India*, pp. 334, 425-428. For the English East India Company in India in the 17th century, see John Keay, *The Honourable Company; a History of the English East India Company* (New York, 1991), pp. 1-217.

[71] Its early history is covered in Volume Five of this history, Chapter 4.

China (1517-1715)

A world away from India, two worlds away from Europe, the vast and populous empire of China stood like a colossus bestriding the Orient. So isolated was China, so long had been the development of its civilization, so fixed had become the concept that the Chinese emperor ruled all mankind so long as he retained the favor of Heaven, that China from its unification by Shih Huang-ti in the third century B.C. had firmly believed that it was the only civilized country on earth. The existence of the West had been only barely and occasionally known, and when briefly learned was quickly forgotten. India was better known, though still not well, chiefly because of the remarkable surge of interest in Buddhism that came to China in the period of political instability that intervened between the fall of the Han dynasty in the early third century of the Christian era, and the rise of the T'ang dynasty at the end of the sixth century. Chinese Buddhist pilgrims visited India in the early seventh century and left accounts of their experiences and impressions which were sufficiently widely read to have been preserved for our examination.[72]

Alone among civilizations in history, the Chinese were to a great extent agnostic and unconcerned with religion, except for ancient rites and superstitions, mostly involving the dead. Confucius, who was an ethical philosopher and not a religious leader, summed up their attitude when he said "respect the spirits and keep a safe distance from them." Along with Buddhism, there was the vague concept of the "Tao" or Way, sometimes philosophical, more often magical or occult, a collection of ancient lore whose purported founder is not believed by many Chinese scholars to have actually existed.[73] Consequently China provided an extraordinary missionary opportunity, the most promising in the whole non-Christian world, as it was by far the largest, since China has always been the most populous country on earth.

Christianity had reached China in the seventh century, in one of the most remarkable efforts in all of missionary history, by Syrian and Mesopotamian Christians who took the name "Nestorian" to shield themselves from the wrath of the pagan Persian king who persecuted all Catholics as agents of his great political rival, the Roman Emperor. Actually most of them were not full-blown Nestorian heretics, but quite orthodox doctrinally. They planted the Faith in China and converted highly placed persons, so that it was maintained for almost two hundred years, until crushed by the persecution of Emperor Wu Tsung, begun in 845 before he poisoned himself with a Taoist "elixir of immortality."[74] By the middle of the sixteenth century, when St. Francis Xavier waited in vain on

---

[72] The best guide to the exceedingly difficult history of early Buddhism in China, well documented but mostly lacking in chronological hitching posts, is E. Zürcher, *The Buddhist Conquest of China; the Spread and Adaptation of Buddhism in Early Medieval China* (Leiden, 1959). For the Chinese Buddhist pilgrim Hiuen Tsang, who spent fifteen years in India (630-645), see Smith, *Oxford History of India*, pp. 180, 182, 222.

[73] Lao-tse; see Volume One, Chapter 7 of this history.

[74] See Volume Two of this history, pp. 231-234, 296-297, 344.

the island of Sancian, hoping somehow to gain admission to this tightly closed empire, the very memory of these first Christian evangelists in China had perished, along with that of the Franciscan travellers who had crossed the vast empire of the Mongols linking East and West, in the thirteenth and early fourteenth centuries.[75]

In the fourteenth century the Mongols had conquered China, first the north and then the south. The north had previously been ruled by another tribe of invaders, the Khitai, whose kings called themselves the Kin ("Golden") dynasty. They were subjugated early in the century by the great Mongol conqueror Genghis Khan, and ruled during most of the second half of the thirteenth century by Genghis' grandson Kublai Khan. It was to Kublai's capital of Peking[76] (which he built) that Western travellers came, all the way across the Eurasian land mass. The most famous of these travellers, Marco Polo, published an account which survived; Columbus believed him, though many did not. Marco Polo described the kingdom of Kublai Khan and called it "Cathay" from the Khitai who had ruled it before the Mongols. It was not until the early seventeenth century that Europeans finally realized that Cathay, about which they had heard so much in song and story, was in fact China.[77]

By 1279 Kublai Khan and his great general Bayan "of the hundred eyes" had conquered all of China. He now saw himself (and his Chinese subjects saw him) as lord of the world. He listened politely to the Christian missionaries who came to his court, but gave no indication of serious interest in conversion. In 1294, obese and alcoholic, he died after a reign of 34 years, and had no successor nearly comparable to him in dominating power.[78]

During the first half of the fourteenth century, China slid into increasing chaos as Mongol rule became more fiction than fact. A Buddhist rebellion began, led by men identified by their headgear as Red Turbans. By 1352 the Red Turbans had gained control of most of central China except for the largest cities

---

[75] See Volume Three of this history, p. 322.

[76] Now usually written Beijing. Transliteration from the Chinese herein follows the older Wade-Giles rather than the new Pinyin system. Pinyin was imposed by the Chinese government in the 1970's, in an assertion of linguistic and journalistic imperialism, totally without regard to the fact that the Pinyin transliteration does not conform to the English alphabet. The utterly aberrant use of the "x" and the "q" render Pinyin for English speakers a kind of code, necessitating consultation of a key. Such a system has no precedent and no legitimate place in Western linguistic use. The majority of Western historical scholarship on China used the Wade-Giles system, and the distinguished *Cambridge History of China*, cited repeatedly herein, continues to use it even in its recently published volumes.

[77] *Ibid.* See below, this chapter and section, for mention of the astonishing overland journey of Portuguese Jesuit lay brother Benedict de Goes early in the 17th century that finally proved the identity of Cathay and China. The best account of Kublai Khan and his domain is Morris Rossabi, *Khubilai Khan; His Life and Times* (Berkeley CA, 1988). As usual, I use the more familiar form of his name.

[78] Rossabi, *Khubilai Khan*, pp. 87-90, 93-94, 226-228. See Volume Three of this history, p. 322.

and had found a leader, who had been a Buddhist monk and had survived alone when all the rest of his peasant family starved to death in the famine following the great Yellow River flood of 1344. His name was Chu Yan-chang—a tall, frighteningly ugly man of immense talent and glacial will, a Chinese history-maker. For fifteen years he fought his way to power over the whole immensity of the Celestial Empire, defeating warlords, Mongol chiefs, and would-be new emperors one after the other. He had the support of most Buddhists; he gained the support of the Confucian elite, as the only person who could restore order. On January 23, 1368 he proclaimed himself Emperor, naming his dynasty Ming ("brilliant") and taking the appropriate reign title Hung-wu ("vast militance"). Claiming the Mandate of Heaven, this peasant's son offered the prescribed imperial sacrifices to Heaven and Earth, vowed to restore law and order throughout China, and sent envoys to Korea, Japan, and Vietnam demanding tribute.[79]

He ruled in unchallenged power for thirty years. But he made one mistake, caused by his limited Chinese world-view, which might have destroyed all he had built. In 1397 he sent an embassy which addressed the immensely powerful Timur (Tamerlane), ruler of most of central Asia, as his vassal. Timur was no man's vassal. In 1404 he marched on China with 200,000 men. The Hung-wu Emperor in his prime might have stopped him; but now he was dead, and no one else was likely to. China was saved by the Grim Reaper; the winter of 1404-05 in central Asia was the coldest in the memory of man, and the 69-year-old conqueror died on the march.[80]

The Hung-wu Emperor's retiring and scholarly grandson succeeded him as the Chien-wen ("Establishment of Civic Virtue") Emperor; his surviving sons were all passed over. One of them, the Prince of Yen, refused to accept this. In 1399 he seized Peking, and after three years of constant war also took Nanking. On July 17, 1402 he became the Yung-lo ("Increased Joy") Emperor.[81]

He was one of China's greatest Emperors, even if not fully a match for his history-making father. From the beginning of his reign he showed a strong interest in extending his power overseas. In its first full year he ordered Fujian

---

[79] Edward L. Dreyer, *Early Ming China, a Political History, 1355-1435* (Stanford CA, 1982), pp. 18-39, 63-64, 85, 116; *Cambridge History of China*, VII, 11, 39-40, 44-45, 57. The Chinese practice of assigning names to reigns is at first sight very confusing to the Western reader; but once an imperial dynasty has been established, it seems better to use them than the given name of the ruler, which scarcely appears in any records after his coronation. Therefore each of the Ming emperors will be referred to herein only by his regnal name. (To add to the confusion, an emperor also received a third name after he died, but this posthumous name will be ignored in this brief survey.) For a good explanation of the content and meaning of the official Chinese veneration of Heaven and its relation to the Emperors, see *Cambridge History of China*, VIII (2), 848-849.

[80] Dreyer, *Early Ming China*, pp. 66, 83-84, 100-106, 145, 177; *Cambridge History of China* VII 139-142, 173-174, 223, 259; VIII (2) 867, 899, 904, 955, 960. See Volume Three of this history, pp. 457-458.

[81] Dreyer, *Early Ming China*, pp. 152, 157-158, 161, 164-167, 169; *Cambridge History of China* VII, 181, 195, 198-199, 200-201.

province to produce 137 ships, five other southern provinces to produce two hundred more, and 188 flat-bottomed ships to be refitted for service on the high seas. By 1405 he had a fleet of 62 "treasure ships" and 255 smaller ships ready to deploy. The "treasure ships" were the largest wooden ships ever built, 444 feet long and 186 feet wide, with nine masts, 12 enormous square sails, thousand-pound anchors, watertight compartments, balanced rudders (not developed in Europe until the 18th century), and 24 bronze cannon, crewed with 28,000 men. Nothing in the world of the fifteenth century could stand for a moment against such giant ships. They dwarfed Prince Henry the Navigator's venturesome little caravels, developed later in the century. This overpowering fleet was put under the command of the physically imposing eunuch Cheng Ho, who first took it on a long voyage through the China Sea and the Straits of Malacca to India, stopping at Java, Sumatra, Malacca, Ceylon, and the port of Calicut in southern India where Vasco da Gama would land at the very end of the century. All these places were claimed as vassal tributary states to China, and all hastened to send gifts to the Yung-lo Emperor, including exotic objects and strange animals. By 1407 over 1,680 ships had been constructed or refitted for long ocean voyages.[82]

In 1409 Cheng Ho returned to the Indian Ocean with 48 treasure ships and 30,000 men. He restored King Vijaya Bahu VI of Ceylon to power, who consequently acknowledged himself tributary to China. The expedition reinforced Chinese domination of the crucially located city of Malacca. Thus many of the places the Portuguese came to rule after Vasco da Gama's epochal voyage at the end of this century were brought under the sway of the Chinese Empire at this time. If Chinese naval power had been preserved to the end of the century, the whole history of the world, or at least of the Orient, might have been very different.[83]

In 1412 the Yung-lo Emperor ordered a fourth immense naval expedition, with 63 vessels and nearly 29,000 men. Its destination this time was the Muslim Middle East, specifically the Iranian port of Ormuz at the narrowest point in the Persian Gulf, later a prize of the Portuguese conquerors. Cheng Ho was again in command, escorting ambassadors home from 18 countries outside of China which had acknowledged Chinese supremacy. After passing through the Maldive Islands and into the Arabian Sea, this expedition not only reached Ormuz, but then turned south to the Horn of Africa, where they reached Mogadishu in Somalia and obtained a giraffe from Kenya, presented with great fanfare to the Yung-lo Emperor. The Chinese government officials convinced themselves it had bowed to his august presence. In 1417 another naval expedition commanded by Cheng Ho retraced the route of the expedition of 1413-14, again reaching Africa, this time going as far south as the city of Mombasa on the coast of Kenya, where da Gama was later to depart from the African coast for India. Cheng Ho's

---

[82] Louise Levathes, *When China Ruled the Sea; the Treasure Fleet of the Dragon Throne*, 1405-1433 (New York, 1994), pp. 75-76, 80-82, 87, 10; *Cambridge History of China*, VII, 232-233.

[83] Levathes, *When China Ruled the Sea*, pp. 103-10007, 116-118; *Cambridge History of China* VII, 233.

expedition of 1419 brought back lions, leopards, camels, ostriches, zebras, rhinoceroses, antelopes and another giraffe for the curiosity-loving Emperor. But the Chinese were not interested in exploring unknown coasts. Full knowledge of the coasts along which they sailed was common property of navigators of India and of the Muslim Middle East.[84]

In 1421 the Yung-lo Emperor formally dedicated Peking as the capital of the Chinese empire, and sent out another fleet, which split at Sumatra, with part of it continuing on once more to the Middle East and the Horn of Africa. But in his last years (he was now in his sixties and ailing) the Yung-lo Emperor was fighting the Mongols, still dangerously capable warriors. Returning to Peking from Mongolia, the Yung-lo Emperor died, apparently of the effects of several strokes. His very non-military eldest son, a dedicated student of the Confucian classics, ascended the throne as the Hung-hsi ("vast splendor") Emperor in 1424; but the splendor he sought did not include treasure ships. He ordered their voyages stopped immediately and forbade the building of any more, calling it an unnecessary expense. A year later he suddenly died at 47 and was succeeded by his son, the Hsan-te ("Propagating Virtue") Emperor. He temporarily revived the great fleets, sending Cheng Ho on his last expedition, to Vietnam, Indonesia, Malacca, Ceylon, and Calicut and Cochin in India. Appropriately enough, the great Chinese admiral died on his ship in the Indian Ocean during that final voyage. In 1435 the Hsan-te Emperor died suddenly and young, succeeded by his son who was only seven years old. The palace eunuchs who soon established their domination over the boy Emperor had no interest whatsoever in far voyaging. The construction of oceangoing ships was halted in China and the total number of ships reduced by half. It was never to be resumed on a large scale. The opportunity for China to become the leading naval power in the world, similar to Great Britain in the 19th century, was not to be realized.[85]

With the successors of the Yung-lo Emperor began the great moral decline of Chinese Buddhism, recognized by Buddhist as well as Western scholars and historians.[86] The Chinese court was increasingly dominated by eunuchs. Mutilated so that they could serve without temptation in the imperial harem with thousands of women, they tended to be profoundly selfish since they could have no families, interested only in the power and wealth they could acquire by any means they found available. In 1451 began the sale of Buddhist ordinations as a means of raising additional funds for the imperial treasury which they controlled. In 1477 the logs of Cheng Ho's naval expeditions were destroyed by the vice-president of the Ministry of War, hoping to foreclose any attempt to revive them. If they had been revived and gone farther down the east African coast, they could

---

[84] Levathes, *When China Ruled the Sea*, pp. 137-142, 149-151; *Cambridge History of China* VII, 235.

[85] Dreyer, *Early Ming China*, pp. 181, 183, 222, 225-226, 236; Levathes, *When China Ruled the Sea*, pp. 151, 163-164, 170-175; *Cambridge History of China* VII 227-228, 235-236, 241-242, 272, 278, 283, 303-307.,

[86] *Cambridge History of China* VIII (2), 895-896, 919.

have met Bartholomew Dias at the Cape of Good Hope in 1488. But it was not to be.[87]

In 1511 Malacca, still considered to be under the protection of the Chinese empire and still visited occasionally by Chinese ships, was taken by the great Portuguese commander Afonso de Albuquerque.[88] Thus did the bold Western seamen first come to the attention of the Chinese, who had discarded the only effective means of dealing with them when they dismantled their mighty navy. In 1514 came the first Portuguese voyage to China, captained by one Jorge Alvares, of which nothing but the fact is known. The next year there followed Rafael Perestrello, an Italian living on Portuguese Madeira, who told his countrymen (rather too optimistically) that the Chinese wanted friendship and trade with the Portuguese. In 1517 the Portuguese sent an official embassy to the Chinese Emperor on a fleet of eight ships commanded by Fernao Pires de Andrade, who sailed into the Canton River but was not permitted in the city. After a month of waiting for permission that never came, he sailed up to the city anyway, firing cannon salutes that terrified the Chinese. Local officials allowed trading, and Fernao Pires de Andrade came back with "a very rich cargo." But his brother Simon, who followed him to Canton in 1519, built a fort there without permission, knocked an imperial official's hat off, set up and used a gallows, and kidnapped children of some of the Chinese traders to sell them as slaves. In consequence of the behavior of Simon de Andrade and in view of the Portuguese conquest of Malacca, the Portuguese ambassador was coldly received in Peking. When the Emperor died the next spring, in 1521, only 29 years old but hopelessly alcoholic, the Portuguese ambassador was thrown into prison (where he died) and all foreigners were ordered to leave China at once. The Portuguese in particular were regarded by the imperial authorities as pirates, and attacked and punished as such.[89]

Nearly twenty years passed before there was significant new contact between the Portuguese and China. Then in 1539 Portuguese merchants came to the island of Ning-po off the coast, a pirate stronghold, to trade. They continued active on some of the offshore islands for the next twelve years, until St. Francis Xavier first arrived at Sancian island in 1551. As already described, he died there the next year without ever having been able to enter mainland China. In 1552, the year of St. Francis Xavier's death, two Portuguese merchants, arriving on the Kwangtung coast near Canton, persuaded (or bribed) the responsible Chinese official there to allow Portuguese trading in return for payment of duties, entirely without the knowledge or approval of the Emperor. In 1557 the

---

[87] *Cambridge History of China* VII 322-329, 338-339; VIII (2), 895; Levathes, *When China Ruled the Sea*, p. 179

[88] For the conquest of Malacca see Volume Three of this history, pp. 699-703.

[89] *Cambridge History of China* VII, 411, 433-434, 436-437, 441; VIII (2), 336-340; Jayne, *da Gama and Successors*, pp. 227, 229; R. S. Whiteway, *The Rise of Portuguese Power in India, 1497-1558* (Patna, India, 1979), pp. 338-340. For the Portuguese in the Indian Ocean in the first decade of the 16th century, see Volume Three, Chapter 15 of this history.

Portuguese seized Macao, on a narrow peninsula south of Canton harbor. The neck of the peninsula was walled off from the mainland, and the Chinese officials decided to give the Portuguese control of it, since the enclosing wall would keep them out of the rest of the mainland, though they were granted permission to trade in Canton two or three months out of the year. By 1562, when the first Jesuits arrived in Macao, the new town had nearly a thousand Portuguese, with two small churches.[90]

In 1565 the Chinese imperial government refused to receive a Portuguese ambassador, demanding to know why the Portuguese had not yet yielded back Malacca to them, while missionary François Pérez was repeatedly refused entry into China by officials in Canton because he knew no Chinese. That year the first Jesuit residence was established in Macao, Pérez perforce going there. In 1565 and 1566 piracy was almost completely suppressed along the east coast of China by a major campaign initiated by the Chia-ching Emperor. However, he died in 1567, like several of his predecessors, from the effects of drinking Taoist "elixirs of immortality." He was succeeded by his eldest surviving son as the Lung-ch'ing Emperor, but he appears to have been retarded and was unable to speak in public. The defeat of the pirates caused maritime trade to be reopened; a customs office was established at the request of the governor of Fukien, and the city of Yeh-kang near modern Amoy in Fukien was designated as the port through which the permitted maritime trade should pass. In 1568 a Spanish Jesuit, Juan Bautista Ribeira, later to be secretary to Jesuit general St. Francis Borgia, landed without permission on the coast of China, though he did not know the language. He was caught and sent back to Europe, where he reported the penetration of China to be impossible except by armed invasion. Such an invasion was also advocated by his fellow Jesuit missionary Melchior Nunes Barreto.[91]

In 1573 the handicapped Lung-ch'ing Emperor died and was succeeded by his ten-year-old half-brother as the Wan-li Emperor. He was a bright, intelligent child, much attracted to Buddhism, but as he passed through his adolescent years he was increasingly corrupted by the availability of unlimited gratification of his every desire. He became absorbed in his harem and increasingly under the control of his eunuchs. He became so fat that he was ashamed to appear in public, and completely stopped doing so. He held the Dragon Throne for no less than 47 years in apparent security, but at his death in 1620 the Manchu people directly north of China had been mostly united by the great warrior Nurhachi, and had defeated a Chinese army against odds of two to one in the Battle of Siyanggiayan in Manchuria in 1619. Meanwhile the most honest and upright

---

[90] *Cambridge History of China* VII 491, 496, 498; VIII (2) 343-345; Jayne, *da Gama and Successors*, p. 231.
[91] *Cambridge History of China* VII, 504, 512-513, 559; VIII (2) 345; George H. Dunne, S.J., *Generation of Giants; the Story of the Jesuits in China in the Last Decades of the Ming Dynasty* (Notre Dame IND, 1962), pp. 15-16; Michael Cooper, S.J., *Rodrigues the Interpreter; an Early Jesuit in Japan and China* (New York, 1974), p. 270.

government officials had formed the Tung-lin Academy to try to improve public administration.[92]

In the same year of 1573 when the Wan-li Emperor's long reign began, Alessandro Valignano was appointed superior of all the Jesuit missions in the Orient, with the title of Visitor. In 1574 he sailed from Lisbon with 41 Jesuits. In the following year Pope Gregory XIII made Macao a diocese, suffragan to Goa and covering all of China and Japan, and appointed to it the Portuguese Jesuit Melchior Carneiro.   And in 1577 Valignano, visiting Macao after reviewing the then very promising missionary prospects in Japan, declared that Jesuit missionaries in China must familiarize themselves with Chinese customs and civilization, living as Chinese. He wrote to the Jesuit general: "The only possible way of penetration will be utterly different from that which has been adopted up to now in all the other missions in these countries."[93]

In 1577 a young Italian named Matteo Ricci was received in private audience by Pope Gregory XIII, along with several other Jesuit missionaries. He had been superbly educated by the great St. Robert Bellarmine and the mathematician and astronomer Christopher Clavius, who had been the primary maker of the Gregorian calendar. Assigned to India, he set out immediately from Italy to Portugal. The fleet on which he embarked left Lisbon harbor in March 1578, rounded the Cape of Good Hope in June, and arrived in Goa in September—one of the fastest early passages of that famous route. In 1579 Jesuit Father Matthew Ruggieri arrived in Macao from Goa and, in accordance with the orders of the far-sighted Valignano, began intensive study of Chinese, probably the most difficult major language in the world, with its many homophonic words and four tones for each syllable. Valignano's vision was by no means universally shared.[94] Ruggieri testifies to the immense importance of this Jesuit Visitor for Oriental missionary work as follows:

> If Father Alessandro Valignano were not here, I do not know what would happen to this business of the conversion of China. I write this because I hear certain ones say: "What is the sense of this Father occupying himself with this sort of thing when he could be of service in the other ministries of the Society? It is a waste of time for him to learn the Chinese language and to consecrate himself to a hopeless enterprise."[95]

---

[92] *Cambridge History of China* VII, 514-515, 531, 540, 543, 553-556, 579-t8e, 591; VIII (2) 364, 799-800; Vincent Cronin, *The Wise Man from the West* (Garden City NY, 1957), pp. 124-125, 164.

[93] *Cambridge History of China* VIII (2) 793; Dunne, *Generation of Giants*, p. 17 (quote); D'Sa, *History of the Catholic Church in India*, I, 130; Chappoulie, *Indochine*, I, 5. Valignano's approach to the Oriental missions, first put in practice by Matteo Ricci, began to bear fruit about twenty years before Roberto de Nobili applied it to India (see previous section, this chapter).

[94] Cronin, *Wise Man from the West*, pp. 27-29, 47-48; Dunne, *Generation of Giants*, p. 24. For the Gregorian calendar see Chapter Seven, above.

[95] Dunne, *Generation of Giants*, p. 24.

So was the first necessity of real missionary work—speaking the native language at least reasonably well—overlooked or explicitly rejected by the Portuguese and even the Jesuits at Macao. Valignano would not tolerate such blindness. He declared that Chinese converts should not be pressured to live just like the Portuguese, as many of them did in Macao as in the rather similar enclave of Goa in India. He removed the Jesuit superior at Macao, sending him to Japan, and provided an unusual degree of autonomy for Jesuit missionaries working outside Macao, inside the Chinese Empire. As yet there were no such missionaries. But in 1582 Matteo Ricci arrived in Macao, ordered there personally by Valignano, and plunged immediately into the study of Chinese and the preparation of the first formal description of China and its culture by a Westerner, which Valignano had directed him to write. In 1583 Ricci and Ruggieri, now speaking Chinese well enough to be able to make themselves understood, went to the Chinese city of Shiu-hing, in which the local governor allowed them to stay because of his special interest in Ricci's skills as a mathematician and clockmaker. Settling in Shiu-hing with their interpreter Philip, a Christian born of Chinese parents in Macao, Ricci and Ruggieri at first wore the gray robe of Buddhist monks, but soon saw the consequence when the governor approved their building a house, but not a church, saying there were plenty of Buddhist pagodas where they could worship. Eventually Ricci adopted the distinctive mandarin dress, with enthusiastic endorsement from Valignano.[96]

In 1584 Ricci and Ruggieri successfully survived what could have been a very serious incident. A boy who had been throwing stones at their new house was caught by Ricci's Indian servant. Despite the fact that he was released less than three hours later, the story was spread that he had been given a drug to make him mute and had been imprisoned in the missionaries' house for three days, with the purpose of selling him as a slave in Macao. The local examining magistrate, who served as a judge, heard the evidence. Three men clad in the purple uniforms of mandarins (graduates) stepped forward to confirm the accuracy of the missionaries' account. The magistrate had the offending boy given thirty strokes with the terrible bamboo cane with which Chinese judges inflicted their penalties. Shortly after that, in the spring of the year, Ricci baptized his first Chinese, a young man on the point of death. In the fall he published a translation of the Ten Commandments into Chinese, and then a translation, with revisions to fit China, of the Latin catechism, a book of 78 pages marked with the IHS emblem of the Jesuits and entitled "A True Account of God." The 1,200 copies of the first printing were soon sold out, and more were required. In 1583 Ricci declared: "I can now converse [in Chinese] with everyone without an interpreter and can write and read fairly well."[97]

In 1585, in far-distant Rome, Pope Gregory XIII very wisely (as later events were to show) restricted missionary activity in China to Jesuits, who had

---

[96] *Ibid.*, pp. 19-21, 25, 32-33; Cronin, *Wise Man from the West*, pp. 39, 41, 50-51, 102; *Cambridge History of China* VIII (2), 363, 794-795, 797.

[97] Cronin, *Wise Man from the West*, pp. 63-69, 72-73; Dunne, *Generation of Giants*, p. 29; *Cambridge History of China* VIII (2), 796 (quote).

in fact been the only order so far to seriously attempt it. Ruggieri, not completely in sympathy with the new missionary method, returned to Macao, ostensibly for consultation with Valignano. Ricci, remaining in Shiu-hing, made instruments and clocks to attract the Chinese, along with globes of the world and accurate sundials. In mid-summer a young Portuguese named Anthony de Almeida arrived as Ricci's new assistant, replacing Ruggieri. About 50 adult Chinese had now been converted—a very small but real beginning. In 1588 a petition calling for Ricci's expulsion was drawn up by a hundred influential Cantonese, but rejected by the leading officials of Shiu-hing. Before the end of that year Valignano sent Ruggieri to Rome to persuade the Pope to send his own embassy to the Ming Emperor. Because of the confusion caused by the succession of four Popes in less than 18 months (1590-92), Ruggieri was not able to accomplish his mission, and disappears from the China story.[98]

In the spring of 1589 Ricci and Almeida baptized 18 more Chinese, including their first woman convert. (Chinese women were very difficult to approach, being kept most of the time at home and physically prevented from walking much by the cruel binding of their feet when they were little girls.) In August of that year the missionaries were allowed to take residence in the city of Shao-chou in the northern part of Kwangtung province, where the next year Ch'ü T'ai-su, brilliant son of a great poet and historian who had squandered his inheritance on alchemy, became the first Chinese scholar to select Ricci as his master. At the end of the year they were joined by two Chinese Christians whom Valignano had made candidates for Jesuit lay brotherhood. In 1592 Ricci prepared a Latin translation of four of the Chinese classics and the first to Latinize the name of the great ethical philosopher Kung Fu-tze to Confucius.[99] He had now come to the first clear understanding by a Westerner of the religious situation in China, which he rightly thought uniquely favorable to evangelization.

The earliest religion of the country contained far less magic and far fewer logical errors than any primitive creed known to Ricci. A single, omnipotent, supreme being was worshipped as Heaven, together with various subsidiary protective spirits of stars, mountains, rivers, and the four corners of the world. Virtue pleased, vice displeased Heaven, which rewarded or punished men in this world according to their deeds. So reverent was religious awe that only the Emperor and high officials might perform sacrifice, and the people never attributed to Heaven or other spirits the reprehensible conduct with which Egyptians, Greeks and Romans defiled their gods. The primitive religion no longer existed in its original form. Over a thousand years before Ricci's arrival, its beliefs and practices had already become partially incorporated in three main sects, to one or more of which most Chinese now claimed to belong. Of these the most flourishing, the most highly esteemed and boasting the largest number of

---

[98] Cronin, *Wise Man from the West*, pp. 80-82; Dunne, *Generation of Giants*, pp. 30, 231; *Cambridge History of China* VIII (2), 796.

[99] Cronin, *Wise Man from the West*, pp. 82, 92-96, 101-102; Dunme, *Generation of giants*, p. 31.

great books was Confucianism, the national philosophical system of China, professed—at least in public—by the majority of graduates [mandarins], and preserving the essentials of the primitive theology, in particular the Emperor's sacrifice to Heaven, more as a state religion than a vital creed. It had been handed down in the most curious fashion, not consciously chosen or proclaimed, but imbibed through education, the essential criterion for passing state examinations being a thorough knowledge of the works of Confucius.[100]

In 1595 Ricci tried but failed to reach Peking. During the summer he wrote probably his most famous book in Chinese, "On Friendship," followed by "The Art of Memory." These two Chinese works in particular established his reputation as a mandarin, which remained with him for the rest of his life.[101]

In June 1598 the persevering Ricci returned to Nanking with an old acquaintance, Wang Chun-ming, who was going to Peking for the Emperor's birthday. Accompanied by Jesuit missionary Lazzaro Cattaneo and Brother Sebastian, Ricci travelled up the Grand Canal and arrived at the port for Peking in September, from which he travelled to the capital by sedan chair, the proper conveyance for a mandarin. He stayed at the home of a mandarin who had previously supported him. Ricci was unable even to give his presents to the Emperor (to say nothing of seeing him personally) because suspicion of foreigners at the Ming court had been sharply increased by the recent war with Japan's great conqueror Hideyoshi (who had just died, though knowledge of his death may not have reached Peking when Ricci was there). So he left Peking disappointed, before the end of the year.[102] In 1599 he wrote:

> As for what you tell me about the desire to hear of a great movement of conversions in China, know that I and all the others who reside here do not think of anything else day or night, and it is for this purpose that, having left our country and our dear friends, we are here, clothed and shod in Chinese style, speaking, drinking, eating and living according to the customs of China.[103]

Ricci returned to Nanking on horseback, and was visited by its highest mandarins. One of them gave him this splendid praise: "This father is modest and asks for nothing; he finds his pleasure in practicing virtue and honoring heaven; every morning and evening resolving to guard his thoughts, words, and actions." In April he vanquished the Buddhist monk Huang San-hui in argument, challenging him to create something when he said that man can be made into God. Ricci bought a house in Nanking that nobody else wanted because it was reputedly haunted. In August he wrote to Girolama Costa in Rome saying, with a profoundly wise realism: "Our credit and reputation have so grown that it can be

---

[100] Cronin, *Wise Man from the West*, pp. 57-58.

[101] *Ibid.*, pp. 102-104, 108-113, 118-120; Dunne, *Generation of Giants*, pp. 39-41, 44, 47; *Cambridge history of China* VIII (2), 798-799.

[102] Cronin, *Wise Man from the West*, pp. 121-125; Dunne, *Generation of Giants*, pp. 50, 54-55, 58; *Cambridge History of China*, VIII (2), 364, 799-800.

[103] Dunne, *Generation of Giants*, p. 124.

said that we have doubled our gains in China this year . . . [but] this is not a time for harvesting, or even for sowing, but for clearing the soil."[104]

In the spring of 1600 the second edition of Ricci's world map in Chinese was published, with a laudatory preface by the Ministry of Civil Appointments. His greatest future convert, Hsü Kuang-ch'i, visited him in Nanking and had his first discussions with him. In May Ricci set out again for Peking, but was intercepted on his way by the corrupt eunuch Ma T'ang. On inspecting Ricci's baggage, Ma T'ang found three crucifixes, objects which inspired horror in many Chinese; he accused Ricci of attempted fetish killing of the Emperor, and filed charges against him. Meanwhile, back in Rome, Pope Clement VIII reversed Gregory XIII's order confining the Chinese mission to the Jesuits, a well-meant but disastrous action that ultimately led to probably the worst mistake in Catholic missionary history.[105]

In January 1601 the Wan-li Emperor, having heard of Ricci's wonderful clocks, granted him a special license not only to come to Peking but to present gifts to him. Ricci came bearing paintings of Christ and the Blessed Virgin Mary, a breviary with gold-thread binding, a polychrome glass cross, an atlas, two clocks, two prisms, a clavichord, mirrors, sand clocks, the Four Gospels in Chinese, and a "unicorn" (rhinoceros) tusk. He had an elaborate memorial drafted by a mandarin skilled in such work, explaining how he had come from the Far West to live in China, having heard of its good government, and wished to be accepted as a Chinese citizen and imperial subject. He explained that his education in the West was comparable to that of China and entitled him to the robes of a graduate (mandarin). The Wan-li Emperor was delighted, especially with the clocks. When one of them ran down, Ricci was specially summoned to the Forbidden City, with its multitudinous courtyards and elaborate dragon decorations, to wind it. Cleverly he said that he would need several days to regulate the clock and teach the imperial officials how to tend it, and used that time to become well known at court, where he was a great curiosity but also much and sincerely admired by leading Chinese whose culture and language he had so thoroughly adopted. Ricci never saw the Wan-li Emperor personally, for this Emperor had never showed himself to anyone but his wives and some of his eunuchs for many years; but he had Ricci's portrait painted, and in response to his request for information about the rulers of the Far West, Ricci gave him a picture showing the Pope and the kings and queens of Europe. Ricci was invited back into the palace to teach music and the clavichord. He demonstrated the eight-tone European musical scale, unknown in China, and played madrigals on the clavichord.[106]

---

[104] *Ibid.*, pp. 56, 62-64 (second quote on 64), 67 (first quote); Cronin, *Wise Man from the West*, pp. 125-126, 132-138, 140; *Cambridge History of China* VIII (2), 800.

[105] Cronin, *Wise Man from the West*, pp. 140-148, 150-153; Dunne, *Generations of Giants*, pp. 68, 74-76, 254. This mistake was the Chinese rites decision of 1704 (see below).

[106] Cronin, *Wise Man from the West*, pp. 155-168.

Late in February Ricci was arrested on specious charges by the Ministry of Rites. Though promptly acquitted, he was then sent to the Castle of the Barbarians, where ambassadors from many foreign countries were kept in rather uncomfortable quarters. Conversing with these ambassadors, he found one from Muslim Turkestan who knew of Europe, and called China Khitai (Cathay), convincing Ricci that Cathay and China were identical. Ricci's mandarin friends were outraged that he was kept in such a place, and he was treated with increasing honor to make up for it. However, he was disappointed that the Wan-li Emperor did not appear for a scheduled audience with him.[107] In March Ricci went to the Acting Minister of Rites saying:

> We have come to preach the law of the Lord of Heaven in the Middle Kingdom [China] by command of our superiors, and to Peking in order to offer gifts to His Majesty in gratitude for having been allowed to remain so many years in his country. We desire no office, nor a return for our presents; only permission to remain as before in the Middle Kingdom, either in Peking or in some other city that His Majesty may designate.[108]

In May Ricci was released from the Castle of the Barbarians, and informed by the Wan-Li Emperor's eunuchs that he might remain in Peking. Ricci had free entry into the palace to regulate the clocks, and began to discuss Christianity with mandarins close to the throne, who were much impressed both by him personally and by his good standing with the Emperor. He was now a recognized figure in the academic and social world of the mandarins, known as Li Ma-tou, the closest Chinese could come to pronouncing his Italian name. He described the charitable works of the Church in Christian countries, and the universal Christian practice of monogamy, which Chinese tended to admire very much in the abstract but find exceedingly difficult to practice.[109]

There were now three missionary houses in China outside Peking: at Nanking, Nan-ch'ang, and Shao-chou. In 1602 Ricci received a report on them from young Sicilian Jesuit Nicholas Langobardo, who was to remain in China as a missionary until he died there at the age of 95. Conversions were being made, though very slowly. In an elitist society like China, the increasing prestige of "Li Ma-tou" as a mandarin was bound to help his cause. In 1603 Ricci baptized the brilliant Hsü Kuang-chi, who was rising rapidly in this group, as "Paul;" he soon became the native Christian leader in China. In that same year Ricci published his most ambitious Chinese book about Christianity, an apologetic dialogue entitled "True Meaning of the Lord of Heaven," using arguments from Chinese classics and tradition to show the unity of mankind and the basic similarities between China and the West despite all their superficial differences, and advocating a return to the early monotheism of China, in the days of Confucius.

---

[107] *Ibid.*, pp. 171-175, 178-179; Dunne, *Generation of Giants*, pp. 79-80.
[108] Cronin, Wise Man from the West, p. 176.
[109] *Ibid.*, pp. 179-182; Dunne, *Generation of Giants*, p. 83.

This apologetic was brilliantly conceived and went through several editions. Li Ma-tou was actually becoming famous as a Chinese writer.[110]

Also in 1603 the great Jesuit Visitor Alessandro Valignano came back from Japan to Macao, where he dedicated its new church, but split the missions in Macao completely away from the missions inside China proper. He promised to send some missionaries intended for Japan, at that time a field of great promise, to China instead. He gave permission for three young Chinese, born of Christian parents at Macao, to become Jesuits. He made the first ruling on the question of Chinese rites for the dead, saying (with Ricci but against Langobardo) that they were not inherently idolatrous or superstitious, but simply a traditional way of honoring the dead, like our custom of placing flowers on a grave, without expecting the dead to smell them! At the end of 1602 Valignano had sent Jesuit lay brother Benedict de Goes from India on an incredible journey, no less than to cross central Asia from India to China and establish once and for all whether Cathay and China were the same. In February 1603 de Goes set off from the Mogul capital of Lahore for Kabul in Afghanistan. In September he joined a caravan to Chinese central Asia, crossing the Hindu Kush and the Pamirs, which had defied even Alexander the Great, until he reached the town of Yarkand (in Sinkiang, or Chinese Turkestan), where he heard Cathay mentioned as a caravan destination. But no caravan to Cathay was permitted to leave for a year; de Goes had to wait. The next year he crossed the grim Takla Makan desert, and fell in with a party of Muslims travelling westward as he was travelling east, to tell him they were on their way back from Cathay after staying at the Castle of Barbarians in Peking. In the fall of 1605 de Goes crossed the Gobi desert to the Chinese frontier garrison town of Suchow, where he heard Cambaluc, the version of the name of Kublai Khan's capital used by Marco Polo, used for Peking. In April 1606 he wrote to Ricci that he had established the identity of Cathay and China. The letter did not arrive until November, but Ricci promptly sent a Chinese Christian and Jesuit candidate, baptized Juan Fernandes, to help de Goes. Late in March he arrived in Suchow, to find de Goes gaunt and emaciated, having been robbed of all his money and therefore unable to buy food. He died in April, faithful to the last. His deathbed message for Ricci was: "You should never trust the Mohammedans; as for the journey, it is very long, difficult and dangerous, and I advise no one to undertake it again." None did, until Sven Hedin and Aurel Stein at the turn of the twentieth century.[111]

In 1605 missionary Alfonso Vagnoni wrote from Nanking: "Incredible is the reputation which good Father Matteo Ricci enjoys among the Chinese, and the extent to which he is visited by important personages and esteemed throughout the whole empire of China. . . . He captivates everyone by the graciousness and suavity of his manners, by his conversation and by the solid

---

[110] Cronin, *Wise Man from the West*, pp. 193-196; Dunne, *Generation of Giants*, p. 60; *Cambridge History of China* VIII (2), 799.

[111] Cronin, *Wise Man from the West*, pp. 186-188, 219-233; Dunne, *Generation of Giants*, p. 102; Cooper, *Rodrigues the Interpreter*, p. 271.

virtue which his life exhibits."[112] Valignano again endorsed Ricci's view of the permissibility of the ordinary Chinese rites honoring ancestors, pointing out that Confucius had taught them yet professed total agnosticism about life after death. However, the solemn rites for Confucius himself were held idolatrous. That year the Buddhists demanded Ricci's exclusion from the capital, but the Wan-li Emperor would not let him go, since he was still fascinated by the clocks and wanted Ricci to be available to keep them in good working order. Ricci then wrote a Christian critique of Buddhism called the "Twenty-five Sentences," remarkable for its courtesy and gentleness in dealing with the false Buddhist doctrines.[113] Convert Paul Hsü wrote at the end: "Today we have the True Man [Ricci], learned and great, who brings our moral code to completion and protects our court; is he not a treasure even more precious [than the nest of the ancient phoenix]? Let us praise him to the heights."[114] By the summer of that year, when Ricci bought a large house in Peking with the aid of loans from his mandarin friends, there were over 200 Christians in Peking and about a thousand nation-wide.[115]

In 1606 the great Jesuit leader Valignano died at 65, leaving behind 130 missionaries and 250,000 converts in Japan, having transformed the concept of missionary work in the civilized countries of the Orient and provided a model for Ricci while invariably giving him support. Immediately after Valignano's death a controversy exploded in Macao between its bishop and an apostolic delegate, who excommunicated each other. The bishop's supporters blamed the Jesuits, and some of them spread to the Chinese the story of a Jesuit plot to conquer China with the aid of the Portuguese and the Japanese (feared in China for their martial prowess). Many Chinese in Canton believed the story, and Kwangtung province was put in a state of defense. Brother Francis, one of the first two native Chinese Jesuit lay brothers, lay ill with malaria at Canton. The rumors about prospective foreign aggression swirled through the city. A renegade Christian exposed Brother Francis. He was tortured and twice severely beaten, which caused his death. He was China's first martyr.[116]

In 1607 Ricci and Paul Hsü collaborated on a Chinese translation of the first six books of Euclid—heavy going for the Chinese, whose mathematical education was greatly lacking at many points. In that year Ricci received a new missionary companion, the zealous Italian Jesuit Sebastian de Ursis, sent to him by Valignano before he died. De Ursis became a close friend and invaluable co-worker. In 1608 Ricci published another apologetic dialogue in Chinese, "Ten Truths Contrary to Common Opinion," in which he discussed the value of time, the problem of evil, the advantage of reflecting on death and the Judgment, the wisdom of silence, the rationale of fasting, the benefits of self-examination, the

---

[112] Dunne, *Generation of Giants*, p. 92.

[113] *Ibid.*, pp. 288-292, 294; Cronin, *Wise Man from the West*, pp. 202-204.

[114] Cronin, *Wise Man from the West*, p. 204.

[115] *Ibid.*, pp. 210-211.

[116] *Ibid.*, pp. 211-212; Dunne, *Generation of Giants*, pp. 118-119; *Cambridge History of China* VIII (2), 350.

folly of seeking to know the future through charms and oracles (the Chinese were particularly prone to this superstitious folly), and the miserable state of the avaricious rich man. It was considered a masterpiece and went through many printings. In August Ricci's friend, geographer Li Chih-tsao, joined him in Peking. He had been helping the Christians for some years, but had not been baptized because he would not give up polygamy. Now he sent away all his concubines but one, whom he selected for his wife. She and all her family became Christians along with him. Li was given the Christian name of Luke, and established the first Chinese Sodality of the Blessed Virgin Mary. Also in August, Ricci wrote to his brother that there were already more than two thousand Christians in China, among them many scholars. At that same time a new Christian community was established in Shanghai by Lazzaro Cattaneo, and made rapid progress in conversions largely due to the presence in it of Paul Hsü; there were a hundred in its first year.[117]

In 1609 Ricci received a permanent exemption from taxes on his house, indirectly acknowledging his official right to live in Peking. But his health had begun to decline under the constant strain of his apostolate. Feeling this, he began and completed in the course of that year a history of the missions in China, an absolutely indispensable volume on which all accounts of their early days are based. Ricci wrote to Jesuit vice-provincial Francisco Pasio, saying that the apostolate in China should be completely separated from Macao and carried on "prudently, without fanfare, and with good books and reasoned arguments, proving to the scholars the truth of our doctrine."[118]

On May 11, 1610 Ricci died a holy death in Peking, saying prophetically to his missionary associate de Ursis: "I leave before you a door open to great merits, but not without numerous dangers and much labor." Longobardo succeeded him as head of the Jesuit mission to China. Ricci's body lay in state in his new church in Peking. Large crowds including some of the leading mandarins of China came to honor him. The Wan-li Emperor granted him a lot in a cemetery where only the greatest Chinese had been buried, under a hexagonal brick chapel with a plaque reading: "To one who loved righteousness and wrote books. To Li Ma-tou the Far Westerner, from Huang Chi-shih, Governor of Peking." At Easter of the next year (1611) Yang T'ing-yen, an elderly and influential mandarin, was converted after many discussions. He put away his second wife, was baptized "Michael" in his full official ceremonial dress, and became an ardent Christian, converting many of his family and relatives and writing tracts explaining the tenets of Christianity and the incompatibility of Christianity with Buddhism. Along with Paul Hsü and Luke Li, he became one of "the three pillars of the Catholic Church in China."[119]

---

[117] Cronin, *Wise Man from the West*, pp. 213-214, 217-28, 238-243; Dunne, *Generation of Giants*, pp. 98-101, 104-105, 112.

[118] Dunne, *Generation of Giants*, pp. 87 (quote), 243; Cronin, *Wise Man from t he West*, pp. 243-246.

[119] Cronin, *Wise Man from the West*, pp. 253-254 (first quote on 254); Dunne, *Generation of Giants*, pp. 106-107, 109-110, 112-114 (second quote on 112-113). A later

Matteo Ricci, one of the very few greatest missionaries who ever lived, had laid a solid foundation for the Faith among a people who nowhere had known it. But with the strong sense of history and tradition characteristic of the Chinese people, the question was asked of the missionaries with increasing urgency: Why did we not hear about Christianity earlier? Why is it all new and strange to us? Had God forgotten us for all the centuries of our ancestors?

The answer came in 1623 with the extraordinary discovery of the "Nestorian monument," a long inscribed tablet in Chinese emanating from the Syrian mission to China in the seventh and eighth centuries, just short of a thousand years before. The Chinese had totally forgotten these missionaries and the religion they taught. Now they had written proof that the Gospel had been preached in China in the far-distant days of the T'ang dynasty. Luke Li, the former Li Chih-tsao, declared: "Nine hundred and ninety years ago this doctrine [Christianity] was preached [in China]; amidst the constant vicissitudes of the world, the ever unchanging Providence of God raised up wise men who knew no obstacle. Now this holy stone so providentially preserved has suddenly come to light. . . . Buried for so many years, this treasure seems to have waited only for the propitious moment." Jesuit missionary Manoel Dias Sr. wrote to the general of the Jesuits in Rome announcing the discovery of the tablet. But hostility to the Jesuits was rising, and they were actually accused of faking it, though its authenticity is now universally recognized by scholars.[120]

In 1613 Langobardo, now chief of the Jesuit China mission, sent Nicholas Trigault, who had been two years on the China mission, to Rome for permission for Mass to be said in Chinese, and for the priest to keep his head covered while saying it, since in China, exactly opposite to the West, an uncovered head was regarded as a sign of disrespect. He reached Rome in October of the following year and presented these petitions to the aged Jesuit general Aquaviva, who immediately approved them and passed them on to the Roman College, which in turn quickly passed them to the Pope, with the special favorable recommendation of St. Robert Bellarmine. In extraordinarily fast action, Pope Paul V approved both requests in January 1615, also giving the missionaries permission to translate the whole Bible into Chinese—a task of enormous difficulty. A week later, however, General Claudio Aquaviva of the Jesuits died, and tragically the Chinese Mass was never brought to reality. In this year Ricci's personal history of the China mission, translated into Latin from Chinese, was published in Rome, bringing his extraordinary accomplishments to the attention of all Christendom.[121]

Back in China, a persecution was launched against the Christians by Shen Ch'üeh, vice-president of the Board of Rites at Nanking, with the support of the president of the Board of Rites in Nanking. Shen submitted a memorial to the

---

book by Michael Yang on the incompatibility of Christianity and Buddhism bore the imaginative, intriguing title "The Owl and the Pheasant Cannot Harmonize."

[120] Dunne, *Generation of Giants*, pp. 193-198 (quote on 196). See Volume Two of this history, pp. 296-297, for this tablet, which was deposited in Sianfu.

[121] Dunne, *Generation of Giants*, pp. 162-165, 169, 175-176.

declining Wan-li Emperor calling the Christians "contemptible rats" and "barbarian dogs" and urging their immediate expulsion from China. The leading converts came vigorously to their defense, and the Emperor made no response to the memorial. Nevertheless in Nanking Shen had all the Jesuits in the region arrested, including the head of the mission there, Alfonso Vagnoni, who was put in a cage. Finally an imperial order was obtained ordering the expulsion of all foreign Christians. It was not universally enforced; Langobardo stayed at Paul Hsü's home, and several other Jesuit missionaries were harbored by Chinese Christians. The expulsion edict was never published in Hangchow, where most of the Jesuits remaining in China gathered, and in 1619 baptized 277 new Christians, despite Shen's proclamation solemnly forbidding anyone to honor "Jesus, whom the barbarian preachers of this religion claim to the Lord of Heaven become man." Vagnoni and his associate Semedo were released from their cages. Imprisoned again when they reached Canton, the prefect released them in days.[122]

These were the last years of the Wan-li Emperor, who was no longer able to govern. In 1616 successful Manchu leader Nurhachi proclaimed himself emperor of China; and though he was never recognized as such within China itself, the dynasty he began eventually defeated the Mings and took over China; it is called the Ch'ing dynasty. Overwhelmed by the Manchu threat, the repulsively obese Emperor who for many years had literally seen no one but women and eunuchs, died unmourned in 1620. His successor, the T'ai-ch'ang Emperor, died amid rumors of poison after just one month on the Dragon Throne. He in turn was succeeded by a 14-year-old boy, the T'ien-ch'i Emperor, who was "physically weak, poorly educated, and perhaps mentally deficient." Paul Hsü resigned his office rather than work under him, since the boy Emperor was totally dominated by his eunuchs. About the same time Paul Hsü answered a letter from Cardinal St. Robert Bellarmine, saying how much joy the Faith had brought to them, asking for prayers, and concluding with best wishes for Bellarmine's health and happiness.[123]

In 1622 the Mings were badly defeated by the Manchus in the north, and a rebellion broke out in the province of Shantung led by the White Lotus Society. The Calvinist Dutch, whose power in Oriental waters had been rapidly rising, made a full-scale attack on Macao in June, but the Portuguese heroically counter-charged them and blew up their magazine with well-aimed cannon shot. A newly arrived Jesuit missionary who was to take Ricci's place at Peking, the German Adam Schall, personally took a Dutch officer prisoner in this battle. In September Shen Ch'üeh fell from power and the persecution of Christians which he had undertaken ceased, although some Christians were accused of being members of the rebel White Lotus Society. They denied it despite torture and

---

[122] *Ibid.*, pp. 128-138 (first two quotes on 132), 143-145 (third quote on 145), 148; *Cambridge History of China* VIII (2), 365.

[123] Dunne, *Generation of Giants*, pp. 152-156, 179; *Cambridge History of China* VII, 583, 591-595 (quote on 595).

beatings. One of them, a carpenter, died as a result of his beating: the second martyr in China.[124]

In 1623 two particularly influential Christian converts, Paul Hsü and Luke Li, urged the T'ien-ch'i Emperor (or rather, the eunuch Wei Chung-hsien, who completely dominated the government while this Emperor lived) to have the Portuguese from Macao train his soldiers in the use of Portuguese cannon against the invading Manchus, who had nothing even resembling cannon. Jesuit missionary chief Langobardo arrived in Peking, accompanied by the much younger, ardent Adam Schall, and were accommodated under the orders of the Board of War since their presence was thought to facilitate despatch of the Portuguese artillery. When the guns and gunners arrived, they were given an imperial audience. In October Schall accurately predicted a lunar eclipse, bringing him fame as a learned man; the next year he published a book in Chinese on eclipse prediction, formally presented to the Board of Rites by Paul Hsü.[125]

Nurhachi had steadily expanded his realm in Manchuria, in 1625 establishing his capital at Mukden, one of the few cities in Manchuria of that time. But in the summer of that year the European cannon finally arrived at the fighting front, and the Manchus were driven back more than a hundred miles, followed by a major Chinese victory over Nurhachi at Ningyüan near the Liao River, largely due to the cannon. Nurhachi died in September, but left a brood of sons to carry on his work. In 1626 a major revolt broke out in the rich western province of Szechwan. In the following year the revolts spread from Shensi province in the north to Kwangsi province in the south, while organized pirates ravaged the coast. In September the T'ien-ch'i Emperor, whose health had never been good, died at the age of 21. All his five children had died in infancy, so his legitimate successor was his eldest surviving brother, who took office immediately as the Ch'ung-chen Emperor. Though only 16, he showed immediate positive leadership, restoring many of the officials with Tung-lin connections he had purged in the past two years.[126]

In August 1628 the pirate chief of the southeast coast surrendered to the new governor of Fukien province and agreed to help him suppress piracy on that coast. In the fall Han K'uang, a Tung-lin supporter, returned to Peking as chief grand secretary of the Empire and continuation the restoration of Tung-lin officials and the removal of their enemies. The great Christian convert Paul Hsü was rising steadily in influence; in 1629 he became vice-president of the Nanking Board of Rites, and arranged a competition for predicting a solar eclipse in June in which Chinese and Muslim efforts failed, while the Europeans succeeded.

---

[124] Dunne, *Generation of Giants*, pp. 159-161, 183-185; *Cambridge History of China* VII, 601, 603; VIII (2), 351, 365; Cooper, *Rodriguez the Interpreter*, p. 316; Israel, *Dutch in the Hispanic World*, p. 120.

[125] *Cambridge History of China* VIII (2), 352; Dunne, *Generation of Giants*, pp. 186-187, 199-200; Cooper, *Rodrigues the Interpreter*, p. 336.

[126] *Cambridge History of China* VII, 608-612; Dunne, *Generation of Giants*, pp. 185-187, 204-205, 208; Cooper, *Rodrigues the Interpreter*, pp. 334-335.

Consequently the Ch'ung-chen Emperor decreed a reform of the calendar and specifically approved several Jesuits to work on calendar reform, as part of the Calendrical Bureau headed by Paul Hsü.[127]

Near the end of 1628 a Portuguese military expedition headed by Gonçalvo Teixeira Correa set out from Macao with ten heavy cannons, seven of bronze and three of iron. They were certainly needed. In December 1629 the Manchus broke through the Great Wall of China[128] and approached Peking, taking the city of Ku-an just thirty miles to the south of it. The Chinese general in the area was arrested, falsely charged with treason, and executed by the uniquely Chinese method of slicing, "the death of a thousand cuts." On Ash Wednesday 1630 Teixeira and his big guns arrived in Peking, where they were received with great enthusiasm and caused the invading Manchus to withdraw from the Peking area. The immediate threat seemed ended, and the Portuguese artillery unit was not actually deployed, though the Portuguese were highly praised in a memorial written by Paul Hsü and a substantial Portuguese force, consisting of about 350 men, was sent to support the gunners, being transported in 19 decorative barges provided by the Emperor. But the Manchus, in a major military victory took the northern fortress of Talingho, and in January 1632 a mutiny broke out in the Chinese garrison of Shantung province. The army there was commanded by a Christian convert, Ignatius Sun, who was seized and imprisoned, and later executed by the Ming government for having permitted the mutiny to happen. The Portuguese tried to fight the mutineers; they were overwhelmed, and Teixeira was killed. The rebellion was put down by the next year, but the gunners of Europe had shown they were not invincible. Meanwhile Luke Li, a convert of Ricci and one of "the three pillars of the Chinese Church," died, leaving Paul Hsü as the most important remaining convert. Tragically for the Church, he died in 1633, shortly after rising to the highest position in the Chinese Empire next to the Emperor himself, the office of chief grand secretary. He died a holy death, making three confessions and being anointed.[129]

In 1634 the Jesuits created a new calendar for China, which ensured their place in Peking for a long time. In January of that year the first Franciscan missionary to China, Antonio Caballero a Santa Maria, arrived in Nanking, where he was promptly seized, bound, and sent back on a boat to Canton. In November the first Dominican arrived in Canton. Other Franciscans and Dominicans were soon arriving, with little to no preparation in Chinese culture and practices. They scorned the Jesuit adaptations, criticizing particularly the

---

[127] *Cambridge History of China* VII, 613-614; VIII (2), 365; Dunne, *Generation of Giants*, pp. 208-209.

[128] Contrary to the myth of its ancient origins, the Great Wall of China, to keep out the northern barbarians, was built almost entirely by the Ming dynasty, beginning in 1474. It consisted of a line of interconnected fortifications several hundred miles long. More ancient fortifications were connected by the wall built in the late 15th century. See *Cambridge History of China* VII, 392, 401.

[129] *Ibid.* VII, 616-618, 626; VIII (2), 352; Dunne, *Generation of Giants*, pp. 67-68, 215-223; Cooper, *Rodrigues the Interpreter*, pp. 338-339, 342-346, 350.

failure to enforce Sunday observance; there was no sabbatarian tradition whatever in China. In 1636 they compiled the result of an interrogation of 11 Chinese Christians as a basis for charges against the Jesuit missionary practices of cultural adaptation. The next year two Franciscans went to Peking, where they stayed in Adam Schall's residence. They were horrified by a painting of Christ and the Apostles with shoes (Chinese considered that shoes should always be worn by distinguished people, and abominated bare feet) and claimed the Jesuits made sacrifices to a statue of the Emperor and concealed the realities of the Crucifixion—charges which were blatantly and provably false. Stirred up by other Franciscan and Dominican missionaries, who harangued crowds in the street in Foochow in 1638, an official persecution of all Christians was begun, with some of the friars welcoming it as a chance for martyrdom. The outspoken Adam Schall declared: "It is better to die in bed than to become a martyr in this fashion." The next year they roundly criticized the Jesuits not only for not enforcing Sunday observance, but for baptizing women without salt and oil, and for not preaching that Confucius and all the ancient kings were in Hell! The great Jesuit missionary Giulio Aleni, who had recently (1635) written a book in Chinese entitled "Sacred Explanation of the Life of Christ, Illustrated with Pictures" and including a depiction of the Crucifixion, was forced to leave Foochow. The venom of the Franciscan and Dominican missionaries against the Jesuits grew with every additional proof of how little they knew about China. They complained not only to Jesuit authorities but to De Propaganda Fide in Rome, which also had little knowledge of China. In 1639 Jesuit superior Francisco Furtado wrote to Pope Urban VIII expressing great concern over the threat to the Jesuit missions in China posed by the activities of the newly arrived Franciscans and Dominicans, who were inexperienced in dealing with the Chinese and engaged in much inflammatory public preaching. He urged that the Chinese mission be confined to Jesuits, but this was not done.[130]

In the fall of 1638 Manchu armies devastated north China as far as Shantung province, attacking some sixty Chinese cities and killing the Ming commander in this area. The Ch'ung-chen Emperor levied increased taxes, weakening the economy further. Famines, bad weather, and major floods created mass starvation, hordes of beggars, infanticide and cannibalism. On April 9, 1640 the great Jesuit missionary Alfonso Vagnoni died on station at age 74, leaving behind him 102 Christian communities and more than 8,000 Christians, including over 200 mandarins. The next March a rebel leader operating in western Honan province where lack of food was acute, captured the old Chinese capital of Loyang and a "notoriously profligate" imperial prince who was executed, dismembered and eaten to demonstrate the rebels' hatred for the imperial family which continued to luxuriate while they starved. The imperial court was still split between friends and enemies of the Tung-lin faction; efforts

---

[130] Dunne, *Generation of Giants*, pp. 239-241, 245-247, 250-253, 256-260, (quote on 259), 269-276, 298; *Cambridge History of China* VIII (2), 366. It is Catholic doctrine that mortal men cannot know which specific individuals are in Hell.

to form a common front toward the rebels and the Manchus were unsuccessful. As winter came on, the Ming supreme commander in the north was trapped by the Manchus under Prince Abahai and forced to surrender in March 1642. All Ming control anywhere beyond the Great Wall was lost. By 1644 the chief grand secretary had been forced to commit suicide, the troops' pay was five months in arrears, and the imperial granaries and rice stores were virtually empty. The Ch'ung-chen Emperor issued a desperate call for immediate aid from all commands in the empire, but there was virtually no response. With the rebels closing in on Peking and the failure of an attempt to escape, the Emperor hanged himself in a pavilion in the palace compound, after ordering his Empress to do the same and trying to kill his 15-year-old daughter, but only cutting off her hand. The rebel chief proclaimed himself Emperor, but Manchu Prince Dorgon defeated him and took Peking, establishing the new Ch'ing dynasty in China in the person of a six-year-old Emperor to whom he was Regent. Adam Schall defended the Jesuit residence in Peking, wielding a sword with good effect. Nevertheless he found favor with Prince Dorgon, who in the fall made him Director of the Bureau of Astronomy.[131]

Support for the Ming cause remained strong in the south, but the Manchus let no grass grow under their feet. In November 1644, having learned the weakness of the surviving Ming authority, Prince Dorgon launched simultaneous campaigns, each headed by one of his brothers, against the rebel headquarters in Sian and against Nanking, now capital of what was left of the Ming empire. Prince Dorgon and his brothers refused all Ming attempts to negotiate with them. In January 1645 Manchu forces under Prince Dodo crossed the Yellow River in northwest Honan, taking the old imperial cities of Loyang and K'ai-feng and receiving the surrender of several Ming commanders. He crossed a high pass and forced a rebel leader to flee from Sian. A Ming loyalist made a brave stand at the city of Yang-chou, but it was overrun and horribly sacked in May, with its commander captured and executed. On June 1 the Manchu army crossed the great Yangtze River shrouded by darkness and heavy fog; a week later Nanking surrendered to them without a fight. On June 24 the triumphant Manchus proclaimed their rule, which included a general amnesty, cancellation of all new taxes, harsh punishments for official corruption, tax remissions for areas submitting to them without resistance, restoration of confiscated property, and preservation the government school system and the civil service examinations. A month later they ordered the entire male population of China to wear their hair as the Manchus did, tightly bound and braided into a long queue. Widespread attempts to defy this edict were repressed by massacres of the defiant ones.[132]

Over the next 14 years Ming resistance, though it still existed, gradually declined. After Canton was lost to the Manchus in 1647 (following which another chief grand secretary committed suicide) the Ming faded steadily until

---

[131] *Cambridge History of China* VII, 629-632, 634, 636-641, 644; Dunne, *Generation of Giants*, pp. 305-306, 317, 320-322, 325.

[132] *Cambridge History of China* VII, 652, 656-658, 660-663. The famous Chinese "pigtail" or queue is therefore not Chinese at all, but Manchu.

their Emperor was finally driven out of China to Burma in 1659. The Manchus pursued him even there. The Burmese king delivered him up to them, and he was executed. Some of the Jesuits stayed with him for a long time, even writing to Rome asking for prayers to restore him and the Ming dynasty. But the Ming dynasty star had set; the future in China lay with the Manchus of the Ch'ing dynasty.[133]

Adam Schall in Peking soon established himself firmly with them. He was their resident calendar expert, but much more than that. In 1651, when the unusually mature twelve-year-old Shun-chih Emperor took charge of his government, Schall was close at hand. The boy called him "Grandpa" and gave him the greatest respect, specifically directing that he not be required to perform the ritual protestation (kowtow) before him, and celebrating his 18th birthday at Schall's house. In 1659 he declared Schall Imperial Chamberlain and made him a mandarin of the first class, first division. Schall was genuinely fond of the young Emperor and spent long hours discussing the Christian Faith with him. Naturally he hoped to convert him to Christianity. This was the best—and the only really good—opportunity for such a conversion in the history of the Chinese Empire. Schall believed that the Shun-chih Emperor accepted Christianity with his head, but not with his heart. Its prohibition of polygamy stood in the way, as with so many other Chinese.[134]

During this time Schall was under heavy personal attack from the hostile Franciscans and Dominicans, as well as from some Jesuits. In 1648, when China was still in chaos, several Jesuits were captured by Chang Hsien-chung, known as the "Yellow Tiger" and infamous for his atrocities. They were held in great danger to their lives for several months. They blamed Schall for not doing more to secure their release, and five of them, including even old Langobardo who should have known better, petitioned the Jesuit vice-provincial to expel Schall from the Society. They even condemned his holding office as head of the Astronomical Bureau under the Chinese Emperor. The personal bias of this vendetta was obvious, and by 1651 Langobardo had come to see it; he urged that the two Jesuits most hostile to Schall be removed from Peking because they were injuring Christianity there. In 1652, hearing of this unseemly squabble, Jesuit General Piccolomini wrote that Schall was not going to be dismissed from the Society of Jesus no matter what his accusers said, and the matter was closed. In 1654 Schall wrote to the general saying that he had not defended himself against these calumnies because of his complete faith in the Providence of God. In 1664 the Pope himself ruled that there was nothing wrong with Schall holding the Chinese office of head of the Astronomical Bureau.[135]

In 1660 the Shun-chih Emperor's favorite consort died, after he had hounded her young husband to suicide in order to have her. She had been strongly Buddhist, and he had her buried with full Buddhist rites, ordering about

---

[133] *Ibid.*, VII, 679-680, 692, 707-710; Dunne, *Generation of Giants*, p. 234.

[134] Dunne, *Generation of Giants*, pp. 325, 347-348.

[135] *Ibid.*, pp. 326, 328, 332-333, 335-336, 338.

thirty of her entourage to die with her.[136] Obviously he had rejected the Christian teachings Schall had given him. But the young Emperor still had great respect for Schall. On July 28 he stated:

> Your law [Christianity] is already widely spread. Through your exertions the science of astronomy has become known. Thus do you labor for the Empire. Should not the heart of the Emperor rejoice? You know how the Empire should be governed.[137]

There was still hope for his conversion, with the enormous effects it would undoubtedly have, if only it happened. But on February 2, 1661 the Shun-chih Emperor died of a sudden attack of smallpox. Schall tried but failed to achieve a deathbed conversion, but did prevail upon him to name his six-year-old son as his successor. This was the K'ang-hsi Emperor, one of the very greatest of all the Chinese Emperors, who began to rule on his own in 1668—three years after Schall had died. The K'ang-hsi Emperor was the first—and last—to give explicit permission for Christianity to be preached through the whole of China, after reading Ricci's famous "Treatise on the True Idea of God."[138]

At Schall's death in 1666 there were approximately a quarter of a million Christians in China.[139] They included a substantial number of mandarins. Mainly because of Schall's presence in Peking with the Manchu Emperor, it had been possible to bridge the fall of the Ming dynasty and the advent of the Manchu Ch'ing. Christian influence was well established. With the K'ang-hsi Emperor's full permission for evangelization, its future seemed secure. It would take time to spread throughout the most populous nation on Earth, but it seemed in the seventeenth century that China had unlimited time.

Back in 1615 Pope Paul V had approved a request to translate the Mass into Chinese, but most unfortunately it had never been acted upon. Nothing was done to implement it for more than sixty years. When in 1671 Belgian Jesuit Frans de Rougemont sent a memorial to Rome asking for renewal of the permission, Pope Clement X referred it to De Propaganda Fide, which pigeonholed it. An accurate translation of the missal and breviary was not available until 1678, in which year De Propaganda Fide failed to act on another memorial asking for the Mass in Chinese. Finally in 1688 three Chinese priests were ordained, fulfilling the gloomy prophecy of the Jesuit vice-provincial in China in 1637 that "it will be impossible for a long time, and perhaps to the end of the century, to institute a Chinese clergy." It is hard to imagine how anyone, and especially a perceptive Jesuit who knew China, could have thought the learned and highly cultured

---

[136] *Ibid.*, pp. 352-353.

[137] *Ibid.*, p. 353.

[138] *Ibid.*, pp. 96, 334-336, 353, 363-365, 367; Cronin, *Wise Man from the West*, pp. 255-256.

[139] Cronin, *Wise Man from the West*, p. 256.

products of China's classical education system to be unfit for the priesthood. But the vice-provincial's position went unchallenged, so far as is known.[140]

This was bad enough, but very substantial progress in evangelizing China could have still been made in spite of it, as had happened, slowly but surely, from the time of Ricci's arrival to the death of Adam Schall. The K'ang-hsi Emperor was on record as permitting and even encouraging it. But now the Franciscan and Dominican attacks on the Jesuits' China mission bore evil fruit. Among their charges against the Jesuits was that they permitted their converts to continue practicing the ordinary rites commemorating the dead.[141] De Propaganda Fide heard in 1656 an excellent presentation of the Jesuit case that these were simply customs, not manifestations of a false religion, by the Jesuit scholar Martin Martini, and permitted Christian converts to continue to perform them. But the Franciscans and Dominicans would not let the issue die. Increasingly fevered debates on it raged.[142] The Jesuits appealed to the K'ang-hsi Emperor, who responded (not as a Christian, for he was never that, but as a believer in truth):

> Honors are paid to Confucius not as a petition for favors, intelligence or high office but as to a Master, because of the magnificent moral teaching which he has left to posterity. As for the ceremony in honor of dead ancestors, it originates in the desire to show filial piety. According to the customs observed by Confucians, this ceremony contains no request for help; it is practiced only to show filial respect to the dead. Souls of ancestors are not held to reside in the tablets [kept in honor of ancestors]; these are only symbols which serve to express gratitude and keep the dead in memory, as though they were actually present.[143]

This should have settled the matter once and for all. But the agitation went on. The Popes, knowing little of China and not sure whom to trust among the missionaries, wavered and evaded taking a stand. Hostility to the Jesuits as "elitist" helped arouse opposition to them. In 1704 nine Italian cardinals assembled to decide what was now called "the Chinese rites controversy." A week later all Chinese practices honoring the dead were banned for Christians, an action confirmed by the bull "*Ex illa*" of Pope Clement XI in 1715. Henceforth, no Chinese convert to Christianity would be allowed to honor his ancestors in any of the traditional ways.[144]

It was probably the most disastrous single decision in the history of Catholic Church evangelization. Eventually it was explicitly repealed, but only

---

[140] Dunne, *Generation of Giants*, pp. 172, 174-175.

[141] There were extraordinary rites much more clearly idolatrous, which the Jesuits never allowed their converts to perform.

[142] Dunne, *Generation of Giants*, pp. 255, 265, 298-299; Cronin, *Wise Man from the West*, p. 258.

[143] Cronin, *Wise Man from the West*, pp. 258-259

[144] *Ibid.*, pp. 259-260; Dunne, *Generation of Giants*, p. 299.

in 1939, far too late.[145] The surge of conversions in China, still continuing at the turn of the 18th century, stopped almost completely. Many converts obeyed the new Church law, with what suffering can only be imagined; but most Chinese could not be persuaded to enter a religion that forbade them from honoring their ancestors, seen as a very important duty in virtually every Chinese household, and most especially of the Confucian mandarins, who could now no longer be Christians. A splendid missionary opportunity in the world's most populous nation, without a clearly formed national religion to be overcome and moral teachings that could easily be adapted to Christianity, was lost. The Church had turned decisively away from millions of souls.[146]

But God did not forget them. In the 19th century He tried again. By that time Protestant missionaries were active in China, passing out badly translated versions of the New Testament. One of them was casually picked up by a young man named Hung Hsiu-chüan. He found it hard to read. But it caught his attention, particularly when he was deeply depressed by repeated failure to pass the all-important civil service examinations. Despite its bad Chinese, he read it over and over, and came to understand much (though by no means all) of its teaching. He had no guide, no interpreter; he was totally on his own. In good time he proclaimed his faith, in the heart of China, where no missionaries were then to be found. He called himself Christ's "younger brother," which has scandalized many. But it has always been Christian teaching that Christ, while truly God, is brother to all of us, a man like us in all things but sin—just as his Mother is also our Mother. Hung Hsiu-chüan set out to bring China into the Heavenly Kingdom (*T'ai-p'ing*) of Christ. He almost succeeded. He was finally defeated, in significant part, by Western armies.[147] It was the second great lost opportunity in the history of the China mission, rivalling the first—the Chinese rites decision—in importance. The Church awaits its third missionary opportunity in China, which all Christians of good will should pray will be better handled than the first two.

---

[145] By then the Chinese Empire had fallen (1911) and China was desperately searching for the "secret" of the West—what had enabled the West to develop what China finally realized was the most advanced civilization in the world. That "secret," of course, was Christianity; but the intellectuals of the West no longer knew it. When they were asked to send spokesmen to explain to the Chinese the reasons for the superiority of Western civilization, they sent Bertrand Russell and John Dewey, an atheist and a pragmatist, respectively. China listened to them. To a considerable extent as a result, at the turn of the millennium she remained one of the world's last four Communist nations.

[146] Dunne, *Generation of Giants*, pp. 299-301.

[147] For Hung Hsiu-chüan and his Heavenly Kingdom, see especially Jen Yu-wen (or Chuwen), *The Taiping Revolutionary Movement* (New Haven CT, 1973) and Jonathan Spence, *God's Chinese Son* (New York, 1996).

Japan (1552-1873)

On September 23, 1542 three Portuguese castaways from a Chinese junk, blown east by a typhoon, landed at tiny Tanageshima island off the southern Japanese island of Kyushu. No European had ever been in Japan before; unlike India and China, except for Marco Polo's vague reports of "Cipangu" it had been totally unknown to the West. By 1544 word of the discovery had spread among the far-ranging Portuguese, and their trading vessels began to appear on the southern Japanese coast. The Japanese immediately made it clear that what the Portuguese had that they wanted most was not glassware or clocks or anything like that, which had been the desire of the Chinese, but firearms: the arquebus, or primitive musket. China had developed gunpowder, but without harnessing it to a weapon. The Japanese had never known it. They coveted muskets and began to obtain them in quantity, so as better to carry on their favorite activity, killing one another. The Chinese had long been familiar with them, as ravaging pirates on the eastern seas, and feared and despised them for their ferocity and blood lust.[148]

Indeed, they were the most completely militaristic people in all the history of civilization, who before the end of the 16th century were already actively contemplating the conquest of all the world known to them.[149] No Western nation ever seriously contemplated the conquest of Japan, or was ever able to obtain real protection for their people in Japan. In the twentieth century Japan defeated Russia, and then in the Second World War gained control of all of east Asia down to Australia, after destroying the American battle fleet at Pearl Harbor. In 1945, at the end of that war, with the aid of the atom bomb, for the one and only time they were conquered. Their character appears to have changed since then. Before that, since at least the twelfth century, it never did.

In December 1547 Portuguese captain Jorge Alvares, who had sailed to China and Japan, met St. Francis Xavier in Malacca and described Japan to him. It was an extraordinarily beautiful country, he said, with marvellous scenery, radiant flowers, intensively cultivated soil, a great abundance of fish, but very few domestic animals. The people were warlike, very inquisitive, proud, and punctilious in their etiquette. Their principal religion was Buddhism. Large communities of Buddhist monks dotted the countryside. Many if not most of these monks were known for their open practice of sodomy.[150]

In his two years in Japan, already recounted, St. Francis Xavier saw a great opportunity for the conversion of these intelligent, cultured, industrious and apparently hospitable people. He went joyfully to an audience with their revered emperor, hoping to convert him. But he was astonished to discover that the

---

[148] George Sansom, *A History of Japan* (Stanford CA 1958-63), II, 217-218, 363-364; *Cambridge History of Japan*, Volume IV ("Early Modern Japan," ed. John Whitney Hall (New York, 1991), p. 302; Charles R. Boxer, *The Christian Century in Japan* (Berkeley CA, 1967), pp. 25-26, 255.

[149] See the discussion of the ambitions of Hideyoshi, below.

[150] Boxer, *Christian Century in Japan*, pp. 32-36.

emperor had no power, did not rule. We do not know what he thought of that discovery, but we do know that he was not in Japan long enough to see the gulfs of darkness that lay behind their apparent light.[151]

A number of outstanding Jesuit missionaries followed him; we will tell some of their story below. By far the most important was Alessandro Valignano, an Italian Jesuit who was sent to Japan as Visitor Provincial to the Jesuit missions throughout the Orient. He arrived in Japan in 1579, just forty years old, a man of extraordinary perception and original thought, the first to see clearly that missionaries to civilized pagan countries must take special care to live like natives in order that their message should not be dismissed because of accidentals. Valignano had been primarily responsible for launching the mission of Matteo Ricci in China. Now in Japan he "insisted on the urgent need for the Jesuits to study and speak Japanese well, and issued instructions concerning language studies. He strictly enjoined on them the necessity of adaptation to Japanese customs and way of life, and discussed in some detail the rules of etiquette which the Jesuits were to observe in their dealings with Japanese."[152] His initial enthusiasm resembled that of St. Francis Xavier, but he soon began to realize the enormous obstacles that the mission to Japan was confronting. A year after his arrival there, he wrote a lengthy report on them:

> [The Japanese] are the most warlike and bellicose race yet discovered on the earth . . . they will kill a man not only on the smallest excuse but merely to try the edge of their swords. . . . Such is their cruelty that often the very mothers when they have brought forth a child will put their foot on its chest and kill it, simply because they cannot nurture them. Similarly many men kill themselves by cutting their intestines with a dagger. . . . They are the most false and treacherous people of any known in the world; for from childhood they are taught never to reveal their hearts, and they regard this as prudence and the contrary as folly, to such a degree that those who lightly reveal their mind are looked upon as nitwits, and are contemptuously termed single-hearted men. Even fathers and sons never reveal their true thoughts to each other, because there can be no mutual confidence between them in word or deed; for when they are most determined to do evil to someone, the more outward compliments they pay him. Thus when they wish to kill somebody, just when they are about to do so, they show him more politeness and kind words, in order the better to effect their intention; and in truth they cannot live with one another in any other way. For this reason, and because Japan is divided between so many lords and fiefs, it is continually torn by civil wars and treasons, nor is there any lord who is secure in his domain.[153]

Valignano mentioned their approval of sodomy, particularly in the Buddhist monasteries (which were also, in total contradiction to the professed pacifist

---

[151] See section of this chapter entitled "St. Francis Xavier," above.

[152] Michael Cooper, S.J., *Rodrigues the Interpreter; an Early Jesuit in Japan and China* (New York, 1974), pp. 52-53 (quote). For a sketch of Valignano's career in Japan see Boxer, *Christian Century in Japan*, pp. 72-74.

[153] Boxer, *Christian Century in Japan*, pp. 74-75.

ideals of Buddhism, armed camps which played a major role in political and military affairs). Despite all this, he went on to say hopefully that when the Christian Faith was preached to them, the Japanese were "most apt to be taught and to adopt our holy law, and to produce the finest Christianity in all the East."[154]

For some of them, that was to be proved very true. But it never proved true for enough of them.

The Japan which the Jesuit missionaries reached in the sixteenth century was in fact an almost perfect example of what Pope John Paul II has taught us to call "the culture of death." It was, and remained at least until 1945, the cruelest civilized society known to history, with the one exception of Aztec Mexico with its human sacrifices.[155] The primary theme of its existence was always death— death in battle, ceremonial suicide when defeated in battle, abortion, infanticide, and sodomy. A year later, in 1581, Valignano would make this still more explicit, in his "Advertisement and Advice on the Customs of Japan."

> They are very cruel and quick to kill, because for the most insignificant reason they kill their subjects, and do not think more of cutting a man down the middle than if it were a dog; so much that many of them, when they can do it without danger to themselves, in encountering some poor individual will split him in half, for no better reason than to test how their swords cut. And in their wars they plague and destroy the population by fire and flow of blood, without sparing even the temples of their idols; and they even go so far as to kill themselves with the greatest of ease, slashing themselves in the guts, whether it be for the sake of vexation or to avoid capture at the hands of their enemies. And what is most cruel and contrary to the order of nature, the very mothers often kill their children, either while still in the womb by taking something to induce abortion, or after birth in suffocating them by trampling on the throat; and that only to avoid the bother of bringing them up, or with the excuse of poverty and inability to support so many children.[156]

Later, in a remarkable insight, Valignano pointed to a major source of all these evils, "that they are not all as before subject to the Dayri [Emperor], who was their natural and true sovereign; since they rose against him, rendering Japan divided among so many lords who are neither natural nor legitimate, therefore continue the everlasting wars among them, for each endeavors to acquire for himself as much territory as he can."[157]

In fact the Japanese governmental system was—and remained at least until 1945—unique. The Emperor was exalted to the skies, all major official acts were done in his name, the ancient Shinto ritual which was almost the only other form

---

[154] *Ibid.*, p. 76.

[155] See Chapter One, above.

[156] George Elison, *Deus Destroyed; the Image of Christianity in Early Modern Japan* (Cambridge MA, 1973), p. 74.

[157] *Ibid.*, p. 44.

of religion in Japan besides the debased Japanese Buddhism made him the high priest of the nation and virtually a god; but he had no power, and everybody knew it. The turn away from actual rule by the emperor began soon after the imperial capital was moved from Nara to Heian-kyo (present Kyoto) in Japan's central Yamato plain at the end of the eighth century. The Fujiwara clan gained dominance over the emperors and repeatedly intermarried with the imperial family, putting them in position to act as regents for child emperors. In the course of the ninth and tenth centuries, this proved so attractive and effective a way for them to rule that the practice developed of forcing the resignation of the Emperor when or shortly after he reached adulthood, to be succeeded by another child and therefore another Fujiwara regent. When this system had developed in primitive France in the eighth century, with the Carolingian "mayors of the palace" exercising actual power while long-haired Merovingian kings held the royal title, Pope Zachary intervened to tell the Catholic French that he who had the power should reign, and the Carolingians succeeded as the kings of France. But the Japanese had no Pope.[158]

When the Fujiwara began to decline, an even stranger system developed. A boy would be proclaimed emperor, reach adulthood, and then abdicate in favor of his minor son as titular emperor and become the "cloistered emperor," as such exercising some real power. So the emperor gained power by first proclaiming himself not the emperor. This weird system (called *insei*) continued until the late twelfth century, when the two most powerful military clans in Japan clashed in the famous Gempei War. The Minamoto were victorious, the Taira defeated, and total power fell into the hands of Minamoto leader Yoritomo, who declared he would exercise it from his army encampment (*bakufu*) which he set up at Kamakura near present Tokyo. The powerless emperors in Kyoto agreed to endorse whatever Yoritomo did. In 1192 Yoritomo took the title "Shogun," meaning commander-in-chief of all armies.[159]

But Yoritomo had killed so many of the members of his own family that after he died at 52 in 1199 from being thrown from his horse, there were not enough relatives left to found an enduring dynasty. The Hojo family took over from the Minamoto. In 1318 one of the few straightforward and genuinely heroic figures in Japanese history, Go-Daigo, took the scorned office of emperor at the age of thirty with a vow that he would never abdicate, but would restore true imperial rule.[160] The families and clans worked against him, but Go-Daigo defied them all. In a magnificent letter to the Kamakura *bakufu* in 1324, he wrote:

---

[158] Sansom, *History of Japan* I, 99-102, 113, 123, 141-142, 155-158. See Volume Two, Chapter 11 of this history.

[159] *Ibid.*, I, 154, 199-201, 204, 207, 267, 275, 289, 303, 319, 324, 331-332, 342, 346, 348, 352-353.

[160] Andrew E. Goble, *Kenmu; Go-Daigo's Revolution* (Cambridge MA, 1996), pp. 18-19.

I address the imperial prince shogun: the imperial wrath is severe. The shogun is not lord of the realm, yet has succeeded to the powers of government. This is most immoral. . . . I am the lord of this entire country. All below are in receipt of the favors of the court. To constrict me is certainly equivalent to dwelling in the shade and snapping off the foliage, or to drawing water from a stream and forgetting the source. . . . This is in accord with what is ordained by Heaven. . . . Bent trees detest straight rope; base scoundrels fear righteous government. The reason is that purity is like a mirror. This is something which small people cannot attain.[161]

Go-Daigo had thrown down the gauntlet to the convoluted, fraudulent political system he had inherited, flinging his straight rope around the bent trees. The next year he sent the first official Japanese embassy to China in five hundred years.[162] He continued to refuse abdication absolutely, and fought to the end against his thronging enemies, who were determined to preserve and continue the Japanese system of political deceit. In 1332 Go-Daigo was exiled to desolate Oki Island, almost alone. But the next year he escaped from the island by hiding under bales of dried fish, assembled an army whose leaders finally saw him as their natural lord, and fought his way back to power in Kyoto. But he was only able to do this by the support of the great warlord Ashikaga Takauji, whom he nevertheless refused to appoint as shogun, and who eventually betrayed and defeated him. Go-Daigo remained at large, still fighting, until he died in 1339, after naming his son his successor and urging his followers to continue the struggle to restore a real empire that he had begun. But they lost.[163] Ashikaga Takauji founded a new shogunate, which for more than a century was very like the one Go-Daigo had destroyed.

In view of the character of Japan, Go-Daigo's attempted revolution might not have changed it fundamentally. History shows us that imperial power can certainly also be abused. But an essential part of the pernicious political system that had developed in Japan was avoidance of responsibility, of always acting in another's name rather than one's own. In five hundred years, only Go-Daigo had challenged that system; and he challenged it on Alessandro Valignano's premises.

Ashikaga rule in turn degenerated, until the Onin War of 1467-1477 threw Japan into virtual anarchy. Now the shoguns had scarcely more power than the emperors. Every warlord's hand was against every other.[164] The warlords were

---

   [161] *Ibid.*, pp. 68-69.

   [162] Sansom, *History of Japan* II, 9.

   [163] *Ibid.*, II, 37-45, 47, 49, 51-56, 59, 61, 64-67, 71; Goble, *Go-Daigo's Revolution*, pp. 99-104, 123-129, 134-139, 141-144, 154-155, 176, 208-209, 222-223, 246-248, 250-255, 257-259, 261, 270.

   [164] Sansom, *History of Japan*, II, 218-228; Mary Berry, *Hideyoshi* (Cambridge MA, 1989), pp. 16-17.

called *daimyos*.[165] There were between two and three hundred of them. When the Jesuit missionaries arrived, their internecine conflicts were reaching a climax.

The year after St. Francis Xavier's departure from Japan, Jesuit missionaries established a residence at Funai in the province of Bungo on the northern coast of Kyushu. They were favored by the local *daimyo*, Otomo Yoshisige (later known as Sorin, who did not accept baptism until many years later) and made it their headquarters. When Jesuit Father Gaspar Vilela arrived in Japan in 1554, he found only about 500 Japanese Christians. But by 1557 a Jesuit hospital, headed by a Portuguese doctor, had been established at Funai and Father Cosmas de Torres had converted 2,000 people in the large city of Yamaguchi, only to see its pro-Christian *daimyo* overthrown in a rebellion so that Father Torres and many of his converts had to flee to Bungo for refuge. But he never stopped evangelizing; in the course of 1558 he baptized about 1,300 people on two islands just off Kyushu. In 1559 Father Vilela was received in audience by Shogun Ashikaga Yoshiteru as a priest from India, who obtained assurance that as such he would be exempt from taxes and service required of Japanese and, implicitly, allowed to preach his faith.[166]

The Jesuits had learned from St. Francis Xavier's sad experience that the emperor had no power. Now they were to learn that the shogun no longer had power either. No law in Japan ran beyond the boundaries held by each *daimyo*. In August 1561 Father Vilela was excluded from the capital of Kyoto by the vehemently anti-Christian lord Matsunaga. But Bungo held firm in the defense of Christians under Otomi Yoshisige (Sorin), who was highly praised in a report of missionary Father Gago, and the extraordinary Japanese preacher Brother Laurence was continuing his apostolate there. Another *daimyo* in Kyushu, Omura Sumitada, gave the Jesuits a specific license to preach Christianity in his domain, and port privileges in Yokoseura. He was baptized Bartholomew in June 1563, the first avowedly Christian *daimyo*. In the province of Nara near the capital that year, two judges—an astronomer and a Confucian scholar (Confucian teachings were now coming to Japan for the first time, and were far more compatible with the Christian faith than Buddhism)—along with the man who had requested them to examine Christianity with a view to forbidding it, were baptized.[167]

Because of the fierce reputation of Japanese pirates and the increasing Japanese absorption with their civil wars, trade between China and Japan, never vigorous, had almost stopped. The Portuguese boldly took it over. They now

---

[165] The Japanese language differs fundamentally from all the Indo-European languages in having no number, so it is technically incorrect to write *daimyos* as a Western plural, and most histories of Japan do not do so. But the ambiguities for a Western student in following the Japanese practice justify this use of the plural for clarification.

[166] Michael Cooper, S.J., *Rodrigues the Interpreter; an Early Jesuit in Japan and China* (New York, 1974), p. 45; Boxer, *Christian Century in Japan*, p. 78; *Cambridge History of Japan*, IV, 315-318, 322; Elison, *Deus Destroyed*, pp. 85-86.

[167] *Cambridge History of Japan* IV, 319-320, 323; Boxer, *Christian Century in Japan*, pp. 99-100; Elison, *Deus Destroyed*, pp. 88, 126.

had on the Pacific shores of Asia a number of the giant merchant ships called carracks. In August 1563 a carrack (called by the Japanese "Great Ship") came to the newly baptized Bartholomew's little port of Yokoseura. It bore large quantities of Chinese silk, prized but not made in Japan. As wealth from this trade began to flow into the coffers of *daimyo* Bartholomew, jealous lords attacked him and drove him into the wilderness, burned Yokoseura, and seized Jesuit Fathers Louis Frois and Cosmas de Torres as hostages. But the Christians were making conversions with unexpected speed. Otomo Yoshisige, lord of Bungo, was leaning more and more toward Christianity; another *daimyo* named Takayama Zusho was baptized along with his son Ukon; and Brother Laurence was preaching in the capital city with great success—he brought 73 of the local samurai into the Church, including some of the principal vassals of leading general and feudal lord Nagayoshi.[168]

This raised the question, to be agitated for decades by opponents of the Jesuits and frequently alluded to in varying tones of disapproval by modern historians, of whether many or even most of the Japanese were converting to Christianity in the hope of getting the annual Great Ship to come to a harbor in their domain and so gain great material profit. Jesuit Father Louis Frois had no doubt that this was a help in the evangelization of Japan:

> It was a sign of the grace of Divine Providence that the traffic and trade between the Japanese and Chinese in their junks had stopped. Instead, only the one yearly China Ship came with the Portuguese and their wares; and because of this very favorable opportunities arise for our purpose, which is the conversion of souls.[169]

Extensive discussion of this question and sarcasm about it in almost all modern histories of Japan is vitiated by the fact that major human actions, especially conversion to a new faith, are usually taken for a variety of motives, in a mixture known only to God, not to historians. Furthermore, most modern historians have no understanding of anyone like Father Frois who genuinely makes "the conversion of souls" his chief objective, and think that a desire for profit and influence through trade is always a much more probable motive. From this distance of time and space, especially with the paucity of records, we are in no position to speculate on the motives of converts unless they later gave up the Christian Faith for political and monetary advantage. Bartholomew, Francisco, Takayama Zusho, and his heroic son Ukon held fast to the Faith to the end. It provided a way out of the blood lust of the Japanese culture of death. In the next century, over four thousand Japanese died for it in the most terrible persecution of which history has record. As they dangled head down over the hellish horror

---

[168] *Cambridge History of Japan* IV, 261-262, 320-321, 324; Sansom, *History of Japan* II, 291-292; Elison, *Deus Destroyed*, pp. 91, 126-127.
[169] Elison, *Deus Destroyed*, p. 86.

known as "the pit," filled with human excrement, they were hardly thinking of trade advantages.[170]

In January 1565 Shogun Ashikaga Yoshiteru ceremonially received Jesuits Fathers Vilela and Frois. In June he was murdered by rebellious vassals under Matsunaga Hisahide, who promptly expelled the Christians from Kyoto. Yoshiteru's son Yoshihide fled for his life. He died in a few months, succeeded by Yoshiaki. Compelled to recognize that he no longer ruled effectively any part of Japan, Shogun Yoshiaki went to the one man who was showing promise of establishing effective centralized power in Japan for the first time in a hundred years, the brilliant, ruthless young warrior Oda Nobunaga. Oda was eager to use both the shogun and the emperor as his "fronts." In November 1568 he entered Kyoto in triumph with the shogun in his train. One of his first acts was to rebuild the palace of the utterly powerless Emperor Ogimachi, who fawningly replied by addressing him as "famous general, with no peer in any age." The next year Oda built another palace for Shogun Yoshiaki. Oda was winning battles not so much because of his generalship, as because of his rapid development of the military potential of the muskets brought by the Portuguese.[171]

At this point there were still only six Jesuit Fathers in Japan, but they were making astonishing progress. Nagasaki, then a small village of only 1,500 people, became entirely Christian. More than a thousand of Bartholomew's retainers were converted by Father Vilela in 1569. In the time-honored practice of the Church in dealing with temples to false gods, followed in the conversion of the Roman empire and again in this very 16th century in the conversion of Mexico, a Buddhist temple in Bartholomew's territory was burned and the foundations laid for what was to become the great Cathedral of All Saints. In April Oda Nobunaga and Father Frois, who was exceptionally fluent in the difficult Japanese language, met on a bridge. The meeting was arranged by Dario of the now Christian Takayama family. Oda showed no particular interest in adopting the Christian faith himself—that would have required a very large change in the conduct of his life—but was pleased to hear the Christian condemnations of Japanese Buddhism, which he despised for their independent armed monasteries and regarded as a major obstacle to his conquest of Japan. He gave the Jesuits a license to preach in the capital city of Kyoto. When someone expressed concern that Emperor Ogimachi, influenced by Buddhists, was trying to prohibit Christian preaching, Oda responded with the blunt cynicism for which he was famous: "Do not worry about the Emperor or the Shogun, because I am in complete control of everything. Only do what I tell you, and you can go where you like." In 1570 he made this equally clear to Shogun Yoshiaki himself,

---

[170] All the histories used in this research, except Jesuit Cooper's *Rodrigues the Interpreter*, are characterized by considerable to virulent hostility to Christianity, which at least plays some part in leading them to conclude that the desire for Western trade was the chief motivation of conversions in Japan. For the great persecutions of the 17th century, see below.

[171] Sansom, *History of Japan* II, 234-272, 278-279, 340; Elison, *Deus Destroyed*, p. ix; Berry, *Hideyoshi*, pp. 43, 45.

directing him to sign several articles, of which the fourth read: "Insofar as the affairs of the realm have been fully entrusted to Nobunaga, all judgments shall be rendered—regardless of those concerned—in accord with his perceptions and without consultation of the Shogun."[172]

Father Frois was naturally elated by the favorable impression he seemed to have made on the man who was now the most powerful in Japan. But such a man, a notable practitioner of almost all the vices which characterized Japan during this and preceding centuries, could never be a reliable foundation for spreading the Faith unless and until he accepted it, which he showed no sign of doing. In 1570 Jesuit Father Cosmas de Torres, who had been chief of the Japanese mission, died and was succeeded by the unimaginative Portuguese Francisco Cabral. In 1571 the annual Portuguese "Great Ship" anchored in Nagasaki harbor, which proved well adapted to navigation and trade, and its Christian ruler granted the Jesuits a sizeable tract of land in the town. Father Vilela headed for home on the return voyage of this carrack, after no less than 17 years of service in Japan. There were now about 30,000 Christians in Japan out of a population of about 20 million. In 1571 another *daimyo*, Amakusa Shigehisa, was baptized as Miguel. In the same year Oda stormed the great Buddhist monastery of Hiyei-zan and burned it to the ground, indiscriminately killing monks, laymen, women and children. Fighting Buddhist monks of the Honganji monastery joined with warlords frightened by Oda's rising power to attack Kyoto, and defeated Oda's army. Even the puppet shogun turned against him. But in December 1572 Oda won the decisive Battle of Mikatagahara and a few months later deposed the shogun without replacing him, marking the end of the checkered history of the Ashikaga shogunate.[173]

Meanwhile three of the Christian *daimyos* decided to require baptism of many of their subjects, and it does not appear that the Jesuit Fathers tried hard enough to dissuade them. Bartholomew decreed thousands of these coerced "conversions" in 1574, and destroyed many Buddhist temples and Shinto shrines in his Kyushu domain. In 1576 *daimyo* Arima Yoshisada was baptized as André and immediately ordered the baptism of some 12,000 of his subjects. In 1577 Christian *daimyo* Miguel (formerly Amikusha Shigehisa), required the baptism of all of his approximately 10,000 subjects, destroyed their Buddhist temples, and replaced them with churches. In 1576 the first Mass was said in the newly opened Church of the Assumption at Kyoto, and fourteen more Jesuit missionaries arrived in Nagasaki on the "Great Ship" in July 1577. Then in 1578, *daimyo* Otomo Yoshisige (Sorin) of Bungo, who had hosted St. Francis Xavier as a young man and was a lifelong Zen Buddhist, after 27 years finally broke with his vices, put away his anti-Christian first wife, and was baptized Francisco along with his current mistress, who became his wife Julia. Most of

---

[172] Boxer, *Christian Century in Japan*, pp. 58-62, 95-96, 100 (first quote on 62); Elison, *Deus Destroyed*, p. 93; Berry, *Hideyoshi*, p. 44 (second quote).

[173] Cooper, *Rodrigues the Interpreter*, pp. 39, 45, 176; Boxer, *Christian Century in Japan*, pp. 70-71, 78, 100-101; *Cambridge History of Japan* IV, 326-327, 333; Sansom, *History of Japan* II, 234, 285-286; Berry, *Hideyoshi*, pp. 46-47.

his 70,000 subjects became Christians, and he destroyed many Buddhist temples and Shinto shrines. He actually wrote to Rome asking for the beatification of St. Francis Xavier.[174]

But in a society so full of violence, still more violence by Christians was the last thing the people needed, and Christ ever reminds us that "those who take the sword shall perish by the sword." The newly baptized Francisco of Bungo was badly defeated in the Battle of the Mimikawa River in December 1578 and lost substantial territories, though he did retain Bungo itself. In Bartholomew's domain there were now over 50,000 Christians, though many of these were probably not sincere converts. Takayama Ukon succeeded to his father's inheritance in the Takatsuki domain. By 1580, after Valignano had arrived, there were a total of about 150,000 Christians, ministered to by 20 European Jesuit missionary priests and a larger number of brothers (including many Japanese, who for the most part were not yet allowed to be ordained), and no less than two hundred churches. Valignano himself baptized Arima Harunobu, formerly a persecutor of the Church, as Protasio, and he immediately destroyed more than forty Buddhist temples and pledged full support to the Jesuits, giving them land for a school in his territory. But the Christians in Japan were still not really strong enough to be taking such measures. In June 1580 Bartholomew turned over to them full governmental powers (civil and criminal jurisdiction) in the entirely Christian city of Nagasaki, which they promptly fortified. At the end of 1580 Valignano established a novitiate at Uzuki in Bungo. Half the first students there were native Japanese. In 1582 he took four well-born Japanese Christian youths with him to Rome, but there still was no broad-based effort to ordain Japanese.[175]

On June 21, 1582 Oda Nobunaga, now 49 and controlling more than half of the provinces of Japan, residing temporarily in the Honnoji Buddhist monastery which he had seized, was suddenly attacked by his own troops and killed (or committed suicide). One of his chief lieutenants, Hideyoshi, assaulted the rebels before the month was over, cut off the head of their leader, Akechi Mitsuhide, and placed it before the corpse of Oda Nobunaga.[176] One could hardly ask for a better depiction of Japan's culture of death than rebel Akechi's severed head gazing with its dead eyes on Oda Nobunaga's ravaged body.

The next month Hideyoshi took over full control of Kyoto, ruling according to Japanese political tradition in the name of Oda Nobunaga's three-year-old grandson. Hideyoshi was the most potent and ambitious conqueror in Japanese history. He built on Oda's achievements and completed them. In 1584 he won

---

[174] *Cambridge History of Japan*, IV, 327-328, 333, 335-336, 338-339; Cooper, *Rodrigues the Interpreter*, pp. 43-44, 46; Elison, *Deus Destroyed*, pp. 28, 92; Boxer, *Christian Century in Japan*, p. 112.

[175] *Cambridge History of Japan* IV, 329-330, 334, 339-341, 343; Sansom, *History of Japan* II, 294-295, 298; Cooper, *Rodrigues the Interpreter*, pp. 19, 47-48, 50, 54-55, 58, 129; Elison, *Deus Destroyed*, pp. 27-28, 64, 81, 94-95, 98.

[176] Sansom, *History of Japan* II, 307-309; Boxer, *Christian Century in Japan*, pp. 71-72; Elison, *Deus Destroyed*, pp. 82-83; Berry, *Hideyoshi*, pp. 2, 41, 72.

the decisive Battle of Shizugatake against the members of Oda Nobunaga's family who had refused to accept his leadership. The leader of these foes, Shibata Katsuie, not only killed himself after the battle, but also stabbed his wife and daughters. In 1585 Hideyoshi was officially designated Regent and was planning soon to complete the subjugation of the southern island of Kyushu and the still independent province of Odowara in central Japan, allying himself with several of the Christian *daimyos*. In May of the following year Jesuit vice-provincial Gaspar Coelho and Father Louis Frois called on Hideyoshi at his Osaka castle. There he told them that, as soon as he had completed the conquest of Japan, he would begin a massive invasion of Korea, through which he would march on no less an enterprise than the conquest of China, a land which he had never seen nor really knew. He would do this, he said, not to add to his kingdoms and powers, of which he had already enough, but "solely. . . to immortalize himself with the name and fame of his power." Though Valignano had strictly charged the Jesuits in Japan not to become involved in its bloody politics, the imprudent Coelho hastened to assure Hideyoshi that two Portuguese carracks would be placed at his service for the transportation of his soldiers, plus other Portuguese ships from India. Hideyoshi told him that when he conquered China he would order all of its people to become Christians.[177]

Coelho's approval and encouragement of this immoral and madcap scheme has been generally recognized as the greatest single error committed in the Jesuit attempt to evangelize Japan. Not only did it link the Christian Church closely with wholly unprovoked aggression, but it gave Hideyoshi every reason to think that if the Fathers could promise so much political and military help to him, they could also marshal it against him. In the deceitful world of Japanese politics, suspicion was as good as truth. In 1587 Hideyoshi led to Kyushu an enormous army of 200,000, many armed with Western muskets, and won a complete victory, arriving in triumph July 12 at the Kyushu port of Hakata. Just two weeks earlier, as a kind of portent, Bartholomew, the first Christian *daimyo*, died. The Jesuits had already had to transfer their college and novitiate in Bungo (at Funai and Uzuki) to Yamaguchi because of the assaults of Bartholomew's enemies on his domain.[178]

Japan under Hideyoshi fulfilled all of Machiavelli's evil dreams about the prince. In the morning of July 24, 1587 Hideyoshi invited the misguided Father Coelho to meet him in Hakata, told him he would allow him to build a church there, and was taken aboard a Portuguese ship with great good fellowship. Later that very same day, he issued an edict which took the missionaries totally by surprise, bitterly condemning them, comparing them to the politically ambitious

---

[177] Berry, *Hideyoshi*, pp. 73-75, 77, 83-84, 88-89 178-179, 207-208 (quote); Sansom, *History of Japan* II, 346-347; *Cambridge History of Japan* IV, 267, 348; Boxer, *Christian Century of Japan*, pp. 140-141; Elison, *Deus Destroyed*, pp. 112-114; Cooper, *Rodrigues the Interpreter*, pp. 67-68.

[178] Sansom, *History of Japan* II, 321-323, 354-356; *Cambridge History of Japan* IV 343, 352-353, 357; Berry, *Hideyoshi*, pp. 89-90; Boxer, *Christian Century in Japan*, p. 145; Cooper, *Rodrigues the Interpreter*, p. 61.

and very worldly Buddhist monks, and ordering their expulsion from the country. He took back Nagasaki from Jesuit rule, and demanded that Takayama Ukon abjure his faith; but he would not.[179]

But Hideyoshi did not yet really mean it. His purpose was more to frighten the Jesuits than to actually remove them. No less than 120 of them assembled at Hirado in January 1588, but only three actually left the country on the annual Great Ship, while the remainder dispersed to the territories of the Christian *daimyos*, where they could continue their work of evangelization if they proceeded quietly and prudently. At the end of 1589 Hideyoshi set in motion the invasion of Odawara province with an army of the same size that had conquered Kyushu. Odawara surrendered unconditionally to him in August 1590; he now ruled the whole of Japan. Valignano learned of his anti-Christian edict when he stopped at Macao in China in July 1588. Nevertheless he pressed on, landing at Nagasaki in July 1590, to find that Coelho had died two months before. Coldly he commented that if Coelho had been still alive when he arrived, he would have "punished him severely" for ignoring his explicit instructions to stay out of Japanese politics, and for all his actions contrary to the policy and orders of the Society of Jesus.[180]

On March 3, 1591 Hideyoshi received Valignano not as a missionary, but as an accredited representative of the Viceroy of India, along with the four Japanese who had gone to Rome. He paid them great honor. On the following day he summoned the excellent Jesuit interpreter Rodrigues to regulate his new clock, and asked him many questions about Europe and India, while expounding his plans for the conquest of China. But at the end of the month, returning to Kyoto after a brief absence, he declared that though he wanted to encourage trade with the Europeans, he did not want their missionaries in Japan preaching against the Buddhist and Shinto religions and destroying their temples and shrines, and especially he did not want to see them converting *daimyos*. On September 12 he officially permitted ten missionaries to remain in Nagasaki pending a reply to his letter to the Viceroy of India, but ordered them not to proselytize. But he had made his point that the continued presence of the missionaries in Japan was dependent solely on his fragile good will. In 1592 died the famous half-blind Christian minstrel, Brother Laurence, a convert of St. Francis Xavier.[181]

Steadily Hideyoshi's megalomania grew. By 1592 he was madly declaring that he intended to conquer India as well as Korea and China, and had written at the end of the previous year to the Spanish governor of the Philippines

---

[179] Sansom, *History of Japan* II, 347-348; *Cambridge History of Japan* IV, 360-363; Boxer, *Christian Century of Japan*, pp. 145-148; Berry, *Hideyoshi*, pp. 91-93; Elison, *Deus Destroyed*, pp. 115-118, 124; Cooper, *Rodrigues the Interpreter*, pp. 61-62.

[180] Sansom, *History of Japan* II, 324-328; Boxer, *Christian Century in Japan*, pp. 149-150, 153, 172-173; Berry, *Hideyoshi*, pp. 94-95; Conrad Totman, *Tokugawa Ieyasu, Shogun* (Union City CA, 1983), pp. 54-56; Cooper, *Rodrigues the Interpreter*, pp. 72-73; Elison, *Deus Destroyed*, p. 134.

[181] Cooper, *Rodrigues the Interpreter*, pp. 75-78, 83, 85, 87-89, 91-93, 177; Sansom, *History of Japan* II, 349; Boxer, *Christian Century in Japan*, p. 153.

demanding his immediate submission: "You should bear the banner of surrender and come to submit. If, creeping and crawling along, there is any delay, it will be necessary promptly to attack." In April 1592 he assaulted Korea with 225,000 men and 700 ships, an apparently irresistible force hurled against a much smaller and less militaristic country.[182]

But in this maximum crisis for their nation, Korea produced an admiral named Yi Sun-Sin, who has been compared to Horatio Nelson, the British victor at the Nile, Copenhagen, and Trafalgar.[183] Yi deployed a fleet of heavy-timbered, metal-spiked "turtle ships" lying very low in the water, the likes of which no Japanese had ever seen. Japanese naval communications and transportation were severely disrupted. When Chinese soldiers began to arrive, the conquest ground to a halt. Hideyoshi never came in person to command his army. In May 1593 the Japanese forces evacuated the Korean capital of Seoul, and by summer most of the their troops had returned home, ignominiously defeated.[184]

In the spring of 1593 four Franciscan friars left the Philippines for Japan; later in the year three more came to join them. Incorrectly believing they had permission to do so, they built a church in Kyoto. Evangelization was proceeding quite well despite Hideyoshi's edict against the Christians and the fact that conversions could no longer be forced; it was estimated there were 300,000 Christians in Japan by 1596, with 60,000 baptized in the nine years since Hideyoshi's edict. A bishop arrived at Nagasaki from Europe in August 1596; one of his first acts was to excommunicate the Franciscan friars for coming to Japan without permission. Hideyoshi saw the depth of hostility between the Christian orders and resolved to play one against the other. His suspicions of dark designs by the Christian missionaries were renewed when the Manila galleon *San Felipe* was wrecked on the island of Shikoku, broken up, and its cargo confiscated, including a large quantity of arms and ammunition. Attempting to recover his cargo, the ship's captain threatened to call on the long arm of Spain's king Philip II, while his pilot was supposed to have said (no one knows whether he actually did) that Western conquest followed the missionaries. Furthermore, two more Franciscan friars were on the ship and survived its wreck. In December 1596 Hideyoshi allowed some Jesuits to remain in Japan, but arrested the six Franciscans in Kyoto, mutilated their faces, and sent them to Nagasaki for execution along with a native group including three Jesuit brothers, one of whom was Paul Miki. A total of seven Europeans led by St. Peter Baptist and 19 Japanese Christians including Paul Miki shed their blood for Christ in this

---

[182] Sansom, *History of Japan* II, 353-354; *Cambridge History of Japan* IV, 270-273; Boxer, *Christian Century in Japan*, pp. 261-262; Berry, *Hideyoshi*, p. 212 (quote).

[183] See Volume Five of this history, Chapter 10.

[184] Sansom, *History of Japan* II, 353, 357-358; *Cambridge History of Japan* IV, 277-278; Berry, *Hideyoshi*, pp. 213-214, 225,

first mass martyrdom in Japan, on February 5, 1597. Like St. Peter, they were crucified upside down.[185]

In March 1597 Hideyoshi ordered a new attempt to conquer Korea and invade China from there. The Japanese proceeded with terrible cruelty, killing every Korean official they captured and every member of his family. Japanese received credit for Korean heads cut off by collecting the noses (just one army presented 18,350 noses). They pushed to within fifty miles of Seoul, but Chinese reinforcements stopped them short of it. Hideyoshi again ordered most of the Jesuits expelled, except for Rodrigues the interpreter and a few others. Talking to Rodrigues, Hideyoshi said that he had heard that the Spanish empire was built up by its missionaries, with the Philippines as an example. In September senior Jesuits met and decided that in view of the continuing official hostility to the missionaries in Japan, they should close their school at Arima and their college at Amakusa, never stop in one place more than two weeks, wear Japanese dress, and exercise "the greatest caution"—but not leave the country unless explicitly and personally forced to do so. There were still 46 Jesuit priests and 79 Jesuit brothers in Japan. In Korea in October, peerless Admiral Yi Sun-sin was returned to command after his incompetent replacement was killed in battle, and once again turned the tide of the invasion. In the summer of 1598 Hideyoshi recalled most of his army for the second time, leaving 60,000 of his best troops to hold the area around Pusan. That summer Valignano began his third, last and longest visit to Japan.[186]

Hideyoshi, 62, was now a dying man, and in mid-August 1598 called the five greatest noblemen among his supporters to form a council of regency for his only surviving son, Hideyori, just five years old. They all took an oath of loyalty to the boy. Oaths of loyalty which stand in the way of the exercise of power are perilously weak even in countries whose moral and ethical systems are much superior to Japan's. The strongest of these five noblemen, Tokugawa Ieyasu, who was most completely to betray his trust, betrothed Hideyori to his two-year-old granddaughter. Hideyoshi died on September 18, after a last fruitless plea to the five nobles to keep their word.[187]

In March 1599 the long-serving Jesuit missionary Father Organtino held Holy Week services in Kyoto despite all the edicts against Christians, and Rodrigues the interpreter persuaded the governor of Nagasaki not to do anything about it. In his annual report to Rome, Valignano praised the late Hideyoshi for arranging for the momentarily undisputed succession of his little son, and for

---

[185] Sansom, *History of Japan* II, 312, 350, 363-364, 374; Cooper, *Rodrigues the Interpreter*, pp. 114, 116, 126-129, 132-133, 135-139, 154-158, 160; Berry, *Hideyoshi* pp. 225-227; *Cambridge History of Japan* IV, 364-365; Boxer, *Christian Century in Japan*, p. 166; Elison, *Deus Destroyed*, p. 137.

[186] Sansom, *History of Japan* II, 312, 339, 360; *Cambridge History of Japan* IV, 287-287, 290-291; Cooper, *Rodrigues the Interpreter*, pp. 142-146, 169; Berry, *Hideyoshi*, p. 233; Boxer, *Christian Century in Japan*, p. 73.

[187] Sansom, *History of Japan* II, 368-369; Berry, *Hideyoshi*, pp. 234-235; Cooper, *Rodrigues the Interpreter*, pp. 183-185.

setting up the five-man regency.[188] It is strange that the man who saw so clearly the terrible vices of Japan's indigenous culture still could not see how far they extended.

In 1600 Ieyasu began his move toward power. He attacked one of the other regents, who controlled the second largest domain in Japan (Ieyasu's was the largest) and had gained possession of young Hideyori. At the Battle of Sekigahara in September Ieyasu suborned one of his opponents' generals and as a result won the battle decisively. Betrayal was "the name of the game" in Japan. Defeated regent Mori Terumoto turned over Osaka castle to Ieyasu, which he made the strongest fortress in Japan. There were still Christian *daimyos*. They fought on both sides, but stood out because of their refusal when captured to commit suicide in proper Japanese fashion.[189]

Meanwhile, in the spring of 1600, a Dutch ship named *Liefde*, which had sailed more than half way around the world through the Straits of Magellan, was wrecked on the rocky coast of Japan, with only 24 survivors of an original crew of 110, in the last stages of starvation and dehydration. One of these survivors was a tough and adaptable Englishman, Will Adams, who knew some Portuguese. He acquired fluent Japanese very quickly and thereby was soon able to talk directly to Ieyasu. He told him that his Protestant England was in constant conflict with Spain and Portugal, which he alleged were using their evil Catholic religion to conquer the world. Ieyasu came to trust Adams, and in 1601 took him into his service, building warships which attacked Spanish and Portuguese ships. But in time-honored Japanese fashion Ieyasu nevertheless pretended friendship with the Spanish and Portuguese missionaries, authorizing the Jesuits to live in Kyoto, Osaka, and Nagasaki and thereby implicitly cancelling Hideyoshi's expulsion edict. In September 1601 he made Rodrigues the interpreter his commercial agent at Nagasaki; in October he gave audience to the Franciscan Jeronimo de Jesus and agreed to send a message to Manila expressing good will toward the Franciscans (known enemies of the Jesuits) and a desire for more trade.[190]

In 1602 Francisco, son of Christian *daimyo* Antonio Murayama, was ordained in Nagasaki, one of the first few Japanese to receive holy orders. This was commendable, but not rapid progress 23 years after Valignano had called for adaptation of the missionaries to Japanese customs and culture and had held open at least the possibility of the ordination of native priests. In August Valignano called a Jesuit meeting to discuss the fiscal difficulties of the mission. There were now no less than 127 Jesuits in Japan, of whom 70 were priests, mostly European. This was a great many men to support on the very limited income the

---

[188] Cooper, *Rodrigues the Interpreter*, p. 192; Boxer, *Christian Century in Japan*, p. 179.

[189] Sansom, *History of Japan* II, 392-395; Totman,*Tokugawa Ieyasu*, pp. 71-72, 75, 77-78, 81; Cooper, *Rodrigues the Interpreter*, pp. 193-194.

[190] Sansom, *History of Japan* II, 402-403; Totman, *Tokugawa Ieyasu*, pp. 15-16, 18-19, 85; Cooper, *Rodrigues the Interpreter*, pp. 195, 199-200, 205; Boxer, *Christian Century in Japan*, pp. 205-206.

Jesuits obtained from their share in the trade of the "Great Ship" which on several occasions was wrecked or captured, while money sent to them from Europe often did not arrive. In January 1603 Valignano held another meeting to discuss making Japan and China a separate Jesuit province from that of far-distant India. Five days later he left Japan forever. He was to be sorely missed in the coming years.[191]

In February Ieyasu took the title of shogun and declared his intention to restore the *bakufu*, "which Nobunaga had flouted and Hideyoshi ignored, if not destroyed." That same month he summoned Rodrigues the interpreter to court and gave him high favor. Ieyasu made the Christian *daimyo* Antonio Murayama governor of Christian Nagasaki. But Rodrigues had not lived in Japan from the age of sixteen for nothing. He visited Ieyasu's honest and upright confidential advisor Honda Masazumi, who warned him that Ieyasu continued to be anti-Christian at heart and did not want any of the *daimyos* to become Christians. In 1604 Ieyasu issued a rather vague and mild anti-Christian edict, which was not strictly enforced. There were now about 750,000 Christians in Japan, with an average annual increase of five or six thousand.[192]

But now came an ominous sign: in 1605 Christian *daimyo* Omura Sumitada, saying that the Fathers had cheated him out of land in Nagasaki, expelled all of them from his domain, denounced his faith, and became a persecutor of the Christians.[193] In that same year, a well-educated Japanese convert named Fabian Fucan published a Christian apologetic which included a penetrating indictment of Japanese Buddhism:

> The claim that the land is put at peace by virtue of the gods' power is without foundation. Even more unreasonable is the claim that it is put at peace by the majesty of Buddha's law. That is because Buddhism, in the final analysis, is a doctrine which preaches the absolute void, and considers good and evil undifferentiated, perniciousness and righteousness the same. How can the claim that our mind is of void and that there is no master over punishment or bliss be construed into a basis of peace? Quite the contrary; here is the origin of revolt and perturbation. . . . Beginning with the wars between the houses of Minamoto and Taira, steeped in pride, through the Shokyu Disturbance, all the way down to our times, you will find in the histories nothing but assault in one place, battle at another. About more recent events, you can hear from men advanced in years; the rout of such-and-such a year, the uprising of another, here a conflagration, there a demolition. That's all you'll hear. Peace by benefit of the Buddhas and gods, indeed! What period in our country's history can be designated that?[194]

---

[191] Boxer, *Christian Century in Japan*, pp. 182, 274; Cooper, *Rodrigues the Interpreter*, pp. 200-201, 203.

[192] Sansom, *History of Japan* II, 396-397 (quote on 396), 399-401; Boxer, *Christian Century in Japan*, pp. 184, 187; Cooper, *Rodrigues the Interpreter*, pp. 202-203; Totman, *Tokugawa Ieyasu*, pp. 87, 113.

[193] Boxer, *Christian Century in Japan*, p. 186.

[194] Elison, *Deus Destroyed*, pp. 52-53.

Fabian Fucan understood as well as Alessandro Valignano the sources and character of the cultural evil in Japan. Yet the man who could write these words apostatized from the Faith just two years later, and was to become the author of the most comprehensive attack on Christianity in Japan in the 17th century, grimly entitled *Deus Destroyed*, published in 1620.[195]

In 1609 the Portuguese "great ship," a carrack named *Madre de Deus* commanded by André Pessoa, arrived at Nagasaki with a particularly rich cargo of Chinese silk. Two Dutch ships arrived shortly afterward in nearby Hirado. Ieyasu gave the Dutch the first audience. Blaming Pessoa for the killing of forty Japanese in a riot at Macao, Ieyasu ordered his arrest. The carrack beat off several Japanese attacks, but then caught fire, whereupon Captain Pessoa blew himself up with his ship, which went down with all its cargo and most of its crew. Many Japanese greatly admired his self-immolation; but this was not the face Christianity needed to present in this most militaristic of countries. Rodrigues the interpreter, who had been Shogun Ieyasu's agent in Nagasaki, was expelled from Japan two months later. Christian *daimyo* Arima Harunobu was dispossessed of his lands in 1612 and executed. Eight of his samurai were Christians. Three of them held to the Faith despite his attempts to persuade them to give it up, and were publicly martyred. Thousands of Japanese Christians witnessed the martyrdom, praying and singing hymns to honor it. Four of the other five, who had denied the Faith, returned to its affirmation.[196] In September 1612 Ieyasu wrote to the Spanish governor of the Philippines:

> The doctrine followed in your country differs entirely from ours. Therefore, I am persuaded that it would not suit us. . . . It is best, therefore, to put an end to the preaching of your doctrine in our soil.[197]

At the beginning of 1614, now past 73 and ruling through his son Hidetada who now had the title of Shogun, Ieyasu requested an eminent Buddhist monk named Suden to write a new edict against the Christians, entitled "Statement on the Expulsion of the *Bateren*" [the pejorative Japanese word for foreigners]. This document declared that Christians had come to Japan "hoping to spread their evil doctrine without permission, to confound true religion, change the political order of the realm, and make it their own." Not only were foreign missionaries to be expelled, but every Japanese was to be enrolled in one of the Buddhist sects. Those who had become Christians must give up their newfound Faith. Ieyasu made it clear that this edict was to be strictly enforced, as it was until he died in 1616, and then by Hidetada and later by his son Iemitsu. Ieyasu declared, in response to protests: "If Christianity spreads, the people of the realm become

---

[195] *Ibid.*, pp. 155-159; Boxer, *Christian Century in Japan*, pp. 337-338.

[196] Sansom, *History of Japan* II, 312. 403; Boxer, *Christian Century in Japan*, pp. 271-272, 279-285, 314-315, 330, 342; Cooper, *Rodrigues the Interpreter*, pp. 261-267; Totman, *Tokugawa Ieyasu*, p. 105.

[197] Totman, *Tokugawa Ieyasu*, pp. 137-138.

rebellious. Therefore, to stamp out the evil at its source, not a single Portuguese will be permitted to remain in the country." Shortly afterward he informed the spokesman from the annual "Great Ship" that he wished to continue this trade, but was resolved to expel the missionaries forever.[198]

In Nagasaki, home to 20,000 Christians, there were fervent religious processions, often led by Christian *daimyo* Antonio Murayama and his family, with flagellations and pledges of faith even unto martyrdom. The missionaries compiled exhortations to martyrdom. On October 27, 1614 Japanese officials took formal possession of all Christian churches and convents in the country. Many of the bodies in Christian cemeteries were reburied secretly to avoid profanation. In that very same month the Jesuits held the first congregation in the newly designated province of Japan and recommended against making Japanese converts either Jesuit priests or brothers. Since the very next month most of the European missionaries were shipped out of Japan (88 of 115), there could hardly have been a worse-timed action. In 1615 the heroic Christian *daimyo* Takayama Ukon died in Manila. Meanwhile Ieyasu and Hidetada had consolidated their rule by capturing and burning Osaka castle, which had fallen into the hands of Hideyoshi's son Hideyori, now grown to manhood. Its garrison contained many Christians. Ieyasu had broken his regency oath, as oaths were so often broken in Japan. Hideyori and his mother died by their own hands. In 1616, after his father's death, Hidetada reissued his anti-Christian edicts and continued their vigorous enforcement.[199]

Forty-nine priests, almost all European, remained in Japan. In 1617 Christovao Ferreira, assistant superior of the Jesuit residence in Kyoto, took his final vows and travelled widely, administering the sacraments, finally making his way to Nagasaki. In April of that year a Jesuit and a Franciscan were martyred at Omura. In October 1619 55 Christians were burned to death on the dry bed of the Kamo River in Kyoto, including children as young as five who cried out: "Jesus, receive our souls!" In 1620 Ferreira became procurator of the Jesuits remaining in Japan. He is said to have heard 1,300 confessions while walking the beaches of Nagasaki at night. In 1622 there were three great martyrdoms, the first in August before at least 30,000 people, many of them Christians singing the "Magnificat" and "Te Deum Laudamus," while the martyrs said "*sayonara*" (the Japanese farewell) from the top of the piles of wood which would become their funeral pyres. The second great martyrdom was at Nagasaki in September. Ten Dominicans, nine Jesuits, three Franciscans, and 32 laymen were burned after horrible tortures. The third great martyrdom was at Edo (now Tokyo) in November, in which Father de Angelis, who had been the first missionary to go to the northernmost Japanese island of Hokkaido, perished with 49 companions.

---

[198] *Ibid.*, pp. 140 (first quote), 157 (second quote); Sansom, *History of Japan* II 312, 404; *Cambridge History of Japan* IV, 367; Boxer, *Christian Century in Japan*, pp. 317-320, 325-326.

[199] Boxer, *Christian Century in Japan*, pp. 323-327, 330-332; *Cambridge History of Japan* IV, 368; Sansom, *History of Japan* II, 398, 404; Totman, *Tokugawa Ieyasu*, pp. 177, 188; Dunne, *Generation of Giants*, pp. 166-167.

But nearly 40 Western missionaries were still in Japan, along with just one Japanese priest.[200]

In 1623 Shogun Hidetada announced his retirement and the succession of his sadistic son Iemitsu, a vehement enemy of the Christians. Before the year was out Iemitsu burned 50 more Christians at Edo. The Jesuits had actually recorded 17,000 baptisms in Japan *after* the full persecution began in 1614. But a native clergy, now almost nonexistent, was desperately needed since because of their physical differences European missionaries could not escape detection for long in Japan, while native priests could have done so. In 1630 De Propaganda Fide issued a statement favoring the ordination of natives in the Orient, and urged Pope Urban VIII to "take energetic measures with the view of preparing the way for the creation of indigenous bishops and priests in northern Asia." But it was far too late now to do this for Japan. Christianity might have been impossible to suppress in Japan if there had been a major effort to prepare and ordain Japanese priests in the fifty years that had elapsed since the first arrival of Jesuit Visitor Valignano. What they might have done was demonstrated by the Japanese Jesuit priest Pedro Casui Kibe, who after ordination in Rome in 1620 and a series of fantastic adventures during his long return, landed in Japan disguised as a merchant and worked among the people for nine years before he was captured and martyred.[201]

At this point, in the 1630's, the persecution reached a level of horror which in some ways exceeds that of all other Christian martyrdoms. Most martyrdoms in the history of the Church have been the work of one particular sovereign or a temporary, angry faction in a city or region. They burst out, then subside. But in Japan the persecution was deliberately intended to destroy Christianity altogether, and it was carried on by three able rulers in succession without a break: Ieyasu, Hidetada, and Iemitsu. When in 1631 and 1632 five European missionaries were taken to the hot sulphur springs of Unzen, slashed by knives, had scalding corrosive water poured into the cuts, and then were brought for burning at the stake, every one stood fast, crying *"Viva la fe de Christo!"* ("long live the faith of Christ!"). Infuriated by such unbreakable spirit, Iemitsu and his men developed the Satanic torture called "the pit," in which the victims were hung upside down from a gallows over a pit filled with excrement. A simple hand gesture signifying willingness to apostatize would release the victim instantly from the incredible torment. In October 1633 Christovao Ferreira apostatized after five hours of hanging in the pit; but Juliao Nakaura, a priest who had been one of the four Japanese taken to Rome by Valignano, held firm to the

---

[200] Boxer, *Christian Century in Japan*, pp. 327, 332, 335-336, 342-343, 349-350, 358; Elison, *Deus Destroyed*, p. 188.

[201] Boxer, *Christian Century in Japan*, pp. 336-337; *Cambridge History of Japan* IV, 368; Elison, *Deus Destroyed*, pp. 180, 197; Carlos Merces de Melo, S.J., *Recruitment and Formation of the Native Clergy of India*, p. 211.

end. The following June the new Jesuit vice-provincial for Japan, Sebastian Vieira, endured the pit until death finally released him.[202]

Shogun Iemitsu now issued the series of Sakoku ("Closed Country") edicts which cut Japan off from all the rest of the world, except for a handful of carefully guarded (and non-Catholic) Dutch traders at Nagasaki. Japanese were prohibited on pain of death from travelling abroad, except to Pusan in Korea. They were forbidden to construct seagoing ships. The final Sakoku edict ended the lucrative trade with China carried by the Portuguese. A delegation sent from Macao to ask for some easement of this total ban was killed to the last man in 1640, and their ship was burned with all its cargo.[203]

Shogun Iemitsu was about to mount a major invasion of the increasingly Catholic Philippines[204] when a rebellion broke out in the Shimabara peninsula of Kyushu in December of 1637, where many of the people had been Christian though most had recanted the Faith under duress. They cried out "Jesus!", "Maria!", and "Santiago!" as they marched, and carried banners in Portuguese saying "Praised be the Most Holy Sacrament!" The rebellion caused the projected invasion of the Philippines to be abandoned. The largely Christian rebels killed 13,000 of Iemitsu's soldiers, but were finally shut up in the castle of Hara. A Dutch warship bombarded it from the sea. It was carried by storm in the spring of 1638 after its defenders had almost entirely run out of food.[205]

In the summer of 1639 the last survivors of the original mission to Japan— two Spanish Franciscans, one Italian Jesuit, and two Japanese—were captured in northern Japan. The Italian Jesuit and one of the Japanese apostatized under torture. The two Spanish Franciscans stood firm at the stake, and the Japanese priest Pedro Kasui Kibe perished in the pit. The apostate Jesuit Ferreira was there, trying to induce them all to repudiate their faith as he had done; but the staunch three would not.[206]

In all there were over four thousand martyrs, all but about 70 of them Japanese. Not even the most evil society can crush all aspiration for the divine and the holy. These four thousand Japanese shed their blood freely, enduring the most fiendish tortures that Satan could inflict, rather than deny Christ. But the massive power of the government, marshalled by the Tokugawa successors of

---

[202] Boxer, *Christian Century in Japan*, pp. 352-353, 390; Elison, *Deus Destroyed*, pp. 190-191. The suggestion in some histories that Ferreira was very old and sick are incorrect. He was in his fifties and, so far as we know, in good health. He lived in Japan for no less than 25 years after his apostasy and actually wrote a book in Japanese against the Christian Faith in 1636, calling the First Commandment "the root of rebellion and the inception of the reign's overthrow" (Elison, *op. cit.*, p. 190).

[203] Boxer, *Christian Century in Japan*, pp. 372-373, 384-385; *Cambridge History of Japan* IV, 296, 300, 369; Elison, *Deus Destroyed*, pp. xi, 193-194.

[204] See section on "Southeast Asia," below, this chapter.

[205] Boxer, *Christian Century in Japan*, pp. 373-374, 377-383; Elison, *Deus Destroyed*, pp. 220-221.

[206] Boxer, *Christian Century in Japan*, p. 390; Elison, *Deus Destroyed*, pp. 190-191, 196.

Ieyasu and Iemitsu, crushed them so thoroughly that they disappeared from sight. Vast quantities of propaganda against Christians and Christianity was distributed; Christians became stock villains in plays and other stage performances. In 1658 a handbook was published on the persecution of Christians, sneering at the inability of the Christian God to protect his people. In that year some six hundred hidden Christians were found near Nagasaki; 411 were martyred, 77 died in prison, and only 99 apostatized. In 1665 all *daimyos* were ordered to establish local inquisitions against Christians. By now it had become completely impossible for any European Catholic to come to Japan and keep his liberty.[207]

Still some Japanese Christians survived—without priests, without the Mass, with every head of family obliged to appear once a year in a Buddhist temple or before a magistrate and declare his membership in a Buddhist sect and sign an avowal of the membership of all his family in that sect. Virtually all printed Christian books had been confiscated, but some still circulated in manuscript, notably a ten-chapter summary of Catholic doctrine and a treatise on contrition. (The hidden Japanese had no priests to confess to, so had to rely on perfect contrition at the moment of death.) They memorized the prayers that St. Francis Xavier had first taught them—the Our Father, the Hail Mary, the Apostles' Creed, the Ten Commandments, the Salve Regina, the Confiteor, and the fifteen mysteries of the Rosary—said them often, and never forgot them. Every secret Christian community had a catechist who led the recitation of prayers and taught Christian doctrine, and one or several baptizers, who passed on from generation to generation the exact Latin words of the baptismal ritual. Holy pictures, crosses and crucifixes, Christian medals, rosaries and statues were preserved as priceless treasures. In formerly Christian areas, all the people were required to trample on a picture of Christ or of Our Lady every year. The hidden Christians complied with this requirement of the government because the only alternative was a horrible death in the pit. Periodically some of them were discovered, still staunch in the Faith. Over 500 Christians were found in Bungo from 1660 to 1691; 486 were killed or died in prison, while just 24 were still living in prison in 1691. The last mass martyrdom occurred in Mino province as late as 1697, with 35 victims.[208]

After American Commodore Matthew Galbraith Perry opened Japan to American trade in 1854, the Catholic French, with the assistance of American Consul-General Townsend Harris, were able five years later to obtain permission to trade in Japan, with the right to build churches for their people in Japan and to administer cemeteries. The ceremony of trampling on pictures of Christ and Our Lady was abolished. French priests began to appear in Japan. One of them was Father Petitjean. On March 17, 1865, he saw gathered in front of his closed church a group of about fifteen men, women and children, their demeanor

---

[207] Boxer, *Christian Century in Japan*, pp. 337-338, 358, 360-361, 388, 395-397; *Cambridge History of Japan* IV, 370; Johannes Laures, S.J., *The Catholic Church in Japan* (Tokyo, 1954), pp. 178-179.
[208] Laures, *Catholic Church in Japan*, pp. 174-175, 185, 194-197.

showing great reverence. He opened the church and entered, the Japanese following.[209]

> Three middle-aged women approached him, knelt down beside him, and one of them, laying a hand on her breast, said to him in a whispered voice: "All of us have the same heart as you." "Indeed?" asked the astonished priest. "Where do you come from?" "We are all from Urakami, where nearly all have the same heart." Then one of the women asked: "Where is the statue of Santa Maria?" Instead of giving an answer, Petitjean conducted the group to the altar of the Blessed Virgin. All knelt down with him and wept for joy, exclaiming: "Yes, this is indeed Santa Maria! Behold her divine Infant in her arms!"
>
> Then they asked a lot of questions. One of the women remarked: "We celebrate the Feast of the Lord on the 25th day of the cold month. We were told that at midnight of that day He was born in a stable. Then He grew up to manhood in poverty and suffering to die for us on the cross in his 33rd year. At present we are in the season of sorrow. Have you also these feasts?"
>
> "Yes," the priest answered, "we have today the seventeenth day of Lent."[210]

It had been two hundred and thirty-two years since Jesuit superior Christovao Ferreira had apostatized in the pit. After all that enormous lapse of time, no less than nine generations, there remained 1,300 Christians in Urakami alone, and nearly 14,000 throughout Japan. The preservation of the Faith so long underground by so many is unique in the history of Christianity.[211]

The Japanese, forced to face the fact of immense Western material preponderance, were now determined to enter into the modern world at any cost. After the Meiji imperial restoration, a top-level Japanese embassy to Europe and America headed by Prince Iwakura Tomomi was very coldly received by almost every Christian country, because about 3,400 of the hidden Japanese Christians had been deported following their discovery (all had actually been subject to execution under still existing laws). The nations of the West, then still truly Christian (Protestant as well as Catholic), made it clear that they would do nothing to help Japan unless and until the persecution ceased. Therefore, so it did, by imperial edict in the year 1873. The deported Christians were all returned to their homes.[212]

Still the great majority of the Japanese population remained and remains pagan. [Many Japanese Christians gathered in Nagasaki, site of the great martyrdoms, in the early years of the twentieth century. Most of them died under the second U.S. atomic bomb. In no country have the faithful borne so great and terrible a cross for Christ, for so long, as in Japan.]

---

[209] *Ibid.*, pp. 206-210.

[210] *Ibid.*, pp. 210-211.

[211] *Ibid.*, pp. 212-214, 227

[212] *Ibid.*, pp. 223-226.

[In a culture where trust and constancy was almost unknown, the four thousand Japanese martyrs testified to it for all ages. If Japan has been truly cleansed of its worst evils by defeat in World War II, as seems to be the case, it is may well be due to prayers offered before the Face of God by its martyrs of the seventeenth century, ever since then in Heaven.]

Southeast Asia (1513-1671)

So, despite the immense promise seen for conversions in the Orient by St. Francis Xavier, the three great Oriental civilizations of India, China, and Japan proved for the most part impossible to penetrate. With India already almost half Muslim and therefore unreachable by missionaries, and with the native Hindu religion and philosophy fundamentally antithetical to Christianity, only the spectacular example of St. Francis Xavier and the very slow progress of a Roberto de Nobili could make missionary headway—and then never very much, in view of the vast number of people in India and the division of the country into multitudinous separate states. In China, as St. Francis Xavier realized at the end of his life, prospects were best and the consequences of success most world-shaking. No one will ever know if China could in fact have been converted in the 17th and 18th centuries, but be that as it may, the Church itself made such conversion impossible by its misguided ruling against the Chinese rites for the dead. In Japan, though the people were much more open initially to conversion than either in China or in India, the dominant characteristics of the government and the culture—rampant militarism and utter ruthlessness—literally destroyed the missions and drove the few Japanese Christians deep underground. So all three of these missionary efforts (compared to that which converted the Roman empire, the barbarians around it, Armenia, Georgia, Ethiopia, and the Americas) must be pronounced failures, except of course for the souls that were saved in the course of them. However, the evangelization of Black Africa in the 19th and 20th centuries and of Korea in the 20th century show how much can be accomplished by missionaries in non-Western countries.

But at the same time as the largely unsuccessful missionary efforts in India, China and Japan, there was an immensely successful effort in the great archipelago named for Philip II of Spain, the Philippines; and a more successful effort than anywhere else in Asia, in the country later to be known as Vietnam. Hardly a word on the evangelization of Vietnam is found in books in English—only the French, who accomplished it, have written about it. The Philippines were American territory for more than forty years, and there is a little more information about their evangelization by the Spanish, but not much. Yet these were the two greatest success stories of the Church's Oriental mission, and very much deserve to be told.

Southeast Asia is a vast region, until the Vietnam war in the late 20th century very little known to Americans, and in Europe known only by the countries that administered parts of it: France for Vietnam and Indo-China, Britain for Burma and Malaya and Singapore and North Borneo, the Netherlands for Indonesia, Spain for the Philippines. Siam (later called Thailand) remained free of Western control. The region as a whole, except for the Philippines, is thickly jungled and very hot, but fertile. Its cultures were very alien to the West, and its rulers totally absolute. The native religions were a mix very difficult to penetrate (except in the Philippines, where most people were still primitive animists when the Spanish arrived). Burma, Siam, and Cambodia and Laos in Indo-China were fervently Buddhist, with some Brahman Hinduism thrown in. In Cambodia the great city of Angkor had been built originally to glorify the Hindu god Shiva, but in the twelfth and early thirteenth century became Buddhist.[213] Indonesia also had both the Hindu Shiva worship and Buddhism, mixed with Tantric (magical) cults. Kublai Khan, the Mongol Emperor of China, had tried but failed to extend his domination over the great kingdom of Madjapahit in Java at the end of the thirteenth century.[214] Malaya, most of Indonesia (including the principal Spice Islands), and substantial parts of the large southern Philippine island of Mindanao had become Muslim during the 150 years before the Europeans arrived, when traders from Arabia, Persia, and Muslim India began appearing in ever greater numbers in this region, with Muslim missionaries from India afterwards remembered for their zeal to make converts.[215]

As always, Muslims proved almost impossible to convert. Buddhism proved almost equally resistant to Christianity, which was never able to gain a significant foothold in Burma, Siam, Laos, or Cambodia—all strongly Buddhist nations.[216] Vietnam was different, being not so strongly Buddhist and markedly influenced by Confucianism, which had much in common with the natural law recognized by the Christians. It did not help that the initial penetration of and discoveries in Southeast Asia were mostly made by far-ranging Portuguese and Spanish seeking above all their individual fortunes; the missionaries they sent out almost all went to India, China, and Japan, leaving a bare handful for Southeast Asia.

The work of evangelizing Southeast Asia began in the Moluccas or Spice Islands in the east of Indonesia, originally reached by the Portuguese in 1513, just two years after the great Portuguese viceroy Afonso de Albuquerque had

---

[213] D. G. E. Hall, *A History of Southeast Asia*, 3rd ed. (New York, 1968), pp. 100-106, 114-115, 118-121, 126. Angkor was abandoned by its original Khmer inhabitants and taken over by the Siamese in 1389 (*ibid.*, p. 130).

[214] *Ibid.*, pp. 72-73, 77-80.

[215] *Ibid.*, pp. 88, 243-244; Donald F. Lach, *Southeast Asia in the Eyes of Europe; the Sixteenth Century* (Chicago, 1968), p. 573, 578, 596; E. S. de Klerck, *History of the Netherlands East Indies* (Amsterdam, 1938, 1975) I, 147-149, 153-154.

[216] For the earlier ineffectual missionary attempts, which even later attained very little success, see Hall, *History of Southeast Asia,* p. 255 and Lach, *Southeast Asia in the Eyes of Europe*, pp. 562, 565, 567-568 (for Cambodia); Lach, *op. cit.*, pp. 537, 558 (for Burma and Siam). The Dominican Silvestre de Azevedo in 1583 attempted to use Ricci's methods in Cambodia, but received no support in doing so except from the great Jesuit Valignano; the vicar of Malacca excommunicated him for five years (Dunne, *Generation of Giants*, pp. 231-232).

established firm Portuguese control of the very strategically situated port of Malacca on the Indian Ocean side of Malaya.[217]   In the Moluccas Islam had already established several footholds, but was not yet in full control over the many islands and their primitive peoples, though they had mastered the two richest ones, Ternate and Tidore.   There were consequently many people not yet Muslim whom the missionaries, including St. Francis Xavier himself, could and did reach.[218]   A substantial number of conversions were made in the Moluccas and a substantial number of Christians remain there to this day (especially on the island of Amboina, where a Jesuit brother named Fernandes had baptized over 1,300 people himself in the mid-sixteenth century, before he was drowned).[219] But the conquest of that region by the Dutch East India Company in the early seventeenth century made the open avowal and practice of Catholicism very difficult, while the Dutch themselves made virtually no effort to propagate Protestant Christianity.[220]

The great archipelago of the Philippine Islands, lying northeast of Indonesia, was discovered in the first round-the-world voyage by Ferdinand Magellan, already recounted.   He was killed there.[221]   Though the Spanish expeditions of Loaysa, Saavedra and Villalobos passed along some islands of the Philippines in 1526, 1528 and 1542-43 respectively, no attempt was made by any to secure the islands or plant a colony.[222]   But in 1565 several ships journeyed from now fully converted Mexico to the Philippines under the joint command of a bold and brilliant Spanish *hidalgo* named Miguel López de Legazpi and the remarkable Augustinian friar Andrés de Urdañeta, who had sailed with Loaysa and Saavedra and become the world's most experienced Pacific pilot, but was now on fire to spend his last years converting those who had never heard the name of Christ.[223]

---

[217] Hall, *History of Southeast Asia*, p. 243.   For Afonso de Albuquerque and the conquest of Malacca, see Volume Three, Chapter 15 of this history.

[218] See section on "Saint Francis Xavier," above.

[219] Lach, *Southeast Asia through the Eyes of Europe*, pp. 616-617.

[220] De Klerck, *History of the Netherlands East Indies* I, 203-205, 207, 209-210; Hall, *History of Southeast Asia*, pp. 249-250.   By 1611 Dutch Governor-General Both had set up a Dutch Council for India and sailed to the Moluccas to make his permanent headquarters there (De Klerck, *op. cit.* I, 214-215).   In that same year Dutch navigator Hendrik Brouwer discovered a much faster route to Indonesia across the southern Indian Ocean from the Cape of Good Hope rather than north to India and then south to Indonesia. In 1616 Dirk Hartog, sailing this new route, discovered western Australia, and Dutch navigators Willem Schouten and Isaac Le Maire were the first to round Cape Horn and sail on to the west (Frank Sherry, *Pacific Passions* [New York, 1994], pp. 193-194, 201-204, 206-207).

[221] See Chapter One, above.

[222] Lach, *Southeast Asia in the Eyes of Europe*, pp. 599, 624, 640-643; Hall, History of Southeast Asia, p. 249.

[223] Hall, *History of Southeast Asia*, p. 248; Sherry, *Pacific Passions*, pp. 92-99.   For an excellent summary of Urdañeta's amazing career and the achievements of the Legazpi

Legazpi had brought with him four hundred hard-bitten Spanish soldiers, the best in the world. He landed where Magellan had landed, at the city and island of Cebu, where a small image of Our Lady had been preserved from Magellan's visit. Urdañeta began immediately the missionary work for which he had come. Before Legazpi died in 1572, he had secured full Spanish control of the central Philippine (Visayan) islands of Cebu, Panay, Leyte and Mindoro and the fertile central plain of the largest island, Luzon, where he founded the city of Manila as the capital of the Philippines, on a great bay that formed an ideal natural harbor. Beginning in the next year, an annual galleon sailed from Manila to Mexico loaded with Chinese silks and other valuable trade goods from China. The infant colony prevailed over a vicious attack by the Chinese pirate Limahong in 1574.[224]

The people of the Philippines were considerably more primitive than those in the rest of Asia whom the missionaries had encountered—more like the native Americans—but they lacked many of the worst vices of the native Americans. They spoke a variety of languages, among which the best known was Tagalog, spoken widely in Luzon. Except for the southernmost island of Mindanao, Islam had not reached them, nor Buddhism anywhere. They were generally friendly, intelligent and cooperative. The Spanish saw at once the dimensions of the missionary opportunity in what was to become the only Catholic country in Asia. In 1577 the first Franciscans arrived, soon followed by the Augustinians, Jesuits and Dominicans. Philip II decided to appoint a bishop for Manila, the Dominican Fray Domingo de Salazar, as early as 1579, just eight years after the city was founded. The voyage from Spain was slightly more than halfway around the world. Bishop Salazar arrived at Manila in September 1581, accompanied by two Jesuit priests (Antonio Sedeño and Alonso Sánchez) and a scholastic, the brother of the famous Catholic philosopher Francisco Suárez. Immediately (before the end of the year of his arrival) Bishop Salazar called the first diocesan synod at Manila. Its initial action was to forbid the Spanish from holding any Filipino slaves. This was a very good beginning.[225]

Bishop Salazar was certainly not letting any grass grow under his feet. In 1583, just two years after his arrival, he was writing to Philip II urging the establishment of a Jesuit college in Manila. It took the better part of a year one-way for a letter from the Philippines to reach Madrid; but by 1585 Philip II replied heartily endorsing the planned college, which came into being in 1596. In 1586 a Dominican province was established on Luzon. The Augustinians already had 27 mission houses established in regions with a population of about 300,000, approximately half of whom were actually under Christian instruction, while the Franciscans had the spiritual care of about 200,000. Jesuit priest Alonso Sánchez

expedition, see Samuel Eliot Morison, *The European Discovery of America; the Southern Voyages* (New York, 1974), pp. 492-495.

[224] Hall, *History of Southeast Asia*, p. 248; H. de la Costa, S.J., *The Jesuits in the Philippines, 1581-1768* (Cambridge MA, 1961), pp. 11, 21; *Cambridge History of China* VIII (2), 354-355.

[225] da Costa, *Jesuits in the Philippines*, pp. 5-6, 9-10, 23, 25.

was especially impressed with how readily the Filipino children took to the new faith, with its colorful processions and happy songs. He said the future of evangelization in the Philippines lay with them; how right he was! Most of them were fully and sincerely converted by the time they had reached adulthood. In 1586 Governor de Vera called a general *junta* of leaders of the Philippines, both lay and ecclesiastical, at which the prior of the Augustinian monastery in Manila strongly objected to indiscriminate Spanish use of forced native labor.[226]

In 1587 one of the two pioneer Jesuit priests in the Philippines, Alonso Sánchez, was granted an interview of no less than two hours by Philip II, despite his being in the midst of his gigantic effort to equip and launch the Spanish Armada. Sánchez pointed out the glowing promise of the Philippine Islands and their open-hearted people, but explained the problems arising out of their immense distance from Spain, the consequences of the resulting constant shortage of Spanish money and soldiers (the most serious being the almost complete lack of defenses), the severity of the temptation for the governor to accumulate his own fortune at the expense of the colony, and the failure of the Spanish landholders, the *encomenderos*, to attend to the religious instruction of their people. In March 1588, on the very eve of the departure of the Spanish Armada, Philip II appointed a special commission to examine the Philippine situation and Sánchez's recommendations. The commission included the great Archbishop of Mexico Pedro Moya de Contreros. In August Sánchez brought the commission's recommendations to Philip II: that the colony, despite its distance and cost, be maintained and defended by four major forts and a wall around Manila. It was to gain revenue from a 3% duty on all merchandise entering or leaving the Philippines, and to have a monopoly of the Manila galleon trade, in addition to a substantially expanded royal subsidy.   Not only did Philip II approve all this, but he even asked Sánchez himself to select the man whom he believed would be most fit to govern the Philippines. Sánchez's choice was Gómez Pérez Dasmariñas, who arrived in the Philippines in 1590 and the next year began construction of the wall around Manila, which he completed in 1593. Meanwhile Sánchez had gone on to Rome, where he met with Jesuit General Aquaviva to plead for the continuance and expansion of the Jesuit mission in the Philippines despite its great cost, for the establishment of a college and a seminary at Manila, for more Jesuits to be sent there, and for it no longer to be subordinate to the Jesuit province of Mexico.   Aquaviva approved the establishment of the college in Manila and Jesuit mission stations with resident missionaries throughout the far-flung islands.   In 1590 two new Jesuit missionaries arrived, and the Jesuit community in Manila began serious study of the Tagalog language; while in the mission stations, in accordance with Sánchez's recommendation, they worked primarily through the children. But most of the Filipinos were grateful for the Spanish presence. In May 1592 the "householders and common folk" of Manila wrote to Philip II that great progress

---

[226] *Ibid.*, pp. 59-61, 63, 75-81, 174; Ludwig von Pastor, *History of the Popes*, Vol. XXI (St. Louis, 1952), p. 183.

had been made in their protection, administration and trade by Governor Dasmariñas. In 1593 the Dominicans printed the first book in the Tagalog language, a summary of Christian doctrine. In that same year Alonso Sánchez died in Spain, his magnificent work done. Though almost unknown, he is one of the great missionaries in the history of the Church. Seventy million Filipinos are Catholic today in substantial part due to him.[227]

The turn of the seventeenth century brought the Dutch, who quickly consolidated their hold on Indonesia and made repeated efforts to drive the Spanish out of the Philippines as well. But the Spanish resisted with iron determination, supported by their converted Filipinos. The only allies the Dutch could find in the islands were on Mindanao and Palawan and the Sulus, which alone were partly or mostly Muslim. Time and again the superior Dutch ships would attempt to take or burn Manila or to blockade its bay. Time and again they were driven off, even when the Spanish had no warships in the bay and had to build them or convert merchant ships for war. During the 1630's, when Spain was coming to so much grief in Europe and other parts of the world, losing its status as the world's leading power, the Spanish and their Filipino allies held firmly to their islands and even expanded their rule to the Muslim islands in the south. A great fort was established at highly strategic Zamboanga on the southern tip of Mindanao. Governor Sebastián Hurtado de Corcuera (1635-44), who has been called "the last conquistador," won two splendid victories which guaranteed full Spanish control of all of the Philippines. In 1635, at the height of Muslim raids on the Visayan islands, Jesuit Provincial in the Philippines (they were now a separate province in the Jesuit order) Juan de Bueras, reviewing the effects of the raids and the martyrdom of three Jesuit Fathers during them, said "let us be patient and endure, keeping our gaze fixed on the eternal reward that awaits God's faithful servants."[228]

The following description of the Jesuit mission at Salang near Manila shows how effectively the missionaries to the Philippines worked with the native children:

> Every day at dawn the church bell rings for all the children to come to church. Thence they go in procession through the town, chanting the catechism in their native tongue. The passing of the procession, so numerous (there are as many as 200 boys) and so devotional, is a constant delight to the beholder. They return to the church, where they recite the principal points of Christian doctrine and answer questions on them. Then they hear Mass, after which they betake themselves to school. Some learn their first letters, others are further exercised in the catechism; no one is permitted to work on the farm or help his parents until he is first solidly grounded in the faith. On

---

[227] da Costa, *Jesuits in the Philippines*, pp. 35, 88-91, 94-99, 106, 120-124, 136, 140-141. A second Jesuit college was established in Cebu in 1606, and the Dominican College of Santo Tomás was founded in Manila in 1611 (*ibid.*, pp. 276, 352).

[228] *Ibid.*, pp. 254 (for the establishment of the separate Jesuit province of the Philippines), 302-350 (quote on 324-325), 377-403.

Sundays all the people, young and old, attend a catechism lesson in the church.[229]

In 1623, following the canonization of St. Ignatius of Loyola and St. Francis Xavier, Archbishop García Serrano of Manila (there were now five dioceses in the Philippines) made their feasts holy days of obligation, since their followers the Jesuits had done so much for the Philippines. There was one great failure of the extraordinarily successful Philippine mission: its refusal throughout the 17th and 18th centuries to ordain native priests, though native catechists were widely used from 1601.[230] But so deeply and strongly did the missionaries build that they overcame even that obstacle. There is no more Catholic country in the world today, not even Ireland or Poland, than the Philippine Islands.

The other great Oriental evangelization, though not nearly as sweeping and thorough as that of the Philippines, brought between 15 and 20 per cent of the population of Vietnam, on the east coast of the great Southeast Asian peninsula, into the Church. These were not enough conversions to make Vietnam a Catholic country, but they did create a Catholic community large and committed enough so that it could never be destroyed or reduced to insignificance, as to a large extent were the Catholic communities in India, China and Japan. It was still playing a major role in the tumultuous history of Vietnam during the second half of the twentieth century.

In Vietnam, as nowhere else but in Canada (where the circumstances were very different),[231] the French were the primary evangelizers. The first missions there were begun mainly by refugees from Japan after Ieyasu's 1614 edict against Christianity. In 1624 six Jesuits came from Rome, including the man who above all may be called the apostle of Vietnam: Alexander of Rhodes, who labored in that forgotten land for almost exactly thirty years, becoming the first European to fully master its language. Just six months after arriving in South Vietnam, he was able to preach in Vietnamese. Later he wrote books of religious instruction in the language and devised an alphabet for it using Western letters. In 1626 he was received with special honors in Tonkin (North Vietnam) by its ruler Trinh Trang, and began his missionary work there. Some years later, in 1640, Alexander was made head of the entire Vietnam mission. Driven out of Vietnam in a small boat in September of that year, he fearlessly returned in December. Banished again in 1641, he returned early in 1642. In July 1644 the Vietnamese convert and catechist baptized André was martyred—the first martyr in Vietnam. The next year Alexander was arrested in the Vietnamese capital of Hue by order of the Emperor of Vietnam. The Christian wife of one of his chief councillors persuaded the Emperor not to kill him, but he was told to leave Vietnam, never to return. He promptly escaped and returned to preaching, catechizing and

---

[229] From the Jesuit annual letter from the Philippines for the year 1614, reprinted in *ibid.*, pp. 369-370. In December of that year began the flow of Christian refugees from Japan. They were received with a "charity approaching veneration" (*ibid.*, p. 363).

[230] *Ibid.*, pp. 127, 233-234, 289, 365.

[231] See fourth section, "French North America," in Chapter 12, above.

confessing, baptizing 92 persons in just three weeks. By this time there were already about fifty thousand Christians in Vietnam, and two hundred churches had been built in the country.[232]

In the summer of 1649 Alexander of Rhodes returned to Rome to plead for bishops for the growing number of converts in Vietnam. In the following year he met with the cardinals of De Propaganda Fide to tell them that at least 300 priests were needed in Vietnam and that it was imperative that a native clergy be ordained. De Propaganda Fide decided to propose to then Pope Innocent X a full hierarchy for Indo-China, with recommendations of specific archbishops and bishops, but the Pope did not immediately act on their request. In 1653 Alexander published a book in which he said there were already 300,000 baptized Christians in Tonkin (North Vietnam) alone. That year three French priests were approved as bishops for Vietnam, and the wealthy Duchesse d'Aiguillont promised an annual subsidy to them. By now this mission was catching fire in the Catholic imagination of the French. It was strongly endorsed by St. Vincent de Paul. The Archbishop of Reims and four more French bishops volunteered to go to Vietnam. In 1655 a fund for the maintenance of French bishops in Vietnam was formally set up by the Assembly of the Clergy of France, with the continuing support of St. Vincent de Paul.[233]

In 1656 Christmas was publicly celebrated in South Vietnam and Holy Week 1657 in North Vietnam. By that year there were four large churches in Hanoi and 414 chapels throughout the realm. Local catechists, living under a strict monastic rule and using Alexander of Rhodes' books in Vietnamese on the Faith, prepared catechumens for baptism and the reception of the Blessed Sacrament. In 1658 was formed in France the *Société des Missions-Étrangères*. Pope Alexander VII approved François Pallu and Pierre Lambert de la Motte as bishops for Vietnam, Pallu in the north and La Motte in the south. This marked a decisive break with the tradition of the Spanish and Portuguese royal *padronado* in non-Western lands, whereby one or the other had to approve all episcopal appointments in their area. Portugal, which had revolted from Spain in 1640 and made an increasingly precarious claim to its old colonial lands, protested vigorously, but to no avail; in 1663 Pope Alexander VII issued a brief praising the missionary work of the Jesuits in Vietnam and confirming their independence of the Portuguese authorities. The new ruler of North Vietnam, Trinh Tac, tried to suppress Christianity by decree, but unlike the Japanese he was not powerful and ruthless enough to do it. Some missionaries were expelled or not allowed to enter, including Bishop Pallu (who went to Siam, while keeping well informed on French missionary progress in Vietnam). But two French Jesuits—Borgès and Tissanier—were allowed to remain in Vietnam. In the single year 1659 they baptized 7,300 persons including several great ladies of the court, among whom was one especially favored by Trinh Tac. They were therefore allowed freely to

---

[232] Henri Chappoulie, *Aux origine d'une église; Rome et les missions d'Indochine aux XVIIe siècle* (Paris, 1943) I, 13-14, 22-24, 26-32, 191.

[233] *Ibid.*, I, 3-4, 103-109, 115.

practice their new faith, and in 1660 Trinh Tac told Borgès and Tissanier that he was no longer angry with the Christians.[234]

In November 1663 Trinh Tac became once again hostile to the Christians and forced Borgès and Tissanbier to leave the country; Borgès died on the way out. He had personally baptized more than 20,000 Vietnamese. Several other missionaries were also expelled. There were a few martyrs, but the number of baptisms far exceeded the number martyred or forced to recant their faith. Seeking to follow Alexander of Rhodes' strong recommendations for a native clergy, Pope Alexander VII allowed priests to be ordained in Southeast Asia without even a full knowledge of Latin—a marked and welcome change in the policy of the Church in pagan countries. In the spring of 1666 a catechist in Hanoi wrote to missionary Bishop Pallu in Siam that Trinh Tac's hostility to the Christians had again been appeased and once again missionaries were allowed to come to North Vietnam. Bishop Pallu immediately sent François Deydier, 32 years old, robust, fiery and zealous, learned and dedicated. Deydier left Siam in a Chinese junk, studying the Vietnamese language on his journey. He came to Hanoi, held a meeting of native catechists, and said Mass for Jeanne, aunt of Trinh Tac, whose son was a major counsellor in his government. In February 1668 Deydier sent two especially promising young Vietnamese to Siam, where Bishop La Motte ordained them to the priesthood. In that year the Christians were allowed to celebrate Holy Week openly in Hanoi. In November Deydier blessed a much enlarged Church of the Nativity in that city, where he estimated there were now ten thousand Christians. Trinh Tac continued to waver between persecution and toleration, but he never applied a consistent and universal policy of persecution as the Tokugawa shoguns had done in Japan. Though the French bishops were not able to live and preach and govern the Church openly in Vietnam, missionaries continued to arrive, mostly from France, and baptize in great numbers. Over six thousand Vietnamese entered the Church in the year 1671 alone. In 1670 the first women's religious order was established in Vietnam, and native catechists numbered in the thousands.[235]

The church in France, long crippled by its delay in putting into practice the Tridentine reforms, by Gallicanism, Jansenism, and the power of the French Calvinists, was at last coming into its own. Now that France had displaced Spain as the world's leading power, its clergy were showing that they also were truly Catholic, ready to do their share in extending the Faith to the uttermost parts of the earth.

---

[234] *Ibid.* I, 116-123, 170-171, 195, 197, 201, 205-207, 248-249; Adrien Launay, *Histoire Générale de la Société des Missions-Étrangères* (Paris, 1894), I, 36-61; von Pastor, *History of the Popes* XXXI, 151.

[235] Chappoulie, *Aux origines d'une église* I, 181, 185211, 214-221, 223, 227-229, 235-237, 247, 348.

Bibliography

1. GENERAL HISTORY

Auclair, Marcelle. *St. Teresa of Avila* (Garden City NY, 1959). Thorough and perceptive biography of the great Spanish mystic.

Bangert, William V. *To the Other Towns; a Life of Blessed Peter Favre, First Companion of St. Ignatius* (Westminster MD, 1959). A strangely titled, superficial work of very limited value despite the importance of its subject.

Batiffol, Louis. *The National History of France, Volume III: The Century of the Renaissance* (New York, 1916). Gives only brief treatment to the issues of the sixteenth century that primarily concern the Catholic historian.

Baumgartner, Frederic J. *Henry II, King of France* (Durham NC, 1988). The only good biography of this important sovereign, whose sudden death in a tournament ushered in the Wars of Religion in France.

Beaglehole, J. C. *The Exploration of the Pacific* (Stanford CA, 1966). The standard work on its subject. Good information but very dull reading on an exciting topic.

Beeching, Jack. *The Galleys at Lepanto* (New York, 1982). The best account of this pivotal battle between Christians and Turks.

Beer, Barrett L. *Northumberland; the Political Career of John Dudley, Earl of Warwick and Duke of Northumberland* (Kent State OH, 1973). Adds little to other studies of the period such as Wilbur Jordan's two-volume set on the reign of young Edward I.

Belloc, Hilaire. *Cranmer* (Philadelphia, 1939). Tries to prove, with considerable though not total success, that Cranmer's main purpose as Protestant Archbishop of Canterbury was to abolish the Mass in England.

Benedict, Philip. *Rouen during the Wars of Religion* (Cambridge, England, 1981). Very valuable and thorough regional study.

Bercé, Yves-Marie. *The Birth of Absolutism; a History of France* 1598-1661 (New York, 1992).

Bergendoff. Conrad. *Olavus Petri and the Ecclesiastical Transformation in Sweden* (New York, 1928). Has much information on a rarely studied topic.

Bergin, Joseph. *The Rise of Richelieu* (New Haven CT, 1991).

Bingham, Caroline. *James V, King of Scots* (London, 1971). Contains most of the relatively little that is known about the king of Scotland who was the son of Henry VIII's sister and contemporary with him.

Birt, Henry N. *The Elizabethan Religious Settlement* (London, 1907). Old but indispensable; very thorough.

Black, J. R. *The Reign of Elizabeth* (Oxford, 1936). Part of the lengthy Oxford History of England, one of its first volumes published.

Blickle, Peter. *The Revolution of 1525* (Baltimore, 1981). Thorough account, but tends to be overly influenced by Marxist theory.

Boehmer, Henrich. *Martin Luther: Road to Reformation* (New York, 1957). Covers only the first part of Luther's life and career.

Bradford, Ernle. *The Great Siege* (New York, 1961). Popularized but accurate, comprehensive and inspiring account of the siege of Malta, defended by the crusading Knights of St. John (originally of Jerusalem) by the Turks in 1565.

Bradford, William, ed. *Correspondence of the Emperor Charles V and His Ambassadors at the Courts of England and France* (London, 1850).

Brandi, Karl. *The Emperor Charles V* (Atlantic Highlands NJ, 1965). The best biography of the great Emperor, both scholarly and well-written. The author is a Protestant but has much sympathy and understanding for the very Catholic Charles V.

Bridge, Antony. *Suleiman the Magnificent, Scourge of Heaven* (New York, 1966). Adds little to Merriman's biography; there is just not enough source material.

Brockman, Eric. *The Two Sieges of Rhodes, 1480-1522* (London, 1969). The only thorough coverage of the two great sieges of Rhodes, in 1480 and 1521-22.

Brodrick, James, S.J. *The Origin of the Jesuits* (New York, 1940). Brief but excellent account of the founding of the Jesuit order by one of their finest historians.

_____. *The Progress of the Jesuits, 1556-79* (New York, 1947). Thorough, well-written history of the history of the first years of the Jesuit order after the death of St. Ignatius of Loyola.

_____. *Robert Bellarmine, Saint and Scholar* (London, 1961). Outstanding, comprehensive biography of this great saint in his troubled times. Strongly Catholic viewpoint.

_____. *Saint Ignatius Loyola; the Pilgrim Years* (New York, 1956). Thorough, very well-written biography of St. Ignatius up to the founding of the Jesuits.

_____. *St. Peter Canisius* (Baltimore, 1950). The most extensive of Brodrick's studies, based on St. Peter Canisius' voluminous correspondence. A definitive biography of the Jesuit missionary to Germany in the sixteenth century.

Brook, V. J. K. *A Life of Archbishop Parker* (Oxford, 1962). Reasonably thorough coverage of its uninspiring subject, Matthew Parker, Archbishop of Canterbury under Queen Elizabeth.

Bruce, Marie Louise. *Anne Boleyn* (New York, 1972). Probably the best biography of this extraordinary woman, who was more responsible than anyone else for the English schism.

Brundage, Burr C. *A Rain of Darts; the Mexican Aztecs* (Austin TX, 1972).

Buisseret, David. *Henry IV* (London, 1984). Stresses his military policy and achievements.

Burckhardt, Carl J. *Richelieu and His Age* (London, 1970) 3 vols. The most thorough treatment of its subject.

Cambridge Modern History, Volume III, ed. A. W. Ward, G. W. Prothero and Stanley Leathes (New York, 1934). Far superior to the New Cambridge Modern History, which emphasizes economic interpretations of events at the expense of personalities in history and religious motivations and significance.

Caraman, Philip. *Henry Garnet and the Gunpowder Plot* (New York, 1964). An excellent account of the Gunpowder Plot and Garnet's very slight participation in it. Catholic viewpoint.

Carroll, Warren H. *Our Lady of Guadalupe and the Conquest of Darkness* (Front Royal VA, 1983).

————. *1917: Red Banners, White Mantle* (Front Royal VA, 1981).

————. *The Rise and Fall of the Communist Revolution* (Front Royal VA, 1995).

Casway, Jerrold I. *Owen Roe O'Neill and the Struggle for Catholic Ireland* (Philadelphia, 1984) Along with being an outstanding, thorough biography, this presents much the best history of the Irish rebellion against the Puritan dictatorship in England.

Chamberlin, E. R. *Marguerite of Navarre* (New York, 1974). Popularized history, but excellent, based on good research and with many important insights.

————. *The Sack of Rome* (New York, 1985). Popularized account, very vivid.

Cheyney, Edward P. *A History of England from the Defeat of the Armada to the Death of Queen Elizabeth* (London, 1926) 2 vols.

Collis, Maurice. *Cortés and Montezuma* (New York, 1954).

Cornwall, Julian. *Revolt of the Peasantry 1549* (London, 1977). Thorough and comprehensive on its limited subject.

Cortés, Hernan. *Letters from Mexico*, ed. A. R. Pagden (New York, 1971). The famous letters written by Cortés himself during his conquest of Mexico.

Davies, Norman. *God's Playground; a History of Poland* (New York, 1984). This oddly titled book is the most comprehensive history of Poland in English, but is still disappointingly superficial.

Diaz, Bernal. *Chronicles* (originally entitled *The True History of the Conquest of Mexico*), translations by Maurice Keatinge (New York, 1927) and Albert Idell (New York, 1956). Probably the greatest extended first-person account of fantastic adventure in all historical literature. The principal source of all later accounts of Cortés' conquest of Mexico.

Diefendorf, Barbara B. *Beneath the Cross; Catholics and Huguenots in Sixteenth-Century Paris* (New York, 1991). An excellent, fair and comprehensive study.

Duffy, Eamon. *The Stripping of the Altars; Traditional Religion in England c1400-c1580* (New Haven CT, 1992). A landmark work, showing that a fair and moving portrayal of traditional Catholicism at the time of the

Protestant revolt can still be written and published at the end of the apostate twentieth century.

Dunkley, E. H. *The Reformation in Denmark* (London, 1948). Slight, but the only general coverage of its subject in English.

Edwards, Francis. *Guy Fawkes; the Real Story of the Gunpowder Plot?* (London, 1969). Definitely inferior to Antonia Fraser's book on the same subject— Catholic conspiratorial viewpoint. The uncertainty of the author's conclusions is indicated by the question mark in the title.

Elliott, J. H. *The Count-Duke of Olivares* (New Haven CT, 1986). The only full scholarly biography of this very important figure. Definitive on its subject.

England, Sylvia L. *The Massacre of St. Bartholomew* (London, 1938). Popularized account, but has some merit.

Erlanger, Philippe. *The Massacre of St. Bartholomew's Night* (New York, 1960). Unfortunately full of prejudice, as most accounts of this catastrophe are, but has some good information.

Esson, D. M. R. *The Curse of Cromwell; a History of the Ironside Conquest of Ireland, 1649-53* (Totowa NJ, 1971) Tells the whole dreadful tale with full scholarly apparatus.

Evenett, H. Outram. *The Cardinal of Lorraine and the Council of Trent* (Cambridge, England, 1930). Classic, voluminous, indispensable study of the leader of French Catholicism in the mid-sixteenth century and his vital role in the final success of the Council of Trent.

Falls, Cyril. *Elizabeth's Irish Wars* (New York, 1970). Solid military history of England's Irish wars during Elizabeth's reign.

Ferguson, Charles W. *Naked to Mine Enemies; the Life of Cardinal Wolsey* (Boston, 1958) 2 vols. Fine, perceptive biography.

Feldhay, Rivka. *Galileo and the Church* (Cambridge, England, 1993). Well-balanced treatment of the Galileo case,

Fehrenbach, T. R. *Fire and Blood; a History of Mexico* (New York, 1973). Well-researched and well-written; pulls no punches.

Fichtner, Paula. *Ferdinand I of Austria* (New York, 1982). An inadequate and superficial biography, but the only one we have of this brother of Charles V who succeeded him as Emperor.

Fife, Robert H. *The Revolt of Martin Luther* (New York, 1957). The finest Luther biography, well-researched, well-organized and full of vivid descriptions. Protestant viewpoint, but critical and dispassionate.

Fitzgerald, Brian. *The Geraldines* (New York, 1952). This little-known and quite rare book provides much the best account of the Munster Catholic uprising of the 1580's under James Fitzmaurice Fitzgerald and the Earl of Desmond.

Foley, Albert S., S.J. *St. Regis, a Social Crusader* (Milwaukee, 1941).

Fraser, Antonia. *Cromwell, the Lord Protector* (New York, 1973). Splendid, massive, comprehensive biography of this dominant figure of his age.

_____. *Faith and Treason; the Story of the Gunpowder Plot* (New York, 1996). A thorough, comprehensive, fair treatment of this very important and controversial subject.

_____. *King James VI of Scotland and I of England* (London, 1974). A small book, more an outline than a full biography, but still valuable because of the great abilities of this historian.

_____. *Mary Queen of Scots* (New York, 1983). The first major work, and perhaps the greatest, of this outstanding English historian. Remarkably well-written, judicious, thoroughly researched. Gives an unforgettable presentation of the fantastic life of this tormented woman.

_____. *Royal Charles* (New York, 1979). Much the best biography of King Charles II, with full information on his incredibly adventurous life.

Fuentes, Patricia de, ed. *The Conquistadors; First-Person Accounts of the Conquest of Mexico* (New York, 1963).

Gardiner, Samuel R. *History of England from the Accession of James I to the Outbreak of the Civil War*, Volume I (London, 1884). Classic history of its subject.

Garrisson, Janine. *A History of Sixteenth Century France* (New York, 1995). Adds little to other histories on this subject.

Garsten, Oskar. *Rome and the Counter-Reformation in Scandinavia*, Volume I (Bergen, Norway, 1963). With its subsequent volumes, gradually printed by numerous publishers over many years) this is the only history of its kind, far more detailed than any other in English, but almost unknown. See particularly Volume IV for the full story of Queen Christina, who gave up a crown to become a Catholic.

Geyl, Pieter. *The Netherlands in the Seventeenth Century* (New York, 1961), 2 vols.

_____. *The Revolt of the Netherlands* (London, 1932). Only occasionally useful; Geoffrey Parker's history is much better.

Golden, Richard M. *The Godly Rebellion; Parisian Curés and the Religious Fronde* (Chapel Hill NC, 1981). The only scholarly book on its subject.

Goslinga, Cornelis. *The Dutch in the Caribbean and on the Wild Coast 1580-1680* (Gainesville FL, 1971). Maritime history; the only history found describing in full Piet Hein's capture of the Spanish silver fleet in 1628.

Grell, Ole P., ed. *The Scandinavian Reformation* (Cambridge, England, 1995). A collection of articles of varying and limited value.

Grey, Ian. *Boris Godunov, the Tragic Tsar* (New York, 1973).

Grisar, Hartmann. *Luther* (St. Louis, 1913), 6 vols. The most comprehensive study of Luther in English, from the Catholic viewpoint. Some brilliant insights and profound research, but suffers from poor organization. All six volumes have been translated from the original German into English but are very rare. A one-volume abridgment in English is much more widely available and easier to follow.

Haigh, Christopher. *The Last Days of the Lancashire Monasteries and the Pilgrimage of Grace* (Manchester, England, 1969). Very good on its limited subject.

Haile, Martin. *An Elizabethan Cardinal: William Allen* (London, 1914). This book from a strongly Catholic author comes from another age, but is still very useful.

————. *Life of Reginald Pole* (London, 1910). Even better than his biography of Cardinal Allen.

Halecki, Oscar. *From Florence to Brest (1439-1596*, 2nd ed. (New York, 1968). Perhaps the best work of this great (and believing) Polish Catholic historian, this tells the full story of the last great reconciliation with the Catholic Church, involving millions of separated believers.

Handover, P.M. *The Second Cecil; the Rise to Power 1563-1603 of Sir Robert Cecil, Later First Earl of Salisbury* (London, 1959). The closest we have to a full biography of this chief advisor to James I.

Harbison, E. Harris. *Rival Ambassadors at the Court of Queen Mary* (Princeton, 1940). Excellent on Queen Mary's foreign policy, often overlooked or incorrectly considered identical with Philip II's.

Harrison, G. B., ed. *The Elizabethan Journals, Being a Record of Those Things Most Talked of during the Years 1591-1603* (London, 1938).

Haugaard, William P. *Elizabeth and the English Reformation* (Cambridge, England, 1968). An extensive and relatively objective study.

Hemming, John. *The Conquest of the Incas* (New York, 1970). Nearly definitive on its unpleasant subject.

Hibbert, Christopher. *The House of Medici; its Rise and Fall* (New York, 1980). A useful summary of its broad subject.

Henry-Couannier, Maurice. *St. Francis de Sales and His Friends* (New York, 1964). Most complete coverage of the life of this great and famous saint.

Holt, Mack P. *The Duke of Anjou and the Politique Struggle during the Wars of Religion* (Cambridge, England, 1986). By far the most detailed and factual study of the last years of the Wars of Religion in France.

————. *The French Wars of Religion, 1562-1629* (New York, 1995). A refreshing new look at its subject, the only detailed scholarly coverage of it in English not marked by strong Protestant bias.

Hudson, Winthrop S. *The Cambridge Connection and the Elizabethan Settlement of 1559* (Durham NC, 1980). A very important little book which establishes the major role of Cambridge University and its graduates in the making of the English schism.

Hughes, Philip. *The Reformation in England*, 5th ed., 3 vols. (London, 1963). A classic work of Catholic history, these volumes have many merits, but are somewhat lacking in detailed research, impressionistic rather than comprehensive in their coverage.

Hutton, Ronald. *The Restoration; a Political and Religious History of England and Wales, 1658-1667* (Oxford, 1985). The most complete retelling of this remarkable story.

Iongh, Jane de. *Margaret of Austria, Regent of the Netherlands* (New York, 1953). Popular rather than scholarly, but the only reasonably good biography of this remarkable woman in English.

Israel, Jonathan I. *The Dutch Republic; its Rise, Greatness and Fall* (Oxford, 1995). This thorough and accurate Jewish historian provides a welcome relief from tendentious Protestant histories of its subject, and the long shadow of the bitterly anti-Spanish John Lothrop Motley (whose classic history proved worthless as a source for this history because its rampant Protestant bias made it impossible to trust).

_____. *The Dutch Republic and the Hispanic World, 1606-1661* (New York, 1982). Excellent.

Jaki, Rev. Stanley L. "The Case for Galileo's Rehabilitation," *Fidelity* March 1986. Freely admits that the Church made a major mistake in dealing with Galileo.

Janssen, Johannes. *History of the German People at the Close of the Middle Ages* (London, 1910), Volumes III-X. A superb history of Germany from the advent of Luther to the outbreak of the Thirty Years War from the Catholic viewpoint, based on much original research, far too much neglected by modern scholarship.

Jedin, Hubert. *Crisis and Closure of the Council of Trent* (London, 1967). This little book, hardly more than a pamphlet, is not the history of the last session of the Council of Trent, translated into English, that the thorough researcher is looking for, but little more than an essay generated mostly by the Second Vatican Council, in session when it was written.

———. *A History of the Council of Trent* (St. Louis, 1957), 2 vols. (translation into English unfinished). One of the worst consequences of the Second Vatican Council in Catholic historical scholarship was that it occurred during the translation of Jedin's monumental study of the Council of Trent, causing the publishers to believe it was no longer of importance and so to suspend the translation and publication project with the second volume. All who do not read German are thereby deprived of nearly half a master-work which has no parallel and no substitute.

_____. *Papal Legate at the Council of Trent, Cardinal Seripando* (St. Louis, 1947). Substantially supplements his history of the Council of Trent, including a little of the period not covered by the two volumes of his history of the Council of Trent translated into English.

Jensen, DeLamar. *Diplomacy and Dogmatism; Bernardino de Mendoza and the French Catholic League* (Cambridge MA, 1964). Thorough and perceptive account of the Spanish ambassador to France who played a pivotal role in keeping France Catholic at the climax of the Wars of Religion.

Johnson, Donald S. *Charting the Sea of Darkness; the Four Voyages of Henry Hudson* (Camden ME, 1993). The only scholarly study of Hudson and his voyages.

Jones, Frederick M. *Mountjoy 1563-1606, the Last Elizabethan Deputy* (Dublin, 1958). Full account of the man who won the Nine Years War in Ireland for England.

Jordan, Wilbur K. *Edward VI, the Young King; the Protectorate of the Duke of Somerset* (London, 1968) and *Edward VI, the Threshold of Power* (Cambridge MA, 1970). Comprehensive study of the vitally important years when the boy Edward VI was titular sovereign, toward the end preparing to be king and tyrant.

Kamen, Henry. *Philip of Spain* (New Haven CT, 1997). At long last, a study of this great man by a non-Catholic who nevertheless rejects the black legend.

Kelley, Donald R. *François Hotman, a Revolutionary's Ordeal* (Princeton, 1973). Rather thin and bland biography of one of the most fiery of the French Calvinist ("Huguenot") leaders.

Kingdon, Robert M. *Geneva and the Coming of the Wars of Religion in France, 1555-1563* (Geneva, 1956) and *Geneva and the Consolidation of the French Protestant Movement* (Madison WI, 1957). Strongly Protestant, pro-Calvinist viewpoint, but the best study available on the early growth of Calvinism in France.

Knecht, R. J. *Francis I* (New York, 1982). The best biography of a rather unpromising subject.

Knowles, David. *The Religious Orders in England*, Volume III (Cambridge, England, 1967). Thoroughly researched and well explained conclusion of a monumental work of religious history, covering the 16th century.

Langford, Jerome J. *Galileo, Science and the Church*, 3rd ed. (Ann Arbor MI, 1992). Notably well-balanced treatment of a difficult and controversial subject.

Lehmberg, Stanford E. *The Reformation Parliament, 1529-1536* (Cambridge, England, 1970). Confined strictly to the Parliament, on which only limited data are available, but presents those data very well.

Leon-Portilla, Miguel, ed. *The Broken Spears; the Aztec Account of the Conquest of Mexico* (Boston, 1962).

Loades, David. *The Reign of Mary Tudor*, 2nd ed. (London, 1991). Substantially more thorough coverage of Mary's actual reign than Prescott's biography provides.

Luther, Martin. *The Table Talk of Martin Luther*, ed. Thomas S. Kepler (Grand Rapids MI, 1952). The real Luther, "warts and all," revealed in his own words.

Macdonald, William W. *John Pym* (New York, 1981).

Madariaga, Salvador de. *Hernan Cortés, Conqueror of Mexico* (Chicago, 1955). Splendid biography of the greatest and best of the *conquistadores*.

Mahoney, Irene. *Madame Catherine* (New York, 1975). An attempt at a popularized history of Catherine de Medici, Queen Regent of France, which contains much serious history; but the reader is never sure at what audience the author is aiming.

Major, J. Russell. *The Estates-General of 1560* (Princeton, 1951).

Maltby, William S. *Alba; a Biography of Fernando Alvarez de Toledo, Third Duke of Alba* (Berkeley CA, 1983). Well researched and well written biography of the greatest of the Spanish commanders, but noticeably hostile to its subject.

Mann, Golo. *Wallenstein* (New York, 1976). The most thorough, comprehensive, and thoughtful study of its enigmatic subject.

Manschreck, Clyde L. *Melanchthon, the Quiet Reformer* (New York, 1958). Adequate but not penetrating biography of the author of the Augsburg Confession, the primary Protestant statement of faith.

Martin, A. Lynn. *Henry III and the Jesuit Politicians* (Geneva, 1973). Strongly anti-Catholic but well-researched and therefore valuable for its factual detail, though the Catholic reader cannot help wondering what germane material from the excellent research was left out.

Mattingly, Garrett. *The Armada* (New York, 1959). Unquestionably the finest history of one of the most dramatic encounters in all history, the Spanish Armada with the English navy in 1588. Superbly researched and brilliantly written.

_____. *Catherine of Aragon* (New York, 1941). Though Mattingly was not a Catholic, no one has written with so much sympathy and understanding of Queen Isabel's daughter as this book displays. It tells her tragic story in full and very movingly. Like *The Armada*, it is a rare combination of great scholarship and writing of power, elegance and passion.

Maynard, Theodore. *Queen Elizabeth* (Milwaukee, 1940). Good account of the Queen's last days; Catholic viewpoint.

Maynard, Thomas. *The Crown and the Cross; a Biography of Thomas Cromwell* (New York, 1950). Excellent, somewhat popularized biography by a strongly Catholic writer.

McNeill, John T. *The History and Character of Calvinism* (New York, 1967). The only real history of Calvinism written in English during the twentieth century.

Menéndez Pidal, Ramón. *Historia de España*, Volumes XX-XXIII. Very comprehensive history of the reigns of Emperor Charles V and his son King Philip II in Spanish. Catholic viewpoint.

Merriman, Roger B. *The Life and Letters of Thomas Cromwell* (Oxford, 1902), 2 vols. Product of an earlier age of historical scholarship, of limited value to the modern reader.

_____. *The Rise of the Spanish Empire in the Old World and the New*, Vols. III-IV (New York, 1918). Tries to cover too much, pedestrian style, but very valuable on the periods and events he describes in most detail, such as the *comunero* uprising. Protestant viewpoint.

_____. *Suleiman the Magnificent* (New York, 1944, 1968). Does the best that can be done with the skimpy available data on Suleiman, but shows how thin that data is.

Nessenger, Ernest C. *The Reformation, the Mass and the Priesthood* (London, 1937) 2 vols. Unabashedly Catholic and a bit polemical, this is nevertheless one of the most extensive studies ever done on the invalidity of Anglican orders, essential to understanding this complicated question.

Moberg, Wilhelm. *A History of the Swedish People* (New York, 1973) 2 vols. Not really a history, but a collection of essays of varying value. Though the author has no religion, he greatly admires Catholic rebel Nils Dacke who fought against Gustavus Vasa, and presents the best account of him available in English.

Moody, T. W., F. X. Martin, and F.J. Byrne, eds., *A New History of Ireland*, Volume III "Early Modern Ireland, 1534-1691" (Oxford, 1976). Collective work, useful reference.

Moote, A. Lloyd. *Revolt of the Judges; the Parlement of Paris and the Fronde, 1643-1652)* (Princeton NJ, 1971). Comprehensive study of its subject.

Morison, Samuel Eliot. *The European Discovery of America: the Northern Voyages* (New York, 1971). A master-work.

———. *The European Discovery of America: the Southern Voyages 1492-1616* (New York, 1974). This great historian's last book of history, and one of his best. About a third of it describes Magellan's voyage, which he followed by air, and considers "the greatest human achievement on the sea." Indispensable for Magellan.

———. *Samuel de Champlain, Father of New France* (Boston, 1972). Most complete and imaginative study of its subject, by the great naval historian.

Mousnier, Roland. *The Assassination of Henry IV* (London, 1973). More a general study of Henry IV rather than just an account of his assassination.

Muller, James A. *Stephen Gardiner and the Tudor Reaction* (New York, 1970). Excellent, thorough coverage of this Anglo-Catholic champion.

Naef, Henri. *La conjuration d'Amboise et Genève* (Geneva and Paris, 1922).

Neale, J. E. *Elizabeth I and Her Parliaments* (New York, 1958-), 2 vols. A splendid, classic and definitive history of its subject.

Nugent, Donald. *Ecumenism in the Age of the Reformation; the Colloquy of Poissy* (Cambridge MA, 1974). Despite the trendy modernist title, this is a sound and thorough history replete with important facts.

O'Donnell, Timothy. *Swords Around the Cross* (Front Royal VA, 2000). Most recent comprehensive history of the Nine Years War between Ireland and Britain, written from a strongly Catholic viewpoint.

O'Faolain, Sean. *The Great O'Neill* (Cork, 1942, 1970). Impressionistic sketch of the leader of the Nine Years War, well-written but somewhat short on research.

Oechsli, William. *History of Switzerland, 1499-1914* (Cambridge, England, 1922). Thorough but dull.

Ollard, Richard. *The Escape of Charles II after the Battle of Worcester* (New York, 1966). Comprehensive, detailed account of this nearly incredible episode in history.

Orsenigo, Cesare. *Life of St. Charles Borromeo* (London, 1945). Comprehensive but unfortunately undocumented.

Padden, R. C. *The Hummingbird and the Hawk* (New York, 1970). Study of Aztec civilization from a secular viewpoint which describes at length their practice of human sacrifice.

Palm, Franklin L. *Politics and Religion in Sixteenth-Century France* (Gloucester MA, 1960). A rather shallow biography of a relatively minor figure, Montmorency-Damville, who changed sides from Calvinist to Catholic. Originally written in the 1920's.

Parker, Geoffrey. *The Dutch Revolt*, rev. ed. (London, 1985). Remarkably clear and succinct on a subject much written about, and often confusingly.

_____. *The Thirty Years War* (New York, 1984, 1987). Thorough and penetrating.

Parker, T. H. L. *John Calvin* (Philadelphia, 1975). One of the few good modern biographies of Calvin.

Parmiter, Geoffrey de C. *The King's Great Matter; a Study in Anglo-Papal Relations 1527-1534* (London, 1967). The most valuable book discovered in my research on the years when the English schism happened. Outstanding research, excellent use of sources, clearly written.

Pastor, Ludwig von. *History of the Popes from the Close of the Middle Ages*, 40 vols. (St. Louis, 1950). A landmark in every sense, probably the most extraordinary achievement in historical study for one man in all time. The scholar cannot do better than begin his study of any period between the end of the Council of Constance in 1418 and the end of the 18th century than by a careful reading of von Pastor's chapters or volumes for the period he is researching. Catholic viewpoint.

Payne, Robert and Nikita Romanoff. *Ivan the Terrible* (New York, 1975). The best biography of this extraordinary ruler, though somewhat popularized.

Petrie, Charles. *Don Juan of Austria* (New York, 1967). Adequate biography of the hero of Lepanto, but not of the magnitude and scale he deserves.

Pettegree, Andrew. *Emden and the Dutch Revolt* (Oxford, 1992). Occasionally useful regional study.

Potter, G. R. *Zwingli* (Cambridge, England, 1976). Workmanlike biography of this major Protestant figure who appeared only shortly after Luther but disagreed with him on many important issues.

Prescott, H. F. M. *Mary Tudor* (New York, 1953). Thoughtful, perceptive, well-researched and well-written biography.

Purcell, Mary. *The First Jesuit* (New York, 1956). Popularized, but essentially sound, comprehensive, and well-written.

_____. *The World of Monsieur Vincent* (London, 1963). The best biography of St. Vincent de Paul of France.

Read, Conyers. *Mr. Secretary Cecil and Queen Elizabeth* and *Lord Burghley and Queen Elizabeth* (New York, 1960). Magnificent two-volume biography of Philip II's great opponent in England, the leading Protestant statesman of his day. Read takes the Protestant viewpoint for granted and has nothing but praise for Cecil, but uses such a profusion of documents and quotations that much of the real truth about Cecil still comes through. Indispensable.

_____. *Nr. Secretary Walsingham and the Policy of Queen Elizabeth* (Cambridge MA, 1925) 3 vols. As thorough and almost as valuable as his two-volume study of Cecil, and equally well documented. Together these five monumental volumes comprised Read's life work as a historian.

Redondi, Pietro. *Galileo, Heretic* (Princeton NJ, 1987). Good research, but based on an unprovable hypothesis that Galileo was a heretic on the issue of transubstantiation.

Reid, W. Stanford. *Trumpeter of God; a Biography of John Knox* (New York, 1974). Distinctly Protestant viewpoint; considerably inferior to Jasper Ridley's fine biography of Knox.

Reynolds, E. E. *Campion and Parsons; the Jesuit Mission of 1580-1* (London, 1980). Very thorough treatment of this well-known mission which resulted in Campion's martyrdom.

_____. *The Field Is Won; the Life and Death of St. Thomas More* (Milwaukee, 1968). A much improved revision of his earlier biography of More.

_____. *St. John Fisher.* An adequate biography of the great saint and martyr, often overshadowed by St. Thomas More, but Fisher deserves more.

Ridley, Jasper. *John Knox* (New York, 1968). Presents, on the basis of outstanding research, Knox as a true revolutionary.

_____. *Thomas Cranmer* (Oxford, 1962). A genuinely great biography. Ridley, though definitely Protestant in his viewpoint, surveys Cranmer's numerous tergiversations with a cool and judicious gaze and does not try to apologize for him.

Roberts, Michael. *The Early Vasas; a History of Sweden 1523-1611* (Cambridge, England, 1968). The only book on this period in English, by the only historian writing in English able to do extensive research in Swedish sources.

_____. *Gustavus Adolphus; a History of Sweden 1611-1632* (London, 1953). Definitive, superbly researched.

Roelker, Nancy. *Queen of Navarre: Jeanne d'Albret* (Cambridge, 1968). Excellent, comprehensive biography. Protestant viewpoint.

Ronan, Myles V. *The Reformation in Dublin 1536-58* (New York, 1926). Good presentation of the beginning of English Protestantism in Ireland, in Dublin and the surrounding area.

_____. *The Reformation in Ireland under Queen Elizabeth 1558-80* (London, 1930). Attempts to cover the Protestant penetration of all Ireland, but is episodic and disorganized and does not carry through to the end.

Russell, Conrad. *The Fall of the British Monarchies* (Oxford, 1991).

_____. *Parliaments and English Politics, 1621-9* (Oxford, 1979). Very thorough treatment of its subject.

Sanderson, Margaret H. B. *Cardinal of Scotland: David Beaton* (Edinburgh, 1986). Very thorough research, presents most of the available information about this very important figure, whose murder destroyed the Catholic Church in Scotland.

Scarisbrick, J. J. *Henry VIII* (Berkeley CA, 1970). One of the best of the University of California's "Kings of England" series. Very thorough and factual, does not take sides regarding its subject.

Schurz, William L. *The Manila Galleon* (New York, 1939). This book stands alone in maritime history in English, and remains virtually the only one on its subject.

Seaver, H. L. *The Great Revolt in Castile; a Study of the Comunero Movement of 1520-21* (New York, 1928, 1966). Remains the definitive study of this important rebellion in Spain.

Sharpe, Kevin. *The Personal Rule of Charles I* (New Haven CT, 1992). Extremely detailed.

Sherry, Frank. *Pacific Passions; the European Struggle for Power in the Great Ocean in the Age of Exploration* (New York, 1994). Written by a journalist rather than a historian, this book is however an excellent overall account of early Pacific exploration, fully rivalling Beaglehole's standard work.

Silke, John J. *Kinsale; the Spanish Intervention in Ireland at the End of the Elizabethan Wars* (New York, 1970). The definitive account of the most decisive battle of the Nine Years War.

Sutherland, N. M. *The Huguenot Struggle for Recognition* (New Haven CT, 1980). Three generations removed from James Thompson, it might have been hoped that this historian would have been less biased, but she fully matches him in Protestant orientation and hostility to Catholics, though she has gathered many important facts in this book.

————. *The Massacre of St. Bartholomew and the European Conflict, 1559-1572* (London, 1973). The title is puzzling, since the massacre of St. Bartholomew came at the end rather than the beginning of the period the author covers. Impressively researched in great factual detail, but poorly organized and showing all the anti-Catholic prejudice of her other book on the Huguenots.

Thompson, James W. *The Wars of Religion in France 1559-1576* (New York, 1909). Vehemently Protestant, and though a classic history reveals Protestant bias throughout, especially in the omission of clearly relevant facts. Any researcher of this period must read this book, but he must supplement it extensively.

Thurston, Herbert, S.J. and Donald Attwater. *Butler's Lives of the Saints* as edited, revised, and supplemented by, 4 vols. By far the best source on the lives of the saints.

Vedder, Henry C. *The Reformation in Germany* (New York, 1914). Thorough, solid Protestant study.

Vernadsky, George. *The Tsardom of Moscow, 1547-1682*, 2 vols. (New Haven CT, 1969). Standard history of Russia.

Wade, C. E. *John Pym* (London, 1912).

Walker, Williston. *John Calvin, the Organiser of Reformed Protestantism* (New York, 1960. Old, but very detailed biography of Calvin based on extensive research.

Walsh, William T. *Philip II* (New York, 1937). The *magnum opus* of this great Catholic historian, much better documented than his biography of Queen Isabel, ignored or traduced by conventional historians because of its appearance at points of anti-Semitic prejudice (of which there is actually very little); needs to be used in conjunction with other studies but should not be neglected or overlooked as it so often has been.

Wandel, Lee P. *Voracious Idols and Violent Hands; Iconoclasm in Reformation Zürich, Strasbourg and Basel* (Cambridge, England, 1995). Shows good research, but almost no appreciation of the cultural impact of Protestant iconoclasm such as is displayed by Duffy's outstanding *Stripping of the Altars*.

Wedgwood, C. V. *A Coffin for King Charles; the Trial and Execution of Charles I* (New York, 1964). The final volume in Wedgwood's great history of the English Civil War.

_____. *The King's Peace, 1637-1641* (New York, 1955). Beginning of four superb volumes on the much-described English Civil War, the best modern retelling of its story.

_____. *The King's War, 1641-1647* (London, 1938). The second volume, and the most valuable, in Wedgwood's history.

_____. *Montrose* (London, 1952). Probably the best biography of this striking man.

_____. *The Thirty Years War* (New York, 1961). Classic one-volume history, the best in its field.

_____. *William the Silent* (New Haven CT, 1944). Vividly and brilliantly written, very valuable despite its strong Protestant bias.

Weibull, Curt. *Christina of Sweden* (Stockholm, 1966). Tries to be fair to this often pilloried queen.

Wendel, François. *Calvin; the Origins and Development of His Religious Thought* (London, 1963).

Wernham, R. B. *Return of the Armadas; the Last Year of the Elizabethan War against Spain, 1595-1603* (Oxford, 1994). Definitive in its subject area.

Whitehead, A. W. *Gaspard de Coligny, Admiral of France* (London, 1904. Old and strongly Protestant, but still excellent.

Willson, David H. *King James VI and I* (New York, 1956). The only thorough biography of King James.

Yeo, Margaret. *Reformer: St. Charles Borromeo* (Milwaukee, 1938). A popular Catholic saint's life of some merit.

2. HISTORY OF THE MISSIONS

Aiton, Arthur S. *Antonio de Mendoza, First Viceroy of New Spain* (New York, 1927) Thorough coverage.

Andrien, Kenneth. *Crisis and Decline; the Viceroyalty of Peru in the Seventeenth Century* (Albuquerque NM, 1985). Less broad in its coverage than the title suggests.

Ascensio, Luis, S.J. "The Apparitions of Guadalupe as Historical Events," *CARA Studies on Popular Devotion*, Volume II "Guadalupan Studies," No. 1 (Washington, 1979)

Bancroft, Hubert H. *History of Mexico* (San Francisco CA, 1883). The most extensive treatment of the history of Mexico, in many volumes.

Barbour, Philip L. *The Three Worlds of Captain John Smith* (Boston, 1964). Much the best treatment of its exciting subject.

Basham, A. L. *The Wonder That Was India* (London, 1954) Best presentation of the unique Indian world-view and religions.

Berry, Mary. *Hideyoshi* (Cambridge MA, 1989) Careful study of probably the greatest leader in Japanese history.

Bolton, Herbert E. *Coronado, Knight of Pueblos and Plains* (Albuquerque NM, 1949).

Boxer, Charles R. *The Christian Century in Japan* (Berkeley CA. 1967). The only complete history of the mission to Japan, disfigured for the Christian reader by its alternately hostile and patronizing attitude toward the missionaries.

_____. *Salvador de Sa and the Struggle for Brazil and Angola* (London, 1952)

Brodrick, James, S.J. *St. Francis Xavier* (New York, 1952). Fine, full biography of the greatest missionary in the Church's history.

Burns, E. Bradford. *A History of Brazil*, 2nd ed. (New York, 1980)

Burrus, Ernest H., S.J. "The Basic Bibliography of the Guadalupan Apparitions," *CARA Studies on Popular Devotion*, Volume II: Guadalupan Studies, Nos. 4 (Washington, 1981) and 5 (Washington, 1983).

Callahan, Philip. "The *Tilma* under Infra-red Radiation," *CARA Studies on Popular Devotion*, Volume II: "Guadalupan Studies, No. 3 (Washington, 1982).

Cambridge History of China, Volumes I, VII, VIII. The most complete history of China.

Cambridge History of Japan (New York, 1991), 4 vols.

Caraman, Philip. *The Lost Paradise; the Jesuit Republic in South America* (New York, 1976). Classic account of the Jesuit Indian settlements in Paraguay, the "reductions."

Carroll, Warren H. *Our Lady of Guadalupe and the Conquest of Darkness* (Front Royal VA, 1982)

Chappoulie, Henri. *Aux origines d'une église; Rome et les missions d'Indochine aux XVIIe siècle* (Paris, 1943) The only full account of the founding of the remarkably successful French mission to Vietnam.

Cooper, Michael, S.J. *Rodrigues the Interpreter; an Early Jesuit in Japan and China* (New York, 1974) Detailed study of an important figure in Oriental missionary history.

Costa, H. de la, S.J. *The Jesuits in the Philippines. 1581-1768* (Cambridge MA, 1961). The most detailed and only readily available missionary history of the only Catholic country in Asia.

Cronin, Vincent. *A Pearl to India; the Life of Roberto de Nobili* (New York, 1959) The best single source on the missionary history of India.

_____. *The Wise Man from the West* (Garden City NY, 1957) Comprehensive study of the great missionary to China, Matteo Ricci.

Cuevas, P. Mariano. *Historia de la Iglesia en Mexico* (El Paso, Texas, 1928). The finest and most complete church history of Mexico ever written in any language. Contains original research from Spanish archives on the apparition of Our Lady of Guadalupe.

Davidson, Basil. *The African Slave Trade* (Boston, 1988).

Day, Arthur G. *Coronado's Quest; the Discovery of the Southwestern States* (Berkeley CA. 1948).

De Klerck, E. S. *History of the Netherlands East Indies* (Amsterdam, 1938, 1975) 2 vols.

Demarest, Donald and Coley Taylor. *The Dark Virgin; the Book of Our Lady of Guadalupe* (New York, 1956). Includes most of the evidence of the historical reality of the apparition of Our Lady of Guadalupe in Mexico in 1531.

Dominian, Helen G. *Apostle of Brazil; the Biography of Padre Jose de Anchieta, S.J.* (New York, 1958). Fine biography of a little-known but very important missionary.

Dreyer, Edward L. *Early Ming China, a Political History, 1355-1435* (Stanford CA, 1982). Follows in detail the establishment of Ming dynasty power in China.

D'Sa, M. *History of the Catholic Church in India* (Bombay, 1910) 2 vols. Disappointingly superficial.

Dunne, George H., S.J. *Generation of Giants; the Story of the Jesuits in China in the Last Decades of the Ming Dynasty* (Notre Dame IND,'1962). All that missionary history should be.

Elison, George. *Deus Destroyed; the Image of Christianity in Early Modern Japan* (Cambridge MA, 1973)

Gibson, Charles. *Tlaxcala in the Sixteenth Century* (New Haven CT, 1952). Tells the story of the people in Mexico who first allied with Hernan Cortés, who chiefly suffered under the Aztec practice of human sacrifice.

Goble, Andrew E. *Kenmu; Go-Daigo's Revolution* (Cambridge MA, 1996). Only twice in a thousand years was the attempt made in Japan to restore real political power to the Emperor. Both attempts failed. This book describes and analyzes the first of these attempts, in the fourteenth century.

Hall, D. G. E. *A History of Southeast Asia*, 3rd ed. (New York, 1968). Very comprehensive, a standard historical reference work for its part of the world.

Hemming, John. *Conquest of the Incas* (New York, 1970). The best of the many books on this subject, supported by thorough investigation of the Spanish archives.

_____. *Red Gold; the Conquest of the Brazilian Indians* (Cambridge MA, 1978). Contains some facts not readily attainable elsewhere, but generally a sad example of the "tree-hugging" culture so prominent in the academic world at the time of its publication.

Horgan, Paul. *Great River* (New York, 1954). A well researched and poetically written history of the Rio Grande region.

Jayne, K. G. *Vasco da Gama and His Successors* (London, 1910). Good summary of the history of Portuguese India.

Kearns, J. C. *The Life of Blessed Martin de Porres, Saintly American Negro and Patron of Social Justice* (New York, 1937).

Keay, John. *The Honourable Company; a History of the English East India Company* (New York, 1991).

Kelly, John E. *Pedro de Alvarado, Conquistador* (Princeton NJ, 1932).

Keyes, Frances P. *The Rose and the Lily* (New York, 1961). A dual biography of St. Rose of Lima and Bd. Mariana of Quito.

Klein, Herbert S. *African Slavery in Latin America and the Caribbean* (New York, 1986).

Korth, Eugene H. *Spanish Policy in Colonial Chile; the Struggle for Social Justice, 1535-1700* (Stanford CA, 1968) Reviews in detail the efforts in the Spanish colonies to protect the Indians and their labor from exploitation.

Lach, Donald. *Southeast Asia in the Eyes of Europe; the Sixteenth Century* (Chicago, 1968).

Laures, Johannes, S.J. *The Catholic Church in Japan* (Tokyo, 1954) Gives the amazing story of the survival of Japanese Christianity underground after 250 years of ferocious persecution.

Launay, Adrien. *Histoire générale de la Société des Missions-Étrangères* (Paris, 1894) 2 vols.

Leies, Herbert F. *Mother for a New World; Our Lady of Guadalupe* (Westminster MD, 1964)

Levathes, Louise. *When China Ruled the Sea; the Treasure Fleet of the Dragon Throne, 1405-1433* (New York, 1994). A unique chapter in maritime history.

López Beltran, Lauro. *La Historicidad de Juan Diego* (Mexico, 1981). Makes a powerful case.

_____. *La Protohistoria Guadalupana* (Mexico, 1981).

Maclagan, Edward. *The Jesuits and the Great Mogul* (London, 1932). Describes the unsuccessful attempts of missionaries to penetrate and make conversions in the Mogul empire of India.

Majumdar, Ramesh C., ed. *The History and Culture of the Indian People*, multi-volume.

Markham, Clements. *The Conquest of New Granada* (London, 1912). The only book devoted to this subject.

Martin, Luis. *The Intellectual Conquest of Peru; the Jesuit College of San Pablo, 1568-1767* (New York, 1968).

Means, Philip A. *Ancient Civilizations of the Andes* (New York, 1931). Pedestrian, but remains the best account of South American native civilization.

Merces de Melo, Carlos. *The Recruitment and Formation of the Native Clergy of India* (Lisbon, 1955).

Moraes, George. *A History of Christianity in India, A.E. 52-1542* (Bombay, 1964) The only thorough history of the beginnings of Christianity in India.

Padden, R. C. *The Hummingbird and the Hawk* (New York, 1970). Study of Aztec civilization from a secular viewpoint which describes at length their practice of human sacrifice.

Parkman, Francis. *The Jesuits in North America* (Boston, 1867, 1963). Classic history.

———. *Pioneers of France in the New World* (Boston, 1865, 1905). Classic history.

Pocock, Hugh. *The Conquest of Chile* (New York, 1967). The only book devoted to this subject.

Poole, Stafford. *Pedro Moya de Contreros; Catholic Reform and Royal Power in New Spain* (Berkeley CA, 1987). Thorough study of a comparatively little known but very significant figure in Mexican religious history.

Rawley, James A. *The Transatlantic Slave Trade; a History* (New York, 1981).

Ricard, Robert. *The Spiritual Conquest of Mexico* (Berkeley CA, 1966). The best study on the conversion of Mexico, though nowhere near sufficient emphasis is given to Our Lady of Guadalupe.

Rippy, J. Fred and Jean T. Nelson. *Crusaders of the Jungle* (Chapel Hill NC, 1936). History of the evangelization of northern South America.

Rossabi, Morris. *Khubilai Khan; His Life and Letters* (Berkeley, 1988). The only full biography of the great Mongol khan and Emperor of China in the time of Marco Polo.

Royer, Fanchon. *St. Francis Solanus, Apostle to America* (New York, 1976). Excellent biography of a little-known missionary saint in South America.

Sansom, George B. *History of Japan* (Stanford CA, 1963), 3 vols.

Schurhammer, George. *The Malabar Church and Rome during the Early Portuguese Period and Before* (Trinchinopoly, 1934) Early history of the Thomas Christians of India.

———. *St. Francis Xavier* (St. Louis MO. 1928). By a world-famed expert on St. Francis Xavier, whose breadth of knowledge more than compensates for its lack of scholarly documentation.

Simpson, Lesley B. *The Encomienda in New Spain* (Berkeley CA, 1950).

Smith, Vincent A. *Oxford History of India*, 3rd ed. (Oxford, 1958). The most comprehensive history of India.

Spence, Jonathan. *God's Chinese Son* (New York, 1996) The extraordinary story of the native Christian movement in China founded by Hung Hsiu-chüan, the Taiping ("Heavenly Kingdom").

Talbot, Francis X. *Saint among Savages; the Life of Isaac Jogues* (New York, 1935). The first of two fine volumes about the Martyrs of North America.

————. *Saint among the Hurons; the Life of St. John de Brébeuf* (New York, 1949). The second of two fine volumes about the Martyrs of North America.

Thapar, Romila. *Asoka and the Decline of the Mauryas* (New York, 1961) Excellent coverage of Indian history during the first three centuries before Christ.

Thomas, Hugh. *The Slave Trade* (New York, 1991).

Tibesar, Antonin. *Franciscan Beginnings in Colonial Peru* (Washington, 1953).

Totman, Conrad. *Tokugawa Ieyasu, Shogun* (Union City CA, 1983).

Valtierra, Angel. *Peter Claver, Saint of the Slaves* (Westminster MD, 1960). The most complete account of the extraordinary life of this great saint.

Wahlig, C. J. *Past, Present, and Future of Juan Diego* (Kenosha WI, 1972). The full story of the Guadalupe apparition of the Blessed Virgin Mary.

Wagner, Henry P. *The Life and Writings of Bartolome de Las Casas* (Albuquerque NM, 1967).

Whiteway, R. S. *The Rise of Portuguese Power in India, 1497-1558* (Patna, 1979).

Yu-wen, Jen. *The Taiping Revolutionary Movement* (New Haven CT, 1973) The astonishing history of the native Christian movement in China in the 19th century, without benefit of missionaries.

Zürcher, E. *The Buddhist Conquest of China; the Spread and Adaptation of Buddhism in Early Medieval China* (Leiden, 1959) Very comprehensive study, the only one of its kind.

Index

Note: Dates given after an individual's name are those during which he held the office mentioned, unless marked with b. and d. for born and died. All Popes are identified by their pontifical rather than by their original name. Identical names are listed with Popes first; then cardinals; then bishops alphabetically and chronologically by see; then abbots (and masters and generals of orders) alphabetically and chronologically by monastery or order; then emperors and empresses, then kings and queens, then other rulers alphabetically and chronologically by country, then others. Saints are alphabetized by their first names only. The victor in a cited battle is indicated by the first contender named.